Employment law

an adviser's handbook

Tamara Lewis brings over 25 years' experience of working as a solicitor in the employment unit of the Central London Law Centre and has written and lectured extensively on employment law.

The Legal Action Group is a national, independent charity which campaigns for equal access to justice for all members of society. Legal Action Group:

- provides support to the practice of lawyers and advisers
- inspires developments in that practice
- campaigns for improvements in the law and the administration of justice
- stimulates debate on how services should be delivered.

Employment law

an adviser's handbook

FOURTEENTH EDITION

Tamara Lewis

Legal Action Group
2022

This edition published in Great Britain 2022
by LAG Education and Service Trust Limited
Gatehouse Chambers, 1 Lady Hale Gate, London WC1X 8BS
www.lag.org.uk

WORLD
LAND
TRUST™
www.carbonbalancedprint.com
CBP2250

print ISBN 978 1 913648 32 9
eBook ISBN 978 1 913648 33 6
bundle (print and eBook) ISBN 978 1 913648 34 3

Typeset by Refinecatch Ltd, Bungay, Suffolk
Printed in Great Britain by Hobbs the Printers, Totton, Hampshire

Preface

This book was first written because Thomas Kibling and I were constantly asked to recommend a book which covered the wide range of employment problems in a clear and practical form. There was no obvious book to recommend and we wrote this book to fill the gap. In particular, we have aimed to provide lay advisers, trade union officials and lawyers with a handbook which is a real support in identifying the relevant law and issues of evidence and which can be used as a self-contained guide while running unfair dismissal and discrimination cases. The book therefore devotes as much space to evidence, precedents and checklists as to setting out the law. Due to this practical emphasis, further research may be necessary on the law itself in new, developing, specialist or complex areas.

For a clear overview of the contents and layout of the book, it is best to look at the contents list on pages xi–xvi. Employment law is a large subject, which has simply exploded in recent years, especially as a result of European influence. The book now is almost twice as long as the first edition. It is not possible to cover the whole of employment law and all the rules and permutations in a small textbook. Inevitably there are some omissions and certain topics have been covered in more detail than others. I have tried to deal most thoroughly with subjects which frequently come up for advisers of low-paid workers. Because of its complexity, discrimination law has been treated in the greatest detail. At certain points in the book, I express views on points of law which are untested or could be challenged. I am happy to hear other arguments and I may be proved wrong – it's important always to keep an open mind.

Since 2010, the government has systematically cut back on employment rights, as well as making radical changes to the tribunal system by removing non-legal members from unfair dismissal claims, introducing pre-claim conciliation and most devastatingly, charging fees. In July 2017, the Supreme Court declared the fees order unlawful under both domestic and EU law because it had the effect of preventing access to justice.

A continuing area of uncertainty is the long-term effect of Britain leaving the European Union. The European Union (Withdrawal) Act 2018 effectively converts EU law as it stands immediately before exit into UK law. However, in future such rights will be subject to political change by any majority party in parliament without the bulwark of Europe as a safeguard.

Meanwhile in the UK, the issue of basic employment rights (minimum pay and holidays) for workers in the so-called gig economy continues to attract a great deal of media attention, with test cases regarding the employment status of Uber taxi drivers, couriers and others. Increasing numbers working on zero-hours contracts are also a particularly vulnerable group. Some employment rights are available only to employees working under a contract of employment, others are available to workers generally. In early editions, we used the generic word 'worker'. Since the fifth edition, I have tried to use the appropriate terminology when dealing with each right. However, this can become awkward in some contexts, and it is most important to check the start of each section to see who is covered. Unless specified, where the word 'worker' is used, it is not confined to the definition of 'worker' followed in certain legislation.

The internet is now an invaluable access source for reports, guidance and Codes. As these are often badly sign-posted and hard to find on the host websites, I have tried to give the exact web addresses. Unfortunately these tend to be long and cumbersome and very frequently change. If you find they are out of date, try looking through the sitemap. The internal search engines rarely help, but it sometimes works if you type in the full name of a report. Surprisingly often, the best bet is to type the name of what you want into Google. A fair amount of information is available on the GOV.UK site, although in a simplified form.

Regarding cases and statutory references in the footnotes, 'SI' stands for 'statutory instrument' and can be accessed on the Legislation.gov.uk UK website. Cases with the 'UKEAT' reference can be found on GOV.UK, EAT section. 'IRLR' refers to *Industrial Relations Law Reports*. Most cases at all levels can be found on Bailii, but I only give the Bailii citation where the case is not reported in IRLR or on the EAT's own website. Web addresses for all these are in appendix F.

I should say that all the names used in the case precedents in the appendices are fictional and any resemblance to real names is purely coincidental.

The law is stated as known at 1 October 2021. Where possible, reference has been made to more recent law at proof stage.

Tamara Lewis

While every attempt has been made to ensure the accuracy of the contents of this book, the author can accept no responsibility for advice given in reliance on its contents.

Acknowledgements

The development of Central London Law Centre's employment unit was greatly assisted by a small group of volunteers who showed remarkable commitment over the years. Particular thanks to barristers Nick O'Brien and Martin Westgate for being such staunch supporters of the law centre for a very long time. Sadly the Law Centre eventually became a victim to funding cuts and closed. Thanks also to Thomas Kibling, my first inspiration in employment law, who conceived the idea of this book with me many years ago.

In relation to this book, many thanks to Martin Westgate, Dave Jones and particularly Philip Tsamados for checking various sections over past editions and helping with tricky queries. Thanks also to Vivienne Gay for her invaluable inputs into the equal pay chapter. Any mistakes are nevertheless my own.

Finally I would like to thank all at LAG for their encouragement and support over the years. In particular, my editor, Esther Pilger, who shows remarkable patience and good humour at all points.

Contents

Table of cases

Table of statutes

Table of statutory instruments

Table of EU legislation

Table of international legislation

Abbreviations

AAL	additional adoption leave
ACAS	Advisory, Conciliation and Arbitration Service
ADR	alternative disputes resolution
AML	additional maternity leave
AMRA 1988	Access to Medical Reports Act 1988
APL	additional paternity leave
APL Regs 2010	Additional Paternity Leave Regulations 2010 SI No 1055
AW Regs 2010	Agency Workers Regulations 2010 SI No 93
BAILII	British and Irish Legal Information Institute
BC	Borough Council
BEIS	Department for Business, Energy & Industrial Strategy
BERR	Department for Business, Enterprise & Regulatory Reform
BIS	Department for Business, Innovation & Skills
CAC	Central Arbitration Committee
CBI	Confederation of British Industry
CC	County Council
CCO	continuation of contract order
CJEU	Court of Justice of the European Union
CML	compulsory maternity leave
CPR	Civil Procedure Rules 1998
CRB	Criminal Records Bureau
CRE	Commission for Racial Equality
DAFD	discrimination arising from disability
DBS	Disclosure and Barring Service
DC	District Council
DLA	disability living allowance
DPA 1998	Data Protection Act 1998
DPA 2018	Data Protection Act 2018
DRC	Disability Rights Commission
DSO	direct services organisation
DWP	Department for Work and Pensions
DTI	Department of Trade and Industry
EA 2002	Employment Act 2002
EAT	Employment Appeal Tribunal
EAT PD 2013	Employment Appeal Tribunal Practice Direction 2013

EAT PD 2019	Practice Direction (Employment Appeal Tribunal – Procedure) 2019
EAT Rules 1993	Employment Appeal Tribunal Rules (EAT Rules) 1993
EC	ACAS Early Conciliation
EC Rules 2014	Employment Tribunals (Early Conciliation: Exemptions and Rules of Procedure) Regulations 2014 SI No 254
ECHR	European Convention on Human Rights
ECJ	European Court of Justice
ECSO	Early Conciliation Support Officer
ECtHR	European Court of Human Rights
EDT	effective date of termination
EEC	European Economic Community
EHRC	Equality and Human Rights Commission
EIA	equality impact assessment
EJRA	employer justified retirement age
EOC	Equal Opportunities Commission
EqA 2010	Equality Act 2010
EqPA 1970	Equal Pay Act 1970
ERA 1996	Employment Rights Act 1996
ERelA 1999	Employment Relations Act 1999
ESA	Employment and Support Allowance
ET	employment tribunal
ET and EAT Fees Order 2013	Employment Tribunals and Employment Appeal Tribunal Fees Order 2013 SI No 1893
ET Regs 2013	Employment Tribunals (Constitution and Rules of Procedure) Regulations 2013 SI No 1237
ETA 1996	Employment Tribunals Act 1996
ETO	economic, technical or organisational
ETS	Employment Tribunals Service
EU(W)A 2018	European Union (Withdrawal) Act 2018
EWC	expected week of childbirth
FIA 2000	Freedom of Information Act 2000
FI(S)A 2002	Freedom of Information (Scotland) Act 2002
FSA	Financial Services Authority
FTE Regs 2002	Fixed-term Employees (Prevention of Less Favourable Treatment) Regulations 2002 SI No 2034
GB	Great Britain
GCHQ	Government Communications Headquarters
GDPR	General Data Protection Regulation (EU)
GEO	Government Equalities Office
GP	general practitioner
GRA 2004	Gender Recognition Act 2004
GRC	gender recognition certificate
HMCTS	HM Courts and Tribunals Service
HMRC	HM Revenue & Customs
HMSO	HM Stationery Office
HRA 1998	Human Rights Act 1998
HSE	Health and Safety Executive
ICE	information and consultation of employees

ICE Regs 2004	Information and Consultation of Employees Regulations 2004 SI No 3426
ICO	Information Commissioner's Office
ICR	Industrial Cases Reports
IRLR	*Industrial Relations Law Reports*
ITEPA 2003	Income Tax (Earnings and Pensions) Act 2003
JES	job evaluation study
JSA	jobseeker's allowance
KIT	keeping in touch
LBC	London Borough Council
LIFO	last in, first out
MBC	Metropolitan Borough Council
MHSW Regs 1999	Management of Health and Safety at Work Regulations 1999
MOJ	Ministry of Justice
MP	member of parliament
MPL Regs 1999	Maternity and Parental Leave etc Regulations 1999 SI No 3312
NHS	National Health Service
NI	National Insurance
NIF	National Insurance Fund
NMW Regs 2015	National Minimum Wage Regulations 2015 SI No 621
NMWA 1998	National Minimum Wage Act 1998
OAL	ordinary adoption leave
OML	ordinary maternity leave
OPL	ordinary paternity leave
OPSI	Office of Public Sector Information
PAL Regs 2002	Paternity and Adoption Leave Regulations 2002 SI No 2788
PBL Regs 2020	Parental Bereavement Leave Regulations SI No 249
PCP	provision, criterion or practice
PENP	post-employment notice pay
PHA 1997	Protection from Harassment Act 1997
PI	personal injury
PIDA 1998	Public Interest Disclosure Act 1998
PILON	pay in lieu of notice
PIP	personal independence payment
PPP	Public Private Partnership
PSED	public sector equality duty
PTSD	post-traumatic stress disorder
PTW Regs 2000	Part-time Workers (Prevention of Less Favourable Treatment) Regulations 2000 SI No 1551
PWD	Pregnant Workers Directive 92/85/EEC
RIPA 2000	Regulation of Investigatory Powers Act 2000
ROA 1974	Rehabilitation of Offenders Act 1974
RPI	Retail Price Index
RRA 1976	Race Relations Act 1976
RRO	restricted reporting order
SAP	statutory adoption pay

SAR	subject access request
SDA 1975	Sex Discrimination Act 1975
SERPS	State Earnings-Related Pension Scheme
ShPP	statutory shared parental pay
SIA 1978	State Immunity Act 1978
SML	statutory maternity leave
SMP	statutory maternity pay
SOSR	some other substantial reason
SPL	shared parental leave
SPL Regs 2014	Shared Parental Leave Regulations 2014 SI No 3050
SPLIT	shared parental leave in touch
SSCBA 1992	Social Security Contributions and Benefits Act 1992
SSP	statutory sick pay
TAEN	The Age and Employment Network
TFEU	Treaty on the Functioning of the European Union (Treaty of Rome)
TSO	The Stationery Office
TUC	Trades Union Congress
TULR(C)A 1992	Trade Union and Labour Relations (Consolidation) Act 1992
TUPE Regs 2006	Transfer of Undertakings (Protection of Employment) Regulations 2006 SI No 246
WHO	World Health Organization
WTD	Working Time Directive 2003/88/EC
WTR 1998	Working Time Regulations 1998

Introduction

Terms and conditions of employment

continued

Chapter 1: Key points

- All employees have a contract of employment. Verbal contracts have the same status as written contracts, but are harder to prove.
- Contract terms may be express, implied or inserted by statute. Express terms are written or verbally agreed. Where there is no express term, an implied term may fill the gap. Terms may be implied because they are obvious or by looking at what has happened in practice, but not just because they are reasonable.
- Also, general implied terms apply in most employment contracts, eg the obligation not to destroy trust and confidence.
- Under Employment Rights Act (ERA) 1996 s1, certain contract terms must be put in writing. A written statement of these particulars does not necessarily constitute the contract in itself, but often amounts to strong evidence of what the contract is. Changes in terms should be confirmed in a section 4 statement.
- Contract terms are often varied during employment, but this can only occur by agreement (express or implied). Where the employer tries to enforce changes to the contract without agreement, this is called 'unilateral variation'.
- An employee must respond quickly where the employer tries to impose contract changes unilaterally, otherwise s/he may be taken to have agreed the change by inaction. There are various options for an employee in this situation, but most of them risk dismissal. If an employee is dismissed for refusing to accept a contract change, the dismissal will not necessarily be unfair.
- There are special regulations protecting employees working on fixed-term contracts from unjustified less favourable treatment.
- Temporary agency workers must be given equal access to facilities and knowledge of permanent vacancies; after 12 weeks, they must be given the same basic working conditions as if they were a permanent employee or worker.
- In theory, an employer can be sued for defamation, malicious falsehood or negligent misstatement if s/he writes a misleading or inaccurate reference. In practice, these claims are difficult to bring.
- Under the UK General Data Protection Regulation (GDPR) and the Data Protection Act 2018, workers have access to their own personal data and can seek corrections of inaccurate information held on them.

continued

- Monitoring and privacy at work are covered by various specialist legislation as well as the Human Rights Act 1998 and Part 3 of the Data Protection Code, subject to updating by the GDPR.
- The Freedom of Information Act 2000 provides access to information held by public authorities.

General guide to useful evidence

- The letter of appointment; written contract of employment or statement of particulars under ERA 1996 s1; the staff handbook; any collective agreement (if unionised) or other written procedures; payslips.
- If there is no written contract: the job advertisement; what was said at interview and immediately on starting; custom and practice at the workplace.
- Having established the original contractual agreement, look for any variations which were applicable at the material time: further documents; verbal agreements; changes in practice.

The contract of employment

Overview

1.1   Depending on the circumstances, people may work on a variety of arrangements, eg as self-employed, as a 'worker' or as an 'employee'. As will be clarified throughout this book, their status will affect the extent of their employment rights. Whatever the basis for their employment, they are likely to be working under some kind of contract. Paras 1.1–1.40 of this chapter specifically concern the contractual rights of employees. For the definition of an employee in the context of unfair dismissal law, see paras 6.4–6.12. Every employee has a contract *of* employment, which consists of a number of terms, some of which are express terms, some implied and some statutory. Express terms are those agreed between the employer and employee whether in writing or orally. Implied terms are not expressly agreed but are implied from surrounding circumstances into the contract of employment by the tribunals and courts. Some implied terms are universal (ie they apply to all contracts of employment) and others are implied as a natural consequence of a specific contract of employment, either because the term is so obvious that the employer and employee would have agreed to the term if asked to consider it, or because the contract could not work without the term being incorporated. Statutory terms are inserted into the contract by Acts of Parliament. For example, the 'Equality of Terms' section of the Equality Act (EqA) 2010 inserts an equality clause into contracts.

Express terms

1.2 An express term is one which has been the subject of discussion and acceptance by the employer and employee. These terms are usually put in writing, but this is not necessary.[1] The main express terms are usually found in the letter of appointment or in the written contract of employment. Sometimes they are found in other documents such as the staff handbook, the rule book or collective agreement. Also watch for memos, notices on a notice board, emails and policies on the intranet, although these documents may or may not have contractual status. Payslips can provide good evidence of contractual pay rates and the name of the employer, although they are unlikely to amount to contractual documents in themselves. It would not be unusual for a redundancy policy containing enhanced redundancy terms to be in an employee handbook rather than in the main contract document.[2] Even where a handbook or intranet policy or similar is expressly incorporated into the contract of employment, not every clause within it will necessarily be regarded as contractual. For example, clauses which set out policy or good practice guidelines or minute details of sickness absence procedures might not be suitable ('apt') for incorporation as part of a contract.[3] The main express terms are usually:

- the rate of pay, and how often the employee will be paid;
- the hours of work;
- any terms and conditions relating to holidays and holiday pay;
- sick pay;
- notice pay; and
- the disciplinary rules and grievance procedure.

---

1 Though there is a separate right to have certain terms in writing. See para 1.24.
2 *Allen and others v TRW Systems Ltd* UKEAT/0083/12.
3 There is useful guidance to this complicated area in *Sparks and others v Department for Transport* [2016] EWCA Civ 360; [2016] IRLR 519

Implied terms

1.3   In the absence of express terms, employment contracts need terms to be implied into them in order to make them workable, meaningful and complete. Implied terms of fact are used to fill a gap where there is no express term on a particular point. The courts will imply a term only if it is absolutely necessary to do so, or if it is clear that the employer and employee would have agreed to the term if it had been discussed.[4] The courts will not intervene and imply a term just because it is reasonable or convenient.[5] The idea is to give effect to the parties' presumed intentions. There are four common ways of trying to work out what an implied term might be:

- the 'business efficacy' test;
- the 'officious bystander' test;
- the behaviour of the parties in practice; and
- custom and practice.

1.4   The 'business efficacy' test is where a term is implied to make the contract workable. For example, it is likely to be an implied contract term that a chauffeur holds a valid driving licence, even though this has never been explicitly discussed. The 'officious bystander' test is where a term is so obvious that both parties would instantly have agreed it at the outset, had they been asked. This test works for the driving licence example too. However, these tests do not always give an answer where there is no express term on a point.

1.5   A term can sometimes be implied by looking at what has happened between the particular employee and the employer in practice. This may be called implication by 'past performance' or by 'custom and practice'. For example, if the employer has given seven weeks' holiday every year to the employee without exception this may indicate an unspoken agreement at the outset for seven weeks' holiday. This way of implying a contractual term can be confusing, because behaviour and the contractual position can change over time.

1.6   As well as what has happened with the individual employee, custom and practice across the workplace or the industry may also give rise to an implied term if the custom and practice is reasonable, notorious and certain. 'Reasonable' means that the term is fair, 'notorious' requires the term to be well known, and 'certain' requires the term to be sufficiently precise so that the term is possible to

---

4   See *Lister v Romford Ice and Cold Storage Co Ltd* [1957] 1 All ER 125, HL.
5   *Aparau v Iceland Frozen Foods plc* [1996] IRLR 119, EAT.

state.[6] For example, the employer always closes the factory for a trade holiday and gives all staff paid holidays for that week.[7] Depending on the facts, a policy which is adopted unilaterally by management, eg to pay travel expenses or to give enhanced redundancy pay, can sometimes become implied into an employee's contract by custom and practice.[8]

Universal implied terms

Mutual trust and confidence

1.7 As employment contracts involve personal contact between the parties, it is necessary to have certain terms implied into them so that they can operate smoothly, such as the implied term of mutual trust and confidence. This is the most widely applied and influential of all the implied terms. The employer must not, without reasonable and proper cause, conduct him/herself in a manner calculated or likely to destroy or seriously damage the relationship of trust and confidence with the employee.[9] This term applies to the employee as well. The following are examples of breaches of this implied term by the employer:

- physical or verbal abuse;[10]
- sexual harassment[11] and the failure to support someone who has been the victim of harassment at work;[12]
- imposing a disciplinary penalty when unwarranted or where the disciplinary procedure is not followed.[13]

Breach of the implied term of trust and confidence may cause an employee to resign and claim constructive dismissal.[14]

---

6 *Sagar v Ridehalgh and Sons Ltd* [1931] 1 Ch 310, CA.

7 *Quinn v Calder Industrial Materials Ltd* [1996] IRLR 126, EAT.

8 *Quinn v Calder Industrial Materials Ltd* [1996] IRLR 126, EAT; *Albion Automotive Ltd v Walker and others* [2002] EWCA Civ 946; *Allen & others v TRW Systems Ltd* UKEAT/0083/12; *Peacock Stores v Peregrine, Norman & Matthews* UKEAT/0315/13.

9 *Woods v WM Car Services (Peterborough)* [1982] ICR 693, CA; *Malik v Bank of Credit and Commerce International SA* [1997] IRLR 462, HL as corrected by *Baldwin v Brighton & Hove CC* [2007] IRLR 232, EAT.

10 *Western Excavating (ECC) Ltd v Sharp* [1978] ICR 221; [1978] IRLR 27, CA.

11 *Western Excavating (ECC) Ltd v Sharp* [1978] ICR 221; [1978] IRLR 27, CA.

12 *Wigan BC v Davies* [1979] ICR 411, EAT.

13 *Post Office v Strange* [1980] IRLR 515, EAT.

14 See paras 6.35–6.44.

1.8   In very limited circumstances, employers may use an express term in a way which breaches the implied term of trust and confidence. For example, in one case the employers were in breach of this term when they invoked a mobility clause to insist an employee move workplace to a distant town on extremely short notice.[15] Usually, however, employers are able to rely on express terms, however unreasonable the result.

Not to act arbitrarily, capriciously or inequitably

1.9   There is an implied term that an employer will not treat an employee arbitrarily, capriciously or inequitably without good reason. Failing to give an employee a pay increase without good cause when other employees are given an increase has been held to be a breach of this term.[16]

Good faith and fidelity

1.10   This implied term lasts during employment but not after its termination.[17] Any action by an employee which seriously harms the employer's business will be in breach of this term[18] (although whistleblowing authorised by the Public Interest Disclosure Act 1998 would override this).[19] Likewise, an employer who discloses to a third party information about an employee without good reason or consent will be in breach of this term. Examples are:

- carrying on business in competition with the employer;[20]
- the use of the employer's list of customers including his/her business requirements.[21]

Employees cannot use confidential information for their own personal benefit during their employment.

1.11   The employee may also have agreed express contract terms, eg not to set up in competition after leaving the employment or not to poach staff or customers for a specified period of time. These are known as 'restrictive covenants'. If they are too restrictive in their ambit, they may not be enforceable, because it can be against the

---

15 *United Bank Ltd v Akhtar* [1989] IRLR 507, EAT.
16 *FC Gardiner Ltd v Beresford* [1978] IRLR 63, EAT.
17 *Faccenda Chicken Ltd v Fowler* [1986] IRLR 69, CA.
18 *Boston Deep Sea Fishing and Ice Co v Ansell* (1888) 39 Ch D 339, CA.
19 See para 6.101.
20 *Hivac Ltd v Park Royal Scientific Instruments* [1946] Ch 169; [1946] 1 All ER 350, CA.
21 *Faccenda Chicken Ltd v Fowler* [1986] IRLR 69, CA.

public interest to restrain trade more than is reasonably required to protect legitimate business interests. This is a complex area of law.

Not to disclose trade secrets/confidentiality

1.12   It is implied that the employee cannot disclose, either during employment or after it has ended, the employer's trade secrets or highly confidential information.[22] Most employees will not have access to information which would amount to a trade secret. The true nature of a trade secret is something which the outside world does not or could not ascertain, such as a process or a chemical formula, eg the ingredients of Coca Cola, and not just lower level confidential information which the employer does not want the employee to use after s/he leaves.[23]

To obey reasonable and lawful orders

1.13   The employee is obliged to obey reasonable and lawful orders. Lawful means both a requirement of parliament as well as an order given within the ambit of the employment contract. If the employee is asked to perform a function outside the employment contract which is unreasonable, s/he can, in theory, refuse. The employee needs to be careful because a small degree of flexibility is often taken to be within the contract. Also, if the employee is dismissed for failing to follow a reasonable but non-contractual order, it is still possible that the dismissal will be fair.[24]

Care of employer's equipment

1.14   The employee owes the employer a duty to look after the employer's equipment and machinery. The failure to exercise due care, leading to loss to the employer, could constitute a disciplinary matter. This will arise if the employee has injured a third party, as any claim by the latter will usually be against the employer.

To employ a competent workforce

1.15   The employer owes a duty to employ a competent and safe workforce,[25] safe plant and equipment, to have a safety system at work

---

22   *Faccenda Chicken Ltd v Fowler* [1986] IRLR 69, CA. This is subject to protected whistleblowing, see para 6.101.
23   *Faccenda Chicken Ltd v Fowler* [1986] IRLR 69, CA.
24   See paras 7.57–7.62.
25   *Hudson v Ridge Manufacturing Co* [1957] 2 All ER 229, QBD.

and to pay attention to employees' complaints in relation to safety matters.[26]

To provide a safe working environment

1.16   The employer owes a contractual duty to provide a safe working environment. (There are also detailed statutory rules about health and safety at work.)[27]

To deal promptly with grievances

1.17   The employer is under a duty to give employees an opportunity to have their grievances heard reasonably and promptly.[28]

Statutory terms

1.18   Due to the unequal bargaining power between workers and employers, successive governments have found it necessary to incorporate into the employment contract certain terms protecting workers during, and on termination of, employment, for example minimum notice pay, an equality clause under the EqA 2010 (previously the Equal Pay Act 1970) and the national minimum wage.

1.19   Generally speaking, clauses which exclude an employee's various statutory rights are void, though there are special rules when claims are settled and in respect of employee shareholders.[29]

Varying the terms of employment

1.20   Any term of the employment contract can be varied by consent of the parties (except for certain statutory minimum terms). If the employer tries to vary a term of the employment contract but does not get the employee's consent, that variation is not recognised as lawful.[30] However, the courts and tribunals may treat the employee as having consented to the variation if s/he does not object to the change within a reasonable period of time. It is therefore important that the employee objects to any proposed variation as soon as possible. It is

---

26 *British Aircraft Corporation v Austin* [1978] IRLR 332, EAT.
27 See also chapter 17 for some introductory points.
28 *W A Goold (Pearmak) Ltd v McConnell* [1995] IRLR 516, EAT.
29 See paras 6.109 and 20.273.
30 *Rigby v Ferodo Ltd* [1988] ICR 29; [1987] IRLR 516, HL.

not necessary for the employee to keep repeating his/her objection – once is sufficient if it is clear and unequivocal. However, an objection cannot hold all the options open forever without taking further action.[31]

1.21 Where an employer insists on varying terms without the employee's consent, the employee's refusal to agree will rarely be the end of the matter. The employer may impose the changes anyway, such that the employee's normal options are to resist, resign[32] or, if relevant, sue for any unauthorised deduction from wages or breach of contract. Alternatively, if the change is very radical, an employee may claim that s/he has in reality been dismissed and is now working under an alternative contract.[33] The employee can then claim unfair dismissal, while still working in the new employment. There are other options too, eg claiming discrimination, whether or not the employee actually leaves the employment. A checklist of the options is in appendix A.[34]

1.22 Many of the options may lead to the employee's dismissal. Whether or not an employee will succeed in an unfair dismissal case depends on eligibility to claim and the normal principles of fairness.[35] It does not necessarily follow that dismissal for opposing a change of contract will be unfair. Even if it is, the employee may not get much by way of compensation. In some circumstances, the dismissal will be automatically unfair, eg if on the facts it is due to the employee having asserted a statutory right such as to have written particulars of the terms and conditions of employment or not to have an unauthorised deduction from wages.[36]

1.23 The employer cannot effect a change in the contract simply by notifying the employee that after a period of time the contract will be treated as having been varied. Employers have been known to terminate the original employment contract and offer a new contract which contains the variation as a means of getting round the employee's lack of consent to the variation. This approach is only lawful under the contract if the full contractual period of notice is given to terminate the employment contract and it is clear that the original contract

---

31 Although it is advisable to object clearly, this may not be essential. See *Abrahall and others v Nottingham City Council and another* [2018] IRLR 628, CA.

32 For constructive dismissal, see paras 6.35–6.44.

33 *Hogg v Dover College* [1990] ICR 39, EAT; *Alcan Extrusions v Yates and others* [1996] IRLR 327, EAT.

34 See checklist A25.

35 In particular, see paras 7.74–7.79.

36 See paras 6.71–6.74.

is being terminated. If this happens, the employee may be able to claim unfair dismissal in respect of the first contract and continue to work under the second contract on the new terms. What s/he cannot do is claim unfair dismissal, accept the new contract so that s/he can continue working, and then say that the new terms which s/he has accepted do not in fact bind him/her. Where the employer carries out mass dismissals in this way, the duty to consult trade union or employee representatives regarding collective redundancies also applies.[37]

The right to written particulars of employment

1.24   Workers are entitled to receive at the start of their employment,[38] a written statement of particulars of their employment. This is often known as a 'section 1 statement'.[39] The particulars must include:

- the names of the employer and worker;
- the date on which employment began, including any period of continuous employment with a previous employer;
- rates of pay or methods of calculating pay and frequency of payment;
- hours of work, including normal working hours, compulsory overtime,[40] the days of the week the worker is required to work and, if such hours or days may vary, how that variation will be decided;
- terms relating to holidays, including public holidays, holiday pay and how it will be calculated when the worker leaves the job;
- the worker's job title or a brief description of the work for which s/he is employed;
- place of work, including details of any mobility clause, and the employer's address;
- rules relating to sickness or injury, sick pay and details of any other paid leave;
- pension arrangements;
- any other benefits provided by the employer;
- the length of notice required by each party;

---

37 See para 2.21.
38 Employment Rights Act (ERA) 1996 s1(2).
39 Ie under ERA 1996 s1. Prior to 6 April 2020, only employees had this entitlement.
40 *Lange v Georg Schünemann GmbH* Case C-350/99 [2001] IRLR 244, ECJ.

- if employment is not intended to be permanent, the period for which it is expected to continue, or if a fixed-term contract, its expiry date;
- any probationary period, including its conditions and duration;
- any training entitlement, identifying if it is compulsory and where the employer will not pay the cost of the training;
- any collective agreements which directly affect the terms and conditions of employment;
- certain details[41] if the employee is required to work outside the UK for a period of more than one month;
- the disciplinary rules and procedure;[42]
- the name of a person to whom the employee can apply if s/he is dissatisfied with any disciplinary decision or seeking redress of any grievance relating to his/her employment; and
- any other term which, in view of its importance, is an essential part of the contract.[43]

Where there are no particulars on a point, this should be stated. If there is a change in any of the terms, the employer is required to notify the worker in writing within one month of the change.[44] This is sometimes called a 'section 4 statement'. Employers do not always make this written notification of contract variations, but an agreed variation will nevertheless be valid (provided it can be proved).

1.25   For terms related to disciplinary and grievance procedure, sickness, other paid leave, pension and training, the section 1 statement can refer to another reasonably accessible document. Regarding notice, the statement can refer to the legal position (see para 1.38) or a reasonably accessible collective agreement. The terms related to pensions, training, applicable collective agreements, and the note on disciplinary and grievance procedures can be provided in instalments within two months of the worker starting the job. Where an employer has supplied a written contract of employment or letter of engagement containing all the required particulars within the relevant time, this will be sufficient.[45]

---

41 ERA 1996 s1(4)(k).
42 ERA 1996 s3(1).
43 *Lange v Georg Schünemann GmbH* Case C-350/99 [2001] IRLR 244, ECJ.
44 ERA 1996 s4. Again, this will include all workers who start work on or after 6 April 2020 – Employment Rights (Miscellaneous Amendments) Regulations 2019 SI No 731.
45 ERA 1996 s7A.

1.26   The statement of terms is not itself the contract. It is strong but not conclusive evidence of what the contractual terms are.[46] If no proper statement is supplied as required, the worker can apply to an employment tribunal (ET) during employment or within three months after termination of employment.[47] The application can ask the ET to decide all the particulars which ought to have been given in a statement, or simply one or two specific particulars which have been omitted. The ET cannot award compensation in itself for failure to supply the particulars, but it can award two or four weeks' gross pay (subject to the same cap as for statutory redundancy pay) as extra compensation where the worker has also brought and won certain other claims, eg unfair dismissal (if an employee) or discrimination.[48] Unless there are exceptional circumstances, this award must be made if, at the time such proceedings were started, the employer was in breach of his/her duty to supply a section 1 or section 4 statement.[49]

1.27   In practice, workers tend not to apply to the ET unless there is a dispute over their entitlement, eg to holidays. There is always a risk that the worker will not be happy with the ET's findings on what the true contractual position is. It is is automatically unfair to dismiss an employee, regardless of length of service, because s/he has asked for a section 1 statement.[50]

1.28   The duty on the ET is to decide what has in fact been agreed by the employer and the worker (including any term which needs to be implied), but not to remake a contract or decide what should have been agreed. The ET cannot go as far as interpreting what an agreed contractual term actually means – for that it is necessary to get a declaration in a civil court.[51] The ET may have to make findings as to the terms and conditions of the contract when initially made and then consider whether there have been subsequent variations.

---

46 *Robertson and Jackson v British Gas Corporation* [1983] IRLR 302, CA.
47 ERA 1996 s11.
48 This covers claims listed in Employment Act 2002 Sch 5 (see para 22.38) – essentially those covered by the compensation regime under the ACAS (Advisory, Conciliation and Arbitration Service) Code on Disciplinary and Grievance Procedures.
49 Employment Act 2002 s38. See also the grounds of claim in the ET1 in appendix A.
50 See paras 6.71–6.74.
51 *Southern Cross Healthcare Co Ltd v Perkins and others* [2010] EWCA Civ 1442; [2011] IRLR 247.

Wrongful dismissal

Overview

1.29 Unlike unfair dismissal, which is a statutory right, wrongful dismissal is a contractual claim. It arises when an employer terminates the employment contract contrary to the terms of the contract (eg failure to give proper notice, or breach of another contractual term such as failure to follow the contractual disciplinary procedure).

1.30 The general rule is that either party can end the contract by giving the appropriate notice and without cause or reason. Where an employee has committed an act of gross misconduct, the employer may end the contract without giving notice. What amounts to gross misconduct depends on the facts of each case, but essentially it is deliberate or grossly negligent conduct which would completely undermine the employer's trust and confidence in the employment contract.[52] Some employment contracts define what amounts to gross misconduct; some acts such as theft and physical assault are obvious acts of gross misconduct and do not need stating. Although gross misconduct entitles the employer to dismiss without giving notice, whether the dismissal is fair is a separate question under the general unfair dismissal provisions of the ERA 1996.[53]

1.31 A wrongfully dismissed employee can recover damages for breach of contract. The idea is to put the employee in the position s/he would have been in if the employer had not broken the contract. Where the breach of contract is failure to give proper notice, compensation will usually be the net loss of earnings (pay and other benefits, eg use of a company car) for the notice period, subject to mitigation. The employee is expected to take reasonable steps to reduce his/her loss by seeking alternative employment. Any earnings received in the notice period will be set off against the claim.[54] It is also possible that any jobseeker's allowance received will be set off if it amounted to a net gain; similarly if the employee unreasonably failed to claim it.[55]

---

52 For a useful summary of cases defining gross misconduct, see *Burdett v Aviva Employment Services Ltd* UKEAT/0439/13 and on gross, negligence, *Adesokan v Sainsbury's Supermarkets Ltd* [2017] EWCA Civ 22.

53 See also paras 22.17–22.18.

54 *Cerberus Software Ltd v Rowley* [2001] IRLR 160, CA.

55 *Secretary of State for Employment v Stewart* [1996] IRLR 334, EAT; *Westwood v Secretary of State for Employment* [1984] IRLR 209, HL.

1.32   Employers often give employees notice pay rather than asking them to work their notice. The contract of employment sometimes has a 'PILON' (pay in lieu of notice) clause which says they can do this. This is so that technically there is no breach of contract, which might have other consequences. Either way, if an employer chooses to pay in lieu, the basic pay will be taxable as earnings.[56] Matters of tax are beyond the scope of this book and where there is an issue, advisers should check specialist sources.

1.33   It is not possible to recover compensation for mental distress or injury to feelings caused by the wrongful dismissal,[57] although it might be possible to get stigma damages, but this will only arise in very limited circumstances.[58] It may, however, be possible to claim damages for breach of the implied term of trust and confidence if this takes place before and is unconnected with the dismissal.[59] It may be difficult to know on the facts whether the breach was part of the process of dismissal. For example, distress caused by a lengthy suspension which is followed by a disciplinary process ending with dismissal, may or may not be connected with the dismissal.[60]

1.34   The law is complicated where the wrongful dismissal is because the employer fails to follow a contractual disciplinary procedure prior to dismissal. The employee cannot get general compensation for the breach of procedure, eg for hurt feelings or the lost chance of being kept on, but s/he may be able to claim wages for the length of time it would have taken to go through the compulsory disciplinary procedure.[61]

1.35   If the employer tells the employee that s/he is dismissed without giving the contractually required notice (unless it is gross misconduct) or if the employer fails to follow compulsory requirements in the contract for terminating employment, the employee can refuse to accept that the dismissal has taken effect.[62] The employee probably

---

56 Where termination and the payment took place on after 6 April 2018: Income Tax (Earnings and Pensions) Act (ITEPA) 2003 s401D.

57 *Addis v Gramophone* [1909] AC 488; *Johnson v Unisys Ltd* [2001] IRLR 279, HL.

58 *Bank of Credit and Commerce International SA v Ali* [1999] IRLR 508, Ch D.

59 *McCabe v Cornwall CC* [2003] IRLR 87, CA. But this would be an unusual and technical contract claim.

60 *McCabe v Cornwall CC* [2003] IRLR 87, CA.

61 If considering a claim, read *Edwards v Chesterfield Royal Hospital NHS Foundation Trust; Botham v Ministry of Defence* [2011] UKSC 58, [2012] IRLR 129, regarding the *Johnson* exclusion zone and *Gunton v Richmond LBC* [1980] IRLR 321, CA. The commentary in *Harvey* (see bibliography) is also useful.

62 *Societe General, London Branch v Geys* [2012] UKSC 63; [2013] IRLR 122.

cannot stop the employer then following the contractual rules and carrying out an effective dismissal. However, the extra time can be important if, for example, the employee needs to remain employed for a few more weeks to become eligible for a contractual bonus. A more common scenario is where an employee is dismissed without his/her contractual notice to avoid him/her reaching the necessary length of service to claim unfair dismissal. Unfortunately, it seems that refusing to accept the dismissal and keeping the contract alive will not change the termination date for unfair dismissal purposes.[63] Nor will an employee's compensation for breach of contract include compensation for the lost opportunity of bringing an unfair dismissal claim.[64]

1.36   Claims for breach of contract based on failure to follow disciplinary procedures are hard to prove and should be approached with caution. Most disciplinary procedures are not contractual but offer guidance rather than impose mandatory obligations, and failure to hold a disciplinary hearing or give a warning prior to dismissal will not necessarily be a breach of contract.

1.37   In England and Wales, an employee who has been wrongfully dismissed can claim in the ET, county court or High Court, subject to the value of the claim. The court rules are complex and should be checked.[65] As a rough guide, only high value claims can be started in the High Court. Most claims are started in the county court. There are different allocation tracks for both county court and High Court claims according to the type, value and complexity of the claim. One of these is the small claims track (previously known as 'the small claims court') which covers most claims for damages up to £10,000 (other than certain housing and personal injury claims). There is a more limited costs risk on the small claims track if the employee loses than is the usual position in the civil courts.[66] Alternatively, certain contract claims arising or outstanding on the termination of an employee's employment may be brought in an ET, currently for up to £25,000.[67] In Scotland, a notice pay claim can be brought in the

---

63 See para 6.24.
64 *Harper v Virgin Net Ltd* [2004] IRLR 390, EAT; *The Wise Group v Mitchell* UKEAT/0693/04.
65 See Civil Procedure Rules (CPR) 26.6(3) at: www.justice.gov.uk/courts /procedure-rules/civil/rules/part26#26.6.
66 See CPR 27.14 at: www.justice.gov.uk/courts/procedure-rules/civil/rules /part27#27.1.
67 Employment Tribunals Act 1996 s3; Industrial Tribunals Extension of Jurisdiction (England and Wales) Order 1994 SI No 1623 art 10.

relevant civil court, probably the Sheriff Court. The Sheriff Court operates a 'simple procedure' for claims up to and including £5,000.[68] Alternatively, a claim up to £25,000 can be brought in an ET.[69]

Statutory minimum notice

1.38   ERA 1996 s86 sets out minimum notice periods, though the contract may require more. An employer must give at least:

- one week's notice to an employee who has been continuously employed for one month or more but less than two years;
- one week's notice for each whole year of continuous employment for an employee employed for two years or more, but less than 12 years. For example, an employee employed for five years 11 months, would be entitled to at least five weeks' notice of dismissal;
- 12 weeks' notice for continuous service of 12 years or more. For example, an employee employed for 16 years would be entitled to at least 12 weeks' notice.

An employee employed for one month or more need give only one week's notice when resigning (unless the contract requires longer). Pay for the statutory notice period should be based on the employee's normal wage and not any reduction because s/he was on furlough.[70] In some situations, neither contractual nor statutory notice needs to be given,[71] eg an instant or summary dismissal for gross misconduct or a resignation due to the employer's fundamental breach of contract (constructive dismissal).

1.39   An employee must be paid for the statutory notice period even if s/he is off sick and has exhausted his/her normal entitlement to sick pay; or if s/he is absent due to pregnancy, childbirth, adoption leave, parental leave or paternity leave.[72] Oddly, if the employee has a contractual entitlement to notice which is at least one week longer than the statutory minimum, s/he entirely loses the right to statutory

---

68 For further details, see: www.scotcourts.gov.uk/taking-action/simple-procedure.

69 Employment Tribunals Act 1996 s3; Employment Tribunals Extension of Jurisdiction (Scotland) Order 1994 SI No 1624.

70 ERA 1996 ss87–91 sets out the calculation rules for notice pay. In respect of furlough, see Employment Rights Act 1996 (Coronavirus, Calculation of a Week's Pay) Regulations 2020 SI No 814.

71 ERA 1996 s86(6).

72 ERA 1996 ss87–88.

notice pay in these circumstances.[73] An employee can claim for wrongful dismissal, including the failure to give notice in the ET within three months of the effective date of termination (EDT).

Zero hours contracts

1.40   In recent years there has been a huge increase in what has come to be known as 'zero hours contracts'. This is not a technical term, but is generally used to refer to a contract where no minimum number of hours is guaranteed. Zero hours contracts are particularly heavily used in the care and hospitality sectors. There has been considerable public and political discussion about how to improve the rights of those working on zero hours contracts and this is likely to remain on the agenda. Since 26 May 2015, 'exclusivity clauses' in zero hours contracts have been unenforceable. An exclusivity clause is one which prohibits a worker from doing work or performing services under another contract or arrangement, or which says that the employer's consent is required.[74] Whether workers on zero hours contracts are employees and can claim unfair dismissal depends on the circumstances and is discussed at paras 6.4–6.12.

Fixed-term employees

1.41   The Fixed-term Employees (Prevention of Less Favourable Treatment) Regulations (FTE Regs) 2002[75] implement the EC Fixed-term Work Directive[76] and grant additional rights concerning pay and pensions.

1.42   The FTE Regs 2002 only cover employees, but it may be arguable that the Fixed-term Work Directive also protects other workers.[77] A fixed-term employee is someone who is employed under a contract of employment that will terminate on a specific date, or on completion of a particular task, or when a specific event does or does not happen.[78] This can include employees on short contracts to do seasonal work

---

73   ERA 1996 s87(4); *Scott Company (UK) Ltd v Budd* [2003] IRLR 145, EAT.

74   ERA 1996 s27A.

75   SI No 2034.

76   99/70/EC.

77   See scope defined by the European Court of Justice (ECJ) in *Del Cerro Alonso v Osakidetza-Servicio Vasco de Salud* [2007] IRLR 911, ECJ.

78   FTE Regs 2002 reg 1(2).

(eg agricultural workers or working in children's summer camps, or shop assistants taken on purely for Christmas), and employees employed as maternity or sickness locums. It is still a fixed-term contract, even if it contains a clause allowing the employer or employee to terminate it on notice during its course.[79] A permanent employee is one who is not employed on a fixed-term contract.[80] The FTE Regs 2002 do not apply where the employee is an agency worker.[81] Apprentices and employees on certain government training or work experience schemes are also excluded.[82]

1.43   A fixed-term employee has the right not to be treated less favourably than a comparable permanent employee because s/he is a fixed-term employee as regards contract terms or by being subjected to any other detriment.[83] A comparable permanent employee is someone who, at the time of the less favourable treatment, is employed by the same employer on broadly similar work (having regard to similar levels of qualification and skills), and who is based at the same establishment or if there is no one comparable at the same establishment, then based at a different establishment.[84] Subject to the defence of justification (below), an employer must not give a fixed-term employee less favourable access than a permanent employee to benefits such as Christmas bonuses, free gym membership, travel loans, training courses or occupational pension schemes, or deny him/her promotion opportunities or select him/her first for redundancy, purely because s/he works fixed-term. However, it is not contrary to the FTE Regs 2002 to dismiss full-time employees just short of the qualifying period for unfair dismissal protection, even though no similar action is taken against permanent employees.[85] Where the fixed-term employee does the same work as several permanent employees whose contract terms are different, s/he may choose who to compare him/herself with. It is also unlawful unjustifiably to treat a permanent employee less favourably because s/he was a fixed-term employee in

---

79   *Allen v National Australia Group Europe Ltd* [2004] IRLR 847, EAT.

80   FTE Regs 2002 reg 1(2).

81   FTE Regs 2002 reg 19. The Fixed-term Work Directive also does not apply to agency workers: *Della Rocca v Poste Italiane SpA* C-290/12, CJEU. See para 1.50 onwards regarding discrimination against agency workers.

82   FTE Regs 2002 regs 20 and 18.

83   FTE Regs 2002 reg 3.

84   FTE Regs 2002 reg 2. See para 2.24 regarding 'establishment'.

85   *Department for Work and Pensions v Webley* [2005] IRLR 288, CA.

the past, eg by failing to take account periods of time worked on fixed-term contracts when assessing service-based pay.[86]

1.44   Employers have a defence if the less favourable treatment can be 'justified on objective grounds'.[87] An employer should balance the rights of individual employees against business objectives and consider justification on a case-by-case basis. It is generally thought that treatment will be justified if it is to achieve a legitimate objective, if it is necessary to achieve that objective and if it is an appropriate way to achieve that objective.[88] This is similar to the test used under the EqA 2010 for justifying indirect discrimination. Another way an employer can justify less favourable treatment is if the terms of the fixed-term employee's contract, taken as a whole, are at least as favourable as the terms of the comparable permanent employee's contract.[89] This 'package approach' may not be lawful under the directive.[90] It will also not necessarily amount to less favourable treatment where the pro rata principle applies,[91] eg where an employer pays for annual health insurance and an employee on a six-month fixed-term contract is offered half the subscription cost.

1.45   A fixed-term employee has the right to be informed of any available permanent vacancies. It is sufficient if the vacancy is contained in an advertisement which the employee has a reasonable opportunity of reading in the course of his/her employment.[92] Also, once an employee has been continuously employed on two or more fixed-term contracts for four years, the contract becomes permanent unless keeping the employee on a fixed-term contract is objectively justified.[93] A collective or workforce agreement can modify the rule.[94] Continuous employment for this purpose is calculated in the same way as it is to qualify for unfair dismissal protection,[95] so that certain

---

86 *Valenza and others v Autorità Garante della Concorrenza e del Mercato* C-302-305/11 [2013] ICR 373, CJEU.

87 FTE Regs 2002 reg 3(3)(b).

88 Accepted by the Employment Appeal Tribunal (EAT) in relation to the similarly worded Part-time Workers (Prevention of Less Favourable Treatment) Regulations 2000 SI No 1551 in *Besong v Connex Bus (UK) Ltd* UKEAT/0436/04.

89 FTE Regs 2002 reg 4.

90 The ECJ in *Del Cerro Alonso v Osakidetza-Servicio Vasco de Salud* [2007] IRLR 911, ECJ seems to require a more precise defence.

91 FTE Regs 2002 regs 2(1) and 3(5).

92 FTE Regs 2002 reg 3(6) and (7).

93 FTE Regs 2002 reg 8.

94 FTE Regs 2002 reg 8(5).

95 FTE Regs 2002 reg 8(4); see paras 6.20–6.22.

breaks between fixed-term contracts may be counted in. For example, teachers employed on nine-month or term-time only contracts may be able to claim permanent status after four years if they can show their service through the breaks is continuous by reason of custom and arrangement or as temporary cessation only, and the employer cannot justify keeping them on fixed-term contracts.

1.46   An employee can request a written statement confirming his/her new status as permanent employee or, if this is disputed, explaining the justification for the contract remaining fixed-term.[96] Employees place a great value on being given 'permanent' status, but it is not always as important as they think. Employees qualify for unfair dismissal protection as soon as they build up two years' service, whether they are employed on a permanent or fixed-term contract.[97] Admittedly, having permanent status as opposed to working on a short-term contract may make the employee less vulnerable to dismissal in practice.

Enforcement

1.47   An employee who thinks s/he may have been less favourably treated, may make a written request to the employer to supply written reasons for the treatment within 21 days.[98] If the employer fails to answer or is evasive, the ET may draw an adverse inference in any subsequent tribunal proceedings. If the treatment concerned is dismissal, the employee cannot make a request under the FTE Regs 2002, but can make an equivalent request for written reasons for dismissal under ERA 1996 s92.[99]

1.48   If a fixed-term employee believes s/he has been less favourably treated than a comparable permanent employee, or that his/her rights have been infringed under the FTE Regs 2002 in any other way, s/he can bring an ET claim within three months.[100] Late claims may be allowed if it is just and equitable to do so. The ET has power to make a declaration as to the employee's rights, to order compensation and to make recommendations that the employer take certain action.[101] The amount of compensation will be what the ET thinks is just and equitable having regard to the infringement and any loss

---

96 FTE Regs 2002 reg 9.
97 See para 6.20.
98 FTE Regs 2002 reg 5.
99 FTE Regs 2002 reg 5(4). See para 20.10 for ERA 1996 s92.
100 FTE Regs 2002 reg 7.
101 FTE Regs 2002 reg 7.

attributable to it. No award may be made for injury to feelings for less favourable treatment as a fixed-term employee.[102]

1.49   It is automatic unfair dismissal to dismiss an employee because s/he has done anything under the FTE Regs 2002 including alleging, eg in a grievance, that the employer has infringed the regulations (except where the allegation is false and not made in good faith), bringing ET proceedings, giving evidence or requesting a written statement, or because the employer believes or suspects the employee has done or intends to do any of these things.[103] It is also unlawful to submit an employee to a detriment for these reasons.[104]

Agency workers

1.50   Employment agencies and businesses are regulated by the Conduct of Employment Agencies and Employment Businesses Regulations 2003.[105] There are statutory requirements for the provision of clear written information about terms and conditions before starting the relationship.

1.51   Agency workers can claim unfair dismissal or discrimination, provided they meet the necessary eligibility requirements for those statutory rights, which may be difficult.[106] Some other employment rights explicitly cover agency workers. This section is about equal treatment of agency workers compared with the hirer's permanent workers.

1.52   The Agency Workers Regulations (AW Regs) 2010[107] were passed in order to implement the EU Agency Worker Directive.[108] They came into force on 1 October 2011. Some key aspects of the AW Regs 2010, which the directive left to national discretion, were based on a formal agreement between the Trades Union Congress (TUC) and Confederation of British Industry (CBI). The AW Regs 2010 are complicated to read. The Department for Business, Energy & Industrial Strategy (BEIS) has issued *Agency Workers Regulations*

---

102 FTE Regs 2002 reg 7(10). This applies only to reg 3 claims.
103 FTE Regs 2002 reg 6.
104 FTE Regs 2002 reg 6.
105 SI No 3319, and to a lesser extent, by the Employment Agencies Act 1973.
106 See para 6.13 regarding unfair dismissal and paras 12.18–12.19 regarding discrimination.
107 SI No 93.
108 2008/104/EC.

2010: Guidance (updated October 2019).[109] This guidance has no legal status, but may help in understanding the law. The following is only a brief summary, and the AW Regs 2010 need to be consulted if running a case.

1.53   The AW Regs 2010 protect agency workers supplied by a temporary work agency[110] to work temporarily for and under the direction of a hirer.[111] 'Temporary' means 'not permanent' and probably excludes arrangements of indefinite duration.[112] In case-law concerning agency workers in other contexts, the hirer tends to be referred to as an end-user, though this is not a legal term. The AW Regs 2010 do not cover situations where the agency or the hirer is a client or customer of a profession or business carried on by the worker.[113]

1.54   It helps to appreciate that the AW Regs 2010 do not operate like other rights, eg for fixed-term employees (see above). There is no general right not to be discriminated against as an agency worker. Instead, there are very specific rights to equal terms on certain matters. Indeed, in some respects, it is permitted to treat agency workers more favourably, eg by paying them more.[114]

1.55   Under reg 5, agency workers who meet the qualifying period are entitled to certain of the same basic working and employment conditions as if they had been directly recruited by the hirer, whether as an employee or as a worker. The relevant terms and conditions are those related to pay, the duration of working time, night work, rest periods and annual leave.[115] The 'duration of working time' does not mean the length of the working week or even the length of particular shifts, but it does cover any maximum number of hours the employer sets for a particular shift.[116] 'Pay' (both amount and timing) includes certain bonuses, commission and holiday pay, but not the amount of detail on a payslip. There are various excluded payments, eg

---

109   Available at: https://assets.publishing.service.gov.uk/government/uploads/ system/uploads/attachment_data/file/841981/agency-workers-regulations- 2010-guidance.pdf.

110   As defined by AW Regs 2010 reg 4.

111   AW Regs 2010 reg 3(1).

112   *Moran v Ideal Cleaning Services Ltd* [2014] IRLR 172, EAT.

113   AW Regs 2010 reg 3(2).

114   *(1) Angard Staffing Solutions Ltd (2) Royal Mail Group Ltd v Kocur and another* UKEAT/0105/19 and 0209/19 – discussed at para 1.59.

115   AW Regs 2010 reg 6(1). On hours, see *Kocur v (1) Angard Staffing Solutions Limited, (2) Royal Mail Group Limited* [2019] EWCA Civ 1185.

116   *(1) Angard Staffing Solutions Ltd (2) Royal Mail Group Ltd v Kocur and another* UKEAT/0105/19 and 0209/19; *Kocur v Angard Staffing Solutions Ltd and another* [2019] EWCA Civ 1185; [2019] IRLR 933.

occupational sick pay, pension, redundancy pay and payment in respect of maternity leave.[117] The overtime rate and when it is triggered (eg after working a 39 hour week) is covered, but the opportunity to work overtime is not.[118] The fact that an agency worker is paid a higher hourly rate does not mean that the other terms can be less favourable.[119]

1.56   The agency worker satisfies the qualifying period when s/he has worked in the same role with the same hirer at some stage during each of 12 continuous weeks during one or more assignments.[120] An 'assignment' means the period of time that the worker is supplied by one or more agencies to the hirer.[121] The worker is taken to have worked 'in the same role' unless s/he has started a new role with the same hirer which has work or duties which are substantively different to the previous role and the agency has told the worker in writing of the type of work involved in the new role.[122] Usually if a worker stops working for the hirer and goes back again later, s/he will have to start counting the 12 weeks all over again. But in some situations, s/he can add in his/her previous work for the hirer,[123] eg where the break is for no more than 6 weeks or for any leave to which the worker is entitled under his/her contract or statute including annual leave and maternity leave. There are specific rules where the worker cannot complete the assignment due to pregnancy, maternity, adoption or paternity leave.

1.57   Once the qualifying period is achieved, the worker becomes and remains entitled to the same basic working and employment conditions until s/he stops working in the same role for that hirer or there is a break which is not covered by the previously mentioned rules.[124] Unusually, the AW Regs 2010 include anti-avoidance provisions. Where the structure of a worker's assignments with a particular hirer suggest the hirer or the agency intended to prevent the worker from acquiring reg 5 rights, the qualifying period will be deemed to have been completed at the time when it would have been completed had

---

117 AW Regs 2010 reg 6(2)–(3).

118 *(1) Angard Staffing Solutions Ltd (2) Royal Mail Group Ltd v Kocur and another* UKEAT/0105/19 and 0209/19.

119 *Kocur v (1) Angard Staffing Solutions Limited (2) Royal Mail Group Limited,* UKEAT/0181/17. This point was not appealed to the Court of Appeal.

120 AW Regs 2010 reg 7(2) and (4).

121 AW Regs 2010 reg 2.

122 AW Regs 2010 reg 7(3).

123 AW Regs 2010 reg 7.

124 AW Regs 2010 reg 7(8).

no such measures been taken.[125] The AW Regs 2010 set out factors to be taken into account when deciding whether the most likely explanation for the structure of the assignments is such an intention, eg the number and length of assignments and breaks in between and the number of different roles worked by the agency worker.[126] An example where the pattern of assignments might indicate a deliberate attempt to avoid a worker acquiring sufficient qualifying service would be where a single agency worker is given a series of 11-week assignments with seven-week breaks in between and no obvious 'innocent' reason why this should have happened.

1.58   As well as the reg 5 entitlement, after 12 weeks, to the same basic working and employment conditions, agency workers have certain other rights from day one. During an assignment, an agency worker must be treated no less favourably than a comparable worker in relation to the collective facilities and amenities provided by the hirer, eg access to the canteen, childcare facilities and transport services.[127] Unlike reg 5 rights, the worker must compare him/herself with an actual comparator, usually an employee or worker of the hirer who works at the same establishment and is engaged in the same or broadly similar work.[128] It is not unlawful to treat an agency worker less favourably if so doing can be objectively justified.

1.59   During an assignment, an agency worker also has the right to be told by the hirer of any relevant vacant posts, so that (in theory) s/he has the same opportunity as a comparable permanent employee or worker to get a permanent job with the hirer.[129] The agency worker does not have an equal right actually to apply for the vacancies, so this entitlement to information is only useful in making sure the worker does not miss an opportunity which is in fact openly advertised.[130]

1.60   An agency worker who believes the hirer or the agency may have infringed his/her rights under the AW Regs 2010, can make a written request for a written statement within 28 days containing information about the treatment in question.[131] In any subsequent ET case for breach of the AW Regs 2010, a tribunal can draw an adverse inference if it believes the agency or the hirer deliberately, and without

125 AW Regs 2010 reg 9(1).
126 AW Regs 2010 reg 9(5).
127 AW Regs 2010 reg 12.
128 See AW Regs 2010 reg 12(4) for details.
129 AW Regs 2010 reg 13.
130 *Coles v Ministry of Defence* UKEAT/0403/14; *(1) Angard Staffing Solutions Ltd (2) Royal Mail Group Ltd v Kocur and another* UKEAT/0105/19 and 0209/19.
131 AW Regs 2010 reg 16.

reasonable excuse, gave an evasive or equivocal reply or failed to answer altogether.

1.61   It is unlawful to subject an agency worker to a detriment because s/he has brought a claim under the AW Regs 2010, given evidence or information in connection with such a claim, requested a written statement, alleged that the agency or hirer has breached the AW Regs 2010, refused or proposed to refuse to forgo a right conferred by the AW Regs 2010 or otherwise done anything under the AW Regs 2010.[132] It is not unlawful if the allegation was false and not made in good faith. This protection is similar to the law of victimisation under the EqA 2010. It is also automatic unfair dismissal to dismiss an agency worker who is an employee for any of those reasons.

1.62   An agency worker can bring a tribunal claim if his/her rights under the AW Regs 2010 are infringed by the hirer or the agency.[133] The claim must be brought within three months of the infringement or if there is a series of infringements, within three months of the last one. An ET can consider a late claim if it is just and equitable to do so. If the worker wins the case, the ET can make a declaration and a recommendation that the respondent take certain action for the purpose of reducing the adverse effect on the worker of the unlawful actions.[134] The ET can also order any compensation which it considers just and equitable, which in respect of some of the rights must be no less than two weeks' pay.[135] Where the ET found the agency or hirer was in breach of the anti-avoidance provisions, it may make an additional award up to £5,000. No compensation is awarded for injury to feelings.

References

1.63   There is usually no obligation on an employer to provide a worker with a reference on termination of the employment contract. An exception is where a reference is required by a regulatory body such as the Financial Services Authority (FSA) to ensure that financial services are only handled by authorised and competent persons.

1.64   If an employer does provide a reference to a third party, that employer owes a duty of care to the person to whom the reference is

---

132 AW Regs 2010 reg 17.
133 See AW Regs 2010 regs 14 and 18 for details.
134 AW Regs 2010 reg 18(8).
135 See AW Regs 2010 reg 18 for details.

provided. Furthermore, a corresponding duty is owed to the worker who is the subject matter of the reference. It is necessary for the reference to be true, accurate and fair. Also the reference must not give an unfair or misleading impression overall, even if the discrete components are factually correct.[136]

1.65   A worker can sue an employer if s/he has suffered loss due to a negligent reference, either for breach of an implied term of the contract or in negligence.[137] The duty imposed on the employer is to ensure that the reference is fair, just and reasonable and the author of the reference should take all reasonable care to ensure that there is no misstatement. Negligent misstatement is where the employer, honestly but carelessly, makes a false statement of fact or opinion in the reference or in any other communication to a new employer.[138] Employers should confine unfavourable statements about the employee to those matters into which they had made reasonable investigation and had reasonable grounds for believing to be true.[139] It is also possible to sue an employer for defamation or malicious falsehood in the provision of a reference.

1.66   In practical terms, it can be difficult for a worker to do anything if s/he suspects a bad reference has been given. It may be hard to obtain a copy of the reference, even from the proposed new employer. There is no right of access under the Data Protection Act (DPA) 2018 to a confidential reference.[140] Any claim for a negligent or false reference would usually only be enforceable in the county court or High Court. If s/he has been unable to get the reference any other way and has sufficient grounds, the worker may be able to get pre-action disclosure. Realistically, the worker will probably not want to bring a case in the civil courts. Sometimes the best and simplest thing to do is to send a solicitor's letter to the former employer warning him/her of the consequences of unjustified references. This may prevent the employer doing it again.

1.67   An employer may give a discriminatory reference or victimise a worker by giving an adverse reference or no reference because the worker alleged discrimination during his/her employment or brought a case after leaving.[141] The advantage of a discrimination claim, if it

136 *Bartholomew v Hackney LBC* [1999] IRLR 246, CA.
137 *Spring v Guardian Assurance plc* [1994] IRLR 460, HL.
138 *McKie v Swindon College* [2011] EWHC 469 (QB).
139 *Cox v Sun Alliance Life Ltd* [2001] IRLR 448, CA.
140 DPA 2018 Sch 2 Part 4 para 24.
141 See para 13.76 regarding victimisation and references.

can be brought, is that it is run in an ET, and it may be possible to get details and even a copy of the reference, through the non-statutory questionnaire procedure[142] before starting any case.

1.68 These days, many employers give a purely factual reference confirming dates of employment and job title, to avoid any possibility of action being taken against them. Unfortunately such a reference can be of limited value to the worker. Because of the above difficulties, it is usually important to obtain an agreed reference as part of any settlement negotiated on an unfair dismissal or discrimination case.

Data protection

The legal framework

1.69 Data protection is required by the General Data Protection Regulation (GDPR)[143] and the Data Protection Act (DPA) 2018 (plus some specialist statutory instruments). The DPA 2018 and GDPR replaced the previous DPA 1998 and EC Data Protection Directive from 25 May 2018. Roughly 80 per cent of the law has not changed, but there are some differences, particularly in strengthening of individuals' rights over their own data. The EU GDPR has been retained in domestic law as the UK GDPR alongside an amended version of the DPA 2018. There is an Information Commissioner whose role is to uphold information rights in the public interest. The Information Commissioner's Office (ICO) has power to advise, take enforcement action and issue codes and guidance. The ICO's website is very informative and has detailed guidance, although much of it has still to be updated to reflect the GDPR changes.[144] At the time of writing, the best starting point is the 'Guide to Data Protection', which provides an overview of the new legislation, and the 'Guide to the UK GDPR', which takes you through the detailed rules.[145] The ICO's

---

142 See para 21.48.
143 EU Reg 2016/79.
144 At: https://ico.org.uk.
145 See: https://ico.org.uk/for-organisations/guide-to-data-protection/ introduction-to-data-protection/ and https://ico.org.uk/for-organisations/ guide-to-data-protection/guide-to-the-general-data-protection-regulation-gdpr/.

Employment practices code[146] has not yet been updated and therefore needs to be read very carefully. However, it still contains much good practice. The Code has four parts: Part 1 concerns recruitment and selection; Part 2 concerns employment records; Part 3 concerns monitoring at work; and Part 4 concerns medical information. The Code does not constitute the law, but it provides useful guidelines on how the ICO will interpret the law.

1.70   The data protection rules are detailed and complex. The following is intended only as a summary of the main data protection rules which may be applicable in an employment context. It is advisable to consult the ICO website before taking any action. Note also that the government intends to make amendments in certain areas.

1.71   The DPA 2018 and GDPR provide data protection controls in all fields of life. They contain a lot of jargon which cannot be avoided. The 'data controller' is the person who decides the purposes and means of processing personal data. The 'processor' is the person responsible for actually processing the data on the controller's behalf. In the employment field, the data controller is usually a senior decision-maker and the processor might be someone more junior. The 'data subject', whose rights are protected, may be a job applicant, trainee, existing employee or other worker. 'Processing' data or information includes collecting, recording, storing, using, altering, retrieving, destroying and disseminating data.[147]

Which data is protected

1.72   Data protection law covers personal data stored on automated systems, eg computers, CCTV or telephone logging systems, or paper records filed in an organised way. Unstructured paper records held on individuals by a public authority are an exception and do count as personal data. This is so that the rules on 'freedom of information' can work (see para 1.91 below). However, this information is exempt from most GDPR rules.[148]

1.73   'Personal data' means data related to a worker who can be identified from the data alone or taken together with other information which the employer has. Information which can identify a worker

146 See: https://ico.org.uk/media/for-organisations/documents/1064/the_employment_practices_code.pdf. The ICO has consulted over how to update its guidance to reflect changes in working life over the last few years.
147 GDPR Art 4.
148 DPA 2018 ss21(2) and 24.

could for example be a name, number or an online identifier such as an IP address or cookie identifier.[149] It is not enough that the data simply refers to the worker. It must concern the individual in some way. Relevant factors would be whether the data is directly about the individual or his/her activities; what the data is processed for; and what the effect of processing the data might be on the individual. It would include an expression of opinion about the worker or indication of someone's intentions towards him/her, eg a manager's view on a worker's promotion prospects.[150] There is detailed guidance on what is 'personal data' on the ICO website.[151]

The data protection principles

1.74   At the heart of the GDPR, there are six key data protection principles, with which employers must comply.[152] The controller is responsible for and must be able to demonstrate compliance with these principles. Failure to comply can lead to substantial fines. In summary, the principles are:

1) **Lawfulness, fairness and transparency:** to process personal data fairly, lawfully and transparently. The lawful grounds for processing data are set out below.

2) **Purpose limitation:** to collect the data for specified, explicit and legitimate purposes. The data must not be further processed in a way which is incompatible with those purposes.

3) **Data minimisation:** the data should be adequate, relevant and limited to what is necessary for the purpose.

4) **Accuracy:** data should be kept accurate and up-to-date. Every reasonable step should be taken to erase or update without delay where data is inaccurate. This links to the rights of individuals to have inaccurate data rectified (see para 1.83 below).

5) **Storage limitation:** data from which individuals are identifiable should be kept for no longer than is necessary for its purpose. It can be kept longer, eg for statistical purposes, subject to safeguards. How long an employer should keep data depends on the reason it is needed. The Information Commissioner says employers should

---

149 GDPR Art 4(1).
150 This was the position under DPA 1998 s1(1). *Common Services Agency v Scottish Information Commissioner* [2008] UKHL 47.
151 At: https://ico.org.uk/for-organisations/guide-to-data-protection/guide-to-the-general-data-protection-regulation-gdpr/what-is-personal-data/.
152 GDPR Art 5.

review the information they keep about workers once the workers have left the employment. Employers will need to keep enough information to deal with reference requests and pension, for example, but should delete information they are unlikely to need, such as personal contact details and former addresses. Employers also should not normally keep recruitment applications of unsuccessful candidates past the tribunal time-limits for bringing a claim.

6) **Integrity and confidentiality:** data should be processed in a way which ensures appropriate security of the data including against accidental loss or destruction and unauthorised processing.

1.75   As stated above, the data controller needs to have a lawful basis for processing the data. This must be at least one of the six grounds set out in GDPR Art 6, ie:

a) the worker has given consent to the processing of his/her personal data for one or more specific purposes. The GDPR operates a high standard for consent. Consent must be explicit and entail a positive opt-in. It must also be possible to withdraw easily at any time. Consent must be freely given. This is unlikely to be the case if it is a condition of employment, so a paragraph in the contract of employment stating that the worker has given consent may well not be enough;

b) processing is necessary for the performance of the employment contract, eg bank account information or sickness absence data so that statutory sick pay can be paid;

c) processing is necessary for compliance with a legal obligation of the employer;

d) processing is necessary in order to protect the vital interests of the worker or someone else;

e) processing is necessary for the performance of a task carried out in the public interest;

f) processing is necessary for the purposes of the legitimate interests of the employer or a third party, except where such interests are overridden by a worker's fundamental right to privacy. This does not apply where a public authority is processing data to perform its official tasks.

1.76   Processing of special categories of personal data – ie data revealing racial or ethnic origin, political opinions, religious or philosophical beliefs, trade union membership, sexual orientation or sex life – or the processing of genetic data, biometric data, or data concerning health, is prohibited unless it falls within one of the exceptions in GDPR Art 9. These include:

- where the worker has given explicit consent;
- where processing is necessary for an employer to carry out specific obligations or exercise specific rights;
- where it is necessary to establish, exercise or defend legal claims.

Workers' rights

The right to be informed (privacy information)

1.77　Workers have the right to be informed, at the time that their employer collects personal data from them, of certain privacy information. This includes information as to the identity and contact details of the data controller; the purposes and legal basis for the processing; the recipients or categories of recipients of the data; the period for which data will be stored or criteria used to decide that period; and the existence of any automated decision-making with meaningful information about the logic involved and the significance for the worker. The worker must also be told about his/her right to request access to data, rectification, erasure or restriction of processing, to withdraw consent if the employer was relying on consent, and to complain to a supervisory authority. Employers can put some of this information on their website as long as workers are told of this and it is easily accessible. If personal data is collected from other sources, the worker must be told within a reasonable period and no later than one month later. Certain exemptions apply.

Access to the data

1.78　Workers have a right of access to their own personal data, eg they may ask for their computerised personnel information. The request can be made to anyone in the organisation, and it can be made verbally or in writing. Although employers may, as good practice, have a standard form on which requests can be made, a request is still valid if it is not made on such a form. Such requests are called 'subject access requests' (SARs), but the worker need not use that term. The employer is not generally allowed to charge unless the request is 'manifestly unfounded or excessive', particularly because it is repetitive, in which case the employer can charge a reasonable administrative fee or refuse to act on the request.[153] The information

153 GDPR Art 12.

must be provided without undue delay, and in any event, within one month of the request. This can be extended by two further months if it is necessary because of the complexity and size of request.[154] The information must be provided in a concise, transparent, intelligible and easily accessible form.[155]

1.79   Where the data reveals information about any other individual including an individual who is the source of the information (eg the author of an appraisal or reference), the employer can conceal his/her identity or, if that is impossible, withhold the data. This is the position unless the individual consents or it is reasonable for the employer to dispense with his/her consent.[156] It may be unreasonable of the employer to refuse to dispense with consent where s/he has not even tried to get it. In addition, workers are not entitled to see employment references given or received in confidence by their employer.[157]

1.80   There are other exceptions to the right of access including documents which are legally privileged (ie confidential documents between the employer and legal advisers), and information revealing the employer's intentions in any situation where s/he is negotiating with the worker and revealing the information would be likely to prejudice the negotiations.[158] There is no right to data processed for management planning if it would prejudice the conduct of the business, eg confidential plans regarding future staff reorganisations.[159]

1.81   There are special rules regarding whether data relating to the worker's health needs to be disclosed if it would be likely to cause serious harm to the physical or mental health of the worker or anyone else's.[160]

1.82   It is permitted for employers to disclose personal data to others if it is necessary for the purpose of, or in connection with, actual or prospective legal proceedings or for obtaining legal advice or for establishing, exercising or defending legal rights or because required by a court or tribunal order.[161] This can be important, for example,

---

154 GDPR Art 12.
155 GDPR Art 12.
156 See DPA 2018 Sch 2 Part 3 paras 16–17.
157 DPA 2018 Sch 2 Part 4 para 24.
158 DPA 2018 Sch 2 Part 4 para 23.
159 DPA 2018 Sch 2 Part 4 para 22.
160 DPA 2018 Sch 3 Part 2 para 5; GDPR Art 15.
161 DPA 2018 Sch 2 Part 1 para 5.

where employers use the GDPR and DPA 2018 as a reason not to answer pre-litigation questions.[162]

Correcting inaccurate data

1.83   It is contrary to the 'accuracy' data protection principle to hold inaccurate data (see para 1.70 above). Workers have the right to have inaccurate personal data rectified without undue delay and, taking account of the purpose of the processing, to have incomplete data completed.[163] 'Inaccurate' means incorrect or misleading as to any matter of fact.[164] Opinions are inevitably subjective and are unlikely to count as inaccurate data as long as it is clear that they are opinions. Time limits for dealing with requests are the same as for responding to subject access requests (see para 1.78 above). The fees position is also the same. A worker can ask for the processing of the data to be restricted while its accuracy is being sorted out.[165]

The right to restrict processing or have data erased

1.84   Workers can ask their employer to restrict the processing of their data in certain circumstances, eg where accuracy is being verified when they have contested it (as mentioned in the preceding paragraph) or the employer no longer needs the data for processing purposes but the worker wants it for a legal claim.[166] Workers also have the right to have their personal data erased or 'forgotten' in certain circumstances, eg it has been unlawfully processed or consent was required and the worker withdrew it, or processing is no longer necessary.[167] Even then, the right to erasure does not apply in certain circumstances, eg the data processing is necessary to comply with a legal obligation or for the establishment, exercise or defence of legal claims.

Automated decision-making and profiling

1.85   Workers have the right not to be subject to a decision based solely on automated processing (including profiling) which has legal or similar

---

162 See para 21.49 on this.
163 GDPR Art 16.
164 DPA 2018 s205.
165 GDPR Art 18.
166 GDPR Art 18.
167 GDPR Art 17.

effects, eg e-recruiting decisions without human intervention.[168] This restriction does not apply if the worker gives explicit consent or (except for special category data), if it is authorised by law or necessary for entering or performing the contract of employment. There are various safeguards even when the restriction does not apply, eg that the employer carry out a Data Protection Impact Assessment and individuals must be given certain meaningful information and have the right to contest the decision with human beings. Note that this is an area where the government may change the law.

Criminal records

1.86   As a general rule, employers must not require existing employees or job applicants to supply records of criminal convictions, unless it is in the public interest or required or authorised by law.[169] Where it is proper for employers to know if a worker has a criminal record, they can do so with the worker's consent through the Disclosure and Barring Service (DBS), which has replaced the Criminal Records Bureau (CRB). To avoid employers circumventing the safeguards built into the DBS process, it is a criminal offence in certain circumstances for an employer to require employees or job applicants to use their subject access rights under the GDPR and DPA 2018 to gain access to information about their convictions and cautions and to pass it on to the employer. Details of the DBS are on the GOV.UK website.[170]

Enforcement

1.87   If any of the data protection principles are not complied with, the worker can either go directly to court or approach the Information Commissioner. The rules are set out in Part 6 of the DPA 2018. The ICO has powers to carry out assessments and issue enforcement notices. It can also issue substantial penalty notices.

---

168 GDPR Art 22.
169 See DPA 2018 s184 for precise scope of this.
170 Details of the DBS service are available at: www.gov.uk/government/
     organisations/disclosure-and-barring-service.

Monitoring at work

1.88   Some employers may monitor their workers – eg by CCTV, by opening emails, examining logs of internet websites visited, checking telephone logs for calls to premium lines, and even arranging video evidence outside the workplace to check whether a worker is genuinely sick. It is potentially a breach of the first data principle in the GDPR[171] to carry out this monitoring. In theory it could also breach the Human Rights Act 1998 (see below). However, there does not seem to be an absolute right not to be monitored, especially if the worker has been informed in advance that monitoring will take place. Part 3 of the Data Protection Code concerns monitoring at work and provides useful guidelines, although it does not amount to the law in itself.[172] Also bear in mind that the Code has not, at the time of writing, been updated to incorporate the GDPR and DPA 2018. The Code seeks to balance the rights of workers with the needs of employers.

1.89   The Code stresses that workers have a legitimate expectation to a degree of privacy in the workplace. Monitoring of private information is intrusive and should be avoided if possible. Even a ban on private email and internet use does not in itself allow the employer to access messages that are clearly private. Any monitoring which is carried out should be for a clear purpose and, ideally, justified by an impact assessment. This means the employer should have, formally or informally, weighed up his/her business needs against the adverse impact of monitoring and alternative ways of meeting the needs. Workers should be made aware of the nature, extent and reasons for any monitoring, except in exceptional circumstances where covert monitoring is justified, eg where there are grounds for suspecting criminal activity. The Code notes that continuous video and audio monitoring is particularly intrusive and only justifiable in rare situations, eg where security is a particular issue. Employers should also avoid opening workers' personal emails as this is especially intrusive. Workers should be told if their emails are to be opened and checked in their absence. If workers are to be monitored on their use of telephones, emails and internet, there should be a clear policy as to the permitted use of such systems (eg how much personal use is allowed; what kind of use is prohibited) and the penalties for breaching the policy. For a worker's rights if the GDPR and DPA 2018 are not

---

171 See para 1.70.
172 Available at https://ico.org.uk/media/for-organisations/documents/1064/the_employment_practices_code.pdf.

complied with, see para 1.87. Most employers will not like the prospect of the Information Commissioner investigating their data arrangements. A threat by workers to request a Commissioner assessment may be a useful way to persuade an employer to reduce or abandon the idea of monitoring.

1.90   Article 8 of the European Convention on Human Rights (ECHR) (respect for private and family life) and possibly Article 10 (freedom of expression) may provide protection in some circumstances. Interception of calls made on a worker's office telephone without his/her prior knowledge is a breach of the right to privacy.[173] Covert or even open video surveillance of people in their workplace is a considerable intrusion into their private life and can be a breach of Article 8 unless there is an extremely good reason and appropriate safeguards.[174] Proportionate monitoring or surveillance for disciplinary purposes may or may not be a breach of Article 8, depending on these factors: whether the employer has given advance notification of the monitoring and its nature; the extent of monitoring and the degree of intrusion into the employee's privacy; the employer's justification, which needs to be stronger if the monitoring is particularly intrusive; the consequence of the monitoring for the individual; whether it is possible to devise a less intrusive monitoring system; and whether the employee is provided with adequate safeguards These principles will be relevant in an unfair dismissal case where an employee is dismissed for improper use of telephone, email or internet or on the basis of evidence obtained by surveillance.[175] For the use in ET cases of evidence obtained from covert surveillance, see para 3.25. The law on privacy is a developing area and the above is just a brief introduction.

Freedom of information

1.91   The Freedom of Information Act (FIA) 2000 and the Freedom of Information (Scotland) Act (FI(S)A) 2002 came into effect on

---

173 *Halford v United Kingdom* [1997] IRLR 471, ECtHR.

174 Some key cases in the ECtHR are *López Ribalda and others v Spain* App Nos 1874/13 and 8567/13, [2020] IRLR 60, ECtHR; *Antovic and Mirkovic v Montenegro* App No 70838/13, ECtHR, available at: https://hudoc.echr.coe.int/eng#{%22fulltext%22:[%22antovic%22],%22documentcollectionid2%22:[%22GRANDCHAMBER%22,%22CHAMBER%22],%22itemid%22:[%22001-178904%22]}; *Barbulescu v Romania* App No 61496/08, Grand Chamber, ECtHR; [2017] IRLR 1032.

175 See para 7.69.

1 January 2005. The FIA 2000 applies to public authorities in England, Wales and Northern Ireland, UK government departments, parliament and the Welsh and Northern Ireland assemblies. The FI(S)A 2002 applies to Scottish public authorities, the Scottish Executive and Scottish Parliament. It is similar to the FIA 2000, but gives slightly better rights.

1.92 FIA 2000 Sch 1 lists the public authorities to which it applies and this list is updated every October. Some authorities are listed by category and others are precisely described. The list includes central and local government, the health sector, the education sector, the Employment Tribunals Service (ETS) and the police. The UK Information Commissioner has produced very useful guidance notes on her website[176] and the Scottish Information Commissioner also has a helpful site.[177] There is also interesting information on the website of the Campaign for Freedom of Information.[178]

1.93 Under FIA 2000 s19, all public authorities must produce a publication scheme, which sets out what kinds of information the public authority will proactively make available, how it can be accessed and the cost. Very often these schemes are published on the authorities' websites. The scheme must be approved by the Information Commissioner.

1.94 A member of the public can request any information held by the public authority,[179] whether or not it appears on the published scheme. 'Information' is wider than 'data' covered by the DPA 2018 and GDPR. It covers information which is recorded in any form, including paper records, handwritten notes, computer information and information on audio cassettes and videos. Information which is purely in the knowledge of the authority but unrecorded is not covered.

1.95 A request should be in writing, state clearly what information is required, and state the name of the applicant and an address for correspondence.[180] The request should be sent to someone appropriate, eg the authority's freedom of information officer, if it has one, or the chief executive. The authority must respond as soon as possible and no later than 20 working days after receiving the request.[181] The

---

176 See www.ico.org.uk.
177 See www.itspublicknowledge.info/home/AboutSIC/AboutCommissioner. aspx.
178 See www.cfoi.org.uk.
179 FIA 2000 s1 gives the general right of access.
180 FIA 2000 s8.
181 FIA 2000 s10.

response must either provide the information or explain why it has not been provided, quoting an exemption under the FIA 2000.

1.96   There are two categories of exempt information: information which is absolutely exempt and information which is exempt if the authority can prove the public interest in keeping it exempt is greater than the public interest in its disclosure. Absolute exemptions include information contained only in court documents, personal data about the applicant (because there is a right of access under the DPA 2018 and GDPR) or about another individual, if disclosure would breach the DPA 2018 and GDPR, and information whose disclosure would be a breach of confidence at common law. Public interest exemptions include information covered by legal professional privilege and information whose disclosure is likely to prejudice commercial interests. It is advisable to look at the full list of exemptions before making a request.[182]

1.97   Broadly speaking, the authority may charge a fee of £25 per hour, but it cannot charge (except for photocopying and post) for requests costing less than £450 to answer (£600 for requests to central government). If it costs more than these figures to search out the information, the authority can either charge or refuse to supply the information altogether.[183] In Scotland, the maximum fee is £15/hour with no charge at all for the first £100 and thereafter only ten per cent of charges over £100 and up to £600.[184]

1.98   If a request is refused, it is possible to apply for an internal review of the decision (reviews are compulsory only in Scotland). If the review also fails, the Information Commissioner can be asked to review the decision.

1.99   Workers or trade unions may be able to use freedom of information requests to get information from public authorities which they cannot get in any other way. The FIA 2000 does not place restrictions on how the information supplied under it may be used, although certain types of confidential information may be exempt from disclosure. However, if the information sought by the worker concerns him /herself, s/he must apply under the DPA 2018 and GDPR, which involves a different procedure.[185]

---

182 FIA 2000 Part II.
183 FIA 2000 s12. For ICO guidance on fees see https://ico.org.uk/for-organisations/guide-to-freedom-of-information/refusing-a-request/.
184 For details of possible charges in Scotland, see: www.itspublicknowledge.info/Law/FOISA-EIRsGuidance/Fees_and_charging/ChargingFOISA.aspx.
185 See para 1.75.

Collective consultation and trade union rights

Chapter 2: Key points

- It is unlawful to subject a worker to a detriment including dismissal for joining or not joining a trade union or participating in trade union activities in various ways.
- A worker must not be offered an inducement to join or not join a trade union or to surrender trade union rights.
- It is unlawful to compile or sell a blacklist of people who are or have been trade union members or involved in trade union activities. Individuals can bring claims if they are discriminated against as a result of such a list.
- Trade union officials, learning representatives and members are entitled to time off for trade union duties or activities in strictly defined circumstances.
- An employer must inform and consult the trade union or, if none, employee representatives, when proposing to make redundant or substantially change the terms and conditions of 20 or more employees.
- An employer must inform and consult the trade union or, if none, employee representatives, prior to a transfer of an undertaking.
- The Information and Consultation of Employees Regulations cover wider areas of consultation with employees.
- Under these regulations, employers with at least 50 employees must set up an information and consultation mechanism if requested by two per cent of employees.

Inducements related to trade union membership

2.1   It is unlawful for an employer to make a worker an offer for the purpose of inducing him/her to become or not to become a trade union member, or not to take part in trade union activities or, as a trade union member, not to use its services at an appropriate time.[1] This includes a member consenting to a trade union raising a matter on his/her behalf. It is also unlawful for an employer to make offers which, if accepted, would mean that the worker's terms of employment, or any of those terms, will not or will no longer be

---

1 Trade Union and Labour Relations (Consolidation) Act (TULR(C)A) 1992 s145A.

determined by collective agreement negotiated by the union, where that is the employer's sole or main purpose.[2]

2.2   Before the introduction of this legislation, the House of Lords had said it was lawful for an employer to offer pay increases only to staff who agree to sign personal contracts and relinquish their right to union representation in pay negotiations.[3] However, the European Court of Human Rights (ECtHR) said that, by allowing employers to use financial incentives to induce employees to surrender important union rights, the UK was in breach of Article 11 of the European Convention on Human Rights (ECHR).[4] The ECtHR said it is the essence of the right to join a trade union that employees should be free to instruct or permit the union to make representations to their employers or take action in support of their interests on their behalf. If workers are prevented from doing so, their freedom to belong to a union for the protection of their interests becomes illusory. As a result of this case, the government made the above changes to the law in 2004.

Detriment or dismissal for trade union reasons

Overview

2.3   It is unlawful to refuse a person employment because s/he is or is not a trade union member. This includes the way s/he manifests his/her membership, ie his/her trade union activities.[5] In addition, it is unlawful for an employer to subject a worker to a detriment including dismissal or to fail to confer a benefit which would otherwise be conferred, because of the worker's refusal to accept an inducement as set out in para 2.1. It is also unlawful to subject a worker to a detriment by any act or deliberate failure to act for the purpose of:

---

2   TULR(C)A 1992 s145B. For how to interpret this, see *Kostal UK Ltd v Dunkley and others* [2021] UKSC 47. NB the time limit runs from the offer, eg an offer letter, not from any later letter simply imposing changed terms: *Scottish Borders Housing Association Limited v Caldwell* EA-2020-SCO-000084-SH.

3   *Wilson v Associated Newspapers; Palmer v Associated British Ports* [1995] IRLR 258, HL.

4   *Wilson and National Union of Journalists v United Kingdom; Palmer, Wyeth and National Union of Rail, Maritime and Transport Workers v United Kingdom; Doolan and others v United Kingdom* [2002] IRLR 568, ECtHR.

5   TULR(C)A 1992 s137(1); *Jet2.com Ltd v Denby* UKEAT/0070/17; [2018] IRLR 417, EAT.

- preventing or deterring the worker from being or seeking to become a member of a trade union, or penalising him/her for doing so;[6]
- preventing or deterring the worker from taking part in the activities of a trade union at an appropriate time, or penalising him/her for doing so;[7]
- preventing or deterring the worker from making use of the services of his/her trade union at an appropriate time, or penalising him/her for doing so;[8]
- compelling the worker to become a member of a trade union or a particular trade union.[9]

2.4   Where the worker is an employee, it is automatically unfair to dismiss him/her or select him/her for redundancy if the sole or principal reason for dismissal is that the employee:

- was or proposed to become a member of a trade union;[10]
- had taken part in or proposed to take part in the activities of a trade union at an appropriate time;[11]
- had made use of or proposed to make use of his/her trade union's services at an appropriate time, including giving consent to the union to raise a matter on his/her behalf, or the trade union raised a matter on his/her behalf with or without his/her consent;[12]
- had refused to accept an inducement as set out at para 2.1.[13]

2.5   There is only protection for activities which the worker did, or services which s/he used, at the 'appropriate time'. Appropriate time is defined as a time which is either outside a worker's working hours or is within hours at a time which, in accordance with arrangements agreed with, or consent given by, the employer, it is permissible for the worker to take part in union activities.[14] Working hours are those hours which the worker is contractually required to be at work. Lunch and tea breaks are usually outside working hours.[15]

---

6   TULR(C)A 1992 s146(1)(a).
7   TULR(C)A 1992 s146(1)(b).
8   TULR(C)A 1992 s146(1)(ba).
9   TULR(C)A 1992 s146(1)(c).
10   TULR(C)A 1992 s152(1)(a).
11   TULR(C)A 1992 s152(1)(b).
12   TULR(C)A 1992 s152(1)(ba) and (2B).
13   TULR(C)A 1992 s152(1)(bb).
14   TULR(C)A 1992 ss152(2) and 146(2).
15   *Post Office v Union of Post Office Workers and another* [1974] ICR 378, HL.

2.6   The protection on taking part in the activities of an independent trade union applies even if the union is not recognised. The type of protected activity depends on whether it is a union official or ordinary member claiming the protection. Both officials and members would need to be acting within union rules and approved practices for their role. Depending on their role, protected activities could be recruitment and organisation, acting or being involved in grievances and complaints,[16] meetings and voting, and organising industrial action.[17] See below as regards actually participating in industrial action.

2.7   Employers sometimes try to argue that the reason for dismissal is not that the worker was carrying out trade union activities but the way s/he was carrying them out. This is a dangerous distinction which could in theory undermine the protection. However, the way trade union activities are carried out is not relevant to whether they are in fact trade union activities, unless the way they are carried out is dishonest or in bad faith or for some extraneous cause.[18] So the normal rhetoric and hyperbole one would expect when a union tries to recruit should fall within the scope of 'activities'. On the other hand, the contents of a speech made at a trade union recruiting meeting could fall outside the term 'trade union activities' if they were malicious, untruthful or irrelevant to the task in hand.

Industrial action

2.8   There are special rules regarding whether a worker dismissed while taking industrial action can claim unfair dismissal.[19] In addition, under TULR(C)A 1992 s146, a worker must not be subjected to a detriment for taking part in industrial action – or in order to prevent or deter him/her from doing so. This includes action during working hours. It

---

16 *Brennan and Ging v Ellward (Lancs) Ltd* [1976] IRLR 378, EAT. See also special rules on the right to representation at para 22.39 onwards.

17 *Britool Ltd v Roberts and others* [1993] IRLR 481, EAT. But see *Crowther v British Railways Board* EAT 762/95. See also para 6.90 for health and safety representatives.

18 *Bass Taverns Ltd v Burgess* [1995] IRLR 596, CA; *Mihaj v Sodexho Ltd* UKEAT/0139/14; *Morris v Metrolink RATP Dev Ltd* [2018] EWCA Civ 1358; [2018] IRLR 853.

19 See paras 6.126–6.129 regarding TULR(C)A 1992 s238A.

would cover, for example, the employer taking disciplinary action; however, an employer still need not pay a worker for days on strike.[20]

Time off for trade union duties and activities

Officials

2.9   Regard must be had to the revised Advisory, Conciliation and Arbitration Service (ACAS) *Code of Practice 3 on time off for trade union duties and activities* (2010), which aims to aid and improve the effectiveness of relationships between employers and trade unions. The Code of Practice may be taken into account by employment tribunals (ETs) when considering a claim which concerns the subject matter of the Code.[21] ACAS has also produced a non-statutory guide – *Trade union representation in the workplace*. The Code and the guide are available via links on the ACAS website.[22]

2.10   An employer must allow an employee who is an official of an independent trade union to take paid time off during working hours to carry out his/her union duties.[23] The duties are:[24]

- negotiations connected with collective bargaining matters set out in TULR(C)A 1992 s178(2) in respect of which the union is recognised;
- the performance on behalf of employees of functions related to the collective bargaining matters set out in section 178(2) which the employer has agreed may be so performed by the union;
- receipt of information and consultation for collective redundancies or the Transfer of Undertakings (Protection of Employment) Regulations (TUPE Regs) 2006.[25]

---

20   This is based on an interpretation and slight extension of TULR(C)A 1992 s146(1)(b) to comply with ECHR Article 11. See *Mercer v (1) Alternative Future Group Limited (2) Pritchard – and – Secretary of State for Business, Energy & Industrial Strategy (Intervener)* UKEAT/0196/20; [2021] IRLR 620 for its precise scope. See also *Ryanair DAC v Morais and others* EA-2021-000275 regarding whether this is confined to 'protected' industrial action as in TULR(C)A 1992 s238A.

21   TULR(C)A 1992 ss168 and 170.

22   At: www.acas.org.uk/acas-code-of-practice-on-time-off-for-trade-union-duties-and-activities and www.acas.org.uk/acas-guides-on-trade-union-and-employee-representation.

23   TULR(C)A 1992 ss168–169.

24   TULR(C)A 1992 s168.

25   SI No 246.

The matters set out in TULR(C)A 1992 s178(2) include terms and conditions or physical conditions of employment; disciplinary issues; work allocation; trade union membership and facilities; machinery for negotiation, consultation and other procedures. Para 13 of the ACAS Code gives guidance on the scope of these.

2.11 Employers must also allow a trade union official paid time off for industrial relations training[26] relevant to carrying out his/her duties.[27] This training must be approved by the Trades Union Congress (TUC) or by the official's own trade union.[28] Section 2 of the ACAS Code provides further guidance as to the type of training covered.

2.12 The amount of time off for duties or training must be reasonable in all the circumstances. The ACAS Code provides guidance as to what is reasonable. Regard must be had to the size of the organisation, the production process, the need to maintain a public service, and safety considerations. The test is objective and requires the balancing of the competing interests of both parties.[29]

2.13 Where time off is given during working hours the employee is entitled to be paid and the employer cannot allow time off if the employee agrees it will not be paid.[30]

2.14 Note also that the Employment Relations Act (ERelA) 1999 entitles a worker, where there is a reasonable request, to be accompanied by a work colleague or trade union official at disciplinary and grievance hearings.[31] The companion must be allowed reasonable paid time off during working hours to attend the hearing.[32] A trade union official must be certified by the union as being capable of acting as a worker's companion.

Members

2.15 An employee who is a member of a recognised independent trade union is entitled to a reasonable amount of unpaid time off to take part in any activities of the union or activities in relation to which s/he is acting as a representative of the union.[33] Section 3 of the ACAS Code gives examples of union activities, eg meeting and voting on the

26 TULR(C)A 1992 s168.
27 TULR(C)A 1992 s168(2).
28 TULR(C)A 1992 s168(2).
29 *Chloride Silent Power Ltd v Cash* EAT 95/86.
30 *Beecham Group Ltd v Beal* [1983] IRLR 317, EAT.
31 ERelA 1999 ss10–15, particularly s10(7). See also paras 22.39–22.42.
32 ERelA 1999 s10(6)–(7). See para 22.40.
33 TULR(C)A 1992 s170(1).

outcome of negotiations with the employer; meeting full-time officials to discuss workplace issues; voting in strike ballots and union elections; representation at the union's annual conference or regional committees. Industrial action is excluded.[34]

Remedies

2.16   An employee can complain to an ET about the failure to permit time off for trade union duties or activities, or, in the case of trade union duties, failure to pay for any time off which is permitted.[35] The claim must be presented within three months of the refusal or failure to pay.[36] Where there has been a failure to give time off, the ET can award compensation which it considers just and equitable.[37]

Time off for union learning representatives

2.17   Employees who are members of an independent trade union recognised by the employer can take reasonable paid time off to undertake the duties of a union learning representative, provided the union has given the employer written notice that the employee is a learning representative and has undergone sufficient training for the role.[38] Activities covered include providing information and advice about learning or training matters and analysing needs, promoting the value of training and learning, arranging it and consulting with the employer. Learning representatives are also allowed reasonable paid time off to undergo training relevant to their functions.[39] The ACAS Code[40] gives further guidance.

Blacklisting of trade unionists

2.18   After long delays, legislation outlawing blacklisting of trade unionists was at last passed in 2010 by the Employment Relations Act 1999

---

34   TULR(C)A 1992 s170(2).
35   TULR(C)A 1992 ss168(4), 170(4) and 169(5).
36   TULR(C)A 1992 s171.
37   TULR(C)A 1992 s172(2).
38   TULR(C)A 1992 ss168A and 170.
39   TULR(C)A 1992 s169.
40   See para 2.9.

(Blacklists) Regulations 2010.[41] The Department for Business, Innovation and Skills (now the Department for Business, Energy & Industrial Strategy (BEIS)) issued guidance, though this has no special legal status, *The blacklisting of trade unionists.*[42]

2.19   The regulations make it unlawful to compile, use, sell or supply a 'prohibited list'. A 'prohibited list' is a list which contains details of people who are or have been members of trade unions or people who are taking part or have taken part in trade union activities, eg by attending union meetings, writing for a union newsletter, standing for office or participating in official industrial action. The list must have been compiled with a view to being used by employers or employment agencies for the purposes of discrimination on grounds of trade union membership or activities in relation to recruitment or the treatment of workers.

2.20   An individual can bring an ET case if an employer dismisses him/her or refuses to employ him/her or subjects him/her to some other detriment for a reason related to a prohibited list, eg because the employer has found out that s/he is a trade union member. Cases can also be brought against employment agencies for refusing their services for that reason. Cases must be brought within three months of the action complained of, or later, if it is just and equitable to do so. The rules are a little complicated and should be checked regarding compensation limits according to whether the claimant is a worker or an employee and whether the claim concerns detriment or dismissal.

The statutory duty to consult in respect of collective redundancy dismissals

2.21   TULR(C)A 1992 ss188–198 contain rules regarding consultation with trade union or employee representatives where redundancies of 20 or more employees are proposed. The relevant sections in TULR(C)A 1992 are intended to implement the Collective Redundancies Directive.[43]

2.22   Certain employees are completely excluded, eg those in Crown employment (working in a government department, etc), the police

---

41   SI No 493.

42   March 2010, available at: www.gov.uk/government/uploads/system/uploads/attachment_data/file/252698/10-773-blacklisting-guidance.pdf.

43   98/59/EC consolidating previous directives.

and the army.[44] Employees on fixed-term contracts are no longer included within the redundancy consultation requirements unless it is proposed to cut short their contracts as opposed to simply not renewing them when they expire.[45] Redundancy in this context includes dismissals for any reason not related to the individuals concerned, eg reorganisation or in order to harmonise terms and conditions, as opposed to dismissals for redundancy in the normal sense (as in paras 8.2–8.8).[46] Therefore, consultation is required where the employer proposes to vary employees' contracts in order to offer new contracts on different terms.[47] It will also be required where the proposal is to redeploy staff following redundancy on substantially different contracts.[48] Where there is a simultaneous TUPE transfer, the TUPE consultation rules also apply (see para 2.31 onwards). In addition, a prospective transferee who proposes redundancies can start redundancy consultation before the transfer takes place if it gives a written notice to the transferor and the transferor agrees.[49]

2.23 Consultation must take place with the appropriate representatives of any employees who may be affected by the proposed dismissals or by measures taken in connection with those dismissals.[50] This means the representatives of the recognised trade union, or if there is none, correctly elected employee representatives.[51] Affected employees could include employees who are not going to be made redundant, but who may experience a change in their working conditions as a result of the redundancies. There are rules covering the position where there is no trade union and employee representatives have not been elected.[52]

2.24 The duty arises when an employer is proposing to dismiss as redundant 20 or more employees at one establishment within a period of 90 days or less.[53] Volunteers who were selected for redund-

---

44 TULR(C)A 1992 ss273, 280, 274 and 282 respectively.

45 TULR(C)A 1992 s282.

46 TULR(C)A 1992 s195(1); *GMB v Man Truck & Bus UK Ltd* [2000] IRLR 636, EAT.

47 *GMB v Man Truck & Bus UK Ltd* [2000] IRLR 636, EAT; *TGWU v Manchester Airport plc* (2005) 755 IRLB 16, EAT.

48 *Hardy v Tourism South East* [2005] IRLR 242, EAT.

49 TULR(C)A 1992 ss198A–198B, introduced in January 2014.

50 TULR(C)A 1992 s188(1).

51 TULR(C)A 1992 ss188(1B) and 188A(1).

52 See TULR(C)A 1992 ss188, 188A and 189.

53 TULR(C)A 1992 s188(1).

ancy can be counted in.[54] There is no precise legal definition of what an 'establishment' under TULR(C)A 1992 is, but it can be (and often is) something less than the whole organisation.[55] Employers sometimes try to avoid their consultation obligations by claiming that the employees are spread across several establishments, arguing that different buildings, departments or even floors are separate establishments. The Court of Justice of the European Union (CJEU) has given some general guidance in a few cases:

- Essentially, an 'establishment' is the unit to which the employees to be made redundant were assigned to carry out their duties.
- An establishment need not have any legal, economic, financial, administrative or technological autonomy, or even geographical separation. Nor does it need to have a management that can independently choose to make collective redundancies. It may be enough if, for example, it is a distinct entity with a certain degree of permanence and stability, which is assigned to perform one or more given tasks and which has a workforce, technical means and a certain organisational structure allowing for the accomplishment of those tasks.[56]
- Each case should be looked at on its facts and tribunals are likely to make findings which encourage consultation.
- Although not essential, geographical separation, permanence, exclusivity of employees, and managerial and administrative independence are still relevant factors.
- An individual's place of work may be the best guide, but not in the sense of a particular office or even a particular building, but a wider idea of workplace, eg a group of buildings or a factory complex.[57] A useful rule of thumb may be what an employee would say if asked where s/he works. For example, the 'establishment' in which a university laboratory assistant works may well be the particular campus where s/he is located, and for a teacher, a school within the area of an education authority may well be an

---

54 *Optare Group Ltd v Transport and General Workers Union* UKEAT/0143/07; [2007] IRLR 931, EAT.

55 *USDAW and another v WW Realisation 1 Ltd, in liquidation, Ethel Austin Ltd and Secretary of State for Business, Innovation and Skills; Lyttle and others v Bluebird UK Bidco 2 Limited; Rabal Cañas v Nexea Gestión Documental SA and another* Case C-80/14, Case C-182/13, Case C-392/13, [2015] IRLR 577, CJEU.

56 *Rockfon A/S v Special arbejderforbunet i Danmark, acting for Nielsen and others* [1996] IRLR 168, CJEU; *Athinaiki Chartopoiia AE v Panagiotidis and others* Case C-270/05, [2007] IRLR 284 CJEU.

57 *City of Edinburgh Council v Wilkinson* [2011] CSIH 70; [2012] IRLR 202 on the meaning of 'establishment' in equal pay legislation.

establishment in itself. The fact that the education authority holds certain central management powers over its schools does not mean that any given school is not a separate 'establishment'.

- It is inevitable – and therefore not necessarily significant – that an organisation retains some central powers over its various establishments.[58] It does not stop a place being an independent establishment that the employees employed there have mobility clauses in their contracts. On the other hand, if staff are peripatetic, eg music and drama staff employed by a council to visit and carry out their duties at several schools, the 'establishment' may be wider, such as the council's education and leisure service.

2.25   Consultation must begin in good time and in any event, where the employer is 'proposing' to dismiss 100 or more employees, at least 45 days before the first dismissals take effect; where the employer is proposing to dismiss at least 20 but fewer than 100 employees, then at least 30 days before.[59] The period of 45 days was reduced from a period of 90 days by the coalition government in April 2013. A dismissal takes effect in this context when notice is given.[60] The obligation to consult does not start when an employer is simply thinking about the possibility of redundancies. The employer must have a fixed, clear, albeit provisional intention to make redundancies.[61] Consultation must also be completed before notice of any dismissal is given.[62]

2.26   Consultation is supposed to be with a view to reaching agreement.[63] This means negotiation.[64] It is strongly arguable that for meaningful consultation to take place, it should start as early as possible. Employers do not need to consult on the economic decisions forming the background to redundancies, eg decisions to close certain branches of a chain.[65] However, where the closure decision

---

58   *City of Edinburgh Council v Wilkinson* [2011] CSIH 70; [2012] IRLR 202; *Renfrewshire Council v The Educational Institute of Scotland* UKEATS/0018/12; [2013] IRLR 76, EAT. Both these cases should be read for their guidance.

59   TULR(C)A 1992 s188(1A).

60   *Junk v Kühnel* [2005] IRLR 310, ECJ.

61   *UK Coal Mining Ltd v National Union of Mineworkers* [2008] IRLR 4, EAT. See also *Keeping Kids Company (in compulsory liquidation) v Smith* UKEAT/0057/17; [2018] IRLR 484, EAT, Arguably the wording of the Collective Redundancies Directive 98/59/EC means the obligation starts sooner, when the employer 'contemplates' redundancies, but more recent UK and CJEU case-law suggests there is little difference.

62   *Junk v Kühnel* [2005] IRLR 310, ECJ.

63   TULR(C)A 1992 s188(2).

64   *Junk v Kühnel* [2005] IRLR 310, ECJ.

65   *Securicor Omega Express Ltd v GMB* [2004] IRLR 9, EAT.

would inevitably lead to redundancies, that might be different.[66] In the *Nolan* case, the Court of Appeal asked the CJEU to clarify whether the Collective Redundancies Directive requires an employer to consult over a strategic decision which will inevitably lead to redundancies, or only once such a decision has been made.[67] Unfortunately, the CJEU was unable to decide the case because the directive does not apply to the dismissal of staff from a military base, which is what happened in *Nolan*. At some point, the UK courts will have to make a decision, but currently it is unresolved.[68]

2.27   Consultation must at least cover ways of avoiding or reducing the numbers of dismissals and mitigating the consequences of the dismissals.[69] To be meaningful, it should take place when the proposals are still at a formative stage; the representatives must have sufficient information and adequate time in which to respond; and the employer must give conscientious consideration to the response.[70] However, the employer cannot be forced to agree with the representatives or change any plans. Employers must ensure consultation covers the topics required. It is not enough simply to provide the opportunity to consult.[71]

2.28   For the purposes of consultation, the employer must disclose in writing to the representatives:

- the reason for the redundancy proposals;
- the numbers and descriptions of the workers whom it is proposed to dismiss as redundant;
- the total number of workers employed at the establishment in question;
- the proposed method of selection; the manner in which the dismissals are to be carried out; and
- the proposed method of calculating the redundancy payments.

---

66 *UK Coal Mining Ltd v National Union of Mineworkers (Northumberland Area) and another* UKEAT/0397/06 and 0141/07; [2008] IRLR 4, EAT.

67 *USA v Nolan* [2010] EWCA Civ 1223 and [2012] IRLR 1020, CJEU, as to the meaning of *Akavan Erityisalojen Keskusliitto Alek RY and others v Fujitsu Siemens Computers OY* [2009] IRLR 944, ECJ.

68 The Court of Appeal held the matter over when the case returned to it: [2014] IRLR 302, CA.

69 TULR(C)A 1992 s188(2); *Middlesbrough BC v TGWU and another* [2002] IRLR 332, EAT.

70 *R v British Coal Corporation and Secretary of State for Trade and Industry ex p Price* [1994] IRLR 72, DC; *Middlesbrough BC v TGWU and another* [2002] IRLR 332, EAT; *TGWU v Ledbury Preserves (1928) Ltd* [1986] IRLR 492, EAT.

71 *(1) Kelly (2) Jackson v The Hesley Group Ltd* UKEAT/0339/12.

The employer must also disclose:

• the number of temporary agency workers under its supervision and direction;
• the parts of its undertaking where they are working; and
• the type of work they are carrying out.[72]

Where there is no trade union and the employees have failed to elect representatives after being invited to do so, the employer must give each affected employee this information.[73] The obligation to consult does not wait until the employer is able to supply all the required information; flexibility is essential, and the employer can and must add information as it arises during the consultation process.[74]

2.29   The employer must also give BEIS written notification of his/her proposal to make 20 or more employees redundant at least 30 days before, and 100 or more employees redundant at least 45 days before.[75] The employer must give copies of the notice to the trade union or employee representatives. Failure to notify is a criminal offence.

2.30   Employers are excused from the duty to consult or provide information only in special circumstances, eg a very sudden disaster. However, tribunals are unlikely to consider it special circumstances where there have been financial difficulties over a long period, or where redundancies would seem to be inevitable. Even if special circumstances exist, the employer must still do as much as is reasonably practicable.[76]

Collective consultation on TUPE transfers

2.31   The employer's duty to consult on a transfer is similar, although not identical, to the duty to consult on mass redundancies. The EC Business Transfers Directive[77] is implemented by the TUPE Regs 2006.[78]

---

72 TULR(C)A 1992 s188(4).
73 TULR(C)A 1992 s188(7B).
74 *Akavan Erityisalojen Keskusliitto Alek RY and others v Fujitsu Siemens Computers OY* [2009] IRLR 944, ECJ.
75 TULR(C)A 1992 s193.
76 TULR(C)A 1992 s188(7).
77 Now EC Directive 2001/23 consolidating previous directives.
78 Transfer of Undertakings (Protection of Employment) Regulations (TUPE Regs) 2006 – see chapter 10 on TUPE Regs 2006 generally.

2.32   The employer of any affected employees must inform and consult 'appropriate representatives'. The affected employees may be those of the transferor or transferee, whether or not employed in the undertaking to be transferred, who may be affected in some way by the transfer or measures taken in connection with it.[79] The appropriate representatives are either the trade union or, if there is none, correctly elected employee representatives.[80] If the employees fail to elect any representatives within a reasonable time, the employer must give each affected employee the relevant information.[81] Where the employer has fewer than ten employees, there are no appropriate representatives and the employer has not invited employees to elect employee representatives, the employer can comply with his/her obligations by treating each affected employee as if s/he were an appropriate representative.[82]

2.33   The employer must provide the following information long enough before the transfer occurs to enable consultation to take place:[83]

- the fact of the transfer, its approximate date and the reasons for it;
- the legal, economic and social implications of the transfer for the affected employees; the legal implications need not be correct as long as the employer expresses a genuinely held view and doesn't just shut his/her eyes to the legal implications (though it is unlikely to excuse a complete failure to inform or consult that an employer genuinely believes TUPE does not apply);[84]
- whether the employer envisages taking measures in relation to the affected employees and if so, what these are;
- if the employer is the transferor, s/he must also pass on any measures which the transferee envisages. The transferee must give the transferor this information.[85]

---

79 TUPE Regs 2006 reg 13(1).
80 TUPE Regs 2006 regs 13(2) and (3) and 10A.
81 TUPE Regs 2006 reg 13(11); *Howard v Millrise t/a Colourflow (in liquidation) and another* [2005] IRLR 84, EAT; *Hickling t/a Imperial Day Nursery and others v Marshall* UKEAT/0217/10.
82 TUPE Regs 2006 reg 13A, for transfers on or after 31 July 2014.
83 TUPE Regs 2006 reg 13(2).
84 *Royal Mail Group Ltd v Communication Workers Union* [2009] EWCA Civ 1045; [2009] IRLR 1046.
85 TUPE Regs 2006 reg 13(2)(d) and (4).

The above information must include suitable information regarding the use of temporary agency workers, ie the number working for the employer, the kind of work they are doing and where.[86]

2.34   The obligation to inform is wider than the obligation to consult. There is no obligation on employers to consult with regard to the fact and reasons for the transfer. However, if employers envisage they will take measures in connection with the transfer, they must consult with a view to seeking the representatives' agreement. 'Measures' can involve administrative arrangements or anything else done which is not simply an inevitable consequence of the transfer.[87] For example, an arrangement by the transferor to make a payment in lieu of accrued holiday or a change of pay date would be a 'measure', whereas the mere fact that the transferee would now be paying wages as opposed to the transferor would not. It is unnecessary for a 'measure' to be one which would cause the employees any disadvantage.[88]

2.35   Employers should consider and reply to any representations made by the representatives, giving reasons if they reject the suggestions.[89] It appears that there is no duty on the transferee to consult with the transferred employees after the transfer, which does seem to undermine the duty to consult.[90] Note that the obligation to inform exists even if there will never be an obligation to consult because the employer does not envisage taking any measures.[91] Moreover, the information must still be provided sufficiently well in advance for any voluntary consultation to take place.[92]

2.36   As with redundancy consultation, delay or failure to consult can only be justified in special circumstances, which will be hard for the employer to prove.[93]

---

86   TUPE Regs 2006 reg 13(2A).
87   *Todd v (1) Strain and others (2) Care Concern GB Ltd (3) Dillon and others* UKEATS/0057/09; [2011] IRLR 11.
88   *Todd v (1) Strain and others (2) Care Concern GB Ltd (3) Dillon and others* UKEATS/0057/09; [2011] IRLR 11.
89   TUPE Regs 2006 reg 13(6) and (7).
90   *UCATT v AMICUS and others* UKEATS/0007/08 and *AMICUS and others v UCATT and others* UKEATS/0014/08.
91   *Todd v (1) Strain and others (2) Care Concern GB Ltd (3) Dillon and others* UKEATS/0057/09; [2011] IRLR 11; *Cable Realisations Ltd v GMB Northern* [2010] IRLR 42, EAT.
92   *Cable Realisations Ltd v GMB Northern* [2010] IRLR 42, EAT.
93   TUPE Regs 2006 reg 13(9); *Clarks of Hove v Bakers' Union* [1979] 1 All ER 152.

Remedies for failure to consult on redundancies or transfers

2.37 If the employer fails to inform or consult, the remedy is to complain to an ET. If the appropriate representative is the trade union, then the complaint is made by the trade union, and otherwise, by the employees' representative.[94] The remedy is in two stages. The first stage is a declaration that the employer has failed to consult and an ET may award compensation to each affected employee.[95] The second stage applies if the employer fails to pay, in which case the individual employee must apply to an ET.[96] Where there is no trade union, if the employer has failed to take the correct steps in relation to the election of employee representatives, an individual employee can claim compensation for failure to inform or consult.[97]

2.38 Where an ET declares that there has been inadequate consultation on collective redundancies, it can make a protective award, ordering the employer to pay remuneration to individual employees for the protected period. This period starts when the first dismissal takes effect (or the date of the ET award if earlier), and lasts for as long as the ET thinks just and equitable having regard to the seriousness of the employer's default. It cannot exceed 90 days' pay.[98] There are a few circumstances in which an award cannot be made, eg for unreasonably refusing an offer of suitable alternative employment by the employer.[99] The purpose of the award is to ensure consultation takes place, and not to compensate individual workers. In deciding how much to award, the emphasis is therefore on the extent of the

94 TULR(C)A 1992 s189(2); TUPE Regs 2006 reg 15(1). An individual cannot claim on behalf of other redundant employees – *Independent Insurance Co Ltd (in provisional liquidation) v (1) Aspinall (2) O'Callaghan* UKEAT/0051/11.

95 TULR(C)A 1992 s189(2); TUPE Regs 2006 reg 15(7)–(9).

96 TULR(C)A 1992 s192; TUPE Regs 2006 reg 15(10). Recoupment will apply to the redundancy protective award if the employee needs to claim under s192 because of non-payment by the employer: Employment Protection (Recoupment of Jobseeker's Allowance and Income Support) Regulations 1996 SI No 2349.

97 TULR(C)A 1992 s189(1)(a); TUPE Regs 2006 reg 15(1)(a). *Hickling t/a Imperial Day Nursery and others v Marshall* UKEAT/0217/10. An individual cannot claim on behalf of other redundant employees – *Independent Insurance Co Ltd (in provisional liquidation) v (1) Aspinall (2) O'Callaghan* UKEAT/00512/11.

98 TULR(C)A 1992 ss189(4) and 190. This is calculated in accordance with ERA 1996 s220: TULR(C)A 1992 s190(2) and (5). Strangely, the 90-day maximum protective award was not reduced to 45 at the same time as the reduction in the consultation period.

99 See TULR(C)A 1992 s190(4) and (6) and s191 for the exceptions.

employer's failure to consult, whether it was deliberate and whether legal advice was available.[100] Where there has been no consultation at all, the starting point is to consider the 90-day maximum (regardless of the minimum statutory consultation period applicable) and to reduce it only if there are appropriate mitigating circumstances.[101] The award is not confined to 30 days simply because the employer was proposing to dismiss fewer than 100 employees.[102] Mitigating circumstances could be that the employer had already discussed matters with the union at an earlier stage, or that the employer would have been unable to consult for 30/45 days anyway, because it very suddenly became insolvent.[103] However, insolvency is not in itself a reason not to make a protective award.[104]

2.39   Where there is a failure to give information or consult under the TUPE Regs 2006, an ET can order the employer to pay appropriate compensation to individual employees up to a maximum of 13 weeks' pay for each employee. This is gross pay which is not subject to any statutory cap.[105] As with the protected award for failure to inform and consult in collective redundancies, the purpose is to provide a sanction against the employer, not to compensate the employees. Therefore the employees need not show they have suffered any actual financial loss. The starting point is again the maximum award, which may then be discounted according to the seriousness of the employer's failure.[106] A maximum award is unlikely to be appropriate where an employer has given some inform-ation, albeit inadequate, and where the measures requiring consulta-tion are of very limited significance.[107] If the transferor did not tell

100 *Susie Radin v GMB* [2004] IRLR 400, CA.
101 *Susie Radin v GMB* [2004] IRLR 400, CA; *Leicestershire CC v UNISON* [2006] IRLR 810, CA; *Hutchins v Permacell Finesse Ltd (in administration)* UKEAT/0350/07; *Todd v Strain and others* [2011] IRLR 11, EAT.
102 *TGWU v Morgan Platts Ltd (in administration)* EAT/646/02; *Hutchins v Permacell Finesse Ltd (in administration)* UKEAT/0350/07.
103 *Amicus v GBS Tooling Ltd* [2005] IRLR 683, EAT; *AEI Cables Ltd v (1) GMB (2) UNITE (3) individual claimants* UKEAT/0375/12.
104 *Smith and another v Cherry Lewis Ltd (in receivership)* [2005] IRLR 86, EAT.
105 *Zaman and others v Kozee Sleep Products Ltd t/a Dorlux Beds UK* [2011] IRLR 196, EAT.
106 The principles set out in relation to compensation for failure to consult in collective redundancies in *Susie Radin v GMB* [2004] IRLR 400, CA, apply equally to TUPE consultation – *Todd v (1) Strain and others (2) Care Concern GB Ltd (3) Dillon and others* UKEATS/0057/09; [2011] IRLR 11, EAT. See also TUPE Regs 2006 reg 16(3).
107 *Todd v (1) Strain and others (2) Care Concern GB Ltd (3) Dillon and others* UKEATS/0057/09; [2011] IRLR 11.

the representatives of its affected employees about any measures envisaged by the transferee (see para 2.33), compensation can only be claimed directly against the transferor, even if the reason is that the transferee failed in its duty to inform the transferor what it planned to do. This seems unfair, but if the transferor wants to hold the transferee responsible, it can make the transferee party to the tribunal proceedings by serving a notice under reg 15(5). The tribunal can then order any compensation against the transferee. This means the affected employees (via their representatives) must make the claim against the transferor even if they believe the transferee is the one at fault.[108]

Information and Consultation of Employees Regulations

2.40   The Information and Consultation of Employees Regulations (ICE Regs) 2004[109] came into force on 6 April 2005, to implement the EC Directive on Information and Consultation in the Workplace.[110] The regulations apply to undertakings with 50 or more employees.[111] An undertaking means a public or private undertaking carrying out an economic activity, whether or not operating for gain.

2.41   Except in unionised workplaces, there will usually be no existing mechanisms for information and consultation to take place. There are two ways under the ICE Regs 2004 for starting negotiations to set up such mechanisms. Either the employer voluntarily starts negotiations to set up an ICE agreement[112] or two per cent of the employees (subject to a minimum of 15 and maximum of 2,500) put in a written request for an agreement.[113] Where there is a valid pre-existing agreement,[114] eg a trade union collective agreement which satisfies the conditions, and fewer than 40 per cent of employees have requested an ICE agreement, the employer has the option of balloting the workforce as to whether they endorse the request for a new ICE agreement, or – in effect – would prefer to leave things as they are.

---

108 *Allen and others v Morrisons Facilities Services Ltd* [2014] IRLR 514, EAT.
109 SI No 3426.
110 No 2002/14.
111 ICE Regs 2004 reg 3.
112 ICE Regs 2004 reg 11.
113 ICE Regs 2004 reg 7.
114 Meeting the requirements of ICE Regs 2004 reg 8(1); *Stewart v Moray Council* [2006] IRLR 592, EAT.

Even if the workforce votes for a new ICE agreement, any collective agreement would remain in force for other purposes. The Central Arbitration Committee (CAC) adjudicates on breaches of the general rights in the ICE Regs 2004 and has issued guidance for employers and employees.[115]

2.42　　The ICE Regs 2004 seemed to represent a culture change in the UK, where traditionally worker representation is carried out through trade union recognition. It was feared that the ICE Regs 2004 would undermine trade unions in unionised workplaces by setting up alternative structures, and that ICE representatives without trade union experience would not be sufficiently experienced or supported to negotiate effectively. In practice, the threats to trade union organisation seem to have come more from the increasing fragmentation of the workforce through factors such as privatisation, use of agency workers and the gig economy, than specifically because of the ICE Regs 2004, which are very little used.

---

115 *Guidance: The Information and Consultation Regulations – A Guide for Employers and Employees to the role of the Central Arbitration Committee (CAC) for these regulations* (17 September 2020) at www.gov.uk/guidance/the-information-and-consultation-regulations.

European law and
human rights

Chapter 3: Key points

- European Union (EU) law has greatly influenced certain areas of employment law, eg TUPE, collective consultation, equal pay, pregnancy rights and discrimination.
- EU law derives from the treaties and charters and from directives. Domestic courts and tribunals must interpret national law consistently with EU law as far as possible and in some cases, must disapply conflicting national law.
- Where EU law applies, cases can be referred by member states to the European Court of Justice (ECJ) to lay down guidelines. Post Brexit, the UK can no longer make referrals to the ECJ.
- Following implementation period (IP) completion day (11 pm 31 December 2020), there is a body of 'retained' EU law, most notably:
  - the right to equal pay under Treaty on the Functioning of the European Union (Treaty of Rome) (TFEU) Article 157;
  - rights under EU directives which had been recognised by the ECJ or any UK court or tribunal prior to this date.
- Apart from the Supreme Court, Court of Appeal and Inner House of the Court of Session, UK courts/tribunals must follow retained case law. They can choose to have regard to what the ECJ says in future, but they are not bound by it.
- UK legislation enacted after IP completion day will take precedence over retained EU law.
- The UK is a signatory to the European Convention on Human Rights (ECHR). Decisions about the meaning and applicability of the ECHR are made by the European Court of Human Rights (ECtHR) in Strasbourg. Cases can be taken against the UK direct to the ECtHR, but it is likely to be expensive.
- Under the Human Rights Act (HRA) 1998, employment tribunals and courts must take account of applicable ECHR rights when deciding cases under UK law. The government has in the past indicated it wants to abolish the HRA 1998.
- The Charter of Fundamental Rights of the European Union is part of EU law but does not apply in the UK post Brexit.

European Union law

Introduction

3.1   Over the years, the law of the European Union (EU) had become increasingly influential in the employment field, most obviously in the fields of discrimination, transfers of undertakings and health and safety. When so many employment rights had been repealed since 2010, the existence of minimum European protection had become an important safeguard.

3.2　The advantage of EU law is that its ambit is often wider than the equivalent UK legislation. The extent to which individuals in the UK could rely on EU law which conflicted with 'domestic' law (ie the law of England, Wales, Scotland or Northern Ireland) was already complicated prior to Brexit. There is now an extra layer of complexity in working out the post-Brexit position. The following is only a brief and simplified outline and where issues arise, readers will need to research further.

Retained EU law

3.3　On 31 January 2020 ('exit day'), the European Union (Withdrawal) Act (EU(W)A) 2018 repealed the European Communities Act 1972. A transition period called the 'implementation period' (IP) then ran until 11 pm on 31 December 2020 ('IP completion day'). The EU(W) A 2018 preserves these categories of EU law as they stood on IP completion day:

1) EU derived domestic legislation,[1] eg the Equality Act 2010 which implemented various EU directives;
2) Direct EU legislation operative immediately before IP completion day, but not EU directives.[2] It includes the EU GDPR;[3]
3) Directly effective rights which individuals could enforce in courts and tribunals under an EU Treaty, eg the right to equal pay under Article 157 of the Treaty on the Functioning of the European Union (TFEU);
4) 'Any rights, powers, liabilities, obligations, restrictions, remedies and procedures' which were recognised and available in domestic law immediately before IP completion day. This includes rights under EU directives provided they had been recognised by the European Court of Justice (ECJ) or any UK court or tribunal in a case decided before IP completion day.[4]

This 'retained EU law' takes precedence over any UK legislation enacted prior to IP completion day. However, any UK legislation

---

1　EU(W)A 2018 s2(1).
2　EU(W)A 2018 ss3 and 20.
3　See para 1.69 above.
4　EU(W)A 2018 s4.

enacted on or after IP completion day will take precedence over retained EU law.[5]

3.4   The ultimate authority on EU law is the Court of Justice of the European Union (CJEU), which comprises the ECJ and the General Court. In practice, the ECJ makes most of the employment-related decisions.

3.5   Where a question arises as to the interpretation or applicability of EU law, any national court or tribunal of a member state can ask the ECJ to give a preliminary ruling if they are unsure what EU law requires. The referring court/tribunal asks the ECJ a series of questions relevant to the principles in its case. The ECJ's judgment takes the form of answers to those questions. The ECJ then sends the matter back to the referring court/tribunal for it to apply the guidelines to the facts of the particular case. Before it reaches a decision, the ECJ seeks an opinion from an Advocate General. The opinion tends to get published before the final judgment and is usually, but not always, followed by the court. It is worth reading the Advocate General's opinion in a case because it often provides more insight into the ECJ's thinking than the rather terse judgments of the court. There is now a large body of ECJ case-law developed from cases referred by the various member states, in areas such as equal pay, pregnancy and transfers of undertakings.

3.6   After IP completion day, UK courts and tribunals can no longer make referrals to the ECJ for rulings on points of principle, and future decisions by the ECJ will no longer be binding in the UK. Nevertheless, domestic courts and tribunals can still 'have regard to' what the ECJ says in the future.[6] Moreover, domestic courts and tribunals must still follow retained EU and domestic case law, ie cases decided prior to the IP completion day. However, the Supreme Court, High Court of Judiciary in Scotland when sitting as a court of appeal, the Court of Appeal in England and Wales (and in Northern Ireland) and the Inner House of the Court of Session in Scotland can all depart from retained case law where it appears right to do so – basically this is in the same circumstances that the Supreme Court would depart from its own decisions in the past (which is unusual).[7]

---

5 EU(W)A 2018 s5.

6 EU(W)A 2018 s6 deals with interpretation of retained EU law.

7 EU(W)A 2018 s6; European Union (Withdrawal) Act 2018 (Relevant Court) (Retained EU Case Law) Regulations 2020 SI No 1525 regs 3–5.

3.7   Given the body of retained law, it is likely to be necessary to understand how EU law works for some years. The following provides a broad overview.

Direct and indirect effect

3.8   Equal pay law is contained in an EU Treaty, but most EU equality law is set out in a large number of directives and subsequent interpretations by the CJEU in case-law. What happens if UK domestic law and EU law conflict on a point?

3.9   EU law has 'indirect effect'. In applying national law, and in particular a national law specifically introduced to implement an EU measure, national courts are required to interpret domestic law in the light of the wording and purpose of the relevant EU directive. This is sometimes referred to as the 'Marleasing principle'.[8] It may mean that UK courts and tribunals must imply extra words into the national legislation, provided these are compatible with the underlying thrust of the legislation and do not go against its grain.[9]

3.10   Where a provision has 'direct effect' it may also be possible to rely directly on the EU measure and, if necessary, conflicting UK law must be disapplied. This would be important where the domestic legislation just cannot be interpreted in a way which is consistent with EU law. To have 'direct effect', the provision of EU law must be clear and precise, unconditional and unqualified, and not need any further implementing measures.[10] A provision with 'horizontal direct effect' can be directly relied on by workers bringing cases against private or public sector employers. A provision which has 'vertical direct effect' applies in that way only when the worker is claiming against the government or an emanation of the state (see below).

---

8   *Von Colson and anor v Land Nordrhein Westfalen* [1984] ECR 1891, ECJ; *Pickstone v Freemans* [1988] IRLR 357, HL; *Litster v Forth Dry Dock and Engineering Co* [1989] ICR 341; [1989] IRLR 161, HL; *Finnegan v Clowney Youth Training Programme* [1990] IRLR 299, HL; *Marleasing SA v La Commercial Internacional de Alimentacion SA* [1992] 1 CMLR 305, ECJ; *Webb v EMO Air Cargo (UK) Ltd* [1993] IRLR 27, HL.

9   Taking principles from a Human Rights Act (HRA) 1998 case, *Ghaidan v Godin-Mendoza* [2004] UKHL 30; [2004] 3 All ER 411. A useful summary and example is *Rowstock Ltd and another v Jessemey* [2014] EWCA Civ 185; [2014] IRLR 36. Also see *Bear Scotland Ltd and others v Fulton and others* [2015] IRLR 15, EAT.

10   *Van Gend en Loos v Nederlandse Administratie der Belastingen* 26/62 [1963] ECR 1; [1963] CMLR 105, ECJ.

The Treaty of Rome and its articles

3.11   The European Economic Community (EEC)[11] was established by the Treaty of Rome 1957 and it is this treaty which provides the original basis for the establishment of employment rights. On 1 May 1999, the Treaty of Amsterdam came into force, renumbering the articles of the Treaty of Rome and making other amendments. On the whole, the treaties impose obligations on member states which are enforceable only by other member states. However, some key articles are directly applicable and have horizontal direct effect as well as vertical direct effect (see above). This means they can be used in claims brought by individual citizens of the member states, even though they may not have been implemented by the relevant member state. If necessary, such articles override conflicting national law.

3.12   Under the Treaty of Rome, the articles with direct effect were Article 119 requiring men and women to receive equal pay for equal work, and Article 48 prohibiting discrimination in work on grounds of nationality against nationals of other member states. An example of the application of a treaty provision with horizontal direct effect is when the Court of Appeal disapplied the requirement under the former Equal Pay Act 1970 to have a male comparator, in a case where a woman was paid less on grounds of pregnancy.[12]

3.13   The Treaty of Rome has been amended several times and the articles renumbered. Most importantly for employment law, Article 119 was renumbered as Article 141 (when it was expanded to include a reference in the treaty to equal treatment for the first time) and is now Article 157 of the (renamed) TFEU.[13] Article 48 was renumbered Article 39 and is now Article 45.

Directives

3.14   The European Parliament, together with the Council and the Commission, can make regulations, issue directives and make recommendations.[14] Examples of important directives issued over the years are:

---

11 Subsequently renamed the EU.
12 *Alabaster v Barclays Bank plc and the Secretary of State for Social Security (No 2)* [2005] IRLR 576, CA; and see para 5.11.
13 Available at: http://eur-lex.europa.eu/legal-content/EN/TXT/?uri=CELEX: 12016E157.
14 Treaty of Rome Article 288 (formerly Article 249 and before that, Article 189).

- Directive 76/207/EEC on the implementation or the principle of equal treatment for men and women as regards access to employment, vocational training and promotion, and working conditions. This was known as the Equal Treatment Directive.[15] In 2006 it was consolidated with other directives relating to gender into the Recast Directive.[16]
- Directive 2001/23/EC safeguarding employees' rights on transfers of undertakings, businesses or parts of businesses. This is known as the Business Transfers Directive.[17]
- Directive 93/104/EEC (now contained in 2003/88/EC) concerning certain aspects of the organisation of working time. This is known as the Working Time Directive.[18]
- Directive 2000/43/EC on equal treatment between persons irrespective of racial or ethnic origin. This is known as the Race Discrimination Directive.
- Directive 2000/78/EC establishing a general framework for equal treatment in employment and occupation. This is known as the General Framework Directive or the Framework Directive.

A member state must implement the contents of a directive into its own national law by a given date. Unlike certain articles of the Treaty, directives usually have only vertical direct effect.

What is an emanation of the state?

3.15   A useful definition of 'emanation of the state' is in *Foster v British Gas*,[19] where the ECJ said that the Equal Treatment Directive could be used by individuals employed by any body made responsible by the state for providing a public service under the control of the state and which has special powers for that purpose. An 'emanation of the state' includes local government, health authorities,[20] the police,[21] the Post Office and nationalised industries.[22] In some circumstances, privatised industries may remain an 'emanation of the state'. A useful case

---

15 See para 13.8.
16 No 2006/54.
17 See para 10.2.
18 See para 4.71.
19 [1991] IRLR 268, HL.
20 *Marshall v Southampton and South-West Hampshire AHA* [1986] IRLR 140, ECJ.
21 *Johnston v Chief Constable of the Royal Ulster Constabulary* [1986] IRLR 263, ECJ.
22 *Foster v British Gas* [1991] IRLR 268, HL. But see also *Doughty v Rolls-Royce plc* [1992] IRLR 126, CA.

is *Griffin v South West Water Services Ltd*.[23] In stating that a privatised water company was an emanation of the state, the court emphasised that it is the service, not the body, which needs to be under state control. The *Foster* case gives indicators as to when an employer may be considered an emanation of the state, but these will not always apply, for example, it is not necessary to be under the control of central government.[24] The governing body of a voluntary aided school can be considered an emanation of the state for these purposes.[25]

Working abroad

3.16   There have been a number of cases in recent years regarding the territorial scope of domestic employment rights, ie can workers apparently based or working abroad bring claims such as unfair dismissal, discrimination and holiday pay? This is an extremely complicated area, with rapidly developing case-law. The Court of Appeal in *Hottak* has now said that the same rules on territorial jurisdiction apply to claims under the Equality Act 2010 as they do to unfair dismissal claims (see para 6.16).[26] Previously it was suggested that where the employment contract is governed by English law and the employment right in question derives from a European directive, workers should be allowed to make a claim regardless of any restrictions in domestic rules about territorial scope.[27]

The Charter of Fundamental Rights

3.17   The Charter of Fundamental Rights of the European Union (2000/ C364/01) only started to gain recognition as a potential source of legal protection relatively recently. The Charter contains 54 Articles which are said to be the core values of the EU. The Charter has the same status as the EU Treaties, and certain Charter rights have been

---

23 [1995] IRLR 15, ChD.
24 *NUT v Governing Body of St Mary's Church of England (Aided) Junior School* [1997] IRLR 242, CA.
25 *NUT v Governing Body of St Mary's Church of England (Aided) Junior School* [1997] IRLR 242, CA.
26 *R (Hottak) v Secretary of State for Foreign and Commonwealth Affairs* [2016] EWCA Civ 438; [2016] IRLR 534.
27 *Bleuse v MBT Transport* UKEAT/0339/07; [2008] IRLR 264 approved by the Court of Appeal in *Duncombe and others v Secretary of State for Children, Schools and Families* [2009] EWCA Civ 1335. However, the matter did not need to be decided in the Supreme Court and Lady Hale observed that it would need to be decided by the CJEU – see [2011] UKSC 36; [2011] IRLR 298.

held to have horizontal direct effect.[28] However, the Charter does not form part of domestic law following IP completion day. There is potential uncertainty regarding the position where the ECJ relied on the Charter as part of its reasoning in a decision which was otherwise within the scope of retained case-law.[29]

Human rights

Introduction

3.18   The HRA 1998 was passed in order to incorporate the ECHR[30] into domestic law. It came into force on 2 October 2000. The government has in the past indicated that it would like to repeal the HRA 1998. It remains to be seen whether this will be feasible and what difference it will make. As long as the UK remains a signatory to the ECHR, individuals can claim against the UK directly in the European Court of Human Rights (ECtHR) in Strasbourg. Such claims are not dependent on the HRA 1998. The ECHR was ratified by the Labour Government in 1951 and came into force in 1953.

3.19   Taking a case direct to the ECtHR is generally unfeasible because of the costs involved and unfamiliar procedure. As long as the HRA 1998 remains in place, it should rarely be necessary, because the HRA 1998 requires UK courts and tribunals to interpret domestic legislation so far as is possible to give effect to the rights imposed by the articles of the ECHR, and to take into account any relevant decision of the ECtHR.[31] Where it is not possible to do so, the domestic legislation remains unaltered thereby preserving parliamentary sovereignty. However, ECHR rights can generally be enforced directly against public authorities.[32] The Equality and Human Rights Commission (EHRC)[33] has a remit to promote human rights, but no power to take up individual cases.

---

28 *Rugby Football Union v Consolidated Information Services Ltd (formerly Viagogo Ltd)* [2012] UKSC 55; [2013] 1 CMLR 56; *Benkharbouche v Embassy of the Republic of Sudan and another* [2015] EWCA Civ 33; [2015] IRLR 301.

29 See EU(W)A 2018 s5 for its full effect.

30 European Convention for the Protection of Human Rights and Fundamental Freedoms 1950 ('the Convention').

31 HRA 1998 ss2, 3; *Ghaidan v Godin-Mendoza* [2004] UKHL 30, illustrates how this works in practice. For general principles, see also *X v Y* [2004] EWCA Civ 662, [2004] IRLR 625.

32 See para 3.28.

33 See para 12.3.

The Articles of the Convention

3.20   The HRA 1998 incorporates Articles 2–12 and 14 of the ECHR, but not Article 13.[34] The Articles which have been most relevant in the employment field include:

- Article 4 (the right not to be held in slavery and to be protected against forced or compulsory labour);
- Article 5 (the right to liberty and security of the person);
- Article 6 (the right to a fair and public hearing within a reasonable period of time);
- Article 8 (the right to respect for private and family life);
- Article 9 (freedom of thought, conscience and religion);[35]
- Article 10 (the right to freedom of expression); and
- Article 11 (the right to peaceful assembly and the freedom of association with others).

3.21   Importantly, Article 14 declares:

> The enjoyment of the rights and freedoms set forth in this Convention shall be secured without discrimination on any ground such as sex, race, colour, language, religion, political or other opinion, national or social origin, association with a national minority, property, birth or other status.

There is a defence of objective justification. 'Other status' could include any category, eg sexual orientation, age, education or trade union status. Article 14 does not give a free-standing right not to be discriminated against in any sphere of employment. It only forbids discrimination in areas covered by the other ECHR rights. The Council of Europe has adopted Protocol 12 to the ECHR, which does give a free-standing right against discrimination. Unfortunately, past governments have been unwilling to sign and ratify the protocol on grounds that it is 'too general and open-ended'.

3.22   Many of the rights and fundamental freedoms under the ECHR are qualified, ie have exceptions. For example, Articles 8–11 may be subject to restrictions on a number of grounds 'in accordance with the law' or 'prescribed by law' which are deemed 'necessary in a democratic society', eg for public safety, for the protection of health or morals, or for the protection of the rights and freedoms of others. There should be a fair balance between protecting individual rights and the interests of the community at large. This is called the prin-

---

34   HRA 1998 s1.
35   See paras 14.120–14.128.

ciple of 'proportionality'.[36] Many cases have failed because of the exceptions.

3.23　Article 6 has been used to challenge the conduct of court and tribunal processes. This is because 'public authorities' are defined to include courts and tribunals.[37] Article 6 starts by saying:

> In the determination of his civil rights and obligations . . . everyone is entitled to a fair and public hearing within a reasonable time by an independent and impartial tribunal established by law.

Article 6 does not usually apply to internal disciplinary hearings, though it may apply where the outcome may have a substantial influence or effect on the determination in a second set of proceedings of the worker's right to practice his/her profession.[38] In such exceptional cases, it can be a basis for arguing there is a right to legal representation at an internal disciplinary hearing. The UK rules on state immunity preventing employees at diplomatic missions from claiming in courts and tribunals may breach Article 6.[39]

3.24　Under Article 6, a worker may be able to challenge certain tribunal procedures, eg an unreasonable refusal of a postponement[40] or failing to make necessary adjustments to ensure disabled claimants or those with language difficulties are able to give evidence to the best of their ability. Article 6 has been used successfully to challenge the appearance of bias where an employer's representative at an Employment Appeal Tribunal (EAT) hearing was a part-time judge at the EAT. He had previously chaired a panel where one of the current lay members had also sat as a lay member.[41]

3.25　Article 8 is one of the most frequently called upon articles. Article 8(1) states:

36　*Hill v Governing Body of Great Tey Primary School* UKEAT/0237/12; [2013] IRLR 274, EAT gives useful guidance at para 45 on how to approach the exceptions.

37　HRA 1998 s6(3)(a). See para 3.29.

38　*R (G) v Governors of X School and Y City Council (interested party)* [2011] UKSC 30; [2011] IRLR 756. See also *Mattu v The University Hospitals of Coventry and Warwickshire NHS Trust* [2012] EWCA Civ 641; [2012] IRLR 661 and *Kulkarni v Milton Keynes Hospital NHS Trust and the Secretary of State for Health* [2009] EWCA Civ 789, for additional points although the main aspects of the latter are overturned by *G*.

39　*Benkharbouche v Secretary of State for Foreign and Commonwealth Affairs; Secretary of State for Foreign and Commonwealth Affairs and another v Janah* [2017] UKSC 62; [2018] IRLR 123.

40　*Teinaz v Wandsworth LBC* [2002] IRLR 721, CA. Also see para 20.144.

41　*Lawal v Northern Spirit Ltd* [2003] IRLR 538, HL.

Everyone has the right to respect for his private and family life, his home and his correspondence.

This right is qualified by Article 8(2), which allows an exception if it is 'in accordance with the law and is necessary in a democratic society in the interests of national security, public safety or the economic well-being of the country, for the prevention of disorder or crime, for the protection of health or morals, or for the protection of the rights and freedoms of others'. The right to respect for private life includes sexual activity, eg the ECtHR said that the discharge of lesbians and gay men from the armed forces and investigations into their homosexuality were breaches of Article 8.[42] However, where an employee is dismissed for sexual activity in a public place, this does not fall within Article 8 because it does not concern privacy.[43] Even where Article 8 does apply, it may be a justified interference with employees' privacy to dismiss them if knowledge of their sexual activities has become public and could impair their ability effectively to carry out their duties.[44] Article 8 has also proved useful in connection with the rights of transgender people to legal recognition of their gender reassignment.[45] Where the employer obtains evidence for an ET case by covert tape-recordings infringing the worker's right to privacy, Article 8 may clash with the right to have all the evidence heard so as to have a fair trial under Article 6. Similar issues arise where the worker does not want to disclose private medical records. The ET will usually allow the evidence to be used if needed for a fair trial.[46] Considerations under Articles 6, 8 and 10, taken together are very relevant to whether a tribunal should make an order restricting publicity in a sexual harassment or similar cases.[47]

3.26   Article 9 is another important article, which frequently comes up in relation to workers' rights to express their private religious and other beliefs, especially where this might clash with the rights of others.[48] Two high-profile cases in recent years were taken directly to

---

42 *Smith and Grady v United Kingdom* [1999] IRLR 734; 88 EOR 49, ECtHR.

43 *X v Y* [2004] IRLR 625, CA. Activities in a private members club may be considered private in some circumstances: *Pay v United Kingdom* [2009] IRLR 139, ECtHR.

44 *Pay v United Kingdom* [2009] IRLR 139, ECtHR.

45 *Goodwin v United Kingdom* [2002] IRLR 664, ECtHR.

46 See *De Keyser Ltd v Wilson* [2001] IRLR 324, EAT; *McGowan v Scottish Water* [2005] IRLR 167, EAT; *XXX v YYY and another* [2004] IRLR 137, EAT; *Jones v University of Warwick* [2003] EWCA Civ 151.

47 See para 21.62.

48 See paras 14.120–14.128.

the ECtHR. In *Eweida*, the ECtHR supported a person's right to manifest his/her religion at work, provided such manifestation does not clash with the rights and freedoms of others or public safety interests.[49] In *Redfearn*, the ECtHR decided that a worker who is dismissed for belonging to a political party must have the right to have the fairness of that dismissal assessed by an employment tribunal regardless of his/her length of service.[50] This led to legislation removing the qualifying period for bringing unfair dismissal claims regarding dismissal related to an employee's political opinion or affiliation.

3.27   It may be hard to challenge a dress code under Article 10, unless it is extremely unreasonable.[51] However, a code which discriminates between men and women in relation to hair length or wearing trousers may breach Article 10 taken together with Article 14.[52] Article 11 is interesting because it covers the right to join trade unions. In one case, UNISON unsuccessfully challenged restrictions on the right to strike under UK law.[53] There has been a more successful case challenging inducements to workers to surrender their right to union representation.[54]

Who can claim under the Human Rights Act 1998?

3.28   Under the HRA 1998, it is unlawful for public authorities to behave in a manner contrary to the ECHR,[55] except where a public authority is forced to act a certain way because of an Act of Parliament. Workers employed by obvious public authorities such as government departments and local authorities should be able to enforce the ECHR rights directly. Workers employed by bodies 'some of whose functions only are of a public nature', eg Railtrack, the BBC or GP practices which have both NHS and private patients, may not be able to claim. This is because only the public functions of such mixed bodies will be covered and the employment relationship may be seen as a

---

49 *Eweida, Chaplin, Ladele, McFarlane v United Kingdom* [2013] IRLR 231, ECtHR. See paras 14.120–14.125 for more detail.

50 *Redfearn v United Kingdom* [2013] IRLR 51, ECtHR.

51 See *Kara v United Kingdom* [1999] EHRLR 232, ECtHR.

52 A case such as *Smith v Safeway plc* [1996] IRLR 456, CA may now be decided differently. See para 13.9.

53 *UNISON v United Kingdom* [2002] IRLR 497, ECtHR.

54 See para 2.2.

55 HRA 1998 s6.

private function. A service contracted out by a local authority may no longer be carrying out a public function.[56]

3.29   Workers employed exclusively in the private sector cannot enforce ECHR rights directly. However, this is unlikely to make much difference in most cases as courts and tribunals must interpret domestic law consistently with the ECHR as far as possible. For example, ETs should take account of any relevant ECHR rights when deciding unfair dismissal claims. Also, claimants may be able to challenge unfair court or tribunal processes under Article 6.[57] ET claimants should mention the HRA 1998 in their claim form if they want to rely on it or have it taken into account.

3.30   A court can award damages against a public authority which will be assessed in accordance with Article 41 of the ECHR.[58]

---

56 *R (Heather and Callin) v Leonard Cheshire Foundation and HM Attorney General* [2002] EWCA Civ 366; (2002) 5 CCLR 317.

57 See para 3.24.

58 HRA 1998 s8(4).

Wages

Pay and protection of wages

continued

Chapter 4: Key points

- Employers are obliged to pay wages to workers who are willing and able to work their contractual hours, even if the workers are not required to do so. Some contracts have an express term allowing the employer to lay off workers when there is no work and without pay, but such a term is unusual and can only be relied on for a short period of time.
- Increasingly, different contract arrangements are made so that employers are not obliged to offer paid hourly work on a regular basis, eg casual work and zero hours contracts.
- Employers are not allowed to make deductions from wages. There are some exceptions – eg where there is a statutory requirement to make deductions (tax and National Insurance), where it is a term of the employment contract, or where the worker has agreed in writing in advance to the deduction.
- Any deduction made without such authority can be recovered by claiming in the employment tribunal under Employment Rights Act (ERA) 1996 Part II. This is known as a claim for an 'unlawful' or (more correctly) 'unauthorised' deduction from wages.
- The majority of workers are entitled to the national minimum wage. Failure to pay the minimum wage will entitle the worker to recover the shortfall at current rates. The employer will also be committing a criminal offence and can be fined.
- Workers on furlough are still entitled to their full contractual pay unless they agree a reduction. However, they are not entitled to the national minimum wage for unworked hours except when undergoing approved training.
- Under the Working Time Regulations (WTR) 1998, workers are entitled to limits on the hours worked and rest breaks. They are also entitled to four weeks' paid annual leave plus 1.6 weeks' additional annual leave in recognition of bank holidays. Statutory holiday entitlement cannot be substituted by a payment in lieu except on termination of employment. There are special rules where the worker cannot take holiday because s/he is sick, on maternity leave or the employer has effectively prevented him/her from taking it. There are also special carry over provisions where it is not reasonably practical for the worker to take leave because of Covid-related reasons.

continued

- When off sick, most workers are entitled to statutory sick pay (SSP). They will not be entitled to full pay unless they have such a right under their contract. Workers may also be entitled to SSP if self-isolating because of Covid-19.
- Workers are entitled to receive itemised pay statements (usually payslips) at or before each pay day.

General guide to useful evidence

- Contract of employment – documents or evidence of verbal or implied terms.
- The payslips; P45; P60.
- The employer's pay and tax records.

Introduction

4.1   The payment of wages, and the intervals at which payments are made, is a matter of agreement between the employer and worker, although there are some statutory restrictions. There must be no discrimination because of sex[1] or any other protected character-istic under the Equality Act 2010, eg race. There is also a national minimum wage.[2]

4.2   The employer is under a statutory duty to give employees a written statement which includes the scale or the method of calculating wages and the intervals at which wages will be paid, whether weekly or monthly or some other period.[3] The employer is also obliged to give employees written itemised pay statements (usually payslips) at or before the time of payment of wages.[4] The pay statements must set out the gross pay and all deductions made from it. As well as this right to be notified of deductions made, there are restrictions on what kind of deductions employers are allowed to make from wages.[5]

4.3   It is a fundamental term of the employment contract to pay wages, and deliberate failure to do so will entitle the employee to claim

---

1 See chapter 5 regarding equal pay.
2 See paras 4.33–4.54.
3 Employment Rights Act (ERA) 1996 s1(4)(a) and (b). See paras 1.24–1.28.
4 ERA 1996 s8. See paras 4.67–4.70.
5 See paras 4.8–4.25.

constructive dismissal.[6] Mere delay in payment due to unexpected events, accounting mistakes or temporary faults in the employer's technology may not be a fundamental breach of contract unless repeated or unexplained.[7] It is also possible to sue for the wages owing, either in the employment tribunal (ET) as an unauthorised deduction from pay[8] or as a breach of contract in the civil courts (county court or High Court) or, if the contract has terminated, in the ET.[9]

4.4   Unless the contract explicitly says otherwise, the employee is generally entitled to be paid for his/her contractual hours as long as s/he is ready and willing to work. This is so even if for some reason the employer refuses to allow him/her to come in and work, eg due to work shortage or disciplinary suspension. While the employer's obligation in most work situations is to pay the wages contractually agreed, there is usually no obligation to supply work.[10] The employee's obligation is to be willing and able to perform his/her contractual duties. The failure to do so entitles the employer to deduct a sum equal to the proportion of the time when the employee was not willing to work.[11] Increasingly, different contract arrangements are made so that employers are not obliged to offer paid hourly work on a regular basis, eg casual work and zero hours contracts (see para 1.40 for more detail).

Workers

4.5   There are different eligibility requirements for different employment rights. For example, to claim unfair dismissal, it is necessary to be an 'employee' as defined by the Employment Rights Act (ERA) 1996. For other rights, it is only necessary to be a 'worker', which is a much broader category. Nevertheless, when claims are made for matters such as holiday pay, unauthorised deductions or the minimum wage, claimants often find their first problem is to prove they were a 'worker'. The definition of a worker is the same under the ERA 1996

---

6 *Cantor Fitzgerald International v Callaghan* [1999] IRLR 234, CA; and see para 6.35 onwards.

7 *Cantor Fitzgerald International v Callaghan* [1999] IRLR 234, CA.

8 ERA 1996 Pt II.

9 Employment Tribunals Extension of Jurisdiction Orders 1994 SI Nos 1623 (England and Wales) and 1624 (Scotland).

10 *William Hill Organisation Ltd v Tucker* [1998] IRLR 313, CA; *Collier v Sunday Referee Publishing Co Ltd* [1940] 2 KB 647; [1940] 4 All ER 234.

11 *Miles v Wakefield MDC* [1987] IRLR 193, HL.

(s230), the Working Time Regulations (WTR) 1998[12] (reg 2), the National Minimum Wage Act (NMWA) 1998 (s54) and the Part-time Workers (Prevention of Less Favourable Treatment) Regulations 2000[13] (reg 1). It reads as follows:

> A 'worker' means an individual who has entered into or works under . . .
> (a) a contract of employment, or
> (b) any other contract, whether express or implied and (if it is express) whether oral or in writing, whereby the individual undertakes to do or perform personally any work or services for another party to the contract whose status is not by virtue of the contract that of a client or customer of any profession or business undertaking carried on by the individual.

Category (a) is therefore the conventional type of 'employee' who can bring, for example, an unfair dismissal claim. Category (b) refers to other types of worker. In the case-law, they are often referred to as 'limb (b)' workers. Shop workers and betting workers are separately covered under ERA 1996, as are agency workers and home workers under NMWA 1998.

4.6   A worker is different from someone who is truly self-employed. Self-employed individuals can make their own choices as to what work they do and when and where they do it. They work for themselves. Although the practical realities of getting work mean they must satisfy the (often quite stringent) requirements of those who engage their services, ultimately the choices are their own to make.[14] There are three key elements to the definition of a 'worker' in the legislation: (1) there must be a contract between the individual and the 'employer'; (2) the individual must be required to work 'personally' for the employer; and (3) the individual must not be working for someone who is in reality his/her client or customer. As long as these apply, it does not matter that the individual is in business on his/her own account.[15] There are no absolute rules, but often a useful distinction will be the difference between an individual who markets his/her services to the world in general and someone who works in a subordinate position in circumstances where s/he is integrated into the

---

12 SI No 1833.
13 SI No 1551.
14 *O'Brien v Ministry of Justice (formerly Department for Constitutional Affairs)* [2013] UKSC 6; [2013] IRLR 315.
15 *Hospital Medical Group Ltd v Westwood* [2012] EWCA Civ 1005; [2012] IRLR 834.

employer's business.[16] Although there are some borderline situations where it is difficult to know whether or not a person is a worker, the effect of recent case-law is that the definition should widely apply.[17] It is particularly important that the person is required to do the work 'personally'. Therefore, someone is unlikely to be a worker if s/he is completely free to send along substitutes to work in his/her place. However, a limited power of delegation does not necessarily mean that s/he is not a worker.[18] It will depend what kind of restrictions are imposed on the person's right to send substitutes. For example, depending on the facts, someone can still be working 'personally' for the employer if s/he is only allowed to arrange a substitute when s/he is unable (as opposed to unwilling) to do the work, or if a substitute must be a work colleague or can only be provided with the employer's prior approval.[19] In general, when deciding whether someone is a worker, it is important to consider the real position. Although any written contract will be a relevant factor, it is not the starting point, as it may not reflect the true agreement between the parties.[20] All the evidence should be considered. For example, the written contract may say that a person can send along a substitute, but the person may have tried to do so at some point and the employer may have objected.

4.7   The definition of 'worker' excludes people who carry on a business or profession where the other party is a client. This would exclude professionals such as solicitors, doctors and dentists, and also sole traders and taxi drivers. There can be marginal situations where the person is not in one of these obvious categories, yet is

16 'Self-employed' is not a precise legal term for these purposes. Some of the case-law uses the word 'self-employed' only to refer to those who are not 'workers' because they are working for clients/customers of their own business. Confusingly, other case-law describes limb (b) workers also as a type of self-employed. Whatever the label, however, the cases are consistent regarding which arrangements count as 'worker' and which do not.

17 For a recent case on various aspects including whether minimum obligation is required, see *Nursing and Midwifery Council v Somerville* UKEAT/0258/20.

18 This has been established by a number of cases, but summarised by the Court of Appeal in *Pimlico Plumbers Ltd and another v Smith* [2017] IRLR 323, and essentially confirmed by the SC at [2018] IRLR 872. It is important to read the explanatory comments by the CA in *Stuart Delivery Ltd v Augustine* [2021] EWCA Civ 1514.

19 For some examples, see cases in the previous footnote. More historically, see also *MacFarlane and another v Glasgow City Council* [2001] IRLR 7, EAT; *Byrne Brothers (Formwork) Ltd v Baird and others* [2002] IRLR 96, EAT; *James v Redcats (Brands) Ltd* [2007] IRLR 296, EAT.

20 *Autoclenz Ltd v Belcher and others* [2011] UKSC 41; *Uber BV and others v Aslam and others* [2021] UKSC 5; [2021] IRLR 407. Similar issues arise in respect of whether someone is an employee. See paras 6.4–6.12.

working for more than one 'employer' at the same time. This does not necessarily mean the person is treating the employer as a client. A good indicator in many, but not all cases, is to consider the extent to which the individual is integrated into the employer's business.[21] There are special rules regarding partners in solicitors' firms or members of a limited liability partnership (LLP).[22] In a series of high-profile cases over the last few years, private taxi drivers and bicycle couriers have been found to be workers.[23] However, every employment arrangement will be considered on its own facts. The case-law regarding who meets the extended definition of 'employee' under the Equality Act 2010 will also be relevant, as it is now considered to have the same requirements as a 'limb (b)' worker (see para 12.12).

Deductions from pay

The legal framework

4.8   The Wages Act 1986 repealed the Truck Acts which gave workers the right to be paid in cash. It also set out certain protection against deductions from wages. The Wages Act 1986 was repealed and re-enacted in the ERA 1996 Part II. Part II of the ERA 1996 allows employers, if they satisfy the necessary requirements, to make deductions from the pay of workers. The definition of a 'worker', as opposed to someone who is an employee or self-employed, is discussed at paras 4.5–4.7 above. Part II also covers Crown employment (civil servants), but not those employed in the armed forces. Once a deduction is allowed, there is no restriction on its amount unless the worker is employed in retailing. ERA 1996 s13 deals with the employer's right to make deductions from a worker's wages. ERA 1996 s18 additionally limits the size of the deduction that can be made from the wages of retail workers for cash

---

21 *Hospital Medical Group Ltd v Westwood* [2012] EWCA Civ 1005; [2012] IRLR 834. Subject to that, see the useful guidance in *Cotswold Developments Construction Ltd v Williams* [2006] IRLR 181, EAT and *Byrne Brothers (Formwork) Ltd v Baird and others* [2002] IRLR 96, EAT. Most recently, see *Pimlico Plumbers Ltd and another v Smith* [2018] IRLR 872, SC.

22 *Bates van Winkelhof v Clyde & Co LLP and another* [2012] EWCA Civ 1207; [2012] IRLR 992.

23 *Uber BV and others v Aslam and others* [2021] UKSC 5; [2021] IRLR 407; *Addison Lee Ltd v Lange* UKEAT/0037/18 and [2021] EWCA Civ 594; *Dewhurst v CitySprint UK Ltd* ET/220251/2016. Less successfully: *R (Independent Workers of Great Britain) v Central Arbitration Committee and Roofoods Ltd t/a Deliveroo* [2019] IRLR 249, QBD.

shortages and stock deficiencies.[24] However, even the limited protection afforded to retail workers is removed on their final pay day.[25]

Unauthorised deductions from wages

Definition of 'wages'

4.9 For the purpose of ERA 1996 Part II, 'wages' are given a wide definition, covering 'any sums payable to the worker by his employer in connection with his employment, including any fee, bonus, commission, holiday pay or other emolument referable to his employment',[26] including guarantee payments, SSP[27] and statutory maternity pay (SMP).[28] The courts have held that wages do not include notice pay (unless the worker is working out his/her notice or is treated as doing so).[29] Discretionary and ex gratia payments are wages if there is a reasonable expectation that the worker will receive the payment.[30] The definition includes commission that becomes payable after the termination of the worker's contract, provided that it is in connection with the employment.[31]

4.10 Certain payments are expressly excluded from the definition of wages, eg loans and advances on wages, expenses including a car mileage allowance,[32] pensions, allowances or gratuities in connection with the worker's retirement, redundancy payments and benefits in kind. Payment of pension contributions to a pension provider is also not covered.[33]

When deductions can be made

4.11 ERA 1996 Part II prevents the employer from making any deduction from the wages of workers unless it is:

1) authorised by statute.[34] This enables the employer to deduct from wages the PAYE tax and National Insurance payments as required

---

24 ERA 1996 ss17 and 18.
25 ERA 1996 s22.
26 ERA 1996 s27.
27 See para 4.62 for failure to pay SSP.
28 ERA 1996 s27.
29 *Delaney v Staples (t/a De Montfort Recruitment)* [1992] IRLR 191, HL.
30 *Kent Management Services Ltd v Butterfield* [1992] IRLR 394, EAT.
31 *Robertson v Blackstone Franks Investment Management Ltd* [1998] IRLR 376, CA.
32 *Southwark LBC v O'Brien* [1996] IRLR 420, EAT.
33 *Somerset CC v Chambers* UKEAT/0417/12 at para 18.
34 ERA 1996 s13(1)(a).

by law or payments following a court order[35] (maintenance payments, fines, etc);

2) authorised by a 'relevant provision in the contract'. There is no requirement that the term of the contract should be in writing, and the term in question can be an implied rather than express term. However, it is necessary for the employer to have notified the worker in writing of the existence of the term before making the deduction;[36] or

3) previously agreed in writing by the worker that the deduction may be made.[37]

4.12   The worker's consent to the contractual agreement or the deduction cannot be retrospective, ie after the worker's conduct or event leading to the deduction.[38] Where the written consent is to make deductions in respect of stock shortages, it must have been given before the shortage arose.[39] The employer also cannot receive any payment from the worker unless the payment satisfies one of the three conditions above. This prevents the employer recovering payments by demand rather than deduction.

4.13   Even if the above three conditions are absent, the employer is entitled to deduct money:

- for a statutory purpose to a public authority (eg taxes owing to Her Majesty's Revenue & Customs (HMRC));
- as a consequence of a strike or industrial action;[40]
- for any contractual obligation to pay to a third party (eg union dues);[41]
- in satisfaction of a court or tribunal order requiring the worker to pay the employer, where the worker has given prior written consent;[42]
- if the deficiency in payment is attributable to an error of computation. However, a conscious decision not to make a payment because the employer believes that there is a contractual right not to make the payment does not amount to an error of computation;[43]
- in respect of any overpayment of wages and/or expenses.[44]

---

35 Under the Attachment of Earnings Act 1971.
36 ERA 1996 s13(1)(a) and (2).
37 ERA 1996 s13(1)(b).
38 ERA 1996 s13(5)–(6).
39 *Discount Tobacco and Confectionery Ltd v Williamson* [1993] IRLR 327, EAT.
40 ERA 1996 s14(5).
41 ERA 1996 s14(4).
42 ERA 1996 s14(6).
43 *Yemm v British Steel plc* [1994] IRLR 117, EAT.
44 ERA 1996 s14(1).

Overpayments of wages

4.14   Unfortunately, there is a complete bar on bringing a claim for unauthorised deductions where the employer's reason for the deduction is to recover an overpayment of wages.[45] This is so even if the employer has miscalculated how much the overpayment is, or is not entitled to the money for other reasons.[46] However, the ET cannot just refuse to hear a claim on the employer's assertion that the deduction is for an overpayment. If the worker disputes there was an overpayment, the ET must listen to the evidence and decide on the facts whether it occurred. This is different from deciding whether the employer was entitled to deduct the pay as a matter of contract,[47] but practically speaking, the ET may end up deciding the whole issue. Assuming the ET refuses to hear the case because ERA 1996 Part II does not apply, the worker must sue in the civil courts if s/he wants to recover the deducted sum on grounds that the employer was never entitled to it. Alternatively, if the sum is outstanding when his/her employment ends and s/he is an employee, s/he can claim for breach of contract in the employment tribunal.[48] Either way, the worker's claim should be expressed as for his/her unpaid wages and not as for the overpaid sum.

4.15   Very often, the worker accepts the sum was originally overpaid, but has innocently spent the money. Whether the worker will be successful in claiming breach of contract as mentioned above, depends on the following principles. At common law, an employer who overpays a worker by mistake (factual or legal)[49] usually has a good claim to restitution, and is bound to assert this when defending the worker's claim. However, this argument will fail if the worker can prove 'change of position'.[50] The worker must prove that s/he did not realise s/he had been overpaid. To see whether this is credible, it is relevant to look at the size and pattern of the overpayments, how recent they were and whether the payslips were clear. It is also important to show the overpayment was not primarily the worker's

---

45 ERA 1996 s14(1)(a).
46 *Sunderland Polytechnic v Evans* [1993] IRLR 196, EAT; *SIP Industrial Products v Swinn* [1994] IRLR 323, EAT; both rejecting *Home Office v Ayres* [1992] IRLR 59, EAT.
47 *Gill and others v Ford Motor Company Ltd; Wong and others v BAE Systems Operations Ltd* [2004] IRLR 840, EAT.
48 Watch time limits on this. See also para 4.26.
49 *Kleinwort Benson Ltd v Lincoln City Council* [1999] 2 AC 349, HL.
50 *Lipkin Gorman (a firm) v Karpnale Ltd* [1991] 2 AC 548; [1992] 4 All ER 512, HL; *Commerzbank AG v Price* [2003] EWCA Civ 1663.

fault, eg because s/he gave some misleading information to the employer. Finally, the worker must show s/he has changed his/her position in reliance on the money, eg made purchases s/he would not normally have made. The older but similar argument of estoppel (if still valid) may be more beneficial where the worker changed his/her position only in respect of part of the overpayment. The law in this area is complex and developing. The full legal position should be checked, as the above represents only a general summary.

What amounts to a deduction?

4.16   Where the total amount of any wages that are paid by an employer to a worker is less than the total amount of the wages that are properly payable to the worker on that occasion, the amount of the deficiency will be treated as a deduction made by the employer from the worker's wages, even where there is a 100 per cent deduction.[51] Any unauthorised deduction from any of the different types of 'wages' or a non-payment of them,[52] such as the failure to pay SSP, SMP or accrued holiday pay,[53] is recoverable in the ET. However, if there is an issue regarding entitlement to SSP and SMP, this is a matter for HMRC rather than the ET.[54]

Retail workers

4.17   Those working in retail employment are given additional protection regarding the amount of any deductions on account of cash or stock deficiencies.[55] This assumes the deductions are allowed at all under the general rules above. During the worker's employment, the employer can deduct no more than ten per cent of the gross wage due on any given pay day, and can only continue to recover up to ten per cent in the following weeks until the full sum is recovered. In the final week of employment any amount which remains outstanding can be recovered by the employer.[56] Deductions other than for cash or stock shortages are not subject to this ten per cent ceiling.

---

51   *Delaney v Staples* at the Court of Appeal stage – [1991] IRLR 112, CA.
52   *Kournavos v JR Masterton and Sons* [1990] IRLR 119, EAT.
53   *Greg May (CF and C) v Dring* [1990] IRLR 19, EAT.
54   *Taylor Gordon and Co Ltd v Timmons* [2004] IRLR 180, EAT; *Hair Division Ltd v Macmillan* UKEATS/0033/12-13.
55   ERA 1996 s18.
56   ERA 1996 s22.

4.18   Also, deductions for cash shortages or stock deficiencies may not be made more than 12 months after the employer discovers, or ought reasonably to have discovered, the shortage.[57] This protection was introduced because of the widespread practice of retail employers of deducting cash and stock deficiencies from wages. The worst employers were garage owners, who would hold workers responsible for unpaid fuel bills which were often in excess of the wages owing, resulting in the worker owing money to the employer for the privilege of working!

4.19   Retail employment means employment which involves the carrying out by the worker of retail transactions directly with members of the public and the collection by the worker of amounts payable in connection with retail transactions such as the sale and supply of goods and services.[58] This definition covers workers in shops, banks, building societies, petrol stations, restaurants (waiters and cashiers); homeworkers; those working on the 'lump' in the building trade; and workers involved in the delivery and sale of produce, such as those who do milk rounds.

Remedies and time limits

4.20   The worker can make a claim to the ET asking for a declaration that the employer has made unauthorised deductions and an order that the employer repay the sums deducted.[59] To decide whether there has been an unauthorised deduction, an ET will have to consider the facts and, if necessary, decide what the contract meant.[60] The ET claim must be made within three months of the date of the deduction or, if the worker has made a payment to the employer, of the date when the payment was made.[61] If a worker leaves and a deduction is made from his/her final pay, the time can be counted from the date of the final payslip or payment, even if that is sent some time after the termination date.[62] Even so, it is advisable to lodge the claim within three months of the termination date.

---

57 See the rule in ERA 1996 s18(2) and (3).
58 ERA 1996 s17.
59 ERA 1996 s23.
60 *Agarwal v Cardiff University and another; Tyne and Wear Passenger Transport Executive (t/a Nexus) v Anderson and others* [2018] EWCA Civ 2084; [2019] IRLR 657.
61 ERA 1996 s23(2).
62 *Grampian Country Chickens (Rearing) Ltd v David M Paterson* EAT/1358/00.

4.21   The time limit runs from the latest date on which payment could be made under the contract rather than an earlier date of actual payment.[63] So for example, if commission is due on 1 February but usually paid on 20 January, and the worker wants to claim for an underpayment, the three months runs from 1 February. Again, if given the choice, the worker should play safe and count three months from the earlier date.

4.22   If the employer made a series of deductions, the time limit runs from the last deduction.[64] In this situation, a claim could be made for deductions going back more than three months, eg for an ongoing reduction of wages which has not been agreed. The EAT has said that there cannot be more than three months between each deduction in a series, although the Northern Ireland Court of Appeal disagrees and it is difficult to see how the wording of the legislation supports the EAT's view.[65]

4.23   The ET can extend the time limit if it was not reasonably practicable for the claim to have been made within the three-month period.[66] The extension provision adopts the same form of words as is used for the unfair dismissal provision and it can be assumed therefore that the worker will experience the same problems with ERA 1996 Part II claims as with unfair dismissal claims[67] if the time limit is missed. In addition to the above rules regarding time limits, claims cannot be brought at all in respect of deductions made more than two years before the ET1 is presented.[68] There are limited exceptions, eg in respect of deductions from SSP, SMP and guarantee payments.[69]

---

63 *Group 4 NightSpeed Ltd v Gilbert* [1997] IRLR 398, EAT.
64 ERA 1996 s23(3).
65 *Bear Scotland Ltd and others v Fulton and others; Hertel (UK) Ltd v Woods and others; Amec Group Ltd v Law and others* [2015] IRLR 15, EAT; confirmed by a later EAT in the same case, *Fulton & Baxter v Bear Scotland Ltd*. However, see *Chief Constable of the Police Service of Northern Ireland and Northern Ireland Policing Board v Agnew and others* [2019] NICA 32 for a different view and general guidance on what a 'series of deductions' means. NICA judgments are not binding in England, Wales and Scotland, but are persuasive. UKEATS/0010/16. But see EAT's comments on this in *Pimlico Plumbers Ltd v Smith (No 2)* UKEAT/0211/19, UKEAT/0003/20, UKEAT/0040/20; [2021] IRLR 654.
66 ERA 1996 s23(4).
67 See para 20.49 onwards.
68 ERA 1996 s23(4A) as inserted by the Deduction from Wages (Limitation) Regulations 2014 SI No 3322, for claims made on or after 1 July 2015.
69 The exceptions are those in ERA 1996 s27(1)(b)–(j): see ERA 1996 s23(4B).

The Advisory, Conciliation and Arbitration Service (ACAS) early conciliation procedure applies to wages claims.[70]

4.24 Wages owed may be claimed either under ERA 1996 Part II as a deduction, or as a breach of contract in the county court or High Court (or Scottish equivalent) or, if the contract has been terminated and the worker is an employee, in the ET. There may be advantages in claiming under Part II even though it seems a more artificial concept, eg because employers can launch their own contract claims against an employee who has brought a contract claim, but not against an employee who has brought a Part II unauthorised deduction claim. Also, the employer may have a genuine entitlement to the money, but not to acquire it by helping him/herself out of the pay packet. If that happens and the worker wins his/her unauthorised deductions claim, the employer loses the right to claim in respect of the same sum in the county court or High Court.[71] On the other hand, time limits are shorter under Part II and claims cannot go back further than two years, even for continuing deductions. Further differences between the two venues, ie ET (unauthorised deductions claims) and county court or High Court (breach of contract claims) are set out at para 4.28 below.

4.25 There is an often forgotten entitlement whereby, if the tribunal finds the claim for unauthorised deductions is well-founded, it can order the employer to pay financial compensation for any further financial loss attributable to that deduction.[72]

Employment tribunal claim for breach of contract

Introduction

4.26 Once an employee's employment has ended, s/he can bring a claim in the ET for breach of contract, eg for holiday pay, wages owing or notice.[73] The claim must arise or be outstanding on the termination of employment, and not a result of later events, eg suing for breach of a settlement agreement made some days after termination.[74] It is

---

70 Employment Tribunals Act (ETA) 1996 s18(1)(b); see para 20.16 onwards.
71 *Potter v Hunt Contracts Ltd* [1992] IRLR 108, EAT.
72 ERA 1996 s24(2). Applicable to tribunal claims on or after 6 April 2009.
73 ETA 1996 s3; Employment Tribunals (Extension of Jurisdiction) (England and Wales) Order 1994 SI No 1623; SI No 1624 for Scotland.
74 SI No 1623 art 3(c) and *Miller Bros & F P Butler Ltd v Johnston* [2002] IRLR 386, EAT.

not possible to bring contract proceedings in the ET for compensation arising out of personal injury sustained at work, or claims concerning living accommodation or clauses in restraint of trade.[75] There is a three-month time limit from the end of employment for bringing an ET contract claim unless it is not reasonably practicable to do so within that period. Any claim then brought by the employer against the employee must be made within six weeks of receipt of the employee's ET1. There is a maximum ceiling of £25,000 for a claim in the ET.

4.27   Many claims, for example for wages owing (though not for pay in lieu of notice), could alternatively be brought under ERA 1996 Part II as an unauthorised deduction (see paras 4.20–4.23 regarding time limits). For this, it is not necessary for the worker to be an employee. Since, as we have said, the employer can bring his/her own contract claim if an action is commenced by the employee for breach of contract in the ET, an unauthorised deduction claim will be preferable where there is a choice, except where there are time limit problems.

The difference between employment tribunal and county or High Court claims

4.28   These are some key respects in which a contract claim in the county court or High Court differs procedurally from one in an ET:

- Only an employee can bring a contract claim in the ET and only after his/her employment has ended.
- The time limit in the county court or High Court is normally six years from the breach, whereas in the ET it must be brought within three months of termination, though in some circumstances the cause of action may have arisen in the previous six years.[76]
- The ACAS early conciliation procedure applies to a contract claim in the ET.[77]
- There is no longer a fee for ET claims. There is a fee for running a county court claim (or a sheriff court claim in Scotland), though the latest position should be checked.

75   SI No 1623 arts 3 and 5.
76   SI No 1623 art 7. The time limit for a Scottish contract claim is also longer than in the ET, but readers should check the exact calculation.
77   ETA 1996 s18(1)(g) and (h); see para 20.16.

- Legal costs will only be awarded against an employee in the ET in limited circumstances,[78] but in the county court or High Court costs will normally be awarded to the party who wins (unless it is a case on the small claims track).
- If an employee has a claim in excess of £25,000 and makes an ET claim which is capped at £25,000, s/he cannot claim the balance in the county court or High Court because the matter has already been litigated.[79] S/he cannot get round this by expressly 'reserving' his/her right to go to the civil courts afterwards. If the employee realises s/he has made a mistake and withdraws the tribunal claim before it is decided, s/he may be able to start again in the civil courts, as long as the ET does not make an order dismissing the withdrawn claim.[80] The employee should be sure to ask the ET not to dismiss the claim on withdrawal and explain why.

Furlough

4.29   The Coronavirus Job Retention Scheme was introduced on a temporary basis in an attempt to keep employees employed during the Covid-19 pandemic. The central idea was that the government would subsidise most of the wages of employees who were not working and placed on furlough. Public sector employers were discouraged from using the Scheme. The basis for the Scheme was set out in several Treasury Directions under powers granted by the Coronavirus Act 2020. HMRC, which was responsible for running the Scheme, issued regular and detailed guidance which unfortunately differed from the Treasury Directions in several respects. This made it difficult to understand the exact rules, which were in any event hugely detailed and complicated, as well as frequently changing.

4.30   The Scheme ran, with various permutations, from 1 March 2020 to 30 September 2021. For most of the period, employers were able to claim a grant from the government of 80 per cent of a furloughed employee's pay, but at certain times, that was reduced to 70 per cent

---

78 See para 20.246 onwards.
79 *Fraser v HLMAD Ltd* [2006] IRLR 687, CA.
80 *Verdin v Harrods Ltd* [2006] IRLR 339, EAT; *Sajid v Sussex Muslim Society* [2002] IRLR 113, CA, under the old ET rules of procedure. A fairly recent case reviewing estoppel generally, although not this scenario, is *Nayif v High Commission of Brunei Darussalam* [2015] IRLR 134, CA.

and then 60 per cent subject to a cap of £2,500/month. Initially furloughed employees were not allowed to work at all for their employer, but from 1 July 2020 a flexible furlough scheme was introduced, whereby employees could work part-time and be furloughed for the remaining hours.

4.31   There are these key points to bear in mind:

- There was no legal obligation on an employer to offer furlough to all or any of the workforce, but failure to do so, or unfair selection, could have implications for unfair dismissal and discrimination claims.
- Conversely, workers could not be put on furlough unless they agreed. However, refusal to agree might lead to a fair redundancy, depending on the circumstances of course.
- Unless the worker agreed to a pay cut (or, unusually, there was a right in the contract to lay off without pay), employers were still contractually obliged to pay workers their full wage, even though they could only reclaim 80 per cent (or less) from the government. In practice, there may be difficulty in proving whether a worker's agreement to be furloughed included an agreement, whether express or implied, to be paid only 80 per cent during the furlough period.
- There are complicated rules attempting to protect an employee's right to receive notice pay or redundancy pay etc based on his/her pre-furlough pay levels.[81] These are discussed further in the relevant chapters of this book, but full details are beyond the scope of this book.

4.32   If bringing a claim for pay deductions made while on furlough, it may be necessary to establish the exact furlough rules in place on the relevant dates. As stated above, these varied over time as to the percentage of pay which the employer could reclaim, and whether the worker was allowed to work reduced hours for the employer. This may not directly bear on the fundamental question which is whether the worker agreed to a pay cut, but it may provide important context.

National minimum wage

The legal framework

4.33   The NMWA 1998 introduced for the first time a national minimum wage, although in the past there had been minimum pay for certain

---

81 Employment Rights Act (Coronavirus, Calculation of a Week's Pay) Regulations 2021 SI No 814 and amended in November 2020 by SI No 1292.

vulnerable groups of workers.[82] The law is set out in the NMWA 1998 and the National Minimum Wage Regulations (NMW Regs) 2015.[83] The NMW Regs 2015 replaced the NMW Regs 1999 and various amending regulations. The Department for Business, Energy & Industrial Strategy (BEIS) has issued some useful guidance, although it has no formal legal status.[84]

4.34   There is a Low Pay Commission which advises the government on pay rates. Its reports and pay rates for many years are available on its website.[85] Many commentators feel that the minimum pay rates are set too low and do not do enough to tackle poverty. By contrast, the voluntary 'living wage' campaign in recent years has gradually gathered strength, showing up the inadequacy of the statutory minimum wage. In April 2016, the government introduced a so-called 'national living wage' for those aged 25 or over, thus appropriating the name 'living wage' from the campaign. This still fell below what is now called the 'real living wage'. For example, in April 2021, when the statutory minimum wage was only £8.91/hour for those aged 23 and above, the real UK 'living wage' was assessed at £9.50/hour, and the London living wage at £10.85/hour. Details of the real living wage, which is currently revised every October/November, can be found on the website of the Living Wage Foundation.[86]

4.35   The government plans to reduce the age qualification for the statutory national living wage to those aged 21 and above by 2024. It has also announced an aspiration to bring the hourly rate up to two-thirds of median earnings, but whether this will be sustainable after the Covid-19 pandemic remains to be seen. UNISON has made regular submissions to the Low Pay Commission calling for the national minimum wage to be brought up to the level of a 'living wage'.[87] The Trades Union Congress (TUC) has also made submissions in the past. The following paragraphs in this chapter deal only with the statutory national minimum wage.

---

82 For example, under the Wages Councils.

83 SI No 621.

84 *Calculating the minimum wage*: BEIS (updated 4 August 2021) at www.gov.uk/guidance/calculating-the-minimum-wage.

85 This is now located on the GOV.UK website at: www.gov.uk/government/organisations/low-pay-commission.

86 At: www.livingwage.org.uk/what-real-living-wage.

87 'UNISON evidence to the Low Pay Commission on minimum wage rates for 2022' is at www.unison.org.uk/content/uploads/2021/09/UNISON-evidence-to-the-Low-Pay-Commission-2021-Final.pdf.

Who can claim

4.36   A person qualifies for the national minimum wage if s/he is a worker over compulsory school age who works or ordinarily works in the UK.[88] The definition of a 'worker',[89] as opposed to someone who is an employee or self-employed, is discussed at paras 4.5–4.7 above. Agency workers and home workers are explicitly covered by the NMWA 1998.[90]

4.37   Excluded from an entitlement to a minimum wage are: workers participating in certain government training or work experience schemes; those on work schemes for provision of accommodation to the homeless; those on certain European Union (EU) programmes;[91] those on further education courses interrupted by work experience of no more than one year;[92] live-in au pairs and nannies and companions who are treated as a member of their employer's family with free accommodation and meals;[93] and members of the employer's family who live in his/her home.[94]

Method of calculation and the rates

4.38   The minimum wage is periodically increased. This used to take place in October, but now occurs in April. Past rates can be found on the GOV.UK website.[95] For the year starting 1 April 2021:

- the hourly rate for those aged 23+ (the so-called national living wage) was £8.91;
- the hourly rate for those aged 21–22 was £8.36;[96]
- the hourly rate for those aged 18–20 years was £6.56;[97]

---

88   NMWA 1998 s1.
89   NMWA 1998 s54(3).
90   NMWA 1998 ss34 and 35.
91   See NMW Regs 2015 regs 51, 52 and 54–56 for details.
92   NMW Regs 2015 reg 53.
93   NMW Regs 2015 reg 57(3). See *Nambalat v Taher and another; Udin v Chamsi-Pasher and others* [2012] EWCA Civ 1249; [2012] IRLR 1004 regarding domestic workers.
94   NMW Regs 2015 reg 57(2).
95   At: www.gov.uk/national-minimum-wage-rates.
96   National Minimum Wage (Amendment) Regulations 2021 SI No 329; NMW Regs 2015 reg 4(1)(a).
97   NMW Regs 2015 reg 4(1)(b).

- the hourly rate for those under 18 years (and over compulsory school age[98]) was £4.62;[99] and
- the apprentice rate was £4.30 per hour.[100]

These are all gross sums.

4.39   The NMW Regs 2015 are complicated. They set out in detail how to work out whether the minimum wage has been paid. The worker must calculate the hourly rate s/he is actually paid for the relevant pay reference period by dividing the total paid by the number of hours worked.[101] The pay reference period is a calendar month, or if a worker is paid at shorter intervals, that shorter interval.[102] If a worker has earned pay in one reference period, eg for overtime or commission, but it is not paid until the next, for calculation purposes it is taken as paid in the initial period. There is an online calculator for the national minimum wage at: worksmart.org.uk/tools/minimum-wage-calculator.

How much has the worker been paid?

4.40   Unfortunately it is not as simple as looking at the worker's payslip to ascertain the total paid towards the minimum wage. There are all sorts of payments, bonuses, perks and deductions, which make up a pay packet. The NMW Regs 2015 set out which payments by the employer may and may not be taken into account.[103] The total paid cannot include payments by the employer which represents amounts paid by customers by way of service charge, tip, gratuity or cover charge.[104] The total does include performance allowances, but not other allowances (unless consolidated into pay), eg attendance

---

98   To work out exact school leaving age, see: www.gov.uk/know-when-you-can-leave-school.

99   NMW Regs 2015 reg 4(1)(c).

100   NMW Regs 2015 reg 4(1)(d). For when the apprentice rate applies, see reg 5.

101   NMW Regs 2015 reg 7.

102   NMW Regs 2015 reg 6.

103   NMW Regs 2015 regs 9–15.

104   NMW Regs 2015 reg 10(m); *Nerva v R L & G Ltd* [1996] IRLR 461, CA; *Nerva v UK* [2002] IRLR 815, ECtHR. See also *Annabel's (Berkeley Square) Ltd v Commissioners for Her Majesty's Revenue and Customs* [2009] EWCA Civ 361. The former Department for Business, Innovation & Skills (BIS) issued a voluntary *Code of best practice on service charges, tips, gratuities and cover charges* (October 2009), available in the archives at: http://webarchive.nationalarchives.gov.uk/20090609003228/http://www.berr.gov.uk/files/file52948.pdf.

allowances[105] or reimbursement of expenses.[106] Benefits in kind, eg free meals or luncheon vouchers, cannot be counted towards the employer's payments.[107] The value of free accommodation including provision of related gas and electricity[108] can only be counted to a limited extent (known as the 'accommodation offset'). In the year starting 1 April 2021, this was £8.36/day.[109] If it is a contractual requirement to live in, and not a perk of the job, the value of free accommodation may not be set off at all.[110] Payments made to or deductions by a local housing authority or registered social landlord in respect of provision of accommodation are not deducted from the total pay calculation except where the accommodation is provided in connection with the worker's employment with that authority or landlord.[111] Certain deductions made by employers are not counted as deductions in the calculation of the total paid, eg deductions for the repayment of loans or due to an accidental overpayment of wages.[112] Where the worker works overtime hours during the pay reference period, payments above the basic rate for those hours are not counted.[113] So if the worker's basic contractual rate is below the minimum wage, it cannot be brought above the minimum wage just because s/he regularly works overtime or receives other shift premiums which mean s/he was actually paid above the minimum overall.[114] In the same way, a 'salary premium' for working at a particular time, location or on particular responsibilities, also cannot be counted into basic pay for a salaried worker.[115]

---

105 NMW Regs 2015 reg 10(k).

106 NMW Regs 2015 reg 10(l) and (n).

107 NMW Regs 2015 reg 10(f)–(g).

108 *Leisure Employment Services Ltd v Commissioners for HM Revenue & Customs* [2007] IRLR 450, CA.

109 NMW Regs 2015 regs 9(1)(e), 14–16; National Minimum Wage (Amendment) Regulations 2021 SI No 329.

110 See *Vasquez-Guirado and Vasquez-Howard t/a The Watermeadows Hotel v Wigmore* UKEAT/0033/05, where a hotel worker was required to live in, and be on call in the hotel 24 hours a day.

111 NMW Regs 2015 reg 14(1)(b).

112 NMW Regs 2015 reg 12(2)(b) and (c).

113 NMW Regs 2015 reg 10(j).

114 *Hamilton House Medical Ltd v Hillier* UKEAT/0246/09.

115 NMW Regs 2015 reg 10(o) and reg 21(9).

How many hours have been worked?

4.41 The number of hours which the worker has 'worked' during the pay reference period may not be obvious, and it is important that the correct type of work is identified, because it affects the calculation. There are four types of work under the NMW Regs 2015: 1) time work,[116] 2) salaried hours work,[117] 3) output work[118] and 4) unmeasured work.[119] *Time work* is paid by reference to actual hours worked. *Salaried hours work* is where a worker is entitled to be paid for an ascertainable number of basic hours in a year by an annual salary which is paid in instalments, usually weekly or monthly; and where there is no entitlement to extra payment except for any performance bonus or salary premium. *Output work* is where pay is linked to output but not to time. *Unmeasured work* means any other work, but particularly work where there are no specified hours and the worker is required to work when needed or when work is available.

4.42 Time on call – where a worker must be available at or near the workplace – can be counted as hours 'worked' within time work or salaried hours work (except when the worker lives there).[120] For example, a driver is waiting at the employer's premises to start a journey or a worker is called into a factory to help with an urgent order, but there is a delay in the materials being delivered. Both must be paid for their waiting time. However, if a duty solicitor is on call at home, awaiting urgent calls from a police station, s/he need not be paid while waiting at home.

4.43 There have been many conflicting cases over the years regarding whether sleep-in workers are entitled to be paid the minimum wage for each hour of their sleep-in shift, or only when they are up and doing work tasks. The cases have tended to involve care workers in residential homes and security guards, who are basically given sleeping facilities, allowed to sleep, but expected to respond to emergencies, requests for help, the telephone, and alarms.

4.44 The Supreme Court in the *Royal Mencap* case has now clarified the position. Where an employer provides sleeping facilities, and the main purpose of the shift is to sleep at or near the workplace, with other tasks such as responding to a disturbance only being subsidi-

---

116 NMW Regs 2015 regs 30–35.
117 NMW Regs 2015 regs 21–29.
118 NMW Regs 2015 regs 36–43.
119 NMW Regs 2015 regs 44–50.
120 NMW Regs 2015 regs 32 and 27. Formerly NMW Regs 1999 regs 15(1) and 16(1).

ary, the worker will not be taken to have worked for the entire shift. The worker can only claim the minimum wage for the time when s/he is awake for the purposes of working.[121] It is not enough for workers to be awake for their own purposes. They must be awake specifically for the purpose of carrying out the tasks which the employer has required them to do, such as answering emergency calls, helping night staff when called on, or distributing breakfast. It is unlikely to matter how often or how rarely the worker is disturbed in practice (unless it is so often that the main purpose of the arrangement is not in fact sleeping). It also does not matter that the worker has been asked to sleep on the premises because of regulatory requirements.

4.45   If on the other hand, sleeping is not the main purpose of the arrangement, the fact that the worker is allowed to nap between tasks does not necessarily mean s/he is a sleep-in worker. S/he may on the facts be 'working' throughout the shift and entitled to the minimum wage for all the hours. The Supreme Court in *Royal Mencap* was anxious to stress that it had not considered the type of home-working arrangements which might arise because of Covid-19 restrictions.

4.46   Time on a rest break is *not* counted as time at work.[122] Travelling for work duties, though not to and from work, *is* usually counted as working hours.[123] Where required or approved by the employer and taking place during the working day, time spent training and travelling between the workplace and the training venue is generally treated as hours worked.[124]

4.47   Output and unmeasured work can cause particular difficulties in assessing the number of hours worked. The rules on calculating output work are especially complex.[125] Unmeasured work is either paid for as the total number of hours worked or by reference to a 'daily average' agreement.[126] This is a written agreement between the worker and the employer made before the pay reference period. It determines the average daily number of hours the worker is likely to

---

121 NMW Regs 2015 reg 27(1)(b) and (2), and reg 32. *Royal Mencap Society v Tomlinson Blake; Shannon v Rampersad and another (t/a Clifton House Residential Home)* [2021] UKSC 8.

122 NMW Regs 2015 reg 35(3).

123 NMW Regs 2015 regs 27(3), 34, 39 and 47. Formerly NMW Regs 1999 regs 15(2) and (3), 16(2) and (3), 17(1) and 18(1). *Whittlestone v BJP Home Support Ltd* [2014] IRLR 176, EAT. See para 4.72 regarding when travel to and from work is counted as working time, which may have implications for pay.

124 NMW Regs 2015 regs 19, 33, 38, 46.

125 See NMW Regs 2015 regs 36–43.

126 NMW Regs 2015 regs 45–50.

spend carrying out his/her contractual duties on days when s/he is available to carry out those duties for the full amount of time contemplated by the contract. It must be a realistic average.

4.48   In some cases it may not be clear whether a worker is doing time work or unmeasured work. This can make a big difference to how many hours should be paid for. Unmeasured work probably covers situations such as those where residential care workers sleep on the employer's premises and are on call around the clock, but may be only actively working for a few hours.[127]

4.49   A worker will not usually be entitled to the minimum wage while on furlough for periods that s/he was not working.[128] However, s/he must be paid for hours where s/he is required to undertake training.[129]

Enforcement

4.50   Employers must keep sufficient records to show whether they are paying the national minimum wage.[130] A worker who has reasonable grounds to suspect that s/he has been underpaid has the right to inspect and copy his/her own records.[131] S/he must give his/her employer a 'production notice' requesting production of the relevant records for a specified period and stating whether s/he intends to bring someone with him/her. The employer must then produce the records on reasonable notice at the workplace or at another reasonable location, within 14 days.

4.51   A worker who is paid less than the minimum wage can claim for an 'unauthorised deduction' in the ET[132] or 'breach of contract of employment' in the county court or High Court (or Scottish equivalent). The worker can claim arrears calculated at the minimum wage rates applicable at the time the arrears are determined if these are higher than those applicable at the time the underpayment

127 For some different examples, see *Walton v Independent Living Organisation Ltd* [2003] IRLR 469, CA, and *MacCartney v Oversley House Management* [2006] IRLR 514, EAT.

128 NMWA 1998 s1(1) says someone is entitled to be paid the national minimum wage 'in respect of his work'.

129 Subject to the rules on training.

130 NMW Regs 2015 reg 59 as amended by the National Minimum Wage (Amendment) Regulations 2021 SI 329.

131 NMWA 1998 s10. For the position on transfers of undertakings, see para 10.44.

132 See para 4.8 onwards.

occurred.[133] If an employer suddenly tries to reduce one part of a worker's contractual pay package, eg attendance allowances, to subsidise an increase in the basic hourly rate, this would be an unauthorised deduction from pay even if the overall pay package remained the same.[134]

4.52   As well as individuals taking cases, enforcement can be carried out by HMRC. HMRC officers have power to enter premises, inspect records, interview employers and pass information onto workers. They can issue a 'notice of underpayment' if they find underpayment, requiring the employer to pay the arrears within 28 days.[135] Officers must at the same time also serve a penalty notice imposing a fine of 100 per cent of the total due subject to a minimum of £100 and maximum of £20,000 per worker.[136] The penalty is halved if the employer pays the arrears within 14 days. Employers can appeal against the notice of underpayment or the penalty notice to an ET.[137] If the employer does not comply with a valid notice, the officer may on behalf of the worker present an ET claim for unauthorised deductions or a claim for breach of contract in the civil courts.[138] To register a complaint with HMRC, a form needs to be completed online.[139] There is a 'name and shame' scheme whereby employers who have been issued with a notice of underpayment are named in a press notice unless certain exceptions apply. The scheme was paused for a review in 2018 and restarted in 2020 for employers owing more than £500. A press release in August 2021 named 191 companies for the period 2011–2018.[140] Of named employers, 47 per cent wrongly deducted pay, eg for uniform and expenses, and 30 per cent failed to pay all time worked, eg when workers did overtime. For details of the

---

133 NMWA 1998 s17. This also applies to arrears prior to the amendments to s17 coming into force – Employment Act 2008 s8(8).

134 *Laird v A K Stoddart Ltd* [2001] IRLR 591, EAT and *Aviation & Airport Services Ltd v Bellfield* [2001] UKEAT 194_00_1403.

135 NMWA 1998 s19.

136 NMWA 1998 s19A. The £20,000 maximum applies per worker, as opposed to in total, for pay periods from 26 May 2015 – Small Business, Enterprise and Employment Act 2015 (Commencement No 1) Regulations 2015 SI No 1329.

137 NMWA 1998 s19C.

138 NMWA 1998 s19D.

139 Via a link at: www.gov.uk/pay-and-work-rights under 'Complaints' or directly at www.gov.uk/government/publications/pay-and-work-rights-complaints.

140 See www.gov.uk/government/news/naming-employers-who-fail-to-pay-minimum-wage-to-be-resumed-under-revamped-rules and www.gov.uk/government/news/employers-named-and-shamed-for-paying-less-than-minimum-wage.

enforcement policy generally, BEIS's *Minimum Wage Law: enforcement* (2020).[141]

4.53 It is also a criminal offence not to pay the national minimum wage or not to keep or preserve the prescribed records or to make false records.[142]

4.54 A worker must not be subjected to a detriment including dismissal because s/he is about to qualify for the minimum wage or because s/he takes any action or any action is taken on his/her behalf to secure the minimum wage.[143] If an employee is dismissed, it will be treated as automatically unfair dismissal regardless of his/her length of service.[144] HMRC has no power to assist workers with this type of claim.

Holiday pay

4.55 The Working Time Regulations (WTR) 1998[145] set minimum holiday entitlements for most workers,[146] but it is possible for workers to agree greater holiday entitlements with their employers and these become a contractual right. The worker can take whichever is more favourable in each respect of his/her holiday rights under the contract or WTR 1998.[147] The worker's holiday entitlement must be set out in writing in his/her contract or statement of particulars.[148] See para 4.87 onwards for the general position on holidays including under the WTR 1998.

---

141 At https://assets.publishing.service.gov.uk/government/uploads/system/ uploads/attachment_data/file/923118/national-minimum-wage-enforcement-policy-1-oct-2020.pdf. The latest version of this document plus policies on the social care sector are linked at www.gov.uk/government/publications/ enforcing-national-minimum-wage-law. See also the Low Pay Commission's April 2021 report *Non-compliance and enforcement of the National Minimum Wage* at https://assets.publishing.service.gov.uk/government/uploads/system/ uploads/attachment_data/file/978383/2021_LPC_non-compliance_report.pdf.
142 NMWA 1998 s31.
143 NMWA 1998 ss23 and 24.
144 ERA 1996 ss104A and 108(1)(gg).
145 SI No 1833.
146 WTR 1998 reg 13.
147 WTR 1998 reg 17.
148 ERA 1996 s1 and see para 1.24.

Sick pay

Introduction

4.56   The position regarding sick pay entitlement should be in writing, as it is one of the terms and conditions which must be provided in a written contract or statement of particulars.[149] Regardless of the contractual position, if an employee is leaving, and off sick during his/her statutory notice period, s/he must usually be paid full pay for that period.[150] In 2010, the old system of 'sick notes' was replaced by 'fit notes' whereby GPs in England, Scotland and Wales must issue a 'Statement of fitness for work'. Revised guidance for GPs, employers and employees on fit notes was issued in December 2016.[151] The emphasis is on encouraging everyone involved to think about what adjustments could be made to enable workers to return to work, rather than getting drawn into prolonged sick leave.

Statutory sick pay

4.57   Employees[152] are entitled to statutory sick pay (SSP) from their employers for a period of up to 28 weeks' sickness absence. Employees on fixed-term contracts are included. Some employees are specifically excluded, including those earning below the lower earnings limit, ie normal (average) gross earnings below £120 per week (for the year starting 6 April 2021).

4.58   The employee must be incapable of doing his/her work due to a specific disease or bodily or mental disablement, or certified as a carrier of an infectious disease.[153] S/he must have been incapable of work for at least four consecutive days (including days s/he does not normally work). Two periods can be linked together if separated by no more than eight weeks. S/he should be paid for each qualifying day, ie a day on which s/he is contractually required to work but is off sick. However, the first three qualifying days (known as 'waiting days') are unpaid. If s/he is off sick within eight weeks of an earlier period, s/he need not serve the three waiting days again. The entitle-

---

149 ERA 1996 s1(4)(d)(ii); and see para 1.24.
150 See para 1.39 for the precise rule.
151 Available at: www.gov.uk/government/collections/fit-note.
152 As defined by the Social Security Contributions and Benefits Act (SSCBA) 1992 and the Statutory Sick Pay (General) Regulations 1982 SI No 894.
153 SSCBA 1992 s151.

ment ceases if his/her job comes to an end, although not if the employer dismissed him/her to avoid paying SSP.

4.59　At the time of writing, a person may be entitled to get SSP for every day off work if they are self-isolating because they or someone they live with or in their support bubble has Covid-19 symptoms, or because they have been notified by the authorities that they have been in contact with someone with Covid-19, or because they have been advised to self-isolate prior to surgery. It does not cover having to self-isolate purely after entering or returning to the UK. This position is likely to change at some point.[154]

4.60　SSP is paid at a flat weekly rate – £96.35 is the standard weekly rate for the year beginning 6 April 2021.[155] The daily rate is calculated by dividing the weekly rate by the number of qualifying days in a week. SSP is usually paid through the pay packet in the same way as normal wages.

4.61　Employers can decide how and when they want their employees to notify them of sickness. For entitlement to contractual sick pay, the employers can, within reason, impose any rule they like. For the SSP element, however, they cannot insist that they are notified personally by the employee, as opposed to by a friend or relative. They cannot insist on being contacted more than once a week. Nor can they insist on a medical certificate for the first seven days. For the initial seven-day period, employees must be allowed to self-certify.

4.62　If employers refuse SSP or intend to stop paying it, they should give a written statement (usually on an SSP1 form) explaining why. Workers who are ineligible for SSP or whose SSP runs out may be able to claim Employment and Support Allowance (ESA) instead, which depends on a different set of rules. They may also have an independent entitlement to contractual sick pay. Employees can claim unpaid SSP as an unauthorised deduction from wages under ERA 1996 Part II.[156] If the employer disputes the employee's entitlement to SSP or its amount, a ruling should first be obtained from HMRC.[157]

4.63　SSP and other benefits are not within the scope of this book and the above is only a broad outline. Where the issue arises, specialist advice should be sought. There are full details of the SSP rates, the

---

154　Details from www.gov.uk/statutory-sick-pay at the time of writing.

155　Social Security Benefits Up-rating Order 2021 SI No 162. SSP rates and rules are at www.gov.uk/statutory-sick-pay.

156　See para 4.8 onwards.

157　*Taylor Gordon and Co Ltd v Timmons* [2004] IRLR 180, EAT; *Hair Division Ltd v Macmillan* UKEATS/0033/12-13.

entitlement provisions and the remedies available for non-payment in the excellent *Welfare benefits and tax credits handbook*, which is published annually by the Child Poverty Action Group. The GOV. UK website has useful guidance aimed at employers on how to calculate SSP and the latest rates.[158]

Contractual sick pay

4.64   The SSP provisions are a minimum entitlement when away from work on account of sickness. Many employees are covered by a contractual sick pay scheme which generally makes up the difference between the SSP figure and normal wages for a fixed period of time in any given year. The first three days of sickness are usually also covered. A contractual scheme may have various notification requirements which it is important for the employee to follow, even if some of these will not be valid for the SSP element (see above).

4.65   A contractual sickness procedure is normally set out in writing in the contract of employment. If it is not in writing and was never expressly agreed, it may still be possible to imply a term that the employee is entitled to normal pay for a certain amount of time, eg if the employee has been fully paid in previous years or if all other staff are paid normally when off sick.[159] In the absence of any express term or this kind of implied term, there is no presumption that employees are entitled to the normal rate of pay when off sick.[160]

4.66   If an employee's contract says payment for sickness absence is conditional on management being satisfied the sickness absence is genuine, it is for the employer to make the decision as long as it is in good faith and not perverse. The employer cannot just decide the absence is not genuine without any specific evidence to that effect and merely because the employer's occupational health service disagrees with the employee's GP as to when the employee will be fit to return.[161] On the other hand, if an employer refuses to allow an employee to return to work once the employee is certified as fit by his/her own doctor, s/he must be paid full wages while remaining at home unless the contract says otherwise.[162]

---

158 At: www.gov.uk/calculate-statutory-sick-pay.
159 See paras 1.3–1.6 for implied terms.
160 *Mears v Safecar Security* [1982] IRLR 183, CA.
161 *Scottish Courage Ltd v Guthrie* UKEAT/0788/03.
162 *Beveridge v KLM UK Ltd* [2000] IRLR 765, EAT.

Itemised pay statements

4.67   Employers are obliged to provide employees with an itemised pay statement at or before each pay day.[163] There is no requirement on the employee to request an itemised pay statement. It is an absolute right.[164] Itemised pay statements must include the gross pay, details of all deductions from the gross pay, and the net pay. If the net pay is paid in different ways, the amount and method of payment of each part of the net pay must also be itemised.[165] Where pay varies by reference to time worked, the statement must include the number of hours carried out.[166] If the employer supplies the employee with a written statement of a fixed deduction to be made each pay day (such as the repayment of a season ticket loan), the employer need detail the nature of this deduction only once every 12 months.[167]

4.68   If the employer fails to give an employee an itemised pay statement, or if deductions are made which were not notified, the employee can apply to the ET for a declaration to this effect,[168] and ask the ET to exercise its discretion to make a compensatory award. The declaration is mandatory, but the compensation award is discretionary. The maximum amount of compensation that can be awarded is calculated by taking the date of application to the ET and determining the amount of the unnotified deductions (tax, National Insurance, union subscriptions, etc) on each of the pay days in the 13 weeks prior to the ET application.[169] The ACAS early conciliation procedure applies.[170]

4.69   If the reason why the employer has failed to provide itemised pay statements is due to fraud or dishonest conduct, it is likely that the ET will be more willing to make a high award. The compensation is intended to act as a penalty on the employer for non-compliance and it does not matter whether the employer has accounted for the sums deducted to HMRC and therefore ends up paying twice.[171] The

---

163 ERA 1996 s8.
164 *Coales v John Woods and Co (Solicitors)* [1986] IRLR 129, EAT.
165 ERA 1996 s8.
166 Employment Rights Act 1996 (Itemised Pay Statement) (Amendment) Order 2018 SI No 147 for periods of work starting on or after 6 April 2019.
167 ERA 1996 s9.
168 ERA 1996 s11.
169 ERA 1996 s12(4).
170 ETA 1996 s18(1)(b); see para 20.16.
171 *Cambiero v Aldo Zilli & Sheenwalk Ltd t/a Signor Zilli's Bar* [1997] UKEAT 273_96_0907.

Employment Appeal Tribunal (EAT), in a decision in 1979, allowed a low ET award because the provisions had come into effect only recently and the employer was a busy professional person in sole practice.[172] Twenty years later, the EAT took a stronger position[173] and it is now unusual for employers to get away with such leniency. It is important to stress to the ET that the failure to supply these statements is often indicative of some unlawful practice by an employer: usually the failure to make the appropriate tax and National Insurance returns. It can also cause the employee practical inconvenience.

4.70   Employees who do not get itemised pay statements should check with HMRC to discover whether the employer has been committing a fraud by not paying the requisite tax or National Insurance. If the employer deducted National Insurance contributions but did not pass these on to HMRC, the employee is treated as if the contributions have been paid unless the employee agreed or was negligent.[174]

Working Time Regulations 1998

The legal framework

4.71   The WTR 1998[175] came into force on 1 October 1998 in order to implement European Community (EC) directives on the organisation of working time[176] and protection of young workers.[177] Apart from opting out of the 48-hour week (see below), it is not possible for individuals to contract out of WTR 1998 rights.[178] However, collective or workforce agreements can modify or exclude certain entitlements as set out below. WTR 1998 Sch 1 sets out specific requirements for an agreement to become a workforce agreement.

4.72   'Working time' under the WTR 1998 means any period during which the worker is working, at his/her employer's disposal and carrying out his/her duties plus any period during which s/he is

---

172 *Scott v Creager* [1979] IRLR 162, EAT.
173 *Cambiero v Aldo Zilli & Sheenwalk Ltd t/a Signor Zilli's Bar* [1997] UKEAT 273_96_0907.
174 Social Security (Contributions) Regulations 2001 SI No 1004 reg 60. It is believed this is still the case, but readers should check.
175 SI No 1833.
176 Directives 93/104/EC (now contained in directive 2003/88/EC) and 2000/43/EC.
177 Directives 94/33/EC.
178 WTR 1998 reg 35.

receiving relevant training.[179] It includes overtime, working lunches and travel on the job. Travel to and from work is *not* covered, unless the worker has no fixed or habitual place of work; in that case, travel from home to the first customer appointment and back home from the last customer appointment is likely to be working time.[180] This kind of scenario may well apply to care workers who spend the day going from appointment to appointment arranged by their employer. Whether a worker is entitled to be paid for such time is an untested question, but arguably that might be implied under the contract.[181] Time while the worker is on call at or near the workplace, although not at home, is all working time even if the worker can sleep during periods of inactivity; but if the worker need not attend the workplace and merely needs to be contactable at all times, then working time is usually only for the periods when the worker is actually doing work for the employer.[182] However, there are situations where the restriction on the worker's freedom to engage in other activities means that it is all working time.

Who is covered?

4.73   The WTR 1998 give rights to 'workers'. The definition of a 'worker', as opposed to someone who is an employee or self-employed, is discussed at paras 4.5–4.7 above. Temporary and agency workers are also covered by the WTR 1998.[183] 'Young workers', ie those over compulsory school age[184] but under 18, are also covered, sometimes with greater protections.

---

179 WTR 1998 reg 2.
180 *Federació de Servicios Privados del sindicato Comisiones obreras v Tyco Integrated Security SL and another* C-266/14; [2015] IRLR 935, CJEU.
181 In terms of the national minimum wage, the problem is that the wording of the national minimum wage legislation is quite different and not derived from EU directives.
182 *Sindicato de Médicos de Asistencia Pública (Simap) v Conselleria de Sanidad y Consumo de la Generalidad Valenciana* C-303/98, [2000] IRLR 845, ECJ; *Landeshaupt-stadt Kiel v Jaeger* C-151/02, [2003] IRLR 804, ECJ; *Ville de Nivelles v Matzak* C-518/15, [2018] IRLR 457, CJEU. For an example concerning a residential careworker, see *MacCartney v Oversley House Management* [2006] IRLR 514, EAT. *(1) Truslove (2) Wood v Scottish Ambulance Service* UKEATS/0053/13 provides a useful example of a hybrid situation and discussion of the law.
183 WTR 1998 reg 36.
184 Broadly, 16 years old, but a little more complicated.

4.74   Certain categories of seafarers, sea fishermen and workers on vessels in inland waterways are excluded from the WTR 1998.[185] Mobile staff in civil aviation are excluded from virtually all the WTR 1998 rights except young worker protection.[186] The Civil Aviation (Working Time) Regulations 2004 apply instead.[187] Workers performing mobile road transport activities are excluded from the limits on working hours and night work and from the entitlements to daily and weekly rest periods and daily rest breaks.[188] However, the Road Transport (Working Time) Regulations 2005[189] lay down a 60-hour maximum working week with an average 48 hours over the reference period, plus minimum breaks and rest periods, for certain mobile road workers, including drivers and crew. The rules for who are covered are complex. For any other mobile workers than those described above, there are exclusions on the rest periods and breaks and regarding the length of night working.[190] These other 'mobile workers' are defined under reg 2 as members of travelling or flying personnel by an undertaking which operates transport services for passengers or goods by road or air. Rail workers are not covered by these general exclusions, but they are excluded in certain specific circumstances under reg 21 as mentioned below. Non-mobile transport workers are now generally covered. The reason for the various exclusions is that in most cases they are covered by sector-specific EU directives and have their own domestic legislation, which is similar. For further detail, see WTR 1998 reg 18.[191] There are also additional rules covering workers on cross-border rail services, eg through the Channel Tunnel.

4.75   Domestic servants in private households are excluded from much of the protection, although the entitlement to holidays and rest breaks remains.[192]

4.76   Almost all the protections in the WTR 1998, except for annual leave, do not apply where the worker works on 'unmeasured working time'.[193] It is unclear exactly what 'unmeasured time' means. The

---

185 WTR 1998 reg 18.
186 WTR 1998 reg 18(2).
187 SI No 756.
188 WTR 1998 reg 18(3).
189 SI No 639.
190 WTR 1998 reg 24A.
191 For airline pilots' holiday pay, see *British Airways plc v Williams and others* [2012] UKSC 43.
192 WTR 1998 reg 19.
193 WTR 1998 reg 20(1).

exception is intended to apply where, due to the specific nature of the work done, the duration of the worker's working time is not measured or predetermined, or it can be determined by the worker him/herself. The WTR 1998 give examples as managing executives or other persons with autonomous decision-making powers; family workers; or workers officiating in religious ceremonies. The problem is that in many workplaces, there are unspoken expectations or hidden pressures to work extra hours. The exception should not apply if someone works extra hours because of an excessive workload and unrealistic deadlines, or because his/her colleagues habitually work long hours and s/he feels this is what the employer expects. Some employers have attempted to interpret this exception widely, but advisers should question this. High-powered, self-regulating managing directors should probably be covered, but not junior workers who are pressurised by higher management to work limitless unpaid overtime.

The 48-hour week

4.77   WTR 1998 reg 4(1) imposes a contractual obligation on the employer not to require a worker to work more than an average of 48 hours per week including overtime.[194] The employer also has a duty subject to criminal sanctions to take all reasonable steps to ensure no more than 48 hours per week are worked unless the worker has opted out (see below).[195] The 48 hours is usually averaged over 17 weeks, although for some workers it will be 26 weeks.[196] A collective or workforce agreement cannot modify or exclude the 48-hour ceiling, but in certain circumstances it can extend the period over which hours are averaged.[197] Certain days off are excluded from the calculation of hours worked over the reference period, eg days off sick, on maternity, paternity, adoption or parental leave, or taken as part of the first four weeks' annual leave.[198]

4.78   A worker can make a written agreement with his/her employer to exclude (ie 'opt out' of) the 48-hour limit either for a specified period or indefinitely.[199] The worker is entitled to end the agreement without

---

194 *Barber v RJB Mining (UK) Ltd* [1999] IRLR 308, QBD.
195 WTR 1998 reg 4(2).
196 WTR 1998 reg 4.
197 WTR 1998 reg 23(b).
198 See WTR 1998 reg 4(7) for how an adjustment is made in these circumstances.
199 WTR 1998 regs 4(1) and 5.

the employer's consent on seven days' written notice or any longer notice period specified in the agreement, but no longer than three months.[200] If the worker is dismissed or suffers a detriment for refusing to enter into such an opt-out agreement or for bringing one to an end, s/he can bring a claim to the ET.[201] However, if an employer refuses to allow a worker who has not opted-out to work occasional voluntary overtime, this is not necessarily an unlawful detriment. It depends whether the employer was taking reasonable steps to comply with his/her duty to ensure a worker who had not opted-out did not work more than 48 hours.[202] For an opt-out to be valid, the worker must have expressly and freely consented to work longer hours.[203] Given the inequality of bargaining power, it is doubtful whether the common practice of presenting a worker with an opt-out form to sign on his/her induction leads to free consent.

4.79   If a worker who has been working more than 48 hours decides to exercise the opt-out and reduce his/her hours to 48, an employer can probably reduce his/her pay proportionally, especially if pay is explicitly linked to hours worked.[204]

4.80   Young workers generally must not work more than eight hours each day and 40 hours per week.[205]

Night workers

4.81   Broadly speaking, a night worker is someone who works at least three hours between 11pm and 6am on most working days.[206] Night workers must not work on average more than eight hours in each 24-hour period, averaged over 17 weeks.[207] If the work involves special hazards or heavy mental or physical strain, there is an absolute limit of eight hours in any 24-hour period. There are exceptions to this protection for certain types of job.[208] A collective or workforce agreement can modify or exclude these limits.[209] A worker who is put onto

---

200 WTR 1998 reg 5.
201 ERA 1996 ss45A and 101A. See para 4.115.
202 *Arriva London South Ltd v Nicolaou* UKEAT/0280/10.
203 *Pfeiffer and others v Deutsches Rotes Kreuz, Kreisverband Waldshut eV* [2005] IRLR 137, ECJ.
204 See the obiter comments in *Clamp v Aerial Systems* [2005] IRLR 9, EAT.
205 WTR 1998 reg 5A, subject to regs 27A, 19, 25 and 26.
206 WTR 1998 reg 2.
207 WTR 1998 reg 6.
208 See para 4.85.
209 WTR 1998 regs 23 and 24.

night work must be given the opportunity of a free health assessment before starting such work and at regular intervals thereafter.[210] If a registered medical practitioner advises that a worker is suffering from health problems connected with night work, the employer must transfer the worker to suitable work not at night if that is possible. Young workers must not work between 10pm and 6am or 11pm and 7am except in certain sectors.[211] Mobile workers, if covered at all,[212] are excluded from the night work limits but must have adequate rest.[213]

Rest periods

Overview

4.82   Employers must allow workers to take certain breaks during their working hours. Some mobile workers (if covered at all) are excluded from the normal rest break entitlements but they must be given adequate rest.[214]

4.83   Workers are entitled to a minimum daily rest period of 11 consecutive hours.[215] There are special rules for young workers. Workers are also entitled to a weekly rest period of at least 24 consecutive hours in any given week, which may be given as two 24-hour breaks or one 48-hour break over a fortnight.[216] There are special rules for young workers.

4.84   During the day, workers whose working time is more than six hours are entitled to a rest break of 20 minutes without any interruption and away from the work station.[217] This means one rest break in the working day, not a break every six hours.[218] There are special rules for young workers. A period of 'downtime', where the worker need not work but must remain in radio contact and at the employer's disposal, is not a rest break. Nor can it retrospectively be designated a rest break just because the employer happened not to call on the

---

210 WTR 1998 reg 7.
211 WTR 1998 regs 6A, 27A, 19, 25 and 26.
212 See para 4.74.
213 WTR 1998 reg 24A.
214 WTR 1998 reg 24A, but see para 4.74 for mobile road workers.
215 WTR 1998 reg 10(1).
216 WTR 1998 reg 11.
217 WTR 1998 reg 12.
218 *Corps of Commissionaires Management Ltd v Hughes* UKEAT/0196/08; [2009] IRLR 122, EAT.

worker.[219] There is nothing to say when during the day this break must be given, but as a matter of logic it should be taken during the day and not tagged on to its start or end.[220] It is not enough that the employer allows rest breaks if requested by workers. The employer must take active steps to ensure the working arrangements enable workers to take the break. The failure to do so may amount to a 'refusal' to allow the break.[221] However, this is more a question of not making it impossible to take breaks, as opposed to any obligation to check workers actually take the breaks, let alone an obligation to insist that they do so. There is no requirement under the WTR 1998 that the break must be paid, but there may be an entitlement for paid breaks under the worker's own contract. An employer cannot suddenly insert a break during normal paid working hours and deduct pay for that period. There is also a little tested entitlement to 'adequate' rest breaks where the worker's health and safety is put at risk because of the working pattern, in particular because the work is monotonous or the work-rate pre-determined.[222]

Exceptions

4.85   Certain exceptions exist:

- Shift workers or workers engaged in activities involving periods of work split up over the day, eg cleaning staff, do not have the entitlement to daily and weekly rest periods, although they are entitled to a period of compensatory rest where possible.[223]
- The entitlements to daily and weekly rest periods and to rest breaks during the day as well as the restrictions on the length of night working[224] do not apply:
  - In special areas where continuity of service or production by the worker (as opposed to the employer) may be necessary,[225] eg work in hospitals, prisons, security guards, caretakers, media, gas, water and electricity, urban transport services or refuse collection; or where there is a foreseeable surge of activ-

219 *Gallagher and others v Alpha Catering Services Ltd (t/a Alpha Flight Services)* [2005] IRLR 102, CA.
220 See observations of EAT in *Corps of Commissionaires Management Ltd v Hughes* UKEAT/0196/08; [2009] IRLR 122.
221 *Grange v Abellio London Ltd* UKEAT/0130/16; [2017] IRLR 108.
222 WTR 1998 reg 8.
223 WTR 1998 reg 24.
224 See para 4.81.
225 *Gallagher and others v Alpha Catering Services Ltd (t/a Alpha Flight Services)* [2005] IRLR 102, CA.

ity, eg in tourism or postal services.[226] A 'surge' means an exceptional level of activity beyond the fluctuations experienced within a working day or week.[227]

- To workers on board trains or whose work affects train traffic or timetables.[228]
- Where there have been unusual and unforeseeable circumstances or exceptional events whose consequences are unavoidable.[229]

• In all these circumstances, the worker should be given an equivalent period of compensatory rest. Compensatory rest must be as near in quality, character and value as the standard type of break as possible.[230] Depending on the circumstances, it could for example be the same as a standard break in all respects except that the worker is technically 'on call', provided his/her services are rarely called upon at that time; or when working a double shift, s/he could be given an uninterrupted double break in the second shift. It does not have to be a single continuous 20-minute break provided the total rest has the same value to the worker in terms of contributing to his/her well-being. It could for example be two interrupted breaks of 15 minutes, one-third and two-thirds through a shift.[231] The fact that an employer may need to provide a continuous service, eg provision of a security guard, does not mean that it has to be the same worker who is present throughout – someone else could cover on breaks.[232]

• In exceptional cases, where it is not possible to provide compensatory rest, the employer must afford sufficient protection to safeguard the worker's health and safety.[233] The type of protective measures might be several ten-minute breaks or other steps which are not breaks at all, eg health checks for workers, risk assessments, or rearranging the way work is carried out.[234]

---

226 WTR 1998 reg 21(c) and (d).
227 *Gallagher and others v Alpha Catering Services Ltd (t/a Alpha Flight Services)* [2005] IRLR 102, CA.
228 WTR 1998 reg 21(f).
229 WTR 1998 reg 21(e).
230 *Hughes v Corps of Commissionaires Management Ltd (No 2)* UKEAT/0173/10; [2011] IRLR 100.
231 Network Rail Infrastructure Ltd v Crawford [2019] IRLR 538, CA.
232 *Corps of Commissionaires Management Ltd v Hughes* UKEAT/0196/08; [2009] IRLR 122.
233 WTR 1998 reg 24.
234 *Hughes v Corps of Commissionaires Management Ltd (No 2)* UKEAT/0173/10; [2011] IRLR 100.

- Under WTR 1998 reg 24A, mobile workers[235] are entitled only to adequate rest, ie regular rest periods which are sufficiently long and continuous to ensure they don't damage their health or cause injury to themselves or others.[236]

4.86   An individual worker cannot opt out of his/her entitlement to rest periods and breaks. However, a collective or workforce agreement can modify or exclude these entitlements provided an equivalent period of compensatory rest is given.[237]

Annual leave and bank holidays

Introduction

4.87   The WTR 1998 give workers the right to minimum paid annual leave of 5.6 weeks. For someone working five days per week, this translates into 28 working days' leave. It would be higher for someone working a six-day week, but there is a total overall cap on the statutory entitlement of 28 days.[238] A worker may have a greater contractual entitlement. The Working Time Directive (WTD) only requires workers to be given four weeks' leave, and this is the period which was originally contained in the WTR 1998.[239] The 1.6 weeks' 'additional annual leave' are not in the WTD, but were phased into the WTR 1998[240] from 1 October 2007 to 1 April 2009 in recognition of the eight public and bank holidays (though there happen to be nine in Scotland). There is no right to take the extra eight days on the public/bank holidays in question, nor to get paid extra if required to work on those days, unless the worker has such a right (express or implied, eg by custom and practice) under his/her own contract. The law for such a basic right as holidays has become ridiculously complicated, with many difficulties arising on issues such as whether untaken holidays can be carried over, what happens if a worker is unaware of his/her statutory entitlement and what if s/he is on long-term sick leave. Test cases continue to be run on various factual permutations and many questions remain unanswered. Strangely, because the first four weeks leave are required by the WTD and the additional 1.6 weeks

---

235   Defined in WTR 1998 reg 2.
236   *First Hampshire and Dorset Ltd v Feist and others* UKEAT/0510/06.
237   WTR 1998 regs 23 and 24.
238   WTR 1998 reg 13(3).
239   2003/88/EC. The four-week basic entitlement is in WTR 1998 reg 13.
240   Additional annual leave is at WTR 1998 reg 13A.

are not, there are situations where the value of the first four weeks' holiday is greater than that of the balance. This is explained further below where it arises.

The nature of the entitlement

4.88   Leave entitlement is usually calculated in days or fractions of a day. For example, a worker who works a five-day week is entitled to 28 days' paid leave per year (5 × 5.6); a part-timer who works three days each week is entitled to 16.8 days' paid leave per year (3 × 5.6). If the worker works irregular hours or shifts, the calculation will probably be based on the average number of hours/days worked each week. The position with zero hours contracts is unclear, but possibly a calculation would be based on the average of hours previously worked.[241] There is no longer a provision for rounding up the leave entitlement if it does not work out as exact days. Where a worker changes from full-time to part-time during the year, or vice versa, his/her holiday accrues at the relevant rate for each period. For example, if s/he worked six months on a five-day week and six months on a three-day week, her holiday entitlement for the year would be 14 days (5.6 × 5 divided by 2) + 8.4 days (5.6 × 3 divided by 2) = 22.4 days.[242] If there is no collective or workforce agreement setting the dates of the holiday year and no written agreement between the employer and worker on this point, the leave year for workers employed before 1 October 1998 starts on 1 October; and for other workers, on the anniversary of the start of their employment.[243] In the worker's first year, s/he can only take holiday which s/he has accrued, in this case (confusingly) rounded up to the nearest half day.[244] For example, a worker works five days per week, so his/her holiday entitlement is 28 days (5.6 weeks) per year. After 16 weeks, s/he can take nine days' holiday. This is calculated as follows: (16 divided by 52) × 28 = 8.61, which is then rounded up to 9. In subsequent years, the worker need

---

241 The CJEU cases of *Zentralbetriebsrat der Landeskrankenhauser Tirols v Land Tirol* C-486/08, [2010] IRLR 631, CJEU and *Heimann v Kaiser GmbH* C-229/11, [2013] IRLR 48, CJEU provide some guidance but are not easily applied in practice. However, 'part-year' workers should still be paid 5.6 weeks: see *The Harpur Trust v Brazel* [2019] EWCA Civ 1402 for details. It is believed this is on appeal.

242 This seems to be the effect of *Zentralbetriebsrat der Landeskrankenhauser Tirols v Land Tirol* C-486/08, [2010] IRLR 631, CJEU; *Greenfield v Care Bureau Ltd* C-219/14, [2016] IRLR 62, CJEU.

243 WTR 1998 regs 13(3) and 13A(4).

244 WTR 1998 reg 15A.

not wait until s/he has accrued leave entitlement. Calculations of holiday pay are potentially complicated. If you want to avoid the maths, GOV.UK provides an online calculator.[245]

4.89   Leave must be taken in the leave year in which it is due and this entitlement cannot be substituted by payment in lieu of the holiday except on the termination of employment for the portion of the termination year which has been worked.[246] Under the WTR 1998, untaken holidays cannot be carried over, although the worker may have a contractual entitlement to do this. It is also permitted to carry over some or all of the additional 1.6 weeks' leave to the next holiday year if the employer agrees in a relevant agreement, eg in a collective agreement or the worker's written contract.[247] With this small exception, untaken leave is therefore lost. There is a danger that a worker will be strung along with the employer continually refusing his/her proposed holiday dates until time runs out. Workers in this position should give formal notice in good time to take leave under the WTR 1998.[248] See below for whether workers can claim compensation where they did not try to take holidays or tried and were refused. Also see para 4.109 regarding temporary additional rights to carry over leave because of the Covid-19 pandemic.

4.90   Unfortunately there is nothing in the WTR 1998 which prevents employers specifying when in the year the leave must or must not be taken, or how many days at a time, although the worker may have greater rights under his/her contract. For example, an employer can insist that holidays are taken at an annual Christmas shutdown unless the contract indicates otherwise. The employer must give sufficient notice specifying when the leave must be taken. The notice need not be given in writing. Such notice must be given at least twice as many days in advance of the earliest leave day as the number of days to which the notice relates,[249] eg an employer requiring a worker to take two weeks' holiday at Christmas must give at least four weeks' notice. An employer can require a worker to take his/her holidays during periods when s/he is not working anyway, eg teachers during school holidays.[250] In one case, where oil rig workers worked two weeks offshore followed by two weeks onshore without work obliga-

---

245 See: www.gov.uk/calculate-your-holiday-entitlement.
246 WTR 1998 regs 13(9)(b) and 13A(6).
247 WTR 1998 reg 13A(7).
248 See para 4.91.
249 WTR 1998 reg 15.
250 See comments of the Supreme Court in *Russell and others v Transocean International Resources Ltd and others* [2011] UKSC 57; [2012] IRLR 149.

tions, the Supreme Court said the employer could designate part of the two weeks off as annual leave.[251] The important point was that the workers had whole weeks where they were not required to work and which they could take as holidays. This was not the same as requiring a worker to take leave on his/her normal days off or a part-time worker to take his/her leave on the days of the week when s/he does not work.

4.91   A worker can take leave by giving the correct notice specifying the proposed leave days.[252] It is safer to give such notice in writing, although this is not required under the WTR 1998. The notice must be given twice as many days in advance of the first day proposed for leave as the number of days proposed in total.[253] If the employer objects to leave being taken on those dates, s/he must give counter-notice as many days in advance of the earliest date as the total number of days to which the worker's notice relates.[254] For example, a worker wanting to take three days' leave must give at least six days' notice. Employers wishing to refuse that leave must give at least three days' counter-notice. Note that workers and employers may have agreed a different notification procedure by a relevant agreement under the rules, eg in a collective agreement or the worker's written contract of employment.[255] This can include setting annual holiday dates in the contract or including a contractual term saying an employee who is leaving can be required to take holidays during his/her notice period.[256] Under the WTR 1998, the employer does not need to have a good reason for refusing leave at any particular time.[257]

4.92   Employers cannot unilaterally reduce a worker's pay in order to pay for holidays under the WTR 1998.[258] The practice of 'rolled-up' holiday pay is also unlawful, ie simply increasing the basic wage to cover holiday pay, but not making any payment at the time holiday is taken.[259] Having said that, an employer may set off any sums actually

251 *Russell and others v Transocean International Resources Ltd and others* [2012] IRLR 149, SC.
252 WTR 1998 reg 15.
253 WTR 1998 reg 15(1), (3) and (4).
254 WTR 1998 reg 15(2) and (4).
255 WTR 1998 regs 2(1) and 15(5).
256 *Industrial and Commercial Maintenance Ltd v Briffa* UKEAT/0215-6/08.
257 Except in relation to the extended right to carry over leave due to the effects of Covid-19: see para 4.109.
258 *Davies and others v M J Wyatt (Decorators) Ltd* [2000] IRLR 759, EAT.
259 *Robinson-Steele v R D Retail Services Ltd; Clarke v Frank Staddon Ltd; Caulfield and others v Hanson Clay Products Ltd (formerly Marshall's Clay Products Ltd)* [2006] IRLR 386, ECJ.

paid in advance under transparent and comprehensive arrangements.[260] This effectively allows rolled-up payments by the back door.

4.93   On the termination of employment, a worker is entitled to receive payment for any untaken holiday in the holiday year of termination, calculated proportionally to the leave year.[261] This applies even if s/he has been absent on sick leave all year up to the point of leaving.[262] As explained below, a worker may in very limited circumstances be entitled to pay for untaken holiday in previous years, even if s/he did not ask to carry over his/her holiday at the time. To calculate the amount of leave due on termination in respect of the current leave year, there is a formula in the WTR 1998:

$(A \times B) - C$[263]

where:

A is the number of days annual leave to which the worker is entitled,
B is the proportion of the leave year which has expired at the termination date, and
C is the amount of leave already taken that year.

For example, a worker who works five days each week has a 28-day annual leave entitlement. If s/he leaves nine months into the final holiday year, having taken six days paid leave that year, s/he is owed $((28 \times 9/12) - 6) = 15$ days. Alternatively, the WTR 1998 say that if the worker's contract (or other relevant agreement) specifies the sum which the worker should be paid on leaving in respect of untaken holiday, 'such sum' will apply instead of the statutory formula.[264] This cannot mean no payment at all, so eg a contractual term excluding all payment for untaken holidays if the dismissal is for misconduct will not apply.[265] It is also unlikely that a purely nominal sum would be allowed.[266] In respect of any contractual holiday entitlement over and above the 5.6 weeks, pay in lieu of the untaken holiday will only be payable on termination if there is an express right to it under the

---

260 *Robinson-Steele* [2006] IRLR 386, CJEU; *Lyddon v Englefield Brickwork Ltd* [2008] IRLR 198, EAT. WTR 1998 reg 16(5).
261 WTR 1998 reg 14.
262 WTR 1998 reg 15.
263 WTR 1998 reg 14.
264 WTR 1998 reg 14(3).
265 By analogy with *Witley & District Men's Club v Mackay* [2001] IRLR 595, EAT.
266 Because of ECJ's comments in *Stringer and others v HM Revenue and Customs sub nom Commissioners of Inland Revenue v Ainsworth and Schultz-Hoff v Deutsche Rentenversicherung Bund* C-520/06 and C-350/06, [2009] IRLR 214, CJEU.

contract or a clear term implied by custom and practice. The contract may also choose to provide that such additional entitlement is not payable where there is dismissal for gross misconduct.

4.94   Under the WTR 1998 there is no requirement that workers repay excess holiday taken in the year of leaving unless there is a 'relevant agreement', eg the worker's contract or a workforce agreement, requiring this to be done.[267] It will be an unauthorised deduction under ERA 1996 Part II if the employer deducts the excess from the worker's wages without such an agreement.[268]

4.95   WTR 1998 reg 16 says a worker is entitled to be paid for annual leave at the rate of a week's pay. This is usually the worker's contractual entitlement for normal working hours. If the worker's pay fluctuates, an average is taken over the previous 52 weeks. If the worker received no pay in any of the weeks in that period, paid weeks in the previous year can be taken into account.[269] The daily rate of holiday pay for a salaried worker is calculated by dividing his/her annual salary by the number of working days in the year – not the number of calendar days.[270]

4.96   Read literally, by referring to the 'normal working hours' in the worker's contract, reg 16 could mean that a worker's holiday pay would fall far short of his/her usual pay packet, eg by excluding the overtime, commission or allowances which would normally be earned if the worker was at work (unless the worker's contract explicitly stated that such sums should be included). It has now been established that under the WTD, holiday pay must represent a worker's normal earnings. If pay is variable, what is 'normal' should be assessed over a representative period. Therefore a sum to represent overtime, whether voluntary or compulsory,[271] and commission[272]

---

267 WTR 1998 regs 14(4) and 2(1).

268 *Hill v Chappell* [2003] IRLR 19, EAT.

269 WTR 1998 reg 16 as amended with effect from 6 April 2020 to add subsections 16(3)(e), (f), 16(3A) and (3B). This is only a general summary of the exact rules.

270 *Leisure Leagues UK Ltd v Maconnachie* [2002] IRLR 600, EAT; *Yarrow v Edwards Chartered Accountants* UKEAT/0116/07. Although arguably there is some conflicting case-law, this makes the most sense.

271 *Bear Scotland Ltd and others v Fulton and others; Hertel (UK) Ltd v Woods and others; Amtec Group Ltd v Law and others* [2015] IRLR 15, EAT; *Dudley Metropolitan Borough Council v Willets and others* UKEAT/0334/16; [2017] IRLR 870; *East of England Ambulance Trust v Flowers and others* [2019] EWCA Civ 947; [2019] IRLR 798.

272 *Lock v British Gas Trading Ltd* [2014] IRLR 648, CJEU; *Lock and another v British Gas Trading Ltd (No 2)* [2016] IRLR 946, CA. Strictly speaking, the case only dealt with contractual results-based commission.

must be included if they are 'normally' earned. Broadly regular and predictable overtime will be included, as opposed to if it is only rare and unforeseen. Allowances should also be included in holiday pay if: (i) they relate to personal and professional status, eg allowances relating to seniority length of service and professional qualifications; or (ii) the pay is intrinsically linked to the performance of the tasks which a worker is required to carry out under his/her contract of employment as opposed to payments intended exclusively to cover occasional or ancillary costs, eg an off-base allowance for pilots. Whether an allowance is genuinely intended to cover costs may need investigation.[273] How HMRC treats the payment for tax purposes is irrelevant. It is an employment tribunal's opinion which counts. An allowance in recognition of travel time should be paid as it is intrinsically linked to work. On the other hand, reimbursement of fares or petrol costs would be an ancillary cost which need not be included.[274] Reg 16 should be notionally amended so as to allow this interpretation for the first four weeks of holiday pay.[275] However, because the case-law is based on the requirements of the WTD, reg 16 in its unamended form (ie usually without the addition of voluntary overtime,[276] commission[277] etc) is still likely to apply to the extra 1.6 weeks granted by the WTR 1998.[278]

Untaken holiday: sickness

4.97   The position when a worker is absent for long periods due to sick leave has led to some very complicated case-law, not least because the WTR 1998 are not entirely compatible with principles laid down by

---

273 *British Airways plc v Williams* [2011] IRLR 948, CJEU and applied in *Bear Scotland Ltd and others v Fulton and others; Hertel (UK) Ltd v Woods and others; Amtec Group Ltd v Law and others* [2015] IRLR 15, EAT.

274 *Bear Scotland Ltd and others v Fulton and others; Hertel (UK) Ltd v Woods and others; Amtec Group Ltd v Law and others* [2015] IRLR 15, EAT.

275 *Bear Scotland Ltd and others v Fulton and others; Hertel (UK) Ltd v Woods and others; Amtec Group Ltd v Law and others* [2015] IRLR 15, EAT.

276 *Bamsey and others v Albon Engineering Ltd* [2004] IRLR 457, CA establishes the interpretation of reg 16 in respect of overtime which is not required under the contract both to be given and to be worked. This case was decided before the subsequent cases requiring a notional amendment of reg 16 for at least four weeks' holiday because of the WTD.

277 *Evans v Malley Organisation Ltd t/a 1st Business Support* [2003] IRLR 156, CA. This case was also decided before the subsequent cases referring to the WTD, but again is useful on the likely interpretation of reg 16 in respect of the extra 1.6 weeks.

278 *Bear Scotland Ltd and others v Fulton and others; Hertel (UK) Ltd v Woods and others; Amtec Group Ltd v Law and others* [2015] IRLR 15, EAT.

the Court of Justice of the European Union (CJEU) under the WTD. It should also be remembered that the WTD only covers the basic four-week leave entitlement and is not concerned with protecting the additional 1.6 weeks leave entitlement. The following principles can therefore only be relied on in respect of four weeks' leave.[279] The current position appears to be as follows. Entitlement to annual leave continues to accrue while the worker is absent through sickness.[280] If a worker has been off sick throughout the holiday year or through the last part of the holiday year when s/he still has some leave due, the employer must allow him/her to choose whether to take paid annual leave while on sick leave or at some other time (ie carry it over into future years). If the worker is never able to take the annual leave, eg because s/he leaves the employment in the next holiday year without ever having returned to work, s/he must be paid in lieu for the previous year's leave as well.[281]

4.98   This rolling forward of untaken holiday while a worker remains off sick cannot be indefinite, although it must be allowed for longer than the reference period (usually the holiday year). The EAT has suggested that holiday can be taken no later than 18 months after the end of the holiday year in which it accrued.[282] The idea is that the leave should not lose its connection with its original purpose, ie as a period of rest from work.[283]

4.99   In order to carry forward his/her annual leave entitlement to the next holiday year, it is not necessary for a sick worker to serve a notice or even ask his/her employer to do so.[284] However, if the worker

---

279 *Neidel v Stadt Frankfurt am Main* C-337/10 [2012] IRLR 607, CJEU; *NHS Leeds v Larner* [2012] EWCA Civ 1034; [2012] IRLR 825; *Sood Enterprises Ltd v Healy* [2013] IRLR 865, EAT; *Terveys – ja Sosiaalialan neuvottelujarjesto (TSN) ry v Hyrinvointialan liitto ry (C-609/17); Auto-ja Kuljetusalan Tyontekijaliitto AKT ry v Satamaoperaattorit ry (C-610/17)*, CJEU.

280 Because the entitlement derives simply from being a worker, not from the ability to work: *Kigass Aero Components Ltd v Brown* [2002] IRLR 312, EAT and *Stringer and others v HM Revenue and Customs sub nom Commissioners of Inland Revenue v Ainsworth and Schultz-Hoff v Deutsche Rentenversicherung Bund* C-350/06, [2009] IRLR 214, CJEU.

281 This is based on a combination of cases: *Stringer and others v HM Revenue and Customs sub nom Commissioners of Inland Revenue v Ainsworth and Schultz-Hoff v Deutsche Rentenversicherung Bund* C-350/06, [2009] IRLR 214, CJEU; *Pereda v Madrid Movilidad SA* C-277/08, [2009] IRLR 959, CJEU; *Kigass Aero Components Ltd v Brown* [2002] IRLR 312, EAT (on this point).

282 *Plumb v Duncan Print Group Ltd* UKEAT/0071/15; [2015] IRLR 711, EAT.

283 *Neidel v Stadt Frankfurt am Main* C-337/10 [2012] IRLR 607, CJEU; *KHS AG v Schulte* C-214/10 [2012] IRLR 156, CJEU.

284 *NHS Leeds v Larner* [2012] EWCA Civ 1034; [2012] IRLR 825.

wishes to take his/her paid annual leave while on sick leave, s/he should send his/her employer the appropriate notification, indicating which dates should be considered as annual leave. If s/he is at that time only receiving SSP, s/he should be paid her full pay for the period. It is uncertain whether s/he can claim holiday pay if s/he is already receiving full sick pay. On the one hand, this is very unlikely because it would mean s/he receives double pay for the holiday period; on the other hand, the right to take paid leave becomes meaningless in that situation if s/he is not paid. It is arguable, though untested, that if s/he is in the middle of a limited period of full sick pay, the holiday pay period should be deducted from that total, thus extending her full sick pay by the same amount of time.

4.100   If a worker is unable to take pre-booked sick leave because s/he falls ill, s/he must be allowed to take the leave at a further date.[285] This also applies if the worker falls sick while on holiday,[286] but the worker should have good evidence that s/he was indeed ill at that time.

4.101   The right to carry over annual leave where the worker was off sick is contrary to the clear wording of WTR 1998 reg 13(9) (see para 4.89 above). EU law effectively overrides the WTR 1998 on this point. However, unless there is a relevant agreement, this only applies to the four weeks' holiday entitlement derived from the WTD and not to additional leave.[287]

Untaken holiday: maternity and other special leaves

4.102   The logic of the case-law suggests that entitlement to annual leave also accrues while a worker is absent for any other reason while the contract of employment is still running, eg on statutory maternity leave or parental leave. As well as accruing leave, it also seems that the right to take annual leave is not lost while a worker is absent on various leaves derived from EU law, such as statutory maternity leave[288] or parental leave. If the worker cannot take the leave because of such absence, s/he must be allowed to carry it forward to the next

---

285 *Pereda v Madrid Movilidad SA* C-277/08 [2009] IRLR 959, CJEU.

286 *Asociación Nacional de Grandes Empresas de Distribución (Anged) v Federación de Asociaciones Sindicales (Fasga) and others* C-78/11, [2012] IRLR 779, CJEU.

287 *NHS Leeds v Larner* [2012] EWCA Civ 1034; [2012] IRLR 825; *Sood Enterprises Ltd v Healy* UKEATS/0015/12; [2013] IRLR 865; *Terveys – ja Sosiaalialan neuvottelujarjesto (TSN) ry v Hyrinvointialan liitto ry* (C-609/17); *Auto-ja Kuljetusalan Tyontekijaliitto AKT ry v Satamaoperaattorit ry* (C-610/17), CJEU

288 *Merino Gómez v Continental Industrias del Caucho SA* C-342/01, [2004] IRLR 407, CJEU.

leave year.[289] Where a worker also cannot take her additional 1.6 weeks' leave because she is on maternity leave, it is likely that she should be allowed to carry it over under maternity discrimination law. See chapter 11 regarding the rights of workers on maternity leave and parental leave generally.

Untaken holiday: deterred by the employer

4.103   Apart from the exceptions in the previous paragraphs, on leaving their job, workers cannot claim pay in lieu of untaken holiday prior to the year of termination. A further exception is where a worker has not taken annual leave because his/her employer has refused to pay for it, perhaps due to an incorrect belief that the worker is self-employed and therefore not entitled to it. It is irrelevant whether or not the worker has actually asked to take leave. Unlike the position with sickness, there is no limit on the period in respect of which the worker can carry over and, where appropriate, accumulate leave until termination. This is because it would have been the employer's fault – an employer who does not allow leave to be taken must bear the consequences.[290]

4.104   Indeed, it is not only where the worker is deterred from taking holiday because the employer has said it will be unpaid. There are many subtle ways in which employers can deter workers from taking paid leave, eg by continually refusing requests because of understaffing or by letting it be known that insisting on holiday will not be looked on favourably. The CJEU has now said that any practice or omission by employers that may potentially deter a worker from taking annual leave will count against them. Employers do not have to force their workers to take paid leave, but they must ensure that their workers are in a position to exercise such a right. An employer must ensure, specifically and transparently, that workers are actually in a position to take the paid leave by encouraging them to do so, formally if necessary, and informing them accurately and in good time of their rights. The burden of proof will be on employers to show that they have exercised all due diligence in order to enable workers actually to take holiday. If an employer cannot show this, a

---

289 *Zentralbetriebsrat der Landeskrankenhauser Tirols v Land Tirol* C-486/08, [2010] IRLR 631, CJEU.

290 *King v The Sash Window Workshop* C-214/16, [2018] IRLR 142, CJEU. See para 4.98 for the position on sickness.

worker will be entitled to pay in lieu when s/he leaves the job.[291] On the other hand, if a worker deliberately and in full knowledge of the consequences, chooses not to take holiday, then s/he will not be able to claim pay in lieu when s/he leaves.

4.105　Although workers may be able to claim pay for untaken holiday in previous years in the circumstances described above, this seems only to apply to the position on termination (unless their contract says otherwise). While they are still employed, their right is probably only to carry over the entitlement to the next year.[292]

4.106　The above applies where a worker was deterred from taking holiday altogether. If the worker took unpaid holiday, believing s/he was self-employed, s/he will not be able to carry over a claim for pay for all the previous unpaid years on termination.[293]

4.107　As already stated, any right to claim for untaken holidays in years prior to the year of termination in these circumstances applies to the first four weeks of the statutory entitlement, ie the period covered by the WTD.

Covid-19 related leave issues

4.108　Government guidance during the pandemic stated that workers accrued holiday entitlement in the normal way while on furlough.[294] Holiday pay should be based on the worker's normal pay and not reduced on the basis of any periods paid at 80 per cent while on furlough – at least for the four weeks protected by the EU Directive.[295]

4.109　Where it was not reasonably practicable for a worker to take some or all of his/her annual leave during the relevant leave year 'as a result

291　*Max-Planck-Gesellschaft zur Förderung der Wissenschaften eV v Shimizu* C-684/16. Reported at: https://eur-lex.europa.eu/legal-content/EN/TXT/PDF /?uri=CELEX:62016CJ0684&from=EN. The CJEU relied on both the WTD and the Charter of Fundamental Rights. Subject to the usual technical arguments about the applicability of EU law, UK courts should probably follow these principles.

292　This is suggested both by WTR 1998 reg 13(9) and the apparent view of the CJEU, eg *Federatie Nederlandse Vakbeweging v Staat der Nederlanden* C-124/05 [2006] IRLR 561, CJEU; and *Max-Planck-Gesellschaft zur Förderung der Wissenschaften eV v Shimizu* C-684/16. Reported at: https://eur-lex.europa.eu/ legal-content/EN/TXT/PDF/?uri=CELEX:62016CJ0684&from=EN.

293　*Pimlico Plumbers Limited v Smith (No2)* UKEAT/ 0211/19, UKEAT/ 0003/20, UKEAT/0040/20; [2021] IRLR 654.

294　See *Holiday entitlement and pay during coronavirus (COVID-19)* at www.gov. uk/guidance/holiday-entitlement-and-pay-during-coronavirus-covid-19.

295　See paras 4.95–4.96 above on 'normal' holiday pay.

of the effects of coronavirus (including on the worker, the employer, or the wider economy or society', s/he is entitled to carry the leave forward and take it during the next two leave years.[296] The government suggests that relevant factors as to whether it was practicable may be that the business has faced a significant increase in demand, disruption of the workforce, ability of the available workforce to cover the worker's leave, the worker's own health and need for time off, how much is left of the current leave year, and any impact on wider society.[297] The extra right to carry over only applies to the first four weeks' basic leave entitlement.

4.110 Once leave has been carried over, the employer can only tell the worker not to take it on particular days if the employer has 'good reason to do so'.[298] If the worker leaves before s/he has taken the carried over leave, it should be paid in lieu on termination.[299]

Contractual holidays

4.111 The WTR 1998 provide for a minimum entitlement. There is nothing to prevent an employer agreeing to give additional holidays beyond the legal minimum entitlement, or agreeing that holiday can be carried over or untaken holiday from past years paid on termination. It is an obligation on the employer to give employees within two months of starting employment a statement of particulars including details of any terms and conditions relating to holidays, public holidays and holiday pay.[300]

Enforcement of the WTR 1998

4.112 The statutory enforcement of the working hours is carried out by the Health and Safety Executive (for schools, hospitals and factories, etc) or the local authority (for retail, catering, offices and leisure, etc).[301] Inspectors have power to enter and inspect workplaces, to issue improvement or prohibition notices and, in England and Wales, to

---

296 WTR 1998 reg 13(10).
297 See www.gov.uk/guidance/holiday-entitlement-and-pay-during-coronavirus-covid-19.
298 WTR 1998 reg 13(12). This is a reference to the employer's powers under reg 15(2) – see para 4.91 above.
299 WTR 1998 reg 14(5).
300 ERA 1996 s1(4)(d)(i); and see para 1.24.
301 And in some respects, the Civil Aviation Authority or Vehicle and Operator Services Agency.

prosecute.[302] Breach of the obligations can result in criminal proceedings punishable by a fine. It is also an offence, punishable by a fine or in some cases, prison, to obstruct an inspector. Where an offence by a company is committed with the consent, connivance or neglect of any director, manager or officer, that individual can also be found guilty of the offence and punished.[303]

4.113   As stated at para 4.77, a worker has a contractual entitlement not to be required to work more than 48 hours without his/her agreement. Unfortunately, employers have no obligation to insist workers take rest breaks and holidays (see para 4.84).

4.114   Individual workers can make an ET claim for any refusal to give rest periods and breaks and paid holidays. The ACAS early conciliation procedure applies.[304] It is not enough that the employer has organised shifts in a way which prevents breaks being taken. The employer must actually have refused the breaks.[305] The ET can award compensation according to what is just and equitable having regard to the employer's default and any attributable loss for the worker.[306] However, it cannot order compensation for injury to feelings.[307] More detail with regard to holiday claims is set out below.

4.115   It is unlawful to dismiss or subject a worker to a detriment for insisting on his/her rights under the WTR 1998, eg for insisting on taking breaks or refusing to work more than 48 hours.[308] This protection may be particularly important in the latter case, as it seems a worker cannot claim compensation in an ET for being forced to work more than 48 hours, but can only go to the county court or High Court for a declaration as to breach of contract and, most unlikely, an

---

302 WTR 1998 regs 28–29E, Sch 3.
303 WTR 1998 reg 29B.
304 ETA 1996 s18(1)(b); see para 20.16.
305 *Miles v Linkage Community Trust Ltd* UKEAT/0618/07; [2008] IRLR 602; *Carter v Prestige Nursing Ltd* UKEAT/0014-15/12, though see para 4.84 and n222 on 'refusal'. See also para 4.103 on deterring holidays.
306 WTR 1998 reg 30(4); *Miles v Linkage Community Trust Ltd* UKEAT/0618/07; [2008] IRLR 602 gives guidance.
307 *Santos Gomes v Higher Level Care Ltd* [2018] IRLR 440, CA.
308 See ERA 1996 ss45A and 101A for this and related reasons, and see *McLean v Rainbow Homeloans Ltd* [2007] IRLR 14, EAT. For this type of claim, injury to feelings can probably be awarded – see *South Yorkshire Fire & Rescue Service v Mansell & others* UKEAT/0151/17 (and comments on this case in *Santos Gomes* n307 at paras 51–54). See also para 6.78 on dismissal for asserting statutory rights.

injunction.[309] This is not a practical remedy and it may be simpler for a worker, having made sure s/he is protected, to inform the employer politely and in writing that in accordance with the WTR 1998 s/he is not willing to work more than 48 hours. Obviously a worker needs to tread carefully and be sure of his/her rights before upsetting an employer in this way.

4.116 The employer must keep up-to-date records of workers who have agreed to work longer than 48 hours per week, plus records which are adequate to show that the 48-hour and night work limits are complied with.[310] Records must be kept for two years. It is an offence for an employer not to comply with any of the relevant requirements in the WTR 1998 including the keeping of adequate records.[311]

Enforcing holiday claims

4.117 Apart from the sometimes complex questions of entitlement to holiday pay, there are further difficulties regarding how a claim should be made. The position is most straightforward when a worker has left the employment and simply wants pay for untaken holidays in the year of termination. Payment in lieu is explicitly allowed by the WTR 1998 in such circumstances.[312] and a claim can be made under WTR 1998 reg 30 or as an unauthorised deduction under ERA 1996 s23.[313] Where holiday has been taken but not paid for, a claim can again be made either under WTR 1998 reg 30(1)(b) or as an unauthorised deduction under ERA 1996 s23. Where there is a right to compensation for not being allowed or able to take holiday, compensation can be claimed under WTR 1998 reg 30(1)(a), but probably not under ERA 1996 s23 because there has been no pay deduction in the normal sense. The worker has simply been refused his/her holiday entitlement.[314]

4.118 The time limits for unauthorised deductions claims under ERA 1996 s23 are set out at paras 4.20–4.23 above. The advantage of an unauthorised deduction claim is where non-payment of holidays

---

309 See *Barber v RJB Mining (UK) Ltd* [1999] IRLR 308, QBD. But see *Sayers v Cambridgeshire CC* [2007] IRLR 29, QBD, which states no civil claim can be brought for breach of statutory duty.

310 WTR 1998 regs 4(2) and 9.

311 WTR 1998 reg 29(1).

312 WTR 1998 reg 14(2).

313 *HM Revenue and Customs v Stringer and others sub nom Commissioners of Inland Revenue v Ainsworth and others* [2009] UKHL 31; [2009] IRLR 677.

314 *Sash Window Workshop Ltd and another v King* UKEAT/0057-8/14; [2015] IRLR 348.

extends back up to two years. This is because, where an employer makes a series of deductions, time runs from the last of those deductions. However, in the context of holiday payments, such a series of deductions could be broken by occasional payments, eg if the employer pays in lieu of holiday for the year of termination, but not for earlier years. There is also a problem if the non-payments are more than three months apart.

4.119   If the claim is made under WTR 1998 reg 30, the three-month time limit is counted from when leave should have been allowed to begin, or when payment should have been made, as the case may be. It is subject to any extension if it was not reasonably practicable to get the claim in on time.[315] In some circumstances, if an employer has misled a worker about his/her employment status, this may have made it not reasonably practicable to bring the claim in time.[316]

4.120   Following the decision of the CJEU in *King v The Sash Window Workshop*,[317] it would seem that if there is a right to payment for untaken holidays in previous years, such right crystallises on the date the employment ends and the three months is counted from then. It is arguable whether this avoids the two-year limit on back-claims under ERA 1996 s23. However, the right to payment for previous years does not carry over to termination if the worker actually took the holiday but did not get paid for it.[318]

4.121   It was previously thought that the solution in regard to any time-limit problems with back claims might be to bring a breach of contract claim. However, the government closed off that possibility by stating explicitly that the statutory holiday entitlement does not give any contractual rights.[319] The position is different if the worker has an additional entitlement set out explicitly in his/her contract.

4.122   One other difference between making a reg 30 claim and a section 23 claim may be as to whether compensation is awarded apart from any financial loss. A section 23 claim is solely concerned with the amount of any unauthorised deduction, ie what should have been paid as holiday pay. Similarly, where a complaint under reg 30(1)(b)

---

315 WTR 1998 reg 30(2).
316 It depends. See the discussion in *Pimlico Plumbers Ltd v Smith (No 2)* UKEAT/0211/19, UKEAT/0003/20, UKEAT/0040/20; [2021] IRLR 654.
317 C-214/16, [2018] IRLR 142, CJEU. It is yet to be established whether this principle must be applied to domestic cases, but it is likely.
318 *Pimlico Plumbers Ltd v Smith (No.2)* UKEAT/0211/19, UKEAT/0003/20, UKEAT/0040/20; [2021] IRLR 654.
319 WTR 1998 reg 16(4) as amended by the Deduction from Wages (Limitation) Regulations 2014 SI No 3322 reg 3, with effect from 8 January 2015.

is upheld, ie that the employer has failed to pay some or all of the holiday pay due, the tribunal will order the employer to pay the sum owing.[320] On the other hand, where a claim under reg 30(1)(a) is upheld because the employer has refused to allow the worker to take holiday, the tribunal must make a declaration and can award compensation which it thinks 'just and equitable' in the circumstances having regard to any loss suffered by the worker and the employer's default.[321]

4.123   In general, because of the complexities and uncertainties, it is usually best to claim under both WTR 1998 reg 30(1)(a) and/or (b) and/or for an unauthorised deduction under ERA 1996 s23.

---

320 WTR 1998 reg 30(5).
321 WTR 1998 reg 30(3)–(4). See para 4.114 above.

CHAPTER 5

Equal pay

continued

Chapter 5: Key points

- Sex discrimination in pay or contract terms is covered by equal pay law – previously the Equal Pay Act 1970 and now the 'Equality of Terms' section of the Equality Act (EqA) 2010. Pay discrimination because of other protected characteristics is dealt with as ordinary discrimination under the EqA 2010 in the usual way.
- The woman must compare her pay with that of a man in the same employment employed on like work, work rated as equivalent under a job evaluation study or work of equal value.
- Where there is no comparator within the rules, a woman may be able to claim direct sex discrimination based on a hypothetical comparison if she has the evidence.
- Once the woman proves like work or work of equal value, the burden of proof passes to the employer to prove a material factor defence, ie a genuine reason for the pay differential, which is not tainted by direct sex discrimination.
- If the reason amounts to indirect sex discrimination, the employer must provide objective justification. In other cases, it seems a neutral non-discriminatory reason (however bad) will do.
- Indirect discrimination is the biggest cause of unequal pay. The concept of indirect discrimination in equal pay law is wider than under normal discrimination law.
- Equal value claims are traditionally lengthy and complex. Recently, some large collective private sector claims have been launched.
- Pay audits can be ordered against employers who lose equal pay claims in certain circumstances.
- Private and public sector employers with at least 250 employees must publish annual information on male and female pay differentials. There are also particular requirements in the Scottish and Welsh specific duties.
- EU law has been very influential on equal pay and will continue to be so post Brexit (see chapter 3).

The legal framework

The legislation

5.1 Equal pay law is difficult to understand and apply. European Union (EU) law has been particularly influential in this area, especially the

Treaty on the Functioning of the European Union (TFEU) Article 157 (originally the Treaty of Rome Article 119).[1] This book outlines the key issues so that potential cases may be identified. 'Like work' claims can be relatively straightforward to run in the employment tribunal (ET), but complex and lengthy procedures are involved for 'equal value' claims. An adviser considering running an equal value claim for the first time should talk to someone who has done it before.

5.2　　'Equal pay' law has always referred to discrimination in pay as between men and women, as opposed to any other protected characteristic. Pay discrimination because of age or race, for example, is dealt with in the same way as any other discriminatory action. Although equal pay law most often deals with pay claims including overtime, bonuses, recruitment premiums and sick pay, it also covers sex discrimination in relation to other contract terms,[2] eg a company car or gym membership. Bonus payments usually arise from the contract, but may on the facts be wholly discretionary and therefore not within equal pay law.[3]

5.3　　Originally equal pay law was set out in the Equal Pay Act (EqPA) 1970. It is now contained in Equality Act (EqA) 2010 Part 5 Chapter 3, which is headed 'Equality of Terms' and largely replicates the EqPA 1970, though with some differences. A worker cannot pick and choose whether she wants to bring her claim under the equal pay rules or as ordinary sex discrimination. There are complicated rules set out in EqA 2010 ss70 and 71 as to which (if any) legal protection applies to particular situations. This is important because of the different shape of the law and procedure as between equal pay and ordinary sex discrimination. Most significantly, equal pay law requires a woman to compare her pay or contract terms with an actual male colleague, whereas sex discrimination law only needs a hypothetical comparison. Equal pay cases also tend to be far longer and more complicated than sex discrimination cases. One of the most interesting developments in the EqA 2010 was that, in limited circumstances, it may be possible to bring an ordinary direct sex discrimination claim based on a hypothetical comparator in relation to a pay term (see para 5.60 below).

1　See preface and chapter 3 for the effect of Brexit on the continued availability of EU law to UK workers.

2　EqA 2010 s66.

3　For an example, see *Hoyland v Asda Stores Ltd* [2006] IRLR 468, CSIH.

5.4   The Equality and Human Rights Commission (EHRC) has issued an Equal Pay Code of Practice, which is available on its website.[4] The Code is admissible in evidence in any ET claim for equal pay and, where relevant, it must be taken into account by the ET.

5.5   In 2021, the gender pay gap for all employees, measured as an hourly rate, was 15.4 per cent. The gap has decreased from 27.5 per cent in 1997, but progress has been painfully slow considering that equal pay legislation has been in place for 40 years. Part-timers, who tend to be women, earn far lower hourly rates than full-timers. The gender pay gap for full-timers only was 7.9 per cent. For them, the gap is close to zero up to the age of 40, after which it starts to widen.[5] Over the last fifteen years or so, a large number of claims have been brought, especially in local government and the health service. Unfortunately, the length and cost of equal value claims is such that low-paid individuals cannot afford them. Equal pay cases tend to be collective and backed by trade unions or run by private solicitors on a 'no win, no fee' basis. The unions themselves have struggled to finance the bigger claims. Thousands of equal pay claims have been brought against local government regarding historic pay discrimination. The 1997 'single status' agreement (also known as the 'Green Book') was intended to put manual and white collar workers onto new single pay scales based on principles of equal pay. Unfortunately, a large number of councils did not meet the agreed deadline for implementation of 31 March 2007. Where job evaluations did take place, some staff benefited, whereas others were put on lower grades, although with a level of pay protection to ease the transition. The validity of the pay protection agreements then came under challenge. Similar sweeping changes occurred in the NHS through 'Agenda for Change', with pay scales based on a new job evaluation system. Most of the complicated equal pay case-law in recent years has been in these areas. Regrettably, the scope for negotiated equal pay agreements was weakened after unions became anxious following challenges to collective negotiations brought by some 'no win, no fee' lawyers. The difficulty facing unions is to balance the interests of different groups of members, while persuading employers to accept new equality deals for the future and make generous settlements of past claims at a time when

---

4 At: www.equalityhumanrights.com/en/advice-and-assistance/equality-act-codes-practice.

5 *Gender pay gap in the UK: 2021*, Office for National Statistics (ONS), October 2021 release (ons.gov.uk/employmentandlabourmarket/peopleinwork/earningsandworkinghours/bulletins/genderpaygapintheuk/2021). The Equal Pay Portal also provides useful analysis of statistics (www.equalpayportal.co.uk).

they are short of money. If the interests of underpaid women in the past are undervalued in this equation, it can lead to indirect sex discrimination claims against the union.[6] However, that is not to say that negotiated deals can never be justified. In the last few years, some large-scale equal pay cases have been brought in the retail sector, particularly against certain supermarket chains.

5.6   As part of the public sector equality duty (PSED) under the EqA 2010, public authorities in carrying out their functions must have due regard to the need to eliminate discrimination, which presumably would include eliminating pay discrimination.[7] Public authorities with 250 or more employees must publish annual information on gender pay differentials, and there are also precise requirements under the PSED in the Scottish and Welsh specific duties (see para 5.64 onwards).

Who is covered?

5.7   Equal pay law under the EqA 2010 has wider scope than the unfair dismissal provisions of the Employment Rights Act (ERA) 1996. As well as protecting employees employed on a contract of employment, it covers workers employed under a contract of apprenticeship or a contract personally to do work. Other categories are also covered, eg Crown employees, parliamentary staff, those employed in the armed forces and office holders.[8] Both men and women can claim equal pay under the EqA 2010. For ease of reference, this chapter presumes a woman is bringing the claim.

Using EU law

Article 157

5.8   All UK workers can claim under Article 157[9] in the ET in relation to discrimination in pay. Article 157(3) requires that men and women should receive equal pay for equal work and is expanded by the Recast

---

6 *Allen and others v GMB* [2008] IRLR 690, CA. For a historic overview of the public sector equal pay crisis and the debate about 'no win, no fee' lawyers, see 'The union perspective on equal pay' (March 2008) 174 EOR 13.

7 See para 12.36 onwards.

8 See variously EqA 2010 ss83, 49 and 52.

9 References to Article 157 are to Article 157 of the TFEU. It was formerly numbered 119, then 141 of the Treaty of Rome.

Directive.[10] EU law is generally superfluous because it duplicates rights which exist under UK law. However, in respect of pensions and some other limited matters, EU law may be needed because of exclusions and omissions from the UK legislation. For the effect of Brexit on use of EU law, see chapter 3.

What does Article 157 mean by 'pay'?

5.9 Unlike the EqA 2010, Article 157 does not apply to all terms and conditions, but only to pay. This is important because it affects when EU law can be called upon. Article 157(2) defines 'pay' as:

> ... the ordinary basic or minimum wage or salary and any other consideration, whether in cash or in kind, which the worker receives directly or indirectly, in respect of his employment, from his employer.

This wide definition was confirmed by the European Court of Justice (ECJ) in *Garland v British Rail Engineering*,[11] which added that the consideration may be 'immediate or future, provided that the worker receives it, albeit indirectly, in respect of his employment from his employer'.

5.10 Article 157 can include overtime pay, commission and financial allowances. Non-contractual discretionary payments can also be included, eg voluntary bonuses. Both contractual[12] and statutory redundancy pay[13] fall within Article 157, although payment by the National Insurance Fund when the employer defaults is not covered.[14] Some payments made by employers under a statutory obligation, eg statutory sick pay,[15] may also be within Article 157. Most significantly, Article 157 covers contributions towards and benefits paid under contractual pension schemes, whether supplementary to,[16] or contracted-out from,[17] the state pension scheme. Compensation for unfair dismissal constitutes pay within Article 157.[18]

10 2006/54/EC. This incorporates the former Equal Pay Directive (75/117/EEC) and Equal Treatment Directive (76/207/EEC).
11 [1982] IRLR 111, ECJ.
12 *Hammersmith and Queen Charlotte's Special Health Authority v Cato* [1988] ICR 132; [1987] IRLR 483, EAT.
13 *Barber v GRE Assurance Group* [1990] IRLR 240, ECJ.
14 *Secretary of State for Employment v Levy* [1989] IRLR 469, EAT.
15 *Rinner-Kühn v FWW Spezial-Gebaüdereinigung GmbH* [1989] IRLR 493, ECJ.
16 *Bilka-Kaufhaus GmbH v Weber von Hartz* [1986] IRLR 317, ECJ.
17 *Barber v GRE Assurance Group* [1990] IRLR 240, ECJ.
18 *R v Secretary of State for Employment ex p Seymour-Smith and Perez* [1999] IRLR 253, ECJ.

The comparable man

Requirement for a comparator

5.11   Under equal pay law in EqA 2010 Part 5 Chapter 3 (unlike ordinary sex discrimination law) a woman must usually find an actual man with whom she can compare herself (unless she is complaining of pay discrimination due to pregnancy).[19] However, the EqA 2010 introduced a new exception whereby if a woman has evidence of direct sex discrimination in pay, but cannot find a comparator within the rules, she may be able to make an ordinary direct discrimination claim under EqA 2010 s13 based on a hypothetical comparator (see paras 5.3 and 5.60).

The same employment

5.12   The male comparator must be employed by the same or an associated employer.[20] An employer is an associated employer where one company directly or indirectly has control of the other or where two companies come under the control directly or indirectly of a third person.[21] In the context of an equal pay claim, this can include a limited liability partnership.[22] Under EqA 2010 s79, the comparator must work at the same establishment as the woman. If he does not, he must work at another establishment where common terms apply at the establishments, either generally or as between the woman and her comparator.[23] 'Common terms and conditions' means terms which are substantially comparable on a broad basis, as opposed to the same terms subject only to tiny differences.[24] A tribunal should make a broad comparison – it should not embark on a detailed line by line examination of the terms and conditions to decide this issue.[25]

5.13   The requirement for 'common terms and conditions' does not mean as between the woman and her comparator, but as between the comparator's terms where he is working at the different establish-

19 *Alabaster v Barclays Bank plc and the Secretary of State for Social Security (No 2)* [2005] IRLR 576, CA; and see para 5.63.
20 EqA 2010 s79(3)(a).
21 EqA 2010 s79(9).
22 *Glasgow City Council and others v UNISON claimants* [2014] IRLR 532, CSIH.
23 EqA 2010 s79(3)(b) and (4).
24 *British Coal Corporation v Smith* [1996] IRLR 404, HL, interpreting the slightly different wording in EqPA 1970 s1(6).
25 *Asda Stores Ltd v Brierley and others* [2021] UKSC 10; [2021] IRLR 456.

ment, and the terms and conditions under which he would be employed if he was working at the woman's establishment. Sometimes this is more obvious than at other times, but it is not meant to be a major blockage on equal pay claims. The Supreme Court has described it as a 'threshold' test, simply designed to weed out cases where the comparator's pay is obviously linked to a different location for geographical and also perhaps historical reasons.[26]

5.14   A typical (although not the only) example of where common terms and conditions apply generally is where they are governed by the same collective agreement.[27] For example, in one case female support staff employed by a local authority in schools could compare their pay with that of male local authority staff who were not employed in schools, since they were employed under the same collective agreement on common terms.[28] However, it is not necessary for the same collective agreement to cover the woman and her comparator. In *Asda Stores Ltd v Brierly and others*, the Supreme Court upheld a decision where the claimants and other retail workers did not have collectively negotiated terms at all, whereas the comparators did have collectively negotiated terms.

5.15   It is not necessary for there actually to be any men employed in the comparator's type of job at the claimant's establishment or for any real possibility that men would be employed there in the future. This is known as the 'North hypothetical'.[29] It is not even necessary for it to be feasible to employ men on the comparator's type of job there. The tribunal might find it helpful eg to imagine, where a comparison is made by a woman in retail with a man in a warehouse, what would have happened if the warehouse was put adjacent to the retail store at the woman's establishment. It might be obvious what a comparator terms and conditions would have been in this hypothetical situation if, for example, terms and conditions for his job are set out in collective agreements or elsewhere, without any mention of where individuals are based.

---

26 *Asda Stores Ltd v Brierley and others* [2021] UKSC 10; [2021] IRLR 456. The judgment should be read for its comprehensive guidance on how to approach this issue.

27 *Leverton v Clwyd CC* [1989] IRLR 28, HL. But when reading this case, remember it was dealing with the definition as in EqPA 1970 s1(6).

28 *South Tyneside MBC v Anderson and others* [2007] IRLR 715, CA.

29 *North and others v Dumfries and Galloway Council* [2013] UKSC 45; [2013] IRLR 737. Confirmed in relation to EqA 2010 s79 by *Asda Stores Ltd v Brierley and others* [2021] UKSC 10; [2021] IRLR 456.

5.16   The wider the definition of 'establishment', the more likely it is that the woman will be employed at the same establishment as her comparator, and any residual problems associated with cross-establishment comparisons will not arise. Recent case-law has considered the meaning of the term 'establishment' in connection with collective redundancy consultation (see para 2.21 above).

5.17   EqA 2010 s80(3) says that if work is not done *at* an establishment, it is to be treated as done at the establishment with which it has the closest connection. It is not entirely clear what this means, but possibly it is intended to cover mobile workers or those who work away from any base. For example, a mobile sales rep who works from home but reports to head office might be treated as working at head office.

5.18   Under Article 157 comparisons are not limited to where the man and woman are employed by the same or an associated employer.[30] The test is whether the comparator is employed in the same establishment or service.[31] It is essential that the pay differences can be attributed to a 'single source', as otherwise there is no single body which is responsible for the inequality and can restore equal treatment.[32] Examples where comparisons can be made between different employers are:

1) where statutory rules apply to pay and conditions in more than one undertaking, establishment or service, eg nursing salaries within a national health service;

2) where several undertakings or establishments are covered by a collective works agreement;

3) where terms and conditions are laid down centrally for more than one organisation or business within a holding company or conglomerate.[33]

---

30 *Scullard v Knowles and Southern Regional Council for Education and Training* [1996] IRLR 344, EAT. See also *North and others v Dumfries and Galloway Council* [2013] UKSC 45; [2013] IRLR 737 in the context of EqPA 1970 s1(6) regarding disapplying domestic legislation which stands in the way of EU law.

31 *Scullard v Knowles and Southern Regional Council for Education and Training* [1996] IRLR 344, EAT.

32 *Lawrence and others v Regent Office Care Ltd and others* [2002] IRLR 822, ECJ. A 'single source' of pay and conditions for claimant and comparator is sufficient, and it is not necessary that there is also a single establishment, collective agreement or statutory framework – see *Asda Stores Ltd v Brierley and others* [2019] EWCA Civ 44; [2019] IRLR 335.

33 *Lawrence and others v Regent Office Care Ltd and others* [2002] IRLR 822, ECJ.

The EHRC Equal Pay Code gives as an example where a claimant and her comparator are employed by different education authorities, but pay is set by a national scheme and can be remedied by a single negotiating body.

5.19   As always, the cases very much depend on the factual circumstances. In one case, teachers employed by different Scottish councils were able to compare their pay because the salary scales of both were set by the Scottish Joint Negotiating Committee, a quasi-autonomous body, and the whole structure of education was regarded as a 'service'.[34] With teachers, much will depend on the legal status of the school. Teachers employed by a voluntary aided or academy school are unlikely to be able to compare themselves with local authority employees.[35] On the other hand, if the school is maintained by a local authority with a delegated budget, a comparison probably can be made; although theoretically governors can recommend terms and conditions to the local authority, in reality, it is fanciful to suggest they could force the local authority to appoint someone on an inappropriate pay grade.[36] Moving outside the teaching field, the Court of Appeal said in a 2005 case that it was not permissible to use comparators from different government departments because, although technically they had the same employer (the Crown), power to negotiate and set most aspects of pay was delegated to the individual government departments without any co-ordination between them.[37] However, comments made in recent cases suggest that the higher courts may now be prepared to pay more attention to the closeness of the relationship between superficially autonomous pay sources.[38]

5.20   Workers employed by a direct services organisation established to submit an in-house tender in compliance with the requirements of the Local Government Act 1988 may compare themselves with other employees of the same council provided common terms and conditions apply.[39] It may also be possible for workers employed by an arm's length external organisation which is in reality under the

---

34 *South Ayrshire Council v Morton* [2002] IRLR 256, CSIH.

35 See, eg, *Beattie v Leicester City Council* UKEAT/0386/09.

36 *Beddoes and others v Birmingham City Council* UKEAT/0037-43; 0045-48; 0053-59/10.

37 *Robertson and others v Department for the Environment, Food and Rural Affairs* [2005] IRLR 363, CA.

38 See *Glasgow City Council and others v UNISON claimants* [2014] IRLR 532, CSIH and *North and others v Dumfries and Galloway Council* [2013] UKSC 45; [2013] IRLR 737.

39 *Ratcliffe and others v North Yorkshire CC* EAT 501/92.

practical control of a local authority to compare their pay with that of local authority staff.[40] However, if the work is contracted out to independent contractors, employees transferred to the new employer can no longer compare their pay with that of council staff.[41] Similarly, an agency worker, even if she previously worked for the employer, cannot compare her pay with a directly employed member of staff, assuming there is no single source in control of pay.[42] Note that it is not necessary to establish that there is a 'single source' when making a claim under the EqA 2010, where the simpler section 79 test is satisfied.[43]

5.21   Unlike the former EqPA 1970, the EqA 2010 states explicitly in section 64(2) that the work with which comparison is made need not have been done contemporaneously with the woman's work. It was already established that a woman may compare herself with a predecessor, even one who left long before she started.[44] Under the EqPA 1970, the woman could not compare her pay with that of a successor, because that amounted to making a hypothetical pay comparison, which was not permitted under the EqPA 1970.[45] However, under the EqA 2010, a comparison with a successor may now be possible, either because of the new section 64(2) or because it is relevant evidence supporting a hypothetical comparator (see para 5.60).

5.22   In certain circumstances a man can make a claim contingent on his female comparator's claim against a different man. This is sometimes called a 'piggyback' claim. For example, a male primary school teacher could name as his comparator a female primary school teacher whose pay was the same or less than his, pending resolution of her equal pay claim using a male secondary school teacher who

---

40 *Glasgow City Council and others v UNISON claimants* [2014] IRLR 532, CSIH.

41 *Lawrence and others v Regent Office Care Ltd and others* [2002] IRLR 822, ECJ. But a contractual pay entitlement notionally varied by a sex equality clause in the past could transfer – *Gutridge v Sodexo Ltd and North Tees and Hartlepool NHS Trust* [2009] EWCA Civ 729; [2009] IRLR 721.

42 *Allonby v Accrington & Rossendale College and others* C-256/01 [2004] IRLR 224.

43 *North Cumbria Acute Hospitals NHS Trust v Potter and others* UKEAT/0121/07; [2009] IRLR 176; *Beddoes and others v Birmingham City Council* UKEAT/0037-43; 0045-48; 0053-59/10.

44 *Macarthy's Ltd v Smith (No 2)* [1980] IRLR 210, CA; *Albion Shipping Agency v Arnold* [1981] IRLR 520, EAT; *Kells v Pilkington* [2002] IRLR 693; (2002) 112 EOR 26, EAT.

45 *Walton Centre for Neurology and Neurosurgery NHS Trust v Bewley* [2008] IRLR 588, EAT, overruling *Diocese of Hallam Trustee v Connaughton* [1996] IRLR 505, EAT. The problem is that *Walton* turned on the scope of A157, which would presumably remain binding even under the EqA 2010.

was paid more than them both.[46] Similarly, a male part-timer could make a claim contingent on the success of a female part-timer bringing an equal pay case on grounds of exclusion of part-timers from an occupational pension scheme.[47] Piggyback claims are important because men employed in female-dominated types of job may get paid less along with the women because women's type of work is undervalued.

Comparable jobs

The nature of the comparison

5.23   A woman may compare herself with a man in the same employment if she is doing equal work, ie:

- she is doing work which is like his work, ie work which is the same or broadly similar, and where any differences in the work they actually do are not of practical importance;[48] or
- she is doing work rated equivalent to his in a job evaluation study (JES) which gives the work an equal value in terms of the demands made on a worker – or would do so if the evaluation was not made on a sex-specific system, ie one which in respect of any of the demands sets values for men different from those it sets for women;[49] or
- neither of the two previous categories apply, but she is doing work of equal value in terms of the demand made on each worker by reference to factors such as effort, skill and decision-making.[50]

Where the jobs seem fairly similar (but not identical), it is safer to claim both 'like work' and, in the alternative, 'work of equal value' (assuming no JES applies). Then if the ET decides that some of the differences between the jobs are significant, it can immediately turn to the equal value claim.

46 *South Ayrshire Council v Milligan* [2003] IRLR 153, CSIH. Confirmed and expanded by the EAT in *Hartlepool BC and others v Llewellyn and others; McAvoy and others v South Tyneside BC and others* UKEAT/0006/08; 0057/08; 0058/08; 0168/08; 0276/08.
47 *Preston v Wolverhampton Healthcare NHS Trust* [1997] IRLR 233, CA.
48 EqA 2010 s65(1)(a)–(3).
49 EqA 2010 s65(1)(b) and (4)–(5).
50 EqA 2010 s65(1)(c) and (6).

5.24   The following points should be noted:

- A woman can choose which man she wants to compare herself with and may choose more than one.[51] Choosing more than one man as comparator reduces the risk of losing because the particular man chosen is in some way not typical, eg he has been favoured because he is infirm or red-circled for a non-discriminatory reason. However, the woman should not unreasonably choose too many comparators.

- Even if there is a man in the same employment doing like work or work rated as equivalent under a job evaluation scheme (and getting the same pay), a woman may still compare herself with a different (higher paid) man who is doing work of equal value.[52] This prevents equal pay claims being defeated by the presence of one or two low-paid men in predominantly female areas of work.

- Where there has been a JES which rates the work of the woman as less than that of her comparable man, the woman cannot claim equal value unless there are reasonable grounds for suspecting that the JES was based on a system which discriminates because of sex or is otherwise unreliable.[53]

- A woman may claim equal pay and terms with those of a man whose work is rated lower than hers under a JES, but this does not entitle her to higher pay or better terms than her comparator.[54]

- Under Article 157 a woman in an equal value claim may compare herself with a man whose work turns out to be of less value than hers,[55] although she can only claim pay equal to his. ETs now commonly accept this under the domestic legislation as well.

Like work

5.25   The most straightforward situation where a woman can compare her pay with that of a man in the same employment is if her work is like his work. In deciding whether a woman is doing work like that of her comparator, the ET should consider the matter in two stages.[56]

---

51 See EHRC Equal Pay Code, para 61.
52 *Pickstone and others v Freemans* [1988] IRLR 357, HL.
53 EqA 2010 s131(5) and (6).
54 *Redcar and Cleveland BC v Bainbridge and others* [2007] IRLR 91, EAT; EHRC Equal Pay Code, para 47.
55 *Murphy and others v Bord Telecom Eireann* [1988] IRLR 267; (1988) 19 EOR 46, ECJ, where a woman's work was in fact found to be of higher value than her male comparator's, even though she was paid less.
56 *Capper Pass Ltd v Lawton* [1976] IRLR 366, EAT.

1) *Is the work done by the woman and her comparator the same or broadly similar?* At this stage, the ET should make a general consideration of the type of work and the skill and knowledge required to do it. So, eg women cleaners who clean offices and toilets should easily pass the test when compared with male cleaners who clean offices and urinals.

2) *Are any differences between the work done by the woman and her comparator of practical importance in relation to the terms of employment?* In other words, if the jobs were both done by members of the same sex, would you expect the differences in their tasks to warrant a difference in pay? This involves looking at the nature and extent of any differences and how often they occur.[57] It is important to consider the similarities as well as the differences to avoid a distorted impression. Trivial differences or differences which in the real world are unlikely to be reflected by a pay difference should be disregarded. Differences such as additional duties, level of responsibility, skills, the time at which work is done, qualifications, training and physical effort could be of practical importance.[58] It does not prevent it being 'like work' if the woman is doing more duties or a heavier workload than her comparators.[59]

The ET must look at the tasks actually carried out by the woman and her comparator, rather than to a (perhaps artificially inflated or understated) job description or contract.[60]

5.26   The EHRC Equal Pay Code deals with 'like work' at paras 37–39 and gives examples of 'like work' claims which have succeeded despite small differences in duties. The code says it is for the employer to show that there are differences of practical importance in the work actually performed. In any 'like work' claim, detailed evidence of the work of both the woman and her comparator needs to be presented to the ET. Often it can take an entire day at the ET to draw out all the elements of each job. If there are several women bringing a joint case, it is usually a good idea for each of them to give evidence as to the nature of the job. This reduces the risk of key elements being omitted.

---

57 EqA 2010 s65(3).
58 EHRC Equal Pay Code, para 38.
59 *SITA UK Ltd v Hope* UKEAT/0787/04; EHRC Equal Pay Code, para 38.
60 *Shields v E Coombes (Holdings) Ltd* [1978] IRLR 263, CA.

Job evaluation studies

5.27   A woman can compare her pay with that of a man in the same employment if she is doing work rated equivalent to his in a JES. The EHRC Equal Pay Code deals with JESs at paras 40–47. A JES is a study measuring the relative value of jobs, either solely of the woman and her comparator, or of some or all workers in the same employment. Sometimes a JES is called a job evaluation scheme. For the purposes of the EqA 2010, a JES is a study undertaken with a view to evaluating the jobs of some or all of the workers in terms of the demands made on them by reference to factors such as effort, skill and decision-making.[61] The JES must encompass the woman's job and that of her comparator. Work is rated as equivalent if their jobs are assessed as having the same number of points or within the same job evaluation grade. So where an employer uses a JES which bands job points in advance (eg 210–239 points will be put at grade 5; 240–279 points at grade 6), a woman obtaining, for example, 210 points can demand to be paid equally with a man obtaining anything up to 239 points.[62] In points-based systems, whether or not a small difference in points means there is a material difference in the value of the jobs depends on the nature of the job evaluation exercise.[63]

5.28   Because JESs are measured in terms of demands, it is possible for very different types of job to be rated as equivalent.[64] However, to be valid, a JES must be analytic.[65] An analytic JES is one which evaluates jobs according to a breakdown of demands and characteristics. Factors such as responsibility, working conditions, physical and mental requirements are weighted and measured. A non-analytic JES compares jobs on a 'whole-job' basis, eg by ranking and paired comparisons. The JES must only take into account factors connected with the job requirements as opposed to the person doing the job, eg how well the job-holders are performing is irrelevant.[66]

5.29   The JES must be thorough in analysis and capable of impartial application.[67] EqA 2010 s65(5) says the JES must not be made on a

---

61   EqA 2010 s80(5).
62   *Springboard Sunderland Trust v Robson* [1992] IRLR 261, EAT.
63   EHRC Equal Pay Code, para 41.
64   EHRC Equal Pay Code, para 42.
65   *Bromley and others v H and J Quick* [1988] IRLR 249, CA; EHRC Equal Pay Code, para 43.
66   EHRC Equal Pay Code, para 43.
67   *Eaton Ltd v Nuttall* [1977] IRLR 71, EAT; *Diageo plc v Thomson* (2004) 744 IRLB 12, EAT; EHRC Equal Pay Code, para 43.

'sex-specific system', ie one which sets values for men different from those it sets for women for the purposes of one or more demands.[68] This rather unclear wording presumably refers to the danger that a JES may itself be directly or indirectly discriminatory, eg because it overvalues traditional male skills and attributes, such as physical strength. The EHRC Equal Pay Code points out that historically there has been a tendency to undervalue or overlook qualities inherent in work traditionally undertaken by women, eg caring.[69]

5.30   In summary, where there is an existing JES which is analytic, non-discriminatory and not otherwise unreliable, it can serve two functions:

1) a woman may claim equal pay and other terms and conditions equal to those of a man whose work has been rated as equivalent (or less)[70] under such a JES;[71]

2) where a woman's work has been rated of less value than a man's under such a JES, she will be unable to prove her work is of equal value to his.[72]

Sometimes an employer may commission a JES after an equal value claim has been started in an attempt to block the claim. In order to have any effect, the JES must be completed at the latest by the final hearing, and it is in the ET's discretion whether it is willing to postpone the hearing if the JES is not ready.[73] A 'completed' JES means one which has been accepted by the employers and workers as a valid study, even though it may not yet have been implemented.[74]

Equal value claims

5.31   The hardest type of equal pay claim is one for equal value. It requires imagination to identify possible cases where different jobs can be considered of equal value when broken down into factors such as effort, skill and demand. This is why special experts have traditionally been used on equal value cases to analyse the jobs, but this has led to expensive and lengthy procedures. For these reasons, a few

---

68 EqA 2010 s65(4)(b) and (5).
69 EHRC Equal Pay Code, para 45.
70 *Redcar & Cleveland BC v Bainbridge and others (No 1)* [2007] EWCA Civ 929; [2007] IRLR 984.
71 EqA 2010 s65(1)(b) and (4).
72 EqA 2010 s131(5) and (6).
73 *Avon CC v Foxall and others* [1989] ICR 407; [1989] IRLR 435, EAT.
74 *Arnold v Beecham Group Ltd* [1982] ICR 744; [1982] IRLR 307, EAT.

years ago, the government gave tribunals increased power to make the equal value assessment themselves. In an equal value claim, an analytic comparison must be made comparing the work of the claimant and her comparator on a one-off basis for the proceedings. This is different from a JES, which is usually done for a whole range of jobs across the workplace, thus creating a general ranking system. Most JESs are introduced co-operatively through negotiation between the employer and trade union, whereas an equal value comparison for a tribunal claim is an adversarial process. Examples where jobs have been found of equal value are:

- a group personnel and training officer with a divisional sales trainer;
- a speech therapist with a psychologist;
- a packer with a labourer;
- a Grade A nurse with a joiner;
- a cook, clerical officer and switchboard operator in a hospital with a maintenance assistant.

Equal value procedures are set out at para 5.73 onwards.

The material factor defence

5.32   Even where there is equal work, employers have a defence under EqA 2010 s69 if they prove on a balance of probabilities that the difference between the woman's and the man's pay (or other terms) is because of a 'material factor' which does not involve direct sex discrimination. If the material factor involves indirect sex discrimination, the employer must prove that it is justifiable as a 'of achieving proportionate means to a legitimate aim'.[75] The wording of the defence is similar to that previously in the EqPA 1970, but it is more explicit, partly in order to incorporate some of the case-law which had developed previously. Nevertheless, cases referred to in the following text need to be read with some care, as their interpretation of direct and indirect discrimination was based on the open wording of the EqPA 1970 and not on the more specific defence set out in the EqA 2010. It is also helpful to look at paras 74–90 of the EHRC Equal Pay Code which covers the defence.

5.33   Once the woman has shown there is equal work, the employer must identify the material factor and prove:

75   EqA 2010 s69(1)(b).

- it is the real reason for the difference in pay and not a sham or pretence;
- the lesser pay is due to this reason;
- the factor is 'material', ie significant and relevant;
- the reason is not the difference of sex, whether direct or indirect discrimination.[76]

Therefore, provided the pay difference is for a genuine reason, which is not tainted by any kind of sex discrimination, the employer has a valid defence. It does not have to be a good reason, since the purpose of equal pay law is to eliminate sex discrimination in pay, not to achieve fair wages.[77] It therefore seems likely that a pay difference based on a mistake or a misunderstanding would still be lawful.

5.34 There is an argument, derived from the *Brunnhofer* case,[78] that European law requires more than a neutral explanation, and requires the employer to supply an objective justification for a pay variation even if no indirect sex discrimination is involved. This would be contrary to the EqA 2010. Unfortunately, Employment Appeal Tribunal (EAT) cases have differed over whether *Brunnhofer* really does require objective justification where no indirect discrimination is involved.[79] The later cases say that it does not, and this is now the more widely accepted view.

5.35 As well as personal differences between the workers concerned, such as experience and qualifications, the following are examples of material factors, although whether the defence is made out will depend on the specific circumstances in each case:

- market forces and other economic considerations;
- administrative efficiency;
- geographical differences, eg London weighting;
- unsocial hours, rotating shift and night working.

Some equal value cases have confused matters relevant to evaluating the relative worth of each job such as skill, responsibility, effort, with material factors which would justify a pay difference. The EAT in

---

76 *Glasgow City Council v Marshall* [2000] IRLR 272, HL; EHRC Employment Code, para 78.

77 *Strathclyde Regional Council v Wallace* [1998] IRLR 146, HL.

78 *Brunnhofer v Bank der Österreichischen Postsparkasse* [2001] IRLR 571, ECJ.

79 *Parliamentary Commissioner for Administration v Fernandez* [2004] IRLR 22, EAT; *Sharp v Caledonia Group Services Ltd* [2006] IRLR 4, EAT; *Villalba v Merrill Lynch & Co Inc and others* [2006] IRLR 437, EAT. See also *Armstrong v Newcastle-upon-Tyne NHS Hospital Trust* [2006] IRLR 124, CA, but the Court of Appeal was not referred to the relevant ECJ judgments.

Davies v McCartneys[80] suggested that the employer could use as a defence the very matters which were relevant in determining whether a job was of equal value. This approach has been criticised and is open to doubt: once two jobs have been evaluated as equal in terms of these separate demands, employers ought not to be able to justify a pay difference by saying that they personally value one job more highly. An employer's defence may be based on several factors. Where an employer can only partially justify a pay differential, an ET may accept the justification to that extent.[81]

Not a sex-based explanation: direct discrimination

5.36   As stated above, the employer must prove the material factor defence does not involve treating the woman less favourably than her comparator because of her sex.[82] A defence which amounts to direct sex discrimination cannot be justified.[83] It may be quite easy for the employer to show no direct discrimination was involved. For example, in the absence of any other evidence, the ET is unlikely to find any direct discrimination where the worker compares herself with a man who is obviously more skilled and where there are also many skilled women who receive the higher pay.

5.37   The woman may take it upon herself to prove direct sex discrimination, eg by relying on something she was told or has found out about the true reason for her lower pay; for example, she has heard that the employer believes women will work for less pay than men. Alternatively, the factor put forward by the employer may itself contain an element or history of direct sex discrimination, which is readily apparent or becomes clear on examination, eg in one case[84] a material factor defence of red-circling was rejected because it was based upon previous direct sex discrimination, excluding women from male pay and jobs in the 1960s. It would also be direct discrimination if men,

---

80   [1989] IRLR 429, EAT. This may be only obiter given the actual findings in the case.

81   *Enderby v Frenchay Health Authority and Secretary of State for Health* [1993] IRLR 591; (1993) 52 EOR 40, ECJ.

82   EqA 2010 s69(1)(a).

83   EqA 2010 s69(1)(a); EHRC Equal Pay Code, para 84. *E Coombes (Holdings) Ltd v Shields* [1978] IRLR 263, CA; *Parliamentary Commissioner for Administration v Fernandez* [2004] IRLR 22, EAT. The more explicit wording of the defence in the EqA 2010 than the EqPA 1970 should preclude any problems arising from the obiter comments made in *Strathclyde Regional Council v Wallace* [1998] IRLR 146, HL.

84   *Snoxell v Vauxhall Motors Ltd* [1977] ICR 700; [1977] IRLR 123, EAT.

in jobs which tended to be male preserves, had been paid bonuses precisely because they were men.[85] On the other hand, there may be explanations for paying the woman less which are not because of her sex. For example, if a male employee was put on a higher point on an incremental scale on starting a job because of his greater experience, this may well remain an explanation for the disparity in subsequent years even after the female employee has caught up in terms of experience.[86] Another possibility is that, following a TUPE transfer,[87] women already employed by the transferee find themselves paid less than men who are transferring into the organisation. This may not be direct discrimination, if the genuine reason causing the differential – and for maintaining it is that the men's terms and conditions had to be preserved on transfer.[88] If women were disproportionately affected, it may amount to indirect discrimination, and the employer would have to justify retaining the differential.

5.38   A market forces defence can be acceptable, provided it is not discriminatory. The employer must prove the exact amount of the pay differential which is due to market forces. It is for the employer to show the market dictated the higher pay, not for the woman to show her comparator's pay was too high.[89] A market forces defence can be discriminatory where there is job segregation, since female-dominated jobs tend to be paid less precisely because they are traditionally carried out mainly by women. For example, in *Ratcliffe v North Yorkshire CC*[90] the council's direct services organisation (DSO) reduced the pay of catering assistants (who were almost exclusively female) in order to compete successfully on a compulsory competitive tendering exercise. Three women brought an equal value case comparing themselves with male council workers, such as road sweepers and refuse collectors, whose work had been rated equivalent under a JES. The House of Lords rejected the council's argument that the DSO had to be able to compete on the open market. This

---

85   Bonuses can also be a result of indirect discrimination, eg if paid to manual workers because they are easier to calculate in manual jobs – see *Bury MBC v Hamilton and others* UKEAT/0413-5/09 and UKEAT/0241/09; [2011] IRLR 358.

86   See eg *Secretary of State for Justice (sued as National Offenders Management Service) v Bowling* [2012] IRLR 382, EAT.

87   That is, a transfer under the Transfer of Undertakings (Protection of Employment) Regulations 2006 SI No 246 (TUPE).

88   See eg *Skills Development Scotland Co Ltd v Buchanan and Holland* UKEAT/0042/10.

89   *Cumbria CC v Dow (No 1)* [2008] IRLR 91, EAT.

90   [1995] IRLR 439, HL.

defence was based on sex because the council's competitors could pay less on the open market precisely because such work was done mainly by women.[91]

Unjustifiable indirect discrimination

5.39   The material factor defence also fails if it involves indirect sex discrimination which the employer is unable to justify by showing it is a 'proportionate means of achieving a legitimate aim'.[92] In describing indirect discrimination, EqA 2010 s69(2) refers to a situation where, 'as a result of the factor', the woman and other women doing work equal to hers are put at a particular disadvantage when compared with men doing work equal to hers. This wording is not completely clear and does not easily match all situations covered by the previous case-law. For example, as a result of the ECJ decision in *Enderby*,[93] an employer is required to justify a statistical imbalance in disadvantage even where the factor causing that imbalance cannot be identified.

5.40   In the EqPA 1970, there was no definition of direct discrimination and indirect discrimination at all, so the concepts needed to be developed by case-law. As a result, the concept of indirect discrimination in equal pay, when read together with European legislation and case-law, developed in a way which was broader than ordinary sex discrimination under the Sex Discrimination Act 1975. It is unlikely to be lawful for the EqA 2010 to be interpreted in a way which is more restrictive than previous case-law. Equal pay indirect discrimination can take many forms, but essentially it breaks down into two main categories:

1) The normal type of indirect discrimination recognised in EqA 2010 s19 (see chapter 13) where the employer applies a provision, criterion or practice (PCP) which puts women at a particular disadvantage compared with men, eg paying part-timers a lower hourly rate or paying a higher salary for previous experience in a male-dominated industry. Sometimes the true (and indirectly discriminatory) reason is hidden or not obvious, eg a woman is really being paid less because she cannot work unsocial hours,

---

91   For another example, in a collective bargaining context, see *William Bull Ltd v Wood and others* (2002) 711 IDS Employment Law Brief 7, EAT.

92   EqA 2010 s69(1)(b).

93   *Enderby v Frenchay Health Authority and Secretary of State for Health* [1993] IRLR 591, ECJ.

whereas the employer contends that the pay differential is because she is less competent at her job.

2) *Enderby*-type indirect discrimination, where two groups of workers doing work of equal value receive different pay and there is sufficient statistical disparity in the gender breakdown of each group.[94] For example:

- A job which is carried out almost exclusively by women, or where a significant number are women, is paid less than a job carried out predominantly by men.[95] It does not matter if there are a significant number of men in the disadvantaged group (although this may indicate that the employer will have a defence unrelated to sex).[96]

- The employer uses a pay system which is wholly lacking in transparency (see para 5.41), but the average pay for women is less than the average pay for men.[97]

5.41   It is important that the pay system is clear and easy to understand; this has become known as transparency. A transparent system is one where workers understand not only their rates of pay but the components of their individual pay packets. The ECJ has said that where an employer operates a pay system which is wholly lacking in transparency but appears to operate to the substantial disadvantage of one sex, the onus will be on the employer to explain and justify objectively the differential, even if the individual worker cannot identify why she has been paid less.[98] According to the EHRC Equal Pay Code, where the disadvantaged group is predominantly women and the group of advantaged comparators is predominantly men, it will be hard for an employer to prove there is no unlawful sex discrimination.[99]

5.42   To measure the adverse impact, the tribunal can choose to look at the proportion of men and women disadvantaged by the practice or at the proportion of those advantaged by the practice – whichever realistically tests the issue. The tribunal should consider everyone

---

94 *Bury MBC v Hamilton and others* UKEAT/0413-5/09 and UKEAT/0241/09; [2011] IRLR 358.

95 *Enderby v Frenchay Health Authority and Secretary of State for Health* [1993] IRLR 591, ECJ; *British Road Services Ltd v Loughran* [1997] IRLR 92, NICA.

96 *Bailey and others v Home Office* [2005] IRLR 369, CA.

97 *Enderby v Frenchay Health Authority and Secretary of State for Health* [1993] IRLR 591, ECJ; *Handels-og Kontorfunktionaerernes Forbund i Danmark v Dansk Arbejdsgiverforening* [1989] IRLR 532, ECJ.

98 *Handels-og Kontorfunktionaerernes Forbund i Danmark v Dansk Arbejdsgiverforening (acting for Danfoss)* [1989] IRLR 532, ECJ.

99 EHRC Equal Pay Code, para 86.

affected by the relevant practice, whether positively or negatively, but there is no single suitable pool for comparison in every case.[100]

5.43　To justify indirect discrimination, the employer must show it is a proportionate means of achieving a legitimate aim. The EHRC Equal Pay Code gives examples at paras 89–91. Under the case-law, the employer must prove:

- there is a real need on the part of the undertaking;
- the measures chosen by the employer are appropriate for achieving the objective in question; and
- the measures chosen by the employer are necessary to that end.[101] 'Necessary' does not mean it has to be the only course available to the employer: it just means 'reasonably' necessary.[102] The ET must balance the discriminatory effect against the justification put forward.[103]

5.44　It seems that the justification need not contemporaneously and consciously feature in the employer's decision-making process, and the reason put forward at a tribunal hearing can even be a reason different from the one in the employer's mind at the time the pay was decided upon.[104] Nevertheless, retrospective justification will be harder to prove.[105] Moreover, where a material factor applied at a particular point in time, but no longer applied for the period when equal pay was claimed, it can no longer provide a defence to indirect discrimination.[106] For example, bonus schemes which once were dependent on productivity may by now have become automatic payments; where these were originally negotiated in male job areas (as has tended to happen historically), excluding women in female job areas from equivalent bonuses may no longer be justifiable.[107]

---

100 *Grundy v British Airways PLC* [2008] IRLR 74, CA.

101 *Rainey v Greater Glasgow Health Board* [1987] IRLR 26, HL.

102 *Cadman v Health and Safety Executive* [2004] IRLR 971, CA.

103 *Cadman v Health and Safety Executive* [2004] IRLR 971, CA.

104 *Cadman v Health and Safety Executive* [2004] IRLR 971, CA. *Schönheit v Stadt Frankfurt Am Main* [2004] IRLR 983, ECJ.

105 *British Airways plc v Grundy (No 2)* [2008] IRLR 815, CA.

106 EHRC Equal Pay Code, para 92.

107 *Cumbria CC v Dow (No 1)* [2008] IRLR 91, EAT; *Hartlepool BC and Housing Hartlepool Ltd v Dolphin and others* UKEAT/0007-08/08; [2009] IRLR 168; *Bury MBC v Hamilton and others* UKEAT/0413-5/09 and UKEAT/0241/09; [2011] IRLR 358; *Council of the City of Sunderland v Brennan and others* [2012] EWCA Civ 413; [2012] IRLR 507.

5.45   It is a common defence that the different pay rates were arrived at by independent and distinct collective bargaining processes. This is probably not sufficient justification where the outcome is a disparity between the mainly female group and the mainly male group, even if no direct or indirect discrimination can be identified within each process.[108] Otherwise an employer could easily circumvent the principle of equal pay by using separate bargaining processes.[109] Indirectly discriminatory terms are not justifiable purely because they have been agreed with a trade union – the union negotiators may not have realised their effect.[110]

5.46   Sometimes an employer tries to defend a case on the basis that s/he cannot afford to pay the worker more. This may amount to indirect discrimination if the worker is in a job which tends to be done by women, and if her comparator is in a job mainly done by men. Budgetary considerations alone cannot justify indirect discrimination in pay.[111]

5.47   The ECJ's most explicit guidance on what may be considered justifiable or not in indirect discrimination is in *Danfoss*.[112] In that case, the employer awarded pay increments on the basis of a number of criteria, ie flexibility, quality of work, vocational training and seniority. It was not apparent to the workers precisely how the level of each person's pay had been arrived at, but the net effect was that women were on the whole paid less than the men. The ECJ said that where a pay system is characterised by a total lack of transparency, that is, where it is impossible to tell precisely how each worker's pay level was reached, and where there is a statistical imbalance between the pay of male and female workers, the onus is on the employer to justify the difference.

---

108 *Enderby v Frenchay Health Authority and Secretary of State for Health* [1993] IRLR 591, ECJ and *Strathclyde Regional Council v Wallace* [1998] IRLR 146, HL; *Glasgow CC and others v Marshall and others* [2000] IRLR 272, HL; *Redcar & Cleveland BC v Bainbridge and others (No 1); Surtees and others v Middlesbrough BC; Redcar & Cleveland BC v Bainbridge and others (No 2)* [2008] IRLR 776, CA.

109 See also *Nimz v Freie und Hansestadt Hamburg* [1991] IRLR 222, ECJ; *Kowalska v Freie und Hansestadt Hamburg* [1990] IRLR 447, ECJ. See further the possibly contradictory position of the ECJ in *Specialarbejderforbundet i Danmark v Dansk Industri (acting for Royal Copenhagen A/S)* [1995] IRLR 648, ECJ.

110 *British Airways plc v Grundy (No 2)* [2008] IRLR 815, CA.

111 *Jorgensen v Foreningen AF Speciallaeger* [2000] IRLR 726, ECJ.

112 *Handels-og Kontorfunktionærernes Forbund i Danmark v Dansk Arbejdsgiverforening (acting for Danfoss)* [1989] IRLR 532, ECJ.

5.48   The ECJ then examined each of the criteria. It recognised that proportionally fewer women were likely to score highly on criteria such as flexibility, vocational training and seniority. Therefore, where statistics indicated that women were generally paid less than men on the basis of flexibility or vocational training criteria, the employer must justify the use of each criterion by showing it was 'of importance for the performance of the specific duties entrusted to the worker concerned'.

5.49   The ECJ took a radical position in respect of merit payments. It said that if women were, on the whole, paid less on the basis of 'quality of work', this could not be justified because 'it is inconceivable that the work carried out by female workers would be generally of a lower quality'. In other words, the employer must be directly discriminating.

5.50   In *Danfoss*, the ECJ said the employer need not justify the use of the seniority criterion because that was obviously justifiable. In the subsequent case of *Nimz v Freie und Hansestadt Hamburg*,[113] the ECJ appeared to change its mind. In *Cadman v Health and Safety Executive*,[114] the ECJ largely returned to its position in *Danfoss*. It said that an employer does not usually have to justify using length of service as a determinant of pay because length of service goes hand in hand with experience, and experience generally enables workers to perform their duties better. However, where the woman can provide evidence raising serious doubts as to whether length of service, in the particular circumstances, would lead to better performance, then the employer must still provide detailed justification. The ECJ did not clarify how difficult it would be to fall within this exception.[115]

5.51   EqA 2010 s69(3) says that the long-term objective of reducing inequality between men's and women's terms of work must always be regarded as a legitimate aim. Nevertheless, employers must prove that the steps they have taken were genuinely intended to reduce inequality. Also, the means used must be proportionate.[116] One of the issues related to this concerns pay protection. Agreements negotiated with many local authorities in recent years for new unified pay

113 *Nimz v Freie und Hansestadt Hamburg* [1991] IRLR 222, ECJ.

114 [2006] IRLR 969, ECJ.

115 See *Wilson v Health and Safety Executive and EHRC (intervener)* [2009] EWCA Civ 1074; [2010] IRLR 59 for how the ECJ in *Cadman* should be applied domestically. See para 14.21 for the effect of this decision on age discrimination.

116 EHRC Equal Pay Code, paras 90–91.

scales included several years' pay protection for those whose pay would be reduced under the new scales. However, where a woman has previously been paid less due to historic direct or indirect sex discrimination, it is not necessarily justifiable to deprive her of a sum for pay protection just because her pay is not in reality reduced.[117] Although the purpose of pay protection is to cushion employees against the shock of an actual salary cut, granting it for an extended period to those previously paid higher rates simply perpetuates past inequality. Whether or not it is justifiable in a particular case depends on a variety of factors, eg the extent of the cut, the duration of the protection, the extent to which the employer is trying to eliminate past discrimination, the cost for an employer of equalising up the pay disparities, the industrial relations consequences of imposing pay-cuts and the extent to which the unions insisted on protection as the price for agreeing single status.

Summary

5.52   In summary, the key principles relating to the defence are as follows:

- the onus is on the employer to prove any defence;
- the material factor must be significant and relevant;
- the material factor must not be discriminatory, either directly or indirectly;
- if the factor involves direct discrimination, it cannot be justified;
- if the factor involves indirect discrimination, the employer must objectively justify it;
- where pay is governed by merit, flexibility, training or seniority, the comments of the ECJ in the *Danfoss* case[118] should be borne in mind;
- for service-related pay, see comments of the ECJ in *Cadman v Health and Safety Executive*;[119]
- where the pay system is wholly lacking in transparency, the onus will be on the employer to justify a pay differential which appears substantially to disadvantage one sex.

---

117 *Redcar & Cleveland BC v Bainbridge and others (No 1); Surtees and others v Middlesbrough BC; Redcar & Cleveland BC v Bainbridge and others (No 2)* [2008] EWCA Civ 885; [2008] IRLR 776.

118 *Handels-og Kontorfunktionærernes Forbund i Danmark v Dansk Arbejdsgiverforening (acting for Danfoss)* [1989] IRLR 532, ECJ.

119 [2006] IRLR 969, ECJ.

Part-time workers

5.53   Many ECJ cases concern lower pay and benefits for part-time workers.[120] There is a general recognition that a far higher proportion of women than men are in part-time work and the issue has been whether employers can justify the differential. In the key case of *Bilka-Kaufhaus GmbH v Weber von Hartz*,[121] a German department store (in line with West German state legislation) excluded part-time workers from its occupational pension scheme. The ECJ said that where a pay practice, applied generally, operated to disadvantage more women than men, it would infringe Article 157 (see para 5.1) unless it were objectively justifiable.[122]

5.54   Working full-time is not a justification in itself for receiving greater hourly pay. Nor would the ECJ in *Rinner-Kühn v FWW Spezial-Gebaüdereinigung GmbH*[123] accept as justification an argument that part-timers were less integrated into the business than full-timers. However, it may be justification if an employer can show that for economic or administrative reasons it needs to discourage part-time working.

5.55   In another case, the ECJ has said that a civil service rule whereby job-sharers progress up an incremental pay scale only in accordance with time actually worked and therefore at half the speed of full-timers with equal competence, cannot be justified merely on the grounds of saving costs.[124] Unfortunately it seems that restricting overtime supplements to cases where the normal full-time working hours are exceeded is not unlawful.[125] On the other hand, it can be indirect discrimination (unless justified) to apply a rule that neither part-timers nor full-timers get paid for the first three hours of overtime each month, since this would represent a higher proportion of part-timers' hours.[126] It may also be unlawful, unless justified, to pay a lower hourly rate for overtime than for normal working hours,

120   See also the section on part-time working in chapter 11.
121   [1986] IRLR 317, ECJ. See also *Jenkins v Kingsgate (Clothing Productions) (No 2)* [1981] IRLR 388, EAT.
122   See para 5.43 for more detail on the definition of justification.
123   [1989] IRLR 493, ECJ.
124   *Hill and Stapleton v Revenue Commissioners and Department of Finance* [1998] IRLR 466, ECJ.
125   *Stadt Lengerich v Helmig* [1995] IRLR 216, ECJ.
126   *Elsner-Lakeberg v Land Nordrhein-Westfalen* [2005] IRLR 209, ECJ.

since part-timers could end up working the same amount of hours as their full-time colleagues for less pay.[127]

5.56 Statutory entitlement to certain payments such as redundancy pay, sick pay and unfair dismissal compensation is often subject to requirements, eg length of service or age, which may have indirectly discriminatory effect. There have been several major cases challenging such requirements.[128]

5.57 In addition to the above, it may be contrary to the Part-time Workers (Prevention of Less Favourable Treatment) Regulations 2000[129] unjustifiably to pay a part-timer less than a comparable full-timer.

The sex equality clause

5.58 When an equal pay claim based on an actual comparator succeeds, the way equal pay law operates is to insert an equality clause into the contract of the woman.[130] Each contractual term that is less favourable than the equivalent term in the contract of the comparable man is modified to make it equal. It is irrelevant that, looking at the contracts as a whole, the woman may be said to be equally treated. For example, where a woman receives less basic pay, but better holiday and sick pay, she is nevertheless entitled to have her basic pay increased to the male level.[131] Similarly under Article 157 (see para 5.1), the ECJ has said that the principle of equal pay entails equality in each component of remuneration and does not look at whether the total benefits are the same.[132] In *Degnan*, the Court of Appeal suggested that monetary payments, eg basic pay, fixed bonuses and attendance allowances, should be added together and regarded as a single term.[133] However, this decision should be regarded as a result

---

127 *Voss v Land Berlin* C-300/06 [2008] 1 CMLR 49 (p1313); 847 IDS Employment Law Brief 12, ECJ.

128 *Rinner-Kühn v FWW Spezial-Gebaüdereinigung GmbH* [1989] IRLR 493, ECJ; *R v Secretary of State for Employment ex p EOC* [1994] IRLR 176, HL; *R v Secretary of State for Employment ex p Seymour-Smith and Perez* [1999] IRLR 253, ECJ; *Rutherford and another v Secretary of State for Trade and Industry (No 2)* [2004] IRLR 892, CA.

129 SI No 1551; and para 11.113.

130 EqA 2010 ss64 and 66.

131 *Hayward v Cammell Laird Shipbuilders* [1988] IRLR 257, HL.

132 *Barber v GRE Assurance Group* [1990] IRLR 240, ECJ; *Jämställdhetsombudsmannen v Örebro Läns Landsting* [2000] IRLR 421, ECJ.

133 *Degnan and others v Redcar and Cleveland BC* [2005] IRLR 615, CA.

of its particular facts, as the bonuses and allowances were part of basic pay in that particular workplace – the allowances were paid simply for turning up for work and not necessarily even for completing shifts.[134] More recently, a percentage bonus for working at unsocial times within normal contracted hours was not regarded as part of basic pay. It did not matter if the woman received a higher basic pay rate because this was a separate term.[135] However, the overall picture may be relevant to the employer's defence.[136]

5.59   Once the woman's contract is modified, it remains so even if her male comparator leaves or is promoted or demoted. This means she will be entitled to pay arrears even after her comparator has left his job.[137]

Hypothetical pay comparisons

5.60   Where a woman has evidence of direct sex discrimination in pay, but there is no actual comparator within the equal pay rules, she may be able to make an ordinary direct discrimination claim under EqA 2010 s13.[138] The advantage of such a claim is that a hypothetical comparison can be made, and it avoids all the complexities of usual equal pay procedure. However, the woman cannot just choose to bring a section 13 claim.[139]

5.61   It is difficult to know what level of evidence will be required to persuade an ET that there has been direct discrimination in pay based on a hypothetical comparator. The EHRC Equal Pay Code gives a very simplistic example at para 63, ie where an employer tells a woman that she would be paid more if she were a man. There is no reason why such explicit evidence should be required to succeed in a claim. As discussed in chapters 13 and 16, an inference of direct discrimination can be drawn from a variety of evidence. In an equal pay context, useful evidence may include the treatment of other

---

134 *St Helens & Knowsley Hospital NHS Trust v Brownbill and others* [2011] EWCA Civ 903; [2011] IRLR 815.

135 *St Helens & Knowsley Hospital NHS Trust v Brownbill and others* [2011] EWCA Civ 903; [2011] IRLR 815.

136 *Jämställdhetsombudsmannen v Orebro Läns Landsting* [2000] IRLR 421, ECJ.

137 *Reading Borough Council v James and others* UKEAT/0222/17.

138 See chapter 13 for direct discrimination cases under the EqA 2010.

139 The combined effect of EqA 2010 ss 70–71. The EAT in *BMC Software Ltd v Shaikh* UKEAT/0092/16; [2017] IRLR 1074 confirmed this is only possible where there is no comparator (the case was appealed to the Court of Appeal on a different point).

workers who do not come within the technical definition of an equal pay comparator, but who are employed by the same employer and whose pay is significantly higher, eg where there is a man doing work of only slightly higher value than the woman, but being paid a lot more, or conversely, where the woman is doing obviously higher value work than a man, but is not paid any more than him. It may also be useful evidence if a male successor is paid more than the woman, although it is easy to envisage explanations for that which are not direct discrimination.

Occupational pensions

5.62   Equal pay law also covers pensions. This is a complex area which is outside the scope of this book. It is also a developing area as a result of certain European rulings regarding sex discrimination in pensions based on actuarial factors. The following is a very rough overview. Whereas a sex equality clause is implied into the contracts of men and women doing work of equal value, a sex equality rule is implied into occupational pension schemes.[140] This applies to terms of membership and to the way scheme members are treated. As with non-pension equal pay cases, there is a potential material factor defence.[141] There are also some express exceptions in the EqA 2010 Sch 7. ETs and possibly the courts have jurisdiction to deal with pension claims.[142] Time limits are as set out below for equal pay claims generally.[143] If an ET finds discrimination in terms of membership or in treatment of scheme members, it can make a declaration that the woman has a right to join the scheme and as to terms of membership with retroactive effect.[144] The EqA 2010 tries to address the difficulties which can arise where trustees of an occupational pension scheme do not have power to make sex equality alterations to the scheme.[145] If there has been discrimination in the terms on which a member is treated, the ET can award arrears or damages for a specified period.[146]

---

140 EqA 2010 s67.
141 EqA 2010 s69(4).
142 EqA 2010 ss127–128.
143 EqA 2010 ss129–130.
144 EqA 2010 ss126 and 133.
145 EqA 2010 s68.
146 EqA 2010 s134.

Pregnancy and maternity

5.63   Unfavourable treatment of a woman because of pregnancy or maternity in non-contractual pay or benefits is covered by normal sex discrimination law. In regard to contractual pay and benefits, the woman's position is covered by a 'maternity equality clause'.[147] The idea of a maternity equality clause was new in the EqA 2010, but the rules are those already established by previous case-law. A woman cannot claim equal pay with a man while she is on maternity leave. However, under EqA 2010 s74 a woman is protected regarding some aspects of her pay.[148]

Gathering information on pay

Gender pay reporting

5.64   After several unsuccessful attempts at encouraging voluntary gender pay reporting, in 2017 the government issued regulations requiring public and private sector employers with at least 250 employees to publish annual information regarding pay differentials.[149] The Government Equalities Office (GEO) has issued detailed guidance.[150] The information must be published on the organisation's website and any other website specified by the government for at least three years in a manner which is accessible to the public and other employees. In the private sector, the information must be accompanied by a signed statement of a director or equivalent senior person that the information is accurate. Public authorities listed in the regulations include local government, health trust, publicly funded schools and central government (except for security departments).[151] The information relates to the pay of employees employed at the 'snapshot date'

---

147 EqA 2010 ss72–76.
148 *Gillespie v Northern Health and Social Services Board* [1996] IRLR 214, ECJ. See paras 11.63–11.65 below.
149 Equality Act 2010 (Gender Pay Gap) Regulations 2017 SI No 172; Equality Act 2010 (Specific Duties and Public Authorities) Regulations 2017 SI No 353.
150 On the GOV.UK website at www.gov.uk/guidance/who-needs-to-report-their-gender-pay-gap. Published 14 December 2020 and last updated 1 November 2021. This appears to be based on a guide originally published jointly with ACAS.
151 SI 2017 No 353 Sch 2 lists which public authorities are covered. See GOV.UK guidance at https://www.gov.uk/guidance/who-needs-to-report-their-gender-pay-gap for details of educational bodies covered.

(5 April for private sector employers and 31 March for public author-ities). Public authorities were required to publish their first informa-tion by 30 March 2018, relating to those employed on 31 March 2017. Private employers had to publish their first information within 12 months of 5 April 2017.

5.65   The relevant employees are basically those employed under a contract of employment or of apprenticeship or, unless data is not available, under a contract personally to do work. Part-timers and job-sharers are counted as individuals. The GEO Guidance says agency workers are included as part of the headcount of the agency, not the organisation where they are placed. The GEO Guidance has advised that furloughed employees should be included in the report. Those with topped up wages would be a 'full-pay relevant employee' and those without topped up wages would be a 'relevant employee'. Employers should add a supporting narrative if furlough and Covid-19 affected the gender pay gap.[152]

5.66   The information comprises the difference between the mean hourly rate of male and female employees, the median hourly rate of male and female employees, the mean bonus paid to male and female employees and the median bonus paid to male and female employees. It must also include the proportion of male and female employees who were paid bonus pay, and the proportion of male and female employ-ees in each of four evenly divided pay bands from bottom to top. The regulations set out how to calculate the figures in each of these categor-ies and the GEO Guidance gives further examples. The pay includes basic pay, allowances and shift premiums, but not overtime.

5.67   A private employer's failure to comply with these requirements constitutes an unlawful act under Equality Act (EqA) 2006 s34, in respect of which the EHRC can take enforcement action. Failure by a public authority to comply with the rules would be a breach of the PSED. The EHRC has power to take enforcement action against any employer not complying with their reporting duties.[153] It paused its enforcement action for six months during 2021 due to the pandemic, but encouraged reports still to be submitted by the usual deadline.

5.68   What is strikingly missing from these rules is any requirement to do anything about any pay gap which is revealed by the information. The GEO Guidance recommends an action plan as good practice to

---

152 At www.gov.uk/guidance/the-gender-pay-gap-data-you-must-gather#task-1 and www.acas.org.uk/gender-pay-gap-reporting.

153 Its enforcement strategy is at www.equalityhumanrights.com/en/publication-download/our-litigation-and-enforcement-policy-2019-2022.

redress the gender pay gap.[154] In addition, pay audits are recommended by the EHRC Equal Pay Code at para 163, and there is guidance for large organisations on auditing equal pay on the EHRC website.[155] The GEO has also published statistics for the two years of pay reporting together with related research.[156] The research suggests that roughly half of employers have voluntarily published an action plan. The EHRC has suggested action plans and explanatory narratives should be made compulsory.[157] Moreover, in the public sector it can be argued that the PSED already requires open pay audits.[158] The Scottish special duties require authorities of 150 or more employees to publish information on the gender pay gap within the authority as well as specifying their pay policy in relation to gender, disability and race where there is occupational segregation.[159] The Welsh special duties require authorities to have equality objectives which address the cause of any pay differences as between those with different protected characteristics, and in respect of gender pay differences, they must set out an action plan.[160] In October 2014, tribunals were given power to order compulsory pay audits in certain circumstances where employers have lost equal pay cases (see para 5.89).

Pay secrecy clauses

5.69   Secrecy about pay allows discrimination to continue. One of the innovations in the EqA 2010 was the introduction of a ban on pay secrecy clauses, although this is not quite as effective as it seems at first sight. Under EqA 2010 s77, a contract term which tries to prevent

154 At www.gov.uk/guidance/the-gender-pay-gap-information-employers-must-report#action-plan.

155 Available at www.equalityhumanrights.com/en/multipage-guide/equal-pay-audit-larger-organisations.

156 *Gender Pay Gap Information Regulations: summary of 2017/2018 data* available at: www.gov.uk/government/publications/gender-pay-gap-information-regulations-summary-of-201718-data; *Mandatory Gender Pay Gap Reporting: summary of reported data for 2018/19* at www.gov.uk/government/publications/mandatory-gender-pay-gap-reporting-summary-of-reported-data-for-201819. Data supplied by employers can be searched online at http://gender-pay-gap.service.gov.uk.

157 *Closing the Gender Pay Gap* at: www.equalityhumanrights.com/en/publication-download/closing-the-gender-pay-gap.

158 See para 5.6.

159 Equality Act 2010 (Specific Duties) (Scotland) Regulations 2012 SI No 162 regs 7 and 8.

160 Equality Act 2010 (Statutory Duties) (Wales) Regulations 2011 SI No 1064, W155 regs 11 and 12.

or restrict a person from disclosing information about their pay or other terms is unenforceable. This applies to disclosure to work colleagues, trade union representatives or anyone else, inside or outside of the organisation. In addition, a contract term is unenforceable if it tries to prevent someone seeking disclosure from a colleague or former colleague about the colleague's pay or other terms. A 'relevant pay disclosure' is only protected if it is made for the purpose of enabling the person who makes it or to whom it is made, to find out whether or to what extent there is a connection between pay and having a protected characteristic in relation to the work in question. In other words, a term must not prevent discussion about pay and terms in order to find out whether there is discrimination related to a protected characteristic (not only sex, but any of the protected characteristics, eg race or age). However, a term can still prohibit general chat about pay which is not linked to protected characteristics. Although this at first sight does not seem to matter, it is often through such general pay comparisons that people notice pay discrimination which they would not previously have considered. The restrictive wording of EqA 2010 s77 also means confidentiality clauses in workers' contracts can still be used to prevent them disclosing their pay to competitors. Making or seeking a relevant pay disclosure or receiving information disclosed in a relevant pay disclosure are protected acts for the purposes of the law on victimisation, ie a worker must not be treated unfavourably because s/he has in good faith done these things or because the employer believes s/he has done or may do these things.[161]

Questionnaires

5.70　A discrimination questionnaire procedure has applied to equal pay cases since 2003, working in the same way as in other types of discrimination cases.[162] The statutory procedure was abolished by the Conservative and Liberal Democrat coalition government and replaced by a less structured non-statutory (voluntary) procedure for 'contraventions' on or after 6 April 2014.[163] There was ACAS guidance for the non-statutory procedure, but at the time of writing, the author has been unable to find it online.

161 EqA 2010 s26. For more detail on victimisation, see chapter 13.
162 See paras 21.47–21.48.
163 Enterprise and Regulatory Reform Act 2013 s66 brought into force by the Enterprise and Regulatory Reform Act 2013 (Commencement No 6, Transitional Provisions and Savings) Order 2014 SI No 416 Article 3.

5.71   Some employers may object to disclosing information regarding the pay of other workers on grounds of confidentiality or breach of the General Data Protection Regulation (GDPR). However, information can be disclosed about other workers where they consent or where information is disclosed for the purpose of or in connection with legal proceedings.[164] Anonymity is also a possibility which will be acceptable in some situations.

Trade unions and freedom of information

5.72   In a unionised workplace, another way to find out information about pay practices in the workplace is through the collective bargaining machinery. It is arguable that statistical information regarding pay forms part of the information which an employer must give a recognised union to bargain effectively.[165] In the public sector, a freedom of information request could be made[166] although this may run into problems of confidentiality where precise salaries (rather than bands) of identifiable individuals are sought.

Equal value procedure

Overview

5.73   Traditionally, equal value claims have been long and drawn out, often taking two or more years to complete. Expert evidence and legal representation is almost certain to be used by one or both parties and cases tend to be extremely time-consuming and expensive. For these reasons, equal value cases are usually brought by more than one worker (and sometimes by hundreds or thousands) or with an agreement with the employer that all similarly circumstanced female workers will get the benefit (including back pay) of any favourable decision in a test case.

5.74   In October 2004, changes were made to the procedural rules, with the clear intention of controlling the length of case preparation. It was hoped that the built-in timetables would make considerable improvements on the past, ideally enabling hearings to take place within six to nine months, depending on whether an expert is appointed. However, the evidence suggests that, if anything, procedural

---

164 For further discussion of this, see para 1.69.
165 Trade Union and Labour Relations (Consolidation) Act 1992 ss181–185.
166 See para 1.91 onwards.

changes have slowed things down. Equal value claims remain long, complex and expensive. If the woman has a good 'like work' claim against a different comparator which would lead to the same compensation, it may sometimes be possible to separate the claims and ask the ET to deal with the like work claim first. If it is successful, the equal value claim need not be pursued.

5.75 The procedural steps of an equal value claim are usually as follows, although there may be additional interim hearings if necessary:

- (Claim;[167] response.)
- Preliminary hearing for early case management to decide matters such as whether non-equal pay claims should go ahead first; the identity of the comparators; the scope of the stage 1 hearing and any necessary preparatory orders.
- Stage 1 equal value hearing, mainly to decide whether to appoint an independent expert and make orders for case preparation.
- Stage 2 equal value hearing, only if an independent expert has been appointed, to decide facts on which his/her report should be based.
- The full hearing at which the ET makes its decision.

The steps are set out in more detail below. There are special rules of procedure for equal pay claims in Employment Tribunals Constitution and Rules of Procedure) Regulations (ET Regs) 2013 Sch. 3,[168] but they set out unrealistic timescales.

Stage 1 equal value hearing

5.76 If there is a dispute as to whether the work is of equal value, there will be a stage 1 equal value hearing, which can be heard by an employment judge alone.[169] When the ET notifies the parties of the stage 1 hearing date, it will also set out what will be dealt with at the hearing and the standard case management orders. The tribunal may decide it would be useful to have an ordinary preliminary hearing first to decide on the scope of the stage 1 hearing and necessary orders. For example, the employer may argue that the ET should

---

167 Where claims are brought by several claimants against a single employer, consider whether it is safe to use a single claim form – see *Brierley and others v Asda Stores Ltd; Ahmed and others v Sainsbury's Supermarkets Ltd and another; Fenton and others v Asda Stores* [2019] EWCA Civ 8; [2019] IRLR 327, but ET Rules Sch 1 r9 has since been amended (with effect from 8 October 2020).

168 SI No 1237.

169 Rules for content of the hearing are at ET Regs 2013 SI No 1237 Sch 3 rr3 and 4.

strike out the claim if the claimant's work was rated less than her comparator's under a suitable and non-discriminatory JES.[170] If so, this issue needs to be identified in advance of the stage 1 hearing. An ET can also strike out the claim on any of the usual grounds, eg because it has no reasonable prospect of success.

5.77   Assuming the claim is not struck out, the ET will decide whether to determine the question of equal value itself[171] or to appoint an independent expert to prepare a report. If either party requests, the ET can choose to hear evidence at this early stage regarding whether there is a material factor defence, before deciding whether to appoint an expert. If the ET does decide to appoint an expert, it can change its mind or choose a different expert at any time.[172]

5.78   The ET will make appropriate orders with timescales for the next steps of case preparation. If not already clear, the claimant will be ordered to disclose the name of her comparator(s) or if she is unable to do so, to disclose information which will enable the employer to identify who she is referring to (within 14 days). If possible, the employer must then give the claimant the relevant name(s) (within a further 14 days). The claimant will also be ordered to set out the period within which she wishes the comparison to be made. The tribunal will usually order each party to prepare a job description for the claimant and her comparator(s) and then exchange the job descriptions (within 28 days). Any other relevant facts should also be identified. The employer will be ordered to provide access to the premises within a specified period so that the claimant and her representative can interview any comparator. The idea is then that the parties should then meet or otherwise liaise so that within eight weeks of the stage 1 hearing they can present the tribunal with agreed facts, agreed job descriptions and identify points of dispute.

5.79   If an independent expert is involved, the next stage will be a stage 2 hearing at which the tribunal will supplement the agreed facts with its own fact findings regarding the content of the jobs (see below). If there is no independent expert, it is possible that the next stage will be the full merits hearing. Either way, the tribunal is likely to order that witness statements be exchanged at least eight weeks before the next hearing, and that at least 28 days before the hearing, the parties send the tribunal a statement of agreed and disputed facts and issues with a summary of the reasons for disagreeing. If an independent

170 EqA 2010 s131(5)–(6); para 5.28.
171 EqA 2010 s131(2).
172 EqA 2010 s131(3); ET Regs 2013 Sch 3 r9(4).

expert is appointed, s/he must be copied into all relevant information. It is usually best if s/he is appointed at an early stage, so that s/he can be shown the draft job descriptions and make comments before any agreement between the parties is finalised. S/he should also be invited to attend any meetings between the parties for the purpose of agreeing facts. The ET can order the employer to grant the independent expert access to interview relevant staff or management on the premises.[173]

5.80   Finally, the ET will fix a date for the full hearing or, if an expert is to be appointed, for a stage 2 equal value hearing. In the multiple public sector claims, this indicative timetable is not being met, with the stage of agreeing facts and job descriptions prior to instructing experts taking a very long time, sometimes years.

Stage 2 equal value hearing

5.81   A stage 2 hearing in front of a full ET is held where an independent expert has been appointed.[174] At the stage 2 hearing, the ET will make a decision as to any facts that have not been agreed between the parties and will require the expert to prepare his/her report on the basis only of those facts agreed by the parties or decided by the ET. The ET will usually order the expert to prepare and send his/her report to the ET and parties by a specified date. It will also fix a date for the full hearing. The ET has power at any stage, on its own initiative or at a party's request, to order the independent expert to help the ET in establishing the facts on which s/he will rely in preparing his/her report.[175] This may be useful if the parties cannot agree facts or a party is not legally represented or is withholding information.

The full hearing

5.82   The expert's report will be used as evidence in the full hearing, unless it is not based on the agreed or determined facts. If the ET does not allow in the report, it can appoint a different expert or decide the matter itself. The ET can refuse to allow in evidence or hear arguments put by either party if not previously disclosed to the other as

---

173 ET Regs 2013 Sch 3 r4(1)(c).
174 Rules for conduct of the stage 2 hearing are set out at ET Regs 2013 Sch 3 rr6–7.
175 ET Regs 2013 Sch 3 r5.

ordered or required by the rules.[176] At the hearing, the ET will decide whether the job is of equal value and whether the employer can prove a material factor defence. If the employee wins, the ET may go on to decide remedy there and then.

Expert evidence

5.83   If an independent expert is appointed, the ET will use an expert from the panel of independent experts nominated by ACAS and make contact after the stage 1 hearing. The ET rules set out the duties and powers of the independent expert.[177] The ET sends the parties its brief to the independent expert. The expert will get copies of all the relevant information (see para 5.79) and be available to attend hearings as required. If delays are caused by the conduct of the parties, the expert must inform the ET, which has power to order costs or even strike out the claim or response. The final report is sent to the parties, who can ask the expert written questions to clarify the factual basis of the report. Unless the ET agrees otherwise, the parties have just one opportunity to ask these questions within 28 days of the report being sent, and must copy their questions to each other.[178] The expert must provide written answers within a further 28 days.

5.84   The independent expert's opinion has no special status[179] but an ET may well find it very convincing simply because it is independent. Nevertheless, the ET should form its own decision as to whether the work is of equal value.

5.85   In large trade union backed cases, the parties tend to instruct their own experts. The ET's permission is needed, and the evidence will be restricted to what is reasonably required.[180] If an independent expert is also instructed by the tribunal, the parties' own experts must make their assessment based on the same facts. They must disclose their reports in advance of the hearing and answer written questions within set timescales. Although the ET can choose whether to follow the conclusion of the independent expert, in reality an expert's reasoning and conclusions can only be challenged by another expert. This is why parties usually call their own experts at the hearing. Another advantage is that the tribunal may decide not to appoint an independent

---

176   ET Regs 2013 Sch 3 r8(3).
177   ET Regs 2013 Sch 3 r9.
178   ET Regs 2013 Sch 3 r11.
179   *Tennant Textile Colours v Todd* [1988] IRLR 3, NICA.
180   ET Regs 2013 Sch 3 r10.

expert if there are already two other experts, and this may make the process much quicker than having to wait for ACAS to appoint an independent expert. However, it is expensive to instruct an expert (the ET pays for the independent expert[181]) and s/he will not have the same rights of access to the employer's premises and to interview the woman or her comparators. These matters will need negotiation between the parties, and reciprocal access should be agreed.

Remedies, audits and time limits for claiming

Remedies

5.86   Remedies in equal pay cases involving an equality clause (ie all those except any EqA 2010 s13 hypothetical comparator claims) are different from those applying to other discrimination.[182] In non-pensions cases, if an ET finds there has been a breach of an equality clause, the disputed term in her contract is deemed modified and any beneficial term in her comparator's contract which is not in her own becomes included in her contract (see para 5.58). The ET can also make a declaration as to the rights of the parties and award pay arrears or compensation in relation to any non-pay term.[183] If the employer is able to provide a material factor defence for only part of the pay differential, the claim will succeed, but the remedy will be only for the unjustified part. Under Article 157 (see para 5.1), a part-timer suffering indirect discrimination may have her contract modified so that she receives proportionally the same benefits as full-timers.[184] The ET will need evidence of the differential between the pay of the claimant and her comparator(s) for the whole arrears period. It is advisable to ask the ET at an early case management stage for an order that such information be provided by the respondents. Otherwise by the remedy stage, the information may no longer be available.

5.87   In England and Wales, a woman can claim arrears of remuneration or damages for up to six years from the start of ET proceedings; in Scotland it is only five years.[185] There are special rules where the

---

181 Employment Tribunals Act 1996 s5(2).
182 EqA 2010 s113(6). Part 9 Chapter 4 of the Act deals with equality clause remedies; Chapter 3 deals with remedies for other discrimination generally.
183 EqA 2010 s132.
184 *Kowalska v Freie und Hansestadt Hamburg* [1990] IRLR 447, ECJ.
185 EqA 2010 s132(4)–(5). This can be affected by a later amendment of the claim – see para 5.95.

woman had an incapacity or where the employer deliberately concealed relevant information.[186] Obviously a woman cannot claim arrears for a period before she was employed or before the particular comparator was employed. Where the woman's claim is based on work rated as equivalent under a JES, she cannot claim pay arrears for a period prior to the date of the scheme.[187] For any earlier period, she may have to bring an equal value claim. Remedies in respect of pension cases are more complicated and dealt with by EqA 2010 ss133–134. Bear in mind the potential effect of pre-claim ACAS early conciliation (EC) on arrears as EC delays the start of ET proceedings. Although untested, EC could well impact on the arrears period in certain circumstances, eg if the woman has more recently left or ceased to be underpaid. This may be a reason to bring EC to an early end.

5.88   ETs have power to award interest on pay arrears[188] and are prepared to do so. This partly counters the effect of the delays in the ET procedure, so advisers should always seek interest on any claim or settlement. Interest runs from a date midway between the initial breach of the EqA 2010 and the calculation date by the ET.[189] An award for injury to feelings cannot be made in respect of a breach of an equality clause.[190] Unlike other discrimination claims, there is no power for the ET to make recommendations.

Equal pay audits

5.89   An ET can order employers who lose equal pay cases in the ET to carry out and publish equal pay audits.[191] Micro-businesses with fewer than ten employees immediately before the date of judgment and new businesses which started up in the 12 months prior to the

186 EqA 2010 ss132(4)–(5) and 135.
187 *Redcar & Cleveland BC v Bainbridge and others (No 1); Surtees and others v Middlesbrough Council; Redcar & Cleveland BC v Bainbridge and others (No 2)* [2008] EWCA Civ 885; [2008] IRLR 776.
188 Employment Tribunals (Interest on Awards in Discrimination Cases) Regulations 1996 SI No 2803 as amended (see para 19.40). These regulations are deemed made under EqA 2010 s139, by virtue of Equality Act 2010 (Commencement No 4, Savings, Consequential, Transitional, Transitory and Incidental Provisions and Revocation) Order 2010 SI No 2317 art 21(1).
189 *Redcar and Cleveland BC and another v Degnan and others* [2005] IRLR 179, EAT; see para 19.42 for interest on discrimination awards.
190 By analogy with *Council of the City of Newcastle upon Tyne v Allan and others; Degnan and others v Redcar and Cleveland BC* [2005] IRLR 504, EAT on the EqPA 1970.
191 Equality Act 2010 (Equal Pay Audits) Regulations 2014 SI No 2559 with effect from 1 October 2014.

date of the complaint are exempt.[192] The idea of the audit is to identify action to be taken to avoid equal pay breaches occurring or continuing.[193] Although the ET must order an audit where it finds an equal pay breach, there are so many exceptions that the power is considerably weakened. An audit must *not* be ordered in any of these circumstances:

- if there is no reason to think from the particular breach in the proceedings that there may be other equal pay breaches;
- if it is clear without an audit whether any action is required to avoid future equal pay breaches;
- if the information is already available from an audit in the previous three years; or
- if the disadvantages of an audit would outweigh its benefits.[194]

The ET will set the ambit of the audit, specifying the categories of employee to whom the relevant gender pay information must be included and the relevant period of time. The audit must then:

- include the relevant gender pay information for those employees;
- identify any pay differences between the male and female employees and the reason for the differences;
- include the reasons for any equal pay breach identified by the audit; and
- include the employer's plan to avoid equal pay breaches occurring or continuing.[195]

The ET will specify a date for receipt of the completed audit which is no sooner than three months from the order.[196] If the tribunal does not receive the audit on the ordered date or is not satisfied that it meets the requirements, it will invite the employer to attend a hearing and explain. If the employer has not yet provided the audit, it will be given the opportunity to do so prior to the hearing date.[197] If the tribunal decides after the hearing that there is no audit or it does not comply with the requirements, it must make an order that the employer supply or amend the audit (as applicable) by a new date, and consider imposing a penalty of up to £5,000 if there was no reasonable excuse

---

192 This exemption will cease to apply on 1 October 2024. For more detail on the exemptions, see 2014 SI No 2559 reg 4 and Schedule.
193 EqA 2010 s139A(3).
194 2014 SI No 2559 reg 3.
195 2014 SI No 2559 regs 5–6.
196 2014 SI No 2559 reg 5.
197 2014 SI No 2559 reg 7.

for non-compliance.[198] If the employer continues to fail, there can be additional penalties up to £5,000 on each occasion.

5.90   Once the ET has confirmed the audit is satisfactory, within 28 days the employer must publish the audit by telling everyone who is covered by it where they can get a copy and, if the employer has a website, putting it on the site for at least three years.[199] 'Website' is not defined, but seems to envisage a public site as opposed to an intranet. The ET must be sent evidence that this has been done. Modifications can be made if publication would involve breach of any legal obligation, but an explanation must be sent to the ET. Presumably this means that where there are concerns about breach of confidentiality and data protection legislation, statistics could be published on an anonymous basis. The difficulty sometimes will be that individuals are still identifiable, eg because the employer is small or there are unique job titles.

Time limits

5.91   The time limit for lodging equal pay claims concerning breach of an equality clause or rule is set out in detail in EqA 2010 ss129–130. There is no 'just and equitable' extension rule for late claims of the type available for other types of discrimination claim. Equality clause claims must be brought within the 'qualifying period'. In a 'standard case', this means six months beginning with the last day on which the woman was employed in the employment. A standard case is any case which does not fall within the categories of a 'stable work case', a concealment case or an incapacity case, as described below.[200]

5.92   A woman needs to be careful about arguing that she falls under the 'standard case' category. If her contract is varied in some minor respect during her employment, eg to reduce hours, but she is issued with and signs new contract documentation at that time, her previous employment may be taken to have come to an end for the purposes of triggering the equal pay time limit.[201] It may not be obvious whether a change in contract terms amounts to the imposition of a new contract (thus ending her previous 'employment' and causing time limit problems) or is simply a variation in the existing

---

198 2014 SI No 2559 regs 8 and 11.

199 2014 SI No 2559 reg 9.

200 EqA 2010 ss129 and 130(2).

201 *Slack and others v Cumbria CC, with EHRC intervening sub nom Cumbria CC (No 2)* [2009] EWCA Civ 293; [2009] IRLR 463.

one. It depends on what the parties intended, which may not be easy to work out. The fact that the change is fundamental may indicate a new contract has been imposed, but on the other hand, an employee can expressly or impliedly agree to vary a contract, even fundamentally.[202] If there is no agreement to a variation and the change is fundamental, there is probably a termination and a new contract. However, if a change is not fundamental, it is likely to be a variation unless there was an express agreement to use the mechanism of termination and a new contract.[203]

5.93   In many cases, the simpler solution to such a time limit problem is to say that the woman's continuing employment, despite new contracts with varied terms, amounts to a 'stable work case'. Indeed this may be a better starting point than the 'standard case' category. This is because, in a stable work case, the six months runs from the end of the relationship, not from the end of a particular contract. A stable work case is one where there was a 'stable working relationship' between the worker and the employer, including any time after the terms of work had expired.[204] It is not completely clear what amounts to a stable work relationship, but it basically refers to the nature of the work rather than technicalities regarding whether there were different contracts or not.[205] It can therefore include a situation where the same work is carried out for the same employer over a period of time through a series of successive contracts, whether short or long-term contracts, and whether or not there is a break between them.[206] For example, where such contracts are concluded at regular intervals in respect of the same employment and with the same pension scheme, time would run from the end of such a stable work relationship. An unknown question is whether any change in the

---

202 *Potter and others v North Cumbria Acute Hospitals NHS Trust and others* UKEAT/0385/08; [2009] IRLR 900 illustrates this in the context of Agenda for Change. This case was appealed (see n206), but the Court of Appeal decided the appeal based on a different argument, ie stable employment relationship, and did not analyse whether the EAT's analysis of whether there was a change or termination was correct or not.

203 *Cumbria CC v Dow (No 2)* [2008] IRLR 109, EAT.

204 EqA 2010 s130(3).

205 *North Cumbria University Hospitals NHS Trust v Fox and others sub nom Potter and others v North Cumbria Acute Hospitals NHS Trust and others (No 2)* [2010] EWCA Civ 729; [2009] IRLR 804.

206 *Slack and others v Cumbria CC, with EHRC intervening sub nom Cumbria CC (No 2)* [2009] EWCA Civ 293; [2009] IRLR 463; *North Cumbria University Hospitals NHS Trust v Fox and others sub nom Potter and others v North Cumbria Acute Hospitals NHS Trust and others (No 2)* [2010] EWCA Civ 729; [2009] IRLR 804.

nature of the work or the woman's status breaks a stable work relationship, eg if she moves from fixed-term contracts to a permanent position, or is promoted to a higher grade.[207] It is worth remembering that the 'stable work case' category was called a 'stable employment relationship' under the EqPA 1970, and the case-law developed on the basis of the latter wording, which may be more restrictive. If there are intermittent contracts without a stable work relationship, time runs from the end of each contract.

5.94   There are special rules where the woman had an incapacity or where the employer deliberately concealed relevant information, without which the woman could not reasonably have been expected to start a case.[208] Where there has been a TUPE transfer, the time limit for any claim in respect of the period of employment with the transferor should be counted from the transfer date.[209] This is so even if liability for the underpayment transfers to the transferee under the TUPE rules. However, where the transferee continues to act in breach of an equality clause, eg by inheriting a contractual liability to increase pay to that of a male comparator, time runs from the end of the relevant employment with the transferee with regard to underpay in the post-transfer period.[210] When NHS Trusts are dissolved and the woman's employment is taken over by another body, it is likely that the time limit runs from the dissolution date.[211] There are different time limit rules in armed forces cases.[212]

5.95   Because equal pay claims are so complex, it does happen in the large claims that the correct comparators are not identified in the original tribunal claim form. The problem with amending to add new comparator jobs later is that this is regarded as adding a new cause of action, even if the existing claim is on the same basis, ie like work or work rated as equivalent or work of equal value.[213] However, it seems that if the amendment is only to substitute another named individual carrying out the same or substantially the same job as the

---

207 It is uncertain whether the older case of *Jeffery and others v (1) Secretary of State for Education (2) Bridgend College* UKEAT/0677/05 survives *Slack* (n206).

208 EqA 2010 ss129 and 130(4)–(10).

209 *Powerhouse Retail Ltd and others v Burroughs* [2006] IRLR 381, HL regarding pension entitlement, generally extended by *Gutridge v Sodexo Ltd and North Tees and Hartlepool NHS Trust* [2009] EWCA Civ 729; [2009] IRLR 721.

210 *Gutridge v Sodexo Ltd and North Tees and Hartlepool NHS Trust* [2009] EWCA Civ 729; [2009] IRLR 721. See also para 10.44.

211 *Foley and others v NHS Greater Glasgow & Clyde and others* UKEATS/0007/12 and UKEATS/0008/12.

212 EqA 2010 ss129–130.

213 *Bainbridge and others v Redcar and Cleveland BC (No 2)* [2007] IRLR 494, EAT.

original comparator, there is no new cause of action and the amendment can be allowed.[214] The date from which the arrears period is counted (see para 5.87) will also be affected according to whether or not it is a new cause of action.

5.96   Direct sex discrimination based on a hypothetical comparison as opposed to sex equality clause cases are brought under EqA 2010 s13 and one assumes the time limit rules would be as for direct discrimination generally (see chapter 21). ACAS EC applies to either type of tribunal claim.[215]

5.97   Equal pay cases can in some circumstances be brought in a civil court as opposed to in an ET. This is not usually desirable because of the increased costs involved and because ETs are more familiar with such claims. One of the main reasons for doing so may be if the ET time limits are missed, since civil courts have much longer time limits. However, it is not purely a matter of choice. A court can strike out an equal pay claim if it would 'more conveniently' be brought in an ET.[216] The fact that the shorter tribunal time limits have been missed means a claim cannot be brought more conveniently in an ET and it will probably be allowed as a civil claim, provided there was no deliberate abuse of process going on.[217] Nevertheless, this route should never be relied on as a reason for letting an ET time limit pass. Not only might a court decide that it was an abuse of process to deliberately miss a time limit because of some idea that having a civil court case will lead to a litigation advantage, it is also a more expensive course of action.

214 *Prest v Mouchel Business Services Ltd* [2011] ICR 1345, EAT.

215 See EqA 2010 s140B and para 21.21 below for effect on time limits.

216 EqA 2010 s128. But not the other way round – an ET cannot transfer an equal pay case to the High Court or impose an indefinite stay so the claimants are forced to take that route: *Asda Stores Ltd v Brierley and others* [2016] EWCA Civ 566; [2016] IRLR 709.

217 *Birmingham City Council v Abdullah* [2012] UKSC 47; [2013] IRLR 38.

PART II

Unfair dismissal, redundancy and TUPE

Unfair dismissal: eligibility, fairness and automatic dismissal

continued

Chapter 6: Key points

- Only employees can claim unfair dismissal. To decide whether a worker is an employee, the label and tax position are not conclusive. The key tests are mutual obligation to give and undertake work, and control by the employer.
- Agency workers may or may not be employees of either the agency or the client organisation (end-user). In the latter case, the key test is whether it is necessary to imply a contract between the worker and the end-user to explain their working relationship.
- For ordinary unfair dismissal, employees must have at least two years' service. Certain breaks in service do not in fact break continuity of employment.
- A dismissal may be substantively unfair (why the employee was dismissed) or procedurally unfair (how the employee was dismissed).
- The *Polkey* principle applies, ie it can be an unfair dismissal purely because unfair dismissal procedures were followed (though compensation will be reduced if there is no substantive unfairness – see chapter 18).
- It is not against the law in itself for an employer to fail to follow a relevant part of the Advisory, Conciliation and Arbitration Service (ACAS) Code of Practice on Disciplinary and Grievance Procedures, but the tribunal must take it into account. Compensation can also be increased or reduced by up to 25 per cent for either party's unreasonable failure to follow the Code.
- There are special rules where an employee is dismissed during industrial action, depending on whether or not the action was official. Workers must not be subjected to a detriment to prevent or deter them from going on strike.
- There are a large and growing number of grounds on which dismissal is automatically unfair. Most but not all of these grounds do not require any minimum service.
- It is also unlawful to subject employees to a detriment other than dismissal on most but not all of these grounds.
- In respect of many of these grounds, it is unlawful to subject a worker (as well as an employee) to a detriment other than or including dismissal. This is usually where the substantive right being protected is given to workers generally.

continued

- Many of the grounds for automatic unfair dismissal or detriment are to ensure employees/workers are not victimised for asserting their rights, eg to a minimum wage, under the Working Time Regulations or for payslips. The law and evidence required is similar in some respects to that for victimisation under the discrimination legislation.[1]
- Workers must not be subjected to a detriment because they refuse to work in circumstances of danger, which they reasonably believe to be serious and imminent. This may apply where there are dangers of catching Covid-19.
- Workers must not be subjected to a detriment for whistleblowing in the correct manner.
- This chapter should be read in conjunction with chapter 22 on fair disciplinary procedures.

The legal framework

6.1   The statutory right not to be unfairly dismissed was first introduced by the Industrial Relations Act 1971. It is now contained in the Employment Rights Act (ERA) 1996. The right not to be unfairly dismissed is closely linked to the fair handling of disciplinary hearings. Chapter 22 deals with disciplinaries and grievances.

6.2   The ERA 1996 contains many of the most common statutory employment rights belonging to individuals, apart from the discrimination legislation. As well as unfair dismissal, it includes notice entitlement, redundancy, the rights to payslips and written particulars, unauthorised deductions from wages and some maternity rights. There are separate regulations dealing with such matters as working time, the minimum wage and transfers. Most collective trade union laws and rights of workers to belong to trade unions are contained in the Trade Union and Labour Relations (Consolidation) Act (TULR(C)A) 1992.

6.3   There are a number of codes of practice in employment law issued by various specialist bodies including the Advisory, Conciliation and Arbitration Service (ACAS). Generally speaking, these codes are not legally enforceable in themselves, but provide guidance which the tribunals and courts must take into account. The

---

1 See para 13.58.

ACAS Code of Practice on Disciplinary and Grievance Procedures sets out good practice guidelines for the handling of disciplinary and grievance issues in employment.[2] This code is often referred to in unfair dismissal cases, where procedures prior to dismissal are important (see para 6.64).

Who can claim unfair dismissal?

Eligible categories

Employees and the self-employed

6.4   In order to claim unfair dismissal, a worker must be employed (ie work under a contract of employment or service). A worker who is self-employed (ie working under a contract for services) is not entitled to bring a claim. The distinction between these two types of worker can be extremely blurred and difficult to distinguish.

6.5   Unfortunately, there is no clear guidance given by the tribunals and courts to distinguish between those who are employed and those who are simply a worker or even self-employed. An 'employee' is defined in the ERA 1996 simply as someone who has entered into, or works under, a contract of employment.[3] A 'contract of employment' means 'a contract of service or apprenticeship, whether express or implied, and (if it is express), whether it is oral or in writing'.[4] A checklist which summarises the following text is in appendix A at A14.

6.6   There is no single test which determines whether an individual is an employee, although there have been a large number of cases trying to establish the approach to be adopted to determine this issue. It is not enough that a person looked like an employee, acted like an employee and was treated as an employee.[5] The test is more technical than that. The usual starting point is to consider the three criteria in the *Ready Mixed Concrete* case (admittedly expressed in rather old-fashioned terms):[6]

---

2 The most recent code from 11 March 2015 is available on the ACAS website: www.acas.org.uk/acas-code-of-practice-on-disciplinary-and-grievance-procedures.

3 ERA 1996 s230.

4 ERA 1996 s230.

5 *Heatherwood and Wrexham Park Hospitals NHS Trust v Kulubowila and others* UK/EAT/0633/06; *Tilson v Alstom Transport* [2010] EWCA Civ 1308.

6 *Ready Mixed Concrete (South East) v Minister of Pensions and National Insurance* [1968] 2 QB 497, QBD.

- in consideration of a wage or other remuneration, the 'servant' agrees to provide his own work and skill in the performance of some service for 'his master';
- the servant agrees to be under the other's control to a sufficient degree to make the other a master;
- the other provisions in the contract are consistent with it being a contract of employment.

6.7   There cannot be a contract of employment if there is not at least some level of mutual obligation to supply and perform work. This is often referred to as 'an irreducible minimum of obligation on each side'.[7] For example, even if the employer is not obliged to offer a particular number of hours, s/he must be obliged to offer at least a reasonable amount of work, or to offer work if it becomes available, or to pay a retainer if there is no work. Equally, the individual must be obliged to accept work if it is offered, or at least to accept a reasonable amount of work. It can be difficult to apply these legal principles in practice because it is not always easy to analyse what the contractual obligations are. In one case,[8] butlers who worked in a hotel as 'regular casuals' were not employees, even though they were provided with work on a regular basis, since the hotel was not under an obligation to provide such work. In a later case, power station guides were held not to be employees because the employer had no obligation to provide work and the workers were free to accept or refuse any work which was in fact offered.[9] By contrast, in another case, homeworkers were found to be employees, even though they could decide how much work they took on. This was because they had to accept at least a reasonable amount of work so that it was worthwhile for the delivery drivers to call, and the employer in turn had to provide a reasonable share of the available work to each homeworker.[10] Whether there is sufficient mutual obligation for a worker on a zero hours contract[11] to be an employee is an important question. These cases, although arising before that terminology became widespread, provide useful guidance.

---

7   *Nethermere (St Neots) Ltd v Gardiner* [1984] IRLR 240, CA.

8   *O'Kelly v Trusthouse Forte plc* [1983] ICR 728; [1983] IRLR 369, CA.

9   *Carmichael v National Power plc* [2000] IRLR 43, HL.

10   *Nethermere (St Neots) Ltd v Gardiner* [1984] IRLR 240, CA. For further examples, see *Saha v Viewpoint Field Services Ltd* UKEAT/0116/13 and the helpful *St Ives Plymouth Ltd v Haggerty* UKEAT/0107/08.

11   See para 1.40.

6.8   It is also essential to being an employee that the employer has a sufficient framework of 'control' over the worker, although this can be ambiguous because direct supervision and control is absent in many kinds of employment today.[12] If the worker controls when, where and how s/he performs the work, this degree of autonomy would suggest that s/he is self-employed. However, if the employer has the contractual power to tell the worker when, where and how to perform, it would indicate that the worker is an employee, whether or not the worker has day-to-day control over his/her own work.[13] Personal service is also an essential requirement. As stated in *Ready Mixed Concrete* (see para 6.6), the individual must have agreed to provide his/her own work and skill. This means it is unlikely to be a contract of employment if the individual has an unfettered power to send someone else along to do the work in his/her place, ie a power of 'substitution'. But a limited power to send a substitute, eg only when the individual is unable (as opposed to unwilling) to work and/or only if the substitute is approved by the employer, is not necessarily inconsistent with the individual being obliged to provide personal service.[14]

6.9   Although lack of mutual obligation, an insufficient right of control by the employer, and an individual's right to send substitutes are all factors which are highly likely to prevent there being a contract of employment, the converse does not mean there definitely *is* a contract of employment. The other provisions of the contract must also be consistent with its being a contract of employment. It is useful to look at how integrated the individual is into the business. It is helpful, though not conclusive in itself, if s/he is very much part of the organisation. The employment tribunal (ET) will also look at the purpose of the contract and what the parties intended when they formed it. It is the nature of the agreement and the actual performance of the contract which counts, not simply the label attached to the relationship by the parties. Just because an individual is told by an employer that s/he is self-employed does not mean that is the true legal position. Nor is it conclusive that s/he is paying tax on a self-employed

---

12 *Montgomery v Johnson Underwood Ltd* [2001] IRLR 269, CA.

13 *Ready Mixed Concrete (South East) v Minister of Pensions and National Insurance* [1968] 2 QB 497; and see facts in *White and another v Troutbeck SA* [2013] EWCA Civ 1171; [2013] IRLR 949.

14 *Macfarlane and another v Glasgow City Council* [2001] IRLR 7, EAT; *Byrne Brothers (Formwork) Ltd v Baird and others* [2002] IRLR 96, EAT; *James v Redcats (Brands) Ltd* [2007] IRLR 296, EAT; *Premier Groundworks Ltd v Jozsa* UKEAT/0494/08. Some of these cases concern whether the individual is a 'worker', but the principle regarding personal service is the same.

basis, although that will be one of the relevant factors.[15] The method and mode of payment of wages may also be relevant. If pay is referable to a period of time rather than productivity, this suggests that the individual is more likely to be an employee. S/he is also more likely to be an employee if s/he gets paid sick leave and is subject to the usual disciplinary and grievance procedures.

6.10   The above assumes that it is clear what the contract terms are, but this may not be the case. When deciding what terms have been agreed between the parties, the written contract is not the starting point.[16] Employment contracts are not like other types of contract. The important point is whether individuals qualify for employment rights by meeting the statutory definition of 'worker' and 'employee'. The danger with relying too much on what is in a written contract is that employers are often in a position to dictate the terms. Workers sometimes sign pro forma contracts which are designed to prevent them being an employee, eg by stating there is no mutual obligation to offer or perform work, or that the worker has the right to send along a substitute. This does not mean that the terms of any written agreement should be ignored, because the evidence might show that the parties really did understand and agree to those terms. But the written document is just one factor. The tribunal will look at all the evidence to see what the true nature of the relationship was.[17] This will not necessarily be contained in an explicit verbal agreement, but it can be implied from the circumstances. For example, a contract might state there is a right to send along a substitute, but is that really what the employer agreed, given the nature of the work and the employer's requirements? Or the contract may state that the employee can refuse work at any time, but does the way the business is organised suggest it could really run on that basis? The behaviour of the parties in practice can be a good guide, but it can also be misleading. For example, just because the individual never tried to send along a substitute does not mean s/he did not have the right to do so. It would be far more significant if the individual did try to send along a substitute one day and was refused. That would suggest there was no such agreement in the first place. When deciding whether a written contract is a true reflection of the parties' agreement, tribunals must be realistic and worldly wise. They must be alive to the concern

---

15 *Massey v Crown Life Insurance Co* [1978] ICR 590; [1978] IRLR 31, CA.

16 *Uber BV and others v Aslam and others* [2021] UKSC 5; [2021] IRLR 407.

17 *Autoclenz Ltd v Belcher and others* [2011] UKSC 41; [2011] IRLR 820; *Uber BV and others v Aslam and others* [2021] UKSC 5; [2021] IRLR 407.

that armies of lawyers will simply place clauses denying mutual obligation as a matter of form even when such terms do not begin to reflect the relationship.[18] To override an express clause by proving it is a sham, the tribunal must be convinced that the real agreement was to a different effect, but there does not need to have been any intent to deceive third parties.[19]

6.11   'Contract workers', 'temps', 'casuals', workers on zero hours contracts,[20] people working freelance, agency workers or, less likely, volunteers, may or may not meet the definition of an 'employee'. If these workers are 'employees' and meet the other eligibility requirements (see below), they can claim unfair dismissal. With volunteers, the key factor is whether there is a mutual obligation to provide and attend work, not whether the volunteer has obligations and standards to meet while at work.[21]

Umbrella contracts and intermittent assignments

6.12   Sometimes an employee is not required to work all the time, but only as and when required on individual engagements. Zero hours contracts may fall within this category. In such situations, it is very possible that the individual engagements, once accepted, would in themselves amount to self-contained contracts of employment. For example, a teacher employed on a series of individual short-term contracts can be an employee for the period of each individual contract, even if there is no obligation to grant him/her each new contract.[22] There is no minimum length of such contracts, which could even come into effect on a daily basis.[23] The fact that the employer or employee can terminate the contract during the individual engagement does not in itself prevent it being a contract of employment.[24] The only problem for workers wanting to claim unfair dismissal will

18   *Protectacoat Firthglow Ltd v Szilagyi* [2009] EWCA Civ 98; [2009] IRLR 365.
19   *Autoclenz Ltd v Belcher and others* [2011] UKSC 41; [2011] IRLR 820; *Protectacoat Firthglow Ltd v Szilagyi* [2009] EWCA Civ 98; [2009] IRLR 365; *Consistent Group Ltd v Kalwak and others* [2008] IRLR 505, CA; *Redrow Homes (Yorkshire) Ltd v Buckborough & Sewell* UKEAT/0528/07; [2009] IRLR 34. See also *Fitton v City of Edinburgh Council* UKEATS/0010/07 re secondment.
20   See para 1.40.
21   *Melhuish v Redbridge Citizens Advice Bureau* [2005] IRLR 409, EAT.
22   *Cornwall CC v Prater* [2006] IRLR 362, CA; *Vernon v Event Management Catering Ltd* UKEAT/0161/07.
23   *Augustin v Total Quality Staff Ltd* UKEAT/0343/07. See para 6.13 for the agency worker context.
24   *Drake v Ipsos Mori UK Ltd* [2012] IRLR 973, EAT disapproving *Little v BMI Chiltern Hospital* UKEAT/0021/09.

be acquiring sufficient length of service if the contracts are short and there are gaps in between.[25] The worker then needs to argue either that the rules on continuous service allow for the separate contracts to be added together (see below) or that there is in fact an overarching 'global' or 'umbrella' contract, which covers the time when the employee is not working, as well as the times when s/he is employed on the individual engagements. To be able to prove that the contract of employment continues throughout in this way, there must be 'an irreducible minimum of obligation' which continues through the breaks in work engagements.[26]

Agency workers

6.13   Agency workers may in theory be employees of the organisation to which they are assigned (the 'end-user') or of the agency which assigns them[27] (or neither). If in genuine doubt, the employee should bring a case against both.[28] The usual tests of mutual obligation and control apply when deciding whether the worker is an employee of either party.[29] However, when considering whether the worker is an employee of the end-user, the more important question is whether there is any contract at all between the worker and the end-user. Usually there is no express contract between them, so the issue becomes whether a contract can be implied. A contract can only be implied if it is necessary to do so, to give business reality to the fact that the end-user provides work and the worker carries it out. The problem is that in most cases, this arrangement can be explained by the express agreements between the end-user and the agency, and between the worker and the agency – it is not necessary to imply any contract between the end-user and the worker.[30] It needs some specific words or action to convince a tribunal that the agency

---

25 See para 6.20 onwards regarding length of service required to claim unfair dismissal.

26 For a very clear, fairly recent analysis, see *Stringfellow Restaurants Ltd v Quashie* [2012] EWCA Civ 1735; [2013] IRLR 99.

27 *McMeechan v Secretary of State for Employment* [1997] IRLR 353, CA.

28 Provided this is reasonable, which it usually will be. *Astbury v Gist Ltd* UKEAT/0446/04. But since this case, the Court of Appeal in *James* (n30 below) has clarified the law.

29 *Montgomery v Johnson Underwood Ltd* [2001] IRLR 269, CA; *Brook Street Bureau v Dacas* [2004] IRLR 358, CA; *Bunce v Postworth Ltd t/a Skyblue* [2005] IRLR 557, CA.

30 *James v Greenwich LBC* [2008] IRLR 302, CA; *Wood Group Engineering (North Sea) Ltd v Robertson* UKEATS/0081/06. For another illustration, see *Tilson v Alstom Transport* [2010] EWCA Civ 1308.

arrangements no longer explain the relationship. The fact that the arrangement has been going on for a long time is not enough on its own, as it is explicable by mutual convenience. It may be easiest to imply a contract of employment when agency arrangements are superimposed on an existing direct contractual arrangement.[31] It is useful to look at the written agreements between the agency and the worker,[32] and the agency and the end-user, although it is not enough simply to look at the label applied to the situation in the documents.[33] A contract of employment can be implied between the worker and the end-user even if the contract between the worker and the agency expressly stipulates there is no such contract of employment,[34] but as already explained, it is difficult to imply such contracts.

6.14 A worker can be an employee of an agency in respect of a single assignment or placement, even if s/he is not an employee of the agency overall.[35] If the worker has accepted a series of individual assignments with the same or different end-users, the question then becomes whether s/he can add together the assignments and maintain continuity between any gaps, so that s/he qualifies to claim unfair dismissal against the agency. Where a worker has an express contract of employment with an agency, it is unlikely (though not impossible) that s/he is also an employee of the end-user.[36]

Upper age limit

6.15 There is no longer an upper age limit for claiming unfair dismissal. It used to be possible to force employees to retire at or above the age of 65 or any lower, objectively justifiable, normal retirement age, if the correct procedures were followed. However, those rules were phased out with effect from 6 April 2011.

---

31 Comments of EAT in *James v Greenwich LBC* [2007] IRLR 168, EAT at paras 53–62.
32 Required under the Conduct of Employment Agencies and Employment Businesses Regulations 2003 SI No 3319.
33 *Franks v Reuters Ltd and another* [2003] IRLR 423, CA. See also para 6.7.
34 *Brook Street Bureau v Dacas* [2004] IRLR 358, CA; *Royal National Lifeboat Institution v Bushaway* [2005] IRLR 674, EAT. See also *Cable & Wireless plc v Muscat* [2006] IRLR 354, CA.
35 *McMeechan v Secretary of State for Employment* [1997] IRLR 353, CA. See also *Cornwall CC v Prater* (see n22 above); *Augustin v Total Quality Staff Ltd & Humphries* UKEAT/0343/07. See para 6.8.
36 *Cairns v Visteon UK Ltd* [2007] IRLR 175, EAT.

Working abroad and ship workers

6.16   Employees can claim unfair dismissal if they were working in Great Britain (GB) at the time of their dismissal. A peripatetic employee, eg a pilot with a base in GB, can also be covered. Where an employee lives and/or works for at least part of the time in GB, it is only necessary for his/her connection with the system of law in GB to be 'sufficiently strong' for it to be appropriate for a tribunal to deal with the claim. Where an employee lives and works wholly abroad, s/he can only claim in exceptional circumstances and it is necessary to identify factors which are sufficiently powerful to displace the more obvious connection with the foreign jurisdiction. The employee will need to show s/he has a much stronger connection both with GB and with British employment law than with any other system of law. It is the degree of connection which is relevant. The relative merits of the competing systems of law are irrelevant. An example of an employee who could be covered might be an employee who is posted abroad for the purposes of a business carried on in GB, as opposed to a business carried out abroad albeit for British owners. For example, a foreign correspondent on the staff of a British newspaper, who is posted abroad and lives there for many years but remains nevertheless a permanent employee of the newspaper who could be posted to some other country. Another example could be an employee living and working effectively in a British enclave abroad, eg a military base.[37] Special rules apply to employment on a ship.[38]

Categories excluded from claiming unfair dismissal

Overview

6.17   Employees in Crown employment (eg working for government departments) can generally claim unfair dismissal, though there are some

---

37 These principles are derived from a number of cases, starting with *Lawson v Serco Ltd; Botham v Ministry of Defence; Crofts and others v Veta Ltd and others* [2006] IRLR 289, HL, and developed in particular by *Duncombe and others v Secretary of State for Children, Schools and Families* [2011] UKSC 36; [2011] IRLR 840; *Ministry of Defence v Wallis and Grocott* [2011] EWCA Civ 231; *Ravat v Halliburton Manufacturing & Services Ltd* [2012] UKSC 1; [2012] IRLR 315; and *Creditsights Ltd v Dhunna* [2014] EWCA Civ 1238; [2014] IRLR 953. There is a good summary of the pre-*Dhunna* cases in *Bates van Winkelhof v Clyde & Co LLP and others* [2012] EWCA Civ 1207; [2012] IRLR 992. There is no *Lawson* limitation where the unfair dismissal claim is linked to an EU right: see para 3.16 for more detail.

38 ERA 1996 s199(7).

partial exceptions with regard to certain of the grounds for automatic unfair dismissal in relation to members of the armed services or for employment in the Security Service.[39] Members of the police service are generally excluded.[40] There are certain other special categories.[41] Advisers should check the exact wording of the legislation and up-to-date amendments where any of these exclusions may apply. Special rules also apply to employees of foreign and Commonwealth missions.[42] Whether a church minister is an employee and can therefore claim unfair dismissal depends on the facts and nature of his/her duties and, most importantly, whether there was an intention to create legal relations.[43] Under Article 9 of the European Convention on Human Rights (ECHR) (freedom of religion) a tribunal must take it into account if the church in the particular case does not believe in creating legal relations.

Contracting out

6.18   It is a very important principle that employees cannot agree to give up their right to claim unfair dismissal.[44] The only exceptions are where they have settled their claim through ACAS or in a 'settlement agreement' (formerly called compromise agreement).[45] In addition, there is the controversial category of 'employee shareholders' who can give up their right to claim ordinary unfair dismissal (see para 6.130).

Illegal contracts of employment

6.19   An employment tribunal claim may fail on grounds of 'illegality'. This may be 'statutory illegality' where legislation prohibits the contract or a particular term, or 'common law illegality', where the formation, purpose or performance of the contract involves conduct that is illegal or contrary to public policy and where it is therefore appropriate for the courts to deny enforcement of the contract to one

---

39   For details see ERA 1996 ss191–193.
40   Apart from ERA 1996 s100 dismissals (health and safety) and s103A dismissals (whistleblowing). See ERA 1996 s200.
41   For example, see ERA 1996 s199 regarding mariners.
42   This can be complex due to immunity rules and there is a body of recent case-law.
43   *New Testament Church of God v Stewart* [2008] IRLR 134, CA; *The President of the Methodist Conference v Preston* [2013] UKSC 29; [2013] IRLR 646; *Sharpe v The Bishop of Worcester (in his corporate capacity)* [2015] EWCA Civ 399; [2015] IRLR 663.
44   ERA 1996 s203(1).
45   See para 20.273.

or other party. A tribunal should consider the public interests at stake and consider whether denying the claim would be a proportionate response to the illegality. Potentially relevant factors include the seriousness of the conduct, its centrality to the contract, whether it was intentional and whether there was a marked disparity in the parties' respective culpability.[46] The law on illegality is difficult and inconsistent. It is not helped by the most recent Supreme Court decision on the matter not being an employment case.[47] This section can only offer a few pointers. Where illegality is a potential problem, it is necessary to read the case-law. These are the most common types of illegality in employment cases:

- The most obvious example of statutory illegality is where an employee is not entitled to enter or work in the UK under the immigration rules.[48] This may prevent the worker bringing a claim, but not necessarily if eg the worker was vulnerable, unaware the rules had been broken, and the wording of the immigration legislation does not categorically make the contract void.

- The most typical type of 'common law illegality' is where, with the employee's involvement, there has been a fraud on HM Revenue & Customs (HMRC), eg the employer is not paying the appropriate income tax on the employee's wages. A common indication of a fraud is when wages are wholly or partly in cash and payslips are inaccurate or non-existent. The employee must have known the facts (although not necessarily that anything was against the law). Moreover, the employee must have actively participated in the fraud, not just turned a blind eye.[49]

- It does not make a contract illegal to wrongly describe it as self-employment and to pay tax on that basis, if the parties are in good faith and have not misrepresented the facts to HMRC.[50]

- Where the performance of the employment contract is illegal at certain times, the prohibited period will not count towards the required length of continuous employment for an unfair dismissal claim. An employee must be continuously employed for two years

---

46 *Patel v Mirza* [2016] UKSC 42; [2017] 1 All ER 191.

47 *Patel v Mirza* [2016] UKSC 42; [2017] 1 All ER 191.

48 *Okedina v Chikale* [2019] EWCA Civ 1393; [2019] IRLR 905 is a useful review of the law. See also para 14.85.

49 *Hall v Woolston Hall Leisure Ltd* [2000] IRLR 578, CA. See also *Robinson v Sheikh Khalid bin Saqr al Qasimi* [2021] EWCA Civ 862; [2021] IRLR 774 for the emphasis on proportionality post *Patel*.

50 *Enfield Technical Services Ltd v Payne; BF Components Ltd v Grace* [2008] IRLR 500, CA.

after the end of the prohibited period in order to qualify for the general protection against unfair dismissal.[51]
• The rules on illegality are more flexible for discrimination claims.[52]

Qualifying service

Length of continuous employment

6.20   To claim unfair dismissal, an employee must have been continuously employed for at least two years at the effective date of termination (EDT) of his/her contract of employment.[53] The qualifying period has changed several times in the past. In June 1999, it was reduced from two years to one year, and it was increased back to two years by the coalition government in April 2012. There also used to be a requirement to work at least 16 hours per week to qualify for the right not to be unfairly dismissed. This was found to be indirect sex discrimination contrary to EU law, and the minimum hours requirement was removed in 1995. There is no minimum length of service requirement for dismissals related to an employee's political opinions or affiliation or connected with the employee's membership of a reserve force[54] or for certain automatic unfair dismissals, eg where dismissal is related to pregnancy or maternity.[55]

Weeks which count towards continuous service

6.21   Continuous employment is measured by 'qualifying' weeks.[56] Any week during all or part of which the employee's relations with his/her employer are governed by a contract of employment is a week which counts. If during all or part of a week a worker is away on account of holiday or sickness or other recognised absence, that week will nevertheless count if the contract of employment is still running. Equally, if an employee resigns or is dismissed in one week and re-engaged in the subsequent week, each week counts and continuity is not broken. In certain circumstances, there can also be continuous service once a

---

51   See also *Blue Chip Trading Ltd v Helbawi* UKEAT/0397/08; [2009] IRLR 128 regarding a national minimum wage claim where a student worked excessive hours during term-time contrary to the immigration rules.
52   See para 12.21.
53   ERA 1996 s108(1).
54   ERA 1996 s108(4)–(5).
55   ERA 1996 s99. See para 6.67 onwards for full list of automatic unfair dismissals.
56   ERA 1996 s212(1).

contract of employment is agreed but the start date has not yet arrived,[57] but it may be risky to rely on this. Continuous service is broken by a week that does not qualify with the result that the employee will have to start again in accruing the two years' continuous service.[58] Days spent on a strike,[59] whether official or unofficial, do not count towards continuous service. However, the period on strike does not break continuity either. The effect is simply to push forward the date when the employee's continuous service is considered to have started by the relevant number of days.[60]

Continuity if the employee leaves work and returns

6.22   The period of continuous employment must be of unbroken service except in limited circumstances. As already stated, where an employee is absent from work but the contract continues, there is no problem and continuity is preserved. In some circumstances, even though the contract is terminated because the employee leaves, when s/he subsequently returns to the job continuity is preserved and the weeks of absence will count towards his/her continuity of employment. Continuity is preserved where the contract of employment is not in existence and the employee is absent from work in any of the following circumstances:

- on account of a temporary cessation of work. This is when the employer lays off employees through lack of work.[61] It can also cover regular breaks between contracts, eg teachers who are contracted from September to July every year but not over the summer.[62] Whether a break can be considered 'temporary' may not be clear;[63]
- because of sickness or injury, subject to a maximum of 26 weeks;[64]

---

57   *Welton v Deluxe Retail Ltd (t/a Madhouse (in administration)* UKEAT/0266/12; [2013] IRLR 166.
58   ERA 1996 Pt XIV Chapter 1.
59   Defined in ERA 1996, s235(5). This is a different definition to that used for strike dismissals – see para 6.126 below.
60   ERA 1996 s211(3).
61   ERA 1996 s212(3)(b).
62   *Ford v Warwickshire CC* [1983] IRLR 126, HL. Note that ERA 1996 s212(3)(c) may also help. See also para 1.45 regarding possible entitlement to permanent status after four years.
63   *Fitzgerald v Hall, Russell & Co Ltd* [1970] AC 984, HL; *Flack v Kodak Ltd* [1986] IRLR 255, CA.
64   ERA 1996 s212(3)(a) and (4).

- in such circumstances that, by arrangement or custom, the employee is regarded as continuing in employment for all or any purposes.[65] This can be helpful when, eg, an employer agrees that an employee may leave to visit family overseas and return subsequently to the same employment. At the outset, both parties must regard the employee as continuing in employment for the entire period of the absence.[66] An arrangement cannot be entered after the absence to confer continuity retrospectively.[67] Women taking advantage of child-break schemes need to be extremely careful about the terms of the scheme so they do not lose continuity.[68] Ideally they should simply take unpaid extended leave, without terminating their employment at all;

- the employee is reinstated or re-engaged through ACAS conciliation following dismissal, or a settlement agreement, or as a result of bringing an ET claim, eg through a reinstatement or re-engagement order made by the ET, or as a result of a decision taken arising out of the use of the (now abolished) statutory dispute resolution or age and retirement procedures.[69]

The presumption of continuity

6.23   The period of continuous employment begins on the day the employee starts work[70] and is presumed to continue[71] until the EDT of the contract of employment.[72] The presumption of continuity is very important for employees, since it means that it is for the employer to prove there has been a break which is not recognised by the law as preserving continuity.[73]

---

65 ERA 1996 s212(3)(c).

66 *Curr v Marks & Spencer plc* [2003] IRLR 74, CA.

67 *Welton v Deluxe Retail Ltd (t/a Madhouse (in administration))* UKEAT/0266/12; [2013] IRLR 166.

68 *Curr v Marks & Spencer plc* [2003] IRLR 74, CA; *Bright v Lincolnshire CC* (2003) 707 IRLB 8, EAT.

69 Employment Protection (Continuity of Employment) Regulations 1996 SI No 3147.

70 ERA 1996 s211(1)(a).

71 ERA 1996 s210(5).

72 ERA 1996 s97.

73 ERA 1996 s210(5).

Identifying the effective date of termination

6.24 The EDT is identified in the same way as for time limit purposes[74] except that, for the purposes of calculating length of continuous service, it is artificially extended when the employer fails to give notice. In those circumstances, the EDT is when the minimum statutory notice period, not the contractual notice period, would have expired.[75] The EDT will not be extended if the employee was dismissed without notice on grounds of gross misconduct and s/he had in fact committed gross misconduct.[76] The law on an employee's contractual rights is complicated where an employer, without justification, dismisses him/her without notice and the employee then refuses to accept that the dismissal has taken place. However, from the point of view of the statutory right to claim unfair dismissal, this does not affect the EDT in an unfair dismissal case.[77]

Transfer of the business and associated employers

6.25 Continuity of employment is preserved where there has been a transfer of the business.[78] For the general effect of TUPE, see chapter 10. Continuity is also preserved if, at the time the employee starts work for a new employer, the new employer is an 'associated' employer of the original employer. Companies are associated employers if one company directly or indirectly controls the other, or if both companies are under the control of a third person.[79] Any gap in service between the old and new employers may be preserved by the usual rules (para 6.22 above).[80]

---

74 See para 20.47.

75 ERA 1996 s97(2); *Fox Maintenance v Jackson* [1977] IRLR 306, EAT.

76 *Lancaster & Duke Ltd v Wileman* UKEAT/0256/17; [2019] IRLR 112.

77 See para 1.35 for the contractual argument. For the effect on unfair dismissal, see *Robert Cort & Son Ltd v Charman* [1981] IRLR 437, EAT; *Duniec v Travis Perkins Trading Company Ltd* UKEAT/0482/13.

78 ERA 1996 s218(2) and possibly the Transfer of Undertakings (Protection of Employment) Regulations (TUPE Regs) 2006 SI No 246 reg 4.

79 ERA 1996 ss218(6) and 231. Where one company is in liquidation, see *Da Silva Junior v Composite Mouldings & Design Ltd* UKEAT/0241/08.

80 See *Services for Education (S4E) Ltd v (1) White (2) Birmingham City Council* UKEAT/0024/15 for a scenario where ERA 1996 s218(2) was required rather than the TUPE Regs 2006 because a transfer took place during a temporary break in employment.

'Contract workers', 'casuals', 'temps' and 'zero hours workers'

6.26 With the deregulation of the labour market, workers are employed on an increasingly insecure basis under a number of labels which have no legal meaning. Whether or not 'contract workers', 'casuals', 'temps' and 'zero hours workers' can claim unfair dismissal depends on whether they meet the eligibility requirements set out in this chapter. In particular:

- Are they employees? This is a question of fact having regard, in particular, to the issues of mutual obligation and how much control the employer exercises (see paras 6.4–6.14).
- Do they have the requisite length of service? Remember that a series of fixed-term contracts without a break which counts will be added together.
- Have they been dismissed? Failure to renew a fixed-term contract is a dismissal in law.
- It is no longer possible to exclude the right to claim unfair dismissal on expiry of fixed-term contracts by written waiver clauses.[81] Whether or not the failure to renew a fixed-term contract is in practice fair or unfair, will be subject to the usual reasonableness test (see below). However, it cannot necessarily be assumed that just because the contract was for a fixed-term period, non-renewal is fair.

What is a dismissal?

6.27 To bring a claim for unfair dismissal, the employee must have been dismissed in a way recognised by the ERA 1996.[82] There are various types of dismissal:

- termination by the employer;
- expiry of a fixed-term contract;
- forced resignation;
- resignation amounting to constructive dismissal.

---

81 ERA 1999 s18(6). See para 6.18.
82 ERA 1996 s95.

Termination by the employer

6.28   Usually the employer terminates the employment with or without notice. Notice of dismissal occurs when there is an ascertainable date, not merely advance warning. If an employee resigns simply because s/he has been warned of a future dismissal, s/he cannot claim actual or constructive dismissal.

6.29   Sometimes there is an argument where an employer uses ambiguous words, which the employee may understand as a dismissal, but the employer later denies s/he said at all or that they meant any more than 'Go home for the rest of the day'. If there is a dispute over whether a dismissal has occurred, the onus is on the employee to show on the balance of probabilities that s/he has been dismissed. If the ET cannot decide this issue on the available evidence, the employee's claim will fail.[83] If the employee cannot prove s/he was dismissed, the tribunal will say s/he resigned and has no rights. However, if the employer's behaviour amounted to a fundamental breach of contract, the employee may be able to claim constructive dismissal instead.

6.30   Where the employer's words are ambiguous, the ET will look at the purpose and effect of those words in the light of all the surrounding circumstances and, in particular, the conduct of the parties and what happened before and after the disputed dismissal.[84] The ET must then decide how a 'reasonable' employee would have interpreted the employer's words.[85] On the other hand, if the employer's words clearly indicated a dismissal, and are taken at face value, the dismissal probably stands even if the employer did not mean to dismiss and a reasonable listener would have understood that.[86] The situation is different where the dismissal (or resignation) took place in 'the heat of the moment', for example, as a result of an argument between the employer and employee.[87] If the employer retracts the dismissal soon afterwards, the ET may consider that s/he was entitled to do so and that if the employee refuses to come back, s/he has in fact resigned. The period of time in which a party may retract depends on the circumstances, but usually it should be shortly afterwards.

83 *Morris v London Iron and Steel Co* [1987] ICR 855; [1987] IRLR 182, CA.
84 *Tanner v D T Kean Ltd* [1978] IRLR 110, EAT.
85 *J & J Stern v Simpson* [1983] IRLR 52, EAT.
86 But the case-law is conflicting on this.
87 *Martin v Yeoman Aggregates Ltd* [1983] IRLR 49, EAT.

6.31   A similar principle applies where an employee resigns in the heat of the moment and instantly retracts the resignation. If the employer refuses to accept the retraction, the ET may consider the employee to have been dismissed. Similarly, where the employee is immature or of below average intelligence and resigns while under emotional stress, the ET will not necessarily treat those words as constituting a resignation, if the employee never intended it.[88]

6.32   An employee who wants to leave before his/her notice expires, eg to start a new job, must be careful as s/he could lose his/her right to claim unfair dismissal. If his/her employer agrees to the employee leaving early, the dismissal almost certainly still counts as a dismissal in law.[89] If the employer refuses to agree, the employee must give counter-notice in accordance with ERA 1996 s95(2), though it is not completely clear how this works.[90] For where an employee is offered reinstatement after an internal appeal, see para 22.24.

Expiry of a fixed-term contract

6.33   Non-renewal of a fixed-term contract on its expiry is treated as a dismissal.[91] A fixed-term contract is a contract for a specific term and at its commencement the termination date is ascertainable.[92]

Forced resignation

6.34   If the employee resigns as a result of the employer saying that s/he must resign or otherwise be dismissed, this counts as a dismissal.[93] The difficult issue for the ET to decide is whether the resignation was forced. An employee should be wary of resigning in these circumstances, because it may be difficult to prove that s/he was threatened in this way.

---

88 *Barclay v City of Glasgow DC* [1983] IRLR 313, EAT.
89 *McAlwane v Boughton Estates Ltd* [1973] ICR 470, NIRC; *CPS Recruitment Ltd v Bowen and the Secretary of State for Employment* [1982] IRLR 54, EAT.
90 In a redundancy case, s/he must comply with ERA 1996 s136(3)(b).
91 ERA 1996 s95(1)(b).
92 *BBC v Dixon* [1979] ICR 281; [1979] IRLR 114, CA.
93 *Sheffield v Oxford Controls Company Ltd* [1979] IRLR 133, EAT; *Sandhu v Jan de Rijk Transport Ltd* [2007] IRLR 519, CA.

Constructive dismissal

Overview

6.35   There is much confusion among the public about the meaning of 'constructive dismissal'.[94] Constructive dismissal occurs when an employee resigns (with or without giving notice) because of a 'fundamental' or 'repudiatory' breach of the employment contract by the employer. In order to bring an unfair dismissal case, an employee still needs to meet the other eligibility criteria, eg length of service. S/he will also have to prove the constructive dismissal was unfair. Constructive dismissal is usually difficult to prove with lots of pitfalls, and an employee should be very careful about resigning if s/he wants to be able to claim unfair dismissal.

6.36   For constructive dismissal, the employer must have broken the contract and it is not enough that s/he simply acted unreasonably.[95] So, for example, if the employer gives the employee an instruction which is unreasonable but which is allowed by the contract, there is no breach of contract and therefore no constructive dismissal. However, extremely unreasonable behaviour might breach the implied contract term of trust and confidence (see below).

6.37   Before resigning, an employee needs to consider which contract term the employer has broken. This means being sure what the contract says on the point in dispute. Contracts consist of express terms (verbal or written), which are sometimes ambiguously worded, and unwritten implied terms, which can be even more uncertain. Many constructive dismissal claims rely on the employer's breach of one of the generally implied terms, for example:

- not to subject the employee to capricious or arbitrary treatment;
- not to break trust and confidence;
- to take reasonable care for the employee's health and safety.[96]

It can be particularly difficult to know when such an implied term has been broken in practice. Examples of breach of the implied term of trust and confidence could be:

- persistent and unwanted amorous advances towards a female employee;[97]

94   ERA 1996 s95(1)(c).
95   *Western Excavating (ECC) Ltd v Sharp* [1978] IRLR 27, CA.
96   *Flatman v Essex County Council* UKEAT/0097/20. For constructive dismissal and stress, see para 17.11.
97   *Western Excavating (ECC) Ltd v Sharp* [1978] ICR 221; [1978] IRLR 27, CA.

- failure to investigate properly the employee's allegations of sexual harassment;[98]
- undermining a supervisor by reprimanding him/her in the presence of subordinates;[99]
- swearing abusively at the employee, unless such language is commonly used and directed at each other by staff;[100]
- most conduct which amounts to unlawful discrimination under the Equality Act (EqA) 2010, but there will be exceptions;[101]
- suspending an employee without reasonable and proper cause.[102] However, employees need to be very careful on this one because an employer usually needs less justification for suspending an employee and investigating an allegation than for actually taking disciplinary action.

The band of reasonable responses test (see para 6.60) does not apply in constructive dismissal cases to the question whether the employer has broken the implied term of trust and confidence.[103]

Fundamental breach of contract

6.38   The employee cannot resign unless the breach of contract is 'fundamental'. There are no hard and fast rules on this, and it is for the ET to decide what impact the breach has on the contractual relationship of the parties. The working relationship will be relevant and what in one job may amount to a fundamental breach, in another will not. Many constructive dismissal cases arise when an employer tries to vary the employee's contract unilaterally, eg by substantial cuts in pay or changes in hours or shifts. A serious change of contractual job content or demotion can also be fundamental breach. As noted above, in most cases, an act of discrimination by the employer will amount to a fundamental breach of trust and confidence. For example, in one case, an unjustifiable refusal to allow a woman to work part-time on her return from maternity leave together with refusal on grounds that she was a woman amounted to a fundamental breach of trust and confidence.[104]

---

98 *Bracebridge Engineering Ltd v Darby* [1990] IRLR 3, EAT.

99 *Hilton International Hotels (UK) Ltd v Protopapa* [1990] IRLR 316, EAT.

100 *Ogilvie v Neyrfor-Weir Ltd* UKEATS/0054/02.

101 *Amnesty International v Ahmed* [2009] IRLR 884, EAT.

102 *Gogay v Hertfordshire County Council* [2000] IRLR 703, CA; *The Mayor and Burgesses of the London Borough of Lambeth v Agoreyo* [2019] EWCA Civ 322.

103 *Buckland v Bournemouth University Higher Education Corporation* [2010] EWCA Civ 121; [2010] IRLR 445.

104 *Shaw v CCL Ltd* UKEAT/0512/06; [2008] IRLR 284.

6.39   Sometimes a single breach of contract is enough if it is sufficiently serious. Alternatively, the employee can rely on a series of
breaches, where each breach in isolation might not constitute a significant and fundamental breach, but taken together they do. In certain
circumstances, an employee can resign over a relatively insignificant
final straw (see para 6.44 below).

An anticipatory breach

6.40   When an employer breaks a term of a contract with immediate effect,
this constitutes an actual breach. When the employer merely indicates in advance a clear intention to commit a fundamental breach,
this is called an 'anticipatory breach'. An employee who resigns as a
result of an anticipatory breach may claim constructive dismissal.[105]
However, an employee should be careful not to resign prematurely
where the employer has not finally decided to commit the fundamental breach. The employer may still be willing to negotiate. For
example, an invitation to use the grievance procedure in response to
a proposed step will indicate that the employer has made no final
decision. Equally, an employer's statement that, 'I expect you to
co-operate in the manner asked of you', is only a forceful request,
falling short of an actual breach of contract.

When to resign

6.41   Once the employee is sure that the employer has committed an
actual or anticipatory breach, s/he must resign fairly promptly, since
any delay may be taken by the ET as evidence that the employee has
really accepted the employer's conduct. This is known as 'affirming'
the contract or 'waiving' the breach.[106] In theory, delay on its own is
not enough to amount to affirmation, but prolonged delay can
suggest implied affirmation, especially as there may easily be other
indicators. It is not the delay which may be fatal, but what happens
during the period of delay.[107] For example, it may amount to affirmation if the employee does anything to suggest that s/he still wants to
continue the contract, or if s/he asks the employer to take actions
under the contract. However, recognising the realities of the employment situation, an employee can probably perform the contract to a

---

105   *Harrison v Norwest Group Administration Ltd* [1985] IRLR 240, CA.

106   The key case on affirmation is *WE Cox Toner (International) Ltd v Crook* [1981]
   IRLR 443, CA, and there is a useful summary of the principles in *Hadji v St
   Luke's Plymouth* UKEAT/0095/12.

107   *Bashir v Brillo Manufacturing Co Ltd* [1979] IRLR 295, EAT.

limited extent for a temporary period if s/he makes it clear s/he does not accept the breach and wants it remedied.

6.42   How long an employee can afford to delay depends on the facts of each case. A written objection or statement that the employee is 'working under protest' is not enough to keep his/her position open indefinitely. An employee's actions, by staying in the job, and even changing his/her behaviour, speak louder than words. Delay is very risky where the employer's breach has immediate impact on the employee, eg a pay cut, and particularly where the employee has to behave differently to comply with the breach, eg new duties or location. It may be legitimate to object in writing and request a short trial period before resigning.[108] There is less urgency where the breach has no immediate impact, eg a change in retirement age or sick pay entitlement, provided a written protest is made immediately.

6.43   An employee can probably delay long enough to establish the nature of the breach and give the employer an opportunity to change his/her mind, eg by negotiating or taking out a grievance. However, the employee needs to be careful to object in writing from the outset, not to be strung along for too long in pointless negotiations, and if s/he gives an ultimatum, to stick to it.[109] Equally, if the employee has awaited the outcome of a lengthy grievance which is decided against him/her, s/he needs to make up his/her mind very quickly afterwards. It may be possible to avoid affirming while off sick and accepting sick pay, but this depends on the general circumstances, eg the length of the delay, how ill the employee is, whether the sickness was caused by the employer's behaviour, whether the employee is repeating his/her rejection of the breach, whether s/he is carrying out other parts of his/her contract, whether s/he is asking the employer to carry out other parts of the contract etc.[110]

6.44   If an employee has affirmed an earlier breach of trust and confidence, but the employer then carries out another objectionable action, the employee can rely on the totality of the employer's behaviour when deciding to resign. This is known as the 'last straw' doctrine.[111]

---

108 See, eg, *Bevan v CTC Coaches* (1989) 373 IRLIB 10, EAT.

109 *W E Cox Toner (International) Ltd v Crook* [1981] IRLR 443, CA.

110 *El-Hoshi v Pizza Express Restaurants Ltd* UKEAT/0857/03; *Southern v Wadacre Ltd t/a Wadacre Farm Day Nursery* UKEAT/0380/09; *Colomar Mari v Reuters Ltd* UKEAT/0539/13.

111 *Omilaju v Waltham Forest LBC* [2005] EWCA Civ 1493; [2005] ICR 481; *Lewis v Motorworld Garages Ltd* [1985] IRLR 465, CA. Illustrated more recently in *Williams v The Governing Body of Alderman Davies Church in Wales Primary School* UKEAT/0108/19; [2020] IRLR 589.

The final act by the employer may be relatively insignificant, though it cannot be completely trivial and must add something, however slight, to the earlier incidents. It does not have to be unreasonable or even blameworthy by the employer. It is an objective test – a completely innocuous act by the employer cannot be the last straw, even if the employee genuinely interprets it as hurtful.

6.45   It usually works to follow through this checklist:[112]

1) What was the most recent action which triggered the employee's resignation?
2) Has the employee affirmed the contract since that action?
3) If not, was the action sufficient to amount to a repudiatory breach in itself?
4) If not, was it nevertheless part of a series of actions which cumulatively amounted to a repudiatory breach of trust and confidence? If so, it does not matter that there was a previous affirmation.
5) Did the employee resign at least partly in response to that breach?

6.46   When the employee does resign, s/he should make it clear in writing that it is in response to the employer's fundamental breach and not for any other reason. An employee is not prevented from bringing a claim for constructive dismissal because no mention is made at the time of resignation that it is a constructive dismissal, but it may be harder to prove why s/he left.[113]

6.47   The breach of contract need not be the only reason for the employee resigning, but it must be one of the reasons.[114] For example, if the employee resigns partly because s/he believes s/he has been bullied and partly because of a failure to pay her sick pay, s/he can still prove constructive dismissal if a tribunal decides there was no bullying but that the failure to pay sick pay was a fundamental breach of contract.[115] An employee is often reluctant to resign before s/he has found another job and this can cause problems, both because during the delay s/he might affirm the contract, and because it might suggest s/he eventually resigned for a completely different reason. If an employee resigns as a consequence of securing another job, but

---

112 *Kaur v Leeds Teaching Hospitals NHS Trust* [2018] EWCA Civ 978; [2018] IRLR 833.
113 *Weathersfield Ltd v Sargent* [1999] IRLR 94, CA.
114 *Nottinghamshire CC v Meikle* [2004] IRLR 703, CA; *Logan v Celyn House Ltd* UKEAT/0069/12; *Wright v North Ayrshire Council* UKEATS/0017/13; [2014] IRLR 4. All these go further than *Jones v F Sirl & Son (Furnishers) Ltd* [1997] IRLR 493, EAT.
115 *Logan v Celyn House Ltd* UKEAT/0069/12.

the seeking of alternative employment was driven by the fundamental breach, s/he probably can still claim constructive dismissal.[116] Nevertheless it is safest for the employee not to wait too long, as it can then appear that s/he wanted to leave for reasons which are nothing to do with the employer's breach.

6.48 It is up to the employee whether to give notice or not, but it is risky to give longer notice than the statutory minimum or that required under his/her contract, even for financial reasons, since that might be taken as evidence of affirmation.[117]

6.49 Once the employer has committed a fundamental breach of contract, it remains a fundamental breach even if the employer later tries to put it right.[118] The employee can still resign at a later stage as long as s/he has not affirmed by staying in the job after the original breach.

Situations where there is no dismissal

6.50 Where an unforeseen event occurs which makes future performance of the employment contract impossible or radically different, eg terminal sickness or imprisonment, the contract is frustrated and the employee cannot claim s/he has been unfairly dismissed. This is, however, very rare. Employers sometimes try to claim frustration inappropriately, eg in cases of ordinary long-term sickness. Given the change in emphasis towards the treatment of lengthy sickness arising from law prohibiting disability discrimination, frustration in these circumstances should apply less readily. Further, where the employee is disabled, the contract cannot be frustrated if the employer is in breach of a duty to make reasonable adjustments.[119]

6.51 Termination by mutual agreement means the employee cannot claim unfair dismissal or other rights dependent on a dismissal having taken place. It is not always obvious whether a mutual termination has taken place. Voluntary redundancy depends on the facts; it may be a dismissal, although it is likely to be fair.[120] Similarly, early

---

116 *Jones v F Sirl & Son (Furnishers) Ltd* [1997] IRLR 493, EAT.

117 *Cockram v Air Products plc* [2014] IRLR 672, EAT. NB At common law the giving of any notice to terminate the contract would amount to affirmation of it, but this is not the case under ERA 1996 s95(1)(c).

118 *Buckland v Bournemouth University Higher Education Corporation* [2010] EWCA Civ 121; [2010] IRLR 445. Applied recently in a health and safety case: *Flatman v Essex County Council* UKEAT/0097/20.

119 *Warner v Armfield Retail & Leisure Ltd* UKEAT/0376/12.

120 *Burton, Allton and Johnson v Peck* [1975] IRLR 87, QBD; *Birch and Humber v University of Liverpool* [1985] IRLR 165, CA; *Optare Group Ltd v Transport and General Workers Union* UKEAT/0143/07; [2007] IRLR 931.

retirement, unless involuntary, is usually a mutually agreed termination. Employees need to be careful. A dismissal accompanied by a settlement package, however small, may appear later to an ET to indicate a mutually agreed termination. Another situation where there may be no dismissal is where the employer offers reinstatement after an internal appeal. For more detail on this, see para 22.24.

6.52   An employer cannot deprive an employee of the right to claim unfair dismissal by informing him/her in advance that the contract will automatically terminate on the happening of a certain event, eg the worker's late return from holiday. This would effectively circumvent the ET's jurisdiction and is invalid.[121]

What makes a dismissal unfair?

The two stages

6.53   ERA 1996 s98 sets out how an ET should decide whether a dismissal is unfair. There are two basic stages:

1) The employer must show what was the reason, or if more than one, the principal reason, for the dismissal.[122] The reason must be one of the four potentially fair reasons set out in ERA 1996 s98(2) or some other substantial reason of a kind such as to justify dismissal.

2) The ET must then decide in accordance with ERA 1996 s98(4) whether it was fair to dismiss the employee for that reason.

The reason for the dismissal

6.54   The potentially fair reasons are the following:

• a reason relating to the employee's capability or qualification for performing work of the kind s/he was employed to do;[123]
• a reason relating to the conduct of the employee;[124]
• the employee is redundant;[125]

---

121 ERA 1996 s203; and *Igbo v Johnson Matthey Chemicals* [1986] ICR 505; [1986] IRLR 215, CA.
122 ERA 1996 s98(1).
123 ERA 1996 s98(2)(a).
124 ERA 1996 s98(2)(b).
125 ERA 1996 s98(2)(c).

- the employee could not continue to work in the position s/he held without contravention of a duty or restriction imposed by or under an enactment;[126]
- for some other substantial reason of a kind such as to justify the dismissal of an employee holding the position which the employee held.[127]

If the employer cannot show the reason for dismissal, the dismissal will be unfair. If there are several reasons, the employer must establish the principal reason. The dismissal will be unfair if the reason shown is insignificant, trivial or unworthy.[128]

6.55   The reason for dismissal will be the set of facts known to the employer at the time of dismissal or a genuine belief held on reasonable grounds by the employer which led to the dismissal.[129] This usually means that the reason is what is in the mind of the dismissing manager or panel. However, in some circumstances it may include a reason or fact in the mind of an investigating officer or person in the hierarchy of responsibility above the worker, but unknown to the dismissing officer.[130] An employer is not prohibited from giving one reason for dismissal at the time or immediately afterwards and another once ET proceedings have started, although the change may affect the employer's credibility. It is the true reason for the dismissal at the time of the dismissal which is relevant. The ET will be reluctant to accept a change of reason if raised at the hearing for the first time, particularly if it will cause prejudice to the employee and the employee will not have had the fullest opportunity to answer the allegations made.[131]

Was it fair to dismiss for that reason?

ERA 1996 s98(4)

6.56   ERA 1996 s98(4) sets out the statutory test of fairness:

> ... the determination of the question whether the dismissal is fair or unfair (having regard to the reason shown by the employer)–

---

126 ERA 1996 s98(2)(d).
127 ERA 1996 s98(1)(b).
128 *Gilham and Others v Kent CC (No 2)* [1985] ICR 233; [1985] IRLR 18, CA.
129 *Abernethy v Mott, Hay and Anderson* [1974] ICR 323; [1974] IRLR 213, CA.
130 This is a developing area of law and not entirely straight-forward. See *Royal Mail Group Ltd v Jhuti* [2019] UKSC 55; [2019] IRLR 129; *Uddin v London Borough of Ealing* UKEAT/0165/19; [2020] IRLR 332.
131 *Hotson v Wisbech Conservative Club* [1984] ICR 859; [1984] IRLR 422, EAT.

(a) depends on whether in the circumstances (including the size and administrative resources of the employer's undertaking) the employer acted reasonably or unreasonably in treating it as a sufficient reason for dismissing the employee, and

(b) shall be determined in accordance with equity and the substantial merits of the case.

The ET must take into account a number of considerations in deciding the fairness of a dismissal under ERA 1996 s98(4). The relevant factors vary according to the reason for the dismissal.[132] There are also broad considerations which apply to all section 98(4) dismissals. See also chapter 22 regarding fair disciplinary procedures.

Employer's size and administrative resources

6.57   In deciding whether a dismissal is fair, an ET must have in mind the size and administrative resources of the employer. The larger the employer, the greater the obligation to operate proper disciplinary, grievance and consultative procedures. This does not mean small employers can get away with poor employment practices, but they may be able to take a more informal approach.

Equity and the substantial merits of the case

6.58   Equity requires that an employer treats employees consistently; an arbitrary or capricious dismissal will be inequitable. If, on a different occasion, the employer failed to dismiss another employee for a similar offence, the dismissal may well be inequitable and therefore unfair.[133]

Human rights

6.59   If the Human Rights Act 1998 applies because a right under the European Convention on Human Rights (ECHR) is involved in the facts surrounding the dismissal, the ET must consider whether the dismissal was fair having regard to that Convention right.[134] This applies whether the employee was employed in the private or public sector.

The band of reasonable responses

6.60   The real question is not whether the ET would itself have chosen to dismiss the employee in the circumstances, but whether the decision

---

132 See chapter 7.
133 But see para 7.39.
134 See the guidelines in *X v Y* [2004] IRLR 625, CA; and para 3.18 onwards.

to dismiss fell within 'the band of reasonable responses' open to a reasonable employer. The ET must not substitute its own opinion for that of the employer. The ET may think that the dismissal was harsh, but nevertheless within the band of reasonable responses. Within such a band, one employer might reasonably retain the employee whereas another employer might reasonably dismiss him/her. If so, then it is not unfair dismissal, even if the ET would not itself have chosen to dismiss.[135]

6.61　This is a very important concept which results in many claims of unfair dismissal being rejected. It is to be noted that ERA 1996 s98(4) gives no scope or support for this approach. It is a judicial creation, but the case-law is very firmly established on the point and legal challenges have failed.[136] Nevertheless, the Court of Appeal has repeatedly told the Employment Appeal Tribunal (EAT) it must not too readily interfere with ETs' decisions as to whether a dismissal falls inside or outside of the band of reasonable responses.[137] Employers have to be held accountable to some standard and there is a band within which the employer must fall – 'an employer cannot be the final arbiter of its own conduct in dismissing an employee'.[138]

6.62　When deciding whether a dismissal was unfair, it is not for the tribunal to find out the truth about the employee's conduct or capability. Instead, the tribunal has to ascertain what the employer believed, and to decide whether the employer carried out a fair investigation and had reasonable grounds for that belief. This approach was established in a case concerning dishonesty,[139] but it tends to apply to many types of unfair dismissal case. The final question is then whether the sanction was fair. The band of reasonable responses test applies both to the way the investigation was carried out and to the employer's decision regarding the sanction.

---

135 *British Leyland (UK) v Swift* [1981] IRLR 91, CA; *Iceland Frozen Foods v Jones* [1982] IRLR 439, EAT and confirmed in numerous cases including *London Ambulance Service NHS Trust v Small* [2009] EWCA Civ 220; [2009] IRLR 563.

136 *Post Office v Foley; HSBC Bank plc v Madden* [2000] IRLR 827, CA.

137 *Salford Royal NHS Foundation Trust v Roldan* [2010] EWCA Civ 522; [2010] IRLR 721; *Bowater v Northwest London Hospitals NHS Trust* [2011] EWCA Civ 63; [2011] IRLR 331; *Fuller v Brent LBC* [2011] EWCA Civ 267; [2011] IRLR 414; *Graham v Secretary of State for Work and Pensions (Jobcentre Plus)* [2012] EWCA Civ 903; [2012] IRLR 759.

138 *Bowater v Northwest London Hospitals NHS Trust* [2011] EWCA Civ 63; [2011] IRLR 331.

139 *British Home Stores v Burchell* [1980] ICR 303; [1978] IRLR 379; EAT. See para 7.44 for more detail.

6.63   Confusingly, a tribunal may have to make a separate decision in the same case as to the employee's actual conduct for other purposes, eg where a conduct dismissal is unfair, to decide whether the employee in fact contributed to his/her dismissal by his/her conduct,[140] or if there is a notice claim and the employer asserts dismissal was for gross misconduct.[141]

The ACAS Code

6.64   Although it is not against the law in itself to fail to follow any relevant part of the ACAS Code of Practice on Disciplinary and Grievance Procedures, the Code sets standards of sound industrial practice and a tribunal must take it into account.[142] The latest edition of the Code (March 2015) is disappointingly short and basic, setting out minimal standards of good practice. This may be because a tribunal is now able to increase or reduce compensation by up to 25 per cent for any unreasonable failure by the employer or employee respectively to follow the Code's guidance.[143] ACAS has also produced a guidance booklet, *Discipline and grievances at work: the ACAS guide* (July 2020), but this has no formal legal status, and it is hard to know whether a tribunal will find it persuasive.[144] For more detail of the Code and guidance booklet, see chapter 22.

Procedural unfairness

6.65   The key case of *Polkey v AE Dayton Services*[145] established that a dismissal may be unfair purely because the employer failed to follow fair procedures in carrying out the dismissal. This case overturned the previous 'no difference' rule, so that it is now unfair to omit fair procedures even if following them is unlikely to have altered the decision to dismiss. However, compensation will often be reduced if the dismissal was substantively fair, ie for a fair reason.[146] The only exception to *Polkey* is if the employer was reasonable to consider at the time that carrying out such procedures would have been utterly futile. It is very rare that consultation, for example, would be utterly

---

140   *London Ambulance Service NHS Trust v Small* [2009] EWCA Civ 220; [2009] IRLR 563. See paras 18.53–18.55 regarding contributory fault.
141   See para 22.17.
142   TULR(C)A 1992 s207.
143   See para 18.56.
144   Available at: www.acas.org.uk/acas-guide-to-discipline-and-grievances-at-work.
145   [1987] IRLR 503, HL.
146   See para 18.57.

futile. The exception probably envisages circumstances such as making unexpected redundancies following a sudden and unforeseen financial crisis.[147] However, even the appointment of a receiver is something which has usually been foreseen and may not involve closure, so would not usually excuse consultation.

6.66 The House of Lords in *Polkey* gave some guidance on what it considered to be fair procedures. It would not normally be fair to dismiss an employee for incapacity without giving him/her fair warning and an opportunity to improve; in a conduct case, a dismissal would not normally be fair unless the employer fully investigated and listened to what the employee had to say; in a redundancy case, it would not normally be fair unless the employer warned and consulted any affected employees or their representatives, adopted a fair basis for redundancy selection and took reasonable steps to find redeployment.[148] Not all procedural failings will make a dismissal unfair – it is important to consider the fairness of the whole process as a whole.

6.67 Failure to hear an appeal would almost always make a dismissal unfair, as would procedural defects in the appeal, unless these were very minor.[149] On the other hand, a comprehensive appeal process can cure procedural defects in the original dismissal. It is not relevant whether the appeal is by way of rehearing or review, but what is important is whether the disciplinary process as a whole is fair.[150]

Automatically unfair dismissals and detriments short of dismissal

Introduction

6.68 Certain dismissals are not subject to the reasonableness test and are treated as automatically unfair. In most of these cases, there is no minimum service requirement. It is also unlawful to subject an employee to a detriment other than dismissal for most of the automatically unfair reasons. The most common reasons are set out below.

6.69 The list is constantly added to as employees or workers are given new rights which they must be allowed to assert without fear of

---

147 *Spink v Express Foods Group Ltd* [1990] IRLR 320, EAT.
148 *Polkey* [1987] IRLR 503, HL.
149 *West Midlands Co-operative Society v Tipton* [1986] IRLR 112, HL; *Whitbread & Co plc v Mills* [1988] IRLR 501, EAT.
150 *Taylor v OCS Group Ltd* [2006] EWCA Civ 702; [2006] IRLR 613, CA; *Whitbread & Co plc v Mills* [1988] IRLR 501, EAT.

dismissal or detriment. Several of the listed reasons apply to workers generally as well as to employees. This is where the substantive right is given to workers. In such cases, the worker can claim for dismissal as well as action other than dismissal under the general heading of 'detriment'. The law of unfair dismissal does not apply to non-employees, and this is why dismissal of a worker is treated within the word 'detriment'. Detrimental action after the worker has left, eg by providing a poor reference, is probably also unlawful.[151]

Pregnancy and maternity

6.70   It is automatically unfair to dismiss a female employee or select her for redundancy for a reason connected with her pregnancy or maternity.[152] There is no minimum qualifying service.[153] A woman who is dismissed while pregnant but for non-related reasons can claim ordinary unfair dismissal, but only if she has the usual qualifying service. It is also unlawful to subject a female employee to a detriment other than dismissal.[154] The prohibited reasons are those connected with any of the following:[155]

- the employee's pregnancy; or the fact that she has given birth, where the detrimental act takes place during the ordinary or additional maternity leave period, or in the case of dismissal, where it ends the ordinary or additional maternity leave period.[156] Presumably taking time off for antenatal care would be included within this category;
- the fact that she took or sought to take the benefits (eg preserved terms and conditions) of ordinary or additional maternity leave or shared parental leave (SPL), or the employer thought she was going to take SPL.[157] The protection in respect of SPL also applies to 'P' (the person sharing SPL with the mother);[158]

---

151 *Woodward v Abbey National plc* [2006] IRLR 677, CA.
152 ERA 1996 s99 and the Maternity and Parental Leave etc Regulations (MPL Regs) 1999 SI No 3312 reg 20. *Clayton v Vigers* [1990] IRLR 177, EAT and *Atkins v Coyle Personnel plc* [2008] IRLR 420, EAT discuss the meaning of 'connected with'. The EqA 2010 will also apply, see paras 11.1–11.11.
153 ERA 1996 s108(3)(b).
154 ERA 1996 s47C.
155 MPL Regs 1999 regs 19 and 20.
156 MPL Regs 1999 regs 19(2)(a)–(b) and (5) and 20(3)(a)–(b) and (4).
157 MPL Regs 1999 regs 19(2)(d), (e) and 20(3)(d), (e); Shared Parental Leave Regulations (SPL Regs) 2014 SI No 3050 regs 42(1)(a), (b) and 43(3)(a), (b).
158 See para 11.39 onwards regarding SPL.

- the fact that she failed to return after maternity leave when the employer had not notified her of her return date (see para 11.25) or because she considered, undertook or refused to work on the keeping-in-touch (KIT) or shared parental leave in touch (SPLIT) days (see paras 11.66–11.67);[159]
- a requirement or recommendation for a health and safety suspension (see para 11.83);[160]
- if she is made redundant during the ordinary or additional maternity leave period or while taking SPL or adoption leave and not offered any existing suitable alternative vacancy.[161]

6.71　It is not automatic unfair dismissal to dismiss for the above reasons (except those related to SPL)[162] where the employer proves it is not reasonably practicable, for reasons other than redundancy, to allow the woman to return to a suitable and appropriate alternative job, and an associated employer offers such a job, which the woman accepts or unreasonably refuses.[163] The woman may be able to claim unfair dismissal on ordinary principles, but she will need two years' minimum service.

6.72　If a woman is dismissed while pregnant or at the end of her maternity leave, she is entitled to written reasons for her dismissal, whether or not she asks for them, and regardless of her length of service.[164] For more details of pregnancy and maternity rights, see chapter 11.

Other family and domestic entitlements

6.73　It is automatically unfair to dismiss an employee or subject him/her to a detriment other than dismissal for any of the following reasons:

- because s/he took, sought to take or made use of the benefits of adoption leave or paternity leave, or because the employer believed s/he was likely to take adoption leave or paternity leave or because s/he reasonably failed to return on time because the employer did not give the proper notification of the return date or because s/he

159 MPL Regs 1999 regs 19(2)(ee), (eee) and 20(3)(ee), (eee); SPL Regs 2014 regs 42(1)(c) and 43(3)(c), also applicable to 'P' (see para 11.39 onwards).
160 MPL Regs 1999 regs 19(2)(c) and 20(3)(c).
161 MPL Regs 1999 regs 10 and 20(1)(b); SPL Regs 2014 regs 39 and 43(1)(b), also applicable to 'P'; Paternity and Adoption Leave Regulations (PAL Regs) 2002 SI No 2788 regs 23 and 29(1)(b) (see paras 11.61–11.62).
162 The author cannot find any reference to this in the SPL legislation.
163 MPL Regs 1999 reg 20(7) and (8).
164 ERA 1996 s92(4).

worked or refused to work on KIT days;[165] similar exceptions apply as for maternity leave;[166]

• for reasons related to taking time off to accompany his/her partner to antenatal appointments or for pre-adoption appointments;[167]

• because s/he took or sought to take parental leave or time off for care of dependants under ERA 1996 s57A;[168]

• because s/he refused to sign a workforce agreement related to parental leave or because s/he is a workforce representative or candidate;[169]

• for a reason connected to the employee taking parental bereavement leave or its benefits or because the employee was likely to take parental bereavement leave.[170]

There is no minimum service requirement to make these claims.[171] It is not automatic unfair dismissal to dismiss for the above reasons (except in relation to parental bereavement leave)[172] where the employer proves it is not reasonably practicable, for reasons other than redundancy, to allow the employee to return to a suitable and appropriate alternative job, and an associated employer offers such a job, which the employee accepts or unreasonably refuses.[173]

Flexible working

6.74   The right to request flexible working is set out at para 11.121 onwards. It is automatic unfair dismissal to dismiss an employee because s/he has applied for flexible working under the statutory scheme, or brought an ET claim, or alleged the existence of any circumstances which would constitute a ground for bringing such proceedings.[174]

---

165 For exact wording, see Additional Paternity Leave Regulations (APL Regs) 2010 SI No 1055 regs 33 and 34; ERA 1996 s99; PAL Regs 2002 regs 29 and 28.

166 Additional paternity leave (APL) has been replaced by SPL (see paras 11.39–11.47). The SPL protection is in SPL Regs 2014 regs 39 and 43(1)(b).

167 See paras 11.92–11.93 for exact position.

168 ERA 1996 s99; MPL Regs 1999 regs 20(3)(e) and 19(2)(e).

169 ERA 1996 s99; MPL Regs 1999 regs 20(3)(f)–(g) and 19(2)(f)–(g).

170 ERA 1996 s47C and s99(3)(cb); Parental Bereavement Leave Regulations 2020 SI No 249 regs 12 and 13.

171 ERA 1996 s108(3)(b).

172 The author cannot find any reference to this in the relevant legislation.

173 MPL Regs 1999 reg 20(7)–(8); PAL Regs 2002 reg 29(5)–(6); APL Regs 2010 reg 34(5).

174 ERA 1996 s104C.

There is no minimum service requirement.[175] It is unlawful to subject an employee to a detriment other than dismissal for the same reasons.[176]

Part-time working

6.75 Paragraph 11.113 onwards sets out workers' rights under the Part-time Workers (Prevention of Less Favourable Treatment) Regulations (PTW Regs) 2000.[177] It is automatic unfair dismissal to dismiss an employee because s/he has done anything in relation to the PTW Regs 2000, including alleging that the employer has broken the PTW Regs 2000 (unless a false allegation in bad faith), refusing to forgo a right under the PTW Regs 2000, bringing a case or giving evidence for a colleague, or requesting a written statement of reasons why the employer has broken the PTW Regs 2000.[178] It is also automatic unfair dismissal to dismiss an employee because the employer believes or suspects s/he has done or intends to do any of those things. There is no minimum service requirement.[179] A worker who is not an employee also must not be dismissed for those reasons. It is unlawful to subject both employees and workers generally to a detriment other than dismissal for those reasons.[180]

Fixed-term employees

6.76 The rights of fixed-term employees are set out at para 1.41 onwards. It is automatic unfair dismissal to dismiss an employee because s/he has done anything in relation to the Fixed-term Employees (Prevention of Less Favourable Treatment) Regulations (FTE Regs) 2002[181] including alleging that the employer has broken the FTE Regs 2002 (unless a false allegation in bad faith), refusing to forgo a right under the FTE Regs 2002, bringing a case or giving evidence for a colleague, or requesting a written statement of reasons why s/he has been treated contrary to the FTE Regs 2002.[182] It is also automatic unfair dismissal to dismiss an employee because the

---

175 ERA 1996 s108(3)(gi).
176 ERA 1996 s47D; SI No 3207 reg 16.
177 SI No 1551.
178 PTW Regs 2000 reg 7.
179 ERA 1996 s108(3)(i).
180 PTW Regs 2000 reg 7(4).
181 SI No 2034.
182 FTE Regs 2002 reg 6(1) and (3).

employer believes or suspects s/he has done or intends to do any of those things. There is no minimum service requirement.[183] It is also unlawful to subject an employee to a detriment other than dismissal for those reasons.[184]

Agency workers

6.77   It is automatic unfair dismissal to dismiss an agency worker who is an employee because s/he has brought proceedings under the Agency Workers Regulations (AW Regs) 2010,[185] given evidence or information in connection with such proceedings, made a request for a written statement under the AW Regs 2010, alleged that an agency or a hirer has breached the AW Regs 2010, refused or proposed to refuse to forgo a right conferred by the AW Regs 2010 or otherwise done anything under the AW Regs 2010.[186] This does not apply if the allegation made by the agency worker was false and not made in good faith. It is also unlawful to subject an agency worker (whether or not an employee) to a detriment for these reasons. Employees qualify for this protection regardless of their length of service.[187]

Dismissal for asserting a statutory right

6.78   It is automatically unfair to dismiss an employee or select him/her for redundancy for alleging that the employer has infringed a statutory right or for bringing proceedings to enforce such a right.[188] Employees qualify for this protection regardless of their length of service.[189]

6.79   The statutory rights covered include: minimum notice; any right conferred by the ERA 1996 and various rights under the TULR(C)A 1992 which can be enforced in an ET, eg rights to antenatal care, itemised payslips, statements of terms and conditions; the right not to have unauthorised deductions from wages (which can include delays in payment);[190] the right to time off for trade union activities

---

183   ERA 1996 s108(3)(j).
184   FTE Regs 2002 reg 6(2) and (3).
185   SI No 93.
186   AW Regs 2010 reg 17.
187   ERA 1996 s108(3)(q).
188   ERA 1996 ss104 and 105(7).
189   ERA 1996 s108(3)(g).
190   *Elizabeth Claire Care Management Ltd v Francis* [2005] IRLR 858, EAT.

and the right not to suffer action short of dismissal which prevents, deters, penalises or compels union membership; rights conferred by the Working Time Regulations (WTR) 1998[191] and by TUPE Regs 2006.

6.80   As long as the employee's allegation is made in good faith, it does not matter whether s/he is correct in thinking s/he has the right or that it has been infringed. It is also unnecessary for the employee to name the right, as long as s/he has made it reasonably clear to the employer what the right was.[192] However, this protection only applies to allegations that the employer has already infringed the statutory right – not to allegations that the employer is likely in the future to infringe such a right.[193]

6.81   This concept has some similarities to the law prohibiting victimisation for taking up issues under the EqA 2010 and there are likely to be similar difficulties of proving the link between a dismissal and the assertion of a statutory right. It is therefore wise to make any request, eg for payslips or clarification of terms and conditions, in a reasonable manner and in writing.

Health and safety

Overview

6.82   It is unlawful to dismiss employees or subject them to detriments for various kinds of health and safety reasons in ERA 1996, s100. There is no minimum service requirement.[194] There is also enhanced compensation for successful cases.

6.83   Note that whistleblowing protection can also be invoked in some circumstances where a worker is victimised for taking up health and safety issues. Whistleblowing law protects workers (not just employees) who raise concerns about health and safety through the proper channels.[195]

---

191 SI No 1833.
192 *Mennell v Newell & Wright (Transport Contractors) Ltd* [1997] IRLR 519, CA
193 *Spaceman v ISS Mediclean Ltd t/a ISS Facility Service Healthcare* UKEAT/0142/18; [2019] IRLR 512; *Simoes v De Sede UK Limited* UKEAT/0153/20.
194 ERA 1996 s108(3)(c).
195 See para 101 onwards for details. See also chapter 17 on health and safety and stress.

Serious and imminent danger

6.84　It is automatically unfair to dismiss or select for redundancy an employee because, in circumstances of danger which s/he reasonably believes to be serious and imminent:

- s/he refuses to work in the place of work, when s/he cannot reasonably be expected to avert the danger;[196] or
- s/he takes appropriate steps for self-protection or to protect others and does not act negligently in doing so.[197] The reasonableness of the employee's actions will be judged by reference to all the circumstances, including the employee's knowledge and the facilities and advice available to him/her at the time;[198]

It is also unlawful to subject employees to a detriment for these reasons, eg by refusing to pay them. Workers have had the same protection since 31 May 2021.[199]

6.85　There are two initial stages: 1) there must be 'circumstances of danger', and 2) the worker must reasonably believe those circumstances of danger are 'serious and imminent'.[200] It is irrelevant whether the danger was in fact serious and imminent, or whether the employer at the time believed that it was.[201] All that matters is that the worker reasonably believed this.

6.86　'Danger' has a wide meaning, and can include danger of violence from a co-worker, or being put at risk by careless actions of a colleague.[202] The worker can take appropriate steps to 'protect others' as well as him/herself from the danger. This includes members of the public, eg in one case, a chef who was dismissed for refusing to cook food which he considered unfit for human consumption, could bring a claim.[203]

6.87　Historically, there have been few cases on the meaning and scope of the protection. However, successful ET cases have included

---

196　ERA 1996 s100(1)(d).

197　ERA 1996 s100(1)(e) and (3).

198　ERA 1996 s100(2).

199　Employment Rights Act 1996 (Protection from Detriment in Health and Safety Cases) (Amendment) Order 2021 SI No 618. These were issued as a result of *R (on the application of the Independent Workers' Union of Great Britain) v (1) The Secretary of State for Work and Pensions (2) The Secretary of State for Business Energy and Industrial Strategy and The Health and Safety Executive* [2020] EWHC 3050 (Admin).

200　*Edwards & others v The Secretary of State for Justice* UKEAT/0123/14.

201　*Oudahar v Esporta Group Ltd* UKEAT/0566/10; [2011] IRLR 730, EAT.

202　*Harvest Press Ltd v McCaffrey* [1999] IRLR 778, EAT.

203　*Masiak v City Restaurants (UK) Ltd* [1999] IRLR 780, EAT.

dismissals for refusal to drive defective vehicles and a dismissal of a young female employee who refused to take rubbish alone at night to a deserted dump.

6.88   Recently, there has been far greater interest in this legal protection because of issues arising in respect of the Covid-19 pandemic. In theory, workers must not be penalised or dismissed if they refuse to work or take other protective measures because they reasonably believe there are serious and imminent danger of catching Covid-19 or passing it on to others. Whether their belief is reasonable may depend on factors such as the level of the virus in the community at the relevant time, whether they and others have been vaccinated, whether they or others are particularly vulnerable, government guidance at the relevant time, whether there has been a risk assessment, what protective measures the employer has put in place, and whether these are effectively enforced. Scientific and medical evidence may be relevant. It is conceivable that a worker may hold the necessary reasonable belief even if an employer has put all recommended government measures in place.

6.89   It is untested whether the legislation covers danger in travelling into work on public transport. In *Edwards & others v The Secretary of State for Justice*, the EAT accepted it covered a situation where employees were asked to travel on a road which the police or highway authority had closed in snowy conditions.[204] However, this was a slightly different situation in that the refusal was to get on board transport provided by the employer.

Health and safety representatives, and others raising harmful working conditions

6.90   Employees designated with a specific health and safety duty under statute or by agreement with the employer have the right not to be dismissed or subjected to detrimental treatment because they carry out or propose to carry out their health and safety duties.[205] The way in which the designated employee carries out his/her health and safety activities is also protected, unless, possibly, if the representative is acting completely unreasonably, maliciously or irrelevantly to the task in hand.[206] As with trade union dismissals, a health and

---

204 UKEAT/0123/14.
205 ERA 1996 ss100(1)(a)–(b) and 47(1)(a)–(b).
206 *Goodwin v Cabletel UK Ltd* [1997] IRLR 665, EAT; *Sinclair v Trackwork Ltd* UKEAT/0129/20; [2021] IRLR 557.

safety representative who has been dismissed may be entitled to interim relief and enhanced compensation.

6.91   Where there is no health and safety representative at the workplace or it is impracticable for the employee to raise the particular issue through the representative, it is also automatically unfair to dismiss an employee because s/he brings to the employer's attention by reasonable means conditions of work which s/he reasonably believes are harmful or potentially harmful to health and safety.[207] It is also unlawful to subject the employee to any detriment other than dismissal on any of these grounds.[208]

Trade unions and employee representatives

6.92   It is unlawful for an employer to subject a worker to a detriment including dismissal in order to prevent, deter or penalise him/her for joining or not joining a trade union, taking part in its activities, using its services, or refusing to accept an inducement.[209] Where the worker is an employee, it is automatically unfair to dismiss him/her or select him/her for redundancy for any of those reasons.[210] An employee can claim unfair dismissal for these reasons regardless of his/her length of service.[211] Employee representatives are also protected.[212]

The right to be accompanied in disciplinaries and grievances

6.93   The statutory right to be accompanied to disciplinaries and grievances is set out at para 22.39 onwards. It is unlawful to subject a worker to a detriment either because s/he has exercised the right to be accompanied or because s/he has accompanied or sought to accompany another worker.[213] It is also automatic unfair dismissal to dismiss an employee for those reasons. No minimum service requirement applies.[214]

---

207 ERA 1996 s100(1)(c).
208 ERA 1996 s44.
209 TULR(C)A 1992 s146; and see paras 2.1–2.8. See *Serco Ltd v Dahou* [2017] IRLR 81, CA regarding the burden of proof.
210 TULR(C)A 1992 s152.
211 TULR(C)A 1992 s154.
212 ERA 1996 ss47 and 103.
213 Employment Relations Act (ERelA) 1999 s12.
214 ERelA 1999 s12(4).

Not declaring spent convictions

6.94 The Rehabilitation of Offenders Act (ROA) 1974 gives certain workers the right not to disclose previous convictions which are 'spent' as a result of the passage of a specified length of time. The length of time depends on the nature of the conviction, and the rehabilitation period ranges from six months to ten years. It is thought to be automatically unfair to dismiss an employee for failing to disclose a 'spent' conviction.[215] There is still the need to satisfy the qualifying requirements as with ordinary unfair dismissal claims. It is to be noted that exception orders can be made to exclude the protection of the ROA 1974.[216]

Jury service

6.95 It is automatically unfair to dismiss an employee or select him/her for redundancy because of jury service unless the employer told him/her that his/her absence was likely to cause substantial injury to the employer's undertaking and the employee unreasonably refused to apply to be excused from the service.[217] There is no minimum service requirement.[218] It is also unlawful to subject an employee to a detriment other than dismissal for this reason.[219]

Minimum wage, working time and tax credits

6.96 Paragraph 4.71 onwards deals with the WTR 1998[220] and para 4.33 onwards sets out the law on the minimum wage. It is automatic unfair dismissal to dismiss an employee or select him/her for redundancy for any of the following reasons, regardless of length of service.[221] It is also unlawful to dismiss a worker or subject a worker (including an employee) to a detriment other than dismissal:

- because s/he refused or proposed to refuse to comply with a requirement imposed by the employer in contravention of the WTR 1998 or because s/he refused to forgo a right conferred on

---

215 ROA 1974 s4(3)(b).
216 ROA 1974 s4(3)(b); *Wood v Coverage Care Ltd* [1996] IRLR 264, EAT.
217 ERA 1996 s98B.
218 ERA 1996 s108(3)(aa).
219 ERA 1996 s43M.
220 SI No 1833.
221 ERA 1996 s108(3).

him/her by the WTR 1998.[222] There must be an explicit refusal. A refusal cannot be implied from the worker's conduct. For example, it is not enough in itself for a worker who is dismissed for falling asleep while on duty to say s/he was dismissed for taking a rest break under the WTR 1998;[223]

- because s/he brought proceedings against the employer to enforce a right conferred by the WTR 1998 or even just alleged that the employer had infringed such a right.[224] The worker does not need to prove s/he actually has the legal right or that the employer has in fact infringed it, as long as s/he makes the allegation in good faith. The allegation need not specifically mention the WTR 1998 but the worker must be clear what type of right s/he is talking about, eg 'You make me work all day without any breaks' is probably sufficient;[225]

- because s/he failed to sign a workforce agreement or vary any other agreement provided for in the WTR 1998 or for being a workforce representative or candidate for the purposes of the WTR 1998 Sch 1;[226]

- because of qualifying for a minimum wage rate or seeking to enforce the minimum wage, etc;[227]

- because the worker took action to secure the benefit of a tax credit and certain related reasons.[228]

Sunday trading

6.97   Shop workers[229] and betting workers need not work Sundays if they give their employer an opting-out notice. 'Protected' shop and betting workers, ie those employed from the time the Sunday Trading Act 1994 was passed, need not work Sundays unless they provide an opting-in notice.[230] An employee who is an opted-out or protected shop worker or betting worker will be treated as automatically unfairly dismissed if the reason, or where there is more than one

---

222 ERA 1996 ss101A and 45A.
223 *Ajayi and Ogeleyinbo v Aitch Care Homes (London) Ltd* UKEAT/0464/11.
224 ERA 1996 ss45A(1)(e)(f), s104; and see paras 6.78–6.81 above.
225 *Mennell v Newell & Wright (Transport Contractors) Ltd* [1997] IRLR 519, CA.
226 ERA 1996 ss101A and 45A.
227 ERA 1996 s104A; National Minimum Wage Act 1998 s23.
228 ERA 1996 s104B; Tax Credits Act 1999 Sch 3 para 1.
229 Defined by ERA 1996 s232.
230 See ERA 1996 ss36–43 for full details. NB the rules regarding 'protected' shop and betting workers do not apply in Scotland – see ERA 1996 s244(2).

reason the principal reason, for dismissal is the refusal to do shop work or betting work on a Sunday.[231] No minimum service is required.[232] S/he also has the right not to be subjected to a detriment.[233] Apart from these rights, workers unable to work sabbaths for religious reasons may bring a claim for indirect religious discrimination under the EqA 2010.

Trustees of occupational pension schemes

6.98   The dismissal of an employee is treated as automatically unfair if the reason relates to any function discharged as a trustee of an occupational pension scheme.[234] No minimum service qualification is required.[235] The employee also has the right not to be subjected to a detriment other than dismissal.[236]

Dismissal because of the transfer of an undertaking

6.99   It is automatically unfair to dismiss an employee due to the transfer of an undertaking unless the dismissal is for an economic, technical or organisational (ETO) reason entailing changes in the workforce. It is necessary to have at least two years' qualifying service as for ordinary unfair dismissal claims. As mentioned in para 6.79 above, it is also automatically unfair to dismiss an employee for asserting statutory rights conferred by the TUPE Regs 2006. No minimum service is required for such a claim. For more details, see chapter 10 on the TUPE Regs 2006.

Zero hours contracts

6.100 It is automatic unfair dismissal to dismiss an employee on a zero hours contract if the reason or principal reason is that s/he has breached an exclusivity clause or purported exclusivity clause.[237]

---

231 ERA 1996 s101.
232 ERA 1996 s108(3).
233 ERA 1996 s45.
234 ERA 1996 s102.
235 ERA 1996 s108(3).
236 ERA 1996 s46.
237 Exclusivity Terms in Zero Hours Contracts (Redress) Regulations 2015 SI No 2021 reg 2(1).

There is no minimum qualifying service.[238] It is also unlawful to subject an employee to a detriment for that reason or to subject a worker to a detriment including dismissal. A zero hours contract is one where there is no certainty that work will be made available. An exclusivity clause is any provision in the contract which prevents the worker from working for anyone else or under another arrangement, or which requires the employer's consent to do so.[239] See para 1.40 for more detail on zero hours contracts.

Protection for whistleblowers

Overview

6.101   Public inquiries found that in many of the major disasters of the 1990s, workers were aware of the danger but were afraid to speak out. Partially as a response to this, the Public Interest Disclosure Act (PIDA) 1998 introduced a new Part IVA into the ERA 1996 to provide public interest whistleblowers with protection against victimisation. The provisions are complex and should be read closely before taking any action. There is a short checklist in appendix A at A26 which must be read together with this text if a worker is considering blowing the whistle. In recent years, the legislation has rather lost its way, becoming increasingly – and often unsuccessfully – used by individuals seeking to complain about their own work problems, rather than providing solid backing to workers who want to speak out about serious public dangers. In 2013, the Conservative and Liberal Democrat coalition government legislated to try to get things back on track. On the one hand, disclosures would in the future only be protected if they were in the public interest. On the other hand, workers would get protected for making real public interest disclosures even if they were motivated by personal animosity to their employer. There is also a longer standing power for tribunals to pass on information about whistleblowing claims to the relevant regulators where claimants agree.[240] The approved ET1 form asks the claimant at section 10 whether s/he would like this to happen. The charity Protect (formerly Public Concern at Work) provides expert

---

238   Exclusivity Terms in Zero Hours Contracts (Redress) Regulations 2015 SI No 2021 reg 2(5).
239   Exact wording is in ERA 1996 s27A(3)(c).
240   Employment Tribunals (Constitution and Rules of Procedure) (Amendment) Regulations 2010 SI No 131.

advice and has a very practical website.[241] There is a *Whistleblowing: guidance for employers and code of practice* (March 2015), which contains ideas on designing and, more importantly, promoting a whistleblowing policy, and sets out good practice on dealing with disclosures.[242]

6.102 The law covers workers (not just employees), contractors, agency workers, home workers, NHS professionals (even if self-employed) and trainees.[243] There is an extended definition of a 'worker' for individuals supplied by a third party who would not otherwise be employed as a worker. For example, an agency worker who is victimised for whistleblowing by the organisation where s/he is placed could potentially be protected.[244] It is automatic unfair dismissal to dismiss an employee because s/he has made a 'protected disclosure' of information.[245] No minimum service is required.[246] It is also unlawful to dismiss a worker for making a protected disclosure. In addition, a worker (including an employee) has a right not to be subjected to a detriment other than dismissal,[247] eg disciplinary action, lack of promotion or a poor reference after s/he has left.[248] A threat could also amount to a detriment. Workers are also protected against dismissal or detriments because of disclosures made after their employment ended[249] or in their previous employment to their previous employer.[250] In general, whistleblowing law does not protect job applicants. However, an exception is made where NHS

---

241 At: www.protect-advice.org.uk, tel: 020 3117 2520.
242 Access at: www.gov.uk/government/publications/whistleblowing-guidance-and-code-of-practice-for-employers.
243 See ERA 1996 ss43K, 191, 193, 196 and 200 for who is covered and exceptions. Also *Croke v Hydro Aluminium Worcester Ltd* UKEAT/0238/05.
244 The ordinary definition of worker in ERA 1996 s230(3) is extended by s43K. For the meaning of s43K, see *Day v Health Education England and others* [2017] EWCA Civ 329 and *McTigue v University Hospital Bristol NHS Foundation Trust* UKEAT/0354/15; [2016] IRLR 742, which is an example of its application to an agency worker.
245 ERA 1996 s103A.
246 ERA 1996 s108(3)(ff).
247 ERA 1996 s47B.
248 *Woodward v Abbey National plc* [2006] IRLR 677, CA.
249 *Onyango v Adrian Berkeley t/a Berkeley Solicitors* UKEAT/0407/12; [2013] IRLR 338.
250 *BP plc v (1) Elstone (2) Petrotechnics Ltd* UKEAT/0141/09; [2010] IRLR 558.

employers discriminate against job applicants because they have made protected disclosures in the past.[251]

6.103   The disclosure need not necessarily concern wrongdoing by the worker's employer; it can include wrongdoing by a third party, eg fraud or breach of health and safety obligations by a client of the employer.[252]

6.104   Work colleagues can sometimes become upset about the whistleblowing and turn on the whistleblower. It is possible to make a claim in respect of any detrimental actions (including dismissal[253]) carried out by work colleagues in the course of their employment or by authorised agents of the employer. Further, employers will be vicariously liable for such actions, even if they were done without their knowledge or approval, unless they can show they took reasonable steps to prevent such actions happening.[254] This is similar to the vicarious liability rules for discrimination by co-workers under the EqA 2010 although there are some differences.

Content of the disclosure

6.105   The worker must have disclosed information and not simply made an allegation.[255] This distinction can become a problem in a tribunal case, but actually the two categories are closely intertwined and the fact that the worker has made an allegation, does not necessarily mean that s/he has not also disclosed information.[256] The relevant 'information' can be about something that has not been done, eg 'The wards have not been cleaned for two weeks'.[257] But a pure allegation such as 'You are not complying with health and safety requirements' would be too lacking in factual content to amount to information.[258] In some cases, although the disclosure on its own is too vague, sufficient

---

251 ERA 1996 s49B and the Employment Rights Act 1996 (NHS Recruitment – Protected Disclosure) Regulations 2018 SI No 579, into force on 23 May 2018. The regulations set out their own rules on time limits and remedies.

252 *Hibbins v Hesters Way Neighbourhood Project* UKEAT/0275/08; [2009] IRLR 198.

253 *Timis and another v Osipov* [2018] EWCA Civ 2321; [2019] IRLR 52.

254 ERA 1996 ss47B(1A)–(1E) and 48(2). For an analysis of the effect and comparison with EqA 2010 victimisation, see *Timis and another v Osipov*, above.

255 *Cavendish Munro Professional Risks Management Ltd v Geduld* [2010] IRLR 38, EAT.

256 *Kilraine v Wandsworth LBC* [2018] EWCA Civ 1436; [2018] IRLR 846; *Dray Simpson v Cantor Fitzgerald Europe* UKEAT/0016/18.

257 *Millbank Financial Services Ltd v Crawford* [2014] IRLR 18, EAT.

258 *Kilraine v Wandsworth LBC* [2018] EWCA Civ 1436; [2018] IRLR 846,

information is provided by its context, eg a chain of correspondence or where the individual is when s/he makes the disclosure.[259] If the worker wants to rely on the context when bringing a tribunal case, it is important to spell this out in the tribunal claim form.

6.106   The information disclosed must fall within certain categories and it must be disclosed to the correct person in the correct way.[260] A 'qualifying disclosure' means any disclosure of information which, in the reasonable belief of the worker, is made in the public interest and which tends to show one or more of the following:[261]

- that a criminal offence has been, is being or is likely to be committed, eg fraud or assault;
- that a person has failed, is failing or is likely to fail to comply with a legal obligation. This includes a legal obligation contained in the worker's contract of employment and could also include any statutory requirement or common law obligation, eg negligence, nuisance or defamation.[262] In theory, a complaint about an employer's breach of contractual obligations could cover many things, although – as already stated – it must disclose information and not simply amount to an allegation. An even greater difficulty with this category of disclosure might be the requirement that the worker reasonably believe disclosure is made 'in the public interest' (see below). This requirement was introduced in June 2013 as an attempt to stop the proliferation of tribunal claims brought by workers complaining that they had been dismissed or subjected to a detriment because they had complained about the way their employer was mistreating them personally;
- that a miscarriage of justice has occurred, is occurring or is likely to occur;
- that the health and safety of any individual has been, is being or is likely to be endangered, eg risks to hospital patients, train passengers or consumers as well as to work colleagues and the worker him/herself, although in the latter case, bear in mind the 'public interest' requirement;[263]

---

259   *Kilraine v Wandsworth LBC* [2018] EWCA Civ 1436; [2018] IRLR 846.
260   ERA 1996 ss43A and 43B. Several communications taken together can amount to a protected disclosure even if they do not individually: *Norbrook Laboratories (GB) Ltd v Shaw* UKEAT/0150/13; *Dray Simpson v Cantor Fitzgerald Europe* UKEAT/0016/18.
261   ERA 1996 s43A.
262   *Parkins v Sodexho Ltd* [2002] IRLR 109, EAT; *Ibrahim v HCA International Ltd* UKEAT/0105/18; [2019] IRLR 690.
263   See also chapter 17 on health and safety and stress.

- that the environment has been, is being or is likely to be damaged;
- that information tending to show any of the above has been, is being or is likely to be concealed.

6.107   There does need to be sufficiently detailed and specific information to be capable of tending to show any of the above matters.[264] Simply saying that behaviour is 'inappropriate' or 'manipulative' without more facts is unlikely to be enough.

6.108   The worker only needs to believe that the information 'tends' to show the relevant matter – s/he does not have to go as far as believing that the information does actually show such a matter.[265] Moreover, the worker's allegations need not be factually correct, but it must be reasonable for the worker to believe that the factual basis of what is disclosed is true and that it tends to show one of the above-listed matters.[266]

6.109   When making the disclosure, it is not necessary for the worker explicitly to say that s/he believes the information tends to show a particular matter, or even for it to be obvious. However, if the worker does say so, it is easier to prove that is what s/he thought at the time.[267]

6.110   It does not matter that the information is confidential, but the worker must not commit an offence by making the disclosure, eg by breaching the Official Secrets Act 1989.

The public interest

6.111   In *Chestertons v Nurmohamed*, the Court of Appeal gave no precise definition of the meaning of 'public interest', but laid down these guidelines:[268]

- At the time s/he made the disclosure, the worker must have reasonably believed the disclosure was in the public interest. The

---

264   *Kilraine v Wandsworth LBC* [2018] EWCA Civ 1436; [2018] IRLR 846. There is a further illustration in *Williams v Michelle Brown AM* UKEAT/0044/19.

265   *Babula v Waltham Forest College* [2007] IRLR 346, CA; *Twist DX Ltd and others v (1) Armes (2) Armes* UKEAT/0020/30.

266   *Darnton v University of Surrey* [2003] IRLR 133, EAT. See also *Babula v Waltham Forest College* [2007] IRLR 346, CA.

267   *Twist DX Ltd and others v (1) Armes (2) Armes* UKEAT/0020/30 paras 80–87.

268   *Chesterton Global Ltd and another v Nurmohamed* [2017] EWCA Civ 314; [2017] IRLR 837. For further examples and guidance, see *Dray Simpson v Cantor Fitzgerald Europe* UKEAT/0016/18 and *Dobbie v Felton (t/a Feltons Solicitors)* UKEAT/0130/20; [2021] IRLR 679.

tribunal should consider separately (i) did the worker believe this, and (ii) if so, was that belief reasonable?

- The reason why the worker held that belief is not critical. Indeed, the tribunal might later find the worker's belief was reasonable but for different reasons.
- The worker's belief that disclosure was in the public interest need not be his/her predominant motive for making the disclosure. Arguably, it need not form any part of the worker's motivation.
- The relevant question is not whether disclosure actually was in the public interest but whether the worker reasonably believed that it was. There might be more than one reasonable view as to whether the disclosure was in the public interest, and the tribunal must not substitute its own opinion.
- Whether it was reasonable to believe disclosure was in the public interest is something for tribunals to decide on the facts. It is possible for a disclosure to be made in the public interest even if the worker also has his/her own interests in mind. The main idea is to debar disclosures made exclusively in the worker's personal interests. It is not essential for outside interests to be involved – the 'public' can comprise other employees within the organisation employing the worker. Relevant considerations could be, for example, the nature of the interests affected and to what extent; whether the alleged wrongdoing was deliberate or inadvertent; the profile and identity of the person or organisation alleged to have done wrong; and the number of people affected. In the latter case, if those affected were simply other employees with the same personal interests as the worker, it is just about possible that large numbers could convert a private interest into a public one. Although tribunals should be cautious if this last consideration is the only factor, it is likely that where large numbers share similar private interests, other features of the situation will also engage the public interest.

To whom the disclosure is made

6.112   ERA 1996 ss43C–43H set out to whom qualifying disclosures may be made and in what circumstances. It is important to read these carefully, but in general, internal disclosures[269] are more readily protected. For example, a worker who makes disclosure to someone with managerial responsibility only needs a reasonable belief about the malpractice. The same applies to disclosure made to someone

---

269 ERA 1996 ss43C and 43E.

authorised by an employer under a procedure,[270] eg an internal whis-tleblowing procedure, which allows the matter to be raised with a trade union or health and safety representative, an external auditor, a retired director or the employer's lawyers. There is no requirement to have such an internal procedure, but employers may find that it encourages internal disclosure first. During parliamentary debate, the government and the sponsors of the bill consistently expressed the view that trade unions would have a valuable role both in framing such procedures and in being authorised to receive disclosures.

6.113   Disclosures can also be made in certain circumstances to the worker's MP or to a person prescribed by the secretary of state,[271] eg as set out in the Public Interest Disclosure (Prescribed Persons) Order 2014 as periodically amended.[272] It is useful to look at the Department for Business, Energy & Industrial Strategy (BEIS) list on the GOV.UK website for its clear layout and description of the type of matter covered by each prescribed body. The bodies include (as appropriate): the Charity Commissioners; the Care Quality Commission; the NHS Trust Development Authority; the Health and Care Professions Council; Healthcare Improvement Scotland; the Nursing and Midwifery Council; HM Chief Inspector of Education, Children's Services and Skills; Commissioners for HMRC, Revenue Scotland, the Information Commissioner and Scottish Information Commissioner; the General Medical Council; the Food Standards Agency, Food Standards Scotland, the Health and Safety Executive, the Environment Agency and Scottish Environment Protection Agency; the Gas and Electricity Markets Authority (OFGEM); the Water Services Regulation Authority; Audit Scotland; the National Crime Agency; the Independent Office for Police Conduct; the Office of Rail and Road; the Office for Nuclear Regulation; and Welsh Ministers in relation to children's social care.[273]

Disclosure can be made to these bodies even if the matter has not been raised internally first, provided that the worker reasonably believes that the relevant failure falls within a matter for which that

---

270 ERA 1996 s43C(2).

271 ERA 1996 s43F.

272 SI No 2418 for disclosures on or after 1 October 2014 and amended by subsequent Public Interest Disclosure (Prescribed Persons) (Amendment) Orders.

273 Taken from the government guidance list, updated 13 February 2020, at: www.gov.uk/government/publications/blowing-the-whistle-list-of-prescribed-people-and-bodies-2.

body is prescribed and that the information disclosed and any allegation made is substantially true.

Good faith

6.114 In the past, there was a requirement that the disclosure was made 'in
good faith'. Under whistleblowing law, a disclosure was not made in
good faith if the worker had an ulterior motive for whistleblowing, eg
personal antagonism towards his/her manager. The good faith
requirement greatly undermined whistleblowing protection because
a worker with ulterior motives would not be protected from repercussions, even if s/he reasonably believed the disclosed information was
true.[274] The position now is that a worker no longer loses his/her case
if the disclosure was not in good faith, but a tribunal may reduce his/
her compensation by up to 25 per cent if it thinks it just and equitable
to do so. It is for the employer to prove that a disclosure is not in good
faith, and this will require strong evidence.[275] It is common for
workers to be fiercely cross-examined on this aspect and, as people
tend to have mixed motives, it is often problematic.

6.115 Disclosures can be made in the course of obtaining legal advice[276]
and the previous position was that good faith was not required for
this anyway. However, if the lawyer is authorised to pass on the
disclosure, eg by communicating with the employer, then the good
faith rules apply in the usual way. Disclosures to trade union lawyers
would also be covered, but it is less certain whether disclosure to a lay
trade union official for the purpose of getting legal advice is covered.
Trade unions may be best advised to set up specific advice lines to
cover this situation. Disclosure to a trade union official for other
purposes must otherwise fit one of the other categories of protected
disclosure, eg as part of an authorised internal procedure (see above).

Wider disclosures

6.116 Wider disclosures, eg to the media, MPs or police, are protected only
in more limited circumstances, including that they are not made for

---

274 *Street v Derbyshire Unemployed Workers' Centre* [2004] IRLR 687, CA.

275 *Lucas v Chichester Diocesan Housing Association Ltd* EAT 0713/04; *Bachnak v
Emerging Markets Partnership (Europe) Ltd* [2006] UKEAT 0288_05_2701.
Although these cases did not concern compensation, but concerned the
previous law which stated a whistleblowing claim could fail altogether in the
absence of good faith.

276 ERA 1996 s43D.

personal gain.[277] It must be reasonable in all the circumstances to make the disclosure, taking account in particular of the identity of the person to whom disclosure is made, and also the seriousness of the matter, the likelihood of recurrence and the employer's reaction if the matter was previously raised internally.[278] Except where the disclosure relates to a failure of an exceptionally serious nature,[279] the worker must already have made disclosure to his/her employer or reasonably fear a detriment if s/he raises it with his/her employer or a prescribed body, or if there is no prescribed body, s/he must reasonably fear that the evidence will be concealed or destroyed by the employer.[280]

6.117   Any term in an agreement or contract of employment which tries to gag a worker by imposing confidentiality will be void, provided the disclosure is otherwise within the ERA 1996.[281]

6.118   It is for the tribunal to judge whether the worker had made a protected disclosure; it is not a defence for an employer to say s/he felt s/he could safely dismiss the worker because s/he genuinely believed the disclosure was not protected, eg because s/he thought the disclosure was not made in the public interest.[282]

Bringing a case

6.119   When bringing a case, workers should be careful to address each stage of the legal requirements in the tribunal claim and in the evidence.[283] Where the claim is for automatic unfair dismissal due to whistleblowing, there are no complex rules about who has the burden of proof. As with all unfair dismissal claims, the employer must prove the reason for dismissal. If the employee is suggesting that the employer dismissed him/her for whistleblowing, s/he has to produce some positive evidence of that, but s/he does not have to discharge any burden of proof. Having heard the evidence of both sides and making inferences from the primary facts, the tribunal will decide what the reason for dismissal was. If the employer is unable to prove an alternative reason, this may indicate that whistleblowing is the

---

277 ERA 1996 s43G.
278 ERA 1996 ss43H(2) and 43G(3).
279 ERA 1996 s43H.
280 ERA 1996 s43G.
281 ERA 1996 s43J(2).
282 *Beatt v Croydon Health Services NHS Trust* [2017] EWCA Civ 401.
283 *ALM Medical Services Ltd v Bladon* [2002] IRLR 807, CA.

true reason, but not necessarily.[284] However, if the employee does not have sufficient length of service to claim ordinary unfair dismissal, the burden of proof lies on the employee to prove s/he was dismissed for whistleblowing reasons.[285]

6.120   Where the claim is for detriment, the burden of proof is closer to that in discrimination claims, ie once less favourable treatment amounting to a detriment following a protected disclosure has been shown, the employer must prove under ERA 1996 s48(2) on what ground s/he acted and that the protected disclosure was no more than a trivial influence, if any, on the employer's treatment of the whistleblower.[286] This is different from the position on an automatic unfair dismissal claim, where because of different wording in the legislation, it is unlawful only if the protected disclosure was a larger factor, ie it must have been the reason or principal reason for dismissal.

6.121   Remember that the worker needs to show that the employer has subjected him/her to a detriment on the ground that s/he made the initial disclosure. It is not enough to show that if the worker had not made the disclosure, a train of events would not have followed.[287] An employer has not subjected a worker to a detriment simply because the worker becomes distressed when the employer fails to do anything about the allegations, eg out of laziness or inefficiency, as opposed to a deliberate decision to ignore or persecute the worker precisely because s/he made the disclosure.

6.122   What happens if the person who makes the decision to dismiss does not know about the protected disclosure or is not influenced by it, but is influenced by someone else who does know about the disclosure and is hostile towards the worker as a result? An employee can still hold the employer responsible for automatic unfair dismissal in these circumstances if the person manipulating the evidence was the employee's line manager or someone else in the hierarchy of responsibility above the employee.[288] A similar problem arises in discrimination cases.[289] Where this is a possible scenario, it is a good idea also to claim that the input of the manipulative manager is itself a whistleblowing detriment.

---

284 *Kuzel v Roche Products Ltd* [2008] IRLR 530, CA.
285 *Ross v Eddie Stobart Ltd* UKEAT/0068/13.
286 *Fecitt and Public Concern at Work v NHS Manchester* [2012] IRLR 64, CA.
287 *Harrow LBC v Knight* [2003] IRLR 140, EAT.
288 *Royal Mail Group Ltd v Jhuti* [2019] UKSC 55; [2020] IRLR 129, SC.
289 See para 13.24.

6.123   A worker may also be unprotected if the true reason s/he is disciplined is not for making a disclosure, but for taking unauthorised actions to prove the risk s/he is complaining about, eg hacking into a computer to prove data protection may be inadequate.[290]

6.124   Remedies are similar to those for ordinary unfair dismissal except that there is no ceiling on the compensatory award.[291] In detriment cases (though not those involving dismissal of a worker), awards can be made for injury to feelings along the lines of discrimination cases.[292] Interim relief may also be claimed if the ET application is lodged within seven days from the effective date of termination.[293]

Retirement

6.125   It used to be possible to force an employee to retire at the age of 65 or lower objectively justifiable normal retirement age if the employer went through the correct procedures. If the procedures were properly followed, a dismissal could not be challenged as unfair. On the other hand, if an employee was forced to retire but the employer got the procedure wrong, the dismissal would be automatically unfair. These rules no longer apply and are not set out in this edition of the book. See para 14.27 onwards for age discrimination and retirement.

Dismissal during industrial action

6.126   It is automatically unfair to dismiss an employee within the protected period – generally the first 12 weeks of industrial action (with some extensions) because s/he took protected industrial action.[294] This includes later dismissals, where the employee had stopped taking industrial action within the 12 weeks.[295] No minimum service is required.

6.127   After the first 12 weeks, the position is less straightforward. An ET will have no jurisdiction to hear the employee's unfair dismissal claim if all those taking part in the action or affected by the lock-out were also dismissed and none were re-engaged within three

---

290 *Bolton School v Evans* [2007] IRLR 140, CA.
291 ERA 1996 s124(1A).
292 ERA 1996 s49(6); and see para 19.13 onwards.
293 ERA 1996 ss128 and 129.
294 TULR(C)A 1992 s238A(2).
295 TULR(C)A 1992 s239(1).

months.[296] This is designed to protect employees against selective or targeted dismissals. The only exception is if the employee is dismissed for specific reasons related to family, dependant leave, health and safety, working time, employee representatives, whistleblowing or other automatically unfair reasons.[297]

6.128 An employee dismissed while taking part in unofficial industrial action cannot claim unfair dismissal.[298] Broadly speaking, industrial action is unofficial unless some or all of its participants are members of a trade union which has authorised or endorsed the action.[299] There are complicated rules on this. There are the same exceptions as for dismissals on official action.[300]

6.129 The EAT has stated recently that under TULR(C)A 1998 s146, workers must not be subjected to a detriment in order to prevent or deter them from taking part in industrial action or to penalise them for having done so (see para 2.8). It is not entirely clear how this fits with the separate rules set out in the preceding two paragraphs.

Employee shareholders

6.130 Despite massive opposition from the House of Lords, the Conservative and Liberal Democrat coalition government eventually passed legislation creating the status of 'employee shareholders'. The law is contained in ERA 1996 s205A, with effect from 1 September 2013. There is little evidence that it has been taken up.

6.131 In summary, a worker who agrees to become an 'employee shareholder' gives up certain employment rights in return for fully paid-up shares in the employing company which must be worth at least £2,000. The rights which an employee shareholder gives up are: the right to claim unfair dismissal (except for automatic unfair dismissal or a dismissal which would be discriminatory under the EqA 2010); the right to statutory redundancy pay; the right to request time for study or training; and the right to request flexible working (except within 14 days of return from parental leave). It is not possible to give up rights to claim discrimination under the EqA 2010.

---

296 TULR(C)A 1992 s238.
297 TULR(C)A 1992 s238(2A).
298 TULR(C)A 1992 s237(1).
299 TULR(C)A 1992 s237(2).
300 TULR(C)A 1992 s237(1A).

Types of unfair dismissal

continued

Chapter 7: Key points

Capability or qualification dismissals

- Capability dismissals cover sickness, injury and qualification dismissals, as well as dismissals relating to ability to do a job.
- Sickness and injury dismissals fall into two categories: long-term sickness/injury; and intermittent absence from work. The employer has to satisfy different requirements depending on the category.
- With long-term sickness/injury dismissals, the employer should obtain a medical report (to find out the nature and likely duration of the illness/injury) and discuss this report with the employee before dismissing. See also the adjustments suggested under disability discrimination law.
- How long the employer should wait depends on the difficulty of covering the employee's absence, and the prognosis. There should be no rigid rule.
- With a competence dismissal, the test is not whether the employee was actually incompetent, but whether the employer genuinely believed s/he was incompetent, on reasonable grounds, having carried out a proper investigation.
- Only in exceptional cases will a dismissal for a first act of incompetence be fair. The exceptions concern employees who are responsible for the safety of the public, eg as airline pilots or bus drivers. Otherwise, employers should give an opportunity to improve, and offer guidance and support if appropriate.

General guide to useful evidence

- With sickness dismissals, get a copy of all the medical reports. If the employer did not rely on a medical report, get a report from the employee's GP for use at the employment tribunal (ET) hearing.
- If other employees have had more time off and there is any suggestion of inequitable treatment or discrimination, get details of their sickness records. This might be evidenced by the statutory sick pay (SSP) records.
- If the dismissal is due to incompetence, get information on the nature and consequences of the incompetence; check past appraisals.
- Obtain any written sickness and capability procedures.

continued

Conduct dismissals

- It is usually only with acts of gross misconduct that an employer can fairly dismiss for a first offence. Acts of gross misconduct are normally set out in the disciplinary procedure.
- The ET's function is not to determine whether the employee was guilty of the offence. The ET has to determine whether the employer acted reasonably in dismissing the employee. If the employee was not guilty, then it may well be an unfair dismissal, but this is not always the case.
- The test is whether the employer genuinely believed the employee was guilty, on reasonable grounds, having carried out a proper investigation. If so, was dismissal a fair sanction?
- The ET cannot decide what investigation and decision it would have conducted and reached itself. It can only measure what the employer did by the objective standard of any reasonable employer.

General guide to useful evidence

- It is important to get a copy of the disciplinary procedure and check whether the employer followed it.
- Obtain notes of the disciplinary hearing and ask the worker for his/her version. Decide whether it was fairly and properly conducted. Had the decision already been made to dismiss?
- Ascertain the evidence relied on by the employer in deciding to dismiss. Obtain copies of earlier warnings.
- Find out whether any other employees have committed similar acts of misconduct and not been dismissed.

'Some other substantial reason' dismissals

- The most common types of 'some other substantial reason' (SOSR) dismissal are where the dismissal arises out of a reorganisation at the workplace or refusal to agree a variation of contract terms.
- It is necessary for the dismissal to be for a substantial reason. Where the interests of the employer and the employee cannot be reconciled, the tribunal will consider whether a reasonable employer could have dismissed in the circumstances.
- Dismissals due to incompatibility with other employees will be for SOSR.

General guide to useful evidence
- Any evidence to show that it was not prejudicial to the employer to continue to employ the employee will be valuable.
- Find out if any other employees in a similar situation were dismissed.

Capability or qualification dismissals

Introduction

7.1 An employer may claim that a dismissal relates to the capability or qualifications of the employee for performing work of the kind s/he was employed to do.[1] The statutory definition of 'capability' is 'capability assessed by reference to skill, aptitude, health or any other physical or mental quality'.[2] 'Qualification' means 'any degree, diploma or other academic, technical or professional qualification relevant to the position which s/he held'.[3]

Incompetence dismissals

Overview

7.2 An incompetence dismissal is one that is due to the employee's inability to perform the job to the standard expected by the employer. It includes situations where that standard is higher than the norm in the industry.[4]

The reasonableness test: ERA 1996 s98(4)

7.3 It is important to note that the employer need not prove in the employment tribunal (ET) that the employee actually was incompetent. The employer need show only that s/he genuinely and reasonably believed that the employee was incompetent. The test is as follows:

---

1 Employment Rights Act (ERA) 1996 s98(2)(a).
2 ERA 1996 s98(3)(a).
3 ERA 1996 s98(3)(b).
4 *Brown v Hall Advertising* [1978] IRLR 246, EAT.

- Did the employer honestly believe that the employee was incompetent or unsuitable for the job?
- If so, was such belief held on reasonable grounds?
- In forming such a belief, did the employer carry out a proper and adequate investigation? In most cases, this would include giving the employee an opportunity to answer the criticisms.[5]

To show that the employer's belief was reasonable, the ET may accept evidence of the honest views of the employee's managers. Other evidence against the employee may include complaints by customers or other staff, or a drop in sales figures. On the other hand, the employee may be able to prove the employer's belief was unreasonable, eg by showing s/he had above-average sales figures or s/he was understaffed or overworked, or that s/he recently had a good appraisal or a merit pay rise. Remember that since the ET cannot make its own judgment on the level of the employee's competence, the employer only needs enough evidence to show his/her belief was reasonable.

7.4   Other factors are relevant to the fairness of the dismissal. The employer should previously have made the employee aware of his/her dissatisfaction, given reasonable time to improve and warned of the consequences if s/he did not. The amount of time which should be allowed for improvement depends on the facts including the type of job, the level of incompetence, length of service and seniority. An ET usually expects the employer to have taken steps to try to improve the situation, eg by offering support and/or supervision, or re-training, setting targets and monitoring progress. The extent of assistance that should have been offered depends on the employer's size and administrative resources.

7.5   It is rarely fair to dismiss an employee on the basis of one act of incompetence. The exception is where the consequences are so serious that to continue to employ the employee would be too risky and dangerous, eg when a mistake is made by an airline pilot or a coach driver.[6] In this type of situation, dismissal without retraining or being given the chance to improve would usually be fair.

7.6   The ET may also take into account whether the employer had any alternative vacancy which could have been offered to the employee prior to dismissal. An employer will not be expected to create a vacancy or new job for the employee. The failure to offer alternative employment is not an overriding factor in capability dismissals but it

---

5 *McPhie and McDermott v Wimpey Waste Management* [1981] IRLR 316, EAT.
6 *Alidair Ltd v Taylor* [1978] IRLR 82; [1978] ICR 455, CA.

is a relevant consideration, particularly where a large employer had appropriate vacancies which were not offered to the employee.

Aptitude and mental quality dismissals

Overview

7.7 An 'aptitude' dismissal may be because an employee is inflexible at work or is difficult or disruptive or not prepared to adapt.[7] 'Mental quality' would include an employee's lack of drive or having a personality which has a detrimental effect on colleagues' work or on customers.[8] If an employee has not satisfied the necessary standards required by the employer due to carelessness, negligence or idleness, this is more appropriately dealt with as misconduct rather than incapability.[9]

The reasonableness test: ERA 1996 s98(4)

7.8 The employer must show that the employee's inflexibility or other mental quality was detrimental to the business. Prior to dismissal, the employer should have given sufficient and adequate warnings detailing the alleged shortcomings and the employee ought to have been provided with a reasonable opportunity to improve. As usual, the employer's size and administrative resources will be relevant in judging the adequacy of the procedures followed.

Sickness, injury and other health dismissals

Overview

7.9 An employer who dismisses an employee for ill-health or sickness absences may be dismissing on grounds of capability or conduct.[10] It will be a dismissal for conduct if the employer believes that the employee is not ill but is using sickness as an excuse not to work. Since different considerations will be relevant to the fairness of dismissing for conduct, it needs to be established what was the principal reason for dismissal. This section deals with capability dismissals. Note that in some circumstances, an employee may gain protection from the Equality Act (EqA) 2010 in respect of disability discrimination (see chapter 15).

---

7 *Abernethy v Mott, Hay and Anderson* [1974] ICR 323; [1974] IRLR 213, CA.
8 *Bristow v ILEA* (1979) EAT 602/79.
9 *Sutton and Gates Ltd v Boxall* [1978] IRLR 486, EAT.
10 See para 7.52.

The reasonableness test: ERA 1996 s98(4)

7.10   There are two distinct forms of absence from work as a result of ill-health:

1) several intermittent absences, not necessarily for the same reason; and
2) a prolonged continuous absence due to a single medical condition.

The proper steps for an employer to take, prior to dismissing an employee, depend on whether the ill-health was intermittent or continuous. In respect of both situations, it is necessary for the employer to have regard to the whole history of employment and take into account a range of factors such as the nature of the illness, the length of absences, the likelihood of the illness recurring, the need of the employer to have the employee's work done, and the impact on others of the employee's absence.

1) Intermittent absences

7.11   Before dismissing, the employer must have made it clear to the employee what level of attendance was expected. If the employer is dissatisfied with the employee's attendance record, s/he should conduct a fair review of the record and give the employee an opportunity to explain the reason for the various absences.[11] Any warning after the review should make it clear that the employee may be dismissed if there is no improvement. If there is no satisfactory improvement following a warning, dismissal will usually be fair.[12]

7.12   An employer also ought to take into account the following factors:

- the length of absences and periods of good health;
- the likelihood of future absences;
- the nature of the employee's job and the effect of absences;
- the consistent application of the employer's absenteeism policy.[13]

Employees should be gently warned that their absence may lead to dismissal, but genuine illness should not be treated as a disciplinary matter. The employer should handle each case individually in a sympathetic, understanding and compassionate manner.[14]

---

11   *Rolls-Royce v Walpole* [1980] IRLR 343, EAT.
12   *International Sports Co v Thompson* [1980] IRLR 340, EAT.
13   *Lyncock v Cereal Packaging* [1988] IRLR 510, EAT. Inconsistency may also indicate discrimination.
14   *Lynock v Cereal Packaging* [1988] IRLR 510, EAT.

7.13   If there is an underlying medical condition, the employer should usually take medical advice and follow the steps appropriate in cases of long-term sickness (see below).

2) A single period of prolonged absence

7.14   The basic question is whether in all the circumstances the employer could be expected to wait any longer and, if so, how much longer.[15] Each case must be considered on its own facts and an employer cannot hold rigidly to a predetermined period of sickness after which any employee may be dismissed.

7.15   An ET would expect the employer to have found out the true medical position and to have consulted with the employee before making a decision. A medical report on the implications and likely length of illness should generally be obtained from the employee's GP or a company doctor or independent consultant. Where the employer gets a report from a company doctor, the employer should also be willing to consider a report from the employee's own GP or specialist. Whereas the former may be more familiar with working conditions, the latter may be better placed to judge the employee's health.

7.16   The Access to Medical Reports Act (AMRA) 1988 covers workers' access to reports prepared by a medical practitioner who has responsibility for their clinical care.[16] An employer must not apply to a worker's doctor for a report without first getting the worker's written consent, having notified the worker in writing of his/her rights under the Act.[17] Most employers have a standard notification and consent form for this. The worker is entitled to see the report before it is sent to the employer if s/he so requests and to make amendments with the doctor's agreement.[18] The worker must be told of these rights at the time s/he is asked for his/her consent to the obtaining of the report. The employer is supposed to tell the medical practitioner that the worker wants access to the report before it is supplied, but it is advisable for the worker also to remind the doctor of this. If the doctor does not consent to any requested amendments, the worker has the right to attach a personal statement to the report.[19] The doctor must give the worker a copy of the report if requested, except in

---

15 *Spencer v Paragon Wallpapers* [1976] IRLR 373, EAT.
16 AMRA 1988 ss1 and 2.
17 AMRA 1988 s3.
18 AMRA 1988 ss4(1) and 5(2).
19 AMRA 1988 s4.

certain excepted circumstances.[20] A worker may also have rights under the Data Protection Act 2018 or the Access to Health Records Act 1990 to health records held on him/her by the employer or any external doctor working for the employer.

7.17   If an employee refuses to see a company doctor or allow any medical report, s/he increases the risk of being fairly dismissed.

7.18   Once the employer has the report, a meeting should be arranged to discuss its contents with the employee. In general, the employer must take such steps as are sensible in the circumstances to discuss the matter and become informed of the true medical position.[21] Consultation will often throw new light on the problem, bringing up facts and circumstances of which the employer was unaware.[22]

7.19   Unless the medical advice is obviously inaccurate, based on inadequate information or lack of proper examination, the employer is allowed to rely on what the doctor says, as long as the employee gets a chance to comment. If the employee's GP report is more favourable than the employer's own medical report (often from occupational health practitioners), the employer can choose which report to follow if s/he has a good reason for the choice. Obviously, the GP knows the employee better, whereas an occupational health doctor will be more familiar with the work environment. In some cases, the difference could only reasonably be resolved by getting a third opinion from a specialist.

7.20   The employer's decision ought to be based on the following factors:

- the nature and likely duration of the illness;
- the need for the employee to do the job for which s/he was employed and the difficulty of covering his/her absence. The more skilful and specialist the employee, the more vulnerable s/he is to being fairly dismissed after a relatively short absence;
- the possibility of varying the employee's contractual duties. An employer will not be expected to create an alternative position that does not already exist nor to go to great lengths to accommodate the employee.[23] However, a large employer may be expected to offer any available vacancy which would suit the employee. What is reasonable very much depends on the facts;

---

20 AMRA 1988 ss6(2) and 7.
21 *East Lindsey DC v Daubney* [1977] ICR 566; [1977] IRLR 181, EAT.
22 *East Lindsey DC v Daubney* [1977] ICR 566; [1977] IRLR 181, EAT.
23 *Garricks (Caterers) v Nolan* [1980] IRLR 259, EAT.

- whether or not contractual sick pay has run out is just one factor either way;[24]
- the nature and length of the employee's service may suggest the employee is the type of person who is likely to return to work as soon as s/he can, but length of service would not necessarily be relevant in any other way.

7.21   It is important for the employer to have discussions with the employee and for the employee to know when his/her job might be at risk. However, the word 'warning' should be avoided because it is associated with misconduct. The issue relates to the employee's capability, not conduct, and the consequence of a warning may be counterproductive.[25] These days, this can be seen with the common use of staged sickness absence procedures which almost inevitably increase the employee's stress and can set back recovery, especially where the employee has mental ill-health. On the other hand, employers are entitled to be kept informed of the situation and indeed can be criticised if they do not keep in touch. They also need to forewarn an employee if there is a risk of dismissal.

7.22   Sometimes the nature of the illness or injury is such that an employee may never be able to perform his/her contractual duties again or any performance would be radically different from what s/he and the employer envisaged at the outset. If this happens, the contract of employment may be 'frustrated' and just come to an end (see para 6.50). Since the employer will not have actually dismissed the employee, the employee will be unable to claim unfair dismissal or notice.[26] The courts and tribunals are extremely reluctant to say that an employment contract has ended in this way because of the dire consequences for the employee. Further, where the employee is disabled, the contract cannot be frustrated if the employer is in breach of a duty to make reasonable adjustments.[27]

7.23   An employee suffering from long-term ill-health may succeed in a claim for disability discrimination under the EqA 2010, where s/he would have failed in an unfair dismissal claim. The EqA 2010 places greater obligations on the employer, eg to modify the employee's duties or actively find alternative employment.

---

24 *Hardwick v Leeds Area Health Authority* [1975] IRLR 319, EAT; *Coulson v Felixstowe Dock & Railway Co* [1975] IRLR 11, EAT.
25 *Spencer v Paragon Wallpapers* [1976] IRLR 373, EAT.
26 See paras 6.27–6.52 on types of dismissal under the ERA 1996.
27 *Warner v Armfield Retail & Leisure Ltd* UKEAT/0376/12.

7.24   It is not necessarily unfair to dismiss an employee at a time when s/he is still entitled to contractual sick pay. It is just one factor to be taken into consideration. It is unlikely to be fair to dismiss an employee purely because his/her sick pay has run out. Where the employee is still receiving a benefit under a health insurance scheme, the position is unusual. It is likely to be a breach of contract to dismiss him/her while s/he is still receiving that benefit, unless the dismissal is for gross misconduct or for proper and reasonable cause (which cannot be the ill-health itself).[28] It does not automatically mean the employee will win an unfair dismissal claim or a claim for discrimination arising from disability, but it will be a very relevant factor.[29] Some employees have a potential entitlement to an enhanced pension for ill-health retirement. If the employer knows that an employee has incapacity and is likely to be entitled to this, it may well be an unfair dismissal not to take reasonable steps to explore it.[30] On the other hand, it may not be unfair dismissal if it was reasonable for the employer to believe ill-health retirement was not relevant, eg because the employee kept insisting s/he would eventually be fit to return to work.

Ill-health or stress caused by the employer

7.25   If the employee is unable to do the job because of injury or ill-health originally caused by the employer, this does not necessarily mean the dismissal is unfair. The ET can take it into account when considering whether it is reasonable to dismiss in the circumstances, but it is unlikely to be a big factor.[31]

7.26   The employee may have claims against the employer in legal areas outside the employment law field, eg for personal or industrial injuries. For an introduction to employers' duties to do risk assessments and personal injuries claims for stress, see chapter 17. See also para 17.5 regarding the NHS Injury Allowance.

Going on holiday while on sick leave

7.27   Employees may legitimately not be at home during sickness leave. They may be out visiting the doctor or staying with relatives. As long

---

28 *Aspden v Webbs Poultry and Meat Group (Holdings) Ltd* [1996] IRLR 521.
29 *ICTS (UK) Ltd v Visram* UKEAT/0344/15; *Awan v ICTS UK Ltd* [2019] IRLR 212, EAT.
30 *First West Yorkshire v Haigh* [2008] IRLR 182, EAT; *Matinpour v Rotherham MBC* UKEAT/0573/12.
31 See *McAdie v Royal Bank of Scotland plc* [2007] IRLR 895, CA.

as they keep in touch in the way required by their contract or sickness procedure, they need not be available to answer every telephone call. Occasionally employees are dismissed for going on holiday or attending college while off sick. This is not necessarily contradictory, as the employee may be absent due to work-related stress, and a holiday may in fact help.[32] Nevertheless, it is advisable for an employee ask his/her GP whether it is a good idea to go, and then to check with the employer.

Dismissals due to other physical quality

Overview

7.28   An 'other physical quality' would include an injury or loss of faculty which affected the employee's ability to perform the job. Employees may also gain protection from the disability discrimination law under the EqA 2010.[33] Although outside the scope of this book, note that an injury sustained at work may give rise to a personal injury claim against the employer, including compensation for loss of earnings.

The reasonableness test: ERA 1996 s98(4)

7.29   The employer will usually be able to justify dismissal if the injury is such that it is impossible or dangerous for the employee to perform his/her job. Before dismissal, the employer should consult the employee concerning the injury and its consequences for future employment. It may be possible for the employee to retrain or use aids to overcome the loss of faculty. An employer should offer any suitable alternative vacancy.

Qualification dismissals

Overview

7.30   A qualification dismissal is one where an employee loses a qualification or fails to obtain a qualification which was a condition of his/her employment. A common example is disqualification from driving when having a licence is a necessary requirement of the job. This requirement need not be expressly stated in the contract where the job clearly entails driving duties.[34] An employer may also require a

---

32 For example, *McMaster v Manchester Airport plc* (1997) EAT 149/97.
33 See chapter 15.
34 *Tayside RC v McIntosh* [1982] IRLR 272, EAT.

qualification during the employee's employment which the employee does not possess and is unable or unlikely to acquire.

The reasonableness test: ERA 1996 s98(4)

7.31 Where an employee loses a qualification which s/he is required to have under his/her contract or which is necessary for the job, it may be fair to dismiss. The employer would not usually be expected to create an alternative job, but s/he should make an effort appropriate to the size and administrative resources of the enterprise and the availability of vacancies.

7.32 An employer may require new qualifications because of the introduction of new technology or a different mode of operation. It may be fair to dismiss an employee who fails to acquire the new qualification if the employer can justify the need for it. The employer must also act reasonably in the introduction of the requirement, eg by offering retraining. Failure to give an employee a fair and proper opportunity to satisfy the new requirement will make the dismissal unfair.[35] An employer's insistence on certain qualifications may be indirect race, sex or age discrimination contrary to the EqA 2010.[36]

Conduct dismissals

Introduction

7.33 Unlike with capability and qualification dismissals, there is no statutory definition of conduct dismissals. Nevertheless, there are a number of activities which are recognised as potential misconduct and are usually listed in the disciplinary procedure if there is a written contract of employment – for example:

- theft or other dishonesty;
- violence and fighting;
- unauthorised absenteeism[37] or lateness;
- disobedience;
- being under the influence of alcohol or drugs;[38]
- threatening or abusive language;
- misuse of telephone, email or internet;

35 *Evans v Bury Football Club* (1981) EAT 185/81.
36 See para 13.27 onwards.
37 Though this may be a capability issue; see para 7.9 on health.
38 This may also be a capability issue.

- behaviour undermining the implied term of fidelity and good faith.

Some acts of misconduct amount to 'gross misconduct'. The main relevance of this concept is that an employer dismissing for gross misconduct need not give notice under the contract.[39] Unfair dismissal is a separate issue. It may be fair or unfair to dismiss an employee for gross misconduct. However, as gross misconduct involves more serious forms of misconduct, it is more likely to be fair to dismiss for a single act, with no previous warnings.

7.34   Conduct outside working hours might lead to a fair dismissal in some circumstances, where it has relevance for the work situation. Whether a dismissal is fair will depend on a number of factors, such as adverse publicity, implications for the workplace, relevance to the job and whether the conduct outside work could be said to breach the implied term of trust and confidence. A risk of reputational damage from criminal charges, even if not yet proved in court, can be sufficient justification for dismissal, though this should not be assumed, and the type of charge will be relevant.[40] Where relevant, an ET should bear in mind the employee's right to respect for his/her private life under the European Convention on Human Rights (ECHR), but this can be outweighed by the impact on the employer.[41]

Issues of fairness common to many conduct dismissals

7.35   For general principles of fairness in any unfair dismissal case, see paras 6.53–6.68 and chapter 22 regarding disciplinary procedures. An employer should take account of the explanation given by the employee; actions taken in previous similar cases; the employee's disciplinary and general record; and whether the intended disciplinary action is reasonable under the circumstances. The employee's length and nature of service is relevant if it suggests the misconduct was out of character and unlikely to recur. There has been an increasing tendency in recent years for employers to say they are dismissing an employee for 'breach of trust and confidence', when the real reason amounts to misconduct or maybe capability. Employers should not be allowed to avoid the usual stages associated with a

---

39 See wrongful dismissal, summary dismissal and gross misconduct, paras 1.29–1.30.
40 *Leach v The Office of Communications (OFCOM)* [2012] EWCA Civ 959; [2012] IRLR 839; *Lafferty v Nuffield Health* UKEATS/0006/19.
41 For an interesting example, see *Pay v United Kingdom* [2009] IRLR 139, ECtHR. See also para 3.25.

conduct dismissal, simply by giving it a vague generic label of this kind.[42] In misconduct cases, the tribunal should first consider the three stages in the famous *British Home Stores v Burchell* case,[43] and then consider whether it was fair to dismiss for that misconduct. The stages are:

1) whether the employer genuinely believed the employee committed the misconduct in question;
2) whether the employer held that belief on reasonable grounds; and
3) whether the employer carried out a proper and reasonable investigation.

The band of reasonable responses test described at para 6.60 above applies to the evidence relied on and the investigation carried out as well as the decision to dismiss.[44] In other words, it is not for the tribunal to decide how it would itself have carried out the investigation or what evidence it would have found satisfactory. The tribunal must simply decide whether a reasonable employer could have investigated that way and found that evidence sufficient. The following issues frequently arise in conduct dismissals, although some of the principles may be transferable to other types of dismissal:

- fair investigation;
- inconsistency in the treatment of different employees;
- taking account of previous warnings;
- the importance of the disciplinary rules;
- cross-examination of witnesses at the disciplinary hearing.

Fair investigation

7.36   It is very important that the employer follows a fair procedure and investigates properly. The degree of appropriate investigation depends on a number of factors including the complexity of the case,[45] the nature of the offence, the size and administrative resources of the employer[46] and whether the employee confessed to the misconduct or was caught red-handed. Employers are not expected to carry out investigations to the standard required in criminal cases. However, where the consequences for an employee are particularly

---

42   See comments of the Court of Appeal in *Leach v The Office of Communications (OFCOM)* [2012] EWCA Civ 959; [2012] IRLR 839.

43   [1978] IRLR 379, EAT.

44   *Sainsbury's Supermarkets Ltd v Hitt* [2002] EWCA Civ 1588; [2003] IRLR 23.

45   *British Home Stores v Burchell* [1980] ICR 303; [1978] IRLR 379, EAT.

46   ERA 1996 s98(4).

serious, eg where the employee's reputation or ability to work in his/her chosen field is at risk, employers should be particularly careful that they carry out a conscientious investigation.[47] Having said that, ECHR Article 8 (right to respect for one's private and family life) does not add any higher standard of procedural fairness than the usual unfair dismissal test in such cases.[48]

7.37 The employer's disciplinary procedure should be followed in conducting the investigation, or in the absence of a procedure, whatever steps the ET deems fair in order to ensure justice.[49] A failure to follow a contractual disciplinary procedure will often, but not necessarily, result in a finding of unfair dismissal.[50] It's the overall fairness of the procedure followed which counts. Regard will be had to the Advisory, Conciliation and Arbitration Service (ACAS) Code of Practice on Disciplinary and Grievance Procedure, especially if there is no contractual procedure.[51] Any contractual procedure should state what acts of misconduct are considered by the employer to be gross misconduct, the various stages of the procedure itself, the right to be represented and the right of appeal against any decision reached.

7.38 An investigatory officer may go on to hold the disciplinary hearing as long as s/he has not become so involved that s/he cannot be impartial.[52] A person who has been a witness, should not normally hold the disciplinary inquiry, but there are certain exceptions.[53] Furthermore, it is a requirement of the rules of natural justice that an employee knows the allegations made against him/her, that s/he has an opportunity to answer those allegations fully and that the conduct of the investigation and internal hearings is in good faith.[54] The allegations must be clearly put to the employee. It would be unfair, for example, to tell the employee that s/he is facing an allegation of breach of procedures, but to dismiss him/her for dishonesty. An employee

---

47 *A v B* [2003] IRLR 405, EAT; *Salford Royal NHS Foundation Trust v Roldan* [2010] EWCA Civ 522; [2010] IRLR 721; *Crawford and another v Suffolk Mental Health Partnership NHS Trust* [2012] EWCA Civ 138; [2012] IRLR 402.

48 *Turner v East Midlands Trains Ltd* [2012] EWCA Civ 1470; [2013] IRLR 107.

49 See chapter 22 regarding fair procedures.

50 *Stoker v Lancashire CC* [1992] IRLR 75, CA; *Westminster CC v Cabaj* [1996] IRLR 399, CA.

51 At: www.acas.org.uk/acas-code-of-practice-on-disciplinary-and-grievance-procedures.

52 *Slater v Leicestershire Health Authority* [1989] IRLR 16, CA.

53 *Slater v Leicestershire Health Authority* [1989] IRLR 16, CA.

54 *Khanum v Mid-Glamorgan Area Health Authority* [1978] IRLR 215; [1979] ICR 40, EAT.

should only be found guilty of an offence of which s/he is charged.[55] If an investigating officer finds evidence or takes a statement which is helpful for the employee, that evidence should be shown to the employee even if the investigator does not want to rely on it and does not intend to show it to the disciplinary panel.[56] It is also likely to be unfair if the investigating officer withholds relevant facts from the dismissing officer/panel.[57] Delay in the investigation can in itself make a dismissal unfair if it is substantial and there is no good reason for it. It is not essential for the employee to show that s/he has been prejudiced by the delay, though it will be an extra ground of unfairness if s/he has, eg if the result is inability to speak to certain witnesses or faded memories.[58]

Inconsistency

7.39   The ACAS Code says employers should act consistently. This can come up in two ways – either because two employees commit the same offence at the same time, but only one is dismissed; or because other employees have been treated more leniently for the same offence in the past.[59] Both situations are potentially unfair, but in practice, inconsistency rarely makes a dismissal unfair in a particular case. This is partly because any argument about inconsistency only works if the comparable situations really are similar. In reality, few cases are identical.[60] Also, where an employer consciously thinks about the two cases and makes a distinction between them, the dismissal will only be unfair if there was no rational (ie reasonable)[61] basis for the distinction.[62] Employers are allowed considerable flexibility and can choose to become stricter than in the past, provided no one has been misled. Inconsistency is most likely to make a dismissal unfair where leniency in the past has led an employee to believe that a particular offence will be overlooked, or at least that it will not lead to dismissal.[63] If an employer wants to clamp down on certain

---

55   *Strouthos v London Underground Ltd* [2004] IRLR 636, CA.
56   *Old v Palace Fields Primary Academy* UKEAT/0085/14.
57   As an example, see *Uddin v Ealing LBC* UKEAT/0165/19; [2020] IRLR 332.
58   *A v B* [2003] IRLR 405, EAT; *Secretary of State for Justice v Mansfield* UKEAT/0539/09.
59   *Post Office v Fennell* [1981] IRLR 221, CA.
60   *Hadjioannou v Coral Casinos Ltd* [1981] IRLR 352, EAT.
61   *Network Rail Infrastructure v Mockler* UKEAT/0531/11.
62   *Securicor Ltd v Smith* [1989] IRLR 356, CA; *Harrow LBC v Cunningham* [1996] IRLR 256, EAT.
63   *Hadjioannou v Coral Casinos Ltd* [1981] IRLR 352, EAT.

offences, this should be made clear in advance to employees. In some circumstances, inconsistency may also be an indication that there is some other reason for the dismissal entirely.[64] It could even be an indication of discrimination because of a protected characteristic under the EqA 2010. From an unfair dismissal viewpoint, it is not a good reason for treating similar cases differently that different managers dealt with the two incidents.[65] An employee cannot complain of inconsistency in failing to discipline a colleague, if the employer was unaware of the other person's misconduct. Lack of consistency is often argued in front of tribunals, but rarely succeeds. It is more important for the tribunal to consider the individual facts of the particular case and to decide on the usual ERA 1996 s98(4) test whether the dismissal fell within the band of reasonable responses.[66]

Disciplinary rules

7.40 Many written disciplinary procedures contain a set of rules specifying disciplinary offences as well as those which are regarded as gross misconduct. The ACAS Code[67] says that:

- rules and procedures should be clear, specific and in writing;
- employees and where appropriate, their representatives, should be involved in the development of rules and procedures; and
- it is important to help employees and managers understand what the rules and procedures are, where they can be found and how they are to be used.

Unless an offence is very obviously gross misconduct, it will be relevant (though not conclusive) to consider whether it is mentioned in the rules. A written rule effectively operates as a warning. On the other hand, it will be unfair for an employer automatically to dismiss for any offence listed as dismissable within the rules, without considering the circumstances of the individual case.

Taking account of previous warnings

7.41 The ACAS Code recommends that an employee is told how long a warning will remain current. Previous live warnings can be taken into account in a decision to dismiss, even if they concern different offences, although this may affect how much significance should be

---

64 *Hadjioannou v Coral Casinos Ltd* [1981] IRLR 352, EAT.
65 But this may defeat a discrimination claim.
66 *Levenes Solicitors v Dalley* UKEAT/0330/06.
67 ACAS Code, para 2.

attributed to them.[68] It is a question of overall fairness, taking account of the number of previous warnings, the time periods between them, and the nature of the offence each time.[69] When an employer relies on an existing final written warning in deciding that further misconduct warrants dismissal, s/he does not need to reinvestigate whether that warning was fairly given, provided it was given in good faith and there were prima facie grounds for it – that is, it was not issued for an oblique motive and was not manifestly inappropriately issued.[70] Nor should an ET reopen the matter except in the same circumstances.[71] If a warning is subject to an appeal at the time of the later offence, an employer can rely on its existence provided it is also taken into account that an appeal is pending.[72] If the appeal on the previous warning is due to be heard very soon, arguably the employer should wait and deal with the appeal before moving onto the subsequent offence. However, if the previous warning was obviously inappropriate, then it cannot be relied on by the employer even if the employee chose not to appeal against it.[73]

7.42   It is recognised good practice that warnings are disregarded for disciplinary purposes after a specified period, eg six months for a first written warning and 12 months for a final written warning. Many disciplinary procedures also recommend that warnings are disregarded or removed from the file after a period. If the employer has chosen to state that the warning will lapse after a specified period, it is usually unfair subsequently to rely overtly on the lapsed warning in deciding to dismiss, especially where the final offence would not otherwise justify dismissal on its own.[74] However, there are circumstances where the existence of previous warnings can help to make the employer's decision to dismiss reasonable, eg if an employee has a history of re-offending shortly after many previous expired

---

68 *Wincanton Group plc v Stone and Gregory* UKEAT/0011/12; [2013] IRLR 178.

69 *Auguste Noel Ltd v Curtis* [1990] IRLR 326, EAT.

70 *Stein v Associated Dairies Ltd* [1982] IRLR 447, EAT; *Tower Hamlets Health Authority v Anthony* [1989] IRLR 394, CA; *Davies v Sandwell MBC* [2013] EWCA Civ 135; [2013] IRLR 374. The same applies in a capability dismissal – *General Dynamics Information Technology Ltd v Carranza* [2015] IRLR 43, EAT.

71 *Wincanton Group plc v Stone and Gregory* UKEAT/0011/12; [2013] IRLR 178, EAT has a good summary of the legal principles. See also cases in n69 above and *Way v Spectrum Property Care Ltd* [2015] EWCA Civ 381; [2015] IRLR 657.

72 *Tower Hamlets Health Authority v Anthony* [1989] IRLR 394, CA; *Rooney v Dundee City Council* UKEATS/0020/13.

73 *Davies v Sandwell MBC* at EAT stage UKEAT/0416/10.

74 *Diosynth Ltd v Morris Thompson* [2006] IRLR 284, CS. But this is weakened by *Airbus UK Ltd v Webb*, see n75.

warnings.[75] Another example is where the final offence is in itself worthy of dismissal, but the employer would be more lenient to an employee who had never previously been disciplined. *Airbus UK Ltd v Webb*[76] provides a good example. In that case, the company decided it would be reasonable to dismiss five employees for watching TV while on night duty, but if there was a good reason not to dismiss anyone, s/he would be given a lesser penalty. Four employees with good disciplinary records were therefore given warnings, but Mr Webb was dismissed because he had previously been disciplined for doing other things when he should have been working. In fact, he had a final written warning which had expired only three weeks before this further offence. The Court of Appeal said the fact that the employer took account of an expired warning in this way did not mean the dismissal had to be unfair. It depends on what is fair overall. Obviously the fact that a warning has expired is a relevant factor.

Cross-examination at the disciplinary hearing

7.43   Some disciplinary procedures give employees the right to cross-examine witnesses against them at disciplinary hearings. Otherwise, it all depends on the facts whether an employer can act reasonably without allowing the employee to cross-examine witnesses against him/her.[77] It is always important that employees should know the evidence against them but it may be enough if they have been shown witness statements. If the employer is relying on information from an informant who wishes to remain anonymous, it is important that:

- a full statement is taken and shown to the employee;
- the hearing officer interviews the informant and takes careful notes;
- the employer considers whether the informant has any reason to fabricate information against the employee.[78]

---

75 *Stratford v Auto Trail VR Ltd* UKEAT/0116/16.

76 [2008] EWCA Civ 49; [2008] IRLR 309.

77 *Santamera v Express Cargo Forwarding t/a IEC Ltd* [2003] IRLR 273, EAT, clarifying *Ulsterbus Ltd v Henderson* [1989] IRLR 251, NICA.

78 See *Linfood Cash & Carry Ltd v Thomson and another* [1989] IRLR 235, EAT for full guidelines.

Theft and other dishonesty

Overview

7.44 An employee may be dismissed for an act of dishonesty, whether at work or outside work,[79] and whether against the employer, a fellow employee or the public. Dishonesty dismissals often relate to offences peculiar to the working environment such as borrowing money without authorisation, fraudulent expense claims,[80] unauthorised use of the employer's property and clocking offences.[81]

The reasonableness test: ERA 1996 s98(4)

7.45 It is imperative to understand the difference between the criminal law and unfair dismissal law. Many employees feel that the ET is the arena for them to clear their name. Unfortunately the real issue is not whether the employee actually committed the offence but whether, in the circumstances, it was reasonable for the employer to dismiss. An ET may well find that an employee was fairly dismissed for suspected theft, even though by the time of the ET hearing s/he has been acquitted by a criminal court. The employer need not await the outcome of any criminal trial. What counts is whether the employer, at the time of dismissal and having carried out reasonable investigations, genuinely and reasonably believed that the employee committed the theft.[82] Equally, it does not automatically justify a dismissal that an employee has been charged with a criminal offence.

7.46 In order to dismiss fairly for dishonesty, the employer must:

- genuinely believe that the employee was dishonest;
- hold that belief on reasonable grounds; and
- have carried out proper and adequate investigations.[83]

The final question is whether dismissal is a fair sanction and in proportion to the offence. The ET cannot substitute itself for the employer and decide whether it would itself have dismissed or carried out a fuller investigation.[84] It is irrelevant whether the evidence

---

79 *Singh v London Country Bus Services* [1976] IRLR 176, EAT.

80 *John Lewis and Co v Smith* (1981) EAT 289/81.

81 *Engineering Services v Harrison* (1977) EAT 735/77.

82 *British Home Stores v Burchell* [1978] IRLR 379; [1980] ICR 303, EAT.

83 *British Home Stores v Burchell* [1978] IRLR 379; [1980] ICR 303, EAT; *Weddel and Co v Tepper* [1980] ICR 286; [1980] IRLR 96, CA.

84 *Iceland Frozen Foods Ltd v Jones* [1982] IRLR 439, EAT; *Post Office v Foley; HSBC Bank plc v Madden* [2000] IRLR 827, CA; *Sainsbury's Supermarkets Ltd v Hitt* [2003] IRLR 23, CA.

against the employee is insufficient to satisfy an ET of his/her guilt, if by the objective standards of a reasonable employer, the investigation and conclusion was reasonable.[85] What counts is the evidence in front of the investigating and dismissing officers. It does not help to put evidence of the employee's innocence to the ET if the employee chose not to produce that evidence to his/her employer at the time (unless that was due to the employer's failure properly to investigate). For the same reason, it is irrelevant that untruthful evidence from the employee's manager influenced the dismissing officer, if it was reasonable for the dismissing officer to have believed the manager rather than the employee.[86]

7.47   If the employer is unable to ascertain which of a group of employees was guilty of the dishonesty, the employer may fairly dismiss all of them solely on reasonable suspicion, provided that:

- after proper investigation, the employer tries and is unable to identify which employee is guilty;
- the employer genuinely believes, on reasonable grounds, that one or more of the group is guilty; and
- any member of the group was capable of having carried out the dishonest act.[87]

It will be inequitable and unfair to dismiss only some members of the group to which the employer has narrowed things down. However, the more 'suspects' the employer dismisses, the stronger business reasons s/he will need for taking such drastic action.

7.48   It is a matter of fundamental fairness that if the employer dismisses the employee for dishonesty, the charge of dishonesty is put to the employee as opposed to a simple charge of breach of procedures, for example.[88] As to whether dismissal for dishonesty is a fair sanction, the ET cannot substitute its own view. As always, the test is that of a reasonable employer. Relevant factors which an employer should take into account are the employee's length of service and past conduct.[89] An employer may also consider the conduct of an employee after an offence is discovered. For example,

---

85 *Post Office v Foley; HSBC Bank plc v Madden* [2000] IRLR 827, CA.
86 See *Orr v Milton Keynes Council* [2011] EWCA Civ 62; [2011] IRLR 317.
87 *Monie v Coral Racing* [1980] IRLR 464; [1981] ICR 109, CA; *Whitbread and Co v Thomas* [1988] IRLR 43; [1988] ICR 135, EAT.
88 *Strouthos v London Underground* [2004] IRLR 636, CA; *Celebi v Scolarest Compass Group UK & Ireland Ltd* UKEAT/0032/10.
89 *Trusthouse Forte (Catering) Ltd v Adonis* [1984] IRLR 382, EAT; *Strouthos v London Underground Ltd* [2004] IRLR 636, CA.

if the employee persistently lies, that would influence the decision to dismiss.[90]

7.49   Since dishonesty is gross misconduct, dismissal for a single act is usually justified and warnings are not normally appropriate. It is important to emphasise long service and, if relevant, the minor extent of the dishonesty, on the employee's behalf.

Violence or fighting dismissals

7.50   Violence or fighting usually constitutes gross misconduct even if the employer's disciplinary procedure does not explicitly describe it as such.[91] Nevertheless, this does not mean that a dismissal for violence is always fair. An employer must carry out an investigation and take into account all relevant matters,[92] eg the nature and circumstances of the violence, whether it was in public view, the proximity to machinery or dangerous objects,[93] the status of the employees, the length of service[94] and the nature of any provocation. If the fight is between employees with different racial backgrounds, it is also worth checking whether there was any racial harassment provoking the fight.[95]

7.51   The employer should speak to the parties involved and any witnesses. If the employer cannot ascertain who was responsible for the violence, the employer may dismiss all concerned if it was serious.[96] It will not usually help an employee who participated in fighting to say that another employee initiated it.

Dismissals for unauthorised absences or lateness

Overview

7.52   Dismissals for absenteeism may relate to capability and ill-health.[97] Conduct absenteeism is where an employee is absent without authority, and it is usually a form of bad timekeeping. There may also be issues regarding not properly notifying absence under the employer's

90 *British Leyland (UK) Ltd v Swift* [1981] IRLR 91, CA.
91 *CA Parsons and Co v McLoughlin* [1978] IRLR 65, EAT.
92 *Taylor v Parsons Peebles* [1981] IRLR 119, EAT.
93 *Greenwood v HJ Heinz and Co* (1977) EAT 199/77.
94 *Ealing LBC v Goodwin* (1979) EAT 121/79.
95 See chapters 12–14 regarding race discrimination.
96 *Monie v Coral Racing* [1980] IRLR 464, CA.
97 See para 7.9.

sickness procedure (see also para 7.27). A common form of unauthorised absenteeism is where an employee returns late from a holiday.

General absenteeism or lateness

7.53 An employer is rarely entitled to dismiss for a single occasion of lateness or absenteeism. The usual situation is when an employee is frequently late or absent from work. Some large employers set out in the contract of employment an 'expected level of attendance' below which an employee will be dismissed. However, it is not necessarily fair to dismiss an employee who falls below this level. The employer should fairly review the employee's attendance record and the reasons for the absences. Appropriate warnings should be given after the employee has had the opportunity to explain. If there is no improvement, the employee's subsequent dismissal is likely to be fair.[98]

7.54 As well as fairness in procedures, the ET will take into account:

- the employee's age, length of service and performance;
- the likelihood of an improvement in attendance;
- the effect of absences on the business;
- the known circumstances of each absence, eg a temporary domestic problem.[99]

If lateness or absences are caused by a health condition, eg depression or tiredness in the morning, this may be a matter requiring reasonable adjustments under disability discrimination law.[100]

Late return from holiday

7.55 Where an employer has warned the employee in advance that failure to return from holiday on the due date will be treated as gross misconduct, it will be easier to justify a dismissal. Unless the employee can put forward compelling reasons why s/he should not be dismissed, dismissal will be fair.[101] It may well be discriminatory if the employer disregards medical certificates just because they are from abroad. Usually the employer should wait until the employee comes back to work or invite an explanation by post.

7.56 Sometimes an employer informs the employee that if s/he returns late from holiday, s/he will be taken to have dismissed him/herself.

98 *International Sports Co v Thompson* [1980] IRLR 340, EAT.
99 *Post Office v Stones* (1980) EAT 390/80.
100 See chapter 15.
101 *Rampart Engineering v Henderson* (1981) EAT 235/81.

Legally this is not recognised as a resignation or mutual termination. The employee cannot be deprived of the right to claim unfair dismissal in this way.[102]

Disobedience

Overview

7.57 This type of dismissal usually arises when an employee refuses to obey an order or instruction of the employer. The instruction may or may not be one with which the employee is required to comply under the contract of employment.

The reasonableness test: ERA 1996 s98(4)

7.58 The two key considerations are: a) the nature of the employer's instruction; and b) the employee's reason for refusal to comply.

7.59 An employee is entitled to refuse any unlawful,[103] unreasonable or dangerous instruction. Although the starting point is whether the employee is obliged to comply with the instruction under the employment contract, this does not necessarily determine whether a refusal is reasonable.[104] It may be unfair to dismiss an employee who refuses to obey a contractual instruction, or fair to dismiss an employee who refuses to obey a non-contractual order. An employee who fails to co-operate with an employer's request to do non-contractual overtime,[105] to adapt to new technology[106] or otherwise go along with a reorganisation[107] will often be found to have acted unreasonably and to be fairly dismissed.

7.60 Where an employee is required to comply with a contractual term which has not previously been operated and which will cause inconvenience or hardship, the employer must give reasonable advance notice. If no notice is given, an employee may be entitled to refuse to comply with the instruction in the short term[108] on this ground alone.

7.61 The ET must consider also the employee's reason for refusing to obey the instruction, and it should weigh up the competing interests and take into consideration the nature of the contractual relationship

---

102 See paras 6.27–6.52 on what constitutes dismissal under the ERA 1996.
103 *Morrish v Henlys (Folkestone)* [1973] 2 All ER 137; [1973] ICR 482, NIRC.
104 *Redbridge LBC v Fishman* [1978] IRLR 69; [1978] ICR 569, EAT.
105 *Horrigan v Lewisham LBC* [1978] ICR 15, EAT.
106 *Cresswell v Board of Inland Revenue* [1984] 2 All ER 713; [1984] IRLR 190, ChD.
107 *Ellis v Brighton Co-operative Society* [1976] IRLR 419, EAT.
108 *McAndrew v Prestwick Circuits* [1988] IRLR 514, EAT.

between the employer and employee generally. There may be good reason for the employee's refusal, eg a pregnant woman refusing to work close to a VDU screen, a risk to the employee's safety in handling money or a risk of civil liability.[109]

7.62   It can be automatic unfair dismissal to dismiss an employee because s/he refuses to work in a situation of serious and imminent danger.[110]

Dependency on drugs or alcohol or possession of drugs

Overview

7.63   Taking or possessing drugs at work, and sometimes out of work, tends to be treated as gross misconduct. Drinking at work may be treated as misconduct depending on the circumstances and what the contract says. Dependency on drugs or alcohol is now more likely to be treated by an enlightened employer as a medical condition[111] and will not be referred to as an act of misconduct in the disciplinary procedure. The advantage of treating this as a health issue is that the requirements relating to capability dismissals apply. These are more conducive to helping the employee, as medical reports will be obtained and appropriate treatment will be encouraged.

Dependency on alcohol or drugs

7.64   The employer must have a genuine and reasonable belief, based on proper and adequate investigation, that the employee is dependent. The employee should be given the chance to answer the allegations and to obtain a medical or specialist report ifs/he wishes, particularly if the employer treats it as a sickness issue.

7.65   In deciding whether to dismiss, the following factors will be relevant:

- whether the contract of employment or disciplinary procedure treats alcohol/drug dependency as a matter of conduct or capability;
- whether the employee is responsible for the safety of others, eg a coach driver or operator of dangerous machinery. If so, the

---

109 *UCATT v Brain* [1981] IRLR 224, CA.
110 See para 6.84 onwards for details.
111 See para 7.9 onwards for capability/health dismissals and *Strathclyde RC v Syme* (1979) EAT 233/79.

employee should not be permitted to continue on the job. The employer may dismiss or transfer the employee to safer duties;

- whether the employee works in an environment which is potentially dangerous to others or him/herself, eg an electrician. Similar considerations apply; and
- whether there is a risk of adverse publicity or harm to customer relations (which would be a dismissal for 'some other substantial reason').

Taking or possessing drugs in or out of work

7.66   Most employers are uninformed about the different types of drugs and their effects, so summary dismissal is common for using or possessing drugs, particularly when at work. Many ETs take a hard line on any drug-related dismissal.

7.67   It will usually be fair to dismiss an employee for using or possessing drugs in or out of work, when there is a risk of adverse publicity, harm to customer relations or other harm to the employer's business interests.[112] However, if the possession or use of drugs is outside the work environment, not a matter of public knowledge and could not harm the business, the employee may be able to show that dismissal is unfair.[113]

Drinking at work

7.68   This may not be a matter of alcohol dependency at all, and it will not necessarily be misconduct to drink at work. This will depend on whether the contract or disciplinary procedure expressly lists drinking as misconduct or, if not, whether the employee and employer clearly contemplated that it would be misconduct. In certain jobs there is a zero-tolerance policy. This depends on the nature of the job, factors such as proximity to dangerous equipment and custom and practice.

Misuse of telephone, email, internet or social networking sites

7.69   This is increasingly becoming a reason for dismissal. An employee is entitled to be informed clearly in advance as to what his/her employer's policy is on private use of the telephone, email, internet

---

112 This would be a dismissal for 'some other substantial reason'.
113 *Norfolk CC v Bernard* [1979] IRLR 220, EAT.

and social networking sites.[114] There is an issue both as to use of working time and of inappropriate content. If the policy allows 'reasonable' personal use, it should be clear what amounts to 'reasonable' and it should be applied consistently by different managers. An employer could reasonably dismiss for gross misconduct a lead personnel officer who downloaded pornography from the internet on his computer.[115] Downloading, and certainly circulating, pornography may also lead to sexual harassment claims.[116] If an employee uses an unauthorised password to enter a computer known to contain information to which s/he is not entitled, it is gross misconduct regardless of whether s/he has some illegitimate purpose or simply idle curiosity. Having said that, the employer should have clearly notified employees of the rules regarding unauthorised access.[117] Employers who base disciplinary action on material they have only discovered by unauthorised monitoring may be in breach of the right to privacy under ECHR Article 8, although this will not necessarily mean the dismissal is unfair.[118] With regard to *social networking sites*, it is important first to identify what aspect of the employee's social media use caused the employer to dismiss. The reasonableness of the dismissal will be assessed against that reason. It could, for example, be reasonable to discipline or dismiss employees for making comments which are defamatory, which constitute harassment of other employees who read the tweets or messages, which breach confidentiality, or which bring the business into disrepute. Relevant considerations are likely to be the impact or potential impact on other employees, customers, or the public; whether the employer can be identified; whether the connection with the employee posting the messages is clear; and whether the employer had any relevant policies on the matter. Difficulties most often arise where employees imagine they are using social media in a non-work capacity, but they do not adopt privacy settings and/or are followed by co-workers. The right to freedom of expression under ECHR Article 10 needs to be taken into account, and it is strongly arguable that employees should be allowed to make negative comments as long as they are not damaging. ACAS has issued guidance on social media,

---

114 See paras 1.88–1.90 on this and on employer monitoring.
115 *Thomas v Hillingdon LBC* EAT/1317/01.
116 See para 14.136 onwards regarding sexual harassment.
117 *Denco Ltd v Joinson* [1991] IRLR 63, EAT.
118 See para 1.90.

disciplinaries and grievances,[119] which acknowledges employees' confusion over what is permissible and recommends that employers make it clear in advance what kind of online behaviour is not acceptable. It is worth reading the first reported Employment Appeal Tribunal (EAT) case regarding unfair dismissal because of Twitter use, even though it gives no general guidelines: *Game Retail Ltd v Laws*.[120] Although not an unfair dismissal or discrimination case, *Smith v Trafford Housing Trust*[121] is also a useful guide to how such cases may be analysed by tribunals.

Redundancy dismissals

7.70　See chapter 8 for all aspects of redundancy including unfair redundancy dismissals.

Statutory restriction dismissals

7.71　There are very few cases where the employer relies on a statutory restriction as the reason for dismissal. A common example is the loss of a necessary qualification for a job, eg a van driver losing his/her driving licence. The employer must show that the statutory restriction affected the work that the person was employed to perform and that no alternative employment was available. The larger the employer, the greater the duty to try to find an alternative to dismissal. Statutory restriction dismissals can also occur where the worker is not allowed to work because of his/her immigration status.[122] The employer must be right that there would be a breach of a statutory duty or restriction if the employee was allowed to continue to work in the job. It is not enough that the employer genuinely and reasonably, but wrongly, believes that to be the case.[123]

7.72　　　　Consultation on the consequences of the statutory restriction and possible alternatives is very important.[124] Where a restriction does

---

119 Available at: https://webarchive.nationalarchives.gov.uk/ukgwa /20210104113954/https://archive.acas.org.uk/index.aspx?articleid= 3375.

120 UKEAT/0188/14.

121 [2012] EWHC 3221 (Ch); [2013] IRLR 86.

122 For more detail, see section on 'Migrant workers' in chapter 14.

123 *Bouchaala v Trusthouse Forte Hotels Ltd* [1980] IRLR 382, EAT.

124 *Sutcliffe and Eaton v Pinney* [1977] IRLR 349, EAT.

not prevent the employee from doing his/her job but makes it diffi-cult, eg a salesperson losing a driving licence, the employer should consult on what assistance may be possible. Even where continued employment of the employee would be unlawful, eg where a GP has been struck off the medical register, the employer should still consult on the likelihood of the decision being reversed.

Dismissals for some other substantial reason (SOSR)

Introduction

7.73 A dismissal which is not for one of the four potentially fair reasons may still be fair if it is for 'some other substantial reason of a kind such as to justify the dismissal'.[125] The most common SOSR dismissals are for reorganisation including variation of the contract of employment, in order to protect the employer's business interests or as a consequence of the transfer of a business. Other situations where a dismissal might be deemed to be for SOSR are where the interests of the business might suffer as a result of friction at work between two colleagues, or an employee is incompatible and does not fit in, or due to adverse publicity on any matter, eg relating to an employee taking drugs or having a criminal conviction. Note that a 'substantial' reason is one which is not trivial or unworthy but one which would justify the dismissal.[126]

Dismissals due to reorganisation or variation of contract

Overview

7.74 It is sometimes hard to differentiate between a reorganisation and a redundancy situation. An employer may try to claim that the dismissal is because of reorganisation, in order to avoid making a redundancy payment.

7.75 An employee may be dismissed because s/he cannot or will not accept a change in terms and conditions resulting from the reorgan-isation. The employer first needs to prove that the reorganisation or the employee's refusal or inability to fit in with it was a substantial

---

125 ERA 1996 s98(1).
126 *Gilham v Kent CC (No 1)* [1985] IRLR 16, CA.

reason such as could justify dismissal, otherwise the dismissal will be unfair.[127] In practice, it is fairly easy for the employer to meet this initial requirement. An employer is entitled to reorganise the workforce and terms and conditions of employment to improve efficiency and to dismiss an employee who does not co-operate with the changes.[128] It is sufficient to amount to a potentially fair reason for dismissal for the employer to show that the reorganisation is for sound business reasons requiring a change in the employee's terms and conditions.[129] The reorganisation need not be essential. It is very hard for an employee at the ET to challenge the employer's reasons as not being sound and good. The employer needs only to demonstrate the benefits to the business of the reorganisation, perceived at the time of dismissal. If the employer cannot demonstrate these benefits existed and their importance at the time of dismissal, the dismissal will be unfair as the employer will not have established a 'substantial' reason for dismissal.[130]

The reasonableness test: ERA 1996 s98(4)

7.76   Although the ET should consider a number of factors when deciding whether it was fair to dismiss, it primarily looks at the situation from the employer's point of view, ie whether a reasonable employer would make those changes to the employee's terms of employment.[131] The ET considers the competing advantages and disadvantages to the employer and the employee, but the main emphasis in reorganisation or variation of terms dismissals is on the employer's interests which are paramount. Nevertheless, there have been some ET decisions, endorsed by the EAT, indicating that an employer does not have a completely free hand.[132] It is unlikely that an ET would think it fair to cut pay or reduce terms and conditions merely to increase profitability of an already successful business. However, it goes too far to say that significant changes can be made only if the survival of the business is at stake.[133] Whether or not the majority of the workforce have agreed to changes to their terms and conditions will be a

---

127 ERA 1996 s98(1).
128 *Lesney Products and Co v Nolan* [1977] IRLR 77, CA.
129 *Hollister v National Farmers Union* [1979] ICR 542; [1979] IRLR 238, CA.
130 *Banerjee v City and East London Area Health Authority* [1979] IRLR 147, EAT.
131 *Chubb Fire Security v Harper* [1983] IRLR 311, EAT.
132 *Interconnections Systems v Gibson* (1994) 508 IRLB 8, EAT; *Selfridges Ltd v Wayne and others* (1995) 535 IRLB 13, EAT.
133 *Catamaran Cruisers Ltd v Williams and others* [1994] IRLR 386, EAT.

factor.[134] It will also be relevant upon whom in the workforce the cuts fall and whether, for example, management have exempted themselves from the cuts.[135] A change in terms and conditions may also lead to a successful discrimination claim under the EqA 2010, eg for indirect sex discrimination on an introduction of flexi-shifts.

7.77   Consultation plays an important part in all types of dismissal including reorganisation. For options when an employer tries to vary terms and conditions, see paras 1.20–1.23. The practice of dismissing employees and offering new contracts on reduced terms has become increasingly common in recent years and worsened due to the Covid-19 pandemic. Due to parliamentary concerns, the government asked ACAS to carry out a fact-finding exercise to inform its thinking on possible action.[136]

Dismissals to protect employers' business interests

Overview

7.78   There is an implied term of fidelity and good faith in every employment contract which lasts as long as the employee is employed. Some employees also agree to express terms which restrict their future employment in the same industry for a given period. These terms are known as 'restrictive covenants'.

7.79   An employee dismissed for breaking the implied term of good faith and fidelity will be dismissed for SOSR and perhaps also misconduct. In addition, there may be a substantial reason potentially justifying dismissal if:

• an employee refuses to sign a restrictive covenant and the employer is genuinely seeking to protect the business interests;[137] or

• there is a genuine risk arising from an employee's relationship with a competitor.[138]

---

134 For a checklist on variation of terms and conditions, see appendix A at A25.

135 *Garside and Laycock Ltd v Booth* UKEAT/0003/11.

136 ACAS paper: *Dismissal and re-engagement (fire-and-rehire): a fact-finding exercise*, 8 June 2021, at www.acas.org.uk/fire-and-rehire-report/html. See also *Fire and rehire tactics are levelling down pay*, TUC, 25 January 2021, at www.tuc.org.uk/blogs/fire-and-rehire-tactics-are-levelling-down-pay.

137 *RS Components v Irwin* [1973] ICR 535; [1973] IRLR 239, NIRC.

138 *Skyrail Oceanic v Coleman* [1981] ICR 864, CA.

The reasonableness test: ERA 1996 s98(4)

7.80   Where dismissal is for refusing to sign a restrictive covenant, the ET will take into account the necessity of applying it, whether the industry usually requires employers to take this precaution and whether the employee's job was of sufficient importance. The ET will also consider the manner and method of the introduction of the clause and whether it was consistently introduced among other employees.

Other SOSR dismissals

7.81   Where dismissal is due to a personal relationship with a competitor, the ET should take into account the nature of the relationship and its bearing on the work situation. The manner of the employee's dismissal and the degree of notice or warning of impending dismissal are also relevant.[139] If dismissal is due to a personality clash with colleagues, the employer should do all that is reasonable to try to remedy the problem, which might involve transferring the employee.[140] If dismissal is at the behest of a third party, the employer must do its best to avoid or mitigate any injustice to the employee. For example, where employees work for a company providing a service to a local authority or other contracting authority, the authority often reserves the right to veto the continued employment of any of the contractor's staff. If the veto causes injustice to the employee who has not done anything serious enough to warrant dismissal, the contractor should do its best to change the authority' mind or to find alternative employment.[141]

Dismissals on transfer of an undertaking

Overview

7.82   Depending on the facts, a dismissal of an employee on or after the transfer of an undertaking for an economic, technical or organisational (ETO) reason entailing changes in the workforce of either the transferor or transferee is treated either as a redundancy dismissal

---

139 *Skyrail Oceanic v Coleman* [1981] ICR 864, CA.

140 *Turner v Vestric Ltd* [1981] IRLR 23, EAT.

141 Useful cases are *Henderson v Connect (South Tyneside) Ltd* [2010] IRLR 466, EAT; and *Bancroft v Interserve (Facilities Management) Ltd* UKEAT/0329/12.

or as dismissal for a substantial reason of a kind that can justify dismissal.[142]

7.83 Dismissals at the time of a transfer usually arise out of the desire of the buyer or seller or both to reduce the workforce or their terms and conditions so as to make the business a more valuable asset.

The reasonableness test: ERA 1996 s98(4)

7.84 Dismissals connected with a transfer are automatically unfair unless for an ETO reason entailing a change in the workforce. If they are for such a reason, they may be fair or unfair, depending on the facts in the usual way. For more detail, see chapter 10.

---

142 Transfer of Undertakings (Protection of Employment) Regulations 2006 S I No 246 reg 7(3).

CHAPTER 8

Redundancy

continued

Chapter 8: Key points

- Redundant employees have a right to reasonable time off to look for work during the notice period.
- An employee who is dismissed for redundancy may be entitled to statutory redundancy pay.
- An employee who is put on short-time working or laid off without pay may resign and claim statutory redundancy pay if s/he follows the correct procedure.
- Even where there is a genuine redundancy situation, the employee may have been unfairly dismissed.
- A redundancy dismissal may be unfair if there has been inadequate consultation by the employer or unfair selection for dismissal. Larger employers will be expected to have more sophisticated selection criteria than small ones. Criteria should be possible to measure objectively.
- Length of service used to be a common selection criterion, but can be discriminatory.
- The employer is expected to offer any available alternative employment which the employee is capable of doing.
- Where old jobs are replaced by newly designed jobs, particularly at a higher level, the selection process can be more forward-looking and assess whether the employee can do the new job.
- Watch out for direct and indirect discrimination against black and minority ethnic workers, women and pregnant women, or discrimination related to any of the other protected characteristics under the Equality Act 2010, eg disability, sexual orientation, religion or age.
- See interview checklist in appendix A at A4.

General guide to useful evidence

- Get copies of all minutes, notes and memoranda of meetings at which the redundancy dismissal was discussed.
- Get a list of all workers who could have been selected for redundancy; ascertain who was retained. In a discrimination claim, try to discover when they started their employment, why they have been kept on, and how they met the selection criteria.
- Find out all vacancies available shortly before and after the dismissal (including the whole of the notice period) to see whether the worker could have done any of them.

continued

> • Find out from those workers who are still employed, what happened to the worker's job after the dismissal. Was the worker simply replaced? If so, find out who the new worker is, and get a copy of the job advert and the letter of appointment.

Introduction

8.1 An employee who is made redundant may claim statutory redundancy pay. Some employees have a greater contractual entitlement, and much of the public sector has its own schemes. An employee may be able to get additional compensation if s/he has a claim for unfair dismissal and/or discrimination because of one of the nine protected characteristics under the Equality Act (EqA) 2010, ie: age; disability; gender reassignment; marital or civil partnership status; pregnancy or maternity; race; religion or belief; sex; or sexual orientation. An adviser must be careful because the time limits are different for each of these claims. The time limit to claim redundancy pay from the employment tribunal (ET) is fairly relaxed. Within six months of the termination date, the employee must either claim the pay in the ET or make a written claim to the employer or lodge an unfair dismissal claim.[1] However, if the employee wants to claim unfair dismissal or discrimination at the same time, s/he must meet the three-month time limit for these latter claims. The Advisory, Conciliation and Arbitration Service (ACAS) early conciliation (EC) procedure (see para 20.16) applies to all these claims. See appendix A at A4 for an interview checklist applicable to a redundant employee.

The definition of 'redundancy'

Overview

8.2 In broad terms, there are three main redundancy situations:
1) closure of the business as a whole;
2) closure of the particular workplace where the employee was employed; and
3) reduction in the size of the workforce.

1 Employment Rights Act (ERA) 1996 ss164 and 145.

The statutory definitions are a little more complex.[2]

Closure of the business

8.3   Employment Rights Act (ERA) 1996 s139(1) states:

> . . . an employee who is dismissed shall be taken to be dismissed by reason of redundancy if the dismissal is wholly or mainly attributable to–
> (a) the fact that his employer has ceased or intends to cease–
>   (i) to carry on the business for the purposes of which the employee was employed . . .

The closure may be permanent or temporary,[3] eg, closure of a restaurant for refurbishment.

Closure of the workplace

8.4   A dismissal is deemed to be for redundancy if it is attributable wholly or mainly to the fact that the employer 'has ceased or intends to cease . . . to carry on that business in the place where the employee was so employed'.[4] The employee is dismissed for redundancy if dismissed when his/her own workplace closes, even if under the contract s/he could be required to work elsewhere.[5] For example, an employee working in one branch of a restaurant or retail chain is dismissed when his/her branch closes, even though there is a mobility clause in his/her contract.

8.5   The employee needs to be careful if, instead of being made redundant, s/he is instructed to work at a different location or branch. If the employee refuses, s/he may lose his/her redundancy pay because s/he has refused an offer of suitable alternative employment (below). Also, if the employee refuses a move when there is a mobility clause, s/he may be dismissed for misconduct rather than redundancy. There is nothing to stop an employer invoking a mobility clause to avoid redundancy payments.[6] A mobility clause is one which means the worker can be contractually required to move workplace, eg: 'Your place of work is at (*address*). However, you may also be

2 Note there is a different definition of redundancy for the purposes of collective consultation, see para 2.21.
3 ERA 1996 s139(6).
4 ERA 1996 s139(1)(a)(ii).
5 *Bass Leisure Ltd v Thomas* [1994] IRLR 104, EAT; *High Table Ltd v Horst and others* [1997] IRLR 513, CA.
6 *Home Office v Evans* [2008] IRLR 59, CA.

required to work at any other company premises within reasonable travelling distance of your home.'

Reduction of the workforce

8.6 It is a dismissal for redundancy where it is:

... wholly or mainly attributable to . . .
(b) the fact that the requirements of that business–
   (i) for employees to carry out work of a particular kind, or
   (ii) . . . to carry out work of a particular kind in the place where the employee was employed by the employer,
have ceased or diminished or are expected to cease or diminish.[7]

This is where, for whatever reason, the employer wants fewer employees doing a particular kind of work. There need not necessarily be less work to be done.[8] The employer may just have decided to cut costs by reducing staff and making those remaining do more work. As long as the employee is dismissed as a result of the employer's diminished requirements, s/he is dismissed for redundancy, regardless of what kind of work s/he actually did or could be required to do under his/her contract.[9]

8.7 It is obviously a redundancy situation where the employer wants fewer employees overall. It is less clear where the employer retains the same number of employees, but on different work from before. It is redundancy if a particular type of job has disappeared altogether, but if it has simply been altered or modernised, eg, by technology, this may not be the case. The test is whether the changed job requires different aptitudes, skill or knowledge.[10] It can also be a redundancy dismissal if the employer dismisses an employee because there is less work to do and the employee won't accept a cut in his/her hours – for example if a full-time worker is dismissed and replaced by a part-time worker because there is only half as much work to do.[11]

8.8 Finally, an employer may offer a redundant employee another employee's job. The other employee is then treated as dismissed for redundancy.[12] This process is known as 'bumping' and usually

---

7 ERA 1996 s139(1)(b).
8 *McRea v Cullen & Davison Ltd* [1988] IRLR 30, NICA.
9 *Safeway Stores plc v Burrell* [1997] IRLR 200, EAT; *Murray and another v Foyle Meats Ltd* [1999] IRLR 562, HL.
10 *Amos and others v Max-Arc Ltd* [1973] IRLR 285, NIRC.
11 *Packman t/a Packman Lucas Associates v Fauchon* UKEAT/0017/12.
12 *Gimber and Sons v Spurrett* [1967] ITR 308, QBD.

occurs in recognition of long service, though it occurs only rarely now.[13]

Redundancy payments

Introduction

8.9   An employee dismissed on the ground of redundancy is entitled to statutory redundancy pay if s/he meets the necessary eligibility requirements, ie:

- s/he is an employee;
- s/he has at least two years' continuous service; and
- s/he has been dismissed for redundancy.

It may not be clear whether the employee has actually been dismissed. Notifying an employee that his/her post will be deleted is not necessarily the same as terminating his/her contract of employment.[14] The dismissal then needs to be for redundancy reasons. This is presumed, unless disproved, if the employee makes a tribunal claim for a statutory redundancy payment.[15] The employee risks losing his/her redundancy pay if s/he is given notice and leaves before the notice period expires. In such a case, s/he may need to follow the special procedure set out in ERA 1996 s136(3)–(4). The calculation of statutory redundancy pay is set out at para 18.22. There is also a lesser known right whereby a tribunal can order an employer to pay an employee an appropriate amount as compensation if the employee suffers any financial loss as a result of non-payment of his/her redundancy entitlement.[16] Workers who have the status of employee shareholders are unable to claim statutory redundancy pay.[17] The government plans at some stage to bring in regulations to impose an upper limit on the amount public sector employees can be paid in exit payments including redundancy pay, notice pay and ex gratia

---

13   Whether the 'bumped' employee has been unfairly dismissed (see para 8.27) or discriminated against is a separate question.

14   *East London NHS Foundation Trust v O'Connor* UKEAT/0113/19; [2020] IRLR 16 provides practical guidance to help identify whether an employee has been dismissed. This is particularly important in the context of whether the statutory rules on trial periods for alternative employment apply.

15   ERA 1996 s163(2).

16   ERA 1996 s163(5).

17   See paras 6.130–6.131 above.

payments.[18] A cap was briefly introduced in November 2020 and then revoked with retrospective effect in March 2021.[19]

Suitable alternative employment

Overview

8.10   The employee will lose his/her statutory redundancy pay if s/he unreasonably refused an offer of suitable alternative employment.[20]

What constitutes a valid offer?

8.11   The offer of alternative employment must be made before the previous employment ends and the new job must start immediately or within four weeks of the end of that employment. The offer need not be in writing, but it will be for the employer to prove that a suitable offer was made.[21] If the employee says s/he is not interested in receiving any alternative offer and the employer therefore does not make one, the employee will not be taken to have unreasonably refused a suitable offer and will be entitled to a redundancy payment.[22] The offer must set out the main terms of the new job in enough detail to show how it differs from the old one[23] and the starting date should be clear.

8.12   If the employee accepts the offer, s/he is treated for redundancy purposes as never having been dismissed.[24] However, s/he can still claim unfair dismissal from the original job.[25] S/he may want to do this if, eg, his/her pay in the new job is lower.

The statutory trial period

8.13   Where the employee is offered an alternative job as above, s/he can try out the new job, where it differs from the old one, for a trial period

---

18 Small Business, Enterprise and Employment Act 2015 s153A.
19 Restriction of Public Sector Exit Payments (Revocation) Regulations 2021 SI No 197.
20 ERA 1996 s141.
21 *Kitching v Ward* [1967] ITR 464; (1967) 3 KIR 322, DC.
22 *Simpson v Dickinson* [1972] ICR 474, NIRC. Although different rules may apply to collectively agreed and other contractual redundancy schemes, eg in the NHS.
23 *Havenhand v Thomas Black Ltd* [1968] 2 All ER 1037; [1968] ITR 271, DC.
24 ERA 1996 s138(1).
25 *Hempell v W H Smith & Sons Ltd* [1986] IRLR 95, EAT; *Jones v Governing Body of Burdett Coutts School* [1998] IRLR 521, CA.

of up to four weeks.[26] If s/he leaves or gives notice to leave within this period, the original redundancy dismissal stands and s/he can still claim redundancy pay.[27] The trial period starts on the date the employee begins the new job and ends four calendar weeks later, by which time the employee must have decided whether to accept the new job permanently. If the employee works beyond the four-week period, s/he will lose the right to claim redundancy pay. It is irrelevant whether the employee is unable to work the four weeks, eg, because s/he is off sick or the workplace is closed for Christmas.[28] However, an offer of a different alternative job will attract another four-week trial period. The four-week trial period is a strict time limit and can be extended only by agreement for the purpose of retraining the employee; such agreement must be in writing and specify a new date when the trial period will end.[29]

Unreasonable refusal of a suitable offer

8.14 The employer must prove both that the offer was suitable and that the employee's refusal was unreasonable. 'Suitability' tends to mean objective job-related factors such as pay, status, hours and location. The reasonableness of a refusal depends more on the employee's individual circumstances, eg, domestic factors and health. A very common form of alternative offer is of the same job but in a different location. Whether this is a suitable offer which the employee cannot reasonably refuse depends on a combination of factors such as extra travelling time and expense, childcare responsibilities, health and status of the job (the higher the status, the more an ET would expect an employee to travel). If an employee is going to refuse a job because of travel difficulties, it is important that s/he knows precisely what the travel would entail. It may also be helpful at least to try it out. It is not for the tribunal to impose its own view on whether the refusal of the offer was reasonable. Nor is the test whether a reasonable employee would have accepted the offer. It must be looked at from the viewpoint of the particular employee concerned. Did s/he have good reasons for refusing the offer given his/her particular circumstances, even if his/her view might not be shared by others.[30] Moreover, an employee's desire to take

---

26 ERA 1996 s138.
27 ERA 1996 s138(2)(b).
28 *Benton v Sanderson Kayser Ltd* [1989] IRLR 19, CA.
29 ERA 1996 s138(3).
30 *Bird v Stoke-on-Trent Primary Care Trust* UKEAT/0074/11; *Devon Primary Care Trust v Readman* [2013] IRLR 878, CA.

advantage of his/her redundancy rights does not necessarily defeat a claim if s/he has given proper consideration to the job on offer.

Lay-off and short-time

8.15   Normally an employee can claim statutory redundancy pay only if s/he is dismissed for redundancy. This includes constructive dismissal – for example, if s/he resigns due to a fundamental breach of contract, such as being sent home without pay, when under his/her contract this is not permitted. However, there is a problem if an employee has a contract which allows him/her to be temporarily laid off without pay or put on short-time working (ie fewer hours), with a consequent cut in pay. This situation could carry on indefinitely, without the employee being able to sue for his/her lost wages or resign and claim redundancy pay. There are therefore special statutory rules which cover this situation once the employee has been laid off or put on short-time for at least four consecutive weeks or six weeks in a 13-week period. There is a specified procedure involving notices and counter-notices which enables the employee to resign and claim redundancy pay.[31] If the employer has no money to pay the redundancy pay, this can be recovered from the Insolvency Service.[32]

Guarantee pay

8.16   Where an employee is not provided with work on any day when s/he would normally be required to work under his/her contract because of lesser requirements of the employer's business for the employee's type of work, s/he may be entitled to a small guarantee payment from his/her employer. The rules are set out in ERA 1996 ss28–35. This sum is a minimum and is set off against any contractual wages to which the employee is entitled.[33] The maximum amount of guarantee pay in the year starting 6 April 2021 is £30 per day for five days in any three-month period.[34]

---

31   ERA 1996 ss147–150. For a recent case, see *Craig v Bob Lindfield & Son Ltd* UKEAT/0220/15.

32   See para 18.73.

33   ERA 1996 s32.

34   Employment Rights (Increase of Limits) Order 2021 SI No 208. For guidance and latest rates, see GOV.UK website at: www.gov.uk/lay-offs-short-timeworking/guarantee-pay.

Unfair redundancy dismissal

Overview

8.17 A dismissal for redundancy may be automatically unfair on one of the specified grounds, eg selecting a woman for redundancy because she is pregnant.[35] Alternatively, it may be unfair on general principles for one or more of the following reasons:

a) there was no genuine redundancy situation;
b) the employer failed to consult;
c) the employee was unfairly selected; or
d) the employer failed to offer alternative employment.

The Employment Appeal Tribunal (EAT) in *Williams v Compair Maxam Ltd*[36] set out guidelines for the fair handling of redundancy dismissals. It is not necessarily unfair to fail to follow the guidelines in every case, but they do provide a useful standard. For general principles on unfair dismissal, including unfair dismissal on grounds of redundancy, see chapter 6.

No genuine redundancy situation

8.18 An employee cannot challenge whether the employer acted reasonably in creating the redundancy situation. The ET cannot investigate the commercial and economic reasons which prompted a closure or look into the rights and wrongs of the employer's decision.[37] However, an ET is entitled to investigate whether the redundancy situation is in fact genuine.

Failure to consult

8.19 The employer should give as much warning as possible of impending redundancies to enable the union and affected employees to consider possible alternative solutions and if necessary, find alternative employment.[38]

---

35 See para 6.70 onwards.
36 [1982] IRLR 83, EAT; approved by *Robinson v Carrickfergus BC* [1983] IRLR 122, NICA.
37 *James W Cook & Co (Wivenhoe) Ltd v Tipper and others* [1990] IRLR 386, CA; *Moon v Homeworthy Furniture (Northern) Ltd* [1976] IRLR 298, EAT.
38 *Williams v Compair Maxam Ltd* [1982] IRLR 83, EAT.

8.20   The statutory right to collective consultation for redundancies of 20 or more is set out at para 8.43 below. This section is concerned with the right not to be unfairly dismissed and is referring to the significance of consultation in the context of an individual unfair dismissal claim. Consultation is very important in redundancy situations and can take many forms. At one end of the spectrum, it involves collective discussions and meetings with the union; at the other end, it will entail discussions with individual employees who are likely to be made redundant. Failure to consult individually may well make a dismissal unfair, although compensation may be limited if consultation would not have made any difference to the outcome.[39]

8.21   Consultation requires the employer to consider options which would not involve making the employee redundant, including early retirement, seeking volunteers, alternative employment, lay-off and short-time working. The employees and their representatives should be involved in this process. Consultation means more than communicating a decision already made. The Industrial Relations Code of Practice,[40] which has been repealed, provided a good definition of consultation. It defined consultation as jointly examining and discussing problems of concern to both management and employees. It involves seeking mutually acceptable solutions through a genuine exchange of views and information.[41] Furthermore, the courts have held that fair consultation involves consultation when the proposals are still at a formative stage, there is adequate information on which to respond, adequate time in which to respond, and conscientious consideration by an authority of the response to consultation.[42]

8.22   Although failure to follow the statutory rules on collective consultation will not in itself make the dismissal of an individual employee unfair, the failure to consult collectively is one factor which can be taken into account in assessing the reasonableness of the dismissal.[43] On the other hand, even if there has been union consultation, it is normally important that the employer has also consulted the individual employees. Collective consultation tends to concentrate on matters such as choice of selection criteria and how the process will take effect, whereas individuals want the opportunity to

---

39 See para 18.57.
40 1972 para 46.
41 *Heron v City Link-Nottingham* [1993] IRLR 372, EAT.
42 *R v British Coal Corporation ex p Price* [1994] IRLR 72, DC; *Rowell v Hubbard Group Services Ltd* [1995] IRLR 195, EAT.
43 *Williams v Compair Maxam Ltd* [1982] IRLR 83, EAT.

make representations on their own position,[44] eg how they should be assessed against the criteria and suggestions for alternative employment. An employee does not necessarily have to be given his/her particular scores, but it depends on the circumstances. What is important is that s/he is given sufficient information to challenge, correct and supplement the information which the employer may have wrongly taken into account or not known about when making the assessment.[45] Where there is no union or collective consultation, individuals should also get the chance to comment on the process and choice of selection criteria.

Unfair selection

8.23 As a first stage, the employer must choose a fair pool from which to select the redundant employees. Employers have a lot of flexibility in deciding on a pool, provided they apply their mind to it and act from genuine motives.[46] However, it could be unreasonable to restrict the pool artificially, eg, by not including all those doing similar work. It should not be automatically assumed that if a particular post is deleted, the post-holder is the one to go,[47] but in some situations that is the only obvious candidate. Whether a subordinate employee whose post is to be retained should be included in the pool will depend on factors such as: whether the post-holder is willing to accept the more junior role at a reduced salary; the difference in salary between the two posts; the difference in the jobs; the relative length of service of the two employees; and the qualifications of the employee in danger of redundancy.[48]

8.24 Once a reasonable pool is chosen, the employer can choose any reasonable selection criteria, provided these can be objectively measured and are not discriminatory. Ideally the employer should try to agree the criteria with the union, if there is one.[49] It is common these days to use multiple selection criteria, which often include length of

---

44 *Mugford v Midland Bank plc* [1997] IRLR 208, EAT.
45 *Davies v Farnborough College of Technology* [2008] IRLR 14, EAT; *Alexander v Brigden Enterprises Ltd* [2006] IRLR 422, EAT.
46 *Thomas & Betts Manufacturing Ltd v Harding* [1980] IRLR 255, CA.
47 *Fulcrum Pharma (Europe) Ltd v Bonassera and another* UKEAT/0198/10.
48 *Fulcrum Pharma (Europe) Ltd v Bonassera and another* UKEAT/0198/10. See also para 8.27 on bumping.
49 *Williams v Compair Maxam Ltd* [1982] IRLR 83, EAT.

service,[50] productivity (if it can be objectively assessed), timekeeping, the employee's adaptability and the employer's future needs. Length of service is less popular nowadays, especially if it has discriminatory effect. If attendance is one of the criteria, it should be judged over a substantial period, particularly for long-standing employees. It may in some circumstances be unreasonable not to look at the reasons behind each employee's absence,[51] but this would be unusual. Vague criteria such as 'attitude to work' could be unreasonable.[52] Certain criteria may also be discriminatory.[53]

8.25   Having chosen fair selection criteria, the employer must apply these fairly and objectively. A reasonable criterion such as 'merit' can be challenged if it is not judged in an objective manner. Unfortunately, it is hard to challenge the employer's assessment of the employees against the various criteria. An ET is not going to embark on its own exercise of re-marking all the candidates. Rather than checking whether marks were valid, an ET will be looking at the process and how marks were arrived at, ie whether there was a structured scoring process, carried out with an open mind and assessment done by informed managers who relied on solid evidence, eg appraisals, statistics or views of other managers. To challenge an assessment score, the claimant needs strong evidence that it does not make sense, eg giving an extremely low mark for product knowledge to a long-standing salesperson when there has been little change in the design of goods sold.[54] The ET will not order disclosure of the assessment forms of all employees in the selection pool unless it is clear from the tribunal claim why these are relevant and why the redundancy is unfair.[55] Nevertheless, the ET does not simply have to accept the employer's assertion that it has applied its selection criteria fairly.[56] An ET does need to know how the claimant's markings compare with those of the retained employees in deciding whether the employer acted reasonably. Disclosure or additional information regarding all the employees in the redundancy selection pool can

---

50   *Bessenden Properties v Corness* [1974] IRLR 338 [1977] ICR 142, HL. See also para 8.37.
51   *Paine and Moore v Grundy (Teddington) Ltd* [1981] IRLR 267, EAT.
52   *Graham v ABF Ltd* [1986] IRLR 90, EAT.
53   See para 8.35.
54   For examples of unfairness, see *Grant v BSS Group plc* UKEAT/0832/02; *E-Zec Medical Transport Service Ltd v Gregory* UKEAT/0192/08.
55   *British Aerospace plc v Green and others* [1995] IRLR 433, CA. See para 20.123 onwards for principles for disclosure.
56   *FDR Ltd v Holloway* [1995] IRLR 400, EAT.

therefore be relevant.[57] In discrimination cases, an employee may well be entitled to more detailed comparable information.

8.26   The lengths to which the ET expects an employer to go in drawing up and applying criteria will depend on the employer's size and administrative resources.[58] Usually the ET expects a medium or large employer to have adopted a methodical approach, awarding each potentially redundant employee with points against various criteria and dismissing those who score least.[59] This selection process, provided it is consistent and measured objectively, will in most cases justify the dismissal. However, even small employers must show that they used a fair selection method. Although a more forward-looking recruitment-style process may be appropriate where new jobs have been created on a reorganisation,[60] this is unlikely to be appropriate in a traditional redundancy selection process for existing jobs where emphasis is more on assessment of past performance.[61]

8.27   In some circumstances, a tribunal may expect an employer to consider dismissing an employee who works in a non-redundant post to make way for an employee of greater suitability who works in a redundant post.[62] This is called 'bumping'. Whether it is unfair to fail even to consider bumping very much depends on the facts,[63] and the claimant would have to show, not only that there were powerful reasons to prefer him/her over the bumped employee, but that s/he could easily slot in and undertake the bumped employee's work. See para 8.23 where a senior post is deleted and a more junior employee might be dismissed to make way for the senior post-holder. Bumping may be expected if it has happened regularly in the past.[64] Moreover, the bumped employee may be able to claim that s/he has him/herself been unfairly dismissed, again depending on the facts.[65]

---

57 *FDR Ltd v Holloway* [1995] IRLR 400, EAT, stating *British Aerospace plc v Green and others* [1995] IRLR 433, CA should not be taken too literally.

58 ERA 1996 s98(4).

59 *Williams v Compair Maxam* [1982] IRLR 83, EAT.

60 See para 8.32.

61 *Mental Health Care (UK) Ltd v (1) Biluan (2) Makati* UKEAT/0248/12. See also comments in *Gwynedd Council v Shelley Barratt & others* UKEAT/0206/18.

62 *Thomas & Betts Manufacturing Co v Harding* [1980] IRLR 255, CA.

63 *Green v A & I Fraser (Wholesale Fish Merchants) Ltd* [1985] IRLR 55, EAT.

64 *Thomas & Betts Manufacturing Co v Harding* [1980] IRLR 255, CA; and see para 8.8.

65 *Barbar Indian Restaurant v Rawat* [1985] IRLR 57, EAT.

Failure to offer alternative employment

8.28   Employers must take reasonable steps to avoid or minimise redundancy by redeployment within their own organisation.[66] They must therefore look for alternative employment and should offer any suitable available vacancies. Employees at risk of redundancy should usually be given priority over external candidates for suitable vacancies.[67] An employer's duty is not limited to offering similar positions or positions in the same workplace and s/he should consider the availability of any vacancies with associated employers.[68] However, failing to put a redundant employee on a bank of non-employees who have no employment rights is unlikely to make a dismissal unfair, even if the employer uses the bank quite frequently.[69]

8.29   When offering alternative employment, the employer must give sufficient detail of the vacancy and, unless the job functions are obvious, allow a trial period. Failure to do so is likely to make the dismissal unfair.[70] It is up to the employee whether to accept the alternative employment, which might even involve demotion or a reduction in pay.[71] Employers should consult about possibilities and not make assumptions about what jobs an employee would find acceptable.

8.30   Employees who unreasonably refuse a suitable alternative offer will reduce their chances of winning an unfair dismissal case or receiving full compensation if they do win. They will also lose their entitlement to statutory redundancy pay (see above).

8.31   One of the main purposes of consultation is to consider other employment, eg, transfer to another workplace, as an alternative to dismissal. The ET will look at vacancies existing during the consultation period (regardless of whether there was actual consultation) and during the employee's notice period as well as at the time of dismissal itself. For relevant evidence in an unfair redundancy dismissal, see para 9.16.

---

66   *Polkey v AE Dayton Services Ltd* [1987] IRLR 503, HL.
67   Reiterated most recently in *Gwynedd Council v Barratt and Hughes* [2021] EWCA Civ 1322.
68   *Vokes Ltd v Bear* [1973] IRLR 363, NIRC, though later cases have suggested the duty in *Vokes* is too onerous.
69   *Aramark (UK) Limited v Fernandes* UKEATS/0028/19; [2020] IRLR 861.
70   *Elliott v Richard Stump Ltd* [1987] IRLR 215, EAT; *George v Brent LBC* UKEAT/0089/18.
71   *Avonmouth Construction Co v Shipway* [1979] IRLR 14, EAT.

Reorganisation and new jobs

8.32 Where the employer reorganises so that the old roles disappear and are replaced by new jobs, the approach can be different. Whereas traditional redundancy selection involves consultation and assessment of past performance to some degree, appointment to new roles is more forward-looking and can legitimately rely on something like an interview process to assess employees' ability to perform in the new roles.[72] This is especially so if the new job is at a high level and involves promotion. Even if there are sufficient vacancies to match the number of potentially redundant employees, it may well be fair for an employer to make an employee redundant if s/he is unable to meet the standard required for the new job. The tribunal will still look to see whether a fair process was followed and whether there was any indication of bias. A dismissal could be unfair if the new job is very similar to the disappearing job, or if the employer does not abide by a collective agreement to slot in displaced staff without competition.[73] It is also arguable that, even if the employer is entitled to test the redundant employee's capability to carry out the new job, the employee should be assessed before the post is opened up to external applications.[74] Although this different kind of redundancy process is common nowadays where there are public sector reorganisations, the tribunal will still consider whether all aspects of the dismissal (consultation, right of appeal etc) were within the band of reasonable responses.[75]

Redundancy and discrimination

Pregnancy/maternity dismissals

8.33 Selection for redundancy dismissal due to pregnancy, maternity or a related reason is automatically unfair and no minimum qualifying service is required to make a claim. Where a woman is made redundant while pregnant or on maternity leave, but not due to that fact, the

---

72 *Morgan v Welsh Rugby Union* [2011] IRLR 376, EAT. For examples, see also *Asif v Elmbridge BC* UKEAT/0395/11; and *Cumbria Partnership NHS Foundation Trust v Steel* UKEAT/0635/11.

73 *Cumbria Partnership NHS Foundation Trust v Steel* UKEAT/0635/11.

74 *Morgan* and other recent cases do not seem to focus on this question, but it seems a logical extension of the principle to offer redundant employees priority over external candidates for suitable vacancies – see para 8.28.

75 *Green v Barking & Dagenham LBC* UKEAT/0157/16.

normal test of fairness applies. However, a woman made redundant on maternity leave must be offered any suitable available vacancy, however inconvenient for the employer.[76] Failure to do this is automatically unfair dismissal. The same applies to employees on adoption leave or shared parental leave. Redundancy selection due to pregnancy or maternity may also be sex discrimination under the EqA 2010. See para 11.1 onwards regarding pregnancy dismissals.

Race discrimination – direct

8.34   In any case where a black, Asian or other minority ethnic worker, or someone born abroad, has been selected for redundancy, it is worth checking that there has been no direct discrimination. Indications may be the racial composition of those made redundant as compared with those retained. It is essential to ascertain why the employer says the worker has been selected. A common indicator of direct race discrimination is where retained white workers score equally badly or worse on the selection criteria. Direct discrimination may also occur because of other protected characteristics, eg religion, age, sex or sexual orientation. For evidence to prove direct discrimination, see chapter 16.

Indirectly discriminatory selection criteria

8.35   Criteria for selecting which workers are made redundant are frequently indirectly discriminatory.[77] Criteria such as hours worked, flexibility, mobility or attendance records could adversely affect women. Black workers may suffer from criteria based on conduct records, internal appraisals or customer complaints, if they have been subjected to direct discrimination in those areas. Unjustifiable selection of a part-time worker would be a breach of the Part-time Workers (Prevention of Less Favourable Treatment) Regulations 2000.[78] The selection first of workers on temporary or short fixed-term contracts may be unjustifiable indirect race or sex discrimination under the EqA 2010.[79]

---

76 See paras 11.61 and 6.70.
77 See para 13.27 onwards.
78 SI No 1551. See para 11.113 onwards.
79 For example, as in *Whiffen v Milham Ford Girls' School* [2001] IRLR 468, CA; it may also be a breach of the Fixed-term Employees (Prevention of Less Favourable Treatment) Regulations 2002 SI No 2034; see paras 1.41–1.49. See also list of indirectly discriminatory criteria in appendix B.

Last in, first out (LIFO)

8.36   Length of service is still sometimes applied as a means of redundancy selection. Although in many workplaces this requirement clearly disadvantages women, young people and black and other minority ethnic workers, it is a traditional selection method which has often been found justifiable in the past. Where LIFO has an obvious adverse impact, the following approach should be taken to challenge its justifiability:

- The higher the proportion of black and women workers made redundant due to the application of this criterion, the stronger the necessary justification from the employer.[80]
- The employer must show that the use of LIFO serves a real business need. Nowadays employers' main concern is to retain a balanced and flexible workforce.[81] This need is unlikely to be served by overemphasis on length of service.
- Current working practices show that workers are employed increasingly on short-term and temporary contracts and little premium is placed on long service by employers.
- The mere fact that a particular requirement has been widely used in the past does not make it justifiable now. Nor should it be an objective justification that LIFO is or was preferred by certain trade union negotiators.

Use of the criterion may be hard to challenge as indirect age discrimination if it is simply one of several selection criteria, especially as redundancy selection criteria may be considered a 'benefit' in age discrimination law under the EqA 2010, which requires a lower level of justification by the employer.[82]

Redundancy and disability

8.37   A disabled worker may be selected for redundancy because of failure to make reasonable adjustments to allow for his/her disability. For example, s/he may not score well on selection criteria such as hours worked, flexibility, mobility or sickness record. S/he may be unable to fulfil new flexible working practices or multiple duties. The employer needs to make appropriate reasonable adjustments by

80 *Hampson v Department of Education and Science* [1990] IRLR 302, HL.
81 IRS Employment Trends 504.
82 *Rolls Royce plc v UNITE the Union* [2009] EWCA Civ 387; [2009] IRLR 576. See para 14.22.

modifying selection criteria, eg by being careful not to hold it against a disabled worker that s/he has refused to work overtime in the past.

8.38 The employer may be expected to take a more active role in seeking appropriate alternative employment than may be required of an employer under ordinary unfair dismissal law. The duty to make reasonable adjustments applies to any suitable vacancies, eg modifications to equipment or provision of training. Chapter 15 deals with disability discrimination generally.

Preventing discriminatory dismissals

8.39 In rare cases, it may be possible to prevent a public employer embarking on a discriminatory redundancy selection policy by means of an application for judicial review in the High Court; it will be necessary clearly to establish that the policy definitely has discriminatory effect and on a fairly widespread basis.[83] With public authorities, it is arguable that they should carry out an 'equality impact assessment' before deciding what criteria to choose.[84]

Time off to look for work

8.40 An employee who is being made redundant, and who has been continuously employed for at least two years, has the right to reasonable time off during the notice period to look for a new job or make training arrangements for future employment.[85] It is irrelevant whether the employee has turned down an offer of suitable alternative employment.[86] It is not necessary to have concrete job interviews; the time can be used going into job centres, for example. There is no statutory requirement to give the employer proof of where s/he has been, though this may be relevant to whether the time was 'reasonable'.

8.41 There is no set amount of time which the employee can have off. It is a question of what is reasonable, balancing the employer's needs against the employee's. However, the employee is only entitled to be paid for a maximum of two-fifths of a week's pay for time off taken

---

83 *R v Hammersmith & Fulham LBC ex p NALGO* [1991] IRLR 249, DC.

84 See para 12.36 onwards regarding the public sector equality duty.

85 ERA 1996 s52. There are a few excepted professions. See ERA 1996 ss192, 199 and 200.

86 *Dutton v Hawker Siddeley Aviation Ltd* [1978] IRLR 390, EAT.

during the whole notice period. The employer must give the time off during working hours and cannot ask the employee to rearrange his/her hours or make up the time.[87]

Collective consultation

8.42 There are special rules under Trade Union and Labour Relations (Consolidation) Act 1992 ss188–198, whereby an employer must inform and consult with the appropriate representatives of any employees who may be affected by proposed redundancy dismissals or by measures taken in connection with those dismissals. The duty arises when an employer is proposing to dismiss as redundant 20 or more employees at one establishment within a period of 90 days or less. If the employer fails to inform or consult, the trade union or employee representative (as applicable) can bring a claim for compensation on behalf of the employees. This is known as a 'protective award'. Individual employees can only bring a claim for failure to inform or consult if there is no union or elected employee representative. As with all claims, it is important when writing the tribunal claim form to be clear if a claim for failure to inform and consult is being made under the 1992 Act, as distinct from other claims which may also be itemised on the form, eg unfair dismissal. For more detail, see chapter 2.

Redundancy and the Covid-19 pandemic

8.43 Unfortunately, the economic effect of the Covid-19 pandemic is likely to lead to a wave of redundancies. Employers will still need to follow fair and non-discriminatory selection procedures. Broadly speaking, redundancy and notice pay should be calculated on the basis of normal pay and not any reduction in pay during periods of furlough.

8.44 In relation to discrimination, the Equality and Human Rights Commission (EHRC) has advised that certain redundancy selection criteria could indirectly discriminate against groups who have taken disproportionate time off due to coronavirus, eg women who have disproportionately taken on caring responsibilities or disabled employees who have had to shield. Problematic criteria might be sick

---

87 *Ratcliffe v Dorset CC* [1978] IRLR 191, EAT.

leave taken during the pandemic; unpaid leave; productivity during the pandemic; working part-time; previously having been furloughed.[88]

8.45   In terms of unfair dismissal, one uncertainty is to what extent it can be argued that employers should have put employees on furlough (while it was available) rather than making them redundant. As always, the test is whether a reasonable employer could have decided to dismiss. Relevant considerations are likely to be whether the employer might be able to survive an interim shortfall of work or was on the point of collapse anyway; whether there was any longer-term prospect of the employee being able to be offered work; whether the employee was willing to agree furlough and a reduction of pay to the level of the 80 per cent grant; and what was happening with other employees. In one early case,[89] a tribunal found a dismissal unfair because the employer did not even consider placing the employee, a care worker, on furlough. She was made redundant because the amount of live-in work had reduced significantly due to Covid-19 and the company had no immediate work for her to do. The tribunal said this was exactly the type of situation that the furlough scheme had envisaged, and the employer had not explained why furlough was not considered suitable or even considered.

---

88   *Coronavirus (COVID-19) guidance for employers* at www.equalityhumanrights. com/en/advice-and-guidance/coronavirus-covid-19-guidance-employers.

89   *Mhindurwa v Lovingangels Care Limited* ET Case No: 3311636/2020. As an ET case, this is purely an illustration.

CHAPTER 9

Evidence in ordinary unfair dismissal cases

Chapter 9: Key points

- In an unfair dismissal claim, if dismissal is disputed, it is the employee who must prove it had taken place.
- The employer must then prove the reason why s/he dismissed the employee.
- An employee's secret recordings are not always helpful, but the employment tribunal (ET) does have power to listen to them if relevant. If producing a recording, the employee must prepare a transcript of the relevant sections and ask the employer to agree it is accurate in advance of the hearing.
- It may not breach an employee's human rights for an employer to gain evidence by covert surveillance; nor will it necessarily make a dismissal unfair.
- Verbal or written negotiations aimed at settling potential or actual litigation cannot usually be referred to at a tribunal hearing, though it is safer to use the words 'without prejudice' to make sure this is the case.
- Negotiations through the Advisory, Conciliation and Arbitration Service (ACAS), whether during the early conciliation (EC) process or during case preparation, cannot be referred to at a tribunal hearing.
- 'Legal advice privilege' keeps confidential communications between a client and professional legal adviser, even if litigation is not envisaged. This does not apply to employment consultants or other non-lawyers.
- 'Litigation privilege' keeps confidential communications between a client, his/her adviser and third parties, eg witnesses or medical experts, which come into existence for the purpose of actual or contemplated litigation.
- Parties can inadvertently or deliberately lose ('waive') their own right to insist on such confidentiality by referring to something which was said 'without prejudice' or during privileged communications. The other side can insist on maintaining confidentiality.
- The statutory rules on 'protected conversations' keep confidential from ordinary unfair dismissal hearings (though not automatic unfair dismissal or discrimination hearings) offers made and discussions held between an employer and employee before the termination of employment with a view to termination on agreed terms. This can cover conversations which would not otherwise fall into 'without prejudice' or privileged categories.

- Confidentiality on 'protected conversations' will not apply to anything improper which is said or if improper pressure is applied.
- Unlike other types of privilege, confidentiality cannot be waived on 'protected conversations', even if both sides agree.

Burden of proof

9.1   If dismissal is disputed, the burden is on the employee to prove that it occurred. Once dismissal is proved, the employer must show the reason (or if there is more than one reason, the principal reason) for the dismissal and that it was one of the potentially fair reasons set out in Employment Rights Act (ERA) 1996 s98. In cases where the employee claims automatic unfair dismissal, s/he will need to provide evidence which helps prove that the dismissal was for the automatically unfair reason.[1]

What kind of evidence is helpful?

Proving a disputed dismissal

9.2   If the employee seeks advice shortly after dismissal, it is essential to see any letter of dismissal. In any event, the employer should be asked under ERA 1996 s92 for confirmation of the dismissal and the written reasons for it.[2] Where dismissal is during pregnancy, the employers should automatically supply such a statement, whether requested or not, but it is worth asking if they do not.[3]

9.3   If there is a dispute whether the employee was actually dismissed, supporting documents and witnesses will be needed. As early as possible, try to obtain a signed statement plus the name and address of any witnesses to the dismissal. If the employer decided to dismiss before the employee knew about it, any documentary proof will be

---

1   See para 6.119 regarding the burden of proof on whistleblowing dismissals.
2   ERA 1996 s92. Note that to found a claim for compensation for supplying false reasons, those reasons must have been supplied in response to a formal written request: *Catherine Haigh Harlequin Hair Design v Seed* [1990] IRLR 175, EAT. See para 20.11 for details.
3   ERA 1996 s92(4).

helpful, eg a copy of job advertisements which had already appeared for the employee's job.

9.4   If advising on a potential constructive dismissal claim, where the employee must show a fundamental breach of contract, all contractual documents must be obtained. These may comprise a letter of appointment, statement of main terms and conditions under ERA 1996 s1, notices of variation of contract[4] and staff handbook. Also obtain the employee's resignation letter. If s/he resigned without putting anything in writing, it is important to write a letter as soon as possible, setting out what happened, unless it is now so long since the resignation that it would look very odd.

Conduct and capability dismissals

Overview

9.5   In the vast majority of conduct cases and many capability cases, the tribunal will start by considering whether the employer has adequately followed the three stages of the *Burchell* test, and will then consider whether dismissal was a fair sanction.[5] Fair procedures will be part of the consideration on fairness. It is therefore useful to consider what evidence is necessary by reference to these stages. In relation to *Burchell*, try to find out a) from the documents, b) from what the employee knows him/herself, c) from what is written in the employer's ET3, and ultimately d) from questioning the employer's witnesses at the tribunal hearing, what steps the employer took to investigate the alleged offence. You should also try to establish from the same sources what evidence the employer relied on in reaching the decision to dismiss. In general, what is important is what the employer knew or ought to have known, had s/he properly investigated at the time of dismissal. Therefore establish what the employee told the employer, or would have told the employer if s/he had had the chance. Evidence which only emerged after the dismissal or which is brought up for the first time at the tribunal hearing is not relevant to whether the dismissal was unfair unless, for example, the employee was prevented from putting such evidence forward at the time because s/he was not given the chance to answer the allegations.

9.6   There are often disputes about whether the minutes of the disciplinary or appeal hearing are accurate. It is important to keep sight of

---

4   Under ERA 1996 s4.
5   *British Home Stores Ltd v Burchell* [1978] IRLR 379, EAT. See para 7.35.

whether any inaccuracies are important in relation to what a tribunal has to decide. The tribunal will not want to get bogged down in disputes over minor details. On the other hand, the minutes of the disciplinary hearing may provide evidence as to important matters such as what charges were put to the employee, what explanation the employee gave at the time, what other witnesses said on key points and any procedural request, eg for an adjournment. Usually the formal minutes have been taken by the employer and you should obtain a copy. If the employer provides typed minutes, ask for the original hand-written notes too. The employee or his/her witness may also have written their own minutes. Check whether the employer asked the employee at the time to agree the accuracy of the minutes and if so, how long after the disciplinary hearing this happened and whether the employee noted any disagreement. If the employee has not yet seen the minutes, get these as soon as possible, while his/her memory is still fresh and s/he can check their accuracy. Also take a statement from the employee immediately as to the key aspects of the disciplinary and appeal hearings. If there is no serious dispute between the parties as to what was said at the disciplinary and appeal, it is unnecessary to ask the tribunal to read the full minutes. The key points can just be summarised in the witness statements. If there is an important dispute, identify the key sections of the minutes which the tribunal should be asked to read and, if hand-written, make sure they are legible. If not, ask the notetaker to type up the minutes prior to the tribunal hearing. Do not ask the tribunal to read the full minutes, which often consist of pages and pages of repetition, irrelevant side-issues, incoherence and unnecessary detail. See para 9.17 regarding tape recordings of the hearing.

9.7   Regarding fair procedures, the employee should be asked:

- what investigative and disciplinary hearings took place;
- who was present;
- whether s/he was advised s/he could bring a representative;
- how much warning s/he was given of the hearing;
- whether s/he knew what it would be about in advance;
- whether she was shown the key evidence against him/her before the meeting; and
- whether s/he was warned that dismissal was a possible outcome.

Obtain:

- the letters inviting the employee to the disciplinary and appeal hearings;
- any grievance investigation reports; and

- copies of any evidence, eg statements which s/he was given in advance or during the hearing.

Ask the employee at what point in the meeting s/he was told that s/he was dismissed. If the employer said something at the start of the hearing to indicate that the decision to dismiss had already been taken, this would be unfair. It is surprising how often the letter of dismissal has been typed prior to the disciplinary meeting, which is a strong indication that the hearing was a sham. The relevant provisions of the contract of employment or staff handbook should also be examined, in particular check the notice provisions, the disciplinary procedure and, if relevant, which offences are listed as disciplinary matters and what amounts to gross misconduct. Ascertain whether the contractual procedures were in fact followed.

9.8   Check the reasons for dismissal and for rejecting any appeal. These are usually set out in the letter of dismissal and the appeal outcome letter. The tribunal will read the letters, listen to the evidence and consider what were the true reasons. It is then a matter of whether a reasonable employer, relying on the evidence which was before this particular employer, could reasonably have dismissed for those reasons. In connection with the appeal, establish the employee's grounds of appeal from any letter of appeal written by him/her or as put forward verbally in the appeal meeting as recorded in the minutes. Consider whether the appeals officer properly considered the grounds of appeal, as evidenced by his/her areas of questioning at the appeal (again, check the minutes) and the reasons for refusing the appeal, which will probably be set out in a letter.

9.9   One of the considerations relevant to whether dismissal was a fair sanction, may be whether the employee had a clean disciplinary record. Find out whether the employee has received any written or verbal warnings in the past, particularly concerning the matter for which s/he was dismissed. Copies of the written warnings should be obtained. With verbal warnings, check when they were given, by whom and roughly what was said. Under some procedures, verbal warnings are recorded in writing. For dismissals for poor performance, seek documents and information to establish the nature of the criticisms by the employer, whether and when these were taken up with the employee, and obtain relevant letters of complaint or criticism and appraisals. Find out about any training and support offered. Also obtain any evidence proving the employee did carry out good work, eg performance-related bonuses or thank you letters from customers. With sickness, injury, incapability or qualification dismissals, find out what other jobs the employer had available at the relevant time.

Absenteeism and lateness

9.10 Ascertain to what extent the employee was made aware of the employer's dissatisfaction with his/her attendance and whether it was made clear that dismissal would follow a failure to improve. If there was only a general verbal warning, given to a group of employees, clarify from another of those employees what was said and whether it was clear that dismissal might ensue. Get copies of any written individual or collective warnings which the employee mentions.

9.11 Check whether the employer properly reviewed the employee's attendance record prior to giving any warning or dismissal. The employer should have consulted the employee as to the reasons for the absences or lateness. In general, consider whether the employer approached the dismissal of the employee with sympathy and understanding.

Prolonged sickness absence

9.12 If the employer obtained a medical opinion on the employee's state of health, obtain a copy of the report. It is often important also to get a copy of the employer's letter instructing the doctors. Was the employee consulted in respect of the employer's medical report? If so, copies of notes taken of the meeting and a statement from the employee on what was said should be obtained. Ask the employee whether s/he was offered the opportunity of getting his/her own medical report. Get copies of any correspondence with the employee about this.

9.13 Consider the importance of the employee's job and whether the employer could be expected to hold it open any longer. What arrangements were made during the employee's absence? What other short-term solutions were possible?[6] How soon after the dismissal was the vacancy filled?

Injury

9.14 Clarify whether the injury was such as to make the performance of the job impossible. Could the employee, through retraining or the use of

---

6 See chapter 15 if the employee's sickness may amount to a disability.

aids, have continued to do the job?[7] Was there any consultation with the employee on the medical prognosis and what s/he could do? Was the employee warned s/he may be dismissed? Get copies of any correspondence. If the employee seeks advice while still employed, the employer may have a beneficial sickness retirement scheme or medical insurance covering sick pay from which the employee can claim. Also consider whether the employee should take advice in respect of a personal/industrial injury claim if the injury occurred at work.

Qualifications

9.15 Establish whether the qualification was a term of the contract or otherwise a genuine requirement of the job. If not, the employer will find it hard to justify dismissal. If the employer has changed the requirement, why was the change necessary? Are there any other employees doing the same job who do not have the qualifications, and are new employees expected to be qualified? Also, find out whether other jobs were available which the employee was qualified to do at the time of dismissal. Get copies of all correspondence. Finally, consider whether the requirement had a discriminatory effect on the employee (see para 13.27 regarding indirect discrimination).

Redundancy dismissals

9.16 To check whether it was a genuine redundancy, find out whether a new employee has simply replaced the employee in the same job. If relevant, find out what selection criteria were adopted by the employer and how the employee was measured and scored. Were there other employees in similar jobs who were not made redundant? It is important to obtain all internal and external advertisements and vacancy lists relating to suitable vacancies at the time of dismissal and for a short period before and after. These are relevant both to the genuineness of the redundancy (advertisements for the same job) and to the availability of alternative jobs which should have been offered. The employee should be asked what other jobs s/he could and would have done for the employer and whether s/he was consulted about vacancies or doing any other work. Get copies of all correspondence related to the redundancy. See also para 8.27 regarding documents and information relevant to other employees in the selection pool where the employee is claiming unfair selection.

---

7 See chapter 15 for any protection an employee may have if the injury causes a disability.

Recorded evidence and covert surveillance

9.17   Sometimes employees secretly record conversations, meetings or disciplinary hearings with their employer. This is a risky strategy as, if they are found out, it may be a ground for dismissal. There is no public policy reason why a secret recording of a disciplinary hearing should not be heard by a tribunal, since the employer has usually intended that there is a public record of such a meeting in the form of minutes.[8] On the other hand, recordings of the disciplinary panel's private deliberations would not usually be allowed as evidence, except perhaps where they contained the only, or incontrovertible, proof of discrimination.[9] Nevertheless, in one case a tribunal allowed in secret recordings of comments made by members of a grievance panel during a break in the grievance hearing.[10] Ultimately the tribunal has to weigh up the relevance of the evidence against the public policy in allowing deliberations of disciplinary and grievance panels to be kept confidential. Covert recordings by the employee may in rare cases breach the employer's privacy contrary to Article 8 of the European Convention on Human Rights (ECHR) (right to respect for private and family life, home and correspondence),[11] but the tribunal will probably allow in the evidence if it is necessary for a fair hearing.[12] In practical terms, employees need to decide whether it is worth using any secret recordings they have obtained. Usually the tribunal will disapprove of the fact that the employee acted in an underhand manner and the value of the content needs to outweigh the bad impression it makes. There is also a risk that the tribunal will reduce compensation if it thinks the recording was intended to entrap the employer, although these days, it is so easy just to press 'record' on a mobile phone, that it may just be that the employee feels flustered or vulnerable, rather than having any intention to entrap.[13] In the context of a disciplinary hearing, where the employee's main concern is that minutes will not be accurate, it is better openly to ask the

---

8   *Chairman and Governors of Amwell View School v Dogherty* [2007] IRLR 198, EAT.

9   *Chairman and Governors of Amwell View School v Dogherty* [2007] IRLR 198, EAT. For a rare exception, see *Fleming v East of England Ambulance Service NHS Trust* UKEAT/0054/17.

10   *(1) Punjab National Bank (International) Ltd (2) Singh (3) Singh v Gosain* UKEAT/0003/14.

11   See paras 1.90 and 3.25.

12   *Jones v University of Warwick* [2003] 3 All ER 760, CA; *XXX v YYY and another* [2004] IRLR 471, CA.

13   *Phoenix House Limited v Stockman* UKEAT/0284/17 and 0058/18. See paras 18.26, 18.53 and 18.55 regarding deductions for conduct.

employer to make a recording, which can be available to both sides. Bear in mind that recordings can be long, boring and inconclusive. Moreover, the employee does not always perform well in a disciplinary hearing. If a recording is to be used, the employee should prepare a transcript well in advance of the tribunal hearing and ask the employer to agree that it is accurate. If the recordings are very long, the employee should be ready to identify which passages are important, eg because they prove some crucial evidence was given or allegation made, or because they reveal the employer's true state of mind.[14] Evidence to prove misconduct which is obtained by an employer from covert surveillance, in or outside the workplace, also potentially breaches Article 8, but not if the employer acted proportionately. Moreover, even if the tribunal disapproves, it will not make the dismissal unfair if it was fair to dismiss applying the usual test for misconduct dismissals.[15]

Without prejudice, privilege and protected conversations

Without prejudice

9.18   Statements and offers made during negotiations, whether in writing or verbally, are not generally admissible as evidence in tribunals or courts if they were genuinely aimed at settling a dispute. If an adviser or employee wants to ensure the content of settlement discussions cannot be referred to in the tribunal, s/he should write the phrase 'without prejudice' at the top of any settlement letter or say it at the start of any settlement conversation. Even if s/he fails to use the actual words, it is possible that without prejudice privilege may still apply. On the other hand, writing the phrase 'without prejudice' at the top of a letter which is not conducting a negotiation will not have the effect of keeping it off the record.[16] Settlement negotiations through the Advisory, Conciliation and Arbitration Service (ACAS), whether through the early conciliation (EC) process or during case preparation, are also kept private from the tribunal.

---

14   *Vaughan v Lewisham LBC and others* UKEAT/0534/12 is a useful guide to how lengthy recordings should be treated.

15   See *McGowan v Scottish Water* [2005] IRLR 167 and *City and County of Swansea v Gayle* [2013] IRLR 768, plus para 1.90 above.

16   *Faithorn Farrell Timms LLP v Bailey* UKEAT/0025/16; [2016] IRLR 839, EAT provides a useful summary of without prejudice privilege and its exceptions.

9.19   The reason for the without prejudice rule is public policy in encouraging settlement negotiations without parties being inhibited in case the negotiations fall through and they are quoted in the tribunal. It therefore only applies if there is a genuine dispute. There is obviously a dispute if a tribunal case has started, but the mere fact that a worker has brought a grievance may not amount to a dispute because it could in theory be upheld by the employer.[17] Without prejudice privilege can apply before litigation has started provided the parties have contemplated – or might reasonably have contemplated – that litigation will occur if they cannot agree.[18] In rare circumstances, the without prejudice protection will not apply, eg because it would hide an unambiguous impropriety (see para 16.34 for an example) or because both parties have waived privilege. The case-law regarding these exceptions can be complicated and is beyond the scope of this book. The problem with the without prejudice rule is that employees may need to refer to something said to them in without prejudice discussions in order to prove their tribunal case. For example, employees need to be careful about resigning because of something said during without prejudice discussions, because they may find they are unable to refer to this in their constructive dismissal claim.[19]

Privilege

9.20   The law of privilege is important because it keeps certain communications private. It can get very complicated, but here are a few key points. 'Legal advice privilege' protects confidential communications between a client and his/her professional adviser made for the purpose of giving or seeking legal advice, regardless of whether litigation is envisaged. For example, it covers conversations between employers and their solicitors during a disciplinary process. It applies to the advice of solicitors, barristers or other lawyers acting in that capacity and not, for example, to advice given as a friend. It does not apply to advice from non-qualified employment consultants or other non-lawyers.[20] 'Litigation privilege' is different, though both types of

---

17 *BNP Paribas v Mezzotero* [2004] IRLR 508, EAT.

18 *Framlington Group Ltd and Axa Framlington Group Ltd v Barnetson* [2007] EWCA Civ 502; [2007] IRLR 598.

19 *Brodie v Nicola Ward t/a First Steps Nursery* UKEAT/0526/07. For correspondence headed 'without prejudice save as to costs', see para 20.259.

20 *New Victoria Hospital v Ryan* [1993] IRLR 202, EAT; *R (Prudential plc and another) v Special Commissioner of Income Tax and another* [2013] UKSC 1.

privilege can apply in some situations. It protects confidential communications between a client, his/her legal adviser (whether or not a qualified lawyer) and a third party, eg a medical expert or witness, where such communication comes into existence for the dominant purpose of use in connection with actual or contemplated litigation. It is not enough that it is created for another purpose, eg resolving a grievance, where litigation is only vaguely in mind.[21] A party can lose privilege by 'waiving' it, eg by selectively quoting parts of a confidential document or advice to support his/her case.[22] Again, the rules around this are complex and it is best to be careful.

Protected conversations

9.21   The law on 'protected conversations' was introduced in 2013 to keep certain discussions off the record which would not otherwise be caught by the rules on 'without prejudice' negotiations and legal advice or litigation privilege. Under ERA 1996 s111A, evidence of pre-termination negotiations cannot be referred to in unfair dismissal claims. This covers any offer made or discussions held, before the termination of the employment in question, with a view to the employment being terminated on terms agreed between the employer and the employee. In some cases, a tribunal may have to be told what was said in the allegedly pre-termination negotiations in order to decide as a preliminary issue when termination took place. However, once the termination date is decided, the tribunal cannot take into account evidence of any negotiations before the termination date in deciding the rest of the unfair dismissal claim including whether there was a dismissal or constructive dismissal and whether the dismissal was fair.[23] The fact as well as the content of the discussions must be kept off the record. Where there is a gap in open correspondence, employment tribunals (ETs) should proceed on the assumption that there were no communications relevant to their decision on the unfair dismissal claim.[24]

9.22   If the tribunal believes anything said or done in the pre-termination negotiations was improper, or connected with improper behaviour, evidence of the protected conversation can be excluded

---

21 *Howes v Hinckley & Bosworth BC* UKEAT/0213/08.

22 *Brennan and others v Sunderland City Council and others* UKEAT/0349/08 and *Watson v Hilary Meredith Solicitors Limited and Meredith* UKEAT/0092/20 usefully summarise the case-law around waiver, including selective waiver.

23 *Basra v BJSS Ltd* UKEAT/0090/17.

24 *Faithorn Farrell Timms LLP v Bailey* UKEAT/0025/16; [2016] IRLR 839, EAT.

only to the extent that the tribunal thinks just.[25] ACAS has produced a Code of Practice on Settlement Agreements which sets out good practice.[26] It recommends face-to-face negotiations and that an employee is allowed to bring a work colleague or trade union representative. The Code gives guidance as to what might be considered improper, eg:

- bullying and intimidation;
- discrimination;
- putting undue pressure on the other party, such as the employer not giving a reasonable amount of time for consideration of an offer (normally ten calendar days) or telling the employee that s/he will be dismissed if s/he refuses the offer, or the employee threatening to damage the employer's reputation (except where that would be legitimate whistleblowing).

9.23 An example of a protected conversation would be where an employer approaches an employee to say that things are not working out and offers him/her six months' pay if s/he agrees to leave. The employee may turn down this offer, but if s/he is later dismissed and brings an unfair dismissal claim, s/he cannot refer to the fact that this offer had been made at an earlier stage. Nor, for that matter, can the employer refer to it. It would also seem that the employee cannot resign and claim constructive unfair dismissal on the basis that the offer amounted to a breach of trust and confidence, unless there was something 'improper' about the discussion.

9.24 Privilege on the 'protected conversation' cannot be waived and the parties cannot agree that the conversation is put before the tribunal.[27]

9.25 The 'protected conversations' rule only applies to ordinary unfair dismissal claims and not to other claims such as for automatic unfair dismissal or discrimination. Where an employee claims both unfair dismissal and discrimination, it is therefore possible for the protected conversation to be inadmissible for the unfair dismissal claim but admissible for the discrimination claim.[28]

---

25 ERA 1996 s111A(4).
26 *Code of Practice 4: Settlement Agreements (under section 111A of the Employment Rights Act 1996)*, July 2013, available on the ACAS website at: www.acas.org. uk/code-of-practice-settlement-agreements.pdf. ACAS has also produced non-statutory, *Settlement agreements: guidance*. The guidance can be accessed at: www.acas.org.uk/settlement-agreements.
27 *Faithorn Farrell Timms LLP v Bailey* UKEAT/0025/16; [2016] IRLR 839.
28 *Faithorn Farrell Timms LLP v Bailey* UKEAT/0025/16; [2016] IRLR 839.

CHAPTER 10

TUPE

Chapter 10: Key points

- The Transfer of Undertakings (Protection of Employment) Regulations (TUPE Regs) 2006 replaced the TUPE Regs 1981. Further amendments were made in January 2014.
- The TUPE Regs protect employees on transfer of the business in which they are employed.
- Many situations are covered by the TUPE Regs 2006, and a purposive approach should be adopted. The mechanism of the transfer does not matter, provided there is a change of legal person responsible for running the undertaking who acts as employer.
- The TUPE Regs 2006 have two different definitions of transfer: 1) business transfers; and 2) service provision changes. The latter category was explicitly added to the regulations in 2006.
- A 'business transfer' is a transfer of an economic entity (an organised grouping of resources) which retains its identity after transfer.
- A 'service provision change' covers contracting out of services; services reverting in-house; and the transfer of the service between two successive contractors.
- Protected employees are those who are employed immediately before the transfer or who are dismissed in advance because of the transfer, unless their dismissal was for an economic, technical or organisational (ETO) reason entailing changes in the workforce.
- Where part of an undertaking is transferred, an employee must have been assigned to that part, even if s/he has carried out some duties for non-transferred parts.
- It is automatically unfair to dismiss (or constructively dismiss) an employee because of the transfer. It is not automatically unfair if the dismissal is for an ETO reason entailing changes in the workforce, in which case the ordinary test of fairness will apply. The normal eligibility rules for claiming unfair dismissal apply to both situations.
- Where an employee is covered, rights, liabilities and contractual terms transfer, eg wages owed, liability for previous discriminatory acts and continuous service, but the pension situation is complex. Where a term is linked to a collective agreement, the incorporation of the collective agreement for that term does not transfer if the new employer is not a party to the collective bargaining process.

- An agreement to change an employee's terms and conditions is void if it is because of the transfer. There are several exceptions including variations for an ETO reason and changes to collectively agreed terms taking effect more than one year after the transfer if overall the terms are no less favourable.
- There used to be special requirements and guidance for parts of the public sector under the Cabinet Office Statement of Practice and various Codes of Practice. These included safeguards against development of a two-tier workforce. The Statement of Practice has now been revised and the codes for England and Wales have been abolished. However, the Welsh Government has introduced a revised code.
- For collective consultation on transfers, see paras 2.31–2.39.
- It is arguable, but not tested in the higher courts, that workers who are not employees have certain rights on transfer.
- Discrimination law (with no minimum service requirement) applies if the new employer refuses to take on workers or treats them less favourably because of a protected characteristic, eg race or disability.
- Contracting out plays havoc with equal pay protection, since contracted-out employees cannot usually compare their pay with employees retained in-house (see para 5.20).

General guide to useful evidence

- Evidence comparing the nature of the undertaking before and after the transfer by reference to factors such as location, staff, customers, product and service.
- Legal and other documents relating to the transfer and any related transfers of assets and staff. Consultation documents with the trade union/employee representatives. Letters to employees.

The Transfer of Undertakings Regulations

10.1   The Transfer of Undertakings (Protection of Employment) Regulations (TUPE Regs) 2006[1] protect employees' rights on transfer of the business in which they are employed. Where there is a

---

1   SI No 246.

transfer to which the TUPE Regs 2006 apply, the new employer effectively stands in the shoes of the old employer, and employees maintain continuous service for the purpose of all statutory rights. The TUPE Regs 2006 also transfer the existing contractual terms and conditions, as well as any outstanding liabilities and rights.[2] An employee, regardless of his/her length of service, can claim automatic unfair dismissal if s/he is dismissed for asserting his/her statutory rights under TUPE.[3] In practice, however, the most important protection is against unfair dismissal because of the transfer, but employees must have at least two years' service to make such a claim.[4] The TUPE Regs 2006 potentially apply to a transfer from the UK to a business which is based outside the UK and even outside the European Union (EU).[5]

10.2   The TUPE Regs were originally brought in to implement the European Acquired Rights Directive, also known as the Business Transfers Directive.[6] This means they should be interpreted as far as possible in line with decisions of the Court of Justice of the European Union (CJEU) under the directive.[7] The law is difficult and constantly developing through decisions of the courts. The 2006 TUPE Regs made some changes from the earlier 1981 TUPE Regs which they replaced, and in limited respects gave additional rights to those in the directive. Further changes were made in January 2014. There is a guide to the 2006 Regs produced by the then Department for Business, Innovation & Skills (BIS). The guide, which is aimed at employees, employers and representatives, was issued in 2006 and revised in 2014.[8] It is helpful, but it has no legal status.

10.3   An employment tribunal (ET) has said that workers, and not just employees, are also covered by the legislation as a result of the EU

---

2 TUPE Regs 2006 reg 4.

3 See paras 6.78–6.81.

4 The usual qualifying requirements for claiming unfair dismissal apply.

5 *Holis Metal Industries Ltd v GMB and another* [2008] IRLR 187, EAT.

6 Currently 2001/23/EC, which updates and consolidates previous directives.

7 See chapter 3 where there is a conflict between the TUPE Regs and the directive.

8 *Employment rights on the transfer of an undertaking: a guide to the 2006 TUPE Regulations (as amended by the Collective Redundancies and Transfer of Undertakings (Protection of Employment) (Amendment) Regulations 2014) for employees, employers and representatives*, Department for Business, Innovation & Skills (BEIS), January 2014, available at: https://assets.publishing.service.gov. uk/government/uploads/system/uploads/attachment_data/file/275252/bis-14-502-employment-rights-on-the-transfer-of-an-undertaking.pdf.

directive.[9] This is untested in the appeal courts. It raises difficult questions as to which rights would be protected, as presumably workers could not be given rights which ordinarily (aside from TUPE) only employees have.

What is the method of transfer?

10.4 Much of the case-law has concerned when the TUPE Regs apply. This means looking at what form of transfer, as well as what kind of undertaking, is covered. A transfer may occur in many different ways, although the most common means is by a straightforward sale of a business, eg a restaurant chain under a brand name is sold by one company to another with little visible change. It may also take place by some other form of disposition such as granting a lease, franchise, contract or gift, even if ownership of physical property has not been transferred. Note that a share take-over is not in itself a transfer, since ownership remains in the same legal person, ie the company.[10] However, a share sale could be accompanied or followed by a transfer.[11]

10.5 A transfer may take place as a result of a series of transactions[12] provided the business retains its identity, for example:

- A factory is transferred back from a lessee to the owner, who then sells it on to another company.[13]
- An NHS Trust cleaning contract can transfer between two successive contractors (the first contractor hands back the cleaning services at the end of its contract, which are immediately transferred on to the second contractor).

There will be a particular date at which the transfer is considered to take place and the employees' contract rights transfer.[14]

---

9 *Dewhurst and others v Revisecatch Ltd t/a Ecourier and another* ET Case No: 2201909/2018.

10 *Brookes and others v Borough Care Services and another* [1998] ICR 1198, EAT.

11 *Millam v Print Factory (London) 1991 Ltd* [2007] IRLR 526, CA, though this very much depends on the facts.

12 TUPE Regs 2006 reg 3(6)(a).

13 *P Bork International A/S v Foreningenaf Arbedjsledere i Danmark* [1989] IRLR 41, ECJ.

14 *Celtec Ltd v Astley and others* [2005] IRLR 647, ECJ. But see also *Metropolitan Resources Ltd v (1) Churchill Dulwich Ltd – in liquidation (2) Martin Cambridge and others* UKEAT/0286/08; [2009] IRLR 700.

What is a relevant transfer?

10.6   There are two forms of transfer under the TUPE Regs 2006:

1) The first type follows the original definition and case-law under the TUPE Regs 1981 and derives from the EU directive. It is set out from para 10.7 below. Since 2006, this has become known as a 'business transfer'.

2) The second type of transfer, introduced in the TUPE Regs 2006, is referred to as a 'service provision change', and is set out from para 10.13 below.

The 'business transfer' definition can still be used for contracting out by public authorities, as indeed it was prior to 2006, but the 'service provision change' definition more naturally applies to that situation and should have fewer legal problems in doing so.

Business transfers

Overview

10.7   Under TUPE Regs 2006 reg 3(1)(a), a transfer of an undertaking or business occurs when there is a transfer of an economic entity which retains its identity. An 'economic entity' means an organised grouping of resources which has the objective of pursuing an economic activity, whether that activity is central or ancillary.[15] This definition was re-worded in the TUPE Regs 2006 to reflect the case-law which had already developed under the TUPE Regs 1981. There are two stages which must be proved:[16]

1) that the undertaking was a stable economic entity prior to transfer; and

2) that the entity was transferred in a recognisable form.

The following are broad guidelines taken from the case-law as to when TUPE will apply, but the particular facts of every case will be important. It should also be remembered that most of the case-law on the business transfers definition developed before the TUPE Regs 2006 came into force.

---

15 TUPE Regs 2006 reg 3(2).

16 *Whitewater Leisure Management Ltd v Barnes and others* [2000] IRLR 456, EAT; and see *Cheesman and others v R Brewer Contracts Ltd* [2001] IRLR 145, EAT for a useful summary of the principles.

Stage 1: stable economic entity

10.8 The undertaking transferred must be a stable economic entity, but it need not own any tangible assets. For example, it could be a labour-only contract such as the provision of cleaning services or management of a shopping centre. It is not necessary for property to be transferred by the transferee to the transferor.[17] An organised grouping of wage-earners who are specifically and permanently assigned to a common task may amount to an economic entity.[18] Relevant factors to consider are the entity's workforce, management staff, the way work is organised, its operating methods and where appropriate, the operational resources available to it.[19] A single employee such as a cleaner can amount to an entity depending on the facts, eg if the task to be performed is complex and sophisticated and requires careful planning, specification and costings.[20]

10.9 Either the whole undertaking or a severable part of it must be transferred, eg the transfer of one shop in a chain or contracting out a cleaning or catering service. Non-commercial ventures are covered,[21] eg non-profit enterprises, voluntary organisations, free advice centres, charities, NHS trusts[22] and local education services.[23] It can include transfers between subsidiary companies within a corporate group.[24] An administrative reorganisation or transfer of administrative functions between public administrative authorities is not covered.[25] The scope of this exclusion is not entirely clear, but certain intra-governmental transfers may not be covered by TUPE. The rights of public sector employees in these instances are intended to be covered by other means, ie certain case-specific specialist legislation and various public sector Codes.

---

17 TUPE Regs 2006 reg 3(6)(b).
18 *Sánchez Hidalgo v Asociación de Servicios Aser* [1999] IRLR 136, ECJ; *Francisco Hernández Vidal SA v Gomez Pérez* C-127/96, [1999] IRLR 132, ECJ; *Cheesman and others v R Brewer Contracts Ltd* [2001] IRLR 145, EAT.
19 *Sánchez Hidalgo v Asociación de Servicios Aser* [1999] IRLR 136, ECJ; *Francisco Hernández Vidal SA v Gomez Pérez* C-127/96, [1999] IRLR 132, ECJ; *Cheesman and others v R Brewer Contracts Ltd* [2001] IRLR 145, EAT.
20 *Dudley Bower Building Services Ltd v Lowe* [2003] IRLR 260, EAT.
21 *Dr Sophie Redmond Stichting v Bartol and others* [1992] IRLR 366, ECJ.
22 *Porter and Nanayakkara v Queen's Medical Centre (Nottingham University Hospital)* [1993] IRLR 486, HC.
23 *Kenny and others v South Manchester College* [1993] IRLR 265, QBD.
24 *Allen and others v Amalgamated Construction Co Ltd* [2000] IRLR 119, ECJ.
25 *Henke v Gemeinde Schierke and Verwaltungsgemeinschaft 'Brocken'* [1996] IRLR 701, ECJ; TUPE Regs 2006 reg 3(5).

Stage 2: transferred in a recognisable form

10.10   The undertaking must be transferred in a recognisable form from one employer to another. The overall test is whether the business in question retains its identity, this being indicated in particular by the continuation or resumption of its operation by the new employer.[26] The greater the similarity between the business run before and after the transfer, the more likely it is to satisfy this test. So, for example, a chocolate factory which is sold to be converted into a nightclub, would be a mere sale of assets and not of an undertaking. However, the business need not be identical before and afterwards in the way that it is run.

10.11   Case-law has suggested certain guidelines in deciding whether a business has retained enough of its identity on transfer to be covered by the 'business transfers' definition, although no single factor needs to be present in every case and an overall assessment must be made. In weighting factors, the type of undertaking must also be taken into account.[27] Employment tribunals must take a purposive approach, ie remember that the purpose of the TUPE Regs 2006 and the directive is to protect employees. Relevant factors[28] will be:

- the type of business or undertaking concerned; its size is irrelevant;
- whether the business's tangible assets, such as buildings and equipment, are transferred. For example, catering is an activity essentially based on equipment; it is therefore important whether the equipment is transferred.[29] It is not essential that ownership (as opposed to use) of assets is transferred.[30] For example, if a hospital provides a kitchen and equipment for its contract caterers, it is enough if both transferor and transferee use that same equipment.[31] If the business solely comprises services, transfer of assets will be particularly unimportant;

---

26   *Spijkers v Gebroeders Benedik Abbatoir CV* [1986] CMLR 296, ECJ.

27   *Allen and others v Amalgamated Construction Co Ltd* [2000] IRLR 119, ECJ.

28   Sometimes referred to as the *Spijkers* factors. Set out by the European Court of Justice (ECJ) in *Spijkers v Gebroeders Benedik Abbatoir CV* [1986] 2 CMLR 296, ECJ and confirmed in numerous cases including *Dr Sophie Redmond Stichting v Bartol and others* [1992] IRLR 366, ECJ.

29   *Abler and others v Sodexho MM Catering Gesellschaft mbH and Sanrest Großküchen Betriebsgesellschaft mbH (intervener)* [2004] IRLR 168, ECJ.

30   *Allen and others v Amalgamated Construction Co Ltd* [2000] IRLR 119, ECJ.

31   *Abler and others v Sodexho MM Catering Gesellschaft mbH and Sanrest Großküchen Betriebsgesellschaft mbH (intervener)* [2004] IRLR 168, ECJ.

- the value of the intangible assets, eg goodwill, at the time of transfer and whether they are transferred;
- in a labour-intensive undertaking, whether or not the majority of employees are taken over by the new employer;[32] in an undertaking based significantly on tangible assets, whether these have transferred;[33] however, these are just factors – the fact that no assets are transferred in an 'asset-reliant' undertaking, does not necessarily mean there is no TUPE transfer.[34] Indeed, it is not always possible or necessary to characterise a business exclusively as 'labour-intensive' or 'asset-reliant';[35]
- whether customers are transferred;
- the degree of similarity between the activities carried on before and after the transfer;
- the period, if any, during which those activities are suspended.

It does not matter if the new employer intends to integrate the transferred undertaking into his/her own business, provided that immediately after transfer the entity carries on the same activities as before and so retains its identity.[36] To say otherwise would make the TUPE Regs 2006 largely ineffective as every business is likely to wish to integrate any new business it has acquired. However, the ECJ has stated, rather unintelligibly, that if there are organisational changes post transfer, there must still be a 'functional link of interdependence and complementarity between the various elements of production transferred'.[37] It is also possible that an identifiable economic entity is divided into two parts, both of which are transferred. For example, a service providing refuse collection to a whole borough may be divided geographically into the north and south of the borough on transfer to two new contractors. Depending on the facts, this does not necessarily prevent there being a transfer.[38]

10.12   Applying these guidelines tends to be difficult. For example, in one case[39] there was found to be a transfer of an undertaking to provide medical services, although the method of provision would change. The object of the undertaking remained the same, even

---

32 See comments at para 10.14 regarding *Süzen* and contracting out.

33 *Oy Liikenne AB v Liskojärui and Juntunen* [2001] IRLR 171, ECJ.

34 *Balfour Beatty Power Networks Ltd and another v Wilcox* [2007] IRLR 63, CA.

35 *Balfour Beatty Power Networks Ltd and another v Wilcox* [2007] IRLR 63, CA.

36 *Farmer v Danzas (UK) Ltd* (1995) 518 IRLB 14, EAT.

37 *Klarenberg v Ferrotron Technologies GmbH* [2009] IRLR 301, ECJ.

38 *Fairhurst Ward Abbotts Ltd v Botes Building Ltd* [2004] IRLR 304, CA.

39 *Porter and Nanayakkara v Queen's Medical Centre (Nottingham University Hospital)* [1993] IRLR 486, HC.

though the method of achieving that object changed as medical science developed. By contrast, there was no transfer where an NHS Trust hospital shop selling newspapers, magazines, confectionery and flowers was changed on transfer to a major chain convenience store with a much wider range of goods, longer opening hours and a more commercial outlook. The ET considered that the identity of the original shop had been replaced by an entirely new and different concept.[40] These examples are simply illustrative. It is essential to give detailed examination to all the facts.

Contracting out – service provision changes

Applying the business transfers definition

10.13 The principle that the TUPE Regs can cover the contracting out of services, often as a result of a compulsory competitive tendering exercise in the public sector, was well-established prior to the 2006 amendments.[41] Contracting out situations can therefore still be covered under the original 'business transfers' definition. However, the wording of the EU directive and the definition of business transfers is not always adequate to cover the situations which arise. Many problems arose under the 1981 TUPE Regs.

10.14 Applying the business transfers definition, the ECJ in *Süzen* said that an 'entity' cannot be reduced to the activity it is carrying out. An entity's identity also emerges from other factors, eg workforce, management structure, operating methods and resources. Therefore, in a labour-intensive sector, where there is no transfer of significant tangible or intangible assets, there may be no transfer unless the new employer takes over a major part of the employees (in terms of numbers and skills).[42] However, following this decision, the Court of Appeal said repeatedly that the importance of *Süzen* has been overstated. It is still necessary to consider all the facts characterising the transaction in question. The failure to appoint any of the former employees does not point conclusively against a transfer. It is relevant to consider why the employees were not taken on, eg whether it

---

40 *(1) Matthieson (2) Cheyne v United News Shops Ltd* EAT 554/94. Similar issues arise in regard to the service provision change definition: see para 10.17.

41 *Rask and Christensen v ISS Kantineservice A/S* [1993] IRLR 133, ECJ; *Dines and others v (1) Initial Health Care Services Ltd (2) Pall Mall Services Group Ltd* [1994] IRLR 336; [1995] ICR 11, CA.

42 *Süzen v Zehnacker Gebäudereinigung GmbH Krankenhausservice* [1997] IRLR 255, ECJ; *Allen and others v Amalgamated Construction Co Ltd* [2000] IRLR 119, ECJ.

was a deliberate attempt to avoid the TUPE Regs.[43] The intention of the parties and the fact that the transferee tendered on the basis that TUPE applied would also be helpful.[44]

10.15 Under this definition, the undertaking must be a stable economic entity and not one where the contracted service is itself of limited duration, whoever is running it. For example, in one case the transfer of part of a building contract for the construction of a canteen was not covered by the TUPE Regs.[45] It is different where complete works projects are transferred.[46]

10.16 Examples where the original TUPE Regs applied include:

- the contracting out of cleaning services by a bank which had previously employed one cleaner to do the work;[47]
- the transfer of hospital cleaning services from one contractor at the end of its contract to another;[48]
- a college's termination of a catering contract in order to provide its own catering service;[49]
- the contracting out to a college of prison education previously provided by the local education authority;[50]
- the transfer of a subsidy or grant by a public body, eg a local authority, from one advice agency to another with similar aims.[51]

Service provision changes – the 2006 definition

10.17 Subject to specified exceptions, the former Labour government wanted the TUPE Regs to apply to all contracting out situations, without the legal complications and uncertainties set out above. In

43 *ECM (Vehicle Delivery Service) v Cox* [1999] IRLR 559, CA; *ADI (UK) Ltd v Willer and others* [2001] IRLR 542, CA; *RCO Support Services Ltd v UNISON* [2002] IRLR 401, CA.

44 *Lightways (Contractors) Ltd v Associated Holdings Ltd* [2000] IRLR 247, CS.

45 *Ledernes Hovedorganisation, acting on behalf of Ole Rygaard v Dansk Arbejdsgiverforening, acting on behalf of Stro Molle Akustik A/S* [1996] IRLR 51, ECJ. This principle should not be applied too widely: *BSG Property Services v Tuck* [1996] IRLR 134, EAT.

46 *Allen and others v Amalgamated Construction Co Ltd* [2000] IRLR 119, ECJ.

47 *Schmidt v Spar-und Leihkasse der früheren Ämter Bordesholm, Kiel und Kronshagen* [1994] IRLR 302, ECJ.

48 *Dines and others v (1) Initial Health Care Services Ltd (2) Pall Mall Services Group Ltd* [1995] ICR 11; [1994] IRLR 336, CA.

49 *Campion-Hall v (1) Wain (2) Gardner Merchant Ltd* (1996) 561 IDS Employment Law Brief 5, EAT.

50 *Kenny and another v South Manchester College* [1993] ICR 934; [1993] IRLR 265, QBD.

51 *Dr Sophie Redmond Stichting v Bartol and others* [1992] IRLR 366, ECJ.

2006, it therefore introduced an additional definition of a transfer. Under TUPE Regs 2006 reg 3(1)(b), service provision changes are explicitly covered.

10.18   Service provision changes cover any stage of the contracting out or outsourcing process, ie the original grant of a contract, reassignment of the contract to a different contractor, and taking the service back in-house. The definition refers to a situation where 'activities cease to be carried out' by one person (whether the original contracting body or a contractor) and 'are carried out instead' by another person, eg a new contractor or reverting back to the contracting body. It must also be the case that:

i)   immediately before the change, there is an organised grouping of employees, which has as its principal purpose the carrying out of the activities concerned on behalf of the client (the contracting body); and

ii)   the client intends that, following the service provision change, the activities will be carried out by the transferee.[52]

The client must remain the same for the definition to apply.[53] It is possible for a sub-contractor to have the contracting body as its client even though there is no contractual relationship between them and the sub-contractor has only contracted with the contractor.[54] The important question will be whether the sub-contractor was carrying out the activities for the client.

10.19   The advantage of the service provision change wording is that it focuses on whether the activities remain the same, as opposed to whether employees or assets transfer. Minor changes in the way activities will be carried out by the transferee are within the definition.[55] Nor does it matter if the transferee carries out the activities in a new or innovative way, eg by computerisation.[56] The test is 'whether the activities carried on by the alleged transferee are fundamentally

---

52   TUPE Regs 2006 reg 3(3)(a).

53   *Hunter v McCarrick* [2012] EWCA Civ 1399; [2013] IRLR 26; *Taurus Group Ltd v (1) Crofts (2) Securitas Security Services (UK) Ltd* UKEAT/0024/12; *SNR Denton UK LLP v Kirwan and others* [2012] IRLR 966, EAT; *Horizon Security Services Ltd v Ndeze* UKEAT/0071/14; [2014] IRLR 854.

54   *Jinks v Havering LBC* UKEAT/0157/14.

55   *Metropolitan Resources Ltd v (1) Churchill Dulwich Ltd – in liquidation (2) Martin Cambridge and others* UKEAT/0286/08; [2009] IRLR 700.

56   Example given by the government at paras 27–29 of the Public Consultation Document with the draft revised regulations, URN 05/926, at: http:// webarchive.nationalarchives.gov.uk/20090609003228/http://www.berr.gov.uk/ files/file16389.pdf.

or essentially the same as those carried out by the alleged trans-feror'.[57] For example, in one case where the activity was the provision of accommodation for asylum-seekers, a difference in location and the provision of a few extra ancillary services was not enough to make it a different activity.[58] However, in another case, the provision of a hot cooked canteen service was not the same 'activity' as selling sand-wiches at a kiosk.[59] Borderline situations arise when public authorit-ies transfer care from residential homes to the community. It does not matter if the service is split in two after the transfer, but if the service becomes completely fragmented, there may be no service provision change. Depending on the facts, this might apply for example where a service is split amongst a large number of transfer-ees and where the service users are also split and randomly allocated amongst the transferees.

10.20   An 'organised grouping of employees' can comprise one employee.[60] However, the definition does not apply if there is no identifiable employee or group of employees in the first place, eg the client grants a contract for courier services, but prior to this, courier services were carried out by various different couriers on an ad hoc basis, as opposed to a permanent dedicated team. The employees must have been deliberately organised for the purpose of carrying out the activities for the particular client. TUPE may not apply if, for example, call centre workers provide IT support services to callers from a number of different schools without differentiating, but just one of those schools decides to get its support services from a differ-ent organisation. It is not enough that coincidentally a particular group of employees happens to work on tasks benefiting a particular client, eg because shifts coincide.[61] Difficulties may also arise where

---

57 *Metropolitan Resources Ltd v (1) Churchill Dulwich Ltd – in liquidation (2) Martin Cambridge and others* UKEAT/0286/08; [2009] IRLR 700; *OCS Group UK Ltd v Jones and Ciliza* UKEAT/0038/09; TUPE Regs 2006 reg 3(2A). Similar issues arise under the business transfers definition: see para 10.12.

58 *Metropolitan Resources Ltd v (1) Churchill Dulwich Ltd – in liquidation (2) Martin Cambridge and others* UKEAT/0286/08; [2009] IRLR 700. For another example, see *The Salvation Army Trustee Company v Bahi and others* UKEAT/0120/16; [2017] IRLR 410.

59 *OCS Group UK Ltd v Jones and Ciliza* UKEAT/0038/09.

60 TUPE Regs 2006 reg 2(1). *Rynda (UK) Ltd v Rhijnsburger* [2015] EWCA Civ 75; [2015] IRLR 394.

61 *Eddie Stobart Ltd v Moreman and others* UKEAT/0023/11; [2012] IRLR 356; *Seawell Ltd v (1) Ceva Freight (UK) Ltd (2) Moffat* UKEATS/0034/11; [2012] IRLR 802; *Rynda (UK) Ltd v Rhijnsburger* [2015] EWCA Civ 75; [2015] IRLR 394.

a group of employees spend part of their time carrying out the relevant activities, but spend the rest of their time on other activities.[62]

10.21   Contracts which the client genuinely intends to be for single specific events or short-term tasks are excluded, eg organising a conference or transporting schoolchildren to a temporary school location while the usual school building is repaired. What amounts to 'short-term' depends on the overall context, eg a council usually grants school bus driving contracts for five years but on this occasion, a contract is granted for only one year. If there is a change of contractor in the middle of a contract, the question is how long the remainder of the contract is intended to last, not the overall time taken for the project.[63] Remember that the question is how long the client *intends* the task to last at the time of granting the contract, not how long it turns out to last in practice.[64] Useful evidence of the client's intentions might be any time estimate contained in the contract or complaints about delays during the performance of the contract. It is not enough for the client to hope the task will be short-term if it has no control over how long the task will take, eg a council seeking a contractor to look after a person with learning difficulties until the Court of Protection agrees to allow the individual to be moved to a different town.[65] The exclusion applies either in the case of a single specific event or in the case of a task of short-term duration. It is not necessary for both to apply.[66] Contracts wholly or mainly for the supply of goods as opposed to services are also excluded,[67] eg supplying sandwiches to a staff canteen to sell on, as opposed to running the canteen, or providing computer equipment as opposed to a trouble-shooting support service.

Public sector transfers

10.22   The Labour government in the early 2000s issued a number of codes and similar documents to encourage fair treatment of transferred

---

62   For an example of the meaning of 'principal purpose', see *Tees Esk & Wear Valley NHS Foundation Trust v Harland and others* UKEAT/0173/16; [2017] IRLR 486.

63   *Swanbridge Hire & Sales Ltd v Butler and others* UKEAT/0056/13.

64   *Swanbridge Hire & Sales Ltd v Butler and others* UKEAT/0056/13.

65   *Robert Sage Ltd (t/a Prestige Nursing Care Ltd) v O'Connell* [2014] IRLR 428, EAT; *Horizon Security Services Ltd v Ndeze* [2014] IRLR 854, EAT.

66   *Liddell's Coaches v Cook, Gold and Abbey Coaches Ltd* UKEATS/0025/12 – the Scottish EAT disagreeing with the obiter comments of the EAT President in *SNR Denton UK LLP v Kirwan and others* [2012] IRLR 966, EAT.

67   TUPE Regs 2006 reg 3(3).

workers in England and Wales. The codes were subsequently withdrawn by the Conservative and Liberal Democrat coalition except in residual cases where they were incorporated in the terms of existing contracts with external providers., Instead of the codes, the Cabinet Office issued some voluntary good practice principles: *Principles of good employment practice: a statement of principles that reflect good employment practice for government, contracting authorities and suppliers.*[68]

10.23 The Cabinet Office *Statement of practice on staff transfers in the public sector* was revised in December 2013 together with its important annex (revised October 2013): *A fair deal for staff pensions: staff transfer from central government.*[69] The guidance applies directly to central government departments, agencies, the NHS, maintained schools (except where they are covered for other arrangements for local government) and any other parts of the public sector under the control of government ministers where staff are eligible to be members of a public service pension scheme.

10.24 On 2 July 2015, the Welsh Government introduced its own *Revised code of practice on workforce matters* aimed at various public bodies in Wales including councils, fire and rescue authorities, NHS Trusts and the governing bodies of maintained schools.[70] Known informally as the 'Two-tier Workforce Code', this is also aimed at preventing a two-tier workforce. In Scotland, the Scottish Executive and Scottish TUC (Trades Union Congress) agreed a Protocol in 2002 which was similar to the former codes.[71] It is unclear whether this is still in usage.

10.25 The rest of this chapter sets out the general law under the TUPE Regs 2006 and, if relevant, indicates what the remaining codes say on the matter.

10.26 From time to time, legislation affecting transfers of employees between different public sector bodies sets out statutory rules which mirror those of TUPE. For example, in the past when local health authority staff transferred to NHS Trusts. This is important where

---

68 Available at: www.gov.uk/government/uploads/system/uploads/attachment_data/file/62089/principles-good-employment.pdf.

69 The Statement of Practice is available via links at: www.gov.uk/government/publications/staff-transfers-in-the-public-sector. The Fair Deal guidance is available at: www.gov.uk/government/publications/fair-deal-guidance.

70 Available at: https://gov.wales/transferring-public-sector-staff-tupe-code-practice.

71 *Public Private Partnerships in Scotland – Protocol and guidance concerning employment issues,* 2002.

TUPE might not otherwise apply eg because what has occurred is an administrative reorganisation in the public sector (see para 10.9).

Which workers are protected?

10.27 The TUPE Regs 2006 protect employees who are employed by the transferor and assigned to the organised grouping of resources or employees immediately before,[72] ie at the moment of,[73] the transfer. It is irrelevant if the employee is off work at the time of the transfer due to sickness, holidays, maternity leave, etc.[74] The employee will usually transfer if s/he would have been required to work on the transferring activities if s/he had not been absent. Some situations may depend on the facts, eg absence due to a disciplinary suspension where it is unclear if the worker will be returned to the same post; a long-term sickness where the employee is unlikely to return at all; a temporary lay-off because of no work or a gap between contracts.[75]

10.28 Employees dismissed because of the transfer and in advance of it, are deemed to be employed immediately before the transfer, unless the dismissal was for an economic, technical or organisational (ETO) reason entailing changes in the workforce.[76]

10.29 An employee who is dismissed before the transfer, but not because of the transfer, is not employed at the moment of transfer and has no right to transfer, even if an appeal is pending – for example, an employee is dismissed for theft. Nor is there any obligation on the transferee to hear the appeal. The only exception would be in the unusual situation where the employee's contract states that his/her employment is reinstated until the appeal is completed. However, if the appeal is heard at a later stage and is successful, the original dismissal effectively 'disappears', which means the employee was employed after all immediately before the transfer and s/he has TUPE rights against the transferee. Unless the contract says other-

---

72 TUPE Regs 2006 reg 4(1) and (3).
73 *Secretary of State for Employment v Spence and others* [1986] ICR 651; [1986] IRLR 248, CA.
74 *Fairhurst Ward Abbotts Ltd v Botes Building Ltd* [2004] IRLR 304, CA.
75 See eg *Robert Sage Ltd t/a Prestige Nursing Care Ltd v O'Connell* UKEAT/0336-7/13; [2014] IRLR 428; *Jakowlew v Nestor* UKEAT/0431-2/14; [2015] IRLR 813; *Inex Home Improvements Ltd v Hodgkins and others* UKEAT/0329/14; [2016] IRLR 13; *BT Managed Services Ltd v Edwards and another* UKEAT/0241/14; [2015] IRLR 994.
76 *Litster v Forth Dry Dock Engineering Co Ltd* [1989] ICR 341; [1989] IRLR 161, HL; TUPE Regs 2006 reg 4(3). See para 10.34 for the meaning of ETO.

wise, a successful appeal has this effect automatically and it is not necessary for there to be an additional express decision to reinstate.[77]

10.30 Where part of an undertaking is transferred, the TUPE Regs 2006 protect only those employees 'assigned' to that part.[78] An employee may be assigned to the transferred part even though s/he carried out duties for other parts of the transferor's business.[79] An ET must look at all the facts, such as time spent in each part, value given, and allocation of costs and contractual terms. Although time is a big factor, the whole picture is important. For example, an employee who moves around as a trouble-shooter is not necessarily assigned to the transferring part just because s/he happens to have spent the last few months working there. Similarly, an employee who is employed generally to manage contracts is not necessarily assigned to a particular contract because that happens to be the most time-consuming.[80] Employers may try to shift employees around immediately before a transfer so as to get rid of unpopular staff. However, the ET will look at the reality of the situation, and if the employee was assigned only temporarily to the part transferred, s/he will not be part of the transfer.[81]

10.31 Where an employee apparently works in the whole of an undertaking, which is subsequently split and transferred to two or more different transferees, it can be difficult to identify to which part (if any) s/he was assigned. If the employee worked in both parts, his/her contractual rights and obligations will be split in proportion amongst the transferees, but only if this does not worsen the employee's working conditions or damage his/her TUPE rights. It also needs to be practically possible to separate the work. There is no reason in theory why an employee cannot have two employers at the same time, provided the work to be done for each is clearly identifiable, for example there is a geographical split. If this does not work,

---

77 *Bangura v (1) Southern Cross Healthcare Group PLC (2) Four Seasons Healthcare* UKEAT/0432/12. See also para 22.24 below regarding disappearing dismissals; *Salmon v (1) Castlebeck Care (Teesdale) Ltd (In Administration) (2) Danshell Healthcare Ltd and others* UKEAT/0304/14.

78 *Botzen and others v Rotterdamsche Droogdok Maatschappij BV* [1986] 2 CMLR 50, ECJ.

79 *Duncan Webb Offset (Maidstone) Ltd v Cooper and others* [1995] IRLR 633, EAT; *Buchanan-Smith v Schleicher and Co International Ltd* [1996] IRLR 547, EAT; *CPL Distribution Ltd v Todd* [2003] IRLR 28, CA.

80 See, for example, *Williams v (1) Advance Cleaning Services Ltd (2) Engineering and Railway Solutions Ltd (In Liquidation)* UKEAT/0838/04.

81 *Securiplan v Bademosi* [2003] UKEAT 1128_02_0905; TUPE Regs 2006 reg 2(1).

then the transferees will be responsible for any resulting termination of the employment relationship, even if it is because the employee refuses to transfer.[82]

10.32 It is hard to see how this principle will operate in practice. Tribunals have to assess the practical implications of dividing an employee's contract amongst two or more employers. What seems practical initially, may not be as time goes by. A full-time employee may suddenly become a part-time employee in several different jobs. How secure will part-time arrangements be in the longer term? What happens if one employer changes hours of working so that the two jobs can no longer be carried out at the same time? Equally unclear is what type of claim an employee will have if a tribunal decides that a split is not practical. Will it be a claim for automatic unfair dismissal because the dismissal is because of the transfer, or will it be an ordinary unfair dismissal claim?

10.33 Another difficulty arises with employees who did not directly work on the transferring activities, but were in support operations such as training, contract compliance and submitting tenders. Such employees, even in an organisation which exclusively worked for the one contracting authority, may not transfer if a tribunal believes that technically they were not carrying out the activities which transferred. This will usually come down to the definition of the 'activities' which are to be transferred and the work done by the employee.[83]

Dismissal due to the transfer

10.34 It is automatically unfair for the transferor or transferee to dismiss an employee if the sole or principal reason is the transfer.[84] For transfers and dismissals before 31 January 2014, it was also automatic unfair dismissal if the reason was 'connected with' the transfer. The difference between the reason being 'the transfer' itself, and being 'connected with' the transfer, has not been clearly explored by the case-law. It is still difficult to know how much difference removing 'connected with' dismissals makes. The cases referred to below were

---

82 *ISS Facility Services NV v Govaerts and another* C-344/18 [2020] IRLR 639, CJEU; *McTear Contracts Limited v Bennett & others; Mitie Property Services UK Limited; and Amey Services Limited* UKEATS/0023/19.

83 *(1) Edinburgh Home-Link Partnership (2) Morrison (3) McAleavy v The City of Edinburgh Council and others* UKEATS/0061/11.

84 TUPE Regs 2006 reg 7(1) as amended where the transfer and dismissal took place on or after 31 January 2014: 2014 SI No 16 reg 8(2).

largely before this change to TUPE and should be considered with that in mind.

10.35   Dismissals due to redundancy or reorganisation take place with alarming regularity these days, and it can be hard to tell whether the reason is a recent, current or pending transfer. It is important to remember that it is the reason in the employer's mind which counts: the test is not simply whether the dismissal would have occurred had there been no transfer.

10.36   It is possible for a dismissal for a personal reason also to be because of the transfer,[85] eg the transferee feels a particular individual will be difficult to manage.

10.37   Dismissals at the time of the transfer are more likely to be because of the transfer, but not necessarily. A dismissal for, say, stealing money from the till, is unlikely to be because of the transfer (unless it is a sham), even if it happens at roughly the same time. On the other hand, the transfer can still be the reason even if the dismissal takes place some time afterwards. There is no fixed time-period afterwards within which a dismissal will be deemed because of the transfer, and it can be years later if the evidence still suggests the reason was the transfer.[86]

10.38   Similarly, a dismissal can be because of the transfer even if it is carried out by the transferor well in advance. The old case-law on 'connected with' the transfer dismissals said this could include dismissals at a very early stage where a transfer is contemplated but no particular transfer or transferee is yet identified.[87] For example, where a public authority dismisses employees in order to make a service more appealing to contractors, but before any bidding process has started; or where administrators dismiss employees to make a business more saleable, but before they advertise the business as for sale, or before they have identified a prospective purchaser.[88] Having said that, a transfer would probably have to be clearly envisaged and more than a remote possibility. There is the extra uncertainty since 2014 as to whether such dismissals will be covered under the more restricted wording.

---

85 *Hare Wines Ltd v Kaur and another* [2019] EWCA Civ 216; [2019] IRLR 555.

86 See also para 10.53 for a similar issue in the context of variation of terms.

87 *CAB Automotive Ltd v Blake and others* UKEAT/0298/07; *Morris v John Grose Group Ltd* [1998] IRLR 499, EAT; *Spaceright Europe Ltd v Baillavoine and another* [2012] IRLR 111, CA.

88 *Spaceright Europe Ltd v Baillavoine and another* [2012] IRLR 111, CA.

10.39   It is *not* automatic unfair dismissal if the sole or principal reason for dismissal is an ETO entailing changes in the workforce.[89] This should be considered in two stages:

1) First, is the reason economic, technical or organisational?
2) Second, does that reason entail changes in the workforce?

There is no statutory definition of the elements of 'ETO' but economic reasons could relate to the profitability or market performance of the business; technical reasons could relate to equipment or production processes; and organisational reasons could relate to management or organisational structure.

10.40   Any 'economic' reason must relate to the conduct of the business itself and not just be to secure an enhanced sale price.[90] A contracting out situation can create ambiguities and it will depend on the facts of the case. For example, where it is a condition of the contract that a new contractor reduces the contract price by reducing staff, what is the reason for the dismissals of the redundant staff? Is it a cost-saving relating to the conduct of the business which would have happened whether or not there was a transfer, or is it just a way to reduce the cost of the contract to prospective bidders?[91] Another ambiguous situation is where a company is in severe financial difficulties and administrators dismiss employees. It is important to examine the facts carefully to see whether the ultimate objective of the dismissals is to enable the business to continue, even if there is to be a sale, as opposed to dismissing the employees merely to make the business more attractive to purchasers.[92]

10.41   The main restriction on the ETO exception is that it must entail 'changes in the workforce'. It is easy to forget this extra requirement because of the common usage of the phrase 'ETO' to cover the entire exception. However, it is very important – it means that the employer cannot simply alter an employee's contractual terms, eg to harmonise with the existing workforce. The dismissal must be in order to change the overall numbers of the workforce or change job func-

---

89 TUPE Regs 2006 reg 7(1).
90 *Spaceright Europe Ltd v Baillavoine and another* [2012] IRLR 111, CA; *Wheeler v (1) Patel (2) J Golding Group of Companies* [1987] IRLR 211; [1987] ICR 631, EAT; *Gateway Hotels Ltd v Stewart and others* [1988] IRLR 287, EAT. Although see *Whitehouse v Chas A Blatchford and Sons Ltd* [1999] IRLR 493, CA and *Kerry Foods Ltd v Creber and others* [2000] IRLR 10, EAT.
91 See *Whitehouse v Chas A Blatchford & Sons Ltd* [1999] IRLR 493, CA, which is a strange interpretation of a factual situation – see commentary at [1999] IRLR 450.
92 *Kavanagh and others v Crystal Palace FC (2000) Ltd and another* [2014] IRLR 139, CA.

tions[93] or change the place where employees are employed.[94] For example, if an employee is dismissed for redundancy in order to reduce the overall number of employees so as to save costs, that would be dismissal for an economic reason which entails a 'change in the workforce'. If the change is to job function, it is not necessary that the job functions of the whole workforce are changed; it is enough if the dismissal is because of a change in the claimant's role.[95] Such a change must be the objective of the employer's plan, not just a possible consequence. Nor is it enough that there is a parallel change in workforce numbers or job functions at the same time as the employee's dismissal for, say, not agreeing a pay cut. The employee must be dismissed for a reason which entails that change,[96] eg the employee must be dismissed for redundancy or because his/her own job function is changing.[97] A change in job function must be more than a minor change.[98] If the dismissal is by the transferor, the ETO reason must relate to the future conduct of the transferor's business, as opposed to changes in the transferee's workforce.[99]

10.42   If the ETO exception does apply, it does not mean the dismissal is fair. The ordinary principles to decide unfair dismissal claims will apply, as the reason for dismissal is treated as a dismissal for redundancy or some other substantial reason.[100] To claim ordinary or automatic unfair dismissal, the worker must be an employee with at least two years' service[101] and have been dismissed in law. This includes constructive dismissal, dismissal under reg 4(9) (see below) and failure to renew a fixed-term contract.[102]

10.43   An employee may resign and claim constructive dismissal in the usual way if his/her employer is in fundamental breach of contract.[103]

93 *Delabole Slate Ltd v Berriman* [1985] IRLR 305, CA.

94 TUPE Regs 2006 reg 7(3A).

95 *Nationwide Building Society v Benn and others* UKEAT/0273/09; [2010] IRLR 922.

96 *Manchester College v Hazel and another (No 2)* [2014] EWCA Civ 72; [2014] IRLR 392.

97 *Miles v Insitu Cleaning Co Ltd* UKEAT/0157/12.

98 *Miles v Insitu Cleaning Co Ltd* UKEAT/0157/12.

99 *Hynd v Armstrong and others* [2007] CSIH 16; [2007] IRLR 338, CS.

100 TUPE Regs 2006 reg 7(3)(b).

101 Collective Redundancies and Transfer of Undertakings (Protection of Employment) (Amendment) Regulations 1995 SI No 2587. See also chapter 6 for eligibility to claim unfair dismissal; and *MRS Environmental Services Ltd v Marsh and another* [1997] ICR 995, CA.

102 See para 6.26 for the rights of employees on temporary contracts.

103 TUPE Regs 2006 reg 4(11).

Even where the employer has not broken the contract, the employee may claim s/he has been 'dismissed' if the transfer involves, or would involve, a substantial change in working conditions to his/her material detriment.[104] This could include changes in terms and conditions as well as physical working conditions; a change in location allowed by the contract, but leading to a longer and more stressful journey or childcare difficulties;[105] a reduction in the employee's skills and responsibilities or a substantial reduction in his/her bonus.[106] Whether a change is a 'substantial change' depends on the nature and degree of the change. An ET should consider the impact from the employee's point of view and decide whether the employee's position was a reasonable one to adopt.[107] Even if the employee can prove s/he has been 'dismissed' in these situations, the dismissal will not necessarily be unfair, as explained above. Note that notice pay cannot be claimed in respect of a 'material detriment' resignation.[108]

The effect of a transfer

Overview

10.44   Where the TUPE Regs 2006 apply, the new employer stands in the shoes of the old employer for most purposes. The contractual terms and conditions are transferred,[109] as are all the transferor's rights, powers, duties and liabilities under or in connection with the contract.[110] This would include wages owed, keeping wages records for the purposes of the national minimum wage,[111] liability for

---

104 TUPE Regs 2006 reg 4(9).

105 *Tapere v South London and Maudsley NHS Trust* UKEAT/0410/08; [2009] IRLR 972.

106 *Nationwide Building Society v Benn and others* UKEAT/0273/09; [2010] IRLR 922.

107 *Tapere v South London and Maudsley NHS Trust* UKEAT/0410/08; [2009] IRLR 972; *Abellio London Ltd (formerly Travel London Ltd) v (1) Musse and others (2) CentreWest London Buses Ltd* UKEAT/0283/11 and UKEAT/0631/11; [2012] IRLR 360. *Cetinsoy and others v London United Busways Ltd* UKEAT/0042/14 provides a useful contrast.

108 TUPE Regs 2006 reg 4(10).

109 TUPE Regs 2006 reg 4(1).

110 TUPE Regs 2006 reg 4(2).

111 *Mears Home Care Limited v Bradburn & others* UKEAT/0170/18. See para 4.50.

discrimination by the former employer[112] and tortious liability,[113] eg for negligence leading to personal injury. If the transferor had an employers' liability insurance policy, the transferor's right to an indemnity under the policy for any such liability would also transfer.[114] It may also include liability for higher pay arising from an equal pay comparison, even though the employee's comparator has not transferred and no equal pay case was brought prior to the transfer.[115] Alarmingly, where there is a contractual right to have pay rates or other terms set by reference to a collective agreement, and the transferee is not a participant in the collective bargaining process for the relevant term, the contractual incorporation of the collective agreement for that term does not transfer.[116] For example, an employee would continue to be entitled to his/her pay rate at the time of the transfer, but not to any subsequent rises negotiated under the collective agreement. The TUPE Regs 2006 probably also transfer acquired continuous service for statutory employment rights.[117]

10.45 It is impossible to transfer an employee's entitlement to participate in the original employer's profit-share scheme, so what transfers is an entitlement to participate in a scheme of substantial equivalence.[118] On the other hand, if the employee had an express mobility clause with the transferor, eg 'The employee can be transferred to work anywhere within the Trust', this still covers the geographical boundaries of the original Trust after the employee has transferred to a new employer; it is not necessary to operate any concept of 'substantial equivalence' even though the transferor's other locations are

---

112 *DJM International Ltd v Nicholas* [1996] IRLR 76, EAT.

113 *Bernadone v Pall Mall Services Group and others; Martin v Lancashire CC* [2000] IRLR 487, CA.

114 *Bernadone v Pall Mall Services Group and others; Martin v Lancashire CC* [2000] IRLR 487, CA. See TUPE Regs 2006 reg 17 regarding liability where the transferor was not required to hold employers' liability insurance.

115 *Gutridge v Sodexo Ltd and North Tees & Hartlepool NHS Trust* [2009] EWCA Civ 759; [2009] IRLR 721.

116 TUPE Regs 2006 reg 4A following on from the decision of the CJEU in *Alemo-Herron and others v Parkwood Leisure Ltd* C-426/11 [2013] IRLR 744, CJEU.

117 Although this is usually preserved in any event by Employment Rights Act (ERA) 1996 s218(2). See *Services for Education (S4E) Ltd v (1) White (2) Birmingham City Council* UKEAT/0024/15 for a scenario where s218(2) was required when a transfer took place during a temporary break in employment.

118 *Mitie Managed Services Ltd v French* [2002] IRLR 521, EAT.

different from those of the new employer, which makes the clause irrelevant.[119]

10.46   To ensure the transferee is well placed to honour obligations towards the employees, the transferor must give the transferee written 'employee liability information' at least 28 days before the transfer.[120] This comprises, in respect of each employee subject to the transfer:

- the employee's identity and age;
- the particulars required under ERA 1996 s1;[121]
- information regarding any disciplinary action or grievance taken within the previous two years in circumstances where the Advisory, Conciliation and Arbitration Service (ACAS) Code on Disciplinary and Grievance procedures applies;[122]
- information regarding any court or tribunal case brought by the employee within the previous two years or which is likely to be brought; and
- applicable collective agreements.

10.47   The transferor and transferee must make sure they comply with data protection law. It is permitted to disclose the employee liability information under General Data Protection Regulation (GDPR) Article 6(1)(c) because it is necessary for compliance with a legal obligation to which the controller is subject. However, data protection principles must still be complied with, and only necessary information disclosed. For a general overview of data protection legislation, see chapter 1.

10.48   The precise legal position regarding transfer of pensions is beyond the scope of this book. The law is complex and developments in legislation and case-law should be watched. The following is only a broad guide and further research is recommended. Occupational pension schemes are excluded from the TUPE Regs 2006 in so far as they cover old age, invalidity or survivors' benefits.[123] Early retirement benefits paid on dismissal to employees who have reached a

---

119 *Tapere v South London and Maudsley NHS Trust* UKEAT/0410/08; [2009] IRLR 972.
120 TUPE Regs 2006 reg 11.
121 See para 1.24.
122 This is the practical meaning of the section at the moment, though it is worded more widely. See para 22.3 regarding the ACAS Code.
123 TUPE Regs 2006 reg 10. See also Council Directive 2001/23/EC Article 3(4).

certain age do not fall within this category and should transfer.[124] However, benefits payable after normal retirement age, even if the pension first paid benefits before normal retirement age, are considered old age benefits.[125] Accrued pension rights should be preserved,[126] but there is probably no entitlement to continued membership or contributions.[127] Although, with these exceptions, occupational pension schemes do not transfer, the Pensions Act 2004 and the Transfer of Employment (Pension Protection) Regulations 2005[128] have introduced a minimum occupational pension entitlement to transferred employees who had such an entitlement with their employers before the transfer. Unfortunately, there is no requirement that the post-transfer pension is equivalent to the original scheme. Under the revised New Deal agreement for transfers out of central government (see para 10.22), those compulsorily transferred from public service to independent providers will retain membership of their previous employer's pension scheme.[129] This replaces the original New Deal approach that the transferee must provide a broadly comparable private pension scheme.

10.49　　If the TUPE Regs 2006 apply to a particular employee, s/he should usually claim for any transferred rights or unfair dismissal against the transferee, even if s/he never started work for the new employer and was dismissed in advance of the transfer, provided that the dismissal was because of the transfer.[130] However, if the transferor's reason for dismissal was not the transfer or if it was for an ETO reason, the employee may have to sue the transferor. If in doubt as to who to sue – eg due to uncertainty whether the TUPE Regs 2006 apply or the transferor's reason for dismissal or any other complication – it is probably safest to claim in the alternative against the old employer and the apparent transferee.

124　*Beckmann v Dynamco Whicheloe Macfarlane Ltd* C-164/00, [2002] IRLR 578, ECJ; *Martin v South Bank University* [2004] IRLR 75, ECJ.

125　For exact details, see *Procter & Gamble Co v (1) Svenska Cellulosa Aktiebolaget SCA and another* [2012] EWHC 1257 (Ch); [2012] IRLR 733, on appeal.

126　Article 3(4)(b) of 2001/23/EC.

127　*Walden Engineering Co Ltd v Warrener* [1993] IRLR 420, EAT; *Adams and others v Lancashire CC and BET Catering Services Ltd* [1997] IRLR 436, CA.

128　SI No 649.

129　For detail. It is important to read the *Fair Deal for staff pensions: staff transfer from central government*, 2013 at: www.gov.uk/government/publications/fair-deal-guidance.pdf.

130　*Stirling DC v Allan and others* [1995] IRLR 301, CS.

10.50   There are special rules where the transferor is subject to insolvency proceedings. If the proceedings were instituted with a view to the liquidation of the transferor's assets and are under the supervision of an insolvency practitioner, TUPE Regs 2006 regs 4 and 7 will not apply.[131] This means that debts owed to employees will not transfer to the transferee, nor will there be protection against automatic unfair dismissal in respect of dismissal due to the transfer. There has been ongoing uncertainty regarding what kind of insolvency proceedings fit within this exclusion, but broadly speaking it seems that it would include compulsory liquidation or creditors' voluntary liquidation, but not administration. This is because an administrator by definition is not appointed with a view to liquidating assets, even if that is what s/he ends up doing.[132] In situations where insolvency proceedings were opened *not* with a view to liquidating the transferor's assets (eg administration), the National Insurance Fund will pay the transferor's debts up to the limits set under the statutory schemes and only the balance will be due from the transferee.[133] The idea is to help rescue failing businesses. Note that rules regarding different kinds of insolvency are a specialist area and this book can only give a loose guide based on what appears to be the latest case-law.

10.51   An employee's contract of employment and all the rights, powers, duties and liabilities in connection with it, will not transfer if the employee tells the transferor or the transferee that s/he objects to becoming employed by the transferee. His/her employment will simply terminate on the transfer, but s/he will not be treated as having been dismissed and s/he will not be able to claim unfair dismissal or redundancy pay.[134] If the transferor allows the employee to stay on, the employee may have to negotiate new terms and conditions, as his/her old contract of employment will probably no longer apply.[135]

---

131 TUPE Regs 2006 reg 8(7).

132 *OTG Ltd v Barke, Luke and Department of Business Enterprise & Regulatory Reform and others* UKEAT/0320/09; [2011] IRLR 272, disagreeing with *Oakland v Wellswood (Yorkshire) Ltd* UKEAT/395/08; [2009] IRLR 250. See also *Pressure Coolers Ltd v (1) Molloy (2) Maestro International Ltd (3) Secretary of State for Trade and Industry* UKEAT/0272/10, 00479-80/10; *Secretary of State for Trade and Industry v Slater and others* UKEAT/0119/07; [2007] IRLR 928.

133 TUPE Regs 2006 reg 8(1)–(6).

134 TUPE Regs 2006 reg 4(7)–(8), unless reg 4(9) or constructive dismissal applies – see para 10.43.

135 See, eg, *Sunley Turriff Holdings Ltd v Thomson and others* [1995] IRLR 184, EAT.

10.52   An employee, who is employed in the undertaking to be transferred, cannot be forced to stay with the transferor because the TUPE
Regs 2006 will automatically apply. For example, the transferor
cannot prevent employees against their will from transferring by
insisting they remain with the transferor and redeploying them at
the moment of transfer under contractual mobility clauses.[136] It
sometimes happens that employees employed in the business to be
transferred choose to remain with their original employer, but to
work for the transferee on secondment. In such situations, despite
what everyone agrees and believes, it is very likely that the employee's
employment will have automatically transferred to the transferee at
the date of transfer of the business.[137] If the employee then returns to
work for the transferor at the end of the secondment period, this will
probably be deemed a new contract of employment between the
employee and the transferor, which means the employee will lose
his/her continuous service (unless that is preserved by 'custom or
arrangement' – see para 6.22).

10.53   A difficulty can arise regarding the transfer of migrant workers
who require sponsorship under the points-based immigration
system. An employer needs to be licensed to sponsor migrant
workers. If the transferor was licensed but the transferee is not,
presumably the latter must apply for a licence and, if it chooses not
to, its employees who are sponsored migrants will have a limited
amount of time to find a new sponsor. Quite apart from this, transferees must check the documents of all their employees within
60 days of the transfer to check no illegal workers have transferred
contrary to the rules in the Immigration, Asylum and Nationality Act
2006 (see paras 14.83–14.84).[138] Immigration rules frequently change,
and it is advisable to check the latest position. These are some pointers, but immigration rules are not within the scope of this book.

---

136 *Royal Mail Group Ltd v Communication Workers Union* UKEAT/0338/08;
     [2009] IRLR 108. It may be different if such redeployment takes place prior to
     transfer. Note that this point was not appealed before the Court of Appeal in
     the same case.
137 *Celtec Ltd v Astley* [2006] IRLR 635, HL; *Capita Health Solutions Ltd v McLean*
     [2008] IRLR 595, EAT.
138 See *Code of practice on preventing illegal working: civil penalty scheme for
     employers*, January 2019, p11 at: www.gov.uk/government/publications/illegal-
     working-penalties-codes-of-practice-for-employers.

Changing the terms and conditions

Generally

10.54   The TUPE Regs 2006 preserve contractual terms and conditions and prohibit changes due to the transfer. An employer's attempt to impose new terms and conditions, even if s/he has secured the employee's agreement (expressly or by affirmation) will be ineffective if the sole or principal reason for the change is the transfer.[139] So, for example, an employee retained by the new employer, ostensibly on changed terms and conditions, can subsequently insist on his/her pre-transfer terms still applying.[140] The position has become less clear-cut where it is the new employer (the transferee) who later wants to back out of an agreement it has made with the transferring employee. It is probable that, unlike an employee, the transferee cannot later rely on the TUPE Regs 2006 to contend that a variation agreed on a transfer is void. If this is right, there is nothing to stop an employee agreeing additional rights with the transferee and later choosing whether to rely on his/her old term or the agreed new term[141]

10.55   A variation to the contract can be agreed if the reason is not the transfer. It depends on the facts whether the reason for changing terms and conditions is the transfer. It is more likely to be the reason if the purpose of the change is to bring terms and conditions into line with those of existing staff of the transferor, or if the change occurs at the time of the transfer as opposed to much later.[142] On the other hand, if the business was already in financial trouble and the transferor was trying to save money by cutting pay prior to the transfer, the fact that the transferee cuts salaries for the same reason suggests the

---

139   TUPE Regs 2006 reg 4(4).

140   *Foreningen A F Arbejdsledere i Danmark v Daddy's Dance Hall A/S* [1988] IRLR 315, ECJ; *Credit Suisse First Boston (Europe) Ltd v Lister* [1998] IRLR 700, CA; *Martin v South Bank University* [2004] IRLR 75, ECJ. However, it is still a risky strategy.

141   *Regent Security Services Ltd v Power* [2008] IRLR 66, CA. This assumes that *Power*, which was decided under the TUPE Regs 1981, would still apply under the TUPE Regs 2006. There is also some uncertainty whether *Ferguson v Astrea Asset Management Ltd* UKEAT/0139/19; [2020] IRLR 577 makes an agreed variation void under the 2006 Regs where it is the employee who wants to rely on the new term, or whether *Ferguson* only applies to invalidate a manipulative agreement between employee and transferor pre-transfer which was made with a view to imposing more onerous terms on the transferee.

142   Though in *Taylor v Connex South Eastern Ltd* EAT/1243/99 and *London Metropolitan University v Sackur* UKEAT/0286/06, a change made two years later was found to be connected.

contract change is not because of the transfer.[143] The issues are similar to those arising for automatic unfair dismissals (see above) and there is the same change in wording from January 2014 so that changes for reasons 'connected with' the transfer are no longer explicitly made void. The test of whether the reason for the change in terms and conditions is the transfer, is not simply whether it would have happened if there had been no transfer. The proper test is to look at the reason the transferor acted as it did.[144]

10.56 Even if the agreed variation to terms and conditions is because of the transfer, there are some exceptions where it is permitted, for example if the contract allows such a variation.[145] An agreed variation is also allowed if it is for an ETO reason entailing changes in the workforce.[146] The ETO exception is the same as that for transfer-related automatic unfair dismissal (see above). A change in the workforce can be a change in numbers, job function or location.[147] It is also possible to agree a variation to a term incorporated from a collective agreement, provided the variation takes place more than one year after the transfer and the rights and obligations in the employee's contract are overall no less favourable than before.[148] Finally, there is an exception for insolvency situations, where the business is transferred as a going concern. The transferor, transferee or insolvency practitioner is permitted to make a written agreement with trade union or employee representatives to change terms and conditions, even if the reason for the variation is the transfer and not an ETO reason, provided the variation is designed to safeguard employment opportunities by ensuring the survival of the undertaking.[149]

New employees

10.57 One practical problem is that new employees get taken on with less favourable terms and conditions than those of transferred staff,

---

143 See eg *Carlton Care Ltd v Rooney and others* EAT/112/00, although this was under the 1981 TUPE Regs.

144 As illustrations, see *Smith and others v Trustees of Brooklands College* UKEAT/0128/11; *Tabberer and others v Mears Ltd and others* UKEAT/0064/17 and *Hare Wines v Kaur* [2019] EWCA Civ 2016; [2019] IRLR 555. Note also the Court of Appeal's comments re *Smith* at paras 22–23.

145 TUPE Regs 2006 reg 4(5)(b).

146 TUPE Regs 2006 reg 4(5).

147 *Delabole Slate Ltd v Berriman* [1985] IRLR 305, CA; TUPE Regs 2006 reg 4(5A).

148 TUPE Regs 2006 reg 4(5B).

149 TUPE Regs 2006 reg 9; and see BEIS Guidance Note, n8 above.

making the latter less desirable to retain in the long term. UNISON and other unions lobbied hard for legislation to help prevent such a two-tier system after contracting out of the public sector. As a result, where the *Code of Practice on workforce matters in public sector service contracts* ('Two-tier Workforce Code') applies in Wales or (if still in existence) the Scottish Protocol applies,[150] it requires the service provider to consult representatives of the recognised trade union on the terms and conditions to be offered to new recruits. If there is no recognised trade union, consultation will be with elected representatives. The consultation should involve a genuine dialogue. The intention is that contractors and trade unions should be able to agree on a particular package of terms and conditions to be offered to new joiners, in keeping with the terms of the Protocol. In the Welsh Code, 'new joiners' are defined as including existing employees of the transferee as well as newly taken on staff.

10.58   The Protocol and Code say that new employees must be employed on fair and reasonable terms and conditions which are no less favourable overall (apart from pensions) than those of transferred employees. Unfortunately, this does mean that they can have different terms and conditions, some being more favourable and some being less favourable. New joiners must also be offered the same or broadly comparable pension arrangements as transferred employees. Details are at paras 9.5–9.6 of the Protocol. In England, similar principles used to be covered by Local Authority and Public Sector 'Two-tier Workforce' Codes, but as explained above, these have now been withdrawn.

Collective consultation

10.59   There are special rules under TUPE Regs 2006 regs 13–16 whereby the employer of any affected employees must inform and consult about the transfer with either the trade union or, if there is none, with correctly elected employee representatives. If the employer fails to do so, the trade union or employee representative (as applicable) can bring a claim for compensation on behalf of the employees. A maximum of 13 weeks' compensation for each employee can be awarded. The transferor and transferee are jointly and severally liable for any compensation due to failure collectively to consult the trade union or employee representatives about the transfer.[151]

---

150 See para 10.24.
151 See paras 2.31–2.39; TUPE Regs 2006 reg 15(9).

10.60   Individual employees can only bring a claim for failure to inform or consult if there is no union or elected employee representative. As with all claims, it is important when writing the tribunal claim form to be clear if a claim for failure to inform and consult under regs 13 and 15 is being made, as distinct from other claims which may also be itemised on the form, eg unfair dismissal because of the transfer. For more detail, see paras 2.31–2.39.

PART III

Equality and discrimination

CHAPTER 11

Work and family life

continued

Chapter 11: Key points

Pregnancy-related dismissals and discrimination

- Dismissals for reasons connected with pregnancy or maternity leave are automatically unfair. Other detrimental treatment is also unlawful. There is no minimum qualifying service.
- Dismissal or other discrimination due to pregnancy and related reasons such as pregnancy-related sickness is unlawful pregnancy discrimination if it occurs during pregnancy or maternity leave.
- In limited circumstances, eg pregnancy-related sickness occurring after maternity leave, a comparison with a man in equivalent circumstances may be necessary to prove sex discrimination.
- A woman cannot claim full pay while on maternity leave purely because her absence is pregnancy-related.

General guide to useful evidence

- Evidence proving that the detriment or dismissal was for pregnancy or a related reason as opposed to the reason put forward by the employer.
- If comparison with a man is necessary, evidence showing how a man would have been treated in comparable circumstances, eg if he required sick leave.

Maternity rights and family related leave

- Pregnant women are entitled to risk assessments and paid time off if specified risks exist. They are also entitled to reasonable time off for antenatal care. Their partner is entitled to unpaid time off on two occasions to accompany them. Employees adopting children are allowed equivalent time off for meetings in advance of the adoption.
- Every woman who is an employee is entitled to 26 weeks' ordinary maternity leave (OML) followed by 26 weeks' additional maternity leave (AML).
- There are two weeks' compulsory maternity leave (CML) following childbirth.
- The correct notifications must be given before starting leave and if wanting to come back early.

continued

- Maternity leave is automatically triggered by any pregnancy-related absence in the last four weeks before the expected week of childbirth (EWC).
- There are similar rights for adoption leave and new rights for parental order parents in surrogacy arrangements.
- During statutory maternity leave (SML), women are entitled to their normal terms and conditions other than pay.
- There is a right to two weeks' ordinary paternity leave (OPL).
- The mother and her partner or the father can choose to share maternity leave and pay after the first two weeks' compulsory leave for the mother. This is called 'shared parental leave' (SPL).
- There is a new right to two weeks' parental bereavement leave.
- Statutory maternity, paternity, adoption, shared parental, and parental bereavement leave pay are available for those who qualify.
- Employees with one year's service are entitled to a total of 18 weeks' unpaid parental leave to take care of children up to 18. This is not the same thing as '*shared* parental leave' (above).
- Employees are entitled to reasonable unpaid time off as dependant leave to make arrangements when certain emergencies arise with children or other dependants.
- It is automatic unfair dismissal to dismiss an employee and unlawful to subject him/her to a detriment for reasons connected with maternity, parental, dependant or parental bereavement leave (see paras 6.70–6.73). It is also automatic unfair dismissal to dismiss an employee for asserting a statutory right, eg the right to time off for antenatal care.

Part-time and flexible working

- Employees with 26 weeks' continuous service can formally request flexible working under the Flexible Working Regulations 2014, ie a change in their hours or to work from home. Employers can refuse to give permission. As long as the correct procedure is followed, refusal can be challenged only by using other legal rights eg discrimination law if it applies.
- Refusal to permit a woman to work part-time or arrive or leave at certain hours may be unlawful indirect sex discrimination under the Equality Act (EqA) 2010.
- The main issue on part-time working will usually be whether the employer can justify insisting on full-time working.

- It may also be indirect sex discrimination unjustifiably to treat part-time workers less well than full-timers.
- Where part-timers are given less favourable contractual terms and conditions, including pay rates, EqA 2010 Part 5 Chapter 3 ('equality of terms') applies.
- Under the Part-time Workers Regulations 2000, a part-timer (male or female) should not be treated less favourably than a comparable full-timer because she is a part-timer (on a pro rata basis), unless an employer can justify doing so.

General guide to useful evidence

- Find out the employer's justification.
- Evidence to show why part-time working in the job will be satisfactory or even beneficial.

To claim sex discrimination:

- Evidence generally and within the appropriate pool showing that women are at a particular disadvantage compared with men in respect of the particular hours or flexibility requirement.
- Evidence showing that the particular worker has difficulty working full-time or the particular hours or shifts required.

To claim under the Part-time Workers Regulations 2000:

- Evidence regarding the chosen comparator.

Pregnancy-related dismissals and discrimination

11.1   In September 2003, the former Equal Opportunities Commission (EOC) launched a formal investigation into pregnancy discrimination, including discrimination while on maternity leave and on return to work. In June 2005, it published its final report: *Greater expectations: Final report of the EOC's investigation into discrimination against new and expectant mothers in the workplace.* The report said the data it had collected showed that the level of pregnancy discrimination in the workplace was 'appalling'. The EOC was stunned at the number of women who said they had been dismissed, demoted, denied training or promotion, or bullied into quitting, just because of their pregnancy. It estimated that each year, almost half of the 440,000 pregnant women in Great Britain experienced some form of disadvantage at work as a result, and 30,000 were forced out of their jobs. In March 2016, the Equality and Human Rights Commission (EHRC) and the then Department for Business, Innovation & Skills (BIS) published *Pregnancy and maternity-related discrimination and disadvantage: experience of employers* and *Pregnancy and maternity-related discrimination and disadvantage: experience of mothers.*[1] One in five mothers surveyed said they had experienced harassment or negative comments related to pregnancy or flexible working from their employer and/or colleagues; ten per cent of mothers said their employer discouraged them from attending antenatal appointments; and 11 per cent of mothers believed they had been dismissed, made redundant or forced to leave because of pregnancy.[2] Following this, the House of Commons Women and Equalities Select Committee published a report into pregnancy and maternity discrimination at work.[3] It expressed concern that inaction would lead to the same problems in five to ten years' time, and made a number of recommendations. For evidence to prove pregnancy discrimination, see para 16.37.

11.2   Under Employment Rights Act (ERA) 1996 s99 and Maternity and Parental Leave etc Regulations (MPL Regs) 1999[4] reg 20, it is automatically unfair to dismiss a female employee for a number of reasons connected with her pregnancy, maternity or maternity leave (see paras 6.70–6.72). There is no minimum service requirement to claim unfair dismissal for these reasons. A woman is entitled to written reasons if she is dismissed while pregnant or on maternity leave, again regardless of her length of service.[5]

---

1   The 2005 report is available at: www.maternityaction.org.uk/wp-content/uploads/2013/09/eocpregnancydiscrimgreaterexpectations.pdf. The 2016 reports are available via: www.equalityhumanrights.com/en/managing-pregnancy-and-maternity-workplace/pregnancy-and-maternity-discrimination-research-findings.

2   See also *Employers in the dark ages over recruitment of pregnant women and new mothers*, EHRC research published 19 February 2018 at: www.equality human-rights.com/en/our-work/news/employers-dark-ages-over-recruitment-pregnant-women-and-new-mothers.

3   The Committee report and government response are available via links at: old.parliament.uk/business/committees/committees-a-z/commons-select/women-and-equalities-committee/inquiries/parliament-2015/pregnancy-and-maternity-discrimination-15-16/.

4   SI No 3312.

5   ERA 1996 s92(4); see paras 20.11–20.15.

11.3   Women may also claim that dismissal in such circumstances is unlawful pregnancy or maternity discrimination contrary to the Equality Act (EqA) 2010.[6] Where possible, women should usually claim under both statutes, since a successful discrimination claim would lead to additional compensation. Discrimination in pay and contract terms would be covered by EqA 2010 Part 5 Chapter 3.

11.4   Unfavourable treatment of a woman due to pregnancy or maternity is also prohibited by European Union (EU) law. It is covered by the general provisions of Article 157 (formerly 141) and the Recast Directive[7] as well as the Pregnant Workers Directive.[8] For the continued applicability of EU law post-Brexit, see chapter 3.

11.5   Under EqA 2010 s18, it is unlawful to treat a woman unfavourably because of her pregnancy or because of an illness suffered by her as a result of her pregnancy. This applies where the unfavourable treatment, or the decision to carry out the unfavourable treatment, is made in the woman's 'protected period'. The protected period begins with her pregnancy and ends at the end of her statutory maternity leave (SML) period. Where a woman has the right to ordinary maternity leave (OML) and additional maternity leave (AML), this means at the end of the AML period or when she returns to work if sooner. If she does not have the right to OML and AML, the protected period is two weeks from the end of pregnancy, ie the compulsory maternity leave (CML) period. It is well-established in the case-law that no comparison is required either with how a man would be treated in an equivalent situation or with how a non-pregnant woman would be treated. It need only be shown that the discrimination is because of the woman's pregnancy. Although in many situations – for instance, a failed promotion – it is useful as a matter of evidence to compare the way a pregnant woman is treated with the treatment of a non-pregnant comparator, such a comparison does not always work.

11.6   There is no justifiability defence available to the employer for pregnancy-related discrimination. The Court of Justice of the European Union (CJEU) has consistently taken a very firm line on this principle, even when the results seem unfair to the employer. In the leading case of *Webb*,[9] Mrs Webb was taken on for a permanent job, but initially to cover another worker's maternity leave. She was

---

6 Unlike unfair dismissal, discrimination law does not apply only to employees.
7 2006/54/EC para (23) of the Preamble and Article 2(2)(c).
8 92/85/EEC.
9 *Webb v EMO Air Cargo (UK) Ltd (No 2)* [1995] IRLR 645, HL; *Webb v EMO Air Cargo (UK) Ltd* [1994] IRLR 482, ECJ.

dismissed when the employer discovered she could not cover the leave, due to her own maternity leave. Nevertheless, this was unlawful discrimination. In another case,[10] a temporary nurse in a heart clinic applied for a permanent post which was to start immediately. She was eight weeks pregnant at the time. Under German law, pregnant women could not work in an operating theatre for health and safety reasons. Her application was therefore rejected. The CJEU said this was unlawful sex discrimination.

11.7   It is the same if the woman was only employed on a short fixed-term contract,[11] although this may mean she does not get much compensation. Mrs Brandt-Nielsen was employed for a six-month fixed-term contract starting 1 July 1995. In August 1995 she told her employer that she was pregnant with a due date of early November. She was dismissed on the grounds that she had not said she was pregnant when she was recruited. The CJEU said that dismissal of a worker on account of pregnancy was direct sex discrimination whatever the nature and extent of the economic loss incurred by her employer as a result of her pregnancy. This was so even though she had knowingly failed to inform her employer of her pregnancy on recruitment and even though she was unable to work a substantial part of the term of a fixed-term contract.[12] As an employee's pregnancy is not a factor which an employer can lawfully be influenced by, the woman is not obliged to tell her employer that she is pregnant.[13]

11.8   It is pregnancy discrimination for a sick pay scheme to exclude pregnancy-related illness.[14] A woman absent due to a pregnancy-related illness must be paid the same sick pay as anyone else, but she is not entitled to full pay just because she is pregnant, if there is no such entitlement under her contract.[15]

10 *Mahlburg v Land Mecklenburg-Vorpommern* [2000] IRLR 276, ECJ.

11 *Jimenez Melgar v Ayuntamiento de los Barrios* [2001] IRLR 848, ECJ; *Tele Danmark A/S v Handels-og Kontorfunktionærernes Forbund i Danmark acting on behalf of Brandt-Nielsen* [2001] IRLR 853, ECJ.

12 *Tele Danmark A/S v Handels-og Kontorfunktionærernes Forbund i Danmark acting on behalf of Brandt-Nielsen* [2001] IRLR 85, ECJ.

13 *Busch v Klinikum Neustadt GmbH & Co Betriebs-KG* C-320/01, [2003] IRLR 625, ECJ.

14 *Handels-og Kontorfunktionærernes Forbund i Danmark acting on behalf of Hoj Pedersen v Faellesforeningen for Danmarks Brugsforeninger acting on behalf of Kvickly Skive* C-66/96, [1999] IRLR 55, ECJ.

15 *North-Western Health Board v McKenna* [2005] IRLR 895, ECJ; see para 11.64.

11.9   As stated above, it is pregnancy discrimination (without needing
a male comparison) to treat a woman unfavourably due to her pregnancy at any time through her protected period, or to make a decision
during the period, which is carried out afterwards. However, where
the unfavourable treatment is decided upon and occurs after the end
of her maternity leave, the claim is for sex discrimination and a
comparison with a man in a similar position is still necessary, eg
where a woman is dismissed due to a pregnancy-related illness occurring after her maternity leave period.[16] This applies even if the illness,
eg post-natal depression, first arose during maternity leave.[17] Where
a woman is absent through sickness after her maternity leave, she is
entitled to be treated no worse than a man would be treated if sick for
a similar period disregarding the earlier period of absence during
pregnancy and maternity leave.[18] If the woman is suffering from
post-natal depression, depending on its severity and how long it lasts,
she could alternatively consider a disability discrimination claim.[19]

11.10   It is also unlawful to treat a woman unfavourably because she is
on SML or is seeking to take up her rights to SML or has done so.[20]
For more detail regarding discrimination during maternity leave, see
paras 11.63–11.65. A woman who is dismissed because her maternity locum is more efficient may claim pregnancy discrimination
because, had she not been absent, the unfavourable comparison
would not have arisen.[21]

11.11   Dismissal of a female worker because she is undergoing an
advanced stage of IVF treatment, ie between the follicular puncture
and the immediate transfer of the fertilised ova into the uterus,
constituted direct sex discrimination under the former Equal
Treatment Directive (now consolidated into the Recast Directive) and
presumably also under the EqA 2010, without needing to make any
comparisons with how a man would be treated. It will not be 'pregnancy discrimination' until after the transfer of the egg, but either

---

16 *Handels og-Kontorfuntionærernes Forbund i Danmark (acting for Hertz) v Dansk
    Arbejdsgiverforening* [1991] IRLR 31, ECJ; *Brown v Rentokil Ltd* [1998] IRLR 445,
    ECJ.
17 *Lyons v DWP Jobcentre Plus* UKEAT/0348/13.
18 *Brown v Rentokil Ltd* [1998] IRLR 445, ECJ; *Healy v William B Morrison & Sons
    Ltd* (2000) EAT/203/00.
19 See chapter 15.
20 EqA 2010 s18(3) and (4).
21 *Rees v Apollo Watch Repairs plc* [1996] UKEAT 23_93_0502.

way, the woman will be legally protected.[22] Dismissal of a woman at very early stages of IVF treatment, before she is considered pregnant, is potentially sex discrimination (as opposed to pregnancy discrimination). The difficulty then is that a comparison is required with how a man would be treated in an 'equivalent' situation, eg a man needing an equivalent amount of time off.[23]

11.12   Note that men cannot claim sex discrimination if an employer chooses to give special treatment to women in connection with pregnancy or childbirth.[24] However, this only applies if the special treatment goes no further than is reasonably necessary to compensate the woman for any disadvantage occasioned by her being pregnant or on maternity leave.[25] It was not possible under the Sex Discrimination Act (SDA) 1975 for a man to claim pregnancy discrimination if he was treated less favourably because of his partner's pregnancy.[26] It is untested whether such a claim would be possible under the EqA 2010, if not as pregnancy discrimination under section 18, perhaps as associative sex or pregnancy discrimination under section 13.

Maternity leave

Introduction

11.13   The rules regarding maternity leave have always been complex. The law is set out in the ERA 1996 and the MPL Regs 1999.[27] Although the rules are now simpler than in the past, the law is still complex and uncertain in some areas. The following is therefore only a general introduction.

11.14   Historically, a woman risked losing all her rights if she failed to take the correct steps before and after maternity leave. Although there are more safeguards now, even under the current law, there are

---

22 *Mayr v Bäckerei und Konditorei Gerhard Flöckner OHG* [2008] IRLR 387, ECJ concerning the definition of 'pregnancy' for the purposes of the Pregnant Workers Directive.

23 *Sahota v (1) The Home Office (2) Pipkin* UKEAT/0342/09.

24 EqA 2010 s13(6)(b).

25 *Eversheds Legal Services Ltd v De Belin* UKEAT/0352/10 and UKEAT/0444/10; [2011] IRLR 448.

26 *Kulikaoskas v (1) MacDuff Shellfish (2) Watt* UKEAT/0062/09 was referred to the CJEU for guidance, but settled before the hearing, having been supported by the European Commission in written observations.

27 SI No 3312 as amended by the Maternity and Parental Leave etc and the Paternity and Adoption Leave (Amendment) Regulations 2006 SI No 2014.

important rules to comply with. If a woman is refused maternity leave or not allowed to return for a reason related to pregnancy or maternity leave,[28] she may be able to claim unlawful detriment or unfair dismissal under the ERA 1996 as well as sex or pregnancy or maternity discrimination under the EqA 2010.[29] If the woman is dismissed for an unconnected reason, she can claim ordinary unfair dismissal, provided she has at least two years' service. There are advantages in claiming jointly under the ERA 1996 and the EqA 2010, since the EqA 2010 can attract additional compensation. There are other possible claims which may apply, eg it would be automatic unfair dismissal to dismiss the woman for asserting a statutory right such as the right to maternity leave or to time off for antenatal care.[30] Whereas EqA 2010 s18 covers pregnancy discrimination against women who are not employees, the position is unclear on discrimination in connection with maternity leave. This is because the prohibition on maternity leave discrimination is linked to being on SML, which is itself only available to employees. Arguably there is protection for the first two weeks after birth, but even if this is correct, it is inadequate. Female workers (but not employees) discriminated against because of maternity leave can claim sex discrimination under EqA 2010 s13 and argue that, by virtue of EU law, no comparison with a man should be required. Whether this will succeed remains to be tested.

11.15   All women who are employees, regardless of length of service, are entitled to 12 months' SML, comprising 26 weeks' OML and a further 26 weeks' AML. The entitlement depends on having made the correct notifications. There is also a short period of two weeks' CML.

Ordinary maternity leave

Overview

11.16   The first 26 weeks of SML are OML.[31] There is a compulsory leave (CML) period of two weeks after childbirth (and any period where there is a relevant statutory prohibition on the woman working).[32]

---

28 See chapter 6 for full list of automatic unfair dismissals.
29 EqA 2010 s13 or s18.
30 See chapter 6 and para 11.77.
31 MPL Regs 1999 (as amended) reg 7.
32 Four weeks for certain factory workers: Public Health Act 1936 s205.

11.17   OML starts on a date notified by the woman, which she can subsequently vary. It can start earlier, eg if childbirth occurs, or on the first day after the start of the fourth week before the expected week of childbirth (EWC) when she is absent from work wholly or partly because of pregnancy.[33] This means that maternity leave could start automatically, even though the woman does not want it to, just because she is off work through pregnancy-related sickness for an isolated day. However, her employer may be prepared to make an agreement that her leave is not automatically triggered in this way.

The required notifications

11.18   The woman must give notice no later than the end of the fifteenth week before her EWC (or if that is not reasonably practicable, as soon as reasonably practicable afterwards) of:

- her pregnancy;
- the EWC;
- (in writing if her employer so requests) the date she intends her OML to start;[34] this cannot be earlier than the eleventh week before the EWC.

11.19   The woman can change her mind about the date she wants her leave to start, as long as she gives her employer at least 28 days' notice before the date varied or the new date (whichever is earlier), or if that is not reasonably practicable, as soon as is reasonably practicable.[35]

11.20   Where the woman's OML is automatically triggered by a pregnancy-related absence in the last four weeks before the EWC (see above), she must notify the employer (in writing if requested) as soon as reasonably practicable that she is absent due to pregnancy and the date her absence began for that reason. Similarly, if her leave is triggered by giving birth, she must notify her employer (in writing if requested) as soon as is reasonably practicable after the birth that she has given birth and the date on which it occurred. Otherwise she will lose her right to OML.[36]

11.21   If requested by her employer, the woman must produce a certificate from a registered medical practitioner or midwife stating the EWC.[37] The EWC means the week, beginning with midnight

---

33 MPL Regs 1999 reg 6.
34 MPL Regs 1999 reg 4.
35 MPL Regs 1999 reg 4(1A).
36 MPL Regs 1999 reg 4(3) and (4).
37 MPL Regs 1999 reg 4(1).

between Saturday and Sunday, in which it is expected that childbirth will occur.[38]

11.22   If a woman has a premature birth, her maternity leave will start on the day after the baby is born (regardless of any date she has formally noted for maternity leave).[39] The woman is entitled to her full leave if she has given birth to a live baby, even if the baby does not survive very long, or if she has a stillbirth after 24 weeks of pregnancy.[40]

Additional maternity leave

Overview

11.23   The right to AML used to be available only to women who had been employed for at least 26 weeks at the start of the fourteenth week before the EWC. However, women no longer need any qualifying service.[41] AML starts on the day after the expiry of OML and continues for 26 weeks.[42]

The required notifications

11.24   The woman must make the same notifications as for OML. She need not state explicitly that she will be taking AML as it is presumed that she will do so.

Returning from ordinary or additional maternity leave

The return date

11.25   Within 28 days of receiving the woman's notification of when she intends to take her leave (see paras 11.18–11.19), the employer must notify her of the date when her maternity leave period will end.[43] If the woman has notified the employer of a variation in the start date, the employer must notify her within 28 days of the start of her OML of when the maternity leave period will end.[44]

---

38 MPL Regs 1999 reg 2(1).
39 MPL Regs 1999 reg 6(2).
40 MPL Regs 1999 reg 2(1).
41 MPL Regs 1999 reg 4(1).
42 MPL Regs 1999 reg 7(4).
43 MPL Regs 1999 reg 7(6) and (7). See para 6.70 if the woman is dismissed for returning late when she did not receive this notification.
44 MPL Regs 1999 reg 7(6) and (7).

11.26   It is then assumed that the woman will return at the end of her 12 months' leave. If she wants to return early, she must give at least eight weeks' notice. Otherwise her employer can postpone her return for up to eight weeks (though not beyond the end of the relevant maternity leave period).[45] The woman can change her mind about her return date as long as she gives at least eight weeks' notice before her original date or her new date, whichever is earlier.[46] If a woman is unable to return after her leave due to sickness, the normal sick-leave procedures at her workplace will apply. If the woman is dismissed during her SML, but before its expiry, the leave period ends at the time of the dismissal.

11.27   Paras 11.58–11.68 below set out the woman's rights during her maternity leave and the nature of the job to which she is entitled to return.

11.28   If the woman wants to share her maternity leave with her partner, she must bring her normal SML to an end and follow the various notification requirements for shared parental leave (SPL), provided she is eligible. This is set out in paras 11.39–11.47.

Adoption leave

11.29   ERA 1996 ss75A and 75B give employees a right to adoption leave which is very similar to the right to maternity leave. The law is set out in the Paternity and Adoption Leave Regulations (PAL Regs) 2002.[47] The following is only a very brief summary and advisers need to check the regulations. Note that the rules have some slight differences for overseas adoptions. The intended parent of a child born via a surrogacy arrangement who has a parental order, or who has applied or intends to apply for one, (a 'parental order parent') is entitled to take ordinary adoption leave (OAL).[48]

11.30   Since 5 April 2015, it has no longer been necessary for employees to have any minimum service to be entitled to adoption leave.[49] Either

---

45 MPL Regs 1999 reg 11. This is 16 weeks for 'employee shareholders' – ERA 1996 s205A(3)(a). For more detail, see paras 6.130–6.131.

46 MPL Regs 1999 reg 11.

47 SI No 2788 as amended by the Maternity and Parental Leave etc and the Paternity and Adoption Leave (Amendment) Regulations 2006 SI No 2014.

48 Paternity, Adoption and Shared Parental Leave (Parental Order Cases) Regulations 2014 SI No 3096.

49 PAL Regs 2002 reg 15(2) as amended by the Paternity and Adoption Leave (Amendment) Regulations 2014 SI No 2112.

adoptive parent can take the leave but not both. However, the other parent may be able to take paternity leave, or both could take SPL.[50]

11.31 No later than seven days after the date the employee is notified of having been matched with the child, the employee must give the employer notice of the date when the child is expected to be placed with him/her and the date when s/he wishes the leave to begin. The employee can give notice to vary the date once given.[51] Within 28 days of this notification, the employer must write to the employee setting out the date s/he is due to return.[52] If the employer requests, the employee must also provide the employer with documents issued by the adoption agency confirming certain details.[53]

11.32 OAL starts either when the child is placed with the employee or on a date up to two weeks earlier which the employee has notified to the employer.[54] The employee will usually be entitled to 26 weeks of OAL and a further 26 consecutive weeks of additional adoption leave (AAL).[55] If the employee wishes to return earlier, s/he must give at least eight weeks' notice.[56] If the placement is disrupted during adoption leave, eg because it will not take place or because the child dies, the employee will be entitled to eight weeks' leave from the disruption or death, although not beyond the end of the AAL period.[57]

11.33 An employee's rights during OAL and AAL and on return are virtually identical to those for OML and AML (see paras 11.58–11.67).[58]

11.34 Statutory adoption pay (SAP) is available for employees who meet the necessary criteria and who have worked for the employer for at least 26 weeks by the week they were matched with the child.[59] It is payable during adoption leave for a maximum of 39 weeks at

---

50 PAL Regs 2002 reg 8; SPL Regs 2014; and see paras 11.35 and 11.39.
51 PAL Regs 2002 reg 16(4)–(5).
52 PAL Regs 2002 reg 16(7) and (8).
53 PAL Regs 2002 reg 17(3).
54 PAL Regs 2002 reg 16.
55 PAL Regs 2002 reg 20.
56 PAL Regs 2002 reg 25. This is 16 weeks for 'employee shareholders' – ERA 1996 s205A(3)(b). For more detail, see paras 6.130–6.131.
57 PAL Regs 2002 reg 22.
58 PAL Regs 2002 regs 19–21, 23–24 and 26–27.
59 More detail at: www.gov.uk/adoption-pay-leave/eligibility.

90 per cent of weekly pay, subject to a maximum of £151.97 after the first six weeks.[60]

Paternity leave

11.35   The right to ordinary paternity leave (OPL) is set out in ERA 1996 ss80A–80E and the PAL Regs 2002.[61] As with the rights to maternity and adoption leaves, the rules are detailed and the following is only a summary. An employee who is the father of the child or married to or the partner of the child's mother is entitled to paternity leave if he has responsibility for the child's upbringing.[62] Same-sex partners are included.[63] An employee is also entitled to take paternity leave where he is married to or the partner of the child's adopter.[64] An employee taking paternity leave must have been continuously employed for at least 26 weeks ending with the week immediately preceding the four-teenth week before the EWC.[65] There is a right to paternity leave even if the child has died or was stillborn after 24 weeks of pregnancy.

11.36   The employee can take either one week's leave or two consecutive weeks, but not two separate weeks and not individual days.[66] The leave must be taken within 56 days of the child's birth or, if the child is born prematurely, of the EWC.[67] In or before the fifteenth week before the EWC, the employee must give the employer notice of his intention to take paternity leave, specifying the EWC, the length of leave he wishes to take and the start date.[68] He can vary the date by giving 28 days' notification.[69] If it is not reasonably practicable to give

---

60   From 4 April 2021. The Social Security Benefits Up-rating Order 2021 SI No 162 articles 11 and 1(3)(g). Rates may increase annually. Rates can also be found at: www.gov.uk/employers-adoption-pay-leave together with a link to an interactive calculator. If the employee was on furlough, calculation is on the basis of normal earnings – see Statutory Maternity Pay, Statutory Paternity Pay, Statutory Adoption Pay, Statutory Shared Parental Pay and Statutory Parental Bereavement Pay (Normal Weekly Earnings etc) (Coronavirus) (Amendment) Regulations 2020 SI No 450.
61   SI No 2788.
62   PAL Regs 2002 reg 4.
63   PAL Regs 2002 reg 2.
64   See PAL Regs 2002 regs 8–11 for details.
65   PAL Regs 2002 reg 4.
66   PAL Regs 2002 reg 5.
67   PAL Regs 2002 reg 5.
68   PAL Regs 2002 reg 6(1).
69   PAL Regs 2002 reg 6(4) and (5) for details.

these notifications, the employee must give them as soon as reasonably practicable afterwards.

11.37 The employee is entitled to return to the job in which he was employed previously. If he has added the paternity leave onto other statutory absences, eg AAL or parental leave of more than four weeks, then if it is not reasonably practicable to let him return to the same job, he is entitled to return to another job which is suitable and appropriate for him.[70] During OPL, the employee is entitled to the benefit of all his terms and conditions of employment as if he had not been absent, apart from wages or salary.[71] Employees who meet the necessary criteria can claim statutory paternity pay at 90 per cent of weekly pay or £151.97,[72] whichever is less.

11.38 An employee is not entitled to take OPL if he has taken any SPL in respect of the child.[73] Additional paternity leave (APL) no longer exists as it has been replaced by SPL (see below).

Shared parental leave

11.39 The right to SPL arises where a child's EWC or the adoption placement was on or after 5 April 2015.[74] SPL applies where a birth mother wishes to share her maternity leave and pay with 'P', the father of the child or husband or civil or other partner of the mother. The general idea is that a mother who is eligible for SML and statutory maternity pay (SMP) can cut short her leave and pay, and share the balance after the child's birth with P. The mother must still take at least two weeks CML after birth. The mother and P can decide to take the leave at the same time or take it in turns to be off work. SPL replaces the old

---

70 PAL Regs 2002 reg 13(2).
71 PAL Regs 2002 reg 12.
72 From 4 April 2021. The Social Security Benefits Up-rating Order 2021 SI No 162 articles 11 and 1(3g). Rates usually increase annually. The latest rates can also be checked on the GOV.UK website at: www.gov.uk/paternity-pay-leave/pay. Rates may increase annually. If the employee was on furlough, calculation is on the basis of normal earnings – see Statutory Maternity Pay, Statutory Paternity Pay, Statutory Adoption Pay, Statutory Shared Parental Pay and Statutory Parental Bereavement Pay (Normal Weekly Earnings etc) (Coronavirus) (Amendment) Regulations 2020 SI No 450.
73 PAL Regs 2002 reg 4(1A).
74 Shared Parental Leave Regulations (SPL Regs) 2014 SI No 3050 reg 2.

system of APL,[75] although OPL still exists (see para 11.35). It is possible that only one of the mother and P is eligible for SPL. The rules for SPL are painfully detailed and complicated and can only be summarised here. There are similar rights for employees who adopt children and for intended parents of surrogate children. There are two useful and clear guides, although they have no formal legal status: *Employers' technical guide to shared parental leave and pay* (December 2014, updated April 2020) published by the Department for Business, Energy & Industrial Strategy (BEIS);[76] and the Advisory, Conciliation and Arbitration Service's (ACAS's) *Shared parental leave: a good practice guide for employers and employees.*[77] There are also some template forms on the ACAS website which are intended to cover all the information which must be provided at each stage.

11.40 Employees are eligible for SPL if they have been continuously employed for at least 26 weeks by the end of the fifteenth week before the EWC or, if the child is born earlier, would otherwise have reached that number of weeks.[78] They must also remain employed by that employer until the week before they take any period of SPL. A mother is eligible for SPL to care for a child if she has the main responsibility for the child's care at the date of birth (apart from P's responsibility), she is entitled to SML, and she has curtailed her right to SML or has in practice returned to work before the end of her SML. If the mother wants to return to work early, she needs to give at least eight weeks' notice in accordance with the usual rules for returning from maternity leave.[79] Alternatively, she can cut short her entitlement to SML by serving a 'maternity leave curtailment notice'.[80] The effect of this is to make the balance of SML available for SPL. The mother must also give the correct notices and provide evidence as set out below. In

75 Abolished on 5 April 2015: Children and Families Act 2014 s125 brought into force by the Children and Families Act 2014 (Commencement No 3, Transitional Provisions and Savings) Order 2014 SI No 1640 article 6.

76 At: www.gov.uk/government/uploads/system/uploads/attachment_data/file/353019/bis-14-1076-employers-technical-guide-shared-parental-leave-and-pay.pdf.

77 You can find it at www.nct.org.uk/sites/default/files/related_documents/ACAS%20guide%20to%20Shared%20Parental%20Leave.pdf. ACAS's current guidance on its website with templates is at www.acas.org.uk/shared-parental-leave-and-pay.

78 SPL Regs 2014 regs 4, 5, and 35.

79 MPL Regs 1999 reg 11; see para 11.26.

80 Maternity and Adoption Leave (Curtailment of Statutory Rights to Leave) Regulations 2014 SI No 3052 regs 5–6.

addition, P must satisfy the earnings and employment test[81] and, at the date of birth, must have the main responsibility for the care of the child (apart from the mother's responsibility).[82] P's eligibility for SPL has mirror image requirements except that, whereas the mother must be entitled to SML for her own eligibility for SPL, it is sufficient for P's eligibility if the mother was entitled to SML or SMP or maternity allowance.[83] So for example, in the unusual situation where the mother is entitled to maternity allowance but not to SML, P would be entitled to SPL but the mother would not.

11.41   SPL can be taken at any time between the date of birth and the child's first birthday. It must be taken in whole weeks, but it can be taken as one continuous period or broken up ('discontinuous leave').[84] Where the mother returns to work before the end of her SML, the total amount of SPL available is 52 weeks less the number of weeks SML which she has already taken. Where the mother has instead served a maternity leave curtailment notice, it is 52 weeks less the period from the start of her SML to the curtailment date in the notice.[85] There are different rules in the small number of cases where the mother is not entitled to SML. The two weeks CML (four weeks for certain factory workers) must be taken by the mother. The way the SPL is shared between the mother and P depends on the agreement they make between them.

11.42   The mother must give her employer a written 'notice of entitlement' at least eight weeks before she intends to take the first period of SPL.[86] The notice must state her name, P's name, the child's EWC and the actual date of birth, the start and end dates of any SML taken or to be taken by her, the total amount of SPL available, how much SPL she and P each intend to take and an indication of the dates when she intends to take SPL. Ultimately the mother can take SPL on different dates, but the point is to give the employer some idea of what she has in mind. If the child has not yet been born, the mother must notify the date as soon as practicable after birth and in advance of any period of SPL to be taken. The mother must also provide signed declarations from P and herself, essentially confirming their eligibility for SPL. P's declaration must give his/her name and

---

81 SPL Regs 2014 reg 36.
82 SPL Regs 2014 reg 4.
83 SPL Regs 2014 reg 5.
84 SPL Regs 2014 reg 7.
85 SPL Regs 2014 reg 6(1).
86 SPL Regs 2014 reg 8.

address and NI number and give consent to the amount of leave which the mother says she intends to take in the notice of entitlement.[87] In order to take his/her own period of SPL, P must serve his/her own employer with a very similar notice of entitlement and declarations.[88] There are various rules if the mother and P wish to vary the notice of entitlement so as to change the amount of leave each of them intend to take.[89] Within 14 days of her notice of entitlement, the employer can ask the mother for a copy of the child's birth certificate and the name and address of P's employer. P's employer can make a similar request of P. The birth certificate (or a declaration where one has not yet been issued) must be supplied within 14 days of the child's birth. The details of the other person's employment must be provided within 14 days of the request.[90]

11.43   The mother and P must also each give their employer a 'period of leave notice' (informally known as a 'booking notice'), which sets out the start and end dates of each period of requested SPL. The notice can be provided at the same time as the notice of entitlement, but in any event, must be given to the employer at least eight weeks before the earliest date requested in the notice.[91] A notice can contain a request for a continuous block or leave, and provided the correct notifications have been made, the employer cannot refuse the request.[92] Alternatively, the notice can request a discontinuous period, eg four weeks on, four weeks off. Where discontinuous periods of leave are requested in a single booking notice, the employer has two weeks within which to agree or refuse. If the employer refuses, the employee is entitled to take the total amount requested as a continuous period of leave, but there are further detailed rules regarding timing and notification.[93]

11.44   Only three booking notices can be submitted in total, unless the child was born early or late or the employer asks for a variation.[94] After that, it is up to the employer whether to agree further periods of SPL. If the mother and P want to vary the dates notified, they must

---

87 For exact requirements of the declarations, see SPL Regs 2014 reg 8(3).
88 SPL Regs 2014 reg 9.
89 SPL Regs 2014 reg 11.
90 SPL Regs 2014 reg 10.
91 SPL Regs 2014 reg 12.
92 SPL Regs 2014 reg 13.
93 SPL Regs 2014 reg 14.
94 SPL Regs 2014 reg 16.

submit a variation notice, but this falls within the three maximum notices.[95]

11.45 During SPL, an employee is entitled to the benefit of his/her terms and conditions except for remuneration, ie sums payable as wages or salary.[96] However, an employee may well be entitled to statutory shared parental pay (ShPP), provided s/he makes the correct notifications. ShPP is £151.97/week or 90 per cent of the employee's earnings, whichever is lower.[97] The mother will have to curtail her own SMP or maternity allowance. The maximum available ShPP is 39 weeks less the amount of SMP or maternity allowance already taken by the mother including the two weeks' CML. Full details of the eligibility requirements are not within the scope of this book. There is an introductory explanation in the BEIS and ACAS guides. A man on SPL cannot claim sex discrimination just because he is getting paid less on SPL than a birth mother would get paid on SML. He can only claim discrimination if a woman on SPL would have been paid more than a man on SPL.[98] As with SML, there are keeping-in-touch (KIT) days, in this case called 'shared parental leave in touch' (SPLIT) days, and unlike KIT days, there are up to 20 days for each of the mother and P. An employee can work SPLIT days during the period when s/he is taking SPL without bringing it to an end or losing his/her ShPP.

11.46 An employee has the right to return to the job s/he was employed in before his/her absence with the same seniority, pension and similar rights and on terms no less favourable than had s/he not been absent.[99] This is qualified where the employee is absent for a total of more than 26 weeks on SPL added together with certain other statutory leaves or is returning from the last of two or more consecutive periods of relevant statutory leave which included a period of

---

95 SPL Regs 2014 reg 15.
96 SPL Regs 2014 reg 38.
97 From 4 April 2021. The Social Security Benefits Up-rating Order 2021 SI No 162, articles 11 and 1(3)(g). Rates usually rise annually. Latest rates are at: www.gov.uk/shared-parental-leave-and-pay/what-youll-get. If the employee was on furlough, calculation is on the basis of normal earnings – see Statutory Maternity Pay, Statutory Paternity Pay, Statutory Adoption Pay, Statutory Shared Parental Pay and Statutory Parental Bereavement Pay (Normal Weekly Earnings etc) (Coronavirus) (Amendment) Regulations 2020 SI No 450.
98 *Capita Customer Management Ltd; Hextall v Chief Constable of Leicestershire Police* [2019] EWCA Civ 900; [2019] IRLR 695. Similarly, if the employer pays men and women on adoption leave more than men and women on SPL: *Price v Powys CC* UKEAT/0133/20.
99 SPL Regs 2014 regs 40–41.

parental leave of more than four weeks, a period of AML, or a period of AAL. In such situations, if it is not reasonably practicable for him/her to return to his/her job for a reason other than redundancy, s/he is entitled to return to another job which is both suitable for him/her and appropriate for him/her to do in the circumstances.

11.47   As with SML, it is automatically unfair to make an employee redundant during SPL if there is a suitable alternative vacancy.[100] It is also automatically unfair to dismiss the employee because s/he took or sought to take SPL or made use of the benefits of SPL, or because s/he considered, worked or refused to work on SPLIT days.[101] In addition, it is unlawful to subject the employee to a detriment other than dismissal for any of these reasons.[102]

Parental leave

Introduction

11.48   Employees have a limited right to have unpaid leave for the purpose of caring for a child.[103] Confusingly, this is called 'parental leave' and must not be muddled with 'shared parental leave', which is described in the previous paragraphs and concerns sharing maternity leave. There is very basic government guidance on parental leave for employees on the GOV.UK website, though this has no formal legal status.[104] There is no definition in the MPL Regs 1999 of what 'caring for a child' means, but the GOV.UK guidance says the leave can be to look at new schools, settle children into new childcare arrangements, spend more time with your children or with the family generally, eg visiting grandparents. Reasons for the leave need not be connected with the child's health. However, employees need to be careful because these suggestions have not all been legally tested. Leave is unpaid, although income support may be available.

Who is entitled?

11.49   Employees who have been continuously employed for at least one year and who have or expect to have parental responsibility for a child

100 SPL Regs 2014 regs 39 and 43(1)(b). See paras 11.61–11.62.
101 SPL Regs 2014 reg 43.
102 SPL Regs 2014 reg 42.
103 MPL Regs 1999 reg 13.
104 At: www.gov.uk/parental-leave.

are entitled to parental leave while their child is under 18.[105] It is not necessary to have had one year's service at the date the child was born.

Overall scheme: how the entitlement works

Overview

11.50 An employee is entitled to a total of 18 weeks' leave in respect of each child.[106] A part-time employee's entitlement is pro rata.[107] Both parents are entitled to parental leave. The mother can seek to take parental leave immediately after her SML if she wishes.

11.51 During parental leave, an employee is entitled to the benefit of the employer's implied obligation of trust and confidence and any terms and conditions relating to notice pay on termination; compensation in the case of redundancy; and disciplinary or grievance procedures. The employee is bound by the implied term of trust and confidence; the obligation to give notice of termination; the obligation not to disclose confidential information; and not to participate in any other business; and obligations regarding acceptance of gifts and benefits.[108]

11.52 The government had wanted collective or workforce agreements to be made, setting out detailed rules regarding how a parental leave scheme would work, and that such schemes would be incorporated into individual employees' contracts. A collective agreement or workforce agreement cannot agree less than the minimum entitlements, but can be more generous. It can also work out the precise rules as to how and when leave is taken.

11.53 If there is no such collective agreed scheme, a default scheme applies (see below).[109] The default scheme may be less generous than a scheme which could be negotiated by collective agreement. For example, a collective agreement could negotiate more flexible notice requirements than appear in the default scheme. Other examples of more generous terms could include allowing more than 18 weeks in

---

105 MPL Regs 1999 reg 15. Restriction of the entitlement to leave for children under five was removed from 5 April 2015 by the Maternity and Parental Leave etc (Amendment) Regulations 2014 SI No 3221.

106 MPL Regs 1999 reg 14.

107 MPL Regs 1999 reg 14.

108 MPL Regs 1999 reg 17.

109 MPL Regs 1999 reg 16.

total, allowing paid leave, or allowing leave to be taken in single days or in the form of reduced hours working.[110]

The default scheme

11.54　The default scheme is set out in MPL Regs 1999 Sch 2.[111] Better terms may be collectively agreed. The key elements of the scheme are as follows, though for exact details the regulations should be checked. Under the scheme, an employee cannot take more than four weeks in respect of an individual child during a particular year. The employee can only take the leave in one-week blocks (or part-time equivalent), but not in single days.[112] The exception is for a child entitled to a disability living allowance (DLA), armed forces independence payment or personal independence payment (PIP). An employee is not entitled to the leave unless s/he produces, if requested, any evidence to the employer which is reasonably required to establish the employee's responsibility for the child and the child's date of birth or adoption date.

11.55　　The employee must give the correct notice. Except where a baby is yet to be born or adopted, the required notice must specify the dates the leave period will start and end, and give the employer at least 21 days' notice of the start. The employer can postpone this leave if the operation of the business would be unduly disrupted, provided the employer agrees a period of leave of equivalent length may be taken within six months, starting on a date determined by the employer after consulting the worker. The employer must give the employee written notice of such postponement, stating the reason for it, and specifying the new dates. The notice must be given to the employee no more than seven days after the employee's notice was given to the employer.

11.56　　If the employee is an expectant father, he need only specify the EWC and the duration of the leave period. He must give the notice at least 21 days in advance of the EWC. If the child is to be adopted, the employee need only notify the expected week of placement, the duration of the required leave, and again must give notice at least 21 days in advance.

110　Without such agreement, the restricted default scheme will apply to this, eg as in *Rodway v South Central Trains Ltd* [2005] IRLR 583, CA.

111　SI No 3312.

112　*Rodway v South Central Trains Ltd* [2005] IRLR 583, CA.

11.57   An employee can bring an ET claim if his/her employer unreasonably postpones or prevents him/her taking parental leave.[113] The claim must be made within three months of the matters complained of, and the ET can award compensation which it considers just and equitable, having regard to the employer's behaviour and any resultant loss suffered by the employee.[114]

The right to return after maternity or parental leave

Ordinary maternity leave

11.58   A woman is entitled to return to the job in which she was employed before her absence on no less favourable terms and conditions than had she not been absent.[115] Her seniority, pension rights and similar rights must be as if she had not been absent.[116] The 'same job' does not mean the woman has to be allowed to return to literally the same position as before she went onto leave. On the other hand, the employer cannot change her duties or workplace just because that is allowed by the woman's contract. Basically, the tribunal will take account of the normal range of variation in duties and location which occurred before the woman went onto leave. The legislation seeks to ensure there is as little dislocation as reasonably possible in her working life, so as to avoid adding to the burdens which will inevitably exist in her family or private life simply because she has a very young infant making new demands upon her.[117]

Additional maternity leave and/or parental leave

11.59   An employee who takes parental leave as an isolated period of four weeks or less is entitled to return to the job in which s/he was employed before his/her absence. The same applies if his/her parental leave consecutively followed periods of other statutory leave unless it included:

i)   any period of parental leave of more than four weeks; or

---

113   ERA 1996 s80(1).
114   ERA 1996 s80(2) and (4).
115   MPL Regs 1999 regs 18(1) and 18A(1)(a)(ii) and (b).
116   MPL Regs 1999 reg 18A(1)(a)(ii).
117   *Blundell v (1) The Governing Body of St Andrew's Catholic Primary School (2) Assid* UKEAT/0329/06; [2007] IRLR 652, EAT.

ii) any period of statutory leave which when added to any other period of statutory leave (excluding parental leave) taken in relation to the same child means that the total amount of statutory leave taken in relation to that child totalled more than 26 weeks.[118]

Where the employee returns from AML or from more than four weeks' parental leave (whether or not preceded by another period of statutory leave) or from a period of parental leave which is four weeks or less but not within the above categories, the right is again to return to the same job, except that if it is not reasonably practicable to do so, it is only a right to return to another job which is suitable and appropriate for the employee in the circumstances.[119] The position is different where a redundancy situation arises during maternity leave (see para 11.61).[120]

11.60   The employee is entitled to return on terms and conditions (including remuneration) not less favourable than those which would have applied had s/he not taken any maternity or parental leave and with seniority, pension and similar rights treated as if s/he had not been away.[121] On return, the employee should therefore get any payrise awarded during his/her leave. See para 4.102 regarding accrual of statutory annual leave.

Redundancy during maternity, adoption and shared parental leave

11.61   Where, during OML or AML, it is not practicable due to redundancy for the woman's employer to continue to employ her under her existing contract of employment, the woman must be offered any suitable available vacancy with her employer or an associated employer.[122] The terms and conditions (including capacity and place) must not be substantially less favourable than had she continued under the previous contract.[123] It is up to the employer, knowing what it does about the employee, to decide whether the vacancy is suitable. Suitability

---

118 MPL Regs 1999 reg 18(1).
119 MPL Regs 1999 reg 18(2).
120 MPL Regs 1999 reg 18(4).
121 MPL Regs 1999 reg 18A(1). See also reg 18A(2) on employment-related benefit schemes if applicable.
122 MPL Regs 1999 reg 10. For an interesting example in the context of restructuring, see *Sefton BC v Wainwright* [2015] IRLR 90, EAT.
123 MPL Regs 1999 reg 10(3).

includes refers to the terms and conditions as well as the suitability of the job itself.[124]

11.62   The offer must be made before the end of her existing contract of employment and must start immediately on the ending of her existing contract of employment. There are similar rights where an employee on adoption leave or shared parental leave is made redundant.[125] This special right does not apply when a woman's position becomes redundant during pregnancy.

Rights during leave

Overview

11.63   Less favourable treatment of a woman because she is absent on maternity leave is unlawful maternity discrimination under EqA 2010 s18(3) or (4) and the previous domestic and EU case-law.[126] A woman should be told of any job vacancies arising while she is on leave in which she may be interested. Failure to do so could amount to a fundamental breach of trust and confidence entitling her to resign,[127] and may also be pregnancy or maternity discrimination. It is discriminatory to fail to give a woman a performance-related pay assessment because she has been absent on maternity leave.[128] Similarly, a woman must be given the benefit of any pay-rise awarded before or during maternity leave.[129]

11.64   Despite these cases, a woman cannot argue that she should be paid full wages during maternity leave purely because her absence is pregnancy-related.[130] This is because women on maternity leave are

124 *Simpson v Endsleigh Insurance Services Ltd* UKEAT/0544/09.
125 PAL Regs 2002 reg 23 and SPL Regs 2014 reg 39 respectively.
126 *Land Brandenburg v Sass* [2005] IRLR 147, ECJ; *Sarkatzis Herrero v Instituto Madrileno de la Salud* [2006] IRLR 296, ECJ. A recent Employment Appeal Tribunal (EAT) case, *Interserve FM Ltd v Tuleikyte* UKEAT/0267/16; [2017] IRLR 615, takes a narrow view of what 'because' means and EU case-law suggests it must be incorrect with regard to treatment during the protected period. In the light of *Tuleikyte*, where a woman is deprived of pay rises, appraisals etc simply because she is absent while on maternity leave, it may be wise to claim indirect sex discrimination in the alternative.
127 *Visa International Service Association v Paul* [2004] IRLR 42, EAT.
128 *Caisse Nationale D'Assurance Vieillesse des Travailleurs Salariés (CNAVTS) v Thibault* [1998] IRLR 399, ECJ.
129 *Gillespie v Northern Health and Social Services Board* [1996] IRLR 214, ECJ; EqA 2010 s74(8).
130 *Gillespie v Northern Health and Social Services Board* [1996] IRLR 214, ECJ.

in a special position that affords them special protection, but which is not comparable with the position of other workers. The only requirement under EU law is that maternity pay must not fall below an adequate level, ie that of statutory sick benefits.[131] This requirement is normally satisfied by the level of SMP.[132] Even where the contract gives contractual sick pay, but not contractual maternity pay, this is not sex or pregnancy or maternity discrimination.[133] The same applies if there is contractual pay for both sickness and maternity leave, but only the maternity pay must be repaid if the woman fails to return to work for a specified time after her absence.[134]

11.65   A woman on maternity leave is entitled to the benefit of her terms and conditions except for remuneration (and is also bound by obligations) which would apply if she was not absent.[135] This includes non-contractual matters which are connected with her employment.[136] 'Remuneration' refers only to sums payable as wages or salary.[137] This suggests that the woman will still be entitled to benefits in kind, eg health insurance and company cars. If a woman is paid contractual maternity pay, it must be calculated on the basis of any pay increase which she received during her pregnancy or SML (or would have received if she was not on maternity leave).[138] It is discriminatory to deprive a woman of a bonus (whether contractual or discretionary), payable in respect of a period before or after her pregnancy and SML, or in respect of the compulsory leave period (usually two weeks).[139] It seems it is not discriminatory to reduce a woman's contractual bonus in respect of any other period when she was absent on maternity leave.[140] For the position regarding annual

---

131 *Gillespie v Northern Health and Social Services Board* [1996] IRLR 214, ECJ; *Gillespie v Northern Health and Social Services Board (No 2); Todd v Eastern Health and Social Services Board and Department of Health and Social Services* [1997] IRLR 410, NICA.

132 But see *Banks v (1) Tesco Stores Ltd (2) Secretary of State for Social Security* [1999] UKEAT 911_97_1509, where the woman was ineligible even for SMP.

133 *Gillespie v Northern Health and Social Services Board (No 2); Todd v Eastern Health and Social Services Board and Department of Health and Social Services* [1997] IRLR 410, NICA.

134 *Boyle v Equal Opportunities Commission* [1998] IRLR 717, ECJ.

135 MPL Regs 1999 reg 9. Under the EqA 2010, see s74.

136 ERA 1996 s71(5)(a).

137 MPL Regs 1999 reg 9.

138 EqA 2010 s74(1)–(5).

139 EqA 2010 s74(6)–(7) if contractual; if discretionary: *Lewin v Denda* [2000] IRLR 67, ECJ and EqA 2010 s18.

140 *Hoyland v Asda Stores Ltd* [2006] IRLR 468, CtS, though this is untested by the ECJ and *Hoyland* did not concern discretionary bonuses.

leave entitlement, see para 4.102. An occupational pension scheme is deemed to include a maternity equality rule.[141] The law on pensions and equality is very complex and outside the scope of this book. As a rough guide, terms related to membership of the scheme or accrual of rights under the scheme or determination of the amount of benefit under the scheme must treat time when the woman is on maternity leave as time when she is not on leave. In regard to accrual of rights, this only applies during AML for periods where the woman was getting paid SMP or contractual maternity pay. The woman's contributions to the scheme during her leave need only be determined by reference to the amount she is paid while on leave.

Keeping in touch

11.66   An employee can carry out up to ten days' work or training for her employer during her SML without bringing the leave to an end or losing her maternity pay.[142] It is for the employer and employee to agree any additional payments for working those days. The days can be worked singly or in blocks. Any work carried out on a particular day counts as a day's work. The maternity leave period does not get extended if the employee does choose to work any of these days. In addition, reasonable contact can be made from time to time by the woman or her employer, eg to discuss arrangements for the woman's return to work. Contact can be made in any way, eg by telephone, email, letter or in person. What amounts to 'reasonable' presumably depends on all the circumstances – the type of work, any agreement between the woman and the employer before her leave, whether there is important information to communicate, and what the woman feels happy with.

11.67   Neither the employer nor the employee can insist on work being carried out during maternity leave. If a woman is dismissed or otherwise penalised for refusing to do such work, she can claim automatic unfair dismissal or unlawful detriment.[143] No work must be carried out in the two-week compulsory leave period following childbirth.

---

141 EqA 2010 s75. It is recommended that the section is read for its full detail.
142 MPL Regs 1999 reg 12A.
143 MPL Regs 1999 regs 20(3)(eee) and 19(2)(eee).

Statutory maternity pay

11.68   Women who meet the service and earnings qualifying conditions can claim SMP for 39 weeks of their leave period. A woman must have been continuously employed for at least 26 weeks ending with the fifteenth week before her EWC. A woman should give 28 days' notice of when she wants her SMP to begin, in writing if the employer requests. Normally she cannot start receiving SMP until she has reached the eleventh week before her EWC (although she need not still be employed by then). She also cannot receive SMP until she has stopped work entirely for the employer (except for KIT days, which are exempt – see para 11.66). Subject to the above, it does not matter if the woman is made redundant or otherwise leaves the employment before or after her maternity pay period begins. Moreover, if the employer dismisses her before she reaches 26 weeks' service or before the fifteenth week before her EWC, and she can prove this was to avoid liability for SMP, she can still claim, provided she had been employed for at least eight weeks at the time of dismissal. A woman's right to receive SMP is not dependent on whether she intends to return to work after the child is born, and an employer cannot try to recover SMP if she does not return. However, a woman can be required to return the amount of any higher contractual maternity pay if she does not return to work afterwards, if there is a contractual agreement to that effect.[144] SMP is paid at 90 per cent of the woman's average pay, but subject to a weekly maximum of £151.97[145] after the first six weeks. If the woman was on furlough, weekly earnings are calculated by reference to what she would have been paid if not furloughed.[146] Women who do not qualify for SMP may be able to claim maternity allowance. The calculation of SMP must take account of any pay rises between the start of the period over which maternity pay is calculated and the end of maternity leave.[147] The above is a loose overview, without all the detailed rules,

---

144 *Boyle v Equal Opportunities Commission* [1998] IRLR 717, ECJ.

145 From 4 April 2021. Statutory Maternity Pay (General) Regulations 1986 SI No 1960 as amended by the Social Security Benefits Up-rating Order 2021 SI No 162 articles 10 and 1(3)(f). Rates usually increase annually. Latest rates and an interactive calculator are available at: www.gov.uk/maternity-pay-leave/pay.

146 Statutory Maternity Pay, Statutory Paternity Pay, Statutory Adoption Pay, Statutory Shared Parental Pay and Statutory Parental Bereavement Pay (Normal Weekly Earnings etc) (Coronavirus) (Amendment) Regulations 2020 SI No 450.

147 Statutory Maternity Pay (General) (Amendment) Regulations 2005 SI No 729, putting into effect *Alabaster v Woolwich plc* [2004] IRLR 486, ECJ.

and should not be relied on for giving advice in individual cases. Social security benefits are not within the scope of this book and specialist advice must be obtained in this area.

Contractual rights to maternity or parental leave

11.69   Where an employee is entitled to maternity or parental leave and also has a right under his/her contract of employment, s/he cannot exercise each right separately, but may take advantage of whichever right is in any particular respect the more favourable.[148]

Dependant leave

11.70   An employee is entitled to reasonable unpaid[149] time off to take action necessary for any of the following purposes:[150]

   a) to provide assistance on an occasion when a dependant is injured or assaulted, falls ill or gives birth;
   b) to make care arrangements for a dependant who is ill or injured;
   c) in consequence of the death of a dependant;
   d) because of the unexpected disruption or termination of arrangements for the care of a dependant;
   e) to deal with an incident involving the employee's child which occurs unexpectedly while the child is at an educational establishment.

11.71   There is no minimum length of service required for this entitlement. The employee may not have time off to allow him/her personally to provide care beyond the reasonable amount necessary to deal with the immediate crisis.[151] If the dependant has an underlying medical condition which is likely to cause regular relapses, the situation is no longer covered.[152] Time off due to an 'unexpected disruption' to care arrangements is not confined to sudden emergencies, although the time lapse between the employee becoming aware of the future disruption and the date of that disruption may affect whether it is 'necessary' for the employee to take the time.[153] For example, it may

---

148 MPL Regs 1999 reg 21.
149 Unless the contract of employment gives a right to paid leave.
150 ERA 1996 s57A(1).
151 *Qua v John Ford Morrison Solicitors* [2003] IRLR 184, EAT.
152 *Qua v John Ford Morrison Solicitors* [2003] IRLR 184, EAT.
153 *Royal Bank of Scotland PLC v Harrison* UKEAT/0093/08; [2009] IRLR 28.

be necessary to take the leave if an employee has received only two weeks' notice of the unavailability of a childminder, but it is unlikely to be necessary if s/he has had six months' forewarning.

11.72   The employee's time off in consequence of the death of a dependant includes such matters as making arrangements for and attending the funeral, applying for probate and being interviewed by the probate office, but it does not extend to time off for a bereavement reaction by way of compassionate leave.[154] There is a separate entitlement to parental bereavement leave (see below).

11.73   To have the right to dependant leave, the worker must tell the employer, as soon as reasonably practicable, how long s/he expects to be absent and the reason.[155] S/he needs to say enough to indicate the nature of the problem and that something has happened which makes it urgent to leave work, but s/he does not need formally to spell out all the circumstances.[156] The amount of time off which is 'reasonable' depends on the individual circumstances. The employer can take account of the number, length and dates of previous absences, but cannot take account of any disruption or inconvenience caused to the business.[157]

11.74   A 'dependant' means a spouse, civil partner, child, parent or person (other than a tenant, lodger or employee) who lives in the employee's household, eg a grandparent or cohabitee. In relation to the right to time off in categories a), b) or d) above, it also includes anyone who reasonably relies on the employee for assistance or to make arrangements in those circumstances.[158]

11.75   An employee can complain to an employment tribunal (ET) within three months of any refusal of such time off. The ET can award compensation which it considers just and equitable including for resulting loss.[159]

Parental bereavement leave

11.76   An employee who is the bereaved parent of a child is entitled to take up to two weeks' bereavement leave within 56 weeks of the death of

154 *Forster v Cartwright Black* [2004] IRLR 781, EAT.
155 ERA 1996 s57A(2).
156 *Truelove v Safeway Stores plc* UKEAT/0295/04.
157 *Qua v John Ford Morrison Solicitors* [2003] IRLR 184, EAT.
158 ERA 1996 s57A(3) and (4).
159 ERA 1996 s57A(4).

the child.[160] A 'child' means someone under the age of 18 and includes a baby who is stillborn after 24 weeks of pregnancy.[161] Parental bereavement leave can only be taken as two consecutive weeks or in two periods of one week each.[162]

11.77 An employee can take the leave if s/he is the natural parent, adoptive parent, a person with whom the child was placed for adoption, or the partner of a parent or adoptive parent.[163] It also includes a 'parent in fact', ie a person in whose home the child had been living for at least four weeks at the date of death and who had day-to-day responsibility for their care, but not on a paid basis, and not if the child's parent or someone with parental responsibility lived in the same premises. The employee does not need to have any minimum length of service.

11.78 The employee must notify the employer of the date of death or stillbirth, when the leave will start and its length. This need not be in writing. If leave is to start within 56 days of the date of death or stillbirth, notification must be given before the first leave day or as soon as reasonably practicable afterwards. For later leave, the employee must give at least seven days' notice.[164]

11.79 As with maternity, adoption and shared parental leave, employees on parental bereavement leave continues to have the benefit of their terms and conditions except in relation to wages or salary. They also continue to be bound by their contractual obligations except those inconsistent with being on leave.[165] The employee has the right to return to the same job. If the bereavement leave follows other leaves, that right is modified.[166]

11.80 If an employee has 26 weeks' continuous employment ending with the week before the bereavement and meets the minimum earnings condition, s/he is entitled to statutory parental bereavement pay. This is 90 per cent of the employee's weekly pay, subject to a

---

160 ERA 1996 ss 80EA–80EE, applying to bereavements on or after 6 April 2020.
161 ERA 1996 s80EA(9).
162 Parental Bereavement Leave Regulations (PBL Regs) 2020 SI No 249 reg 5.
163 There are a few other categories – see PBL Regs 2020 reg 4.
164 PBL Regs 2020 reg 6.
165 ERA 1996 s80EB(1)(b); PBL Regs 2020 reg 9.
166 PBL Regs 2020 regs 10–11.

maximum of £151.97.[167] The employee needs to give notice to show eligibility.

11.81 ACAS has general guidance on time off for bereavement on its website, including this new right to parental bereavement leave and pay.[168] There is a sample bereavement policy for downloading, which contains considerations of how return to work should be managed.

Detriments and automatic unfair dismissal

11.82 It is automatically unfair dismissal to dismiss an employee for a number of reasons related to the fact that s/he has taken maternity, paternity, adoption, parental, shared parental, dependant or bereavement leave. No minimum qualifying service is required. It is also unlawful to subject an employee to a detriment other than dismissal for any of those reasons. See paras 6.70–6.73 for the reasons and exceptions.

Suspension from work on maternity grounds

11.83 The Management of Health and Safety at Work Regulations (MHSW Regs) 1999[169] together with ERA 1996 ss66–68 implement the health and safety provisions in EU Pregnant Workers Directive Articles 4 and 5.[170] The rules on health and safety suspension appear only to apply to women who are employees.[171] The Health and Safety Executive (HSE) provides some guidance for employers and for expectant mothers.[172]

---

167 From 4 April 2021. The Social Security Benefits Up-rating Order 2021 SI No 162 articles 11 and 1(3)(g). Rates are likely to increase annually. If the employee was on furlough, calculation is on the basis of normal earnings – see Statutory Maternity Pay, Statutory Paternity Pay, Statutory Adoption Pay, Statutory Shared Parental Pay and Statutory Parental Bereavement Pay (Normal Weekly Earnings etc) (Coronavirus) (Amendment) Regulations 2020 SI No 4050.

168 At www.acas.org.uk/time-off-for-bereavement.

169 SI No 3242.

170 92/85/EEC.

171 MHSW Regs 1999 refer to employees (as does the ERA 1996) and although 'employee' is not defined in the 1999 Regulations, it is defined it in the parent Health and Safety at Work, etc Act 1974 s53(1).

172 At: www.hse.gov.uk/mothers/.

11.84   As part of their general duty to carry out risk assessment in the workplace,[173] where employees include women of child-bearing age and the work could involve a risk to the mother or baby, employers must include any risk which might be posed to a new or expectant mother.[174] Once the woman has notified her employer in writing that she is pregnant, has given birth in the previous six months or is breast-feeding, the employer must carry out a specific risk assessment in relation to her. The assessment need not be in writing. Where the risk cannot otherwise be avoided, the employer must alter the woman's working conditions or hours of work.[175] If it is not reasonable to do this or it would not avoid the risk, the employer should suspend the woman from work for as long as necessary.[176] This is the woman's entitlement to a health and safety suspension.[177] However, the woman is entitled to be offered any available suitable alternative work before being suspended.[178]

11.85   Failure to carry out a risk assessment for a pregnant woman can be sex discrimination in itself, but only if the woman's work is of a kind which could put her at risk.[179] If the woman resigns because no risk assessment was done, it may also be constructive dismissal.[180] Conversely, it would be sex discrimination for an employer to impose a change of duties or suspension on an unwilling woman, where it is not necessary because of a low level of risk.[181] In most situations, however, it is the woman who wants an adjustment to be made and the employer who is unsympathetic.

11.86   The woman is entitled to be paid during her suspension, unless she has turned down an offer of suitable alternative work for the relevant period.[182] The work must be of a kind which is both suitable in relation to the woman and appropriate for her to do in the circumstances, and on terms and conditions not substantially less favourable

---

173 See chapter 17.

174 MHSW Regs 16(1).

175 MHSW Regs 16(2) and 18.

176 MHSW Regs 16(3).

177 ERA 1996 s66.

178 ERA 1996 s67(1).

179 *Hardman v Mallon t/a Orchard Lodge Nursing Home* [2002] IRLR 516, EAT; *Madarassy v Nomura International plc* [2007] IRLR 246, CA; *O'Neill v Buckinghamshire CC* UKEAT/0020/09; [2010] IRLR 384, EAT.

180 *Bunning v G T Bunning & Sons Ltd* [2005] EWCA Civ 983.

181 *New Southern Railway Ltd v Quinn* [2006] IRLR 266, EAT; *Chief Constable of Devon and Cornwall Police v Town* UKEAT/0194/19.

182 ERA 1996 s68.

than her normal terms and conditions.[183] The woman must produce a medical certificate confirming her pregnancy within a reasonable time of any written request to do so by her employer.[184]

11.87   The risks covered may include night-working[185] and any physical, biological or chemical agent which carries risk to the health and safety of a new or expectant mother, including the risks specified in Annexes I and II to the Pregnant Workers Directive.[186] Physical risks include:

- extremes of heat and cold;
- prolonged exposure to loud noise;
- manual handling of loads;
- regular exposure to shocks and low-frequency vibration;
- working in tightly fitted workstations;
- excessive physical or mental pressure causing stress and anxiety;
- fatigue from standing and other physical work;
- travelling inside or outside the establishment.

Steps to avoid risks could include:

- ensuring available seating;
- granting longer and more frequent rest breaks;
- adjusting workstations;
- ensuring that hours and volume of work are not excessive and that, where possible, the woman has some control over how her work is organised.

11.88   The provisions regarding fatigue are particularly important, but their scope in practice is untested. An example would seem to be as follows: a woman may find that due to pregnancy-related fatigue, she is unable to work her full hours. Her employer must allow her to work reduced hours on full pay (or, if it sufficed, alter her duties so they were less tiring). If the woman became unable to work at all, she must be suspended on full pay. It would be automatically unfair to dismiss her for these reasons.

11.89   Where a woman is suspended without pay, she may claim her pay from an ET. Where she is on paid suspension but the employer has

---

183 ERA 1996 s67(2).

184 MHSW Regs 18(2).

185 MHSW Regs 17.

186 Guidance on the annexed risks and ways to avoid them is available at: http://eur-lex.europa.eu/LexUriServ/LexUriServ.do?uri=CELEX:31992L0085:EN: HTML. The HSE provides guidance regarding risk assessments for expectant mothers at: www.hse.gov.uk/mothers/ – the 'FAQs' are the most useful.

failed to offer some available suitable alternative work, an ET may award any sum it considers just and equitable, with no ceiling.[187] The time limit for these claims is three months from the date the suspension started.[188] It is automatically unfair to dismiss a woman because of her entitlement to a medical suspension and it is unlawful to subject her to a detriment for that reason.[189] It is also automatic unfair dismissal to dismiss a woman who refuses to work in a situation which she reasonably believes may entail serious and imminent danger and unlawful to subject her to a detriment for that reason.[190] If a woman is injured as a result of the employer's failure to comply with the MHSW Regs 1999, she may sue for damages.[191]

Time off for antenatal care

11.90   A pregnant employee must not be unreasonably refused time off during her working hours to attend an appointment for antenatal care, which has been made on the advice of a medical practitioner, registered midwife or registered health visitor.[192] Apart from on the first appointment, if her employer so requests, the woman must produce a certificate from one of the latter, confirming her pregnancy and a document proving the appointment has been made.[193] Antenatal care probably includes relaxation classes attended on medical advice.[194] If the woman is allowed the time off, she is entitled to be paid for it.[195] Agency workers who have completed the 12-week qualifying period[196] are similarly entitled to time off during an assignment for antenatal care which should be paid at the appropriate hourly rate by the agency.[197] Compensation for unreasonable refusal

---

187   ERA 1996 s70.
188   ERA 1996 s70(2).
189   See para 6.70.
190   See paras 6.84–6.89.
191   SI No 3242 reg 22.
192   ERA 1996 s55(1).
193   ERA 1996 s55(2)–(3).
194   As accepted by an ET in *Gregory v Tudsbury* [1982] IRLR 267, IT.
195   ERA 1996 s56 sets out how the pay should be calculated.
196   ERA 1996 s57ZD(1); see para 1.56 above.
197   ERA 1996 ss57ZA–57ZD.

to allow the time off is double the employee's usual pay for the time she should have been allowed.[198]

11.91   In addition, an employee who is the partner of a pregnant employee (whether her spouse or civil partner or an unmarried partner who lives with her in an enduring family relationship) has the right to unpaid time off during working hours to accompany the pregnant employee while she attends her antenatal appointment on up to two occasions for a maximum of six and a half hours each (including travel and waiting time).[199] The father of the expected child who is not the mother's partner, and prospective parents in a surrogacy arrangement who intend to apply for a parental order, also have this entitlement. If the employer so requests, the employee must provide a written statement confirming the date and time of the appointment, his/her relationship to the pregnant employee or child and confirming that the appointment was made on the advice of a registered medical practitioner, midwife or nurse. The employer cannot ask for the pregnant employee's certificate, as that is her property. Agency workers who have completed the 12-week qualifying period have the same rights to accompany.[200] If the employer refuses the time off, the employee or agency worker can claim compensation which is twice the hourly rate for the number of hours involved.[201] BIS produced a guide for employers, *Time off to accompany a pregnant woman to antenatal appointments: employer guide* (September 2014), which explains the right to accompany in simple terms, though it has no legal status.[202]

11.92   It is automatic unfair dismissal to dismiss an employee for taking time off for antenatal care,[203] or for taking time off to accompany a woman to antenatal care appointments.[204] Similarly it is unlawful to subject an agency worker to a detriment for taking time off for

---

198   ERA 1996 s57(4) for employees and s57ZC for agency workers.

199   ERA 1996 s57ZE.

200   ERA 1996 ss57ZG and 57ZI.

201   ERA 1996 ss57ZF and 57ZH.

202   Available at: https://assets.publishing.service.gov.uk/government/uploads/system/uploads/attachment_data/file/361292/bis-14-1063-time-off-to-accompany-a-pregnant-woman-to-ante-natal-appointments-employer-guide.pdf.

203   Either because this is a reason related to her pregnancy and/or because it would be dismissal for asserting a statutory right under ERA 1996 s104.

204   PAL Regs 2002 reg 29(3)(za) and (zb).

antenatal care or to accompany his/her partner to antenatal care appointments.[205]

11.93   Employees who have been notified by an adoption agency that their child is to be placed for adoption are entitled to take paid time off during working hours to attend up to five appointments of up to six and a half hours each in connection with the adoption or for contact with the child.[206] The appointments must have been arranged by the adoption agency. The employer can ask for documentary proof and a signed declaration. This entitlement does not apply once the adoption placement has happened. Where two prospective parents have been notified, only one of them can take the paid time off. The other is entitled to unpaid time off on two of the occasions.[207] Agency workers have equivalent rights.[208] It is automatic unfair dismissal to dismiss an employee for a reason related to taking time off for such adoption appointments and it is unlawful to subject an employee to a detriment for such reasons.[209] It is also unlawful to subject an agency worker to a detriment for exercising his/her rights to attend an adoption appointment (whether the paid or unpaid entitlement).[210]

11.94   In all these cases relating to leave for antenatal care and adoption appointments, an ET complaint must be made within three months of the relevant appointment. Time may be extended if it was not reasonably practicable to do so.[211] The ACAS early conciliation (EC) procedure applies.[212]

Agency workers and maternity

11.95   Provided they are covered by the EqA 2010,[213] agency workers must not be discriminated against because of their pregnancy. The general rules regarding pregnancy and maternity discrimination generally are set out in the rest of this chapter. So, for example, it would be unlawful pregnancy discrimination if an agency refused to take a

---

205 ERA 1996 s47C(5)(a) and (b).
206 ERA 1996 ss57ZJ, 57ZK and 57ZM.
207 ERA 1996 ss57ZL and 57ZM.
208 ERA 1996 ss57ZN–57ZR.
209 ERA 1996 ss99(3)(ab) and 47C(2)(ab); PAL Regs 2002 reg 28(1)(zc), (zd) and reg 29(3)(zc), (zd).
210 ERA 1996 s47C(5)(c), (d).
211 Variously ERA 1996 ss57(2), 57ZF, 57ZM, 57ZC, 57ZG and 57ZQ.
212 Employment Tribunals Act (ETA) 1996 s18(1)(b); see para 20.16.
213 See chapter 12.

worker on or to offer her placements because she was pregnant, or only offered her short placements for that reason. It would also be pregnancy discrimination if a particular hirer refused to accept a woman on a placement because she was pregnant. The law is more complicated if the agency or hirer refuses to let the woman return to her previous assignment after maternity leave. Although EqA 2010 s18 makes it unlawful discrimination to treat a woman unfavourably because she has taken statutory maternity leave, an agency worker may not have been entitled to take such statutory leave. There may be other arguments which succeed, perhaps relying on sex discrimination under EqA 2010 s13, but these are not explored here.

11.96   Agency workers who have completed the 12-week qualifying period have the same rights as employees to time off for antenatal care and adoption appointments. This is explained at para 11.90. There is also a right to a health and safety suspension on maternity grounds for agency workers who have met the 12-week qualifying period.[214] The protection is very similar to that available for permanent employees (see para 11.90 onwards), save with the additional complication that both the hirer and the agency have duties. The rules are set out in the MHSW Regs 1999[215] regs 16A, 17A, 18A and 18AB; and ERA 1996 ss68A–68D, 69A and 70A. The protection lasts for the duration, or originally intended duration, of the worker's assignment. The duties of the hirer (or end-user) and agency are triggered when the agency worker notifies them that she is pregnant, has given birth within the previous six months or is breastfeeding. Where there is a relevant risk, in the first instance it is for the hirer to alter the worker's conditions or hours if it is reasonable to do so. If there is no suitable reasonable adjustment, the hirer must tell the agency immediately, which will then stop sending the worker to the hirer. The agency must then offer any suitable alternative work on terms and conditions which are not substantially less favourable. The worker is entitled to be paid by the agency for the assignment period unless she was offered suitable alternative work which she unreasonably refused.[216]

11.97   Paras 11.84–11.85 deal with an employer's duty to carry out a pregnancy risk assessment in respect of employees. Case-law prior to the passing of the Agency Workers Regulations 2010 already sugges-

---

214 ERA 1996 s68D; see para 1.56.
215 SI No 3242.
216 For precise rules, see ERA 1996 ss68A–68D and 69A–70A, inserted by the Agency Workers Regulations 2010 SI No 93.

ted that in some circumstances, an employment agency would have the duty to carry out the risk assessment and would be guilty of sex discrimination if it failed to do so.[217] The BEIS guide on the Agency Workers Regulations[218] says that if the nature of the assignment is such that there is a potential risk to health and safety, the agency must ask the hirer to carry out a risk assessment and the hirer must carry it out.

Part-time working and other problematic hours or locations

Introduction

11.98   There is no absolute right to work part-time, though unjustifiable refusal of a request may amount to indirect sex discrimination under the EqA 2010. It may also be indirect sex discrimination under the EqA 2010 unjustifiably to treat a part-timer less favourably than a full-timer, eg in relation to her terms and conditions. The Part-time Workers (Prevention of Less Favourable Treatment) Regulations (PTW Regs) 2000[219] also protect part-timers' terms and conditions. The key differences between the PTW Regs 2000 and the EqA 2010 regarding part-timers are:

- Because of the way the definition of indirect sex discrimination works, the EqA 2010 will mainly protect women.
- Under the EqA 2010, the worker needs to prove it is a particular disadvantage for women generally as well as herself to work full-time. This is irrelevant under the PTW Regs 2000.
- The EqA 2010 and the PTW Regs 2000 both cover discrimination in terms and conditions, but in most situations only the EqA 2010 allows a worker to challenge a refusal to allow him/her to work part-time. However, dismissing a worker for refusing to change from part-time to full-time work would potentially be unlawful under the PTW Regs 2000.
- The PTW Regs 2000 require a comparator.
- The EqA 2010 enables workers to challenge other types of requirement which do not fit in with childcare, eg start or finish times. The PTW Regs 2000 only deal with part-time working.

217   *Brocklebank v Silveira* UKEAT/0571/05.
218   See para 1.52.
219   SI No 1551.

11.99   In many ways, the PTW Regs 2000 are simpler to use than the EqA 2010. However, where possible, a worker should claim both under the PTW Regs 2000 and the EqA 2010. Although more difficult to prove, the advantage of an EqA 2010 claim is that it may attract additional compensation, eg for injury to feelings (though not if it is an equal pay claim).[220] The ACAS EC procedure applies both to sex discrimination claims under the EqA 2010 and to claims under the PTW Regs 2000.[221]

Part-time working and sex discrimination

Is there a right to work part-time?

11.100   There is no absolute right in sex discrimination law to work part-time or to job share. However, a number of cases have accepted that women are adversely affected due to childcare responsibilities when only full-time work is available, and this can be unlawful as indirect sex discrimination. More recently, there has been recognition that workers may need time off to care for adult relatives. The evidence indicates that women are more likely to be carers for adults than men,[222] but there have been few cases on this specific point.

11.101   The main case establishing that refusal to let women work part-time may be unlawful indirect sex discrimination was *Home Office v Holmes*[223] in 1984. The stages of proving indirect discrimination are dealt with at para 13.27 onwards.

Is full-time working a provision, criterion or practice?

11.102   There should be no difficulty in proving that an employer who requires a woman to work full-time is imposing a provision, criterion or practice (PCP) that she do so.[224]

---

220 Not available under the PTW Regs 2000 reg 8(11).
221 Employment Tribunals Act (ETA) 1996 s18(1)(e) and (l); see para 20.16.
222 For example, see *Living longer: caring in later working life*: ONS 15.3.19 at www.ons.gov.uk/peoplepopulationandcommunity/birthsdeathsandmarriages/ageing/articles/livinglongerhowourpopulationischangingandwhyitmatters/2019-03-15.
223 [1984] IRLR 299; [1984] ICR 678, EAT.
224 See *Home Office v Holmes* [1984] IRLR 299, EAT; and *Briggs v North Eastern Education and Library Board* [1990] IRLR 181, NICA, on the wording 'requirement or condition' which is encompassed within 'provision, criterion or practice'.

Is full-time working a disadvantage?

11.103 The woman no longer needs to prove that she 'cannot comply'[225] with the full-time work requirement – she only needs to show that she is put at a 'disadvantage'. Many of the cases under the pre-2001 definition insisted the woman must prove she was completely unable to work full-time, eg because she could not afford or find suitable childcare. These cases ignored the reality that many women wish to work part-time because they feel it makes their children happier or easier to deal with, or because it is a physical and emotional strain to work full-time while bringing up children, or to keep rearranging childcare.

11.104 A few of the very early cases did recognise this. In *Holmes* the ET noted that attempting to fulfil parental responsibilities and work full-time entailed excessive demands on Ms Holmes' time and energy. In *Price*, another early case, the Employment Appeal Tribunal (EAT) stated quite clearly that although a woman 'is not obliged to marry, or to have children, or to mind children; she may find somebody to look after them', but to say that for those reasons she can comply with a requirement to work full-time would be 'wholly out of sympathy with the spirit and intent of the Act'.[226]

11.105 As we have said, under the current definition of indirect discrimination, a woman only has to show that full-time working puts her at a disadvantage. The disadvantage need not be economic, but could for example, include the stress of maintaining practical childcare arrangements or physical tiredness. It does not need to be impossible to comply with a requirement before there is disadvantage. The fact that compliance is possible but only with real difficulty or with additional arrangements having to be made or by shifting the childcare burden onto someone else can still mean there is a disadvantage.[227]

11.106 It is not quite clear whether it is enough that a woman simply wants to spend more time with her child, though *Price* (see above), suggested that it should be. If an ET takes an unsympathetic approach, a woman will be in difficulty if she has demonstrated that, pending the tribunal hearing, she can in fact work full-time without undue difficulty. On the other hand, she will not want to resign if there is a chance that the ET can help her. This is a good reason for asking the ET for an early hearing date on the ground that the woman's job is in jeopardy because she cannot continue working.

225 As in the pre-2001 definition of indirect discrimination.
226 *Price v Civil Service Commission* [1977] IRLR 291, EAT.
227 *Dobson v North Cumbria Integrated Care NHS Foundation Trust* UKEAT/0220/19; [2021] IRLR 729, which concerned weekend working.

Sometimes an employer may agree that she works part-time pending the result. If not, she may have to show the ET that her childcare arrangements could only be sustained in the short term and were causing great stress, expense or inconvenience. A woman could try to avoid this trap by using up her days off to work part-time in practice. Ms Holmes took six months' sick leave. Having said that, maybe this approach is unnecessarily cautious. The former President of the EAT made a useful observation in one of the first cases to look closely at the current definition of indirect discrimination (albeit an age discrimination case).[228] He said that a woman who wished to work part-time for childcare reasons but was forced to work full-time because she would otherwise lose her job, may well be considered at a 'disadvantage' for the purpose of the current definition.

Would it put women at a particular disadvantage?

11.107 The worker needs to show that full-time working would put women at a particular disadvantage compared with men. The EAT has said that tribunals must accept that there is a 'childcare disparity' which means that women are more likely to find it difficult to work certain hours, eg nights, or changeable hours imposed by the employer.[229] If the PCP requires working to such arrangements (or, presumably, working full-time), the group disadvantage is highly likely to follow. Other kinds of fixed hours or arrangements (see para 11.111 below) might not necessarily be more difficult for those with childcare responsibilities and would need to be proved.

Is the requirement justifiable?

11.108 To be justifiable, employers must prove that insisting on full-time working is a proportionate means of achieving a legitimate aim. This depends very much on the facts and practicalities of the particular case. In one old case,[230] for example, a health visitor was permitted to work part-time after maternity leave, provided her hours were spread over five days. The worker objected that this involved her in greater expenses for the same wage. Nevertheless, the EAT found the requirement justified because patients needed regular personal contact and health visitors should be available five days a week for

---

228 *Eweida v British Airways plc* UKEAT/0123/08; [2009] IRLR 78. (The case went to the Court of Appeal, which did not explicitly address this observation.)

229 *Dobson v North Cumbria Integrated Care NHS Foundation Trust* UKEAT/0220/19; [2021] IRLR 729.

230 *Greater Glasgow Health Board v Carey* [1987] IRLR 484, EAT.

consultation with doctors or social workers. On the other hand, there have been many similar cases where tribunals have found employers unjustified in refusing job-share or part-time working in a whole variety of jobs. The crucial point is that a tribunal must not simply consider whether the employer has a good reason for requiring the woman to work full-time; it must balance the employer's reasons against the discriminatory effect on women.[231]

11.109 The increasing move towards part-time and flexible working, backed by enabling legislation, means it is harder for employers than in the past to justify insisting on full-time working or treating part-timers less favourably. In negotiating with her employer or running a case, a woman could point to the Best Practice Guidelines accompanying the PTW Regs 2000.[232]

Common forms of discrimination against part-timers

11.110 The application of the redundancy selection criterion of part-timers first may well be unlawful sex discrimination.[233] Most difficulties facing part-time workers, however, concern less favourable terms and conditions, particularly indirect discrimination in 'pay' in its broadest sense. Because Article 157 (formerly 141) of the Treaty of Rome is binding on all employers,[234] EU law has been very helpful in securing equality of pay, pension contributions, sick pay, etc. Examples of indirect discrimination against part-timers or job-sharers include (subject to justification):

- requiring a longer period of part-time service than full-time service in order to be eligible for promotion;[235]
- on a job-sharer converting to full-time working, placing her on the incremental scale according to actual hours worked in the post in the past, so that she is lower in the scale than had she worked the same number of years full-time.[236]

---

231 For a robust expression of this principle, see *Craddock v Cornwall CC and another* UKEAT/0367/05.

232 See para 11.120.

233 *Clarke v Eley (IMI) Kynoch Ltd* [1982] IRLR 482, EAT.

234 See para 3.3 above regarding retained EU law.

235 For example, see *Gerster v Freistaat Bayern* [1997] IRLR 699, ECJ.

236 *Hill and Stapleton v Revenue Commissioners and Department of Finance* [1998] IRLR 466, ECJ.

Shifts, flexible hours and mobility: sex discrimination

11.111 A requirement that an employee work shifts or flexible hours may indirectly discriminate against a woman because of childcare commitments. Similarly, an employer's attempt to alter a woman's hours (whether or not permitted to do so by her contract), even in a minor way, may be indirect discrimination if, for example, it interferes with her arrangements for collecting her children from school. Conversely, an employer's refusal to allow a woman to arrive or leave half an hour late or early in order to transport her children to and from school, may be discriminatory. In all cases, the main issue is likely to be whether the change or refusal is justifiable. Similar considerations apply with mobility requirements. In one case, where a lone parent was unable to comply with new flexi-rotas due to childcare, the EAT said that employers should consider carefully the impact which a new roster might have on a section of their workforce and take a reasonably flexible attitude towards accommodating a worker's particular needs.[237] The stages of proving an indirect sex discrimination case in these various circumstances will be as set out in the part-time working and job-share section above.

11.112 On the other hand, any assumption made by an employer that women will be less mobile or flexible is directly discriminatory. Interview questions concerning mobility or flexibility, if asked only of female candidates, are likely to lead to poorer interview performance and constitute direct discrimination in the arrangements made for determining who should be offered employment.[238] Similarly, it may be direct sex discrimination to allow a man to work part-time or to be flexible with his hours, but not a woman (or vice versa).

The Part-time Workers Regulations

11.113 The PTW Regs 2000[239] were brought in to implement the EU Part-time Work Directive.[240] As at early 2021, there were over 7.7 million part-time workers in the UK. Prior to the Covid-19 pandemic, there were slightly more. In introducing the regulations, the government at the time said it believed the economy and society would gain as a

---

237 *London Underground Ltd v Edwards (No 2)* [1997] IRLR 157, EAT. Note that this case went to the Court of Appeal on a number of different points.

238 EqA 2010 ss11, 13 and 39(1)(a).

239 SI No 1551.

240 97/81/EC and 98/23/EC.

whole if people were able to achieve a better balance between work and family responsibilities.

11.114 The PTW Regs 2000 are not confined to employees, and cover any individual working under an oral or written contract whereby s/he undertakes to perform work or services personally. It excludes situations where the employer is a client or customer of a business carried out by the individual.[241]

11.115 A part-time worker must not be treated less favourably than a comparable full-time worker on the ground that s/he is a part-timer as regards his/her contract terms or by being subjected to any other detriment.[242] The worker cannot rely on a hypothetical comparator.[243] A comparable full-time worker means someone who, at the time of the less favourable treatment, is employed by the same employer, under the same type of contract and engaged in the same or broadly similar work.[244] The work need not be identical as long as a large amount of it is the same. Comparison must be made with a worker at the same establishment, unless the only comparable worker is at a different establishment. Also, if the worker changes from full-time to part-time working, s/he must not be treated less favourably than beforehand.[245]

11.116 In Scotland, the worker must show that his/her part-time status is the only reason that s/he has been treated less favourably. In England and Wales, the cases are inconsistent as to whether it is sufficient simply for it to be one reason.[246] Once a worker proves less favourable treatment on grounds of being a part-timer, a 'pro rata principle' applies, ie a part-timer must not receive a lesser proportion of a full-timer's pay or other benefit, than the proportion that the number of his/her weekly hours bears to the number of weekly hours of the full-timer.[247] As with the EqA 2010, there is an exception if the employer

---

241 PTW Regs 2000 reg 1(2).

242 PTW Regs 2000 reg 5(1) and (2).

243 *Carl v The University of Sheffield* UKEAT/0261/08; [2009] IRLR 616, EAT.

244 PTW Regs 2000 reg 2. For an analysis of who is a comparable worker, see *Matthews v Kent & Medway Towns Fire Authority* [2006] IRLR 367, HL.

245 PTW Regs 2000 reg 3.

246 *Sharma and others v Manchester City Council* UKEAT/0561/07; [2008] IRLR 336; *Carl v The University of Sheffield* UKEAT/0261/08; *Engel v Ministry of Justice* UKEAT/0303/18. Scottish tribunals are bound by *McMenemy v Capita Business Services Limited* [2007] IRLR 400, CS.

247 PTW Regs 2000 regs 1(2) and 5(3).

can objectively justify less favourable treatment.[248] In addition, a part-timer cannot claim equivalent overtime rates until s/he has worked more hours than the comparable full-timer has worked (excluding absences and overtime) in the relevant period.[249]

11.117　The part-timer can request a written statement detailing reasons for any treatment s/he considers less favourable,[250] though on dismissal she must request written reasons under ERA 1996 s92.[251] It is automatic unfair dismissal to dismiss an employee for requesting such a statement or for claiming any rights under these regulations in good faith.[252] It is also unlawful to subject a worker to a detriment including dismissal.

11.118　A worker can claim compensation from an ET if his/her employer breaches the regulations, but s/he cannot claim for injury to feelings for less favourable treatment as a part-time worker.[253]

11.119　Some examples of the effect of the regulations are that, unless the employer can objectively justify otherwise:

- Current or past part-time status should not constitute a barrier to promotion.
- Part-time workers should receive the same hourly rate as comparable full-time workers.
- Part-timers should not be less favourably treated than full-timers in calculating the rate of sick pay, how long it is paid, or the length of service required to qualify for payment.
- Employers should not discriminate against part-timers over access to pension schemes.
- Part-timers should not be excluded from training.
- Part-timers should not be targeted for redundancy selection.

248　PTW Regs 2000 reg 5(2). For an example of the approach, see *O'Brien v Ministry of Justice (formerly Department for Constitutional Affairs)* [2013] UKSC 6; [2013] IRLR 315.
249　PTW Regs 2000 reg 5(4).
250　PTW Regs 2000 reg 6.
251　See para 20.11 onwards.
252　PTW Regs 2000 reg 7.
253　PTW Regs 2000 reg 8. But it may be possible to claim for injury to feelings for detriments under reg 7.

11.120 At the time of passing the regulations, the government issued Best Practice Guidelines.[254] Although the PTW Regs 2000 give no right to work part-time, the Best Practice Guidelines make useful recommendations which can be used in indirect sex discrimination cases:

- At all levels of an organisation, including skilled and managerial positions, employers should seek to maximise the range of posts designated as suitable for part-time working or job share.
- Larger organisations should keep a database of those interested in job share.
- Employers should actively consider whether it would be appropriate to introduce flexible forms of working, eg term-time working, lunch-time working, flexi-time, homeworking, a parental leave scheme and reduced-hours working.
- Larger organisations should consider whether to provide childcare facilities on site or offer a contribution towards childcare costs.

Flexible working

Overview

11.121 The original right to request flexible working was introduced in 2003 and applied to requests to change hours or work from home for childcare purposes. This was expanded in 2007 to include caring for adult relatives. Since 30 June 2014, it has no longer been necessary that the request be for caring purposes. When negotiating with employers, it is useful to refer to the survey evidence of the benefits to them of flexible working, eg there is an interesting Chartered Institute of Personnel and Development (CIPD) report, *Employee outlook: Focus on commuting and flexible working – Survey report* (April 2016).[255] There is also ACAS guidance on working from home, including during the Covid-19 pandemic, on its website.[256]

---

254 See the then Department for Business, Enterprise & Regulatory Reform (BERR), *Part-time workers. The law and best practice – a detailed guide for employers and part-timers*, URN No 02/1710. This is now archived, but can be found at: http://webarchive.nationalarchives.gov.uk/20081023163153/berr. gov.uk/whatwedo/employment/employment-legislation/employment-guidance/page19479.html.

255 Available at: www.cipd.co.uk/knowledge/fundamentals/relations/flexible-working/employee-outlook.

256 Access via www.acas.org.uk/working-from-home.

11.122   The law is contained in ERA 1996 ss80F–80I and expanded in the Flexible Working Regulations 2014.[257] There is government guidance on the GOV.UK website, though it has no legal status. There is also an ACAS Code of Practice aimed at employers: *Handling in a reasonable manner requests to work flexibly* (June 2014).[258] The code must be taken into account by tribunals when deciding cases under the regulations. The legislation does not give any right to work flexibly, but it makes it easier for an employee to make the request and have it properly considered. Of course, any worker can ask his/her employer for changes in hours or other flexible arrangements without following any statutory procedure. However, if the worker wants to invoke the specific statutory right to make a request, there are certain conditions.

11.123   An eligible employee may apply to his/her employer for a change in his/her terms and conditions of employment regarding hours, time of work or working partly or wholly from home.[259] Any permitted change will be permanent (unless agreed otherwise) and the employee will have no right to revert back to his/her former hours of work. The rules do not offer the option of an employer imposing a trial period: it is either 'yes' or 'no' to the employee's request. However, there is nothing to stop the parties agreeing to a trial period if either of them is unsure whether the change would work.

11.124   The GOV.UK guidance gives examples of different types of flexible working, including:

- part-time working and job share;
- staggered hours;
- homeworking;
- annual hours;
- compressed hours (working the same number of hours over a shorter period); and
- phased retirement.

There are also other possibilities, eg:

- shift-swapping;
- term-time working; or
- slightly reduced hours (such as starting an hour later each day). Working fewer hours will of course usually mean less pay.

---

257 SI No 1398.
258 Available via a link at www.acas.org.uk/acas-code-of-practice-on-flexible-working-requests.
259 ERA 1996 s80F(1).

11.125 Any employee can apply for flexible working provided s/he has at least 26 weeks' continuous service. As already stated, it is no longer necessary that the purpose of the request is to care for children or adult relatives. However, if the request is refused, provided the employer dealt with it in a procedurally correct manner, the employee has no legal rights under this set of rules. Individuals who have the status of 'employee shareholders' cannot use the flexible working procedure, although that does not affect their ability to make other claims if an ordinary request is refused, eg for discrimination.[260]

11.126 An employee cannot make more than one application to the same employer in 12 months.[261] S/he should therefore choose a good time to make the request. The application must be in writing and contain the following information:[262]

- the date of the current application;
- the date of any previous application or confirmation that there has been none;
- a statement that the application is being made under the statutory right to request flexible working;
- the flexible working pattern applied for and the date it should come into effect;
- an explanation of what effect, if any, the employee thinks the proposed change will have on the employer and suggestions as to how the effect may be dealt with.

The employee is not expected to know exactly what the effect on the employer may be. This is just to show s/he has considered the likely impact of the proposed change. A well thought-out application also makes it more likely the employer will agree. The ACAS Code recommends that employers make clear to employees what information should be included in a written request to work flexibly.

11.127 There used to be strict procedural requirements that an employer had to follow when dealing with the request. Now it is only necessary that the employer deals with the application 'in a reasonable manner' and notifies the employee of the decision within three months of the application or any permitted appeal unless any longer period is agreed.[263] What is reasonable is set out in the ACAS Code (above) and must be taken into account by a tribunal when it decides whether the employer has correctly followed the procedure. The ACAS Code

---

260 See paras 6.130–6.131 for more detail of employee shareholders.
261 ERA 1996 s80F(4).
262 Flexible Working Regulations 2014 reg 4; and ERA 1996 s80F(2).
263 ERA 1996 s80G.

recommends these steps: the employer should discuss the request with the employee; consider the application carefully; and inform the employee of the decision as soon as possible; this should be in writing to avoid future confusion. If the request is rejected, the employer should allow the employee to appeal. ACAS says it can be helpful to discuss the decision with the employee to see whether any further facts emerge.

11.128   The rules say that an application will be treated as withdrawn if the employee, without good reason, fails to attend both a first meeting arranged by the employer to discuss the application and the next meeting arranged for that purpose. If the employer has allowed an appeal, the application will be treated as withdrawn if the employee similarly fails to attend a first and rearranged meeting. The employer must notify the employee that s/he has decided to treat the application as withdrawn for these reasons.[264]

11.129   An employer may only refuse the application on one of the specified grounds,[265] ie:

- additional costs;
- detrimental effect on ability to meet customer demand;
- inability to recruit additional staff or re-organise work among existing staff;
- detrimental impact on quality or performance;
- insufficient work during the periods the employee proposes to work;
- planned structural changes.

11.130   As long as the employer's refusal falls within one of these specified grounds and is not based on incorrect facts,[266] the employee cannot challenge the refusal under the flexible working procedure. However, a tribunal is entitled to examine evidence as to the circumstances leading to the refusal in case this indicates the employer was relying on incorrect facts.[267] As the grounds cover almost every situation, the employee's best chance of success will be to persuade the employer to agree the request. The employee should present a well-considered application, showing how the change will not harm the business and may in fact benefit the employer. It may be helpful to cite some of the positive case studies set out in the guidance for employers mentioned above.

264 ERA 1996 s80G(1D).
265 ERA 1996 s80G.
266 ERA 1996 s80H(1)(b).
267 *Commotion Ltd v Rutty* [2006] IRLR 171, EAT.

11.131 It is also important to consider whether the employee has other rights, eg under his/her contract or under discrimination law. For example, it may be direct race discrimination if the employer refuses a request from a black worker to adjust hours when s/he has agreed a similar request by a comparable white worker. Or it may be indirect sex discrimination if the employer unjustifiably refuses a woman's request to change her hours for childcare reasons.[268] Similarly, a refusal to allow adjustments in hours to care for elderly parents could be indirect age discrimination. A worker may also have a right to reduce or adjust hours as a reasonable adjustment for his/her disability.[269]

Enforcement

11.132 An employee can bring a tribunal claim if the employer:

- failed to deal with the flexible working application in a reasonable manner;
- did not notify the decision within three months or any agreed extension;
- wrongly treated it as withdrawn; or
- if a decision to reject the application was based on incorrect facts or an impermissible ground.[270]

No claim can be brought if the application has been agreed or withdrawn.[271] The claim cannot be brought until the employer has notified the decision (or appeal decision, if the employer allowed an appeal). If the employer has not notified any decision, the employee must wait until the deadline for giving such decision has expired.[272] A claim regarding an incorrect notification that the employee has withdrawn his/her application can be made immediately. The tribunal claim must be made within three months of the date when the employee was first allowed to make a claim in these different situations. Late claims will be allowed only if it was not reasonably practicable to claim in time and they have been presented within a further reasonable period.[273] If the ET finds the claim well-founded,

---

268 See para 11.98 onwards. Note also that costs alone are unlikely to be an acceptable defence under the EqA 2010.
269 See para 15.43.
270 ERA 1996 s80H.
271 ERA 1996 s80H(2).
272 ERA 1996 s80H(3)–(3C).
273 ERA 1996 s80H(5)–(6).

it can order reconsideration of the application and award such compensation as is just and equitable up to eight weeks' pay.

11.133   It is unlawful to subject someone to a detriment because s/he has made or proposed to make an application for flexible working under this procedure, or brought an ET claim, or alleged the existence of any circumstances which would constitute a ground for bringing such proceedings, and it is automatic unfair dismissal to dismiss someone for any of those reasons.[274] The ACAS EC procedure applies to all these claims.[275]

---

274 ERA 1996 ss47E and 104C.
275 ETA 1996 s18(1)(b); see para 20.16.

Discrimination overview

Chapter 12: Key points

- The Equality Act (EqA) 2010 replaced the previous discrimination legislation in respect of discriminatory actions on or after 1 October 2010.
- It covers the protected characteristics of age; disability; gender reassignment; marital or civil partnership status; pregnancy and maternity; race; religion or belief; sex; and sexual orientation.
- The Equality and Human Rights Commission (EHRC) has a remit to oversee all discrimination and human rights law. It has issued a statutory Code of Practice on Employment ('the EHRC Employment Code') and a statutory Code of Practice on Equal Pay.
- Those working abroad under contracts which have some connection with English law can probably use the EqA 2010, though this is a difficult area.
- The EqA 2010 has wider scope than unfair dismissal law. It covers job applicants, apprentices, employees, former employees, contract workers and those working on a contract personally to do work, though not for a client or customer of their own business. Volunteers will not usually be protected.
- An employer must not discriminate in recruitment, treatment of people at work, dismissal or post-dismissal matters such as references. These are called 'prohibited actions' or 'acts of discrimination'.
- Unless they took all reasonable preventative steps, employers are vicariously liable for the actions of their employees carried out in the course of their employment or for acts of their agents. Individual employees and agents can also be liable.
- There is a public sector equality duty. In carrying out their functions, including their employment function, public authorities must have due regard to their duty to eliminate discrimination and advance equality of opportunity.

The legal framework

The Equality Act 2010 and previous legislation

12.1   The Equality Act (EqA) 2010 consolidated and updated the previous legislation covering unlawful discrimination, including:

- Equal Pay Act (EqPA) 1970;
- Sex Discrimination Act 1975;
- Race Relations Act 1976;
- Disability Discrimination Act (DDA) 1995;
- Employment Equality (Religion or Belief) Regulations 2003;
- Employment Equality (Sexual Orientation) Regulations 2003;
- Employment Equality (Age) Regulations 2006.

The EqA 2010 applies to any discriminatory actions on or after 1 October 2010, or where an action which was unlawful discrimination prior to 1 October continued on or after that date.[1] It is important to be careful when relying on case-law under the old legislation that the wording in the EqA is the same. Although the legislation changed very little on employment discrimination apart from a few developments in relation to disability, there were some small changes elsewhere.

12.2 The EqA 2010 covers discrimination outside employment as well as employment, although only employment situations are within the scope of this book. The Act attempts to use plain English, but that is not always helpful. Because it covers so much, the wording can sometimes be clumsy and it is hard to find your way around. The contents list at the beginning of the Act is very helpful in this respect, as is the index of defined expressions in Schedule 28, right at the end.

Equality and Human Rights Commission

12.3 The Equality and Human Rights Commission (EHRC) started up in October 2007. The EHRC replaced the Commission for Racial Equality (CRE), the Disability Rights Commission (DRC) and the Equal Opportunities Commission (EOC) (now sometimes referred to as the 'legacy commissions'), and took on additional responsibility for religion, sexual orientation and age discrimination and for human rights. The EHRC cannot give legal assistance to individuals on human rights cases unless there is also an equality dimension, but it does have power to hold formal inquiries or take judicial proceedings to prevent breaches of the Human Rights Act (HRA) 1998. The powers, budget and staff numbers of the EHRC have been severely reduced on more than one occasion since 2010.

---

1 Equality Act 2010 (Commencement No 4, Savings, Consequential, Transitional, Transitory and Incidental Provision, and Revocation) Order 2010 SI No 2317 article 7.

Codes of Practice

12.4   The EHRC has issued two statutory Codes of Practice, one on Employment and one on Equal Pay.[2] The Codes apply to England, Scotland and Wales. The Codes do not impose legal obligations in themselves and they do not purport to be an authoritative statement of the law. However, they can be used in evidence in legal proceedings. Tribunals must take into account any provision in the Codes which appears relevant to them.[3] The importance of the Codes has been confirmed by the higher courts.[4]

12.5   The EHRC says the main purpose of its Employment Code is to provide a detailed explanation of the Act, which should help tribunals, lawyers, trade union representatives, human resources (HR) departments and everyone else. At over 300 pages, the Code is a somewhat daunting document. However, it is full of helpful examples and is usefully divided into two: chapters 1–15 contain the explanation of the Act; and chapters 16–19 set out recommended good practice for employers.

12.6   The other document with statutory effect is the *Guidance on matters to be taken into account in determining questions relating to the definition of disability*.[5] This document is discussed further in chapter 15 in this book. When deciding whether a worker is disabled within the meaning of the EqA 2010, a tribunal must take account of any relevant guidance in this document.[6]

EU legislation and international instruments

12.7   Chapter 3 of this book sets out the framework of European Union (EU) law. In the case of discrimination law, this derives from the Treaty of Rome (now renamed the Treaty on the Functioning of the European Union) and a series of directives. In particular, there is the Recast Directive (2006/54/EC) which deals with sex discrimination; the Race Discrimination Directive (2000/43/EC) and the General Framework Directive (2000/78/EC), which covers age, disability,

---

2   Issued under Equality Act (EqA) 2006 s14. Both Codes are available on the EHRC website: www.equalityhumanrights.com.

3   EqA 2006 s15(4).

4   See paras 16.29–16.31.

5   Available at https://assets.publishing.service.gov.uk/government/uploads/system/uploads/attachment_data/file/570382/Equality_Act_2010-disability_definition.pdf.

6   EqA 2010 Sch 1 para 12.

sexual orientation and religion and belief. The full titles of these are set out in chapter 14.

12.8 An overview of the relationship between European directives and national rights is explained in chapter 3. Although much has changed post Brexit, it is important for understanding retained EU law to look at how the relationship worked previously. As far as possible, the EqA 2010 had to be interpreted consistently with EU law.[7] There was also an important 'non-regression' principle in the directives, which meant that implementation of the directives could not result in a diminution of rights already established in UK law.[8]

12.9 In recent years, the higher courts had started to seek guidance from international conventions protecting equality, where important and difficult points of principle were involved. The recitals to the General Framework Directive and the Race Discrimination Directives refer to various conventions to which all member states are signatories, ie: the Universal Declaration of Human Rights; the United Nations Convention on the Elimination of All Forms of Discrimination against Women; the International Convention on the Elimination of all forms of Racial Discrimination; the United Nations Covenants on Civil and Political Rights and on Economic, Social and Cultural Rights; and the European Convention for the Protection of Human Rights and Fundamental Freedoms. When interpreting the meaning of the EU directives, it is therefore sometimes necessary to consider the wider conventions on which they appear to be based. In the *JFS* case,[9] for example, in deciding that direct race discrimination included discrimination against a person because of the ethnicity of someone from whom they were descended, Lord Mance noted that the International Convention on the Elimination of all forms of Racial Discrimination 'to which the United Kingdom is party and to which Directive 2000/43/EC recites that it was intended to give effect' defined racial discrimination to include discrimination based on 'descent'.[10] Similarly, in *Grainger plc and others v Nicholson*,[11] when deciding on the scope of a protected

---

7 As established by *Marleasing SA v La Commercial Internacial de Alimentacion SA* [1992] 1 CMLR 305, ECJ.

8 This was part of the reason for the successful judicial review in *Equal Opportunities Commission v Secretary of State for Trade and Industry* [2007] IRLR 327, HC.

9 *R (E) v Governing Body of JFS and The Admissions Appeal Panel of JFS and others* [2009] UKSC 15; [2010] IRLR 136.

10 See also the debate re whether 'caste' is covered – para 14.74.

11 UKEAT/0219/09; [2010] IRLR 4.

'belief' under the EqA 2010, the Employment Appeal Tribunal (EAT) looked at cases decided by the European Court of Human Rights (ECtHR), referring to the fact that the ECHR was cited as a source in the General Framework Directive. Of course the ECHR must also be considered as a result of the HRA 1998 which, so far, survives Brexit.[12]

12.10   An introduction to the effect of Brexit and the ongoing interpretation of the EqA 2010 in the light of retained EU law is set out in chapter 3.

Working abroad

12.11   The EqA 2010 forms part of the law of England, Scotland and Wales. Unlike the previous legislation, the EqA 2010 does not set out its territorial scope. The problem arises where a worker works partly or wholly outside Great Britain (GB). The tribunal will have to decide by reference to the case-law whether there is a sufficiently close link between the employment relationship and GB. According to the EHRC Employment Code, relevant factors will be where the employee lives and works, where the employer is established, where tax is paid and what laws govern the employer relationship in other respects.[13] However, it is a bit more complicated than that. The general principles in respect of unfair dismissal claims were set out in the key case of *Lawson v Serco Ltd* and expanded in subsequent cases.[14] The Court of Appeal has now said that the same rules on territorial jurisdiction apply to claims under the EqA 2010 as they do to unfair dismissal claims.[15]

Who is covered?

Overview

12.12   The EqA 2010 is wider in scope than the Employment Rights Act (ERA) 1996. It protects job applicants, apprentices, employees, former employees, contract workers and those working on a contract

---

12   See chapter 3.

13   See EHRC Employment Code, paras 10.70–10.72, and EqA 2010 ss81–82 regarding ships, hovercraft and off-shore work.

14   *Lawson v Serco Ltd; Botham v Ministry of Defence; Crofts and others v Veta Ltd and others* [2006] IRLR 289, HL and see para 6.16 above.

15   *R (Hottak) v Secretary of State for Foreign and Commonwealth Affairs* [2016] EWCA Civ 438; [2016] IRLR 534. See comments at para 3.16.

personally to do work.[16] This latter category is sometimes known as a 'contract for services'. It is defined more widely than being employed as an employee under a contract of employment, which is required to claim unfair dismissal.[17] One of the key differences is that a mutual obligation to provide and do work is very important for there to be a contract of employment, but is not necessary for there to be a contract for services.[18] There have been a number of cases regarding what it means to be employed 'under a contract personally to do work' in the EqA 2010. It is now established that this is essentially the same as being a 'worker' for the purposes of the Working Time Regulations 1998 etc (see paras 4.5–4.6). In other words, it is not only necessary to be employed under a contract to work personally, but the other party to the contract must not be a client or customer of a business run by the claimant. In a few cases, this has been described as being in a relationship of subordination with the employer, as opposed to a genuinely independent provider of services. However, 'subordination' is just one factor.[19] In one case brought by court interpreters, the Court of Appeal said it was relevant to take into account that the individuals were only working on an assignment by assignment basis as a factor indicating a lack of subordination even during the period of the assignment.[20] However, working on intermittent assignments does not necessarily mean that a person is not employed during the assignment. The situation of interpreters working for courts on a case-by-case basis might be seen as very different from, for example, special needs teachers employed from time to time for particular pupils. The latter are more likely to be in the necessary relationship of subordination for the duration of their assignment.

12.13 Volunteer workers are not routinely covered,[21] though they may be able to claim in some circumstances, eg if in reality they are obliged to work under a contract and they receive pay as opposed to

16 EqA 2010 s83.
17 See paras 6.4–6.12 regarding the meaning of 'employee' under the ERA 1996 for unfair dismissal purposes.
18 *Muschett v HM Prison Service* [2010] EWCA Civ 25; [2010] IRLR 451.
19 *Bates van Winkelhof v Clyde & Co* [2014] IRLR 641, SC; *Jivraj v Hashwani* [2011] UKSC 40; [2011] IRLR 827; *Halawi v WDFG UK Ltd (t/a World Duty Free)* [2014] EWCA Civ 1387; [2015] IRLR 50; *Windle v Secretary of State for Justice* [2016] EWCA Civ 459; [2016] IRLR 628; *Pimlico Plumbers Ltd and another v Smith* [2018] UKSC 29; [2018] IRLR 872.
20 *Windle v Secretary of State for Justice* [2016] EWCA Civ 459; [2016] IRLR 628, CA.
21 *X v Mid Sussex Citizens Advice Bureau and another* [2012] UKSC 59; [2013] IRLR 146.

reimbursement of expenses.[22] Unpaid interns may be covered by the provisions on vocational training.[23]

12.14   Employment as a member of parliamentary staff and Crown employment, eg employees in government departments, are covered.[24] So are members of the police force,[25] and personal and public office holders.[26] Armed service personnel are partly covered, subject to certain procedural requirements.[27] There are exceptions for age and disability, and discrimination against women or transsexuals is allowed in certain respects if it is a proportionate means of ensuring combat effectiveness.[28] Depending on the facts, church ministers may be protected as employees[29] or personal office holders. Discrimination is permitted in certain circumstances where employment is for the purpose of an organised religion.[30]

12.15   Employment agencies must not discriminate in their provision of services.[31] Any person providing or making arrangements for the provision of training facilities is also covered.[32] This protects trainees on work experience and work placement programmes.

12.16   Firms must not discriminate in relation to who is admitted to partnership or how partners are treated.[33] Barristers must not discriminate against pupils or tenants, nor must anyone discriminate in which barristers they instruct.[34] Trade unions must not discriminate in access to membership or against members, for example, in the way they offer access to benefits or services.[35]

22   *South East Sheffield Citizens Advice Bureau v Grayson* [2004] IRLR 353, EAT. But this must be read subject to *X v Mid Sussex Citizens Advice Bureau and another* [2012] UKSC 59; [2013] IRLR 146.

23   See para 12.15; plus comments of Lord Manse in *X v Mid Sussex Citizens Advice Bureau and another* [2012] UKSC 59; [2013] IRLR 146.

24   EqA 2010 s83(2).

25   EqA 2010 ss42–43.

26   See EqA 2010 ss49–52 for details. There are exclusions in Sch 6 para 1(1).

27   EqA 2010 ss83(3) and 121.

28   See EqA 2010 Sch 9 para 4 for details.

29   *Percy v Church of Scotland Board of National Mission* [2006] IRLR 195, HL.

30   See chapter 14.

31   EqA 2010 ss55 and 56(d), (e).

32   EqA 2010 ss55, 56.

33   EqA 2010 ss44–46.

34   EqA 2010 s47.

35   EqA 2010 s57.

Contract workers

12.17 The protection of contract workers has become increasingly important with the fragmentation of the labour market. Broadly speaking, contract workers are those who are employed by one organisation ('the employer') but supplied to do work for another ('the principal') under a contract between the two.[36] The contract worker need only be employed by the employer in the wide sense meant by the EqA 2010, ie on a contract personally to do work. Precisely who can be considered as a contract worker depends on the facts, but it will often cover workers supplied by an employment agency to work for a different company,[37] workers supplied by concessionaires to work for department stores in specific concessions, and workers employed in contracted-out services.[38] The importance of the protection is that it means a worker who is discriminated against by the principal, as opposed to his/her employer, still has a legal claim.

Agency workers

12.18 Workers who are placed by agencies with end-users may want to bring a discrimination case against the end-user. To do so, they must either be employed by the end-user under a contract of employment or contract personally to do work, or must be a 'contract worker' under EqA 2010 s41.[39] The difficulty for an agency worker is that there is rarely any contract at all between him/her and the end-user.[40] The 'contract worker' route is usually more successful, although for that to work, the worker must first be employed by the agency (and then supplied to work for the end-user). Following the case of *Muschett*,[41] a general misapprehension seems to have arisen that agency workers cannot bring discrimination claims. This is not correct, and each case must be tested on its facts as to whether the

---

36 EqA 2010 s41.

37 *BP Chemicals Ltd v Gillick* [1995] IRLR 128, EAT.

38 The key case is *Harrods Ltd v Remick* [1997] IRLR 583, CA. See also *MHC Consulting Services v Tansell* [1999] IRLR 677, EAT where the supply went through a third party (an agency); *Jones v Friends Provident Life Office* [2004] IRLR 783, NICA and *Leeds City Council and another v Woodhouse and another* [2010] EWCA Civ 410; [2010] IRLR 625.

39 See previous paragraph.

40 See para 6.13 in the context of unfair dismissal.

41 *Muschett v HM Prison Service* [2010] EWCA Civ 25; [2010] IRLR 451. It is also important to read the EAT decision at UKEAT/0132/08, as some issues stopped there.

worker was in fact employed on a contract personally to do work by the agency and if so, whether the remainder of the conditions necessary to be a 'contract worker' apply.[42]

12.19   The worker's claim may in addition – or alternatively – be against the agency itself. It depends on who has carried out the alleged discrimination. A claim can be made against the agency if the worker was employed by the agency under a contract of employment or a contract personally to do work. Or, if applicable, it may be easier to claim under EqA 2010 s55, which makes employment service-providers responsible for discrimination in their services.

Protected characteristics

12.20   The EqA 2010 introduced a new piece of jargon: 'protected characteristic'. The following protected characteristics are covered by the Act and must not form the basis for discrimination: age; disability; gender reassignment; marital or civil partnership status; race; religion or belief; sex; and sexual orientation.[43] Pregnancy and maternity are also protected characteristics, though they are dealt with slightly separately within the EqA 2010.[44] All the protected characteristics were covered by the previous legislation. More detail on the meaning of each of these protected characteristics and linked discrimination is in chapters 14 and 15.

Illegal contracts

12.21   In unfair dismissal law, an employee may be unable to bring a claim if s/he knew about an illegality in his/her contract and actively participated in it, eg accepting cash payments under the counter, which were not recorded on his/her payslips.[45] In a discrimination case that is based on a statutory tort as opposed to the contract of employment, illegality of the contract is less of a problem. As long as facts giving rise to the claim are not so inextricably bound up with the worker's illegal conduct that allowing him/her to win his/her claim would

---

42 For a useful and positive example where an agency worker was able to sue the end-user, see *Camden LBC v (1) Pegg (2) Ranstad Care Ltd (3) Hays Specialist Recruitment t/a Camden Agency for Temporary Supply* UKEAT/0590/11.

43 Set out in EqA 2010 ss4–12.

44 EqA 2010 s18.

45 See para 6.19.

seem to condone the conduct, the worker can still bring a claim.[46] An employer's defence of illegality would therefore succeed only in quite extreme circumstances. For example:

- In one case, a worker could potentially bring a sexual harassment claim, even though s/he was employed on an illegal contract because her work permit had not yet come through. The EAT commented that there is nothing intrinsic about being an employee that leads to sexual harassment or freedom from it. The fact of employment may have given rise to a practical opportunity for the acts to be committed, but that does not mean the harassment was in any sense necessary, causative or inextricably linked with the employment itself.[47]

- As another example, a woman was allowed to bring a pregnancy dismissal claim even though she knew HM Customs & Revenue (HMRC) was being defrauded and she had done nothing about it. Her acquiescence in the employer's illegal performance of the contract was in no way linked with her sex discrimination claim, which concerned a dismissal for redundancy and incapability after the employer discovered she was pregnant.[48]

On the other hand:

- A rare case where the illegality defence succeeded was where an asylum-seeker, unknown to his employer, was in breach of his conditions of leave to remain. He was not allowed to claim race discrimination when he was dismissed. The illegal conduct was completely down to the worker and amounted to a criminal offence.[49]

There is inevitably some subjectivity in considering whether the illegality defence should succeed. The underlying test always involves public policy and whether it is proportionate to deprive the individual of the right to bring a case:[50]

---

46   *Hall v Woolston Hall Leisure Ltd* [2000] IRLR 578, CA.

47   *Wijesundera v (1) Heathrow 3PL Logistics Ltd (debarred) (2) Natarajan (debarred)* UKEAT/0222/13. Note that its reference to *Hounga v Allen and another* [2014] UKSC 47; [2014] IRLR 811 is prior to the Supreme Court decision, and therefore the suggestion that a dismissal must always be inextricably linked is wrong.

48   *Hall v Woolston Hall Leisure Ltd* [2000] IRLR 578, CA.

49   *Vakante v Addey and Stanhope School and others* [2004] EWCA Civ 1065; [2004] 4 All ER 1056. Although this case has to be considered in the light of *Patel v Mirza* [2016] UKSC 42; [2017] 1 All ER 191.

50   *Patel v Mirza* [2016] UKSC 42; [2017] 1 All ER 191.

- In *Hounga*,[51] a domestic servant from Nigeria was allowed to bring a race discrimination claim regarding her dismissal even though she had participated with her employer in lying on her visa application and entering the country illegally.[52] The Supreme Court said there were no public policy considerations in favour of the illegality defence barring a claim. Ms Hounga did not profit from her unlawful conduct in entering the contract; she was awarded compensation for injury to feelings due to her dismissal, in particular its abusive nature. Nor was the integrity of the legal system compromised by apparently encouraging Ms Hounga to enter an illegal contract. On the contrary. To allow the illegality defence would encourage similar employers to enter illegal contracts. Even if there was any public policy in barring the claim, it was outweighed by another public policy which was to protect victims of trafficking.[53]

Prohibited actions

Overview

12.22   Unlike the law on unfair dismissal, the law on discrimination covers all aspects of employment, including recruitment, promotion and dismissal. Employers must not discriminate:

- in the arrangements made for determining who should be offered employment;
- in the terms on which employment is offered;
- in refusing to offer employment; and
- in access to opportunities for promotion, transfer, training or any other benefits, facilities or services.[54]

Finally, it is prohibited to discriminate by:

- dismissing a worker or subjecting him/her to a detriment.

12.23   Dismissal includes failing to renew a fixed-term contract and constructive dismissal.[55] The general principles of constructive dismissal are set out in chapter 6. For a constructive dismissal to be

---

51   *Hounga v Allen and another* [2014] UKSC 47; [2014] IRLR 811.
52   *Hounga v Allen and another* [2014] UKSC 47; [2014] IRLR 811.
53   See para 14.85 for further comments on trafficking.
54   EqA 2010 s39(1) and (2) in relation to direct and indirect discrimination; s39(3) and (4) in relation to victimisation; s41 applies to contract workers.
55   EqA 2010 s39(7).

an act of discrimination, the repudiatory breach of contract over which the employee resigns needs to be discrimination. If the employee resigns over a number of incidents, only some of which are discriminatory, the question is whether the discriminatory matters sufficiently influenced the overall breach of contract. If so, it does not matter if the last straw is not itself an act of discrimination.[56]

12.24 'Subjecting' the worker to 'any other detriment' basically means putting the worker at a disadvantage.[57] However, a worker is unlikely to win a discrimination case on a trivial matter. The worker must show that 'by reason of the act or acts complained of a reasonable worker would or might take the view that s/he had thereby been disadvantaged in the circumstances in which s/he had thereafter to work'. It could include a disciplinary warning, demotion, or offensive remarks, though the latter is likely to be covered by the specific offence of harassment.[58] If a worker complains about the content of an advertisement which has apparently excluded him/her from getting a job, s/he does need to have a genuine interest in accepting the job if offered. Otherwise it will not be a disadvantage.[59] An unjustified sense of grievance cannot amount to a detriment, but there need not be any physical or economic consequences. The test is whether the worker's opinion that the treatment was to his/her detriment is a reasonable one to hold.[60]

12.25 Sex discrimination in pay and other contract terms is generally dealt with under separate rules which previously existed in similar form under the EqPA 1970.[61] The rules are now in EqA 2010 Part 5 (employment) Chapter 3 (equality of terms). Chapter 5 of this book provides more detail on this and para 5.3 discusses the difficult borderline between sex discrimination and equal pay cases.

---

56 *De Lacey v Wechseln Ltd (t/a The Andrew Hill Salon)* UKEAT/0038/20; [2021]0038/20.

57 *Jeremiah v Ministry of Defence* [1979] 3 All ER 833; [1979] IRLR 436, CA. Here, men were required to work in a dustier part of the factory than women.

58 See para 13.81.

59 *Keane v Investigo and others* UKEAT/0389/09; (1) *Berry v Recruitment Revolution (2) Berry v PTS Consulting (UK) Ltd (3) Berry v Wells Tobias Recruitment (4) Berry v Ruston Hemmings and Carson Gray Recruitment* UKEAT/0190/10; 0419/10; 0420/10; 0421/10.

60 *Shamoon v Chief Constable of the RUC* [2003] IRLR 285, HL.

61 EqA 2010 ss70 and 71 are designed to prevent equal pay claims being brought as ordinary sex discrimination, with one exception dealt with in chapter 5 above.

Discrimination against former employees

12.26   Direct or indirect discrimination against a former employee taking place after his/her job has ended is covered, provided the discrimination arises out of and is closely connected with the former employment relationship.[62] Examples could be giving a discriminatory reference, refusal to return the worker's property, or conducting a post-dismissal appeal in a discriminatory way. Harassment and failure to make reasonable adjustments in respect of a former employee are also prohibited.[63] Post-termination victimisation is also covered, even though the EqA 2010 is poorly drafted on this point.[64] This is important because workers often complain of difficulties getting a fair reference after they have left because they have brought a discrimination case.

Vicarious liability

12.27   Employers are liable for the discriminatory acts of workers, which are carried out in the course of their employment, regardless of whether they knew or approved those acts,[65] unless they took all reasonable preventative steps.[66] It is no use taking remedial steps after the discrimination happens, eg by sacking a manager who has discriminated against the worker. To avoid liability for the original discrimination, the employer must have taken steps to prevent such discrimination happening in the first place. There is little case-law on how much an employer needs to do preventatively to be able to use this defence, but it will involve more than simply having a paper 'equal opportunities' policy. The real question is likely to be whether such a policy is effectively implemented, eg by proper training, refreshers and monitoring.

12.28   The scope of employers' liability is a particularly important issue in harassment claims. This is partly because harassment is often carried out by work colleagues and not approved of by management at all. Also, harassment often occurs outside 'the course of employment', eg at social meetings unrelated to work. Issues then arise as to whether incidents occurring at leaving drinks, Christmas parties,

---

62 EqA 2010 s108(1).
63 EqA 2010 s108(2) and (4).
64 *Rowstock Ltd and another v Jessemey* [2014] EWCA Civ 185; [2014] IRLR 368.
65 EqA 2010 s109(1) and (3).
66 EqA 2010 s109(4).

work trips etc are 'in the course of employment'. This is discussed further in the section on harassment.[67]

12.29   Also, 'principals' are liable for any action done by their agents with their authority.[68] Again this applies whether or not the action was done with the principal's knowledge or approval.[69] It is not necessary that the agent was given authority to discriminate. It is enough that s/he was given authority to do a particular act, which could be done in a lawful or in a discriminatory way.[70] For example, if an agent had authority to terminate an employee's contract, the employer (the principal) would be responsible if the agent did so on a discriminatory basis.

12.30   It can be difficult to know whether a person actually is an agent because they are not always called an agent at the time. This is a subject dealt with under the general common law, which is itself complex, and until recently, there have been few employment cases on the matter.[71] In one case, the Commissioner of the Metropolitan Police was liable for any discrimination against one of his civilian employees carried by an officer of a different police force who was responsible for line managing her, the officer acting as an agent for the commissioner.[72] Another example of the kind of situation which might be covered would be where an external consultant is taken on to deal with a company's accounts, using the company's notepaper when dealing with outside customers and authorised to give instructions to staff in the accounts department. Such a consultant would probably be an agent and, if s/he made racist remarks to the company's bookkeeper while doing this work, the company would be liable unless it had taken all reasonable preventative steps. Arguably, a worker's employer is also vicariously liable for discrimination against the worker carried out by an agency worker who is exercising

---

67 See para 13.81.
68 EqA 2010 s109(2).
69 EqA 2010 s109(3)–(4).
70 *Lana v Positive Action Training in Housing (London) Ltd* [2001] IRLR 501, EAT; *Victor-Davis v Hackney LBC* UKEAT/1269/01; *Mahood v Irish Centre Housing Ltd* UKEAT/0228/10; *Kemeh v Ministry of Defence* [2014] EWCA Civ 91; [2014] IRLR 377; *Unite the Union v Nailard* [2018] EWCA Civ 1203; [2018] IRLR 730.
71 It is advisable to read *Kemeh v Ministry of Defence* [2014] EWCA Civ 91; [2014] IRLR 377; *Unite the Union v Nailard* [2018] EWCA Civ 1203; [2018] IRLR 730 for the latest employment case-law on the subject, as the scope of vicarious liability is ever-widening.
72 *Commissioner of Police of the Metropolis v Weeks* UKEAT/0130/11.

authority or controlled by the employer.[73] On the other hand, where a worker is discriminated against by the employee of a contractor engaged by his/her employer, the situation is more difficult. The contractor's employee is unlikely to be an agent for the worker's employer (the 'principal') as his/her authority to take actions will mainly derive from his/her employment contract with the contractor and s/he is unlikely to be authorised by the principal to act on its behalf towards third parties.[74]

12.31   There are statutory provisions on where employers' liability lies in the case of the police.[75]

Liability of individual discriminators

12.32   In a situation where an employer is liable for discriminatory actions carried out by its agents or by workers who it employs, the individual agent or worker is also legally liable for his/her actions.[76] It makes no difference if the employer can avoid liability because it had taken all reasonable preventative steps.[77] However, the individual is not legally responsible for his/her discriminatory actions if s/he had reasonably relied on a statement by the employer or principal that such actions would not be discriminatory.[78]

Aiding discrimination

12.33   It is unlawful knowingly to help someone else discriminate against or harass a worker.[79] 'Aiding' involves something more than merely tolerating an environment in which discrimination can occur.[80] A person who aids someone do a discriminatory action is treated as if s/he has done that action him/herself. It is not unlawful if the helper

---

73 See the rather unspecific comments made by the EAT in *Mahood v Irish Centre Housing Ltd* UKEAT/0228/10 at para 67. Though also bear in mind the general principles in *Kemeh v Ministry of Defence* [2014] EWCA Civ 91; [2014] IRLR 377.

74 *Kemeh v Ministry of Defence* [2014] EWCA Civ 91; [2014] IRLR 377.

75 EqA 2010 ss42, 43.

76 EqA 2010 s110.

77 EqA 2010 s110(2).

78 EqA 2010 s110(3).

79 EqA 2010 s112(1). EHRC Employment Code, paras 9.25–9.30.

80 *Gilbank v Miles* [2006] IRLR 538, CA.

reasonably relied on a statement that the action for which the help was given was not unlawful discrimination. It is a criminal offence knowingly or recklessly to make such a statement.[81]

Public sector equality duty

Background

12.34 It is worth considering the history of the public sector equality duty (PSED), to see how the specific duties have been weakened over time in England, though not in Scotland and Wales. The first public sector duty was introduced by the Race Relations (Amendment) Act 2000. This resulted from the MacPherson Report following the Stephen Lawrence inquiry. Under Race Relations Act 1976 s71, a positive duty was placed on a public authority in carrying out its functions to have:

> . . . due regard to the need–
> (a) to eliminate unlawful race discrimination; and
> (b) to promote equality of opportunity and good relations between persons of different racial groups.

This included the authority's employment functions. Specific duties for public authorities were set out in regulations.[82] Authorities were required to publish a Race Equality Scheme and to review their list of functions, policies and proposed policies for relevance to the general statutory duty every three years. Monitoring was required of existing staff, job applicants and staff applications for training and promotion. Authorities with 150 or more full-time staff were also required to monitor disciplinaries, grievances, performance appraisals, training and leavers. Results had to be published annually.

12.35 From 6 April 2007, a similar gender equality duty came into effect under Sex Discrimination Act 1975 s76A. This covered pay as well as other areas of employment. The disability equality duty came into effect on 5 December 2006. As with the race and gender duties, many public authorities were subject to specific duties which included publishing a Disability Equality Scheme and revising the scheme every three years. Disabled people were required to be involved in all aspects of the development of the scheme.

81 EqA 2010 s112(2), (3).
82 Race Relations Act 1976 (General Statutory Duty) Order 2001 SI No 3457; Race Relations Act 1976 (Statutory Duties) Order 2001 SI No 3458.

The public sector equality duty under the Equality Act 2010

Overview

12.36   On 5 April 2011, a new PSED came into force in England, Scotland and Wales replacing the previous race, gender and disability duties. The duty covers the protected characteristics of age; disability; gender reassignment; pregnancy and maternity; race; religion or belief; sex; and sexual orientation. The duty applies to the public authorities set out in EqA 2010 Sch 19 and includes government departments, local government, the police, the NHS and various educational bodies.[83] Non-public authorities which nevertheless exercise a public function must comply with the duty when exercising that function.[84] A public function is a function which is considered a function of a public nature for the purposes of the HRA 1998.[85]

12.37   The general duty is set out in EqA 2010 s149, which states:

(1) A public authority must, in the exercise of its functions, have due regard to the need to–
   (a) eliminate discrimination, harassment, victimisation and any other conduct that is prohibited by or under this Act;
   (b) advance equality of opportunity between persons who share a relevant protected characteristic and persons who do not share it;
   (c) foster good relations between persons who share a relevant protected characteristic and persons who do not share it.

12.38   The general duty under EqA 2010 is very similar to the previous general duties, with one important improvement. It talks about the need to 'advance' equality of opportunity, not merely to 'promote' it as in the previous duties. In particular, this involves having due regard to the need to remove or minimise disadvantages suffered by people who share a relevant protected characteristic; to take steps to meet the different needs of people who share a relevant protected characteristic compared with others; and to encourage those who share a relevant protected characteristic to participate in activities where their participation is disproportionately low.[86] In endeavouring to

---

83 EqA 2010 s150. The Sch 19 list was amended by the Equality Act 2010 (Public Authorities and Consequential and Supplementary Amendments) Order 2011 SI No 1060 and a composite list is available via a link at: www.gov.uk/government/publications/equality-act-2010-schedule-19-consolidated-april-2011.

84 EqA 2010 s149(2).

85 EqA 2010 s150(5); see para 3.28. This is not particularly clear-cut.

86 EqA 2010 s149(3).

foster good relations, authorities should particularly have regard to the need to tackle prejudice and promote understanding.[87]

12.39 It is important to note that this duty goes further than simply avoiding unlawful discrimination. It contains positive obligations to 'advance equality of opportunity'. Compliance with the duty may involve treating some people more favourably than others, but not in a way which is otherwise prohibited by the Act.[88]

12.40 In addition to the general duty, England (plus non-devolved bodies in Scotland and Wales), Wales and Scotland each have their own specific duties. The Welsh Assembly has produced fairly progressive specific duties which involve requirements for producing and regularly reviewing written equality objectives; comprehensive monitoring; carrying out and publishing equality impact assessments (EIAs) on proposed policies and practices, and considering whether to make compliance with the general duty part of the award criteria on procurement.[89] The Scottish Parliament has also produced a progressive set of specific duties which include authorities involving people with the relevant protected characteristics when preparing equality objectives, taking into account any impact assessments when developing new policies, monitoring recruitment retention and development of employees and provisions on recruitment.[90] The English specific duties[91] are weaker than their Scottish and Welsh equivalents, and are also less specific than the race, gender and disability special duties under the previous legislation. Every four years, public authorities must prepare and publish one or more 'specific and measurable' equality objectives, which they think they should achieve in order to meet the EqA 2010 s149 general duty. Authorities must also publish annual information to demonstrate their compliance with the section 149 general duty. Although the English duties seem very vague, the general duty in section 149 is strongly worded. Arguably a fair amount of 'information' would need to be published under section 149 to 'demonstrate' an authority's compliance with that duty across its functions.

---

87 EqA 2010 s149(5).
88 EqA 2010 s149(6).
89 Equality Act 2010 (Statutory Duties) (Wales) Regulations 2011 SI No 1064 W.155.
90 Equality Act 2010 (Specific Duties) (Scotland) Regulations 2012 SI No 162.
91 Equality Act 2010 (Specific Duties and Public Authorities) Regulations 2017 SI No 353, replacing the Equality Act 2010 (Specific Duties) Regulations 2011 SI No 2260 with only minor amendments.

12.41   The EHRC has published 'technical guidance' on the PSED in each of England, Scotland and Wales. The EHRC had originally planned to produce statutory codes, but the government said it would not lay these before parliament. The EHRC has instead produced the text as non-statutory 'technical guidance'. The EHRC says this guidance will still be 'a formal, authoritative and comprehensive legal interpretation of the duty'. There are separate guides for England, Scotland and Wales.[92] The EHRC also produced guidance on *Coronavirus (COVID-19) and the equality duty*.[93]

Enforcement

12.42   Individuals cannot bring private law claims against public authorities for failing to comply with the PSED.[94] However, the EHRC[95] – or indeed other interested individuals or groups of individuals – can bring a judicial review against an authority which has breached the general duty. The EHRC also has power to conduct assessments and to issue compliance notices.[96] The EHRC website contains updates from its monitoring of the duties.[97]

12.43   In terms of individual discrimination cases, an employer's failure to follow its public sector duty, including any failure to carry out an EIA before introducing a policy under challenge, may be particularly relevant to whether it can justify indirect discrimination or whether it is reasonable to make an adjustment for a disabled worker.[98]

---

92   *Technical guidance on the public sector equality duty: England*, 2014, updated Febuary 2021 is at: www.equalityhumanrights.com/en/publication-download/technical-guidance-public-sector-equality-duty-england; *Technical guidance on the public sector equality duty: Scotland*, 2016, updated May 2021 is at: www.equalityhumanrights.com/en/publication-download/technical-guidance-public-sector-equality-duty-scotland; and *Technical guidance on the public sector equality duty: Wales*, 2014 is at: www.equalityhumanrights.com/en/publication-download/technical-guidance-public-sector-equality-duty-wales.

93   At www.equalityhumanrights.com/en/advice-and-guidance/coronavirus-covid-19-and-equality-duty-0.

94   EqA 2010 s156.

95   EqA 2006 s30.

96   EqA 2006 ss31 and 32.

97   At: www.equalityhumanrights.com/private-and-public-sector-guidance/public-sector-providers/public-sector-equality-duty/monitoring-and-enforcement. A review of action taken by Welsh Authorities is at: www.equalityhumanrights.com/sites/default/files/publication_pdf/PSED_examples_report_english.pdf.

98   See paras 13.27 and 15.90 for indirect discrimination and para 15.43 for reasonable adjustments.

Equality impact assessments

12.44 Possibly the most effective aspect of the public sector duties has been the development of EIAs. Apart from in the Welsh and Scottish specific duties, there is no explicit requirement under the old or new legislation to carry out EIAs. However, it follows on logically from the nature of the general duty. If an authority is going to be able to have due regard to the need to eliminate discrimination in the exercise of all its functions, one would think it needs to assess the impact of its proposed plans in advance. Ultimately it will be for the courts to decide whether an authority has gathered sufficient information in advance and has applied its mind to the impact of its proposals.

12.45 There have been a number of very interesting judicial review cases, where the courts have quashed decisions made by public authorities because they did not have 'due regard' to the need to promote equality of opportunity.[99] The cases have generally been in non-employment scenarios. They indicate that, whether or not there is a formal EIA, there cannot be 'due regard' if the decision-makers have not fully informed themselves of the facts, which entails collecting and considering sufficient information regarding the people directly and indirectly affected by the proposed policy and understanding the nature of any likely impact. The cases stress that advance consideration is required – not an assessment after the event to justify a concluded decision. Further, making assumptions before actually carrying out an impact assessment that one is unnecessary because there is no obvious evidence of a discriminatory impact, puts the cart before the horse.[100]

12.46 The public sector equality duty is a continuing duty and must be fulfilled before and at the time when a particular policy is being considered. It must be exercised with rigour and an open mind, not as a tick-box exercise. If the necessary information is not available, there is a duty to acquire it, which might involve further consultation with appropriate groups.[101]

12.47 In the employment field, it would seem good practice to carry out an EIA as a preliminary step before introducing new policies on

99 For example, see *R (C) v Secretary of State for Justice* [2008] EWCA Civ 882; *R (Kaur and Shah) v Ealing LBC* [2008] EWHC 2062 (Admin); *R (Watkins-Singh) v Governing Body of Aberdare Girls High School* [2008] EWHC 1865 (Admin); *R (Harris) v Haringey LBC* [2010] EWCA Civ 703.

100 *R (on the application of Edward Bridges) v The Chief Constable of South Wales Police and others* [2020] EWCA civ 1058.

101 *R (Bracking) v Secretary of State for Work and Pensions* [2013] EWCA Civ 1345 sets out the key legal principles.

matters such as sickness and attendance; holidays; customer complaints procedures; access to training; operation of grievance procedures; new terms and conditions; restructuring; and pension proposals. Unions are in a good position to ask employers for EIAs of proposed actions, eg cuts and redundancies, in terms of the impact on the service as well as on the workforce.

What is discrimination under the law?

continued

Chapter 13: Key points

- The definitions of 'direct discrimination', 'indirect discrimination', 'victimisation' and 'harassment' apply to all the 'protected characteristics' under the Equality Act (EqA) 2010 except pregnancy and maternity which have their own rules.

Direct discrimination

- Direct discrimination is less favourable treatment because of a protected characteristic.
- It includes discrimination because of the protected characteristic of someone else, eg someone with whom the worker is associated. It also includes discrimination where the worker is wrongly perceived to have a particular protected characteristic.
- There is no justification defence to direct discrimination except for direct age discrimination.

General guide to useful evidence

- An actual comparator without the relevant protected characteristic who has been treated better in similar circumstances.
- Evidence discrediting the employer's likely explanation of events.
- Indications of prejudice by the relevant decision-makers (not legally essential, but can strengthen the case).
- Statistics as to the position and treatment of workers generally within the workplace by reference to the relevant protected characteristics.

Indirect discrimination

- Indirect discrimination is where the employer applies a provision, criterion or practice (PCP) which puts the worker at a disadvantage and puts others with the same protected characteristic at a particular disadvantage.
- Whether there is a particular disadvantage is usually considered within an appropriate 'pool', ie a relevant section of the community.
- Statistics or other evidence can be used to prove particular disadvantage.
- It is not indirect discrimination if the employer can prove the PCP was objectively justified, ie a proportionate means of achieving a legitimate aim.

continued

General guide to useful evidence

- Statistics or other evidence showing people with the same relevant protected characteristic as the worker would tend to be disadvantaged by the particular PCP.
- Evidence showing the worker is disadvantaged by the PCP.

Victimisation

- It is victimisation to subject a worker to a detriment because s/he has done a 'protected act', eg complained about discrimination in some way.
- It does not matter if the worker was wrong in believing there was discrimination, as long as the complaint was made in good faith.

General guide to useful evidence

- Evidence that the worker has done the protected act and that the employer was upset about it.
- Evidence showing the worker was treated better before doing the protected act or that another worker who has not done a protected act has been treated better in similar circumstances.

Harassment

- Harassment is unwanted conduct related to a protected characteristic with the purpose or effect of violating a worker's dignity or creating an intimidating, degrading, humiliating or hostile environment.
- A worker can be harassed by conduct directed at someone else. The harassment need not relate to the worker's own protected characteristics.
- The conduct must be unwanted. The fact that the worker has put up with harassment for a long time does not mean it is not unwanted.
- It is also unlawful harassment to subject a worker to unwanted conduct of a sexual nature or to treat him/her less favourably because s/he rejected or submitted to sexual harassment.
- If the harasser or management treat the worker less favourably because s/he complains about harassment, this may be further harassment or direct discrimination or victimisation if what is done meets those definitions.

continued

- An employer will be responsible for any direct discrimination in his/her response to a worker's complaint about harassment by third parties, eg members of the public. An employer's inaction may also amount to harassment in itself.
- A failure by the employer to investigate a complaint of harassment may well be fundamental breach of contract, so that the worker can resign and claim constructive dismissal.[1]
- Civil or criminal claims regarding harassment by the public may also be possible, but are difficult and expensive.

General guide to useful evidence

- Evidence proving that the harassment occurred, eg visits to a GP, people the worker told at the time, first-hand witnesses, text messages or emails, worker's diary, groundless disciplinary action brought by the harasser against the worker.
- Evidence of any efforts to inform management and the response.
- Evidence showing the harassment was unwanted.
- Evidence of any substantial preventative measures taken by the employer, eg equal opportunities training of staff.

Other

- It is unlawful to instruct, cause or induce discrimination. If subjected to a detriment as a result, either the worker given the instruction or the potential 'victim' of the discrimination can bring a claim.
- Multiple discrimination claims can be brought where more than one protected characteristic is involved, but workers should think very carefully about whether there is sufficient evidence in each case. A focused case with strong evidence is better than a large number of vague allegations.
- Where evidence suggests discrimination is because of two combined protected characteristics, a claim can be made separately based on each protected characteristic individually.
- Claims based on more than one protected characteristic should have specific evidence that each is involved.
- There are numerous exceptions where discrimination is allowed, including for 'occupational requirements' and positive action. There are strict conditions for these.

continued

---

1 But constructive dismissal claims are difficult. See chapter 6.

> • More detail on each aspect of this chapter is set out in respect of the separate protected characteristics in chapters 14 and 15.

Overview

13.1 The following types of discrimination apply to all the protected characteristics[2] under the Equality Act (EqA) 2010 except pregnancy and maternity which have their own rules:

- direct discrimination;
- indirect discrimination;
- victimisation;
- harassment.

In addition, there is the concept of instructing, causing or inducing discrimination, which has some overlap with victimisation and direct discrimination. There are two further definitions of discrimination applicable to disability, which are explained in chapter 15: discrimination arising from disability; and failure to make reasonable adjustments. The EqA 2010 refers to all these as 'prohibited conduct'.

13.2 One feature of the EqA 2010 compared with the previous legislation is that it tends to use the word 'discrimination' to refer to direct discrimination and indirect discrimination, but excluding victimisation. Each type of discrimination has a precise legal meaning, which is set out below. Note that 'institutional racism' is not a legal concept and it is not helpful to refer to it.[3] In summary, the meaning of each form of discrimination is as follows:

1) *Direct discrimination* is where one worker is treated differently from another because of a protected characteristic. Where the direct discrimination is because of the worker's own protected characteristic, it is usually helpful to ask the question: 'Had this worker been of a different race/sex/religion/age etc, would the employer have treated him/her the same way?'

   If different requirements are imposed on workers according to their race/sex/religion/age etc, this is direct discrimination. For example: If an employer required all male workers to be more than six feet tall and all female workers to be more than five feet

---

2 See para 12.20.

3 *Commissioners of Inland Revenue v Morgan* [2002] IRLR 776, EAT; *Hendricks v Commissioner of Police for the Metropolis* [2003] IRLR 96, CA.

tall, a male job applicant of five feet five inches, who was therefore refused a job, would suffer direct discrimination.

There is no justification defence to direct discrimination (except for direct age discrimination). There are exceptions for occupational requirements and for positive action (see below).

2) *Indirect discrimination* is where an apparently neutral provision, criterion or practice (PCP) is applied, which puts or would put workers who share a particular protected characteristic at a disadvantage compared with others who do not have that protected characteristic. For example: An employer requires all workers to be more than six feet tall. Women would be at a disadvantage compared with men when applying for a job. A female job applicant below six feet would suffer indirect discrimination.

PCPs which can be objectively justified are not unlawful indirect discrimination.

3) *Victimisation* is where a worker is treated badly because s/he has previously complained of discrimination, given evidence for another worker in a discrimination case, or done any other 'protected act'. For example: An employer sacks a worker because s/he complained of race discrimination.

The employer has a defence if the worker made a false allegation and did not act in good faith.

4) *Harassment* is unwanted conduct related to a protected characteristic which has the purpose or effect of violating the worker's dignity, or creating an intimidating, hostile, degrading, humiliating or offensive environment.

This chapter sets out the general principles in relation to each of these definitions. It is important to read this chapter first – then for further detail in relation to their application to particular protected characteristics, see also chapter 14. European Union (EU) legislation and case-law is heavily influential in the discrimination field. For the consequences of Brexit, see chapter 3.

Direct discrimination

Overview

13.3   Direct discrimination is the most obvious form of discrimination. It entails less favourable treatment because of any of these protected characteristics: age; disability; gender reassignment; marital or civil partnership status; race; religion or belief; sex; and sexual orientation.[4] Segregating a person on racial grounds is regarded as less favourable treatment.[5] It is not unlawful under the EqA 2010 to treat someone less favourably because they are not married or not a civil partner.[6] It is permitted to treat a woman more favourably than a man in connection with pregnancy or childbirth.[7] It is also permitted to treat disabled workers more favourably because of their disability.[8] With limited exceptions, unfavourable treatment of women due to pregnancy or maternity is treated under its own rules in EqA 2010 s18.[9]

13.4 The definition of direct discrimination in EqA 2010 s13 states:

(1) A person (A) discriminates against another (B) if, because of a protected characteristic, A treats B less favourably than A treats or would treat others.

13.5 The definition in previous legislation referred to less favourable treatment 'on grounds of' the protected characteristic in question, as opposed to 'because of'. The EqA 2010 replaced the phrase 'on grounds of' with 'because of' purely out of a desire to use plain English. It does not appear to have changed the meaning of the definition as developed by the case-law over a long period.

13.6 Direct discrimination is best thought of in terms of comparative treatment. Comparisons between a worker with a particular protected characteristic and one without that protected characteristic must be made where there is no material difference between the circumstances relating to each case.[10] This is so that the comparison is significant. A worker claiming race discrimination, for example, will usually have a stronger case if s/he can point to an actual person of a different race who was treated more favourably in similar circumstances. However, it is not essential to find an actual comparator if it can be shown that the employer 'would have treated' someone of a different race more favourably. This is called a 'hypothetical comparator'.

---

4 EqA 2010 s13.
5 EqA 2010 s13(5). Separate but equal treatment of men and women can be direct discrimination against both – see *HM Chief Inspector of Education, Children's Services and Skills v Interim Executive Board of C School* [2017] EWCA Civ 1426; [2018] IRLR 334.
6 EqA 2010 s13(4).
7 EqA 2010 s13(6)(b).
8 EqA 2010 s13(3).
9 See para 11.9 for more detail.
10 EqA 2010 s23.

13.7   A possible example of direct sex discrimination is where an employer does not appoint a woman with appropriate qualifications and experience for a job. If the woman was not appointed because she was a woman, then direct discrimination has occurred. This is so regardless of whether an actual man with similar or lesser qualifications and experience has applied and been appointed, although the woman would find it harder to prove her case if there was no actual comparable man.[11]

13.8   Although it is necessary under the definition of direct discrimination for the tribunal to find that the employer has treated the worker less favourably than s/he has treated or would treat a comparator, sometimes this question can only be answered by first considering why the worker has been treated as s/he has.[12] For example, if the evidence suggests that the reason why a female worker has been treated unfavourably is because of her sex, it usually follows that the employer would have treated a hypothetical male comparator better.[13]

13.9   In certain cases it is impossible to make a literal comparison with how someone of the opposite sex would be treated, eg unfavourable treatment of pregnant women[14] or cases concerning dress and appearance. Where women are not allowed to wear trousers or men are required to cut their hair, there is no discrimination if workers of the opposite sex have been required to meet comparable or equivalent standards of smartness.[15] So far, the Human Rights Act (HRA) 1998 does not appear to have helped on this issue.[16]

13.10   The protected characteristic need not be the only basis for the employer's actions. It is enough if the protected characteristic was

---

11 See chapter 16 for evidence to prove direct discrimination.

12 *Shamoon v Chief Constable of the Royal Ulster Constabulary* [2003] UKHL 11; [2003] IRLR 285.

13 *Aylott v Stockton-on-Tees BC* [2010] EWCA Civ 910; [2010] IRLR 994.

14 No comparison with a man is required for pregnancy discrimination. See para 11.1 onwards.

15 See *Schmidt v Austicks Bookshops* [1977] IRLR 360, EAT; *Smith v Safeway plc* [1996] IRLR 456, CA; *Department for Work and Pensions v Thompson* [2004] IRLR 348, EAT. Note the different approach taken by the Northern Ireland High Court in *McConomy v Croft Inns Ltd* [1992] IRLR 561, NIHC. The Equality and Human Rights Commission's (EHRC) Employment Statutory Code of Practice deals with sex discrimination in dress codes at paras 17.41–17.42. (available at: www.equalityhumanrights.com/en/publication-download/employment-statutory-code-practice). The government has now issued non-statutory guidance for employers: *Dress codes and sex discrimination: what you need to know*, available at: www.gov.uk/government/publications/dress-codes-and-sex-discrimination-what-you-need-to-know.

16 See para 3.27.

'an important factor' or 'had a significant influence on the outcome'.[17] For example, if an employer failed to recruit a black job applicant partly because she was black and partly because she was inexperienced, that would still be direct race discrimination.

Perception and association

Overview

13.11   The definition of direct discrimination refers to less favourable treatment of a worker because of 'a' protected characteristic. This wording means it need not be because of the worker's own protected characteristic. Unlawful direct discrimination should therefore include less favourable treatment:

- because of the protected characteristic of someone with whom the worker is associated, eg a friend or relative – this is known as *discrimination by association*;
- because of the protected characteristic of people who the worker does not even know, eg potential users, customers or clients;
- because the employer wrongly perceives the worker to have a protected characteristic – this is often known as *discrimination by perception*.

13.12   This type of discrimination does not appear to apply to marriage and civil partnership,[18] or pregnancy[19] and maternity. Where there is discrimination because of perception or association in relation to pregnancy, it may be possible to bring a direct sex discrimination claim.

Discrimination by association

13.13   As the definition of direct discrimination is less favourable treatment because of 'a' protected characteristic, it includes discrimination against a worker because of someone else's protected characteristic. This might be someone with whom the worker is associated, such as a friend or relative. For example, an employer refuses to recruit a

---

17   *Owen & Briggs v James* [1982] ICR 618; [1982] IRLR 502, CA; *Nagarajan v Agnew* [1994] IRLR 61, EAT. Although these cases were interpreting the old phrasing of direct discrimination ie 'on grounds of'.

18   EqA 2010 s13(4).

19   Though this may be tested in respect of pregnancy and maternity. See para 11.12. Also, a claim for sex discrimination by association may work – see EHRC Employment Code, para 3.18.

Christian worker because she has Muslim friends. The phrase 'discrimination by association' is not spelled out in the EqA 2010, and it is best avoided, even though it is referred to in the EHRC Employment Code at paras 3.18–3.19. The concept of 'association' is more limited than the actual wording of the EqA 2010 (as the next paragraph illustrates) and leads to difficult and irrelevant questions such as what 'associated' means.

Discrimination because of the protected characteristic of people not associated with the claimant

13.14   The EHRC Employment Code gives the example of a worker treated less favourably because s/he campaigned on behalf of others with a particular protected characteristic, eg a non-disabled worker is not shortlisted for an internal job because s/he has helped set up an informal staff network for disabled workers.[20] Another example where discrimination against a worker may be because of the protected characteristic of someone else is where a worker is dismissed because s/he refused to carry out a discriminatory instruction to exclude black or Asian customers.[21] These examples are direct discrimination as they involve less favourable treatment 'because of disability' or 'because of race', albeit not the disability or race of the worker who is discriminated against. In many situations of this kind, the law on victimisation may more obviously apply, provided a 'protected act' can be identified (see para 13.58).

Discrimination by perception

13.15   Although the phrase 'discrimination by perception' is also not spelled out in the EqA 2010, again it is thought to be covered because of the way the definition of direct discrimination is worded. The EHRC Employment Code refers to it explicitly at para 3.21. Discrimination by perception could occur, for example, where an employer treats a worker less favourably because of a wrong assumption that the worker is of a certain age, nationality or religion, or that s/he is gay.

---

20 EHRC Employment Code, para 3.20.
21 *Showboat Entertainment Centre Ltd v Owens* [1984] IRLR 7, EAT; *Zarczynska v Levy* [1978] IRLR 532, EAT; *Weathersfield Ltd t/a Van & Truck Rentals v Sargent* [1999] IRLR 94, CA. See also *Lisboa v (1) Realpubs Ltd (2) Pring (3) Heap* UKEAT/0224/10.

The employer's state of mind

13.16   Employers often tell the employment tribunal (ET) that they are not personally prejudiced and insist that they acted with the best of intentions in everything they did. However true, this is irrelevant.[22] What counts is what the employer does, not his/her motives.

13.17   The key question is 'the reason why' the employer treated the worker in the way s/he did. Was it because of a protected characteristic or for some other reason? If the employer did treat the worker less favourably because of a protected characteristic, the employer's motive for doing so is irrelevant. There cannot be a 'good' motive for discriminating. For example, if an employer treats a black worker worse than s/he would treat a white worker, this is direct race discrimination in any of the following situations:

- the employer intended to treat the black worker worse out of personal racial prejudice or malice;
- the employer intended to treat the black worker worse, but out of a non-malicious or even benevolent motive;
- the employer in fact treated the black worker worse but without realising it, ie *unconscious discrimination*;
- the employer was acting on stereotyped assumptions about members of the relevant racial group.

The House of Lords made a very important statement about stereotyping in the *Roma Rights Centre*[23] case:

> The object of the legislation is to ensure that each person is treated as an individual and not assumed to be like other members of the group, whether or not most members of the group do have such characteristics. If a person acts on racial grounds, the reason why he does so is irrelevant. The person may be acting on belief or assumptions about members of the sex or racial group involved which are often true and which if true would provide a good reason for the less favourable treatment in question, but what may be true of a group may not be true of a significant number of individuals within that group.

13.18   A striking example of the employer's motive being irrelevant was a case where Amnesty International was found guilty of direct race

---

22   The key cases on this are *R v Birmingham CC ex p EOC* [1989] IRLR 173, HL; *James v Eastleigh BC* [1990] IRLR 288, HL; *Swiggs v Nagarajan* [1999] IRLR 572; (1999) EOR 51, HL; *R (E) v Governing Body of JFS and The Admissions Appeal Panel of JFS and others* [2009] UKSC 15; [2010] IRLR 136, SC.

23   *R (European Roma Rights Centre and others) v Immigration Officer at Prague Airport and another* [2005] IRLR 115; (2005) 139 EOR 26, HL.

discrimination, even though its motives were apparently benign.[24] Amnesty decided not to promote a worker of Sudanese origin to the position of researcher for Sudan because of the serious political and ethnic tensions between the North and South of that country. It felt that she would not be seen as impartial because of her ethnic origin, which would compromise Amnesty's reputation for neutrality and also endanger her own safety when travelling there. Nevertheless, the decision was unlawful.

13.19   Other examples of direct race discrimination where the employer was not personally prejudiced are: where a head teacher refused to appoint a teacher because the pupils wished to be taught English by someone of English national origin, and where a Pakistani worker was not re-employed because the employer feared industrial unrest among fellow Pakistani workers resulting from an earlier incident between him and a white foreman.[25] These examples concern direct race discrimination, but the principle is the same regarding all the protected characteristics.

13.20   There is a long-established 'but for' test, which usually helps to identify direct discrimination.[26] The question is whether the worker, *but for* his/her race or sex or other protected characteristic, would have been treated differently by the employer. For example, if a well-qualified woman fails in her job application, the question is whether the employer would have recruited her if she was a man with the same qualifications. The advantage of this test is that it focuses on actions not motives and the ET need not try to assess the employer's state of mind.

13.21   Unfortunately, the beautifully clear 'but for' test has been questioned in many cases in recent years, which prefer to look at 'the reason why' the employer has acted as s/he has.[27] This alternative test rather begs the question, and does not provide much help in practice for analysing evidence. Even worse, it potentially misleads advisers and tribunals into wrongly looking for conscious racial etc motives. Arguably, the attack on the 'but for' test arises from a distortion or extension of its formulation. The original test is expressed in the active tense, ie '*but for* the worker's protected characteristic, would the employer have treated him/her the same way?' This

---

24   *Amnesty International v Ahmed* UKEAT/0447/08; [2009] IRLR 884, EAT.

25   *Din v Carrington Viyella* [1982] IRLR 281, EAT.

26   *R v Birmingham CC ex p EOC* [1989] IRLR 173, HL; *James v Eastleigh BC* [1990] IRLR 288, HL.

27   This view was rejected by the majority in *James v Eastleigh BC* [1990] IRLR 288, HL.

formulation should answer any objections that it goes too far. However, in several of the cases where it has been criticised, it has effectively been looked at passively, ie *'but for* the worker's protected characteristic, would the same thing have happened to him/her?' This latter formulation is incorrect because factors other than the employer's discriminatory reason could affect the outcome.

13.22　　It is also interesting that many of the original cases which attacked the 'but for' test concerned either victimisation (under its pre-EqA 2010 definition, which had a different legal definition to direct discrimination), or the treatment of women in relation to sexual relationships at work (which may be better suited to the definition of harassment).[28] A full discussion of the pros and cons of the 'but for' test and the extent to which it is still useful is beyond the scope of this book. However, in the vast majority of cases, the 'but for' test (correctly formulated), is still a safe way of identifying direct discrimination.

13.23　　*Unconscious discrimination* is hard to prove, but it is a concept which the law recognises. The cases tend to have been concerned with race discrimination, but again, the same principles apply to discrimination because of any of the protected characteristics. The Court of Appeal has talked about the possibility of 'a conscious or unconscious racial attitude which involves stereotyped assumptions about members of that [racial] group'.[29] The most explicit and enlightened guidance on this point was given by the House of Lords in *Nagarajan v London Regional Transport*.[30] Although the case concerned victimisation, the guidance was intended also to apply to direct discrimination:

> All human beings have preconceptions, beliefs, attitudes and preju-dices on many subjects. It is part of our make-up. Moreover, we do not always recognise our own prejudices. Many people are unable, or unwilling, to admit even to themselves that actions of theirs may be racially motivated. An employer may genuinely believe that the reason why he rejected an applicant had nothing to do with the applicant's race. After careful and thorough investigation of the claim, members of an employment tribunal may decide that the proper inference to be drawn from the evidence is that, whether the employer realised it at the time or not, race was the reason why he acted as he did . . . Members of racial groups need protection from conduct driven by unrecognised prejudice as much as from conscious and deliberate discrimination.

28　Although the scope of the harassment definition also has difficulties.
29　*West Midlands Passenger Transport Executive v Singh* [1988] IRLR 186, CA.
30　[1999] IRLR 572, HL.

Unfortunately, some ETs have failed in the past to understand that much discrimination occurs due to unconscious stereotyping, for example, unconsciously undervaluing the performance or capability of a black worker. ETs may find that racial discrimination has not occurred because they believe in the 'honesty' of the employers' witnesses. Yet a manager who honestly believes a black worker is not fit for promotion may nevertheless have reached a different 'honest' view of a white worker, when confronted with the same objective evidence.[31] In some cases, it may be worth explicitly drawing the above passage to the ET's attention at the outset of a hearing.

13.24　　Another issue which can arise is where the reason why the decision-maker treats the worker as s/he does is not because of any particular protected characteristic, but because the decision-maker is innocently acting on tainted information. In such a case, the decision-maker has not committed direct discrimination in his/her own actions, although the person supplying the tainted information may have done so.[32] For example, a managing director dismisses a worker because he has received a poor appraisal from the worker's line manager. Unknown to the managing director, the line manager has assessed the worker less favourably because of the worker's age. The discriminatory action is the giving of the appraisal by the line manager, not the dismissal by the managing director. If the appraisal directly led to the lost job, compensation might well include loss of earnings arising from the dismissal. However, it is important from the point of view of evidence and time limits to make the correct analysis.

Defences to direct discrimination

13.25　With the exception of direct age discrimination, an employer is unable to argue that direct discrimination was justified. Once an employer has treated a worker less favourably because of a protected characteristic, there cannot be a good reason for doing so.

13.26　　In specified circumstances, direct discrimination is permitted, eg where an 'occupational requirement' exception applies or 'positive action' is allowed. These exceptions are set out partly below (from para 13.131) and partly in chapter 14. Direct age discrimination is

---

31　See para 16.19.

32　*CLFIS (UK) Ltd v Reynolds* [2015] EWCA Civ 439; [2015] IRLR 562. See para 6.122 above for the position with a whistleblowing dismissal: it is uncertain how *Royal Mail Group Ltd v Jhuti* [2019] UKSC 55; [2020] IRLR 129, SC, might affect the *CLFIS* principle.

also allowed if the employer can justify it by showing the less favourable treatment was a proportionate means of achieving a legitimate
aim.[33] More detail of this defence is at para 14.10 onwards.

Indirect discrimination

Overview

13.27   Indirect discrimination is a more difficult concept for practitioners
and tribunals alike. The definition of indirect discrimination was
introduced in the Race Relations Act (RRA) 1976, as it was recognised that the law against direct discrimination did not go far enough
to eliminate institutionalised disadvantage in the workplace. The
great difficulty of indirect discrimination is that it is not always easy
to detect, and advisers need to be particularly alert.

13.28   Indirect discrimination occurs where there is apparently equal
treatment of all workers, but the effect of certain requirements and
practices imposed by the employer puts workers with a certain
protected characteristic at a particular disadvantage. For example, a
requirement that all job applicants speak fluent English, while
applied equally to everyone, would disproportionately bar people
born in non-English-speaking countries from employment.

13.29   It may be important to stress to tribunals that the prohibition on
indirect discrimination does not reduce standards or entail any kind
of reverse discrimination. This is a common misconception. If a
discriminatory requirement or practice can be justified, then it is not
unlawful. The law simply prohibits unjustifiable requirements and
practices which have a discriminatory effect.

The definition

Equality Act 2010 s19

13.30   Historically, the definition of indirect discrimination has been
through a number of changes. The earlier case-law is based on the
older definitions, so it is important to understand this. The changes
in the definition have made a difference in what needs to be proved.
The definition of indirect discrimination is now contained in EqA
2010 s19 and reads as follows:

---

33   EqA 2010 s13(2).

(1) A person (A) discriminates against another (B) if A applies to B a provision, criterion or practice which is discriminatory in relation to a relevant protected characteristic of B's.

(2) For the purposes of subsection (1), a provision, criterion or practice is discriminatory in relation to a relevant protected characteristic of B's if—

   (a) A applies, or would apply, it to persons with whom B does not share the characteristic,

   (b) it puts, or would put, persons with whom B shares the characteristic at a particular disadvantage when compared with persons with whom B does not share it,

   (c) it puts, or would put, B at that disadvantage, and

   (d) A cannot show it to be a proportionate means of achieving a legitimate aim.

The relevant protected characteristics are: age; disability; gender reassignment; marriage and civil partnership; race; religion or belief; sex; and sexual orientation.[34]

Identifying the provision, criterion or practice

13.31 The first stage in the definition is that the employer must have applied a 'provision, criterion or practice' (PCP) to the worker. A PCP covers more situations than the original wording of indirect discrimination, which referred to discriminatory 'requirements and conditions'. Almost anything done by an employer will count as a PCP, eg mandatory or preferred selection criteria for jobs, promotion or redundancy; conditions for training or overtime opportunities; rules about when holidays can be taken; imposition of certain hours or working patterns. Examples of PCPs relevant to different protected characteristics are given in chapter 14 and appendix B. See also paras 15.45–15.46 concerning disability reasonable adjustments for a further discussion of what PCP means.

13.32 It is not always easy to identify which is the relevant PCP imposed by the employer. Formulating the PCP wrongly can make the difference between winning and losing a case.

Establishing group disadvantage

1) The pool

13.33 The PCP must be one which 'puts, or would put' people with whom the worker shares the relevant protected characteristic at a particular disadvantage when compared with those who do not share that

---

34 EqA 2010 s19(3).

characteristic. For example, if the worker is a woman, the PCP would put women at a particular disadvantage compared with men. The comparison of the impact of the PCP must be made where there is no material difference between the circumstances relating to those with and without the relevant protected characteristic.[35]

13.34   The question is, within what section of the community should the comparison be made?[36] This is known as a 'pool'. Should the effect of the disadvantage be measured on those with and without the relevant protected characteristic in the general workforce? Or should it be measured in society generally? Or only among those in a particular town or a specific workplace or with appropriate qualifications?[37] The appropriate 'pool' will depend on the facts of each case and which section of the public is likely to be affected by the requirement.[38] It will depend on the type of discrimination involved, as well as what evidence is available.[39] In general, the pool should consist of the group which the PCP affects or would affect, either positively or negatively.[40] The pool has to test suitably the discrimination complained of. There is no point bringing into the equation people who have no interest in the advantage or disadvantage in question.[41] For example, in one case, teachers who had returned to teaching after retirement while in receipt of a pension could only acquire further pensionable service if they returned on a full-time rather than a part-time basis. The correct pool for assessing whether this rule had disparate impact on women was retired teachers, not all teachers.[42] Taking another example, in recruitment cases the appropriate pool will often be those who, apart from the discriminatory requirement, have the required qualifications for the post.[43]

35 EqA 2010 s23.
36 Question 6 in *Raval v DHSS and the Civil Service Commission* [1985] ICR 685; [1985] IRLR 370, EAT.
37 *Pearse v City of Bradford MC* [1988] IRLR 379, EAT; *Price v The Civil Service Commission* [1978] ICR 27; [1977] IRLR 291, EAT.
38 *London Underground Ltd v Edwards (No 2)* [1998] IRLR 364, CA.
39 *Eweida v British Airways plc* [2010] IRLR 322, CA.
40 EHRC Employment Code, para 4.18; *Essop and others v Home Office (UK Border Agency); Naeem v Secretary of State for Justice* [2017] UKSC 27; [2017] IRLR 558.
41 *Somerset CC and Secretary of State for Children, Schools and Families v Pike* [2009] EWCA Civ 808; [2009] IRLR 870.
42 *Somerset CC and Secretary of State for Children, Schools and Families v Pike* [2009] EWCA Civ 808; [2009] IRLR 870.
43 *Jones v University of Manchester* [1993] IRLR 218, CA.

13.35   The outcome of the comparison exercise may well vary according to the pool chosen. The ET's selection of the appropriate pool is a matter for its discretion.[44] The important point is not to define the pool so narrowly that it is misleading because it incorporates discrimination. For example, in one case[45] only those who had been resident in the EU were eligible for lower college fees. It would have been misleading to choose as a pool, people who had actually applied to the college, because many would have been deterred from applying.

2) Measuring disadvantage

13.36   Indirect discrimination is concerned with whether a PCP, requirement or condition adversely affects those with a certain protected characteristic more than others. The original definition of indirect discrimination required comparing proportions of people who were affected. This suggested a statistical exercise and much case-law has developed around that. The looser wording in the EqA 2010, allows other kinds of evidence to prove particular disadvantage, eg evidence from an expert witness,[46] or from the claimant and other individuals in the disadvantaged group.[47] Nevertheless, statistics have retained a central role. The EHRC Employment Code explains how to carry out a statistical comparative exercise at paras 4.21–4.22.

13.37   Comparing proportions (fractions or percentages) of those affected rather than absolute numbers makes a difference. For example, a Spanish national may claim indirect discrimination because s/he cannot speak fluent English as his/her potential employer requires. The appropriate comparison is not the total number of Spanish people who cannot speak fluent English as against the total number of non-Spanish people who cannot speak fluent English. The proper comparison is the proportion of all Spanish people who cannot speak fluent English as against the proportion of all non-Spanish people who cannot do so. The calculation could be done as follows:

A = The total number of Spanish people within the chosen pool (eg 100)

B = The number of Spanish people within the pool who cannot speak fluent English (eg 95)

C = The total number of non-Spanish people in the pool (eg 100,000)

---

44 *Kidd v DRG (UK)* [1985] IRLR 190, EAT.
45 *Orphanos v Queen Mary College* [1985] IRLR 349, HL.
46 EHRC Employment Code, paras 4.13–4.14.
47 *Games v University of Kent* [2015] IRLR 202, EAT.

D = The number of non-Spanish people in the pool who cannot speak fluent English (eg 10,000).

13.38 It would be meaningless to look at absolute numbers and compare the actual number of Spanish people in the pool who cannot speak fluent English with the even larger number of non-Spanish people in the pool who cannot do so, since there are far fewer Spanish people in the world anyway. Therefore proportions are calculated, ie:

B is divided by A; and
D is divided by C

to get the fractions to be compared. Percentages can be calculated by multiplying each fraction by 100. In this example, 95 per cent of Spanish people in the pool compared with ten per cent of non-Spanish people in the pool are disadvantaged by the fluent English requirement.

13.39 A racial group can comprise two or more distinct racial groups.[48] For example, a black British person could describe him/herself as black or as British or as black British for the purposes of his/her claim. Presumably also, a Spanish national could fall into the group of those with Spanish nationality or those with nationality of a European country, or those with nationality of a country which does not have English as its first language. The choice of 'category' may affect the statistical outcome. Following the example in the previous paragraph, since many workers of nationalities other than Spanish also could not meet a fluent English requirement, comparing the statistics as they affect Spanish people versus non-Spanish people may be misleading. It may be more accurate to describe the Spanish worker as 'from a non-English-speaking country' and compare the extent to which workers from a non-English-speaking country, as opposed to workers from an English-speaking country, would be disadvantaged by such a requirement. Note that the comparison cannot simply be made between Spanish workers and workers from a non-English-speaking country: a comparison must be made between those of a particular racial group against everyone else.

13.40 As already stated, it is not enough that the worker him/herself is at a disadvantage. Some identifiable section of the workforce, even a small one, must also share the disadvantage.[49] The PCP need not put everyone with the relevant protected characteristic at a disadvantage, but how much of a discrepancy needs to be shown in the impact on

---

48 EqA 2010 s9(4). EHRC Employment Code, paras 2.46–2.49.
49 *Eweida v British Airways plc* [2010] IRLR 322, CA.

those with the relevant protected characteristic and on those without the relevant protected characteristic? The case-law developed under the older definitions of indirect discrimination is useful where statistics are involved, but may now be considered too rigid in certain respects. The emphasis now is on simply showing that an identifiable group with the relevant protected characteristic has been particularly disadvantaged. If not many people with the relevant protected characteristic are disadvantaged, that may be relevant mostly to whether the PCP is justifiable[50]

13.41   Looking at it statistically, the older cases said the disparate impact should be analysed in terms of those potentially affected; it does not matter if the practice under attack has no relevance to the vast bulk of humanity.[51] Thus a difference of one or two per cent with very small percentages potentially affected or unaffected would be no less significant than a difference between 30 and 60 per cent. A useful measure of what amounts to a significant difference used to be the '4/5 ths' or '80 per cent' rule, which was commonly used in the US. If the smaller percentage is less than 80 per cent of the larger percentage, the difference is significant. However, UK courts have rejected the idea of following any rigid rule or formula, suggesting that ETs simply apply a common-sense approach.[52] The Court of Justice of the European Union (CJEU) has said that the significance of statistical comparisons should be assessed by reference to factors such as the number of individuals counted and whether they illustrate purely fortuitous or short-term phenomena.[53] A lesser disparity which persisted over a long period could be sufficient.[54] An ET can take into account the make-up and overall numbers of the workforce under consideration; the fact that no one without the relevant protected characteristic is similarly disadvantaged, and the inherent likely effect of the requirement or condition under challenge.[55]

---

50 In particular, note the development of this issue in indirect religious discrimination cases although where Article 9 of the ECHR is involved, that fact that only small numbers are disadvantaged should not affect justification. See paras 13.52 and 14.112.

51 *R v Secretary of State for Education ex p Schaffter* [1987] IRLR 53, QBD.

52 *R v Secretary of State for Employment ex p Seymour-Smith and Perez* [1995] IRLR 464, CA; *McCausland v Dungannon DC* [1993] IRLR 583, NICA. Most helpful is *London Underground Ltd v Edwards (No 2)* [1998] IRLR 364, CA.

53 *Enderby v Frenchay Health Authority and Secretary of State for Health* [1993] IRLR 591, ECJ.

54 *R v Secretary of State for Employment ex p Seymour-Smith and Perez* [1999] IRLR 253, ECJ.

55 *Chief Constable of Avon & Somerset Constabulary v Chew* EAT/503/00 at para 36.

13.42   It can make a big difference whether the impact of a PCP is assessed by comparing those who are advantaged by it (eg who can comply with it) as opposed to comparing those who are disadvantaged by it (eg who cannot comply or who suffer a detriment). Although the original definition and case-law measured those who are advantaged, the current definition clearly indicates the measure should be those who are disadvantaged.

13.43   It is not legally necessary to prove the reason why the group is disadvantaged (although that might be evidentially useful in some cases where there are no statistics, to show those with a certain protected characteristic are at a particular disadvantage compared with others). Nor is it necessary to prove that such reason is the same as the reason why the worker is disadvantaged, as long as it is a 'corresponding' (essentially the same) disadvantage.[56]

The PCP puts or would put the worker at that disadvantage

13.44   The PCP must put the worker at a disadvantage, eg s/he does not get a job because s/he does not satisfy a particular selection criterion. It is also unlawful if the PCP 'would put' the worker at a disadvantage. For example, a woman sees a job advert which states 'full-time workers only should apply'. The woman was suitable for the post and would otherwise have applied, but she is unable to work full-time because of childcare. The woman can claim indirect sex discrimination, even if she has not actually applied for the job (although it is usually much easier to bring a case if a worker actually applies and waits to see whether she is rejected).[57]

13.45   A 'disadvantage' is not defined by the EqA 2010, but as well as obvious disadvantages, it could include a denial of an opportunity or choice, deterrence, rejection or exclusion.[58] A worker need not suffer actual loss, economic or otherwise, and it is probably enough that a worker can reasonably say s/he would have preferred to be treated differently. An unjustified sense of grievance will not count. In relation to religious practices, the test is whether someone can comply 'consistently with the customs and cultural conditions of the racial group'.[59] For example, a Sikh man could in theory comply with a

---

56   *Essop and others v Home Office (UK Border Agency); Naeem v Secretary of State for Justice* [2017] UKSC 27; [2017] IRLR 558.

57   But to win his/her claim, the worker needs to be genuinely interested in the job or the advert will not amount to a detriment – see para 12.24.

58   EHRC Employment Code, para 4.9.

59   *Mandla v Lee* [1983] IRLR 209; [1983] ICR 385, HL.

requirement that he wear no turban – he need only take it off. However, in practice he could not comply and would be disadvantaged.

13.46   As stated above, the worker must be put at the 'corresponding' disadvantage to the group, not a different disadvantage.[60] For example, if an older worker's disadvantage is inability to pass a certain test, older job candidates as opposed to younger candidates must also have disproportionately failed the test.

13.47   The relevant time to measure whether the PCP causes a disadvantage is the date on which the worker suffers a detriment because of its application.[61] For example:

- In one case, a woman of Asian origin who qualified as a teacher in Kenya could not comply with a requirement for a clerical post of having English O-level. It was irrelevant that she had the ability to gain an O-level and could in the past or in the future have obtained one. At the time that the requirement was applied, she could not meet it.[62]
- In another case,[63] part-timers were selected first for redundancy. At the time of the redundancy dismissals, the claimant was a part-time worker. It was irrelevant that she could have changed to full-time working several years ago once her children had grown up, since she had not in fact done so and at the time of the selection, she was still a part-timer.

Justifiable as a proportionate means of achieving a legitimate aim

13.48   The final question is whether the employer can prove that the PCP is justifiable or, to use the wording of the current definition in the EqA 2010, 'a proportionate means of achieving a legitimate aim'.[64] The concept of justifiability is central to the law on indirect discrimination. In practice there are numerous, often hidden, PCPs with discriminatory effect in every workplace. The possibility of bringing a successful case often turns on whether the PCP is justifiable. In theory, the aim need not have been articulated or even realised by the

---

60 *Essop and others v Home Office (UK Border Agency); Naeem v Secretary of State for Justice* [2017] UKSC 27; [2017] IRLR 558.
61 *Clarke v Eley (IMI) Kynoch Ltd* [1982] IRLR 482, EAT.
62 *Raval v DHSS and the Civil Service Commission* [1985] ICR 685; [1985] IRLR 370, EAT. For a more recent example, see *Games v University of Kent* [2015] IRLR 202, EAT.
63 *Clarke v Eley (IMI) Kynoch Ltd* [1982] IRLR 482, EAT.
64 EHRC Employment Code, paras 4.25–4.32 discusses the justification defence.

employer at the time when the measure was first adopted. It can be an ex post facto rationalisation,[65] but if it was not thought of at the time, it is less likely to amount to a convincing justification.

13.49 Justifiability is very much a question of fact. At one time an employer needed to produce only what right-thinking people would consider were 'sound and tolerable reasons' for applying a requirement.[66] Now it is not so easy. It is for the tribunal to make its own judgment, upon a fair and detailed analysis of the working practices and business considerations involved, as to whether the PCP is justified. Unlike the test for unfair dismissal, it is not enough for the employer's decision to be within a band of reasonable responses.[67]

13.50 What an ET would consider justifiable requires 'an objective balance between the discriminatory effect of the condition and the reasonable needs of the party who applies the condition'.[68] An employer must show that:

- the requirement was objectively justifiable regardless of race or sex (or whatever is the relevant protected characteristic);
- the requirement served a real business need of the employer;[69] and
- the need was reasonable and objectively justifiable on economic or other grounds, eg administrative efficiency; it is not sufficient that the particular employer personally considers it justifiable.[70]

13.51 There are two stages to the employer's defence. The employer must show:

1) that s/he had a legitimate aim; and
2) that applying the PCP was a 'proportionate' means of achieving that aim. It is important not to forget this second part of the justification test. The central concept of 'proportionality' involves

---

65 *Seldon v Clarkson Wright & Jakes (a partnership)* [2012] UKSC 16; [2012] IRLR 590.
66 *Ojutiku and Oburoni v MSC* [1982] ICR 661; [1982] IRLR 418, CA.
67 *Hardys & Hansons plc v Lax* [2005] IRLR 726, CA.
68 *Hampson v Department of Education and Science* [1989] IRLR 69, CA. There is a useful summary of the law on justification in *Homer v Chief Constable of West Yorkshire Police* [2012] UKSC 15; [2012] IRLR 601.
69 *Bilka-Kaufhaus GmbH v Weber von Hartz* [1987] ICR 110; [1986] IRLR 317, ECJ; *Rainey v Greater Glasgow Health Board* [1987] ICR 129; [1987] IRLR 26, HL.
70 *Bilka-Kaufhaus GmbH v Weber von Hartz* [1987] ICR 110; [1986] IRLR 317, ECJ; *Rainey v Greater Glasgow Health Board* [1987] ICR 129; [1987] IRLR 26, HL. (Note that these were equal pay cases.) *Hampson v Department of Education and Science* [1990] IRLR 302, HL.

balancing the effect of the PCP with the employer's needs. These questions should be asked:

a) Is the objective sufficiently important to justify limiting a fundamental right (ie the right not to be discriminated against)?
b) Is the measure rationally connected to the objective?
c) Are the means chosen no more than is necessary to accomplish the objective?[71]

13.52 Even if the employer's aims are legitimate, it may not be enough for the employer to show that the PCP is the only way of achieving those aims. In some situations, the ends simply cannot justify the means. It is therefore always important to finish by looking at the overall balance between the ends and the means.[72] The impact on workers sharing the protected characteristic generally is part of this balancing exercise. Generally speaking, the greater the impact of the PCP on the affected group (considering numbers affected and the amount of damage), the harder it is to justify.[73] The impact on the particular worker bringing the claim may also be part of the balancing exercise, although possibly only to the extent that it is typical of the impact on the group generally.[74] Also, where the worker has a concurrent right under the European Convention on Human Rights (ECHR), weighing the impact on the individual may be a stronger factor.

13.53 The relevant EU directives are worded differently from the definition of justification in the EqA 2010. Instead of referring to 'a proportionate means of achieving a legitimate aim', they state that the means of achieving the aim must be 'appropriate and necessary'. EU case-law, as well as the directives, also requires the employer to show the PCP was 'reasonably necessary'.

13.54 Examples of factors which may justify a discriminatory requirement are: hygiene; safety; consistency of care; consistency of management; and important economic and administrative considerations. Each case will depend on its precise facts and the principle of balance.

---

71 *R (Elias) v Secretary of State for Defence* [2006] IRLR 934, CA.
72 *Akerman-Livingstone v Aster Communities Limited (formerly Flourish Homes Limited)* [2015] UKSC 15.
73 Confirmed in various cases including recently, *MBA v Mayor and Burgesses of Merton LBC* [2014] IRLR 145, CA. *University of Manchester v Jones* [1993] IRLR 218, CA and more.
74 The case law rarely refers to balancing the effect on the claimant specifically, but see *University of Manchester v Jones* [1993] IRLR 218, CA and *Allonby v Accrington & Rossendale College* [2001] IRLR 364, CA. See para 14.101 for a further discussion in the context of religious discrimination.

13.55 Many reasons given by employers involve costs considerations. If the employer's reason for imposing a discriminatory PCP is solely because it would be more expensive not to discriminate, this will not be a legitimate aim. However, it is permissible for costs to be part of the picture. This is often referred to as 'costs plus' by lawyers. The 'plus' factor is pretty wide and it tends to mean simply that there is a wider context. For example, it can be a legitimate aim to reduce expenditure as a result of resource pressures in order to balance the books. Even if the aim is legitimate, however, the nature and extent of the financial pressures should be examined when considering if imposing the PCP was proportionate.[75] For more discussion of this in the context of justification to direct age discrimination, see para 14.12.

13.56 Often employers lose sight of their aims when imposing discriminatory requirements. Where an employer seeks to justify a PCP, it is worth establishing first what business need the employer claims to have, and then examining whether the imposition of the requirement serves (or is necessary to serve) that need at all. A public authority's failure to follow its public sector equality duty (PSED) may be relevant to whether it can justify indirect discrimination.[76]

13.57 Once it is shown that there is a discriminatory PCP, it is for the employer to prove that it is justifiable.[77] This can be forgotten by an ET who may expect the claimant to show why the PCP is not justifiable and to suggest alternative ways for the employer to achieve the needs. Obviously it is helpful if workers can show how employers could meet their needs by taking action with less discriminatory effect, but workers should not be required to provide such evidence. There have been a number of cases in recent years concerning the justification of indirect discrimination in the relatively newer areas of age and religious discrimination. These are reported in more detail in chapter 14, but what is interesting is the number of times a case is overturned on appeal because, although the tribunals have found the employers' aims to be *legitimate,* they have failed to focus their minds on whether the means used were *proportionate.* The tribunal must make a critical evaluation and demonstrate this in its reasoning.[78]

75 See *Heskett v The Secretary of State for Justice* [2020] EWCA Civ 1487; [2021] IRLR 132, where the Court of Appeal reviews the case-law on 'costs plus'.

76 *R (Elias) v Secretary of State for Defence and Commission for Racial Equality* [2005] IRLR 788, QBD.

77 See para 16.44 on the burden of proof.

78 *Hardy & Hansons plc v Lax* [2005] EWCA Civ 846; [2005] IRLR 726; applied recently in *Ryan v South West Ambulance Services NHS Trust* UKEAT/0213/19; [2021] IRLR 4.

Victimisation

The legal meaning of victimisation

13.58   It is unlawful to victimise a worker because s/he has done a 'protected act'.[79] Basically this means a worker must not be punished
because s/he has complained about discrimination in one way or
another. For example, a worker is made redundant on a pretext
because s/he recently took out a grievance complaining of race
discrimination. As long as the worker does not make her complaint
in bad faith, s/he must not be victimised, even if s/he is wrong to
suggest discrimination had occurred. However, giving false evidence
or information or making a false allegation is not considered a
'protected act' if it was done in bad faith.[80] The key question is
whether the worker honestly believed in the truth of his/her allegation. As long as s/he was honest, it does not matter if s/he had some
ulterior motive for accusing the employer of discrimination.[81]

13.59   A 'protected act' means:[82]

a) bringing proceedings under the EqA 2010 or previous discrimination legislation;
b) giving evidence or information in connection with such
proceedings;
c) doing any other thing for the purposes of or in connection with
the EqA 2010 or previous discrimination legislation; or
d) making an allegation (whether explicitly or not) that the employer
or someone else has breached the EqA 2010 or previous discrimination legislation.

In relation to pay, it is a protected act to seek or make a relevant pay
disclosure or to obtain information in such a disclosure.[83] It is also
unlawful to victimise a worker because it is suspected that the worker
has done or may do a protected act.

13.60   Note that victimisation of a worker who complains of sexual
harassment may fall under the definition of further harassment

---

79   EqA 2010 s27.
80   EqA 2010 s27(3).
81   Unlike the concept of 'good faith' in whistleblowing claims (see para 6.114).
Saad v Southampton University Hospitals NHS Trust UKEAT/0276/17; [2018]
IRLR 2007.
82   EqA 2010 s27(2)(a)–(d).
83   EqA 2010 s77(4). See para 5.69 onwards regarding pay disclosures.

under EqA 2010 s26(3),[84] as opposed to the main victimisation provisions. It may be unclear on the facts which definition should apply. If in doubt, the worker should claim in the alternative under both sections.

13.61   The primary purpose of the victimisation provisions is to ensure that workers are not penalised or prejudiced because they have taken steps to exercise their statutory rights or are intending to do so, and that they are not deterred from their fundamental right to challenge discrimination in the tribunals.[85] This protection is particularly important for workers who risk dismissal by bringing up controversial issues, but do not have the requisite length of service to qualify for a claim of unfair dismissal.

13.62   The law protects workers complaining about discrimination against themselves as well as workers speaking out on behalf of others. For example, a white worker must not be victimised for supporting a black worker who has brought a grievance of race discrimination. Similarly, a trade union representative could claim victimisation if s/he is put under particular pressure by the employer when s/he takes up discrimination cases.[86] It is also unlawful to victimise a worker because someone else has carried out a protected act, eg s/he is a member of a trade union which has spoken out vociferously about racism.[87] Some people might call this 'victimisation by association', but it is unnecessary to introduce that additional concept, which tends to lead into irrelevant questions such as what 'association' means and how close the 'association' must be.

Proving victimisation

13.63   Unfortunately, it can be hard to prove that victimisation has taken place. A worker must prove three things:

1) s/he has done a 'protected act' (or the employer believes s/he has done or may do a protected act);
2) the employer has subjected the worker to a detriment;

---

84   See para 14.144.
85   *Chief Constable of West Yorkshire Police v Khan* [2001] IRLR 830, HL; *Coote v Granada Hospitality Ltd* [1998] IRLR 656, ECJ; *St Helens MBC v Derbyshire and others* [2007] UKHL 16; [2007] IRLR 540.
86   S/he may also be able to claim discrimination for taking up trade union activities. See para 2.1 onwards.
87   *Thompson v London Central Bus Co Ltd* UKEAT/0108/15; [2016] IRLR 9.

3) the reason the employer has subjected the worker to a detriment is because the worker has done that protected act, ie the employer was motivated by it (even if unconsciously).[88]

1) The protected act

13.64 Paragraph 13.59 above sets out the different types of 'protected act'. The precise scope of doing anything 'for the purposes of or in connection with' the EqA 2010 is uncertain. The taking up of a public authority's obligations under the public sector equality duty by trade union officials or in-house equality trainers may well be 'protected acts'. Other examples of 'protected acts' could be encouraging a colleague to take up a discrimination case; issuing a press statement referring to breaches of the EqA 2010; or approaching the EHRC. Victimisation law protects those raising discrimination issues formally or informally, not purely in ET proceedings.

13.65 Where a 'protected act' consists of a verbal complaint of discrimination, the employer may deny that there ever was such a complaint. It is therefore advisable that any complaint of discrimination or statement of intention to bring proceedings or to give evidence should be put in writing at the time. If appropriate, such written statement should be accompanied by a reminder to the employer of the right not to be victimised under the relevant sections. Whether the complaint is made verbally or in writing, the worker needs to be clear that s/he is talking about discrimination rather than general unfairness. If the worker did not clearly allege discrimination, a claim could still be made (if applicable) on the basis that the employer suspected s/he was doing so. If relying on this argument, it should be set out in the ET1.

2) Subjected to a detriment

13.66 A 'detriment' is any disadvantage,[89] eg dismissal, non-promotion or refusal of a reference. Victimisation does not always take the obvious form of dismissing or disciplining a worker. It may take many less obvious and more subtle forms, for example:

• pressurising a worker to drop an allegation of discrimination or threatening him/her if s/he goes ahead;

---

88 *Chief Constable of West Yorkshire Police v Khan* [2001] IRLR 830, HL; *Swiggs v Nagarajan* [1999] IRLR 572, HL; *St Helens MBC v Derbyshire and others* [2007] IRLR 540, HL. Note that some aspects of *Khan* related to the old definition.

89 See para 12.24; and EHRC Employment Code, paras 9.8–9.9.

- writing direct to the worker (even though s/he is represented) and to his/her work colleagues, warning of the risk that if the worker's ET claim succeeds, staff may lose their jobs and service-users suffer (this is as distinct from a reasonable although firm attempt to persuade a claimant to settle his/her claim);[90]
- withdrawing or reducing trade union facilities to a shop steward who is gathering evidence for a discrimination or equal pay claim;
- refusing holiday leave requests on the desired dates;
- writing a poor reference or refusing to provide one at all.[91]

13.67   If the detriment amounts to harassment, a claim must be made as a harassment claim under EqA 2010 s26 rather than a victimisation claim.[92]

3) Because of the protected act

13.68   As a matter of evidence, it is often difficult to prove that the reason the employer has subjected the worker to a detriment is because the worker has done a protected act. For example, an employer dismissing a worker because s/he has made an allegation of racial harassment may purport to do so because his/her work is poor. There is no fixed time between the protected act and the act of victimisation, but the closer in time the two events occur, the easier it is to show a link between them.

13.69   The wording of the definition of victimisation differs slightly from that in the previous legislation, and it is no longer necessary for the worker to compare his/her treatment with that of a worker who has not done a protected act. Nevertheless, such a comparison may still be useful evidence to prove the reason why the worker was subjected to the detriment.

13.70   The EHRC Employment Code says a protected act need not be the *only* reason for the detrimental treatment; it is enough if it is *one of* the reasons.[93] This is consistent with the law on direct discrimination, where the protected characteristic need only be an important factor in the discrimination.[94]

13.71   Employers often say they are not punishing the worker for doing the protected act, but for some other aspect of the worker's behaviour. The difficulty is where the line should be drawn. It is unlikely

---

90   *St Helens MBC v Derbyshire and others* [2007] IRLR 540, HL.
91   See para 12.26 regarding victimisation after dismissal.
92   EqA 2010 s212.
93   EHRC Employment Code, para 9.10.
94   See para 13.10.

to be victimisation if an employer disciplines or dismisses a worker, not because s/he complained of discrimination, but because s/he expressed his/her complaint in a violent manner or because s/he telephoned the managing director at 3 am to talk about it. On the other hand, tribunals should recognise that workers often express their complaints in an apparently unreasonable way because they feel upset. It would be contrary to the purpose of the victimisation law if employers could take steps against workers simply because they had used intemperate language or made inaccurate statements when making their complaint. An employer who objects to 'ordinary' unreasonable behaviour of that kind should be treated as objecting to the complaint itself. Tribunals should not distinguish between the fact of the complaint and the way it is made except in clear cases.[95]

13.72   If the worker complains of discrimination which would not be covered by the EqA 2010, even if s/he proved it happened, s/he may not be protected.[96] For example, a black worker who is dismissed for complaining of a racial assault which took place outside the course of employment (and therefore not covered by EqA 2010) may not be able to complain of victimisation.[97]

Steps in the litigation

13.73   A difficult question arose under the old definition of victimisation as to whether it was unlawful victimisation if the employer was merely taking steps to protect his/her position in discrimination litigation. The cases resolved this tricky issue by stating that, although such steps may be action 'by reason of' the protected act, they did not necessarily amount to a 'detriment'. The question is whether a reasonable litigant would regard the employer's conduct as detrimental. An employer's reasonable conduct defending his/her position in litigation cannot reasonably be regarded as a detriment.[98] In the *Khan*

---

95 *Martin v Devonshires Solicitors* UKEAT/0086/10; [2011] ICR 352; *Page v Lord Chancellor and another* [2021] EWCA Civ 254; [2021] IRLR 377.

96 *Waters v Commissioner of Police of the Metropolis* [1997] IRLR 589, CA. This would seem to be the position under s27(2)(c), although arguably s27(2)(d) could apply (see para 13.59).

97 Although s/he could claim direct discrimination if a white worker bringing an equally serious complaint would not have been dismissed.

98 *Pothecary Witham Weld and another v Bullimore and another and Equality and Human Rights Commission (intervener)* UKEAT/0158/09; [2010] IRLR 572, EAT summarising the effect of *Chief Constable of West Yorkshire Police v Khan* [2001] IRLR 830, HL and *St Helens MBC v Derbyshire* [2007] UKHL 16; [2007] IRLR 540 under the old definition.

case, which was brought under the former RRA 1976,[99] Sgt Khan brought a race discrimination case in the ET regarding his failed promotion. Before the ET hearing, he applied for another post. When asked for a reference, his Chief Constable replied: 'Sgt Khan has an outstanding tribunal application against the Chief Constable for failing to support his application for promotion. In light of that, the Chief Constable is unable to comment any further for fear of prejudicing his own case before the tribunal.' Sergeant Khan claimed victimisation. The House of Lords said there was no doubt that had Sgt Khan not brought his original ET case, he would have been supplied with a reference. However, the reason for the Chief Constable's refusal of a reference was simply to preserve his position in the pending litigation. It was not motivated by the fact in itself that Sgt Khan had brought a race discrimination case. The House of Lords said the test that would usually work was to ask whether the employer would still have refused the reference request if the litigation had finished, whatever the outcome. If the answer was no, then it would usually follow that the reason for the refusal was the current existence of the proceedings – not the fact that the worker had brought them in the first place.

13.74   This decision does not mean that employers have a free hand to victimise workers as long as an ET case is running.[100] The point here was that the content of any reference was precisely the matter awaiting adjudication in the existing ET case. The Chief Constable, having taken legal advice, refused the reference because he feared prejudicing his own case before the ET.

13.75   It is not possible to bring a case alleging that the content of evidence given by witnesses in previous ET proceedings amounts to victimisation, eg contending that a witness gave false and hostile evidence because s/he was upset that the worker brought a discrimination claim. This is because witness evidence attracts judicial immunity.[101] For the same reason, a worker cannot claim victimisation in respect of what an employer says in documents written for the

---

99 [2001] IRLR 830, HL.
100 See *St Helens MBC v Derbyshire and others* [2007] UKHL 16; [2007] IRLR 540, where the House of Lords is anxious to ensure *Khan* is not misinterpreted.
101 *Parmar v East Leicester Medical Practice* UKEAT/0490/10; [2011] IRLR 641. For a useful summary of the law on judicial proceedings immunity, see *Singh v (1) The Governing Body of Moorlands Primary School (2) Reading BC* [2013] EWCA Civ 909; [2013] IRLR 820. See also the discussion in *Aston v The Martlet Group Limited (Formerly Jim Walker and Company Limited t/a I-Ride)* UKEAT/0274/18.

tribunal proceedings, or because the employer refused to disclose documents or applied for costs. But this does not mean a worker has no remedy if the employer behaves badly during proceedings – s/he can apply for the employer's tribunal response to be struck out or for costs, or s/he can seek extra compensation for injury to feelings and aggravated damages.[102] It may also be possible to claim victimisation if the employer unlawfully pressurised a witness to give evidence against the worker.[103]

References

13.76 If an employer refuses to give a reference or writes an unfavourable reference because the worker has done a protected act, this is likely to be victimisation. The worker may also have a victimisation claim against a potential new employer, if the latter withdraws a job offer or fails to offer a job because of the bad reference. However, this will only apply if the new employer knows or is told about the protected act, for example because the former employer has mentioned in the reference that the worker has made a discrimination claim. The fact that the prospective employer acted unlawfully by withdrawing a job offer because of the original employer's discriminatory reference does not stop the original employer being liable for his/her own discriminatory comments. The worker can claim victimisation against both parties if the evidence is available.[104]

Conclusion

13.77 As is apparent from all of the above, the difficulties in proving causation severely limit the effectiveness of the victimisation provisions in practice. Even so, it is often easier to prove victimisation than direct discrimination in the ET. Victimisation is a major practical problem in the workplace, but tends to be overlooked as an industrial relations issue. It is remarkable how often equal opportunities policies and training deal with direct and indirect discrimination but fail to address victimisation.

102 *South London & Maudsley NHS Trust v Dathi* [2008] IRLR 350, EAT. Also see paras 19.14 and 19.23.
103 *Singh v (1) The Governing Body of Moorlands Primary School (2) Reading BC* [2013] EWCA Civ 909; [2013] IRLR 820.
104 *Bullimore v Pothecary Witham Weld Solicitors and another (No 2)* UKEAT/0189/10; [2011] IRLR 18.

Instructing, causing or inducing discrimination

13.78   Under EqA 2010 s111, it is unlawful for an employer to instruct, cause or induce (directly or indirectly) someone else to discriminate against a worker. If either the worker, or the person who is instructed, caused or induced to take action, is subjected to a detriment as a result of the employer's conduct, s/he can bring a tribunal claim. It does not matter whether the person instructed etc actually caries out the unlawful act. For example, a GP instructs his receptionist not to register any patient with an Asian name. If the receptionist fails to follow the instruction and is subjected to a detriment as a result, she can bring a claim against the GP.[105] The EHRC also has power to bring proceedings.

13.79   An EqA 2010 s111 claim can only be made where the relationship between the person giving the instruction and the person receiving the instruction is such that the former would be in a position to discriminate against the latter under EqA 2010 Parts 3–7, eg the person giving the instruction to the worker is the worker's employer or, if the worker is a contract worker, s/he is the principal.[106] This is a worrying limitation. For example, if a company instructed a job agency not to send along any pregnant job applicants or temps, it is unclear how the company would be in a position to discriminate under EqA 2010 Parts 3–7 against the job agency. If this is correct, a pregnant worker who was excluded could not claim against the company under section 111, though she could still claim against the job agency if it agreed to discriminate against her under EqA 2010 s55, and against the company, if the job agency was its agent under section 109.

13.80   The scope of EqA 2010 s111 is little tested because under previous legislation only the equality commissions could bring this type of claim.[107] In addition, the previous wording, eg under RRA 1976 s30, extended to instructions from a person with whose wishes the recipient was accustomed to act. There may be more potential for section 111 than is immediately apparent, but at the moment it seems that such a claim will only be needed in limited circumstances where the more conventional definitions of discrimination do not apply to the

---

105 EHRC Employment Code, para 9.16. This example might also be direct discrimination and/or victimisation.
106 EqA 2010 s111(1) and (7). Part 5 of the EqA 2010 is the employment part.
107 With one exception in relation to age.

situation. For a fuller description of this right, see EHRC Employment Code paras 9.16–9.24.

Harassment

Overview

13.81　Until various changes to discrimination law made during 2003 as a result of the EU Race Discrimination and General Framework Directives,[108] there was no explicit definition of harassment in the discrimination legislation. Nevertheless, harassment was unlawful under those statutes as a form of direct discrimination and a large body of case-law developed. Some of this old case-law will still be applicable, but most of it will be too restrictive as the specific definition of harassment is worded more widely than the definition of direct discrimination.

13.82　Employers are liable for harassment under EqA 2010 s40. The definition of harassment in EqA 2010 s26(1) states:

> (1) A person (A) harasses another (B) if–
> (a) A engages in unwanted conduct related to a relevant protected characteristic, and
> (b) the conduct has the purpose or effect of–
> (i) violating B's dignity, or
> (ii) creating an intimidating, hostile, degrading, humiliating or offensive environment for B.

13.83　The relevant protected characteristics are: age; disability; gender reassignment; race; religion or belief; sex; and sexual orientation. Although the harassment provision does not explicitly apply to marriage, civil partnership, pregnancy or maternity, harassment for those reasons could be claimed as direct marriage or civil partnership discrimination or unfavourable treatment because of pregnancy or maternity.[109]

13.84　The harassment need not be related to the worker's own protected characteristic. A worker may also claim harassment in these situations:

- Remarks not directed at the worker: For example, racist jokes are made in the workplace about black people; a black worker can

---

108　Council Directives 2000/43/EC and 2000/78/EC, respectively.

109　EqA 2010 s13 and s18 respectively. EqA 2010 s212(5) is probably unnecessary, since the Act omits these protected characteristics from the definition of harassment rather than 'disapplies' them.

claim harassment even if the jokes are not actually directed at him/her.

- Remarks about other people: For example, offensive remarks are made at a work presentation about Muslim people; there are no Muslim workers in the room, but a non-Muslim worker finds the remarks offensive.
- Harassment by association: For example, a worker has a child who is undergoing gender reassignment; the worker's colleagues repeatedly make offensive remarks about this.
- False perception: For example, an Indian worker of the Hindu religion is subjected to Islamophobic abuse because of a false perception that she is Muslim.
- Where, for example, a worker is subjected to homophobic 'banter' even though his colleagues know he is not actually gay.[110]

13.85   Harassment also covers a situation where the conduct does not take place because the worker, or anyone else, has the protected characteristic, but it is nevertheless related to the protected characteristic. For example, a female worker previously had a relationship with her boss. After it breaks down, her boss becomes upset because he believes she is having a relationship with someone else and he continually makes offensive remarks about this. The boss's conduct is not because of the worker's sex, but because he suspects she is having a relationship, which arguably is related to her sex.[111]

Conduct 'related to' a protected characteristic

13.86   Unlike direct discrimination, it is not necessary to compare the treatment of the worker with the treatment of a comparator who does not have the same protected characteristic.[112] Also, as explained above, harassment need not be 'because of' the worker's protected characteristic. It is enough that it is simply 'related to' it. There have been few cases on precisely what 'related to' means. The wording suggests that the harassment needs only be connected with the protected characteristic as opposed to caused by it. For example, it may cover a situation where a male manager enters women's toilets to shout at a female cleaner who he believes to be skiving, when he would have done the same thing to a male cleaner. In practice, the words 'related to' rather than 'because of' could make a big difference in certain

110   *English v Thomas Sanderson Ltd* [2008] EWCA Civ 1421; [2009] IRLR 206.
111   Example similar to EHRC Employment Code, para 7.10.
112   *Wandsworth NHS Primary Care Trust v Obonyo (No 1)* UKEAT/0237/05.

situations, though it is generally untested how close the connection has to be.[113] It is the discriminator's own conduct which must be related to the relevant protected characteristic. It is not enough, for example, simply that the employer has failed to look into a complaint of sexual harassment; there must be something about the employer's own conduct which is 'related to' sex, eg a manager failed to investigate because he does not take women seriously.[114]

Direct discrimination or harassment?

13.87 Where a claim is made for harassment, the treatment of the worker cannot also be a 'detriment'.[115] This prevents a finding that a worker has been subjected both to harassment and direct discrimination in respect of the same treatment. Although 'harassment' is traditionally understood as meaning behaviour such as verbal or physical abuse, the legal definition is much wider. 'Unwanted conduct which violates a worker's dignity or creates a hostile etc environment' could presumably include actions such as oppressive disciplinary action, which would normally be covered by the definition of direct discrimination. It may be especially tempting to claim under the heading of 'harassment' in those tricky cases where the wider definition is helpful. If in real doubt as to which definition is most appropriate, it may be best to claim in the alternative, eg 'In the events described above, I have been subjected to harassment contrary to EqA 2010 s26 and s40(1) and/or direct discrimination contrary to EqA 2010 s13 and s39(2)(d)'.

Unwanted conduct

13.88 It is crucial to prove that the behaviour was unwanted. Harassers often try to suggest that black workers don't mind racist banter, or that women are happily flirting back. It is often argued that because the worker has put up with the conduct for a long time, it is not really unwanted. The EAT has given this short shrift:

113 For examples where it may make a difference, including the toilet example, see *Equal Opportunities Commission v Secretary of State for Trade and Industry* [2007] EWHC 483 (Admin); [2007] IRLR 327, concerning the former definition of harassment under the Sex Discrimination Act 1975. These examples are cited with approval in *UNITE the Union v Nailard* UKEAT/0300/15; [2016] IRLR 906.

114 *UNITE the Union v Nailard* [2018] EWCA Civ 1203; [2018] IRLR 730. See para 13.108 onwards for further discussion of this.

115 EqA 2010 s212(1) – interpretation of 'detriment'.

> One of the lay members of this Tribunal has observed that there are
> many situations in life where people will put up with unwanted or
> even criminal conduct which violates their personal dignity because
> they are constrained by social circumstances to do so. A classic
> example . . . is that of the battered wife who for the sake of the chil-
> dren may remain at home, permitting herself to be subject to viol-
> ence, none of which she wishes, but all of which she endures . . .
> Putting up with it does not make it welcome, or less criminal. It is
> therefore not completely beyond the scope of reason to think that
> women in this particular situation should behave as they did.[116]

13.89   If the worker has joined in some offensive banter, there can be a
number of explanations for this. Maybe the worker is trying to laugh
along and make him/herself less of a target. Or maybe the worker is
retaliating. Either way, it can still be the case that the words said to
the worker are unwanted. Also, (looking ahead to para 13.91), it is
still possible that the words were intended to violate the worker's
dignity or, even if not intended, reasonably had that effect. It is even
possible that the parties were harassing each other. On the other
hand, if there is evidence that all concerned were genuine friends, it
may mean the conduct was not unwanted or that it is not reasonable
to consider it had the unlawful effect.[117]

13.90   If the harasser continues or intensifies the harassment or otherwise punishes the worker after s/he complains to the harasser or to
management of the harassment, this may be unlawful victimisation
as well as further harassment.

Purpose or effect

13.91   The definition of harassment covers unwanted conduct which has
either the 'purpose' or the 'effect' of violating a worker's dignity or
creating an intimidating, hostile, degrading, humiliating or offensive
environment. It is important to note that where the conduct does not
have that 'purpose', ie where it is unintentional in that sense, it is not
necessarily unlawful just because the worker feels his/her dignity is
violated etc. To decide whether the conduct has an unlawful 'effect', a
tribunal must take into account the other circumstances of the case
and whether it is reasonable for the conduct to have that effect, as

---

116 *(1) Munchkins Restaurant Ltd and (2) Moss v Karmazyn, Kuylle, Rivas, and
Kralova* UKEAT/0359/09 and 0481/09 at para 23.

117 See *Thomas Sanderson Blinds Ltd v English (No 2)* UKEAT/0316/10 and *Grant
v HM Land Registry and Equality and Human Rights Commission (intervener)*
[2011] EWCA Civ 769; [2011] IRLR 748 for a discussion of these possibilities.

well as the perception of the worker bringing the claim.[118] The starting point is whether the worker did in fact feel that his/her dignity was violated or that there was an adverse environment etc, but it is only unlawful if it was reasonable for the worker to have that feeling or perception; nevertheless, the very fact that the worker genuinely had that feeling should be kept firmly in mind.[119] The EHRC Employment Code suggests that relevant circumstances could include the worker's personal circumstances, eg his/her mental health or capacity, cultural norms or previous experience of harassment, and also the environment in which the conduct takes place. On the other hand, a tribunal is unlikely to find unwanted conduct has an unlawful effect if it considers the worker is hypersensitive and other people subjected to the same conduct would not have been offended.[120] These difficulties are avoided if it can be shown that the harasser's 'purpose' was to create the adverse environment. In that case, there is no objective test of whether it was reasonable for the worker to feel his/her dignity was violated etc. Indeed, if there was a campaign of unpleasant conduct designed to humiliate the worker, it would not even matter if that purpose was not achieved,[121] although it would still need to be unwanted.

13.92　　If the unwanted conduct stopped as soon as the worker complained about it, the employer may argue this is relevant to whether the conduct had the 'purpose or effect' of violating the worker's dignity etc. This may depend in part on the type of conduct and whether it was obviously of a kind which could be unwanted. For a further discussion of this in the context of sexual harassment, see para 14.143 onward.

13.93　　Finally, it is important to remember that the definition of harassment envisages something more than being upset or angry; the words 'intimidating, hostile, degrading, humiliating or offensive' envisage a far more serious effect.[122] The conduct also has to create such an 'environment', ie state of affairs. Although 'violating dignity'

118　EqA 2010 s26(4).

119　*Richmond Pharmacology v Dhaliwal* [2009] IRLR 336, EAT; *Thomas Sanderson Blinds Ltd v English (No 2)* UKEAT/0316/10. These cases were on the definition in the previous legislation, which placed slightly more emphasis on the worker's perception.

120　EHRC Employment Code, para 7.18.

121　*Grant v HM Land Registry and Equality and Human Rights Commission (intervener)* [2011] EWCA Civ 769; [2011] IRLR 748.

122　*Grant v HM Land Registry and Equality and Human Rights Commission (intervener)* [2011] EWCA Civ 769; [2011] IRLR 748.

does not necessitate the creation of an 'environment', the word 'violate' is stronger than simply 'hurt'.[123]

Sexual harassment

13.94   As well as the general definition of harassment, there are two additional definitions relevant to sexual harassment: i) unwanted conduct of a sexual nature; and ii) where the worker is subjected to further unwanted conduct because of his/her rejection of or submission to previous harassment (see para 14.139 onwards for details).

Vicarious liability

Overview

13.95   As explained in chapter 12, the employing organisation is legally responsible for any discriminatory action carried out by one employee against another, provided that the action is carried out in the course of employment. This is often called 'vicarious liability'. The organisation is vicariously liable even if it did not instruct, authorise, approve or even know of the discrimination. The question of vicarious liability is most often disputed by employers in harassment cases, where they want to avoid responsibility for what the harasser has done.

13.96   When is a discriminatory act carried out outside the course of employment? The most important case on this issue is *Jones v Tower Boot Co Ltd*,[124] where Mr Jones was subjected to a number of horrific incidents of verbal and physical racial abuse. These took place in work time and on work premises. The employers argued that they could not be liable for such clearly unauthorised acts carried out by fellow employees. The Court of Appeal disagreed, saying that the words 'in the course of employment' should be given their natural meaning. The whole point was to widen the net of responsibility beyond the guilty employees themselves, by making employers additionally responsible.

13.97   Discrimination carried out in work time and on the premises by fellow employees therefore seems to be covered, even if it is extremely serious and wholly unrelated to the employment, eg physical assault. However, harassment often takes place out of work time or during rest breaks. It will then be for each ET to decide on the facts whether

---

123   *Richmond Pharmacology v Dhaliwal* [2009] I RLR 336, EAT and *Betsi Cadwaladr University Health Board v Hughes and another* UKEAT/0179/13.
124   [1997] I RLR 168, CA.

it took place during 'the course of employment'.[125] An incident which occurs during a chance meeting between work colleagues at a supermarket, for example, would almost certainly not be covered.[126] Similarly, an incident when one employee visits another where s/he is living outside work hours and on a purely social basis will probably not be covered.[127] On the other hand, harassment during business trips, office Christmas parties, organised leaving parties or a social gathering of work colleagues in the pub immediately after work, may well be 'in the course of employment'.[128] It will depend on the circumstances whether an offensive Facebook post is done in the course of employment, eg who belongs to the Facebook group, is the workplace identifiable, does it refer to a particular employee who can be identified, and are the contents of the post circulated at work?[129]

The employer's defence

13.98 The employer is responsible regardless of whether s/he knew or approved of the unlawful act, unless s/he 'took all reasonable steps' to prevent the discriminator from discriminating.[130] It is for the employer to prove this defence and it is a high bar.[131] It is important to remember that the employer's responsibility is to take preventative action; it is not a defence that the employer acted promptly once s/he discovered the discrimination, eg by sacking the harasser (although this may prevent liability for further discrimination).

13.99 The tribunal should go through these stages when assessing the defence: 1) Did the employer take any preventative steps at all? 2) If so, were those steps reasonable? 3) Were there any further reasonable steps which the employer should have taken?[132] The likely effectiveness or ineffectiveness of any step is a factor, although not the only factor. If a step would have had no real prospect of preventing discrimination, it is unlikely to be considered reasonable. On the

---

125 *Jones v Tower Boot Co Ltd* [1997] IRLR 168, CA.

126 *Chief Constable of the Lincolnshire Police v Stubbs* [1999] IRLR 81, EAT.

127 *Waters v Commissioner of Police of the Metropolis* [1997] IRLR 589, CA.

128 *Chief Constable of the Lincolnshire Police v Stubbs* [1999] IRLR 81, EAT.

129 *Forbes v LHR Airport Limited* UKEAT/0174/18 – this contains a good summary of previous cases on 'course of employment'.

130 EqA 2010 s109(4).

131 *Waters v Commissioner of Police of the Metropolis* [1997] IRLR 589, CA; *Allay (UK) Limited v* Gehlen UKEAT/0031.20.

132 *Canniffe v East Riding of Yorkshire Council* EAT/1035/98; [2000] IRLR 555 on the equivalent defence under the Sex Discrimination Act 1995.

other hand, it's not necessary that a step would have been 'more likely than not' to have prevented discrimination.[133]

13.100   This defence does not often succeed. A written equal opportunities policy is unlikely to suffice unless it is very actively implemented. Brief and superficial training is unlikely to be effective or long-lasting in preventing discrimination or harassment; training should not be allowed to go stale – thorough and forcefully presented training is more likely to be effective and last longer.[134] As one ET put it when allowing the defence: 'Harassment [in the workplace] is a live issue, not a dead letter.'[135]

Employer's reaction to a complaint of harassment

Overview

13.101   In some cases, particularly in small organisations, the perpetrator is in reality the employer and there is no one more senior for the worker to turn to. In many cases, however, the perpetrator is a colleague or intermediate manager and the worker may complain about his/her treatment to more senior management. As protection against victimisation, it would be wise to make the complaint in writing.

13.102   The employing organisation will not only be vicariously liable for the harassment itself, but it may also be guilty of direct discrimination and/or victimisation in the way it reacts to the complaint. The discrimination could occur both in the way the complaint is investigated (or not investigated) and also in the subsequent reaction, eg transfer or dismissal of the worker.

Is the employer's reaction direct discrimination?

13.103   To show direct race discrimination, for example, it is necessary to prove that the employer would not have reacted the same way if a worker of a different race had brought an equivalent complaint; eg the complaint would have been treated more seriously and investigated more thoroughly and the worker would have been kept better informed. Further, s/he would not have been transferred or dismissed as a consequence. It is not necessary to have evidence of any such

---

133   *Allay (UK) Limited v Gehlen* UKEAT/0031/20 reviews and attempts to reconcile the authorities on this aspect.

134   See eg *Allay (UK) Limited v Gehlen* UKEAT/0031/20.

135   *Graham v Royal Mail and Nicholson* (1994) 20 EOR DCLD 5, ET. Though see the research report on women in the Royal Mail during the 1990s referred to in (1999) 83 EOR 3.

comparable incident in the past, although it may make it easier to prove. As with any direct race discrimination case, the ET can infer from the evidence generally that a complaint from a white person would have been dealt with in a more favourable manner.

13.104 The tribunals have been undecided about what is a sensible actual or hypothetical comparison for this. Is the question how the employer would have treated a white worker complaining of: a) racial harassment by a colleague or manager; b) non-racial harassment or violence from a colleague or manager; or c) any serious grievance? The first option does not seem to be a helpful comparison because it is far less common for such a situation to occur in most workplaces. The second or third scenarios provide a more logical comparison, but even then, it is not really comparable as there is not the same stigma attached.

Is the employer's reaction victimisation?

13.105 Whether or not the employer can be accused of direct discrimination in the handling of and response to the complaint, his/her treatment of the worker may amount to victimisation, ie penalising him/her for raising the issue. See para 13.72 for further comments.

13.106 In specific circumstances, a worker may be able to claim unlawful detriment or dismissal in relation to health and safety if s/he is penalised by his/her employer for complaining about harassment. A whistleblowing claim may also be possible.[136] These other claims may be useful where the victimisation provisions of the discrimination legislation do not apply, eg because the harassment was not based on one of the protected characteristics.

Constructive dismissal

13.107 As well as any discrimination claim, if an employer commits a repudiatory or fundamental breach of contract, an employee may resign and claim constructive unfair dismissal[137] provided s/he meets the unfair dismissal eligibility requirements. What amounts to a repudiatory breach is a question of fact, but in the key case of *Western Excavating (ECC) v Sharp*,[138] Lawton LJ said that:

---

136 See automatic unfair dismissal in relation to health and safety and also in relation to whistleblowing in chapter 6.

137 See para 6.35 onwards.

138 [1978] IRLR 27; [1978] ICR 221, CA.

Persistent and unwanted amorous advances by an employer to a female member of his staff would . . . clearly be such conduct . . .

In *Bracebridge Engineering v Darby*,[139] the employer's failure to treat seriously and fully investigate the worker's allegations of assault clearly amounted to a repudiatory breach of the implied term of trust and confidence and the obligation not to undermine the confidence of female staff.

Harassment by the public or third party harassment

Overview

13.108 Discrimination by members of the public is often referred to as 'third party harassment', the member of the public being the third party. An employer is not vicariously liable under discrimination law for third party harassment. However, an employer may be guilty of discrimination in his/her reaction to harassment by the public or a complaint about it. For example, it may be direct discrimination to ignore racial harassment from the public against a black member of staff but to take action when a white worker makes an equivalent complaint. In addition, failure to take appropriate action may entitle an employee to resign and claim constructive unfair dismissal.

13.109 Under EqA 2010 s40(2) employers were explicitly made liable for 'third party harassment' as if they had carried it out themselves. This was introduced initially into the Sex Discrimination Act 1975 following a judicial review brought by the then Equal Opportunities Commission (EOC).[140] In 2013 the coalition government decided to repeal section 40(2) despite 71 per cent of respondents to its consultation opposing repeal.[141] The government accepted that third party harassment occurs, but felt it was wrong that employers should be made legally responsible for it. This ignored the fact that employers were only legally responsible if they had failed to take reasonably practicable preventative steps. The government has now indicated

---

139 [1990] IRLR 3, EAT.
140 *Equal Opportunities Commission v Secretary of State for Trade and Industry* [2007] EWHC 483 (Admin); [2007] IRLR 327.
141 By the Enterprise and Regulatory Reform Act 2013 s65, for harassment on or after 1 October 2013 – Enterprise and Regulatory Reform Act 2013 (Commencement No 3, Transitional Provisions and Savings) Order SI No 2227.

that it may reintroduce employers' liability in relation to third party harassment, at least in relation to sexual harassment.[142]

13.110 As things stand, employers can only be responsible under the EqA 2010 for harassment by the public or other third parties if their own action or inaction means they themselves have carried out an act of harassment or other type of discrimination.[143] For example, it would be direct race discrimination if an employer said 'I am not going to deal with that customer's abusive remark because the sales person is black' or if an employer dealt with complaints about abuse from service users more seriously when the victim was a white staff member than when it was a black staff member. Or it could be indirect race discrimination to fail to ensure every incident of racial abuse by patients is recorded on an organisation's incident reporting forms because non-white staff members are more likely to be subjected to racial abuse than white staff members.[144] An employer's failure to take preventative or remedial action could be harassment provided the inaction (as opposed to the original harassment) was 'unwanted conduct' and that the inaction was 'related to' the protected characteristic. Usually that means the reason for the inaction must have been because of a protected characteristic. For example, just because an employer fails to do anything about a woman's complaint of sexual harassment does not mean that that inaction is 'related to' sex. It might simply be a result of laziness or inefficiency. On the other hand, the evidence might suggest the employer's attitude is in itself related to sex. Finally, the inaction (again, as opposed to the harassment by the third party) must violate the worker's dignity or create the offensive environment.

13.111 Where the employer cannot be made liable for third party harassment under the EqA 2010, it is a question of exploring claims in the civil or criminal courts (see below).

Harassment by an agency worker

13.112 One legal difficulty which can arise is where a worker is harassed by an agency worker who is placed with his/her employer. The worker can only claim against his/her own employer in limited circum-

---

142 *Consultation on sexual harassment in the workplace: government response,* July 2021 at www.gov.uk/government/consultations/consultation-on-sexual-harassment-in-the-workplace/outcome/consultation-on-sexual-harassment-in-the-workplace-government-response.

143 *Unite the Union v Nailard* [2018] EWCA Civ 1203; [2018] IRLR 730.

144 *Bessong v Pennine Care NHS Foundation Trust* UKEAT/0247/18; [2020] IRLR 4.

stances. This is because an employer is only vicariously liable for someone who s/he employs or uses as an agent.[145] Unfortunately, it is unusual for an agency worker to fit into these categories. If the agency worker repeatedly harasses the worker and the employer knows this, the worker may be able to claim against his/her employer in the same way that s/he can if harassment is by a member of the public (see the preceding paragraph). The worker cannot claim against the agency if s/he has no legal relationship with it under the EqA 2010.

Civil or criminal claims outside the discrimination legislation

Overview

13.113 Sometimes due to the limitations of the discrimination legislation, other legal claims in the civil courts may be appropriate. These can also apply where the harassment, eg assault or general bullying, is not based on a protected characteristic. Usually an ET claim under the EqA 2010 is preferable. It offers a simpler, quicker and less formal procedure. Moreover, as an industrial court, the ET may be more willing than a county court or High Court to understand and believe the claim (although this may be too optimistic a view). In addition, in most situations, the costs risk of losing in the county court or High Court makes it an unrealistic option. However, advisers may want to explore options such as trade union or (infrequently) EHRC support, or whether the worker has legal protection insurance. There may also be the option of a conditional fee arrangement ('no win, no fee') with after-the-event (ATE) insurance against costs risks. The following suggestions are not a full list of civil and criminal possibilities.

Common law claims

13.114 Where the harassment involves physical contact, particularly if there is a severe assault, the worker may have a claim for damages at common law in civil assault against the perpetrator. Even where there is no physical contact, a claim in tort may be possible where the perpetrator intentionally inflicts injury (physical or psychiatric) by his/her words or actions.[146] An employee can also claim against his/her employer for negligence if the employer fails to protect him/her

---

145 EqA 2010 s109. See paras 12.29–12.30.
146 *Burris v Adzani* [1995] 1 WLR 1373, CA.

against victimisation or harassment which causes physical or psychiatric injury.[147] The employer will not be liable unless s/he knows or ought to know that harassment is taking place and fails to take reasonable steps to prevent it.[148] Common law claims are an underused remedy, and the possibility should not be overlooked. The advantage of such claims is that it is unnecessary to prove the assault was because of a protected characteristic. Longer time limits also apply. It may also help if the assault was by a member of the public or otherwise outside the course of employment. The disadvantages are set out in the previous paragraph.

Protection from Harassment Act 1997

13.115 Although the Protection from Harassment Act (PHA) 1997 was not designed for employment situations, it can apply. The following is a summary of the provisions in relation to England and Wales. For the slightly different provisions in Scotland, see PHA 1997 ss8–16. Under PHA 1997 s1 a person must not pursue a course of conduct which s/he knows or a reasonable person would know amounts to harassment of another person.[149] A 'course of conduct' means conduct on at least two occasions.[150] This needs to be carried out by the same person or if more than one, there must be some link, eg they are acting in concert or one is acting under instructions from the other.[151] Harassment is not defined except to say that it includes alarming the person or causing the person distress and the conduct can include speech.[152] The conduct is not unlawful if it was reasonable in the particular circumstances.[153] Presumably, therefore, reasonable disciplinary action, although causing distress, would be excluded. On the other hand, a series of unjustified warnings may on the facts amount to harassment.

13.116 Under PHA 1997 s4 it is also an offence to cause another person on at least two occasions to fear that violence would be used against him/her. There is an exception for reasonable self-defence.[154]

---

147 *Waters v Commissioner of Police of the Metropolis* [2000] IRLR 720, HL. See also chapter 17 regarding stress.

148 *Waters v Commissioner of Police of the Metropolis* [2000] IRLR 720, HL.

149 PHA 1997 s1(1) and (2).

150 PHA 1997 s7(3); *Banks v Ablex Ltd* [2005] IRLR 357, CA.

151 *Dowson and others v The Chief Constable of Northumbria Police* [2009] EWHC 907 (QB).

152 PHA 1997 s7.

153 PHA 1997 s1(3)(c). There are also other exceptions.

154 PHA 1997 ss2(2) and 4(3)–(4). Together with other exceptions.

13.117   The worker can claim against the individual harasser or, in some circumstances, against the employer. The concept of vicarious liability under PHA 1997 is different from that under the discrimination legislation. Nevertheless, an employer can be vicariously liable under the PHA 1997 for harassment carried out by his/her employees, provided there is sufficiently close connection between the work the harasser is employed to do and the harassment.[155] Depending on the facts, it is likely that the employer would be vicariously liable for a manager harassing a subordinate, and possibly, for harassment by a colleague at the same level working in the same team.[156] If harassment is by a third party, eg an independent contractor, the worker may similarly be able to sue the third party's employer.

13.118   Breach of PHA 1997 s1 or s4 is a criminal offence liable to imprisonment or a fine.[157] A civil claim can also be made for damages for financial loss and anxiety.[158] The High Court or county court can also issue an injunction restraining the perpetrator from continuing to harass.[159]

13.119   The PHA 1997 may be very helpful where the harassment is not covered by the discrimination legislation, eg because it cannot be proved that it is because of a protected characteristic or because it took place off work premises and possibly outside the course of employment, or was perpetrated by a member of the public. The other great advantage is the potential to obtain a restraining injunction, which is not available under the EqA 2010 in the ET. Although the time limits are longer, it will usually be important to act quickly, especially if an injunction is sought. The disadvantage of the PHA 1997, as with all non-ET claims, is the more formal procedure and the costs risks. The scope of the PHA 1997 for use in employment cases is still being tested.

Criminal prosecution

13.120   Criminal prosecution is outside the scope of this book. Workers do sometimes invite the police to prosecute for criminal assault where physical harassment has taken place, but there are difficulties in following this route. The facts are harder to prove due to the stricter

---

155   *Majrowski v Guy's and St Thomas's NHS Trust* [2006] IRLR 695; November 2006 *Legal Action* 13, HL.

156   See, for example, *Vaickuviene and others v J Sainsbury plc* [2012] CSOH 869.

157   PHA 1997 s3(2).

158   PHA 1997 s3(3).

159   Advisers should check the exact position on this.

rules of evidence and the criminal standard of proof. Moreover, the worker is simply a witness in a police action and loses control of the process. An unsuccessful criminal case is likely to jeopardise any parallel civil claim.

Bullying

13.121 Bullying or harassment, even if it is not attributable to a protected characteristic, is now recognised as a workplace problem in itself. If the bullying is carried out by the employer or if the employer fails to deal adequately with a complaint, an employee may be able to resign and claim constructive unfair dismissal.[160] If the bullying is serious, the worker may also be able to bring a civil or criminal claim as set out above.[161]

Multiple discrimination

Introduction

13.122 The term 'multiple discrimination' is not used in the EqA 2010, but it is used to refer to any circumstances in which discrimination occurs because of more than one protected characteristic. There are three different kinds of multiple discrimination:

1) ordinary multiple discrimination;
2) additive discrimination;
3) intersectional or combined discrimination; a subcategory of this is dual combined discrimination.

These terms, apart from 'dual combined discrimination', are used for the purpose of this book and by some academics, but have no universally agreed meaning. The importance of having sufficient evidence to prove discrimination on each of the protected characteristics claimed cannot be stressed too heavily. It is better to bring a claim focusing only on one or two protected characteristics where there is strong evidence, than to weaken the overall effect by adding numerous different protected characteristics without testing whether each one stands up to close examination.

---

160 Subject to the usual rules.
161 For example, see *Green v D B Group Services (UK) Ltd* [2006] EWHC 1898 (QB); [2006] IRLR 764.

Ordinary multiple discrimination

13.123 Ordinary multiple discrimination refers to a situation where a worker has been discriminated against because of one protected characteristic on one occasion and a different protected characteristic on another occasion. For example, a worker is refused promotion because she is a woman and a few months later, she is made redundant because she is black. No special legal difficulties arise, but the worker needs sufficient evidence to support each claim. A common form of ordinary multiple discrimination occurs where a worker is initially subjected to harassment because of one protected characteristic, eg racial harassment, and as a result, develops a severe depression. In itself, this remains a single protected characteristic claim, ie for racial harassment, and the compensation will include compensation for injury to feelings and health. However, if the employer then treats the worker unfavourably because of his/her depression or fails to make a necessary reasonable adjustment, there could be a further act of disability discrimination. For this, the depression needs to meet the definition of disability.[162]

Additive discrimination

13.124 Additive discrimination occurs when an employer discriminates independently because of two different protected characteristics at the same time. For example, an employer refuses to promote a worker because she is a woman (the employer never promotes women) and quite separately, because she is over 50 (the employer only promotes younger workers). Again, there is no legal difficulty in this kind of claim, but there must be sufficient evidence.

Intersectional or combined discrimination

13.125 Intersectional or combined discrimination occurs where an employer discriminates against a worker because s/he has a particular combination of protected characteristics. For example, the employer fails to promote a woman over 50. The evidence shows that the employer has promoted plenty of women. It is just that they are all under 50. The employer has also promoted many workers over 50. It's just that they all men. It is the combination of 'older woman' which the employer discriminates against. Intersectional or combined discrim-

162 See chapter 15.

ination usually involves only two protected characteristics but can in theory involve more. For example, a young Muslim man is subjected to harassment because of unfounded stereotyped fears that he is a terrorist. This kind of stereotyping would not have occurred if he was female or not Muslim or even an older Muslim man.

13.126   It is generally thought that a legal finding of intersectional/ combined discrimination cannot be made under the normal definition of direct discrimination in the EqA 2010 as a result of two cases under the previous legislation: *Bahl v The Law Society* and *Network Rail Infrastructure Ltd v Griffiths-Henry*.[163] These cases concerned direct discrimination claims involving two protected characteristics, race and sex. It is arguable that neither case presented a strong evidential basis for such a finding, so the courts did not confront the issue head on. It is untested whether the CJEU would consider that the European directives require protection for intersectional/combined discrimination. The wording of the directives seems only to cover discrimination based on a single characteristic, though interestingly, paragraph (14) of the preamble of the Race Discrimination Directive states that:

> In implementing the principle of equal treatment irrespective of racial or ethnic origin, the Community should . . . aim to eliminate inequalities, and to promote equality between men and women, especially since women are often the victims of multiple discrimination.

13.127 If a worker believes that s/he has been discriminated against because of an intersection of characteristics, the way to claim legally therefore is on the basis of each protected characteristic separately. For example, the young Muslim man could claim religious discrimination and/ or sex discrimination and/or age discrimination. This is possible because it is not necessary for direct discrimination that the protected characteristic is the exclusive reason for the employer's treatment. It is enough if it is an important factor.[164] The actual or hypothetical comparator can incorporate the other protected characteristics. For example, for the age discrimination claim, the comparator would be an older Muslim man.

13.128   One of the difficulties with making a claim for intersectional/ combined discrimination as such is identifying an appropriate comparator. In theory, the comparator is any person who does not have all of the relevant protected characteristics. Unfortunately, such a comparator is not as significant as in single protected characteristic claims, because the more favourable treatment of such a comparator

163 [2004] IRLR 799, CA and [2006] IRLR 865, EAT respectively.
164 See para 13.10.

is consistent with a number of explanations. For example, if a black woman complains of intersectional/combined discrimination, her comparator could be a white woman, a black man or a white man. Each of those are equally consistent with the discrimination having been based on just one protected characteristic alone. The best evidence to prove intersectional/combined discrimination will therefore be several comparators or other evidence entirely, eg remarks or evidence of stereotyping associated with the combined group.

Dual combined discrimination

13.129   'Combined discrimination: dual characteristics' was specifically made unlawful under EqA 2010 s14, but the coalition government decided not to bring this into force. Nevertheless, claims for direct discrimination based on the combination or intersection of two protected characteristics can still be brought on the basis explained above.

Indirect combined discrimination

13.130   The combination of two different PCPs being applied at the same time may disadvantage a worker because of his/her combination of characteristics. An interesting example of this concerned a female soldier of St Vincentian national origin in *Ministry of Defence v DeBique*.[165] The army's requirement that soldiers be available on a 24/7 basis was aggravated because Ms De Bique's potential child-carer was a foreign national, who could not stay with her long-term. The EAT said:

> The nature of discrimination is such that it cannot always be sensibly compartmentalised into discrete categories. Whilst some complainants will raise issues relating only to one or other of the prohibited grounds, attempts to view others as raising only one form of discrimination for consideration will result in an inadequate understanding and assessment of the complainant's true disadvantage. Discrimination is often a multi-faceted experience.

Exceptions

13.131   The EqA 2010 sets out a number of exceptions where discrimination is permitted. Some of the key exceptions applicable to all protected

---

165 UKEAT/0048-0049/09; [2010] IRLR 471.

characteristics are set out below. Exceptions which relate only to certain protected characteristics are set out in chapter 14.

Occupational requirements

13.132 It is not discrimination for an employer to require a worker to have a particular protected characteristic if the employer can show that, having regard to the nature or context of the work:

- it is an occupational requirement;
- the application of the requirement is a proportionate means of achieving a legitimate aim; and
- the worker to whom the employer applies the requirement does not meet it (or the employer has reasonable grounds for not being satisfied that the worker meets it).[166]

13.133 This exception applies to discrimination in recruitment arrangements and job offers; access to promotion; transfer or training or any other benefit, facility or service; and dismissal.[167] The exception also applies if a principal refuses to allow a contract worker to work.[168] Examples of occupational requirements are given in relation to each protected characteristic in chapter 14. The scope of occupational requirements should be interpreted very narrowly as it is an exception to the prohibition of discrimination. However, occupational requirements can be used in certain situations as a form of positive action, eg where a person with a particular protected characteristic is best equipped to provide care or advice services to others with the same protected characteristics. It may be relevant whether the employer already employs other workers with the needed protected characteristic on the same duties.

National security

13.134 An employer may discriminate for the purpose of safeguarding national security, as long as it is proportionate to do so.[169]

---

166 EqA 2010 Sch 9 para 1(1); EHRC Employment Code, chapter 13.
167 EqA 2010 Sch 9 para 1(2). The exception does not apply to dismissal in relation to sex – Sch 9 paras 6–7.
168 EqA 2010 Sch 9 para 1(2)(b).
169 EqA 2010 s192.

Statutory authority

13.135 There are various exceptions for statutory authority, which apply where certain other legislation requires different treatment because of a protected characteristic. Very generally, it is not age, disability or religion and belief discrimination if an employer does anything pursuant to a statutory requirement.[170] For example, an employer can lawfully dismiss a disabled worker if health and safety regulations leave him/her with no choice.[171] The statutory authority exception no longer applies to race discrimination,[172] except in some circumstances in relation to nationality and residency requirements.[173] Differential treatment based on sex or pregnancy and maternity is permitted if it is required to comply with laws protecting women who are pregnant or who have given childbirth or against risks specific to women.[174]

Insurance and pensions

13.136 There are complicated exceptions in relation to both insurance and to pensions. These are outside the scope of this book.

Positive action

13.137 Positive action under the EqA 2010 is voluntary. In certain circumstances, an employer is allowed to take steps to assist disadvantaged groups which would otherwise be discriminatory against everyone else. In addition, public authorities may wish to use positive action to help them comply with their public sector duty.[175] The EHRC is keen to encourage positive action and devotes chapter 12 of its Employment Code to explaining how it works.

13.138   An employer can take positive action if s/he reasonably thinks that:

- people who share a particular protected characteristic suffer a disadvantage connected to that characteristic; or

---

170 For exact wording and scope, see EqA 2010 Sch 22 para 1(1); EHRC Employment Code, para 13.49.
171 Example in the Explanatory Notes.
172 RRA 1976 s41(1) was not replicated in the EqA 2010.
173 EqA 2010 Sch 23 para 1; EHRC Employment Code, para 13.54.
174 EqA 2010 Sch 22 para 2. See also chapter 11.
175 EHRC Employment Code, para 12.34. The public sector duty is set out in chapter 12.

- people who share a particular protected characteristic have different needs from those who do not have that protected characteristic; or
- participation in an activity by people who share a particular protected characteristic is disproportionately low.[176]

The employer can then take any action which is a proportionate means of achieving the aim of enabling or encouraging those people to overcome or minimise the disadvantage or to participate in the activity or to meet their needs. For example, an employer can target job adverts at particular disadvantaged groups, by using specialist media outlets and stating in the adverts that people from the targeted group are welcome to apply. An employer can also provide open days or training opportunities exclusively for those with particular protected characteristics.

13.139   Discrimination at the point of recruitment or promotion is only allowed in very limited circumstances, ie in what has come to be known as a 'tie-break' situation.[177] An employer can choose to give preference through the recruitment process, including in the decision as to who to appoint, to a worker from a disadvantaged group. This is only permitted where the worker is as qualified as the other candidate to be recruited or promoted. Also, the employer's action must be a proportionate means of achieving the aim of enabling or encouraging people with the relevant protected characteristic to overcome or minimise the disadvantage of the relevant group. The employer must not have a policy of treating people who share the relevant protected characteristic more favourably than those who do not share it. It is not entirely clear what 'as qualified' means and whether it means the favoured candidate must be as good in every respect as the other candidate or simply have the minimum requirements for the job.

---

176 EqA 2010 s158.
177 EqA 2010 ss158(4) and 159.

CHAPTER 14

Protected characteristics

continued

Chapter 14: Key points

- The Equality Act (EqA) 2010 covers the following *protected characteristics*: age; disability; gender reassignment; being married or in a civil partnership; pregnancy and maternity; race; religion and belief; sex; and sexual orientation. These were all covered by the previous legislation.
- There is a defence to direct age discrimination – but not to direct discrimination because of any of the other protected characteristics. The defence is the same justification defence as applies to indirect discrimination generally, except that the aims must be of a public interest nature.
- There are a number of exceptions particular to age discrimination, eg regarding redundancy payments, the minimum wage and benefits based on length of service.
- The default retirement age has been abolished. Enforced retirement is direct age discrimination unless it can be justified as a proportionate means of achieving a legitimate aim.
- The protected characteristic of 'gender reassignment' protects those who have undergone, are undergoing or propose to undergo a process for reassigning their sex. It is no longer necessary for that process to be under medical supervision.
- Workers who have a gender recognition certificate (GRC) should generally be treated as belonging to their acquired sex.
- 'Race' includes colour, nationality, national or ethnic origin and possibly caste.
- A wide range of 'religions and beliefs' are covered, even if the belief is very personal to the individual concerned. Beliefs can be scientific, religious or other; they can potentially include vegetarianism, environmentalism and pacifism. A belief must have a level of cogency, seriousness and cohesion and must be worthy of respect in a democratic society.
- 'Sexual orientation' means orientation towards the same sex or the opposite sex or both.
- The general principles in chapter 13 should be read before this chapter. See chapter 15 for more detail on disability, and chapter 16 for evidence to prove discrimination.

Introduction

14.1 An overview of discrimination law, showing who is covered and the protected characteristics, is set out in chapter 12. Chapter 13 explains the definitions of the different types of discrimination. This chapter expands on the meaning of each protected characteristic and provides examples of how the definition of discrimination will apply in respect of each. The official statistics show that cases started in the employment tribunals (ETs) following the introduction of fees in 2013 fell dramatically in respect of each protected characteristic compared with the previous year. Since fees were removed in July 2017, the number of cases has greatly increased.

Age

Historical and European contexts

14.2 In 2000, the European Council issued a Directive Establishing a General Framework for Equal Treatment in Employment and Occupation.[1] This is known as the 'General Framework Directive' or sometimes the 'Framework Employment Directive' or the 'Equal Treatment Framework Directive'. The directive forbids discrimination in employment on grounds of sexual orientation, religion, disability and age. In order to implement the directive in respect of age, the Employment Equality (Age) Regulations 2006[2] came into force on 1 October 2006. These have since been replaced by the Equality Act (EqA) 2010. For an introduction to the effect of Brexit on the applicability of EU law, see chapter 3 above.

14.3 Until the Equality and Human Rights Commission (EHRC) came into being in 2007, there was no organisation with a statutory remit to oversee the working of age discrimination law. Nor were there any statutory codes, although the Advisory, Conciliation and Arbitration Service (ACAS) had issued some guidance for employers.[3] In the financial year 2019/20, 2,434 age discrimination claims

---

1 2000/78/EC.
2 SI No 1031.
3 Current ACAS guidance on age discrimination is available at: www.acas.org.uk/acas-guide-on-age-discrimination.

were started.[4] In July 2018, the House of Commons Women and Equalities Committee published its Inquiry Report into *Older people and employment*.[5] The Committee concluded (para 28):

> Ageism remains a significant problem within British society and is affecting the ability of people to continue working into later life, despite long-standing laws against age discrimination. Discrimination in recruitment is a significant problem and the public sector is not leading the way in the retention of older workers when it should be.

The protected characteristic of age

14.4   'Age' is a protected characteristic under EqA 2010 s5. It covers workers of a particular age or age group. The law protects workers of all ages against discrimination because of their age. There used to be exceptions for retirement, but these no longer apply.[6]

Direct age discrimination

14.5   The definition of direct discrimination and general principles are explained in chapter 13. It is important to read those paragraphs before reading this chapter. Direct age discrimination occurs where a worker is treated less favourably because of his/her age. For example, an employer selects the oldest workers for redundancy.

14.6   Unlike all the other protected characteristics, there is a potential justification defence to direct age discrimination. Employers can justify direct discrimination if they can prove the less favourable treatment is a proportionate means of achieving a legitimate aim. This is the same wording as for the defence available for indirect discrimination cases in relation to all the protected characteristics, although case-law has established some additional requirements when justifying direct age discrimination. See paras 14.10–14.14 for further comments on the defence.

---

4   Issued as quarterly statistics, but set out for the full year. See 'Main tables (January to March 2021)' at www.gov.uk/government/statistics/tribunal-statistics-quarterly-january-to-march-2021.

5   See: https://publications.parliament.uk/pa/cm201719/cmselect/cmwomeq/359/359.pdf.

6   See para 14.27 onwards.

Discrimination because of perceived age

14.7 It is also unlawful to treat someone less favourably because of his/her apparent age, eg an employer refuses to recruit a worker because s/he guesses the worker is of a certain age, or because s/he mistakenly thinks the worker is older than the worker in fact is, or because the worker looks younger than s/he is and the employer fears customers or clients will not take the worker seriously.

Indirect age discrimination

14.8 The definition of indirect discrimination is set out in respect of all the protected characteristics in chapter 13. In respect of age, it is where a worker is put at a disadvantage because of the application of a provision, criterion or practice (PCP) which also puts or would put those of the same age group at a particular disadvantage compared with others. The worker can choose to describe his/her own age group as appears appropriate.[7] For example, a worker aged 55 could describe his/her 'age group' as '55', 'over 50', '50–60' etc. Obviously the choice of age groups will be determined by the evidence available to show disparate impact on those of the worker's age.

14.9 An example of indirect age discrimination would be where an employer requires job applicants to have lengthy prior experience. This would put younger candidates at a disadvantage as they have had less time to acquire such experience. Alternatively, an employer wants recent graduates for a job. This would exclude the majority of older candidates. A requirement which works to the comparative disadvantage of employees because they are closer to retirement age would also be indirect discrimination unless justified. It is unrealistic to differentiate between age and retirement.[8] For a list of possible indirectly discriminatory requirements on age grounds, see appendix B. It is also useful to read the recent *Ryan v South West Ambulance Services NHS Trust*[9], which applies the stages of indirect discrimination as explained by the Supreme Court in *Essop*.[10]

---

7 EqA 2010 s5(2).

8 *Homer v Chief Constable of West Yorkshire Police* [2012] UKSC 15; [2012] IRLR 601.

9 UKEAT/0213/19; [2021] IRLR 4.

10 *Essop and others v Home Office (UK Border Agency); Naeem v Secretary of State for Justice* [2017] UKSC 27; [2017] IRLR 558.

The defence to direct and indirect age discrimination

14.10   As mentioned above, an employer can defend a case of direct or indirect age discrimination by showing that the treatment or PCP is a proportionate means of achieving a legitimate aim. This derives from Article 6 of the General Framework Directive, which states that a difference of treatment on age grounds is not unlawful if it is objectively and reasonably justified by a legitimate aim, and if the means of achieving that aim are appropriate and necessary. The directive (unlike the EqA 2010) goes on to give examples of potentially justifiable differences of treatment. If any of these examples are quoted against the worker, remember that they are only examples, they do not appear in the EqA 2010, and must still be justified on the facts of the particular case.

14.11   Because it is unique to have a defence available to direct discrimination, there has been uncertainty whether direct age discrimination cases ought to be harder to justify than indirect discrimination cases, despite the wording of the defence being the same. In its final consultation on the original Age Regulations, the then government said, 'treating people differently on grounds of age will be possible but only exceptionally and only for good reasons'.[11] The case-law does not suggest that direct age discrimination can only be justified in exceptional circumstances, but logically one would expect there to be a high threshold where the employer acts on generalisations about people of a certain age rather than considering an individual's particular circumstances and capabilities. On a judicial review brought by the National Council on Ageing (operating through its membership organisation, Heyday), the High Court asked the Court of Justice of the European Union (CJEU) to comment on the defence to direct age discrimination. The CJEU stated that the defence need not be restricted to a precise list of potential grounds for justification such as is contained in Article 6 of the directive.[12] The CJEU went on to say that, allowing a certain degree of flexibility, employers can only justify direct discrimination if it is in pursuit of legitimate aims of a 'public interest nature'. A further discussion of this in the context of enforced retirement is at paras 14.31–14.36. Subject to how the law

---

11   *Equality and diversity: coming of age*, Department of Trade and Industry (DTI) consultation, July 2005.

12   *R (Incorporated Trustees of the National Council on Ageing (Age Concern England)) v Secretary of State for Business, Enterprise and Regulatory Reform* C-388/07 [2009] IRLR 373, CJEU.

continues to develop regarding permitted defences to direct age discrimination, the following observations may apply to direct or indirect age discrimination.

14.12   The issue of whether saving costs can amount to a defence to indirect discrimination in respect of any of the protected characteristics is discussed at para 13.55. This question is equally relevant to direct age discrimination, and it is interesting that many of the cases do concern age discrimination. Employers can take costs into account provided other factors also apply and it is not simply a question of it being more expensive not to discriminate. So in the age discrimination context, it is unlikely to be justifiable to fail to offer a redundant employee redeployment solely because this will take him/her past the age of 50, thus giving him/her an entitlement to an expensive early retirement pension should s/he be made redundant in the future.[13] There have been a few extreme cases in recent years in the field of age discrimination and redundancy pay or pensions, where the courts have thought it justifiable for an employer to bring forward a redundancy termination date so as to avoid giving a worker an 'undeserved windfall'.[14] However, in most run-of-the-mill situations, it should be difficult to justify cutting short the normal stages of a redundancy selection process in order to deprive an older employee of a pension. One would expect the redundancy budget to include covering those employees who happened to hit the age for pension entitlement.[15] On the other hand, where the aim is to break even in the face of reduced budgets, it could be justifiable to have indirectly discriminatory arrangements for access to voluntary redundancy / early retirement schemes.[16] In summary, there are various ways in which an employer might treat a worker less favourably on redundancy because s/he is near retirement or pension age,[17] and the key question will be whether the employer can show the treatment was justified.

13   For example, see *Tower Hamlets LBC v Wooster* UKEAT/0441/08; [2009] IRLR 980.

14   See *Woodcock v Cumbria Primary Care Trust* [2012] IRLR 491, CA, but its facts are unusual and rather extreme. See comments of SC in *O'Brien v Ministry of Justice (formerly Department for Constitutional Affairs)* [2013] UKSC 6; [2013] IRLR 315 for a stronger view against costs, albeit in a different context.

15   *Sturmey v Weymouth and Portland BC* UKEAT/0114/14.

16   *HM Land Registry v Benson* UKEAT/0197/11; *Heskett v The Secretary of State for Justice* [2020] EWCA Civ 1487.

17   Eg by not offering workers over 50 the opportunity of applying for voluntary redundancy – *Donkor v Royal Bank of Scotland* UKEAT/0162/15; [2016] IRLR 268.

14.13　Another controversial area is whether customer preference or corporate image is an acceptable defence to age discrimination. Where this is based on stereotypes and used to justify direct discrimination, it should be challenged as not being a legitimate public interest aim. Defences such as health and safety or proximity to retirement age, although more superficially attractive, may well be based on assumptions and generalisations about the health and abilities of workers of a certain age, and how long workers of any age are likely to remain in a particular job. If a certain level of health or fitness is genuinely needed for a job, it is better that an employer applies a medical or fitness test to all job candidates, rather than make assumptions that workers over a particular age will not be suitable. A general health test may still be indirectly discriminatory, in that it may disproportionately screen out older workers, but it will be fairer than a directly discriminatory rule, in that it assesses the actual individual. 'Last in, first out' (LIFO) may be justifiable indirect discrimination as one of several redundancy selection criteria but probably not as the sole criterion.[18]

14.14　The onus is on the employer to prove the defence, but the worker should be ready to challenge the employer's justification and demand proof of any assumptions made about the link between age and performance. Cases have revealed that a great deal of stereotyping around age still exists.

Harassment: age

14.15　The general law on harassment in respect of all characteristics is set out at para 13.81 onwards. Examples of harassment involving age – deliberate or unintentional – could be teasing; offensive jokes; hostile or patronising remarks; exclusion from team meetings or social occasions; remarks about physical appearance linked to age; being made to do menial tasks and run errands; bullying; and making someone feel they ought to leave. Of course, the worker may be happy with a certain level of joking and banter, especially on occasions such as birthdays. However, if it is unwanted and if it is reasonable to consider that it creates a humiliating or offensive environment etc, remembering the seriousness of those words, then it is unlawful.

18　*Rolls Royce plc v UNITE the Union* [2009] EWCA Civ 387; [2009] IRLR 576 upholding the High Court's decision at [2009] IRLR 49, QBD.

Exceptions: Where age discrimination is allowed

14.16 EqA 2010 Sch 9 sets out most of the exceptions where discrimination is permitted. Part 2 of the Schedule contains further exceptions which apply only to age. The main exceptions applying specifically to age discrimination are set out below.

Occupational requirements

14.17 The occupational requirement exception applicable to all protected characteristics is set out in chapter 13. In relation to age, an example may be a TV production company requiring a young or young-looking actor to play the role of a young person in a film. It is important that stereotyped assumptions regarding age are not used when applying the occupational requirement exception. For example, requirements that staff in leisure industries be of an age which matches the targeted customer group are not necessarily a proportionate means of achieving a legitimate aim.

Armed forces

14.18 The rules against age discrimination do not apply to service in the armed forces.[19]

Minimum wage

14.19 An employer may pay a worker a lower hourly rate because of age if the worker is in a lower national minimum wage band than his/her comparator and the worker is paid less than the national living wage, ie the rate for adults aged 23 and above.[20] For example, in the year starting 1 April 2021, waiter A (aged 19) falls within the 18–20 band (minimum rate £6.56 per hour). Waiter B (aged 26) is within the national living wage band (minimum rate £8.91 per hour). An employer is entitled to pay B £10.00 per hour and pay A, because he is younger, £7.00 per hour. However, if the employer pays A £9.00 per hour, the exception does not apply, because A is now paid more than the national living wage rate. Waiter A can claim direct discrimination and the employer will have to justify the pay difference in the usual way.

---

19 EqA 2010 Sch 9 para 4; EHRC Employment Code, paras 13.21–13.23 (available at: www.equalityhumanrights.com/en/publication-download/employment-statutory-code-practice).

20 EqA 2010 Sch 9 paras 11–12; National Minimum Wage Regulations (NMW Regs) 2015 SI No 621 reg 4 defines 'single hourly rate' as the national living wage rate.

Benefits based on length of service

14.20   EqA 2010 Sch 9 para 10[21] exempts certain benefits based on length of service. It is common for employers to give pay increments or other enhanced benefits, eg longer holiday entitlement, for each year of employment. This indirectly discriminates against younger workers. The EqA 2010 permits these enhancements for the first five years of a worker's service. After that, an employer must justify applying length of service criteria to pay or benefits, but the usual objective test for justification does not apply. The employer need only show that it reasonably appears to him/her that the service criterion fulfils a business need. The previous legislation gave examples such as rewarding experience and loyalty and increasing motivation. These were only examples, but are still likely to apply.

14.21   Service requirements can also discriminate against other workers who are less likely to build up long service eg women because of career breaks, or black workers because of previous discrimination. Indirect discrimination cases can therefore be brought in relation to other protected characteristics. The *Cadman* test case, which was brought under the former Equal Pay Act (EqPA) 1970, concerned what level of justification is necessary for pay increments which indirectly discriminate against women.[22] The decision in that case indicated that although justification is usually self-evident, it can be challenged in special circumstances. It is interesting to consider whether that means the general service-related benefits exemption in relation to age, which does not allow for consideration of special circumstances in individual cases, could be challenged as contrary to European law.

14.22   The Schedule 9 para 10 exemption does not include any benefit awarded to a worker because s/he has stopped working for the employer,[23] eg redundancy pay. However, redundancy selection criteria could be considered a 'benefit' and would be covered, presumably because the worker has not yet been selected for dismissal. This means that criteria such as LIFO, which disadvantage younger workers, require a lower standard of justification in relation to indirect age discrimination.[24] However, if LIFO also discriminated against women or black workers, it would need proper justification under the usual test in relation to indirect sex or race discrimination, since

---

21   Formerly Employment Equality (Age) Regulations 2006 reg 32.
22   See para 5.50.
23   EqA 2010 Sch 9 para 10(7).
24   *Rolls Royce plc v UNITE the Union* [2009] EWCA Civ 387; [2009] IRLR 576.

there is no equivalent exemption for service-related benefits for those protected characteristics.

Redundancy payments

14.23 Direct and indirect age discrimination in the calculation of redundancy pay is permitted in certain circumstances. Details are set out at para 18.23.

Life assurance

14.24 It is not age discrimination for an employer to provide a worker with insurance cover or a related financial service which ends at the age of 65 or any later state pensionable age. Nor is it age discrimination only to provide such insurance or service to workers below that age.[25]

Childcare benefits

14.25 It is not age discrimination for an employer to provide childcare facilities only in respect of children of certain ages.[26] This includes paying some of the costs and helping the parent to find a carer or spend more time caring for the child him/herself.

Pensions

14.26 Certain discrimination in pensions is permitted, but this is a very complex area and beyond the scope of this book.[27]

Retirement

14.27 Until abolished on 1 October 2011 (with some transitional provisions), a default retirement age of 65 used to apply. Provided an employer followed the correct statutory procedures, an employee (though not other kinds of worker) could be forced to retire at 65 and would be unable to claim age discrimination or unfair dismissal. This is no longer the case. The usual rules of unfair dismissal and age discrimination now apply if an employee is forced to retire.

---

25 EqA 2010 Sch 9 para 14. Applicable from 6 April 2011 – Employment Equality (Repeal of Retirement Age Provisions) Regulations 2011 SI No 1069.

26 EqA 2010 Sch 9 para 15.

27 See EqA 2010 s61 and Sch 9 para 16; the Equality Act (Age Exceptions for Pension Schemes) Order 2010 SI No 2133 as amended by the Equality Act (Age Exceptions for Pension Schemes) (Amendment) Order 2010 SI No 2285.

14.28   It is direct age discrimination to dismiss a worker or force him/her to retire because s/he has reached a certain age, unless this can be objectively justified. This applies whether an employer is applying a general normal retirement age or is just making a decision in respect of an individual worker. Primarily it is the general rule which has to be justified since, if it is, its application to the individual will usually also be justified.[28] The term 'EJRA' (employer justified retirement age) is sometimes used to refer to a situation where an employer imposes a contractual retirement age in place of the abolished default retirement age. Employers following this route will need to justify doing so as a proportionate means of achieving a legitimate aim.

14.29   In the key case of *Seldon v Clarkson Wright & Jakes and Secretary of State for Business Innovation and Skills*,[29] the Supreme Court analysed various CJEU cases and gave guidelines as set out in paras 14.32–14.34 below on what an employer must prove to justify imposing a retirement age.

14.30   The Supreme Court (SC) said that in order to justify direct age discrimination, the employer's aims must be of a public interest nature consistent with the UK's social policy objectives, as opposed to purely individual reasons particular to an employer's situation, such as cost reduction or improving competitiveness. Two different kinds of legitimate objective have been identified by the CJEU. The first kind can be summed up as 'inter-generational fairness', eg facilitating access to employment by young people; enabling older people to remain in the workforce; sharing limited opportunities to work in a particular profession fairly between the generations; or promoting diversity and the interchange of ideas between younger and older workers. The SC felt this aim was comparatively uncontroversial.

14.31   The SC said that the second kind of aim which the CJEU believes is legitimate can be summed up as 'dignity', eg avoiding the need to dismiss older workers on the grounds of incapacity or underperformance, thus preserving their dignity and avoiding humiliation, or avoiding the need for costly and divisive disputes about capacity or underperformance. The SC felt that the assumptions underlying these objectives look suspiciously like stereotyping. However, the CJEU has said that the avoidance of unseemly debates about capacity is capable of being a legitimate aim.

---

28 *Seldon v Clarkson Wright & Jakes and Secretary of State for Business Innovation and Skills* [2012] UKSC 16; [2012] IRLR 590.
29 [2012] UKSC 16; [2012] IRLR 590.

14.32   The SC said it is not enough that the employer's aim falls into these categories and is capable of being a legitimate aim. It still has to be legitimate in the particular circumstances of the case. For example, improving the recruitment of young people in order to achieve a balanced and diverse workforce is in principle a legitimate aim. However, if there is in fact no problem in recruiting the young, and if the real problem is in retaining the older and more experienced workers, then it may not be a legitimate aim for the business concerned. Avoiding the need for performance management may be a legitimate aim, but if in fact the business already has sophisticated performance management measures in place, it may not be legitimate to avoid them for only one section of the workforce. Similarly, it may be a legitimate aim to protect public-sector workers nearer retirement from the effect of changes in their pension scheme, but only if the government can show that older workers really would be more badly affected than younger workers.[30]

14.33   Following *Seldon*, it is important to remember that the defence to direct age discrimination does not stop with whether the employer's aim is legitimate. The means used must also be proportionate. Even if an employer can justify imposing a retirement age, it does not mean that the particular retirement age selected is proportionate. On the other hand, the retirement age used by the employer will not be disproportionate purely because an age slightly higher or lower would have been equally justifiable.[31]

14.34   It is useful to follow through this little checklist when considering whether an employer has justified applying a retirement age to a worker:

- Identify the employer's aim in applying the retirement age.
- Consider whether this is genuinely the employer's aim or a false reason put forward for the purpose of defending the case.
- Consider whether the aim is generally capable of being a legitimate social policy aim.
- If so, consider whether the aim was legitimate in the particular circumstances of the case.
- If so, consider whether applying the retirement age rule (including the particular age chosen) was a proportionate means of achieving that aim.

---

30 *The Lord Chancellor and Secretary of State for Justice and another v McCloud and Mostyn and others; Sargeant v London Fire and Emergency Planning Authority and others* [2018] EWCA Civ 2844; [2019] IRLR 477.

31 *Seldon v Clarkson, Wright & Jakes (No 2)* [2014] IRLR 748, EAT.

14.35   As anticipated by the SC in *Seldon*, many of the justifications put forward in tribunals for imposing a retirement age to date have included the need for workforce planning; encouraging staff retention by making available promotion routes; and maintaining a 'collegiate' atmosphere by enabling older workers to retire with dignity rather than having to take them up on deteriorating performance. All of these reasons would need proving in the context of the particular workplace, both in terms of legitimate aims and in terms of proportionate means. In most organisations these days, staff turnover is relatively high (unlike perhaps the level of turnover among partners in professional firms, where the test cases to date tend to have occurred). It therefore seems unlikely that older workers staying on past a predictable retirement age have much or any impact on promotion vacancies or workforce planning. The exception might be a very small employer with long-serving staff.[32]

14.36   As for the 'collegiate' atmosphere, that would be an argument against dismissing employees of any age for a variety of reasons connected with performance. It is not usually something which concerns employers or is thought to damage the employer's organisation. Moreover, the assumption that older workers will have greater performance difficulties than younger workers and that they should be deprived of the same opportunity for performance management reeks of stereotyping. The question is whether it is proportionate to make a whole workforce retire at a particular age just to avoid putting a few individuals through a capability procedure.

14.37   This is an area where unfounded stereotypes can easily creep in. The research report cited by the High Court in *Heyday* pointed out that, except in a very limited range of jobs, work performance does not deteriorate with age, at least up to age 70.[33] In the light of that, the High Court said that if employers had adverse perceptions of employees between 65 and 70, it was likely these were precisely the result of stereotypical thinking. More recently, the House of Commons Select Committee Report on *Older people and employment* said:

---

32 See *Air Products plc v Cockram* [2018] EWCA Civ 346; [2018] IRLR 755, CA and *Professor Pitcher v The Chancellor Masters and Scholars of the University of Oxford and another; The Chancellor, Masters and Scholars of the University of Oxford v Professor Ewart* EA-2020-000128-RN for a discussion of the level of evidence needed by employers to justify age discrimination.

33 *Retirement ages in the UK: a review of the literature* – DTI Employment Relations Research Series 13, Pamela Meadows, cited in *R (Age UK) v Secretary of State for Business, Innovation and Skills* (the 'Heyday' case) [2009] EWHC 2336 (Admin).

There are four main misconceptions that seem to underpin employer bias against older workers: that younger workers cost less; that younger workers are likely to be more productive; that younger workers will provide the employer with more years of work; and that older people need to leave work in order to 'make way' for younger people. We heard evidence refuting all of these stereotypes.[34]

14.38 When considering justifications for age discrimination, it is worth remembering the warning of the House of Lords against stereotyping (albeit racial) in the *Roma Rights Centre* case.[35] Regarding unfair dismissal, a retirement dismissal will probably now be a dismissal for 'some other substantial reason' (SOSR), whether or not it is fair will presumably depend on the considerations discussed above.

Disability

14.39 Disability is covered in chapter 15.

Gender reassignment

Historical and European contexts

14.40 Discrimination because of gender reassignment was previously covered by the Sex Discrimination Act (SDA) 1975, although the EqA 2010 made a step forward by removing the requirement that gender reassignment be a medical process. In its 2016 report on *Transgender equality*,[36] the Women and Equalities Parliamentary Select Committee pointed out that the terms 'gender reassignment' and 'transsexual' in the EqA 2010 'are outdated and misleading, and may not cover wider members of the trans community'. The Select Committee recommended that the protected characteristic should be amended to that

---

34 House of Commons Women and Equalities Committee Report: *Older people and employment*, Fourth report of session 2017–2019 at para 17, available at: https://publications.parliament.uk/pa/cm201719/cmselect/cmwomeq/359/359.pdf.

35 *R (European Roma Rights Centre and others) v Immigration Officer at Prague Airport and another* [2005] IRLR 115, HL. See para 13.17 above.

36 The Women and Equalities Committee *Transgender equality inquiry*, 14 January 2016 and government response are both available via links at: https://old.parliament.uk/business/committees/committees-a-z/commons-select/women-and-equalities-committee/inquiries/parliament-2015/transgender-equality/

of 'gender identity'. The government has rejected this idea, as it did when the same issue arose on the passage of the EqA 2010 through parliament. This leaves the unsatisfactory position whereby workers who are discriminated against because they are non-binary, non-gendered or gender fluid are not clearly protected, although a recent ET decision has suggested the protection may be wider (see below). Meanwhile, the Select Committee recognised that high levels of transphobia are experienced by individuals on a daily basis. A survey of 410 trans workers in 2021 indicated that 25 per cent had experienced transphobic discrimination from work colleagues and 17 per cent from managers, an improvement from 2016, but with higher figures over preceding years.[37] Sixty-five per cent had still felt the need to hide their gender status or history at work. A Trades Union Congress (TUC) survey in 2017 found similar levels of discrimination and bullying. It said that 30 per cent of trans respondents had had their transgender status outed against their will. In a 2018 survey, one in three employers were prepared to admit that they were less likely to hire a transgender worker.[38]

The protected characteristic of gender reassignment

14.41 A 'transsexual person' under the EqA 2010 is someone who has the protected characteristic of gender reassignment. Under EqA 2010 s7, a worker has the protected characteristic of 'gender reassignment' if s/he is 'proposing to undergo, is undergoing or has undergone a process (or part of a process) for the purpose of reassigning the person's sex by changing physiological or other attributes of sex'. Unlike the previous position under the SDA 1975, it is not necessary that such a process be under medical supervision. The EHRC Employment Code gives the example of a person born physically female, who decides to spend the rest of his life as a man. He lives as a man but does not seek medical advice because he successfully passes as a man without the need for any medical intervention. He would have the protected characteristic of gender reassignment.

---

37 *Trans employee experiences survey: Understanding the trans community in the workplace* (2021): research conducted by Totaljobs, available at www.totaljobs. com/advice/trans-employee-experiences-survey-2021-research-conducted-by-totaljobs.

38 *The cost of being out at work* (TUC), available at: www.tuc.org.uk/sites/default/ files/LGBTreport17.pdf; *Transphobia rife among UK employers as 1 in 3 won't hire a transgender person* by Crossland Employment Solicitors, June 2018, available at: www.crosslandsolicitors.com/site/cases/transgender-discrimination-in-UK-workplaces.

14.42   It is strongly arguable that for the purposes of sex discrimination law, a trans person must be regarded as having the sexual identity of the gender to which s/he has been reassigned.[39] This should certainly be the position if the worker has acquired a gender recognition certificate (GRC) under the Gender Recognition Act (GRA) 2004. The GRA 2004 enables trans people to obtain legal recognition of their acquired gender on obtaining a full GRC by a Gender Recognition Panel.[40] This means that the person should be treated entirely as of his/her acquired gender from then on (with very limited exceptions). GRA 2004 ss1–3 set out the basis on which a certificate will be issued. The GRA 2004 was passed following comments by the European Court of Human Rights (ECtHR) that to deny this right could be a breach of European Convention on Human Rights (ECHR) Article 8 (the right to respect for private life).[41]

14.43   In its 2016 report, the Women and Equalities Parliamentary Select Committee recommended that the government update the GRA 2004, stating that it was pioneering but is now dated. It said its medicalised approach pathologises trans identities and runs contrary to the dignity and personal autonomy of applicants. In view of evidence of underuse of the GRA 2004, the government did eventually consult on its reform in August 2018. In September 2020, the government finally announced its response and that no change would be made to the criteria for legal gender recognition.[42] The Women and Equalities Committee then launched a further inquiry into reform of both the GRA 2004 and the EqA 2010, including the question whether reforms are needed to better support the rights of gender-fluid and non-binary people.[43]

39 See *A v Chief Constable of West Yorkshire Police and another* [2004] IRLR 573, HL.

40 The panel is part of HM Courts and Tribunals Service and its guidance on applying for a certificate is available via links at: www.justice.gov.uk/tribunals/gender-recognition-panel.

41 *Goodwin v UK* [2002] IRLR 664, ECtHR. But see paras 13.132–13.133 re the OR defence under EqA 2010 Sch 9 para 1, which arguably may apply in exceptional circumstances.

42 Consultation details are at: www.gov.uk/government/consultations/reform-of-the-gender-recognition-act-2004. The response is at www.gov.uk/government/speeches/response-to-gender-recognition-act-2004-consultation and a House of Commons Research Briefing at https://commonslibrary.parliament.uk/research-briefings/cbp-9079/.

43 *Women and Equalities Committee launches new inquiry into Gender Recognition Act reform and more*, 28 October 2020 at https://committees.parliament.uk/work/658/reform-of-the-gender-recognition-act/news/120336/women-and-equalities-committee-launches-new-inquiry-into-gender-recognition-act-reform-and-more/.

14.44   Meanwhile in *Taylor v Jaguar Land Rover*,[44] an ET decided that 'gender reassignment' could encompass a non-binary or gender fluid person. It said this (at para 178):

> We thought it was very clear that Parliament intended gender reassignment to be a spectrum moving away from birth sex, and that a person could be at any point on that spectrum. That would be so, whether they described themselves as 'non-binary' i.e. not at point A or point Z, 'gender fluid' i.e. at different places between point A and point Z at different times, or 'transitioning' i.e. moving from point A, but not necessarily ending at point Z, where A and Z are biological sex. We concluded that it was beyond any doubt that somebody in the situation of the Claimant was (and is) protected by the legislation because they are on that spectrum and they are on a journey which will not be the same in any two cases. It will end up where it does. The wording of section 7(1) accommodates that interpretation without any violence to the statutory language.

The ET's reasoning would appear also to apply to other trans identities, though not someone who simply performed drag without any change of their gender identity. The *Taylor* case is likely to be influential, but it has not been appealed so it remains with no precedent value.

14.45   Where there is uncertainty regarding whether a worker will be protected under the protected characteristic of 'gender reassignment', it may also be possible to argue such discrimination is sex discrimination, on an extended definition of 'sex' or that it is based on perception that they might undergo or have undergone gender reassignment, but this is an untested area.

14.46   When running a legal case, it will usually be desirable to avoid the term 'transsexual' as far as possible so as to avoid the risk of offence. Where necessary to refer to the statute, it can be said that a worker has the protected characteristic of gender reassignment. As already indicated, for many, 'trans' or 'transgender' are preferred terms. However, be aware that these terms can cover all those who feel their gender identity does not match the single gender assigned to them at birth, regardless of whether they wish to undergo gender reassignment. Advisers need to understand exactly what a worker means when referring to themselves as a trans person. This may be relevant to how well the law fits the circumstances.

14.47   For an introduction to the latest issues around gender identity, see the latest update of the judiciary's Equal Treatment Bench Book,

---

44   ET 1304471/2018.

chapter 12 ('Transgender people').[45] UNISON and the Scottish Transgender Alliance have produced an excellent guide, *Gender identity: an introductory guide for trade union reps supporting trans members.*[46] An ACAS Research Paper, *Supporting trans employees in the workplace*[47] has useful good practice advice, as does the government guidance for employers: *Recruiting and retaining trans gender staff: a guide for employers.*[48]

Direct discrimination because of gender reassignment

14.48   The definition of direct discrimination and general principles are explained in chapter 13. It is important to read those paragraphs before reading this chapter. In the context of gender reassignment, it is unlawful to treat a worker less favourably because s/he proposes to undergo, is undergoing or has undergone gender reassignment. The comparison is with the way the employer treats or would treat a worker who has not undergone, is not undergoing and does not propose to undergo gender reassignment. Alternatively, it may be appropriate to compare the worker's treatment with that of a person of the worker's original sex.[49] In addition, it would be discriminatory to treat a worker's time off for gender reassignment less favourably than a routine sickness absence.[50] It may also be discriminatory to treat such absence less favourably than an absence for some other cause would be treated, eg paid or unpaid leave, but this depends on whether it is reasonable to do so.

---

45   Google 'Equal Treatment Bench Book' and look for the 2021 edition. This should provide you with the latest update.
46   Available at: www.unison.org.uk/content/uploads/2017/06/23488.pdf. See also *How to be a good ally to trans people at work* at https://southwest.unison.org.uk/content/uploads/sites/4/2020/11/How-to-be-a-good-ally-to-trans-people-at-work.pdf.
47   Available at: http://m.acas.org.uk/media/pdf/6/f/Supporting-trans-employees-in-the-workplace.pdf.
48   Available via a link at: www.gov.uk/government/publications/recruiting-and-retaining-transgender-staff-a-guide-for-employers. See also *The workplace and gender reassignment: Guide for staff and managers*, produced by a:gender (the Civil Service transgender support network) (2016) at: www.gov.uk/government/publications/the-workplace-and-gender-reassignment.
49   See *A v Chief Constable of West Yorkshire Police and another* [2004] IRLR 573, HL.
50   EqA 2010 s16.

Harassment: gender reassignment

14.49   Harassment in relation to all the protected characteristics is set out from para 13.81 onwards. There are three definitions of harassment which can apply to gender reassignment: the general definition; unwanted conduct of a sexual nature; and harassment because of rejection of submission to the conduct.[51] For more detail on these, see paras 14.136–14.144 in relation to sex.

Exceptions

Occupational requirements

14.50   The occupational requirement exception applicable to all protected characteristics is set out in chapter 13. In the case of gender reassignment, it only applies to a requirement not to be a 'transsexual person'.[52]

Religious requirements

14.51   An employer may apply to a worker a requirement not to be a 'transsexual person', if s/he can show:

- the employment is for the purposes of an organised religion;
- the application of the requirement engages the compliance or non-conflict principle; and
- the worker to whom the employer applies the requirement does not meet it (or the employer has reasonable grounds for not being satisfied that the person meets it).[53]

14.52   The 'compliance principle' occurs where the requirement is applied so as to comply with the doctrines of the religion. The 'non-conflict principle' applies where, because of the nature or context of the employment, the requirement is applied so as to avoid conflicting with the strongly held religious views of a significant number of the religion's followers. This exception should only be used for a limited number of posts, eg ministers of religion and a small number of other posts, including those which exist to promote or represent the religion.[54] It is unlikely to cover jobs such as cleaners, or even teach-

---

51 EqA 2010 s26.
52 EqA 2010 Sch 9 para 1(3)(a). It's unclear whether this exception applies to someone with a gender recognition certificate.
53 EqA 2010 Sch 9 para 2.
54 EHRC Employment Code, paras 13.12–13.15.

ers in religious schools. The term 'for the purposes of an organised religion' does not mean 'for the purposes of a religious organisation' such as a faith school.[55] This exception applies to discrimination in recruitment arrangements and job offers; access to promotion, transfer or training or any other benefit, facility or service; and dismissal.

Armed forces

14.53   The armed forces can require a person not to be transsexual if that is a proportionate means of ensuring combat effectiveness.[56]

Marriage and civil partnership

Historical and European contexts

14.54   Discrimination because of marriage and civil partnership was previously covered by the SDA 1975.

The protected characteristics of marriage and civil partnership

14.55   Under EqA 2010 s8, a worker has the protected characteristic of marriage or civil partnership if s/he is married or a civil partner.

Direct marriage or civil partnership discrimination

14.56   The definition of direct discrimination and general principles are explained in chapter 13. It is important to read those paragraphs before reading this chapter. It is unlawful to discriminate against a worker because s/he is married or a civil partner. The evidence needs to show that the discrimination is specifically because of the individual's marital (or civil partnership) status and not simply because the worker is involved in a close relationship akin to marriage, eg a cohabiting partner.[57] For example:

---

55   On similar exception in previous legislation, see *R (Amicus – MSF section and others) v Secretary of State for Trade and Industry and Christian Action Research Education and others* [2004] IRLR 430, QBD.

56   For precise scope of exception, see EqA 2010 Sch 9 para 4.

57   *Hawkins v Atex Group Ltd and others* [2012] IRLR 807, EAT.

- An employer refuses to offer a married woman a job because s/he assumes the woman will soon want children, and this assumption would not have been made if the woman was unmarried.
- A church employer dismisses a clergyman because he is having difficulties within his marriage and this damages its promotion of marriage as an important institution.[58]
- A police officer's appointment to a particular division is rescinded because the law means she would be unable to give evidence against her spouse, who is Chief Superintendent in the same division, in any criminal proceedings.[59]

14.57   There have been conflicting Employment Appeal Tribunal (EAT) cases as to whether it is direct marriage discrimination to treat a worker less favourably because s/he is married to a particular person. The latest and most probably correct view is that the answer is no – not if the real reason for the less favourable treatment is the close association between the couple.[60]

14.58   It is not unlawful under the EqA 2010 to discriminate against workers because they are unmarried or not a civil partner.[61] Discrimination against a worker because s/he is divorced does not appear to be covered, but discrimination against a worker because s/he is married and in marital difficulties could be discrimination if the evidence shows that the employer would not have minded so much if an unmarried worker was in relationship difficulties.[62]

Indirect marriage or civil partnership discrimination

14.59   The definition of indirect discrimination is set out in respect of all the protected characteristics in chapter 13.

Harassment: marriage and civil partnership

14.60   The specific definition of harassment does not cover harassment related to marriage or civil partnership. If such harassment occurs,

---

58   *Rev Gould v Trustees of St John's Downshire Hill* UKEAT/0115/17.
59   *Chief Constable of the Bedfordshire Constabulary v Graham* [2002] IRLR 239, EAT.
60   *Hawkins v Atex Group Ltd and others* [2012] IRLR 807, EAT, disagreeing with *Dunn v Institute of Cemetery and Crematorium Management* UKEAT/0531/10.
61   EqA 2010 s13(4).
62   *Rev Gould v Trustees of St John's Downshire Hill* UKEAT/0115/17.

it will be necessary to rely on the usual definition of direct discrimination.

Exceptions

Occupational requirements

14.61 The occupational requirement exception applicable to all protected characteristics is set out in chapter 13. In the case of marriage and civil partnership, it only applies to a requirement not to be married or a civil partner.[63]

Religious requirements

14.62 An employer may apply a requirement not to be married or a civil partner, or not to be married to or the civil partner of a person who has a living former spouse or civil partner, or a requirement relating to the circumstances in which a marriage or civil partnership came to an end. For this, the employer must show that:

- the employment is for the purposes of an organised religion;
- the application of the requirement engages the compliance or non-conflict principle; and
- the worker to whom the employer applies the requirement does not meet it (or the employer has reasonable grounds for not being satisfied that the person meets it).[64]

14.63 The 'compliance principle' occurs where the requirement is applied so as to comply with the doctrines of the religion. The 'non-conflict principle' applies where, because of the nature or context of the employment, the requirement is applied so as to avoid conflicting with the strongly held religious views of a significant number of the religion's followers. This exception should only be used for a limited number of posts, eg ministers of religion and a small number of other posts, including those which exist to promote or represent the religion.[65] It is unlikely to cover jobs such as cleaners, or even teachers in religious schools. The term 'for the purposes of an organised religion' does not mean 'for the purposes of a religious organisation'

---

63 EqA 2010 Sch 9 para 1(3)(b).
64 EqA 2010 Sch 9 para 2.
65 EHRC Employment Code, paras 13.12–13.15.

such as a faith school.[66] This exception applies to discrimination in recruitment arrangements and job offers; access to promotion, transfer or training or any other benefit, facility or service; and dismissal.

Pregnancy and maternity

14.64 The law on pregnancy and maternity operates a little differently from that in respect of the other protected characteristics. It is therefore dealt with separately at chapter 11.

Race

Historical and European contexts

14.65 The first Race Relations Act was passed in 1965, after Lord Brockway had unsuccessfully presented a race relations bill to parliament on nine occasions. Race discrimination in employment was not covered until the 1968 Race Relations Act, and even then, individuals could not bring their own cases in tribunals. They had to go through what was then the Race Relations Board. The first time individuals could directly claim in tribunals was with the Race Relations Act (RRA) 1976. The RRA 1976 was modelled on the Sex Discrimination Act of the previous year. The RRA 1976 remained in force until replaced by the EqA 2010.

14.66 The Commission for Racial Equality (CRE) took over from the Race Relations Board, with a remit to oversee the operation of the RRA 1976. The CRE has now been replaced by the Equality and Human Rights Commission (EHRC). The CRE issued various Codes of Practice under the RRA 1976. These have been replaced by single codes applying to all the protected characteristics and are referred to elsewhere in this book.

14.67 In 2000, the European Council issued a Directive on Equal Treatment Between Persons Irrespective of Racial or Ethnic Origins.[67] This is known as the 'Race Directive', 'Race Discrimination Directive'

---

66 On similar exception in previous legislation, see *R (Amicus – MSF section and others) v Secretary of State for Trade and Industry and Christian Action Research Education and others* [2004] IRLR 430, QBD.

67 2000/43/EC.

or the 'Race Equal Treatment Directive'. For the relationship between EU and national law and the effect of Brexit, see chapter 3 above. In the 2018 calendar year, 3,324 race discrimination claims were started.[68] From December 2021, practitioners can apply to the EHRC for financial support for cases tackling race discrimination.

The protected characteristic of race

14.68 Under EqA 2010 s9, 'race' is one of the protected characteristics and includes colour, nationality and ethnic or national origins. These terms appeared in the RRA 1976 and have been explained further by the case-law.

14.69 There are seven essential characteristics which a group must have to fall within the meaning of 'ethnic group' under the EqA 2010.[69] In summary, these are:

1) a long shared history;
2) its own cultural tradition;
3) a common language;
4) literature;
5) religion;
6) a common geographical origin; and
7) being a minority or oppressed group within a larger community.

It does not matter if the size of a particular ethnic group has diminished due to intermarriage or lapsed observance, provided there remains a discernible minority.[70]

14.70 Jewish and Sikh people are considered 'ethnic groups' and therefore within the protected characteristic of 'race', but Rastafarian[71] and Muslim[72] people are not. However, they all fall within the EqA 2010 under the protected characteristic of 'religion' (see above). Roma people and Irish Travellers are also 'ethnic groups'. Discrimination against 'Travellers' generally may refer to all those of a nomadic way of life but could amount to indirect discrimination against those of

---

68 Issued as quarterly statistics, but set out for the full year. See Annex C, table C.2, available at: www.gov.uk/government/statistics/tribunals-and-gender-recognition-certificate-statistics-quarterly-october-to-december-2018.
69 *Mandla v Lee* [1983] IRLR 209, HL.
70 *Commission for Racial Equality (CRE) v Dutton* [1989] IRLR 8, CA.
71 *Dawkins v Department of the Environment* (1993) 49 EOR 377 and [1993] IRLR 284, CA.
72 *Nyazi v Rymans* (1988) EAT 6/88.

Romany origin.[73] Discrimination because of ethnic origin also includes discrimination because of a worker's descent or lineage.[74]

14.71   The meaning of 'national origins' is ambiguous. Does it mean a worker's nationality at birth, when that has changed? Or does it mean the nationality of the parents or grandparents of a British worker? Or is it entirely separate from the concept of nationality? The Court of Session has suggested that it includes 'nations' with a historical or geographical meaning but which cannot confer citizenship as such, eg a worker discriminated against specifically as English, although s/he is a British national.[75]

14.72   A British national from Northern Ireland who is discriminated against on the ground of being 'Irish' is covered by the EqA 2010.[76] English-speaking Welsh people are not considered a different racial group from Welsh-speaking Welsh people.[77] If a worker is discriminated against in England, for example, because s/he is from Scotland, Wales or Northern Ireland, s/he should probably claim race discrimination on grounds of national origins as opposed to nationality or ethnic origin.[78] Vulnerable immigration status is not protected in itself because it does not exactly equate with nationality. Many non-British nationals living and working in Britain do not have vulnerable immigration status.[79]

14.73   For the purposes of the EqA 2010, a particular racial group may comprise two or more distinct racial groups.[80] For example, a person of Cypriot nationality could claim s/he has suffered discrimination not only as a Cypriot, but as a non-British national or (in the past) as someone not of EU nationality.[81]

14.74   Under EqA 2010 s9(5) there is a power for ministers to issue regulations to include caste within the definition of 'race'. The decision

73 *CRE v Dutton* [1989] IRLR 8, CA. Roma origin is considered ethnic origin under EU law – *Chez Razpredelenie Bulgaria Ad v Komisia Za Zashtita Ot Diskriminatsia* C-83/14 [2015] IRLR 746, CJEU. The Irish Government recognised the ethnic status of Irish Travellers in March 2017.

74 *R (E) v Governing Body of JFS and The Admissions Appeal Panel of JFS and others* [2009] UKSC 15; [2010] IRLR 136.

75 *BBC Scotland v Souster* [2001] IRLR 150, CS.

76 *Bogdenie v Sauer-Sundstrand Ltd* (1988) 383 IDS Brief 15, EAT.

77 *Gwynedd CC v Jones and Doyle* EAT/554/85; [1986] ICR 833.

78 *BBC Scotland v Souster* [2001] IRLR 150, CS.

79 *Onu v Akwiwu and another; Taiwo v Olaigbe and another* [2016] UKSC 31, [2016] IRLR 719.

80 EqA 2010 s9(4).

81 *Orphanos v Queen Mary College* [1985] IRLR 349, HL.

whether to do this was originally made dependent on evidence that came to light in a government-sponsored survey conducted by the National Institute of Economic and Social Research. This reported in December 2012, finding evidence of various kinds of caste discrimination and harassment. For some time, the government resisted calls from the EHRC and various campaign groups to make caste discrimination unlawful. Eventually the government was pressurised by the House of Lords into amending section 9(5) so as to make it compulsory to issue regulations prohibiting caste discrimination, but no timescale was fixed.[82] In March 2017, the government issued a consultation reopening the question whether caste discrimination should be explicitly included in the EqA 2010 or left to the case-law. In July 2018, the government announced its decision not to legislate on the basis that few cases have occurred and it is difficult to arrive at a definition for 'caste'.[83] It prefers to leave it to the case-law to bring caste within the definition of 'ethnic origins' (as below). Many commentators do now feel that caste discrimination can already be challenged within the definition of 'race' in that it amounts to discrimination by reason of descent (see para 14.70). Interestingly, the UN's International Convention on the Elimination of All Forms of Racial Discrimination, ratified by the UK in 1969, defines racial discrimination as including descent. A UN general comment states that discrimination based on 'descent' includes discrimination against members of communities based on forms of social stratification such as caste and analogous systems of inherited status.[84] The EAT has said in the only test case so far that EqA 2010 s9 does not currently cover 'caste' but there may be factual circumstances where the term 'caste' applies, and which come within the term 'ethnic origins' in that the group is determined in part by descent and is of a sufficient quality to be described as 'ethnic'.[85]

---

82 Enterprise and Regulatory Reform Act 2013 s97 amending EqA 2010 s9(5).

83 *Caste in Great Britain and equality law: consultation response*, available at: www.gov.uk/government/consultations/caste-in-great-britain-and-equality-law-a-public-consulation.

84 CERD, General Recommendation No 29. See also the informative House of Commons Library Briefing Paper *The Equality Act 2010: caste discrimination* by D Pyper, 3 August 2018 at: https://researchbriefings.files.parliament.uk/documents/SN06862/SN06862.pdf.

85 *Chandhok and another v Tirkey* [2015] IRLR 195, EAT.

Direct race discrimination

Overview

14.75   The definition of direct discrimination and general principles are explained in chapter 13. It is important to read those paragraphs before reading this chapter. An example of direct race discrimination would be if an employer gave a black worker a final written warning for reading football websites in work time, but did not discipline a white worker for the same offence. If the employer could not provide an innocent explanation, this would suggest the reason for the less favourable treatment was the worker's colour.

14.76   Segregating a worker from others because of his/her race is also direct race discrimination.[86]

Not the worker's own race

14.77   As explained in chapter 13, it is unlawful to directly discriminate against a worker because of the race of someone else. For example, a white worker is excluded from outings entertaining clients because s/he has a black boyfriend/girlfriend, or is refused promotion because s/he is friendly with black members of staff. It is also unlawful to treat a worker less favourably because s/he refuses to discriminate against black customers. However, this principle does not extend to making it unlawful to take account of racial considerations in all situations. For example, it is not in itself direct race discrimination for an employer to dismiss a worker for racially abusing a colleague or customer because of their race.[87]

Indirect race discrimination

14.78   The definition of indirect discrimination is explained in chapter 13. An example of indirect race discrimination would be if an employer required job candidates to speak fluent English. This would disadvantage those born and brought up in non-English speaking countries. It is unlikely to be justifiable unless fluent English was needed for the job.

14.79   The type of PCPs which commonly cause indirect race discrimination are listed in appendix B. PCPs to watch out for include language

---

86   EqA 2010 s13(5).
87   *Redfearn v Serco Ltd t/a West Yorkshire Transport Service* [2006] IRLR 623, CA.

requirements, qualifications, experience, duration or area of residence.

14.80   Certain dress requirements and other rules which indirectly discriminate because of religion may also amount to indirect race discrimination. Before religious discrimination was made unlawful in 2003, it was important that such claims could be brought as indirect race discrimination. For example:

- a rule against wearing turbans may indirectly discriminate against Sikhs;
- a requirement that a manager work on Saturdays may indirectly discriminate against Jewish workers;[88]
- a rule that no holidays are taken over summer peak periods and therefore not on Eid may indirectly discriminate against workers of Asian national origin.[89]

Harassment: race

14.81   The general law on harassment in respect of all characteristics is set out at para 13.81 onwards. In the context of the protected characteristic of race, harassment could include racist remarks directed towards a worker because of his/her own race or made in the worker's presence about other workers of a different race.

Migrant workers

General treatment at work

14.82   Where migrant workers are permitted to work in the UK, they have the same protection against discrimination as everyone else. They also have the same entitlement to other employment rights. In some situations, employers may deprive migrant workers of basic rights such as the minimum wage or rest breaks and limits on working hours under the Working Time Regulations 1998 on an assumption that they are less aware of their rights or less able to take them up than British nationals.[90] However, it is uncertain whether a race discrimination claim can be brought on these grounds (as well as any claims under the relevant legislation such as the National Minimum

---

88 *Tower Hamlets LBC v Rabin* [1989] ICR 693, EAT.

89 *J H Walker Ltd v Hussain* [1996] IRLR 11, EAT.

90 SI No 1833. This is an area which has been taken up the Anti-Trafficking and Labour Exploitation Unit.

Wage Act 1998). If the tribunal finds that the mistreatment is due to the claimant's vulnerable immigration status, that does not in itself amount to direct race discrimination.[91] It is necessary to bring evidence to show the less favourable treatment is because of the worker's particular nationality or race as opposed to his/her 'vulnerability'. This is clearly a severe gap in the law, especially where migrant workers are victims of trafficking or modern slavery.

Getting work – consequence of immigration rules

14.83 The rules making employers liable for employing illegal workers may have repercussions for non-British workers who are entitled to work. The *Code of practice on preventing illegal working: civil penalty scheme for employers* (1 July 2021) sets out very clearly what employers are expected to do.[92] Basically, employers may be liable for a substantial civil penalty in respect of every illegal migrant they have employed unless they have a 'statutory excuse' defence, ie they have taken the correct steps to verify and keep copies of relevant documentation (passports, work permits, residence cards etc). An online right-to-work check can now be carried out in most circumstances. A pre-employment check must be carried out before work starts, and a further check when any time-limited right to work expires. It may well be race discrimination to make assumptions about who needs to prove their right to work and who does not. Employers are therefore advised to check everyone's documents at the point of recruitment. The Code also sets out details of temporary changes to the method of conducting checks from 30 March 2020 to 31 August 2021 (extended to 5 April 2022) because of the Covid-19 pandemic.[93] The Home Office has issued a statutory Code of Practice, which may be taken into account in any tribunal race discrimination claim: *Code of practice for employers: avoiding unlawful discrimination while preventing illegal working* (May 2014). The Code is available on the GOV.UK website.[94]

91 *Onu v Akwiwu and another; Taiwo v Olaigbe and another* [2016] UKSC 31; [2016] IRLR 719.

92 July 2021 update as laid before parliament, at: www.gov.uk/government/ publications/illegal-working-penalties-codes-of-practice-for-employers.

93 Updated advice at www.gov.uk/guidance/coronavirus-covid-19-right-to-work-checks?fbclid=IwAR0Rssw6n56zwLFAUcWUJ3pogBJq6SS-5rn5xhg6qh_ l7sXFlnr7SphPNqs.

94 Updated 6 April 2020. At: www.gov.uk/government/publications/right-to-work-checks-code-of-practice-on-avoiding-discrimination.

14.84   Immigration law is beyond the scope of this book, but there are other occasions where it interrelates with employment rights. There have been a number of cases where an employer has dismissed an employee who is actually entitled to work, because the employee has not produced the supporting documentation fast enough when requested. This cannot be a fair dismissal for 'breach of statutory restriction', whatever the employer reasonably and genuinely believes, because there is in fact no breach. It could potentially be a fair dismissal for 'some other substantial reason', but the employer will need good evidence to show s/he was acting reasonably in such circumstances.[95] Moreover, it may be unlawful race discrimination to refuse to employ a worker who needs a work permit on a mere assumption that the Home Office would be unlikely to grant a work permit.[96] Equally, it may be race discrimination to avoid employing workers of certain nationalities altogether on the assumption that there will be difficulties regarding their work status. For the position on transfers of businesses under the TUPE Regulations 2006,[97] see para 10.53.

Illegal contracts

14.85 If a migrant worker knows s/he does not have the right to enter or work in the UK under the immigration rules, s/he will probably be working illegally. S/he may well be unable to claim unfair dismissal or any other employment rights based on the contract of employment. However, if the employee is not culpable, eg s/he is a vulnerable foreign national who has been brought to the UK for exploitation, s/he may still be able to make such claims.[98] Where the worker has been a victim of trafficking,[99] it may also be useful in relevant circumstances to refer to the Council of Europe Convention on

---

95 It is worth reading *Baker v Abellio London Ltd* UKEAT/0250/16; [2018] IRLR 186 and *Afzal v East London Pizza Ltd (t/a Domino's Pizza)* UKEAT/0265/17; [2019] IRLR 119.

96 *Osborne Clarke Services v Purohit* UKEAT/0305/08; [2009] IRLR 341.

97 Transfer of Undertakings (Protection of Employment) Regulations 2006 SI No 246.

98 The law is complex on illegality. See *Okedina v Chikale* [2019] EWCA Civ 1393; [2019] IRLR 905, where the employee was unaware she was in breach of the rules, and for a clear legal overview. See also a general introduction to illegality at para 6.19 above.

99 The International Labour Office (ILO) *Operational indicators of trafficking in human beings*, September 2009 can be found at: www.ilo.org/wcmsp5/ groups/public/---ed_norm/---declaration/documents/publication/ wcms_105023.pdf.

Action against Trafficking in Human Beings. Article 15 says that victims of trafficking must have the right to civil compensation. It could be argued that this is only realistically available in an employment tribunal and rules about illegal contracts should not stand in the way. It is also worth noting that legal aid may be available for cases brought by victims of trafficking and modern slavery if they have victim status under the National Referral Mechanism.[100] The position with illegal contracts in discrimination claims is sometimes easier as they are not directly based on the contract of employment, but it is still not straightforward.[101]

Exceptions

Occupational requirements

14.86   The occupational requirement exception applicable to all protected characteristics is set out in chapter 13. For example, a council could decide to recruit a worker of Somali origin to visit older people from the Somali community in their homes to encourage them to take up health services. This would probably be allowed because it would be necessary for the post-holder to have good knowledge of Somali language and culture if the council does not have a Somali worker already in post who could take up the duties.[102]

Religion or belief

Historical and European contexts

14.87   As mentioned above, in 2000, the European Council issued a Directive Establishing a General Framework for Equal Treatment in Employment and Occupation.[103] This 'General Framework Directive' forbids discrimination in employment on grounds of sexual orientation, religion, disability and age. In order to implement the directive in respect of religion and belief, the Employment Equality (Religion and Belief) Regulations 2003[104] came into force on 1 December 2003. These have since been replaced by the EqA 2010. For an introduction

---

100 The legal aid position is difficult to ascertain, so it is worth checking.
101 See para 12.21.
102 Example in EHRC Employment Code, para 13.09.
103 2000/78/EC.
104 SI No 1660.

to the effect of Brexit on the applicability of EU law, see chapter 3 above.

14.88   In the financial year 2020/21, 733 religious or belief discrimination claims were started.[105] ACAS has issued some very practical *Guidance: Religion or belief discrimination: key points for the workplace* (August 2018), although it has no formal legal status.[106]

The protected characteristic of religion and belief

14.89   Religion and belief are protected characteristics under EqA 2010 s10. These include a lack of religion or belief.[107] 'Belief' means any religious or philosophical belief.[108] The EHRC Employment Code says at paras 2.43–2.54 that 'religion' includes the more commonly recognised religions in the UK such as the Baha'I faith, Buddhism, Christianity, Hinduism, Islam, Jainism, Judaism, Rastafarianism, Sikhism, and Zoroastrianism. However, a religion need not be mainstream or well known to gain protection, as long as it has a clear structure and belief system. Other ancient religions, eg Druidry, Paganism and Wicca, as well as fringe religions and membership of religious cults, would also seem to be covered, as is membership of the Spiritualist Church.[109]

14.90   Originally the Employment Equality (Religion or Belief) Regulations 2003 referred to 'religious or *similar* philosophical belief' (emphasis added). In 2007, this was amended to remove the word 'similar'. The current definition in EqA 2010 also omits this word. The government insisted that the word 'similar' was superfluous and its removal had no significance, but it did open the way for a wider interpretation of 'belief'. Philosophical belief discrimination is no less protected than religious discrimination. Philosophical beliefs may be just as fundamental or integral to a person's individuality and daily life as are religious beliefs.[110]

105 Issued as quarterly statistics, but set out for the full year. See 'Main tables (January – March 2021) at www.gov.uk/government/statistics/tribunal-statistics-quarterly-january-to-march-2021.

106 Available at www.acas.org.uk/sites/default/files/2021-03/religion-belief-discrimination-guide.pdf.

107 EqA 2010 s10(1).

108 EqA 2010 s10(2).

109 *Greater Manchester Police Authority v Power* UKEAT/0434/09.

110 *GMB v Henderson* UKEAT/0073/14; [2015] IRLR 451.

14.91   Philosophical belief cannot be a matter of casual opinion. The key case of *Grainger plc and others v Nicholson*[111] set out guidelines for deciding whether a belief is covered by the EqA 2010, ie:

i)   The belief must be genuinely held.

ii) It must be a belief and not an opinion or viewpoint based on the present state of information available.

iii) It must be a belief as to a weighty and substantial aspect of human life and behaviour.

iv) It must attain a certain level of cogency, seriousness, cohesion and importance.

v)   It must be worthy of respect in a democratic society, be not incompatible with human dignity and not conflict with the fundamental rights of others.

The requirements should not be set at too high a level. 'Substantial' in guideline iii) just means 'not trivial'. 'Cohesion' in guideline iv) simply means intelligible and capable of being understood.[112] In arriving at these guidelines, the EAT considered case-law under the ECHR, particularly Article 9 (freedom of thought, conscience and religion) and Article 2 of Protocol 1.[113]

14.92   The nature of an individual's beliefs in any particular case need to be considered. However, beliefs in pacifism, vegetarianism, ethical veganism,[114] total abstinence from alcohol, environmentalism[115] and humanism are potentially covered. It does not matter whether the philosophical belief is based on science as opposed to religion, eg a belief in Darwinism.[116] Membership or non-membership of the Masons may also be considered a belief.[117] A belief in a political philosophy or doctrine could constitute a belief covered by the EqA 2010, eg a belief in the philosophies of Socialism, Marxism, Communism

---

111 UKEAT/0219/09; [2010] IRLR 4.

112 *Harron v Chief Constable of Dorset Police* [2016] IRLR 481, EAT.

113 See chapter 3 regarding the Human Rights Act (HRA) 1998 and the ECHR.

114 For an example only at ET level, see *Casamitjana Costa v The League Against Cruel Sports* ET case No: 3331129/2018 at www.gov.uk/employment-tribunal-decisions/mr-j-casamitjana-costa-v-the-league-against-cruel-sports-3331129-2018.

115 *Grainger plc and others v Nicholson* UKEAT/0219/09; [2010] IRLR 4. Decided on the same wording in the Employment Equality (Religion or Belief) Regulations 2003.

116 *Grainger plc and others v Nicholson* UKEAT/0219/09; [2010] IRLR 4.

117 *Gibson v Police Authority for Northern Ireland and others* FET 15 September 2006, case no: 00406/00, although as an ET level case in Northern Ireland, it is only illustrative.

or free-market Capitalism.[118] Mere affiliation with or belief in a political party is unlikely to be covered, as distinct from a belief in a political philosophy aligned with such a party.[119]

14.93 It does not matter that no one else shares the religious or philosophical belief in question.[120] A religious belief can be intensely personal and subjective. As long as a belief is asserted in good faith, it need not be shared by others for it to be a religious belief, nor need it be a mandatory requirement of an established religion. For example, a Christian worker may believe she ought to wear a cross visibly over her clothing, even though she knows it is not required by scripture or as an article of faith.[121]

14.94 In general, people are allowed to believe what they like, however offensive, shocking or even disturbing to others. Criterion v) above from the *Grainger* case would therefore only exclude the most extreme beliefs akin to Nazism or totalitarianism.[122] There was much recent publicity surrounding the *Forstater* case, where the EAT said that belief that sex was immutable and binary (sometimes known as gender-critical belief) was a protected belief. However, the fact that a religion or belief is protected is not the end of the story. In *Forstater*, the EAT was at pains to stress that it does not mean those with gender-critical beliefs can indiscriminately and gratuitously refer to trans people in terms other than they would wish. Depending on the circumstances, such conduct could be discrimination against or harassment of a trans person. Most religion or belief discrimination claims depend not so much on whether the religion or belief is protected, but on whether the employer's treatment of the worker is discriminatory. That is a different – and difficult – question, as is discussed below.

Direct religion or belief discrimination

14.95 The definition of direct discrimination and general principles are explained in chapter 13. It is important to read those paragraphs before reading this chapter. Direct discrimination is where the worker is

---

118 *Grainger plc and others v Nicholson* UKEAT/0219/09; [2010] IRLR 4; *GMB v Henderson* UKEAT/0073/14; [2015] IRLR 451.

119 See comments of Burton J in *Grainger* (previous note).

120 *Grainger plc and others v Nicholson* UKEAT/0219/09; [2010] IRLR 4.

121 *Eweida v British Airways plc* UKEAT/0123/08; [2009] IRLR 78. NB this case went to the Court of Appeal, but not on this point. See also para 14.120 onwards for the human rights aspect of this.

122 *Forstater v CGD Europe and others (Index on Censorship and another intervening)* UKEAT/0105/20; [2021] IRLR 706.

treated less favourably because of religion or belief. It includes situations where the discriminator is of the same religion as the worker, but discriminates against the worker because of the latter's lack of religious belief on an aspect of an otherwise shared faith.[123] The EqA 2010 also covers discrimination against a worker because of someone else's religion or belief (or lack of religion or belief), eg because the worker has Muslim friends or because s/he refuses to carry out an employer's instruction to discriminate against Muslims. However, the EAT has said that the EqA 2010 does not cover discrimination against a worker because of the discriminator's own religion or belief.[124]

14.96   There is a difference between where a worker is less favourably treated simply because s/he holds or manifests a protected belief, and where s/he is less favourably treated because s/he has manifested the belief in some objectionable way. The latter is not direct religion or belief discrimination because the employer's reason for acting is the objectionable manifestation, eg removing a non-executive director of an NHS Trust from post because he expressed views on the national media which risked putting off gay people with mental health difficulties from using the Trust's services.[125]

14.97   There have been cases where workers have been dismissed because they have expressed religious views uninvited to service-users or customers of the employer. Such dismissals will not necessarily be unfair where workers have been warned of the organisation's policy and there is a good reason for it. It is also unlikely to be religious discrimination unless the employer would not have dismissed a worker of a different religion or no religion in equivalent circumstances. Dismissing a worker for promoting his/her religion is not direct religious discrimination in itself. There is a distinction between manifestation of a religious belief and inappropriate promotion of that belief.[126]

14.98   Obviously, restricting freedom of speech about deeply held beliefs cannot be done lightly, and whether it is justified depends on the facts. But under both the EqA 2010 and the ECHR, the freedom to

---

123 *Gan Menachem Hendon Limited v De Groen* UKEAT/0059/18; [2019] IRLR 410.

124 *Gan Menachem Hendon Limited v De Groen* UKEAT/0059/18; [2019] IRLR 410. See commentary in IRLR highlights as to whether the EAT was correct in believing it had to follow *Lee v Ashers Baking Co Ltd* [2018] IRLR 1116, SC on this point.

125 *Page v NHS Trust Development Authority* [2021] EWCA Civ 255; [2021] IRLR 391.

126 *Chondol v Liverpool City Council* UKEAT/0298/08; *Wasteney v East London NHS Foundation Trust* UKEAT/0157/15; [2016] IRLR 388; *Kuteh v Dartford and Gravesham NHS Trust*, [2019] EWCA Civ 818; [2019] IRLR 716.

express religious or other beliefs cannot be unlimited. There are circumstances in which it is right to expect those who work for an institution, especially in a high-profile position, to accept some limitations on how they express their beliefs in public on particularly sensitive matters.[127]

Indirect religion or belief discrimination

14.99 The definition of indirect discrimination is set out in respect of all the protected characteristics in chapter 13. Any unjustifiable restriction on religious practices, eg dress requirements or Sabbath working, may be indirect religious discrimination.[128]

14.100 To prove indirect discrimination, a worker only needs to prove s/he was manifesting his/her religion and not that s/he was actually at a disadvantage because s/he believed s/he must follow the practice required.[129] S/he does, however, need to show some level of group disadvantage, ie that the employer's rules disadvantage not only him/her but also some others of the same religion or belief. This may be a problem where the worker holds a very subjective and personal belief which is not strictly speaking part of the requirements of his/her religion. For example, in *Eweida*, a Christian worker believed she should wear a cross visibly over her clothes, but was unable to prove that other Christians would hold the same views. It would not be enough if she could find one or two other like-minded souls who shared this belief. It must be possible to make some general statements which would be true about a religious group such that an employer ought reasonably to be able to appreciate that any particular PCP may have disparate adverse impact on the group. It is necessary to find some identifiable section of the workforce, even a small one, which would suffer the same disadvantage as the claimant.[130] Despite the subsequent decision of the ECtHR in *Eweida*,[131] where for the purposes of deciding if Ms Eweida's human rights were breached, it was not necessary to prove group disadvantage, the Court of Appeal

---

127 *Page v NHS Trust Development Authority* [2021] EWCA Civ 255; [2021] IRLR 391. For a discussion of human rights in this context, see para 14.120 onwards.

128 See appendix B and paras 14.118–14.126 for examples.

129 This is the effect of interpreting the EqA 2010 compatibly with the ECtHR. See *Eweida v British Airways plc* [2010] IRLR 322, CA; and paras 14.118–14.119.

130 *Eweida v British Airways plc* [2010] IRLR 322, CA.

131 For more detail, see paras 14.123–14.124.

has said it is not possible to interpret the EqA 2010 to avoid this requirement in an indirect discrimination claim.[132]

14.101 If a worker does prove individual and group disadvantage, the burden of proof will shift to the employer to justify applying the PCP as a proportionate means of achieving a legitimate aim. Although generally the more people who would be affected by a PCP, the harder it is to justify, this is not the case where a worker's right to manifest his/her religion under ECHR Article 9 applies. This is because the justification defence under the EqA 2010 must be read compatibly with Article 9. What matters is weighing up the worker's rights against the employer's legitimate aims. Paradoxically, it may even help the worker if few others would be affected by the PCP because his/her religious belief is unusual, since it might be easier for an employer to accommodate the worker if there are only a few other employees holding the belief than a large number.[133]

14.102 There can be difficulties where a worker does not want to perform certain duties because of his/her religion and this clashes with the rights of other protected groups, eg women or gay workers. Where a public employer wants to promote equal opportunities in its services, it may well be justifiable indirect discrimination for it to dismiss a worker who refuses to provide certain services, such as civil partnership ceremonies, for religious reasons.[134] Similarly, a provider of counselling services is likely to be justified in dismissing a worker who will not provide sexual counselling to same-sex couples.[135] Unless evidence shows otherwise, it is also unlikely to be direct discrimination, because the employer would probably also have dismissed someone not of that religion who similarly refused to provide the services in question.

Harassment: religion or belief

14.103 Harassment in relation to all the protected characteristics is set out from para 13.81 onwards. In relation to religion and belief, the ACAS Guidance says it can include bullying, nicknames, threats, intrusive or inappropriate questions, insults, excluding someone, unwanted

---

132 *MBA v Mayor and Burgesses of Merton LBC* [2014] IRLR 145, CA. The Court of Appeal in *Gray v Mulberry Company (Design) Ltd* [2019] EWCA Civ 1720; [2020] IRLR 29 agreed (para 41).

133 *MBA v Mayor and Burgesses of Merton LBC* [2014] IRLR 145, CA. See also *Trayhorn v SOS Justice* UKEAT/0304/16 on the issue of group disadvantage.

134 *Ladele v Islington LBC and Liberty (intervenor)* [2010] IRLR 211, CA.

135 *McFarlane v Relate Avon Ltd* [2010] IRLR 196, EAT and [2010] IRLR 872, CA.

jokes and/or gossip. It is no defence to say the behaviour was unintended or that the comments were 'banter'.

14.104　Harassment may not be targeted at the individual but may consist of a general culture, eg which tolerates the telling of religious jokes. The harassment need not be because of the worker's own religion or belief; it can be because of that of a friend, relative or work colleague. Examples of harassment, deliberate or unintentional, could be:

- anti-Muslim remarks or so-called 'jokes' and 'banter' referring to terrorist attacks, or demonstrating general prejudice towards Muslims as a group (Islamophobia);
- allowing excessive expression of overt football allegiances where these are a proxy for sectarian rivalry, eg as may happen in Glasgow as between Celtic and Rangers fans;
- harassing Jewish workers because of their (perceived) support for Israel; allowing hostility towards the State of Israel to develop into an atmosphere of anti-Semitism;[136]
- a devout Christian haranguing colleagues for being insufficiently religious.

Exceptions: Where religion or belief discrimination is allowed

Occupational requirements

14.105　The occupational requirement exception applicable to all protected characteristics is set out in chapter 13.

Religious ethos

14.106　An employer with an ethos based on religion or belief may require a worker to be of a particular religion or belief if the employer can prove that, having regard to that ethos and to the nature or context of the work:

- it is an occupational requirement;
- the application of the requirement is a proportionate means of achieving a legitimate aim; and

---

136 On this sensitive issue, there is an interesting discussion in the report of the House of Commons Home Affairs Committee on *Antisemitism in the UK*, October 2016, available at: www.publications.parliament.uk/pa/cm201617/cmselect/cmhaff/136/136.pdf.

- the worker does not meet that requirement (or the employer has reasonable grounds for not being satisfied that the worker meets it).[137]

14.107 This exception applies to discrimination in recruitment arrangements and job offers, access to promotion, transfer or training or any other benefit, facility or service, and dismissal. The need for the requirement to be 'proportionate' suggests that whereas, eg a Roman Catholic school may be able to insist on its teachers being Roman Catholic, it may not be able to so insist with cleaners or gardeners.

Special situations

Dress codes and appearance

14.108 The ACAS Guidance has a section on dress code and appearance. Many religions have obligations in terms of dress and appearance. How people dress will depend on their level of observance. Examples of religious dress are as follows:

- As part of the five Ks of their faith, strictly practising male Sikhs do not shave or cut their hair, which is covered with a turban. They wear a 'Kara' (metal bracelet) and a 'Kirpan' (short ceremonial sword under clothing).
- Many Sikh women cover their hair with a scarf ('dupattah' or 'chooni').
- Rastafarians wear uncut hair, plaited into dreadlocks. They often wear a hat (usually red, gold and green).
- Muslim men usually wear western shirts and trousers (not shorts), though a few may wear traditional dress. Some men will keep their heads covered at all times. Many Muslim men also grow a beard, which is considered obligatory within some schools of thought.
- Muslim women may dress modestly, covering arms and legs. Some may wear a 'hijab' (headscarf). More unusually, in some communities, women may wear a 'burqa' or 'chador', which covers them from head to ankle and conceals the shape of their body. Muslims may wear jewellery signifying marriage or religious devotion.
- Many Hindu women wear modest dress, covering their legs, eg a sari or top over loose trousers. They often wear a 'bindi' (a red dot on the forehead). Many married women wear a necklace ('mangal sutra') or other wedding jewellery, eg bangles or nose rings, as well as a wedding ring.

137 EqA 2010 Sch 9 para 3.

- Some Hindu men wear a small tuft of hair ('shikha') similar to a ponytail, although this is often hidden under the remaining hair.
- Orthodox Jewish men keep their head covered at all times, usually wearing a skullcap ('kappel', 'kippah' or 'yarmulke'). Orthodox women will dress modestly, avoiding trousers or short sleeves and skirts. They may cover their heads with a scarf.

14.109   Differential rules may amount to direct discrimination, eg if the employer allows a Jewish man to wear a kappel but does not allow a Muslim woman to wear a headscarf (or vice versa). If an employer applies a general rule that, eg, no one can wear a head covering (whether for religious reasons or otherwise), there is unlikely to be direct discrimination.

14.110   Employers imposing rigid dress codes forbidding jewellery, head-wear, beards or long hair for men, or who impose uniforms with short sleeves or skirts, may indirectly discriminate against members of certain religious groups. Whether or not it is unlawful will usually depend on the employer's reason for imposing the rule. Reasons such as safety or hygiene are the most likely justification, but there are non-discriminatory ways around most difficulties. In one well-publicised case,[138] the EAT upheld an ET decision that it was justifiable to require a bilingual support worker to remove her veil when teaching school pupils, so that children could receive optimal communication from visual clues. This is not to say that an employer could justify refusing to allow the veil in other jobs. Headscarves are a different matter and it is hard to think of many jobs where a prohibition would be justifiable. Although the CJEU recently stated that it would be justifiable for an employer to tell a Muslim woman she could not wear a veil in a public-facing role as part of a cross-the-board 'neutrality' policy applied for business reasons, this was in relation to employment in Belgium and France.[139] In the UK, there is not the same tradition of secularism in the public arena. Moreover, the weight given to business reasons as a justification is contrary to the ruling of the ECtHR in *Eweida* (see para 14.100). Note that the Employment Act 1989 exempts turban-wearing Sikhs from any statutory requirements to wear safety helmets at work. This exception

---

138 *Azmi v Kirklees Metropolitan Council* [2007] IRLR 485, EAT.

139 *Achbita v G4S Secure Solutions NV* C-157/15; [2017] IRLR 466, CJEU; *Bougnaoui v Association de défense des droits de l'homme (ADDH) and Micropole SA* C-188/15, [2017] IRLR 447, CJEU. More recently, the CJHEU took a similar but more nuanced approach to justification in two German cases: *IX v WABE eV* Case C-804/18; *MH Muller Handels GmbH v MJ* Case C-341/19.

must not be taken as discrimination against any non-Sikh. It is also unjustifiable indirect discrimination for an employer to insist that a Sikh wear a safety helmet, provided the employer has no reasonable grounds for believing the person would not wear a turban at work at all times. These exceptions do not apply if the Sikh is working in an occupation involving response to fire, riot or other hazardous situations.[140] For the position regarding the wearing of a veil in a tribunal hearing, see para 21.79.

Prayer breaks

14.111 Observant Muslims need to pray five times per day at fixed times. The times are: dawn; just after midday; mid-afternoon; immediately after sunset; and at night, just before going to bed. The number of occasions which fall at work therefore depends on the worker's shifts and the season. The prayer breaks take about ten minutes on each occasion, the same time it may take any worker to make coffee, have a chat or go to the toilet. Devout Hindus may also pray three times per day: at sunrise, noon and sunset.

14.112　Unjustified refusal to allow time off to pray will be indirect discrimination. It is difficult to see how such a refusal could be justified, although if the employer refuses to allow any workers to take breaks of any kind, the worker may have to offer to make up the time. It is helpful that a worker is entitled to at least one 20-minute break away from the work station after six hours under the Working Time Regulations 1998 (see para 4.84). If the employer allows other workers to take breaks for different reasons, eg cigarette breaks, refusal of a prayer break may also be direct discrimination.

14.113　Employers are probably not required to provide a prayer room, but if there is an available quiet space, it would almost certainly be discriminatory not to allow the worker to use it. The ACAS Guidance makes some recommendations about enabling prayer at pages 14–15.

Sabbath working

14.114 Workers may need certain days off for religious holidays (para 14.116) or because of the Sabbath. The Muslim holy day is Friday and many Muslim men try to attend midday prayer at a mosque every Friday. For Jewish people, the Sabbath ('Shabbat') is Saturday, but it starts at sundown on Friday. Observant Jews must arrive at home before

---

140 Employment Act 1989 ss11 and 12. The employer's liability for injury to the worker is as a consequence restricted.

Sabbath begins, which means leaving work in the early afternoon during winter. A requirement to work Friday, Saturday or Sunday may therefore indirectly discriminate against certain workers. Whether or not such a requirement is justifiable is likely to depend on the nature of the job and whether other arrangements can be made.[141]

14.115 There are also long-standing rules under the Employment Rights Act (ERA) 1996, allowing shop and betting workers to refuse to work on Sundays (see para 6.97).

Religious holidays and time off

14.116 Every religion has a range of holidays of varying importance. Each individual will have his/her own feelings as to which holidays s/he feels obliged to observe. Very often the holidays are part of a cultural as well as a religious tradition, and there are social and family pressures to observe the day, even if the individual is not particularly religious. The dates of the holidays can be hard to ascertain in advance, as many follow the lunar year. Jewish holidays start at sundown the previous evening. Advance dates of Jewish holidays can be found on specialist websites.[142]

14.117 Some religious holidays are as follows:

- The two most important festivals for Muslims are Eid-al-Fitr, which marks the end of Ramadan; and Eid-al-Adha, of which the exact date depends on a sighting of the new moon and is not known far in advance. 'Eid' means festival. Muslim workers would need at least one day off on each occasion to celebrate appropriately.
- Major Hindu festivals include Divali (or Deepavali) in October/ November; which marks the end of the Hindu year; Holi (in February/March); Raksha bandhan (in August); and Navratri (in September/October).
- The main Sikh festivals include the Birthday of Guru Nanak (in October/November); Vaisakhi, the New Year festival, normally on 13 April; and Bandhi Chhord (October/November), at the same time as Divali – many Sikhs celebrate both.
- There are 13 key days which a minority of observant Jews would follow. The most important and universally observed dates requiring time off work are Yom Kippur (the Day of Atonement) and Rosh Hashannah (the New Year). These fall in September/

---

141 For an example where a Sunday-working requirement was justified, see *Mba v Mayor and Burgesses of Merton LBC* [2014] IRLR 145, CA. For the position under the HRA 1998, see para 14.120 onwards.

142 For example: www.jewishgen.org/jos/.

October. Pesach (or Passover), near Easter, and Chanukah, near
Christmas, are also commonly celebrated. Other holidays include
Sukkot, Shavuot and Tish'ah B'av.
- Greek Orthodox Easter is a different date from that usually
observed for Easter by other Christian religions.

14.118   Not all religious holidays require time off work, but most do.
Difficulties arise when employers object to granting time off, saying
that the worker has benefited from time off over Christmas and
Easter. This is rather unfair when such holidays are traditional bank
holidays for all workers regardless of their religion. In most circumstances, refusal to allow the worker time off for a religious holiday
would be discriminatory. It should not be underestimated how
important many of these religious holidays are to the individual and
his/her family. The question is whether the time should be paid or
unpaid, or whether it should come out of the worker's annual holiday
entitlement. Legally, this is difficult to answer. Requiring the time to
come out of existing holiday entitlement is arguably indirect discrimination, because the worker is disadvantaged by using up one of his/
her holiday days to meet religious obligations, which may not even
be of a recreational or festive nature (eg a fast day). It all depends on
whether a tribunal would think such an arrangement was justifiable.
The best solution may be to allow paid leave. Arguably this discriminates against those who are not of a religion requiring additional
holidays, but it is doubtful this is a comparable situation. It is thought-
less, unfair and possibly discriminatory to fix social events, important meetings or one-off training on important religious holidays.
Dates should routinely be checked in advance.

Sources of further information

14.119   The Muslim Council of Britain has produced *Muslims in the workplace – a good practice guide for employers and employees.*[143] The Board
of Deputies of British Jews has published *The Employer's guide to
Judaism.*[144]

---

143   March 2005. Available at: www.mcb.org.uk/wp-content/uploads/2014/06/
Muslims-in-the-Workplace.pdf. Though the law is out of date, the practical
examples are still useful.
144   2004, revised 2015, available at: www.bod.org.uk/wp-content/uploads/2021/
01/Employers-Guide-to-Judaism2.pdf.

Religion, belief and human rights

14.120 Under the HRA 1998, the tribunals and higher courts must interpret the EqA 2010 so far as is possible to give effect to the rights imposed by the articles of the ECHR.[145] Articles 9 (freedom of thought, conscience and religion) and 10 (freedom of expression) are particularly relevant to religion and belief discrimination. Article 11 (the right to freedom of association with others) may also be relevant. In recent years there has been a few religion and belief cases taken directly to the ECtHR in Strasbourg where employees have lost their discrimination claims in the domestic courts.[146] This is really only a practical option where there is financial backing from some kind of organisation or campaign group.

14.121 Article 9 says that everyone has the right to freedom of thought, conscience and religion, and to manifest their religion or belief in public or private in worship, teaching, practice and observance. Not every action which is inspired, motivated or influenced by a religion or belief constitutes a 'manifestation' of it. The act in question must be 'intimately linked' to the religion or belief. There needs to be 'a sufficiently close and direct nexus between the act and the underlying belief'.[147]

14.122 The freedom to manifest one's religion or beliefs is a qualified right, ie under Article 9(2) it is subject to such limitations as are prescribed by law and are necessary in a democratic society in the interests of public safety, for the protection of public order, health or morals, or for the protection of the rights and freedoms of others.

14.123 The most notable religion and belief case decided in recent years by the ECtHR was brought jointly by four Christian employees: Eweida, Chaplin, Ladele and McFarlane.[148] All of these had ultimately lost their claims in the UK courts for indirect religious discrimination under the EqA 2010 because the employers' requirements had been found to be justifiable.[149] However, Ms Eweida had primarily lost because she could not prove any group disadvantage, ie although she was personally disadvantaged because she was not allowed to

---

145 See chapter 3 for a general overview to the ECHR and the HRA 1998.

146 Most notably *Eweida v United Kingdom* 48420/10, [2013] IRLR 231 ECtHR and *Redfearn v UK* [2013] IRLR 51, ECtHR.

147 48420/10, [2013] IRLR 231 ECtHR. Discussed and applied in [2021] EWCA Civ 255.

148 *Eweida, Chaplin, Ladele, McFarlane v UK* [2013] IRLR 231, ECtHR.

149 See para 14.102 on *Ladele* and *McFarlane*.

wear a cross visibly over her uniform, she was unable to prove that any other Christians would take that as a disadvantage.

14.124   The ECtHR considered whether there was a breach of Article 9. The issue of group disadvantage did not arise because of the different wording of Article 9 compared with the stages of indirect discrimination under the EqA 2010 (see comments at para 14.100). Under Article 9, the key questions were whether the employees were 'manifesting' their beliefs and if so, whether interference with their right to do so was allowed under the wording of Article 9(2). The ECtHR rejected the approach it had taken in the past, which said that if there is a problem reconciling working hours with religious belief, a worker can simply find alternative employment.[150]

14.125   The ECtHR upheld Ms Eweida's claim, essentially because it thought the UK courts had given too much weight to the employer's (British Airways (BA)) reasons (corporate image) for not letting her wear her cross. The cross was discreet, it did not detract from corporate image, and anyway, BA had allowed others to wear turbans and hijabs, and it had subsequently decided to amend its uniform code, which showed the rule had not been of crucial importance. By contrast, the ECtHR thought the UK courts were entitled to say the employer was justified in insisting Ms Chaplin remove her cross because of health and safety risks on a hospital ward.

14.126   As for Ms Ladele and Mr Macfarlane, the employers were also justified in their actions. The UK courts had a great deal of discretion in striking a balance between competing Convention rights, and it was important to avoid discrimination against people because of their sexual orientation.

14.127   The ECtHR decisions in these religious cases may provide useful guidance which can be applied to whether indirect religious discrimination under the EqA 2010 is justified. For example, more weight was given by the ECtHR to health and safety reasons for imposing a uniform code than corporate image. It was also very keen to avoid discrimination against people because of their sexual orientation. The ECtHR also said that it is not conclusive – although it is a factor to be considered whether a worker has taken on a job knowing in advance of the restriction on their religious practices or whether the issue only arises unexpectedly later.

14.128   Article 9 requires that, when assessing justification, a tribunal should take into account the impact of the PCP on the individual. The incorporation of this into the EqA 2010 is discussed more fully

150 For example, see *Copsey v WBB Devon Clays Ltd* [2005] IRLR 811, CA.

at para 14.101. It may also be significant that, whereas indirect discrimination law weighs the discriminatory impact against the employer's needs, Article 9 weighs it against the needs of the community generally. It seems that there must be a slight shift in emphasis in any evaluation under the EqA 2010 if a worker's human rights are to form part of the equation.

Sex

Historical and European contexts

14.129 Discrimination because of sex was previously covered by the SDA 1975. Sex discrimination in pay and contract terms was dealt with by the EqPA 1970. The EqPA 1970 was structured quite differently from the SDA 1975. These separate structures are retained in the EqA 2010.[151]

14.130 Until replaced by the EHRC in October 2007, the body with a remit to oversee the operation of the SDA 1975 and the EqPA 1970 was the Equal Opportunities Commission (EOC). The EOC issued various Codes of Practice under the SDA 1975. These have now been replaced by single codes applying to all the protected characteristics and are referred to elsewhere in this book.

14.131 The longest tradition of European discrimination law has been in the field of sex discrimination and equal pay. The key legislation is:

- Article 157 of the Treaty of the Functioning of the European Union (formerly Article 119 of the Treaty of Rome, then Article 141), which lays down the principle of equal pay for equal work.
- The Recast Directive. This came into effect on 15 August 2006. Its full name is the Directive on Equality between Men and Women in Matters of Employment and Occupation (Recast).[152] It consolidated the seven previous directives dealing with equality between men and women in employment, including the Equal Treatment Directive[153] and the Equal Pay Directive,[154] together with interpretative case-law. The individual directives which it replaced were repealed with effect from 15 August 2009.

---

151 Chapter 5 deals with equal pay.
152 2006/54/EC.
153 76/207/EEC.
154 75/117/EEC.

For an introduction to the effect of Brexit on the applicability of EU law, see chapter 3 above.

14.132   In the financial year 2020/21, 5,172 sex discrimination claims were started, excluding equal pay claims, but including claims for discrimination related to marriage, civil partnership and gender reassignment.[155]

The protected characteristic of sex

14.133   Under EqA 2010 s11, 'sex' is a protected characteristic and means being a man or being a woman.

Direct sex discrimination

14.134   The definition of direct discrimination and general principles are explained in chapter 13. It is important to read those paragraphs before reading this chapter. Dress codes are referred to in para 13.9. It is not sex discrimination against a man to give a woman special treatment in connection with pregnancy or childbirth.[156] However, this only applies if the special treatment goes no further than is reasonably necessary to compensate the woman for any disadvantage occasioned by her being pregnant or on maternity leave.[157]

Indirect sex discrimination

14.135   The definition of indirect discrimination is set out in respect of all the protected characteristics in chapter 13. Indirect sex discrimination most commonly arises in the context of employment requirements which interfere with childcare, eg requirements for full-time working, flexible hours and mobility. These are discussed in chapter 11. Note also that the Part-time Workers (Prevention of Less Favourable Treatment) Regulations 2000 prohibit discrimination against part-timers, regardless of their sex or marital status.[158] Length of service requirements also tend to disadvantage women, who may build up less service due to childcare breaks.

---

155 Issued as quarterly statistics, but set out for the full year. See 'Main tables (January – March 2021)' at www.gov.uk/government/statistics/tribunal-statistics-quarterly-january-to-march-2021.

156 EqA 2010 s13(6)(b).

157 *Eversheds Legal Services Ltd v De Belin* UKEAT/0352/10 and UKEAT/0444/10; [2011] IRLR 488.

158 See chapter 11.

Harassment: sex

Overview

14.136 Sexual harassment in the workplace has gained increased attention over the past few years, partly as a result of the #MeToo movement. In July 2018, the House of Commons Women and Equalities Committee published a report on *Sexual harassment in the workplace*[159] suggesting that it is an everyday common occurrence, with the vast majority of incidents never reported. EHRC research has also reported on the lack of consistent effective action by too many employers.[160] The EHRC has produced *Preventing sexual harassment at work: a guide for employers* (January 2020) and *Sexual harassment and harassment at work – Technical guidance* (January 2020).[161] In July 2021, the government published a response to its consultation on sexual harassment in the workplace.[162] It plans to produce guidance for employers and also to support the EHRC in producing a statutory code of practice on sexual harassment. The government also says it will legislate to introduce workplace protections against third-party harassment. Non-disclosure agreements on settling tribunal claims are a particular problem in sexual harassment cases. ACAS has published guidance discouraging their routine use.[163] On a different but related topic, the government intends to look at ways to support workers in the workplace who have been subjected to domestic abuse.[164]

159 At: https://publications.parliament.uk/pa/cm201719/cmselect/ cmwomeq/725/725.pdf. The government's response is at https://publications. parliament.uk/pa/cm201719/cmselect/cmwomeq/1801/1801.pdf.

160 *Turning the tables: ending sexual harassment at work*, EHRC, 27 March 2018 is available at: www.equalityhumanrights.com/en/publication-download/ turning-tables-ending-sexual-harassment-work. See also the TUC's *Still just a bit of banter? Sexual harassment in the workplace in 2016* at: www.tuc.org.uk/ sites/default/files/SexualHarassmentreport2016.pdf.

161 Both available via links at https://equalityhumanrights.com/en/publication-download/sexual-harassment-and-harassment-work-technical-guidance.

162 *Consultation on sexual harassment in the workplace: government response*, July 2021 at www.gov.uk/government/consultations/consultation-on-sexual-harassment-in-the-workplace/outcome/consultation-on-sexual-harassment-in-the-workplace-government-response.

163 At www.acas.org.uk/acas-publishes-new-guidance-on-non-disclosure-agreements-ndas.

164 *Workplace support for victims of domestic abuse: review report*, 14 January 2021 at www.gov.uk/government/publications/workplace-support-for-victims-of-domestic-abuse/workplace-support-for-victims-of-domestic-abuse-review-report-accessible-webpage.

14.137   The law on harassment in relation to all the protected characteristics is set out from para 13.81 onwards. There are three definitions
of harassment which can apply to gender:

a) the general definition applicable to all protected characteristics;

and then two further definitions applicable only to sex and gender
reassignment:

b) unwanted conduct of a sexual nature; and
c) harassment because of rejection of submission to the conduct.

Chapter 7 of the EHRC Employment Code deals with harassment.

The general definition: conduct related to sex

14.138 The general definition of harassment refers to unwanted conduct
related to sex which has the purpose or effect of violating the worker's
dignity or creating an intimidating, hostile, degrading, humiliating
or offensive environment for the worker.[165] The meaning of this is
discussed generally at para 13.81 onwards, which should be read
first.

Conduct of a sexual nature

14.139 The second definition of harassment is unwanted conduct of a sexual
nature which has the same purpose or effect as in the general definition.[166] This definition obviously overlaps to a large extent with the
general definition. The EHRC Employment Code says conduct of a
sexual nature can cover verbal, non-verbal or physical conduct including unwelcome sexual advances, touching, forms of sexual assault,
sexual jokes, displaying pornographic pictures or sending emails
with material of a sexual nature.[167]

14.140   As already discussed at para 13.91, where the conduct is not done
with the purpose of violating the worker's dignity etc, it will still be
unlawful if it has that effect. However, in the latter case, it is not
simply a question of whether the worker felt his/her dignity violated
etc. It is also a question of whether it is reasonable for the conduct to
have that effect, taking account of the circumstances as well as the
worker's own perception.[168] This rather controversial test is designed
to prevent situations where a 'hypersensitive' worker might be upset

165 EqA 2010 s26(1).
166 EqA 2010 s26(2).
167 EHRC Employment Code, para 7.13.
168 EqA 2010 s26(4).

by something which no one else would consider to be offensive in any way.

14.141 There have been few reported cases regarding when it would be 'reasonable' for sexual harassment to have the unlawful effect on the worker. Most of the case-law was decided before the specific definition of harassment was introduced into the SDA 1975, at a time when harassment needed to fit within the definition of direct discrimination causing an unlawful detriment. Many of the principles in those earlier cases would still apply, but it is important always to remember the difference in the wording of the definitions, the fact that the specific offence of harassment is more widely defined than direct discrimination, and also the difference in the definition between cases where the harasser's purpose was to cause the unlawful effect and those where it was not.

14.142 With that cautionary note, some of the older cases regarding what amounts to a 'detriment' may be useful when considering what kind of conduct a tribunal would think a worker was reasonable to be upset by. A single incident of harassment can amount to a detriment 'provided it is sufficiently serious'. A one-off racist or sexist remark can be made worse by the surrounding circumstances, eg an offensive or demeaning sexual comment made by a junior employee to a supervisor in front of others could be unlawful.[169] Where there is a series of incidents, it is important not to look at each one separately, since there can be a cumulative effect which exceeds the sum of each incident.[170] Incidents trivial in themselves can acquire a measure of seriousness if they appear to be recurrent.[171] Once a man has shown unwelcome sexual interest in a female employee, other incidents which would normally appear quite unobjectionable, eg asking to look at personal photographs, can take on a different significance.[172]

Unwanted

14.143 A big issue which tends to arise in harassment cases, and particularly acutely on sexual harassment claims, is whether the conduct was indeed 'unwanted'. It may be easier for a woman to prove it was

---

169 *Insitu Cleaning Co Ltd v Heads* [1995] IRLR 4, EAT.
170 *Reed and Bull Information Systems Ltd v Stedman* [1999] IRLR 299, EAT.
171 *Scott v Commissioners of Inland Revenue* [2004] IRLR 713, CA, obiter.
172 *Reed and Bull Information Systems Ltd v Stedman* [1999] IRLR 299, EAT.

unwanted if she objected at the time, but there are many reasons why she may not have done so.[173]

Harassment because of rejection of or submission to the conduct

14.144 The third definition of harassment is where the worker is treated less favourably because s/he rejected or submitted to unwanted conduct of a sexual nature or that is related to gender reassignment or sex.[174]

Exceptions

Occupational requirements

14.145 The occupational requirement exception applicable to all protected characteristics is set out in chapter 13, though in relation to sex, it does not cover dismissal. Occupational requirements may be used to preserve decency and privacy, eg a gym could require a changing room attendant to be of the same sex as the users of that room. Similarly, a women's refuge could require all its staff members to be women.[175]

Religious requirements

14.146 An employer may apply a requirement to be of a particular sex, if s/he can show:

- the employment is for the purposes of an organised religion;
- the application of the requirement engages the compliance or non-conflict principle; and
- the worker to whom the employer applies the requirement does not meet it (or the employer has reasonable grounds for not being satisfied that the person meets it).[176]

The 'compliance principle' occurs where the requirement is applied so as to comply with the doctrines of the religion. The 'non-conflict principle' applies where, because of the nature or context of the employment, the requirement is applied so as to avoid conflicting with the strongly held religious views of a significant number of the

---

173 See discussion at paras 13.88–13.90. Note that the obiter comments in the final para of *Reed and Bull Information Systems Ltd* (see previous footnote) on whether conduct is 'unwelcome' may have some relevance to 'purpose or effect' in the current definition, but not to whether conduct is unwanted.

174 EqA 2010 s26(3).

175 EHRC Employment Code, para 13.8.

176 EqA 2010 Sch 9 para 2.

religion's followers. For example, an orthodox synagogue could require its rabbi to be a man. This exception should only be used for a limited number of posts, eg ministers of religion and a small number of other posts, including those which exist to promote or represent the religion.[177] It is unlikely to cover jobs such as cleaners, or even teachers in religious schools. The term 'for the purposes of an organised religion' does not mean 'for the purposes of a religious organisation' such as a faith school.[178] This exception applies to discrimination in recruitment arrangements and job offers; access to promotion, transfer or training or any other benefit, facility or service; and dismissal.

Armed forces

14.147　The armed forces can require a person to be a man if that is a proportionate means of ensuring combat effectiveness.[179]

The menopause and work

14.148　Despite increased publicity over the last couple of years, the menopause often remains a taboo subject in the workplace, with few workplace policies covering the subject, and many women leaving their jobs because they cannot get the adjustments they need or do not feel able to ask. There is also evidence that where women do raise the matter, they can frequently be met with embarrassment, ignorance, inappropriate humour and sometimes hostility.

14.149　The menopause usually occurs between the ages of 45 and 55, but it can happen much earlier, and can typically last around four years. There is also a period of hormonal change leading up to the menopause known as the perimenopause, which can last several years in itself. The majority of women are unwilling to disclose menopause-related health problems to their managers, because of embarrassment, fear about how they will be seen, or lack of confidence that any help will be forthcoming. A 2019 survey conducted by BUPA and the Chartered Institute for Personnel and Development (CIPD) found that three in five menopausal women were negatively affected at work, and that almost 900,000 women in the UK left their jobs

177　EHRC Employment Code, paras 13.12–13.15.
178　On similar exception in previous legislation, see *R (Amicus – MSF section and others) v Secretary of State for Trade and Industry and Christian Action Research Education and others* [2004] IRLR 430, HC.
179　For precise scope of exception, see EqA 2010 Sch 9 para 4.

because of menopausal symptoms.[180] There have been many useful and practical guides from both sides of industry.[181] ACAS has issued guidance on the *Menopause at work*.[182]

14.150 The menopause is not a protected characteristic under the EqA 2010 and there is no piece of employment legislation specifically addressing it. This is the subject of some concern and in July 2021, the House of Commons Women and Equalities Committee launched an Inquiry to consider whether enough is being done in legislation and workplace practices.[183] In the meantime, women can only use existing employment law, most notably the law against sex, disability and age discrimination. This is an awkward fit and does not always match the facts and issues.

14.151 Menopause is not a disability. It is a natural life process. However, many menopausal symptoms, when sufficiently severe, fit the legal definition of disability in the EqA 2010. The section on the menopause in chapter 15 sets out some of the common symptoms of the menopause and considers how disability discrimination law may help. The following paragraphs discuss how sex and/or age discrimination law may apply.

14.152 It could be direct sex or age discrimination or sex or age-related harassment:

- to treat physical or mental health difficulties caused by the menopause less seriously or sympathetically than equivalent ill health of a male or younger female employee, eg failing to get an Occupational Health report;
- to use the term menopausal as if it is some kind of insult when talking about women of a particular age;

---

180 Cited by the Women and Equalities Committee when launching *Inquiry: Menopause and the workplace* at https://committees.parliament.uk/work/1416/menopause-and-the-workplace/.

181 Including *A guide to managing menopause at work – guidance for line managers*, CIPD / BUPA, May 2021 at www.cipd.co.uk/Images/line-manager-guide-to-menopause_tcm18-95174.pdf; *The menopause in the workplace – A toolkit for trade unionists*, Wales TUC Cymru at www.tuc.org.uk/sites/default/files/Wales_TUC_menopause_Toolkit.pdf; *Menopause and the workplace*, NHS Employers at www.nhsemployers.org/articles/menopause-and-workplace; *The menopause is a workplace issue: guidance and model policy*, UNISON at www.unison.org.uk/content/uploads/2019/10/25831.pdf.

182 At https://webarchive.nationalarchives.gov.uk/ukgwa/20210104111010/https://archive.acas.org.uk/index.aspx?articleid=6752.

183 *Inquiry: Menopause and the workplace* at https://committees.parliament.uk/work/1416/menopause-and-the-workplace/.

- to make or allow comments such as 'she is menopausal' or 'it must be that time of the month' when trying to suggest a woman is being irrational or difficult; but when a man behaves that way, just saying 'he must be having a bad day';
- to make constant remarks without any knowledge of a particular woman's situation, attributing matters to the menopause, eg when seeing an older woman sweat on a very hot day or when wearing heavy uniform, making jokes about hot flushes;
- not to promote or give particular projects to an older woman because of an assumption that she is or will soon be in the menopause and will be performing poorly as a result. For example, an older woman without menopausal symptoms reported in the *Guardian* that she received comments like 'I am worried about you because you're in your late 40s; you won't be able to do the night shift because you'll be menopausal and won't be sleeping and will be tired all the time'.[184] Although many women are severely affected by menopausal symptoms when at work, many others only have minor symptoms or none that cause any notable difficulty. It can be equally discriminatory to make negative comments and assumptions, regardless of whether a particular woman is in fact in the menopause or having any adverse effects.

14.153 It could be indirect sex discrimination, eg unjustifiably to require a menopausal worker to wear close-fitting, heavy or synthetic uniform or to work in a hot environment with no fans. Dismissing a woman because of capability or conduct issues which the woman says relate to her menopausal symptoms, without fairly taking that into account, may be unfair dismissal.

Sexual orientation

Historical and European contexts

14.154 In a TUC survey at the end of 1998 of 440 lesbian, gay and bisexual (LGB) workers, 44 per cent said they had suffered discrimination at work because of their sexuality. In the public sector trade union UNISON's survey in 2003, 52 per cent of its lesbian or gay members said they had experienced harassment for that reason. Yet despite

---

184 Examples given in *Guardian* article 17 August 2021: '*My bosses were happy to destroy me*' – *the women forced out of work by menopause* at www.theguardian.com/society/2021/aug/17/my-bosses-were-happy-to-destroy-me-the-women-forced-out-of-work-by-menopause.

evidence of the desperate need, no government was prepared to legislate against such discrimination until the intervention of Europe. A 2014 report by the Economic and Social Research Council said that LGB people were twice as likely to be bullied at work as their heterosexual colleagues.[185] According to a 2015 report by Stonewall, 26 per cent of LGB staff in health and social care services said they had personally experienced bullying or poor treatment from colleagues in the previous five years as a result of their sexual orientation.[186] A survey by the TUC in 2017 showed that while there were some positive experiences, bullying and harassment by colleagues, managers and customers were still rife. In addition, 23 per cent of gay workers had been outed against their will, 62 per cent had heard homophobic or biphobic remarks or so-called jokes directed at others and 28 per cent had had such comments directed towards themselves. Over half of those responding said the experience of discrimination and harassment had affected their mental health.[187] In a 2019 TUC survey, seven out of ten LGBT workers said they had experienced at least one type of sexual harassment at work, and almost one in eight LGBT women reported being sexually assaulted or raped at work; black, Asian and minority ethnic LGBT women were the most likely to be targeted.[188] Workplace research shows that whether, how and when to 'come out' at work is difficult for LGB workers to manage for a variety of reasons, not only because of fear of harassment, but because of uncertainty as to what reception they might receive.[189]

14.155   In 2000, the European General Framework Directive[190] came into effect, prohibiting discrimination in employment on grounds of sexual orientation as well as religion, disability and age. In order to implement the directive in respect of sexual orientation, the Employment Equality (Sexual Orientation) Regulations 2003[191] came

185 *The ups and downs of LGBs' workplace experiences: discrimination, bullying and harassment of lesbian, gay and bisexual employees in Britain,* Hoel, Lewis and Einarsdottir, 2014 at www.plymouth.ac.uk/uploads/production/document/path/11/11004/Hoel__Lewis_and_Einarsdottir__2014_.pdf.

186 *Unhealthy attitudes: the treatment of LGBT people within health and social care services,* 2015 at www.stonewall.org.uk/resources/unhealthy-attitudes-2015.

187 *The cost of being out at work: LGBT+ workers' experiences of harassment and discrimination,* 2017 at www.tuc.org.uk/research-analysis/reports/cost-being-out-work.

188 *Sexual harassment of LGBT people in the workplace,* TUC, April 2019 at www.tuc.org.uk/sites/default/files/LGBT_Sexual_Harassment_Report_0.pdf.

189 See eg *The ups and downs of LGBs' workplace experiences: discrimination, bullying and harassment of lesbian, gay and bisexual employees in Britain,* n187.

190 See para 12.7.

191 SI No 1661.

into force on 1 December 2003. For the anticipated effect of Brexit on the applicability of EU law, see chapter 3 above.

14.156　Until the EHRC came into being in 2007, there was no organisation with a statutory remit to oversee the working of sexual orientation discrimination law. Nor were there any statutory codes. There is now the EHRC Employment Code which relates to all the protected characteristics. In the financial year 2020/21, 438 sexual orientation discrimination claims were started.[192]

The protected characteristic of sexual orientation

14.157　Under EqA 2010 s12, 'sexual orientation' is one of the protected characteristics and means a person's sexual orientation towards people of the same sex, or towards those of the opposite sex or towards people of either sex. Sexual orientation discrimination covers discrimination against a worker because of his/her sexual orientation. It also covers discrimination because of the manifestation of that sexual orientation, eg a worker's appearance, places they visit or people they associate with.[193]

Direct sexual orientation discrimination

Overview

14.158　The definition of direct discrimination and general principles are explained in chapter 13. It is important to read those paragraphs before reading this chapter. When making a comparison with how an employer treats a colleague of a different sexual orientation, it is not a relevant difference between the circumstances of the worker and his/her colleague that one is a civil partner or married to someone of the same sex and the other is married to someone of the opposite sex.[194] It is not direct sexual orientation discrimination to treat someone less favourably because they support gay marriage. Many heterosexual people can and do also support gay marriage. The

---

192　Issued as quarterly statistics, but set out for the full year. See 'Main tables (January to March 2021)' at www.gov.uk/government/statistics/tribunal-statistics-quarterly-january-to-march-2021.

193　EHRC Employment Code, para 2.66. See also *R (Amicus – MSF section and others) v Secretary of State for Trade and Industry and Christian Action Research Education and others* [2004] IRLR 430, HC.

194　EqA 2010 s23(3)–(4); EHRC Employment Code, para 3.31 gives an example, though the code was written before amendments to s23 when same-sex marriage became possible.

comparison is with how the employer would treat a person who was not gay in similar circumstances.[195]

Not the worker's own sexual orientation

14.159   It is unlawful to discriminate because of a perception of the worker's sexual orientation, whether this is correct or false. A worker who is discriminated against because of a false perception that s/he is gay would therefore be protected. It also means that a worker may not need to disclose his/her actual sexual orientation when bringing an ET claim.[196] Discrimination against a worker because of someone else's sexual orientation is also covered, eg because s/he has gay friends or because s/he refuses to carry out an employer's instruction to discriminate against gay men or lesbians.[197]

Indirect sexual orientation discrimination

14.160   The definition of indirect discrimination is set out in respect of all the protected characteristics in chapter 13.

Harassment: sexual orientation

14.161   The general law on harassment in respect of all characteristics is set out at para 13.81 onwards. The TUC says the most common form of discrimination faced by lesbian and gay workers is harassment, and the majority of successful tribunal claims have concerned this. Harassment may comprise intentional and obvious bullying, or unintentional or subtle behaviour. It may involve nicknames, teasing, name-calling or other behaviour which is not intended to be malicious, but nevertheless is upsetting. It may not be targeted at the individual but may consist of a general culture, eg which tolerates the telling of homophobic jokes. Harassment can be based on the sexual orientation of the worker or of someone else, eg a friend or relative. It is also unlawful to harass someone on the misconception that they are gay or even using homophobic abuse when knowing perfectly well that they are not gay.[198]

---

195   *Lee v Ashers Baking Company Ltd and others* [2018] UKSC 49; [2018] IRLR IRLR 1116, SC.
196   However, workers bringing sexual orientation discrimination claims should probably work on the basis that they may in practice have to disclose their sexual orientation at some stage.
197   *Lisboa v (1) Realpubs Ltd (2) Pring (3) Heap* UKEAT/0224/10.
198   *English v Thomas Sanderson Ltd* [2008] EWCA Civ 1421; [2009] IRLR 206.

14.162   Examples of harassment, deliberate or unintentional, could be:

- 'outing' (ie revealing the sexuality of) a lesbian, gay or bisexual worker for malicious reasons or against his/her wishes;
- spreading rumours that a gay man has HIV just because he takes sick leave or loses weight (though one would hope this particular stereotype is less common now);
- where lesbian, gay or bisexual workers complain of harassment, accusing them of being oversensitive, having no sense of humour or bringing it on themselves by hiding (or revealing) their sexual orientation.

The fact that a gay worker has 'come out' does not mean that remarks or references to his/her sexuality thereafter cannot constitute discrimination. For example, subsequent remarks could be vicious or designed to embarrass the worker. However, it is difficult for a worker who has come out to certain colleagues, without asking them to keep it confidential, to say it is unlawful harassment if they then pass on that information in a non-malicious manner to other colleagues. Although a gay worker in that position may be upset that s/he was unable to take control of how and when s/he came out to the other colleagues, the definition of harassment requires more than being upset; it requires that the worker has had his/her dignity violated or that s/he has been subjected to an intimidating, hostile, degrading, humiliating or offensive environment.[199]

14.163   When the law against sexual orientation discrimination was introduced, much was made of the possible conflict with the law against religious discrimination. For example, can a worker be prevented from making homophobic observations if these are an expression of his/her religious views? In practice, this kind of case has rarely arisen. Making gratuitous offensive remarks is likely to be unlawful harassment. However, although some religions have strong views about sexual orientation, most do not advocate persecution of people because of their sexual orientation. Everyone has the right to be treated with dignity and respect in the workplace, whatever his/her race, sex, age, disability, religion or sexual orientation. Workers need not be friends, but they should treat each other professionally. What has been a greater problem is where some workers, because of their religious beliefs, have refused to provide civil partnership services or sexual counselling to same sex couples. The tribunals and appeal courts have found the dismissal of workers refusing to provide such

---

199 *Grant v HM Land Registry and Equality and Human Rights Commission (intervener)* [2011] EWCA Civ 769; [2011] IRLR 748.

services is not direct religious discrimination (where anyone else refusing to provide such services would also be dismissed) or indirect discrimination (where it is justifiable in view of the employer's ethos and commitment to equal opportunities for its client group).[200]

Exceptions

Occupational requirements

14.164   The occupational requirement exception applicable to all protected characteristics is set out in chapter 13.

Religious requirements

14.165   An employer may apply a requirement related to sexual orientation, if s/he can show:

- the employment is for the purposes of an organised religion;
- the application of the requirement engages the compliance or non-conflict principle; and
- the worker to whom the employer applies the requirement does not meet it (or the employer has reasonable grounds for not being satisfied that the person meets it).[201]

The 'compliance principle' occurs where the requirement is applied so as to comply with the doctrines of the religion. The 'non-conflict principle' applies where, because of the nature or context of the employment, the requirement is applied so as to avoid conflicting with the strongly held religious views of a significant number of the religion's followers. For example, an evangelical church could require its ministers to be heterosexual. This exception should only be used for a limited number of posts, eg ministers of religion and a small number of other posts, including those which exist to promote or represent the religion.[202] It is unlikely to cover jobs such as cleaners, or even teachers in religious schools. The term 'for the purposes of an organised religion' does not mean 'for the purposes of a religious

---

200 *Ladele v Islington LBC and Liberty (intervener)* [2010] IRLR 211, CA; *McFarlane v Relate Avon Ltd* [2010] IRLR 196, EAT and [2010] IRLR 872, CA. For the approach of the ECtHR see para 14.126.

201 EqA 2010 Sch 9 para 2.

202 EHRC Employment Code, paras 13.12–13.15. For an example of the exception applying to the withdrawal of a qualification to practise as a chaplain in an NHS Trust to a Church of England Priest because of his same-sex marriage, see *Reverend Canon Pemberton v Right Reverend Richard Inwood, former acting Bishop of Southwell and Nottingham* [2018] EWCA Civ 564; [2018] IRLR 542.

organisation' such as a faith school.[203] This exception applies to discrimination in recruitment arrangements and job offers, access to promotion, transfer or training or any other benefit, facility or service, and dismissal.

Benefits dependent on marital status

14.166 It is not unlawful sexual orientation discrimination to provide married people and civil partners access to benefits, facilities or services to the exclusion of others.[204]

Special considerations

14.167 Given that not all LGB workers choose to be 'out' to their managers, this would have implications for the nature of workplace policies, the purpose of monitoring, and the willingness of individuals to complain about discrimination or harassment. In the years since 2003, many employers have taken steps to make their workplaces more LGB-friendly. The EqA 2010 does not explicitly require employers to monitor sexual orientation, but the Welsh and Scottish Specific Duties require collating information on employees by reference to all the protected characteristics. How sexual orientation should be monitored and for what purpose are difficult questions given that, unlike with race and gender, workers may choose to hide their sexual orientation at work. There is guidance in the EHRC Employment Code at paras 15–20.

14.168 The statutory entitlements to dependant, parental, adoption and 'paternity' leave are all available where there are same-sex partners. Any additional benefits offered by the employer in internal policies should state that they are equally available to same-sex partners, eg compassionate and bereavement leave; parental and adoption leave; carers' leave; perks such as private healthcare insurance, free travel and discounts on company goods. Granting benefits only to those with heterosexual partners would probably be direct discrimination.

---

203 On similar exception in previous legislation, see *R (Amicus – MSF section and others) v Secretary of State for Trade and Industry and Christian Action Research Education and others* [2004] IRLR 430, HC.

204 EqA 2010 Sch 9 para 18.

CHAPTER 15

Disability

Chapter 15: Key points

- There is a complex definition of disability under the Equality Act (EqA) 2010. It can often cover workers who would not be seen by themselves or their employers as disabled, eg those with back injuries, depression and other temporary health problems.
- It is often necessary in a case to prove a worker has a disability even where that seems obvious.
- HIV, multiple sclerosis and cancer are deemed a disability on diagnosis. Those registered as blind or partially sighted are also automatically covered.
- Long Covid is potentially a disability, depending on its length and severity.
- Although the menopause should not be considered a disability, menopausal symptoms can sometimes meet the legal definition and thus gain the protection of disability discrimination law.
- Failure to make reasonable adjustment is at the heart of the EqA 2010. Employers are expected to make risk assessments and take proactive steps to assist a worker where reasonable adjustment is needed.
- An employer is not obliged to make reasonable adjustments if s/he does not know and cannot reasonably be expected to know the worker has a disability and that adjustments are required.
- Discrimination arising from disability (DAFD) involves discrimination because of something connected with the worker's disability. There is a potential justification defence.
- *Direct discrimination* means less favourable treatment because of disability. There is no justification defence.
- *Indirect disability discrimination* can be claimed where applicable, though it will only rarely be needed, as the duty to make reasonable adjustments covers most situations.
- *Victimisation* is where a worker is punished for complaining about discrimination.
- Public authorities must comply with the public sector equality duty (PSED) which includes a duty in respect of disability (see chapter 12).
- Guidance for running a discrimination case is at chapter 21. Evidence to prove disability discrimination is in chapter 16. Checklists are in appendix A.

Introduction

15.1　An overview of discrimination law, who is covered and the protected characteristics are set out in chapter 12. Chapter 13 explains the definitions of the different types of discrimination. This chapter expands on how the law applies in the case of disability. The other protected characteristics are covered in chapter 14.

Meaning of disability

Historical and European contexts

15.2　After several attempts at private members' bills, disability discrimination was finally made unlawful by the Disability Discrimination Act (DDA) 1995. The employment provisions did not come into force until December 1996.

15.3　　Until replaced by the Equality and Human Rights Commission (EHRC) in October 2007, the body with a remit to oversee the operation of the DDA 1995 was the Disability Rights Commission (DRC). The DRC issued various Codes of Practice under the DDA 1995. These have now been replaced by unified codes applying to all the protected characteristics. Most important for the purposes of this chapter is the EHRC's Employment Code.[1]

15.4　　In 2000, the European Council issued a Directive Establishing a General Framework for Equal Treatment in Employment and Occupation.[2] This is known as the 'General Framework Directive' or sometimes the 'Framework Employment Directive' or the 'Equal Treatment Framework Directive'. The directive forbids discrimination in employment on grounds of disability as well as a number of the other protected characteristics. For an introduction to the effect of Brexit on the applicability of EU Law, see chapter 3.

15.5　　On 8 June 2009, the UK ratified the UN Convention on the Rights of Persons with Disabilities together with the optional protocol. This was also approved by the EU in 2009 and where possible, the law must be interpreted consistently with the Convention.[3] To date it is

---

1　See chapter 12. EHRC Employment Statutory Code of Practice, available at: www.equalityhumanrights.com/en/publication-download/employment-statutory-code-practice.

2　2000/78/EC.

3　*HK Danmark (on behalf of Ring) v Dansk almennyttigt Boligselskab and another* C-335/11 and C-337/11, [2013] IRLR 571, CJEU.

not clear that this will create any additional rights in terms of the employment sphere except in relation to the definition of 'disability' (see para 15.34). It is also useful in relation to the duty of courts and tribunals to make reasonable adjustments (see para 21.73).

15.6   In the 2020/21 financial year, 7,430 disability discrimination claims were started.[4] Although disabled people are now more likely to be employed than they were in 2002, they are still significantly less likely to be in employment than non-disabled people. Mid 2018, for example, 51.3 per cent of working-age disabled people were in employment compared to 81.4 per cent of working-age non-disabled people.[5] There have been a large number of research reports and good practice guides in the last few years, particularly regarding mental health in the workplace. Particularly important is ACAS guidance on *Supporting mental health at work* and *Thriving at work: The Stevenson/Farmer review of mental health and employers.*[6]

The protected characteristic of disability

Overview

15.7   'Disability' is a protected characteristic under Equality Act (EqA) 2010 s6. Except in obvious cases, one of the most important and difficult issues is whether a worker falls within the definition of 'disability' in the EqA 2010. Far more people are covered than may be realised. The EqA 2010 definition is very wide, and it is also important to remember that many disabilities are invisible. In addition, the definition includes many workers with long-term ill-health, which would not conventionally be seen as a 'disability'. It is dangerous to generalise about when the definition applies and each case will depend on a close examination of its facts. A worker with a back impairment or depression, for example, may or may not be covered by the EqA 2010, depending on the duration and severity of the problem. It is necessary to go through the stages of the statutory definition. Whether the worker is recognised as disabled in other

---

4   Issued as quarterly statistics, but set out for the full year. See 'Main tables (January to March 2021)' at www.gov.uk/government/statistics/tribunal-statistics-quarterly-january-to-march-2021.

5   House of Commons Library Briefing Paper 7540, November 2018: 'People with disabilities in employment'.

6   Both 2017. Respectively at: www.acas.org.uk/supporting-mental-health-workplace and www.gov.uk/government/uploads/system/uploads/attachment_data/file/658145/thriving-at-work-stevenson-farmer-review.pdf.

contexts, eg for the purposes of social security benefits, requires a different legal test.[7]

15.8 A 'disabled person' under the EqA 2010 is a person who has a 'disability'. Section 6(1) reads:

> A person (P) has a disability if–
> (a) P has a physical or mental impairment, and
> (b) the impairment has a substantial and long-term adverse effect on P's ability to carry out normal day-to-day activities.

Each element of this definition should be separately considered.[8]

15.9 It is essential to have a copy of the 2011 Office for Disability Issues guidance, *Equality Act 2010: Guidance on matters to be taken into account in determining questions relating to the definition of disability*, which provides guidelines for applying the definition.[9] The Guidance has similar status to statutory codes. When deciding whether a worker is disabled, a tribunal must take it into account if it is relevant.[10] The Employment Appeal Tribunal (EAT) has encouraged employment tribunals (ETs) to refer explicitly to any relevant provision of the EHRC Employment Code or the Guidance.[11] This chapter should be read together with chapter 16 on evidence to prove disability discrimination.

15.10 Although far more conditions are covered by the EqA 2010 than advisers or workers may at first realise, there is no doubt that many workers with obvious disabilities have struggled to prove they are within the Act. Employers frequently refuse to admit that a worker has a relevant disability once a case starts. The effect of this and the detailed stages of the definition, has led to some seemingly obvious cases being excluded. The EAT stressed in *Goodwin*[12] that although the Guidance should be looked at in deciding whether someone has a disability, it should not be used as an obstacle if it is obvious that they do. The Guidance is for cases where it is not obvious that a worker has a disability, not in the majority of cases where it is clear that s/he does.[13]

---

7 *Hill v Clacton Family Trust Ltd* [2005] EWCA Civ 1456; [2005] All ER (D) 170 (Oct).
8 See checklist A15 in appendix A.
9 Available at www.gov.uk/government/uploads/system/uploads/attachment_data/file/570382/Equality_Act_2010-disability_definition.pdf.
10 EqA 2010 Sch 1 para 12 and s6(5).
11 *Goodwin v The Patent Office* [1999] IRLR 4, EAT.
12 *Goodwin v The Patent Office* [1999] IRLR 4, EAT.
13 Guidance, para 3.

15.11   Workers with multiple sclerosis, HIV or cancer,[14] or those registered with a local authority or certified by a consultant ophthalmologist as blind, severely sight impaired, sight impaired or partially sighted,[15] are deemed disabled without the need to prove the stages of the definition. The type of cancer or stage at which it has reached is irrelevant. Pre-cancerous skin cancer will still be covered if cancerous cells are present, however superficially.[16]

Physical impairment

15.12   'Physical impairment' includes sensory impairment and severe disfigurement, although not tattoos or ornamental body piercing. Provided all aspects of the definition are met, conditions such as ME (chronic fatigue syndrome),[17] epilepsy and back disorders can be covered. Seasonal allergic rhinitis, for example hay fever, is expressly excluded, unless it aggravates another condition,[18] eg asthma. Addictions to alcohol, nicotine or other substances are also not covered unless the addiction was originally the result of administration of medical treatment or medically prescribed drugs.[19] It is not necessary to consider how a physical or mental impairment was caused. So for example, depression[20] or liver disease resulting from alcohol dependency, would count as an impairment.[21]

15.13   The concept of 'impairment' is not defined by EqA 2010. It does not equate with a clinical condition – it is a functional concept rather than a medical one, ie focussing more on adverse effects.[22] Indeed, sometimes it can be hard to distinguish an impairment from its effects. An impairment can be something which results from an illness or which is the illness itself, ie it can be cause or effect.[23] A worker can therefore have a physical impairment where s/he genuinely suffers physical symptoms, even if these result from psycholo-

---

14 EqA 2010 Sch 1 para 6.
15 Equality Act 2010 (Disability) Regulations 2010 SI No 2128 reg 7.
16 *Lofty v Hamis t/a First Café* UKEAT/0177/17; [2018] IRLR 512, EAT.
17 *O'Neill v Symm & Co Ltd* [1998] IRLR 232, EAT.
18 SI No 2128 reg 4.
19 SI No 2128 reg 3.
20 *Power v Panasonic UK Ltd* [2003] IRLR 151, EAT.
21 Guidance, paras A3 and A7.
22 *Ministry of Defence v Hay* [2008] IRLR 928, EAT.
23 *McNicol v Balfour Beatty Rail Maintenance Ltd* [2002] IRLR 711, CA.

gical distress rather than any organic physical cause.[24] In such a case, the psychological condition may also amount to a mental impairment. The underlying cause of an impairment may be hard to establish; effects can be physical and mental, and physical effects can be caused by a mental impairment as well as vice versa.[25] It also seems that a person can be regarded as having had a disability if s/he has suffered from a combination of impairments with different effects, to different extents, over periods of time which have overlapped, even though none of the individual impairments had sufficient adverse effect on their own.[26]

Mental impairment

15.14 'Mental impairment' can include impairments such as learning disabilities, dyslexia and autism, as well as mental illnesses. In each case, to amount to a 'disability', every stage of the definition must be met. The original requirement in the DDA 1995 that a mental illness be clinically well-recognised was removed in December 2005. It is no longer necessary to name a precise condition which is recognised by a respected body of medical opinion, eg by being listed in the World Health Organization's (WHO's) international classification of diseases. However, it is still necessary to provide evidence of a particular impairment and its effects (though note comments in the previous paragraph).

15.15 Workers suffering from schizophrenia, bipolar disorder or severe psychoses will usually be covered. With regard to depression, workers may also be able to claim that ordinary clinical depression is covered, but it will depend on the circumstances and it should be distinguished from a worker simply feeling fed-up or stressed by adverse circumstances or life events.[27] With depression, it is often easiest to start by looking at the severity of the effects and then consider afterwards whether there is an impairment. If the adverse effects of the stress or depression have lasted 12 months or more, it is likely there is a mental impairment. However, the worker's ability to carry out day-to-day activities must be affected. It is not enough on its own that

24 *McNicol v Balfour Beatty Rail Maintenance Ltd* [2002] IRLR 711, CA; *College of Ripon & York St John v Hobbs* [2002] IRLR 185, EAT. See also *Millar v Inland Revenue Commissioners* [2006] IRLR 112, CS; *Walker v Sita Information Networking Computing Ltd* UKEAT/0097/12.

25 Guidance, para A6.

26 *Ministry of Defence v Hay* [2008] IRLR 928, EAT.

27 The key case on depression is *J v DLA Piper UK LLP* UKEAT/0263/09; [2010] IRLR 936.

s/he feels unhappy about a work situation, even over a prolonged period.[28] It is also important that the depression meets other aspects of the definition of disability, eg it must have a substantial adverse effect for as long as 12 months (although it would still have a long-term effect if it was likely to recur). Similarly, a reaction to bereavement may be an ordinary response to adverse life events or may have developed into an impairment.[29]

15.16   Personality disorder is another area which may or may not amount to an impairment, and where it may be helpful (although not essential) first to consider the effect on day-to-day activities.[30] Certain personality disorders are specifically excluded, for example, a tendency to set fires or steal, to physical or sexual abuse, voyeurism or exhibitionism.[31] Where a worker displays an excluded disorder as a result of a non-excluded impairment, the question is why s/he has been discriminated against. For example, a worker who is dismissed for committing indecent exposure as a result of depression is protected only if the dismissal is wholly or partly for the depression as opposed to wholly for the exhibitionism.[32]

Affecting normal day-to-day activities

15.17   The impairment must affect the worker's ability to carry out normal day-to-day activities. Under the DDA 1995, it was necessary to show that the affected abilities fell into one of several categories, ie:

- mobility (including ability to stand);
- manual dexterity;
- physical co-ordination;[33]
- continence;
- ability to lift, carry or move every-day objects;[34]
- speech, hearing or eyesight;
- memory or ability to concentrate, learn or understand;[35] or
- perception of the risk of physical danger.

28 *J v DLA Piper UK LLP* UKEAT/0263/09; [2010] IRLR 936; *Herry v Dudley Metropolitan Council* UKEAT/0100-1/16.

29 *Igweike v TSB Bank PLC* UKEAT/0119/19.

30 For a discussion of this, see *Khorochilova v Euro Rep Limited* UKEAT/0266/19.

31 Equality Act 2010 (Disability) Regulations 2010 SI No 2128 reg 4(1).

32 *Edmund Nuttall Ltd v Butterfield* [2005] IRLR 751, EAT; *Wood v Durham County Council* UKEAT/0099/19. See also the example at para A13 of the Guidance.

33 Now see Guidance, para D18.

34 Now see Guidance, para D18.

35 Now see Guidance, para D19, which includes ability to remember things and to organise one's thoughts.

Ability to understand included understanding of normal social inter-action and the subtleties of human non-factual communication.[36] The need to fit within these categories was removed by the EqA 2010 because not all affected activities comfortably fitted within them. However, the list may still be a useful starting point for checking some of the effects of an impairment.

15.18 Section D of the Guidance, together with its appendix, provides useful guidelines and illustrations as to what are 'normal day-to-day activities'. A general overview is given at para D3. The activity must be one which is carried out by many people on a daily or frequent or fairly regular basis, although not necessarily by a majority of people.[37] Travel by tube or aeroplane is a normal activity,[38] as is taking exams.[39] An activity is still normal if it is only normal for one sex.[40]

15.19 Highly specialised work or leisure activities or those which require a high level of attainment are not considered 'normal day-to-day' activities.[41] The Guidance gives as examples inability to play a musical instrument to a high level of achievement or to play a particular sport to a high level of ability, such as would be required for a professional footballer. This suggests that playing a piano or guitar, or engaging in tennis, swimming or park football at a basic hobby level, should be considered a normal day-to-day activity. Indeed, it is hard to see how such activities are not normal for many people. Presumably normal day-to-day activities would also be affected if, because of an impair-ment such as depression, a worker lost enthusiasm for doing any kind of hobby at all. However, to be safe, workers should give as many examples as possible of the effects of their impairment and not restrict these to hobbies. In many cases, the impairment which restricts the worker's ability to engage in such hobbies, also affects other normal day-to-day activities involving manual dexterity, mobil-ity and so on.

15.20 Difficulty carrying out specialised work activities raises similar issues. For example, in one old case, a garden centre worker was unsuccessful because although he could not lift heavy bags of soil as

---

36 *Hewett v Motorola Ltd* [2004] IRLR 545, EAT, a case concerning Asperger's syndrome. Guidance, para 17 covers communication difficulties.

37 Guidance, para D5.

38 *Abadeh v British Telecommunications plc* [2001] IRLR 23, EAT.

39 *Paterson v The Commissioner of Police of the Metropolis* UKEAT/0635/06; [2007] IRLR 763, EAT.

40 *Epke v Commissioner of Police of the Metropolis* [2001] IRLR 605, EAT; Guidance, para D5.

41 See Guidance, paras D8–D10.

required by his job, he could still lift everyday objects.⁴² On the other hand, the Court of Justice of the European Union (CJEU) has said it is a disability under the directive where a worker's impairment hinders his/her full and effective participation in professional life.⁴³ It remains to be clarified whether this includes an inability to do the worker's chosen profession, however specialised. Certainly, an inability to do a work activity which is common to many jobs, would be covered, eg using a word processor, answering the telephone, interacting with customers,⁴⁴ standing for long periods of time,⁴⁵ lifting and moving cases weighing up to 25kg⁴⁶ or taking assessments or exams.⁴⁷ It is also possible that an impairment which causes difficulty carrying out specialist tasks, might also hinder the worker in doing normal daily activities. The Guidance gives an example of a watch repairer who cannot carry out his job because of tenosynovitis. Although watch repair may not be an example of a normal day-to-day activity, the restricted movement in his hands means he also cannot prepare invoices and count and record daily takings. The latter are normal day-to-day activities. Adverse effects on normal activities such as mobility, which occur only when working at nights, would also be covered because many people do work nights.⁴⁸ All this still leaves open the question as to whether workers are disabled if they have a disability which prevents them doing a very specific chosen profession, but which does not interfere with any normal work or day-to-day activity.⁴⁹

---

42 *Quinlan v B&Q plc* [1998] UKEAT 1386_97_2701.
43 *Chacón Navas v Eurest Colectividades SA* [2006] IRLR 706, ECJ, applied by the EAT in *Paterson v The Commissioner of Police of the Metropolis* UKEAT/0635/06; [2007] IRLR 763; *HK Danmark (on behalf of Ring) v Dansk almennyttigt Boligselskab and another* C-335/11 and C-337/11, [2013] IRLR 571, CJEU. See para 15.34 for more detail of the EU definition.
44 See also Guidance, para D10.
45 *Aderemi v London and South Eastern Railway Ltd* UKEAT/0316/12.
46 *Banaszczyk v Booker Ltd* UKEAT/0132/15; [2016] IRLR 273, EAT.
47 *Paterson v The Commissioner of Police of the Metropolis* UKEAT/0635/06; [2007] IRLR 763, EAT.
48 *Chief Constable of Dumfries & Galloway Constabulary v Adams* UKEATS/0046/08; [2009] IRLR 612.
49 See *Sobhi v Commissioner of Police of the Metropolis* UKEAT/0518/12 for perhaps the clearest illustration of reliance on the EU definition, where there is thought to be no substantial adverse effect on day-to-day activities.

Substantial effect

15.21 The Guidance at section B expands on the meaning of 'substantial' adverse effect. It is unnecessary that a worker is completely unable to carry out the activity, but the effect must be more than minor or trivial.[50] A substantial effect could include where a worker can carry out the activity, but only for short periods of time or more slowly than usual[51] or only in a particular way[52] or under certain environmental conditions.[53] It may be that a worker can carry out the activity, but it is tiring or painful to do so.[54] Alternatively, the worker may have been medically advised to refrain from the activity altogether.[55] An ET should also recognise that someone is disabled even if s/he can get around a problem, eg by using a shoulder bag when s/he is unable to carry a bag in his/her hand.[56] An ET should not place too much emphasis on the way a worker appears to cope at the hearing because this can be misleading.[57]

15.22 A worker may tell an adviser or the tribunal that his/her day-to-day life is unaffected by his/her disability. This can be misleading. A worker may play down the effect of his/her disability.[58] Or it may be that a worker has rearranged his/her life to avoid carrying out a certain activity and feels that s/he is coping. Some coping and avoidance strategies work to a certain extent, but break down in certain circumstances, eg when the worker is under stress.[59] Equally, a worker would still be disabled if s/he had to take abnormal steps to avoid things which might trigger adverse effects. The Guidance at para B7 suggests that where reasonable avoidance steps could stop the effects of an impairment being substantial, there may come a point where a person is not disabled.[60] This is a dangerous idea, which could undermine the

---

50 EqA 2010 s212(1).
51 See Guidance, para B2. *Banaszczyk v Booker Ltd* UKEAT/0132/15; [2016] IRLR 273.
52 See Guidance, para B3.
53 See Guidance, paras B11 and D20–D21.
54 See Guidance, para D22. See also *Leonard v Southern Derbyshire Chamber of Commerce* [2001] IRLR 19, EAT.
55 See Guidance, para D22.
56 *Vicary v British Telecommunications plc* [1999] IRLR 680, EAT.
57 *Leonard v Southern Derbyshire Chamber of Commerce* [2001] IRLR 19; May 2001, EAT; *Morgan v Staffordshire University* [2002] IRLR 190, EAT; *Mahon v Accuread Ltd* UKEAT/0081/08.
58 *Goodwin v The Patent Office* [1999] IRLR 4, EAT.
59 Guidance, paras B9–B10.
60 Guidance, paras B7–B8.

protection of disability discrimination law. The examples given by the Guidance do suggest a high threshold, eg a person with chronic back pain could reasonably be expected to avoid going skiing, but not to modify more normal activities which might exacerbate symptoms, such as shopping. It is also important to bear in mind that if the worker's coping/avoidance measures amount to medical treatment, the impairment should be assessed as it would be if such measures were not taken. This is discussed further at para 15.28.

15.23　　To assess whether an effect is substantial, comparison is made, not with the population at large, but with how the worker would carry out the activity if s/he did not have the impairment.[61] The focus should be on what the worker cannot do, or cannot do without difficulty; as opposed to what s/he can do.[62]

15.24　　The appendix to the Guidance lists examples of circumstances where it would and would not be reasonable to regard the adverse effect on a person's ability to carry out day-to-day activities as substantial. These are only indicators, not rigid tests.[63] In each case, the example is given on the basis that it is the only effect of the impairment. It is also possible that a person is affected in a minor way in a number of different activities and the cumulative effect is substantial.[64] It is important to remember that the list is only illustrative, it is not exhaustive. Advisers should elicit as many examples as possible from the worker, both from within the list and additional to it. Remember also that a physical impairment may have mental effects, and a mental impairment may have physical manifestations.[65] It is important always to remember the statutory wording and that the effect need only be something more than minor or trivial. The appendix to the Guidance can be misleading and place the threshold too high because, as we shall see in the next two paragraphs, on the one hand it gives examples where the effect is substantial and on the other hand, it gives examples where the effect is not substantial. This gives the impression that there is a sliding scale between substantial effects and trivial effects, but there is not. The effect of the impair-

---

61　*Paterson v The Commissioner of Police of the Metropolis* UKEAT/0635/06; [2007] IRLR 763.

62　*Goodwin v The Patent Office* [1999] IRLR 4, EAT; *Vicary v British Telecommunications plc* [1999] IRLR 680, EAT; *Leonard v Southern Derbyshire Chamber of Commerce* [2001] IRLR 19, EAT.

63　Guidance, paras D12–D14.

64　Guidance, para D13.

65　Guidance, para D15.

ment is either trivial/minor, or it is not, in which case it is substantial and covered by the definition.[66]

15.25 The appendix's examples of where it would be reasonable to regard an impairment as having a *substantial adverse effect* on normal day-to-day activities include:

- difficulty getting dressed, preparing a meal or eating;
- difficulty using transport, whether because of physical restrictions or as a result of a mental impairment;
- difficulty using steps, or ability to walk only a short distance without difficulty, eg because of pain or fatigue;
- difficulty carrying objects of moderate weight with one hand, eg a shopping bag or small piece of luggage;
- difficulty hearing and understanding another person speaking clearly on the telephone;
- persistent and significant difficulty reading or understanding written material, eg because of a mental impairment or learning difficulty or visual impairment;
- difficulty understanding or following simple verbal instructions;
- difficulty operating a computer, eg because of a physical impairment or a learning disability;
- behaviour which challenges other people, making it difficult for the person to be accepted in public places;
- persistent general low motivation or loss of interest in everyday activities;
- persistent difficulty taking part in normal social interaction;
- compulsive activities or behaviour; difficulty adapting after a reasonable period to minor changes in a routine;
- difficulty concentrating;
- intermittent loss of consciousness.

15.26 Examples given where it would *not* be reasonable to regard the effect as substantial include:

- inability to move heavy objects, eg a large suitcase or heavy piece of furniture;
- experiencing some discomfort as a result of travelling, eg by car or plane, for more than two hours;
- experiencing some tiredness or minor discomfort as a result of walking unaided for one mile;
- minor problems with writing or spelling;
- inability to reach typing speeds standardised for secretarial work;

66 *Aderemi v London and South Eastern Railway Ltd* UKEAT/0316/12.

- inability to concentrate on a task requiring application over several hours;
- inability to hold a conversation in a very noisy place, eg a factory floor or alongside a busy main road;
- inability to undertake activities requiring delicate hand movements, eg picking up a pin or threading a small needle.

15.27   Severe disfigurement is deemed to have 'substantial' adverse effect.[67]

15.28   The fact that medical treatment or medication controls or corrects the impairment is irrelevant (except for someone whose sight impairment is corrected by glasses or lenses).[68] The effect without the correcting measures should be assessed. So, for example, a worker is still protected, even if his/her epilepsy is controlled by medication or his/her depression is controlled by counselling sessions with a clinical psychologist.[69] Plates and pins inserted into an ankle some time previously should also be taken into account if they continue to give support.[70] The test is whether the impairment is 'likely'[71] to have substantial adverse effect if the medication or controlling measures were not taken. The EAT has suggested that an ET should consider both the effect of a worker's impairment while on medication and the 'deduced effects' but for the medication.[72] This is obviously difficult, and medical evidence may be needed. A controversial case in 2015 suggested that although following a particular diet on medical advice might amount to medical treatment, eg for a person with diabetes, simply avoiding sugary drinks would not be sufficient to amount to a 'particular diet'; it would just be a reasonable avoidance step as envisaged in para B7 of the Guidance. It is difficult to follow the logic of this case and it certainly should not be taken to mean that individuals with type 2 diabetes or, for that matter, severe food allergies, can never be covered by the definition of disability.[73]

---

67 EqA 2010 Sch 1 para 3. Guidance, paras B24–B26.
68 EqA 2010 Sch 1 para 5.
69 See *Kapadia v Lambeth LBC* [2000] IRLR 14, EAT and [2000] IRLR 699, CA.
70 *Carden v Pickerings Europe Ltd* [2005] IRLR 720, EAT.
71 For the meaning of 'likely' when used in the EqA 2010, see observations in the next paragraph.
72 *Goodwin v The Patent Office* [1999] IRLR 4, EAT.
73 *Metroline Travel Ltd v Stoute (debarred)* [2015] IRLR 465, EAT; see also the IRLR commentary in its highlights; Guidance, paras B7, B10, B12 and B14; and para 15.22 above. Since then, *Taylor v Ladbrokes Betting and Gaming Ltd* UKEAT/0353/15 (not an easy case to read) suggests type 2 diabetes could be a disability if the medical evidence supports the definition.

15.29 A worker with a progressive condition, eg motor-neurone disease or muscular dystrophy, is deemed disabled as soon as the condition has any effect on the worker's ability to carry out day-to-day activities, even if the effect is not yet substantial. The worker must prove that it is likely that at some stage in the future, the progressive condition will lead to an impairment with a substantial adverse effect.[74] 'Likely' simply means 'could well happen', which is a lower threshold than 'more probable than not'.[75] If the condition has not yet had any effect at all, the worker is not protected.[76] This causes real problems for workers who are discriminated against by their employers simply because they have been diagnosed with a condition, but who are not covered by the EqA 2010 until the condition starts to affect any of their day-to-day activities.

15.30 It does not matter whether the activity which is initially affected, but not substantially, is different from the activity which will in future be substantially affected, if both arise from the same impairment.[77] It also does not matter if the adverse effect is indirectly caused by the impairment, eg the impairment is an immune disorder, but it is the resultant infections which cause the substantial adverse effect on the worker's ability to carry out normal day-to-day activities.[78]

15.31 Tattoos and body piercings for decorative or other non-medical purposes are not considered to have a substantial adverse effect.[79]

Long-term effect

15.32 The EqA 2010 does not protect those with short-term or temporary disability. To be considered long-term, the effect of the impairment must already have lasted or be likely to last at least 12 months or for the rest of the worker's life.[80] 'Likely' means it could well happen.[81] It

---

74 EqA 2010 Sch 1 para 8. Also see para 16.55 on evidence. The footnoted comments of Underhill LJ in *Chief Constable of Norfolk v Coffey* [2019] EWCA Civ 1061 provide an argument that the initial effect may only need to be very minor.

75 *SCA Packaging Ltd v Boyle* [2009] UKHL 37; [2009] IRLR 746. Guidance, para C3.

76 EqA 2010 Sch 1 para 8(1)(b).

77 *Kirton v Tetrosyl Ltd* [2003] IRLR 353, CA.

78 *Sussex Partnership NHS Foundation Trust v Norris* UKEAT/0031/12.

79 Equality Act 2010 (Disability) Regulations 2010 SI No 2128 reg 5.

80 EqA 2010 Sch 1 para 2.

81 See para 15.29. The definition was confirmed in a third case, *Fag og Arbejde, acting on behalf of Kaltoft v Kommunernes Landsforening, acting on behalf of the Municipality of Bullund* C-354/13, [2015] IRLR 146, CJEU.

is the effect which must be long-term, not just the underlying medical condition.[82] If the effect has not yet lasted 12 months at the time of the discriminatory actions, the tribunal must assess whether at that point it was likely it would go on to do so.[83] The tribunal has to look at the facts and circumstances existing at the date of discrimination. It is not a question of what has actually happened since then. If a secondary condition is likely to develop out of an original impairment, this can be taken into account when deciding whether the effect of the original impairment is likely to be long-term.[84] Where the disability is one which can be treated and cured, it is relevant to consider when this might happen.[85]

15.33   If an impairment ceases to have substantial adverse effect but such effect is likely to recur more than 12 months after the first occurrence, the substantial adverse effect is treated as continuing.[86] This covers workers with impairments with fluctuating or recurring effects, eg rheumatoid arthritis or a recurrent depressive disorder.[87] Conditions which recur only sporadically or for short periods (eg epilepsy or migraine) can still be covered, depending on the facts. Again, the likelihood must be assessed as it existed at the date of the discrimination and not in the light of what has actually happened by the time of the tribunal hearing.[88] The tribunal can consider medical evidence obtained after the event, as long as it relates to the circumstances at the time. For the meaning of 'recurring or fluctuating effect' see the Guidance, section C.

The EU definition

15.34   The EU directive does not define 'disability', so the only guidelines we have derive from primarily two CJEU cases, *Chacón Navas* and *HK Danmark*.[89] In the latter case, the CJEU said that, as the EU has

---

82   *The Guinness Partnership v Szymoniak* UKEAT/0065/17.

83   *All Answers Ltd v Mr W and Ms R* [2021] EWCA Civ 606; [2021] IRLR 612.

84   *Patel v (1) Oldham MBC (2) The Governing Body of Rushcroft Primary School* UKEAT/0225/09; [2010] IRLR 280. See also Guidance, para C2.

85   *Anwar v Tower Hamlets College* UKEAT/0091/10.

86   See EqA 2010 Sch 1 para 2(2); Guidance, para C6. Again, 'likely' means 'could well happen' – see para 15.29.

87   *Crossingham v European Wellcare Lifestyles Ltd* [2006] All ER (D) 279 (Oct), EAT.

88   *Richmond Adult Community College v McDougall* [2008] IRLR 227, CA.

89   *Chacón Navas v Eurest Colectividades SA* [2006] IRLR 706, ECJ; *HK Danmark (on behalf of Ring) v Dansk almennyttigt Boligselskab and another* C-335/11 and C-337/11; [2013] IRLR 571, CJEU.

approved the UN Convention on the Rights of Persons with Disabilities, the directive must be interpreted consistently with the Convention as far as possible. Article 1 of the Convention says:

> Persons with disabilities include those who have long-term physical, mental, intellectual or sensory impairments which in interaction with various barriers may hinder their full and effective participation in society on an equal basis with others.

The CJEU confirmed in *HK Danmark* that it does not matter if the impairment is caused by an illness, whether curable or incurable. Nor does it matter whether the worker has contributed to the onset of his/her disability.[90] Echoing the UN Convention, the CJEU said (para 53):

> ... the concept of 'disability' must be understood as referring to a limitation which results in particular from long-term physical, mental or psychological impairments which in interaction with various barriers may hinder the full and effective participation of the person concerned in professional life on an equal basis with other workers ...

This applies not only to the impossibility of exercising a professional activity, but also to a hindrance to the exercise of such an activity.[91] UK law cannot provide lesser rights than in the directive, but it can of course choose to provide greater rights and a wider coverage. As stated above, the CJEU's wording is useful in that it indicates that a measure of whether a worker is disabled is the effect on participation in professional life, regardless of whether there is an adverse impact on other normal day-to-day activities.

Past disability

15.35 A worker who has recovered from a past disability is protected if s/he is discriminated against in connection with that disability.[92]

Pre-employment health and disability enquiries

15.36 The EqA 2010 introduced a ban on enquiries about health and disability before a job has been offered. Such enquiries were thought to be

---

90 *Fag og Arbejde, acting on behalf of Kaltoft v Kommunernes Landsforening, acting on behalf of the Municipality of Bullund* C-354/13 [2015] IRLR 146, CJEU.
91 *Fag og Arbejde, acting on behalf of Kaltoft v Kommunernes Landsforening, acting on behalf of the Municipality of Bullund* C-354/13 [2015] IRLR 146, CJEU.
92 EqA 2010 s6(4).

the main reason why disabled job candidates often failed to reach the interview stage, and they were also a disincentive in them applying for jobs. With certain exceptions, employers are not allowed to ask job candidates questions about their health or whether they have a disability until they have offered a job (on a conditional or unconditional basis) or put the candidate into a pool of successful candidates to be offered a job when one becomes available.[93] This includes questions about previous sickness absence.[94] The questions must not be asked at any stage of the application process and the candidate must not be referred to an occupational health practitioner or asked to fill in an occupational health questionnaire before any offer is made.[95] If a disabled worker volunteers health information during an interview, the employer still needs to avoid discussing the matter further (unless within one of the exceptions set out below). The rules also apply in respect of contract workers and to job agencies.[96]

15.37   Employers can make offers conditional on health or disability checks. So once the offer has been made, an employer can make enquiries and there is always the risk that the offer will be subsequently withdrawn. However, any change of heart by the employer would be more obviously disability-related at that stage (although not necessarily so) and subject to the usual rules on disability discrimination.

15.38   The EHRC can bring proceedings against an employer who makes unlawful pre-employment health enquiries.[97] It is especially worth drawing it to the EHRC's attention if a large employer persists with making pre-employment health and disability enquiries. An individual job candidate cannot bring a disability discrimination claim purely because such an unlawful enquiry was made, but s/he can bring a claim in respect of any discriminatory action taken by the employer as a result of information contained in his/her response to the question, eg if the employer fails to offer the candidate the job because it was clear from the candidate's answer that s/he was disabled. In such a case, the fact that the employer made a pre-employment health or disability enquiry reverses the burden of proof.[98] The employer would then have to explain why s/he had not offered the job, and if the explanation was unconvincing, the tribunal

93   EqA 2010 s60(1), (10) and (13).
94   EHRC Employment Code, para 10.25.
95   EHRC Employment Code, paras 10.25–10.26.
96   EqA 2010 s60(11).
97   EqA 2010 s60(2).
98   EqA 2010 s60(4); see chapter 16 regarding the burden of proof in discrimination cases generally.

would find disability discrimination. Unfortunately, the burden of proof only shifts where the claim brought by the job candidate is for direct discrimination,[99] which considerably reduces the effectiveness of the protection, since job candidates are probably more likely to be rejected from a job because of discrimination arising from disability (DAFD) than from direct discrimination. In a DAFD case, therefore, a candidate would still need to establish a prima facie case to make the burden of proof shift, though there is no reason why an ET could not take it into account if an employer who knew the rules deliberately flouted them.

15.39   There are exceptions so that an employer can make pre-employment health and disability enquiries where necessary to monitor the diversity of job applicants[100] or to find out whether the candidate will be able to undergo an interview or other job assessment or will need reasonable adjustments to that process.[101] However, questions about reasonable adjustments needed for the job itself should not be asked until after a job offer is made (unless relating to a function which is intrinsic to the job, as explained below). The employer can also ask necessary questions for positive action purposes under EqA 2010 s158[102] or where the employer has decided that, having regard to the nature or context of the work, it is a justifiable occupational requirement that the successful candidate have a particular disability.[103]

15.40   Potentially the most problematic exception is that the employer can ask questions necessary to establish whether the candidate can carry out a function which is intrinsic to the work concerned.[104] Where the employer reasonably believes s/he would have a duty to make reasonable adjustments for that candidate in relation to the work, this means a function which is intrinsic once the employer has complied with that duty.[105] It is not clear what 'intrinsic' means. The EHRC suggests in the EHRC Employment Code that this means only functions necessary to a job. It gives as an example, an employer recruiting a scaffolder could ask questions relating to a candidate's

99 EqA 2010 s60(11).
100 EqA 2010 s60(6)(c).
101 EqA 2010 s60(6)(a) and (12).
102 EqA 2010 s60(6)(d); EHRC Employment Code, para 10.33.
103 EqA 2010 s60(6)(e) and (8); EHRC Employment Code, para 10.34.
104 EqA 2010 s60(6)(b).
105 EqA 2010 s60(7).

ability to climb ladders and scaffolding to a significant height.[106] The Code says this exception should be applied narrowly.[107]

15.41   The prohibition on pre-employment and disability health enquiries does not apply where it is necessary to vet applicants for reasons of national security.[108]

Disability discrimination

Forms of disability discrimination

15.42   There are six forms of unlawful discrimination in relation to disability:

1) failure to make reasonable adjustments;[109]
2) direct discrimination;[110]
3) DAFD;[111]
4) harassment;[112]
5) indirect discrimination;[113]
6) victimisation.[114]

The definitions of direct discrimination, indirect discrimination, victimisation and harassment are common to all the protected characteristics under the EqA 2010.

Failure to make reasonable adjustments

15.43   The duty on employers to make reasonable adjustments is at the heart of disability discrimination law. A failure to make reasonable adjustments constitutes unlawful discrimination.[115] The duty divides into three similar categories which are framed as 'requirements':

1) Where the employer applies a *provision, criterion or practice* (PCP) which puts a disabled person at a substantial disadvantage compared

---

106 EHRC Employment Code, para 10.36.
107 EHRC Employment Code, para 10.38.
108 EqA 2010 s60(14).
109 EqA 2010 ss20–21.
110 EqA 2010 s13.
111 EqA 2010 s15.
112 EqA 2010 s26.
113 EqA 2010 s19.
114 EqA 2010 s27.
115 EqA 2010 s21.

with people who are not disabled. The employer must then take such steps as are reasonable to avoid the disadvantage.[116]

2) Where a *physical feature* puts a disabled person at a substantial disadvantage compared with people who are not disabled. Again, the employer must take such steps as are reasonable to avoid the disadvantage, eg by removing or altering the feature.[117]

3) Where a disabled person would, but for the provision of an *auxiliary aid*, be put at a substantial disadvantage compared with people who are not disabled. The employer must then take such steps as are reasonable to provide the auxiliary aid.[118]

15.44 A disabled worker is not entitled to a reasonable adjustment simply because s/he is disabled. S/he must be put at a substantial disadvantage by a PCP or physical feature of the premises or lack of an auxiliary aid, compared with a non-disabled worker. The reason for the comparison is to establish whether it is because of the worker's disability that s/he is put at the disadvantage.[119] The purpose of the adjustment is then to address that disadvantage. A 'substantial' disadvantage means one that is more than minor or trivial.[120] It is not necessary to show that the PCP would also put other workers with the same disability at a disadvantage.[121] Moreover, if a PCP is more likely to bite on disabled workers, it is irrelevant that non-disabled workers would also be disadvantaged by the PCP if they could not comply with it.[122]

15.45 The phrase 'provision, criterion or practice' may be familiar from the definition of indirect discrimination, and it means the same thing in both contexts.[123] It can cover formal and informal policies, rules, requirements and arrangements, eg attendance and training policies; selection criteria for recruitment, promotion and redundancy; job duties and deadlines. A dismissal is not a PCP in itself, but it might be the result of a different PCP, eg a requirement to be fit for

---

116 EqA 2010 s20(3).
117 EqA 2010 s20(4) and (9).
118 EqA 2010 s20(5).
119 EHRC Employment Code, para 6.16.
120 EqA 2010 s212(1).
121 *Pulman v Merthyr Tydfil College Ltd* UKEAT/0309/16; *Chief Constable of Lincolnshire Police v Weaver* UKEAT/0622/07. This is different from indirect discrimination.
122 *Griffiths v Secretary of State for Work and Pensions* [2015] EWCA Civ 1265; [2016] IRLR 216; see also para 15.67.
123 *Ishola v Transport for London* [2020] EWCA Civ 112; [2020] IRLR 368. For indirect discrimination generally, see para 13.31 onwards.

work.[124] A PCP can include imposing an expectation or a strong request.[125]

15.46   Although 'provision criterion or practice' should be interpreted widely, it does not apply to every decision or to every act of unfair treatment by an employer. The PCP must be capable of being applied to other people, even if that has not actually happened. Also, the word 'practice' suggests repetition, eg the employer has acted that way more than once, or the evidence suggests the employer would act that way again in future if a similar situation arose. It is not impossible for a one-off decision or action to be a practice, but it depends on the facts.[126] For example, if an employer repeatedly fails to investigate a worker's grievances, this is likely to be a 'practice'. But if, on a one-off occasion, in a very particular context, an employer has not investigated a worker's grievance, this might be unique to the circumstances and not a 'practice', because there is no indication it would happen again, either with that worker or with any other.

15.47   Workers sometimes try to fit the employer's treatment awkwardly into the phrase PCP, when the other two reasonable adjustment categories would fit the situation much more easily.[127] A 'physical feature of the premises' can be temporary or permanent and includes internal and external features such as steps, exits, parking areas, doors, toilets, lighting and ventilation, floor coverings, furniture and signs.[128] An 'auxiliary aid' is something which provides support or assistance to a disabled person, eg a specialist piece of equipment, or an auxiliary service[129] such as a support worker or sign language interpreter.[130]

15.48   In the employment field, there is no open-ended duty to make adjustments. The duty is owed only to a particular disabled worker or job applicant if s/he is put at a disadvantage by workplace practices or features. A worker who fails to get a job or who is not promoted or trained or who suffers any other detriment as a result of an employer's failure to make reasonable adjustments may bring a discrimination case. There is no duty under the EqA 2010 or under European law[131]

---

124 *Fox v British Airways PLC* UKEAT/0315/14.
125 *United First Partners Research v Carreras* [2018] EWCA Civ 323.
126 *Ishola v Transport for London* [2020] EWCA Civ 112; [2020] IRLR 368.
127 *Mallon v Aecom Ltd* UKEAT/0175/20.
128 EHRC Employment Code, paras 6.11–6.12.
129 EqA 2010 s20(11).
130 EHRC Employment Code, para 6.13.
131 *Coleman v Attridge Law* C-303/06 [2008] IRLR 722, ECJ.

to make reasonable adjustments to enable a non-disabled worker to look after a disabled relative.[132]

15.49 The EHRC Employment Code says that any reasonable adjustments should be implemented in timely fashion.[133] This is a very important point. It is a common feature of disability discrimination cases that the necessary adjustments have taken an extremely long time to put into place, often leading to a breakdown of the working relationship. Failure to make reasonable adjustments can, if sufficiently serious, amount to a fundamental breach of the implied term of trust and confidence, entitling an employee to resign and claim constructive dismissal.[134]

15.50 Failure to make a reasonable adjustment can never be justified.[135] It is for the tribunal to decide, using an objective test, whether it thinks that an adjustment would have been reasonable. It is not simply a matter of what the employer reasonably thinks.[136]

The employer's knowledge

15.51 The employer is under no duty to make reasonable adjustments if s/he does not know and cannot reasonably be expected to know that the worker has a disability and does not know and cannot reasonably be expected to know that the worker is likely to be placed at a substantial disadvantage as a result.[137] A worker may not have to tell an employer that s/he is disabled, but if s/he needs adjustments to be made, s/he would be wise to tell the employer clearly in writing that s/he is disabled and any adjustment s/he thinks may help. Although an employer has a duty to make reasonable enquiries based on information given to him/her, there is no absolute onus on the employer to make every enquiry possible.[138] When disability discrimination law first came into force, early cases suggested, rather

---

132 *Hainsworth v Ministry of Defence* [2014] EWCA Civ 763; [2014] IRLR 728. Though there must not be direct discrimination against such a worker on the ground that s/he has a disabled relative. See paras 15.78–15.79. Indirect sex discrimination law may also help regarding caring requirements, see para 11.100 onwards.

133 EHRC Employment Code, para 6.32.

134 *Greenhof v Barnsley MBC* [2006] IRLR 98, EAT.

135 When reading older cases, bear in mind that the law changed on this point on 1 October 2004.

136 *Smith v Churchills Stairlifts plc* [2006] IRLR 41, CA.

137 EqA 2010 Sch 8 para 20(1). See also *Eastern & Coastal Kent Primary Care Trust v Grey* UKEAT/0454/08; [2009] IRLR 429.

138 *Ridout v T C Group* [1998] IRLR 628; (1998) 82 EOR 46, EAT; *O'Neill v Symm & Co Ltd* [1998] IRLR 233, EAT.

alarmingly, that employers did not always need to take a very proactive approach in finding out whether a worker was disabled. However, ETs are likely now to have higher expectations of employers. The Code says employers must do all they can reasonably be expected to do to find out if someone has a disability and is likely to need reasonable adjustments.[139]

15.52   An employer cannot just rely on a statement by an occupational health doctor that a worker is not disabled. Responsible employers have to make their own judgment. This involves asking occupational health specific medical questions which are relevant to the definition and not just making a general enquiry. For example, does the worker have an impairment; which day-to-day activities are adversely affected; is the effect likely to be long-term? Having said that, an employer can still give great weight to an informed and reasoned occupational health report.[140]

15.53   With regard to job applicants, an employer is not subject to the duty to make reasonable adjustments if s/he does not know and could not reasonably be expected to know that a disabled person was or might be a job applicant.[141]

Types of adjustment

15.54   Chapter 6 of the EHRC Employment Code[142] deals with the duty to make reasonable adjustments. It says a good starting point is for the employer to conduct a proper assessment in consultation with the disabled worker of what adjustments may be required.[143] Failure to carry out such an assessment or even to think about the possibility of adjustments is almost certainly not a breach of the duty to make reasonable adjustments in itself.[144] It is always necessary for a tribunal to decide that there is a particular practical adjustment which should have been carried out. However, if employers fail to consult, they seriously risk failing to take appropriate steps through ignorance.

---

139 EHRC Employment Code, para 6.19.
140 *Gallop v Newport City Council* [2013] EWCA Civ 1583; [2014] IRLR 211, CA; *Donelien v Liberata UK Ltd* [2018] EWCA Civ 129; [2018] IRLR 535, CA.
141 EqA 2010 Sch 8 para 20(1)(a).
142 See paras 12.4–12.5.
143 EHRC Employment Code, para 6.32.
144 *Mid Staffordshire General Hospitals NHS Trust v Cambridge* [2003] IRLR 566, EAT; *Southampton City College v Randall* [2006] IRLR 18, EAT; apparently superseded by *Tarbuck v Sainsbury's Supermarkets Ltd* [2006] IRLR 664, EAT and *Spence v Intype Libra Ltd* UKEAT/0617/06. Cases since have followed the *Tarbuck* view.

15.55   The EHRC Employment Code makes suggestions (with examples) as to the type of steps which employers may have to take, eg:

- adjusting premises;
- providing information in accessible formats;
- acquiring or modifying equipment;
- providing a reader or interpreter;
- modifying procedures for testing and assessment;
- adjusting hours of work or training;
- allowing time off for rehabilitation, assessment or treatment;
- allowing a period of disability leave;
- providing training or mentoring for the disabled worker or someone else;
- providing supervision or other support; reallocating some duties;
- assigning the disabled worker to a different workplace or allowing home working;
- transferring him/her to fill an existing vacancy;
- permitting flexible working;
- modifying disciplinary or grievance procedures;
- adjusting redundancy selection criteria and modifying performance-related pay arrangements; or
- employing a support worker and participating in supported employment schemes.[145]

Many of these suggestions were previously set out in the DDA 1995, but the EqA 2010 does not give any examples of adjustments. Presumably the reason was to keep an already very long Act concise. In any event, it should not make any difference legally whether the examples are in the statutory Code or in the Act. Adjustments are not confined to those needed to enable a worker to function in his/her job; they include countering a disadvantage in terms and conditions.[146]

15.56   The duty to make reasonable adjustments is unique to the protected characteristic of disability and it is central to the effectiveness of disability discrimination law. In the key case of *Archibald v Fife Council*,[147] the House of Lords said that disability discrimination law was different from sex and race discrimination law in that employers are required to take steps to help disabled people, which they are not required to take for others:

---

145 EHRC Employment Code, para 6.33.
146 *Chief Constable of Lincolnshire Police v Weaver* UKEAT/0622/07.
147 [2004] IRLR 651, HL.

The duty to make adjustments may require the employer to treat a disabled person more favourably to remove the disadvantage which is attributable to the disability. This necessarily entails a measure of positive discrimination.

The House of Lords Select Committee on the Equality Act 2010 and Disability reported in 2016 that a significant problem is employers' failure to understand that making adjustments may involve giving a disabled person more favourable treatment. Employers often tell disabled employers that they 'cannot show any favouritism' to them. The Committee said this is an unsuitable one-size fits all approach. In addition, understanding is also low on hidden disabilities. The Committee said many employees are told by their employer that they cannot have any adjustments because they do not have a physical disability.[148]

When is an adjustment reasonable?

15.57   In considering whether an employer has met any duty of reasonable adjustment, the ET must apply an objective test. Although it should look closely at the employer's explanation, it must reach its own decision on what steps were reasonable and what was objectively justified. Sometimes it may be necessary for an employer to make more than one adjustment.[149]

15.58   Factors which are particularly relevant in deciding whether it was reasonable for the employer to have made the necessary adjustment are the extent to which the adjustment would prevent the disadvantage, the practicability of the employer making the adjustment, the employer's financial and other resources, the availability of financial or other assistance to make the adjustment, and the cost and disruption entailed. These factors are set out in the EHRC Employment Code.[150]

15.59   Sometimes friends and family might be prepared to help a disabled person, eg they may be willing to help a dyslexic person who has difficulty completing an online application form. But if it is otherwise reasonable for an employer to make an adjustment, other people should not be expected to do so, just in order to save the employer the trouble.[151]

---

148 *The Equality Act 2010: The impact on disabled people*, HL Paper 117, published 24 March 2016, available at: www.publications.parliament.uk/pa/ld201516/ ldselect/ldeqact/117/117.pdf.
149 EHRC Employment Code, para 6.32.
150 At para 6.28. They originally appeared in the DDA 1995.
151 *Mallon v Aecom Ltd* UKEAT/0175/20.

15.60   Employers cannot require disabled workers to pay any of their costs in complying with the duty.[152] Research suggests that adjustments are not necessarily expensive. There may also be financial assistance available, eg grants under the Access to Work Scheme[153] as well as advice and information from specialist bodies, eg the Royal National Institute for the Blind (RNIB) and the Work Coaches at the local Jobcentre Plus offices. When considering the reasonableness of an adjustment, the cost of not making the adjustment may also be a relevant factor, eg it may be more expensive to medically retire a worker than make the needed adjustments to keep him/her in work.

15.61   It is not necessary that a particular step is guaranteed to work – it is enough if there is a prospect of it working; it does not even need to be a 'real prospect' or a 'good prospect'.[154] However, the likelihood of the proposed adjustment preventing the disadvantage to the worker is still a factor affecting whether it is reasonable.[155] It may also affect compensation.[156]

Examples of adjustments

15.62   When running a case, a worker needs to make some suggestions as to what adjustments should have been made.[157] The following are some examples of possible adjustments given in the EHRC Employment Code.[158] Note that whether it is reasonable to expect the employer to make such adjustments will depend on all the facts of the case. Possibilities are:

- allowing the worker to work flexi-time to enable additional breaks to overcome fatigue or changing the worker's hours to avoid travel on public transport during rush hours;
- where no reasonable adjustment can keep the worker in his/her original post, transferring him/her to an available suitable alternative post with retraining and modified equipment;

---

152 EqA 2010 s20(7).

153 Details on the GOV.UK site at: www.gov.uk/access-to-work.

154 *Leeds Teaching Hospital NHS Trust v Foster* UKEAT/0552/10. This goes further than *HM Prison Service v Beart* [2003] IRLR 238, CA, but the latter was only looking at whether a 'substantial possibility' was sufficient compared with a guarantee.

155 This is suggested by the Employment Code, para 6.28, which adopts the factors previously set out in DDA 1995 s18B(1)(a).

156 *Redcar and Cleveland Primary Care Trust v Lonsdale* UKEAT/0090/12.

157 See paras 16.63–16.64.

158 At para 6.33.

- ensuring a worker with autism has a structured working day and making sure other workers co-operate with this arrangement;[159]
- discounting periods of disability-related absence when selecting for redundancy;
- allowing a phased return to work with a gradual build-up of hours.

15.63   Depending on the facts, the duty may require moving the worker without competitive interview to a post at a slightly higher grade.[160] If an employee needs redeployment as a result of his/her disability, s/he must be given equal priority (at least) with other categories of redeployee, eg redundant employees.[161] It would also be a reasonable adjustment before dismissing a worker to consult him/her regarding his/her continued prospects for employment.[162] It does not necessarily excuse an employer from making a reasonable adjustment that disciplinary action which may lead to dismissal is pending.[163] It depends on the difficulty of effecting the adjustment, the likelihood of dismissal and the fairness of the disciplinary process. An employer may be under a duty to make physical arrangements for the worker to go to the toilet or to accommodate an external carer to help the worker do so. However, this does not go as far as a duty actually to provide carers to attend to a worker's personal needs.[164] Reasonable adjustments have to enable a worker to work, and not just be steps on the way. So just as it is not a reasonable adjustment to carry out a risk assessment (see para 15.54), it is not a reasonable adjustment to pay the worker to do non-productive work merely by way of rehabilitation.[165] This is to be distinguished from allowing a phased return to work with reduced and less pressurised tasks which nevertheless do amount to work done for the employer. This latter scenario is a commonly required adjustment.

15.64   Although it is a common reasonable adjustment to relocate a worker into a suitable existing vacancy, an employer would rarely be required to create an entirely new job. However, there could be some circumstances where it was appropriate, eg if the employer was in the middle of a reorganisation where many new jobs were being

159 EHRC Employment Code, para 6.35.
160 *Archibald v Fife Council* [2004] IRLR 652, HL.
161 *Kent CC v Mingo* [2000] IRLR 90, EAT.
162 *Rothwell v Pelikan Hardcopy Scotland Ltd* [2006] IRLR 24, EAT.
163 *HM Prison Service v Beart* [2003] IRLR 238, CA.
164 *Kenny v Hampshire Constabulary* [1999] IRLR 76, EAT. Although this was on the arguably narrower wording in the Disability Discrimination Act 1995.
165 *Salford NHS Primary Care Trust v Smith* UKEAT/0507/10.

designed. It would also be extremely unusual to expect an employer to require a non-disabled worker to swap jobs with a disabled worker, but it might be feasible in a workplace where an employer frequently instructs workers to change jobs and where the non-disabled worker has no real objection to the move.[166] In certain circumstances, it may be a reasonable adjustment to maintain a worker's pay at the original level, even though moving him/her to a lower grade job.[167] After all, other types of adjustment may involve a cost to the employer. Nevertheless, this will not be an adjustment which is routinely ordered by a tribunal and may depend on the amount of differential and period of protected pay.

15.65   It will rarely be a reasonable adjustment to pay full sick pay which has otherwise run out in respect of disability-related absences, especially if the original sick pay was generous.[168] However, it may be a reasonable adjustment to pay a worker fully if s/he is off sick due to the employer's failure to make a reasonable adjustment which would enable him/her to return to work.[169]

15.66   There is no absolute rule that disability-related absences must be disregarded for the purpose of totting-up and triggering a review process or dismissal under a sickness absence procedure. To what extent disregarding disability-related absences for this and other purposes may be a reasonable adjustment depends on the facts of the particular case. However, it is likely an ET would expect employers at least to consider disability-related absences separately from other sick leave and to think about each case separately, rather than have a general all-purpose total target.

15.67   Where a worker is unhappy about being subjected to a sickness absence procedure or its consequences, it is important to think carefully about how to formulate the PCP. 'Application of the Attendance Policy' is vague and likely to lead to difficulties.[170] Where a worker is disciplined or dismissed for poor attendance under a sickness absence procedure, the relevant PCP is usually that s/he had to maintain a certain level of attendance at work in order not to be subject to the risk of disciplinary sanctions. Although both disabled and non-disabled workers would suffer stress and anxiety if they were ill in circumstances which might lead to disciplinary sanctions,

---

166 *Chief Constable of South Yorkshire Police v Jelic* UKEAT/0491/09; [2010] IRLR 744.

167 *G4S Cash Solutions (UK) Ltd v Powell* UKEAT/0243/15; [2016] IRLR 820.

168 *O'Hanlon v Commissioners for HM Revenue and Customs* [2007] IRLR 404, CA.

169 *Nottinghamshire CC v Meikle* [2004] IRLR 703, CA.

170 See eg *Martin v City and County of Swansea* UKEAT/0253/20.

a disabled worker is at a substantial disadvantage if s/he is more likely because of his/her disability to be unable to meet the attendance requirement.[171] The worker could alternatively or additionally bring a claim for DAFD if s/he was disciplined, dismissed, made redundant, not promoted etc because of his/her disability-related sickness record (see below). The issue would then be whether the employer could justify his/her actions. See para 7.24 above for dismissals where contractual sick pay is still due or where there are benefits under health insurance schemes or there is a possibility of ill-health retirement.

15.68   Provision of awareness training for other employees in relation to the worker's disability could also be a reasonable adjustment.[172] Indeed, in some cases a reasonable adjustment will not succeed without the co-operation of other workers. Subject to confidentiality, the employer must make sure this happens. The EHRC Employment Code says it is unlikely to be a defence to a claim for reasonable adjustments that other staff were obstructive or unhelpful, and the employer must at least try to deal with such behaviour.[173]

15.69   Special rules exist where an employer may need to alter premises which s/he occupies under a lease.[174]

Contract workers

15.70   The duty to make reasonable adjustments applies both to the employer and to the principal of any contract worker.[175] The period of time that the worker is likely to be placed with the principal will be relevant to what adjustments it would be reasonable for the principal to have to make.[176]

Direct disability discrimination

15.71   The definition of direct discrimination and general principles are explained in chapter 13. It is important to read those paragraphs before reading this chapter. In the context of disability, direct discrim-

---

171 *Griffiths v Secretary of State for Work and Pensions* [2015] EWCA Civ 1265; [2016] IRLR 216; *Perratt v The City of Cardiff Council* UKEAT/0079/16. Think carefully about the formulation.

172 *Simpson v West Lothian Council* EATS/0049/04.

173 EHRC Employment Code, para 6.35.

174 Equality Act 2010 (Disability) Regulations 2010 SI No 2128 regs 9–12; EqA 2010 Sch 21.

175 EqA 2010 s41(4). See para 12.19 for the meaning of 'contract worker' under the EqA 2010.

176 EHRC Employment Code, para 11.13.

ination occurs where an employer treats a disabled worker less favourably because of his/her disability than s/he treats or would treat a worker who was not disabled or who did not have that particular disability. For example, a disabled worker is sacked because his/her total sickness absence amounts to three months, whereas a non-disabled worker who is off sick for three months is not sacked. This suggests the employer has treated the disabled worker less favourably because s/he is disabled, unless the employer can prove a credible reason for the different treatment which is unrelated to disability. It is still possible, though harder, to prove direct discrimination where there is no comparator, eg no one else has been off sick for three months.[177]

15.72   Stereotypical assumptions made about a worker because of his/her disability may also be direct discrimination, eg failing to recruit a disabled worker because of an assumption that s/he will take excessive time off sick,[178] or an overreaction to a worker's behaviour because of stereotyped views of mental illness.[179] In *Coffey*, the employer made a stereotypical assumption that a police officer with hearing loss was not capable of front-line duties.[180]

15.73   It can also be direct disability discrimination to treat a person less favourably because of their particular disability as opposed to someone with a different disability.[181]

15.74   As with all direct discrimination claims, there must be no material difference between the circumstances relating to the worker and his/her actual or hypothetical comparator.[182] In the case of direct disability discrimination, these circumstances include the abilities of the worker and the comparator.[183] For example, a disabled worker with arthritis is not selected for a job because s/he types too slowly. The comparator is a non-disabled worker who types at the same pace as the disabled worker.

---

177 See chapter 16 for types of evidence relevant to proving direct discrimination.

178 *Tudor v (1) Spen Corner Veterinary Centre Ltd (2) Tschimmel* (2006) 809 IDS Employment Law Brief 19; (2006) 787 IRLB 4, ET is an interesting ET level example of a directly discriminatory assumption.

179 *Aylott v Stockton-on-Tees Borough Council* [2010] EWCA Civ 910; [2010] IRLR 994.

180 *Chief Constable of Norfolk v Coffey* [2019] EWCA Civ 1061 at paras 61–78.

181 *VL v Szpital Kliniczny im dra J Babińskiego Samodzielny Publiczny Zakład Opieki Zdrowotnej w Krakowie* CJEU, C-16/19.

182 See para 13.6.

183 EqA 2010 s23(2)(a). Covered by the EHRC Employment Code at paras 3.29–3.30.

15.75   Sometimes it is difficult to identify the relevant circumstances of the appropriate comparator. For example, in *Aylott*, a worker with bipolar affective disorder was dismissed because of his attendance record. The correct comparator would be a person who did not have the conduct and performance difficulties which were in fact caused by the worker's disability.[184] The Court of Appeal in *Aylott* and in *Coffey* suggested it is easier to start by asking *why* the claimant has been treated as s/he has. If it is because of his/ her disability, eg because of stereotyping, it usually follows that a hypothetical comparator without that disability would have been treated better.

15.76   The importance of direct discrimination, as opposed to discrimination arising from disability, is that there is no justification defence available to the employer. Sometimes it can be hard to identify which type of discrimination took place. For example, has the employer refused to recruit a worker because the worker is in fact unable to do certain duties due to his/her disability (discrimination arising from disability) or because the employer wrongly assumes that a worker with such a disability would be unable to do the duties (direct discrimination/ stereotyping)?

15.77   Note that it is not discrimination against a non-disabled person to treat a disabled person more favourably because of his/her disability.[185]

Associative disability discrimination

15.78   As with other protected characteristics,[186] it is unlawful to directly discriminate against a worker because s/he is associated with someone else who has a disability. For example, a worker is not invited to a business dinner with clients, where everyone is attending with their partners, because her partner is disabled. The word 'associative' does not appear in the EqA 2010, so it is important not to become preoccupied with what it means. The Act simply says that the employer must not treat a worker less favourably because of 'a' protected characteristic. That would include the protected characteristic (disability) of other people.

15.79   Unfortunately, the scope of this protection has been widely misunderstood. It is far more limited than it appears, and it does not give a general right to time off to care for disabled relatives. If the complaint is that the employer has refused, or otherwise penalised

---

184 *Aylott v Stockton-on-Tees BC* [2010] EWCA Civ 910; [2010] IRLR 994.
185 EqA 2010 s13(3).
186 See para 13.13.

the worker for taking time off to care for a disabled relative, the actual or hypothetical comparator is a worker who took or wanted to take time off to care for a non-disabled relative. This is well illustrated in the *Coleman* case,[187] which established the right to claim associative disability discrimination under the DDA 1995 and the General Framework Directive. Ms Coleman complained that that her employers did not allow her the same flexibility regarding her working hours to look after her disabled son, as they did her colleagues, who were parents of non-disabled children. She said she was described as lazy when she requested time off to look after her son, whereas parents of non-disabled children were allowed time off. If proved by the evidence, this would be direct associative discrimination. On the other hand, if an employer refused everyone time off for childcare, whether or not their child was disabled, this would not succeed as a disability discrimination claim.[188]

Discrimination because of perceived disability

15.80　It is unlawful to directly discriminate against a worker because of his/her perceived disability.[189] This is fairly straightforward with most of the other protected characteristics, but is difficult to apply in disability cases. What exactly is it that the employer must have wrongly perceived? It is fairly clear-cut if an employer makes an entirely false assumption that a worker has a disability when the worker actually has no impairment whatsoever. For example, an employer has misunderstood something which was said, or has jumped to conclusions through overheard conversations or stereotyped ideas, eg that a worker has HIV or mental health difficulties. This would seem to be covered.

15.81　However, how does it work in other situations? The EAT has said it is not to do with whether the employer understands the law or not. It is to do with whether the employer (wrongly) perceives the worker to have an impairment with the necessary elements of the legal definition. For example, an employer does not recruit a worker because s/he wrongly perceives that the worker's hearing loss is severe enough to have an adverse effect on her ability to carry out day-to-day activities or that it is likely in the future to become so severe.[190]

---

187 *EBR Attridge Law v Coleman (No 2)* UKEAT/0071/09; [2010] IRLR 10, EAT; *Coleman v Attridge Law* C-303/06 [2008] IRLR 722, ECJ.

188 It is also worth considering indirect sex discrimination claims where caring requirements are involved. See para 11.100 onwards.

189 See para 13.15.

190 *Chief Constable of Norfolk v Coffey* [2019] EWCA Civ 1061.

Discrimination arising from disability

15.82   The definition of DAFD was new to the EqA 2010, replacing the previous concept of disability-related discrimination in the DDA 1995 whose effectiveness was eroded by the case of *Mayor and Burgess of Lewisham LBC v Malcolm*.[191] The definition of DAFD was designed to cover the same ground as disability-related discrimination, but to avoid the technical problems exposed by the *Malcolm* case.

15.83   Under EqA 2010 s15(1):

> A person (A) discriminates against a disabled person (B) if–
> (a) A treats B unfavourably because of something arising in consequence of B's disability; and
> (b) A cannot show that the treatment is a proportionate means of achieving a legitimate aim.

Unlike with the definition of direct discrimination, it is not necessary to compare the worker's treatment with that of a comparator. It is only necessary to show the worker was treated 'unfavourably', ie that s/he was put at a disadvantage.[192] The 'consequence' of a disability includes anything which is the result, effect or outcome of the disability, eg inability to use certain equipment at work.[193] Another example might be if a partially-sighted worker was dismissed for making computer-entry errors, when those mistakes were because s/he could not see the computer screen properly. There is a tendency to misunderstand DAFD. The question is *not* simply whether the treatment of the worker caused him/her difficulty because of his/her disability. The starting point is why the employer treated the worker as s/he did, eg the employer dismissed the worker because the worker was unable to type sufficiently fast. The next question is whether that reason was something arising in consequence of the worker's disability, eg the reason the worker typed slowly was as a result of his/her arthritis.[194] The employer need not be aware that the 'something'

---

191 [2008] UKHL 43; [2008] IRLR 700. Applied to employment by *Child Support Agency (Dudley) v Truman* UKEAT/0293/08; [2009] IRLR 277.

192 For a discussion of 'disadvantage', see *Williams v The Trustees of Swansea University Pension & Assurance Scheme and another* [2018] UKSC 65; [2019] IRLR 306. In that case, it was not unfavourable treatment to calculate an early retirement pension based on reduced salary because the worker had reduced hours as a reasonable adjustment for his disability. If he was not disabled, he would not be getting a pension at all.

193 EHRC Employment Code, para 5.9.

194 *Pnaiser v NHS England* UKEAT/0137/15; [2016] IRLR 170 at para 31 sets out the stages of the EqA 2010 s15 definition. This is confirmed by *West v The Royal Bank of Scotland PLC* UKEAT/0296/16 at para 25.

arises in consequence of the worker's disability.[195] Note that if there are several reasons for treating a worker unfavourably, it is sufficient if only one of them was something arising from his/her disability, provided that reason was a 'significant (ie more than trivial) influence'. It need not be the only or main reason.[196]

15.84   It is useful to consider again the example where an employer dismisses a disabled worker because s/he has been off sick for three months. If the employer would have dismissed the worker for three months' absence, whether or not s/he was disabled, the employer has not directly discriminated against the disabled worker. However, if the disabled worker's absences were as a result of his/her disability, the dismissal would be DAFD. A DAFD claim is less attractive than a direct discrimination claim to a worker, because the employer has the possibility of proving the dismissal is justified as a proportionate means of achieving a legitimate aim.

15.85   Note that the 'something' must arise 'in consequence of' the disability. This is a looser connection than 'because of' the disability.[197] The 'something' may arise from the worker's disability in different ways. These examples have been found to be DAFD:

- Giving a worker a negative reference because of her absence record, where the absences were due to her disability.[198]
- Dismissing a worker because she could not decide whether to accept a new shift until a medical report into her disability was received.[199]
- Treating a worker unfavourably because of a genuine but wrong belief that she was falsely claiming to be sick, when in fact her absence was due to disability-related sickness.[200]
- Excluding workers from a bonus because the scheme automatically excluded workers who had a formal warning for sickness

---

195 *City of York Council v Grosset* [2018] EWCA Civ 1105; [2018] IRLR 746, CA.

196 *Pnaiser v NHS England* UKEAT/0137/15; [2016] IRLR 170; *Baldeh v Churches Housing Association of Dudley & District Ltd* UKEAT/0290/18. Though it may mean a reduction in compensation if the unfavourable treatment might have happened for the other reasons anyway.

197 *Sheikholeslami v University of Edinburgh* UKEATS/0014.17; [2018] IRLR 1090, EAT.

198 *Pnaiser v NHS England* UKEAT/0137/15; [2016] IRLR 170.

199 *T-Systems Ltd v Lewis* UKEAT/0042/15.

200 *Hall v Chief Constable of West Yorkshire Police* UKEAT/0057/15; [2015] IRLR 893.

absence. The claimants, who were disabled, had each received a warning for absences which were disability-related.[201]

- Dismissing a worker for losing his temper over a non-accessible training venue, even though being short-tempered was not in itself caused by his disability.[202]
- Taking action against a worker because of something she has done as a result of anxiety arising from her disability. Generally, a worker's genuine but false belief that certain workplace conditions will aggravate her physical disability is not something arising from her disability, However, it may become so if that belief arises from the pain or stress of the disability.[203]

The justification defence

15.86   It is a defence to DAFD if the employer can prove the unfavourable treatment was a proportionate means of achieving a legitimate aim. This wording is the same as used for the objective justification of indirect discrimination in relation to all the protected characteristics (see para 13.48 onwards). In particular, it is important not to forget the 'proportionate means' part of the defence so that, eg, in a dismissal case, the tribunal should balance the prejudice to the worker of losing his/her job against the employer's legitimate aim.[204] If the treatment is the automatic result of applying a rule or policy, it is usually the rule or policy which must be justified. However, this rarely applies to disability cases involving attendance management because attendance management policies generally allow for a series of responses to individual circumstances. The tribunal should therefore consider each discretionary step taken by the employer and whether it is justified.[205]

15.87   It is hard to see how DAFD could be justified if the employer has not made relevant reasonable adjustments. For example, if a typist is dismissed for typing too slowly because of arthritis, this is unlikely to be justifiable if s/he could have reached acceptable typing speeds had the employer obtained accessible keyboards. Similarly, dismissing a

---

201 *Land Registry v Houghton and others* UKEAT/0149/14.

202 *Risby v Waltham Forest LBC* UKEAT/0318/15.

203 See *Sheikholeslami v University of Edinburgh* UKEATS/0014/17; [2018] IRLR 1090, EAT; and *iForce Limited v Wood* UKEAT/0167/18.

204 As an example, see *Baldeh v Churches Housing Association of Dudley & District Ltd* UKEAT/0290/18. The EAT in *Stott v Ralli Ltd* EA-2019-000772-VP suggests the impact on other disabled people is not usually relevant to s15 justification.

205 *Buchanan v Commissioner of Police of the Metropolis* UKEAT/0112/16; [2016] IRLR 918.

worker because s/he cannot return to work as a result of failure to make reasonable adjustments is almost bound to be unjustifiable DAFD. The reverse does not necessarily hold true – just because there are no reasonable adjustments which the employer could have made, does not necessarily mean that the unfavourable treatment of the worker was justifiable DAFD.[206]

The employer's knowledge

15.88   DAFD is not unlawful if the employer can prove s/he did not know, and could not reasonably have been expected to know, that the worker had the disability.[207] There is no explicit requirement that the employer was aware of the effects of the disability.

Harassment

15.89   The general law on harassment in respect of all characteristics is set out in chapter 13.

Indirect discrimination

15.90   The definition of indirect discrimination is explained in chapter 13. Indirect discrimination did not apply to disability prior to the EqA 2010. It was not thought necessary because of the easier and more targeted concept of reasonable adjustments.

15.91   When applying the definition of indirect discrimination to disability, it must be shown that the PCP puts the worker and others who have the *same* disability at a particular disadvantage.[208] It is unclear how closely defined the disability needs to be for these purposes. One example of indirect disability discrimination would be if an employer's office was located on the second floor of a building with no lift. This would disadvantage a disabled worker who was unable to climb stairs. It would also disadvantage other workers who were unable because of the same disability to climb stairs. It would then be a question of whether the employer could objectively justify the location of the workplace.

15.92   A worker unable to climb stairs could equally claim failure to make reasonable adjustments, provided the employer knew of his/her disability. Indeed, it is hard to think of many examples where it

206 See comments in *Griffiths v Secretary of State for Work and Pensions* [2015] EWCA Civ 1265; [2016] IRLR 216 and *Pulman v Merthyr Tydfil College Ltd* UKEAT/0309/16.
207 EqA 2010 s15(2).
208 EqA 2010 s6(3)(b).

would be necessary to claim indirect discrimination, as opposed to failure to make reasonable adjustments. Loosely speaking, in both cases, it is necessary to show the employer has applied a PCP to the worker which has put the worker at a disadvantage. In the case of indirect discrimination, it is also necessary to show that the PCP puts or would put other disabled people at a particular disadvantage. This is a difficult stage in indirect discrimination cases, but not necessary at all in reasonable adjustment claims, where only the worker bringing the claim needs to be affected. Then in an indirect discrimination case, an employer has a defence if s/he can prove applying the PCP was objectively justified as a proportionate means of achieving a legitimate aim. This defence is not available to employers in reasonable adjustment claims, though the employer is only required to take such steps as are 'reasonable'.

15.93   It is also possible for indirect discrimination to apply where a PCP puts workers with a particular disability at a disadvantage compared with workers who have a different disability.[209]

15.94   Possibly one situation where an indirect discrimination claim may prove advantageous over a reasonable adjustment claim is where the employer is not aware that the worker is disabled or needs a reasonable adjustment. Although knowledge is required for the reasonable adjustment obligation to apply, it is not explicitly required for indirect discrimination. It may be that there are other examples which are not immediately apparent. Cautious advisers may want to claim indirect discrimination in the alternative if they identify potential difficulties with a reasonable adjustment claim, but this needs to be balanced against the added complexities of such a claim. Another use of the concept of indirect discrimination may be as a negotiating tool where employers are proposing to make workplace changes which are likely to disadvantage workers with certain disabilities.

Victimisation

15.95   The law on victimisation is set out in chapter 13. There are no special considerations applicable to disability.

---

209 For a situation which might arise, see *VL v Szpital Kliniczny im dra J.Babińskiego Samodzielny Publiczny Zakład Opieki Zdrowotnej w Krakowie* CJEU, C-16/19.

Deciding on the relevant claim

15.96   There are so many different types of disability discrimination that it can become confusing to decide which ones apply to a particular set of facts. The best approach is first to identify the apparently discriminatory actions by the employer, eg failure to promote, disciplinary action, dismissal; and then to test each definition of discrimination against each action, looking for the most natural fit. However, when making a final decision on how to put the claim, it is important not to lose sight of the wood for the trees. It is easy to bury a good claim by listing too many small incidents and covering every option out of anxiety, when the evidence to prove some types of discrimination is weak.

15.97   Where a worker's complaint is about a specific action, such as failure to promote or dismissal, the most obvious claim (subject to evidence) is usually that such action amounted to direct discrimination or DAFD. It is often uncertain whether the evidence suggests direct discrimination or DAFD, in which case, an 'and/or' claim can be made. Remember the advantage of direct discrimination is that there is no justification defence available to the employer. The disadvantage is usually that it is harder to prove.

15.98   A DAFD claim can often be looked at through a different perspective as a claim for failure to make reasonable adjustments. For example, if a worker is demoted because s/he cannot do his/her job, which in turn is because a reasonable adjustment has not been made, his/her claim could also be for the failure to make the reasonable adjustment as opposed to for the demotion. The compensation would include financial loss arising from the demotion. Similarly, a disability-related dismissal due to the worker's absence on sick leave could amount to a failure to make reasonable adjustments if adjustments such as allowing a staged return to work or offering alternative employment would have avoided the dismissal.[210] In cases like this, it is usually best to claim both DAFD and/or failure to make reasonable adjustments. This is because the reasonable adjustment claim may not quite fit the exact circumstances.[211] There is also a potential time limit risk in that the failure to make adjustments may have

---

210   *Fareham College Corporation v Walters* UKEAT/0396/08 and 0076/09; [2009] IRLR 991, EAT.

211   See also para 15.67.

occurred some time before the later demotion or dismissal or other action.[212]

15.99   In other situations, the claim is very obviously for failure to make reasonable adjustments and nothing else. Often such claims will also amount to indirect discrimination, but this may add an unnecessary complexity if a reasonable adjustment claim will cover the situation.

Exceptions

Occupational requirements

15.100 The occupational requirement exception, where in certain circumstances it is not unlawful for an employer to require a worker to have a particular protected characteristic, is set out in chapter 13. In disability cases, this exception is less important because an employer is in any event permitted to treat a disabled worker more favourably because of his/her disability than a non-disabled worker.[213] However, the exception may be useful in relation to special treatment for those with a particular disability.

Supported employment

15.101 Some charities are permitted to provide employment only to people with a particular disability in order to help them gain employment.[214]

Armed forces

15.102 The rules against disability discrimination do not apply to service in the armed forces.[215]

Special cases

Long Covid

15.103 As at 1 August 2021, an estimated 970,000 people were experiencing self-reported long Covid. Of those 40 per cent were experiencing the symptoms over a year after the first (suspected) infection. Of working

---

212 See para 21.14 regarding time limits; and appendix A at A19 for an illustration.
213 EqA 2010 s13(3).
214 EqA 2010 s193(3); EHRC Employment Code, para 13.48.
215 EqA 2010 Sch 9 para 4; EHRC Employment Code, paras 13.21–13.23.

adults, 38 per cent said it had negatively affected their ability to work.[216]In TUC research, workers reported that they were faced with disbelief and suspicion, with employers questioning the impact of their symptoms and sometimes challenging whether they had long Covid at all.[217] ACAS has advice for employers and employees on its website.[218] There is also useful information from the NHS.[219]

15.104   Long Covid, also known as post-Covid-19 syndrome, may in some cases meet the definition of disability. Common symptoms include difficulty sleeping, fatigue, shortness of breath, difficulty concentrating, brain fog and memory problems, palpitations and dizziness, joint pain / muscle ache, depression and anxiety, loss of appetite, loss of smell, earache and feeling sick. This could cause substantial adverse effects on day-to-day activities such as difficulty completing housework, other tasks, or a full work day due to tiredness, difficulty walking or climbing stairs, difficulty eating a normal meal, reluctance to socialise etc. The effects often fluctuate. One key issue may be whether the substantial effects are long-term. If they have not yet lasted 12 months, are they 'likely' to go on to do so? This may be hard to prove with an illness which is still not fully understood, but general statistics from the Office of National Statistics (ONS) as to the usual duration of long Covid together with a specific medical report may be helpful.

15.105   Reasonable adjustments may include flexible working, breaks, recording Covid-related absence separately from other sick leave, and delaying capability procedures. Both ACAS and the TUC recommend as good practice that employers focus on making adjustments rather than whether or not an individual has a disability and can make legal claims.

216 *Prevalence of ongoing symptoms following coronavirus (COVID-19) infection in the UK: 2 September 2021* at www.ons.gov.uk/ peoplepopulationandcommunity/healthandsocialcare/conditionsanddiseases/ bulletins/prevalenceofongoingsymptomsfollowingcoronaviruscovid19 infectionintheuk/2september2021. The ONS regularly publishes updated statistics. The 38 per cent figure is taken from the previous release.

217 *Workers' experiences of long Covid: A TUC report* at www.tuc.org.uk/research-analysis/reports/workers-experiences-long-covid.

218 *Long COVID – advice for employers and employees* at www.acas.org.uk/long-covid.

219 *Long-term effects of coronavirus (long COVID)* at www.nhs.uk/conditions/ coronavirus-covid-19/long-term-effects-of-coronavirus-long-covid/.

The menopause

15.106 Difficulties faced by many menopausal women at work have long been a taboo unaddressed subject. In recent years, the issue has gained publicity and some claims for disability or sex discrimination have been brought in tribunals. Unfortunately, the law is not designed to address menopause discrimination, and it is a poor fit. For an introduction to the menopause and work, see the section on the menopause in chapter 14. That section looks at whether sex and/or age discrimination law can apply. However, pending new targeted legislation, disability discrimination law will often be the most useful where a woman is badly affected.

15.107 The menopause is not a disability, but its symptoms can fit the legal definition where they are sufficiently severe and long-lasting. Every woman will be differently affected in terms of type and seriousness of symptom. Common symptoms include hot flushes and body temperature swings; night sweats; difficulty sleeping; tiredness and lack of energy; difficulty concentrating or memory problems; heavy and unpredictable periods; bladder infections; headaches including migraines; dry eyes; feelings of stress; depression and anxiety; panic attacks; crying spells; mood swings and irritability; loss of confidence and feelings of isolation.

15.108 In terms of the definition of disability, the following are examples of potential substantial adverse effects on ability to carry out normal day-to-day activities:[220]

- substantial difficulty sleeping;
- difficulty concentrating, eg because of tiredness or severe migraines;
- difficulty engaging in normal conversation because of tiredness or distraction of hot flushes;
- persistently wanting to avoid people, eg because of embarrassment;
- reduced ability to socialise because of accumulated tiredness;
- persistent low motivation, eg because of depression (depression can be covered as a disability in itself);

220 By way of example, see these ET cases which found menopausal symptoms to be a disability: *Donnachie v Telent Technology Services Ltd* ET No:1300005/2020 at www.gov.uk/employment-tribunal-decisions/miss-j-donnachie-v-telent-technology-services-ltd-1300005-2020; *Daley v Optiva* ET No:1308074/2019 at www.gov.uk/employment-tribunal-decisions/mrs-d-daley-v-optiva-1308074-slash-2019. See also the examples in *Rooney v Leicester City Council* EA-2-2—000070-DA; EA-2021-000256-DA where the EAT said the ET had wrongly focused on what the claimant *could* do and had not explained why the facts did not amount to a disability.

- difficulty using the computer because of tiredness or headaches;
- difficulty completing housework because of lack of energy;
- difficulty carrying out activities associated with toileting;
- difficulty using transport, eg because of a frequent need for the lavatory;
- difficulty lifting full shopping bags because of muscle weakness and cramps;
- inability to stay awake through a film;
- a combination of various effects.

15.109   A woman needs to show any effects are substantial, which means not trivial. This may require spelling it out. An occasional inability to sleep or very minor infrequent hot flushes may not be considered sufficient. If the symptoms are lessened by HRT, then the relevant effect is what it would be without the HRT.

15.110   Depending on how a woman is affected by the menopause, reasonable adjustments could include:[221]

- Sleep disruption: allowing short-term absence, temporary shift swaps, ad hoc home working, and flexible hours.
- Hot flushes / daytime sweats: desk fans, adjusted air conditioning, desk near window, drinking water, adapted uniform (looser / natural fabrics), limiting time on duties which require personal protective equipment (PPE).[222]
- Headaches / fatigue: quiet areas to work, access to private rest areas, regular breaks, flexible break times, temporary adjustment to duties.
- Heavy / irregular periods / urinary problems: easy access to washrooms, more frequent toilet breaks, extra uniform, ad hoc home working.
- Loss of confidence / anxiety / loss of concentration: quiet time when needed, quiet workspace, homeworking, agreed protected time to catch up with work.

---

221 These and other suggestions in the very useful *A guide to managing menopause at work – guidance for line managers*, CIPD / BUPA, May 2021 at www.cipd. co.uk/Images/line-manager-guide-to-menopause_tcm18-95174.pdf. Also see suggestions in *The menopause in the workplace – A toolkit for trade unionists*, Wales TUC Cymru www.tuc.org.uk/sites/default/files/Wales_TUC_menopause_Toolkit.pdf.

222 See *Menopause and the workplace*, NHS Employers at www.nhsemployers.org/articles/menopause-and-workplace regarding heat stress from wearing PPE.

15.111 Unjustifiably dismissing a woman because of conduct or capability which arises from her menopause could be discrimination under section 15.[223] Bearing in mind that some women may be reticent to mention to their managers that they have menopausal symptoms, remember that it will be necessary to establish that the employer had the requisite knowledge for disability discrimination claims (see above).

---

223 See *Davies v Scottish Courts and Tribunals Service* S/4104575/2017 at https:// assets.publishing.service.gov.uk/media/5afc31a8ed915d0de80ffd2c/Ms_M_ Davies_v_Scottish_Courts_and_Tribunals_Service_4104575_2017_Final.pdf as an example, though as an ET level case, it has no precedent value.

Evidence in discrimination cases

Chapter 16: Key points

- Once the claimant proves facts from which a tribunal *could* conclude there was discrimination in the absence of an explanation, the burden of proof moves to the employer to prove s/he did not discriminate.
- It is not necessary to apply the two-stage burden of proof in obvious cases.
- Where appropriate, the employment tribunal (ET) must take account of the employer's failure to follow a relevant part of the discrimination Codes in deciding whether the employer has a case to answer.
- Employers rarely admit discrimination and often deny it, even to themselves.
- The ET can infer direct discrimination from a variety of factors, eg a pattern of incidents, racist remarks, inadequate explanations, statistics, wholly unexplained unreasonable behaviour, and most importantly, actual or evidential comparators.
- The best evidence is an actual comparator, ie another worker of a different race, sex, religion, age, sexual orientation or without a disability, who has been treated differently (ie better) in comparable circumstances.
- A hypothetical comparison can be made where there are no actual comparators or only evidential, ie loosely comparable, comparators.
- In indirect discrimination cases, it is important to produce statistics or other evidence showing the adverse impact of the provision, criterion or practice (PCP), in all relevant pools.
- In disability discrimination cases, medical evidence is often necessary to prove the worker has a disability under the Equality Act (EqA) 2010.
- Specialist websites are useful sources of information regarding the effect of a disability and possible reasonable adjustments.
- Medical evidence is usually necessary to claim compensation for injury to health (personal injury) in discrimination cases. See also paras 19.27–19.35 for necessary evidence on this.

The burden of proof in discrimination cases

16.1   The standard of proof in discrimination cases is the normal civil standard, namely whether, on the balance of probabilities (ie 'more likely than not'), discrimination occurred. The employment tribunal (ET) should be reminded of this at the hearing.

16.2   As a result of various European Union (EU) directives, the burden of proof shifts onto the employer once the worker has proved a 'prima facie' case.[1] The burden of proof is set out in Equality Act (EqA) 2010 s136 which, to paraphrase, reads as follows:

> If there are facts from which the ET could decide, in the absence of any other explanation, that the employer contravened the provision concerned, the ET must hold that the contravention occurred. However, this does not apply if the employer shows that s/he did not contravene the provision.

16.3   The Court of Appeal in *Igen Ltd and others v Wong; Chamberlin Solicitors and another v Emokpae; Brunel University v Webster*[2] set out guidance on the stages which an ET should follow. Although the guidelines were expressed in terms of a sex discrimination case under the former Sex Discrimination Act (SDA) 1975, the same principles apply under the EqA 2010 to all forms of discrimination, subject to the qualifiers set out below. The Court of Appeal said the ET must go through a two-stage process: At stage 1, the claimant must prove facts from which the ET *could* conclude, in the absence of an adequate explanation from the respondent (employer), that the respondent had discriminated against the claimant. In deciding whether the claimant has proved these facts, the ET can take account of the respondent's evidence. At stage 2, the respondent must prove s/he did not commit that discrimination. Although there are two stages, ETs will generally wish to hear all the evidence in one go, including the respondent's explanation, before deciding whether the requirements of each stage are satisfied. The full guidelines are as follows.

1)   Pursuant to SDA 1975 s63A,[3] it is for the claimant[4] who complains of sex discrimination to prove, on the balance of probabilities, facts from which the tribunal could conclude, in the

---

1   See para 16.5.
2   [2005] IRLR 258, CA.
3   The equivalent section on burden of proof under the SDA 1975.
4   Despite the different wording of EqA 2010 s136, it is still the claimant who must prove these facts: *Ayodele v Citylink Ltd and another* [2017] EWCA Civ 1913; [2018] IRLR 114; *Royal Mail Ltd v Efobi* [2021] UKSC 22; [2021] IRLR 811.

absence of an adequate explanation, that the respondent has committed an act of discrimination against the claimant which is unlawful by virtue of Part II or which by virtue of section 41 or section 42 of the SDA 1975 is to be treated as having been committed against the claimant. These are referred to below as 'such facts'.

2)   If the claimant does not prove such facts, s/he will fail.

3)   It is important to bear in mind in deciding whether the claimant has proved such facts that it is unusual to find direct evidence of sex discrimination. Few employers would be prepared to admit such discrimination, even to themselves. In some cases, the discrimination will not be an intention but merely based on the assumption that 'the claimant would not have fitted in'.

4)   In deciding whether the claimant has proved such facts, it is important to remember that the outcome at this stage of the analysis by the tribunal will, therefore, usually depend on what inferences it is proper to draw from the primary facts found by the tribunal.

5)   It is important to note the word 'could' in SDA 1975 s63A(2).[5] At this stage, the tribunal does not have to reach a definitive determination that such facts would lead it to the conclusion that there was an act of unlawful discrimination. The tribunal is looking at the primary facts before it to see what inferences of secondary fact could be drawn from them.

6)   In considering what inferences or conclusions can be drawn from the primary facts, the tribunal must assume that there is no adequate explanation for those facts.

7)   These inferences can include, in appropriate cases, any inferences that it is just and equitable to draw in accordance with section 74(2)(b) of the SDA 1975 from an evasive or equivocal reply to a questionnaire or any other questions that fall within section 74(2) of the SDA 1975.[6]

8)   Likewise, the tribunal must decide whether any provision of any relevant Code of Practice is relevant and, if so, take it into account in determining, such facts pursuant to section 56A(10) of the

---

5   'Could' also appears in EqA 2010 s136.

6   This referred to statutory questionnaires under the SDA 1975 and was subsequently applied to EqA 2010 s138 and the statutory questionnaire procedure. The statutory procedure and s138 has now been repealed as explained in para 21.47 below.

SDA 1975.[7] This means that inferences may also be drawn from any failure to comply with any relevant Code of Practice.

9) Where the claimant has proved facts from which conclusions could be drawn that the respondent has treated the claimant less favourably on the ground of sex, then the burden of proof moves to the respondent.

10) It is then for the respondent to prove that s/he did not commit, or as the case may be, is not to be treated as having committed, that act.

11) To discharge that burden it is necessary for the respondent to prove, on the balance of probabilities, that the treatment was in no sense whatsoever on the grounds of sex, since 'no discrimination whatsoever' is compatible with the Burden of Proof Directive.[8]

12) That requires a tribunal to assess not merely whether the respondent has proved an explanation for the facts from which such inferences can be drawn, but further that it is adequate to discharge the burden of proof on the balance of probabilities that sex was not a ground for the treatment in question.

13) Since the facts necessary to prove an explanation would normally be in the possession of the respondent, a tribunal would normally expect cogent evidence to discharge that burden of proof. In particular, the tribunal will need to examine carefully explanations for failure to deal with the questionnaire procedure[9] and/ or code of practice.

16.4 Note that stage 1 of the burden of proof (guidelines 1)–8)) requires the claimant to prove facts from which the tribunal *could* conclude that the respondent *has* committed an act of discrimination – not simply that the respondent *could have* committed an act of discrimination. Regarding stage 2 of the burden of proof (guidelines 9)–13)), it is not necessary for the tribunal to go as far as rejecting the respondent's explanation; the respondent will not have discharged the burden of proof if the tribunal simply says it was not persuaded by its explanation.[10]

---

7 Equality Act (EqA) 2006 s15(4) deals with inferences from failure to follow a code.
8 Directive 97/80/EC of 15 December 1997.
9 See n6 above regarding the questionnaire procedure.
10 *Pothecary Witham Weld and another v Bullimore and another and Equality and Human Rights Commission (intervener)* UKEAT/0158/09; [2010] IRLR 572.

16.5   Although the burden of proof is on the claimant at stage 1, the tribunal should take account of all evidence that is in front of it, not only evidence produced by the claimant.[11]

16.6   What facts are sufficient to potentially suggest discrimination in the absence of an adequate explanation from the employer (stage 1)? This is often referred to as having a 'prima facie' case. Ideally, the worker can identify an actual comparator of a different race, sex, etc who has been treated differently or better in similar circumstances.[12] However, by way of an example, it may not be enough to shift the burden of proof simply that a white comparator was promoted to a post for which a black worker had applied. It seems the black worker would also have to have met the stated requirements of the post and was at least as well qualified as the white comparator.[13] Other examples where it may be legitimate for an ET to find a prima facie case so that the burden of proof shifts are:

- where a black woman is not selected for one of five posts following a reorganisation in circumstances where all the successful candidates are white men with whom she is equally qualified. It may be different if a number of equally qualified white candidates have also been rejected;[14]
- where a woman is allocated only three projects out of over 200 following her gender reassignment, compared with a large allocation previously;[15]
- where an employer dismisses a black employee for an offence which has equally been committed by his/her white colleagues; has failed to investigate his/her allegation of race discrimination and has been evasive in replying to his/her questionnaire;[16]
- where an employer asks an employee rhetorically whether it is his age that caused him not to be able to work to expectations and comments that 'you can't teach an old dog new tricks', even if there is no other evidence of age discrimination in the criticism of the employee's performance;[17]
- where on closure of one site, two employees in their 30s are offered transfer to vacancies on another site; the claimant who is

11 *Royal Mail Group Ltd v Efobi* [2021] UKSC 22; [2021] IRLR 811.
12 See paras 13.6 and 16.19 onwards on comparators.
13 *Dresdner Kleinwort Wasserstein Ltd v Adebayo* [2005] IRLR 514, EAT.
14 *Network Rail Infrastructure Ltd v Griffiths-Henry* [2006] IRLR 865, EAT.
15 *EB v BA* [2006] IRLR 471, CA.
16 *Dresdner Kleinwort Wasserstein Ltd v Adebayo* [2005] IRLR 514, EAT. See n6 regarding the questionnaire procedure.
17 *James v Gina Shoes Ltd and others* UKEAT/0384/11.

aged 64 is not offered a third vacancy, which is eventually filled by external recruitment; and the decision-maker falsely tells the tribunal that he had offered the claimant a transfer which the claimant refused.[18]

16.7   The Court of Appeal in *Madarassy* said that the mere fact of a difference in protected characteristic and a difference in treatment will not be enough to shift the burden of proof. There needs to be 'something more'. There has to be enough evidence from which a reasonable tribunal could properly conclude, if unexplained, that discrimination has (not could have) occurred.[19] The need for 'something more' is often raised by employers defending discrimination claims, but it is a vague concept. If too much 'more' is required, the shifting burden of proof will not operate as intended by the EU directives. The better treatment of a comparator is usually good evidence if the circumstances are such that one would have expected the worker and the comparator to have been treated the same way. Perhaps those circumstances constitute the required 'more'. So, for example, if a 57-year-old employee is dismissed for poor performance, while a younger employee is retained, this fact alone is highly unlikely to shift the burden of proof for a case of age discrimination. However, if the evidence indicated that the performance of the employee and his comparator was at a similar level, this could be the 'more' which makes the burden of proof shift. Or to take another example, it may not be enough to shift the burden of proof on sex discrimination that a woman has been disciplined for misconduct, whereas a male colleague has not. However, if the employer was aware that they had both committed the same offence, that might be sufficient to constitute the required 'more'. Arguably, to require any further indicators of sex discrimination in that scenario would make the shifting burden of proof redundant. See also the examples in the previous paragraph.

16.8   Where there is no actual comparator or overt racist, sexist or ageist remarks etc, the prima facie case needs to be established from other evidence,[20] eg a woman who is well-qualified for a job and meets the person specification, is not even interviewed. Further examples of the type of evidence which could lead to an inference of discrimination are set out in the rest of this chapter.

---

18 *Hussain v Vision Security Ltd & another* UKEAT/0439/10.
19 *Madarassy v Nomura International plc* [2007] IRLR 246, CA.
20 *Shamoon v Chief Constable of the RUC* [2003] IRLR 285, HL.

16.9   In deciding whether stage 1 of the burden of proof has been met, although the ET must disregard the employer's explanation, it can take into account other evidence from the employer which discredits or puts the claimant's facts into context, for example, evidence that the alleged discriminator treats all employees equally badly.[21]

16.10   Some employers argue after the claimant's evidence at the ET hearing that it is not necessary for them to provide any explanation because stage 1 has not been met. However, discrimination cases are best looked at as a whole. The ET will usually want to hear the employer's evidence and explanation and the worker should have the opportunity of questioning the employer's witnesses.[22] Very often a claimant may not be sure what lies behind something that concerns him/her and it can only be decided after evidence has been given.[23]

16.11   In indirect discrimination cases, the claimant must point to a provision, criterion or practice (PCP) with discriminatory impact which disadvantages him/her and others sharing the same relevant protected characteristic. Once this is shown, if the employer seeks to claim that a discriminatory practice is justifiable, it is for the employer to prove it is a proportionate means of achieving a legitimate aim. Note the above comments regarding the wording of EqA 2010 s136 in relation to the burden of proof.

16.12   The shifting burden of proof is very important where it is uncertain if there is enough evidence to prove discrimination. However, it is artificial and unnecessary where the evidence is very clear one way or another.[24] One of the problems with the burden of proof is the question whether an employer's unconvincing or lack of explanation can be a matter which helps shift the burden of proof. The wording of section 136 suggests possibly not. However, if the tribunal looks at all matters together, albeit with the burden remaining on the claimant, a poor or contradictory explanation should be able to go into the mix from the outset. Unfortunately the key cases are difficult to reconcile and do not explicitly state the effect of not applying section 136 in this context.[25]

21 *Laing v Manchester City Council* [2006] IRLR 748, EAT; *Madarassy v Nomura International plc* [2007] IRLR 246, CA.

22 *JSV Oxford v DHSS* [1977] IRLR 225, EAT; *Laher v Hammersmith and Fulham LBC* [1994] EAT/215/91.

23 The Court of Appeal approving the Employment Appeal Tribunal (EAT) in *Balamoody v UKCC for Nursing, Midwifery and Health Visiting* [2002] IRLR 288, CA.

24 The Supreme Court in *Hewage v Grampian Health Board* [2012] IRLR 870, confirmed by *Royal Mail Group Ltd v Efobi* [2021] UKSC 22; [2021] IRLR 811 discourages use of the burden of proof where the evidence is obvious.

25 These are the author's current thoughts on this difficult issue.

Helpful kinds of evidence in discrimination cases

Direct discrimination

Introduction

16.13　In *King*,[26] the Court of Appeal said that as direct evidence of discrimination is rarely available, the necessary evidence will 'usually depend on what inferences it is proper to draw from the primary facts'. In other words, the ET must look for clues and draw conclusions. The concept of the ET drawing 'inferences' is central to running a discrimination case. Since such an indirect approach is necessary, a wide range of evidence may seem relevant. Choosing which evidence to use in a case is important. A good case can become discredited by taking weak points. Excessive and inconclusive evidence clouds the real issues and lengthens the hearing.

Other acts of discrimination

16.14　Every act of discrimination within the three months prior to lodging an ET1[27] may form the basis of a claim. However, acts or indicators of discrimination falling outside the time limit may be mentioned in the claim purely as evidence in support of the discriminatory acts founding the claim.[28] For clarity, it should be stated which acts form the basis of the claim. Earlier alleged acts of discrimination will usually be helpful only if they took place relatively recently and relate to the same managers. Acts of discrimination or evidence of discriminatory attitudes occurring after the acts founding the claim are also admissible as supporting evidence of a tendency to discriminate.[29] Indicators from a time before or after a particular decision, eg not to promote, may indicate that an ostensibly fair decision was made because of a protected characteristic.[30] Workers would be well advised not to overload their claims with too many incidents, whether forming the basis of the claim or supporting evidence. There is a great danger that the best evidence will get lost in the welter of information, and cases become very long and expensive, with increasing costs risks if

---

26　*King v Great Britain-China Centre* [1991] IRLR 513, CA.

27　Claim to ET.

28　*Eke v Commissioners of Customs and Excise* [1981] IRLR 334, EAT; *Qureshi v (1) Victoria University of Manchester (2) Brazier* EAT/484/95, approved and quoted at length in *Anya v University of Oxford* [2001] IRLR 377, CA.

29　*Chattopadhyay v Headmaster of Holloway School* [1981] IRLR 487, EAT.

30　*Anya v University of Oxford* [2001] IRLR 377, CA.

they lose.[31] When considering whether to add in a further incident, the worker should think about how much that incident, in itself or added together with other incidents, helps prove the key discrimination. Does it add anything? If the main incidents do not convince the tribunal, will adding this one make any difference?

16.15   Where the worker mentions a number of out-of-time incidents as evidence supporting the claim, the ET should not look at each incident in isolation to decide if it was itself discriminatory. In such a case, it is important to draw the ET's attention to the Employment Appeal Tribunal's (EAT's) guidance in *Qureshi v (1) Victoria University of Manchester (2) Brazier*.[32] The ET should find the primary facts about all the incidents and then look at the totality of those facts, including the employer's explanations, in order to decide whether to infer the acts complained of in the ET1 were because of the protected characteristic. To adopt a fragmented approach 'would inevitably have the effect of diminishing any eloquence that the cumulative effect of the primary facts might have' as to whether actions were because of the protected characteristic.

The employer's explanation

16.16   The employer's likely explanation for what has happened must be anticipated, as it will have to be discredited. If, for example, a worker has clearly committed a dismissable offence or is obviously the least qualified and experienced for an appointment or promotion, then it will be extremely difficult to prove unlawful discrimination, even if it could be shown that the employer was generally prejudiced against workers with the same protected characteristic. The issue is less favourable treatment and if, for example, a man would similarly have been dismissed for the same offence, it is irrelevant that the employer was pleased to have the opportunity to dismiss a woman.

16.17   Where the alleged act of discrimination is dismissal, the ET may wonder whether the case is an attempt to claim unfair dismissal for a worker without the necessary qualifying service. It must therefore be remembered that the ET is not interested in whether or not the dismissal was fair, but whether it was on the discriminatory ground.[33] Direct discrimination is not about unfair treatment, it is about different treatment. However, unreasonable conduct by an employer is not

---

31 See para 20.246 regarding costs.
32 EAT/484/95. The guidance is set out in detail and approved by the Court of Appeal in *Anya v University of Oxford* [2001] IRLR 377, CA.
33 *Glasgow CC v Zafar* [1998] IRLR 36, HL.

completely irrelevant. An inference of unlawful discrimination can be drawn from the employer's inability to explain unreasonable treatment of the worker.[34] Also, in some cases it can be argued that the dismissal was so patently unfair as to be irrational unless explained by hidden grounds. An ET should not assume without evidence that the employer behaves equally badly to employees of all races etc.[35] Even so, it is advisable for the claimant to prove that the employer is not normally unreasonable with other workers or to show some further evidence indicating unlawful discrimination. ETs should take care before accepting an employer's explanation that the reason for the less favourable treatment of the claimant is general inefficiency or poor administration.[36] This could be a mask for direct discrimination. Tribunals can also infer discrimination from untrue or inconsistent explanations.[37]

16.18   Discrimination cases are more than usually dependent on the quality of the employer's evidence at the hearing, which makes their outcome hard to predict. Much will depend on how well the employer's explanation stands up to cross-examination. Any contradiction between different witnesses for the employer, or between the explanation given at the hearing and that in any contemporaneous document or in the tribunal defence, may well lead the ET to infer discrimination was because of a protected characteristic. However, it will not usually be enough simply to discredit the employer's version of events; some other indication of unlawful discrimination will also be required.

16.19   When listening to the employer's explanation, the ET should not simply consider whether the witnesses sound credible or honest. A witness can be credible, honest – and mistaken.[38] The fact that the employer had a genuine belief that the claimant was guilty of misconduct does not mean s/he has discharged the burden of proving s/he did not discriminate. That would fail to appreciate the insidious nature of discrimination.[39] Witnesses do not generally advertise their

---

34 *Bahl v The Law Society* [2004] IRLR 799, CA; *Igen Ltd and others v Wong; Chamberlin Solicitors and another v Emokpae; Brunel University v Webster* [2005] IRLR 258, CA; *Chief Constable of West Yorkshire v Vento* [2001] IRLR 124, EAT.
35 *Anya v University of Oxford* [2001] IRLR 377, CA.
36 *Komeng v Sandwell MBC* UKEAT/0592/10.
37 See comments of EAT in *Veolia Environmental Services UK v Gumbs* UKEAT/0487/12.
38 *Anya v University of Oxford* [2001] IRLR 377, CA. Applied to Disability Discrimination Act (DDA) 1995 cases by *Williams v YKK (UK) Ltd* [2003] EAT/408/01.
39 *Dresdner Kleinwort Wasserstein Ltd v Adebayo* [2005] IRLR 514, EAT.

prejudices.[40] Indeed, very little discrimination today is overt or even deliberate.[41] Witnesses can be unconsciously prejudiced.[42]

16.20   An ET should recognise that an employer may discriminate against one minority ethnic group even though s/he may not discriminate against another. The fact that a person is married to a black woman, for example, is not indicative of whether he would racially abuse an Irish worker.[43] There is no legal reason why a manager could not discriminate against a worker of the same racial group as him/herself, but it is a factor to be taken into account.[44] The ET will no doubt be wondering why such discrimination would have happened. However, it is quite possible to envisage that a black businessperson may hire a white salesperson in order to appeal to white customers; or that a black junior manager may feel isolated and under pressure to be accepted within a white dominant organisation.

Comparative treatment

16.21   The central concept in direct discrimination is that of actual or hypothetical comparative treatment. The question is whether the worker was less favourably treated than an actual or hypothetical comparator without his/her relevant protected characteristic. Such comparison must be made where there is no material difference in the circumstances of the case of the worker and the comparator.[45] For example, if a female police constable fails her probation on grounds of dishonesty, the comparator is an actual or hypothetical male police constable who has his probation confirmed, despite having committed the same kind of dishonesty. Obviously if an actual worker without the relevant protected characteristic can be identified who, in similar circumstances, was treated more favourably, then the case will be much stronger. It then becomes a question of whether the employer can provide a credible innocent explanation for the different treatment. The circumstances of the claimant and of his/her comparator need not be precisely the same and it is up to the tribunal to decide whether the situations were in fact comparable.[46]

---

40   *Glasgow CC v Zafar* [1998] IRLR 36, HL.
41   *Anya v University of Oxford* [2001] IRLR 377, CA.
42   *Swiggs v Nagarajan* [1999] IRLR 572, HL; and para 13.23.
43   *Robson v Commissioners of the Inland Revenue* [1998] IRLR 186, EAT.
44   *Graham v Barnet LBC* [2000] EAT/221/99.
45   EqA 2010 s23.
46   *Hewage v Grampian Health Board* [2012] UKSC 37; [2012] IRLR 870.

16.22   In most cases it is impossible to find a real life comparator where all the relevant circumstances are the same, so the ET must consider how a hypothetical comparator would have been treated.[47] Indeed, even where the worker has real comparators, it is safest also to claim that, in the alternative, s/he was less favourably treated than a hypothetical comparator would have been. A hypothetical comparator is simply someone who is the same as the worker in all relevant ways except that s/he is of a different race, sex, age, etc. To decide how a hypothetical comparator would have been treated, it is necessary to look at all the evidence pointing to race, sex, age, etc discrimination – eg dubious remarks, inadequate explanations and general statistics. In particular, the ET can look at how the employer has treated others in loosely similar but not identical circumstances.[48] As long as the ET understands that these comparisons are not being put forward as actual comparators, it is perfectly legitimate to use them as 'building blocks' in constructing how the hypothetical identical comparator would have been treated.[49] Sometimes the term used for these less precise comparators is 'evidential comparators'.[50] Using the example above, it would be useful to look at a male police constable who had passed his probation when there was evidence that he was not competent at the job. Although incapability is not the same as dishonesty, it would be one indicator of whether the employer is generally lenient towards men as opposed to women.

16.23   Where an actual comparator or even a loosely similar comparator is found, try to anticipate the employer's explanation for treating him/her better than the worker. For example, the explanation could be differences in:

• relevant experience;
• relevant qualifications;
• prior disciplinary record;
• status;
• whether an internal or external candidate for a post.

16.24   In a recruitment case, if a Jobcentre or recruitment agency was involved, it should be asked what job description or advert the

---

47   *Balamoody v UKCC for Nursing, Midwifery and Health Visiting* [2002] IRLR 288, CA; *Chief Constable of West Yorkshire v Vento* [2001] IRLR 124, EAT; *Shamoon v Chief Constable of the RUC* [2003] IRLR 285, HL.

48   *Chief Constable of West Yorkshire v Vento* [2001] IRLR 124, EAT; *Shamoon v Chief Constable of the RUC* [2003] IRLR 285, HL.

49   *Chief Constable of West Yorkshire v Vento* [2001] IRLR 124, EAT.

50   *Shamoon v Chief Constable of the RUC* [2003] IRLR 285, HL.

employer supplied. Where someone fails to gain a post after inter-view, despite having equal or better qualifications and experience than the person appointed, it is common for the employer to say that the successful candidate interviewed better. This is extremely difficult to contradict. All notes made by the interview panel in relation to each candidate during or after the interviews should be obtained. Also, while the interview is still fresh in his/her mind, the worker should note down the questions and answers as near verbatim as possible.

16.25   It may be relevant to know how the employer generally treats male and female workers or workers from different racial groups etc, in circumstances other than those of the alleged discriminatory act. It may be that an employer generally speaks more politely to white workers than to black workers, or that black workers are penalised for arriving late to work whereas white workers are not. In *West Midlands Passenger Transport Executive v Singh*,[51] the Court of Appeal said that evidence of discriminatory treatment against a group may be more indicative of unlawful discrimination than previous treatment of the particular worker, which may be due to personal factors other than discrimination. Sometimes it is appropriate, as in *Singh*, to request statistics showing comparative treatment of groups of workers.

16.26   It may also be helpful to show that the worker has been treated differently from an expected norm, eg the employers have not followed their own written disciplinary or grievance procedure on this occasion.

Statistics

16.27   Statistics showing that a group with particular protected characterist-ics tend to get treated less favourably may be very helpful, though it does not necessarily follow that an individual within the group has been discriminated against on any particular occasion. The *Singh* case established the potential importance of statistical evidence in cases of direct discrimination. The Court of Appeal said:

> Direct discrimination involves that an individual is not treated on his merits but receives unfavourable treatment because he is a member of a group. Statistical evidence may establish a discernible pattern in the treatment of a particular group.[52]

---

51 [1988] IRLR 186, CA.
52 *West Midlands Passenger Transport Executive v Singh* [1988] IRLR 186 at 188, CA.

Mr Singh claimed racial discrimination in his failure to gain promotion to the post of senior inspector. The court said that if statistics revealed a regular failure of members of a certain group to gain promotion to certain jobs and an under-representation in such jobs, it may give rise to an inference of discrimination against members of the group.

16.28 Statistics can be obtained by way of additional information or disclosure.[53] These procedures are more important now that the statutory questionnaire procedure has been abolished.[54] If statistical evidence is not available because, for example, an employer has not monitored the workforce and applications for employment and promotion, the ET could be invited to draw an adverse inference from this fact. In reality, although monitoring is recommended by the Equality and Human Rights Commission Employment Code (see below) and encouraged by the higher courts,[55] it is unlikely an ET will draw an inference from failure to monitor unless there is something surprising about it. It may be different in respect of public authorities who should be monitoring as good practice under the general public sector equality duty (PSED) and explicitly under the Welsh and Scottish specific duties.[56]

Failure to follow the Codes of Practice

16.29 The Equality and Human Rights Commission (EHRC) Employment and Equal Pay Codes of Practice are admissible in evidence and an ET must take into account relevant provisions of the Codes in determining any question in the proceedings.[57] Part 2 of the EHRC Employment Code makes many recommendations on good practice, eg in recruitment and promotion procedures and addressing workers' needs while at work. In cases concerning discrimination in all these areas, the employer's practices and procedures should be examined to see whether the guidelines of the codes have been followed.

---

53 See chapters 20 and 21.
54 See para 21.47 below.
55 Monitoring was approved by the Court of Appeal in *Singh* [1988] IRLR 186, CA and by the EAT in *Carrington v Helix Lighting* [1990] IRLR 6, EAT.
56 The public sector equality duty is explained in chapter 13.
57 The Employment Code is available at: www.equalityhumanrights.com/en/publication-download/employment-statutory-code-practice and the Equal Pay Code is available at: www.equalityhumanrights.com/en/publication-download/equal-pay-statutory-code-practice. Equality Act 2006 s15(4); *Igen Ltd and others v Wong; Chamberlin Solicitors and another v Emokpae; Brunel University v Webster* [2005] IRLR 258, CA; *Noone v North West Thames Regional Health Authority* [1988] IRLR 195, CA.

16.30   Interesting parts of the Equality and Human Rights Commission Employment Code include paras 17.44–17.51 on language in the workplace; paras 17.33–17.38 on annual leave policies; and appendix 2, which encourages monitoring by employers. Paragraphs 17.94–17.97 of the Code deal with grievances and it is strongly recommended that employers properly investigate complaints of discrimination. The ET's attention should be drawn to those provisions, where the worker has complained of discrimination at some stage during his/her employment, including the final disciplinary hearing, and has been ignored.

16.31   An ET should not infer that discrimination has occurred purely from an employer's failure to follow his/her own equal opportunities policy,[58] but poor practice in recruitment procedures is likely to be a significant factor.

Racist (and equivalent) remarks / overt indications of prejudice

16.32   Although prejudice need not be present to prove discrimination,[59] it strengthens the case if it is demonstrably present, eg because racist remarks have been made. Difficulties often arise because it is only the worker's word and s/he can be accused of making up such remarks while giving evidence. It is therefore important that any crucial remarks are mentioned in the ET1 form from the start.

16.33   Another difficulty is that certain words, 'jokes' or actions may not be taken as indicative of a racist, sexist or ageist, etc attitude by the ET. Even if they are, a tribunal will not automatically conclude that prejudiced attitudes lead to discriminatory treatment. In an appointment or promotion case, an employer's comment that someone 'who would fit in' was wanted should be regarded as a danger signal.[60] In certain cases, racist or similar comments may themselves constitute one of the acts of discrimination basing the claim.[61]

16.34   Things said by an employer in a 'without prejudice' negotiation can sometimes be very revealing. Normally, without prejudice discussions are kept off the record from the ET,[62] but the rule will not apply if 'unambiguous impropriety' took place, eg racist remarks were

---

58 *Qureshi v Newham LBC* [1991] IRLR 264, EAT.
59 See para 13.16 onwards.
60 *Baker v Cornwall CC* [1990] IRLR 194, CA at 198; *King v The Great Britain-China Centre* [1991] IRLR 513, CA.
61 Provided they amount to harassment. See para 13.81 onwards.
62 See paras 9.18–9.19.

made during the conversation.[63] However, that only applies where words were said which were unambiguously discriminatory, as opposed to more neutral words which could be interpreted as evidence of a discriminatory attitude.[64]

Previous complaints of discrimination

16.35 Documented previous complaints of unlawful discrimination against relevant managers should constitute useful evidence, particularly if the employer has failed to investigate such allegations. There are many and obvious reasons why a worker may not complain of discrimination while still employed. Nevertheless, a worker who alleges that discrimination has been occurring for some time is likely to be heavily cross-examined on why s/he did not complain at the time, the implication being that s/he has made it up after the event. The worker should be prepared to answer this question at the hearing. For the same reason, even if discrimination has not previously been mentioned, it is advisable for a worker to raise it at any dismissal hearing.

16.36 Where a worker during employment seeks advice in respect of discrimination, legal proceedings will usually be regarded as a last resort. However, s/he should be advised of the risks of not recording the allegation in writing, should some issue of discrimination ultimately end up in the ET. If appropriate, the employer's attention could be expressly drawn to the prohibition on victimisation in the legislation. The worker may also risk having compensation reduced under the Advisory, Conciliation and Arbitration Service (ACAS) Code on Disciplinary and Grievance Procedures if s/he wins a later discrimination case, if s/he unreasonably did not bring a grievance first.

Pregnancy

16.37 Useful evidence to prove pregnancy discrimination includes: remarks indicating the employer or relevant manager is unhappy about the pregnancy; a generally unhelpful attitude to time off for antenatal care or discussions about maternity leave and return; less favourable treatment of the woman compared with other staff; different treatment of the woman compared with how she was treated on similar issues before she became pregnant; a generally unfavourable environment in the workplace or in the woman's own department towards pregnant

---

63 On both points, see *BNP Paribas v Mezzotero* [2004] IRLR 508, EAT.
64 *Woodward v Santander UK plc (formerly Abbey National plc)* UKEAT/0250/09; [2010] IRLR 834.

women or mothers of young children. Various reports into pregnancy discrimination in recent years are useful evidence of a wider pattern.[65]

Indirect discrimination

Proving others of the worker's group are disadvantaged

16.38 Traditionally, statistical evidence is necessary in an indirect discrimination case to prove that the PCP particularly disadvantages those with a certain protected characteristic. Changes in the wording of the definition of indirect discrimination over the years mean that other types of evidence to prove disadvantage may sometimes be acceptable, eg expert evidence and research reports. Nevertheless, where possible, it is usually advisable still to present statistical evidence, as alternative methods may be less convincing.[66] The ET can take account of its own knowledge and experience in determining whether a PCP has disparate impact.[67] In indirect sex discrimination cases, the EAT has said that a woman does not need to prove the 'childcare disparity', ie that women bear the greater burden of childcare responsibilities, and that this can limit their ability to work certain hours, eg nights or changeable hours. However, a woman will still need to prove that the particular type of flexible working arrangement in question would put women at a disadvantage compared with men.[68] Certain arrangements might not be more difficult for people with childcare responsibilities. Generally it is best to play safe – an ET may unexpectedly insist on evidential proof of apparently obvious facts, so always come prepared. It is well-established that determining the correct pool for comparison of the impact on people of different groups is a question of fact for the ET.

16.39 The ET may choose a pool not anticipated by the worker and catch him/her unprepared. It may be possible to avoid this difficulty by agreeing a pool with the employer prior to the hearing or even asking the tribunal to decide the matter at a preliminary hearing. However, it is wise to prepare statistics on all the potential pools. Clearly some pools will be more helpful than others, and less helpful pools which the ET might choose should therefore be anticipated

---

65 See para 11.1.
66 See paras 13.36–13.43.
67 *Briggs v North Eastern Education and Library Board* [1990] IRLR 181, NICA.
68 *Dobson v North Cumbria Integrated Care NHS Foundation Trust* UKEAT/0220/19; [2021] IRLR 729. See also para 11.107 above.

with, if possible, explanations as to why they are misleading or irrelevant, for example, because they incorporate discrimination.

Where to find statistics or other evidence on impact

16.40   As stated above, statistics need to be gathered to show adverse impact within every likely pool for comparison. The statistics must relate to those with and without the relevant protected characteristic within each of the possible pools. One of the difficulties with indirect discrimination cases is that statistics are rarely available to meet the exact purpose. Where directly relevant statistics are not available, other statistics or evidence, from which the relevant facts may be inferred, should be used.

16.41   Statistics on any workplace pool may be obtainable by asking the tribunal for an order for additional information, eg as to how many of the existing workforce, by reference to sex, work part-time or full-time and how many women left after having children.

16.42   Statistics and evidence can be obtained from various sources, eg the Low Pay Commission, the Child Poverty Action Group, Stonewall, Carers UK, the Fawcett Society, the Women's Resource Centre, the Muslim Council of Britain, the Board of Deputies of British Jews, the Trades Union Congress (TUC), trade unions and university research departments, libraries, the Joint Council for the Welfare of Immigrants and community groups. The EHRC may advise on available reports and statistical sources and has publications on its website.[69] Official statistics are available from the Office for National Statistics (ONS) and also on the GOV.UK site.[70] Labour Force Surveys contain detailed statistics on patterns of full-time and part-time work by single and married men and women.[71] Local authority social services should have statistics on childcare facilities and take-up. Carers UK has information and statistics regarding carers on its website, including research into the general profile of caring, and employment and caring.[72] The official statistics are another route to access information on carers. The (usually) annual Modern Families Index published by Working Families looks at how families combine work and family

---

69 See: www.equalityhumanrights.com.
70 At: www.ons.gov.uk/employmentandlabourmarket/peopleinwork /employmentandemployeetypes/bulletins/uklabourmarket/latest and at: www.gov.uk/government/statistics. Searching 'labour market 'on the site gets you a useful set of links.
71 Regional surveys may show large regional variations in patterns of working women.
72 At: www.carersuk.org.

life.[73] There are also reports on the effect on working mothers of the Covid-19 pandemic, including loss of childcare and the burden of home-schooling.[74] Research reports or articles in specialist publications such as the *Nursing Times* on the position of black workers in the NHS, are useful for direct and indirect discrimination cases.

16.43   Where there is no statistical or research evidence precisely on the point required, verbal evidence from 'experts' or respected members of the community may be useful.

Justifiability

16.44   The greater the discriminatory effect, the better the justification the employer needs. Although the onus is on the employer to justify the PCP, it is still useful for the worker to produce evidence of the extent of its discriminatory effect. It will also be useful if the worker is able to put forward any reasonable alternative ways with less discriminatory effects by which the employer could have achieved his/her objectives. The EHRC Employment Code provides guidance on what should be considered unjustifiable in a variety of situations.

Victimisation

16.45   The worker first needs to establish that the 'protected act' took place. This may be difficult if his/her complaint of discrimination was made verbally. In order to show that the worker was victimised as a result, it is useful to prove that the employer's behaviour towards the worker was different before and after doing the protected act. It is worth doing a chronology of the key facts. The timing of events is particularly revealing in victimisation cases. It is also helpful to prove that the employer has treated the worker less favourably than s/he has treated other workers (who have not made allegations of discrimination) in similar circumstances. This is the same concept of comparators as for direct discrimination cases.[75] Although in victim-

---

73   The 2019 report is available at: www.workingfamilies.org.uk/publications/mfi2019_full/. This was the seventh annual index.

74   See eg *TUC poll: 7 in 10 requests for furlough turned down for working mums*, 14 January 2021 at: www.tuc.org.uk/news/tuc-poll-7-10-requests-furlough-turned-down-working-mums and *Six months of COVID-19: The pandemic, working parents, and Working Families*, Working Families, Autumn 2020 at: https://res.cloudinary.com/workingfamilies/images/v1616492652/20-11-25-Working-Families-COVID-19-impact-report-six-months-in/20-11-25-Working-Families-COVID-19-impact-report-six-months-in.pdf?_i=AA.

75   See para 16.21 onwards.

isation cases it is no longer legally required to compare the worker's treatment with that of a comparator, it is still useful evidence to help prove the reason why the worker has been subjected to a detriment is because of the protected act.

Witnesses

16.46 The principles are the same as in other ET cases. However, there is little doubt that independent witnesses in discrimination cases (particularly if they do not have the same relevant protected characteristic as the worker) can vastly increase the chances of success. If witnesses are called on any point of detail, the adviser should check what they will say if asked whether they believe unlawful discrimination has taken place. Witnesses may not understand what amounts to discrimination under the law. Although it is only a matter of their opinion, it will harm the worker's case if his/her witnesses consider that discrimination has not occurred.

Helpful kinds of evidence in disability discrimination cases

Introduction

16.47 In addition to the general content of this chapter, there are additional considerations which are relevant to disability. The EHRC Employment Code applies to disability as it does to all the protected characteristics. Chapters 5 and 6 of the Code cover the two definitions which are unique to disability ie discrimination arising from disability and failure to make reasonable adjustments. In relation to proving whether the worker has a disability, the Office for Disability Issues *Guidance relating to the definition of disability* must also be taken into account.[76] Chapter 15 in this book refers in detail to the provisions of the guidance.

---

76 *Equality Act 2010: Guidance on matters to be taken into account in determining questions relating to the definition of disability* (May 2011), available at: https://assets.publishing.service.gov.uk/government/uploads/system/uploads/attachment_data/file/570382/Equality_Act_2010-disability_definition.pdf. EqA 2010 Sch 1 para 12; s6(5). *Goodwin v The Patent Office* [1999] IRLR 4, EAT.

Proving the disability

Overview

16.48   In most cases, the worker will need to prove that s/he has a disability as defined by the EqA 2010. The employer's first response in defending a case is almost always to deny that the worker has a disability within the meaning of the Act and to require him/her to prove it. Even if the employer concedes that the worker has a disability, it is not guaranteed that the tribunal will accept that this is the case, though it will be unusual not to. There are further hidden dangers when an employer does make a concession. It is important to pin down in writing exactly what disability the employer concedes the worker had and for what time period. There is also the risk that the worker forgets s/he still has to prove the effect of his/her disability on his/her ability to do the job. This will not only need detailed evidence from the worker but may also still require medical evidence. For the law on each stage of the definition, see paras 15.8–15.33. See also the checklist on the definition of disability in appendix A. The following is a guide to gathering evidence by reference to the stages of the definition, bearing in mind the developing case-law.

Mental impairment

16.49   Since December 2005, it has no longer been necessary to prove that a mental illness is clinically well-recognised. Nevertheless, it is still important to get medical evidence of the impairment and its effects, and it is usually helpful (though no longer essential) if a well-recognised illness can be identified. Workers and their GPs tend to use words like 'anxiety', 'stress' and 'nervous debility'. These are the names of symptoms, but not necessarily of impairments in themselves. Simply producing copies of medical certificates using such vague terms at the ET will not be enough. Note also that the ET must not try to judge for itself whether the worker has a mental illness from the way s/he gives evidence on the day.[77] Quite apart from any risk of suspected but non-existent play-acting by the claimant, symptoms of mental illness can fluctuate and tribunal members are not psychiatric experts. Evidence of mental impairment apart from illness, eg learning difficulties, can be provided by an educational psychologist or other suitable expert, not only by doctors.[78]

---

77   *Morgan v Staffordshire University* [2002] IRLR 190, EAT; *Leonard v Southern Derbyshire Chamber of Commerce* [2001] IRLR 19, EAT.

78   *Dunham v Ashford Windows* [2005] IRLR 608, EAT.

Substantial adverse effect on ability to carry out day-to-day activities

16.50 The worker must prove that the impairment has a substantial adverse effect on his/her ability to carry out normal day-to-day activities. Remember that this means 'normal' activities and not specialised hobbies. Specialist work activities may or may not be covered, so it is best to get as many examples as possible on activities in and outside work. A good starting point is to go through paras D11–D17 of the Guidance[79] and its appendix with the worker, discussing the examples of what may and may not have substantial adverse effect. Do not stop with those examples. They should give the worker and the adviser ideas for other examples. Although it is an undesirably negative approach, the more examples of things the worker cannot do, the easier it is to prove disability. Explain to the worker that unfortunately this is how the law works.

16.51 It is not simply a question of what the worker cannot do at all. There is also an adverse effect if s/he can only do certain activities with difficulty, eg in pain, extremely slowly, with great tiredness or in an unusual way. For example, a worker may be able to walk up ten steps, but only if s/he pauses for breath at each step. Or a worker may be able to carry a bag, but only if it is on his/her shoulder rather than in his/her hand. Any effect which is not minor or trivial is relevant.[80]

16.52 As already stated in relation to mental impairment, there is a risk that a tribunal will reach the wrong conclusions regarding the effects of a worker's disability from observing the way s/he looks or behaves at the hearing. It is important to anticipate and ask the worker to explain any potentially misleading impressions, eg the fact that the worker sits for a long period while giving evidence, does not mean that s/he is not in pain, or s/he may have taken painkillers. An ET should not disregard the uncontradicted evidence of a medical expert without good reason.[81] Equally, it should be very cautious about substituting its observations for what is stated in the report of a jointly-instructed expert.[82]

16.53 Do not make assumptions that because the worker has a well-known disability, the ET will accept s/he is disabled or assume that s/he cannot do certain activities. Most disabilities have a huge range of effects on the individual, from extremely mild to very severe. Each

---

79 See para 15.9.
80 See para 15.24 above.
81 *Kapadia v Lambeth LBC* [2000] IRLR 699, CA.
82 *Mahon v Accuread Ltd* UKEAT/0081/08.

worker must be consulted as an individual. However, it does help if the adviser has some knowledge, to ask the right questions. Introductory knowledge can often be gained from the many excellent websites of specialist organisations. Such organisations can be found by doing an internet search, eg using an internet search engine, typing in the name of the disability 'AND organisation'.

16.54   Remember that a worker is covered whose symptoms are controlled by medication or other medical treatment if, apart from that treatment, his/her impairment would have substantial adverse effects.[83] It is particularly important to get clear medical evidence to prove such 'deduced' effects. It is not enough for the worker to make his/her own speculation in the ET as to what would happen if the treatment stopped.[84]

Progressive conditions

16.55   A worker with a progressive condition is covered as soon as there are any symptoms, provided s/he can prove it is 'likely' that s/he will go on to develop a substantial adverse effect.[85] It is not enough for the worker simply to prove s/he has a progressive condition such as rheumatoid arthritis. Such a condition will not necessarily become serious for every individual. The best way to prove it is likely to become serious is to get a medical report on the worker's own condition. This can be difficult, especially if using the doctors treating him/her, as they may not want to be negative. When getting medical evidence, tell the doctors what is the correct legal threshold for 'likely', ie it only means it 'could well happen'. It need not be 'more probable than not'.[86] In some cases, it will be enough to provide statistical evidence showing how the condition in question usually develops. However, it is risky to rely on this alone without reference to the worker's own particular circumstances.

Medical evidence

16.56   It has become unusual now to run a disability discrimination case without the use of medical evidence. This does make the procedure more expensive and time-consuming. See para 21.81 for the position on getting the cost of a report covered by the ET. Usually it is suffi-

---

83   See para 15.28.
84   *Woodrup v Southwark LBC* [2003] IRLR 111, CA.
85   See para 15.29.
86   See para 15.29.

cient to produce a report, without bringing the doctor to the ET hearing. However, if there is a difference of opinion between doctors separately instructed by the worker and the employer, it may be a disadvantage not to have oral evidence. Where a jointly-instructed expert's report has confirmed the worker's symptoms, the worker should not be cross-examined at the hearing on the basis that s/he is exaggerating his/her symptoms without forewarning, so s/he has a chance to ask the expert to attend.[87]

16.57 The EAT has set out guidelines for getting medical evidence in *De Keyser Ltd v Wilson*.[88] The key points are:

- it is preferable for an expert to be jointly instructed by the employer and worker;
- if one side cannot afford to share the cost of a joint expert, so that the other side goes ahead and instructs their own expert, it is still a good idea if both sides agree the terms of instruction;
- the letter instructing an expert should set out in detail the questions which s/he should answer and avoid partisanship;
- the ET may set a timetable for instructing experts and getting their reports (this needs to be a generous timetable as doctors are busy people and cannot be forced to keep to deadlines);
- if each side instructs their own expert, the experts should be encouraged to meet on an off-the-record basis and agree as many issues as possible. (It is rather unrealistic to expect this to happen, both in terms of the experts' time and willingness, and the costs to the parties.)

16.58 With these guidelines in mind, the ET will often set an extensive and contingent timetable at an early stage for establishing whether the worker has a disability, eg:

1) by a certain date, the worker will disclose to the employer his/her medical records;
2) within 14 days thereafter, the employer will state whether s/he admits the worker had a disability at the material time;
3) if not, a joint expert will be instructed and a timetable is set out for agreeing on an expert, writing the instructions, getting the report back, asking further questions and getting the answers;
4) within 14 days of getting the final answers, the employer will state definitively whether s/he concedes disability.

---

87 *Mahon v Accuread Ltd* UKEAT/0081/08.
88 [2001] IRLR 324, EAT.

If it is still a matter of dispute, there will either be a preliminary hearing exclusively to decide if the claimant was disabled or it will be decided as part of the full hearing. To avoid delays, the ET will usually require the other steps of case preparation (disclosure etc) to continue at the same time as the gathering of medical evidence.

16.59   It is a matter of judgment on each case which is the most appropriate course. When asking a doctor to provide a report, remember that the letter of instructions to the doctor may have to be disclosed to the employer and the ET. Make sure the letter does not appear biased. Bearing in mind what the law requires to be proved, ask the doctor a series of precise questions as to his/her medical assessment. A doctor can only advise on medical aspects of a case, not on an interpretation of the law.[89] Ask the doctor to state on what basis s/he knows the worker and is aware of his/her condition. Enclose a written authority from the worker to write the report. It will normally also be necessary to agree to pay the doctor's reasonable costs, but check what these are first. A sample letter to a doctor is in appendix A at A18.

16.60   Although the EAT sets an ideal of a jointly instructed expert, it is still common for each side to call their own expert. This is especially so where the worker wants to get a medical report from the doctor who has been treating him/her. The worker needs to decide whether to get a report from his/her GP or specialist consultant or from an independent specialist who s/he has not met before. In the latter case, the independent specialist could be jointly instructed (as mentioned above). The worker's choice depends partly on the nature of the evidence and the seriousness of the case. It is usually tempting for workers to use their own doctors or specialists, but this is not always a good idea. A GP can confirm the history of his/her treatment of the worker and what s/he was told at the time, but may not have specialist knowledge of the particular condition, and may not be seen as independent. Sometimes workers' own doctors are reluctant to give bad news, and they create a falsely optimistic (or self-protective) report, which does not help workers prove their true situation. They may also rely on sketchy and out-of-date notes. On the other hand, a worker's own doctor or specialist obviously has credibility from having seen the worker over a period of time and it may be unnecessary for the worker to attend a special examination. GPs are perfectly well qualified to give evidence about whether a worker has depression and their evidence should not be ignored by an ET, although it

89   *Vicary v British Telecommunications plc* [1999] IRLR 680, EAT.

may have less weight than that of an expert consultant.[90] Remember also that if the worker produces a report, it is quite likely that the employer will in turn want to get his/her own report. This will mean that the worker has to attend an examination with a possibly hostile doctor.

16.61   If there is a preliminary hearing to discuss case management and no expert has yet been instructed, the ET is most likely to follow the *De Keyser* guidelines (see para 16.57) and suggest the employer and worker jointly instruct an independent doctor and share the expense. If this happens, make sure that the selection of the doctor is not made solely by the employer; that the doctor has not had other dealings with the employer; and that the doctor's instructions are in neutral terms and come equally from each party. Finding an independent medical expert can be difficult. A consultant with the relevant speciality can usually be found by asking the GP or one of the teaching hospitals, but this may not be the best route. The expert must also be willing and able (ideally with experience) to write a suitable report; reliable in terms of timescale; and not too expensive. There are some directories of experts, for example provided by the Law Society of Scotland.[91]

16.62   Having said all this, a worker may choose not to get medical evidence to prove his/her disability and its effects, and simply to rely on his/her own evidence. It is not the tribunal's job to insist on the worker getting medical evidence,[92] but it is of course a risk for a worker not to back up his/her own assertions with more independent and perhaps more accurate evidence regarding the effects of an impairment. A tribunal may be tempted to help the worker out by ordering the employer, who has more resources, to pay for a medical expert, but this is not permitted.[93] If an employment judge orders the claimant to get a medical report, the tribunal administration may be willing to pay the doctor's fees up to a certain amount (see para 21.81).

---

90 *J v DLA Piper UK LLP* UKEAT/0263/09; [2010] IRLR 936.
91 At: www.lawscot.org.uk/members/business-support/expert-witness/. See other possibilities on Inner Temple Library's Access to law at www.accesstolaw.com/general-resources/expert-witnesses/.
92 *City Facilities Management (UK) Ltd v Ling* UKEAT/0396/13.
93 *City Facilities Management (UK) Ltd v Ling* UKEAT/0396/13.

Reasonable adjustments

16.63 It is best to take a methodical approach when trying to persuade a tribunal that the employer has failed to make reasonable adjustments. This is because the ET needs to identify:

1) the PCP or physical feature of the premises which is causing the worker difficulty;
2) the nature and extent of the disadvantage suffered by the worker;
3) any non-disabled comparators who are not placed at a disadvantage (where appropriate);
4) proposed adjustments and to what extent they might alleviate the disadvantage.[94]

To make sense of these stages, it is necessary to analyse with sufficient detail the elements of the worker's job and the effect of the disability on carrying out each of the relevant tasks. The idea of step 3 is to show that the reason the worker is at a disadvantage is the effect of the PCP etc on his/her disability. It should not be necessary to find an actual non-disabled comparator in similar circumstances to prove this point.[95] When running a tribunal case (though not necessarily at the time the problem at work arose), the worker must give at least a broad idea of what kind of adjustments would have been useful, so that the employer knows what allegation s/he has to meet.[96] Once it is established that there is an arrangement causing the worker a substantial disadvantage because of his/her disability, s/he needs to identify a potentially reasonable adjustment. When s/he has done that, the burden of proof is reversed for the employer to prove s/he did not fail in his/her duty to make reasonable adjustments. The amount of detail which the worker needs to give to reverse the burden of proof depends on the nature of the disability – a subtle disability requiring specialised adjustments would require more than basic detail.[97]

16.64 Although the worker needs only give a broad idea of potential adjustments, his/her case will be stronger if s/he can put forward several specific and sensible suggestions. Specialist organisations will have ideas and their websites can be useful. Medical experts and the Work Coaches or Access to Work Advisers based at Jobcentres

---

94 *The Environment Agency v Rowan* [2008] IRLR 20, EAT. See checklist and examples in appendix A at A17.
95 See EHRC Employment Code, para 6.16.
96 *Project Management Institute v Latif* [2007] IRLR 579, EAT.
97 *E A Gibson Shipbrokers Ltd v Staples* UKEAT/0178/08 and UKEAT/0179/08.

may also help. The Access to Work Advisers can also give information regarding what grants the employers could have obtained to pay
for adjustments.[98] If the worker was off sick at the time, it is also
worth looking at the fit notes supplied by his/her GP and any 'Fit for
Work' documentation as these may have made suggestions for reasonable adjustments.[99]

Remedies and compensation

16.65   Medical evidence could be needed on several aspects of assessing
compensation. In terms of loss of earnings, the question is when a
worker would have returned to work, and for how long, had s/he not
been discriminated against. With progressive diseases, a doctor may
need to assess for how long the worker could continue in employment, even assuming all reasonable adjustments were made.

16.66   Where the worker has lost his/her job and cannot find a new job,
statistical or expert evidence may be necessary to prove difficulties on
the job market for people with the relevant disability. For this, it is
worth checking the websites of specialist organisations. The worker
also needs to prove what efforts s/he has in fact made to get a new
job. Where the worker is so distressed by the manner of his/her
dismissal or other unlawful treatment by the employer that it interferes with his/her ability to get a new job, medical evidence should be
obtained as confirmation.

16.67   The worker will also need to provide evidence of his/her injury to
feelings, as in all discrimination cases. If the worker has seen his/her
GP with resulting depression, a GP report should be obtained. If the
worker has suffered psychiatric damage to his/her health, an expert
medical report is essential.[100]

Injury to feelings, mitigation and other evidence

16.68   Although the *Vento* bands for injury to feelings[101] tend to focus on the
seriousness of the discriminatory actions, the real issue in assessing
the award is the level of the worker's hurt feelings. The two tend to

98 For details of Disability Employment Advisers, see: www.jobcentreguide.co.uk/
jobcentre-plus-guide/34/disability-employment-advisors; and for Access to
Work, see: www.gov.uk/access-to-work.
99 See paras 7.23–7.24.
100 See paras 19.27–19.35.
101 See paras 19.16–19.17.

go together, but not necessarily. The worker should explain how his/ her feelings were affected by what happened. Medical reports are not essential for ordinary injury to feelings claims, but the worker is likely to be awarded a higher sum if s/he did visit his/her GP with distress resulting from the discrimination and a GP's report can be obtained. To claim compensation for more serious injury to health, eg psychiatric damage, a formal medical report will be essential.[102] The Judicial College gives guidelines regarding psychiatric damage in personal injury cases, which may be useful for discrimination cases too.[103] Many of the principles relevant to obtaining medical evidence in a disability discrimination case will also be relevant to proving injury to feelings or health where there is discrimination because of other protected characteristics (see paras 16.56–16.62).

16.69   Sexual harassment cases usually cause severe injury to feelings, sometimes amounting to post-traumatic stress disorder (PTSD). General research reports and statistical evidence of the level of sexual harassment of women at work and its effects may also be useful. To prevent an ET taking a pregnancy dismissal case less seriously than other forms of discrimination, a report from the worker's own GP plus any expert evidence that this can be a time when women feel particularly vulnerable, would be helpful.[104] See para 21.81 regarding the possibility of the tribunal covering the costs of a GP report.

16.70   Women who are pregnant or with young babies, as well as black and other minority ethnic or disabled workers, may find it harder to obtain new employment. This can be relevant to the level of compensation in dismissal cases including unfair dismissal. As well as detailed evidence of the particular worker's attempts to find fresh employment, reference to the general problems of the subject group may be of assistance.[105]

16.71   The EAT has said that compensation in discrimination cases where no upper limit applies cannot be dealt with briefly and informally. Careful preparation will be necessary for a remedies hearing. With disability discrimination cases, a medical expert may well be required as to the worker's likely future health, since this would be relevant to an assessment of future loss of earnings.[106]

---

102 *Sheriff v Klyne Tugs* [1999] IRLR 481, CA; and paras 19.27–19.35.

103 See paras 19.29–19.32 for areas requiring evidence.

104 See para 11.1 for research reports.

105 Jobcentres are sometimes willing to write a letter on the general job prospects facing the worker.

106 *Buxton v Equinox Design Ltd* [1999] IRLR 158, EAT.

Chapter 17: Key points

- Employers should make a risk assessment of risks to the health and safety of their employees.
- In extreme cases, an employee subjected to severe stress at work may be able to resign and claim constructive unfair dismissal.
- In discrimination cases under the Equality Act (EqA) 2010, a worker can claim compensation for psychiatric injury caused by discriminatory treatment.
- A worker can bring a personal injury claim in the civil courts for physical or psychiatric injury caused by stress at work, but it is hard to win such cases.
- In some circumstances, stress may amount to a disability and gain the protection of disability discrimination law under the EqA 2010 (see chapter 15).
- There is evidence that Covid-19 has adversely affected physical and, in particular, mental health.
- NHS Injury Allowance may be available for NHS staff who temporarily lose income due to an injury or health condition caused by their NHS employment.
- Workers must not be subjected to a detriment because they refuse to work in circumstances of danger, which they reasonably believe to be serious and imminent. This may apply where there are dangers of catching Covid-19. This is covered in chapter 6.

Introduction

17.1   Health and safety at work is generally beyond the scope of this book. The following is a brief introduction to some areas which overlap with employment law. Note that, although this chapter is within Part III of this book, health and safety is not considered an 'equality' or 'discrimination' area within employment law.

17.2   All employers have a duty to take reasonable care for the health and safety of their employees. This is a general common law duty as well as a specific statutory duty under the Health and Safety at Work Act 1974.[1] Breach of this duty may enable employees to resign and claim constructive unfair dismissal. A breach of the implied duty to

---

1 Section 2.

take care of an employee's health and safety may or may not be a 'fundamental' breach.[2] The actual or potential risk to the employee is likely to be an important factor. It is also possible for a breach to become more serious over time because the risk increases or because actual harm is caused. See para 17.11 for constructive dismissal and stress.

17.3 Alternatively, where a worker has suffered physical or psychiatric damage, s/he may be able to claim compensation in the civil courts in contract or tort. Such claims are known as personal injuries claims. These claims are hard to bring because legal aid is not usually available. Most private solicitors will not take on stress cases in particular, unless the worker has trade union funding, legal expenses insurance, agrees a conditional fee arrangement ('no win, no fee') or pays privately.

17.4 For civil claims in the context of harassment at work, see para 13.113 onwards.

17.5 Staff employed within the NHS may be able to claim NHS Injury Allowance if they temporarily lose income due to an injury, disease or other health condition which is wholly or mainly attributable to their NHS employment.[3]

Risk assessments

17.6 Under the Management of Health and Safety at Work Regulations (MHSW Regs) 1999,[4] an employer must 'make a suitable and sufficient assessment of the risks to the health and safety of his employees, to which they are exposed while they are at work'.[5] An employer with five or more employees must record any significant findings in the assessment and note any groups of employees identified as especially at risk.[6] An employer must also assess the health and safety risks of people not in his/her employment arising out of or in connection with the conduct of the business.[7]

---

2 See *Flatman v Essex County Council* UKEAT/0097/20 where an employer failed to provide manual handling training.
3 For details, see the NHS Employers' website at www.nhsemployers.org/articles/nhs-injury-allowance-guidance.
4 SI No 3242.
5 MHSW Regs 1999 SI No 3242 reg 3(1)(a); for risk assessments and pregnancy, see paras 11.83–11.89.
6 MHSW Regs 1999 reg 3(6).
7 MHSW Regs 1999 reg 3(1)(b).

17.7   Risk assessments should include the risk of employees developing stress-related illness as a result of their work.[8]

17.8   Employees also have a responsibility to tell their employer of any situation which would represent a serious and immediate danger to health and safety or about any shortcomings in the employer's health and safety arrangements.[9] In support of this responsibility is the protection against detriment or dismissal for raising such issues in the appropriate way.[10]

Stress

17.9   The Health and Safety Executive (HSE) defines stress as the adverse reaction people have to excessive pressure or other types of demand placed on them. The HSE says stress is a serious problem. In recent years, it has commissioned research which indicates that up to five million people in the UK feel 'very stressed' by their work, with about half a million experiencing work-related stress at a level they believe is making them ill. In 2019/20, nearly 39 million working days were lost due to work-related ill-health, including 17.9 million for stress, depression or anxiety.[11] This was even before Covid-19 had any real impact. There can be a variety of causes of work-related stress, eg excessive workload, dissatisfied customers, bullying, dangerous working conditions, and traumatic nature of work. The HSE has published Management Standards, which are a useful measure for assessment and support. Details of the HSE research, Management Standards and other guidelines are available on its website.[12]

17.10   A worker who has suffered psychiatric damage caused by stress at work may be able to claim compensation in contract or tort. These claims are heard in the county court or High Court (or Scottish equivalent).

17.11   In theory, an employee who is subjected to severe stress at work can resign and claim constructive unfair dismissal. S/he could claim breach of the implied terms of trust and confidence, and the

---

8 See the Health and Safety Executive Management Standards, Step 1 at: www.hse.gov.uk/stress/standards/step1/index.htm.

9 MHSW Regs 1999 reg 14(2).

10 ERA 1996 ss44, 100 and 43A. See paras 6.82–6.91.

11 At www.hse.gov.uk/statistics/dayslost.htm.

12 At: www.hse.gov.uk/stress/index.htm.

employer's duty to provide a safe working environment. However, such a claim may be difficult to prove.[13]

17.12   A worker who wins a discrimination case in the employment tribunal (ET) may claim compensation for injury to feelings, which includes injury to health caused by the unlawful acts of discrimination.[14]

Disability discrimination

17.13   A worker who has a stress-related illness, whether or not it is caused by his/her work, may fall within the definition of a disabled person under the Equality Act (EqA) 2010. If so, his/her employer must make any reasonable adjustments required, eg reducing workload or hours or allowing a staged return to work.[15]

The Covid-19 pandemic

17.14   Around one in five adults experienced some form of depression in early 2021, more than double that observed prior to the Covid-19 pandemic.[16] Mental health has been adversely affected by isolation; anxiety about contracting the virus or about friends and family; bereavement – often without the chance to say goodbye; fears about job security; fears about returning to work; and financial concerns.[17] Physical and mental health has been affected by poor work-life balance; home-working with heavy computer use and poor ergonomic work stations; reduced exercise; irregular hours; combining work with other family responsibilities. Those with pre-existing mental health conditions have been particularly affected. For some employees, there are also the effects of long Covid.[18]

13   For an example regarding an excessive workload, see *Marshall Specialist Vehicles Ltd v Osborne* [2003] IRLR 672, EAT.

14   See para 19.27.

15   See chapter 15 for more details.

16   At www.ons.gov.uk/peoplepopulationandcommunity/wellbeing/articles/ coronavirusanddepressioninadultsgreatbritain/januarytomarch2021#main-points.

17   See CIPD guide: *Coronavirus (COVID-19): Mental health support for employees* at www.cipd.co.uk/knowledge/culture/well-being/supporting-mental-health-workplace-return.

18   See chapter 15.

17.15   In the 2020 NHS annual survey, 44 per cent of staff reported feeling unwell as a result of work-related stress, up from 40 per cent in 2019. Caring for patients during the pandemic has taken a significant toll on health and social care staff, contributing to stress and burn out. Common work-related stressors are anxiety about exposure to the virus during the commute or at the workplace; bringing the virus home to family members; changing work patterns and loss of control over usual working routine.[19]

17.16   Disability discrimination law may provide some protection where workers' health is severely affected by the pandemic or by contracting long Covid (see chapter 15).

17.17   Workers must not be subjected to a detriment because they refuse to work in circumstances of danger, which they reasonably believe to be serious and imminent. This may apply where there are dangers of catching Covid-19. This is covered in chapter 6.

19   *Supporting our NHS people experiencing stress,* NHS Employers, 22 July 2021 at www.nhsemployers.org/articles/supporting-our-nhs-people-experiencing-stress.

PART IV

Remedies and procedures

CHAPTER 18

Unfair dismissal remedies

Key points

- An employment tribunal can order re-employment (reinstatement or re-engagement) but cannot force the employer to take the employee back. It can only award more compensation, ie an 'additional award', if the employer refuses (unless it was impracticable to re-employ).
- In practice, few re-employment orders are sought or made.
- Unfair dismissal compensation normally comprises a basic award and a compensatory award.
- The basic award is based on age, years of service and gross pay (subject to a £538 weekly maximum for dismissals from 6 April 2020, and £544 maximum for dismissals from 6 April 2021).
- The compensatory award is subject to an overall ceiling (£88,519 for dismissals in year starting 6 April 2020 and £89,493 for dismissals from 6 April 2021). There is a further cap of 52 weeks' gross pay if lower. The compensatory award mainly comprises loss of earnings and pension. The latter can be valuable but complex to calculate.
- The compensatory award may be reduced for contributory fault, failure to mitigate or procedural-only unfairness. There is a strict order in which any such deductions must be calculated.
- The compensatory award may be increased or reduced by up to 25 per cent for the employer's or employee's failure to follow guidance in the Advisory, Conciliation and Arbitration Service's (ACAS's) Code of Practice on Disciplinary and Grievance Procedures.
- There is recoupment of certain benefits claimed by the employee. The employer deducts these from the compensatory award and reimburses the Department for Work and Pensions (DWP).
- Compensation for injury to feelings is not awarded for unfair dismissal.
- There is a minimum basic award and/or no ceiling on the compensatory award in a few special areas.
- Where the employer is insolvent, the state pays limited debts to the employee.
- A week's pay for the purposes of the basic award, additional award and statutory redundancy pay is calculated on the basis of a furloughed employee's normal wage and not any reduced furlough wage.
- For discrimination remedies, see chapter 19. See para 20.279 regarding tax on termination.

Introduction

18.1   An employment tribunal (ET) which finds unfair dismissal cannot force an employer to take the employee back, although it can make an order for reinstatement or re-engagement and award extra compensation (an 'additional award') if the employer refuses to comply. Re-employment orders are unusual. Most employees who win unfair dismissal cases get financial compensation. This consists of a *basic award* and a *compensatory award*.

18.2   An employee is entitled to have an ET decide whether s/he has been unfairly dismissed, even if his/her employer offered a financial settlement equal to the maximum possible award.[1] However, there may be a costs risk if the employee rejects a very large offer, particularly if the employer is prepared to admit s/he has unfairly dismissed the employee.

Reinstatement and re-engagement

Introduction

18.3   If the employee wins his/her case, the ET must explain its powers to order reinstatement or re-engagement and ask the employee if s/he wants re-employment.[2] This duty exists even if the employee did not indicate a desire for re-employment on his/her tribunal claim form. An ET's decision on compensation will not necessarily be invalid if it failed to ask about re-employment, but it may be invalid if the failure led to injustice.[3]

18.4   If the employee does now want to get his/her job back, the ET will decide whether to order reinstatement or re-engagement or neither. If neither of the re-employment orders is practicable or desired by the employee, the ET will make an award of compensation.[4] It was envisaged when ETs were first introduced that re-employment orders would be the primary remedy. Realistically, however, the parties tend not to want to work with each other again after the conclusion of an ET hearing, making re-employment orders rare.

---

1   *Telephone Information Services Ltd v Wilkinson* [1991] IRLR 148, EAT and Employment Rights Act (ERA) 1996 s94. It is uncertain whether the change in costs rules since this case was decided would alter the position – see para 20.246 onwards on costs.
2   ERA 1996 s112(2).
3   *Cowley v Manson Timber Ltd* [1995] IRLR 153, CA.
4   ERA 1996 s112(4). See para 18.16.

What are reinstatement and re-engagement orders?

18.5 Under an order for reinstatement, the employer must treat the employee in all respects as if s/he had not been dismissed.[5] The ET will decide the date when the employee will return to work and the amount of the missing wages and benefit that the employer must pay for the period between dismissal and reinstatement, including restoring any rights that the employee would have acquired during the period of absence. Notice pay or other ex gratia payments and any earnings from a new employer will be deducted.[6]

18.6 An order for re-engagement is more flexible. The ET can decide the employee must be engaged by the employer, its successor or an associated employer in employment comparable to previously or in other suitable employment.[7] On making an order, the ET needs to specify the terms on which re-engagement will take place, including the employer's identity, the nature of the employment and its pay, the date when the employee will start work and the amount payable by the employer in respect of any benefit including pay which the employee might reasonably have expected to have had but for the dismissal, giving credit for notice pay, ex gratia payments and new earnings.[8] The employee is entitled to put forward his/her views on the terms of the order.[9]

18.7 Except where the ET takes into account any contributory fault by the employee (see para 18.53), an order for re-engagement should be on terms which are, so far as is reasonably practicable, no less favourable than an order for reinstatement would have been.[10] This means that (apart from this exception) with both types of order, an employee should get all his/her back pay between the date of termination and the date of re-employment. Even if the dismissal is unfair only on purely procedural grounds and there would normally be a percentage reduction in the compensatory award on the *Polkey* principles, there can be no such reduction of back pay if a re-employment order is made.[11]

---

5 ERA 1996 s114.
6 ERA 1996 s114(4).
7 ERA 1996 s115(1).
8 ERA 1996 s115(2) and (3).
9 ERA 1996 s116(3)(a).
10 ERA 1996 s116(4).
11 *Arriva London Ltd v Eleftheriou* UKEAT/0272/12. Regarding *Polkey* reductions, see para 18.57.

18.8   Where re-employment has been ordered, the ET cannot reduce the back pay for the employee's failure to mitigate, eg failure to look for another job.[12] This contrasts with the position on the compensatory award, where an employee does not want re-employment.[13] Again, unlike the ordinary position with a compensatory award, there is no upper limit on the back pay which can be ordered.

18.9   ETs sometimes like to avoid making orders by pressing the parties to agree certain steps. This can cause difficulties when one or other side does not stick to the agreement. In the case of re-engagement, an ET must make an order and not simply order the employer 'to offer to re-engage' on specified terms.[14]

Will the employment tribunal order re-employment?

18.10   In exercising its discretion whether to order re-employment, an ET must first consider reinstatement and if it decides not to order that, then it must consider re-engagement.[15] In both cases, the ET must take into account:[16]

- whether the employee wants an order and what type of order;
- whether it is practicable for the employer to comply with an order;
- whether it would be just to make an order if the employee has caused or contributed to some extent to the dismissal.

At this stage, the ET only needs to make a provisional assessment of whether it is practicable to re-employ the employee, and this should encourage the ET to be positive.[17] The ET can reconsider after it has made an order, if the employer refuses to re-employ on grounds of practicability.

18.11   The practicability of re-employment is assessed as at the date when it would take effect, not at the date of dismissal, and not necessarily even at the date of the remedies hearing.[18] It is not a bar to getting a re-employment order that the employee has meanwhile got another job.[19] The fact that the dismissal was found to be unfair only

---

12 *City and Hackney Health Authority v Crisp* [1990] IRLR 47, EAT.

13 See para 18.34.

14 *Lilley Construction Ltd v Dunn* [1984] IRLR 483, EAT.

15 ERA 1996 s116(1) and (2).

16 ERA 1996 s116(1) and (3).

17 *Timex Corporation v Thomson* [1981] IRLR 522, EAT; *Port of London Authority v Payne and others* [1994] IRLR 9, CA.

18 *Rembiszewski v Atkins Ltd* UKEAT/0402/11.

19 *Arriva London Ltd v Eleftheriou* UKEAT/0272/12.

on procedural grounds is not a reason in itself why re-employment should not be offered.[20] However, the background circumstances as to why the dismissal was not substantively unfair may be relevant to the practicality of re-employment, eg if the worker was dismissed for a lengthy sickness absence, which was only unfair because the employer failed to consult. 'Practicable' means more than just possible. The order must be capable of being carried into effect with success.[21] It is unlikely to be practicable to re-employ if the working relationship has completely broken down.[22]

18.12   An employment relationship has to work in human terms. As a matter of common sense, it is unlikely to be practicable for an employee to return to work for an employer who does not have confidence in him/her, either because of the employee's previous conduct or because the employer feels the employee cannot do the job to the required standard. It is not for the tribunal to decide whether the employer is right to hold that opinion. However, the employer cannot just assert that s/he lacks trust and confidence in the employee. S/he must prove that his/her view is genuine and rational. If the objection is based on a minor matter or something that happened a long time ago, this may suggest the belief is not genuine or not rational.[23]

18.13   It will also not be practicable if no suitable job is available. The employer does not have to dismiss others to make way for the employee.[24] For re-engagement, the tribunal will look at comparable or suitable vacancies which exist at the date of the remedies hearing. It does not have to consider vacancies which have arisen since dismissal but have been filled by the time of the remedies hearing. However, in respect of reinstatement to the employee's former job, a tribunal should not take it into account that an employer has engaged a permanent replacement unless it was not practicable to get the dismissed employee's work done otherwise, or the replacement was engaged after a reasonable period during which the employee had not indicated s/he wanted re-employment, and it was no longer reasonable to cover the work other than with a permanent

20 *The Manchester College v Hazel and Huggins* UKEAT/0642/11; [2013] IRLR 563; *Arriva London Ltd v Eleftheriou* UKEAT/0272/12.

21 *United Lincolnshire Hospitals NHS Foundation Trust v Farren* UKEAT/0198/16 usefully reviews the authorities.

22 *ILEA v Gravett* [1988] IRLR 497, EAT; *Central & North West London NHS Foundation Trust v Abimbola* UKEAT/0542/08.

23 *Kelly v PGA European Tour* [2021] EWCA Civ 559; [2021] IRLR 575.

24 *Freemans plc v Flynn* [1984] IRLR 486, EAT; *Kelly v PGA European Tour* [2021] EWCA Civ 559; [2021] IRLR 575.

replacement.[25] This is a good reason for noting it on the tribunal claim if the employee wants re-employment or, even better, writing a letter immediately after dismissal, putting the employer on notice.

The employer refuses to comply with the order

18.14 The ET's order for reinstatement or re-engagement will have set a start date. If the employer refuses to comply with the order, there will be another compensation hearing. At this hearing, the onus will be on the employer to prove that it was not practicable to re-employ after all.[26] Obviously it will be hard for the employer to convince the ET, when s/he was unable to prevent the ET making the order in the first place.

18.15 If the ET is satisfied that it was not practicable to re-employ, it will order compensation for unfair dismissal in the usual way (see para 18.16).[27] But if the ET still believes re-employment was practicable, it will also award an 'additional award' of no less than 26 weeks' and no more than 52 weeks' pay.[28] A week's pay[29] is paid gross[30] and is subject to the same weekly maximum as the basic award.[31] In this latter situation, the usual ceiling on the compensatory award can be exceeded to the extent necessary to ensure that, added to the additional award, the total is not less than the back pay which would have been payable had the employer re-employed.[32] This is to ensure an employer has no financial incentive for avoiding re-employment.

---

25 ERA 1996 s116(5) and (6).

26 ERA 1996 s117(4).

27 ERA 1996 s117(3)(a).

28 ERA 1996 s117(3)(b).

29 Calculated in accordance with the rules at ERA 1996 ss220–227 at the employee's normal rate and not any reduced rate while on furlough: Employment Rights Act 1996 (Coronavirus, Calculation of a Week's Pay) Regulations 2020 SI No 814.

30 The author can find no authority for this, except for the general wording of the ERA 1996 provisions regarding compensation which refer to the amount payable under the contract of employment and by analogy to the basic award. See *Secretary of State for Employment v John Woodrow & Sons (Builders) Ltd* [1983] IRLR 11, EAT.

31 ERA 1996 s227(1)(b). See para 18.19.

32 ERA 1996 s124(4). *Parry v National Westminster Bank plc* [2005] IRLR 193, CA.

Compensation

Introduction

18.16   Compensation consists of two elements: the *basic award* and the *compensatory award*. Although it is relatively easy to make an approximate assessment of the value of an employee's claim for settlement purposes (apart from any lost pension element), it is surprisingly difficult to work out and prove the exact sums with the precision necessary for an ET hearing. See appendix A for a compensation checklist, sample calculation and model schedule of loss.

The basic award and redundancy payment

Basic award

18.17   The basic award was introduced to compensate employees for the loss of job security following dismissal. The basic award is calculated broadly in the same way as a redundancy payment.[33]

18.18   The basic award is calculated by reference to the period ending with the effective date of termination[34] during which the employee has been continuously employed. It allows for one-and-a-half weeks' pay for each year of employment in which the employee was not below the age of 41, one week's pay for each year of employment when the employee was below 41 but not below 22, and half a week's pay for each year of employment below the age of 22. A maximum of 20 years' employment will be counted. The table at appendix E can be used to calculate a basic award or redundancy pay.

18.19   A week's pay is gross pay subject to a maximum figure[35] which is index-linked to the retail price index (RPI). It is increased annually. For dismissals from 6 April 2020, the upper limit was £538. This was increased to £544 for dismissals from 6 April 2021.[36] If the employee was paid below the national minimum wage, the basic award must be calculated on the basis of that minimum.[37] If there are fixed working hours, a week's pay is the amount payable by the employer under the contract of employment. If the employee's pay varies with

33 ERA 1996 s119 (basic award) and s162 (redundancy pay).
34 See para 20.46; ERA 1996 s97.
35 ERA 1996 s227(1)(a). The ceiling is the same as that for statutory redundancy pay.
36 ERA 1996 s227(1); Employment Rights (Increase of Limits) Order 2019 SI No 324.
37 *Paggetti v Cobb* [2002] IRLR 861, EAT.

the amount of work done ('piece rate') the amount of a week's pay is calculated by reference to the average hourly rate of pay over the last 12 weeks of employment,[38] and where there are no normal hours, a week's pay will be the average weekly pay over the last 12 weeks of employment. Roughly speaking, the 12 weeks are counted back from the termination date.[39] There are slightly complicated rules to ensure that the calculation is based on the employee's normal wage and not any reduced rate while on furlough.[40]

18.20   The basic award may be reduced if the employee:

- behaved before the dismissal or before the notice was given in such a way that it would be just and equitable to do so;[41]
- received a redundancy payment, whether paid under statute or otherwise;[42]
- received an ex gratia payment, unless it would have been paid in the future, even if the dismissal had been fair;[43] or
- unreasonably refused an offer of reinstatement, in which case the ET will reduce the basic award by such amount as it considers just and equitable.[44]

18.21   A minimum basic award[45] applies in certain cases, eg dismissal due to trade union membership or activities;[46] for being a health and safety representative or carrying out such duties; for being a trustee of an occupational pension scheme, or an employee representative for the purposes of collective redundancy or Transfer of Undertakings (Protection of Employment) Regulations (TUPE Regs) 2006[47] consultation or a workforce representative under the Working Time Regulations.[48] The minimum award is reviewed annually. For dismissals in the year starting 6 April 2020 it was £6,562 and for dismissals in the year starting 6 April 2021 it was £6,634.[49]

---

38 ERA 1996 s222(3).
39 For precise timing, see ERA 1996 ss222(4), 226(3) and 97.
40 Employment Rights Act 1996 (Coronavirus, Calculation of a Week's Pay) Regulations 2020 SI No 814.
41 ERA 1996 s122(2).
42 ERA 1996 s122(4).
43 *DCM Optical Clinic plc v Stark* UKEAT/0124/04.
44 ERA 1996 s122(1).
45 Before any reduction under ERA 1996 s122.
46 Trade Union and Labour Relations (Consolidation) Act (TULR(C)A) 1992 s156.
47 SI No 246.
48 ERA 1996 s120.
49 Employment Rights (Increase of Limits) Order 2021 SI No 208.

Statutory redundancy pay

18.22   Employees often think that redundancy payments will be higher than they are. As noted above, statutory redundancy pay is calculated in the same way as the basic award. The payment is calculated by a combination of age; years of service; and weekly gross pay (subject to the weekly maximum),[50] roughly speaking at the termination date.[51] The relevant date is similar to the effective date of termination.[52] It is easiest to use a table such as that reproduced at appendix E to work out the figure by which weekly pay must be multiplied. There is also a simple interactive ready reckoner available on the GOV.UK website.[53]

18.23   The statutory calculation discriminates in favour of older employees both directly and indirectly on age grounds, but the government decided this was justifiable because older workers find it much harder to obtain new employment. The Equality Act (EqA) 2010 allows employers to pay an enhanced contractual redundancy payment, provided this applies to the whole scheme, by lifting the ceiling on a week's pay or multiplying the weekly amount by more than one year for each year's service or multiplying the total by a certain number.[54] If an employer wishes to give an enhanced redundancy payment calculated on any other basis, s/he needs to justify the age discrimination in the usual way.[55] It may well be justifiable for an employer to adopt a redundancy pay scheme which discriminates directly or indirectly on age grounds if the purpose is to reward loyalty, help older workers who are vulnerable in the job market or to encourage turnover so as to facilitate career progression of younger staff.[56] Similarly, it may be justifiable for an employer to take account of immediate entitlement to a pension.[57] But in all cases, an employer

---

50 Which is the same as the weekly ceiling for the unfair dismissal basic award – see para 18.19. Note that a week's pay is based on the employee's normal rate and not any reduced rate while on furlough: Employment Rights Act 1996 (Coronavirus, Calculation of a Week's Pay) Regulations 2020 SI No 814.

51 In fact a combination of the 'relevant date' under ERA 1996 s145 and the 'calculation date' under s226.

52 See para 20.46 and ERA 1996 s145.

53 At www.gov.uk/calculate-your-redundancy-pay; and see appendix E.

54 EqA 2010 Sch 9 para 13.

55 See chapter 14 regarding age discrimination.

56 *MacCulloch v Imperial Chemical Industries plc* UKEAT/0119/08; [2008] IRLR 846.

57 *Loxley v BAE Systems Land Systems (Munitions and Ordnance) Ltd* UKEAT/0156/08; [2008] IRLR 853.

does need to prove with evidence that the means chosen to achieve the legitimate aim were proportionate. There are great dangers that stereotyped assumptions can be made, eg as to at what age employees' job performance deteriorates.

18.24　On making a redundancy payment, the employer must give the employee a written statement indicating how the amount was calculated.[58] If the employer is insolvent and will not pay, the employee can apply to the Redundancy Payments Office for payment out of the National Insurance Fund (NIF).[59] S/he can also do this if the employer simply fails or refuses to pay and s/he has taken all reasonable steps (other than legal proceedings) to get payment from the employer.

18.25　Any sum received as contractual redundancy pay will be set off against the statutory amount.

The compensatory award

18.26　The idea of the compensatory award is to compensate the employee for the financial loss suffered as a result of being dismissed, including expenses incurred and loss of fringe benefits.[60] The point is to compensate the employee, but not to award him/her a bonus, and not to penalise the employer. The ET must award what it considers to be 'just and equitable' having regard to the loss and it has wide discretionary powers. The tribunal must not take into account the employer's financial circumstances and whether it has enough money to pay the award.[61]

18.27　The compensatory award is subject to an overall ceiling which is revised annually. For dismissals in the year starting 6 April 2020, it was £88,519 and in the year starting 6 April 2021, it was £89,493.[62] There is a further cap of 52 weeks' gross pay, if this is lower than the overall ceiling.[63] This additional cap, introduced by the coalition government in July 2013, substantially increases the risk that employees who have been unfairly dismissed through no fault of their own are not fully compensated for their financial loss. The ceilings do not apply to dismissals for health and safety or whistleblowing reasons[64]

58　ERA 1996 s165(1).
59　ERA 1996 s166 and para 18.73. Contact details via www.gov.uk/government/organisations/insolvency-service.
60　ERA 1996 s123(1) and (2).
61　*Tao Herbs & Acupuncture Ltd v Jin* UKEAT/1477/09.
62　Employment Rights (Increase of Limits) Order 2019 SI No 324.
63　ERA 1996 s124(1ZA).
64　Under ERA 1996 ss100 and 103A, see also s124(1A).

or to compensation for unlawful discrimination.[65] When employees hear about the ceiling, they tend to expect it is the sum they will get. This does not necessarily follow. Statistics are available on average awards made by tribunals, but this is also a poor guide. It is important that employees understand that the compensatory award is worked out by reference to a number of set factors, the most important of which is probably their loss of earnings and pension.

18.28   The compensatory award often includes compensation under these headings:

- loss of earnings;
- loss of fringe benefits;
- loss of pension;
- expenses for job-hunting or, rarely, the cost of setting him/herself up in business[66] or moving to find employment;[67]
- loss of statutory rights.

When an ET makes an award, it must set out the heads of compensation, so that everyone can understand how it arrived at the total figure.[68]

Compensation for injury to feelings

18.29   Compensation for injury to feelings and other non-economic loss cannot be awarded for unfair dismissal cases.[69] Injury to feelings and aggravated damages can be awarded to an employee who wins his/her case for detriment short of dismissal on grounds related to trade union membership or activities,[70] or for other cases concerning detriment short of dismissal,[71] eg due to whistleblowing[72] or for taking up

---

65 See chapter 20.
66 *Hill v Roland Berger Technics Ltd* [1982] IRLR 498, EAT.
67 *Co-operative Wholesale Society Ltd v Squirrell* (1974) 9 ITR 191, NIRC; *Nohar v Granitstone (Galloway) Ltd* [1974] ICR 273, NIRC.
68 *Norton Tool Co Ltd v Tewson* [1972] IRLR 86, EAT.
69 *Dunnachie v Kingston upon Hull City Council* [2004] IRLR 727, HL.
70 *Cleveland Ambulance NHS Trust v Blane* [1997] IRLR 332, EAT.
71 ERA 1996 s49. Note that awards for injury to feelings are not made where an employee is dismissed or a worker's contract is terminated for these reasons. See para 6.68 onwards for full list of detriments.
72 *Virgo Fidelis Senior School v Boyle* [2004] IRLR 268, EAT.

a right under the Working Time Regulations. The *Vento* guidelines[73] apply to the size of any injury to feelings award.[74]

Loss of earnings

1) Past and future loss

18.30   Usually the largest part of an employee's compensatory award is the amount for loss of earnings. In theory, the ET will award loss of earnings from the effective date of termination (EDT) until the hearing date ('past loss') and thereafter until the ET decides that the loss would have stopped or it becomes too speculative to award any further loss ('future loss'). If the employee has obtained a new job at a lower rate of pay, the ET will estimate how long s/he is likely to be earning less, and award the difference. Once a new job is secured which is as well or better paid, the compensation calculation will usually stop at that point, rather than the higher pay eating into the earlier losses, but ultimately it is up to the tribunal.[75]

18.31   Where the employee was dismissed[76] without notice or pay in lieu, s/he will be awarded loss of earnings through the notice period. Any earnings from a new job need not be deducted.[77] Similarly, even if s/he did get paid in lieu of notice, s/he need not set off any higher earnings in the notice period against his/her claim for loss of earnings after the notice period.[78] This should not be confused with a wrongful dismissal claim for unpaid notice, where earnings during the notice period would be set off.[79] Further, an employee will not be awarded loss of earnings for unfair dismissal through the notice period if s/he would have been off sick and only receiving statutory sick pay (SSP) at that time.[80] However, if the employee only has a statutory notice entitlement, a way round this might be a wrongful

---

73 See para 19.16.
74 *Hackney LBC v Adams* [2003] IRLR 402, EAT; *Virgo Fidelis Senior School v Boyle* [2004] IRLR 268, EAT. See para 19.16 for *Vento* guidelines in context of discrimination claims.
75 *Whelan v Richardson* [1998] IRLR 114, EAT; *Dench v Flynn & Partners* [1998] IRLR 653, CA.
76 Though not constructively dismissed. *Stuart Peters Ltd v Bell* [2009] EWCA Civ 938; [2009] IRLR 941.
77 *Norton Tool Co Ltd v Tewson* [1972] IRLR 86, NIRC; *Voith Turbo Ltd v Stowe* [2005] IRLR 228, EAT.
78 *Voith Turbo Ltd* [2005] IRLR 228, EAT. But see *Morgans v Alpha Plus Security Ltd* [2005] IRLR 234, EAT.
79 See para 1.31.
80 *Burlo v Langley and another* [2007] IRLR 145, CA.

dismissal claim for full pay for the notice period, since special rules apply (see para 1.39).

18.32   If the employee has not found a new job, the ET, in assessing how long s/he is likely to remain unemployed, will take into consideration the employee's age[81] and personal characteristics,[82] and the availability of work in the locality. Owing to the speculative nature of this part of the award, it is important to present compelling and persuasive evidence; this should include the opinion of the local jobcentre or other job agencies and the efforts made to secure employment.

18.33   Future loss of earnings will not be awarded after a date on which an ET decides the employee would not continue to have been employed anyway, eg if three months after his/her dismissal, the employer closed down. Or there may come a point where an employee would have become too ill to work. But the date of such ill-health should not be an automatic cut-off for loss of earnings because the tribunal needs to consider what would have happened had s/he not been unfairly dismissed, eg how long the employment would have continued prior to dismissal; what statutory or contractual pay and benefits the employee would have received meanwhile; whether s/he would have returned to work or what his/her notice entitlement would have been.[83]

18.34   Employees cannot assume that the ET will award all of their past loss of earnings, ie up to the date of the ET hearing. Employees have a duty to 'mitigate' their loss,[84] ie to try to find a new job and not simply to sit back and await compensation from the tribunal. This is a real problem in practice. It is crucial that an adviser informs employees at the outset that this is how compensation works and that they should look for fresh employment and keep records of all their attempts, including copies of letters written, diary notes of appointments, screenshots of on-line applications and responses, and hard copies of emails (as these tend to be deleted). It would be wise for employees to register with a local or specialist job agency, read specialist press and apply for vacancies. The ET will be unsympathetic to employees who did not even try to get another job, eg due to fear of a bad reference. It is better that employees apply for a job and if they get rejected on grounds of poor references, they could write to their

81   *Isle of Wight Tourist Board v Coombes* [1976] IRLR 413, EAT.

82   *Fougère v Phoenix Motor Co* [1976] IRLR 259, EAT.

83   *Wood v Mitchell SA Ltd* UKEAT/0018/10.

84   ERA 1996 s123(4).

ex-employer about this, reminding the employer that they are trying to mitigate their loss and possibly, ask for an open reference.[85]

18.35 The ET will expect a degree of flexibility from employees as time goes on if they are getting nowhere. Employees need not necessarily accept the first job which is offered, if it is on low pay, since they may be acting reasonably in mitigating their loss by looking for a job with equivalent pay to previously.[86] For a period of time, it is unreasonable to expect an employee to lower his/her sights, but after a while, it may be reasonable for him/her to accept a job of lesser pay and status.[87] There is always a risk that if an employee is offered a job and turns it down because of low pay or other unsuitability, the ET may decide to stop awarding compensation from the date of the offer. If the tribunal does reduce compensation for failure to mitigate, it should try to work out when it says the employee should have got a new job and at what pay, rather than simply apply a broad percentage deduction.[88]

18.36 When employers lose cases, they tend to fight very hard on the issue of compensation and go to the ET armed with evidence of suitable available vacancies. If there is a potential problem, it may be useful to take the case of *Wilding v British Telecommunications plc*[89] to the ET, as a corrective to the ET being too tough on the employee. The Court of Appeal set out these guidelines in *Wilding*:

- It is the duty of an employee to act as a reasonable person who was not expecting compensation from the former employer.
- The onus is on the employer as the wrongdoer to show that the employee failed to mitigate.[90]
- If the employee turned down a job offer, eg from the former employer, the test is whether the employee acted unreasonably, taking into account all the circumstances.
- The court or tribunal must not be too stringent in its expectations of the employee, who is, after all, the injured party.

18.37 The ET must take the employee's age, health and other personal circumstances into account in deciding whether s/he has failed to

---

85 See also paras 1.63–1.68 on references.

86 *A G Bracey Ltd v Iles* [1973] IRLR 210, EAT.

87 *Orthet Ltd v Vince-Cain* [2004] IRLR 857, EAT.

88 *Gardiner-Hill v Roland Berger Technics Ltd* [1982] IRLR 498, EAT; *Hakim v The Scottish Trade Unions Congress* UKEATS/0047/19.

89 [2002] IRLR 524, CA. *Cooper Contracting Ltd v Lindsey* UKEAT/0184/15 usefully reinforces these principles.

90 See also *Bessenden Properties Ltd v Corness* [1974] IRLR 338, CA.

mitigate.[91] The ET should not refuse to award compensation for loss of earnings because the claimant is unfit to work, if the claimant's ill-health was caused by the dismissal.[92] However, in a constructive dismissal case, the claimant cannot get compensated in the ET – as opposed to making a civil claim – for loss of earnings resulting from ill-health caused by the employer's conduct prior to dismissal.[93] This unpractical outcome is because the loss of earnings would, strictly speaking, have been caused by the employer's actions during the employment and not by the dismissal itself. Depending on the situation, it may be reasonable for an employee to mitigate his/her loss by setting up in business[94] rather than immediately looking for a job with a new employer. It may also be reasonable to undergo retraining or study in order to change careers and improve long-term earning capacity, but there must be good reasons to make this choice in the particular case.[95]

18.38   If the employee gets a new job but has been dismissed or resigned by the time of the ET hearing, it will depend on the facts whether the ET will order the original employer to pay compensation for lost earnings beyond the date when the new job started.[96] If the new job did not last long and was always unsuitable, it could be argued that the employee finding him/herself out of a job again is all part of the loss arising from the original dismissal. A reasonable but unsuccessful attempt to mitigate does not break the link between the original dismissal and the resulting loss.[97] However, a longer period of new employment, where the employee loses the job through his/her own fault, probably would break the link.

2) Calculating the weekly loss

18.39   The calculation is based on how much the employee would have earned had s/he remained in the old job, including regular overtime, bonuses and the employer's pension contributions[98]. The employee

---

91   *Fougère v Phoenix Motor Co Ltd* [1976] IRLR 259, EAT.

92   *Dignity Funerals Ltd v Bruce* [2005] IRLR 189, CS.

93   *GAB Robins (UK) Ltd v Triggs* [2008] IRLR 317, CA; *Countrywide Estate Agents and others v Turner* UKEAT/0208/13.

94   *Gardiner-Hill v Roland Berger Technics Ltd* [1982] IRLR 498, EAT.

95   *Orthet Ltd v Vince-Cain* [2004] IRLR 857, EAT.

96   *Dench v Flynn & Partners* [1998] IRLR 653, CA; *Cowen v Rentokil Initial Facility Services (UK) Ltd (t/a Initial Transport Services)* UKEAT/0473/07.

97   *Witham Weld v Hedley* UKEAT/0176/95. See also *Hakim v The Scottish Trade Unions Congress* UKEATS/0047/19.

98   *University of Sunderland v Drossou* UKEAT/0341/16; [2017] IRLR 1087.

needs to produce evidence of this. The ET must take account of likely pay rises (even if not contractual), including anticipated overtime payments.[99] The award will be greater where the increase is certain rather than probable. If the employer can show that overtime would have diminished or ceased, the award will be reduced accordingly. If the employee would have been unable to work for the original employer anyway because of sickness and would only have been entitled to statutory sick pay (SSP), then s/he will not be awarded loss of earnings for that period if she could get the same level of benefits when out of work.

18.40 Unlike the basic award, the award for loss of earnings is calculated net of tax and National Insurance (NI) contributions. If the employee was paid below the statutory minimum wage, the calculation of lost earnings must be based on the minimum wage.[100]

Loss of fringe benefits

18.41 The compensatory award includes an element for the loss of fringe benefits in respect of both the immediate and the future loss period. The value of these can be hard to quantify, though it is usually the cost to the employee of replacing them. The following fringe benefits have been taken into consideration by ETs:

- entitlement to holiday pay;
- tips or other gratuitous payments which would have been earned during the compensatory period;[101]
- the loss of a company car, which is usually assessed by reference to the AA guidelines on car running costs;[102]
- cheap loans (ie the value in comparison with bank loans);[103]
- accommodation, if it is free or subsidised;
- medical insurance, which is assessed by reference to the cost to the employee of acquiring the same medical protection.

Loss of statutory rights

18.42 Loss of long notice entitlement, maternity rights and the right to claim unfair dismissal should be reflected in the compensatory

---

99 *York Trailer Co v Sparks* [1973] IRLR 348, NICA.
100 *Paggetti v Cobb* [2002] IRLR 861, EAT.
101 *Palmanor v Cedron Ltd* [1978] IRLR 303, EAT.
102 At www.theaa.com/driving-advice/driving-costs/running-costs.
103 *UBAF Bank v Davis* [1978] IRLR 442, EAT.

award. The loss of unfair dismissal protection[104] is now usually compensated at or just below the level of the current maximum on a week's redundancy pay,[105] ie currently around £500. This tends to be known as an award for 'loss of statutory rights'. The ET is unlikely to make this award if the employee has already been employed in a new job for two years by the time of the hearing. In addition, if the employee has built up a long statutory minimum notice period, s/he can also claim for the fact that s/he will have to start again in any new job. This award is usually valued at half of the entitlement to the statutory notice which had been acquired, calculated as a net sum.[106] This means no more than a six-week multiplier, ie half the maximum statutory notice period.[107] The reason for the reduction is to reflect the double contingency that the employee will get a new job and then that s/he will be dismissed before acquiring a similar level of notice entitlement. It can be difficult to claim this latter award, and advisers should take copies of the case-law with them to the ET.[108] Employers – and even tribunals – sometimes argue that the employee has already been paid his/her notice pay and should not get a double award. This is misconceived. The point is to compensate an employee for being vulnerable in his/her new job – just as an employee has already had his/her unfair dismissal claim in respect of the old job, but still routinely gets awarded a sum for loss of statutory rights.

Loss of pension rights

18.43   If the employee had an occupational pension with his/her employer, the pension loss caused by the dismissal needs to be added into the compensatory award. In limited situations, an employee may also suffer some loss of state pension. Unfortunately pension loss is the hardest to quantify, yet may be the most valuable part of the employee's claim. The burden of proof is on the employee to prove the loss, so s/he must obtain the necessary pension documents from the employer when preparing the case and work out how to quantify the loss.

18.44   The latest (4th) edition of *Employment tribunals: principles for compensating pension loss* is extremely helpful. This clear and detailed

---

104 *Head v S H Muffet* [1986] IRLR 488, EAT.

105 See para 18.19.

106 *Daley v Dorsett (Almar Dolls)* [1981] IRLR 385, EAT.

107 *Arthur Guinness Son & Co v Green* [1989] IRLR 288, EAT.

108 *Daley v Dorsett (Almar Dolls)* [1981] IRLR 385, EAT and *Arthur Guinness Son & Co v Green* [1989] IRLR 288, EAT in particular, as the latter post-dates the unhelpful comments in *Head v S H Muffet* [1986] IRLR 488, EAT.

guide, referred to as the 'Principles', was written by a group of Employment Judges and published in August 2017.[109] Presidential Guidance says that tribunals are expected to have regard to the 'Principles' when calculating pension loss.[110] Having said that, the 'Principles' are not statutory, and if the parties put forward a credible alternative with supporting evidence, the tribunal should listen.[111] It is beyond the scope of this book to give practical guidance to calculating pension loss. The following is simply an introduction to the main concepts.

18.45 If pension loss is likely to be substantial, it may be worth getting expert advice from an actuary on the value of lost rights. An alternative approach would be to obtain quotations for the cost of replacing the lost pension. Calculations need to be made as to what pension the employee is now likely to receive and what pension s/he would have received had it not been for the dismissal. Insurance companies can quote for topping up the pension to the latter level.

18.46 The way to calculate financial loss differs according to whether the employee was employed on a 'defined benefit' scheme (eg a final salary or career average revalued earnings (CARE) scheme) or a 'defined contribution' scheme (money purchase).

18.47 In a defined contribution scheme, the amount of pension is based on the investment of sums contributed by the employee and employer over a number of years. In a final salary scheme, the amount of pension is based on a proportion of the employee's earnings at the leaving date for each year of service, eg 1/60 or 1/80 per year worked. In recent years, final salary schemes have become far less common. Where they still exist, the pension is now usually based on 'pensionable pay' (which can be less than the full salary) and 'career average' pay (known as a CARE scheme) rather than final pay.

18.48 Where an employee leaves a defined contribution scheme early, eg due to dismissal, s/he retains the value of the sums invested to the termination date, but loses the prospective value of further contributions from the employer. There may also be a financial penalty for

---

109 The full 'Principles', a shorter 'Basic guide', 'Presidential guidance pension loss' and 'Presidential guidance pension loss (3rd addendum 2021)' are all at www.judiciary.uk/publications/employment-rules-and-legislation-practice-directions/. The latest (3rd) revision of the principles refers to the effect of furlough at para 4.28.

110 At www.judiciary.uk/wp-content/uploads/2013/08/presidential-guidance-pension-loss-20170810.pdf.

111 *Port of Tilbury (London) Ltd v Birch and others* [2005] IRLR 92, EAT. Although the version of the Principles used at that time was not supported by Presidential Guidance.

leaving early. The financial loss is therefore fairly easy to calculate. The position is more complicated with a final salary or other defined benefit scheme. The early leaver will usually be entitled to a deferred pension, but one which will be of lesser value than had s/he not been dismissed. The difference can be hard to quantify and will depend on the approach taken by the tribunal.

18.49   The ET 'Principles' recommend two approaches to calculating pension loss: 'simple' and 'complex'. The ET need not follow either approach, but it must explain its reasons for rejecting both or for choosing one of them. The 'simple approach' will almost always apply to a defined contribution scheme. This involves adding up the amount of the employer's pension contributions for the period of loss. The employee's own pension contributions are not included because, as a result of the dismissal, the employee has not had to pay those. There is more detail of this approach starting at para 4.17 of the 'Principles' and there are sample calculations in its appendix 3.

18.50   The 'simple' approach to calculation will sometimes also be appropriate for a defined benefit scheme, eg where the period of loss is relatively short, say 6–12 months as a rule of thumb, or where the statutory cap on the unfair dismissal award means it is not worth the cost and effort of calculating full pension loss the 'complex' way. To use the 'simple' approach, it will be necessary to find out the rate of the employer's contribution to the defined benefit scheme. The 'Principles' explain more about using the 'simple' approach for defined benefit schemes at paras 5.30–5.40.

18.51   Many cases involving defined benefit schemes will not be suitable for the 'simple' contributions-based calculation method. The 'complex' approach then involves using the Ogden tables and/or expert evidence. The 'Principles' explain the 'complex' approach for defined benefit cases at para 5.41 onwards, including 'seven steps' for making calculations based on the Ogden tables.

Adjustments to the compensatory award

18.52   Payments under any private or occupational pension scheme which the employee decides to take early as a result of the dismissal are not set off against the compensatory award.[112]

18.53   If the ET finds the dismissal was to any extent caused or contributed to by any action of the employee, it can reduce the compensat-

---

112 *Knapton and others v ECC Card Clothing Ltd* [2006] IRLR 756, EAT.

ory award proportionally as it thinks fit.[113] This is known as 'contributory fault' and the ET usually makes a percentage reduction, eg 25 per cent or 50 per cent, but in very rare cases, it can deduct 100 per cent. There are two separate questions: 1) did the employee's conduct cause or contribute to the dismissal? and 2) if so, by how much would it be 'just and equitable' to reduce the compensatory award? Even if the tribunal believes the employee's conduct was completely responsible for the dismissal, it will not necessarily be just and equitable to reduce the compensatory award by 100 per cent.[114] The employee's conduct must have been culpable or blameworthy. This does not necessarily include merely unreasonable conduct – it depends on the extent of the unreasonableness.[115] The biggest risk of a reduction for contributory fault is where the employee has been dismissed for misconduct, but it is also possible with dismissals in other categories if the employee has acted in a blameworthy way, eg his/her actions have led to a breakdown in trust and confidence.[116] Potentially, actions arising from an employee's alcoholism could also amount to contributory fault.[117] Contributory fault for incompetence would be rare, unless the employee was deliberately lazy or negligent.[118] The compensatory award in a constructive dismissal claim can theoretically also be reduced for contributory fault, although it will be unusual.[119] Compensation cannot be reduced for post-dismissal misconduct.[120] It is the tribunal's view of the claimant's behaviour and whether it amounts to contributory fault which counts, not the employer's.[121]

18.54 The decision to reduce the award and the degree of contribution is discretionary and can only be challenged before the Employment Appeal Tribunal (EAT) if it is legally perverse (ie no ET properly

---

113 ERA 1996 s123(6). There is no equivalent section in the EqA 2010 and contributory fault is unlikely to apply to findings of discrimination: *(1) First Greater Western Limited (2) Linley v Waiyego* UKEAT/0056/16.

114 *Lemonious v Church Commissioners* UKEAT/0253/12; *Steen v ASP Packaging Ltd* UKEAT/0023/13.

115 *Nelson v BBC (No 2)* [1979] IRLR 346, CA. For a recent example, see *Wheeley v University Hospitals Birmingham NHS Trust* UKEAT/0259/18, where 'inappropriate' behaviour was not necessarily 'blameworthy'.

116 *Tolley v Scofield* UKEAT/0324/16.

117 *Sinclair v Wandsworth LBC* UKEAT/0145/07.

118 *Slaughter v C Brewer & Sons* [1990] IRLR 426, EAT.

119 *Polentarutti v Autocraft Ltd* [1991] IRLR 457, EAT; *Frith Accountants Ltd v Law* [2014] IRLR 510, EAT.

120 *Mullinger v Department for Work and Pensions* UKEAT/0515/05.

121 *Steen v ASP Packaging Ltd* UKEAT/0023/13.

directing itself could have reached the same decision). Such a challenge is very difficult to succeed in, though the employee must have been given the opportunity to give evidence on the matter in the ET. The ET must also identify the conduct which has been taken into account and explain why it is blameworthy.[122]

18.55   There is nothing to stop a tribunal reducing compensation both for contributory fault and on the *Polkey* principle (see para 18.57). However, a tribunal should first consider the *Polkey* deduction, and this may affect how much it thinks it is just and equitable to deduct for contributory fault.[123] As well as reducing the compensatory award for contributory fault, the ET can reduce the basic award for conduct before the dismissal, where it would be just and equitable to do so.[124] In the case of the basic award, it is not necessary that such conduct actually caused or contributed to the dismissal. Nevertheless, if an employer does reduce the compensatory award for contributory fault, it is likely that it will also reduce the basic award by the same percentage.

18.56   If the employer or employee unreasonably fails to follow the Advisory, Conciliation and Arbitration Service (ACAS) Code of Practice on Disciplinary and Grievance Procedures,[125] the compensatory award may be increased or decreased by up to 25 per cent respectively.[126] Another type of statutory adjustment can be made by a tribunal in whistleblowing cases. If the tribunal believes the disclosure was not made in good faith, it may reduce the worker's compensation by up to 25 per cent if it thinks it just and equitable to do so.[127]

18.57   So-called 'Polkey reductions' are more common than those for contributory fault. A dismissal may be unfair for procedural reasons only, even though the actual reason for dismissal is fair.[128] In such cases, the compensatory award may be reduced by a percentage to reflect the likelihood that the employee would still have been dismissed, even if fair procedures had been followed. A percentage

---

122 *Lindsay v General Contracting Ltd t/a Pik a Pak Home Electrical* (2002) 686 IRLB 8, EAT; *Wheeley v University Hospitals Birmingham NHS Trust* UKEAT/0259/18.

123 *Rao v Civil Aviation Authority* [1994] IRLR 240, CA.

124 See para 18.20; and ERA 1996 s122(2), although the wording is wider.

125 Available at: www.acas.org.uk/acas-code-of-practice-on-disciplinary-and-grievance-procedures. TULR(C)A 1992 s207A; details in chapter 22.

126 See para 22.5 for more detail of criteria which may affect the percentage adjustment.

127 See para 6.114.

128 See para 6.65.

reduction can be as high as 100 per cent, although the ET might still award loss of earnings for the time it would have taken to go through proper procedures. Most often a reduction will be in the area of 25–50 per cent. A tribunal should not automatically assume that just because the dismissal was for gross misconduct, the employer would definitely have dismissed the employee, even if fair procedures had been followed (though it makes it more likely).[129]

18.58   It is often difficult to decide whether unfairness is 'procedural' or a matter of substance. Either way, the tribunal must consider this question of whether and when the employee would have been dismissed if the employer had acted fairly. Sometimes this is obvious, eg the employee would have left anyway in six months' time, eg because of retirement or closure of the workplace. It is also fairly obvious where the only unfairness in a redundancy dismissal is the failure to consider alternative employment, but there were no suitable available vacancies anyway. But sometimes it is less clear what would have happened, eg if the dismissal was only unfair due to unfair redundancy selection criteria, would the employee still have been selected for redundancy if fair criteria had been used? A tribunal must not refuse to make a percentage reduction just because there is an element of speculation – a degree of uncertainty is an inevitable feature of the exercise. On the other hand, if the evidence is such that the whole exercise of trying to reconstruct what might have been, is riddled with uncertainty, no deduction should be made.[130]

18.59   A tribunal can only reduce compensation to reflect the fact that the employee would have been dismissed anyway at some later point, if such dismissal would have been a fair dismissal. It also assumes the employer would not have generally acted unlawfully towards the employee in any way which might impact on the continuation of his/her employment, eg by subjecting the employee to oppressive working conditions which would cause the employee to go off sick and then dismissing him/her for sickness absence.[131]

18.60   If the employer ought to have started consultation much earlier, when s/he first knew redundancy was likely, and as a result, the employee loses time when s/he could have started looking for a new job, compensation can extend to pay for that lost time.[132]

129 *Singh v Glass Express Midlands Ltd* UKEAT/0071/18.
130 See *King v Eaton Ltd (No 2)* [1998] IRLR 681, CS; *Software 2000 Ltd v Andrews and others* [2007] IRLR 568, EAT; *Virgin Media Ltd v Seddington and Eland* UKEAT/0539/08.
131 *Acetrip Limited v Dogra* UKEAT/0238/18.
132 *Coney Island Ltd v Elkouil* [2002] IRLR 174, EAT.

Order of deductions and adjustments

18.61   The order of the various deductions, and the imposition of the overall ceiling,[133] makes a big difference to the final award. There have been several cases on what order should be followed. The ET should approach the calculation as follows:[134]

- Calculate the loss which the employee has sustained in consequence of the dismissal insofar as the loss is attributable to action taken by the employer. For example, loss of earnings and pension, and job-hunting expenses.
- Deduct all sums paid by the employer as compensation for the dismissal, eg pay in lieu of notice[135] or an ex gratia payment, but exclude at this stage any redundancy pay to the extent it exceeds the basic award. Also deduct earnings in a new job.[136]
- Any *Polkey* reduction (para 18.57) should then be made.
- Increase or reduce the sum by up to 25 per cent for failure to comply with a relevant part of the ACAS Code on Disciplinary and Grievance Procedures.[137]
- Add two or four weeks' pay if, when proceedings were begun, the employer was in breach of his/her duty to give the employee a written statement of employment particulars or change under ERA 1996 s1 or s4.[138]
- Make any reduction for contributory fault.
- Deduct any redundancy payment to the extent it exceeds the basic award.
- If part of the award will be taxable (eg if the taxable amount is over £30,000), gross it up.[139]
- If the sum calculated in accordance with the above is in excess of the statutory ceiling, the final stage is to reduce it to bring it down to the statutory maximum.[140]

---

133 See para 18.27.
134 *Digital Equipment Co Ltd v Clements (No 2)* [1998] IRLR 134, CA read together with the EAT's decision at [1997] IRLR 140 and updated to incorporate ERA 1996 s124A.
135 *Heggie v Uniroyal Englebert Tyres Ltd* [1999] IRLR 802, CA.
136 Though see para 18.30.
137 ERA 1996 s124A; TULR(C)A 1992 s207A(5); para 18.56.
138 ERA 1996 s124A; Employment Act 2002 ss31(5) and 38; and see para 1.26.
139 Tax can be complicated and is outside the scope of this book.
140 *Leonard and others v Strathclyde Buses* [1998] IRLR 693, CS.

Recoupment

18.62 Any income support, jobseeker's allowance (JSA), income-related employment and support allowance (ESA) or universal credit received by the employee should not be set off against the sum awarded by the ET. However, the effect is the same from the employee's point of view, because the employer must repay the sum to the Department for Work and Pensions (DWP) before passing on the balance of the award to the employee.[141] This is known as recoupment. The ET will ask the employee whether s/he has received these benefits and, if so, its judgment will set out two figures: the monetary award (ie the total compensation awarded) and the prescribed element.

18.63 The prescribed element is the amount awarded for loss of earnings between the dismissal date and the final ET hearing, subject to any reductions made, eg for contributory fault. It will also be reduced proportionately if the statutory cap had to be applied to the overall award.[142] The judgment will specify the amount of the prescribed element and the period to which it relates. The ET must send a copy of the judgment with these details in a recoupment notice to the DWP when sending the judgment to the parties.

18.64 On receiving the judgment, the employer can immediately pay the balance of the monetary award to the employee. S/he must not pay the prescribed element until s/he has received a recoupment notice from the local DWP or notification that no recoupment applies. The notice should be served on the employer within 21 days of any reserved judgment or the conclusion of the hearing or nine days of an oral judgment, whichever is later.[143] The employer then pays the recouped amount back to the DWP and the balance of the prescribed element to the employee. The employee gets a copy of the notice and should notify the local office in writing if s/he disagrees with the amount of benefit stated as paid. It almost always takes the DWP much longer to serve the recoupment notice and it may be necessary to write to the relevant office, reminding it of the timescale in the regulations. If the delay continues, the employee could use the DWP's complaints procedure.

18.65 Because of recoupment, if the employee was receiving a large amount of income support, income-based JSA, ESA or universal

---

141 Employment Protection (Recoupment of Jobseeker's Allowance and Income Support) Regulations 1996 SI No 2349 as amended by 2010 SI No 2429.
142 *Mason v Wimpey Waste Management Ltd* [1982] IRLR 454, EAT.
143 SI No 2349 reg 8.

credit, his/her claim could be worth very little. In particular, where the employee has claimed mortgage interest as part of his/her income support or income-based JSA, recoupment may swallow most of the award. If the case is settled before the hearing, the recoupment provisions do not apply. It is in the interests of both parties to settle and to reach an agreement on compensation, bearing in mind that there will no recoupment on the settlement sum. The parties often agree to split the difference on the amount which would have been recouped. It is safer if the settlement is for a single figure and does not itemise the specific claims that are being settled, such as notice pay, holiday pay, wages, etc just in case the recoupment provisions could be applied as a result, although this is unlikely. Housing benefit paid following the dismissal is not deducted.[144]

Interest

18.66   Interest is payable on ET awards and runs from the day after the decision unless the award was paid in full within 14 days.[145] Where there is an appeal whose outcome does not affect the level of compensation, the interest still accrues from that date. Where the appeal alters the award of compensation, interest runs on the altered award but still from the original decision (or, for claims presented before 29 July 2013, from 42 days afterwards). Unfortunately, if an ET has only made a decision on liability, which is appealed by the employer, no interest can run until a decision on compensation is made, usually not until the appeal has been disposed of.

18.67   Interest runs on a daily basis on unpaid parts of the award and the rate is that applicable from time to time under the Judgments Act 1838 s17. The ET decision will stipulate the applicable interest rate (eight per cent at the time of writing).

Interim relief

18.68   The law gives special protection in respect of certain dismissals, especially where these relate to whistleblowing or to acting as a workplace representative of various kinds. As well as a minimum basic

---

144 *Savage v Saxena* [1998] IRLR 182, EAT.
145 Employment Tribunals (Interest) Order 1990 SI No 479 as amended for claims presented on or after 29 July 2013.

award and no ceiling on the compensatory award (in some cases)[146] there are also provisions for interim relief.

18.69   Where an employee is dismissed (though not selected for redundancy) for certain reasons, s/he can claim interim relief.[147] The reasons include dismissal for:

- whistleblowing;
- trade union membership or activities;
- taking on the role and activities of a health and safety representative;
- being a trustee of an occupational pension scheme;
- being an employee representative for collective consultation on redundancies or TUPE;
- being a workforce representative under the Working Time Regulations.

Interim relief is not available for ordinary unfair dismissal or discrimination claims.[148]

18.70   Interim relief hearings happen very fast. The employee must apply for interim relief together with his/her tribunal claim for unfair dismissal by the end of seven days following the effective date of termination.[149] The ACAS early conciliation (EC) procedure need not be followed.[150] If the dismissal is for trade union membership or activities, s/he must also produce a certificate from an authorised union official.[151] The ET must then decide the issue as soon as possible, giving the employer at least seven days' notice of the hearing.

18.71   If the ET decides it is likely that the employee will succeed in his/her unfair dismissal case at the eventual hearing, it can order interim relief, ie reinstatement or re-engagement (if the employer agrees) or otherwise a continuation of contract order (CCO).[152] 'Likely to succeed' means having a pretty good chance of success.[153] A CCO orders the employer to pay the employee's wages and other benefits from dismissal until the eventual ET decision or settlement. The payments are not repayable, even if the employee ultimately loses.

---

146 See paras 18.21 and 18.27.
147 ERA 1996 s128.
148 *Steer v Stormsure Ltd* [2021] EWCA Civ 887; [2021] IRLR 762.
149 ERA 1996 s128(2); TULR(C)A 1992 s161(2).
150 See para 20.16.
151 TULR(C)A 1992 s161(3).
152 ERA 1996 ss129–130; TULR(C)A 1992 ss163–164.
153 *Taplin v C Shippam Ltd* [1978] IRLR 450, EAT.

Enforcement

18.72   If an employer does not pay an ET award or compensation under a settlement or compromise agreement, it is possible to enforce payment directly in the county court or High Court (England and Wales) or sheriff court (Scotland).[154] This removes the need to register the judgment and pay a fee first. There is guidance on the different systems in England and Wales and in Scotland on the GOV.UK site.[155] Settlements and compromise agreements are enforced by bringing a claim in the county court or High Court, as appropriate, usually for damages for breach of contract. This has also been simplified in respect of non-payment of ACAS settlements (with some exceptions).[156] Following research showing a high level of unpaid tribunal awards, High Court Enforcement Officers were given power to recover tribunal awards and settlements.[157] An unpaid claimant can also ask the Department for Business, Energy & Industrial Strategy (BEIS) to impose a penalty for non-payment and publicly name the employer. Details of the schemes and how to apply are on the GOV.UK website.[158] Although the penalty goes to the government and not the claimant, the threat of a fine and public naming may persuade some reluctant employers to pay.

Employer insolvency and debts covered by the state

18.73   If the employer becomes insolvent, certain debts can be claimed from the state. These include unpaid wages up to eight weeks; up to six weeks' holiday pay in the previous 12 months; and statutory notice pay.[159] All these are subject to a weekly limit, which was £544 where

---

154 Tribunals, Courts and Enforcement Act 2007 s27.

155 At www.gov.uk/employment-tribunals/if-you-win-your-case.

156 For details, see Tribunals, Courts and Enforcement Act 2007 s142.

157 See *Employment tribunal & ACAS awards*, at https:// thesheriffsoffice.com/ services/high-court-enforcement/employment-tribunal-awards-acas-settlements.

158 A form to have the employer fined and named is at www.gov.uk/government/ publications/employment-tribunal-penalty-enforcement. Details of the naming scheme are at www.gov.uk/government/publications/employment-tribunal-naming-scheme-guidance.

159 ERA 1996 ss182–186. Notice pay can be claimed online at www.gov.uk/ claim-loss-notice and wages, holiday and commission at www.gov.uk/ claim-redundancy.

the employer became insolvent on or after 6 April 2021 or, in the case of notice pay, when the employment terminated if later.[160] Statutory redundancy pay and any ET basic award (though not the compensatory award) can also be recovered.[161] An application needs to be made to the Insolvency Service[162] or, in some cases, the employer's representative. Generally speaking, the Insolvency Service will only pay if the employer is insolvent and not just because s/he has stopped trading. However, redundancy pay is also reimbursed where the employer simply refuses to pay and the employee has taken all reasonable steps to recover the payment from the employer.[163] For more details, see the GOV.UK website.[164] To check whether the employer is an insolvent company, a search can be done on the Companies House WebCheck site.[165] If the company is in administration or receivership, the employee ought to have been informed of the position by the administrators/receivers. See para 10.50 for the position regarding the transfer of an insolvent business.

Financial penalties

18.74   ETs can impose a financial penalty on an employer where the worker has won any of his/her claims and the tribunal feels that the employer's breach of the worker's rights had some 'aggravating features'.[166] No examples are given in the legislation, but presumably this envisages situations such as where a worker wins a claim for outstanding wages against an employer who constantly fails to pay what is due. In 'Employment Tribunals' Powers: Tribunal user guidance on use and application',[167] BEIS suggests deliberate breaches of the law or being motivated by malice would be aggravating features and that employers with dedicated human resources (HR) departments are more likely to be at risk. The penalty must be 50 per cent

160 Employment Rights (Increase of Limits) Order 2019 SI No 324; ERA 1996 s185.

161 ERA 1996 s166 and s182 respectively.

162 See www.gov.uk/claim-redundancy.

163 ERA 1996 s166.

164 See *Your rights if your employer is insolvent* at www.gov.uk/your-rights-if-your-employer-is-insolvent which includes details of how to claim.

165 See para 20.44.

166 Employment Tribunals Act 1996 s12A.

167 Published February 2019. Available via a link at www.gov.uk/government/publications/employment-tribunals-powers-their-use-and-application.

of any award made to the worker subject to a minimum of £100 and maximum of £20,000. This was increased from £5000 on 6 April 2019. The tribunal must consider the employer's ability to pay and may choose not to make an award at all.

18.75   According to the government, the idea of introducing financial penalties was to incentivise employers not to behave badly. When negotiating with employers who refuse to pay wages which are obviously due, it may be worth reminding them that they may find themselves facing a fine as well as the money owed if they persist in dragging their heels.

Discrimination remedies

Chapter 19: Key points

- When a worker wins a discrimination case, the employment tribunal can make recommendations and award compensation.
- Compensation consists of financial loss, injury to feelings and interest. Exemplary damages can be awarded only in exceptional circumstances.
- Injury to feelings can comprise separate awards for hurt feelings, aggravated damages and injury to health.
- Injury to health compensation is compensation for personal injury and the principles for its calculation are similar to those for personal injury claims (for physical or psychiatric injury) in the civil courts.
- There are special considerations related to the duty to mitigate when awarding loss of earnings in pregnancy dismissal cases.
- In some cases, there may be an adjustment of compensation because of a breach of the Advisory, Conciliation and Arbitration Service (ACAS) Code of Guidance on Disciplinary and Grievance Procedures.

General guide to useful evidence

- Payslips, contract documents, information regarding any new employment, and other evidence regarding financial loss.
- Report from GP and/or consultant psychiatrist regarding injury to feelings and/or health, visits and treatment, prognosis, recommendations for and cost of future treatment.
- Evidence from the worker, doctor or other relevant witness regarding each of the factors in the Judicial College guidelines for personal injury.
- Evidence of any conduct by the employer leading to aggravated damages. This evidence was probably given during the hearing on liability, but must now be highlighted.
- See also paras 16.65–16.71.

Introduction

19.1   When an employment tribunal (ET) has made a finding of unlawful discrimination, it may make:[1]

1 Equality Act (EqA) 2010 s124(2).

- a declaration of the rights of the parties in respect of the matter to which the complaint related;
- an appropriate recommendation;
- an order for compensation.

Where an ET finds unintentional indirect discrimination, before ordering compensation, it must first consider whether to make any recommendations.[2] This must not be taken as an obstacle to awarding proper compensation for unintentional indirect discrimination.[3] The purpose of the rule is therefore puzzling, but it may be a legacy of wording in pre Equality Act discrimination legislation. There are different remedies in equal pay cases and in respect of discrimination in occupational pension schemes.[4]

Recommendations

19.2   The ET may recommend that, within a specified period of time, the employer take action to obviate or reduce the adverse effect on the claimant of any matter to which the claim related.[5] The Equality Act (EqA) 2010 expanded recommendations so they could also apply to reduce the adverse effect of discrimination 'on anyone else', but the power to make these 'wider recommendations' was abolished for cases started on/after 1 October 2015.[6] If, without reasonable excuse, the employer fails to comply with the recommendation insofar as it relates to the claimant, the ET can award compensation or additional compensation.[7] The ET cannot insist on a recommendation being carried out. Nor can an ET recommend a pay rise, as this should be

---

2   EqA 2010 s124(4) and (5).
3   *Wisbey v Commissioner of the City of London Police and another* [2021] EWCA Civ 650; [2021] IRLR 691.
4   EqA 2010 s126.
5   EqA 2010 s124(3).
6   Deregulation Act 2015 s2 and 2015 SI No 994 articles 11, 13 and Schedule. There was little support for abolishing wider recommendations and the House of Lords Select Committee on the Equality Act 2010 and Disability has called for them to be reinstated with a view to preventing discrimination experienced by the claimant from happening to others: *The Equality Act 2010: The impact on disabled people*, March 2016, available at: www.publications.parliament.uk/pa/ld201516/ldselect/ldeqact/117/117.pdf.
7   EqA 2010 s124(7).

covered by an award of compensation. Recommendations cannot be made in respect of equal pay claims.[8]

19.3   Examples of recommendations are: that the employer makes a full written apology to the claimant; that s/he provides a reference in agreed terms; that s/he removes discriminatory documents, warnings, adverse reports, etc from the claimant's personnel file; or that s/he notes on it that the claimant has been discriminated against previously.

An interesting example of a recommendation approved by the Employment Appeal Tribunal (EAT) was that an employer interview separately a number of individuals implicated by the ET's decision and discuss with them those parts of the decision that affected them as individuals.[9] In another case, the ET ordered that a letter clearing the name of the claimant (a teacher) be sent to the parents of all the school children.[10] Nevertheless, in such situations, it would usually be better if the letter was targeted simply at the parents who knew the teacher or knew s/he had been criticised. It is important that recommendations, particularly those concerning equal opportunities steps to be taken by the employer, are very precisely described. The following are recommendations made by tribunals in real cases:[11]

- The employer to arrange disability awareness training for all managers.
- The employer to train all staff on equal opportunities and to consider appointing a diversity champion. Progress on these issues to be reported to the claimant within three months of the judgment.
- In a disability discrimination case where the ET found it would have been a reasonable adjustment to discount disability-related absences for the purpose of an attendance policy:

  i) the employer to review and implement policies on capability, absence management and equal opportunities;

---

8 EqA 2010 s113(6). Though see paras 5.89–5.90 regarding pay audits and there may also be an exception for pay claims brought under EqA 2010 s71 – see chapter 5.

9 *Chief Constable of West Yorkshire Police v Vento (No 2)* [2001] IRLR 124, EAT. This point does not seem to have been appealed to the Court of Appeal.

10 *The Governing Body of St Andrews Catholic Primary School and others v Blundell* UKEAT/0330/09.

11 See 190 EOR 26. Another example is in *Lycée Français Charles de Gaulle v Delambre* UKEAT/0563/10.

    ii) the claimant's disability-related absences in future to be recorded separately from other absences and not counted as part of the attendance policy;

    iii) no previous disability-related absences to be counted in with future non-disability-related absences under the attendance policy;

    iv) the claimant's disciplinary record to be expunged;

    v) serious and sympathetic consideration to be given to the claimant's requests for unpaid leave for rest and rehabilitation on the claimant giving as much notice as possible and in accordance with occupational health advice.

19.4   The ET is hampered in what it can recommend. In the case *Noone v North West Thames Regional Health Authority (No 2)*,[12] the ET recommended that if another post of consultant microbiologist became available, the health authority should seek the secretary of state's permission to dispense with the normal NHS advertising requirements and offer the post to Dr Noone. The Court of Appeal rescinded the recommendation because it undermined fair recruitment procedures to the detriment of the NHS, the professions concerned with it, the public and would-be applicants for the post.

19.5   Two other recommendations proposed by the health authority were substituted. These were that the health authority draw to the attention of any future appointments committee considering an application by Dr Noone the provisions of the then Race Relations Act (RRA) 1976 and remind them that Dr Noone's previous application had failed on the ground of race. In *Noone*, the Court of Appeal was influenced by the fact that there was a statutory obligation to advertise vacancies within the NHS. However, in a later case against British Gas, the EAT relying on *Noone* objected to a recommendation that the claimant was promoted to the next suitable vacancy.[13] Both cases were decided a long time ago and arguably are incorrect, as they fail to take full account of the obligation under EU law to give a full remedy for discrimination. The suggestion that it would be impermissible positive discrimination to slot the claimants into the next suitable available post misses the point, which is that doing so would be a remedy for the previous discrimination which has been found.[14] There is an extra argument in disability discrimination cases that direct discrimination in favour of a disabled person against a

---

12 [1988] IRLR 530, CA.

13 *British Gas plc v Sharma* [1991] IRLR 101, EAT.

14 This view has been put forward by Robin Allen QC.

non-disabled person is permitted (see para 15.77). An ET is also hampered in other ways. It cannot recommend that a manager write a letter of apology making statements with which s/he does not agree, eg saying that the criticisms s/he had previously made of the claimant were unfounded and that the claimant had always been capable and hard-working.[15] It does not matter that the ET disagreed with this assessment.

19.6   Now that the power to make wider recommendations has been removed, the question is what kind of actions might obviate or reduce the adverse effect of the discrimination on the claimant as opposed to only benefiting other employees. It is usually accepted that improving equality policies and introducing training is of benefit also to the claimant as long as s/he is still employed. The training need not be confined to those with direct contact with the claimant since everyone working in a substantial organisation needs to understand the effect of diversity, and training is most effective when started from the top down.[16] The main doubts concern what recommendations can be made if the claimant has left the employment. It may be possible in some cases to argue that the introduction of anti-discrimination training and other good equal opportunities policies will still alleviate the effect of the discrimination on the claimant because s/he will take some consolation from knowing that something has been done. This would require specific and convincing evidence from the claimant.

19.7   Since wider recommendations cannot now be made, there may be other ways of encouraging employers to improve their practices, eg through the intervention of the Equality and Human Rights Commission (EHRC) or as part of a public authority's public sector equality duty (PSED).[17] Sometimes negotiated settlements can include action which an employer agrees to undertake. Not only will this not be subject to some of the above limitations, but it will also be enforceable.

---

15 *The Governing Body of St Andrews Catholic Primary School and others v Blundell* UKEAT/0330/09.

16 *Lycée Francais Charles de Gaulle v Delambre* UKEAT/0563/10.

17 See chapter 13 regarding the PSED.

The award of compensation

Overview

19.8   Unlike for unfair dismissal, there is no upper limit on the compensatory award. An award of compensation should comprise all loss[18] directly caused by the act of discrimination including past and future loss of earnings, loss of opportunity and injury to feelings.[19] The overriding principle laid down by the Court of Justice of the European Union (CJEU) is that compensation must enable the loss and damage actually sustained as a result of the discrimination to be made good in full in accordance with the applicable national laws.[20]

19.9   Loss of earnings may be claimed where appropriate, eg the discriminatory action is dismissal or refusal to promote to a higher paid post. Where a candidate is not short-listed for interview, an ET may award compensation representing loss of opportunity, so that the potential loss of earnings will be reduced by a percentage representing the likelihood of the candidate actually obtaining the job had s/he not been discriminated against. In dismissal cases, the tribunal can take account of any evidence that it may take the claimant longer to get another job than otherwise because of the stigma associated with having brought a discrimination claim in the minds of potential new employers.[21] As with unfair dismissal cases, a tribunal can reduce compensation for a discriminatory dismissal to reflect the chance that the claimant would have been dismissed even if s/he had not been discriminated against. For example, an employer discriminates by assessing a worker badly against redundancy selection criteria, but even if the worker had been scored fairly and without discrimination, s/he would still have scored less than others.[22] However, this type of reduction in compensation would be unusual in other types of discrimination case, because it is not normally possible to say what would have happened to a worker had s/he not

---

18   EqA 2010 s124(2)(b) and (6). As the EqA 2010 creates a statutory tort, the loss need not to be reasonably foreseeable – *Essa v Laing* [2004] IRLR 313, CA on similar wording in the RRA 1976 case.

19   EqA 2010 s124(6) read with s119(4).

20   *Marshall v Southampton and South West Hampshire Area Health Authority (No 2)* [1993] IRLR 445, ECJ.

21   *Chagger v Abbey National PLC and another* [2009] EWCA Civ 1202; [2010] IRLR 47; *Small v The Shrewsbury and Telford Hospitals NHS Trust* [2017] EWCA Civ 882, although a whistleblowing case, shows where it might be important.

22   *Chagger v Abbey National PLC and another* [2009] EWCA Civ 1202; [2010] IRLR 47.

been discriminated against. It is very unlikely that a deduction would be made for contributory fault in a discrimination case.[23]

19.10   Discrimination cases sometimes attract awards for lengthy future loss of earnings, either because the discrimination has caused psychological damage or because workers covered by the legislation tend to be those who, for various reasons, will find it harder to find a new job. Expert evidence will usually be necessary to prove such lengthy loss is likely. It is only in exceptional cases that a tribunal will calculate loss of earnings up to retirement, eg where there is strong evidence that the worker's career prospects are permanently damaged and s/he will never get such a good job again. Usually an employment tribunal should award loss of earnings only up to the point when there is a more than 50 per cent chance that the worker will find a new job at the same earnings as previously.[24] Unfortunately, where it is appropriate to award lengthy future loss, complexities have crept into the calculation of lengthy future loss from personal injury cases. Employers argue there should be a discount for the value of receiving a large capital sum up front ('accelerated receipt').[25] Conversely, an ET can award a premium of approximately 2.5 per cent for delayed payments. This is particularly appropriate in a case where some items have been discounted for accelerated payments. It is not the same as an award for interest (potentially at a much higher rate).[26] Also, in rare cases, calculations may be made by reference to the 'Ogden tables' to represent the risk of mortality. General guidance can be found in *Facts and Figures 2021/22* (updated annually).[27] The Ogden tables should not be used unless a career-long loss of earnings has been established.[28] Even then, they should only be used as a starting point and the tribunal also needs to take into account other contingencies which are not in the tables,[29] eg whether at some stage the worker would have stopped working for the original employer for other reasons, and what would have happened then.

---

23 *(1) First Greater Western Limited (2) Linley v Waiyego* UKEAT/0056/16.

24 *Wardle v Credit Agricole Corporate and Investment Bank* [2011] EWCA Civ 545.

25 *Kingston upon Hull CC v Dunnachie; HSBC Bank plc v Drage* [2003] IRLR 384, EAT; *Bentwood Bros (Manchester) Ltd v Shepherd* [2003] IRLR 364, CA.

26 *Melia v Magna Kansei Ltd* [2005] IRLR 449, EAT.

27 Sweet & Maxwell, 8th edn, updated May 2021. This annual publication usually contains a copy of the Ogden tables. The tables themselves can be accessed free online at www.gov.uk/government/publications/ogden-tables-actuarial-compensation-tables-for-injury-and-death.

28 *Kingston-upon-Hull CC v Dunnachie (No 3); Drage v HSBC Bank plc* [2003] IRLR 843, EAT.

29 *Rudd v Eagle Place Services Ltd* UKEAT/0151/09.

This must all depend on the evidence. It is irrelevant if the worker would have left but only for a higher paid job.[30] The tribunal also needs to bear in mind that if the claimant had left the job at some time in the future in quite different circumstances, this may not have led to the problems in securing alternative employment that s/he has encountered because of the discrimination on this occasion.[31] If the Ogden tables are used, the party wanting to use them should submit a schedule well in advance, say 14 days after the employer's tribunal response (ET3), and the other party should submit a counter schedule within 14 days afterwards.[32]

19.11   Where there are findings of discrimination against more than one respondent for the same discrimination – eg against the employing organisation and the individual discriminator – the ET should usually make a single award of compensation on a 'joint and several' basis, ie so that the full award can be claimed by the claimant from either respondent.[33] This is particularly important if one or other respondent is or becomes insolvent. The old practice of making separate awards against individual respondents is no longer considered lawful. If the respondents want to work out between themselves how to share out the award, the one who pays out to the claimant can go to court to recover a contribution from the other. However, this is not the claimant's problem. A manager can be personally liable, not only for his/her own discriminatory actions, but for those of other staff if s/he has consciously encouraged a discriminatory atmosphere.[34]

19.12   Unlike with unfair dismissal awards, there is no government recoupment in respect of benefits on discrimination awards. Certain statutory benefits can be deducted from the award made, but not housing benefit.[35] Large ET awards in connection with termination

---

30 *Chagger v Abbey National PLC and another* [2009] EWCA Civ 1202; [2010] IRLR 47; *Wardle v Credit Agricole Corporate and Investment Bank* [2011] EWCA Civ 545.

31 *Chagger v Abbey National PLC and another* [2009] EWCA Civ 1202; [2010] IRLR 47, CA.

32 *Kingston-upon-Hull CC v Dunnachie; Drage v HSBC Bank plc* [2003] IRLR 384, EAT – though the EAT's suggestion of 14 days is a little early. See also *Birmingham City Council v Jaddoo* UKEAT/0448/04.

33 *Hackney LBC v Sivanandan and others* [2013] EWCA Civ 22; [2013] IRLR 408.

34 *Gilbank v Miles* [2006] IRLR 538, CA.

35 *Olayemi v (1) Athena Medical centre (2) Okoreaffia* UKEAT/0140/15. The position regarding deduction of other benefits can be complicated.

of employment will usually be taxable where they exceed £30,000.[36] If the award comprises past and future loss of earnings, which have been calculated net of tax by the ET, the worker is in effect taxed twice on the same sum. To compensate the worker properly, the ET should award a grossed up figure. An award for injury to feelings in connection with termination is now taxable except for psychiatric injury.[37] By contrast, awards for injury to feelings during employment are usually not taxable.[38] Tax can be complicated on high discrimination awards, and is not within the scope of this book.

Injury to feelings and aggravated damages

Introduction

19.13   Unlike in ordinary unfair dismissal cases, an ET may make an award for injury to feelings where it finds unlawful discrimination. Injury to feelings are awarded to reflect the degree of hurt felt by the particular claimant as a result of the discrimination. This can include upset, frustration, worry, anxiety, mental distress, fear, grief, anguish, humiliation, unhappiness, stress, depression, affront, bitterness, shock and so on.[39] It can also cover loss of a chosen career which gave job satisfaction.[40] It is not necessary that the claimant realised at the time that the discriminatory action which upset him/her, eg the failed promotion or dismissal, was due to discrimination.[41] However, it is probable that a worker's feelings will be even more hurt if s/he did realise this. Injury to feelings need to be proved, although usually this is not difficult.

19.14   There is sometimes extra compensation for 'aggravated damages', ie where a worker's sense of injury is 'justifiably heightened by the

---

36   Income Tax (Earnings and Pensions) Act 2003 ss401 and 403. See also para 20.279. But readers should research the exact position. *Harvey on industrial relations and employment law*, LexisNexis, has a useful introductory section on tax (see appendix F).

37   Income Tax (Earnings and Pensions) Act 2003 s406 starting with the tax year 2018/9, rendering *Moorthy v Commissioners for HM Revenue and Customs* [2018] IRLR 860, CA of historic interest.

38   See, for example *Yorkshire Housing Ltd v Cuerden* UKEAT/0397/09; *A v Commissioners for HM Revenue and Customs* [2015] UKFTT 189 (TC).

39   Referred to at various times by *Vento v Chief Constable of West Yorkshire Police (No 2)* [2003] IRLR 102, CA; *Ministry of Defence v Cannock* [1994] IRLR 509, EAT.

40   *Ministry of Defence v Cannock* [1994] IRLR 509, EAT.

41   *Taylor v XLN Telecom Ltd and others* UKEAT/0385/09; [2010] IRLR 499, EAT.

manner in which or motive for which' the employer did the wrongful act.[42] In *Alexander*,[43] the Court of Appeal said:

> ... compensatory damages may and in some cases should include an element of aggravated damages where, for example, the defendant may have behaved in a high-handed, malicious, insulting or oppressive manner in committing the act of discrimination.

In practice, ETs have awarded compensation for aggravated damages in a range of circumstances (see below).

19.15   Historically, in England and Wales, aggravated damages have not been aggregated with and treated as part of the damages for injury to feelings.[44] More recently, the EAT has said it does not matter whether they are put under the heading of 'injury to feelings' as long as they are separately considered and identified.[45] Either way, it is sensible to list them separately in the claimant's schedule of loss.[46] In Scotland, aggravated damages cannot be awarded as a separate head of damages, but the injury to feelings award can include an element in recognition of this aspect.[47] In very limited circumstances, an ET can award 'exemplary damages', ie an award which is purely to punish the employer.[48]

The size of the injury to feelings award

19.16   The size of the award is largely in the ET's discretion. After many years of uncertainty, the Court of Appeal laid down guidelines in the important case of *Vento v Chief Constable of West Yorkshire Police (No 2)*.[49] The Court of Appeal identified three broad bands for injury to feelings, as distinct from compensation for injury to health:[50]

• A top band, normally between £15,000 and £25,000, for the most serious cases, eg a lengthy campaign of harassment. Only in the most exceptional case should an award for injury to feelings exceed £25,000.

---

42 *Alexander v The Home Office* [1988] IRLR 190, CA; *Commissioner of Police of the Metropolis v Shaw* [2012] IRLR 291, EAT. For examples, see para 19.23.
43 [1988] IRLR 190, CA.
44 *Scott v Commissioners of Inland Revenue* [2004] IRLR 713, CA; *Virgo Fidelis Senior School v Boyle* [2004] IRLR 268, EAT.
45 *Commissioner of Police of the Metropolis v Shaw* [2012] IRLR 291, EAT.
46 See appendix A at A30, model 3 for a sample.
47 *D Watt (Shetland Ltd) v Reid* EAT/424/01.
48 See para 19.37.
49 *Vento v Chief Constable of West Yorkshire Police (No 2)* [2003] IRLR 102, CA.
50 See para 19.27.

- A middle band between £5,000 and £15,000 for serious cases which do not merit the top band.
- A lower band of £500–£5,000 for less serious cases, eg where the act of discrimination is an isolated or one-off occurrence. Awards of less than £500 should generally be avoided altogether.

19.17　Tribunals should take into account inflation since these guidelines were set in 2003. In addition, in England and Wates, damages for injury to feelings (including any aggravated damages) should be increased by ten per cent under *Simmons v Castle* unless the case was funded by a conditional fee arrangement ('no win, no fee') entered before that date.[51] There is now annual Presidential Guidance which adjusts the *Vento* bands to allow for inflation and *Simmons v Castle*.[52] For claims issued on or after 6 April 2021: £900–£9,100 is the recommended lower band; £9,100–£27,400 is the middle band; and £27,400–£45,600 is the upper band. The most exceptional cases can exceed £ 45,600. These rates are inclusive of the *Simmons v Castle* ten per cent. They will be uprated if necessary every April. The Presidential Guidance sets out a formula for inflation for claims presented prior to 11 September 2017. In Scotland, if an ET decides that *Simmons v Castle* does not apply, it should reduce the bands accordingly, but it must explain why it believes that to be the case. Regarding the description of the *Vento* bands, these should not be rigidly applied as the real issue is the level of hurt feelings suffered by the worker. For example, a one-off occurrence could have sufficiently serious effects for the middle or upper band to apply.[53] As previously stated, the bands relate only to injury to feelings, and any award for aggravated damages and injury to health would be separate and additional.

19.18　ETs still have an enormous amount of discretion in how much they award, and the EAT will rarely interfere if the correct band is chosen.[54] It is, therefore, very hard for advisers to predict the size of an award as, for example, one ET may legitimately award £10,000 on

---

51　*Simmons v Castle* [2012] EWCA Civ 1288. Its applicability to both injury to feelings and psychiatric damage was confirmed by the Court of Appeal in *Pereira De Souza v Vinci Construction UK Ltd* [2017] EWCA Civ 879.

52　Presidential Guidance on various matters including *Vento* uprating is accessible at: www.judiciary.uk/publications/employment-rules-and-legislation-practice-directions/.

53　See *Base Childrenswear Limited v Lomana Otshudi* UKEAT/0267/18 and *Hackney LBC v Sivanandan and others* UKEAT/0075/10 respectively.

54　*Da'Bell v National Society for Prevention of Cruelty to Children* UKEAT/0227/09; [2010] IRLR 25.

a middle band case, where another might award almost double that on the same set of facts.

19.19　　One of the first cases to go to the EAT was *(1) Armitage (2) Marsden (3) HM Prison Service v Johnson.*[55] The case merely illustrates when an ET is entitled (if it chooses) to make a high award. Mr Johnson, a black prison auxiliary, was awarded £20,000 for injury to feelings for a campaign of racial harassment lasting 18 months, plus £7,500 aggravated damages for the employer's rejection of his grievance and putting it down to a character defect. The employer's investigation, instead of providing a remedy for the wrongs suffered by the worker, added to his injury. Further, £500 was also awarded against two prison officers personally (which now should not happen – see para 19.11). The EAT decided the ET was entitled to award £28,500 (even if it was then a little on the high side) for such a serious (although not the worst possible) case of discrimination. Adjusted for inflation and *Simmons v Castle,* arguably this award would now equate to around £40,000. The EAT said that, in general, injury to feelings awards should bear some broad similarity to the range of awards in personal injury cases. It should also relate to the value of the sum, in terms of purchasing power or earnings, in real life.

19.20　　The EAT in *Tchoula,*[56] a case decided before *Vento,* also provides an interesting overview. The EAT reviewed a large number of the ET awards to date and divided them into higher and lower categories. The interesting thing about *Tchoula* is that although the EAT reduced the worker's award for injury to feelings and aggravated damages from £27,000 to £10,000, it awarded as much as £10,000 for what it considered to be a lower category case. Although Mr Tchoula did suffer considerable injury to feelings, the discrimination had not contributed to his marriage breakdown nor caused depression. The discrimination lasted only over a period of days, and although he had lost his job and the opportunity to continue in the security industry, he wanted to better himself anyway. £10,000 would have been in the middle of the original *Vento* band, so arguably equating to £17,500 nowadays.

19.21　　The EAT refused to overturn another large ET award of £20,000 for injury to feelings and £5,000 aggravated damages (1997 figures) in *Chan v Hackney LBC.*[57] Mr Chan was forced into medical retirement after months of sustained pressure. The EAT said it was

---

55 [1997] IRLR 162, EAT.
56 *ICTS (UK) Ltd v Tchoula* [2000] IRLR 643, EAT.
57 EAT/120/97.

legitimate to take into account the treatment of Mr Chan outside the time limit as context for the impact on his feelings of the acts of race discrimination within the time limit. In 2019, the EAT refused to overturn a total award of £21,000 (injury to feelings plus aggravated damages) for an employee dismissed in the early stages of her career in a job which she plainly considered her vocation, where both the fact and manner of her dismissal caused significant distress.[58]

19.22   Factors which lead to high awards tend to be a long period or numerous incidents of discrimination; false accusations made in public; loss of a valued job or career; a particular vulnerability of the worker, eg due to age or work environment; and most importantly, evidence of severe injury to health and feelings or family difficulties. Harassment of a pregnant woman could lead to a high award where it causes additional stress because it threatens the well-being of the unborn child.[59] One-off acts of discrimination or only short periods of harassment will not necessarily fall into the lowest *Vento* band as the overall seriousness should be taken into account.[60]

19.23   Aggravating factors may be conscious victimisation,[61] ignoring or mishandling a grievance or appeal, a character attack on the worker, lying about the true reason for dismissal, and failing to apologise.[62] It could also, depending on the facts, lead to aggravated damages to promote the discriminator while the worker's harassment grievance has not yet been fully investigated.[63] The employer's behaviour in the ET proceedings will also be relevant,[64] including repeated unmerited threats of costs in the correspondence. If an employer unreasonably disputes that a disabled worker is disabled under the EqA 2010, thus requiring him/her to go through unnecessary medical examinations, this could lead to an award of aggravated damages.

19.24   It is advisable not to take it for granted that the ET will appreciate the likely impact of the discrimination on the worker's feelings, but

---

58   *Base Childrenswear Limited v Lomana Otshudi* UKEAT/0267/18. She was also awarded a further £3,000 for three months' medical depression caused by her dismissal.

59   *Gilbank v Miles* [2006] IRLR 538, CA.

60   For example, see *Wallington v S & B Car Hire Kent Ltd* EAT 0240/03; *Carney v Rouf and another* EAT 0353/04 and *Base Childrenswear Limited v Lomana Otshudi* UKEAT/0267/18.

61   *ICTS (UK) Ltd v Tchoula* [2000] IRLR 643, EAT.

62   For many of these features, see *Base Childrenswear Limited v Lomana Otshudi* UKEAT/0267/18.

63   *British Telecommunications plc v Reid* [2004] IRLR 327, CA.

64   *Zaiwalla & Co v Walia* [2002] IRLR 697, EAT; *Base Childrenswear Limited v Lomana Otshudi* UKEAT/0267/18.

to give explicit evidence on this from the worker and other witnesses including medical evidence where appropriate.

19.25   Unfortunately ET practice in the size of injury to feelings awards is extremely variable and difficult to predict. Some ETs clearly believe they are awarding a large sum when they award, say, £10,000 for serious injury. It is therefore important to draw the ET's attention to the higher awards, especially in comparable cases, and to the bands in *Vento*. Awards made by other ETs, unless appealed, have no precedent value when considered in isolation. But it is not at all helpful to look at reports of average awards, as these tend to keep the figures low and ignore the factors in the particular case.[65] Media reports are highly misleading as they often report settlements rather than ET awards and, in any event, tend to include figures for the entire compensatory award, which may consist primarily of loss of earnings.

19.26   Although it is hard to appeal against an award for injury to feelings on the grounds that it is too low, where there is strong evidence of injury and an extremely low award, this should be considered. Where there have been a number of acts of discrimination, particularly if there is victimisation as well as direct discrimination or if there is discrimination based on different characteristics (eg race and disability), the tribunal should separately consider the injury to feelings arising from each action rather than taking a loose overview.[66] Having considered these elements separately, a tribunal must still stand back and look at the global figure, ensuring there is no double counting and that the overall award is not disproportionate.

Injury to health (personal injury)

19.27   Injury to feelings, when it becomes sufficiently severe, can be considered as an injury to health. It is now common in serious cases to argue for injury to health as a separate category. It does not matter exactly where the line is drawn, and 'stress and depression' can be included in injury to feelings, but the ET will not allow 'double

---

65 It is hard work finding employment tribunal statistics these days. Those that are online are poorly organised and mislabelled. *Tribunals Statistics Quarterly: April to June 2020* at: www.gov.uk/government/statistics/tribunal-statistics-quarterly-april-to-june-2020 has a link to *Employment Tribunal and Employment Appeal Tribunal tables 2019 to 2020*, which gives compensation tables for every year going back to 2007/08. However, these do not seem to include sums awarded for injury to feelings.

66 *Al Jumard v Clwyd Leisure Ltd* UKEAT/0334/07; [2008] IRLR 345.

recovery', ie the worker to be compensated twice for the same injury.[67] In setting its bands of compensation for injury to feelings, *Vento*[68] did indicate that injury to health was a separate matter.

19.28   Unfortunately, seeking compensation for injury to health in an ET is not a simple matter, because traditionally, claims for damage to health are brought as negligence or contract claims in the civil courts.[69] An ET can award compensation for any personal injury caused by the discrimination.[70] This means that if the discrimination has seriously damaged the worker's health, physically or psychiatrically (and not solely his/her feelings), a claim for damages for personal injury (ie injury to health) must be added to any discrimination case which is brought. Examples could include nervous breakdown, severe depression or post-traumatic stress syndrome. If a worker omits to add such a claim, but his/her discrimination case is decided by the ET or settled, s/he will very probably be unable to make any future personal injury claim arising from the discriminatory actions by the employer.[71] This is because the issue could and should have been argued in front of the ET – an employer is entitled to know that all claims have been dealt with in one place, so there is some finality to the issues.

19.29   Employment lawyers have had to become familiar with the basic principles of quantifying damages in personal injury cases, especially those related to psychiatric illness. A formal medical report is strongly advisable for making such a claim. Although an expert report may not be essential if there is other evidence as to injury (eg occupational health (OH) reports and witness evidence), the award is likely to be lower.[72] In personal injury cases, there is a vast body of reported awards for pain and suffering caused by different injuries. These are collated and set out in such sources as *Kemp & Kemp: Quantum of damages*[73] and formulated into guidelines by the Judicial College: *Guidelines for the assessment of general damages in personal injury cases.*[74]

---

67   *HM Prison Service v Salmon* [2001] IRLR 425, EAT.

68   *Vento v Chief Constable of West Yorkshire Police (No 2)* [2003] IRLR 102, CA.

69   See also chapter 17 on stress.

70   *Sheriff v Klyne Tugs (Lowestoft) Ltd* [1999] IRLR 481, CA.

71   *Sheriff v Klyne Tugs (Lowestoft) Ltd* [1999] IRLR 481, CA. Advisers should read *Sheriff* for its implications.

72   *Hampshire CC v Wyatt* UKEAT/0013/16.

73   Published by Sweet & Maxwell (looseleaf): www.sweetandmaxwell.co.uk.

74   These can be purchased as a book published by Oxford University Press or accessed through various subscriptions. 16th edn due Autumn 2021. Editions before the 11th were issued by the Judicial Studies Board (JSB).

19.30 The Judicial College guidelines are often referred to in the ET when assessing injury to health in discrimination cases. Chapter 4 of the 2019 guidelines (15th edn) deals with psychiatric and psychological damage and lists the following factors to be taken into account:

- the claimant's ability to cope with life, education and work;
- the effect on the claimant's relationships with family, friends and those with whom s/he comes into contact;
- the extent to which treatment would be successful;
- future vulnerability;
- prognosis;
- whether medical help has been sought;
- where the injury results from sexual and/or physical abuse, there is usually a significant aspect of psychiatric or psychological damage, but this is only part of the injury for which damages should be awarded. Also relevant is whether there has been an abuse of trust. Another distinguishing feature is that there may have been a long period during which the effects of the abuse were undiagnosed, untreated, unrecognised or even denied. Aggravated damages may be appropriate.

19.31 The guidelines put awards into four categories, with estimates of the current value of awards in each category, ie: severe (£51,460–£108,620); moderately severe (£17,900–£51,460); moderate (£5,500–£17,900); and less severe (£1,440–£5,500). Cases of work-related stress resulting in a permanent or long-standing disability preventing a return to comparable employment are likely to be moderately severe. Where there is marked improvement by the hearing and a good prognosis, the case is likely to be moderate. These categories are useful, but they are not meant to be rigid – the facts may not fit exactly into one or other category.[75] There are also specific categories for post-traumatic stress disorder (PTSD). When arguing for a certain sum in the ET, it may be useful to find some cases in *Kemp & Kemp* within the relevant range, which are similar to the claimant's case. As with awards for injury to feelings, compensation for personal injury should be increased by ten per cent to reflect the decision in *Simmons v Castle*.[76] The above figures are given here with the ten per cent uplift as calculated in the guidelines.

---

75 *Hampshire CC v Wyatt* UKEAT/0013/16.
76 See para 19.17 and n51.

19.32   There are well-established principles in personal injury law regarding what should happen in cases where the claimant has a vulnerable personality or a pre-existing condition caused by other factors.[77] This is rather complex, but can be broadly summarised as follows:

- *The eggshell skull or personality principle*: If the injury to the claimant is greater than normal because s/he has a vulnerable personality, the employer is nevertheless responsible for all the injury caused, even though it was unforeseeable.
- *The aggravation or exacerbation principle*: If the claimant already had some symptoms arising from a pre-existing illness, the employer is only liable for the additional injury s/he has caused.
- *Pre-existing risk of injury*: If the claimant had a pre-existing condition which made it likely s/he would have gone on to suffer a similar psychiatric illness even if the unlawful act had not occurred, his/her compensation will be reduced by a percentage to reflect that possibility.
- *The acceleration principle*: If the claimant had a pre-existing condition, but the symptoms occurred sooner due to the unlawful act, the employer is only liable for losses during the 'acceleration period'.

19.33   In all these situations, it is important to provide evidence as to what the claimant's condition and prognosis would have been, had s/he not been discriminated against. When considering an award for loss of earnings, a tribunal may make a percentage deduction to reflect the likelihood that the worker would shortly have become unable to work in any event, eg because s/he has a history of regular episodes of depression. If a worker's injury to feelings or health is caused partly by actions which the ET has found to be unlawful discrimination, partly by actions which the ET has found are not unlawful discrimination and partly by other factors altogether, compensation for the injury will only be in respect of the actions found to be unlawful discrimination. However, this applies only if the injury is 'divisible', ie if it is possible to ascertain which part of the injury to feelings is caused by the unlawful discrimination. In practice, it can be very difficult to differentiate between feelings caused by a number of events occurring close together in time which have all profoundly distressed the worker. If the injury is not 'divisible', the discriminator whose act has been a proximate cause of the injury must compensate

---

77 For a detailed source on this, see *Butterworths Personal Injury Litigation Service*, www.lexisnexis.co.uk.

for all of it.[78] It is therefore possible for there to be different levels of deduction (if any) on loss of earnings and on compensation for injury to feelings and health. For example, in *Sadler v Portsmouth Publishing and Printing Ltd*,[79] the claimant had a significant history of depressive episodes prior to her illness caused by sexual harassment. Based on medical evidence, the ET found the claimant had a 33 per cent chance of becoming ill anyway due to her pre-existing condition. Further, her current illness was caused 80 per cent by her underlying condition and made worse by the sexual harassment by 20 per cent. The ET applied both discounts to the award for personal injury (injury to health) and to the award for loss of earnings. The EAT said this was incorrect: only the 80 per cent could be deducted from the personal injury award and only the 33 per cent could be deducted from the financial losses.

19.34 Note that the ET can only deal with the personal injury claim where it is attached to a discrimination claim. If the worker brings no discrimination claim, s/he would take his/her claim for personal injury in the county court or High Court in the usual way.[80]

19.35 Despite the practical difficulties, there are some advantages in bringing such cases in the ET. It can be difficult to find solicitors willing to do cases on conditional fee arrangements ('no win, no fee') unless the claim is substantial or the worker has legal expenses insurance. In the ET, at least the worker has access to a relatively less expensive and less formal procedure. Also, under discrimination law it is only necessary to prove the psychiatric injury was directly caused by the act of discrimination.[81] It is not necessary to show the type of injury was reasonably foreseeable. This is helpful where a worker is more badly hurt by, say, a single act of discrimination, than anyone might have expected.

---

78 The best recent summary of the key principles is in *BAE Systems (Operations) Limited v Konczak* [2017] EWCA Civ 1188; [2017] IRLR 893. See also *Hampshire CC v Wyatt* UKEAT/0013/16, *Olayemi v (1) Athena Medical Centre (2) Okoreaffia* UKEAT/0140/15, *Malcolm v Dundee City Council* UKEATS/0050/13 and *Thaine v London School of Economics* UKEAT/0144/10.

79 UKEAT/0280/04.

80 See chapter 17 for a brief introduction to health and safety, and stress.

81 *Essa v Laing Ltd* [2004] IRLR 313, CA. The case relates to the RRA 1976, but presumably also applies under the other discrimination statutes and regulations.

Exemplary damages

19.36 Exemplary damages are awarded to punish a wrongdoer. They are usually awarded in cases involving wrongful arrest and false imprisonment, but they can in theory also be awarded in employment discrimination cases.[82] The key case of *Rookes v Barnard*[83] established that exemplary damages can be awarded in any of three situations:

1) where there has been oppressive, arbitrary or unconstitutional action by servants of the government; or
2) where the defendant's conduct has been calculated to make profit which will exceed the compensation payable; or
3) where statute says they can be awarded.

19.37 In a case against the Ministry of Defence (MOD) in 2010,[84] the EAT said exemplary damages could be awarded on the basis of the first category, ie 'oppressive, arbitrary or unconstitutional action by servants of the government'. However, the factual basis for the ET's award, ie the failure of the Army to provide a mechanism for redress of Ms Fletcher's complaints, though deplorable, was not sufficiently oppressive to meet the high test for exemplary damages. The EAT said its view might have been different if the tribunal had instead based its award on the army's use of disciplinary action to victimise Ms Fletcher for pursuing her complaints. Moreover, had an award of exemplary damages been appropriate (which it was not), the appropriate level on the facts would have been £7,500, not £50,000.

Compensation for pregnancy discrimination

19.38 In the 1990s, many cases were brought against the MOD by servicewomen formerly discharged on grounds of pregnancy. Compensatory awards tended to be very high, mainly because they referred back to many years of lost earnings and concerned unique difficulties for wives of service personnel in finding fresh employment. A few cases laid down some guidelines applicable to assessing compensation,

---

82 *Kuddus v Chief Constable of Leicester Constabulary* [2001] UKHL 29, established the possibility. Though apparently not in Scotland – *Black v North British Railway Company* 1908 SC 444.

83 [1964] AC 1129, HL.

84 *Ministry of Defence v Fletcher* UKEAT/0044/09; [2010] IRLR 25.

including the MOD cases specifically and pregnancy discrimination cases generally.[85]

19.39   Points made by the cases include the following:

- In awarding compensation for loss of earnings after birth, an ET should consider the chance that a woman would not have returned to work anyway, taking account of work and family demands.[86] It would not be exceptional or even unusual to assess the chance of a woman's return as 100 per cent.[87] Evidence as to what the woman did in fact do, having been dismissed, does not necessarily mean she would have done the same had she not been dismissed.[88]

- The order of deductions where a woman mitigates her loss by obtaining new employment at lesser pay is first to deduct her new earnings from the sum she would have received had she remained in her original employment and then to make any deduction assessed to reflect the chance she would not have returned to her original employment.[89]

- Concerning the duty to mitigate,[90] a woman must actively seek employment six months after the birth of her child if she wishes to obtain compensation for loss of earnings after that date.[91] However, expectations of what a worker should do to find work should not be unreasonable, as she is the wronged party.[92] Furthermore, an ET is entitled to take into account its own knowledge and experience of difficulties in the labour market facing women with young children.[93]

- The burden of proving failure to mitigate is on the person alleging it, ie the employer. If no evidence is given on the failure to mitigate, eg what steps should have been taken and when, the ET

---

85 See *Ministry of Defence v Cannock* [1994] IRLR 509, EAT, as improved and modified by a different EAT in *Ministry of Defence v Hunt* [1996] IRLR 139, EAT. Also see *Ministry of Defence v Wheeler, Donald, Nixon and Joslyn* [1998] IRLR 23, CA.

86 *Ministry of Defence v Cannock* [1994] IRLR 509, EAT.

87 *Ministry of Defence v Hunt* [1996] IRLR 139, EAT.

88 *Ministry of Defence v Hunt* [1996] IRLR 139, EAT.

89 *Ministry of Defence v Wheeler, Donald, Nixon and Joslyn* [1998] IRLR 23, CA.

90 See para 18.34.

91 *Ministry of Defence v Cannock* [1994] IRLR 509, EAT; *Ministry of Defence v Hunt* [1996] IRLR 139, EAT at para 11.

92 *Ministry of Defence v Hunt* [1996] IRLR 139, EAT at para 11.

93 *Ministry of Defence v Hunt* [1996] IRLR 139, EAT at para 85.

cannot fill the gap by making assumptions about when the worker could have found fresh employment.[94]

- An ET should not allow a woman to be questioned on whether the pregnancy was planned or unplanned.

Interest

19.40   An ET has a discretion whether to award interest, although arguably the decision in *Marshall v Southampton Area Health Authority (No 2)*[95] suggests it must always be awarded. The rules should be referred to for the precise calculation method.[96] However, broadly speaking, interest on an injury to feelings award runs from the date of the discrimination and, for past financial loss, runs from a date midway between the act of discrimination and the date of calculation by the ET. The interest rate is that fixed from time to time by Judgments Act 1838 s17 (in England and Wales) or by Sheriff Courts (Scotland) Extracts Act 1892 s19 (in Scotland).[97] Since July 2013, this has been eight per cent.[98] To calculate interest on injury to feelings, multiply the daily rate by the number of days between the discrimination and the hearing. To find out the daily rate, divide the amount of the injury to feelings award by 365 and multiply by the interest rate, eg eight per cent. To calculate interest on financial loss, multiply the daily rate by half the number of days between the discrimination and the hearing. To find out the daily rate, divide the sum awarded for financial loss by 365 and multiply by the interest rate. If the rate of interest has varied during the period for which it must be calculated, the ET may apply a median or average rate for the sake of simplicity.[99] Interest is not awarded on future financial loss.[100]

---

94 *Ministry of Defence v Hunt* [1996] IRLR 139, EAT at para 2. Though it is still wise to bring evidence of efforts to mitigate.

95 [1993] IRLR 445, ECJ.

96 Employment Tribunals (Interest on Awards in Discrimination Cases) Regulations 1996 SI No 2803. These regulations are deemed made under EqA 2010 s139, by virtue of Equality Act 2010 (Commencement No 4, Savings, Consequential, Transitional, Transitory and Incidental Provisions and Revocation) Order 2010 SI No 2317 article 21(1).

97 Employment Tribunals (Interest on Awards in Discrimination Cases) (Amendment) Regulations 2013 SI No 1669.

98 The eight per cent under section 17 was set by the Judgment Debts (Rate of Interest) Order 1993 SI No 564 article 2.

99 Employment Tribunals (Interest on Awards in Discrimination Cases) Regulations 1996 SI No 2803 reg 3(3).

100 Employment Tribunals (Interest on Awards in Discrimination Cases) Regulations 1996 SI No 2803 reg 5.

19.41   An ET must consider whether to award interest, even if it is not invited to do so,[101] and in its written reasons must set out how interest was calculated or, if none has been awarded, explain why not. It is a good idea to include interest in the Schedule of Loss.[102]

19.42   Interest on unpaid awards runs from the day after the date of the award unless full payment of the award is made within 14 days of the relevant decision day.[103]

ACAS uplift

19.43   The Advisory, Conciliation and Arbitration Service (ACAS) Code of Guidance on Disciplinary and Grievance Procedures sets out good practice guidelines for the handling of disciplinary and grievance issues in employment. An ET may increase or reduce an employee's compensation by up to 25 per cent in any successful case for discrimination[104] (as well as unfair dismissal and other specified areas), because of the employer's or employee's unreasonable failure to follow the Code. If a tribunal has awarded aggravated damages because of the same procedural failings, it needs to avoid double-counting. It therefore needs to allow for that, either when assessing the amount for aggravated damages or when assessing the uplift for breach of the Code.[105] The facts of the particular case need to fall within the areas covered by Code recommendations. An example where the Code might apply in a discrimination context would be where an employee's dismissal for misconduct was found to be because of his/her race and the employer had failed to follow the recommended procedures for disciplinary action. The Code does not apply and there is therefore no adjustment to compensation for workers who are not employees. For a further discussion of the Code and its application, see chapter 22.

---

101 Employment Tribunals (Interest on Awards in Discrimination Cases) Regulations 1996 SI No 2803 reg 2(1)(b); *Fasuyi v Greenwich LBC* EAT/1078/99.

102 See example in appendix A at A30, model 3.

103 Employment Tribunals (Interest on Awards in Discrimination Cases) Regulations 1996 SI No 2803 reg 8.

104 Trade Union and Labour Relations (Consolidation) Act 1992 s207A and Sch A2.

105 *Base Childrenswear Limited v Lomana Otshudi* UKEAT/0267/18.

Costs against the employer

19.44   Costs may be awarded against either party on the same basis as in unfair dismissal actions.[106] However, the statistics show that costs are far more frequently awarded against unsuccessful workers in discrimination cases than against unsuccessful employers.[107]

Enforcement

19.45   For information regarding what to do if the employer refuses to pay the award or settlement, see para 18.72.

---

106 See para 20.246 onwards.
107 See para 21.94.

CHAPTER 20

Running an unfair dismissal case

continued

Chapter 20: Key points

- Winning an unfair dismissal case is mostly about the quality of the evidence, which is gathered during case preparation.
- It is essential that a detailed statement is taken from the employee as soon as possible while memory is fresh.
- Before starting a case, an employee must make an early conciliation (EC) notification to the Advisory, Conciliation and Arbitration Service (ACAS). This affects tribunal time limits. A claim cannot be started without the ACAS certificate number on the form unless an exemption applies.
- A case is started when the employee's written claim on the standard ET1 form arrives at the Central Office, nominated tribunal or has gone through online. Time limits are very strict.
- Fees are no longer payable. Those who paid fees in the past should be able to get a refund from the government.
- The employee or other person bringing the case is called 'the claimant'. The employer or other person against whom the claim is brought is called 'the respondent'.
- In England and Wales, the tribunal will usually send out standard case management orders with the tribunal claim or when the employer's response is received.
- In addition, the employee should ask the employer for any extra relevant documents and additional information. If these are not supplied voluntarily, the tribunal must be asked for an order.
- Contemporaneous documents are usually more influential evidence than witnesses.
- It is best to contact possible witnesses at an early stage, while they are still enthusiastic, and take a signed statement. A witness order can be obtained if a relevant witness will not come to the tribunal without one. It is generally unwise to force a reluctant witness to come.
- If the employee is ordered to supply any documents or additional information to the employer, s/he must comply with the order in time. Otherwise costs may be ordered against him/her, or the claim may be struck out.
- The employment tribunal (ET) must give at least 14 days' notice of the final hearing and of any preliminary issues to be dealt with at a preliminary hearing. Once a hearing date is fixed, it is extremely difficult to get it changed.

continued

- Some hearings may now be conducted over a video platform due to pandemic restrictions or subsequent backlogs. This requires special preparation.
- If a representative is noted on the ET1, all correspondence will go to the representative. Make sure the employee is kept informed and told the hearing date. If no representative is noted, make sure the employee gets in touch whenever s/he receives a letter and, in any event, every few weeks.
- Every case is allocated an officer from ACAS, who will get in touch regarding possible settlement. Conversations through ACAS should not be disclosed to the ET.
- There are many advantages in settling a case, provided it is for a reasonable sum. It avoids recoupment (see para 18.62) and can include wording for an agreed reference.
- An employee must try to get a new job (even if less well paid) and keep records of all attempts. If the employee does not try very hard, s/he may not be awarded much compensation.
- The employee and any witnesses for either side give oral evidence at the tribunal. In England and Wales especially, evidence in chief is almost always contained in witness statements which are read by the tribunal to itself. Witness statements are usually exchanged 7–14 days before the hearing.
- Costs can be ordered against a party for various reasons including unreasonable conduct or that his/her case had no reasonable prospects of success.
- On the whole, this chapter refers to 'employees' rather an 'workers' as it is primarily concerned with unfair dismissal claims, but the procedures tend to apply generally.
- For quick reference to unfamiliar terms, readers may find the Glossary at appendix D useful.
- There is a checklist of the basic procedural steps in appendix A at A1 which cross-refers this chapter.

Preliminary steps

Initial steps

20.1   At the outset it should be established what the employee wants to achieve. If the employee only wants his/her job back or a good reference or payment of outstanding wages, holiday or notice pay, it is not usually advisable to commence a claim for unfair dismissal. Nothing is more likely to alienate the employer. On the other hand, starting a claim may be the only way to induce a settlement which incorporates the monies owing and includes an agreed reference. Unfortunately, if the case does not settle, an employment tribunal (ET) cannot order a good reference to be given, even if the employee wins.

20.2   If the priority is to get the employee's job back, negotiations with the employer should start immediately, possibly with the intervention of a third party, eg another employee. The greater the delay in starting negotiations, the less the likelihood of success. If an employee simply wants a good written reference or payment of monies owed, a telephone call or polite letter should be the first step. Only if the employer refuses, should the employee threaten ET proceedings. Where a stronger approach is necessary, it is sometimes effective to send a draft tribunal claim under cover of a 'without prejudice'[1] letter proposing settlement. There is also the possibility that a negotiation can take place through the Advisory, Conciliation and Arbitration Service (ACAS) early conciliation (EC) scheme (see below).

20.3   Before the employee decides to start a case, s/he should be advised on his/her chances of success, what is involved and the likely compensation. The employee should be warned that it is particularly important that s/he makes efforts to find a new job, as otherwise his/her compensation will be reduced for 'failure to mitigate'.[2] S/he must keep records of all efforts to find work (see para 18.34). If the employee's case is extremely weak, but s/he seems determined to go ahead anyway, s/he needs to be advised that there is a risk that costs will be awarded against him/her if s/he loses. Costs are not routinely ordered in tribunal claims and the fear of an award should not be a general deterrent, but nevertheless there are some circumstances where the employee is at risk and needs to be forewarned. Needless to say, it is important that misconceived cases are identified and advised not to be started in the first place. An employee should also be told that judgments (apart from judgments withdrawing a case) go onto the online register (see para 21.61 onwards regarding the register, privacy and anonymity).

20.4   As soon as an employee comes for advice, the adviser should work out and diarise the last day for lodging a tribunal claim. In practice, the significant dates will usually be the last day on which ACAS

1   See para 9.18 and Glossary, appendix D.
2   See para 18.34.

must be notified under the EC procedure and the further deadline following issue of the certificate. The employee should also make a note. Once ET proceedings are started, they move very quickly. It can take as little as three months from the date the tribunal claim is lodged to the hearing. If information and documents need to be gathered, the gathering process must be started immediately. All time limits and dates for chasing up requests made to the employer should be diarised. The tribunal claim form is often known as an 'ET1'.

Collecting information before lodging the ET1

20.5 Before starting the claim, the adviser should get copies of all relevant documents in the employee's possession, eg:

- a statement of the main terms and conditions of employment and/or contract of employment;
- staff handbook;
- works rules;
- letter of appointment;
- letter of dismissal;
- P45 (which should state the leaving date);
- payslips;
- warning letters; and appraisal reports.

There may well be other relevant documents.

20.6 It is very important to obtain all documents which may form the employment contract (see para 1.2). If the employee signed any statement, document or letter during employment, it is essential to see this prior to lodging the ET1 if at all possible. It may contain information relevant to the strength of the case.

20.7 The terms of the contract will be particularly vital in relation to a constructive dismissal claim, where the employee must show a fundamental breach of contract. If, eg the employee relies on a change of workplace as such a breach, but the contract contains a mobility clause, there will be no breach of contract and the claim will fail.

20.8 Once all the employee's documents are gathered, it is good practice for the adviser to take a full statement of all the material facts, concentrating on the reason for dismissal and the events immediately preceding it. The old-fashioned word for this is a 'proof'. The final disciplinary hearing leading to dismissal is usually very important and the adviser should obtain a near verbatim account while the employee's memory is relatively fresh. Probe the employee on the facts, particularly on the weaknesses. The names and addresses of possible witnesses to significant incidents should be collected. It is usually easier to establish names and addresses at an early stage than months later when a witness needs to be written to.

20.9   The employee should sign and date the statement and keep a copy. It should be explained that the statement is only for private use as the adviser's working document. If the adviser does not have time to take a neat statement at this stage, s/he should at least take full and systematic notes covering all the issues. However, since witness statements[3] eventually need to be written in most cases, it may save time in the long run to take notes in the shape of a statement and type these up from the outset. It also helps if any other adviser has to pick up the file to cover holidays etc.

The first letter and written reasons for the dismissal: Employment Rights Act 1996 s92

20.10   Before starting the claim, the employee should write to the employer requesting written reasons for the dismissal. The first letter to the employer is important.[4] As well as requesting information which will be instrumental in the conduct of the case and its final outcome, it creates an initial impression on the employer which may encourage settlement later on. The employee should ask for any key documents which s/he needs at this stage, although this is not the time to ask for absolutely everything relevant to running a case, and the employer cannot be compelled to provide documents before a case starts.[5] The employee may have no contractual documents and be uncertain whether any exist. The employer should therefore at least be asked for copies of the relevant procedures and the employee's contract or statement of particulars of employment.[6] This will help in working out what sums are owing, eg for holiday or notice pay, and may also contain information needed to assess whether the dismissal was unfair.

20.11   If the employee has at least two years' minimum service, s/he is entitled to receive an adequate and truthful statement of the reasons

---

3 See paras 20.186–20.196.
4 See appendix C at C3 for an example.
5 See paras 20.123–20.127 re disclosure once a case has started.
6 See para 1.24.

for dismissal if s/he asks for them.[7] This is often referred to as 'section 92 written reasons' or 'written reasons for dismissal'. If asked for reasons, the employer must supply them within 14 days of the employee's request. In order to prove that a request was made, it is best to make it in writing and send it by recorded delivery or email.

20.12 If the employer unreasonably fails to supply written reasons within 14 days, or supplies reasons which are inadequate or untrue, the employee is entitled to compensation of two weeks' gross pay.[8] It seems that there is no upper limit on a week's pay.[9] It is not enough for an employer to acknowledge the request within the 14 days and supply reasons later unless, eg the person taking the decision to dismiss was on holiday. Note that the test is whether the employer unreasonably 'failed' to provide written reasons, not whether s/he unreasonably 'refused' to do so, which would be harder to prove. The wording of the legislation was changed in 1993 to replace the word 'refused' with 'failed' and, if reading any of the older case-law, that change of wording must be borne in mind.

20.13 The written reasons must be adequate so that it is clear to the employee and to anyone else why the employee was dismissed and upon which of the potentially fair reasons for dismissal[10] the employer relies.[11] The purpose of the right is to make the employer state truthfully the reason for dismissing. The reason need not be truthful in the sense of an accurate judgment about the claimant. It only needs to be the employer's true reason for dismissal. Any statement given by the employer is admissible in unfair dismissal proceedings and will be important in determining the fairness of the dismissal.[12] Moreover, in deciding whether to award compensation for inadequate or untrue reasons, the ET is not concerned with whether the reasons given were intrinsically good or bad.[13] If the reason was bad, the dismissal will doubtless be unfair, but there will be no award for the written reasons claim.

20.14 The time limit for a claim for failure to supply adequate and true reasons is the same as for unfair dismissal. Even if reasons are supplied within 14 days, an Employment Rights Act (ERA) 1996 s92

---

7 ERA 1996 s92.
8 ERA 1996 s93(2).
9 By omission from ERA 1996 s227.
10 Under ERA 1996 s98(2); see para 6.54.
11 *Horsley Smith & Sherry v Dutton* [1977] IRLR 172, EAT.
12 ERA 1996 s9(5).
13 *Harvard Securities v Younghusband* [1990] IRLR 17, EAT.

claim should usually be added to the unfair dismissal claim (see ET1 in appendix C for an example). You can never be sure what will emerge during the unfair dismissal hearing about the truth of the reasons given.

20.15   It is important to remember that no compensation can be claimed if the employer does not provide written reasons or provides inadequate or untrue reasons, unless the employer was asked to provide them in the first place. However, women dismissed while pregnant or on maternity leave are entitled to written reasons, whether or not they request them, and regardless of their length of service.[14] This is logical because they can claim unfair dismissal for reasons related to pregnancy or maternity, even if they do not have the necessary length of service for ordinary unfair dismissal claims. If the reasons are not supplied, a claim should be made in the usual way. Even though it is not necessary in a pregnancy/maternity case, it is probably still worth asking the employer for reasons where they are not volunteered.

ACAS early conciliation

20.16   The introduction of EC and the attempted introduction of fees were just two of a number of radical changes to employment law and the tribunal system introduced by the Conservative and Liberal Democrat coalition government in the period 2010–2015. These included an increase in the unfair dismissal qualifying period to two years; removal of non-legal members from tribunal panels hearing unfair dismissal claims; and the end of payment by the tribunal system of witness expenses.

20.17   It is now compulsory to go through the ACAS EC procedure unless one of the exceptions applies. This section regarding EC needs to be read together with the section on time limits and procedure for starting a tribunal claim below. There is a broad outline of the EC scheme on the ACAS website, but remember that it is only general non-technical guidance and has no legal status.

20.18   The EC scheme applies to 'relevant proceedings' in the ET.[15] These are mainly set out in a list in Employment Tribunals Act (ETA) 1996 s18(1). Virtually all employment rights are covered, including claims for unfair dismissal; written reasons for dismissal; notice pay;

14   ERA 1996 s92(4).
15   ETA 1996 s18A(1).

discrimination; equal pay; redundancy pay; collective redundancy consultation; unauthorised deductions from pay; pay slips; statutory holiday entitlement; less favourable treatment of part-timers and fixed-term employees; flexible working; time off for antenatal care; agency workers' rights; and detriments due to whistleblowing or related to pregnancy and maternity. The scheme also applies to the right to be accompanied to a disciplinary or grievance hearing,[16] and to failure to inform or consult on a TUPE transfer.[17] There are a number of obscure rights which are not covered by the scheme. The one which you are most likely to come across is an application to the secretary of state for payment where the employer is insolvent.[18] Employers' contract claims are also not covered.

20.19 Even if the claim is covered by the EC process, the claimant has a choice whether or not to make an EC notification if one of the following circumstances apply, ie where:[19]

- The employee wants to make a claim with someone else on the same form, and the other person has already notified ACAS under the EC rules.
- The claim form includes claims which are not covered by the EC procedure.
- The employee can show that the prospective respondent has already contacted ACAS in relation to a dispute, the employee has not notified ACAS in relation to that dispute and the proceedings on the claim form relate to that dispute.
- It is an unfair dismissal claim and the tribunal claim will be accompanied by an application for interim relief.
- The claim is against the Security Service, Secret Intelligence Service, or the Government Communications Headquarters (GCHQ).

If the employee decides to enter the EC process in these circumstances, ACAS must follow the procedure in the usual way.

20.20 Assuming the EC procedure applies, employees will be blocked from starting a tribunal claim if they have not first obtained a certificate from ACAS in relation to the relevant respondents. The only way

---

16 Employment Relations Act 1999 s14 read with ETA 1996 s18(1)(b).
17 Transfer of Undertakings (Protection of Employment) Regulations (TUPE Regs) 2006 SI No 246 reg 16(1).
18 See para 18.73.
19 ETA 1996 ss18A(7) and 18B(2); Employment Tribunals (Early Conciliation: Exemptions and Rules of Procedure) Regulations (EC Rules) 2014 SI No 254 reg 3.

to get an ACAS certificate is to follow the EC process. Employees cannot be forced to negotiate, but they must at least make the initial notification to ACAS. The procedure is set out in the Early Conciliation Rules of Procedure (EC Rules) 2014, which are contained in the Schedule to the Employment Tribunals (Early Conciliation: Exemptions and Rules of Procedure) Regulations 2014.[20]

20.21   The employee is known as the 'prospective claimant'. As a first step, s/he must notify ACAS by telephone or, preferably, by using the online form on the ACAS website[21] or by posting a hard copy to the ACAS address which is on the form. ACAS will acknowledge the form by email (if the claimant gave an email address) or by post. Employees should make sure they get confirmation of safe receipt straight away. The only compulsory information on the form is the name and address both of the prospective claimant and of the prospective respondent (ie the employer or other person against whom the employee intends to make a claim).[22] The employee does not need to say what his/her claim will be about. An EC certificate can cover future events, provided there is some loose connection with the claim, eg an employee notifies ACAS about events at work which are making her unhappy, but only resigns because of those events after the EC certificate is issued, and then brings a constructive dismissal claim.[23]

20.22   It is important that the employee gets the name of the prospective respondent right. If the employee invokes EC against a prospective respondent with one name and ultimately issues a tribunal claim against a respondent with a different name, the tribunal claim may not be allowed.[24] If the prospective claim will be against more than one respondent, the claimant can now put all the names on a single EC form.[25]

20 SI No 254.

21 Available via a link on: www.acas.org.uk/earlyconciliation.

22 EC Rules 2014 Schedule rr1–3.

23 *Compass Group UK & Ireland Ltd v Morgan* [2016] IRLR 924, EAT.

24 Employment Tribunals (Constitution and Rules of Procedure) Regulations (ET Regs) 2013 SI No 1237 Sch 1 r12(2A) amended from December 2020; see paras 20.60, 20.77 and 20.79.

25 EC Rules 2014 Schedule r4. Amended by the Employment Tribunals (Constitution and Rules of Procedure)(Early Conciliation: Exemptions and Rules of Procedure) (Amendment) Regulations 2021 SI No 1037 with effect from 1 December 2021.

20.23 On receiving the form, ACAS will try to contact the employee. If ACAS cannot make contact with the employee, they will keep trying for a while, but eventually they will give up and issue a certificate.[26] Once contact is made, if the employee does not want to take up the offer of EC, ACAS will issue a certificate immediately.[27] ACAS will also issue an immediate certificate if the employer is insolvent. It is not the role of ACAS to assess the strength of the case or to discourage weak cases.

20.24 Provided the employee wants to try negotiation, an ACAS conciliator will then contact the prospective respondent. If the conciliator is unable to make contact with the prospective respondent, or if the prospective respondent is uninterested in EC, the conciliator will issue a certificate.[28] Respondents sometimes complain later at the tribunal that ACAS did not get in contact with them. The most likely explanation is that ACAS were unable to make contact and having failed to do so after making reasonable attempts, were entitled to give up.[29]

20.25 If both sides want to negotiate, the conciliator has up to six weeks from when ACAS was originally notified by telephone or receipt of the form.[30] If a settlement is reached, ACAS will record it on a COT3 form. If negotiations collapse during the EC period or if no settlement has been achieved by the end of the period, the conciliator must issue an EC certificate.[31]

20.26 The EC certificate is a crucial document. Until it is issued, the claimant cannot start his/her tribunal claim. The certificate records the name and address of the prospective claimant (the employee) and the prospective respondent; the date of receipt of the written or telephone EC notification; the date of issue of the certificate, ie the date it is sent, a statement of the method by which the certificate is sent; and the unique reference number given by ACAS to the certificate.[32] The certificate will be emailed to the employee or if s/he has no email address, it will be posted.[33] If ACAS has had contact with the prospective respondents, they should be sent a copy too. This does

26 EC Rules 2014 Schedule rr5(3) and 7(1); ETA 1996 s18A(4)(a).
27 EC Rules 2014 Schedule r7(1); ETA 1996 s18A(4)(a).
28 EC Rules 2014 Schedule rr5(3) and 7(1); ETA 1996 s18A(4)(a).
29 EC Rules 2014 Schedule r5(2).
30 EC Rules 2014 Schedule r6(1). Previously this was one calendar month with the possibility of a two-week extension.
31 EC Rules 2014 Schedule r7; ETA 1996 s18A(4).
32 See example in appendix C.
33 EC Rules 2014 Schedule r9.

not always seem to happen, which can cause problems. The ACAS conciliation period extends the time limits for starting a tribunal claim,[34] and if the respondents do not see the dates on the certificate, they tend to challenge the claim as out of time in the tribunal. To avoid this problem, some tribunals send a copy of the certificate to the respondents.

20.27   In rare instances, a prospective respondent may contact ACAS first, eg an employer who anticipates that the employee is about to bring a tribunal claim. ACAS is obliged to try to conciliate of this happens.[35] If the employee is uninterested in negotiating or no settlement is agreed, the employee can go ahead and make a tribunal claim without having notified ACAS him/herself. This is because one of the exceptions applies.[36] It is important to be very careful about the rules in this situation. The wording of the exception causes uncertainties in practice, especially where more than one respondent is involved.

Fees

20.28   In 1968, the Donovan Report recommended that labour tribunals be set up to provide 'an easily accessible, speedy, informal and inexpensive procedure' for the settlement of employment disputes. As a result, the jurisdiction of Industrial Tribunals was extended to cover a variety of employment rights. In 1998, Industrial Tribunals were renamed Employment Tribunals.

20.29   One of the most radical and controversial changes to the tribunal system in recent years was the attempted introduction of fees. Until the Conservative and Liberal Democrat coalition government introduced fees on 29 July 2013, workers could bring cases in an ET and appeal to the EAT without paying a fee. Fees were then charged until their abolition following *R (UNISON) v Lord Chancellor*[37] in July 2017.

20.30   After the introduction of fees, there was a dramatic and persistent fall in the number of claims brought in ETs. Comparing the figures preceding the introduction of fees with periods immediately before

---

34   See para 20.56 onwards.
35   ETA 1996 s18B.
36   EC Rules 2014 reg 3(1)(c). See para 20.19.
37   [2017] UKSC 51; [2017] IRLR 911.

the UNISON decision, there was a long-term reduction in ET claims of 66–70 per cent.

20.31   Following a long fight by UNISON, which brought a judicial review against the government challenging the fees, the Supreme Court decided that the Fees Order was unlawful under both domestic law (going back to Magna Carta) and EU law, because it had the effect of preventing access to justice. The landmark judgment, *R (UNISON) v Lord Chancellor*,[38] makes essential reading. The Supreme Court noted that, for some people, the fees were simply unaffordable. Even for those who could afford them, they were so high that they in practice prevented people from pursuing claims for small amounts and non-monetary claims. The Supreme Court said that, where households on low to middle incomes can only afford fees by sacrificing the ordinary and reasonable expenditure required to maintain what would generally be regarded as an acceptable standard of living, the fees cannot be regarded as affordable.

20.32   The Supreme Court rejected the government's underlying assumption that the administration of justice is merely a public service like any other, that courts and tribunals are providers of services to the 'users' who appear before them, and that the provision of those services is of value only to the users themselves. It said the constitutional right of access to the courts is inherent in the rule of law. In a very important passage, the Supreme Court highlighted the democratic importance of access to the courts (para 68):

> At the heart of the concept of the rule of law is the idea that society is governed by law. Parliament exists primarily in order to make laws for society in this country. Democratic procedures exist primarily in order to ensure that the Parliament which makes those laws includes Members of Parliament who are chosen by the people of this country and are accountable to them. Courts exist in order to ensure that the laws made by Parliament, and the common law created by the courts themselves, are applied and enforced. That role includes ensuring that the executive branch of government carries out its functions in accordance with the law. In order for the courts to perform that role, people must in principle have unimpeded access to them. Without such access, laws are liable to become a dead letter, the work done by Parliament may be rendered nugatory, and the democratic election of Members of Parliament may become a meaningless charade.

20.33   The Supreme Court went on to say that the idea that bringing a claim before a court or a tribunal is a purely private activity and provides no

38 [2017] UKSC 51.

broader social benefit is untenable. Access to the courts is not of value only to the particular individuals involved. That is most obviously true of cases which establish principles of general importance, but it is more than that:

> People and businesses need to know, on the one hand, that they will be able to enforce their rights if they have to do so, and, on the other hand, that if they fail to meet their obligations, there is likely to be a remedy against them. It is that knowledge which underpins everyday economic and social relations. That is so, notwithstanding that judicial enforcement of the law is not usually necessary, and notwithstanding that the resolution of disputes by other methods is often desirable.

20.34　ETs immediately stopped charging fees on the decision of the Supreme Court, and the government set up a system for reimbursing fees which had been paid in the past. Over 22,000 applications for refunds have been received and £18.5 million repaid. The system for reclaiming fees is set out on the GOV.UK website.[39] Since the abolition of fees, the numbers of cases presented to the tribunal have hugely increased although, at the time of writing, they have not yet reached pre-fees levels.[40] The Covid pandemic is likely to have affected and to continue to affect case numbers, initially with a reduction in cases presented and then a likely increase after furlough protection stops and redundancies are made.

The employment tribunal website

20.35　HM Courts and Tribunals Service (HMCTS), an agency of the Ministry of Justice, is responsible for the administration of civil and criminal courts and tribunals in England and Wales and non-devolved tribunals in Scotland. Information regarding employment tribunals is hosted on GOV.UK. The best place to start is the page headed, 'Make a claim to an employment tribunal',[41] and follow the links.

39　See: www.gov.uk/employment-tribunals/refund-tribunal-fees. Refund statistics in *Tribunal Statistics Quarterly, January to March 2021* at www.gov.uk/government/statistics/tribunal-statistics-quarterly-january-to-march-2021/tribunal-statistics-quarterly-january-to-march-2021#employment-tribunals.

40　Annual statistics from 2007/8 to 2019/20 are in the Employment Tribunal and Employment Appeals Tribunal Annual Tables' available via a link at www.gov.uk/government/statistics/tribunal-statistics-quarterly-april-to-june-2020.

41　At: www.gov.uk/employment-tribunals.

The ET Rules of Procedure

20.36   Although this chapter is concerned with running unfair dismissal cases (and therefore refers to 'employees' throughout), the procedural rules are basically the same with all ET cases. However, different cases and types of claim do vary in length and complexity. Additional points relevant to discrimination cases are in chapter 21, and to equal pay claims in chapter 5.[42]

20.37   The current procedural rules regarding the preparation and hearing of cases in England, Wales and Scotland are contained in the Employment Tribunals (Constitution and Rules of Procedure) Regulations (ET Regs) 2013 (also referred to in this chapter as the '2013 rules').[43] Until 2004, there were separate rules for Scotland, which has developed certain different practices in its tribunals. Although there is great similarity, there are some practical differences which may not be covered by this book. It should also be checked that such differences in Scotland which are referred to here still reflect the position. Power over the operation and management of ETs in Scotland is devolved to the Scottish Government. It is therefore possible that changes will be made in the future to rules for Scotland.

20.38   As well as the procedural rules, the President of the Employment Tribunals (England and Wales) and the President of the Employment Tribunals (Scotland) have power to issue practice directions and presidential guidance on certain topics.[44] This includes presidential guidance for England and Wales on general case management. Different guidance may be issued for tribunals in England and Wales and for Scotland by the respective Presidents. Tribunals must have regard to such guidance, but they are not bound to follow it as a matter of law.[45] The guidance is intended to assist both the parties and the tribunals and to help promote consistency.

---

42 See also paras 18.68–18.71 regarding interim relief.

43 SI No 1237. The procedural rules and practice directions can be accessed at www.gov.uk/employment-tribunals, click 'Legislation' (under 'Contents), then 'rules and processes'. This takes you through to an updated set of the procedural rules with all the amendments as at 6 October 2021.

44 Available via links, for England and Wales at: www.judiciary.gov.uk/ publications/employment-rules-and-legislation-practice-directions/ and for Scotland at: www.judiciary.gov.uk/publications/directions-for-employment-tribunals-scotland/.

45 ET Regs 2013 Sch 1 r7.

20.39   Under the 2013 rules, tribunals have great powers and flexibility to make decisions, but this is balanced by fair process, notification and consultation of parties. The 'overriding objective'[46] of the rules is often referred to. Its purpose is to enable tribunals to deal with cases fairly and justly. This includes, so far as is practicable:

- ensuring the parties are on an equal footing;
- dealing with the case in ways which are proportionate to the complexity and importance of the issues;
- avoiding unnecessary formality and seeking flexibility in the proceedings;
- avoiding delay, so far as compatible with proper consideration of the issues; and
- saving expense.

The parties and their representatives are supposed to assist the tribunal in achieving the overriding objective. In addition, the 2013 rules introduced a specific requirement that the parties co-operate with each other as well as with the tribunal.

20.40   An ET must give effect to the overriding objective when exercising its procedural powers. This is constantly referred to by the tribunal when making decisions as to what orders should be made for documents and information, and in deciding the length and conduct of the hearing.

20.41   The overriding objective was introduced in 2001. There are considerable resource pressures on the tribunal system, partly due to constantly expanding areas of employment law and partly due to financial cuts which the justice system has faced along with the rest of society since 2010. Everyone agrees it is important that external resource pressures do not corrode the objectives of justice. The EAT has recognised, albeit in the context of a discrimination case, that there can be a tension between what expedition requires and what fairness requires. If so, in the end, justice should be preferred to expedition.[47] Article 6 (the right to a fair hearing) of the European Convention on Human Rights (ECHR) is also an important safeguard.[48]

---

46 ET Regs 2013 Sch 1 r2.
47 *Senyonjo v Trident Safeguards Ltd* UKEAT/0316/04. See also EAT's comments in *Sodexho v Gibbons* [2005] IRLR 836, EAT.
48 See paras 3.23–3.24.

The tribunal claim (ET1)

Starting a case

20.42　A case is started when the employee (known as the 'claimant')[49] presents a written claim on an approved ('prescribed') form containing the necessary information.[50] This is known as the 'claim',[51] but it is also often referred to by the number of the standard form, ie 'ET1'. Much information can be obtained from the HMCTS website, which contains the approved ET1 form and various guidance notes and leaflets.[52]

20.43　Claimants are encouraged to use the online submission service, which is also available in Welsh. Alternatively, a hard copy of the claim form can be printed off the website and posted to the appropriate Central Office (the addresses are on the HMCTS website under 'Make a claim by post'). It may be permissible to deliver the claim by hand to certain tribunals, but it is best to check the latest rules for that.

20.44　An employee needs to think carefully before starting a case, if s/he is unsure that s/he will want to see it through. Although technically s/he can withdraw at any time, the longer the case goes on, the greater the risk that costs will be awarded against him/her for unreasonable conduct if s/he casually withdraws having put the employer through a lot of unnecessary expense.[53] It is also worth checking whether the employer is insolvent or unlikely to pay any award. Although some debts are covered by the state, these will be relatively small sums.[54] A Company Search can be carried out on the WebCheck service of Companies House.[55] When the company name is typed in, the website shows a list of companies with similar names. Click on the company number of the correct name (in the left-hand column) and the correct page will open. It tells you if the company has been dissolved and, if not, when accounts were last filed, which is usually a good indicator of the employer's financial health. The site may be a few weeks behind actual events.

49　Until 1 October 2004, known as the 'applicant'.
50　ET Regs 2013 Sch 1 rr8 and 10. See para 20.41.
51　Until 1 October 2004, known as the 'originating application'.
52　Start at: www.gov.uk/employment-tribunals.
53　See para 20.246 onwards on costs.
54　See para 18.73.
55　Go to Companies House at www.gov.uk/government/organisations/ companies-house and click on 'Find company information'.

Time limits

20.45   The time limit for lodging an unfair dismissal claim is within three months from dismissal, which is far shorter than that for other civil claims. The time limit is strictly enforced, with an extension only in exceptional circumstances. This section must be read together with para 20.56 onwards regarding the effect of ACAS EC on time limits.

20.46   The period of three calendar months runs from the effective date of termination (EDT). This means three calendar months less one day.[56] If the EDT is 18 May, the claim must be presented on or before midnight on 17 August.[57] Where EC applies (see below), ACAS must be notified by that time limit and the claim must then be presented to the tribunal within a set period after the ACAS certificate is issued. It is always risky to leave presentation of the claim to the last minute, because things tend to go wrong. It is legitimate to expect first-class post to arrive on the second day after posting, provided that it is not a Sunday or bank holiday.[58] If it is unexpectedly delayed, this may be a ground for allowing a late claim, but it is extremely risky to rely on this. If using the interactive online form on the HMCTS website and it does not go through, the claim will not be presented unless it can be proved it arrived at least at the server hosting the website.[59]

20.47   For time limit purposes, the EDT means:

- when the contract is terminated by notice, the date that the notice expires;[60]
- when the contract is terminated without notice, the date on which termination takes effect.[61] With a summary dismissal for gross misconduct, this will be the last day worked.

However, where there is no gross misconduct and notice is required, if the employer pays money in lieu of notice, the EDT can be ambiguous. Either the employer has terminated the contract of employment with immediate effect and made a payment in lieu of notice, or the

---

56 *Pruden v Cunard Ellerman Ltd* [1993] IRLR 317, EAT; *Joshi v Manchester City Council* UKEAT/0235/07; *Wang v University of Keele* UKEAT/0223/10.

57 *Post Office v Moore* [1981] ICR 623, EAT.

58 *Consignia plc v Sealy* [2002] IRLR 624, CA; *Coldridge v HM Prison Service* UKEAT/0728/04 and 0729/04; *Miah v Axis Security Services Ltd* UKEAT/0290-0292/17.

59 The case-law, which concerned the previous interactive system, seems to conflict on this. *Tyne and Wear Autistic Society v Smith* [2005] IRLR 336, EAT; *Mossman v Bray Management Ltd* UKEAT/0477/04.

60 ERA 1996 s97(1)(a).

61 ERA 1996 s97(1)(b).

employer has terminated the contract from the end of the notice period, but does not require the employee to attend work in the interim. The dismissal letter or P45 may indicate which is the case. Usually when the employer pays in lieu of notice, the EDT is the last day actually worked and it is safest when calculating time limits to work from this date. Indeed, it is a useful rule of thumb to present the claim within three months of the last day worked (unless the employee is off sick or on holiday during his/her last weeks). By doing this, the claim will always be in time. If the employee is absent due to sickness or holiday at the end of his/her employment, the EDT takes place when the contract of employment actually terminates.

20.48 Where a dismissal is communicated by letter, the EDT is the date the employee actually reads the letter, not the date it is written, posted or delivered (unless the contract of employment explicitly says otherwise). If the employee does not immediately read the letter, eg because s/he is on holiday or even because s/he deliberately avoids reading it, the EDT is when s/he would in the circumstances have had a reasonable opportunity of doing so.[62] Playing it safe, it is best just to count time from the date of the letter. If the employer notifies the employee's solicitors or advisers of the dismissal before writing direct to the employee, it is possible that the date the solicitors or advisers were notified is the dismissal date.[63] Another uncertain situation can arise where the employer says, verbally or in writing, words to the effect: 'You are dismissed. I am giving you three months' notice. You will be paid, but please do not come into work.' Unless there is something in the employee's contract of employment or other external circumstances which says otherwise, notice in that instance would start to be counted on the next day.[64] So for example, in the absence of any indication that it should be otherwise, if the employee received three months' notice on 3 November, this would start to be counted on 4 November and the termination date would be 3 February.[65] Strictly speaking, any ambiguity in the dismissal letter which could mislead the employee as to the termination date should be interpreted by the tribunals against the writer of the letter

---

62 *Newcastle upon Tyne Hospitals NHS Foundation Trust v Haywood* [2018] UKSC 22; [2018] IRLR 644; *Gisda Cyf v Barratt* [2010] IRLR 1073, SC.

63 *Robinson v Dr Bowskill and others practising as Fairhill Medical Practice* UKEAT/0313/12.

64 *Wang v University of Keele* UKEAT/0223/10. This is a very useful case to read on the calculation of time limits generally.

65 *Wang v University of Keele* UKEAT/0223/10.

(the employer) and in favour of the employee.[66] Nevertheless, to repeat, the law and factual scenarios can be varied and complex; in all circumstances it is best to calculate time limits based on the earliest possible date and not to leave things to the last day.

Late claims

20.49   Exceptionally, the ET will allow a late claim provided it was not reasonably practicable to present the claim in time, and it was presented within such further period as the ET considers reasonable.[67] It is for the employee to show that it was not reasonably practicable to present the claim in time.[68] A tribunal should give the test a liberal interpretation in favour of the employee.[69] Nevertheless, it is very difficult to make unfair dismissal claims out of time.

20.50   Physical or mental[70] disability or ill-health can be a good reason for missing a time limit, depending on the circumstances and timing.

20.51   It may be that the employee missed the deadline because s/he was unaware of the right to claim unfair dismissal or how to do so or what the time limits were. What is relevant is the employee's state of mind and the extent to which s/he understood his/her position.[71] Ignorance will be an acceptable excuse only if the ignorance or mistaken belief is itself reasonable. It will not be reasonable if the employee did not make reasonable enquiries in the circumstances.[72] If the employee knows s/he has employment rights, s/he would normally be expected to have asked about those rights and therefore have found out about time limits.

---

66 *Wang v University of Keele* UKEAT/0223/10 referring to previous case-law on this 'contra preferentem' rule.

67 ERA 1996 s111.

68 *Porter v Bandridge* [1978] ICR 943; [1978] IRLR 271, CA.

69 *Marks & Spencer plc v Williams-Ryan* [2005] IRLR 563, CA; *Lowri Beck Services Ltd v Brophy* [2019] EWCA Civ 2490.

70 *Schulz v Esso Petroleum Co Ltd* [1999] IRLR 488, CA; *Imperial Tobacco Ltd v Wright* UKEAT/0919/04; *Lowri Beck Services Ltd v Brophy* [2019] EWCA Civ 2490.

71 *London International College Ltd v Sen* [1993] IRLR 333, CA; *Palmer and another v Southend-on-Sea BC* [1984] IRLR 119, CA; *Marks & Spencer plc v Williams-Ryan* [2005] IRLR 563, CA.

72 *Wall's Meat Co Ltd v Khan* [1978] IRLR 499, CA; *Porter v Bandridge* [1978] ICR 943; [1978] IRLR 271, CA.

20.52   Ignorance of a fact which is crucial to a claim can make it not reasonably practicable,[73] eg if a redundant employee finds out only after the expiry of the time limit that s/he was immediately replaced by someone else.

20.53   Employees cannot just await the outcome of their appeal against dismissal if it has not been decided within the ET time limit. The mere fact of a pending appeal is rarely in itself sufficient grounds to make it not reasonably practicable to get the claim in on time, if the employee is – or should have been – aware of the time limits. However, if an employee is reasonably ignorant of the relevant time limits, and as a result awaits the outcome of an internal appeal before investigating the possibility of a tribunal claim, an ET *may* decide it was not reasonably practicable to get a claim in on time.[74] Equally, if the employee has been told by ACAS to go through the internal procedure first and there has been no discussion about time limits for starting a claim, some ETs may allow a late claim if the employee acts promptly once the appeal is decided.[75] A genuine and reasonable misunderstanding of the EC procedure leading to the rejection of an employee's original claim and the consequential lateness of a second, corrected, claim, could make it not reasonably practicable to have presented the corrected claim in time.[76]

20.54   It is unlikely that the employee can rely on the fact that it was his/her solicitor who wrongly put in a late claim on his/her behalf[77] – his/her remedy is to sue the solicitor for negligence. However, if a solicitor simply gave wrong advice and the employee retained responsibility for lodging the claim form, the employee may be able to argue that it was not reasonably practicable for him/her to get the claim in on time.[78] If the employee was misled by the advice of a

---

73 *Cambridge and Peterborough NHS Foundation Trust v Crouchman* UKEAT/0108/09.

74 *John Lewis Partnership v Charman* UKEAT/0079/11.

75 *DHL Supply Chain Ltd v Fazackerley* UKEAT/0019/18.

76 *Adams v British Telecommunications plc* UKEAT/0342/15; *Software Box Ltd v Gannon (debarred)* UKEAT/0433/14.

77 *Dedman v British Building and Engineering Appliances Ltd* [1973] IRLR 379, CA; see also *Northamptonshire CC v Entwhistle* UKEAT/0540/09; [2010] IRLR 740, though the EAT in *Remploy Ltd v Brain* UKEAT/0465/10 believes *Dedman* did not lay down a rigid rule. There is a useful review of the authorities in *El-Kholy v Rentokil Initial Facilities Services (UK) Ltd* UKEAT/0472/12.

78 *Royal Bank of Scotland v Theobald* UKEAT/0444/06. Although this distinction was doubted by the EAT in *Ashcroft v Haberdashers Aske's Boys School* UKEAT/0151/07; [2008] IRLR 375 and *Remploy Ltd v Brain* UKEAT/0465/10.

Citizens Advice Bureau, it will depend on who gave the advice within the Bureau and in what circumstances.[79]

20.55   Even if the employee shows that it was not reasonably practicable to present the claim in time, s/he must do so within a further reasonable period. The employee must act promptly once s/he discovers that the claim is out of time.[80]

The effect of early conciliation on time limits

20.56   Where the ACAS EC process applies, there is an extension of time limits. The idea is that the time taken for the EC process is added on to the usual tribunal time limit. This is done by not counting the period starting with the day after 'Day A' and ending with 'Day B'.[81] 'Day A' is the day when the claimant first contacted ACAS under the EC process. 'Day B' is the day when the claimant received or, if earlier, is treated as receiving, the EC certificate. Where the certificate was emailed, it is deemed to have been received on the date it was sent.[82] If it was sent by post, it is deemed received on the day when it would be delivered in the ordinary course of post.[83] For example, the claimant is dismissed on 12 February 2021. The original unfair dismissal time limit would be 11 May 2021. The claimant notifies ACAS on 5 March 2021 (Day A). The claimant is not interested in negotiating and the ACAS certificate is issued and emailed to the claimant on 9 March 2021 (Day B). The period to be discounted is 6 March–9 March 2021 inclusive (four days). The extended tribunal time limit is 15 May 2021 (11 May + four days).

20.57   If the extended tribunal time limit would expire during the period starting with Day A (notification of ACAS) and ending one month after Day B (receipt of the certificate), the new time limit will expire instead one month after Day B. 'One month after' means the corresponding date in the next calendar month, eg if Day B is 30 June 2021,

---

79 *Marks & Spencer plc v Williams-Ryan* [2005] IRLR 563, CA. Regarding advice from employment consultants generally, see *Ashcroft v Haberdashers Aske's Boys School* UKEAT/0151/07; [2008] IRLR 375.

80 *Golub v University of Sussex* (1981) 13 April, unreported, CA; *James W Cook & Co (in liquidation) v Tipper and others* [1990] IRLR 386, CA.

81 ERA 1996 s207B. This is often referred to as 'stopping the clock'.

82 If the email is sent to an invalid email address, eg because of a mistake where a dot is put, it is not deemed to have arrived: *Galloway v Wood Group UK Limited* UKEATS/0017/18.

83 EC Rules 2014 Schedule r9(3).

the time limit will expire on 30 July 2021.[84] This ensures that a claimant has at least one month after receiving the ACAS certificate (or being deemed to receive it) to present the tribunal claim. The one month is a minimum period, not a maximum.[85] If EC is started and completed early, there may well be longer than one month left to present a claim after the certificate is issued. For example in an unfair dismissal claim:

- The EDT is 20 June 2021, Day A (notification of ACAS) is 22 July 2021 and Day B (receipt of the certificate) is 22 August 2021.
- There are 31 days from the day after Day A to Day B inclusive.
- The new time limit is 20 October 2021, ie the original unfair dismissal time limit of 19 September 2021 plus 31 days. It is not 22 September 2021 (one month after Day B).

20.58 There is a further permutation, where the original time limit would not even have started to run before the EC notification is made and/or EC certificate is issued. This could happen, for example, with an unfair dismissal case where a claimant works a lengthy notice period. The claimant might make his/her EC notification to ACAS as soon as s/he is given notice and prior to the termination date. If the certificate is also issued before the usual tribunal time limit would start to be counted, it seems likely there is no extension to allow for any conciliation period.[86] Test cases on how the time limit extension operates are still coming through and should be watched.

20.59 Overall, the claimant therefore needs to keep two dates in mind. First, the original time limit applying to unfair dismissal, or whatever is the employment right in question. ACAS must be notified before that time limit expires. Second, the extra time for submitting a claim to the tribunal following receipt of the ACAS certificate. If the claimant is late at either of these stages, the tribunal will have to decide whether to allow a late claim in the usual way. A claimant cannot try to get around the problem by notifying ACAS again of EC and getting another EC certificate. Only time taken for conciliation under the first certificate will count for the purposes of extending the

---

84 *Tanveer v East London Bus & Coach Co Ltd* UKEAT/0022/16. Where there is no such date in the following month, eg Day B is 31 January, it is likely the time limit is the last day of the following month ie 28 Feburary (or 29 February in a leap year) – see *Dodds v Walker* [1981] 1 WLR 1027 HL which is quoted in *Tanveer*.

85 *Luton BC v Haque* UKEAT/0180/17.

86 *Commissioners for HM Revenue and Customs v Serra Garau* UKEAT/0348/16.

tribunal time limit.[87] If the claimant fails to notify ACAS within the original time limit, but does so subsequently, s/he will not get the benefit of any extension under the rules. The time limit for presenting the claim to the tribunal will remain as it always was, regardless of the length of any conciliation.[88]

Drafting the tribunal claim

20.60   Under the ET Regs 2013, the following information must be set out in a tribunal claim:[89]

- The employee's name and address. The employee is called the 'claimant'. If there is more than one claimant, the name and address of each must be entered on the form.
- The employer's name and address. The employer is called the 'respondent'.
- The ACAS EC number for each named respondent, or confirmation that the claim does not start any 'relevant proceedings' or that one of the EC exemptions applies.

20.61   As already stated, claimants must use an approved ('prescribed') tribunal form (ET1). The current approved form can be found as a pdf on GOV.UK.[90] It can be printed off and completed by hand or completed online and then printed. Alternatively, an application can be made interactively. Unlike the pdf, the interactive form does not have numbered paragraphs.

20.62   The respondent in an unfair dismissal claim will be the claimant's employer. This is often a company (check headed notepaper and any written contract), though it can also be an individual with a trading name, eg 'Bill Roberts trading as Cactus Developments' or an unincorporated association. If uncertain about the precise name or address of an employing company, a search can be done on the Companies House website.[91]

---

87   *Commissioners for HM Revenue and Customs v Serra Garau* UKEAT/0348/16.

88   *Pearce v (1) Bank of America Merrill Lunch, and others* UKEAT/0067/19.

89   ET Regs 2013 Sch 1 r10.

90   Access the approved ET1 form at: www.gov.uk/employment-tribunals/ make-a-claim by clicking 'download and fill in a claim form' under 'make a claim by post' half way down the page and then download the form. Alternatively, for the online process, click the 'Claim online' box then 'Start a claim' at the bottom of the page.

91   See para 20.62 regarding a Company Search; and para 20.79 regarding matching the name on the ACAS certificate.

20.63 An employee who is employed by an unincorporated association is employed by its management or executive committee, not by all the members of the association. ETs will usually accept a claim which simply names the association as respondent, but strictly speaking it should name the members of the committee when the cause of action arose, eg when the employee was dismissed. Sometimes a claim is made against a representative respondent, ie a member of the committee, who is sued both in his/her own name and as a representative of the committee. However, questions may arise as to the right of other members to be kept informed and to have their say, and also as to whether it is necessary to name all the individuals in order to be able to enforce against any one of them.[92] An even more difficult area concerns teachers and support staff working in schools, where quite technical questions can arise as to whether they are employed for the purposes of the unfair dismissal claim by the local education authority or the governing body of the school. This is an area where specialist legislation can apply and is beyond the scope of this book.[93]

20.64 A claimant can make several claims on a single ET1 form, for example a claim for unfair dismissal, notice pay and written reasons for dismissal; or for race discrimination and unfair dismissal.[94] At section 8.1 of the pdf form (page 8 of the interactive form), the claimant is asked to tick one or more boxes indicating the type of claim s/he is bringing. It is very important to spell out more details of any box that has been ticked when going on to complete section 8.2.

20.65 At section 8.2 of the pdf form (page 9 of the interactive form), claimants are asked to set out the background and details of their claim or claims. It is important to remember that the tribunal claim will probably be the first document read by the employment judge or ET panel before the hearing starts and it will give them a strong early impression of the merits of the case. It is, therefore, foolish to give only very brief details of the claim.[95] A well written ET1 can also assist the case preparation to run more smoothly, eg by making a

---

92 For this potentially complicated area, it is important to read *Affleck v Newcastle Mind* [1999] IRLR 405, EAT and *Nazir and Aslam v Asim and Nottinghamshire Black Partnership (Debarred)* UKEAT/332/09.

93 Some useful cases in recent years are *Butt v Bradford MDC* UKEAT/0210/10; *Beattie v Leicester City Council* UKEAT/0386/09; *Jones v Neath Port Talbot County BC* [2011] EWCA Civ 92.

94 See appendix C for a sample form.

95 See also para 20.71 regarding problems in amending a claim later.

preliminary hearing less likely, eliciting a more detailed response from the employer, making it easier to obtain interim orders from the tribunal and improving the chances of settlement.

20.66 The ET1 should state all the key facts and dates, but without going into laborious detail. It is not supposed to be a full witness statement.[96] It should be more of a summary, which gives a reader an overview of what happened and why it is thought to be unlawful. The essentials are usually:

1) the legal basis for the claim, eg unfair dismissal or race discrimination;
2) the act or omission complained of, eg dismissal or lack of promotion;
3) who carried out the action complained of;
4) when it occurred;
5) why the claimant is complaining about the relevant action; and
6) anything affecting remedy.[97]

As a very rough rule of thumb, details of an unfair dismissal claim should not normally need more than two pages and the events should usually be described in chronological order. Details which run to over 15 or 20 pages and read more like a witness statement, even if they are written clearly, are unnecessarily lengthy. An ET cannot simply refuse to accept a claim form because it is too long,[98] but it may get rejected on initial consideration if the details are so incoherent that it cannot sensibly be responded to by the employer.[99]

20.67 It helps when completing the form to think about the relevant law and therefore what issues are relevant or irrelevant. For example, if the employer is a large company, this should be stated in the ET1, since the tribunal must consider fairness in the light of the employer's size and administrative resources.

20.68 In an unfair dismissal case, it is best to complete the ET1 bearing in mind what the employer must do for a dismissal to be fair. The claimant can then draw attention to what the employer ought to have done but did not. For example, in a conduct case, it is of little assistance to focus on the employee's innocence of the misconduct or to

---

96 The EAT gave guidance strongly encouraging more succinct drafting in *C v D* UKEAT/0132/19.
97 *Fairbank v Care Management Group; Evans v Svenska Handelsbanken AB (Publ)* UKEAT/0139-41/12.
98 *Fairbank v Care Management Group; Evans v Svenska Handelsbanken AB (Publ)* UKEAT/0139-41/12.
99 ET Regs 2013 Sch 1 r27; see para 20.100.

refer to matters occurring after dismissal, eg the police's decision to drop charges. What is relevant is the employer's genuine and reasonable belief at the time of dismissal, whether the employer had reasonable grounds for that belief, and the extent of the investigations into the employee's guilt including the opportunity afforded to the employee to offer an explanation. The ET1 should focus on these points, eg highlighting inadequacies in the investigation. If there are obvious weaknesses in the case, they cannot be hidden and it may be best to refer to them in the ET1 and offer as convincing an explanation as possible. For the above reasons, it is almost always better for an adviser who understands the law to write the ET1 rather than ask the claimant to write his/her own, even if the adviser intends to amend it. Sample tribunal claims are in appendix A, but these should not be copied slavishly. Every case is unique.

20.69 At section 9 of the pdf form and page 10 of the interactive form, claimants are asked what outcome they would prefer if they are successful. This includes asking for their job back if they win their unfair dismissal claim. Although a claimant can change his/her mind later, it improves his/her chances of getting a reinstatement order if s/he has indicated at the outset that that is what s/he is seeking. The form also asks claimants to set out how much financial compensation they are claiming and how they calculated the sum, insofar as they are able to do so. Although this may be difficult for claimants to do, it is helpful for them to understand from the outset how compensation is calculated for the types of claim they are making and the limitations of the tribunal's powers. The option of recommendations only applies to discrimination claims (see chapter 19).

20.70 If the adviser puts him/herself down as the claimant's representative, s/he will receive all the correspondence from the ET and employer, and s/he must keep the claimant informed. The ET will expect the adviser or someone else from the adviser's organisation to represent the claimant at hearings unless notified otherwise. If the adviser is not noted as representative on the form, correspondence goes to the claimant, who must be forewarned to keep in close touch with the adviser, even if nothing happens for four or five weeks. An adviser can later take over the running of a case, simply by writing to the ET and to the employer to notify them of this.

Amending the tribunal claim

20.71 A tribunal claim can be amended at any time, but the claimant needs the tribunal's permission. In deciding whether to allow an amendment, the ET must take account of all the circumstances and balance the hardship and injustice of refusing the amendment against that of allowing it.[100] Where the amendment is to add new facts and grounds, the ET must decide if the new claim is in time and, if not, whether the amendment should now be allowed. If the claim arises out of the same facts as the original claim but simply adds factual details or attaches a new legal label, the ET should very readily allow the amendment even if outside the time limit.[101] For example, a claimant may describe a sequence of events leading to a dismissal which s/he labels as unfair under the EqA 2010. The same facts could also support a claim of ordinary unfair dismissal under the Employment Rights Act 1996, provided s/he was eligible. On the other hand, if the amendment is to introduce an entirely new cause of action dependent on quite different facts, it is more difficult. The greater the difference between the factual and legal issues raised by the new claim and the old, the less likely it is that an amendment will be allowed, but it is always a matter for the tribunal's discretion.[102] It is important to remember that whether the new claim would be out of time if it were a free-standing claim (including whether the test for extending time for the relevant claim would be satisfied) is only one factor.[103] Other factors would be why the new claim was not originally included and how late in the day the amendment is sought.

20.72   By far the most important consideration is the balance of hardship and injustice of allowing the amendment as against refusing it. The tribunal should think about the real practical consequences. If the amendment is refused, how severe will be the consequences for the party seeking it? If it is allowed, what will be the practical problems for the other party in responding. The tribunal should focus on reality rather than assumptions. Representatives should actually find out whether witnesses can still remember the events, whether documents have been destroyed etc. They should not argue that they would be prejudiced by the amendment if that is not really true. If there is no real prejudice caused by the amendment, it will often be appropriate to consent to it.[104]

---

100 *Selkent Bus Co Ltd v Moore* [1996] IRLR 661, EAT; *Transport and General Workers Union v Safeway Stores Ltd* UKEAT/0092/07.

101 *Selkent Bus Co Ltd v Moore* [1996] IRLR 661, EAT; *Transport and General Workers Union v Safeway Stores Ltd* UKEAT/0092/07.

102 *Transport and General Workers Union v Safeway Stores Ltd* UKEAT/0092/07.

103 *Transport and General Workers Union v Safeway Stores Ltd* UKEAT/0092/07 reviews the authorities on this.

104 *Vaughan v Modality Partnership* UKEAT/0147/20; [2021] IRLR 97.

20.73 The result of allowing a new claim to be added by an amendment is that it takes effect from the date when permission to amend was given. The ET must make a separate decision on whether it is time-barred under the usual rules for late claims. This may be decided at the same time as the amendment is allowed (usually at a preliminary hearing) or it may be left to the final hearing if for example it is dependent on evidence as to whether there was continuing discrimination. It is even possible for the decision on both amendment and time limits to be left to the final hearing.[105]

20.74 As well as legal difficulties, claimants can sometimes be discredited in terms of evidence if they appear to have changed their mind from what they originally wrote in the tribunal claim. Overall, it can be difficult for several reasons to amend a claim out of time. It is therefore important for an adviser to spend enough time with the claimant at the outset to identify and evaluate all possible claims.

20.75 An ET has power to order an additional party to be joined at any time,[106] eg in a TUPE case where it becomes clear that the other party to the transfer should be joined, or in a discrimination case, when it is necessary to join an individual discriminator. See para 20.85 regarding whether it is necessary to go through ACAS EC prior to adding a new party.

Procedure for accepting the claim

20.76 On receiving the claim, the tribunal decides whether to accept it. If everything is in order, the claimant will be sent a standard acknowledgment form. A copy of the claim will be sent to the respondent, who has 28 days to respond. The case will be allocated a case number, which must be quoted on all correspondence or telephone contact with the tribunal. The acceptance of the claim form does not mean the tribunal has accepted that time limits have necessarily been complied with. Any problem with time limits is likely to come up later in the process.

20.77 All or part of the claim will be rejected if the form does not include all the required information (see para 20.60) or if an employment judge considers it is written in a way which cannot sensibly be

---

105 *Galilee v Commissioner of the Metropolis* UKEAT/0207/16; *Reuters Ltd v Cole* UKEAT/0258/17.
106 ET Regs 2013 Sch 1 r34.

responded to or that it is otherwise an abuse of process.[107] It may also be rejected if there is no jurisdiction to hear the claim, although some jurisdictional issues may only come up later. If all or part of the claim is rejected on any of these grounds, the form will be returned to the claimant with a written explanation for the decision and information on how to apply for a reconsideration of the rejection.[108] A fresh claim form will also be enclosed. If the claimant does nothing, his/her claim will not be started.

20.78 The claimant can apply for a reconsideration of the decision to reject the form within 14 days of the date that the rejection notice was sent. The claimant must either explain why the original decision was wrong or must rectify the defect leading to the rejection of the form.[109] If the claimant wants a hearing to decide whether the claim should now be allowed, s/he should say so. Otherwise, a judge will decide the matter on the basis of the papers. If a judge has decided to allow the claim, no hearing will be held anyway. Any hearing which is held on this point will be with the claimant alone. If the original rejection was correct, but the defect is subsequently rectified, the claim will be treated as presented on the date that the defect was rectified. This could cause problems with time limits for starting a claim.

20.79 One reason why the claim form may be rejected is if there is no ACAS certificate number unless it is indicated one of the exceptions applies. The claim will also be rejected if an EC exemption is claimed which does not in fact apply. A tribunal has no general discretion to allow in claims just because there are exceptional circumstances.[110]

20.80 The ACAS certificate number must be entered accurately on the ET1, as the claim may be rejected if there is a mistake. However, tribunals now have more power than previously to allow a mistake in the number if a judge thinks it would not be in the interests of justice to reject the claim.[111] This is different from the position if the number is left out altogether, in which case the claim must be rejected (see above).

20.81 Another possibility is that the claimant has named two respondents on the ET1, but has only obtained one certificate, and that certi-

---

107 It is doubtful whether the ET can use ET Regs 2013 Sch 1 r12(1)(b) following *Trustees of the William Jones's Schools Foundation v Parry* UKEAT/0088-9/16 but the claim could be dismissed under the r27 procedure – see para 20.100.

108 ET Regs 2013 Sch 1 r10(2) or r12(3).

109 ET Regs 2013 Sch 1 r13.

110 For an early example, see *Cranwell v Cullen* UKEATPAS/0046/14.

111 ET Regs 2013 Sch 1 r12(2ZA) from 8 October 2020.

ficate only names one respondent.[112] In that case, the tribunal will reject the claim as against the respondent without the certificate.

20.82   A tribunal may also reject a claim if the name of the claimant or respondent on the ACAS certificate is different from their name on the tribunal form. However, a judge can decide that it would not be in the interests of justice to reject the claim where the claimant made an error in relation to a name or address.[113] Before 8 October 2020, a judge could only overlook 'minor' errors, but the word 'minor' has now been removed from the rules.

20.83   All the circumstances are likely to be relevant when considering if it is in the interests of justice to reject a claim because of such an error. The most important factors are likely to be whether the claimant was aiming at the same entity and whether in practice, ACAS was able to get in touch with the claimant's employer. Other relevant factors might be whether the claimant had been given clear documents during his or her employment with the employer's name, whether there was reason for confusion eg because of different trading names or multiple companies in a group, and whether the claimant was represented at the time of contacting ACAS. Simple spelling mistakes or typos are very unlikely to be a problem. If the claimant gave ACAS the name of an individual instead of the employer, it may depend on the individual's role in the organisation, whether ACAS made contact with the organisation, and whether the claimant was trying to refer to the employer.

20.84   Relying on a judge to overlook an error is risky. Every effort should be made to give ACAS the correct name in the first place. If the problem is that the claimant is unsure as to who is the correct employer or who else should be named as a respondent, it is usually safest to notify ACAS under each possible name.

20.85   If the tribunal does reject the claim for any of these reasons, the claimant can apply for reconsideration in the usual way. S/he could try to argue, if applicable, that the decision to reject was wrong because it was not in the interests of justice to do so. Or s/he could remedy the defect by entering EC immediately with the correct name, obtaining a certificate and presenting the tribunal claim again. The problem with the latter route is that the date of presentation of the claim will be taken as the date when the claim is presented afresh,

---

112 Even before the rule change allowing a claimant to name more than one respondent in his/her EC notification, an ACAS certificate which named several respondents was effective: *De Mota v ADR Network and another* UKEAT/0305/16.

113 ET Regs 2013 Sch 1 r12(1)(f) and (2A).

which may well cause time limit problems. In a case where one claim is accepted because there is a certificate and it is only a claim against a second respondent which is rejected, a further option is to ask the tribunal to allow an amendment of the claim to add the second respondent back in. The EC process does not apply to an amendment and the usual considerations regarding whether an amendment is allowed would apply, taking into account the reasons why the claimant failed to get a certificate in the first place for the second respondent and any adverse effect on the latter as a result of losing the opportunity for EC, although bearing in mind that there is no obligation on the claimant to negotiate anyway.[114]

The employer's response (ET3)

20.86 The employer must send the tribunal his/her response[115] to the claim on an approved ('prescribed') response form (usually known as an ET3). The employer must give his/her full name and address and state whether s/he intends to resist any part of the claim.[116] In an unfair dismissal case, the employer will have to prove the reason for dismissal and that it was one of the potentially fair reasons.[117] The ET3 should therefore provide an indication as to what the employer's reason was. If the employer does not give sufficient details, so that the claimant does not fully understand what the employer's defence is, a letter should be written to the ET pointing this out and requesting additional information.

20.87 Employers must present their response to the ET within 28 days of the date they were sent a copy of the claim.[118] The response will be rejected if it is received outside the time limit (or any extension of time granted within the time limit) unless an application for an extension of time has already been made or the response is accompanied by such an application.[119] An employer whose response has been rejected for these reasons or for not supplying the minimum required information can apply within 14 days for a reconsideration of the decision, explaining why the rejection was wrong or rectifying

---

114 *Science Warehouse Ltd v Mills* [2016] IRLR 96, EAT. See also paras 20.71–20.75 for rules on amendment generally.
115 Previously called 'Notice of Appearance' or IT3.
116 ET Regs 2013 Sch 1 r17.
117 ERA 1996 s98; para 6.54.
118 ET Regs 2013 Sch 1 r16(1).
119 ET Regs 2013 Sch 1 r18.

the notified defect.[120] The judge will decide the application on the papers unless the employer has requested a hearing (except if the judge has decided to allow the application anyway).

20.88   Where the employer applies for an extension of time to submit the ET3, s/he must give the reasons and, if the time limit has already passed, s/he must attach a draft ET3 or explain why it is not possible to do so. The application must be copied to the claimant, who will have seven days to write in with any objections to the time extension.[121] An employment judge can decide on the basis of the papers, rather than holding a hearing, whether to allow the late ET3. The relevant considerations include whether there has been an explanation for the delay, the quality of any explanation, the strength of the employer's defence to the claim and the prejudice to each side if the ET allows or refuses an extension.[122]

20.89   Time limits on submitting an ET3 are not as strict as time limits for submitting an ET1. There is a reason for this. The ET1 time limits come from the original statutory rights and are a matter of the ET's jurisdiction. The ET3 time limits are purely a matter of procedure. Tribunals often do give permission for ET3s to be submitted one or two weeks' late if the employer makes a request before the time limit is up and has a good reason for needing more time, eg because detailed information has to be gathered to answer a long and detailed ET1, or because the relevant manager who knows about the case is on holiday.

20.90   If no ET3 is received in time or allowed out of time, an employment judge will issue a judgment if it is possible to do so properly on the available material, essentially the ET1 plus any extra documents which the judge might ask for. This is known as a 'rule 21' judgment (under the previous slightly different rules, it was known as a default judgment). The judge must be satisfied on the papers and taking what the claimant says as undisputed fact, that the necessary factual elements exist to make out the legal claim.[123] If not, a hearing will be fixed. The respondent will be entitled to notice of any hearings and decisions, but unless an extension of time is granted, will only be allowed to participate in any hearing to the extent allowed by the

---

120 ET Regs 2013 Sch 1 r19.
121 ET Regs 2013 Sch 1 r20.
122 *Grant v ASDA* UKEAT/0231/16.
123 See guidance in *Limoine v Sharma* UKEAT/0094/19.

judge.[124] There is presidential guidance for England and Wales on rule 21 judgments.[125]

20.91   It is fairly ominous if there is no ET3, or if an attempted ET3 is not accepted by the tribunal and the employer does not bother to apply for a reconsideration. This tends to suggest that the employer has no intention of paying any award and may well be on the way to insolvency.

20.92   If a response is submitted and accepted, the ET sends a copy on to the claimant. It is then that the further preparatory stages can take place. All the information in the ET3 should be checked with the claimant, listing what points are not accepted. Check all the small details on the ET3 form as well as the grounds on which the employer intends to resist the claim. If the employer's reasons for justifying the dismissal are vague or unclear, it may be wise to ask for additional information (see para 20.116 onwards).

Contract claims against the claimant

20.93   As explained in para 4.26, in certain circumstances, an employee whose employment has terminated can bring a contract claim in an ET, eg for notice pay. If s/he does so, it is possible that the employer will bring his/her own contract claim against the employee. This used to be called a 'counterclaim' but strictly-speaking that is not a legally accurate description of the position, and the 2013 rules just refer to 'an employer's contract claim'. The subject of the employer's contract claim does not need to relate in any way to the content of the employee's contract claim. It is important to bear in mind that the employer's contract claim has a life of its own. If the claimant later withdraws or settles his/her own contract claim, the employer's contract claim may continue (unless that is also withdrawn or settled).

20.94   Any contract claim made by the employer must be part of the employer's response to the claimant's ET1 containing a contract claim. There is a specific section 6 on the ET3 if the employer is making such a claim. The tribunal will notify the claimant that there is an employer's contract claim when sending the ET3 to him/her.

---

124 ET Regs 2013 Sch 1 r21.
125 Available via a link at: www.judiciary.gov.uk/publications/employment-rules-and-legislation-practice-directions/.

The claimant must in turn submit a response to the employer's contract claim within 28 days.[126]

Case management

Overview

20.95 Case management is concerned with preparing the case for the hearing, eg collecting information and documents from the other side and fixing hearing dates.[127] These steps are sometimes known as interim or interlocutory matters. In non-discrimination cases, this preparation is usually dealt with in correspondence directly between each side and if necessary, the ET is asked for an order if agreement cannot be reached. The parties are asked on the claim and response forms to indicate their preferred method of communication. Email is now the most popular method, especially given disruption to office space caused by the Covid-19 pandemic, although some documents cannot be sent electronically. Parties should check their emails every day if they want to communicate this way, as they are sometimes required to comment on matters, respond to orders or attend preliminary hearings on very short notice.

20.96 In discrimination cases or other cases which are particularly large or complex, the ET usually holds one or more preliminary hearings, where these matters are dealt with orally in discussion with an employment judge.[128] Some regions hold preliminary hearings on the telephone where the only matters to deal with relate to case management. Since the Covid pandemic, the vast majority of case management preliminary hearings have been conducted by telephone or video (see paras 20.228–20.234 regarding remote hearings generally).

20.97 Once the ET1 and ET3 are submitted, generally no further special forms or formats are used by the parties. Any correspondence with the other side or the ET simply takes the form of an ordinary letter or email. Although no legalistic formats are required, there are certain conventions which tend to be followed. The ET does not want to get into lengthy correspondence to and fro with the claimant. It is important to remember that the case is not argued on paper. The claimant definitely does not, for example, provide a written response to the

---

126 The rules are set out in ET Regs 2013 Sch 1 rr23–25.
127 See appendix A at A1 for the stages of running a basic ET case.
128 In Scotland, readers need to check the latest practice.

ET3 or to any additional information provided by the employer. The opportunity to put his/her own account of events is shortly before the hearing, when s/he writes his/her witness statement (see para 20.186). In the meantime s/he is simply gathering information from the employer by means of answers to written questions (called 'additional information') and documents, and s/he is providing information if requested by the employer. Any correspondence between a party and the ET will be copied to the other party (apart from initial requests for a witness order).

20.98   The ET has general case management powers. In England and Wales, ETs have traditionally been more proactive than in Scotland. An ET can make orders at any stage in the proceedings, either on paper or at a preliminary or other hearing. An order can be made either because one of the parties has applied or on the tribunal's own initiative.[129] Where an order is made based on the paperwork and in the absence of the parties, the parties will have the opportunity to object (see para 20.128 onwards). It is common for the ET to make orders regarding the provision of additional information, written answers, witness statements and documents.[130]

20.99   Legal officers have now been appointed to carry out certain case management functions which previously only employment judges. Parties are able to apply within 14 days of any decision for it to be considered afresh by an employment judge.[131]

Initial consideration of the claim and response forms

20.100 The 2013 rules specifically require tribunals to consider the file as soon as possible after acceptance of the ET3 with a view to confirming there are arguable complaints and defences within the tribunal's jurisdiction and giving case management orders.[132] If an employment judge thinks the ET has no jurisdiction to consider all or part of a claim or that the claim has no reasonable prospects of success, the tribunal will write to the parties setting out the judge's view and reasons for it, and ordering that the claim or part claim will be dismissed on a particular date unless the claimant has supplied a written explanation before that date as to why it should not be

---

129 ET Regs 2013 Sch 1 r29.
130 Though such orders are less common in Scotland.
131 Employment Tribunals (Constitution and Rules of Procedure) (Early Conciliation: Exemption and Rules of Procedure) (Amendment) Regulations 2020 SI No 1003 regs 10A and 10B.
132 ET Regs 2013 Sch 1 r26.

dismissed.[133] For example, the letter might say that the judge is think-ing of striking out an unfair dismissal claim because the employee does not appear to have two years' continuous service. It is essential that the claimant takes such a letter seriously and responds within the time limit set, addressing the particular reasons which the judge has given. If the claimant does not send in a written explanation by that date, the claim will automatically be dismissed and the parties will be notified. If the claimant does send in written comments by the relevant date, a judge will read them and either decide on the paperwork whether to allow the claim, or will fix a hearing with the claimant to discuss the matter. The employer can attend and particip-ate if s/he wants.

20.101   There are equivalent rules if a judge thinks the response or part of it has no reasonable prospect of success.[134] If the whole response is dismissed, the consequences will be as if no ET3 was ever presented (see para 20.90). It is relatively unusual for the tribunal to write this kind of letter to the parties. Therefore, if the claimant receives such a letter, s/he should realise it means his/her position looks very weak on paper. It is an important reason why the claimant should try to get good advice at the outset as to his/her chances of success and to get assistance in writing the ET1 in a way which highlights a sensible legal and evidential basis for his/her claim.

20.102   As an alternative to this specific initial consideration process, an employment judge who has doubts about the strength of all or part of a claim, rather than ask the claimant for any written comments, may go straight to a preliminary hearing at which it will be decided whether to strike out the claim for having no reasonable prospects of success or to order a costs deposit on grounds of having little reasonable prospects of success. This type of hearing has become increasingly common, mainly for cases involving allegations of whistleblowing or discrimination without any obvious evidential foundation. The grounds and procedure for striking out in this way are discussed further at paras 20.111 and 20.165 onwards and for deposit orders at para 20.167 onwards. The important point to remember is that if the tribunal arranges this kind of preliminary hearing, the case on the ET1 probably looks very weak indeed. This is either because the claimant has a good case but the ET1 has been written badly, or because the claimant has no evidence to support his/her gut feeling that s/he has been treated unlawfully. Even if the claimant escapes without a strike out or deposit, it does not mean

---

133 ET Regs 2013 Sch 1 r27.
134 ET Regs 2013 Sch 1 r28.

the claim is strong and it does not mean there is no risk of having costs awarded against him/her if s/he ultimately loses. On the contrary. The claimant should listen very carefully to what the judge says because if s/he has escaped a strike out or deposit warning by the skin of his/her teeth, s/he could still end up paying the employer a lot of money by way of costs at the end of the day.

20.103   One other possibility, whether or not the claimant receives an initial consideration letter or is asked to attend this kind of preliminary hearing, is that it is not the whole claim which looks weak, but only parts of it. The claimant may have one or two reasonable claims buried among a mass of peripheral complaints. Again, this is particularly common in whistleblowing or discrimination claims where there is a temptation to list a large number of incidents as unlawful detriments instead of keeping them in the background and concentrating on only a few major incidents which have a financial value and the best chance of being proved.

Likely stages of case preparation

20.104 If none of the above difficulties arise, the usual preparation stages can be summarised as follows (more details will be set out later in this chapter):[135]

- In England and Wales, either with the acknowledgment of claim form or when the ET3 is sent to the claimant, a tribunal is likely to send out a letter with a table setting out the standard case management orders.[136] Typically this will order the following steps to be taken on certain dates or within a certain number of weeks:
  - that the claimant sends the employer a schedule of loss;
  - mutual disclosure of documents;
  - agreement of a trial bundle;
  - exchange of witness statements.

  Sometimes this is referred to as a 'case management timetable' or 'case management directions'. A hearing date may also be notified at this stage. Where claims are more complicated, eg a whistleblowing or discrimination claim, the tribunal may instead notify the parties of a preliminary hearing to deal with case management.

---

135 See also appendix A at A1 for a checklist of all the main procedural steps.
136 See appendix C at C6 for an example.

- Promptly following receipt of the ET3, the claimant should write to the employer asking for any additional information or written answers which s/he needs. In a straightforward unfair dismissal claim where the employer has provided a detailed ET3, this may not be necessary.
- After disclosure of documents on the date set in the tribunal's case management timetable, if the claimant believes the employer has omitted important documents which are in the employer's possession, s/he should immediately write to the employer asking for these to be provided within a certain timescale, normally 14 days.[137]
- If the employer does not supply the requested information and documents, the claimant should write to the ET, explaining this and asking for an order. This letter is copied to the employer together with a letter informing the employer that s/he must send any objections to the tribunal as soon as possible.
- The ET may send the employer an order to supply the additional information or documents by a certain date, usually in 14 days' time. A copy of the order is sent to the claimant. Alternatively, the ET may refuse to make an order or cut down the information requested.
- If the order is not complied with, the ET can be asked to make an order for costs or to strike out all or part of the employer's ET3 or to debar the employer from defending altogether. Striking out is unusual on this ground, but it can happen where there has been a continual failure to comply with orders.[138]
- Some orders for additional information or documents warn the employer that 'unless' the order is complied with on time, the ET3 will automatically be struck out.[139] If the original order did not contain this warning, an ET cannot strike out without first writing to the employer, inviting him/her to give reasons why s/he should not be struck out.[140] The employer then tends to supply the ordered information.
- The employer can ask the tribunal to vary or set aside the original order for documents etc, especially if s/he had no chance to comment before the order was made.[141] The application must be

---

137 See appendix C at C8 for an example.
138 See ET Regs 2013 Sch 1 r37(1)(c); and para 20.111 onwards.
139 ET Regs 2013 Sch 1 r38. These are called 'unless orders'.
140 ET Regs 2013 Sch 1 r37(2).
141 ET Regs 2013 Sch 1 r29.

copied to the claimant, who must be notified of his/her right to object.[142]

- Each of the above steps regarding disclosure and additional information can happen in reverse if the employer wants to ask the claimant for more information.

- After disclosure of documents, one of the parties has to put the most important documents together into a file or 'trial bundle' (in Scotland, known as a bundle or inventory of 'productions') which will be used at the final hearing. A copy must be supplied to the other party on the ordered date and extra copies brought to the tribunal on the day of the hearing.

- Witness statements must then be exchanged on the date ordered.

- In Scotland, there is less likely to be a standard set of case management orders from the tribunal. This makes it particularly important that the claimant takes the initiative on receiving the ET3 and writes to the employer asking for disclosure of all relevant documents, whether helpful to the employer's case or not, as well as any required additional information and written answers. Witness statements are unlikely to be used unless specifically agreed.

Timescales in any orders against the claimant should be taken extremely seriously, as ETs have been known to order costs against claimants who have failed to comply or even to strike them out for continuous failure. It is no defence that the representative is inexperienced or, for example, a very busy trade union official.

20.105   Although the ET is likely to have sent out standard case management orders at an early stage, it is recommended that, on receiving the ET3, the adviser should write to the employer asking for any additional information which s/he requires. Do not delay in writing this first letter. It is important to allow enough time to prepare the case. Many steps need to be taken after getting documents and information from the employer, including discussing these with the claimant, writing witness statements and agreeing a trial bundle. Some ETs fix hearing dates very quickly and the claimant may not have left enough time to gather the information needed. Although the employer should always be asked for the information voluntarily first, there is a risk in delaying going for an order if the information is not supplied within, say, 14 days. If there is a real indication that the information is coming shortly, then it is worth waiting, because there is always the fear that the ET will refuse to order some of the requested information. On the other hand, there is a risk of getting

142 ET Regs 2013 Sch 1 r30.

strung along by the employer for a long period, at the end of which no information is volunteered and time has run out to get an order.

20.106　Good case preparation is vitally important to the successful outcome of a tribunal case. The claimant must make sure s/he does get all relevant documents from the employer, because documents often contain the most revealing evidence. S/he must ensure s/he understands the employer's defence well in advance of exchange of witness statements, so that s/he can address any relevant points in his/her witness statement. S/he needs to know what is said about the reason for dismissal and the procedural steps which were followed. S/he needs to make sure s/he gets the employer's witness statements in enough time to read them closely and prepare cross-examination for the hearing. Efficient case preparation may also put pressure on an employer which leads to a good settlement. If the claimant keeps to all the time limits and chases the employer regarding any delays, settlement may come to be seen by the employer as an attractive option.

20.107　Having said that, case preparation can become very argumentative, with one or both parties not sticking to time limits and the other party complaining to the tribunal. This is very stressful and can lead to a downward spiral ending in costs or even strike out. In some circumstances, it may be useful to remind the employer that the 'overriding objective' now says parties must co-operate with each other (see para 20.41). Both sides need to apply common sense. If the claimant knows s/he cannot meet a deadline for a good reason, it is a good idea to ask the employer in advance for a short extension of time and explain why. Then s/he must keep to the new date. Similarly, if the employer asks for a short extension, it usually pays off to agree, as long as it does not cause any major problems by getting too near to the date of the final hearing. There is nothing unusual or suspicious about small delays in the case management timetable. If agreement cannot be reached, ask the tribunal well in advance for a time extension, explaining why. Do not get into the habit of asking for extra time at every stage. That creates a bad impression, and the tribunal will start saying no.

20.108　The tribunal's main focus will be on ensuring that the case is well prepared in good time for the final hearing. It will not want to get involved in squabbles between the parties and mutual recriminations about non-compliance with orders. Although it can be frustrating, it will rarely help the claimant win his/her case to point out that the employer has been obstructive in case preparation. The tribunal will be primarily concerned with whether there can be a fair hearing on the appointed day. The key issue is usually whether each party has had sufficient time – which may not mean a great deal of time – to read each other's documents and witness statements and find his/her way around the trial bundle.

20.109   It is helpful to understand how much discretion and flexibility tribunals have under the 2013 rules. The idea is that, rather than get bogged down in rigid rules restricting what they can do, tribunals are free to focus on the realities of fair case preparation. The aim is to get both parties to a fair hearing where they are in a position to argue their case properly. The tribunal will not be happy if one party's failure to abide by case management orders costs the other party unnecessary time and money.

20.110   These are some of the key generic rules in the ET Regs 2013:

- Sch 1 r29: The tribunal can make case management orders and send these to the parties at any stage, on its own initiative or at the request of a party. It can also vary or set aside earlier case management orders where that is 'necessary in the interests of justice', especially where an affected party had no chance to comment before the order was made. Variation of an order will only be 'in the interests of justice' if there has been a material change in circumstances since the order was made or the order was based on misleading facts or for other exceptional reasons.[143] The reason for this restriction is to give parties some certainty during case preparation, by preventing matters being endlessly reopened.

- Sch 1 r30: Either party can apply for a case management order in writing or at a hearing. If applying in writing, the party must tell the other party to send any objections to the tribunal as soon as possible. If the claimant is notified of an application by the employer, s/he should therefore ensure s/he writes to the tribunal with any objection by return and marked 'urgent' as the tribunal may not wait very long before deciding the matter.

- Sch 1 r92: Whenever a party sends any communication to a tribunal (except for an application for a witness order), s/he must send a copy to the other party and let the tribunal know this has happened, eg by writing 'cc' at the foot of the letter to the tribunal or copying the other side into an email. The tribunal can decide no such notification is necessary in the interests of justice.

---

143   *Serco Ltd v Wells* UKEAT/0330/15. See also *Hart v English Heritage (Historic Buildings and Monuments Commission for England)* [2006] IRLR 915, EAT. where a potentially significant point had not previously been argued.

- Sch 1 r70: As mentioned above, rule 29 allows case management orders to be varied in certain circumstances. Rule 70 contains a slightly more formal process for judgments to be 'reconsidered'.[144] The demarcation between orders and judgments is not always clear, but essentially a judgment is a decision which makes the final decision regarding liability, remedy or costs, and a 'case management order' is any other decision relating to the conduct of the proceedings.[145] A decision to strike out all or part of a claim or response is a 'judgment'.
- Sch 1 r5: The tribunal can extend or shorten any time limit, including retrospectively.
- Sch 1 r6: Any failure to comply with a tribunal order or procedural rule does not in itself invalidate the proceedings. The tribunal can react in various ways, eg by varying or waiving the requirement; by striking out the claim or response; by restricting a party's participation in the proceedings; or by awarding costs.

Striking out

20.111   At any time, on its own initiative or on the application of either party, an ET may strike out all or part of a tribunal claim or response on grounds that it is scandalous or vexatious or has no reasonable prospect of success, or that the way the claimant or employer is conducting the proceedings is scandalous, unreasonable or vexatious.[146] It can also strike out for non-compliance with an order or because the claim or response is not being actively pursued or because it is no longer possible to have a fair hearing of the claim or response. Before striking out, the ET must give the relevant party the opportunity to give reasons in writing or, if requested, at a hearing, why the order should not be made.[147]

20.112   Striking out is a very serious step and should not be taken lightly.[148] It should be rare in whistleblowing or discrimination cases to strike out on the ground of no reasonable prospect of success, as these issues are particularly fact-sensitive and dependent on evidence being heard.[149] Where striking out is considered for procedural

---

144 See para 20.236 for more detail.
145 ET Regs 2013 Sch 1 r1(3).
146 ET Regs 2013 Sch 1 r37(1).
147 ET Regs 2013 Sch 1 r37(2).
148 *De Keyser Ltd v Wilson* [2001] IRLR 324, EAT; *Blockbuster Entertainment v James* [2006] EWCA Civ 684.
149 *North Glamorgan NHS Trust v Ezsias* [2007] EWCA Civ 330; [2007] IRLR 603.

abuses, the crucial issue is whether a fair trial is still possible and whether a lesser sanction may be appropriate.[150] A striking out order is unlikely to be made if it is still possible to have a fair hearing, eg because by the time the ET threatens to strike out, the employer finally produces the ordered information and documents.[151] A rare exception occurred in one case where the employer ignored various interim orders and eventually produced a lengthy witness statement on the first day of the hearing, having previously served no witness statements. The EAT agreed that the ET was entitled to strike out the employer's defence, because the employer had gained an unfair advantage by having already seen the claimant's witness statements, and also because there was no guarantee that the claimant's pro bono representative would still be available if the hearing was postponed for the claimant to deal with the unexpected witness statement.[152] In general, however, striking a party out for non-compliance with procedures should only be a last resort, where a fair hearing is no longer possible; a more appropriate step in a serious case may be for a tribunal to issue an 'unless order' (see next paragraph), which at least acts as a warning to the party of the consequences of continuing not to co-operate.[153]

20.113   An 'unless order' under ET Regs 2013 Sch 1 r38 is more draconian than a normal order – it is an order which states that unless it is complied with, the claim or response (as relevant) will be struck out on the date of non-compliance without the need for a hearing or to give notice to the relevant party. This will be an automatic strike-out without the tribunal exercising its discretion any further. The tribunal will give the parties written notice that the strike-out has occurred.

20.114   The ET can be asked to set aside a strike-out arising from an 'unless order' if it is in the interests of justice to do so.[154] A party must write to the tribunal within 14 days of the date the notice of strike-out was sent. The ET may make a decision on paper unless the party requests a hearing. If a claim or response is struck out in the normal way, ie not as a result of an 'unless order', the tribunal can be asked to reconsider under rule 70 (assuming a strike out is a judgment, but if not, to vary the order under rule 29).

---

150 *Bolch v Chipman* [2004] IRLR 140, EAT.
151 *National Grid Company plc v Virdee* [1992] IRLR 555, EAT.
152 *Premium Care Homes Ltd v Osborne* UKEAT/0077/06.
153 *Abegaze v Shrewsbury College of Arts & Technology* [2009] EWCA Civ 96; [2010] IRLR 238; *Girvan v Humberside Probation Trust* UKEAT/0197/09.
154 ET Regs 2013 Sch 1 r37(2).

20.115   When the tribunal decides whether to overturn the striking-out, the sort of factors which are relevant are the reason for the procedural failure, and in particular: whether it is deliberate; the seriousness of the procedural failure; the prejudice to the other party; and whether a fair trial remains possible.[155] It will be more difficult to overturn a striking out which followed an 'unless order', because the party was put squarely on notice of the importance of complying with the order. However, this is just one factor.[156]

Requesting additional information and written answers

20.116   As explained below, it is important to get all relevant and useful documents which are in the employer's possession. If the ET3 is vague or there is some unknown information which is not contained in documents, the claimant can ask written questions and obtain written answers. This is often referred to as asking for 'additional information'.[157]

20.117   Where the employer asks that the claimant give more detail of what s/he is claiming, this is often referred to as giving 'particulars' or 'particularising' the claim ('specification' in Scotland). Equally, employers might be asked to 'particularise' their response where their ET3 is very vague. This jargon dates back to a time when asking a party to spell out parts of his/her claim or response was called 'requesting further and better particulars'.

20.118   One important function of the claimant seeking additional information is to make sure s/he understands the employer's defence and can prepare to answer it. The claimant should ask for clarification of vague statements in the ET3, eg if the employer says in the ET3: 'We warned the claimant on numerous occasions as to her conduct at work', a relevant request for information would be: 'Please state in respect of each warning the date when the claimant was warned, by whom, and the nature of the warning given'.

20.119   As well as questions relating to matters set out by the employer in the ET3, the claimant can also ask questions to clarify any issue likely to arise for determination or to ascertain information relevant to the claim. For example, where the claimant was dismissed for fighting at

---

155 *Thind v Salvesen Logistics Ltd* UKEAT/0487/09.
156 *Thind v Salvesen Logistics Ltd* UKEAT/0487/09.
157 The tribunal can make these orders under ET Regs 2013 Sch 1 rr29 and 30.

work, s/he could ask: 'What action was taken against the other person involved in the fight?'[158]

20.120   The claimant should not ask too many detailed questions. The aim is not to conduct the whole case on paper. Cross-examination is usually reserved for the full ET hearing. It is best just to ask three or four very important questions (if any). If the employer refuses to answer on the ground that 'You are not entitled to this because you have asked for evidence about matters not contained in the ET3', a good reply (if applicable) would be that the questions are relevant to the issues arising for determination and will save time at the hearing if established in advance.

20.121   If the employer will not answer the questions voluntarily, the claimant needs to ask the tribunal for an order under Sch 1 r30.[159] As already stated, an ET may be reluctant to order too much additional information if it is unnecessary at this stage of case preparation and would be expensive or time-consuming for the employer to answer. So the temptation to ask for too much should be avoided unless it is necessary because of the vagueness of the ET3.

20.122   All the above points will apply in reverse if the employer asks the claimant for additional information regarding the ET1. If the ET1 is well written and explains the basis for the claim, especially in the case of an ordinary unfair dismissal claim, it should not be necessary to provide extra detail. However, in a more complex case, eg for automatic unfair dismissal based on whistleblowing, the claimant may not have clearly identified when s/he says s/he blew the whistle or to whom. It is a natural reaction to resist giving extra information unless ordered to do so by the tribunal. Sometimes, this is because of a concern that it would give too much away to the employer before the employer has committed him/herself to an account of events which s/he may not be able to prove. On the other hand, the questions may be fair enough and be likely to be ordered by the tribunal, in which case it is sensible to prepare the answers in any event, in case an order is made that they be supplied at short notice.

Disclosure

20.123   Disclosure is the method by which the claimant can find out about and obtain documents which are in the employer's possession. The old-fashioned legal word for this is 'discovery'. In Scotland, it is called

---

158   For a further example, see appendix C at C8, question 2.
159   See para 20.128 onwards.

'recovery'. Strictly speaking, an order for disclosure only obliges the employer to produce a list of the requested documents. This is combined with an order for inspection, which allows the documents to be seen and copies taken at the claimant's expense. In practice, the ET usually simply asks the employer to send a list and copies to the claimant and to allow inspection of the originals if requested. This is useful because the employer tends not to ask for copying costs in this situation and s/he can always be asked to bring the originals to the hearing. If there is any suspicion at all about whether documents are genuine or have been manipulated, the originals should be inspected at this stage. This will involve a visit to the offices of the employer or employer's representative. Because so much communication has occurred by email as a result of the pandemic, it has become common for employers to provide the documents electronically. If the claimant finds it difficult to look at documents on a computer screen, s/he should ask for hard copies.

20.124　　All courts tend to prefer documents to witnesses and the ET is no exception. This is particularly true of contemporaneous documents. Cases are often won or lost on the strength of the documents before the ET, and it is essential that all relevant documents are available at the hearing. The practice regarding disclosure has become more formal than it used to be. An ET can order such disclosure and inspection as might be granted by a county court, or, in Scotland, by a sheriff.[160] In England and Wales, this means as set out by Part 31 of the Civil Procedure Rules (CPR) 1998.[161] The ET's standard case management timetable in England and Wales commonly states something like this:

> By (date) the claimant and the respondent shall send each other a list of any documents that they wish to refer to at the hearing or which are relevant to the case. They shall send each other a copy of any of these documents if requested to do so.[162]

It may be worth waiting for the date set in the tribunal's original case management timetable to see what the employer volunteers, but an adviser should specifically ask the employer for any important additional documents which are not disclosed and which s/he believes the employer has. In Scotland, a party's duty is to disclose the

---

160　ET Regs 2013 Sch 1 r31.

161　Available at: www.justice.gov.uk/courts/procedure-rules/civil.

162　In Scotland the position is looser. Practice Direction 1 for Scotland requires legally represented parties to send a list of documents to be relied on at the hearing to the other side no later than 14 days before the hearing.

documents on which s/he intends to rely 14 days before the hearing.[163] This is very late if there is going to be any dispute. If the claimant wants to prepare sooner and be sure s/he sees all the documents in the employer's possession (not just those which the employer wants to use), s/he needs to ask specifically at an earlier stage, ideally on receiving the ET3.

20.125　The ET may be more ready to order disclosure than additional information, although it will not allow wide-ranging and speculative requests. The documents must be relevant and must also be necessary for the fair disposal of the case. A document is relevant if it helps prove the claimant's case or damages the employer's case.[164] These principles apply even if the documents are confidential, although a tribunal may then be willing to focus on what is really necessary, eg by ordering partial disclosure or allowing certain information to be 'redacted' (blacked out).[165]

20.126　In unfair dismissal cases, it is usually relevant to seek disclosure of all contractual documents or statements of terms and conditions and any personnel file and written warnings relied on. If the claimant has a long history of grievances, disputes and disciplinary action, it may be unwise to ask for the whole personnel file, and it is better just to specify documents which are relevant to the current claim. The employer should disclose relevant electronic documents, including emails, word-processed documents and databases, which may be stored on servers and back-up systems and even 'deleted'. The claimant needs to agree with the employer in what form such documents should be disclosed (printed out, via email, etc).[166] If tampering is suspected of documents which have been created on computer, ask for these to be emailed to the claimant's/representative's office. The dates that documents were generated can often be checked electronically. Finally, it is always a good idea to request: 'any other documents in the employer's possession, power or control which are relevant to the case, whether helpful to the employer or not'. The ET will usually order this category of documents and it prevents the employer holding back useful documents or surprising the claimant with unseen documents on the day of the hearing. Letters between

---

163 Practice Direction 1 for Scotland.

164 *Compagnie Financière du Pacifique v Peruvian Guano Co* (1882) 11 QB 55, CA.

165 *Nassé v Science Research Council; Vyas v Leyland Cars* [1979] IRLR 465, HL; *Plymouth City Council v White* UKEAT/0333/13. In a trade union context, see *Dhanda v TSB Bank PLC* UKEAT/0294/17.

166 CPR Practice Direction (PD) 31B gives guidelines for the civil courts on electronic disclosure.

the parties or to ACAS concerning possible settlement of the claim must not be produced on disclosure or put before the ET unless each party expressly agrees.[167] See paras 9.20–9.25 for when documents are 'privileged' and therefore not shown to the other side.

20.127 Under the usual case management timetable in England and Wales, a claimant is also ordered to disclose relevant documents. Normally s/he has nothing which the employer does not also have, but tribunals expect the claimant to disclose correspondence relating to efforts to find a new job ('mitigation'). This can be updated just before the hearing by inclusion in the trial bundle. Especially in discrimination cases, employees sometimes have diaries which they wrote at the time. A diary probably has to be disclosed, but check whether it contains 'privileged' information (eg notes of legal advice) and whether it was written at the time or only after the case started as an aide-mémoire. Where there are tape recordings, text messages or electronic documents, consider whether these need to be produced in the tribunal in their original form and if so, how. Also check whether transcripts are necessary and who will prepare and pay for them.[168]

Applying for an order

20.128 If the employer will not voluntarily supply the requested documents and information or takes too long in doing so, it is necessary to apply for an order. Do not delay in applying. If the application is made too close to the hearing, an order is unlikely to be made, either because of slow ET administration, or because it is decided to leave matters to the hearing date. The procedure is set out in ET Regs 2013 Sch 1 r30. To apply for an order, the claimant must write to the ET, setting out what s/he wants by way of additional information, documents, etc. S/he should send a copy of the original request to the employer and indicate the employer's response. Unless it is obvious, it may be useful to explain very briefly why the questions are relevant and how they fit with the 'overriding objective' (see para 20.39). Make the letter to the tribunal short and clear, and number each request. Give the tribunal all the necessary information in one letter. Do not expect the tribunal to start cross-referring numerous documents in order to work out what is being asked for.

20.129 At the same time as writing to the ET, the claimant must send the employer a copy of the letter to the tribunal. The letter to the employer

167 Or otherwise waives privilege. See paras 9.19–9.21.
168 See para 9.17.

must state that any objection to the application must be sent to the ET as soon as possible.[169] The claimant must confirm in writing to the ET that this requirement has been complied with. The simplest way to do this is for the claimant to write 'cc (the respondent)' at the foot of the letter to the ET. The ET may not wait very long for the employer to send in an objection if time is pressing. Indeed, the ET has power to decide no such notification was necessary in the interests of justice.

20.130   The order will usually be considered by the ET on the paperwork, although if a preliminary hearing is already scheduled, the request may well be considered then.

20.131   The request for an order will be considered by an employment judge. It is not unusual for a request to be refused or reduced. This can be a real concern because it is hard to challenge. If the document or information is important, the ET can be asked to change its mind regarding its decision to refuse an order on grounds that it is necessary in the interests of justice.[170] It is best to do this as soon as possible and put forward some additional arguments. The ET cannot change an earlier decision which has affected the parties' preparation of their cases unless there has been a material change in circumstances.[171] This is to ensure that procedural decisions are not endlessly reopened by the parties.

20.132   If an order is made, the employer can ask the ET to withdraw or vary it, especially if s/he had no reasonable opportunity to make comments in advance.[172] Whether it is the claimant or the employer who asks the tribunal to change its mind, the application should be sent to the other side under Sch 1 r30.[173] If the tribunal refuses to withdraw the order and the employer fails to comply with it, the claimant should write informing the tribunal of this (unless s/he has agreed a small time extension with the employer).[174] The tribunal can then be asked to strike out the employer or to issue an 'unless order' or to award costs.

20.133   In procedural terms, the ET cannot be asked formally to 'reconsider'[175] a case management order or refusal to make an order, but as already explained, it can simply be asked to change its mind under

169 ET Regs 2013 Sch 1 r30(2).
170 ET Regs 2013 Sch 1 r29; see para 20.110.
171 See para 20.110.
172 ET Regs 2013 Sch 1 r29.
173 See para 20.110.
174 See para 20.107 regarding a sensible approach to case preparation.
175 Ie under ET Regs 2013 Sch 1 r70.

Sch 1 r29 if appropriate. It is also possible to appeal to the EAT if the ET will not change its mind, but only if there is an error of law or perversity and the claimant's case is clearly prejudiced. Appeals concerning orders, or refused orders, for documents or additional information are very rare and would not normally be embarked upon unless the matter was of central importance.

20.134   The same procedure applies in reverse if it is the employer who wants an order against the claimant.

Orders against third parties

20.135 The ET has power to order a third party to disclose documents or provide additional information.[176] For example, an employment agency could be ordered to provide documents relating to the wording of a job advertisement if that was not in the employer's possession.

Witness orders

20.136 A claimant can apply for a witness order requiring the attendance of any person as a witness[177] if that person can give relevant evidence which is necessary (because it is disputed) and s/he will not attend voluntarily.[178] A witness can also be ordered to produce documents. This is useful where documents are held by someone other than the employer, who will not provide copies voluntarily. A request for an order should be sent to the ET in good time for the hearing, setting out the name and home or work address of the witness. It should very briefly summarise why the evidence is relevant and necessary and state that the witness is not prepared to attend the hearing voluntarily.[179] Unlike requests for case management orders, the letter sent to the ET asking for a witness statement is not routinely copied to the employer, though in exceptional circumstances the ET can ask the employer's views.[180] If the ET issues a witness order, it will send it direct to the witness, and must notify each side that an order has been made and the name of the witness. A witness who fails to attend

---

176 ET Regs 2013 Sch 1 r31 states that an order can be made against 'any person'.
177 ET Regs 2013 Sch 1 r32.
178 *Dada v Metal Box Co* [1974] ICR 559; [1974] IRLR 251, NIRC.
179 See appendix C at C11 for an example.
180 ET Regs 2013 Sch 1 r92. *Christie v Paul, Weiss, Rifkind, Wharton & Garrison LLP & others* UKEAT/0137/19 where the witness had signed a non-disclosure agreement.

can be fined up to £1,000 unless the witness successfully applies to the ET before the hearing for the order to be set aside.

20.137   An order should be obtained only if the witness is co-operative, but does not want to attend without an order (usually to protect the witness, so that the witness can tell his/her employer that s/he is not attending the hearing voluntarily, or because s/he is in a new job and cannot get the time off). A witness who does not want to attend at all, or who is forced to do so, is almost invariably a bad witness. Apart from anything else, it will be hard to get a statement from an unwilling witness in advance of the hearing, so there is no certainty as to what s/he will say. Nor is it a good idea for the claimant to call an unhelpful management witness simply in order to cross-examine him/her. First of all, it is a general rule of evidence that a party cannot cross-examine his/her own witness on the basis that the witness is not telling the truth, unless the tribunal gives the party permission to treat the witness as 'hostile'. This has a technical meaning. It does not mean simply unfriendly, but essentially that the witness is deliberately not telling the truth in order to damage the party's case. The ET may not be bound by such a rule, but it may well take the same approach. Second, the idea that the claimant can successfully cross-examine a hostile witness underestimates the damage that witness's evidence is likely to do to the claimant's case in the first place, and usually overestimates what the claimant is likely to achieve through cross-examination. Even if a witness is friendly and willing to come, it is important to think about how his/her evidence is relevant to the issues in the case, and whether s/he might say anything which is positively unhelpful when questioned by the employer. Finally, remember that whether or not a claimant's witnesses come voluntarily, a tribunal may order the claimant to pay their expenses (see para 20.265).

Hearing dates and postponements

20.138   The legal jargon for fixing a hearing date is 'listing'. In Scotland, the ET usually consults each side about availability before fixing a hearing date, although readers should check this is still happening. The normal practice in England and Wales is for the ET to fix the date and then send each side a notice of hearing. These days, many tribunals send out a date for an unfair dismissal hearing at the same time as acknowledging receipt of the ET1 and copying it to the employer.[181] Each party must receive at least 14 days' notice of the full

181 See appendix C at C6 for an example.

hearing.[182] Reasonable notice must be given of any preliminary hearing, and if it involves any preliminary issues, notice must be at least 14 days and specify what the preliminary issues are.[183] Advisers should read the notice of hearing carefully to check what kind of hearing is referred to. Sometimes parties fail to realise that the notice is calling them to a preliminary hearing and not the full hearing.

20.139   The standard notice is likely to list an unfair dismissal case for a one-day hearing and invite parties to write in if that is not long enough. It is important to make the correct time estimate, as it is highly undesirable for a case to go part-heard (ie to start and not finish) as the follow-up date may not be for some time afterwards. Remember that a one-day hearing is not very long when it has to include time for the tribunal to make its decision. It may only allow three hours for evidence (ie reading the witness statements, swearing witnesses in, cross-examination, re-examination and ET questions) and closing speeches. As a very rough rule of thumb, this is just long enough for about three very short witnesses including the claimant – or two witnesses if the witness statements are fairly long.

20.140   The notice of hearing may tell the parties that if they feel the allocated time is not long enough, they should write in to say so with their reasons and time estimate within 14 days. If the parties do not write in with any objection, they should come prepared to fit into the scheduled time.

20.141   If the date fixed by the tribunal is inconvenient, a postponement (technically known as an 'adjournment') should be requested immediately. If there is a case management preliminary hearing, dates are often fixed on the spot, so it is important to come with diaries and a note of dates to avoid for at least six months ahead for all witnesses.

20.142   If a date is notified by letter (as opposed to in any preliminary hearing), it is essential to check immediately with the claimant and other witnesses that they can attend. It is extremely hard to get a postponement, even with both parties' consent, unless eg a key witness is ill or unavailable or not enough days have been allocated. The ET may be unsympathetic if it is only a representative who is unavailable and may suggest that another representative can surely be found. Small voluntary sector organisations or trade union lay representatives need to explain the realities of how representation is

182 ET Regs 2013 Sch 1 r58.
183 ET Regs 2013 Sch 1 r54, amended with effect from 6 October 2021 by the Employment Tribunals (Constitution and Rules of Procedure) (Early Conciliation: Exemptions and Rules of Procedure) (Amendment) Regulations 2021 SI No 1037.

organised. Otherwise, there is a risk that the person who suffers will be the low-paid claimant who cannot afford to pay for alternative representation and whose case may be harmed by losing the adviser who has been involved from the beginning. There have been a few successful appeals against such refusals in discrimination cases where law centres and other voluntary advice centres have been involved.[184]

20.143   Due to the pressures on the ET system to process cases quickly, there have been a number of cases where postponements have been found to be unreasonably refused. In certain circumstances, inadequate and late disclosure of documents by the employer may be a ground for postponement, but only if it prevents the claimant from dealing with his/her claim properly.[185] A postponement is unlikely on this ground unless it causes real problems. It is quite common for a few extra documents to be produced by the employer at the last minute.

20.144   In a key case under the Human Rights Act 1998,[186] the Court of Appeal said that although a postponement is a discretionary matter for the tribunal, some postponements must be granted if not to do so amounts to a denial of justice. To comply with the right to a fair trial under ECHR Article 6,[187] if a party is unable to be present through no fault of his/her own, s/he must usually be granted a postponement, however inconvenient to the ET and other side. The onus is on the party wanting a postponement to prove a genuine need for it. Having said that, if medical evidence indicates the claimant will never be fit to attend a hearing, there will come a point where the tribunal can refuse a postponement or strike the case out because continuing to wait will be pointless and will eventually make a fair trial impossible.[188] In one case, the EAT overturned an ET's last-minute decision to extend the length of a hearing, where it meant that each side would lose the barrister they had instructed. The EAT said the tribunal's worthy consideration of trying to get the case heard

---

184 *Christou v Morpheus and Symes* [1999] UKEAT 498_99_2704; *Yearwood v Royal Mail* [1997] UKEAT 843_97_1107; *De Souza v British Telecom and Lyon* EAT/400/96.

185 *Eastwood v Winckworth Sherwood* UKEAT/0174/05 sets out guidelines.

186 *Teinaz v Wandsworth LBC* [2002] IRLR 721, CA. For an illustration, see *Chang-tave v (1) Haydon School (2) Marchand* UKEAT/0153/10.

187 See paras 3.23–3.24.

188 *Riley v The Crown Prosecution Service* [2013] EWCA Civ 951. *Ukoro v Independent Workers' Union of Great Britain and others* UKEAT/0128/19 is a useful recent example of these issues.

quickly, bearing in mind the dismissal was over a year earlier, had wrongly taken precedence over a joint well-reasoned application to postpone made responsibly by represented parties.[189]

20.145   To improve the chances of persuading an ET to grant a postponement, or a successful appeal otherwise, it is important generally to conduct the case promptly and efficiently, to request any necessary postponement as soon as the problematic date is notified, to explain fully in a letter to the ET why the postponement is needed and why it will harm the claimant's case if the representative is unavailable. If a holiday was booked prior to the notice of hearing going out, documentary evidence should be provided of the booking and holiday dates. It is also helpful to indicate available future dates as flexibly and imminently as possible.[190] The employer needs to be notified of the application to postpone in the usual way.[191] In any event, it is worth telephoning the employer first to try to get an agreement for the postponement.

20.146   Where a postponement is requested because the claimant is medically unfit to attend, it is crucial to get a strong letter from the claimant's doctor, specifying exactly the nature of the health condition concerned, stating that the claimant cannot attend the hearing and explaining how his/her ill-health prevents him/her from doing so. It is not enough for the doctor to say that the claimant is unfit to attend work, since that is a different matter. The letter or report should not use vague words like 'stress' and 'anxiety', but should be clear about symptoms, their causes and severity.[192] It is also useful if the doctor adds information derived from his/her own observations as opposed to apparently repeating only what the claimant has told him/her. If possible, the doctor should give some indication of the claimant's prognosis and when s/he will be fit to attend. Doctors often do not realise the importance of addressing specific issues in their letter. It is essential to explain to them exactly what is needed and why. If the ET has doubts, it can ask for further medical evidence. However, it is absurd to criticise a party for not attending the hearing to give evidence of his/her condition when a doctor has advised him/her on medical grounds not to attend.[193]

---

189 *Chancerygate (Business Centre) Ltd v Jenkins* UKEAT/0212/10 and 0213/10.
190 *Tillingbourne Bus Co Ltd v Norsworthy* [2000] IRLR 10, EAT indicates relevant considerations for the ET.
191 ET Regs 2013 Sch 1 r30. Also see para 20.110.
192 *Andreou v Lord Chancellor's Department* [2002] IRLR 728, CA.
193 *Teinaz v Wandsworth LBC* [2002] IRLR 721, CA.

20.147 Where possible, it is advisable to make any postponement request well in advance of the hearing. Once the hearing date is imminent, the ET clerks should be chased to ensure the application is put in front of a decision-maker as soon as possible. Do not assume that marking an email 'urgent' will suffice. If the request is left too late, it is more likely that the ET will defer the decision to the tribunal on the day. This is problematic because everyone must come ready to go ahead and costs can be wasted if the postponement is agreed. It also makes it less likely that the request will be granted. The ET has a discretion to order that the claimant pay the costs of the respondent if caused by the postponement.[194] Also see the special rules where a postponement request is made less than seven days before the hearing is due to start (para 20.149).

20.148 If the adviser knows in advance of any notice of hearing that there will be problems with certain dates, s/he should write and inform the ET before the dates are set.

20.149 There are particular difficulties in getting a postponement where the application to postpone is made less than seven days before the hearing, or where two or more postponements have been granted in the same proceedings on an application by the same party and that party applies for a further postponement.[195] In either of those situations, the tribunal may only order a postponement if:

a) all other parties consent to the postponement and either it is practicable and appropriate for the purposes of giving the parties the opportunity to resolve their disputes by agreement, or it is otherwise in accordance with the overriding objective; or

b) the application was necessitated by an act or omission of another party or the tribunal; or

c) there are exceptional circumstances.

The ET will give reasons, though these may be very brief, for agreeing or refusing a postponement request where this is a disputed matter.[196] Before applying for a postponement, it will be useful to read the relevant Presidential Guidance.[197]

---

194 See para 20.246 onwards on costs.
195 ET Regs 2013 Sch 1 r30A.
196 ET Regs 2013 Sch 1 r62(1) and (4).
197 Written before the additional restrictions were introduced, but still generally applicable. Available via links for England and Scotland respectively at: www.judiciary.gov.uk/publications/employment-rules-and-legislation-practice-directions/ and: www.judiciary.gov.uk/publications/directions-for-employment-tribunals-scotland/.

Preliminary hearings – overview

20.150 Occasionally the tribunal may arrange a preliminary hearing. There are two types of preliminary hearing. The most common type simply deals with case management, ie the steps needed to get the case ready for hearing. The other type is to decide preliminary issues such as whether the claim was brought in time or whether someone bringing an unfair dismissal claim was an 'employee' as opposed to self-employed. For most routine unfair dismissal claims, preliminary hearings of either kind will be unusual.

20.151   The 2013 rules state that a preliminary hearing can be fixed for the tribunal to do one or more of the following:[198]

a) conduct a preliminary consideration of the claim with the parties and make case management orders;[199]

b) decide any preliminary issue, eg whether the unfair dismissal claim was started within the time limits or whether the claimant was an employee or had two years' service;[200]

c) consider whether the claim or response should be struck out under Sch 1 r37;[201]

d) make a deposit order;[202]

e) explore the possibility of settlement or alternative dispute resolution including judicial mediation.

20.152 The letter notifying the preliminary hearing will set out what will be covered. The hearing will be held in private, ie without access to the press or public, except for any part of the hearing involving issues in category b) or c). If there are such issues, the tribunal has power to direct that the whole hearing is held in public.[203]

20.153   Category e) is there to encourage parties to settle their disputes without going to a final hearing. It does not mean that the tribunal will conduct a mediation service at the preliminary hearing, but that it may discuss with the parties whether they have explored the possibilities. The parties should not be required to go into details of any negotiations which have already taken place, since these are likely to

---

198 ET Regs 2013 Sch 1 r53.
199 See paras 20.154–20.160.
200 See paras 20.161–20.164.
201 See paras 20.111 and 20.165–20.166 for grounds for strike out under ET Regs 2013 Sch 1 r37.
202 See paras 20.167–20.172.
203 ET Regs 2013 Sch 1 r56.

be 'privileged' (off the record).[204] Nor should the claimant be expected to tell the tribunal how much s/he would accept by way of settlement, nor the employer to tell the tribunal how much s/he would be prepared to offer. Nevertheless, where both parties are open to the idea of settlement, it can be useful if the tribunal prompts a discussion. There is also a little used judicial assessment procedure which may encourage negotiation (see para 21.54). A very good opportunity to reach an early agreement is to suggest a quick chat in the waiting room after the preliminary hearing is completed.

Preliminary hearings – case management

20.154   Category a) in the list at para 20.151 is simply concerned with case management. If no category b), c) or d) matters are involved, the preliminary hearing will be conducted informally before an employment judge sitting alone, attended by each party or his/her representatives, at which the preparation of the case is moved on. It will be a private hearing.

20.155   Case management preliminary hearings are unlikely to be fixed in the vast majority of unfair dismissal or pay claims. They tend to be arranged to help with the management of large complex cases, eg with multiple claimants or involving claims of automatic unfair dismissal and pre-dismissal detriments such as occur in whistleblowing claims. Most tribunal regions will also routinely list a preliminary hearing to carry out case management in discrimination cases.[205] There can be more than one preliminary hearing in a case, but this is uncommon because it leads to additional expense for the parties to attend.

20.156   The judge will usually start by identifying a 'list of issues' for the case. The word 'issues' is confusing because it is used in other contexts. However, a 'list of issues' has a specific meaning. It is a technical idea which involves breaking down the key legal – and sometimes factual – stages which will need to be decided by the tribunal to arrive at its final decision. There are examples in appendix A.[206]

20.157   The hearing will also deal with all or any outstanding procedural issues that have not been resolved in correspondence, eg disclosure of documents, fixing hearing dates, or ordering that cases be heard

---

204 See para 9.18 onwards.
205 See para 21.50.
206 See appendix A at A24. The use of a 'list of issues' is only just starting to be introduced in Scotland.

together. The tribunal's orders on those matters are often called 'directions'.

20.158   A preliminary hearing dealing only with case management is likely to take anything from 45 minutes to three hours depending on the complexity of the issues, the clarity of the original ET1, how much is already agreed between the parties and whether the parties are represented.

20.159   Once the ET has sent notification of this kind of preliminary hearing, it is worth trying to agree as much as possible with the employer's representative regarding which documents will be disclosed, when to exchange witness statements, etc. This reduces the chances of getting unsatisfactory orders from the tribunal and may even obviate the need for the preliminary hearing altogether. If agreement cannot be reached, the claimant should come to the hearing with a typed draft list of issues and the orders s/he is seeking. Ideally these should be sent to the employer and tribunal in advance. This gives the claimant (especially if unrepresented) more chance of getting what s/he wants out of the preliminary hearing. Tribunals usually send out a 'case management agenda' form to be completed in advance of the preliminary hearing which asks what each party proposes. It is common for the employment judge to encourage the parties to agree arrangements voluntarily. It is a good idea to be co-operative where possible, but if one of the judge's suggestions would seriously harm the claimant's case, and the claimant wants to preserve the right to appeal, then s/he should not agree, and the judge should be required to make an order.

20.160   Preliminary hearings concerned only with case management are sometimes conducted by telephone conferencing. In the past, this was usually where both parties were represented and had agreed the issues and directions, or in certain regions where long travel distances were involved. Since Covid, nearly all preliminary hearings have usually been conducted this way (see para 20.229). The conference call is set up by the ET, though the parties may be asked to dial in.

Preliminary hearing – preliminary issues

20.161   Category b) in the list at para 20.151 above concerns preliminary issues. This should not be confused with a 'list of issues' as described above. Category b) refers to issues which can be decided before the final hearing, eg as to whether the claimant had two years' service. A preliminary hearing which will cover this ground is more formal and it will be a public hearing, at least the part concerned with those issues. The preliminary issues will be considered by an employment judge alone, unless a party makes a written request that the hearing is conducted by a full tribunal panel. In that case, it will be for an employment judge to decide whether it would be desirable to have a full panel.[207]

20.162   The outcome of the preliminary issues is usually very important to the claimant as it tends to concern whether the ET has jurisdiction to hear his/her case. For example, preliminary hearings are often held where there is a dispute over whether the claimant has been employed for at least two continuous years; was an employee; worked under an illegal contract; commenced proceedings within the time limit; etc. Many of these hearings can be quite lengthy and complex, particularly if they concern TUPE issues or, in a discrimination case, whether the claimant has a disability as defined by the EqA 2010. A full-blown preliminary hearing covering these sorts of issues could take half a day to a full day. On the other hand, preliminary hearings concerning time limits on late unfair dismissal claims tend to be very short, maybe lasting only an hour.

20.163   A preliminary hearing dealing with preliminary issues often takes the form of a full hearing with witnesses and trial bundles, except that it tends to be much shorter. Preparation is as for a full hearing, except that the evidence is collected relating to the preliminary issue alone. If the claimant and any other witnesses are to give evidence, it is normally a good idea to prepare witness statements even if the ET has not made any order to do so. Unless the entire claim is knocked out by the preliminary issues, the employment judge will usually go on to deal with case management arrangements. The claimant should be prepared for this.

20.164   It is not always sensible and cost-effective to hold a preliminary hearing on a preliminary issue. Sometimes, the evidence needed to address the preliminary issue overlaps awkwardly with the evidence relevant to the substantive case. There is also a risk that fact-findings will be made at the preliminary hearing based on inadequate evidence, because it was unclear that certain matters would arise. Such fact-findings could then bind the ET at the final hearing. Or, a preliminary hearing may be suggested to resolve an issue which, even if decided against the claimant, will not save any time because there will still be other outstanding claims covering the same ground. The ET sometimes consults the parties about whether to order a prelim-

207 ET Regs 2013 Sch 1 r55.

inary hearing. If there is no prior consultation, write in promptly when one is ordered if you have any concerns.

Preliminary hearing – striking out and costs deposits

20.165 A preliminary hearing may also be arranged to decide whether to strike out all or part of a claim or response under category c) in para 20.151 above. This part of the preliminary hearing must be held in public. Very often the possibility of making a costs deposit order under category d) is considered at the same time. The grounds for strike out are set out at para 20.111 above. Again, it is unusual for such a preliminary hearing to be held on an ordinary unfair dismissal claim. It is more likely with a complex automatic unfair dismissal claim such as whistleblowing or in discrimination cases.

20.166 Unlike preliminary issues, whether to strike out a claim (or response) for having no reasonable prospect of success is often decided purely on the basis of 'representations' or 'submissions' (ie comments) by the representatives or unrepresented parties, rather than having evidence and listening to witnesses and cross-examination, but there is no absolute rule. Strike-outs for this reason have traditionally been ordered only where there are no factual disputes on key points or where the case is hopeless even if the claimant's version of the facts is proved. Where important facts are disputed, a tribunal should not make impromptu fact-findings or assumptions about which facts will be proved without hearing evidence properly at a full hearing.[208] On the other hand, it may be that the alleged facts can be conclusively disproved by an unambiguous document. Or, a tribunal can decide to listen to evidence on one or two key factual disputes and make fact-findings which will enable it to decide whether there are reasonable prospects of success.[209] It is important to be prepared. The claimant should read the notice of preliminary hearing carefully to see what will be covered, and take notice of any case management orders, eg to bring witness statements or written submissions to the preliminary hearing regarding the strike-out issue.

20.167 Strike-outs are appropriate in extreme cases where there is no reasonable prospect of success. Alternatively, if the ET considers that any complaint or response to that complaint has little reasonable

---

208 *North Glamorgan NHS Trust v Ezsias* [2007] EWCA Civ 330; [2007] IRLR 603; *Tayside Public Transport Co Ltd t/a Travel Dundee v Reilly* [2012] IRLR 755, CS.

209 *Eastman v Tesco Stores Ltd* UKEAT/0143/12 under the 2004 rules, but the same principle would apply.

prospect of success, it can give a costs warning and order the claimant or employer (as applicable) to pay a deposit of £1,000 as a condition of being permitted to continue with that complaint or response to it.[210] For example, a claimant may have brought a claim for unfair dismissal and age discrimination. If the ET thinks the unfair dismissal claim is fair enough, but the age discrimination claim has little reasonable prospect of success, it can order the claimant to pay a deposit as a condition of continuing with the discrimination claim. In theory, several deposits could be ordered, each one applying to different complaints. For example, the claimant may have brought a claim that, as a result of whistleblowing, she was given an unwarranted warning for poor timekeeping; she was not given an office mobile phone; and eventually she was dismissed. A tribunal may decide there is little reasonable prospect of success in proving the warning was the result of whistleblowing because there was documentary evidence that the claimant was persistently late, and there is little reasonable prospect of proving the failure to give her a phone was due to whistleblowing, since other people also were not given an office mobile phone. However, the complaint that she was dismissed for whistleblowing may appear to be reasonably arguable. The tribunal could then order a £1,000 deposit if the claimant wishes to continue with the disciplinary action complaint and another £1,000 if she wishes to continue with the mobile phone complaint.

20.168   The ET must make reasonable enquiries of the party's financial means to pay the deposit and must take such information into account when deciding the amount of the deposit.[211]

20.169   The tribunal will send out a deposit order, giving fairly brief reasons for making the order and will notify the party of the potential consequences of the order. The order and accompanying notes will set out the date for payment and how payment should be made. If the claimant does not pay the deposit within the set time limit, the claim (or particular allegation, as applicable) is automatically struck out.[212]

20.170   If the claimant decides to pay the deposit and persist with the complaint, s/he will get the deposit back if s/he ultimately wins his/her case on the particular point; or if s/he loses, but for different reasons to those given for making the deposit. On the other hand, if the complaint is eventually decided against him/her for substantially the same reasons as those given for making the deposit order, the

210 ET Regs 2013 Sch 1 r39.
211 ET Regs 2013 Sch 1 r39(2).
212 ET Regs 2013 Sch 1 r39(4).

deposit will be paid over to the employer. Moreover, the claimant will be treated as having acted unreasonably unless the contrary is shown.[213] This means s/he will be at great risk of having costs awarded against him/her beyond the amount of the deposit. The same rules apply in reverse if a deposit is awarded against the employer.

20.171 Whether or not a deposit has been required, any costs ultimately ordered can substantially exceed £1,000. Costs may be awarded against an unsuccessful party even if there has been no preliminary hearing dealing with possible deposit orders, but there is an increased likelihood of costs for unreasonably persisting with the case where a hearing was held and a deposit was required.[214] A party should not think that they have a good case just because they have escaped strike-out and only have a deposit order against them. The law makes it very difficult for tribunals to strike out cases even if they look weak. The award of a deposit is a very serious warning that prospects do not look good at all.

20.172 If a preliminary hearing is fixed to consider whether a complaint should be struck out as having no reasonable prospect of success or a deposit ordered because the complaint has little reasonable prospect of success, the claimant should sit down and think very carefully about the legal and evidential strength of the case. It may be that the preliminary hearing is to consider the entirety of the claim or maybe only some complaints within the claim. In the latter case, the claimant should consider whether s/he has allowed her ET1 to become clogged up with too many peripheral issues. The best way to prevent these issues being fixed for a preliminary hearing is to write a good ET1, which demonstrates a sound understanding of the law, is focused on the key complaints, and makes only relevant points.

Combined cases and lead cases

20.173 Where similar issues of fact or law are concerned, the ET may order that cases brought by different claimants against the same employer be considered together. This is sometimes loosely referred to as 'consolidation'. The ET can do this of its own accord or on application by either party. The ET can choose a lead case where two or more claims give rise to common or related issues of fact or law.[215] Each

---

213 ET Regs 2013 Sch 1 r39(5).
214 ET Regs 2013 Sch 1 r39(5)(a). See para 20.246 onwards on costs generally.
215 ET Regs 2013 Sch 1 r36.

party will have the opportunity to argue for or against consolidation and careful consideration should be given to whether tactically it would help the individual cases or save costs. The commonest instances of consolidation are for multiple redundancy or equal pay claims. Separate claims by the claimant made in separate ET1 forms at different times can also be combined. For example, in a discrimination case, there may be an initial ET1 regarding the original discrimination and a further ET1 if the claimant is subsequently dismissed, claiming victimisation and unfair dismissal.

Preparation for the hearing

Trial bundles

20.174 ETs expect a joint bundle of documents to be agreed with the employer. This is referred to as an 'agreed trial bundle'. Tribunals are trying to get away from jargon by calling it a 'file'. In Scotland, it is called an inventory or bundle of 'productions'. The 'trial bundle' is the set of relevant documents which the parties want to refer to at the hearing. The documents are usually put into one or more ring files or lever-arch files. If there are only a handful of documents, a treasury tag will do. The documents put into the trial bundle should already have been shown to each other at the earlier disclosure stage, but can now be whittled down to what is really necessary. The trial bundle usually contains the ET1 and ET3; selected correspondence from the case preparation, eg letters with additional information; and documents which each side think are relevant for the tribunal to see. Witness statements should be kept separate.

20.175   Trial bundles should be short and relevant. Not every document produced on disclosure needs to go into the bundle. It is a waste of money to add and copy pages of unnecessary documents, and large files are also hard to work with at the hearing. Having said that, if either party insists on certain documents going into the bundle, they should normally be included. The parties are supposed to co-operate with each other on this. If agreement really cannot be reached on the content of the entire trial bundle, as much as possible at least should be agreed and the claimant's representative should prepare his/her own small bundle of any additional documents which the respondents will not agree to insert. In this instance, it is strongly advised that the claimant's representative prepare cross-examination from the page numbering of the agreed bundle so far as possible, and not from any documents duplicated in his/her own bundle. It will be confusing for the representatives and annoying for the tribunal if each party is working entirely from different bundles with different numbering for the same documents.

20.176 Each party should bring to the tribunal their own copy of the joint bundle and one or other will need to bring five extra copies (for a full ET panel) or three (for an employment judge sitting alone). These copies are for the tribunal panel/judge plus one copy for the witness stand and an additional copy to be available for any member of the public or press to look at while sitting in the hearing. The bundle should have the ET1 and ET3 at the front and then the documents in chronological order, numbered on each page and indexed at the front. Sometimes, the ET orders the employer to prepare the joint bundle and bring the extra copies, but it is always better to prepare the trial bundle oneself. However tempting it is to agree to an offer from the employer's representative to do the work (and bear the costs), this can mean getting the bundle at the very last minute and in a shape which is not user-friendly.

20.177 Most tribunals expect the parties to bring the trial bundles with them on the day, and will not accept them ahead of time unless there is a particular reason agreed with the tribunal – eg the tribunal intends to start reading documents and indeed witness statements on the first day of a long hearing or, for reasons related to disability, a party cannot carry the bundles with him/her on the day. Although tribunals are at the moment still working from hard copy bundles when the hearing takes place in the tribunal building, they do sometimes ask for any electronic copy to be provided for their private use.

20.178 If the hearing is to be conducted over a video platform (see para 20.228 onwards), the tribunal will want electronic bundles and witness statements to be prepared. It is important to prepare the bundles so that the numbering on the documents matches the numbering on the computer. This may require having the index separately. PDF-XChange is a useful software for opening pdf bundles as it has an effective bookmark function. It is recommended to bookmark key documents in advance.

20.179 Participating in a hearing over a video platform and looking at electronic bundles and witness statements at the same time is very difficult. Many witnesses and parties, and even some representatives, will not have access to a second computer screen or will find it difficult to work in this way. It is therefore important that anyone who wants also has a hard copy bundle and witness statements to work from.

Evidence related to compensation

Overview

20.180   The claimant should disclose to the employer before the hearing and put into the trial bundle details of all efforts made to secure new employment – eg letters, emails, copies of advertisements, details of employment agencies contacted, jobcentre information about jobs applied for and expenses. If the claimant wins and only wants compensation, the ET will want to know that s/he has made genuine efforts to obtain another job and 'mitigate' his/her loss.[216] In addition, the claimant should come prepared with a calculation of both net weekly and gross weekly earnings with the previous employer and those in any new employment. It may be necessary to explain how these figures were arrived at and provide documentary evidence.

20.181   The ET clerk will also want to know for recoupment purposes, details of the benefit office dealing with the claimant's claim for jobseeker's allowance (JSA), income support or universal credit. Where it has been particularly hard to gain new employment due to the way dismissal took place, a report from a doctor or employment agency may help. If other factors caused difficulties – eg the claimant's age, disability, race or having a young child – specialist evidence and reports will be useful.

Schedule of loss and mitigation or statement of remedy

20.182   It is now common for the ET to order the claimant to provide a statement of what remedy s/he is claiming and a schedule of his/her losses to date. The purpose of this is to increase the chances of a negotiated settlement by focussing the claimant's mind on what a tribunal realistically can award and indicating to the employer what the claimant is looking for. The schedule of loss often has to be provided very early in the case preparation, and updated shortly before or at the hearing. There is no standard format for such a schedule or agreement on how detailed it should be, though some tribunal regions send out a precedent. Essentially it should contain details of the claimant's estimate of what s/he would be earning had s/he not been dismissed; the date of any new job and its pay; and any other losses, eg pension rights or job-hunting expenses. It should contain the heads of compensation claimed, eg loss of statutory rights. Some ETs expect the claimant to fill in details which are

216 See para 18.34.

matters for the ET's discretion, eg the number of weeks' future loss of earnings which is claimed. It is probably safer simply to write 'Future loss @ £00 [specify sum] for the number of weeks which the ET decides'. Where the schedule is used at the hearing in complex cases, it is a nice idea to add two extra columns for the ET to complete – one to contain the employer's contentions under each heading, and the final column to contain the ET's decision. Various model schedules of loss are in appendix A. Some ETs also ask for 'mitigation' to be included in the schedule. This means a list of the steps taken by the claimant to mitigate his/her loss by finding another job,[217] eg a list of job applications (with date and mode of application) and interviews attended.

Other preparation

20.183 In England and Wales, witness statements should be prepared for each witness, signed and dated, and exchanged with the employer in advance of the hearing (see below). Each side should bring three (or five if a full panel) extra copies of their own witness statements to the hearing for the ET judge/panel, witness box and to be read in the room by any member of the public who is watching the hearing. The witness statements should not be added into the trial bundle. Each witness should be told where and when to attend the ET. It is a good idea to explain the procedure to witnesses and to show them a copy of the trial bundle or at least the key documents, so that they understand the context of the case and see any documents on which they might be cross-examined. The adviser should prepare for his/her role as representative and in particular note down the key points on which s/he wants to cross-examine the employer's witnesses. The adviser ought to be able to anticipate what the employer will say at the hearing, especially if witness statements have been exchanged in advance. The adviser should also meet the claimant and go through any unexpected points in the employers' witness statements.

20.184 If an adviser has not run a case before, it is a good idea to visit another ET hearing to see what happens. The claimant may find this useful too. Arrive before 10 am when the hearings start and ask the clerk at reception which would be the most relevant case to watch, or look on the list of cases on the notice board, which indicate by initials the legal issues involved. For example, 'UDL' means unfair dismissal. The clerks are usually very helpful if asked for assistance. It may be a

217 See para 18.34.

good idea to telephone late afternoon the previous day to check there will be an open case to watch. While there are a large number of video hearings due to the Covid-19 pandemic (see para 20.228 onwards), it is also possible to watch a hearing over a video platform, but recording is prohibited.

20.185   If a party or witness needs any adjustments because of disability or vulnerability, ensure the tribunal and other side know as soon as possible. The tribunal also needs to be given good notice if an interpreter is required. See chapter 21 on these matters.

Witness statements

Overview

20.186   ETs in England and Wales now routinely expect the parties to provide written 'witness statements' for their witnesses and this is likely to be contained in the standard set of case management orders. Except in exceptional circumstances, witness statements will stand as those witnesses' evidence in chief. The witness will rarely be required to read the statement out loud and the tribunal is likely to take time out at the start of the hearing to read the witness statements to itself. Where it is said that the witness statements will be 'taken as read', this means the tribunal will read the witness statements to itself in this way.

20.187   The witness will therefore not give her evidence verbally in question and answer format to his/her own representative. S/he will immediately be cross-examined by the other representative, although as explained later in this chapter, the claimant's representative can usually ask a few 'supplementary questions' first. The purpose of written statements is to speed up the proceedings and to let the parties know in advance what the evidence is going to be. ETs expect all the parties' evidence to be in the witness statements apart from any new issues arising from the other side's witness statements. The ET will get annoyed if the claimant or employer's witness statements are sketchy and too many extra questions are asked which could have been included in the first place. In complex cases, to avoid any extra verbal questions, some ETs order that further or supplementary witness statements are exchanged within seven days of the exchange of the original witness statements. However, this does seem rather clumsy and excessive in terms of paperwork. If it does happen, be careful to include all evidence in the statements as the ET is unlikely to allow any supplementary questions at the hearing.

20.188   Usually there has been some agreement between the parties or suggestion (or an order) by the ET that the witness statements should be exchanged seven or 14 days in advance of the hearing. It may have been ordered in a standard ET case management timetable, or otherwise the adviser could suggest this at the time of requesting additional information and documents. The agreed trial bundle should be completed before the witness statements are exchanged, so that there are no surprise documents produced by the employer after the claimant has set out his/her full story. This is also necessary if page references for key documents are to be inserted in the witness statements.

20.189   It is important to exchange witness statements simultaneously with the employer, so there is no risk of last-minute alterations. It is usually best to suggest the employer deliver his/her statements by messenger and the claimant will hand over his/her own witness statements to the messenger by way of exchange. Alternatively it can be done by return of fax or email. If attaching to an email, make sure 'track changes' is not visible when the statement is printed out!

20.190   It may not be possible to get a witness statement in advance where a witness has been compelled to attend by a witness order or only traced at the last minute. Although an ET may be reluctant to exclude evidence from a witness altogether if there is no statement, it may ask for one to be written up on the spot, and may order costs if time is wasted as a result.

20.191   Although technically an ET can choose to read and take account of a written and signed witness statement where the witness does not come to the hearing, such an approach is not very effective or persuasive because the evidence cannot be tested in cross-examination. The ET often says it will 'go to its weight', ie the ET will read the witness statement, but is unlikely to place much reliance on it. It would therefore be unusual for a party to use a witness statement without calling the witness to attend. Witness statements are rarely used in Scotland, although more than they used to be. In whistleblowing and discrimination claims, the judge will discuss with the parties whether to use witness statements.

How should a witness statement be written?

20.192   Ideally a witness statement should be set out clearly, with typed and numbered short paragraphs, and subheadings to break up the text. Where documents are referred to, the page number(s) in the trial bundle should be noted in brackets. If there are documents which are particularly helpful, it is advisable to further highlight the page references, so they do not get overlooked, or the adviser should make a separate list of key documents for the tribunal.[218] Wide margins and double-spacing are useful to enable annotations to be made by the ET panel and representatives, as evidence is given during the hearing. Dates and names should always be stated in full.

20.193   The witness's evidence should be written in a logical order, usually explaining a few important background details first and then telling the story chronologically. This is very important. It is not helpful to the tribunal if the statement jumps around or is structured by answering points in the ET3. Care should be taken with accuracy and consistency of detail. Always bear in mind what are the relevant legal and factual issues, and provide the evidence which is relevant to those. For example, in an unfair dismissal case, draw attention to lack of warnings or inadequate investigation; in a discrimination case, always draw attention to different treatment.[219] If there are problem areas, as a matter of tactics it may be useful to lessen the impact of cross-examination by dealing with those areas in the statement. Statements should not be too long. Remember that the tribunal will have to read and absorb a number of witness statements and documents. As an extremely approximate rule of thumb, a claimant's witness statement in an ordinary unfair dismissal case may not need to be any longer than 3,500–6,000 words. The important thing is to focus on the key issues, so they do not get forgotten in a mass of detail.

20.194   Ensure that the claimant fully agrees with the content of the statement and that s/he understands all the words used. Try to use the words and expressions that the claimant usually uses him/herself to describe the events. It is unwise to ask the claimant to write his/her own statement with a view simply to tidying it up – such a statement may be poorly structured, include irrelevant information and exclude relevant information.

20.195   Tell the claimant in advance that there is nothing wrong with an adviser having written the statement in consultation with him/her. Otherwise, if asked directly at the hearing whether s/he wrote the statement, the claimant may become anxious and not tell the truth.

20.196   Where the witness statement needs to be written in a different language, see para 21.68.

---

218 See para 20.198.
219 See appendix C at C1 for a sample unfair dismissal witness statement and appendix A at A20 and A21 for discrimination examples.

Interpreters and witness expenses

20.197 The position regarding claims for witness expenses and provision of interpreters is the same for all types of tribunal claim and is set out in chapter 21 at para 21.80. See also para 20.265 below regarding costs orders for witness expenses.

Reading lists

20.198 In long cases with a large number of documents and several witness statements – eg some constructive dismissal or whistleblowing dismissal cases – tribunals may ask for a 'reading list' at the outset. Even in short cases, tribunals may find it useful to be offered a brief list. Although many documents are routinely cross-referred in a witness statement by way of confirmatory evidence of the sequence of events, they do not necessarily add any evidence crucial to the outcome of the case. Tribunals would therefore often prefer the parties to produce a combined list of the most essential documents to read at this stage. If such a list has not been agreed with the other side, the claimant can still proffer his/her own list. These are not the only documents which the tribunal will read. The representatives can ask witnesses and the tribunal to look at many other documents during cross-examination. However, these are the documents which it is helpful to look at before the case starts, eg the dismissal or resignation letter, the letter of appeal and the appeal outcome letter. It is advisable to keep this list short and essential. It is not usually necessary to ask tribunals to read lengthy minutes or transcripts of disciplinary and appeal meetings. This can take a long time. If there is no serious dispute about what was said in the disciplinary or appeal, its character and content can briefly be described in the witness statements rather than asking the ET to read laboriously through pages of dialogue. If it is disputed that certain important things were said at such a meeting, then take the opposition witness to the relevant passage during cross-examination, or ask the tribunal to read certain passages.

The hearing

Arrival

20.199 On the day of the hearing, arrive early and check in with the clerk at reception. The clerk will indicate whether the case has been allocated to a particular tribunal panel/employment judge or whether the case is unallocated, ie 'floating' or a 'floater'. The cases are usually also listed on a notice board in the reception area. Allocated cases usually start at 10 am. An unallocated case joins a queue and will be heard by the first ET to come free. This may involve a long delay. Many cases float each day. Some tribunals have press in attendance, who sit in on the hearings. In particularly sensitive cases, it is possible to ask the tribunal at any stage to make an order to protect privacy. For details, see paras 21.56–21.61.

20.200   If a party fails to attend or to send a representative in his/her place, the ET can go ahead and decide the claim or dismiss it in his/her absence. The ET must first consider any information it has about the reason for the party's absence and make any enquiries which are practicable.[220] Usually this means the ET should try to telephone the missing party.[221]

20.201   Claimants and respondents normally have separate waiting rooms and, in many tribunals, there are a number of private meeting rooms available for use. Visit the employer in the respondents' waiting room to sort out any last-minute problems and to see what witnesses are there. This is often an opportunity to discuss settlement. Give the employer's representative copies of any cases that will be referred to in the closing speech. The clerk will visit each side in their waiting rooms to collect the trial bundles and witness statements for the employment judge or ET panel and witness box. If there is any doubt whether a witness will be called, hold back the relevant witness statement in case the ET reads it first. It used to be the practice that the names and references of any cases to be referred to in closing were also given to the clerk together with copies of the cases. This is unusual now, but may be useful if there is a crucial case which you would like to alert the tribunal to from the outset.

20.202   The clerk will ask whether the witnesses will swear or affirm when giving evidence. 'Affirming' is a formal, non-religious, promise to tell the truth. If witnesses require any holy book other than the New Testament, the clerk should be told at this point, eg the Old Testament, or Torah for Jewish witnesses; the Koran for Muslims and the Bhagavadgita (or 'Gita') for Hindus. Some witnesses may prefer to affirm rather than invoke a religious book in this context or, for example, where they do not have facilities to wash first. Where it

---

220 ET Regs 2013 Sch 1 r47.
221 *Cooke v Glenrose* UKEAT/0064/04; [2004] IRLR 866; *Euro Hotels (Thornton Heath) Ltd v Alam* UKEAT/0006/09.

is preferable not to touch a Holy Book because of pandemic precautions, or where an oath is sworn at home on a video hearing, the Judicial College's Equal Treatment Bench Book advises that it is unnecessary for the witness to hold or have the religious book.[222] See paras 21.65–21.71 regarding accessibility of tribunals to people wearing religious dress or with a disability.

20.203　The time before the hearing starts can be used to clear up last-minute queries and to calm the claimant and witnesses. Cases often settle on the morning of the hearing, so the representative should have in mind what the claimant wants, and terms of settlement, and should bring precedents for settlements and consent orders, and a calculator. If part of the settlement would be an agreed reference, which is common, a draft should have been prepared in advance.[223]

Composition of the ET panel

20.204　In the past, the vast majority of tribunal cases could only be heard by a three-person panel. One of the first changes to ETs made by the Conservative and Liberal Democrat coalition government was to remove the absolute requirement for full panels on unfair dismissal claims from 6 April 2012. The position now is that an employment judge will hear an unfair dismissal claim alone unless s/he decides there should be a full tribunal panel having regard to the likelihood of a factual dispute or legal issue of a kind which would make it desirable for there to be a full panel and the views of the parties.[224] In practice, it is unusual for the parties to seek, or for judges to order, a full panel. Certain other claims were already heard by a judge sitting alone before April 2012 on the same basis, eg claims for breach of contract, payslips, a section 1 statement of particulars, unauthorised deductions from pay, or leave entitlement under the Working Time Regulations 1998. If any of these claims is heard at the same time as a claim which still requires a full panel, then a full panel will hear all the claims.

222　At chapter 9. For more about the Equal Treatment Bench Book, see paras 21.65–21.75 below. See also the Presidential Guidance on remote and in-person hearings (England and Wales), para 19.4 via a link at www.judiciary. uk/publications/employment-rules-and-legislation-practice-directions/.

223　See paras 20.268 onwards regarding settlements, including paras 20.274–20.275 for settlements reached at the tribunal.

224　ETA 1996 s4(3) as amended by the Employment Tribunals Act 1996 (Tribunal Composition) Order 2012 SI No 988.

20.205   Full panels are now compulsory only for a few types of case, most notably discrimination claims under the EqA 2010 and claims for unlawful detriment, eg for whistleblowing. Rather strangely, a claim by an employee for automatic unfair dismissal for whistleblowing need not routinely be heard by a full panel because it is an unfair dismissal claim, but a claim for a detriment short of dismissal, such as a disciplinary warning due to whistleblowing, or for the termination of a worker's employment (which technically is a 'detriment' claim rather than an 'unfair dismissal' claim, because only employees can claim unfair dismissal) must still be heard by a full panel. Therefore, a whistleblowing claim for dismissal and pre-dismissal detriments will be heard by a full panel.

20.206   An employment judge must have been a solicitor, barrister, advocate or legal executive of at least five years' standing. Non employment judges can also now be nominated to sit in ETs. Where a full panel is required, a judge is joined by two non-legal members. These are drawn from each side of industry (employer and employee-orientated background), but are not there to represent an interest group and must take a neutral position in deciding cases. The judge chairs the panel. ET panel decisions can be by a majority, but are usually unanimous.

The employment tribunal's approach

20.207   The original intention was for the hearing of unfair dismissal claims to be expedient, simple and informal. ETs still aim to avoid undue formality. Nevertheless, the formality of a hearing can vary quite widely depending on the nature of the claims, the level of co-operation or hostility between the parties, whether the parties are represented and the approach of any such representatives. Always call the employment judge 'Sir' or 'Madam' and remain seated. The other representative can be addressed by name (Mr/Ms/Mrs . . .), although barristers tend to call each other 'my friend' or 'my learned friend'. The room is set out informally and no one wears a wig and gown. However, the witnesses and representatives should dress smartly and behave appropriately. Remember, it is a court of law and everyone in the room is very visible to the tribunal panel. See para 20.228 onwards, where a witness wants to attend a hearing by video link.

20.208   ETs may decide on the most appropriate procedure for the hearing, taking account of the principles contained in the overriding objective.[225] They are not generally bound by the strict rules regarding admissible evidence applicable in the civil and criminal courts. ETs are allowed to question parties and witnesses so far as appropriate to elicit the issues and clarify the evidence. It should not be taken as an indication of hostility, favouritism or bias that an ET is asking questions as matters proceed. Equally, it is the job of employment judges to keep evidence relevant and to the point. It is quite normal for witnesses to be told more than once to answer the question or speak more concisely and for representatives to be told to keep to issues which are relevant to the legal questions to be decided. Tribunals are also explicitly allowed under the 2013 rules to impose time limits on the time a party may take in presenting evidence, cross-examining the other side's witnesses or making submissions (ie comments on any point, including closing speeches). The ET can prevent the party carrying on beyond the allocated time.[226] It is very common for tribunals to timetable the evidence at the outset of the hearing, eg to say how much time each side will have for cross-examination. Advisers tend to overestimate in advance how much time they will have for cross-examination. Remember that the ET also needs to allow time for reading the witness statements, swearing witnesses in, supplementary questions, re-examination, tribunal questions, final comments and various other issues which might unexpectedly arise.

20.209 Taking all that into account, if the claimant's claim is harmed by unreasonable conduct by the ET, eg refusal to allow crucial evidence to be called, this could be a ground of appeal. The representative should object at the time and ask the ET to note the objection. If there is an appeal, the employment judge's notes, if relevant, will be ordered. An appeal can also be made if it is felt that the ET is biased or any member has a conflict of interest, eg has some connection with the employer or claimant. If it is intended to appeal on any of these points, an objection must usually first be raised in the ET. Because of the potential consequences, the representative should ask for five minutes to consult the claimant privately before making any objection.

20.210 At the start of the hearing, the ET will go through the legal issues to be decided. These are fairly standard in an unfair dismissal claim.[227] It will also deal with any preliminary matters such as

---

225 See para 20.39. ET Regs 2013 Sch 1 r45.
226 ET Regs 2013 Sch 1 r45.
227 See appendix A at A24, para 4 for an example.

arguments about the documents. The parties should normally have written to each other about any outstanding matters a reasonable time before the hearing, so no one is caught by surprise. The ET will want to get on with the case, rather than get involved in arguments between the parties about matters such as late disclosure of documents and witness statements. Unless the claimant is genuinely disadvantaged by very late disclosure, it is best not to raise such matters.

20.211   The ET usually informs the parties at this stage how it wants the hearing conducted and says whether it wants to hear evidence about remedy (efforts to get new employment) at the same time as evidence on liability (the win/lose decision), or only if and when the claimant wins. Where remedy is to be left until after the decision on liability, the ET should also clarify at the outset whether it will decide any issues of *Polkey*,[228] contributory fault (in a conduct dismissal) and ACAS adjustments of compensation as part of its decision on liability.[229] If the ET does not clarify all this, then ask.

The order of events

20.212 It is likely that after these introductory matters, the parties will be asked to stay in their waiting rooms while the ET reads the witness statements and key documents. In a large case where each side is represented, the tribunal may prefer to read each witness statements immediately before hearing from that witness, so it may start by reading the witness statement of the first witness and perhaps the main witness on the other side. On a short case or if one side is unrepresented, it is more likely to read all the witness statements at the outset.

20.213   Once the ET has read the papers, the clerk will fetch everyone back for the hearing to continue. If there is a dispute over whether there was a dismissal, the claimant goes first. Otherwise the employer starts in an unfair dismissal case.[230] Opening speeches were dispensed with many years ago, and now the parties go straight into the evidence. Occasionally in a complex case, a party might voluntarily provide the tribunal with some short written 'opening submissions', perhaps two or three pages long. This is usually an attempt to get the tribunal to see the case in a certain light from the outset.

---

228 *Polkey v A E Dayton Services* [1987] IRLR 503, HL. See para 6.65.
229 See paras 18.52–18.60 for an explanation of these issues.
230 See 'Burden of proof' at para 9.1.

20.214   Assuming the employer starts, s/he will call his/her witnesses first. Each witness will be asked to stand and take the oath or affirm to tell the truth. The witness will then sit and will give his/her 'evidence in chief'. If a witness statement has been prepared, most of the evidence in chief will consist of the statement. By way of introducing the statement, the adviser asks the witness to confirm his/her name and address, that it is his/her statement and that its contents are believed to be accurate and true. Nearly always, the tribunal will have read the statement to itself as already described. However, there may be rare circumstances where the tribunal thinks it a good idea to ask the witness to read out the witness statement. Whether or not the witness statement was pre-read by the ET, the witness's representative is usually allowed to ask some supplementary questions, though not too many.[231] This is partly to deal with any important parts of the employer's case which first appeared in the latter's witness statements and therefore have not been covered in the witness statements of the claimant's own witnesses. It also helps the witness settle in before cross-examination to ask him/her to explain one or two relevant matters in his/her own words.

20.215   In Scotland, witness statements have traditionally been ordered less frequently, and the evidence in chief may be given by the witness answering the representative's questions. This may have changed more recently, and it is best to check the tribunal's orders and current practice.

20.216   The representative must not 'lead' his/her own witness, ie must not ask a question in such a way that it suggests to the witness what the answer should be. For example, s/he must ask: 'What did you do next?' as opposed to: 'Did you then go to see the HR director?' However, if the facts to be established are not in dispute by the other side, the representative can lead, eg: 'I think we all agree that you went on holiday from 1 to 14 August'.

20.217   After the evidence in chief is finished, the claimant's representative can then ask questions. This is called cross-examination and 'leading questions' are permitted. After that, the employer's representative can ask a few more questions, simply clearing up anything that arose in cross-examination. This is called re-examination. Either before or after re-examination, the ET panel usually questions the witness. During cross-examination, the employment judge may also have asked some questions for clarification. In Scotland, the ET panel tends to ask more questions than in England and Wales, but

231 See para 20.184.

there is no absolute rule. The degree of questioning will depend on factors such as the nature of the case, how clearly it is being presented by witness and representative, and the approach of the particular employment judge.

20.218   The same process is followed with each witness. After all the employer's witnesses have given evidence, the claimant is immediately called to give evidence and then any of the claimant's witnesses. In Scotland, witnesses must stay outside the room until after they have given evidence. In England and Wales, witnesses are allowed to sit in the room throughout and usually do. Although there has been an explicit power in the rules since 2004 to request that a particular witness be excluded from the room while others give evidence, this is not frequently done in England and Wales, possibly because parties rarely ask.[232] If there is a break in the middle of a witness's evidence, including an overnight break, the witness will be told that s/he must not discuss his/her evidence with anyone else. It is very important that the witness complies with this rule.[233]

20.219   It is useful to prepare in advance of the hearing a chronology, ie a list of the important dates; as well as a 'cast list', ie a list of the names and job title of the main characters, particularly those who will be giving evidence. These can be handed to the ET and the employer's representative at the outset. Ideally the content would be agreed with the employer's representative in advance, but this rarely happens unless the ET has made a specific order.

The closing speech

20.220 At the end of the evidence, it is customary for each party to make a closing speech to the ET. This is sometimes called 'closing submissions' or 'final submissions'. In England and Wales, the party which started usually addresses the ET last. In Scotland, it tends to be the opposite. The length of the speech depends on the complexity of the case, but the ET should not be bored. In a simple one-day hearing where the ET has just heard all the evidence, a closing speech may not last much longer than 10–15 minutes. The main point of the closing speech is to relate the key points of evidence to the relevant law. If the employer's representative will have the last word, the

---

232 ET Regs 2013 Sch 1 r43.
233 In *Chidzoy v British Broadcasting Corporation* UKEAT/0097/17, a claim was struck out because the claimant talked to a journalist during a break in her evidence.

claimant's should anticipate and deal with the employer's strong points in his/her closing speech.

20.221   It is best to prepare the closing speech in advance, amending it through the course of the hearing to reflect what emerges. If the hearing lasts more than one day, it is useful to produce written submissions or at least a 'skeleton argument', ie an outline of the main points which are expanded verbally in the closing speech. The ET should be reminded of the main issues and related evidence. Where there is a conflict of evidence, it can be suggested why the ET should prefer the claimant's witnesses. Rather than make general points about why the claimant and his/her witnesses are credible and the respondent's witnesses are not, it is more useful to focus on the key factual disputes and say why the tribunal should make each finding which supports the claimant's case.

20.222   If any reported cases are referred to, remember that only the decision of the most senior court on a particular issue is important. Most unfair dismissal cases are decided on their facts and case-law need not be routinely referred to. On the whole, it is not necessary to read extracts from the case-law unless there is an unusual or difficult legal issue. The ET will be familiar with the main cases and legal principles and a key authority may just be referred to by name. Copies of the full case report (from IRLR or ICR or, if unreported, from the EAT website or the Bailii website) should be handed to each member of the ET and employer's representative unless it is a very well-known case such as *Polkey*.[234] Where a case is less commonly referred to, but does contain an important point, then it is recommended that the key paragraphs are read to the ET and not just noted down in written submissions. If references are made to reported cases, advisers should make sure that they fully know and understand them.

20.223   Sometimes there is only enough time at the hearing to finish the evidence and a new date would need to be fixed for closing speeches. Provided the parties agree, the ET may suggest each side send in written closing submissions within seven or 14 days and that the ET's decision then be sent out in writing. The ET should order that the submissions are exchanged between the parties so that each side has the opportunity to comment on the other's submissions.[235]

---

234 *Polkey v AE Dayton Services* [1987] IRLR 503, HL. See para 6.65.
235 *Barking and Dagenham LBC v Oguoko* [2000] IRLR 179, EAT; *Mayor and Burgesses of Haringey LBC v Akpan* EAT/0974/00.

The judgment

20.224   The ET's decision, where the case was heard by a panel, is usually unanimous, although it may be by a majority. As already explained, a judge is likely to have heard an unfair dismissal claim alone. In England and Wales, the ET's judgment is usually given verbally at the end of the hearing, after the tribunal has taken a break of a few hours to reach its decision. The judgment will subsequently be confirmed in writing and sent to the parties. Sometimes the tribunal suggests the representatives wait at the tribunal while the judgment is typed up, so they can take it away with them. If a barrister represents the claimant and the instructing solicitor has not come to the tribunal, the latter must remember to get the hard copy of the judgment from the barrister. The judgment simply states the ET's decision (eg 'the claimant was unfairly dismissed') and may include compensation, a declaration or recommendation (in a discrimination case), and any costs order.[236] It usually fits onto one page, sometimes two. In a complex case or where time has run out, the judgment may be 'reserved', ie made at a later date and sent to the parties. This can mean a wait of a few months. A long and unreasonable delay in providing the judgment, even by as much as a year, will not in itself constitute a ground for appeal. Only in exceptional cases will unreasonable delay amount to a real risk that someone has been deprived of their right to a fair hearing under ECHR Article 6.[237] In Scotland, the ET rarely announces its judgment at the end of the hearing.

20.225   When the judgment is given orally at the end of the hearing, the reasons are usually given orally at the same time, although this is not compulsory. The parties will be told that if they want written reasons, they must ask there and then at the hearing or make a written request within 14 days of the date the judgment is sent to the parties.[238] This time limit can be extended if the ET thinks it appropriate.[239] It is essential to ask for written reasons if planning to appeal. The written reasons are much longer than the judgment. As a rough guide, they may well amount to 7–20 pages in an unfair dismissal case, longer in a discrimination one. They should include the issues relevant to the claim; relevant fact findings; a concise statement of the law; how the law has been applied to the facts to determine the issues; and, if compensation has been awarded, details as to how it has been calcu-

---

236 ET Regs 2013 Sch 1 r61.
237 *Bangs v Connex South Eastern Ltd* [2005] IRLR 389, CA.
238 ET Regs 2013 Sch 1 r62.
239 ET Regs 2013 Sch 1 r5.

lated.[240] When the ET reserves its judgment instead of announcing it at the hearing, it must send it to the parties subsequently together with written reasons.[241]

20.226 It is important not to get confused between the written judgment and the written reasons (if any), which are usually contained in separate documents – both will be needed if the claimant wants to appeal. If written reasons are given at the same time as the judgment (eg because judgment was reserved or because written reasons were asked for at the end of the hearing), they will usually be contained on the same document, ie the start of the document will be headed 'Judgment' and will set out the judgment in a few lines, followed by the heading 'Reasons' and the reasons.

20.227 The tribunal may have taken evidence regarding compensation (remedies) at the same time as it heard evidence relevant to liability (ie whether or not the claimant wins the case). If this was not done, then if the ET decides the dismissal is unfair at the end of the hearing, it may go on to deal with the evidence about compensation, or it may adjourn (ie take a break) and suggest that the parties reach agreement on compensation. The parties may be able to do this immediately by talking in the waiting rooms. If so, any agreement should be written, signed and shown to the ET. The clerk will make copies. Alternatively, the ET may send the parties away, on the basis that settlement discussions will take place outside the ET on another day. As long as the ET has reached a final decision on liability, ie that the claimant was successful, then it should only be the compensation which is settled. Depending on the wording of the agreement, this may prevent the original judgment regarding liability being appealed. Time should not be allowed to drift. If no agreement can be achieved, then the claimant can simply write to the ET asking for a hearing on compensation to be fixed. Delays in setting a date for the compensation hearing can cause financial distress to the claimant and may also deprive him/her of the benefit of interest on an unpaid award. Sometimes there will be concerns about the employer's continuing ability to pay any award. For this reason, even where the ET does not reach a decision at the end of the hearing and reserves its judgment, it may well set a provisional date for a remedies hearing (without prejudging its decision), in case the claimant wins.

---

240 ET Regs 2013 Sch 1 r62(5).
241 ET Regs 2013 Sch 1 r62(2).

Remote hearings

20.228   Hearings can be conducted by electronic communication, including telephone, provided a tribunal considers it would be just and equitable to do so and provided the parties and any members of the public attending the hearing can hear what the tribunal hears and can see any witness as seen by the tribunal.[242] A 'remote' hearing means one which is conducted over an audio or video platform. To ensure open justice where a hearing is wholly remote or only the tribunal panel is in the building, a member of the public or press can observe it by obtaining dial in / log on details from the tribunal administration. It is a criminal offence for anyone to record or broadcast a tribunal hearing without the tribunal's permission.

20.229   Prior to the Covid-19 pandemic, few hearings were held remotely. At most, certain regions held case management preliminary hearings over the telephone, and a witness based abroad might give evidence over a video-link for a hearing otherwise conducted in a tribunal building. The pandemic has transformed practice. Full merits hearings and preliminary hearings deciding preliminary issues as well as judicial mediation have largely been held over video platforms, usually Cloud Video Platform (CVP) or Teams. Case management preliminary hearings have been held by audio conferencing (usually BT Meet Me) and sometimes video. The quality of the hardware and software and the ability of judges and non-legal members to operate it has increased very rapidly. There are Practice Directions on remote hearings from the Presidents of England and Wales and Scotland, supplemented in England and Wales by Presidential Guidance.[243]

20.230   Ongoing safety measures mean that many buildings are not operating at full capacity. Together with backlogs caused by the early lockdowns, it is likely that remote hearings will operate in tandem with in-person hearings (ie hearings in the tribunal buildings) for a few more years. Although the Presidents have said that in-person

242 ET Regs 2013 Sch 1 r46.
243 *Presidential Practice Direction (England and Wales) on remote hearings and open justice,* 14 September 2020 update; *Presidential Guidance (England and Wales) on remote and in-person hearings,* 14 September 2020 update; *Practice Direction: Fixing and Conduct of Remote Hearings,* 11 June 2020; *Remote Hearings Practical Guidance,* 12 June 2020 available via links at www.judiciary.uk/publications/employment-rules-and-legislation-practice-directions/ for England and Wales, and at www.judiciary.uk/publications/directions-for-employment-tribunals-scotland/ for Scotland.

hearings are the ideal to be returned to, the option of holding remote hearings is unlikely to disappear altogether in the future.

20.231 The Presidents issue regular 'road maps' to indicate their plans.[244] The road map for 2021/2 says the default position is that judicial mediations and case management preliminary hearings will be held by telephone or video; preliminary hearings to decide preliminary issues or strike out / deposit orders will default to video as will claims for unpaid wages, holiday pay, redundancy pay etc. Final hearings of unfair dismissal and discrimination claims will vary around the country, with many regions returning in greater numbers to in-person hearings, but London and the South East retaining video hearings for unfair dismissal and still relying heavily on video (including hybrid formats) for discrimination claims. A 'hybrid' format means at least one participant (judge / tribunal member / representative / witness / party / interpreter) joins remotely and at least one is in the building.

20.232 A judge can decide at any stage whether a hearing should be held remotely or in-person and the parties can express their views. The standard claim and response forms now ask whether the parties would be able to participate in a video hearing. Considerations would be whether the venue and travel is safe; the availability of hardware, software and HMCTS staff to facilitate a remote hearing; ability of parties to engage meaningfully with a remote hearing including whether they are legally represented; nature of the evidence; and risks of delay. The personal circumstances, disability or vulnerability of any participant (tribunal panel, interpreter, party, witness etc) may mean that attendance in person is either positively desirable for more effective communication or undesirable because of clinical vulnerability or the need to use public transport.[245]

20.233 There are various practicalities which representatives need to be aware of when preparing for a remote hearing. Many of these are set out in Presidential Guidance.[246] In particular:

- An electronic trial bundle must be prepared in accordance with tribunal requirements and provided to the tribunal. This can be

244 Available via a link at www.judiciary.uk/publications/employment-rules-and-legislation-practice-directions/ for England and Wales, and at www.judiciary.uk/publications/directions-for-employment-tribunals-scotland/ for Scotland.
245 *Presidential Guidance (England and Wales) on remote and in-person hearings* available via a link at www.judiciary.uk/publications/employment-rules-and-legislation-practice-directions/.
246 See previous footnote.

difficult with large bundles, but the tribunal is gradually introducing an electronic uploading facility.

- Electronic witness statements must be provided to the tribunal.
- All parties and witnesses need the electronic trial bundle and witness statements plus hard copies if they do not have a second computer screen which they find easy to use.
- It is rarely suitable for a party or witness to join a video hearing using a smart phone. A decent size screen is usually necessary to see the other participants and certainly any documents which are shown.
- A means of direct communication should be arranged between the representative and the party / witnesses. This cannot be used while the witness is giving evidence, but is important the rest of the time.
- Ensure the party / witness has a quiet space to attend the hearing. If interruptions are inevitable, it is best to tell the judge at the outset.
- Ensure the party / witness understands that they should take the hearing just as seriously and formally as if they were in the building.
- Parties and witnesses will generally be required to keep their cameras on, but to have their audio on mute except when giving evidence.
- See para 20.202 regarding taking a religious oath.
- Be prepared for the hearing to be tiring.

20.234   Interestingly, there are strongly divergent views held within the legal profession, among parties and indeed among judges and tribunal members, regarding whether in-person or remote hearings are preferred. There are obviously pros and cons, even without the extra element of Covid-19 precautions. The advantage of a remote hearing is avoiding the need to travel in and out to the venue. Some parties and witnesses find it less intimidating to attend from home. This might be particularly important, eg, where a claimant bringing a sexual harassment claim wants to avoid being close to the alleged perpetrator, or where a party or witness has a level of anxiety or autism which makes tribunal attendance particularly worrying. On the other hand, communication can be more difficult across a video platform. Again, this may particularly disadvantage witnesses with certain disabilities. For a further discussion of difficulties which may arise and possible adjustments, see guidance in appendix E of the Judicial College's Equal Treatment Bench Book.

Appeals and reconsideration

Overview

20.235 A claimant who is unhappy with the ET's judgment, including any costs order, may be able to ask the ET to reconsider its decision or, alternatively, may appeal to the EAT, or both. Whereas there is a 42-day time limit for lodging an appeal, there is only 14 days to seek a reconsideration. The reconsideration process does not apply to case management orders, though the ET can always be asked to vary its decision under its general case management powers.[247] An appeal to the EAT can be made against judgments or case management orders, eg those which refuse additional information or disclosure or a request to postpone.

Reconsideration by the employment tribunal

20.236 The ET has power on its own initiative or, more commonly, at a party's request, to 'reconsider' any ET judgment where it is in the interests of justice to do so.[248] For example, a claimant may ask the ET to reconsider its decision to reject an unfair dismissal claim, or its decision to award costs against the claimant or, during case preparation, s/he may ask the ET to reconsider a judgment on a preliminary issue, eg that s/he is not disabled, or that all or part of the claim should be struck out.

20.237 'Reconsideration' is a technical term, but it means what it says. Under the pre-2013 procedural rules, the reconsideration process was known as a 'review' and it could only be sought on certain listed grounds. There are no specified grounds in the 2013 rules. Nevertheless, there does need to be some reason why it would be in the interests of justice to change a decision which has already been made. Asking an ET simply to reconsider the same evidence and legal arguments which it has already considered in making its original decision is unlikely to be very effective. Traditionally the kind of reasons which have been an appropriate basis for reconsideration are these:

- New evidence has become available since the conclusion of the hearing, whose existence could not have been reasonably known

---

247 See para 20.110; and ET Regs 2013 Sch 1 r29.
248 ET Regs 2013 Sch 1 r70. A 'judgment' is defined in Sch 1 r1(3).

or foreseen at the time of the hearing and which would have had an important influence on the result of the case.

- An important case in the higher courts has been decided subsequent to the decision in the present case, which changes the relevant legal position.
- The ET made a mathematical error in calculating compensation, or made a decision on compensation without asking the parties for their comments.
- The decision was made in the absence of a party, eg because s/he did not receive notification of the hearing date or because s/he had a very good reason for not attending. However, bear in mind that a party should usually attend a hearing unless the ET has accepted a request for a postponement, and it will be rare for reconsideration to succeed if the party has just failed to turn up.[249]

20.238 If the claimant wants a reconsideration, s/he must apply for it orally at the hearing, or in writing, stating the grounds in full, within 14 days of the date when the relevant judgment was sent to him/her or, if written reasons were sent later, within 14 days of when those reasons were sent.[250] The ET has a general power to extend time limits if appropriate.[251] The first stage is an individual consideration of the application by an employment judge, who will refuse to hold the reconsideration if there is no reasonable prospect of the original decision being varied or revoked.[252] This includes where substantially the same application for reconsideration has already been made and refused, unless there are special reasons. Otherwise, the ET will send out a notice to the parties, setting a time limit for the employer to make comments on the application and seeking everyone's views on whether the application can be decided without a hearing.[253] The judge may choose to set out his/her provisional views on the likelihood of the application succeeding.

20.239   Provided the application was not refused at the first stage, the procedure then moves on to a second stage. The reconsideration will then take place at a hearing unless the judge decides a hearing is not necessary in the interests of justice, having taken into account any response by the employer. If the reconsideration goes ahead without

249 See para 20.138 onwards re hearing dates and postponements.
250 ET Regs 2013 Sch 1 r71.
251 ET Regs 2013 Sch 1 r5.
252 ET Regs 2013 Sch 1 r72(1).
253 ET Regs 2013 Sch 1 r72(1).

a hearing, each side will be given a reasonable opportunity to make further written comments.[254]

20.240   Where practical, the initial consideration at the first stage will be made by the employment judge who made the original decision which the claimant wants reconsidered, or, if it was a full tribunal panel, the judge who chaired the panel. If the procedure moves on to the second stage, the reconsideration will be made by the judge or, as the case may be, the full tribunal which made the original decision.[255]

20.241   The same process applies where it is the employer who applies for a reconsideration. Where the ET proposes to reconsider a decision on its own initiative, all the parties will be told the reasons and will be given a reasonable opportunity to make written comments or attend a hearing.[256]

20.242   On reconsideration, the ET can confirm, vary or revoke its decision and can take a new decision. The ET may order a rehearing before the same or a different tribunal. It is important to read the ET's notification of the reconsideration carefully, as it may move on to a rehearing of the full case on the same day, immediately following a successful reconsideration. Note that clerical errors and accidental slips, eg typos or minor numerical mistakes in calculating compensation, can simply be corrected by the ET under the 'slip rule' without any reconsideration.[257]

Appeal to the Employment Appeal Tribunal

20.243 The employment part of the GOV.UK website provides guidance on how to appeal, and attaches the applicable rules and procedures.[258] The appeal must be lodged within 42 days from the date the written judgment was sent to the parties or in some circumstances, within 42 days of when the written reasons were sent. EAT procedure is not within the scope of this book.

20.244   The EAT will 'sift' the Notice of Appeal to see whether there are reasonable grounds for the appeal and whether some or all of the grounds should be allowed to go ahead to the full hearing. There are various permutations for how the appeal might then be processed. Appeals against ET interim orders will be fast-tracked.

254 ET Regs 2013 Sch 1 r72(2).
255 ET Regs 2013 Sch 1 r72(3).
256 ET Regs 2013 Sch 1 r73.
257 ET Regs 2013 Sch 1 r69.
258 Start with 'Appeal to the Employment Appeal Tribunal (EAT)' at: www.gov.uk/appeal-employment-appeal-tribunal/overview.

20.245   Employees often cannot understand that they may not automatically appeal when they lose. An appeal to the EAT is not a fresh rehearing of the entire case. It is a legal argument between the representatives for each party (or unrepresented litigants), largely based on the pleadings and the ET's decision on the facts. The ET's notes of oral evidence are not normally looked at by the EAT. The appeal is confined to errors of law. Where there is no legal error, the claimant must show that the ET's decision on the factual evidence was legally perverse, ie that no reasonable ET could possibly have come to the same decision. The EAT has described this as the type of decision which would 'provoke astonished gasps from the amazed observer'.[259] It is very hard to show this and the EAT is reluctant to interfere with the ET's general discretion.

Costs

Overview

20.246   How much of a risk are costs? Unlike most civil courts, the ET does not usually order that the unsuccessful party pays the costs of the winner. However, in certain circumstances the ET may order costs, usually because a party is running or defending a hopeless case, or because s/he fails to comply with tribunal orders, or because s/he behaves badly in conducting the case or because his/her poor case preparation leads to unnecessary postponements or adjournments of the hearing. The 'paying party' is the one who is ordered to pay costs and the 'receiving party' is the one to whom costs are paid. Costs orders (expenses orders in Scotland) can be made only for costs incurred while the receiving party was legally represented or represented by a lay representative.[260] 'Legally represented' means having the assistance of someone who has a right of audience in county courts, magistrates' courts or any part of the Senior Courts of England and Wales or who is an advocate or solicitor in Scotland, or a member of the Bar of Northern Ireland or a solicitor of the Court of Judicature there.[261] A qualified solicitor without a practising certificate would not constitute a legal representative.[262] Nor would the costs of a non-legal representative be paid simply because s/he had instructed a

259 *JJ Food Service Ltd v Kefil* UKEAT/0320/12.
260 ET Regs 2013 Sch 1 r75(1).
261 ET Regs 2013 Sch 1 r74(2).
262 *Ramsay and others v Bowercross Construction Ltd and others* UKEAT/0534-5/07.

barrister who did constitute a legal representative (although the costs of the barrister can be paid).[263] It does not matter if the legal representative is employed by the receiving party. A 'lay representative' means having the assistance of someone who is not a legal representative but who charges for representation in the proceedings. If the receiving party was not legally represented, a preparation time order may be made instead.[264] A costs order and a preparation time order cannot both be made in favour of the same party in the same proceedings.[265] Wasted costs orders can also be made personally against some representatives.[266]

20.247 A tribunal can order a respondent to pay the claimant's costs where s/he has not incurred them personally, but they have been incurred by a law centre acting on her behalf.[267] This is because 'costs' are explicitly described in the rules as those incurred by 'or on behalf of' the receiving party. Following this logic, it may also be possible for costs to be ordered in favour of the claimant where his/her case was paid for by another organisation such as the EHRC or a trade union. However, this is untested under the 2013 rules.

20.248 To put costs in context, in 2019/20, ETs made 130 costs awards against claimants. This is a small proportion of the total number of cases dealt with. Of those awards, 60 were in the range £800–£4,000, and 21 were over £10,000. In that time, 47 awards were made against respondents, although generally for much lower sums.[268]

Costs orders

20.249 The ET can order a party (called 'the paying party') to make a payment in respect of costs incurred by the other party ('the receiving party'). 'Costs' include the legal fees, disbursements and expenses incurred by or on behalf of the receiving party while legally represented or represented by a lay representative.[269] The ET has a discretion to

---

263 *Ramsay* UKEAT/0534-5/07 at para 27. But remember that the 2013 rules, unlike the 2004 rules, permit costs orders where a lay representative charges.

264 ET Regs 2013 Sch 1 r75(2).

265 ET Regs 2013 Sch 1 r75(3).

266 ET Regs 2013 Sch 1 rr80–84.

267 *Taiwo v Olaigbe and Olaigbe* UKEAT/0254/12 and 0285/12. Although decided under the 2004 rules, the words 'on behalf of' also appear in the 2013 rules.

268 See statistics in *Employment tribunal and Employment Appeal Tribunal tables 2019 to 2020*, available via a link at www.gov.uk/government/statistics/tribunal-statistics-quarterly-april-to-june-2020.

269 ET Regs 2013 Sch 1 rr74–75; and see para 20.246.

award costs (or make a preparation time order) and must consider whether to do so where it considers that any of the following apply:

- The claim or response had no reasonable prospect of success.[270]
- The paying party, or his/her representative, has acted vexatiously, abusively, disruptively or otherwise unreasonably in bringing the proceedings or part of them.[271]
- The paying party, or his/her representative, has acted vexatiously, abusively, disruptively or otherwise unreasonably in the way the proceedings or part of them have been conducted.[272]
- A party has not complied with an order or practice direction.[273]
- A full or interim hearing is postponed or adjourned at the request of the paying party.[274]
- In an unfair dismissal claim where the claimant told the employer of his/her wish to be reinstated or re-engaged at least seven days before the hearing, if the hearing is postponed or adjourned as a result of the employer's failure, without special reason, to produce reasonable evidence about the availability of the job from which the claimant was dismissed or about comparable or suitable employment. In these circumstances, the costs incurred as a result of the postponement or adjournment must be awarded.[275]

The tribunal can also make a costs order for witness expenses. Note that costs cannot be awarded against an employer just because the employer acted extremely unfairly in dismissing the claimant.[276] The respondent organisation must have been unreasonable in the way it conducted the case or the response must have had no reasonable prospect of success. These are not necessarily the same thing.[277]

20.250 The tribunal must first decide whether any of these categories apply; and second, decide whether to use its discretion to award costs and if so, how much to award.[278] The fact that a party was unrepresented may be relevant both to whether the categories apply (eg has s/

270 ET Regs 2013 Sch 1 r76(1)(b).
271 ET Regs 2013 Sch 1 r76(1)(a).
272 ET Regs 2013 Sch 1 r76(1)(a).
273 ET Regs 2013 Sch 1 r76(2).
274 ET Regs 2013 Sch 1 r76(2).
275 See ET Regs 2013 Sch 1 r76(3).
276 Although this could be grounds for a financial penalty payable to the secretary of state. See para 18.74.
277 *Baillon v Gwent Police* UKEAT/0354-5/14.
278 *Oni v UNISON* UKEAT/0370-1/14; *Radia v Jefferies International* [2020] IRLR 431, EAT.

he been unreasonable?) and whether costs ought in the circumstances to be awarded.[279] It may be relevant that a person representing him/herself is likely to lack the objectivity and knowledge of law and practice brought by a professional legal adviser. However, parties are not immune from costs just because they are representing themselves. They may be found to have acted unreasonably even when proper allowance is made.[280]

20.251 There is a greater risk now than in the past that costs will be awarded against a claimant, whether represented or not. Nevertheless, if a case is run properly, tribunal orders and hearing dates are adhered to, and the case is reasonably arguable, it is unlikely that costs will be awarded. Many of the reported cases where costs have been awarded seem to involve highly unsympathetic and sometimes vindictive behaviour by the claimants (although that may just have been the tribunal's interpretation). Even so, the fact that a tribunal has decided, on the balance of probabilities, that the claimant was not telling the truth about a central plank of his/her claim does not automatically mean that costs will be ordered against him/her.[281] Costs are also a big risk where a case is really hopeless and the claimant persistently ignores advice and warnings. If a letter threatening costs is written by the employer to the claimant, it may increase the risk of costs being awarded if the case is patently very weak and the employer's letter clearly explains to the claimant in a way s/he can understand why it has no reasonable prospects of success and the amount of unwarranted expense which is being caused. A claimant in this situation should take – and listen to – specialist advice. Having said that, employees should certainly not be intimidated out of running legitimate cases because of fear of costs or letters routinely sent by some employers' solicitors threatening costs, even when there is a perfectly arguable case. The Court of Appeal has firmly stated that costs awards remain exceptional in ET proceedings.[282]

20.252 Costs should not be lightly awarded against the claimant for being 'unreasonable' in bringing the claim. The ET rules place a high threshold on the award of costs, and 'unreasonable' should be interpreted in the context of the other words in that rule.[283] The fact that

---

279 *AQ Ltd v Holden* [2012] IRLR 648, EAT. Again, under the old rules, but it seems likely the same principle applies.
280 *AQ Ltd v Holden* [2012] IRLR 648, EAT.
281 *Ladrick Lemonious v Church Commissioners* UKEAT/0253/12.
282 *Lodwick v Southwark LBC* [2004] IRLR 554, CA; *Gee v Shell UK Ltd* [2003] IRLR 82, CA.
283 *Ganase v Kent Community Housing Trust* UKEAT/1022/01.

the claimant's case is relatively weak, does not necessarily mean it is unreasonable or has no reasonable prospect of success, although it is obviously important to be very careful. If faced with a costs application against the claimant at the end of a case which s/he has lost, it is important to explain why the case previously appeared to have reasonable prospects of success. It is worth referring to these comments from the case of *E T Marler Ltd v Robertson*:[284] 'Ordinary experience of life frequently teaches us that that which is plain for all to see once the dust of battle has subsided was far from clear to the contestants when they took up arms.' Where a case seems reasonable at the outset, but its weaknesses emerge during preparation, costs should only be awarded from the point when it becomes apparent that there is no reasonable prospect of success or from when the claimant's behaviour becomes unreasonable.[285]

20.253   It is unwise to lodge an extremely weak case in the tribunal, in the hope that the employer will make a settlement offer and with the intention of withdrawing before the hearing if no offer is forthcoming. The employer would be able to apply for costs for an unreasonable case having been started and conducted up to the date of withdrawal. On the other hand, if the claimant runs a reasonable case and withdraws for good reasons, costs should not be awarded just because s/he has withdrawn. The question is not whether the withdrawal of the claim is in itself unreasonable, but whether, in all the circumstances of the case, the employee has conducted the proceedings unreasonably.[286] Withdrawal can lead to costs savings and it would be unfortunate if claimants were deterred from dropping claims because of a fear of costs ordered due to the withdrawal.[287]

20.254   The ET can order the claimant to pay some or all of the employer's costs (or vice versa). Costs awarded are not confined to those incurred by the employer as a result of the claimant's conduct.[288] The nature, gravity and effect of the claimant's conduct are all relevant factors.[289] The aim is compensation of the party which has incurred expense in

284   [1974] ICR 72, NIRC, as quoted with approval in *Lodwick v Southwark LBC* [2004] IRLR 554, CA.

285   *Ramsay and others v Bowercross Construction Ltd and others* UKEAT/0534-5/07; *McPherson v BNP Paribas (London Branch)* [2004] IRLR 558, CA. These cases considered the wording pre-2013, but the same principle is likely to apply.

286   *McPherson v BNP Paribas (London Branch)* [2004] IRLR 558, CA; see also *Yerrakalva v Barnsley MBC and another* UKEAT/0231/10 at para 7.

287   *McPherson v BNP Paribas (London Branch)* [2004] IRLR 558, CA.

288   *McPherson v BNP Paribas (London Branch)* [2004] IRLR 558, CA.

289   *McPherson v BNP Paribas (London Branch)* [2004] IRLR 558, CA.

winning the case, not punishment of the losing party.[290] While there does not have to be a precise causal relationship between the unreasonable conduct and the costs claimed, any award of costs must, at least broadly, reflect the effect of the conduct in question.[291] Costs should only be awarded on an 'indemnity' basis in very rare cases.[292]

20.255   The ET can order costs up to £20,000 without a detailed assessment being made. Alternatively, whether or not costs are likely to exceed £20,000, the ET can order that all – or a specified part – of the receiving party's costs are paid, with the amount to be assessed by a county court in accordance with the CPR 1998 or in Scotland, 'taxation' can be done by a court auditor, or by an employment judge applying the same principles.[293] The ET can apply a cap to the costs award before referring it for detailed assessment.[294] It is also possible for the parties to agree the amount of costs. Claimants may find it worrying that the ET can order costs as high as £20,000 without detailed assessment. Even in such cases, however, employers are usually required to provide in advance an itemised schedule as to how the costs were incurred. Legal costs should be broken down by the standing and hourly rate of each fee earner and the type of activity, eg telephone, meetings, letters in and out, documents read. The paying party should not be ordered to pay the VAT element on counsel's fees if the receiving party is registered for VAT and could reclaim it as input tax.[295] Where the receiving party is represented by a 'lay representative', the hourly rate payable under a costs order is no higher than that for a preparation time order (see below).[296] However, it still falls under the category of a 'costs' order so the tribunal can order costs in respect of the hearing as well as preparation time.

20.256   The ET may choose to take into account a party's ability to pay when considering whether to make a costs order or preparation time order, and if so, in deciding how much to order.[297] The ET should probably raise the question of the claimant's means itself,[298] but in

---

290 *Lodwick v Southwark LBC* [2004] IRLR 554, CA at para 23.
291 *Yerrakalva v Barnsley MBC and another* UKEAT/0231/10 at para 16.
292 *Howman v The Queen Elizabeth Hospital Kings Lynn* UKEAT/0509/12. Paragraph 6 of the judgment explains the difference between standard and indemnity costs.
293 ET Regs 2013 Sch 1 r78.
294 *Kuwait Oil Co v Al-Tarkait* [2020] EWCA Civ 1752; [2021] IRLR 254.
295 *Raggett v John Lewis plc* [2012] IRLR 906, EAT.
296 ET Regs 2013 Sch 1 r78(2).
297 ET Regs 2013 Sch 1 r84.
298 *Doyle v North West London Hospitals NHS Trust* UKEAT/0271/11.

any event, it is sensible for the claimant to ask the ET to consider his/her means and come prepared with evidence as to what these are, eg bank statements, evidence of rent or mortgage payments, regular outgoings, payslips from any new job or benefit statements. The ET should consider the effect of a very large costs order, eg where the claimant might have to sell his/her house where s/he lives with dependent children.[299] The ET should give brief reasons as to how and why ability to pay has affected its decision on costs.[300] The ET can also take account of the fact that the claimant is represented by a trade union which is likely to pay any costs awarded against its members.[301]

20.257   A party can apply for costs at any time during the proceedings. The application can be made by writing to the tribunal or orally, at the end of a hearing. An application cannot generally be made later than 28 days from the date the final judgment in the case (which may be a remedy judgment if the claimant was successful) was sent to the parties.[302] The paying party must be given a reasonable chance to comment in writing or at a hearing before any order is made against him/her.[303] If costs are awarded against the claimant, s/he is entitled to written reasons for the costs order, provided s/he requests the reasons within 14 days of the date the tribunal sends the judgment on costs.[304] The reason and basis for the costs order should be clearly specified by the ET, particularly when a substantial sum (in the thousands) is awarded[305] and the ET must explain how it calculated the costs.[306]

20.258   Although there is an occasionally used procedure for taking a costs deposit from a party where a case has little reasonable prospect of success,[307] costs may be awarded as set out above regardless of whether a deposit was ever required or even applied for. Nevertheless, if a deposit was ordered and the party has lost, s/he is at greater risk

---

299 *Howman v The Queen Elizabeth Hospital Kings Lynn* UKEAT/0509/12.

300 *Jilley v Birmingham and Solihull Mental Health NHS Trust* UKEAT/0584/06 and 0155/07 at para 44; see also *Herry v Dudley Metropolitan Council* UKEAT/0100-116.

301 *Walker v Heathrow Refuelling Services Co Ltd and others* UKEAT/0366/04.

302 ET Regs 2013 Sch 1 r77.

303 ET Regs 2013 Sch 1 r77.

304 The usual rules on requesting reasons apply. See ET Regs 2013 Sch 1 r62(1); and para 20.204.

305 *Lodwick v Southwark LBC* [2004] IRLR 554, CA.

306 *D36 Ltd v Castro* UKEAT/0853/03 and 0113/04.

307 See para 20.167 onwards.

of a costs award. If the case is lost for substantially the same reasons given in the deposit order, the party will be considered unreasonable in continuing with the claim or response unless proved otherwise.[308] However, the tribunal still has the usual discretion as to whether to award costs and must consider all the circumstances.[309]

20.259   Usually settlement negotiations are 'without prejudice', ie off the record as far as the ET is concerned.[310] However, some employers write a letter headed 'without prejudice save as to costs' or a completely open letter offering a certain sum. They threaten to draw this to the attention of the ET on the question of costs should the claimant lose, or win and get a lesser award. Such letters are adapted from civil court practice, where costs are routinely awarded, and are known as '*Calderbank* offers'. The EAT has said they have no place in the ET system. However, general intransigence or pressing for an unreasonably high award after its excessiveness has been pointed out could amount to unreasonable behaviour and lead to costs.[311] The EAT has said in the past that an employee has an absolute right to have his/her unfair dismissal claim decided and an ET therefore should not award costs simply because the claimant has turned down an open offer of compensation which turns out to equal or exceed the eventual ET award.[312] The position may be different if the employer concedes unfair dismissal. There is some contradiction between this principle and the more recent cases mentioned above considering *Calderbank* offers. Overall, the safest approach is for the claimant to be seen to take a reasonable approach in running the case and in his/her approach to negotiations; there may be a difference between a reasonable unwillingness to settle at all unless unfairness is admitted, and a willingness to settle, but only for ridiculous figures.

Preparation time orders

20.260 A tribunal can make a preparation time order that the paying party makes a payment in respect of the preparation time of another party.

---

308 ET Regs 2013 Sch 1 r39(5).
309 *Oni v UNISON* UKEAT/0370-1/14.
310 See paras 9.18–9.193.
311 *Monaghan v Close Thornton Solicitors* UKEAT/0003/01. See also *Power v Panasonic (UK) Ltd* UKEAT/0439/04 and *Kopel v Safeway Stores plc* UKEAT/0281/02, although the claimants' whole approach was misconceived in those cases.
312 *Telephone Information Services v Wilkinson* [1991] IRLR 148, EAT; *Billany v Knutsford Conservative Club* [2003] UKEAT 0065_03_0807.

An order may be made for preparation time spent by the receiving party (including its employees or advisers) while it was not legally represented.[313] It applies to time spent working on the case, except for time spent at any final hearing. The ET will assess the number of hours spent on preparation, based on its estimate of a reasonable and proportionate time to have spent on the particular case, given its complexity and the number of witnesses and documents, and information on time spent provided by the party claiming costs.[314] The hourly rate goes up by £1 annually each year on 6 April. In the year starting 6 April 2021, it was £41/hour. The grounds for making a preparation time order, principles applicable and procedures followed are otherwise the same as for costs awards (para 20.249 onwards). As already stated, orders for witness expenses fall under the category of 'costs' orders (see below).

20.261   Preparation time orders are intended to acknowledge the cost of tribunals to unrepresented parties and not-for-profit representatives. However, it is a lesser entitlement, both in terms of the hourly rate, and the fact that it excludes time at the hearing itself.

Wasted costs orders against representatives

20.262 An ET can order a representative to pay all or part of the wasted costs of any party and/or witness expenses, if these have been incurred as a result of any improper, unreasonable or negligent act or omission by the representative.[315] An order can also be made where the ET thinks it unreasonable to expect the receiving party to pay costs in the light of any improper, unreasonable or negligent act or omission by the representative occurring after the costs were incurred. These costs are known as 'wasted costs'. It seems that the ET must itself assess the amount of costs awarded and unlike in the case of ordinary costs or preparation time orders, cannot refer large sums to the county court or Sheriff Court for assessment.[316]

20.263   It must be fair to make such an order and a high level of misconduct is required, not simply running a hopeless case or acting unreasonably or negligently in the normal way, but having lent assistance to

---

313 ET Regs 2013 Sch 1 r75(2).
314 ET Regs 2013 Sch 1 r79 sets out the calculation rules.
315 ET Regs 2013 Sch 1 r80.
316 By analogy with *Casqueiro v Barclays Bank plc* UKEAT/0085-6/12 – decided under the old rules, but the principle seems the same.

proceedings which amount to an abuse of the court.[317] This is partly because, due to the confidentiality of communications between a lawyer and his/her client, it can be hard to establish how much the lawyer had been told and how much of the decision-making was down to him/her. If privilege is not waived by the represented party, the tribunal may well not have the necessary evidence to decide if the representative acted negligently and whether the representative's actions (as opposed to the party's) caused unnecessary costs.[318] Orders can be made against legal and non-legal representatives, but not against a representative who is an employee of a party, eg the employer is represented by an in-house solicitor or human resources (HR) manager.[319] A wasted costs order cannot be made against a representative who is not acting for profit with regard to the proceedings, eg a law centre or trade union representative. However, orders can be made against representatives acting on a contingency or conditional fee arrangement ('no win, no fee'). A wasted costs order can even be made requiring a representative to pay wasted costs to his/her own client.[320]

20.264   A wasted costs order can be made by the ET on its own initiative or on the application of any party. A party can apply at any stage up to 28 days after the final judgment (including any remedy) was sent to the parties.[321] The ET must give the representative a reasonable opportunity to comment in writing or at a hearing before making an order and may take account of his/her ability to pay.[322]

Witness expenses

20.265 The government no longer reimburses witnesses for their expenses. The 2013 rules state that a 'costs order' can be made which requires the claimant or respondent to pay the other party or to pay a witness directly in respect of 'expenses' that have been or will be incurred in connection with an individual's attendance as a witness at the ET.[323] It is uncertain whether 'expenses' simply means matters such as

317 For a useful summary of the principles, see *KL Law Ltd v Wincanton Group Ltd* UKEAT/0043/18.
318 *KL Law Ltd v Wincanton Group Ltd* UKEAT/0043/18.
319 ET Regs 2013 Sch 1 r80(3).
320 ET Regs 2013 Sch 1 r80(3).
321 ET Regs 2013 Sch 1 r82.
322 ET Regs 2013 Sch 1 rr82 and 84.
323 ET Regs 2013 Sch 1 r75(1)(c).

fares and if necessary, overnight accommodation, or whether it also includes any loss of earnings.

20.266   An ET can make such an order on its own initiative or on the application of a party or the witness him/herself where a witness has attended or has been ordered to attend to give oral evidence at a hearing.[324] It is not necessary for any of the other grounds for making a costs order to apply, eg that the paying party has acted vexatiously or unreasonably or that his/her case had no reasonable prospect of success. The ET can order a party to pay for his/her own witness or for a witness called by the other party.

20.267   There is no case-law authority regarding the basis on which tribunals should make costs orders in favour of witnesses. Factors taken into account may be the relevance of the witness's evidence; whether the other side could have agreed rather than disputed the evidence; and the overall strength of the case. It is uncertain whether the cost to the witness will also be a relevant factor in deciding whether an order should be made. In particular, whether the paying party caused the witness unnecessary expense, eg by requiring him/her to attend the entire hearing rather than fixing a particular time for his/her evidence (though the latter would need to be with the agreement of the ET and the other side).

Settlement

ACAS, settlement agreements and consent orders

20.268 As an entirely separate matter from early conciliation (see para 20.16) an ACAS officer is attached to most ET claims, including all unfair dismissal or discrimination claims, and has a statutory duty to promote a settlement. The ACAS officer usually contacts each party by letter or telephone and the claimant can choose whether to use him/her as an intermediary or negotiate direct with the employer. Communications to an ACAS officer are not admissible in evidence before the ET, unless the parties expressly agree.[325] Most settlements do not take place until each side has a better idea of the strengths of their case following the stages of case preparation. Many settlements occur shortly before the hearing. The role of ACAS is usually referred to as 'conciliation' and the ACAS officer is a 'conciliation officer'. In recent years, the option of 'mediation' has been introduced, either through ACAS or independent mediators, or judicial mediation through the tribunal. As this is most suited to discrimination claims, it is discussed in more detail at para 21.53.

20.269 The ACAS officer has no duty to see that the terms of a settlement are fair and must not advise on the merits of the claim.[326] There is therefore no need to enter into a discussion about the evidence and it is best to focus on issues of compensation. There is a risk that what is said to ACAS about the claimant's case may be passed on to the employer's representative. Remember that the ACAS officer's job is to encourage settlement – it is not to worry about whether the claimant has secured a good deal. There are many advantages in settling a claim, as it avoids the risk of losing, the unpleasantness of the hearing, the operation of the recoupment provisions and may be the only way to negotiate a good reference.

20.270 A settlement agreement reached through ACAS is recorded on a COT3 form and signed, but it is binding and effective as soon as it is verbally agreed, even if the form is never later signed.[327] It is essential to have clear instructions from the claimant on whether to settle and on what terms and to be absolutely clear to ACAS when any discussion is subject to final confirmation. The COT3 form is used to record the settlement terms and is signed by the claimant and respondent or their representatives. ACAS will not normally rubber-stamp a settlement if reached in direct negotiation with the employer's representative, but will accept some direct communications are necessary to clarify or hurry things along. Once there is a COT3 settlement, the ACAS officer notifies the ET. If the hearing date is very close, check that ACAS has done this and it may even be wise to write to the ET to confirm that an ACAS settlement has been reached.

20.271 Once the tribunal has been notified of a settlement, it sends out a letter stating that it has updated its records and closed its file; the file is kept in archive for one year and then destroyed. The tribunal may not issue an order or judgment in these circumstances. Many employers' representatives are uncomfortable with this and therefore insist on it being part of the settlement terms that the claimant writes to the tribunal asking for his/her case to be withdrawn. The ET will then issue a judgment dismissing the proceedings. This means the

---

326 *Clarke and others v Redcar and Cleveland BC; Wilson and others v Stockton-on-Tees BC* [2006] IRLR 324, EAT.

327 *Gilbert v Kembridge Fibres* [1984] IRLR 52, EAT.

claimant cannot try to issue new proceedings against the employer on essentially the same point. There are two exceptions. First the ET will not dismiss the proceedings if the claimant explicitly reserved the right to bring a further claim on substantially the same matter and had a legitimate reason to do so. This is unusual but it can happen, eg the claimant accidentally made a notice claim in excess of the maximum an ET can award and wanted to withdraw and reissue in the civil courts. Second, the ET also will not automatically dismiss the claim following withdrawal if it believes it would not be in the interests of justice to do so.[328]

20.272 The important point is that the claimant does not agree to withdraw the claim until after the employer has paid the settlement sum. For example, 'the claimant undertakes to write to the tribunal withdrawing the claim within seven days of payment of the settlement sum and meanwhile, the case is adjourned generally'. This preserves the claimant's right to reopen the case if the employer does not pay, or to sue for the agreed sum, whichever s/he thinks will most effectively secure him/her the money. Some employers offer to pay only because they cannot face the idea of a tribunal hearing, but have no intention of actually paying up. The possibility of reopening the case can be important to make such employers honour the settlement.

20.273 Usually a settlement is not binding in respect of ET claims unless it is agreed through ACAS. However, ACAS need not be involved where a 'settlement agreement' is reached directly between the parties. This may happen before or after ET proceedings have been launched. A 'settlement agreement' is a written agreement which relates to the employee's complaint before the ET and states that the employee has received independent advice from a qualified lawyer (a solicitor holding a practising certificate or a barrister who is covered by professional indemnity insurance), a legal executive, officers, officials or employees of an independent trade union who have been certified by the trade union as competent to give advice or an advice centre employee or volunteer who has been certified as competent to give advice. In these circumstances it will be a binding settlement.[329] A 'settlement agreement' used to be called a 'compromise agreement' which was useful, because it distinguished it from ordinary agreements to settle which did not follow the procedural requirements.

20.274 If a settlement is reached at the tribunal, eg on the morning of the hearing, it is important to get it validly written out and signed on the

328 ET Regs 2013 Sch 1 r52.
329 ERA 1996 s203; EqA 2010 s147.

spot. If there are the appropriate representatives, a settlement agreement could be drafted. If not, an ordinary signed agreement could be made, although the employer is unlikely to find this satisfactory. Another option is to ask the tribunal to make a judgment by consent.[330] The parties should write out the agreed terms, sign them and ask the tribunal to make an order. There are two ways to do this – either the terms are set out fully in the tribunal's order; or they are set out in a schedule which is attached to the order. The latter option is preferable as it can contain matters outside the tribunal's jurisdiction, eg agreement to provide a reference, and it should avoid any risk of recoupment.

20.275 The tribunal should then be asked to make a decision that the claim is 'stayed' (or 'adjourned') pending payment. As explained above, this means the claimant can ask for the hearing to be refixed if the employer fails to pay and it maintains the incentive on the employer to comply with the settlement terms. Otherwise, the claimant's only option will be to pursue enforcement through the civil courts.[331] Typical wording for the order could be:

> Terms of settlement having been agreed between the parties, the claim is stayed against the respondent. Liberty for the claimant to restore on or before (*date*)[332] and if no application is received by that date, the claim is dismissed against the respondent upon withdrawal by the claimant.

If the claimant is confident that the employer is willing and financially able to pay, s/he may be prepared to agree immediate withdrawal. Wording then could be:

> Terms of settlement having been agreed between the parties (as annexed), the claim in case number (*insert*) is dismissed on withdrawal by the claimant.

Of course, the actual terms of settlement also need to be written out and the clerk can be asked to make copies for the tribunal and each party.

The settlement terms

20.276 Care should be taken that the employee fully understands the implications and meaning of any settlement before an agreement is

---

330 The ET has specific power to do this under ET Regs 2013 Sch 1 r64.
331 See para 18.72.
332 Usually one week after the payment date.

concluded. If possible, only the particular ET claim should be settled. In practice, many employers insist on a wider settlement, ie that in return for payment of the specified sum, the employee waives any other claim arising out of the contract of employment or its termination. Settlement agreements (although not necessarily COT3s) must precisely itemise the claims to be settled and may not be effective to exclude potential complaints which have not yet arisen or been discussed in any way.[333] As well as explaining to the claimant precisely what a 'full and final' settlement means, it is safest to ask explicitly whether money is owing, eg in respect of wages, bonuses and commission, notice pay or holiday pay. Ask about the claimant's health and whether s/he has had any accidents at work. Whatever his/her reply, there should be an express exclusion for any personal injury (PI) or industrial injury claims.[334] If there seems to be a potential PI claim, the claimant should get advice on this before concluding a settlement. This is because the exclusion may not be sufficient to safeguard his/her right to bring such a claim or the employer may refuse to agree such an exclusion or to exclude any potential PI claims of which the claimant is aware at the time of settlement. It may also be possible to do a global settlement including the value of the PI claim. In addition, there should be an explicit exception for pension rights. ACAS officers often suggest the PI and pension exclusions in their standard wording. If the employer had also made a contract claim against the claimant, this needs to be included in the settlement. Otherwise it may continue even if the claimant settles or withdraws his/her own contract claim.

20.277   If the employer wants a confidentiality clause (sometimes known as an 'NDA' – non-disclosure agreement), exactly what needs to be kept confidential needs to be described, plus any necessary exceptions regarding who the claimant can tell. ACAS has published guidance on non-disclosure agreements, which discourages their routine use.[335]

20.278   It is advisable to specify in the COT3 or settlement agreement a date for payment. The actual wording of an agreed reference should be incorporated, as well as the basis on which it will be supplied.[336] The following considerations should be taken into account:

---

333 *Hinton v University of East London* [2005] IRLR 552, CA; *McWilliam v Glasgow City Council* UKEATS/0036/10.

334 But see para 19.28 where settling discrimination claims.

335 At www.acas.org.uk/acas-publishes-new-guidance-on-non-disclosure-agreements-ndas.

336 See appendix C at C13 for an example.

- Does the claimant wish to ask for an open ('to whom it may concern') reference as well as asking the employer to write a reference in the agreed terms on request?
- Does the claimant wish to suggest that if the employer is asked for a verbal reference, s/he will only provide a written reference, or that s/he will respond verbally with the same content and spirit and without addition?
- Does the claimant wish to suggest that if the employer is asked for a reference which asks specific questions, s/he may not answer at all, or s/he may answer if asked, or only with the claimant's prior written consent, or that s/he will answer with the same spirit and content as the agreed terms and without addition? What should the employer say if asked for more information?
- It should be specified that the reference will be supplied on headed notepaper and duly signed and dated. The claimant may wish to specify who should or who should not deal with reference requests.

It should be remembered that an employer cannot be asked to lie in a reference and can only be controlled so far. Often it is important to preserve some remnants of goodwill to improve the chances of fair behaviour in response to reference requests. Alternatively, it may focus the employer's mind, if s/he has asked for confidentiality, for example, to state that if the spirit or content of the reference agreement is not adhered to, then the claimant will no longer be bound by confidentiality.

20.279   The employers may propose a lengthy and complex settlement agreement with onerous and unsuitable terms. It is essential to understand what these mean and to ensure that the claimant understands and consents.[337] A claimant also needs to be advised of any tax implications and of the effect of receiving a lump sum on any benefits currently claimed. The tax position on settlements may not be straightforward and is entirely beyond the scope of this book. Advisers should seek specialist advice where it is an issue.[338] The following is a very general summary which provides the gist of the tax regime, but does not cover every aspect and does not go into the finer details, exceptions and pitfalls:

- Termination payments, eg for unfair dismissal or for a discriminatory dismissal, are taxable as such. As long as no element of the

337 See appendix A at A29 for a checklist on settlement terms.
338 *Harvey on industrial relations and employment law,* published by LexisNexis, has a very useful introductory section on tax (see appendix F).

payment is taxable under any other rules, there is a £30,000 exemption.[339]

- Some parts of a settlement sum may comprise contractual earnings which are owed, eg outstanding wages or holiday pay, which would be taxable in any event.
- For dismissals after 6 April 2018, if the employee is dismissed without notice or pay in lieu, and subsequently receives a large termination payment, HM Revenue & Customs (HMRC) is likely to view that payment as including notice, and to tax that element.[340]
- If, under the settlement agreement, the employer pays the employee's genuine legal expenses direct to the employee's solicitors, this payment should not be taxable.
- Regarding tax on injury to feelings, see para 19.12.
- Employers sometimes seek indemnities in respect of any tax which unexpectedly later becomes due. If the claimant is in a strong position, s/he should insist that the employer bears the risk of unforeseen tax. If the claimant does agree to provide an indemnity, this certainly should not include an agreement to cover any tax penalties, interest or fines, resulting from the employer's default or slowness in dealing with the matter, or the employer's costs in dealing with HMRC, and the claimant should reserve his/her right to make representations or challenge any liability or assessment with HMRC before the employer pays it.

---

339 Income Tax (Earnings and Pensions) Act 2003 ss401 and 403. See also para 19.12 regarding tax in discrimination awards and settlements.
340 Income Tax (Earnings and Pensions) Act 2003 s402D. This is called PENP – post-employment notice pay – and is calculated according to a formula.

CHAPTER 21

Running a discrimination case

continued

Chapter 21: Key points

- The procedure for running a discrimination case is basically the same as that for running an unfair dismissal case, but with greater emphasis on obtaining evidence. The Advisory, Conciliation and Arbitration Service (ACAS) early conciliation (EC) applies, just as it does for unfair dismissal.
- For many years there was a very important statutory questionnaire procedure. This was replaced by a non-statutory scheme supported by an ACAS Code. Without statutory questionnaires, workers need to think more carefully about how to obtain the necessary evidence.
- There are strict time limits for starting a discrimination claim in the employment tribunal (ET). Where there are several acts of discrimination or different legal claims, it is essential to think separately about the time limit and possible extension for each individual claim, as these may vary.
- Claims can be brought against individual discriminators as well as against the employer.
- Preliminary hearings are usually held in discrimination cases to deal with case management orders, eg what additional information and disclosure is needed. The discussions can be tricky to handle and it is important to be well-prepared.
- The ET can make orders in discrimination and other cases to prevent or restrict public disclosure of the names of parties or witnesses or certain allegations where necessary in the interests of justice or to protect rights to privacy etc. However, the powerful principle of open justice limits what an ET can agree to do.
- The ET should be informed of and accommodate accessibility issues affecting any disabled party, witness or representative. This applies to all types of tribunal case, not just discrimination.
- The claimant usually gives evidence first in a discrimination case. S/he should be prepared for aggressive cross-examination by the respondent's representative.
- For quick reference to unfamiliar terms, readers may find the Glossary at appendix D useful.

Introduction

21.1   In running discrimination cases, the basic principles are similar to those for unfair dismissal, including the Advisory, Conciliation and Arbitration Service (ACAS) early conciliation (EC), dealt with in chapter 20 above. This chapter, which should be read in conjunction with chapter 20, highlights the procedural and technical differences that arise in cases under the Equality Act (EqA) 2010. In addition, where the worker intends to claim compensation for injury to health or needs to prove s/he is disabled for a disability discrimination claim, s/he may need to obtain medical evidence at an early stage (see chapter 16). A person bringing a case is referred to as a 'claimant'. The employer or individual against whom a case is brought is called the 'respondent'.

ACAS early conciliation

21.2   ACAS EC applies to discrimination claims. The rules are set out at paras 20.20–20.27 above. In summary, a claimant must make an EC notification to ACAS and obtain a certificate before s/he can present a tribunal claim. EC affects time limits (see para 20.56 onwards). In effect, a claimant must notify ACAS before the end of the tribunal time limit. S/he must then submit his/her tribunal claim within the required time after the ACAS certificate. The following explanation of tribunal time limits should be read with this in mind.

The tribunal claim (ET1)

The time limit

Overview

21.3   The ET1 tribunal claim must be presented within three months of the act of discrimination – ie, the last day for presentation is three calendar months less one day from the discriminatory act.[1] For example, if the discrimination happened on 5 May, the deadline is 4 August. Earlier incidents can be referred to as supporting evidence.[2]

---

1   EqA 2010 s123(1). As ACAS EC usually applies, this means ACAS should be notified by this deadline.
2   *Eke v Commissioners of Customs and Excise* [1981] IRLR 334, EAT.

If the claimant is still employed when s/he started the tribunal case and further discrimination takes place after that, in theory it should be possible to amend the original ET1 to add the later claims.[3] However, it is probably safer to submit a new ET1 within the time limit and ask for the two cases to be considered together. Having said that, in this situation, the claimant does need to keep a sense of proportion. Submitting the first ET1 may well have upset both the claimant and the employer, and it is easy for the claimant subsequently to become discontented with every unfairness in the workplace. It would not be sensible for a claimant to keep submitting fresh ET1s unless very serious further adverse actions have been carried out, which the claimant can prove are discriminatory. Otherwise, the effect of continually submitting ET1s is likely to destroy the workplace relationship and confuse the major issues in the case.

21.4   The act of discrimination is not always easy to identify, so advisers must be alert about time limits. Time usually runs from when a decision not to promote or appoint is made (not when it is communicated),[4] or from when a warning is given, and not from the end of any appeal or grievance procedure. However, if the failure of the grievance procedure or appeal was itself because of race, religion, sex, sexual orientation, age or related to disability, then that is a further act of discrimination from which another three-month period runs. It is unwise to rely on this to extend time, as usually it is the original action which constituted the discrimination, not the decision on appeal or grievance, which tends to be a rubber-stamping exercise. Therefore, if there is a lengthy appeal or grievance process, it is important not to allow the original incident to fall out of time.

21.5   In some situations, discrimination continues over a period of time, sometimes up to the date of leaving employment. The time for submitting an ET1 then runs from the end of that period.[5] The common, although technically inaccurate, name for this is 'continuing discrimination'. A disciplinary suspension is considered an act extending over a period of time, and a suspension linked with disciplinary proceedings should be viewed as a whole.[6] Similarly, the time-limit on a discriminatory decision to instigate disciplinary proceedings may well not start to run until the disciplinary decision is made.[7]

3   *Okugade v Shaw Trust* UKEAT/0172/05; *Prakash v Wolverhampton City Council* UKEAT/0140/06.
4   *Virdi v Commissioner of Police of the Metropolis and another* [2007] IRLR 24.
5   EqA 2010 s123(3).
6   *Kilraine v Wandsworth LBC* UKEAT/0260/15; [2016] IRLR 422.
7   *Hale v Brighton & Sussex University Hospitals NHS Trust* UKEAT/0342/16.

21.6   Advisers should be careful if relying on showing continuing discrimination for time limit purposes as it is sometimes hard to distinguish it from a single act of discrimination with continuing effects. For example, a failed promotion attempt resulting in continued employment at a lower grade and wage is not in itself continuing discrimination.[8] If a worker is out of time, s/he should make another attempt at promotion on which it may be appropriate to base a claim provided this latest failure also appears discriminatory on the facts. On the other hand, if an employer maintained a conscious or unconscious rule that only workers of a particular race or sex would be promoted to certain posts, that would be continuing discrimination.

21.7   In *Calder v James Finlay Corporation Ltd*,[9] a woman was twice refused a mortgage subsidy from her employer which was available to men. The Employment Appeal Tribunal (EAT) said that although the unsuccessful requests took place more than three months prior to her claim, the rules of the scheme barring women constituted a discriminatory act extending throughout Mrs Calder's employment until she left. Similarly, in *Barclays Bank v Kapur*,[10] the employer kept in force 'a discriminatory regime' throughout the workers' employment in that their past service in banks in Africa was not credited towards their pensionable service. The ET had jurisdiction to hear the claim even though the workers entered the discriminatory scheme several years earlier, which was when the decision not to include their service was taken.

21.8   The *Calder* and *Kapur* cases concerned formal rules which remained in place and were discriminatory. This principle was taken further in *Owusu v London Fire and Civil Defence Authority*.[11] Mr Owusu, a clerical worker, complained of the failure to re-grade him at any stage since his transfer several years earlier and the failure to let him act-up when such opportunities arose (all of which had arisen more than three months before he lodged his tribunal claim). The EAT accepted there could be a continuing act of discrimination if Mr Owusu proved a discriminatory policy, rule or practice (however informal) which, when followed or applied, excluded him from re-grading or acting-up opportunities. However, it would be necessary to prove a linking practice as opposed to a series of one-off decisions, even if they were each discriminatory.

---

8 *Amies v ILEA* [1977] ICR 308, EAT.
9 [1989] IRLR 55, EAT.
10 [1989] IRLR 387, CA; [1991] IRLR 136, HL.
11 [1995] IRLR 574, EAT.

21.9   The *Owusu* case was approved of by the Court of Appeal in *Cast v Croydon College*,[12] which confirmed that there could be a continuing policy or regime, even if it was not formal or written, and even if it was only confined to one post or role. Mrs Cast asked her line manager before she went on maternity leave whether she could return to work afterwards on a part-time or job-share basis. He refused, even though the college had a written policy generally receptive to job-sharing at all levels. Mrs Cast unsuccessfully repeated her request to her manager twice after her return. A few months later she resigned. Subsequently she lodged her ET claim. The ET said that the time limit was three months from the first refusal, before Mrs Cast even went on maternity leave. Mrs Cast's claim was therefore well out of time. The Court of Appeal disagreed. It said that the several refusals of Mrs Cast's request indicated the existence of a discriminatory policy in relation to her post (manager of the college's information centre). This policy continued until Mrs Cast left and her claim was therefore in time, regardless of the date of any particular request and refusal.

21.10   The Court of Appeal also considered the position if there had not been a continuing policy or practice, but simply a succession of independent refusals. Any refusal within the last three months would be in time provided it was the result of a fresh consideration by the employer (even if it was a decision made by the same manager and on the same facts). On the other hand, if the manager simply referred back to his previous decision or expanded on his reasons, this would not be a fresh consideration, and time would run from the earlier decision. Mrs Cast therefore had an alternative argument that the time limit should be counted from the last (and not the first) of her line manager's refusals.[13]

21.11   The most useful case of all is *Hendricks v Commissioner of Police for the Metropolis*,[14] where the Court of Appeal further extended the *Owusu* principle. It said a worker need not be restricted to proving a discriminatory policy, rule, regime or practice, if s/he could show that a sequence of individual incidents were evidence of a 'continuing discriminatory state of affairs'. In other words, Ms Hendricks must prove a general link between the incidents so that they amounted to

12 [1998] IRLR 318, CA.

13 See also *Akhtar v Family Services Unit* (1996) 70 EOR 56, CA, and the slightly different approach in a non-employment case, *Rovenska v General Medical Council* [1997] IRLR 367, CA.

14 [2003] IRLR 96, CA, confirmed by *Lyfar v Brighton and Sussex University Hospitals Trust* [2006] EWCA Civ 1548.

'an act of discrimination extending over a period', as opposed to a succession of unconnected and isolated specific acts. Her case was in fact unusual and extreme. She was complaining of nearly 100 incidents of bullying and harassment by a large number of colleagues over an 11-year period and ongoing discrimination by management in failing to give support and unjust appraisals. If there is continuing discrimination, the continuing act is not broken by absences, eg on holiday or maternity leave during which nothing happens.[15]

21.12   A close sequence of discriminatory actions, eg a series of threats, warnings and abuse, as is common in harassment cases, may well constitute continuing discrimination in the legal sense, although to be safe the ET claim should be submitted within three months of each incident. In practice, it is usually enough if the most serious incidents (and those easiest to prove) are in time. The other actions can still be referred to as supporting evidence. Alternatively, the ET could be asked to exercise its discretion to allow in late claims.

21.13   In sexual harassment cases, time limits are often missed because, for example, the worker goes off sick and then resigns. No further acts of discrimination are likely to have occurred during the worker's absence, but an adviser may mistakenly calculate the three months from the resignation rather than from the last incident at work.[16] Another trap into which advisers can fall occurs where the harassment stops once the worker complains, but the employer takes some time to investigate and the longer-term outcome is unsatisfactory. By the time the worker realises s/he is unhappy with the solution, three months may have passed from the harassment itself.[17]

21.14   A discriminatory act may consist of an omission to do something, eg failure to promote a worker on racial grounds or failure to make a reasonable adjustment. A deliberate omission takes place on the date the discriminator decides on it. In the absence of any evidence to the contrary, this means the date when the discriminator takes any step inconsistent with doing the omitted act or otherwise, the date by which s/he might reasonably have been expected to do the omitted

---

15 *Spencer v HM Prison Service* UKEAT/0812/02; (2004) 132 EOR 27.

16 Although *Spencer v HM Prison Service* (above) may help. Also, in some circumstances, the worker's resignation may amount to constructive dismissal which would be in time, but the technical requirements of constructive dismissal would have to be met.

17 Continuing failure to implement promised remedial measures may amount to continuing discrimination, thus extending the time limit: *Littlewoods Organisation plc v Traynor* [1993] IRLR 154, EAT. The ambit of this decision is unclear and advisers should still be careful, especially given the principles in the following paragraph.

act.[18] This is most likely to come up in disability discrimination cases, where the worker claims for failure to make reasonable adjustments. To be safe on time limits, it would be wise to submit any ET claim within three months of the date when the employer first refuses to make the required adjustment or, if earlier, when it might reasonably be expected that the adjustment would have been made. If in doubt, count the three months from when the employer should first have become aware of the need for the adjustment. As with a sequence of discriminatory actions, it is possible for a sequence of failures to make adjustments to constitute a continuing discriminatory state of affairs.[19] Nevertheless, it is difficult to distinguish a one-off omission where the need for the adjustment continues, from a sequence of omissions. It is therefore safer to count the time from individual omissions as suggested.

21.15 The case-law on time limits and on out-of-time claims (below) shows a reluctance by the higher courts to be rigid about time limits in discrimination cases. But it can still be a source of major difficulty in the ETs. Employers tend to argue fiercely that as many incidents as possible are out of time. Although several of the above cases may come to the rescue where a worker seems to be out of time, it is still far easier to run and prove a case where the relevant incidents occurred within the last three months. For example, the concept of continuing discrimination may seem to rescue a situation, but in fact it is much harder to prove that there is a linking practice, than that discrimination occurred on separate occasions.

21.16 The government has acknowledged that the three-month time limit is too short for many workers who have experienced the trauma of sexual harassment and also for many pregnancy discrimination claims. It has indicated that once normal levels of service are restored following disruption caused by the pandemic, it will look closely at extending the time limit for EqA 2010 claims to six months.[20]

---

18 EqA 2010 s123(3) and (4); *Matuszowicz v Kingston upon Hull City Council* [2009] EWCA Civ 22; [2009] IRLR 288.

19 See eg *Secretary of State for Work and Pensions (Jobcentre Plus) v Jamil and others* UKEAT/0097/13.

20 'Consultation on sexual harassment in the workplace: government response', updated 21 July 2021 at www.gov.uk/government/consultations/consultation-on-sexual-harassment-in-the-workplace/outcome/consultation-on-sexual-harassment-in-the-workplace-government-response.

Claims outside the time limit

21.17   An ET may allow a claim outside the time limit if it is just and equitable to do so.[21] This is a wider and therefore more commonly granted discretion than for unfair dismissal claims. The ET must weigh up the reasons for and against extending time and explain its thinking.[22] The ET's approach should be neither 'strict' nor 'liberal'; it should simply consider all the facts and circumstances.[23]

21.18   For many years, a case called *Keeble* has been taken to mean that an ET should go through a checklist based on the requirements of the Limitation Act 1980 s33. However, the Court of Appeal has now stated very firmly that this is not a rigid checklist and tribunals only need to consider the factors which they think are relevant in the particular case.[24] Having said that, two factors are almost always relevant to consider, ie a) the length and reasons for the delay, and b) whether the delay has 'prejudiced' the employer.

21.19   Regarding the reasons for the delay, if the reason is that the claimant was ignorant of his/her rights, it will be relevant whether that ignorance was reasonable, and whether it continued to be reasonable for the whole period during which the claimant was late. The extent to which the claimant acted promptly and reasonably once s/he knew whether or not s/he had a legal case is likely to be relevant. The steps the claimant took to try and get legal advice, and the nature of the advice s/he received, may also be relevant. A mistake by the claimant's legal adviser should not be held against the claimant[25] and appears to be a valid excuse.

21.20   It may also be relevant if the employer withheld certain information or facts from the claimant, especially if the claimant was asking for certain information to establish whether s/he had a case. Where the delay is because the claimant first tried to resolve the matter through use of an internal grievance procedure, this is simply one consideration for the ET to take into account.[26] If the delay was

---

21 EqA 2010 s123(1)(b).
22 *Osaje v Camden LBC* (1997) EAT/317/96; *Arube v Devon Probation Service* [2001] IRLB 14, EAT.
23 *Chief Constable of Lincolnshire Police v Caston* [2009] EWCA Civ 1298; [2010] IRLR 327.
24 *Adedeji v University Hospitals Birmingham NHS Foundation Trust* [2021] EWCA Civ 23.
25 *Chohan v Derby Law Centre* [2004] IRLR 685, EAT; *Virdi v Commissioner of Police of the Metropolis and another* [2007] IRLR 24, EAT.
26 *Apelogun-Gabriels v Lambeth LBC and another* [2002] IRLR 116, CA; *Vodafone Ltd v Winfield* UKEAT/0016/16.

because the claimant tried to pursue the matter in correspondence before rushing to an ET, this should also be considered.[27]

21.21 Where the claimant has a mental disability, a tribunal may choose to take account of the fact that s/he was reluctant to admit to him/herself that s/he had a disability or that severe depression made it difficult for him/her to make decisions about taking legal action.[28]

21.22 Having said all that, unlike with late unfair dismissal claims, it is not necessary to prove it was 'not reasonably practicable' to get the claim in on time. The reason for the lateness is just one factor to be put into the balance. Although an important factor, the ET should not refuse to allow in a late claim purely because the claimant has no good excuse for the lateness.[29] As we have said, all relevant factors should be considered.

21.23 Moving on to the effect of the delay, the extent to which the strength of the evidence of either party might be affected by the delay will be very relevant. When considering if the employer is 'prejudiced' by the delay, the tribunal will look at whether any harm is done to the employer or to the chances of a fair hearing by the element of lateness. Has it prevented the employer investigating the claim while matters were fresh? Was the employer already aware of the allegation and so not caught by surprise? If an employer says it has lost documents or a witness, how important is that evidence to the matters to be decided?

21.24 An ET may also take into account the apparent strength of the case.

21.25 Where a claim is outside the time limit because a material fact emerges much later, eg the job for which a black worker applied is filled several months later by a white person with lesser qualifications or experience, an ET should consider whether it was reasonable of the claimant not to realise s/he had enough evidence until this happened.[30] Alternatively, it could be argued that the claim is not out of time at all because the act of discrimination has not 'crystallised', ie finally taken place, until the eventual appointment.[31]

21.26 It is often worth trying to get in an out-of-time claim, if the above factors are persuasive, as some ETs are prepared to exercise their discretion favourably. In particular, where there are several discriminatory

---

27 *Osaje v Camden LBC* (1997) EAT/317/96.
28 *Department of Constitutional Affairs v Jones* [2008] IRLR 128, CA and *Carter v (1) London Underground Ltd (2) Transport for London* UKEAT/0292/08 respectively.
29 *Rathakrishnan v Pizza Express (Restaurants) Ltd* UKEAT/0073/15; [2016] IRLR 278.
30 *Clarke v Hampshire Electro-Plating Co Ltd* [1991] IRLR 490, EAT.
31 *Clarke v Hampshire Electro-Plating Co Ltd* [1991] IRLR 490, EAT.

acts, with only the most recent in time, the ET may well grant leave to allow in the earlier acts. This is especially so where the earlier acts will be raised in the case anyway as matters of evidence supporting the latest claim.[32] In this type of case, the ET1 should be clearly drafted so that it is plain that the earlier discriminatory acts are meant to be claims in their own right and not just supporting evidence.

21.27   It is also wise expressly to ask permission in the ET1 for the earlier claims to be allowed in under the ET's discretion. However, whether or not this request is made in the ET1 itself, it should be sought by the claimant's representative at the very latest at the start of the hearing. The onus is on the claimant to seek permission. The ET is not obliged to offer to use its discretion and if nothing is said, the earlier acts may be treated purely as evidence.[33] Frequently, however, the question will already have been dealt with during the preparation of the case.

21.28   The ET may also order a preliminary hearing to make decisions on whether part or all of the claim is in time. However, if the one key incident is in time and the earlier incidents will be heard as evidence anyway, a preliminary hearing on this may not be very useful as it will make no difference to the ground covered by the final hearing.[34] Also, it is usually very difficult to decide whether continuing discrimination may be proved without hearing all the evidence, which cannot be done at a preliminary hearing. The ET is often better able to decide after it has heard all the evidence at the final hearing whether to allow in the earlier incidents as claims in themselves.

Drafting the ET1

Overview

21.29   For details regarding the standard forms (ET1) for tribunal claims, see para 20.60 onwards. At section 9.1 of the standard form, the claimant is asked to state what compensation or other remedy s/he wants if s/he is successful. The checklist seemingly does not give the option of asking for both recommendations and compensation in a discrimination claim, because it refers to 'compensation only'. This

---

32 Chapter 16 on relevant evidence, para 16.14 on other acts of discrimination, and para 21.32 re focusing on the key claims.

33 *Dimtsu v Westminster CC* [1991] IRLR 450, EAT.

34 The EAT in *Sutcliffe v Big C's Marine* [1998] IRLR 428, EAT and the Court of Appeal in *Smith v Gardner Merchant Ltd* [1998] IRLR 510, CA at 512 have both commented against the general desirability of having pre-hearing reviews (now preliminary hearings) in this context.

is presumably an error. The claimant should tick both 'compensation only' and 'recommendation' (assuming s/he wants to keep open the possibility of both).

21.30 At section 8.2 of the current form, the claimant should describe the incidents (with dates) which s/he believes amounted to discrimination. It is not enough just to tick the box for discrimination in section 8.1. For example, if the claimant ticks the box for age discrimination at 8.1, at the very least, s/he should identify the alleged discriminatory action and type of discrimination in section 8.2, eg, 'I was made redundant because I was over 50' or 'I was not promoted because I complained about age discrimination'.

21.31 It is very important to be sure about the extent of the worker's claim and set it out correctly from the outset. The ET may not allow any amendments of the ET1 later, especially to add entirely new grounds.[35] Even if the ET does allow later amendments, the original version of the ET1 will still be visible and any significant changes will damage the claimant's credibility. The safest route is to think through the case and get it right from the outset.

21.32 Because discrimination claims do not only cover dismissal, there may be a large number of employer actions over a period of time which the claimant feels were discriminatory. The claim form should make it clear which actions are part of the claim as opposed to merely supporting evidence. It is sensible to focus on key incidents which have a reasonable chance of being proved and are suggestive of discrimination, as opposed to unfairness alone.[36] Overloading the case with too many complaints going back over several years can weaken a case rather than strengthen it.

21.33 If the worker resigned following several discriminatory actions by the employer, s/he should consider claiming constructive dismissal (see para 12.22) as well as claiming for each of the acts which s/he feels were discriminatory. There are good reasons for claiming both. On the one hand, the constructive dismissal claim may fail for a technical reason, even if the earlier actions were discrimination. On the other hand, although compensation for pre-resignation discriminatory actions could include loss of earnings if the worker can show they led directly to the resignation, it is a more obvious award for a constructive dismissal. Also, the constructive dismissal will usually have taken place at a later date than the matters leading to the resignation, which can be important in respect of time limits.

---

35 See paras 20.71–20.75 for general principles regarding amendments.
36 See chapter 16 for relevant evidence and in particular, para 16.14.

21.34   If the worker is claiming indirect discrimination or victimisation as well as direct discrimination, s/he must specify this.[37] Equally, if s/he is complaining of discriminatory treatment during employment and on dismissal, it needs to be clear whether s/he is saying the dismissal is some form of discrimination or victimisation, or whether it is purely an unfair dismissal. As long as the claimant has clearly described all the relevant facts in a way which makes it clear what s/he is claiming, s/he should be allowed to amend later to add the correct legal label. For example, if the claimant wrote on the ET1 that, during a grievance hearing, s/he alleged sex discrimination in promotion, and that is what led to the subsequent dismissal, s/he should be able to add the label 'victimisation' later. Conversely, there may be difficulty amending if all the claimant has done is describe the discriminatory promotion, his/her complaints and the subsequent dismissal, without making any link.

21.35   If victimisation is claimed, the protected act should be cited. In indirect discrimination claims, because of the uncertainty about which provision, criterion or practice (PCP), and which pool the ET will approve, it is probably best to express the claim in broad or alternative terms.

21.36   All key matters on which the claimant will rely should be mentioned concisely in the tribunal claim with dates. It is important to include any racist, sexist or similarly offensive remarks based on other protected characteristics. However, if claimants do omit to mention historic incidents in their ET1 which provide further supporting evidence of discrimination, they should not be debarred from including such evidence for the first time in their witness statement for the hearing.[38] Nevertheless, this is a dangerous strategy and may lead to an award of costs against them for unreasonable conduct of the proceedings. If unfair dismissal is being claimed in addition to discrimination, this should be added in a separate paragraph specifying in which way the dismissal was unfair, to clarify that it is recognised as a different issue.[39]

21.37   If the claimant has mentioned an actual comparator in the ET1, s/he should still reserve the right to argue that s/he has been less favourably treated than a hypothetical comparator would have been.[40]

---

37 *Office for National Statistics v Ali* [2005] IRLR 201, CA.

38 *Senyonjo v Trident Safeguards Ltd* UKEAT/0316/04.

39 See para 20.60 onwards for drafting an ET1 in unfair dismissal claims.

40 See para 16.17 on comparators and appendix A at A8 for a sample pleading.

Naming individual respondents

21.38 Individuals may be named as respondents in the ET1, as well as the employing organisation. Remember that ACAS must be notified of each respondent and needs to have issued a certificate in respect of each or a single certificate naming more than one respondent.[41] It should be possible to bring a claim purely against an individual,[42] but it is rarely done. Apart from anything else, the employer is more likely to have sufficient funds to pay out any compensation. It is therefore normal to bring a discrimination claim against the employer, but whether any individuals are named as additional respondents depends on several considerations:

- Compensation will be awarded equally against the individual and the employing organisation on a 'joint and several' basis.[43]
- If the employing organisation might escape liability because the employer took all reasonable steps to prevent the discrimination happening,[44] naming individuals ensures that the claim succeeds against somebody. This is the most obvious reason for naming individuals. Therefore, if during the course of the case, the employing organisation accepts vicarious liability for any discriminatory actions of the discriminator, the ET may suggest the claimant withdraws the claim against the individuals. However, as set out below, there are other powerful reasons why the individuals should remain as respondents. An ET cannot strike out the case against individual respondents for this reason alone without the claimant's consent: this is a judicial decision which should be handled appropriately and would require grounds.[45]
- It usually ensures that the named individuals will give evidence at the hearing, so the desirability of their attendance must be considered.
- In sexual harassment cases in particular, it is possible that the employer will require the individual to obtain separate representation in case there is a conflict of interest. The claimant may gain

---

41 See paras 20.22 and 20.81.
42 *Barlow v Stone* [2012] IRLR 898, EAT established this under the former Disability Discrimination Act 1995, and *Hurst v Kelly* UKEAT 0167/13 under the former Sex Discrimination Act 1975. The position would appear clearer (though untested) under EqA 2010 s110 because the wording more directly makes individuals personally liable. The employer must be potentially vicariously liable subject to any reasonable steps defence – see paras 13.95–13.98.
43 See para 19.11.
44 See para 12.27.
45 See para 21.59 on the ET's powers to strike out parts of the claim.

useful additional or conflicting information from separated sources. On the other hand, two separate representatives for the respondents will mean a longer and more expensive hearing.

- In harassment cases, it ensures that the individual perpetrator is personally accountable and unable to hide behind the employer. As stated above, compensation will be awarded equally against the perpetrator in regard to discriminatory actions by that individual. If there is a negotiated settlement, part of the settlement sum may be agreed to be paid by the individual.

- In sexual harassment claims where the claimant cannot face seeing the harasser in the room, it is easier to ask the tribunal to exclude the alleged harasser until s/he gives evidence where s/he is not a named respondent.

- Where there has been deliberate and malicious discrimination, costs may be awarded against an individual respondent for unreasonably defending the proceedings.[46] This is valuable because, where, as is common, the employer supports and funds the individual's case, it can be implied that s/he has underwritten the individual's costs,[47] including those ordered against the individual. However, where the individual is not joined as respondent, unless it can be argued that the principle of vicarious liability extends to vicarious liability for the conduct of proceedings, the employer could avoid a costs order by claiming that s/he was entitled to rely on statements from the individual that s/he (the individual) had not discriminated.

- If the employing organisation is likely to go into liquidation with no funds for unsecured creditors, it ensures that the claim can proceed[48] and that there is a likelihood of recovering money, assuming the named individual has any assets. If the employing organisation goes into liquidation or ceases trading completely unexpectedly and no individual respondent has been named, the claimant can try to join an individual respondent at a later stage.[49]

- Individuals should be named as respondents only if there is a strong case against them, as the ET may be reluctant to make a specific finding against them without clear evidence. Caution

---

46 See para 20.246 onwards on costs.

47 *Bourne v Colodense* [1985] ICR 291; [1985] IRLR 339, CA.

48 Leave from the High Court may be necessary to proceed against a company in liquidation or administration, depending on the type of insolvency or liquidation proceedings.

49 Employment Tribunals (Constitution and Rules of Procedure) Regulations (ET Regs) 2013 SI No 1237 Sch 1 r34.

should be used in naming more than one individual since it is much harder to prove that a number of individuals have each discriminated against the claimant. There may also be a risk of costs if naming certain individuals appears frivolous, vexatious or otherwise unreasonable.

Written reasons for dismissal

21.39 Where the alleged act of discrimination is dismissal, a worker should usually request written reasons under Employment Rights Act (ERA) 1996 s92 provided s/he was an employee and had sufficient service.[50] In discrimination cases this may be a particularly significant piece of evidence. Even if the reply is received within the 14 days, you should always add an ERA 1996 s92 claim to the ET1 since, if the discrimination is proved, there is a possibility that the claimant will receive an award for untrue reasons.

Case management

Additional information and written answers

21.40 The considerations and procedure are the same as for unfair dismissal.[51] However, in discrimination cases it is especially important to secure as much information as possible of the employer's defence and this opportunity should not be lost. This is particularly important now that the statutory questionnaire procedure has been abolished (see below). For example, where the claimant was dismissed for fighting at work, s/he could ask: 'What action was taken against the other person involved in the fight? In the last three years have there been other incidents of fighting at work? If so, when, who was involved, what was their "race" and were they dismissed; if not, what action was taken against them?'

21.41 The employer often asks the claimant to provide very detailed additional information regarding his/her claim. For comments on this, see para 21.51.

---

50 See para 20.11.
51 See paras 20.116–20.122.

Disclosure

21.42　Disclosure of documents is a crucial part of the information gathering process in most discrimination cases.[52] The ET will not permit wide, trawling exercises for helpful evidence. What will be relevant and useful needs to be thought out (see a sample in appendix A at A13). If documents are necessary for disposing fairly of a case or for saving costs, the ET should order their disclosure, even if they are confidential.[53] Where there is a problem about confidentiality, the ET can look privately at the documents to see if they are necessary and to decide whether the same information can be obtained in any other way.

21.43　　If an ET refuses to order disclosure of something important, you should write asking that the decision be varied, explaining why the disclosure is needed and citing any relevant case-law.[54] If really crucial, it may be best to request an oral hearing and to give notice to the employer of the request. The EAT has said that given the evidential difficulties in discrimination cases, tribunals should be generous in orders for disclosure against the employers. Such cases are not the same as normal litigation, where a party must make out a credible case before the process of disclosure begins.[55] If the ET continues to refuse disclosure, unless there are powerful grounds for appeal, it is often best to request the document again during the final hearing, when it becomes clear whether it is relevant. This is feasible in discrimination cases because they tend to last several days.

21.44　　The ET can order disclosure of relevant statistics provided that they are relevant to an issue in the case, eg whether the employer, intentionally or otherwise, operated a discriminatory policy which manifested itself on other occasions and may have manifested itself in respect of the present complaint.[56]

21.45　　The disclosure process usually refers to documents. However, for the sake of convenience, the ET can order that the employer supply a digest of information contained in bulky documents.

52　See also paras 20.123–20.127 for general principles.

53　*Nassé v Science Research Council; Vyas v Leyland Cars* [1979] IRLR 465, HL; *Plymouth City Council v White* UKEAT/0333/13.

54　For example *Enfield LBC and others v Sivanandan* [1999] UKEAT 450_98_0102; *Nassé v Science Research Council; Vyas v Leyland Cars* [1979] IRLR 465, HL if the problem is confidentiality.

55　*Enfield LBC and others v Sivanandan* [1999] UKEAT 450_98_0102.

56　*West Midlands Passenger Transport Executive v Singh* [1988] ICR 614; [1988] IRLR 186, CA.

21.46   Original documents should always be inspected, as tampering can happen in discrimination cases, and a request should also be made that the originals be brought to the hearing. If documents have been electronically generated, it may be worth asking for them to be sent by email, as it may be possible to check the date of creation.

Obtaining comparative and statistical information

21.47   For nearly forty years, effective use of the statutory questionnaire procedure under discrimination law offered an important opportunity to obtain information from the employer. Under this procedure, a worker was able to ask the employer written questions regarding the reasons for his/her own treatment and comparative questions regarding treatment of others with and without the same protected characteristics. Although employers could not be ordered to answer the questions, they were expected to do so, and this was underpinned by EqA 2010 s138(4) which said that an ET could draw an adverse inference from a failure to answer within eight weeks, or from an evasive answer.

21.48   Unfortunately, the former Conservative and Liberal Democrat coalition government decided to repeal EqA 2010 s138 and abolish the statutory questionnaire procedure in respect of all acts of discrimination on or after 6 April 2014.[57] It was replaced by a non-statutory procedure set out in ACAS guidance, which is not used as much as it could be. Although the ACAS guidance appears recently to have disappeared from its website,[58] there is no reason why workers cannot still send a non-statutory questionnaire before or after they start their discrimination case. The advantage of sending it before is that the answers may show whether or not it is worth pursuing a case. This can also be explained to the employer in the covering letter. Sample questionnaires are set out in appendix A, at A9–A12. It is much harder to win a discrimination case where no questionnaire has been submitted.

21.49   Although workers cannot ask for the same level of detailed information as part of the disclosure and information processes, they should still ask at that point for essential information such as comparative information of other candidates on a recruitment, promotion process

---

57 Enterprise and Regulatory Reform Act 2013 s66.

58 The EHRC refers to the procedure at www.equalityhumanrights.com/en/ multipage-guide/responding-questions-discrimination-workplace but, at the time of writing, the author has been unable to find details on the ACAS website.

or redundancy. If the employer objects that certain information is confidential, it may be possible to agree that names of other workers be deleted.[59] However, sometimes it is not possible to disguise the identity of other workers, especially where particular comparators are the subject of enquiry. A particular problem may arise if the employer objects to providing information regarding named comparators due to data protection law.[60] The prime response to this is that disclosure is allowed under Data Protection Act (DPA) 2018 Sch 2 para 5 where it is necessary in connection with actual or prospective legal proceedings or for establishing, exercising or defending legal rights. Further, though this is superfluous, disclosure is allowed where the people referred to give explicit consent. An allegedly worried employer should therefore be invited to seek such consent. The employer may also dispense with such consent where reasonable.[61]

Preliminary hearings – case management

21.50   ETs usually hold preliminary hearings at an early stage in discrimination cases for the purpose of making case management orders (or, in jargon terms, 'giving directions').[62] The aim is normally to clarify the 'issues', sort out what disclosure, additional information and written answers should be ordered, decide on exchange of witness statements, estimate the length of hearing and fix dates. It helps set the agenda if the request for disclosure and additional information is sent to the employer in advance of the preliminary hearing and copied to the ET. Although this rarely happens, an ET does have power at a preliminary hearing to rule that certain witnesses cannot be called at the hearing because they are irrelevant.[63]

21.51   The employment judge will usually start by identifying 'a list of issues'. This has two elements. First, identifying every act of discrimination (and other claim) relied on. It's very important that the worker leaves nothing out. Second, breaking down the legal and sometimes factual issues within each claim. For example, if a claim is that the worker's dismissal was victimisation under EqA 2010 s27, the issues might be: 'Did the worker complain to HR on 5 May 2021 that she

---

59   See para 21.42 for confidentiality in relation to disclosure.
60   See paras 1.69–1.87 and particularly paras 1.79 and 1.82.
61   See para 1.75 above.
62   This type of preliminary hearing was previously called a case management discussion (CMD). See paras 20.154–20.160 for general tactics for case management generally at preliminary hearings.
63   *McBride v Standards Board for England* UKEAT/0092/09.

was being excluded from client meetings because she is Chinese? Was that a protected act? Did the worker make that allegation in bad faith? Was the worker's dismissal on 14 July 2021 because she did the protected act?'.[64] The list of issues should be helpful for everyone in preparing to run and defend the case. It will be a reference point for the tribunal at the final hearing in knowing what needs to be decided, although ultimately it is what is in the ET1 that counts. If the list of issues contains additional allegations, the worker will need permission to amend the ET1 to add those. On the other hand, if anything crucial does not find its way into the list of issues, it needs to be established whether that is an oversight or it has actually been dropped. Ideally all this should be sorted out at the preliminary hearing, but sometimes the position needs to be clarified later.

21.52   At the preliminary hearing, many employers take the opportunity to seek clarification of the case against them and the adviser should go prepared for some tricky questions. It is also common for claimants to be asked to give further written details of exactly what they are saying. This is fair enough if the ET1 is vague or unstructured, but where the claim is already clear, employers still tend to request further detail. The EAT has said there is a difficult balance to be drawn between requiring particularity on the one hand, and going too far, so as to render the proceedings technical, legal and pure matters of form, on the other. ET procedures are designed to give relative ease of access to unrepresented parties to make their complaints. When too much is put in writing, ultimately the trial of an action will dissolve into an examination of a whole series of documents rather than concentrating on the main issues in the case. Everything should be made clear by the time of the full hearing by means of an exchange of witness statements, following full and proper disclosure.[65] If taken by surprise at the preliminary hearing, do not attempt to answer on the spot. Ask for 14 days to supply voluntary additional information. This is particularly important if a representative but not the worker attends the preliminary hearing, as is common. The claimant or adviser may find that statements or explanations made casually at a preliminary hearing find their way into the ET's subsequent order or account of the hearing and cause problems later, eg by artificially narrowing the case. Preliminary hearings in discrimination cases should be prepared for very carefully as they can have a major impact on shaping the case. The employment judge

---

64 For a sample list of issues, see A24 in appendix A.
65 *Enfield LBC and others v Sivanandan* [1999] UKEAT 450_98_0102.

can exert considerable pressure to formulate the issues on the spot, and if the claimant or his/her representative is unprepared or unassertive, the nature of the case can change.

Mediation

21.53   In England and Wales, a tribunal may ask the parties at the preliminary hearing whether they are interested in judicial mediation. If so, the regional employment judge decides whether to send the case for mediation, depending on resources and its suitability for mediation. As a rough guide, cases where the final hearing is likely to last at least three days and which involve discrimination or where the claimant is still employed are the most suitable. The regional employment judge will then hold a telephone preliminary hearing to see whether both sides are genuinely willing to compromise. If so, a date for the mediation will be fixed and existing case management orders will usually be put on hold. The mediation will be carried out by a trained employment judge and tends to last up to a day. The idea is to enable the parties to reach a settlement of the case and agree a way forward if the employee is still employed. The judge's role is to remain neutral and avoid giving advice or expressing any opinion on the merits of the case. His/her function is simply to help the parties find a resolution. If the mediation is unsuccessful, the tribunal proceedings will go ahead with a different employment judge and the contents of the mediation will be kept confidential. The scheme is similar in Scotland.

21.54   As well as judicial mediation, ACAS and private organisations may offer mediation at any stage before or during the proceedings, although unlike the tribunal, they may well charge a fee. Whether or not mediation is a good idea is hard to say. A lot depends on whether the employer is in good faith, what the claimant wants and whether s/he can cope with a tribunal hearing. Settlement can be achieved without a mediation meeting – there is always the normal option of negotiating via the representatives, usually over the telephone, through ACAS. The advantage of a meeting is that both parties come to it with an intention to settle, which makes an agreement more likely. Also, it gives the claimant the feeling that s/he has brought the employer to the tribunal forum and has been heard. The disadvantage is that some employers (or their lawyers) may use the opportunity to weaken the claimant's resolve and effectively circumvent the claimant's representative. Also, a claimant may give too much away. Strictly speaking, if the mediation fails, the employer cannot quote what the claimant said at the mediation to the ET. However, in reality it will be useful for the employer to hear what the claimant says and see how s/he reacts under pressure.

Judicial assessment

21.55   In October 2016, a new 'judicial assessment' procedure was introduced into the tribunals for England and Wales. The procedure, which is purely voluntary, can take place at the first case management preliminary hearing after the usual steps have been taken to define the issues and agree a time-table for case preparation. If a party is interested in judicial assessment, ideally s/he should notify the tribunal in advance of the preliminary hearing by ticking the box on the case management agenda which is usually sent out.

21.56   If both parties and the employment judge agree to hold a judicial assessment, it will take place in the second part of the preliminary hearing. The idea is that the judge will give a confidential practical assessment of the strengths, weaknesses and risks of each side's arguments. This will be based on the allegations rather than on evidence, which will not have been heard. It is not supposed to be a mini-trial and it is not a free advice session. It is just an indication which may help the parties have a more realistic view of the case and sums involved, and may therefore encourage settlement. One useful aspect of judicial assessment might be to explain to both sides the realistic value of the claim if it succeeds.

21.57   It is not anticipated that negotiations and settlement will take place at the judicial assessment. It is not a quick form of judicial mediation. It may be that the outcome of judicial assessment is that the parties ask for a day to be fixed for judicial mediation or that they go away and negotiate directly. The content of the judicial assessment must be kept confidential. It can be referred to in further 'without prejudice' negotiations or at judicial mediation, but not openly. The employment judge will not be involved in the final hearing. More detail is set out in Presidential Guidance.[66]

21.58   Judicial assessment does not seem to have been used much in practice. Clearly there are dangers for a party with a weak case. On the other hand, it might inject a note of realism where one or other party is unrealistic, and it may set the ball rolling on negotiations. Judges are likely to be cautious in what they say, and parties may need to read between the lines.

---

66   For England and Wales, see *Presidential guidance rule 3 – alternative dispute resolution* at: www.judiciary.uk/publications/employment-rules-and-legislation-practice-directions/.

Striking out

21.59   An ET at a preliminary hearing may try to discourage or even strike out some of the claimant's background evidence on grounds that it is irrelevant. This would mean that the claimant could not deal with those matters at the full hearing and would be unable to obtain related disclosure at the preparatory stages. The EAT has said that an ET should be careful not to overstep the line between legitimate case management and oversimplifying the case by striking out proper claims to save time.[67] Although it may be desirable that cases should be kept within proper bounds, the claimant must not be prevented from putting his/her full case. An ET certainly should not refuse to allow in relevant evidence of past acts of discrimination simply to save time.[68] On the other hand, evidence can be excluded if it is not relevant or if its relevance is only marginal, eg evidence of a historic discriminatory culture in the organisation involving entirely different people to those involved in the current claim.[69] The EAT has said it is not generally a good idea for background evidence to be struck out at a preliminary stage since the tribunal at the full hearing is usually the best placed to decide whether evidence is relevant, and it can manage the hearing as it goes along; however, there will be cases where there are real advantages in ruling out irrelevant evidence at an early stage, eg where it will otherwise substantially lengthen the hearing or incur substantial costs for the other party.[70]

21.60   If the ET wishes to strike out some of the claims (as opposed to supporting evidence), it must follow the correct procedure.[71] An ET has power to strike out or amend all or part of a claim on grounds that it is scandalous, vexatious or has no reasonable prospect of success.[72] The claimant must have been given a reasonable chance to argue against the striking out.[73] Where a discrimination case looks extremely weak on the ET1, an ET may be tempted to strike out the whole claim, but this should not occur except in the most obvious case. Discrimination cases are generally fact-sensitive and their

---

67   *Hambly v Rathbone Community Industry Ltd* [1998] UKEAT 746_98_0110.
68   *Senyonjo v Trident Safeguards Ltd* UKEAT/0316/04 would be helpful on this.
69   *(1) HSBC Asia Holdings BV (2) HSBC Holdings plc v Gillespie* UKEAT/0417/10.
70   *(1) HSBC Asia Holdings BV (2) HSBC Holdings plc v Gillespie* UKEAT/0417/10.
71   *Hambly v Rathbone Community Industry Ltd* [1998] UKEAT 746_98_0110.
72   ET Regs 2013 Sch 1 r37.
73   ET Regs 2013 Sch 1 r37(2).

proper determination is vital in a pluralistic society.[74] For general principles on striking out, see paras 20.111 and 20.165 onwards.

Privacy and restrictions on disclosure

21.61 ET hearings are open to the public and reporters are in regular attendance in some tribunals, often arranging for photographers to ambush unwitting claimants as they leave the building. Judgments generally go onto a public register,[75] although not those which simply confirm a case has been withdrawn (often as a result of a settlement).

21.62 ETs have a general power under rule 50 to make suitable orders to protect privacy so far as they consider necessary in the interests of justice or to protect anyone's rights under the European Convention on Human Rights (ECHR or 'the Convention').[76] This raises difficult issues about the balance between ECHR Article 8 (the right to private life), Article 10 (the right to freedom of expression) and Article 6 (entitlement to a fair and public hearing) of the Convention.[77] In theory, an order can be applied for and made in any kind of case, eg where very personal issues are involved such as a claimant undergoing gender reassignment or with certain kinds of disability, or where exceptionally serious allegations of misconduct have been made.[78] However, the vast majority of cases where the issue arises involve sexual harassment or other sexual misconduct.

21.63 Tribunals have a great deal of flexibility in the type of order which they can make. For example, they can order that all or part of the hearing be conducted in private or that the identities of parties, witnesses or other individuals are kept anonymous during the hearing and/or in written records including documents, listing notices and the public register. This can apply for a limited period of time or permanently. However, a tribunal has no power to keep a judgment off the public register (except in national security cases).[79]

---

74 *Anyanwu v South Bank Students Union and South Bank University* [2001] IRLR 305, HL.

75 At: www.gov.uk/employment-tribunal-decisions.

76 ET Regs 2013 Sch 1 r50.

77 See chapter 3; and *Tradition Securities & Futures SA and others v Times Newspapers Ltd and others* UKEATPA/1415/08 and UKEATPA/1417/08; [2009] IRLR 354.

78 A good example where an anonymity order is appropriate is *X v Y* UKEAT/0302/18.

79 *Ameyaw v Pricewaterhousecoopers Services Ltd* UKEAT/0244/18; [2019] IRLR 611. This case also has a useful summary of the law on anonymity.

A tribunal can also make a restricted reporting order (RRO)[80] where the case involves allegations of 'sexual misconduct' (eg a sexual harassment case). This specifies that certain parties must not be publicly identified and can cover the person making the allegation or anyone affected by it. An RRO remains in force (unless revoked earlier) only until the final decision is promulgated. It can also be made permanent where necessary to protect Convention rights.[81] The significance of an RRO as opposed to any other kind of rule 50 order is that it is a criminal offence to publish information in breach of it.[82]

21.64   The tribunal can make a rule 50 order at any stage, either on its own initiative, or on an application by a party or someone else. A party can make a written application or raise it at any preliminary hearing or at the full merits hearing. Any party or other person (including the press) with a legitimate interest who has not had a reasonable opportunity to make representations before an order is made can apply for the order to be revoked.

21.65   Tribunals do not automatically issue rule 50 orders just because one party asks or even if both sides consent. Case-law in recent years, often in non-employment cases, has placed a very strong emphasis on the importance of 'open justice'. It is a general principle of UK constitutional law that justice is administered in public. The starting point is therefore that the principle of open justice is of paramount importance and departing from that can only be justified when it is strictly necessary to secure the proper administration of justice.[83] This might occur if fear of publicity would genuinely deter a worker from bringing a claim. In relation to discrimination claims, the EU directives require member states to provide an effective remedy and make judicial processes 'available' to those claiming discrimination covered by the directives.[84] Having said that, it is important to note that the wording of rule 50 does allow privacy orders to be made in wider circumstances, ie where necessary to protect someone's Convention rights, eg an individual's honour and reputation.[85] Note

---

80 Under Employment Tribunals Act (ETA) 1996 s11 or s12.
81 *F v G* UKEATPA/0659/12; [2012] ICR 246.
82 ETA 1996 s11(2).
83 *A v British Broadcasting Corporation* [2014] UKSC 25; *British Broadcasting Corporation v Roden* UKEAT/0385/14; [2015] IRLR 627.
84 Equal Treatment Directive 76/207/EEC Article 6; General Framework Directive 2000/78/EC Article 9; Race Discrimination Directive 2000/43/EC Article 7. See chapter 3 on EU law post-Brexit.
85 *A and another v X and others* UKEAT/0113/18; [2019] IRLR 620.

also that under the Sexual Offences (Amendment) Act 1992, there must be no publication of any information likely to lead the public to identify a person who is alleged to have been a victim of a sexual offence.[86] There might also be circumstances where it is important to protect vulnerable third parties.[87]

21.66   Ironically, although the reporting restrictions were originally brought in with a view to protecting complainants of sexual harassment,[88] it is very often the alleged perpetrators in such cases who try to obtain an order against the claimant's will. Some claimants have experienced heavy-handed attempts from their employers to silence them from the moment they raised the allegations, as well as intimidation from the harasser not to speak out. By the time they reach an ET, they wish the matter to be out in the open. It is now unlikely that the employer's fear of reputational damage will be enough on its own to prevent an open hearing, although it may be a factor. After all, the situation is no different from that in any other civil or criminal court. If the allegations are false, then the alleged perpetrator will be vindicated through the judicial process.[89] Even with serious unsubstantiated allegations, the public can be trusted to distinguish between an allegation and a finding of guilt.[90] A request for an order that those less directly involved are anonymised is even less likely to succeed, eg managers conducting an investigation, or the employing organisation itself.[91] Any order which is made should also not be too wide-ranging in terms of which incidents are covered.[92]

21.67   When reading the older case-law, bear in mind that ETs' power was more specific prior to 2013. Under the 2004 ET rules, there were two kinds of order: 1) an RRO (see above) in a case involving sexual

---

86 This does not mean simply harassment at work. Section 2 lists what are relevant offences.

87 Eg *F v G* UKEATPA/0659/12; [2012] ICR 246. People named adversely in a judgment who were not parties or witnesses can also ask tribunals to anonymise their name (which may or may not be granted) – see *TYU v ILA Spa Limited* EA-2019-000983-VP.

88 See parliamentary debate in *Hansard* HC, 16 June 1993, vol 226, p951.

89 *Global Torch Ltd v Apex Global Management Ltd* [2013] EWCA Civ 819. But for an example where a permanent RRO should be made, see *(1) EF (2) NP v (1) AB (debarred) and others* UKEAT/0525/13.

90 *Re Guardian News and Media Ltd and others* [2010] UKSC 1; *British Broadcasting Corporation v Roden* UKEAT/0385/14; [2015] IRLR 627.

91 *R v London (North) Industrial Tribunal ex p Associated Newspapers Ltd* [1998] IRLR 569, QBD; *Leicester University v A* [1999] IRLR 352, EAT.

92 *R v London (North) Industrial Tribunal ex p Associated Newspapers Ltd* [1998] IRLR 569, QBD; *Leicester University v A* [1999] IRLR 352, EAT.

misconduct or where there was evidence of a personal nature relating to disability, and 2) in cases involving a sexual offence, there would be a permanent deletion from the Register and other tribunal documents of the identity of those affected by or making the allegations.[93]

Preparation for the hearing

Witness statements

21.68　Well-written witness statements can be very effective in helping to win discrimination cases. As opening speeches are rare, the claimant's witness statement will be particularly important in creating a strong first impression and providing an overall picture of what the case is about. The basic procedure and considerations are set out at paras 20.186–20.196. The following additional tips are useful in writing statements in discrimination cases:

- If the claimant is likely to be the first witness, explain important background at the start of the statement, eg how the workplace is structured, the hierarchy, and the claimant's job.
- The claimant's evidence should be set out clearly, and usually in chronological order, though sometimes it is clearer to group 'themes', eg keeping a history of failed promotion attempts separate from the chronology of a dismissal for alleged misconduct.
- If possible without destroying the sense and logical order, indicate some of the discriminatory elements early in the statement. For example, in a race discrimination case, draw attention to a white dominant work hierarchy or to any racist remarks early on.
- Draw attention to legally relevant facts. For example, in a case of direct race discrimination, always point out where the employer's behaviour is different from the norm.[94] In direct discrimination cases, different treatment is more relevant than unfair treatment.
- In a disability discrimination case, a claimant may face difficult questioning related to the definition of 'disability'. The claimant may not answer properly under the stress of a hearing. It is also well-known that some people play down the effect of their disability. A well-written witness statement addressing each aspect of

---

93　ET Rules 2004 Sch 1 rr49 and 50.
94　See sample extracts from race discrimination witness statements in appendix A at A20 and A21.

the definition, having discussed the matter carefully with the claimant when s/he is not under the pressure of cross-examination in a public forum, may be crucial.

- Include facts relevant to proving the claimant's injury to feelings and, if applicable, health.[95] If the employer has particularly upset the claimant by aggressive behaviour, highlight this, as it will be relevant to aggravated damages.

- The witness statement will be probably read in private by the tribunal panel at the start of the hearing, and it is unlikely that the claimant will be asked to read it again out loud. It is important that it is clear; easy to understand, absorb and remember; and that it does not bury the best points in a mass of unnecessary detail. The length of the statement will depend on the size of the case, but as an extremely rough rule of thumb, the claimant's witness statement in, say, a five-day discrimination case should not be longer than 6,000–9,000 words.

- Ensure that the claimant understands and agrees with the content of his/her statement. Try to use his/her normal way of speaking and avoid jargon. If the claimant's English is very limited, the most practical step is probably to write the statement in English with the assistance of an interpreter. Then ask the interpreter to read it back in the claimant's first language, checking carefully that the content is understood and agreed. Then as a final paragraph, the statement should say that the claimant has had this statement translated back to him/her and that it is accurate. The statement should then be signed by the claimant and also the interpreter.

Preparing the claimant

21.69 It should be clearly explained to the claimant what has to be proved and that the issue is discrimination, not fairness. In particular, it should be stressed that it is necessary to prove that the reason for what happened was the claimant's race, religion, sex, sexual orientation, age or related to disability. Advise the claimant to keep to the relevant incidents, not to quote weak examples or accuse irrelevant people of racism or sexism. Certain cross-examination techniques are very common and the claimant should be warned. In particular, s/he is likely to be asked in respect of all key persons for the employer whether they are (for example) racist or have discriminated. Explain

---

95 See chapter 19 regarding what needs to be proved.

the legal significance of saying that someone may have discriminated and that it is not the same as saying that someone is prejudiced. If the legal issues are not explained, the claimant may find that as a result of being pinned down at the outset, s/he unwittingly makes concessions or gives evidence which (wrongly) appears to contradict how the case has been set out. On the other hand, be careful not to confuse the claimant.

21.70   Most discrimination hearings are traumatic experiences, whatever the results, so the claimant should bring along a friend or relative, especially where s/he may otherwise be the only woman or black person in the room. Sexual harassment cases will be particularly unpleasant, and the claimant should be warned about possible lines of cross-examination.

Accessibility of tribunals and legal advice

Vulnerable witnesses

21.71 The *Presidential Guidance on vulnerable parties and witnesses in employment tribunal proceedings*[96] says that where relevant, parties and the tribunal should consider whether a party's participation in proceedings generally is likely to be diminished because of vulnerability and if so, whether to make appropriate orders to facilitate participation. In particular, this includes a party or witness's mental or physical disability or health condition; domestic circumstances; social and cultural background; age, maturity and understanding; ethnic origin or religious belief (if relevant); and the impact of any actual or potential intimidation. The Guidance encourages active case management and gives examples of measures which might be taken.

21.72   In addition, the Judicial College's Equal Treatment Bench Book[97] is an excellent resource to help both practitioners and judges think about the impact of tribunal proceedings on vulnerable witnesses, and to consider what adjustments might be needed. The suggestions in the Equal Treatment Bench Book are not compulsory. The Bench

---

96 Available via a link at www.judiciary.uk/publications/employment-rules-and-legislation-practice-directions/.

97 The latest version of the current (February 2021) edition is available as a pdf on a link at www.judiciary.uk/announcements/equal-treatment-bench-book-new-edition/#:~:text=%2024%20February%202021%20%7C%20News.%20A%20comprehensive,steps%20which%20should%20increase%20participation%20by%20all%20parties. If you save the pdf, bear in mind that small amendments are made to the ETBB at broadly six-nine month intervals and sometimes in between.

Book only provides good practice guidance for judges. Judges still need to decide what adjustments are appropriate in any case, bearing in mind the evidence as to the individual's needs and the impact on the other side. However, case-law in recent years has endorsed looking at the guidance in the Equal Treatment Bench Book.

Disabled workers

21.73 It is generally accepted that ETs, as an organ of the state, should make necessary reasonable adjustments to ensure that disabled workers have a fair hearing. There is some uncertainty regarding the source of this obligation and whether it derives from the UN Convention on the Rights of Persons with Disabilities as incorporated into UK law by the Equal Treatment Directive, or from common law principles of fairness. There is also the right to a fair hearing under ECHR Article 6, together with Article 14 (non-discrimination). Strictly-speaking, the duty probably does not arise as a service provider under EqA 2010 Part 3 because of the exemptions in the statute. In any event, the legal route does not appear to matter because of the consensus that the obligation exists.[98] The issue is simply how far a tribunal should go in making adjustments. The rights of the other party to the case cannot be completely ignored, but the principle of enabling full access to the tribunal system for everyone is very important indeed.

21.74 The Equal Treatment Bench Book (see above) has separate chapters on physical and mental disability and particularly helpful is the 'Disability: glossary of impairments'. It is also worth reading chapter 2 (Children, young people and vulnerable adults). This focuses on the criminal justice system of ground rules hearings, special measures and intermediaries, but can provide further ideas for adjustments. Most interesting is the case-law which has developed regarding possible adjustments to cross-examination where witnesses are very vulnerable.[99]

21.75 Although, as already stated, the suggestions in the Bench Book are only good practice guidance, the EAT in *Rackham v NHS Professionals Ltd*[100] and the Northern Ireland Court of Appeal in *Galo v Bombardier Aerospace UK*, have encouraged tribunals to consider its

---

98 See eg the discussion in *J v K and another* [2019] EWCA Civ 5.
99 The EAT in *Rackham v NHS Professionals Ltd* UKEAT/0110/15 refers to ground rules hearings as described in the 2013 edition of the Equal Treatment Bench Book.
100 UKEAT/0110/15.

advice in respect of disabled claimants.[101] Many of the recommendations in the Equal Treatment Bench Book would also be relevant to arrangements made by advice agencies, solicitors and barristers when providing advice to disabled clients.

21.76   The Equal Treatment Bench Book recognises that the practical and procedural requirements of the tribunal process are likely to present additional barriers for disabled people, eg physical barriers to access, not just for wheelchair users (eg accessible waiting and hearing rooms, parking facilities, toilets); communication with ET staff and written information in inaccessible formats; difficulties sitting still for long periods of time or without breaks; and for users with learning difficulties or mental health issues, possible difficulty understanding the process or progress of their case and generally additional stress. The EAT in *Rackham* stressed that it is important for tribunals to remember that every individual is different. Adjustments need to be tailored to the needs of the individual and not according to some general idea about what people with a particular disability might need. Considerable value should be placed on the integrity and autonomy of the individual, and they should be listened to. It is not for other people and courts to say what adjustments would be suitable.

21.77   Possible adjustments in the hearing, depending on what is needed, might for example be:

- more breaks, later start times or shorter days;
- slowing down the pace of cross-examination;
- changing the usual order of witnesses;
- arranging for electronic bundles so that they can be enlarged;
- rearranging where everyone sits in the room;
- checking that the room has appropriate light, temperature and noise levels;
- providing a private waiting room for the individual (if available).

Rackham v NHS Professionals Ltd illustrates adjustments which were made for a claimant with Asperger's Syndrome.[102]

21.78   Although a tribunal has ultimate responsibility for ensuring that there is a fair hearing, where a disabled claimant is legally represented, a tribunal is usually entitled to leave it to the professional representatives to take the lead in suggesting what adjustments may be

---

101 [2016] NICA 25, reported at https://judiciaryni.uk/judicial-decisions/2016-nica-25.
102 UKEAT/0110/15.

needed and getting any necessary medical advice.[103] There is a box on the standard claim form inviting the claimant to state any assistance s/he requires if s/he has a disability. Be specific about what is needed and do not assume that the ET will know or ask the right questions. Even then, do not just rely on the tribunal noticing what is written on the form. Raise the matter with the tribunal at an early stage. Advisers should inform the ET well ahead of the hearing about any special requirements which an individual may have. With a party or witness who is deaf, for example, the adviser should discuss the layout and lighting of the ET room, the type of assistance needed for the person's usual mode of communication, and if an interpreter is required, their necessary qualifications. It is worth letting the employer's representative know in advance too. A good time to discuss arrangements would be at any preliminary hearing to discuss case management. Alternatively, the EAT in *Rackham* suggested a dedicated 'ground rules hearing' might be useful where suitable adjustments can be worked out.[104] Although the adjustments which are identified at this early stage should not be set in stone, they can act as a useful baseline. These steps should be taken quickly.

Religious dress

21.79   In general, religious dress should be permitted in the tribunal, although there may be objections if a Muslim woman wishes to wear the veil while giving evidence. The matter should be handled with sensitivity, and careful thought should be given as to whether the veil presents a true (rather than imagined) difficulty. In an ET, fact-findings are usually based on factors other than facial expression, eg documents, corroborating witnesses and the content of what a witness says. Identity can be established in private outside the court room, eg by a female clerk comparing the witness's face with a passport photograph. It is important to check the latest guidance provided by the Judicial College for judges in courts and tribunals in its Equal Treatment Bench Book.[105]

---

103 *Anderson v Turning Point Eespro* [2019] EWCA Civ 815; [2019] 1RLR 731.
104 There is no rigid requirement to hold something called a ground rules hearing; the point is simply that the necessary adjustments are discussed properly at some stage, ideally at a preliminary hearing: *Anderson v Turning Point Eespro* [2019] EWCA Civ 815; [2019] 1RLR 731.
105 See n97.

Interpreters, medical and witness expenses

21.80   Interpreters may be needed for witnesses who do not speak English as a first language as well as for deaf or blind workers. Parties are not generally permitted to bring their own interpreters, but the tribunal will provide an interpreter free of charge if requested. A witness may be able to read English well or speak it reasonably well, but the question is whether s/he can give the best account of his/her evidence without an interpreter.[106] It is important to give the tribunal as much advance notice as possible, especially if a sign-language interpreter is required. In Wales, there is a right to speak Welsh, and the Welsh Language Unit will provide an interpreter if a Welsh-speaking tribunal cannot be arranged.[107]

21.81   Witness expenses are no longer paid by the tribunal. For the ET's power to order one or other party to pay a witness's costs of attending, see paras 20.265–20.267. The tribunal may still pay reasonable charges for the attendance of medical professionals or the production of medical reports where that is essential to the case and if ordered by the ET in advance. It is very important to check this will happen before incurring any expense. Also ask to see any indicative pay rates applied by the tribunal for medical evidence.

Remedy

21.82   Most tribunals these days will expect to deal with both liability and remedy within the period listed for the hearing. This means being fully prepared to deal with compensation and other aspects of remedy if the claimant wins. It is surprisingly common for this aspect of preparation to be less thorough than the rest. The claimant needs to be in a position to prove his/her net and gross weekly pay. In a dismissal case, s/he needs to have details and documentary evidence of the efforts s/he has made to find a new job, and these documents must have been disclosed to the employer and copied for the tribunal. The claimant needs some kind of medical evidence to support his/her claim for injury to feelings and if s/he is claiming personal injury,

106   *Hak v St Christopher's Fellowship* UKEAT/0446/14. See chapter 8 of the Equal Treatment Bench Book regarding witnesses speaking English as a second language or using interpreters.

107   See chapter 8 of the Equal Treatment Bench Book regarding the right to speak Welsh. See also the Presidential Practice Direction (on the use of the Welsh language) available via a link at www.judiciary.uk/publications/employment-rules-and-legislation-practice-directions/.

s/he will probably need a consultant's report. The claimant should also give some advanced thought to what recommendations s/he would like the tribunal to make. If the claimant has suffered severe injury to feelings or personal injury, it may be better to ask the tribunal to confine the first hearing to liability (win or lose) and fix a separate remedy hearing if necessary. This is because a consultant's report will probably be needed, and the claimant will not wish to incur the costs until s/he knows whether s/he has won and on what basis. Separate hearings for liability and for remedy are more common in England and Wales than in Scotland.

The hearing

Start of hearing: preliminary issues

21.83 Sometimes the ET will decide certain issues relating to procedure or jurisdiction immediately before starting the full hearing. It is advisable to warn the employer's representative in advance if the claimant plans to ask the tribunal to make an order for a contentious document, so the employer does not argue that s/he has been caught by surprise. If there are time limit issues, it may be possible to decide these at the outset, but it is more likely that they can only be considered by the tribunal along with its decision on merits after all the evidence has been heard. Where there is a time limit problem, this will usually be picked up by the employer or the tribunal at the outset of the case, if not earlier, and it will be added to the issues to be decided when the tribunal goes over these with the parties. Surprisingly often, the claimant then forgets to say anything more about it. Remember that the claimant must give evidence about why the claim was late, and the claimant's representative should address in his/her closing comments whether there is continuing discrimination and/ or whether the tribunal should exercise its just and equitable discretion.

Opening

21.84 As the burden of proof is on the claimant in a discrimination case, usually the claimant and then his/her witnesses go first. In the past, the party who started gave an opening speech, but this no longer happens except in exceptional circumstances. Some legal representatives offer the tribunal a written opening statement, but this is unnecessary. Where a discrimination claim is combined with one of unfair dismissal, it is unclear who should start, and the ET has the right to govern its own procedure. In order to plan ahead, it is helpful to agree with the employer's representative in advance who should go first. Where everything depends on the employer's explanation for what s/he has done, it may be most sensible if s/he goes first. On the other hand, this may set an agenda which distracts from a sequence of events pointing to discrimination. It may also mean that the employer's witnesses escape grilling on crucial points because these have not yet been highlighted by the claimant's oral evidence.

Strategy

21.85   Although the issues will probably have been clarified at a preliminary hearing (see above), ETs often ask workers' representatives to answer the following sort of question put at the start of the hearing:

- Is it alleged that the worker was discriminated against because s/he is of African national origin or because s/he is black?
- Precisely who are you alleging discriminated against the claimant? In promotion cases, which members of the selection panel are you alleging discriminated?

If necessary, the issues should be kept open by putting matters in the alternative. Some ETs recognise that in a promotion case, for example, the claimant cannot know how a decision was made, who influenced whom, who may have been prejudiced, who may have unconsciously discriminated, etc and permit the claimant simply to say it was some or all of the panel. If an ET insists on the claimant saying which of a selection panel discriminated, unless one panel member clearly had a decisive influence, it may be best to name all panel members, reserving the right to drop the allegations against some. The claimant's representative may also wish to register a formal protest against being forced to take a position, to safeguard the possibility of a later appeal.

21.86   As a general rule, it is best to run cases in a low-key way. Fierce cross-examination and use of emotive words such as 'racist' or 'liar' will usually alienate the ET. In any opening discussion, the ET's expectations should not be needlessly raised. It may be planned to reveal overt prejudice, but legally this need not be shown, so do not promise more than may be possible to deliver. On the evidence, the ET may find it easier to accept that senior managers have acted with benevolent motives or through a desire to have someone who 'fits in' rather than through racial or sexual hostility.

21.87   In most cases, it is not certain whether the act of direct discrimination was conscious or unconscious, intended or not. The ET should not be relied on to understand what unconscious discrimination is or that it can happen. An ET may still look for indications of deliberate discrimination (whether the motives were good or bad) and focus on the honesty and sincerity of the employer's witnesses. This issue must be taken on explicitly. It should be explained that an employer may not be aware that s/he has discriminated and that the proper approach for the ET to take in determining direct discrimination or victimisation cases, ie whether inferences can be drawn from the primary facts, does not require it to make a finding as to whether the unlawful discrimination was conscious or not.[108]

21.88   The main opportunity to make comments will be in the closing speech, although this may be too late if the ET has listened to the evidence with the wrong perspective. Sometimes an ET can be reminded indirectly of the correct approach by the way the employer's witnesses are cross-examined, eg a witness can be asked (if relevant) whether s/he accepts discrimination can sometimes be unconscious.

21.89   On the whole, the fewer people that have to be proved discriminatory or prejudiced, the easier it is to convince an ET, except where the main point is that a whole workplace was hostile towards workers of a particular race or sex. Unless there is extremely strong evidence, probably in the form of a direct witness, any suggestion of a conspiracy or policy in the employing organisation to discriminate should be avoided. As a final note of caution, in running the case, be careful not to lose sight of the main issues in a mass of detail.

Dismissals

21.90   Where an unfair dismissal claim is also before the ET, it usually entails quite different considerations. The issues should be kept separate in any opening comments and in the closing speech.

21.91   Where the worker does not have sufficient service to qualify for claiming unfair dismissal, employers may argue that the discrimination claim is an attempt to circumvent the qualifying period under the ERA 1996. Great care must be taken when running such a case

108 See para 16.19.

not to deal with issues which relate solely to fairness.[109] Constantly draw attention to differences from the norm. Even so, in some circumstances it may be appropriate to argue that an employer's failure to explain his/her reasons for failing to follow disciplinary procedures, inadequate grounds for dismissal, failure to consult, etc are also matters from which an inference of less favourable treatment may be drawn.

No case to answer

21.92   It rarely happens, but it is possible that at the end of the evidence of the claimant and his/her witnesses, the employer may ask the ET to reject the case at that stage on the basis that the claimant has not proved enough facts to shift the burden of proof and receive an explanation from the employer.[110] The ET should be reminded of the decision in *Laher v Hammersmith and Fulham LBC*,[111] that only in the most exceptional cases should the employer not be called to give an explanation. If the ET dismisses the case at that stage, there is a likely basis for appeal.[112]

21.93   Some ETs deal with the matter instead by warning the claimant about the costs of proceeding further. Regardless of whether the ET actually gives a costs warning, claimants' representatives should be aware of the danger of an ultimate award of costs if the ET seems sympathetic to the suggestion that there is no case to answer.

Costs

21.94   Costs can be awarded regardless of whether there was a previous costs warning and deposit. Costs are awarded on the same basis as in unfair dismissal cases,[113] although they seem to be awarded more readily against unsuccessful claimants in discrimination cases. Because of the greater length of the latter, costs tend to be larger.

---

109 Particularly in the light of *Glasgow CC v Zafar* [1998] IRLR 36, HL. See para 16.17.
110 See para 16.2 onwards.
111 [1994] UKEAT 215_91_2005. See also *JS V Oxford v DHSS* [1977] IRLR 225, EAT and see para 16.2 onwards on the burden of proof.
112 See also the view expressed by the House of Lords in *Anyanwu v South Bank Students Union and South Bank University* [2001] IRLR 305, HL in the context of striking out at an interim stage. See para 21.59.
113 See para 20.246.

There is little that can be done about this except to keep the issues within reasonable bounds and to be aware that if a case is clearly going badly, points should not be laboured. If a costs award has to be argued, point out the matters which called for an explanation from the employer and could only be obtained in the forum of an ET hearing. If the employer failed to answer questions contained in a letter before the case was started, point out that this could have provided an early explanation to the claimant. As a matter of public policy, discrimination cases should be heard.[114]

Appeals

21.95 For more detail on the procedure and time limits for appeals to the EAT and ET reconsiderations, see para 20.243 onwards. As with unfair dismissal cases, an appeal to the EAT must usually be lodged within 42 days from the date the written judgment was sent out, or in some circumstances, within 42 days of when the written reasons were sent out. A reconsideration must be requested of the ET within 14 days of the judgment being sent out or, if written reasons were sent out later, then within 14 days of that.

21.96 An appeal can only be lodged if the judgment was wrong in law or perverse on the facts. It is hard to challenge discrimination decisions for perversity, but they can sometimes be appealed for taking the wrong approach. For example:

- The ET must give adequate and intelligible reasons for its decision so that each party knows why s/he has won or lost.[115]
- The ET must make findings of the primary facts and follow them through to a reasoned conclusion. It is not enough simply to set out the relevant evidential issues without deciding what happened, though there need not be a fact finding on every minor issue.[116]
- The ET should not give credence to a witness purely because s/he appears to be honest or truthful, without considering the whole of the evidence in the case. A witness may be credible and honest

---

114 *Anyanwu v South Bank Students Union and South Bank University* [2001] IRLR 305, HL and para 21.64. See also para 20.252 for the quote cited by the Court of Appeal in *Lodwick v Southwark LBC* [2004] IRLR 554, CA.

115 *Anya v University of Oxford* [2001] IRLR 377, CA; ECHR Article 6 (right to a fair trial).

116 *Anya v University of Oxford* [2001] IRLR 377, CA.

but mistaken. ETs must recognise that witnesses can uncon-sciously discriminate.[117]

- The ET must not evaluate a series of allegedly discriminatory incidents in isolation and consider whether each on its own is proved to be discrimination. The ET must also consider any 'eloquence that the cumulative effect of the primary facts might have'.[118]

---

117 See paras 16.19 and 13.23.
118 *Qureshi v (1) Victoria University of Manchester (2) Brazier* [1996] UKEAT 484_95_2305, quoted extensively in *Anya v University of Oxford* [2001] IRLR 377, CA. And see para 16.15.

Disciplinary, dismissal and grievance procedures

Chapter 22: Key points

- The Advisory, Conciliation and Arbitration Service (ACAS) Code of Practice on Disciplinary and Grievance Procedures sets out basic principles of fair practice and natural justice which should form part of the procedures. It is not against the law in itself to fail to follow the Code, but an employment tribunal (ET) must take account of the Code in deciding any unfair dismissal case.
- A tribunal may adjust compensation by up to 25 per cent if one party unreasonably fails to follow the ACAS Code. This applies where employees bring specified cases including unfair dismissal and discrimination.
- It is also important to be familiar with the worker's own disciplinary and grievance procedure.
- An ET case can be brought for unfair dismissal, but not for 'unfair warnings'. Unfair warnings which do not lead to actual or constructive dismissal cannot usually be legally challenged unless they are discriminatory or an unlawful detriment on certain specified grounds.
- Except for gross misconduct, there should not normally be dismissal for a first offence.
- Even on allegations of gross misconduct, fair investigative and disciplinary procedures should be followed.
- Workers have a legal right to be accompanied to disciplinary and grievance hearings.
- Discrimination maybe relevant to disciplinary action or the subject of grievances.
- Be very careful not to miss legal time limits while taking out grievances or appeals.
- This chapter should be read in conjunction with the chapters on unfair dismissal (chapter 20) and discrimination (chapter 21) as appropriate.

Disciplinary action including dismissal

Introduction

22.1   Basic principles of good practice in conducting disciplinary action are set out in the Advisory, Counciliation and Arbitration Service (ACAS) Code of Practice on Disciplinary and Grievance Procedures.

When deciding unfair dismissal cases, the employment tribunal (ET) must take account of any failure by an employer to follow the Code. As well as being relevant to whether a dismissal was unfair, the Code can also affect compensation. In specified cases, including unfair dismissal and discriminatory disciplinary action or dismissal, a successful claimant's compensation may be reduced or increased by up to 25 per cent if s/he or the employer respectively unreasonably failed to follow the Code. More detail of the Code is set out below.

22.2   There may be additional good practice steps set out in the employee's own disciplinary procedure. Where the employee has been or is likely to be dismissed, this chapter should be read in conjunction with the chapters on unfair dismissal. Where discrimination is involved, the discrimination chapters should be read. If disciplinary warnings are unfair, but not discriminatory or unlawful on any other ground (eg detriment for taking up rights under the Working Time Regulations (WTR) 1998) there is generally little an employee can do except register his/her disagreement in writing or in an appeal, so that this is at least noted on the file if matters get worse in the future and s/he is ultimately dismissed. In extreme cases s/he can resign and claim constructive dismissal, but this is not usually advised.

The ACAS Code

22.3   The ACAS Code of Practice on Disciplinary and Grievance Procedures sets out good practice guidelines for the handling of disciplinary and grievance issues in employment. The latest version of the Code (COP 1, 11 March 2015) can be downloaded from the ACAS website.[1] Although it is not against the law in itself for employers to fail to follow the Code, ETs must take this into account when deciding unfair dismissal cases.[2] The Code states explicitly that it does not apply to redundancy dismissals or to non-renewal of fixed-term contracts.

22.4   The Code has always been important for unfair dismissal cases, but it gained new significance in April 2009, when it became linked to the level of compensation. This is because an ET may increase or reduce an employee's compensation by up to 25 per cent in any successful case for unfair dismissal, discrimination or other specified

---

1 Available via a link at: www.acas.org.uk/index.aspx?articleid=2174.
2 Trade Union and Labour Relations (Consolidation) Act (TULR(C)A) 1992 s207.

claims, because of the employer's or employee's unreasonable failure to follow the Code where it applies.[3]

22.5   There have been few appeal cases setting guidelines regarding the degree of percentage uplift for failure to follow the Code. The legislation simply says the tribunal 'may, if it considers it just and equitable in all the circumstances to do so, increase any award it makes by no more than 25 per cent'. One factor likely to affect the size of the uplift is the degree to which the employer was at fault for not knowing about the Code. Another factor might be the consequence of the failure to follow the Code, so that a failure which did not make much difference to the claimant's substantive rights might lead to a lower uplift than a substantial breach, eg failing to give the claimant sufficient information to argue against why s/he should be dismissed. Where the underlying award is large, it means that the percentage uplift will amount to a lot of money. A tribunal must take this into account when deciding how much it is just and equitable to award.[4]

22.6   Examples of recommendations in the Code are:

- employees and, where appropriate, their representatives, should be involved in the development of rules and procedures;
- employers (and employees) should act consistently;
- it is important to carry out investigations of potential disciplinary matters without unreasonable delay;
- where practicable, different people should carry out the investigation and disciplinary hearing;
- if there is to be a disciplinary hearing, an employee should be given sufficient information about the alleged misconduct or poor performance to prepare to answer the case;
- the notification of the disciplinary should advise the employee of his/her right to be accompanied. The companion may be a work colleague or a trade union representative;
- employees should be given the right to appeal against any formal decision made.

22.7   Not all failures to follow the Code may be considered relevant in any particular case. The actual wording of the legislation says compensation may be adjusted where:

- 'the claim to which the proceedings relate concerns a matter to which a relevant Code applies'; and

---

3   TULR(C)A 1992 s207A; in the case of unfair dismissal, the uplift is on the compensatory award, see para 18.56.
4   *Acetrip Limited v Dogra* UKEAT/0238/18.

- the employer or employee has unreasonably failed to comply with the Code 'in relation to that matter'.[5]

So how direct does the connection need to be between the content of the Code and the claim? Clearly a concrete matter such as refusal of the right to appeal could lead to extra compensation if an unfair dismissal claim succeeded for that reason. However, what if the breach of the Code was the failure to involve employees or their representatives in the development of the disciplinary rules?

22.8   Another uncertainty is the type of case to which the Code applies. Its content most obviously refers to disciplinary action related to misconduct or incapability. On the other hand, it only explicitly excludes dismissals for redundancy or non-renewal of fixed-term contracts. What about dismissals for other reasons? The Employment Appeal Tribunal (EAT) has said that the Code applies to all cases where an employee's alleged actions or omissions involve culpable conduct or performance that requires correction or punishment.[6] This means the Code can apply to a dismissal which is ultimately for 'some other substantial reason' such as personality clash or poor work relations, but which one would usually expect to be handled through the disciplinary procedure.[7] On the other hand, it suggests the Code does not apply to dismissals for 'some other substantial reason' (SOSR) not involving culpable behaviour, eg dismissals in order to change terms and conditions. The Code does not apply to an ill-health dismissal, unless there are conduct issues such as a question mark over whether the ill-health is genuine or a failure to follow the employer's ill-health procedures.[8] The Code is unlikely to apply to a dismissal for whistleblowing, because a protected disclosure cannot be a legitimate ground for disciplinary action. However, the disclosure may amount to a grievance as defined by the Code, in which case the Code's requirements regarding grievances would apply.[9]

22.9   The Code refers to the treatment of 'employees', although ACAS says in the introduction that it is good practice to allow all workers

5 TULR(C)A 1992 s207A.
6 *Holmes v Qinetiq Ltd* UKEAT/0206/15; [2016] IRLR 664.
7 *Lund v St Edmund's School, Canterbury* UKEAT/0514/12. There is one EAT case which states that the Code does not apply to SOSR dismissals (*Phoenix House Ltd v Stockman* UKEAT/0264/15; [2016] IRLR 848), but pending any decision by the Court of Appeal, the prevailing view is that in *Lund* and *Holmes*.
8 *Holmes v Qinetiq Ltd* UKEAT/0206/15; [2016] IRLR 664.
9 *Ikejiaku v British Institute of Technology Ltd* UKEAT/0243/19.

(and not just employees) access to disciplinary and grievance procedures. However, the power to adjust compensation for failure to follow
the Code only applies where it is an employee who has brought the
case.[10]

22.10   Unlike the 2004 version which it replaced, the current ACAS
Code is extremely short – under ten pages. By reducing its guidance
to obvious and basic steps, it has lost much of its value in setting
standards. Most of the more subtle guidance has been removed to a
70-page guide: *Discipline and grievances at work: the ACAS Guide.*[11]
The guide sets out extracts from the Code and expands it with more
advice. Tribunals do not need to pay any attention to the guide, and it
is difficult to predict whether it will have any influence in cases.
Nevertheless, ACAS does have recognised status in the field of
industrial relations, and the guide expands on what is usually
regarded as good practice. It may be useful to quote sections from
the guide, for example, during disciplinary hearings.

The employer's disciplinary rules

22.11   Employers should have their own written disciplinary procedure,
which will normally cover the disciplinary rules, and standards of
expected conduct, as well as the procedures to be followed when
disciplining a worker. The rules usually set out unacceptable behaviour in a number of areas, although obviously not every scenario can
be covered. The written rule effectively serves as advance warning to
the employee. Employers sometimes have rules that employees will
be automatically dismissed for certain offences, eg fighting at work,
regardless of the circumstances. Nevertheless, in an unfair dismissal
case, the ET will still expect the employer to have considered the individual circumstances including: whether the employee was aware of
the rule and its seriousness; the employee's general work and disciplinary record; the reason the employee broke the rule on this occasion; and any mitigating factors.

22.12   The disciplinary rules normally list examples of behaviour which
is considered to be gross misconduct (see paras 22.17–22.18).

---

10 TULR(C)A 1992 ss207A and 295; *Local Government Yorkshire and Humber v
    Shah* UKEAT/0587/11 and 0026/12.
11 Available at www.acas.org.uk/acas-guide-to-discipline-and-grievances-at-work.

The disciplinary process: procedural steps

22.13 Employers should follow their own procedure when disciplining the employee, provided it complies with the general standards of fairness set by the ACAS Code. The following stages are generally regarded as good practice:

- The ACAS Code says it is important to carry out necessary investigations of potential disciplinary matters without unreasonable delay, so as to establish the facts.[12] An employee may be asked about an event so long after it occurred that s/he cannot give a proper explanation. This can make a dismissal unfair. The investigation stage may involve holding a preliminary meeting with the employee or may simply entail gathering evidence. The Code advises that where practical, different people should carry out the investigation and the disciplinary hearing in misconduct cases. An investigating or disciplinary officer is entitled to ask for human resources (HR) advice, but HR must not go beyond advice on law, procedure and process. HR should not step into areas of culpability or appropriate sanction, except for advising on consistency.[13]

- Minor cases of misconduct and most cases of poor performance should be dealt with through informal advice and counselling. The manager's objective should be to encourage and help the employee to improve. It is important that the employee understands what the problem is, what needs to be done to improve and over what period, and how his/her performance will be reviewed.

- Where formal disciplinary action is likely, the formal procedure should be followed. There should be a disciplinary hearing at which the employee is given the opportunity to answer the allegations and state his/her case. The ACAS Code says the employee must be informed in writing of the disciplinary hearing and told of his/her right to be accompanied. The notification should give sufficient information regarding the alleged misconduct or poor performance and its possible consequences, to enable the employee to prepare for the hearing. ACAS says it would normally be appropriate to provide copies of any written evidence including any witness statements with the notification.

---

12 Unreasonable delay is just as much breach of the Code as failure to follow a concrete step: *Pereira De Souza v Vinci Construction* [2017] EWCA Civ 879.

13 *Ramphal v Department for Transport* [2015] IRLR 985, EAT. It is different if HR overtly has a decision-making role.

- The ACAS Code says the disciplinary hearing should be held without unreasonable delay while allowing the employee reasonable time to prepare his/her case. At the hearing, the employer should explain the complaint and go through the evidence against the employee. The employee should be given a reasonable opportunity to answer questions and present his/her case.
- If disciplinary action is taken, the employee should be given an explanation why and informed of his/her right of appeal. The ACAS Code says that appeals should be heard without unreasonable delay and, where possible, dealt with by a manager who has not previously been involved in the case.
- Where serious misconduct is alleged, it may be fair to suspend the employee during the investigatory or disciplinary process, although this should be for as short a time as possible and kept under review. Unless the contract says otherwise, suspension should be on full pay. Although employers like to say suspension is a 'neutral' act, it is not. It may not indicate the employer has reached any adverse conclusion, but it can still have damaging effects. An employer should not suspend an employee without reasonable and proper cause to do so.[14]
- Overall, the process should be handled without undue delay and confidentiality should be maintained. The employee should be given records of the hearings.

Forms of disciplinary action

22.14   It is long-established good practice that no employee is dismissed for a first offence unless it amounts to gross misconduct. Therefore the employee should normally have received some warnings before dismissal. It is often thought that the law requires precisely one oral and two written warnings before an employee can be fairly dismissed. This is a myth. If the employee's offence is sufficiently serious, the employer can skip the earlier warnings. However, the usual stages followed would be:

- *Informal action.* This is suitable for cases of minor misconduct or unsatisfactory performance. A quiet word should be enough to deal with the problem. It may be particularly helpful in small

---

14   Otherwise it may amount to constructive dismissal – see *The Mayor and Burgesses of the London Borough of Lambeth v Agoreyo* [2019] EWCA Civ 322; [2019] IRLR 560.

employers where problems can be dealt with quickly and confidentially.

- *First formal action.* The employer can start at this stage for more serious difficulties and it will usually take the form of a first written warning. ACAS says the warning should set out the details of the complaint, the required improvement with timescale, and the right of appeal. The warning should also state that the employee is at risk of a final written warning if there is no improvement. ACAS says the employee should be told how long the warning will remain current. It is common for a copy of the warning to be kept on file but disregarded for disciplinary purposes after a specified period, eg six months. Note that ACAS's suggestion that six months is an appropriate period has been moved from its Code to its informal guide (see above).
- *Final written warning.* The employee can be given a final warning, a) because there is no improvement within the timescale set on the first warning, or b) even if there have been no prior warnings, if the behaviour is serious enough. The warning should give similar details to those required on a first warning, but additionally in this case it should indicate the risk of dismissal if there is no improvement. The final warning should normally be disregarded for disciplinary purposes after a specified period, eg 12 months. Again, ACAS's suggestion that 12 months is an appropriate period is now in its guide but no longer in its Code. For particularly serious misconduct, especially eg where harassment of work colleagues is involved, an employer might give a final written warning for 18 months or even two years.
- *Dismissal.* If the employee repeats offences or fails to improve after a final warning or if s/he commits gross misconduct, s/he can be dismissed. Alternatively, the employee's contract may allow other sanctions such as a disciplinary transfer or demotion.

Whatever disciplinary procedure applies to the employee, it is likely to set out stages similar to the above. When deciding whether to dismiss an employee, the employer may sometimes be able to rely on the fact that the employee has several live warnings, even if these concern unrelated offences. However, employers should not normally rely on warnings which have lapsed after a specified time under the procedure.[15]

---

15 See paras 7.41–7.42 regarding reliance on previous warnings.

What level of penalty is appropriate?

22.15   In imposing warnings or dismissing the employee, the employer must act reasonably, taking account of all the circumstances. The following factors will be relevant: the employee's length of service and work record; the nature of the job and his/her status; the seriousness of the employee's behaviour; any personal mitigating factors; and the way similar offences by other employees have been dealt with previously.

22.16   Additional factors will be relevant depending on the nature of the offence.[16] It is particularly important not to discriminate because of race, religion, sex, pregnancy, sexual orientation, age, disability or other protected characteristic under the Equality Act (EqA) 2010 during the process. The ACAS Code recommends that, depending on the circumstances, if disciplinary action is contemplated against an employee who is a trade union representative, the case should be discussed at an early stage with an official employed by the union, after getting the employee's agreement.

Gross misconduct

22.17   Particularly serious offences are known as 'gross misconduct'. Gross misconduct (if proved) usually means the employee can be fairly dismissed for a first offence. Fair procedures in the investigation and disciplinary should be followed in the normal way, although compensation for unfair dismissal is likely to be reduced if the employee wins only because of poor procedures. Gross misconduct also means the employer can dismiss without giving notice or pay in lieu. This is called 'summary dismissal'.

22.18   Employers tend to use the phrase 'gross misconduct' very readily and this should not be automatically accepted as correct. Nevertheless, certain types of misconduct would obviously fall under this category, eg: theft; sexual harassment; or physical violence. Other examples are likely to be: falsification of records; serious bullying or harassment; deliberate damage to property; serious insubordination; bringing the employer into serious disrepute; serious infringement of health and safety rules; and serious negligence which causes or may cause loss or damage. The disciplinary procedure applicable to the employee

---

16   See examples in chapter 7.

will probably list examples of what the employer considers gross misconduct, although this is unlikely to be an exhaustive list.

Capability issues

22.19 Depending on the employer's procedures, an employee's failure to perform to the required standard may be dealt with through the normal disciplinary procedure or (often with public sector employers) through a separate capability procedure. Many employers are reluctant to rush to disciplinary action due to poor performance and often prefer several informal counselling meetings. Continuing poor performance by the employee may be due to some underlying domestic or work problems, eg ill-health or being subjected to harassment. Disability discrimination law under the EqA 2010 may apply in some circumstances.

22.20 The employee should not normally be dismissed for a failure to meet work standards unless s/he has been given warnings and an opportunity to improve, with reasonable timescales and targets. However, employers may be able to dismiss for a single error due to negligence with very serious consequences. Case-law suggests this is most likely where there is a danger to the health and safety of others.[17]

Appeals

22.21 The opportunity to appeal against a disciplinary decision is essential to natural justice. The ACAS Code says employees should be informed of their right of appeal, and appeals should be heard without unreasonable delay. The employer's disciplinary procedure usually sets out time limits for lodging and dealing with the appeal.

22.22 The appeal should be heard by someone appropriate, ideally a senior manager, who has not been previously involved in the disciplinary procedure. In small organisations it may not be possible to find such an individual, in which case the person dealing with the appeal should act as impartially as possible. Independent arbitration may be a suitable alternative if agreed by everyone concerned. The employee is entitled to be represented at the appeal hearing. If new evidence arises during the appeal, the employee or his/her

---

17 See paras 7.1–7.32 re unfair dismissal on grounds of capability, particularly para 7.5.

representative should be given the opportunity to comment and it may be necessary to adjourn the appeal to investigate.

22.23   The employee may appeal on a number of grounds – eg procedural irregularities, the penalty was too severe, new evidence has come to light, or it is unfair to believe that the worker had committed the offence or that his/her work was substandard. The employer's appeal procedure may set out a format for the appeal. The ACAS Guide (see para 22.10 above) says the opportunity to appeal against a disciplinary decision is 'essential to natural justice' and an appeal should not result in any increase in penalty as this might deter individuals from appealing. The ACAS Code is less explicit, but its general tenor suggests appeals are supposed to be for the benefit of the employee. It will therefore usually be an unfair dismissal to increase a final written warning to a dismissal on appeal. It will also be a breach of contract for an employer to increase a disciplinary penalty on appeal unless the contractual disciplinary procedure explicitly says that can be done.[18]

22.24   The employee may not want to appeal, feeling it is pointless. However, that is normally unwise. The ACAS Code seems to expect employees to appeal if they are unhappy about the decision. They therefore risk a reduction in their compensation if they win their tribunal case having failed to appeal. However, if the employee does not want his/her job back after dismissal, there are dangers in appealing. This is because the dismissal will usually 'disappear' after a successful internal appeal. If that happens, the employee can no longer bring an unfair dismissal claim. This is the case even if the employer offers reinstatement to a demoted position or imposes a final written warning.[19] In that situation, all the employee can do is resign and claim constructive dismissal, eg if the employer's actions amount to a breach of trust and confidence.[20] However, constructive dismissal claims tend to be difficult to prove. Exceptionally, if the lesser sanctions are explicitly prohibited by the contract, the dismissal will probably still stand.[21] The dismissal does not disappear in the

---

18 *McMillan v Airedale NHS Foundation Trust* [2014] EWCA Civ 1031; [2014] IRLR 803.

19 See *Roberts v West Coast Trains* [2004] IRLR 788, CA; *Patel v Folkestone Nursing Home Ltd* [2018] EWCA Civ 1689; [2018] IRLR 924, CA.

20 *Patel v Folkestone Nursing Home Ltd* [2018] EWCA Civ 1689; [2018] IRLR 924, CA; *Thomson v Barnet Primary Care Trust* UKEAT/0247/12. See also *Salmon v Castlebeck Care (Teesside)* [2015] IRLR 189, EAT.

21 *Piper v Maidstone & Tunbridge Wells NHS Trust* UKEAT/0359/12; *Saminaden v Barnet Enfield and Haringey NHS Trust* UKEAT/0018/08.

different situation where an employer changes his/her mind and offers the job back without having been asked and without the employee having appealed. Such a unilateral change of mind need not be accepted by the employee.

22.25 The employee must be extremely careful not to miss any ET time limits if s/he intends to bring a claim. The ET claim must be lodged within the time limit even if the appeal procedure has not been completed.

Discriminatory disciplinary action

22.26 The employee may be subjected to disciplinary action for a number of discriminatory reasons, eg:

- The employee's manager is angry with him/her because s/he has rebuffed his/her sexual approaches.
- The manager has chosen to bring formal disciplinary proceedings against a black employee for being late. However, when a white employee was equally late, the manager merely had an informal word.
- The employee is accused of inaccurate completion of timesheets. The employee is dyslexic and finds it difficult to complete forms accurately.

22.27 If the employee believes s/he is being subjected to disciplinary action for discriminatory reasons, s/he needs to decide at an early stage whether to say so at the disciplinary. If the employee later brings an ET case for discrimination, s/he may lose credibility if s/he did not raise the issue at the disciplinary. On the other hand, discrimination is a serious issue to raise which is likely to upset the employer. The employee risks being victimised as a result of raising the issue, and work relations may deteriorate badly. Although victimisation is unlawful, it can be hard to prove. The employee needs to consider whether s/he has sufficient objective evidence to prove the discrimination and whether s/he wants to take on this issue.

22.28 If the employee does decide to raise the issue, s/he should do so in writing prior to the disciplinary hearing. An employer may say later that the issue of discrimination was never raised at the disciplinary. There is also a possible risk of reduction in compensation under the ACAS Code if the employee unreasonably fails to raise the issue of discrimination with his/her employer before going to tribunal.

22.29 Regarding discriminatory handling of disciplinary action, see para 22.37.

Grievances

22.30   The purpose of a grievance procedure is to give employees a way to raise issues with the management about their working environment or work relationships. An individual employee bringing a formal grievance, especially if it is on a controversial subject such as discrimination, does risk upsetting his/her manager. The employee needs to be clear about what s/he is trying to achieve. For those interested in mediation, there is an interesting guide: *Mediation: a guide for trade union representatives* from ACAS and the Trades Union Congress (TUC).[22]

22.31   The ACAS Code does not explicitly state that employees must bring grievances where they have concerns, but it gives that impression by saying employees should raise the matter formally where they have been unable to resolve a grievance informally.[23] There is therefore a risk of compensation being reduced if the employee wins any case when s/he had not first brought an internal grievance. It is unclear whether it would be considered a breach of the Code not to attempt an informal grievance before raising a formal one, although the wording does not seem specific enough to make that compulsory, and it would be a harsh requirement.

22.32   If an employee does raise a grievance, s/he has an implied contractual right to have it dealt with promptly.[24] The ACAS Code should also be followed, but it is only triggered where the grievance is in writing.[25] The Code sets out very basic guidance to employers on handling grievances. It says employees should raise grievances formally and without unreasonable delay if they have not been able to resolve the matter informally. The formal grievance should be raised with a manager who is not the subject of the complaint. Employers should deal with grievances consistently and promptly. Employees should appeal where they feel their grievance has not been satisfactorily resolved.

22.33   Employers' grievance procedures often have more than one appeal stage. The stages may entail either one-to-one meetings, where the employee can be accompanied by a colleague or represent-

---

22   This can be ordered at www.tuc.org.uk/publications/mediation-guide-trade-union-representatives. There is also an ACAS and CIPD guide, *Mediation: an approach to resolving work place issues*, at www.acas.org.uk/sites/default/files/2021-03/mediation-an-approach-to-resolving-workplace-issues.pdf.

23   ACAS Code, para 31.

24   See para 1.17.

25   ACAS Code, para 31; *The Cadogan Hotel Partners Ltd v Ozog* UKEAT/0001/14.

ative, or full hearings with witnesses, rather like a disciplinary hearing. The latter model is more common in the public sector where trade union representation is available. Some employers have different grievance procedures for different issues, eg the normal procedure plus different procedures for bullying, discrimination, sexual harassment or collective grievances. They may also have a special procedure for whistleblowing under the Public Interest Disclosure Act 1998.[26]

22.34   Where an employee raises a grievance during a disciplinary process, the ACAS Code simply says the disciplinary process 'may' be temporarily suspended in order to deal with the grievance.[27] If the grievance and disciplinary are related, it 'may be appropriate' to deal with both together. However, if the employer decides to go ahead with a disciplinary hearing on a related matter, and dismisses the employee at a time when a grievance appeal is still outstanding, it will not necessarily be unfair.[28]

22.35   In an ideal world, where grievances concern proposed changes to an employee's working conditions or duties, the 'status quo' will be maintained until the grievance procedure has been completed. However, unless the grievance procedure explicitly says this is the position, the employee will be on weak ground if the employer insists on instructions being followed immediately. The employee cannot unilaterally insist on the status quo if the employer is acting within the contract and agrees to reconsider if the grievance succeeds. In such a situation, it can be fair to dismiss an employee who is refusing lawful instructions to carry out different duties pending the final outcome of the grievance.[29] The position is more complicated if the changes which the employer wishes to make are outside the contract, as one then gets into the realms of an employee's rights on unilateral variation.[30]

22.36   If an employee intends to bring an ET claim regarding the subject-matter of a grievance, s/he must do so within the ET time limit for the relevant legal right (eg discrimination or pay deductions) even if the grievance procedure has not been completed.

---

26 See para 6.101.
27 ACAS Code, para 46.
28 *Samuel Smith Old Brewery (Tadcaster) v Marshall & Marshall* UKEAT/0488/09.
29 *Samuel Smith Old Brewery (Tadcaster) v Marshall & Marshall* UKEAT/0488/09.
30 This is a different subject. See paras 1.20–1.23.

Discriminatory handling of disciplinary or grievance procedures

22.37 Employers may be guilty of further discrimination or victimisation in the way they deal with an employee's grievance related to discrimination, for example by failing to investigate properly or taking an exceptionally long time to deal with the matter, compared with how they would normally deal with a grievance. In addition, it is sometimes necessary with a disabled employee to make reasonable adjustments to the disciplinary process, eg by allowing an interpreter or signer or, for someone with learning disabilities, adopting a particularly informal and unthreatening manner and process.

Checklist: jurisdictions covered by the ACAS compensation regime

22.38 The ACAS compensation regime applies to jurisdictions set out in Trade Union and Labour Relations (Consolidation) Act (TULR(C)A) 1992 Sch A2. Remember that in all cases, the claimant must be an employee. Almost the same jurisdictions are covered by the rules on compensation for failing to provide a section 1 statement of particulars under Employment Act 2002 Sch 5 (see para 1.26). There are a few obscure jurisdictions set out in Sch A2, but the ones you are most likely to come across are:

- discrimination law, ie claims under EqA 2010 and previous equality legislation;
- claims in respect of trade union membership and activities under TULR(C)A 1992 ss145A, 145B, 146, Sch A1 para 156;
- unauthorised deductions from pay (including to recover pay below the minimum wage);
- ET claims which can be made under WTR 1998 reg 30, regarding breaks and annual leave, etc;
- claims regarding detriment for taking up rights in connection with the minimum wage under National Minimum Wage Act 1998 s24;
- redundancy pay;
- unfair dismissal (including most automatic unfair dismissals);
- detriment (action short of dismissal) on any of the grounds listed in Employment Rights Act (ERA) 1996 s48, ie for: whistleblowing; being an employee representative or trustee of an occupa-

tional pension scheme; for pregnancy or maternity; taking up rights in relation to maternity leave, paternity leave, adoption leave, dependant leave, parental leave, parental bereavement leave, flexible working, Sunday working, health and safety, study leave for young workers (special rules), under the WTR 1998, in relation to jury service, tax credits. Chapter 6 gives more detail of the precise protection against detriment under these categories;

• breach of contract arising or outstanding on termination, eg notice pay;

• detriment connected with a prohibited blacklist.[31]

The right to be accompanied to disciplinary and grievance hearings

The statutory right

22.39 Where a worker[32] is invited or required to attend a disciplinary or grievance hearing and reasonably requests to be accompanied at the hearing, the employer must allow the worker to choose a trade union representative or another of the employer's workers to accompany him/her.[33] The choice of companion is up to the worker, not the employer, and, provided the companion falls within the relevant categories, need not be a reasonable choice.[34] This companion may address the hearing and confer with the worker during the hearing. The companion may put and sum up the worker's case and may respond on the worker's behalf to any view expressed at the hearing, but s/he may not answer questions on behalf of the worker.[35] A disciplinary hearing means a hearing which could result in a formal warning or the taking of some other action.[36] Previous editions of the ACAS Code on Disciplinary and Grievances Procedures considered that hearings or meetings which could only result in informal warnings and/or counselling would not be covered. The current Code does not explicitly address this point. However, some 'informal'

---

31 This is not in Employment Act 2002 Sch 5, though double-check if you have a case.

32 This entitlement is not confined to employees.

33 Employment Relations Act (ERelA) 1999 s10.

34 *(1) Toal (2) Hughes v GB Oils Ltd* UKEAT/0569/12; [2013] IRLR 696, EAT; *Roberts v GB Oils Ltd* UKEAT/0177/13.

35 ERelA 1999 s10(2B)–(2C).

36 ERelA 1999 s13(4).

warnings take on the characteristics of formal warnings and do attract the right to representation, eg where the informal warning is in writing, with a specified time before lapsing, and can be taken into account if further offences are committed.[37] A purely investigatory, as opposed to disciplinary, meeting is unlikely to be covered.[38] A meeting held to inform workers of their impending redundancy also would not be covered.[39]

22.40   The employer must allow a worker to take time off during working hours to accompany another of the employer's workers.[40] If the chosen person cannot attend the proposed time for the hearing, the employer must postpone the hearing to any reasonable time suggested by the worker within five working days of the original date.

22.41   The ACAS Code of Practice on Disciplinary and Grievance Procedures[41] not only refers to this right but adds that employees should be advised of their right to be accompanied, when notified of a disciplinary hearing. This means there may be a compensatory uplift of up to 25 per cent where, eg, the employee wins a case of unfair dismissal or discriminatory disciplinary action, and the employer had not advised of the right or permitted the employee to be accompanied. Remember also that the worker's own disciplinary policy, especially in unionised industries, may give similar rights to representation, but without the restrictions.

22.42   A worker can complain to an ET if the statutory right is denied. The ET can award compensation of up to two weeks' pay.[42] A worker must not be subjected to any detriment because s/he has tried to exercise this right or has accompanied another worker. It would also be automatically unfair dismissal to dismiss an employee for this reason.[43]

22.43   Note that the statutory right to be accompanied under ERelA 1999 s10 is technically a separate right from the right not to be unfairly dismissed. It is very likely that an employer's failure to comply with section 10 will make any dismissal unfair, but that does not automatically follow. Moreover, an employer can still act unfairly in procedural terms even if s/he has not broken the section 10 rules,

37   *London Underground Ltd v Ferenc-Batchelor; Harding v London Underground Ltd* [2003] IRLR 252, EAT.
38   *Skiggs v South West Trains* [2005] IRLR 17, EAT.
39   *Heathmill Multimedia ASP Ltd v Jones and Jones* [2003] IRLR 856, EAT.
40   ERelA 1999 s10(6).
41   See para 22.3.
42   ERelA 1999 s11.
43   ERelA 1999 s12.

eg if his/her refusal to postpone the disciplinary hearing for more than five days so that the worker's representative can attend is unreasonable.[44]

The right to legal representation

22.44 Workers do not usually have the right to legal representation in an internal disciplinary or grievance unless explicitly given that right in their own contract of employment. However, a worker may have such a right as a result of Article 6 of the European Convention on Human Rights[45] (right to a fair trial) where the outcome of the internal disciplinary could affect his/her right to practise his/her profession in the future.

44 *Talon Engineering Ltd v Smith* UKEAT/0236/17; [2018] IRLR 1104, EAT.
45 See para 3.23.

APPENDICES

Running employment tribunal cases: checklists and samples

continued

A1 STAGES OF THE BASIC PROCEDURE

This is a summary and should be read together with chapters 20–21 as applicable.

1 Interview worker; take statement; check all documents; check time limits and diarise.

2 If appropriate, request written reasons for dismissal and await reply. (See para 20.10.)

3 In a case under the Equality Act (EqA) 2010, send employer a non-statutory questionnaire and chase up any failure to reply. (See para 21.2.)

4 Except in unusual cases where Advisory, Conciliation and Arbitration Service (ACAS) Early Conciliation (EC) does not apply, notify ACAS under the EC procedure within the tribunal time limit for starting a case. (See para 20.16.)

5 Where EC fails, obtain EC certificate from ACAS and start tribunal case within necessary time period thereafter. (See para 20.56.)

6 Start case by taking or sending the claim (ET1) to the appropriate tribunal office or submitting it online. (See para 20.43.)

7 The ET will send an acknowledgement with a case number and stating whether the claim has been accepted. Subsequent correspondence with the ET goes to the relevant regional office.

8 The ET will send the ET1 to the employer and will send a copy of the employer's response (ET3) to the worker's representative or to the worker direct, if unrepresented. Expect this roughly four weeks after the acknowledgement (time limits apply). Diarise likely date ET3 is due and query with ET (or consider asking for a 'rule 21' judgment) if not then received.

9 When the ET3 is received, write to the employer asking for any necessary additional information and any key documents. Set a time limit, usually 14 days. (See para 20.104.)

10 If the information is not received, write to the ET with a copy of the request and ask for an order. Copy the ET application to the employer and tell the ET this has been done. The ET will send any order it makes to the employer and a copy to the worker's representative.

11 If the employer does not supply the information as ordered, write to the ET asking that the employer be requested to show cause why the ET3 should not be struck out.

12 In England and Wales, the ET will probably send out a standard case management letter at an early stage (often at stage 7 or 8), setting timescales for disclosure, exchange of witness statements, preparation of a schedule of loss etc. (See appendix C at C6 for an example.) Diarise the steps set out by the ET and prepare well in advance. This does not replace the need to make any specific requests and stages 9–11 above may still apply. (See para 20.104.)

13 In a discrimination case, chase up any failure to answer the non-statutory questionnaire.

14 The ET will notify each side of the hearing date, either when forwarding the ET1 to the employer (stage 8) or after the ET3 is received. Minimum 14 days' notice must be given. Inform ET immediately if the date is unsuitable.

15 An ACAS officer will be allocated to the case at the start and will contact the worker's representative and the employer. This is separate from the EC process before a case starts. Negotiation can be through ACAS or direct with the employer. Once an agreement is concluded, it becomes binding if each side has confirmed it verbally with ACAS. ACAS then tells the ET that the case has been settled. (Check that ACAS has done this.) Alternatively, a binding settlement is reached when authorised representatives sign a settlement agreement (formerly called compromise agreement). (See para 20.268 onwards.)

16 If using ACAS, the officer will send a COT3 form for signature. This contains the agreed terms of settlement. Make sure that the worker at all stages knows the terms. If there is no settlement, the case will go to hearing. ACAS is unlikely to be accessible for any settlement agreed on the day of the hearing, but the ET should be asked to make an order in the agreed terms.

17 In good time for the hearing, write to the ET to request any witness orders that are wanted. (See para 20.136.)

18 Prior to the hearing, prepare trial bundles in agreement with the employer. Each page of the bundle should be numbered. Make sufficient copies or ask the employer to. (See para 20.174 onwards.)

19 If it has been ordered or there is agreement to do so, exchange witness statements with the other side. (See para 20.186.)

20 During the hearing, the ET will either hear evidence relating to liability and remedies (compensation etc) all at once or, more usually, will start by hearing evidence just on liability and then listen to evidence on compensation if the worker wins. Be prepared for both.

21 At the end of the hearing, the ET will give its judgment or reserve judgment and write to the parties later. If ET gives oral judgment, request written reasons at the hearing or within the specified time limit afterwards if thinking of appealing. But bear in mind that written reasons go on the public register.

22 Remember and diarise time limits for reconsideration (14 days) and appeal (42 days) if unsuccessful.

23 If successful, diarise when the money from the judgment or settlement is due and chase/enforce as appropriate. Interest runs from the date of the award if unpaid within 14 days.

Variations:

a) The ET may hold a preliminary hearing simply to discuss case management arrangements (especially in discrimination cases) with the representatives at any stage (or with the parties, if they are unrepresented), just to sort out what needs to be done, eg, whether an order should be made for additional information, disclosure of documents etc. (See para 21.50.)

b) The ET may hold a preliminary hearing on issues of 'jurisdiction' at an early stage which is prepared for and conducted like a full hearing except that it is confined to the jurisdictional or preliminary issue, eg, in an unfair dismissal case, whether the claimant is an employee or in a disability discrimination case, whether the worker has a 'disability'. Alternatively, such issues may be left to the full hearing. (See para 20.161.)

c) The ET may hold a preliminary hearing, usually at an early stage, at which the claims or individual allegations may be struck out because they have no reasonable prospects of success or a costs deposit ordered because they have little reasonable prospect of success. (See para 20.165.)

d) Equal value cases under the EqA 2010 – the basic procedure applies but there are also additional special steps (see chapter 5).

e) Any preliminary hearings and/or the full hearing may be held 'remotely' ie on a vide platform (or by telephone conferencing for a purely case management preliminary hearing). If so, the tribunal will want electronic documents, but witnesses will still find it better to be given hard copy documents.

A2   INITIAL INTERVIEW WITH WORKER SEEKING ADVICE ON DISMISSAL

1   Check what worker wants.

2   Check whether correct contractual/statutory notice was given or pay in lieu (unless gross misconduct).

3   Check whether any outstanding wages or holiday pay are due.

4   Check date of dismissal and time limits for possible ET claims/ACAS EC notification. Inform worker and diarise. Where there is a claim of discrimination, prepare a brief chronology, note and diarise the time limit of the last act of discrimination, if it is a continuing act of discrimination, and the earliest act of discrimination if there are several self-contained acts.

5   Check whether worker qualifies for unfair dismissal (sufficient continuous service, status as employee, whether s/he was 'dismissed').

6   If applicable and if worker qualifies, consider redundancy pay claim.

7   Check possibility of unlawful discrimination (no continuous service required; need not be an 'employee' working under a contract of employment).

8   Where likely, eg, where there is a sex discrimination issue, check for unequal pay.

9   Check pay slips. If worker was given none, consider claim for failure to give itemised pay statements. Ask tax authorities and Department for Work and Pensions (DWP) to investigate contributions record so that credited contributions can be requested if necessary. Consider risk of illegal contract.

10 Obtain all relevant documents from worker and take full statement.

11 If appropriate, write initial letter to employer requesting written reasons for dismissal, P45 and monies due.

12 Consider whether anything can be done immediately to secure a good open reference.

13 Check whether worker has appealed.

14 Advise as to social security benefits or refer on for this advice.

A3   INTERVIEW OF WORKER WITH RACE (OR SEX) DISCRIMINATION CLAIM

The following list suggests points that should be established by an adviser when interviewing a worker with a potential race discrimination claim. It can be adapted for sex discrimination cases. The suggestions are for guidance only and should not be followed rigidly. In each case, the facts and what needs to be proved must be carefully considered.

- What are the key discriminatory actions by the employer which the worker is complaining about, eg lack of promotion, disciplinary action, dismissal?
- Find out whether the worker believes his/her treatment is because of his/her race or the race of someone else. Ask the worker why s/he thinks s/he was dismissed/disciplined/not promoted or appointed. This helps establish whether the worker believes it is race discrimination, although it may be necessary to ask more overtly. It also helps draw out any non-discriminatory explanation for the employer's conduct.
- Unless it is obvious, establish what is the worker's nationality, ethnic or national origin (as relevant under the EqA 2010), ie what 'racial' group is the employer discriminating against?
- Explore the evidence: ask what makes the worker think s/he has been discriminated against. Explain that this is a good question to draw out evidence indicating discrimination.
- Is there an actual comparator? Is there is a direct comparison with a white worker who has been treated more favourably in comparable circumstances?
- Establish who made the relevant decisions and what is the decision-making hierarchy; establish whether any discriminatory patterns among the workforce can be attributed to the same decision-makers (eg, the expression of prejudice by a senior manager is relevant only if that manager has some control over this worker's fate). Avoid 'conspiracy theories', eg, accusing too many senior managers and staff of racism.
- Expressly ask the worker whether any racist remarks were made by any relevant manager, either directly to the worker or in his/her hearing.
- Ask whether relevant managers demonstrated prejudice in any other way, eg, by differential treatment of staff according to their 'race'.
- Try to establish patterns. Patterns in the way the worker has been treated by certain persons in the past compared with how staff of a different racial group, eg, white, are treated, and in the way other staff of the same 'racial' group are treated and their position in the workforce.
- Establish now rather than later if there are any holes in the patterns, eg, if the managers accused have in the past made senior appointments of persons in the same 'racial' group as the worker, or if others of the same 'racial group' are generally highly placed in the employing organisation. Also look at who appointed/promoted the worker in the past and why, if it is the same manager who is now discriminating.
- Assess whether there are non-racial explanations for events, eg, the person promoted above the worker was better qualified or the worker was unpopular for reasons unconnected with his/her 'race'.

- If there is a history of discrimination, establish when it started and explore whether the start date makes sense, eg because a new manager took over or because it was the first time a promotion situation arose.
- Ask whether the worker ever alleged race discrimination and whether that can be proved. Ask for details and the employer's reaction. (This is relevant to credibility of the worker, and of the employer if no action was taken, and to any victimisation claim.)
- Ask if the employer has an equal opportunities policy and whether it was ever brought to the worker's attention.
- Establish whether direct or indirect discrimination, or both, is possible.
- Establish whether victimisation took place, ie, whether the worker alleged discrimination in the past and/or during incidents leading to dismissal and/or in any disciplinary hearing prior to dismissal.
- Watch out for other forms of discrimination, eg, sex discrimination – in addition to or instead of race discrimination.
- Establish all acts of discrimination within the last three months (eg, failed promotion applications; unfair appraisals; warnings; dismissal). These can be the basis of the claim.
- Establish all acts of discrimination or evidence of prejudicial attitudes throughout the worker's employment. (Although these cannot usually form the basis of a claim if more than three months ago, they can be supporting evidence for the main claim. It is also possible that a sequence of incidents would amount to a continuing act of discrimination.) Be careful not to include everything which in hindsight the worker thinks was unfair. Focus on incidents which indicate different treatment.
- Establish evidential strength – witnesses, documents and matters from which inferences could be drawn.
- Establish what information could be usefully obtained on a non-statutory questionnaire. Ask worker about distribution (and treatment – promotions/dismissals, etc) of workers of different racial groups in the workforce.
- Establish what the worker wants (particularly if still employed).

A4   INTERVIEW OF WORKER WHO HAS BEEN MADE REDUNDANT

A worker who has been made redundant may choose only to ask his/her adviser about the level of redundancy pay. However, s/he may have other rights, depending in part on whether s/he is an employee. The following list suggests suitable areas for exploring and should be read in conjunction with chapter 8.

1   Reasonable time off with pay during notice period to look for fresh employment.
2   Redundancy pay:
   • Check worker is eligible for statutory redundancy pay (employee; at least two years' service etc).
   • Check the calculation.
   • Check if s/he has a greater contractual entitlement and any applicable NHS/local government schemes.
   • May s/he lose the right to redundancy pay because s/he unreasonably refused an offer of suitable alternative employment made before the expiry of his/her contract?
   • May s/he lose the right to redundancy pay if s/he has left before the expiry of his/her notice period?[1]
   NOTE: There are rules as to the procedure to be followed if the worker wants to leave early without losing his/her pay.
3   Unfair dismissal:
   • Check worker is eligible to claim (employee; sufficient continuous service; has been dismissed in legal sense). Be careful to check that a dismissal has taken place as opposed to an agreed termination, eg, in some early retirement/ voluntary redundancy situations.
   • Would the worker win? A redundancy dismissal may be unfair if:
      – there was no genuine redundancy situation and the employer had other reasons for dismissing the worker;
      – unfair selection criteria were used, or they were unfairly applied;
      – the employer did not consider alternative employment;
      – poor procedures were followed and there was no consultation with the individual or union.
   • If the worker was made redundant after failing to obtain an alternative post on a reorganisation, the dismissal may be unfair if:
      – the employer had agreed a matching policy with the union, but failed to follow it;
      – the new post was anyway very similar to the worker's previous post;
      – the assessment process used was unsuitable or not marked fairly;
      – there was no consultation at the outset with any recognised union as to a fair process;
      – the worker was denied the right of appeal.
   • How much compensation is the worker likely to receive?
   NOTE: If the worker received a large contractual or voluntary redundancy payment or if s/he obtained a new job very quickly, his/her unfair dismissal claim may be worth little or nothing.

---

1   See rules in Employment Rights Act (ERA) 1996 s136(3)–(4).

4   Was the worker selected for redundancy for an automatically unfair reason (see chapter 6)? For example, if the worker was dismissed for a reason related to pregnancy or maternity, this may be automatic unfair dismissal, which does not require her to have had any minimum length of service.

   NOTE: If the worker is made redundant while on maternity leave, she must be offered any suitable vacancy.

5   Unlawful discrimination:
   • Check eligibility. (Much wider than for unfair dismissal or statutory redundancy pay.)
   • Has the worker been selected for redundancy because of his/her race, religion, sex, gender reassignment, sexual orientation, age, disability, or because she is pregnant or has taken maternity leave?
      – Have objective criteria been used and objectively applied?
      – Would the worker have been selected if s/he had been of a different race, religion, sex, sexual orientation, age, or not disabled? (If not, it may be direct discrimination.)
   • Has the worker been selected on an indirectly discriminatory criterion which cannot be justified, eg, LIFO (last in, first out); part-timers first; 'temps' or 'casuals' first; where these groups are disproportionately black or female?
   • Have reasonable adjustments been made to the redundancy selection procedure or criteria so that a disabled worker is not put at a disadvantage, eg by discounting disability-related absences from a selection criterion based on attendance record?
   • Has the worker been selected for redundancy because of recent complaints about discrimination or harassment which have upset the employer? This would be victimisation.
   • Is access to or calculation of the redundancy payment package discriminatory?

6   Redundancies on a transfer:
   • Consider whether or not the Transfer of Undertakings Regulations (TUPE) apply.
   • Consider whether claim should be made against new or old employer.

7   Trade union or employee representatives' consultation.
   • For collective redundancies.
   • Where the Transfer of Undertakings Regulations apply.

   NOTE: Any claim for breaking consultation rules is brought by the trade union or, if no union is recognised, by appropriate employee representatives on behalf of the employees. If there is no trade union and no employee representatives were elected, an individual may be able to claim.

A5 INITIAL INTERVIEW OF WORKER WITH POSSIBLE SEXUAL HARASSMENT CLAIM

This is a sensitive area, with difficulties of law, evidence and the worker's feelings. The checklist below suggests that the information which needs to be obtained to make an informed judgment about whether the worker can bring a legal case (or even risk speaking out). It may be best not to ask all the questions in the first interview, but to fix another meeting the next day or very soon after, to speak in more detail.

The last part of the checklist suggests how such an interview should be conducted. The same questions will not always be appropriate. The adviser must be thorough in his/her questioning and listen carefully to the answers. This is to ensure that the worker is consistent throughout any grievance and ET case which s/he may take. Explain to the worker some of the legal complexities so s/he understands why you are asking the questions.

1 Questions to find out background information:
   - The harasser's job title and working relationship with the worker.
   - The nature of the working day. How often the worker has contact with the harasser.
   - The general office situation, layout and presence of other workers.
   - The worker's start date and disciplinary record. [This is sensitive: explain the question about the worker's record is only to see how vulnerable s/he is if management raise the issue.]

2 Questions about the harassment:
   - When the harassment started.
   - Details and dates of the harassment (verbal and physical). [This requires a sensitive approach as the worker may be embarrassed, particularly with a representative of the opposite sex.]
   - Establish what is normal acceptable office behaviour and where the line is drawn.
   - Are there witnesses? Has the worker kept a diary? Has s/he seen/told his/her GP; any recruitment agency; family, friends or acquaintances?
   - Has the harasser done the same thing to other workers? Have others complained to management?
   - Has the worker said explicitly to the harasser or made it clear in any other way that s/he does not welcome the behaviour? [Many kinds of behaviour are obviously unwelcome and it is not essential that the worker has said as much to the harasser, but it is helpful if s/he has. Note that although this is important information to know, it is extremely sensitive as the worker may feel s/he is to blame if s/he has not said anything to the harasser. Therefore, do not ask this question until late in the interview when confidence is built. This also gives the worker time to raise it him/herself, which is preferable. If it is necessary to raise the issue first, be sure to give prior reassurance that it would be understandable if the worker had not felt able to say anything.]
   - If the worker did tell the harasser, how and when did s/he do so and what was his/her reaction?

- Has the worker raised the matter with anyone in management or told anyone else before? [This question also needs prior reassurance.]

3   Action:
- What does the worker want to do? [This is the most important question of all, and however bad the situation is, it is not up to the adviser to impose a solution. Discuss the options including taking a grievance, going to the ET plus time limits, informal approach to the harasser, doing nothing but keeping a diary.]

4   Taking a sensitive approach:
- Take the matter seriously and give it the necessary time.
- Be friendly and supportive but formal. Do not be authoritarian or too informal. Both could replicate the harasser's behaviour.
- Take a clear role and explain why sensitive questions are asked before asking them.
- In the first interview, allow the worker to give a broad picture before going back (in this interview or a subsequent interview) to ask for more detail.
- Do not try to get all the information in the first interview – focus on building confidence (although you must find out enough to ensure you do not miss a legal time limit). Ask more sensitive questions and deal with possible counter-allegations in later interviews after confidence in the adviser has been established.
- To maintain confidence, arrange swift follow-up interviews at the first interview. This is also essential before memories fade and witnesses lose interest.
- In case the worker is embarrassed, offer the opportunity to write down what has happened before discussing it. [NOTE: this is not a substitute for spending time talking to the worker.]
- If possible, offer the worker the chance to talk to an adviser of the same sex. [NOTE: this must not be seen as if the representative is not interested or concerned about the matter.]
- Provide reassurance that the worker is entitled to feel upset, that the harasser has behaved unacceptably and that the worker has done nothing wrong.
- Reassure the worker on confidentiality and that nothing will be done without his/her permission. It is important to take notes, but ask permission first.
- Discuss various options, taking account of what the worker wants, offering appropriate support whatever s/he decides. Take a participative and consultative approach. Address any fear of reprisals.
- Raise with the worker his/her feelings and health and direct him/her to sources of support. The adviser should not attempt to act as an amateur counsellor or suggest the worker needs counselling/psychiatric help in a way which could be understood as meaning the adviser thinks there is something wrong with the worker. Suggestions of sources of support are not an alternative to concrete remedial action.

DO NOT:
- Make assumptions.
- Suggest that the worker could be to blame in inviting the harassment.

- Blame the worker for not confronting the harasser or telling the union or management earlier.
- Suggest that the worker may be misinterpreting events or being oversensitive.
- Express any view as to the effect on the harasser or the harasser's spouse/partner if the worker makes an allegation.
- Pressurise the worker into taking any form of action.
- If the adviser is a union representative, s/he should not say that s/he knows the harasser and is surprised s/he has acted in that way, or express concern that the harasser is a worker of the same union.

A6 INTERVIEW OF WORKER DISMISSED FOR POOR WORK, WITH A VIEW TO ASSESSING POTENTIAL CLAIMS FOR (A) UNFAIR DISMISSAL; (B) DISMISSAL IN FACT BECAUSE SHE IS PREGNANT; OR (C) DISMISSAL IN FACT BECAUSE S/HE IS BLACK

The following list suggests areas for questioning common to many dismissals on grounds of capability or conduct and is designed to highlight the additional questions necessary where discrimination due to pregnancy or race is suspected. Note that questions concerning discrimination are designed to find out if the worker has been treated differently, not just unfairly. The list is for guidance only.

Unfair dismissal

1   Questions to test eligibility, eg, length of continuous service, whether the worker is an employee.

2   Questions to establish the sequence of events and disciplinary process followed leading up to dismissal.

3   Obtain documents worker has: contract of employment; disciplinary / capability procedure; dismissal letter; other letters relating to the events leading to dismissal; previous warning letters; previous appraisals.

4   Questions to establish the worker's previous work record: previous disciplinary / capability hearings; warnings (alive or lapsed); verbal criticisms; appraisals; thank-you letters.

5   The worker's job and duties. The hierarchy and other staff in his/her department.

6   The nature of the allegations against the worker and his/her response – in the disciplinary / capability hearing and, if different, to you.

7   If relevant, any training the worker has had. Has s/he recently been promoted? If so, what was his/her experience prior to promotion and is s/he being given support and guidance?

8   Dates of all relevant facts plus date of dismissal. (Relevant to show the pattern of events but also for time limits.)

9   What does the worker want to do?

Pregnancy dismissal – extra questions to unfair dismissal list

1   Note that the worker does not need to be an employee in the unfair dismissal sense or to have any minimum service to claim pregnancy discrimination.

2   Does the worker think dismissal was due to her pregnancy? If so, what makes the worker think that? (This is a useful question, but explain that it is useful to know what she has in mind and that she is not being disbelieved.)

3   Questions to establish whether and when the employer and relevant manager knew the worker was pregnant, eg:
   • When is the baby due?
   • When did the worker tell the employer she was pregnant? Who did she tell? Was it verbal or in writing?
   • Has the worker had time off for pregnancy-related ill-health? If so, when and who did she tell?

- Has the worker had time off for antenatal care? Have there been discussions about maternity leave or benefits? With whom? When?
4 Questions to establish if the employer or relevant manager is hostile towards the worker's pregnancy, eg:
  - In any of the above discussions or at any other time, has the employer expressed any irritation about time off or any other aspect of the pregnancy?
  - What did the employer say when the worker first told him/her of her pregnancy?
  - Has there been any problem getting time off for antenatal care?
  - Has the employer/manager's behaviour or attitude towards the worker changed in any way since s/he found out the worker was pregnant?
  - What is the employer's general attitude towards pregnant workers? What about the particular manager(s) the worker is now dealing with?
5 Questions to establish either that the worker has not performed poor work at all or that other non-pregnant workers have performed equally poor work (or done worse things), yet have not been dismissed. Also ask:
  - How readily does the employer usually discipline or dismiss workers?
  - What sort of offences are usually considered dismissable?
  - Compare the disciplinary procedure applied to the worker with any written procedure and with the normal practice adopted by the employer.
6 Where the pregnancy discrimination falls short of dismissal, eg, disciplinary action or non-promotion, ensure the worker seeks advice on maternity-related matters, eg, how to preserve her right to return after maternity leave, maternity benefits, rights to time off for antenatal care, if relevant, rights to health and safety suspension.
7 Regarding what the worker wants to do, will she want to return to work there after her maternity leave? (This may affect how the matter is handled.)
   NOTE: Adverse treatment due to pregnancy may also be sex discrimination. For this a worker need not be an employee.
   Also watch for dates of all adverse treatment as time limits for sex discrimination will run from each detrimental act.

Race discrimination – extra questions to unfair dismissal list
1 Note that the worker need not be an employee in the unfair dismissal sense or to have any minimum service to claim race discrimination.
2 Does the worker believe s/he has genuinely been dismissed for poor work or for some other reason?
3 Does the worker think s/he would have been dismissed if s/he was white? If so, what makes the worker think that? (This is a useful question, but explain that it is useful to know what s/he has in mind and that s/he is not being disbelieved.)
4 Questions regarding the ethnic breakdown of the workforce and particularly of the relevant managers.
5 Questions to compare the general treatment of black and white workers, eg, as to the level of disciplinary action and dismissals; recruitment; promotion; general day-to-day behaviour by management. Has anyone else complained of race discrimination previously?

6   Questions to establish either that the worker has not performed poor work
      at all or that other white workers have performed equally poor work (or done
      worse things), yet have not been dismissed. Also ask:
      - How readily does the employer usually discipline or dismiss workers?
      - What sort of offences are usually considered dismissable?
      - Compare the disciplinary procedure applied to the worker with any written
        procedure and with the normal practice adopted by the employer.

7   Questions about the previous treatment of the worker, eg, has the worker
      been subjected to different or racist treatment or remarks? Has the worker
      previously alleged race discrimination – if so, when and what happened?

8   Dates of all material incidents because the race discrimination time limit
      runs from each act of discrimination.

9   See also checklist A3 above for interviewing workers generally with potential
      race discrimination claims.

A7 ET1: DIRECT AND INDIRECT RACE DISCRIMINATION; UNFAIR DISMISSAL

Sample details of unfair dismissal and race discrimination claim for para 8.2 of ET1 form

1　The respondent operates a chain of fast-food restaurants in central London. The claimant worked as manager at various branches since his engagement in 2012. At the time of his dismissal, the claimant was working at the Piccadilly branch.

2　The claimant is of Algerian national origin.

3　On 5 November 2020, the claimant was told that his employment would be terminated by reason of redundancy on the closure of his branch on 17 November 2020.

4　The claimant was not consulted at any time prior to his dismissal as to the possibility of employment at any of the respondents' other restaurants. Other staff in the claimant's branch who were white and of British national origin were redeployed within the respondents' organisation.

5　During a conversation in September 2020, the respondent's area manager told the claimant that the respondent had started to 'professionalise' its operation and bring in managers with catering qualifications from recognised UK colleges.

6　Having regard to the size and administrative resources of the respondent, the claimant's dismissal was unfair. The claimant was unfairly selected for redundancy. Furthermore, the respondent failed to consult with the claimant concerning the possibilities of alternative employment and failed to offer such employment.

7　Furthermore, the claimant was directly discriminated against in his dismissal because of his race contrary to sections 9 and 13 of the Equality Act 2010.

8　Further or in the alternative, the claimant was subjected to indirect discrimination in his dismissal contrary to sections 9 and 19 of the Equality Act 2010 in that the respondents required that he hold a UK catering qualification.

A8 ET1: DIRECT RACE DISCRIMINATION AND VICTIMISATION; UNFAIR DISMISSAL

Sample details of unfair dismissal and race discrimination claim for para 8.2 of ET1 form

1 The claimant was employed as a project officer with the respondent council in March 2019. The claimant is black British.

2 In March 2020, one year after the claimant's appointment, a white British project officer (Sally Ward) was engaged. Ms Ward had the same grade, pay and job title as the claimant.

3 Throughout her employment, the claimant received only administrative tasks, and was not permitted to write publicity or represent the department at external meetings. In contrast, Ms Ward was given those opportunities.

4 On 30 May 2021, the claimant complained to the head of the department, Alex Stern, that her immediate supervisor was giving the best work to the white project officer, whereas she was becoming deskilled. The claimant stated she believed the differential treatment was on grounds of her race. Mr Stern did not take any action as a result of this complaint and appeared to be angry.

5 On 25 July 2021 the project officers were reduced from two to one and the claimant was made redundant.

6 The claimant suffered direct discrimination because of race contrary to sections 9 and 13 of the Equality Act 2010:

(a) in the nature of the work which she was allocated;

(b) in Mr Stern's failure to deal with her complaint;

(c) by making her redundant.

7 Further or in the alternative, the claimant was victimised contrary to section 27 of the Equality Act 2010 as a result of complaining about race discrimination as set out at paragraph 4 above in that she was made redundant.

8 In these respects, the claimant compares her treatment with that of Ms Ward and/or with that of a hypothetical comparator.[2]

9 Further or alternatively, the claimant was unfairly dismissed.

---

2 This is a reminder to the ET that if the comparison with Ms Ward does not stand up, the claimant can still claim she has been less favourably treated than a hypothetical comparator.

A9 NON-STATUTORY QUESTIONNAIRE: RACE DISCRIMINATION (DISMISSAL)

See paras 21.47–21.48 regarding non-statutory questionnaires. In this example, the summary of complaint at paras 1–6 could also stand as the grounds of an ET1.

Summary of complaint

1   I am of Asian ethnic origin. I started working for the respondent in its West End branch on 6 January 2020. I was promoted to manager in April 2020. Throughout my employment, I received no warnings of any kind.

2   On 11 May 2021, I was dismissed. I believe this was discrimination. The reason I was given for my dismissal was that I had claimed taxi fares during the tube strike without permission.

3   In the past I had been given travel fares in difficult travel circumstances and I had also given out fares to others. I understood this was in accordance with company policy. There was no secrecy involved, the petty cash slips were signed by myself and sent to head office, and the money was given to me by the chief cashier.

4   A new area manager was appointed in January 2021. On several occasions he told me to get more white staff in the shop. My deputy manager and I were both of Asian background. About half of the remaining staff were white. I told the area manager that I was not prepared to discriminate. I said that when vacancies arose, I could only appoint the best applicants.

5   In April 2021, my deputy manager was suddenly demoted to the position of salesperson. Then on 9 May 2021 I was called to a disciplinary hearing regarding my claim for taxi fares. The disciplinary was conducted by the area manager and personnel. I told them I believed this was race discrimination. On 11 May I received a letter notifying me of my dismissal. I subsequently appealed to the regional manager. Again I told him I believed it was race discrimination. My appeal was rejected on 20 May 2021.

6   I believed I was dismissed because I am of Asian ethnic origin and/or because I made allegations of race discrimination.

7   Do you agree with my description of events? If you do not, please would you set out your version?

Questions

1   Please state who decided to dismiss me, when and each and every reason.

2   Please state who was consulted, when and their views.

3   Please state who decided to reject my appeal and the reasons.

4   Please state who was consulted, when and their views.

5   Please state all investigations made into my allegation of race discrimination (a) during my disciplinary hearing, and (b) during my appeal. In each case, please state what investigation was made, by whom and when, and what was the finding.

6   Please confirm in relation to the allegation against me regarding claiming taxi fares:
(a) that it is accepted I only claimed taxi fares on tube strike days;

(b) whether it is contended that I was not entitled to the fares at all or whether it is contended that I needed permission;

(c) if the latter, whether permission would have been granted had I asked;

(d) please clarify any other respect in which I allegedly broke company policy over claiming the fares;

(e) please state whether the said policy is verbal or written. If written, please supply a copy. If verbal, please state how and when it was communicated to me;

(f) please state what is the company's policy regarding when travel can be claimed and the mechanisms. Please include who has authority to give fares to each level of staff.

7 Please state all members of staff who have been given taxi fares on any occasion (i) during the tube strikes over the last three years, or (ii) for any other reason, by reference to:

(a) race;*

(b) job title and location;

(c) on whose authorisation;

(d) the reason for using the taxi;

(e) date and nature of any disciplinary action taken against them for using taxis.

8 Please state all staff dismissed from London branches since 1 January 2021. In each case please state: (a) race,* (b) job title and location, (c) nature of offences leading to dismissal, and (d) date of dismissal.

9 Please state all disciplinary action, short of dismissal, taken against London staff since 1 January 2021. In each case, please state:

(a) race;*

(b) job title and location;

(c) date and level of action; and

(d) nature of offence.

10 With regard to the demotion of my deputy manager, please state:

(a) who took the decision and for what reasons; and

(b) who was consulted and their views.

11 Please state all staff taken on since 1 January 2021 in London branches by reference to:

(a) race;*

(b) job title;

(c) location placed; and

(d) date taken on.

12 Please state all employees as at the date of this questionnaire above the level of branch manager in the company by reference to:

(a) race;*

(b) job title;

(c) start date; and

(d) location.

* For 'race' please state under the following categories: (a) colour (b) nationality (c) national origins (d) ethnic origins.

A10 NON-STATUTORY QUESTIONNAIRE: RACE DISCRIMINATION (REDUNDANCY)

See paras 21.47–21.48 regarding non-statutory questionnaires. This summary of complaint is not written in a form appropriate for the grounds of an ET1.

Summary of complaint

I am Black British. I was one of 200 engineers employed across three sites in the council's maintenance department. On 10 April 2021, I was made redundant together with 21 other engineers across all the sites. I have a clean disciplinary record and my appraisals have always been excellent. I have not been offered alternative employment.

Do you agree with my description of events? If you do not, please would you set out your version?

Questions

1 Please state the redundancy selection procedure adopted for the April 2021 redundancies including the dates of all decisions and consultations and the persons involved.

2 Please state the redundancy selection criteria used, stating in the case of each criterion:
   (a) when it was decided to use that criterion and by whom;
   (b) the reason for using that criterion;
   (c) how the criterion was to be measured and by whom;
   (d) how the criterion was weighted.

3 Please state whether a decision was made in advance as to how many engineers should be made redundant. If so, when was the decision made, by whom and how many engineers?

4 Please list all engineers employed by the council immediately before the redundancy selection procedure. Initials can be used rather than full names. Please indicate which one is myself. For each engineer, please state:
   (a) their race;*
   (b) their job title, grade and location;
   (c) their start date;
   (d) whether or not they were made redundant;
   (e) the reasons why they were or were not selected for redundancy;
   (f) their score on each of the redundancy selection criteria;
   (g) whether they applied for redeployment;
   (h) details of any job offers made to them for redeployment;
   (i) whether or not they were in fact redeployed and if not, why not.

5 Please list all technical or engineering vacancies from 1 January 2021 to date by reference to job title, grade, location, date vacant, date filled.

6 Please list all staff taken on to work as engineers for the three years prior to the date of this questionnaire by reference to:
   (a) their race;*
   (b) their start date;
   (c) their job title, grade and location.

7   Please state all staff dismissed from (i) the Engineering and Maintenance Department, and (ii) the rest of the council in the three years prior to the date of this questionnaire by reference to:
(a) their race;*
(b) their job title, grade and location;
(c) the dismissal date;
(d) the reason for dismissal.

8   (Since it is a public sector employer) Did you carry out an equality impact assessment before deciding upon your redundancy selection procedure and criteria? If so, when was it carried out? Who was involved? Of what did it comprise? What conclusions were reached?

* For 'race' please state under the following categories: (a) colour (b) nationality (c) national origins (d) ethnic origins.

A11 NON-STATUTORY QUESTIONNAIRE: PREGNANCY

See paras 21.47–21.48 regarding non-statutory questionnaires. This is a sample questionnaire in a case of dismissal of a pregnant woman, ostensibly on grounds of capability/conduct, but suspected to be due to pregnancy.

Summary of complaint

1   I have worked as Assistant Manager for Winfield Shoes in their Nottingham Branch since 12 October 2016. Throughout my employment, I received no warnings from my employers, written or verbal.

2   On 20 October 2020, I informed my manager, Tessa Hennessy, that I was pregnant. On 21 November 2020, I was off sick. I telephoned Jane Baxter of personnel and explained that I would not be in because I felt sick due to my pregnancy.

3   On 24 November 2020 I was sent a letter requiring me to attend a disciplinary hearing on 26 November 2020. This came out of the blue and was a complete shock to me.

4   At the disciplinary meeting held on 26 November 2020 I was dismissed. The reasons given to me were poor supervision of staff, poor time-keeping and taking too many personal phone calls. These allegations were untrue. My appeal to the managing director on 3 December 2020 also failed. I believe I was dismissed due to my pregnancy.

5   Do you agree with my description of events? If you do not, please would you set out your version?

Questions

1   Do you accept that I told Tessa Hennessy on or about 20 October 2020 that I was pregnant? If not, when does Tessa say she first found out I was pregnant and how does she say she found out?

2   Do you accept that I told Jane Baxter on 21 November 2020, when I telephoned in sick, that I was pregnant? If not, what does Jane Baxter say I told her?

3   Please list every person within the company who knew before my dismissal that I was pregnant. In each case, please state when and how they had found out.

4   In respect of the decision to dismiss me, please state:
(a) who took the decision and when;
(b) who was consulted and what were their views;
(c) every reason for my dismissal.

5   In respect of the decision to reject my appeal, please state:
(a) who took the decision and when;
(b) who was consulted and what were their views;
(c) every reason for rejecting my appeal.

6   Please set out every alleged instance with dates of (a) poor staff supervision, (b) poor time-keeping, and (c) receiving personal telephone calls.

7   Please set out the company policy regarding taking personal telephone calls.

8   (a) Was it a verbal or written policy? (b) When was it introduced?

9   Please state all dismissals and disciplinary action by the company since 1 January 2017, stating in each case:
    (a) job title and location of person dismissed;
    (b) age of any children under five years;
    (c) sex of person dismissed and whether pregnant or on maternity leave at the time;
    (d) date and nature of disciplinary action; and
    (e) nature of offence.

10 Please state all staff employed in the company as at 27 November 2020 by reference to:
    (a) job title/location;
    (b) age of children under 5;
    (c) sex;
    (d) dates when pregnant or on maternity leave during employment with you (indicating which).

11 Please state all staff who have become pregnant or gone onto maternity leave since 1 January 2017 by reference to:
    (a) job title/location;
    (b) dates of pregnancy or maternity leave (indicating which);
    (c) if applicable, termination date and reason for leaving.

Notes for readers:

With reference to questions 1 to 3: In post-dismissal correspondence, the managing director denied that the company knew the complainant was pregnant prior to her dismissal. If this happens or if it is possible that the company will deny knowledge, then questions should be asked to pin down its position.

It will not always be appropriate to ask such blunt questions, but on these facts, it is possible that early questions will get a truthful answer. If there has been no prior indication from the employer that s/he will deny knowledge, it may be better not to encourage denial by such questions. Instead, if the summary of complaint sets out when the complainant did tell the employer, then the employer's response should contain any denial.

A12 NON-STATUTORY QUESTIONNAIRE: SEXUAL HARASSMENT

See paras 21.47–21.48 regarding non-statutory questionnaires. This is a sample questionnaire in sexual harassment case.

Summary of complaint

I worked for the council in its Homeless Persons Unit. From September 2017, I was sexually harassed by her supervisor, Mr Briggs. [*Cite incidents.*] On 13 February 2021, the complainant informed personnel of the harassment. An investigation was carried out, during which I was instructed to remain off work. On 1 March 2021, I was told that the outcome of the investigation was inconclusive.

On 9 April 2021, I was required by Mr Briggs to attend a disciplinary hearing for poor work performance. I was issued with a final written warning. I believe Mr Briggs did this because I had told HR about the harassment.

Do you agree with my description of events? If you do not, please would you set out your version?

Questions

1 Please state all steps taken to investigate my allegations including all meetings and interviews with dates and persons involved.
2 In relation to every member of staff spoken to as part of the investigation, please state:
   (a) their name;
   (b) who spoke to them and on what date(s) and time(s);
   (c) whether anyone else was present;
   (d) what they were told about the allegations;
   (e) what they were asked and what they responded;
   (f) whether statements were made and their dates. (If so, please supply copies.)
3 Please state fully every finding of the council as a result of the investigation, indicating who made each finding and on what basis and on what date.
4 If any of my allegations were disbelieved, please state which and give reasons.
5 Was any action taken against Mr Briggs or any advice given to him following the investigation? If so, please specify.
6 Please state when Mr Briggs was first informed of my allegations and by whom.
7 Please state whether Mr Briggs was suspended during the investigation and if so, when.
8 With regard to Mr Briggs, please state (a) his start date, and (b) his job title and location throughout his employment with dates.
9 Please state all warnings or other disciplinary action taken against Mr Briggs at any stage in his employment including any informal counselling, giving in each case:
   (a) its date;
   (b) the level of warning;
   (c) who decided upon it;
   (d) the offence to which it related.

10 Please state all grievances, formal or informal, taken against Mr Briggs by any member of staff during his employment, in each case giving:
   (a) the date;
   (b) the nature of the grievance;
   (c) whether male or female complaining; and
   (d) the outcome of the grievance.

11 Please state whether any other allegations of sexual harassment have been made by any council employee in the last six years, formally or informally. If so, please state:
   (a) the date;
   (b) the name and sex of the alleged perpetrator;
   (c) whether the perpetrator was disciplined;
   (d) the job title and location of the employee making the allegation;
   (e) the sex of the employee making the allegation;
   (f) whether s/he remained with the council. If not, when did s/he leave and why. (Please also give details if s/he was transferred to another job within the council.)

12 Please state the number of staff in the department as at 1 March 2021 by reference to:
   (a) gender; and
   (b) job title and grade.

13 Please state all staff in the department in the last three years who have resigned, been disciplined or dismissed. In each case please state:
   (a) whether male or female;
   (b) whether resignation, dismissal or disciplinary action and date;
   (c) if resignation, reason given;
   (d) if dismissal or disciplinary action, nature of offence.

14 With regard to the decision to issue me with a final written warning, please state:
   (a) who made the decision and when;
   (b) whether anyone else was consulted. If so, when and what were their views;
   (c) every reason for the warning;
   (d) in relation to the criticism of my work, please specify precisely what was wrong with my work, giving dates and details.

A13 RACE DISCRIMINATION CLAIM: REQUEST FOR DISCLOSURE IN PROMOTION CASE

Sample list of documents to request as disclosure in a case of alleged race discrimination in promotion or job application where the claimant failed to obtain a post after interview. For the format of requests for disclosure and orders, see appendix C.

1   Score sheets and all other notes made at any time by the members of the short-listing and interview panels relating to the candidates who applied for and were appointed to the post.

2   All documents including application forms which were before the shortlisting and interview panels for the said post.

3   Any memorandum or report written to or by any member of the interview panel relating to each of the said appointments.

4   All references written on behalf of the claimant and the successful candidate.

5   Any other notes, memoranda, letters, e-mails or documents relating to the selection process for the post, including job description and person specification.

6   The advertisements placed for the post.

7   Any rules or regulations governing procedures for the appointment of employees of the respondents.

8   Any documents relating to the respondents' equal opportunities policy.

9   All other documents in the respondent's possession or control which are relevant to the case, whether of assistance to the respondent or the claimant.

A14 CHECKLIST: IS THE CLAIMANT AN EMPLOYEE FOR THE PURPOSES OF CLAIMING UNFAIR DISMISSAL?

There is no absolute test which applies to all circumstances, but the following checklist, read in conjunction with chapter 6, may help.

- There must be an express or implied contractual agreement between the parties.
- There must be an irreducible minimum of obligation on each side to offer and accept work.
- The employer must have a sufficient right of control over what work is done and how. However, what happens in practice can be misleading.
- The individual must be obliged to do the work him/herself, but it does not necessarily matter if s/he has a very restricted right to send substitutes.
- There must be nothing else which suggests the individual is not an employee.
- The individual is not necessarily an employee just because there is mutual obligation, sufficient control and an obligation to do the work personally. The contract must still appear to be a contract of employment. It is helpful if the individual is well-integrated into the employer's business, in terms of how s/he fits in internally and how s/he is seen externally.
- The labels attached to the relationship by the parties, ie whether or not the individual is called an employee, and the pay and tax arrangements, are relevant factors, but not conclusive.
- Where the individual accepts several separate assignments or engagements from a particular employer but does not have to be offered or to accept work in between the assignments, the individual may still be working under a contract of employment for the duration of each assignment. S/he will still need sufficient continuous service to claim unfair dismissal, which will depend on the rules covering breaks in service (see para 6.22).
- Applying these principles, agency workers may in theory be an employee of the end-user or the agency or neither. It is unusual to be an employee of the end-user because there is not usually any contract (express or implied) directly between the individual and the end-user.
- When trying to work out what the contract terms are, eg whether there is any mutual obligation or right to send substitutes, any written contract will be the starting point. However, if the claimant believes the written contract does not represent the reality of the situation, the tribunal will look at all the circumstances to ascertain what the real agreement between the parties was.

A15 CHECKLIST ON THE DEFINITION OF 'DISABILITY' UNDER EQUALITY ACT 2010 SECTION 6

NOTE: Unless the worker is obviously covered by the legal definition, it will be important carefully to interview him/her with the following checklist in mind. See also paras 15.7–15.35.

- Check that the worker has an 'impairment' which is either physical or mental.
- Check whether it is a condition which is deemed a disability on diagnosis (HIV; cancer; Multiple Sclerosis; certified visual impairment).
- Check that none of the excluded conditions apply.[3]
- Check that the impairment has adverse effects on the worker's ability to carry out normal day-to-day activities.[4]
- Check the affected activity is a 'normal' activity as opposed to, for example, a highly specialised hobby or specialist work activity (though normal hobbies and work activities should be covered).[5]
- The focus should be on what the worker cannot do, not on what s/he can do.[6]
- Check whether the worker's ability to carry out the normal activity is 'substantially' affected, ie, the effect is clearly more than trivial.[7]

NOTE: It is unnecessary that the worker is completely unable to carry out the activity. For example, it is sufficient that:

  – the worker can only carry out the activity more slowly than usual;
  – the worker can only carry out the activity in a particular way;[8]
  – it is tiring or painful to carry out the activity;[9]
  – the worker has medical advice not to attempt the activity.[10]

- Remember that the worker may have 'played down' the true effect of his/her disability on his/her daily life, or may have adjusted his/her life to avoid the need to carry out the activity.[11]
- Remember that if the worker has a progressive condition, s/he is protected as soon as that condition has any adverse effect, even if that effect is not yet substantial.[12]
- Consider whether the worker can only carry out an activity without substantial adverse effect due to medical treatment or an aid (except for glasses correcting eyesight).[13]

---

3 Equality Act 2010 (Disability) Regulations 2010 SI No 2128; paras 15.16 and 15.31 above.
4 *Guidance*, Section D.
5 See paras 15.19–15.20 above.
6 *Goodwin v The Patent Office* [1999] IRLR 4, EAT.
7 *Goodwin v The Patent Office* [1999] IRLR 4, EAT; EqA 2010 s212(1). For examples, see appendix to the *Guidance*.
8 *Guidance*, para B3.
9 *Guidance*, para D22.
10 *Guidance*, para D22.
11 *Goodwin v The Patent Office* [1999] IRLR 4, EAT; para 15.22 above.
12 EqA 2010 Sch 1 para 8. See also para 15.29 above.
13 EqA 2010 Sch 1 para 5. See also para 15.28 above.

- Note: if the worker has a severe disfigurement, it is treated as having substantial adverse effect on normal day-to-day activities, unless this is a tattoo or ornamental body-piercing.[14]
- Consider whether the substantial adverse effect of the impairment on the activity is long-term, ie, for 12 months or the rest of the worker's life.[15]
- Remember that impairments with recurring substantial effects may be covered, even though the effect is only for a short period at any one time.[16]
- Consider whether it is necessary to seek medical advice or obtain medical evidence on the above matters.[17]

---

14 EqA 2010 Sch 1 para 3. *Guidance*, paras B24–B26. Equality Act 2010 (Disability) Regulations 2010 SI No 2128 reg 5.

15 EqA 2010 Sch 1 para 2. See also para 15.32 above.

16 EqA 2010 Sch 1 para 2(2). See also para 15.32 above.

17 See sample letter at A18 below.

A16 DISABILITY DISCRIMINATION UNDER THE EQUALITY ACT 2010 – OVERALL CHECKLIST

Note: This checklist cannot cover every aspect of the law and should be read together with chapter 15.

- Is the worker eligible to claim under the EqA 2010?
  - Check the worker is an employee of the kind covered by the EqA 2010 or a job applicant or 'contract worker'.[18]
  - No minimum length of service is required.
  - Check the worker has a disability under the EqA 2010 s6.[19]
  - Check the worker's condition is not specifically excluded.[20]
- Has the employer treated the worker less favourably because of disability? This would be direct discrimination.[21]
- Has the employer treated the worker unfavourably because of something arising in consequence of the worker's disability?[22]
  - Why did the employer dismiss, discipline, fail to promote or treat the worker badly in any other way?
  - Was that reason because of something arising in consequence of the worker's disability, eg because of his/her attendance record which has disability-related absences?
  - If so, can the employer prove the treatment was a proportionate means of achieving a legitimate aim (taking account of any obligation to make reasonable adjustments)? If not, this would be discrimination arising from disability (DAFD).
  - Did the employer know the worker had a disability? If not, could s/he reasonably have been expected to know?
- Has the employer discriminated by failing to comply with a duty of reasonable adjustment?[23]
  - Did the employer know or should s/he have known that the worker had a disability and that an adjustment may be required?
  - Was the worker put at a disadvantage because of the failure to make reasonable adjustments?
  - Was that disadvantage because of the worker's disability?
  - Was the disadvantage more than minor or trivial?
  - Consider possible adjustments which may assist the worker.[24] (Discuss with the worker, the worker's GP and any relevant specialist organisation.) Is it reasonable to expect the employer to have made the adjustment?
- Has the worker been subjected to indirect discrimination?[25]

---

18 See para 12.12 above.
19 See Checklist at A15.
20 See Checklist at A15.
21 EqA 2010 s13. See paras 15.71–15.81 above.
22 EqA 2010 s15(1). See paras 15.82–15.88 above.
23 EqA 2010 s21. See paras 15.43–15.70 above.
24 See A17 below.
25 EqA 2010 s19. See paras 15.90–15.94 above.

- Has the worker been harassed?[26]
- Has the worker been victimised, ie, discriminated against for complaining of discrimination under the EqA 2010?[27]
    - How and when did the worker complain of discrimination?
    - Did the employer dismiss or treat the worker badly in any other way as a result?
    - Will the employer say the worker's allegation was false and made in bad faith? (If the employer can prove that, the worker will lose.)
- If the worker was a job applicant, did the employer make any enquiries about his/her health, health record or disability before making a job offer?[28] If so, did the employer directly discriminate against the worker based on information given in his/her answer?
- Overall, consider what medical and other evidence may be necessary.
- Can the cost of medical evidence be covered? Can full costs be recovered from the ET?
- Is the worker willing and able to bring an ET case?
- What outcome would the worker want?
- Note time limits for starting an ET case/notifying ACAS under the EC rules.
- Ensure the worker complies with any relevant part of the ACAS Code on Disciplinary and Grievance Procedures, eg by bringing a grievance.
- Consider writing a non-statutory questionnaire.
- Does the worker have any other legal claims, eg, unfair dismissal?
- When writing the ET1, if the facts allow, state the case as under EqA 2010 s13 and/or s15 and/or ss20–21.[29] This is the most likely combination, though other definitions could apply. Do not add definitions which could not apply to the facts and evidence, eg think carefully about whether the facts and evidence could prove direct discrimination (s13), or whether the case is really only about DAFD (s15) and reasonable adjustments (ss20–21).

---

26 EqA 2010 s26.
27 EqA 2010 s27.
28 EqA 2010 s60. See also paras 15.36–15.41 above.
29 See sample at A19 below.

A17 DISABILITY DISCRIMINATION – STAGES OF REASONABLE ADJUSTMENTS

The requirement on employers to make reasonable adjustments is to ensure that disabled workers are not put at a disadvantage due to their disability. If a disabled worker is having difficulties at work or not performing well, it is important to show that this is because of his/her disability rather than an unconnected reason, eg s/he is just not very good at his/her job. It is necessary to consider what it is about the job duties or workplace that causes the difficulty. This also requires considering the exact effect of the worker's disability. Stages 2 or 3 below are likely to reveal if the disadvantage is unconnected with disability. The wording of the definition in the EqA 2010 is rather clumsy, but it is necessary to follow the stages set out below:[30]

1 Identify the substantial disadvantage suffered by the worker, eg inability to carry out certain work or to carry it out to a required standard or sitting or standing; having difficulty working particular hours or under certain circumstances. Where it is specific aspects of the worker's role which cause the difficulty, the duties must be identified in sufficient detail to pinpoint the nature and extent of the disadvantage, eg if completing paperwork is a difficulty, the disadvantage might be described as 'inability to complete paperwork legibly by hand'. The disadvantage must be substantial, ie more than minor or trivial.

2 Identify what it is about the work requirements or workplace or lack of equipment which has caused the disadvantage, ie the provision criterion or practice applied by or on behalf of the employer or the physical feature of the premises and/or the lack of an auxiliary aid. For example, the employer requires work to be done of a certain kind or to a certain standard or in a particular way, or requires the worker to attend full-time between certain hours. As at stage 1, where the problematic provision, criterion or practice (PCP) is carrying out certain duties, these need to be identified in sufficient detail to identify the problem, eg it may not be completing paperwork which causes a difficulty, but it may be the need to complete it by hand.

3 If appropriate, identify a non-disabled comparator (actual or hypothetical) who is not disadvantaged by such PCP or physical feature or lack of an aid. This is a rather artificial step caused by the clumsy wording of the legislation and should not be viewed the same way as comparators in direct discrimination cases. The idea is simply to show that the reason the worker is at a disadvantage is due to his/her disability as opposed to other reasons. It usually involves simply saying that a hypothetical person without the disability *and effects of the disability* (but otherwise with the same skills and competence as the worker) would not be disadvantaged by the particular PCP etc. For example, a non-disabled worker would not usually have difficulty completing paperwork by hand. It would not be appropriate to compare the position of a disabled worker who cannot as a result of his/her disability complete paperwork by hand with a non-disabled worker who for other reasons cannot complete paperwork by hand.

---

30 See para 16.63. Note that this reverses the first two stages in *The Environment Agency v Rowan* [2008] IRLR 20, EAT.

4   Make suggestions as to what adjustments would have been reasonable to prevent such a PCP etc disadvantaging the worker.

Example 1

The worker's hours are 9 am to 5 pm, but this involves traveling to and from work during rush hour. This is a problem because the trains are very crowded and the worker has agoraphobia.

Stage 1: The disadvantage is inability to travel during rush hour.

Stage 2: The disadvantage is caused by the employer's PCP that the worker work 9 am to 5 pm.

Stage 3: A hypothetical comparator without agoraphobia (or other disability) would not be put at that kind of disadvantage by being required to travel at rush hour.

Stage 4: Adjusting working hours.

Example 2

The worker has multiple sclerosis, which makes it difficult for her to walk up and down stairs at the office without handrails. She works on the ground floor, so she does not need to use the stairs, but the rest of her department is on the 1st floor.

Stage 1: The disadvantage is inability to use the stairs to visit her colleagues.

Stage 2: The disadvantage is caused by a physical feature of the premises, ie lack of handrails on the stairs.

Stage 3: A comparator who was not disabled would be able to use the stairs.

Stage 4: Putting up handrails or moving the whole department downstairs.

Example 3

The worker has a visual impairment. She finds it difficult to read the computer screen and as a result makes data entry errors. As a result of her errors, she is demoted.

Stage 1: The disadvantage is difficulty reading the computer screen and therefore difficulty making accurate data entries.

Stage 2: The disadvantage is caused by the lack of an auxiliary aid (adapted software). The worker needs to prove that the errors are caused by her visual impairment and that adapted software would prevent the errors.

NOTE: If her errors have nothing to do with her difficulty seeing the screen and are simply caused by inability to add up, her reasonable adjustment claim would fail at this stage.

Stage 3: A hypothetical comparator with the worker's general level of ability but who did not have a visual impairment (or other disability) would not be making the errors.

NOTE: If the worker's errors were due to her inability to add up and not due to her visual impairment, then a non-disabled worker with the same capabilities would have been at the same disadvantage and the worker's reasonable adjustment claim would fail.

Stage 4: Adapted software.

A18 DISABILITY DISCRIMINATION CLAIM UNDER THE EQUALITY ACT 2010 – SAMPLE LETTER TO GP

NOTE that this is not a standard letter. The letter would vary according to the facts and how obvious the worker's disability and symptoms are. In some cases, it will be appropriate to write a shorter letter focusing on very specific points of concern.

Dear Dr [. . .]

Re: [*Client's full name, address and date of birth*]

I am advising Claudia regarding a potential claim against her employers for disability discrimination under the Equality Act 2010. In order for me to assess whether Claudia is covered by the Act, I should be grateful if you would write a Report concerning her condition and covering the following points.

1   Please could you specify the nature of the impairment from which Claudia suffers.

2   Please could you comment on whether Claudia's ability to carry out day-to-day activities is adversely affected to a substantial (as opposed to minor or trivial) degree. It would be very helpful if you could give concrete examples and address activities such as mobility, ability to lift, social interaction [*make suggestions re relevant activities*]. Please note that it is not simply a question of whether Claudia is able to do such activities at all, but whether she has pain or other difficulty in carrying them out.

3   If Claudia's condition is controlled by medication or aids, please could you also state how Claudia's abilities under the above categories would be affected were she not taking any medication.

4   The Act protects workers where the effect of the impairment has lasted at least 12 months or is likely to last for 12 months or for the rest of their life, if less. Recurring effects are also covered, ie, if the effect lasts less than 12 months but is likely to recur. Please could you clarify when the substantial adverse effects started to apply to Claudia and when they ceased or, if they have not yet ceased, when they are likely to cease. When I say 'likely', I simply mean that it could well happen.

5   Claudia has told me that she has particular difficulties with mobility. Could you please especially address this point and let me know whether you would expect her:
(i)   to have any difficulty using public transport;
(ii)   to be able to travel a short journey in a car;
(iii)   to have any difficulty going up or down stairs.
Would the position be any different if she were not taking medication?

6   I attach a brief description of Claudia's job duties and areas of difficulty caused by her impairment. Do you have any suggestions as to adjustments to Claudia's working conditions which may be of assistance to her?

I enclose Claudia's written authorisation for you to disclose the above information to me. Please feel free to telephone should you wish clarification. Please let me know before writing your report if there will be any fee.

NOTE: Where the adviser is aware of an area of difficulty for the claimant, s/ he may wish to guide the doctor further, eg, by reference to the examples in the appendix to the Guidance and paras D11–D17. Paragraph 5 of the letter is an example of this.

If the GP's letter is to be shown to the employer, the worker must think carefully about its implications. If the letter suggests that the worker cannot do the job at all, but no adjustments are feasible, this could lead to difficulties.

The fee should be agreed in advance and you should check who will be responsible for its payment.

A19 ET1: DISABILITY DISCRIMINATION CLAIM (VARIOUS)

Sample details of disability discrimination claim for para 8.2 of ET1 form. In this example, a discriminatory dismissal is pleaded in the alternative under each of EqA 2010 s13 (direct discrimination), s15 (discrimination arising from disability) and ss20–21 (failure to make reasonable adjustments).

1   I worked as a messenger for my employers from 17 May 2015 until my dismissal on 12 May 2021. I was dismissed because I reached 20 days' sickness absence in each of my last three years of employment under the Sickness Monitoring Procedure. However, nearly all my sickness absences were due to bronchial asthma.

2   My employers were a large company employing over 1,000 members of staff. There were ten other messengers who did the same job as I did. If any messenger was absent through sickness, the others would cover the work on overtime. There was also an agency which supplied workers at short notice in emergencies.

3   The messengers were based in a small office with poor ventilation. I told my employers several times that this aggravated my asthma.

4   Apart from my sickness, I have had no warnings throughout my employment. Indeed, I have often been complimented on my good work.

5   I believe that I was dismissed on because of my disability contrary to the Equality Act 2010 s13. I believe a non-disabled worker who reached 20 days' sickness for three successive years would not have been dismissed.

6   Further or alternatively, I was dismissed because of something arising out of my disability contrary to Equality Act 2010 s15 in that nearly all my sick absences were due to my disability.

7   Further or alternatively, I have been discriminated against contrary to sections 20–21 of the Equality Act 2010 by my employers' failure to make adjustments, for example, by (i) basing me in an office with better ventilation, and/ or (ii) discounting my disability-related absences when applying the Sickness Monitoring Procedure to me, and/or (iii) any other reasonable adjustment.

A20 SAMPLE WITNESS STATEMENT IN RACIAL AND RELIGIOUS HARASSMENT CASE

In reality, a claimant's witness statement may be longer than the following example. A description of the claimant's duties should also be added. The following, however, gives an idea of style and content. Note how the statement draws attention to the differences in the claimant's treatment before and after the main discriminator (Ricky Johnson) started and also compares his treatment in detail with that of a white comparator (Peter Scholar). In discrimination cases, different treatment is more significant than unfair treatment.

For a sample witness statement in an unfair dismissal case, see appendix C.

SAYED MEGALI: WITNESS STATEMENT

Background

1   I was born in Egypt and I grew up there. I came to England in 1996. I have British nationality. I am of the Muslim religion. I was employed as a room service waiter in Herberts Hotel for 16 years. I was promoted to supervisor after three years. Then after another three years I became senior supervisor. While I worked at Herberts Hotel, I never had any disciplinary action taken against me nor did I take any grievances.

2   In 2012 I left the job to return to Egypt for family reasons. When I came back to England in 2013, I started working as security guard for various agencies. On 15 October 2015, I started work as security guard for Matts Hotel.

3   I was already well-known in the hotel. I had worked as a casual waiter previously. I got on well with everyone. The hotel asked about me in the catering department before they took me on in security.

4   Robert Keen started one week before me as Chief of Security. Before Ricky Johnson started, I used to get on well with Robert Keen. Ricky Johnson started in July 2019 as Assistant Chief Security Officer. Ricky Johnson and Robert Keen are both white and English. I believe they are of the Christian religion.

Ricky Johnson

5   Ricky Johnson was hostile and abusive from the beginning. If there was any news story about the Middle East or Arabs or if there were Arab guests in the hotel, he used to say, 'Fucking Arabs'.

6   Gradually Robert Keen became more and more hostile to me. For example, Robert Keen kept saying, 'I am fed up with you. Why don't you go back to Egypt?' He never used to talk like that before.

7   Before Ricky Johnson came, Robert Keen was helpful when I wanted to pray. He even said, 'Sayed, I will be in the office for a while, you can go and pray.' He also let me take Fridays as one of my off-days so I could go to the mosque. After Ricky Johnson came, all this stopped, but Robert Keen gave Ricky Johnson every Saturday off so he could watch football.

8   One day in August or September 2019, I saw a PG Tips card with a picture of a monkey put up on the wall where we make tea. Ricky Johnson used to buy the tea. I took it down and threw it away, but a few weeks later, when a new packet of tea was bought, a new monkey card was put up. I asked Ricky Johnson if he put it there. He denied it, but I believe it was him. It never happened before he came.

9   On 30 October 2019, I wrote to the hotel manager (Frank Alexander) taking out a grievance for race and religious discrimination against Ricky Johnson. Mr Alexander acknowledged my letter on 2 November 2019 and said that his secretary would contact me to arrange an appointment to meet.

10 On 14 November 2019, I received a letter from personnel calling me to a disciplinary the next day. I had worked in security for four years and as a casual waiter for the hotel previously. This was the first time I had been called to a disciplinary.

11 The letter said that the disciplinary was because Ricky Johnson said I had shouted and sworn at him. I told personnel at the disciplinary that this was not true. I said that he had made the accusation because I had taken out the grievance of race and religious discrimination. At the end of the disciplinary, personnel decided to take no action.

12 I met Mr Alexander on 28 November 2019 to talk about my grievance. The meeting was for about one hour. Mr Alexander said he would investigate and come back to me, but he never did come back to me about it afterwards.

The new security guard

13 In January 2020, a new security guard, Peter Scholar, was recruited. Peter was white/English and of the Christian religion. Peter was very young, about 22 years old. He had not worked in security for as long as I had. I knew Peter Scholar. He had worked at the hotel for six months in 2019 for an independent security company employed by the hotel's building contractors. His main job was to stop the builders using the staff entrance. He had to search the builders when they went out with a bag. He also patrolled the hotel to keep an eye on the builders.

14 Right from the start, Peter Scholar was treated better than I was in many ways. He was paid more than I, even though we were supposed to be doing the same job. Then in April 2021, he was given a rise and I did not get a rise.

15 In the first week Peter Scholar started, Ricky Johnson took him to a hotel management meeting. All the senior hotel managers go to that meeting every Friday. I have never been taken to it. The previous day I had heard Ricky tell Peter he would take him to the meeting so that he could cover if Robert Keen or Ricky Johnson were not there.

16 Before Peter Scholar started, the hotel's internal telephone directory only listed Robert Keen and Ricky Johnson by name under Security. After Peter started, his name was put on the list too. I was still not named. I was just 'Back Door Security'.

17 When there is an important function in the ballroom, sometimes they need extra security. I was never given a chance to do this. It was always Robert Keen or Ricky Johnson or outside security. I was not asked. But in his first or second week, Peter Scholar was allowed to do a ballroom function.

18 I saw Ricky Johnson show Peter Scholar how to use the computer several times in his first few weeks. Ricky spent more time with Peter than he spent showing me.

19 In February 2021, the number of the safe in the security office was changed. Peter Scholar was given the new number, but I was not. I asked Robert Keen why he changed the safe number. He said it was because there were

important papers there. He would not give me the number. This had never happened before. Later he told Mr Alexander he changed the safe number because of an electronic fault, but he did not say that to me and he did not give me the new safe number until Mr Alexander intervened.

20   In April 2021, Peter Scholar received a pay-rise. Most of the other hotel staff also received a rise – though some did not. Robert Keen and Ricky Johnson also received a rise, so the whole security department except me got a rise. I had received a rise every April since I started. This April I did not get a rise.

21   I have continued to be harassed by Ricky Johnson. [*Give full dates and details of incidents.*] Robert Keen has also started to criticise my work and threaten me with disciplinary action. [*Give full dates and details of incidents.*] Until Ricky Johnson started, Robert Keen had never made any serious criticisms of my work or threatened disciplinary action.

22   Until all this happened, I was never off sick from work, even for one day. All the pressure and harassment for so long have damaged my health. On 5 May 2021, my doctor told me I was not fit for work due to depression. I was off sick for four weeks.

23   I think I have been treated this way because of my Egyptian or Arab origin and also because of my Muslim religion. I also think that I have been victimised because I complained about the harassment.

24   I really did not want to go to the tribunal. I wrote so many letters. I told the hotel I would prefer to sort it out. But in the end they gave me no option. I have found it very hard to go to work over the last few years. Every day I wondered if I was going to get a letter accusing me of doing something wrong or a disciplinary. It is very stressful. In the end, I became very depressed. I have never been depressed before. I am not that kind of person. I have not taken any further grievance because I am afraid it will just lead to me getting harassed further as has happened in the past.

SIGNED . . .
DATED . . . .

A21 EXTRACTS FROM SAMPLE WITNESS STATEMENT OF TRADE UNION OFFICIAL IN SUPPORT OF CLAIMANT'S RACE DISCRIMINATION CASE

As well as establishing the facts and events in which the official was involved, this statement draws attention to all the ways in which the employer's behaviour differed from what normally occurs (with white staff). In discrimination cases, it is more relevant to highlight different behaviour than unfair behaviour. The statement also establishes the basis of experience from which the official is able to generalise and draw distinctions.

1   I am Branch Secretary of the [*name*] trade union, based at [*name*] Council. I have held that position for approximately four years. I have been a member of the local trade union committee since 2001. I have been involved in a multitude of investigations and disciplinaries of council staff as their trade union representative.

2   The housing department, where the claimant works, comprises 120 members of staff. Although approximately one-third of the staff are black or from minority ethnic groups, nearly all the managers are white. The trade union has taken up equal opportunities issues with management on several occasions. [*Describe incidents revealing management in a bad light on equal opportunities policies, but keep concise and relevant.*]

3   I was involved in the events concerning the claimant from the beginning. My first involvement was on [*date*] when the claimant was notified of disciplinary action.

4   [*Describe sequence of events with dates, official's role and how much information was given to the official and/or the claimant by management.*]

5   It is very unusual to have a disciplinary hearing without a prior investigation. Normally the investigation is carried out first and the accused person is told about the investigation and what the allegations are. The disciplinary then takes place if and when the investigation reveals there is enough to justify it. It was also extraordinary not even to know the allegations against the claimant until just before the disciplinary hearing.

6   Another unusual aspect was [*Describe all procedural irregularities which took place*].

7   [*If official has anything useful to say regarding the disciplinary allegations themselves, insert here.*]

A22 ET1: UNFAIR DISMISSAL (CONDUCT) AND WRITTEN REASONS

Sample details of claim for unfair dismissal and failure to give written reasons for dismissal for para 8.2 of ET1 form.

1   I started work for the respondent restaurant in May 2019 as a sous chef. I was never given a written contract.

2   Until 18 July 2021, there were no problems with my employment and I had received no disciplinary warnings of any kind. I took orders from various more senior members of kitchen staff, including the 2nd Head Chef, Basil.

3   Basil's manner in the kitchen was generally to shout and abuse more junior staff. On 18 July 2021, I was joking with some of my colleagues as I worked. Other supervisors would allow us to talk and joke as long as we got the work done. Basil entered the kitchen and poked his finger in the chest of some of my colleagues. He also waved his finger at me and he told us all to 'shut up'.

4   I was upset by his angry manner and I asked him what was wrong. He swore at me in response and I therefore swore back at him. He told us to 'f . . . ing shut up' and to 'f . . . off'. I replied to him 'f . . . off'. I regret doing this, but it was completely provoked by Basil's manner towards me and my colleagues. Also swearing and use of the 'f . . .' word is very common in the kitchen at all levels of staff.[31]

5   Basil then shouted at me to go home. When I did not want to do this, he became more angry and said that I was suspended and to go home and he called security.

6   When I came in on 19 July 2021, I found the head chef, Mo, and tried to explain what had happened. Mo's first response was that I had been there for two years and should know what Basil was like. He said 'Better look for another job'. Then he told me to return the next day at 5 pm. Then when I went in on 20 July 2021, I was handed a letter calling me to a disciplinary hearing on 23 July 2021.

7   When I arrived on 23 July 2021, Mo and Basil were sitting there. Mo said, 'We have decided you are dismissed. We have discussed it and we have decided.' I was stunned. I had only just entered the room. I said, 'I would just like to explain something.' Mo said, 'OK, Carry on.' I said that Basil had sworn at me first. Basil said the supervisor had already told me twice to shut up. I said that had not happened. Basil did not respond. Mo then said, 'OK, thank you, sorry you have to go.' The whole meeting took about two minutes. No questions were asked of me. I did not even get the chance to sit down.

8   I then went to look for the General Manager, who I found at the bar. I told him I had been dismissed. He said he would look into the details. However, I have not heard from him since.

9   On 25 July 2021, I wrote to the General Manager and asked him the written reasons for my dismissal. I have had no response.

---

31 It is best to deal with the fact that the claimant swore in the ET1 and put it in context.

10 I believe I was unfairly dismissed contrary to Employment Rights Act 1996 s98 in that:[32]

    (a) Having regard to usual language in the kitchen and in particular the generally abusive manner of Basil and the fact that he spoke to me initially on 18 July 2021 in an abusive way, there was not a fair reason to dismiss me.

    (b) I had been given no prior warnings regarding my conduct or any other matter.

    (c) There was no proper investigation and I was not given a fair hearing prior to my dismissal. In particular:

        (i)   the allegations against me were not clearly put to me;

        (ii) I was given no proper chance to state my case;

        (iii) I was not listened to with an open mind.

    (d) The General Manager did not look into the matter as he promised me and I was deprived of the opportunity of an appeal.

11 Good practice guidelines in the ACAS Code of Practice on Disciplinary and Grievance Procedures were not followed as set out above.

12 I further request a declaration as to the reasons for my dismissal and compensation pursuant to Employment Rights Act 1996 s92.

---

32 Only set out reasons in this way if confident, since there is the danger of missing something out. If uncertain, and the unfairness is apparent from the facts set out in the grounds – as in this case – it may be sufficient to state, 'for the above reasons, I believe my dismissal was unfair'. The advantage of itemising the unfairness, if you can, is that it may encourage the employer to settle. It may also prevent the tribunal writing to the claimant on an 'initial consideration' on the basis that the claim seems to have no reasonable prospect of success (see para 20.100).

A23 ET1: UNFAIR DISMISSAL (CONDUCT), NOTICE AND RIGHT TO BE ACCOMPANIED

Sample details of claim for unfair dismissal, notice, pay and breach of the right to be accompanied, for para 8.2 of ET1 form.

1   The claimant was employed as a part-time receptionist by the respondent Leisure Clubs from on or about 10 April 2011 until termination on 7 July 2021. She never received any warnings throughout her employment.[33]

2   At the tennis club where the claimant was based, there were two car parks, one for members of the club and one for the staff. As a general rule, staff were asked not to park in the members' car park unless the staff car park was full.

3   In practice, however, staff frequently parked in the members' car park at different times and on occasion left their cars there overnight or for prolonged periods of time. Management were aware of this but took no action.

4   The claimant also used to park her car in the members' car park on occasion, for example, at night or when the staff car park was full, and was sometimes reminded in passing that she should use the staff car park. At no time did the claimant receive a formal verbal or written warning for parking her car in the members' car park.[34]

5   On 26 June 2021 the claimant was driving into the members' car park in order to pick up a member. She was accompanied in her car by a friend. On her way in she met John Armitage, the Finance Director, who was also in his car.

6   John Armitage said something to her, but because both parties were in their cars, the claimant did not hear him properly. She believed he was saying something about the van owned by the health club, which was parked nearby, and she replied to him 'That's a delivery'. She then parked in the members' car park and went into the club to meet the member she was picking up, who was late.

7   The claimant received a letter dated 4 July 2021 which informed her that a disciplinary interview had been arranged to deal with 'continued abuse of the club car park and wilful misconduct towards a Director of the company' relating to the incident with John Armitage.

8   The disciplinary hearing took place on 7 July 2021. John Armitage conducted the interview. The claimant wanted one of her colleagues to accompany her. She was told this was unnecessary.

9   At the meeting, John Armitage explained the reasons why the disciplinary meeting was taking place and said that he had told the claimant not to park her car in the members' car park, which she had then gone on to do. The claimant explained that there had been a misunderstanding about this incident, because she had not understood what he was saying at the time. If she had known what he was saying she would not have deliberately disobeyed him.

10   The claimant was summarily dismissed and did not return to work after that

---

33 Claimants 'forget' about warnings. Make sure she is correct about this statement.

34 As the claimant did in fact use the members' car park, it is best to admit this from the outset and put it in context.

date. She did not appeal this decision because she was very shocked at the time and was not informed of her right to appeal.

11 The claimant was unfairly dismissed. In particular, the respondent:[35]
   (i)   failed properly to investigate the allegations against the claimant;
   (ii)   failed to reach a reasonable conclusion;
   (iii)   failed to have a reasonable belief in the claimant's guilt;[36]
   (iv)   failed to follow its own contractual disciplinary procedures;
   (v)   failed to inform the claimant of her right to appeal the decision to dismiss;
   (vi)   failed to follow the ACAS Code of Practice on Disciplinary and Grievance Procedures;[37]
   (vii)   allowed John Armitage to act as witness, prosecutor and judge;
   (viii) it was not reasonable in all the circumstances for the respondent to dismiss and the dismissal fell outside the band of reasonable responses.

12 The claimant further claims six weeks' pay in lieu of notice.

13 The respondent failed to permit the claimant to be accompanied at the disciplinary hearing contrary to section 10 of the Employment Relations Act 1999 and contrary to the ACAS Code on Disciplinary and Grievance Procedures.[38] The claimant claims compensation.

---

35 See comments at n32.
36 Points (i)–(iii) relate to the steps which the employer should follow in conduct cases according to *BHS v Burchell* [1978] IRLR 379, EAT and see para 7.46.
37 Points (iv)–(vii) are appropriate on the facts of this particular case.
38 See para 22.3.

A24 LIST OF ISSUES FOR DISCRIMINATION CASE (WITH OTHER CLAIMS)

At preliminary hearings to discuss case management, which are usually held in discrimination cases, it is common for the employment judge to make a list of the 'issues' in the case. Essentially, this sets out the claims and their component parts. It is best to go prepared with a 'draft' to hand up to the judge and the other side, to make sure nothing gets left out. Ideally, send the draft to the other side in advance and try to get agreement to the content. The following is an example. The words in square brackets are optional.

1   Did the respondent subject the claimant to direct race discrimination [under the Equality Act 2010 sections 9 and 13] by giving her a written warning on 16 April 2021?

2   Did the respondent subject the claimant to direct race discrimination [under the Equality Act 2010 sections 9 and 13] by dismissing her on 23 May 2021?

3   In respect of the claimant's victimisation claim [under the Equality Act 2010 section 27]:
   (a) Did the claimant allege race discrimination when speaking to her manager on 20 April 2021?
   (b) If so, was that allegation a 'protected act'?
   (c) Did the respondent victimise the claimant by dismissing her on 23 May 2021 as a result of that allegation?

4   In respect of the claimant's unfair dismissal claim:
   (a) Can the respondent prove the reason for dismissal and what is that reason?
   (b) Was it fair to dismiss the claimant for that reason, taking account of the band of reasonable responses?
   (c) Did the respondent fail to follow a relevant part of the ACAS Code on Disciplinary and Grievance Procedures and if so, should there be an adjustment of compensation and in what sum?

5   Did the respondent has made an unauthorised deduction from the claimant's pay [contrary to Part II of the Employment Rights Act 1996] in the sum of £450 representing the claimant's wages for the period 10–23 May 2021?

6   Compensation if the claimant is successful in any of the above claims.

A25 VARIATION OF CONTRACT CHECKLIST

The law is complicated around what an employee can do if the employer tries to impose a change of terms and conditions in the contract of employment. In theory, no change can be made to a contract unless the employee agrees. In practice, what happens if the employer just sacks an employee who refuses to agree? Not only will the employee have no job, s/he may not be eligible to make any legal claims. Even if the employee is eligible to claim, s/he may not win.

It is commonly believed that employers only need to give 90 days' notice of a change. This is not in fact true, the employee's consent is still necessary.

The following is a guide to some important steps when thinking through the employee's legal position.

- Check the worker's employment status. If s/he is not in fact an employee, s/he will have fewer options, as s/he will not have unfair dismissal protection. Discrimination law is not restricted to employees in the sense meant by unfair dismissal law.
- Check the employee's contract of employment. Is its meaning clear? Is the employer really changing the contract or is it a change which the contract allows?

  WARNING: Contract terms may be written, verbal or implied. If written, they may be ambiguous. If unwritten, they may be hard to ascertain or prove.
- Is the employee eligible to claim unfair dismissal if s/he is sacked or resigns due to a contractual change? If not, his/her position is very weak.
- Even if the employee is eligible to make an unfair dismissal claim in such circumstances, is s/he likely to win it?
  - Did the employer adopt fair procedures in implementing the change? (Advance notice; consultation; flexibility)
  - Would the ET think it reasonable for the employer to impose the change? (The ET may conclude that the employer's needs are more important than the negative impact on employees. Are there better alternatives? Have other employees agreed to the change? Are there special circumstances?)
- Is the employee willing to risk losing his/her job over this?
- What is the likelihood of winning a case and what compensation is the employee likely to receive?
- What is the employee's chance of getting a new job? Will s/he get a bad reference?
- Compare the problem of working under the varied contract with any alternative/job prospects.
- Has the employee been discriminated against in the change, directly or indirectly?
  - Is s/he covered by the discrimination legislation? (Note, s/he need not be an employee in the sense needed for unfair dismissal claims or to have been employed for any minimum period.)
  - Is there any indirect sex discrimination, eg, introducing flexi-shifts or other changes interfering with childcare?
  - Is there any indirect race discrimination, eg, introducing duties requiring sophisticated written English skills?

- Are the changes imposed on some staff but not on others? Is this direct discrimination? For example, an employer may make an exception for a white worker unable to work flexi-shifts for health reasons, but refuse to make an exception for a black worker with equally valid reasons.
- Has the employer introduced duties which are hard for a disabled worker to undertake?

WARNING: Although the employee may be able to claim discrimination without resigning from his/her job, s/he may nevertheless be victimised for doing so. Victimisation and intimidation of an employee pursuing a discrimination case should be catalogued, as this too is illegal and may be the ground for a further case.

What can the employee do now?

- Agree the change (orally or in writing).
- Pin down the employer on the nature of the change and the reasons for it, either in correspondence (formal letters; informal emails etc) or through a grievance. The employer's reasoning helps the worker assess the strength of any tribunal claim and may give scope for a negotiated compromise.
- State disagreement with the change and attempt to negotiate.

WARNING: Once negotiation has clearly become futile, the grievance procedure is exhausted, and the employer is still insisting on the change, an employee needs to make up his/her mind swiftly whether or not s/he accepts the change. Otherwise s/he can lose the right to resign because s/he has 'affirmed' (ie, implicitly agreed by inaction).

- Refuse to accept the change. If it amounts to a pay deduction, make a tribunal claim for an unauthorised deduction or, less practically, a civil claim for the pay owed. If it is a change in duties, refuse to carry out the change.

WARNING: These steps risk dismissal. Dismissal for claiming an unauthorised deduction is automatically unfair, but it may be hard to prove that was the reason.

- Resign and claim unfair constructive dismissal. There are many legal pitfalls for this:
  - The employee may not be eligible to claim unfair dismissal.
  - The contract may be unclear; it may be uncertain that the employer has broken it in a fundamental way.
  - The employee may not have resigned quickly enough; if s/he has taken too long to decide, the ET may consider s/he has already accepted the change.
  - The employer's behaviour may not necessarily be considered unfair by the ET.
  - The employee is out of a job and may not get much compensation even if s/he wins.
- Make a discrimination claim if applicable. This can be done whether or not s/he resigns, but it does risk victimisation or dismissal.
- The employee may also be entitled to a redundancy payment if s/he loses her job in circumstances which fit the legal definition of redundancy.
- If the employer imposes the change by dismissing the employee with correct notice and then offering a new contract on different terms, the employee may be able to accept the new contract while claiming unfair dismissal in respect of the old contract.

- If the employer imposes a very radical change, the law may deem this as a dismissal and again the employee can claim unfair dismissal while remaining in the new job.

  WARNING: The employee cannot have it both ways. If s/he accepts the new terms so that s/he can remain in the job, and reserves his/her right to make a claim in respect of the variation/dismissal from the original contract, s/he cannot then renege on the new terms. Otherwise s/he can justifiably be dismissed from the new contract.

- It will be more effective if a large number of employees simultaneously bring legal action. Collective opposition and negotiation will usually be the best bet.

A26 WHISTLEBLOWING CHECKLIST

If a worker wants to 'blow the whistle' or take up potentially controversial issues at work, it is very important to take account of the criteria in the Employment Rights Act 1996, so that s/he has protection if s/he is dismissed or penalised by the employer as a result. The following checklist does not cover all situations. See also the text at paras 6.101–6.124.

1   Check that the worker reasonably believes that the information which s/he proposes to disclose tends to show one of the following has taken or may take place:
    - a criminal offence. Identify the relevant offence;
    - breach of a legal obligation, including an obligation in the worker's own contract of employment. Identify the relevant obligation;
    - miscarriage of justice;
    - danger to health and safety;
    - damage to the environment.
    - information tending to show any matter falling within these categories has been or is likely to be deliberately concealed.

2   Check that the worker believed making the disclosure was in the public interest. If so, was that belief reasonable? (This applies to disclosures made on or after 25 June 2013.)

3   Check that the worker is acting in good faith. (For disclosures on or after 25 June 2013, this will affect compensation. Before that, it will affect whether s/he is protected at all.)

4   Consider what outcome the worker wants.
    - Is s/he willing to accept potential adverse consequences?
    - Unless the complaint is about how s/he has been treated him/herself, does s/he realise s/he will only be a witness in any investigation carried out by the employer?
    - Does s/he realise the employer may choose to do nothing about the disclosed information? This may well be very frustrating, but it is unlikely to amount to unlawful treatment of the worker *because* s/he blew the whistle.

5   Check whether the employer has a policy which states to whom disclosure should be made and what procedure to follow. If not, see 6–8.

6   The worker should initially raise the matter with his/her employer, but exceptionally s/he can make disclosure to someone else if:
    - in all the circumstances it is reasonable to make disclosure to someone else (taking account of their identity);
    - the worker reasonably believes the information/allegations are substantially true;
    - disclosure is not made for personal gain;
    - the worker reasonably believes s/he will be subjected to a detriment by the employer if s/he makes a disclosure to the employer or a prescribed person;
    - there is no prescribed person and the worker reasonably believes it is likely that evidence will be concealed or destroyed if s/he makes disclosure to employer; or
    - it is an exceptionally serious failure.

7   Alternatively the worker can raise the matter initially with a prescribed body if one exists, provided the worker reasonably believes the information/allegations are substantially true.

8   If the matter is not resolved internally or by the prescribed body, the worker can raise the matter with someone else, provided the conditions at 6 above are met.

9   Consider taking advice from 'Protect'.

A27 ASSESSMENT OF COMPENSATION

Unfair dismissal: compensation checklist

NOTE: This checklist refers to the most common elements comprising unfair dismissal compensation, but does not refer to all the variables. It is important to read chapter 18. The checklist is for the private use of the adviser and employee and is not for disclosure to the employer or ET. For that, see schedules of loss at A30 below.

1   Basic award

(a) Calculate according to age, whole years' service, gross weekly pay subject to current weekly maximum.

(b) Check if dismissal was for a reason where a minimum basic award must be made.[39]

(c) Make any deductions for:[40]

  (i)   unreasonable refusal of an offer of reinstatement;

  (ii) misconduct before dismissal;

  (iii) redundancy payments made.

2   Compensatory award

Case-law on the order of adding and deducting items is extremely complex and not all variables have been tested. The following order is a rough guide, but may not be correct in every case.[41]

(a) Calculate how much the worker would have earned net of tax had s/he not been dismissed. Take into account any likely pay rises or overtime. Calculate the loss up to the hearing date and for a reasonable period into the future. Once the worker has obtained a new job at the same or greater pay, stop counting the loss.

(b) Add any other losses, eg, pension, health insurance, company car, free meals or accommodation.

(c) Add expenses incurred as a direct result of the dismissal, eg, the cost of job-hunting.

(d) Add compensation for loss of statutory rights.[42]

(e) Add compensation for loss of statutory right to a long notice period.

(f) If the worker obtained a new job on lower pay, deduct the new net earnings.

(g) Deduct any payments made by the former employer as a result of the dismissal, eg, notice pay or severance payments except, if a redundancy payment is made, the amount by which it exceeds the basic award.

NOTE: Sometimes notice pay exceeds what is actually due under the contract or statute. The extra will probably be set off against the balance of the compensatory award unless the employer explicitly made the payment in respect of the notice period.

(h) Make any percentage deduction under the *Polkey* principle.[43]

---

39 See para 18.21.

40 See para 18.20.

41 See para 18.61.

42 See para 18.42.

43 See para 18.57.

(i) Increase or decrease by up to 25 per cent for employer's or employee's failure to comply with the ACAS Code.[44]

(j) Add two or four weeks' pay if, when proceedings began, employer was in breach of duty to supply section 1 statement of particulars of employment or a section 4 statement of a change in those particulars.[45]

(k) Make any percentage deduction for contributory fault.

(l) Deduct any sum by which a redundancy payment exceeds the basic award.

(m)Apply the overall ceiling on the compensatory award (except where it does not apply).

Remember that although the employer may have to pay the total award, recoupment may well apply and leave the employee with a lesser sum.[46]

3 Additional award

If applicable, see para 18.15.

4 Other legal rights

Extra compensation may be paid for other rights claimed at the same time in the tribunal, eg, discrimination (see below) or failure to give written reasons for dismissal under ERA 1996 s92 (two weeks' pay). Also claim notice. The employee will not get paid for the notice period twice, but s/he may not win his/her unfair dismissal case.

Unfair dismissal compensation: example 1 (ACAS Code correctly followed)

Facts

Roger was dismissed aged 46 on 3 March 2021. He was required to work his notice. Roger had worked 6½ years for his employer. His gross weekly pay was £485. His net weekly pay was £390. He had no pension. Roger found a new job after eight weeks, though initially it only paid £350 net/week. It cost him £50 to look for a job (fares, telephone calls, newspapers). 12 weeks later he was promoted, getting a rise to £410 net/week. At no stage did Roger claim social security benefits.

Roger's case is due to be heard by the tribunal on 8 September 2021, which is exactly 26 weeks from his dismissal date. Considering the facts of his dismissal, he is likely to have a 20 per cent deduction for contributory fault and his conduct prior to dismissal. There may also be a 25 per cent *Polkey* deduction to represent the fact that had proper procedures been followed prior to his dismissal, there is a 25 per cent chance that he would nevertheless have been dismissed on a fair basis.

Calculation of award

Basic award

£485 (below the maximum gross weekly pay for dismissal in the year starting 6 April 2020) x 7½ = £3,637.50 less

---

44 See para 18.56.

45 See para 1.24 regarding this entitlement.

46 See paras 18.62–18.65.

20% deduction for conduct prior to dismissal = £2,910
Basic award = £2,910

Compensatory award
Average net earnings which Roger would have received had he not been
  dismissed = £390/week
(4.3.21 – 28.4.21)[47] 8 weeks' loss of net earnings while out of work (8 ×
  £390) = £3,120
(29.3.21 – 21.7.21) 12 weeks' loss of net earnings while working new job on
  lesser pay (12 × (£390–£350)) = £480
expenses looking for a job = £50
loss of statutory rights = £450
Total loss = £4,100

Deductions
25% Polkey (75% × £4,100) = £3,075
20% contributory fault (80% × £3,075) = £2,460
Compensatory award = £2,460
Total for unfair dismissal = £2,910 + £2,460 = £5, 370

Unfair dismissal compensation: example 2 (serious and flagrant breach of ACAS Code by employer)

Facts
Irina was dismissed on 29 April 2021 aged 36 and required to work her
notice. She had worked with her employer for two years and four months.
She was paid £600 per week gross (£460 per week net). After ten weeks, she
obtained a new job at the same level of pay. She had no job-hunting expenses
and did not claim benefits. The tribunal awards 20% uplift for a very serious
breach of the ACAS Code.

Calculation of award

Basic award
£544 (maximum gross weekly pay for dismissal in the year starting 6 April
  2021) × 2 = £1,088

Compensatory award
Average net earnings Irina would have received had she not been dismissed
  = £460/week
10 weeks'[48] loss of net earnings while out of work (10 × 460) = £4,600
loss of statutory rights = £500
sub-total = £5,100
20% uplift for employer's failure to comply with ACAS Code = £1,020
Total compensatory award = £6,120
Total for unfair dismissal = £7,208 (£1,088 BA + £6,120 CA).

---

47 An easy way to calculate the number of weeks or days between two dates is by using
  the www.timeanddate.com website or on Excel.
48 See previous note.

A28 ASSESSMENT OF COMPENSATION FOR DISCRIMINATION UNDER THE EQUALITY ACT 2010 (NOT APPLICABLE TO EQUAL PAY CLAIMS)

Compensation checklist

1   A single compensatory award with no upper ceiling applies.

2   Financial loss resulting from the discrimination, eg, loss of earnings on dismissal or lack of promotion, loss of pension. (Similar principles to unfair dismissal but may be longer-term future loss of earnings if severity of discrimination has damaged worker's confidence or health.)

3   Compensation for injury to feelings including aggravated damages and compensation for damage to health (personal injury). In rare situations, exemplary damages. Consider these as four separate headings, though the fairness of the total award must be considered and there must not be double-counting.

4   Interest.

5   The award should be grossed up in respect of any element which will be taxed. (This can be complex.)

6   Note that an ET can make recommendations and award extra compensation for failure to comply with them.

A29 SETTLEMENT TERMS CHECKLIST

Negotiating settlements has become increasingly complicated as employers produce more and more detailed and onerous written agreements. These are considerations to bear in mind:

- Generally consider the tax position, especially with large settlements.[49]
- Specify the sum to be paid and that it is free of tax. Do not agree to indemnify the employer for any attendant costs or for any tax s/he may incur as a result of making that payment. If the employer insists, narrow down the scope of the indemnity as far as possible.[50]
- Ensure there is a date for payment and supply of any reference. This should be either a specified date or 'within 14 days of receipt by the employer or if represented, the employer's representative of the COT3/settlement agreement signed by the claimant or his/her representative'. (Ideally get the claimant to sign the COT3 or agreement so there is no dispute later.)
- Specify who the settlement cheque should be made payable to and where it should be sent.
- Attach the agreed wording of the reference. Specify who should supply the reference, that it should be dated and on headed notepaper. Specify whether any other written or verbal reference may be given in any circumstances. Consider whether the worker also wants an open reference.[51]
- If the settlement is expressed to be 'full and final of all claims . . .' ensure it is only 'all claims arising out of the employment or the termination thereof'.
- If the proposed wording suggests 'all claims which the worker has or may have . . .', try to delete the words 'or may have'. Delete words like 'whatsoever'.
- Add 'with the exception of any personal or industrial injuries[52] or pension rights'.
- If the employer suggests a confidentiality clause, check what is made confidential (the settlement terms? the fact of the agreement? the case itself? the whole employment?). Make any necessary exceptions (close relatives; as required by law; prospective employers; bodies such as the Equality and Human Rights Commission).[53]
- Consider whether to ask the employer to retain confidentiality in return.
- Be careful about vague agreements not to make any 'derogatory remarks' or 'adverse comments' about the employer's business. This wording is so wide that it could, for example, prevent casual and minor critical remarks made socially about a retail employer's products. It is especially problematic if the agreement is not to say anything derogatory about unknown associated companies or individuals (employees, directors, shareholders).
- Do not agree to any penalty clause or suggestion that the worker repay the settlement sum if s/he breaks confidentiality. Apart from anything else, this could make the payment taxable. Penalty clauses may or may not be enforce-

---

49 See para 20.279.
50 See para 20.279.
51 See also para 20.278.
52 This exception may not work in respect of injuries caused by acts of discrimination.
53 See para 14.136 regarding non-disclosure clauses in harassment cases.

able, depending on the overall wording of the agreement, but it is unwise to take the risk.[54]

- If the employer adds clauses in restraint of trade ('restrictive covenants'), ensure the worker understands their meaning and effectiveness. These could also make the settlement partially taxable if some of the payment appears to be for agreeing to such covenants.
- If the worker owes any money to the employer or there is any suggestion the employer may wish to sue him or her, ensure that the settlement is full and final of any claims either side may have.
- The worker must not agree to do anything which is outside his/her control, eg ensuring that other people keep matters confidential.
- The worker should not agree to anything where its meaning or consequences are uncertain.

---

54 *CMC Group plc and others v Zhang* [2006] EWCA Civ 408; [2006] All ER (D) 197 (Mar) CA; *Dunlop Pneumatic Tyre Co Ltd v New Garage and Motor Co Ltd* [1915] AC 79; *Murray v Leisureplay* [2005] IRLR 946, CA.

A30 SCHEDULES OF LOSS

As explained at para 20.182, these can be supplied in various forms. The following are just alternative models. The starting point is obviously the actual sums which the worker could claim (see compensation checklist at A27). The claimant would not normally put down any deductions s/he anticipates for Polkey, contributory fault or failure to mitigate. None of the following models contain the complex figures necessary to calculate pension loss.

Model 1: Simple unfair dismissal schedule where claimant has new job at more pay

This is based on the Roger case study (at A27). Note that other claimants may have other losses, eg, loss of pension or loss of a long notice period.

Date of birth: 16 February 1975
Effective date of termination: 3 March 2021
Actual gross weekly pay when employed by respondent = £485
Average net weekly pay when employed by respondent = £390
New job from 27 April 2021 (ie 8 weeks from EDT) @ £350 net/week, rising to £410 net/week after 12 weeks
Hearing date = 8 September 2021 (26 weeks from dismissal)

Basic award
£485 × 7½ = £3,637

Compensatory award
8 weeks'[55] loss of net earnings while out of work (8 × £390) = £3,120
12 weeks' loss of net earnings on new job at lesser pay (12 × (£390–£350)) = £480
Expenses looking for a job = £50
Loss of statutory rights = £450
Total compensatory award = £4,100

Model 2: Simple unfair dismissal schedule where claimant does not have new job

Suppose Roger did not have a new job by the time of the hearing

Basic award
£485 × 7½ = £3,637

Compensatory award
Past loss of earnings
From day after dismissal (4.3.21) to hearing date (8.9.21)[56] inclusive = 26 weeks @ £390 net/week = £10,140
Future loss of earnings
Ongoing loss at £390/week for as long as the ET thinks appropriate (alternatively, Roger could speculate, eg, 18 weeks @ £390/week = £7,020)
Expenses looking for a new job = £50
Loss of statutory rights = £450

---

55 An easy way to calculate the number of weeks or days between two dates is by using the www.timeanddate.com website or on Excel.
56 See previous note.

Model 3: Race discrimination and unfair dismissal model for use at hearing

The following example is more complicated, as is usual in a discrimination case. The act of discrimination was the dismissal, which was also unfair. It is possible, rather than inserting figures for injury to feelings and injury to health (personal injury), to note 'to be assessed by the ET'. Increasingly, however, ETs are asking how much the claimant is seeking. It may also be good tactics to suggest a high (but not unrealistic) figure in the Schedule. Suggesting unrealistic excessive figures, on the other hand, could be counter-productive. In this example, the discrimination has had a very severe impact on the worker's health. See para 19.40 regarding latest interest rates. Note that an easy way to calculate the number of weeks or days between two dates is by using the www.timeanddate.com website or using a formula on Excel. The worker in question did not have a pension.

CLAIMANT'S SCHEDULE OF LOSS

NO	ITEM	CALCULATION	TOTAL	COMMENT FOR ET
1	Basic award	2 whole years' service @ £500/week gross pay	£1,000	
2	Past loss of earnings 19.9.19 – 1.11.20	58 weeks @ £420 net/week	£24,360 net of tax	Loss from dismissal to hearing
3	Interest on past losses 19.9.19 – 1.11.20 (409 days)	£24,360 × 8% = £1,948.80, ÷ 365 × 409 = £2,183.72, ÷ 2 = £1,091.86	£1,091.86	Interest from midpoint date between act of discrimination 19.9.19 and calculation date 1.11.20
4	Future loss of earnings	£420 × 52	£21,840	Medical report says claimant will be fit to return to work in 6–12 months. It is unrealistic to suggest she will find work at once
5	Loss of statutory rights		£500	
6	Job hunting expenses		£50	
7	Injury to feelings		£17,000	The claim falls within the mid range in *Vento (No 2)*

8	Aggravated damages		£5,000	
9	Interest on injury to feelings and aggravated damages	$£22,000 \times 8\% = £1,760 \div 365 \times 409 = £1,972.16$	£1,972.16	Interest from act of discrimination 19.9.19 to calculation date 1.11.20
10	Personal injury		£20,000	Moderately severe psychiatric injury, within range in Judicial College guidelines
11	Interest on personal injury	$£20,000 \times 8\% = £1,600 \div 365 \times 409 = £1,792.87$	£1,792.87	Interest from act of discrimination 19.9.19 to calculation date 1.11.20
12	Costs of recommended cognitive therapy		£2,500	
13	Adjustment for taxation		*Insert figure*	Certain items will be subject to tax
14	TOTAL		*Insert figure*	

Indirect discrimination: possibly discriminatory provisions, criteria or practices

B1 RACE DISCRIMINATION

Qualifications
- formal qualifications
- qualifications only obtainable in Great Britain
- university degree
- qualifications from certain universities or organisations
- English language qualifications

Language/expression/culture/confidence
- English language fluency – written/verbal
- communication skills
- writing skills
- essay-based tests and application forms
- psychometric testing
- culturally-biased testing
- articulation/fluency in interview performance
- acquiring new technical skills knowledge, within short time periods/ without special training (difficult in an unfamiliar language/with foreign technology)

Experience/service/paid employment
- previous kinds of work experience
- previous management experience
- already being at a certain grade/holding a certain high level job
- previous (fast) promotions
- previous width/variation of experience
- length of previous experience or service in certain positions/with the employer/in the industry/with past employer
- previous paid employment/paid relevant experience
- previous steady employment/no periods of unemployment
- having attended refresher/training courses (usually unavailable to night staff who tend to be black/women)
- previous acting-up experience
- being on a permanent contract rather than temporary

Dress
These could also be religious discrimination
- uniform/dress/no turbans
- clean-shaven (eg, affect Sikhs)

Attendance/shifts
- days/hours of work/shifts/flexibility (Sabbaths/religious holidays) (these could also be religious discrimination)
- not taking holiday entitlement at one time (visits to family abroad)
- limited unpaid/compassionate leave (need to visit ill family abroad)

- good attendance record (extended holidays/unpaid leave to visit family abroad)
- late travel home (danger of racial attacks)

Keeping it internal/references in and out/being part of the club
- nomination/recommendation by/reference from particular staff/management for recruitment/promotion
- word of mouth recruitment (knowing existing workers)
- favouring children from existing staff
- internal applications only
- customer satisfaction (liability to racist complaints)
- membership of certain organisations, professional bodies or trade unions/certain (culturally specific) leisure activities or interests
- using standing lists of vacancies
- using applications for one job for purpose of filling a different job

B2 SEX DISCRIMINATION

Many of the criteria set out above would also adversely affect women. Additional criteria and practices which would specifically affect women could be:

Attendance/shifts/flexibility/mobility
- requirements and practices likely to cause difficulty for women – and sometimes for married men – usually due to childcare commitments

Hours
- full-time work (refusal to allow jobshare or part-time working)
- permitting part-time working, but requiring some hours to be worked each day
- overtime or weekend working
- shift-working, especially rotating shifts varying from day to day or week to week
- requirements to work overtime or varying shifts imposed at very short notice
- specified and inflexible start or finish times (interfering with times of taking or collecting children from school or child-minding)
- all year round working (eg, as opposed to term-time only)
- requirements entailing certain (high) attendance levels/limited absences

Mobility
- long journeys to and from work locations (necessitating earlier departures from and returns to home)
- work trips necessitating staying overnight away from home
- relocation (may be unacceptable if woman is not the primary earner in the household)
  NOTE: Flexibility and mobility requirements often do cause women difficulties and should therefore be justified by the employer. However, it would

be direct discrimination if an employer wrongly assumed a woman would be less flexible and treated her less favourably for that reason.

Miscellaneous

- age bars (women may be out of the job market during child-bearing age)
- to have acquired a certain level of experience by a certain age
- certain forms of dress or uniform (eg, may indirectly discriminate against Muslim women)
- late finishing hours (possibly dangerous travel home)
- home visits, eg, to patients or tenants unaccompanied (in some circumstances may be dangerous)

NOTE: Employers should provide a safe system of work for all workers, but should not directly discriminate against women unless allowed by statute (eg, in relation to pregnancy and childbirth).

B3 RELIGIOUS DISCRIMINATION

There will be some overlap with indirect race discrimination.

Dress

- no jewellery
- no head coverings
- cut hair, be clean-shaven
- uniform which may be regarded as immodest

Alcohol and food

- canteen without suitable food options
- work meetings, business trips, outings in unsuitable venues

Attendance and breaks

- requirement to work on Sabbaths or religious holidays
- refusal of prayer breaks or holidays

B4 SEXUAL ORIENTATION DISCRIMINATION

- first choice of holidays to staff with children

B5 AGE DISCRIMINATION

Could adversely affect older workers:

- maximum experience
- recent graduate
- qualifications only recently in existence
- formal qualifications
- high level IT skills
- having no history of unemployment
- mobility

Could adversely affect younger workers:

- minimum length of experience
- long service

B6 SITUATIONS WHERE DISCRIMINATORY PROVISIONS, CRITERIA OR PRACTICES MAY OCCUR

- access to particular jobs – who is shortlisted; who is appointed
- access to promotion – who is eligible; who is shortlisted; who is promoted
- access to acting-up opportunities
- access to training schemes
- earning extra pay – determining the level of basic pay; criteria for rises; performance assessments
- opportunities to earn overtime, additional bonuses and benefits
- grading levels
- entitlement to paid time-off for trade union duties and training.
- eligibility for subsidised mortgages, occupational pensions, company cars and other perks
- rules for when and for how long holidays may be taken
- sick pay entitlement
- who gets selected for redundancy
- eligibility to formal disciplinary and grievance procedures

APPENDIX C

Unfair dismissal case study[1]

This case study should be read in conjunction with chapters 6, 8 and 20.

1   Note that this case study is purely fictional.

C1   WITNESS STATEMENT

When writing a witness statement, bear in mind the relevant law. What makes a redundancy dismissal unfair are failure to consult, unfair selection and failure to offer alternative employment. Any facts which indicate such failings in the employee's case should be highlighted. For guidance on writing witness statements, see para 20.186 onwards.

WITNESS STATEMENT: JENNY PENNANT

Background

1   I started work for Strass Burger House in 2000. I gained my catering qualifications from Huyton Catering College. After I completed College in 1994, I worked in a number of hotels and restaurants as a sous chef. By January 2000 I was working as the head chef of the exclusive Kyverdale restaurant.[2]

2   On 14 December 2000 I received a letter from Arthur Venger of the Strass Burger House offering me a job as head chef at the Felstead restaurant. This was the company's smallest restaurant. Over the next 12 years I worked at several of the company's other restaurants. Each move was a promotion to more prestigious premises, with an increase in pay. My last move was on 19 December 2012 when I was made the head chef of the Ashburton restaurant, the most prestigious and best restaurant in the group.

3   Strass Burger House has 150 restaurants throughout the UK. A substantial number of them are situated in London. The company also has a large head office at 153 Avenal Avenue, London. There is a large personnel department. Arthur Venger is Head of Human Resources.

4   I never had any time off work for sickness during the 21 years of my employment. I never had any disciplinary action taken against me or any warnings about my work. At my last annual appraisal, Mr Venger told me he wished all the workers had the same commitment to the company that I had.

My company car

5   In November 2020, at the time of the annual appraisal and pay increase, I was told that I would get a salary of £35,000 per year as well as a company car. I had been asking for a company car for some time as I often worked late and had no alternative but to catch a taxi home on those occasions. I was told that it would take about a month to get the car.

6   On 20 March 2021 I had an audit meeting. At this meeting I asked Mr Venger about my company car. He told me to 'stop going on about it' as I was becoming 'too expensive for the company'. However, I did ask him again for the car a few times because it had been promised to me.

---

2   When writing a statement for the purpose of an unfair dismissal claim it is important to establish the previous work record (if it is good) and qualifications that the worker has acquired. If the person has worked for a long time for one employer this should be emphasised, particularly in cases of conduct/capability dismissals. Workers should set it out if they are well qualified, have had considerable experience in the industry, have worked for well-known employers, and held important positions in the past. However, give the information concisely.

My dismissal

7   On 28 April 2021 I was given a letter asking me to attend a meeting at 10 am on 30 April 2021, regarding my possible redundancy. At the meeting Mr Venger told me that I was being dismissed on the ground of redundancy because of the economic climate. I was devastated. I had had no idea before getting the letter that the company was thinking of making redundancies or that I might be losing my job.[3]

8   The meeting lasted about five minutes. Mr Venger seemed to be in a hurry. He had obviously made up his mind from the outset and he gave me no opportunity to argue against my redundancy. I tried to enter into a discussion about my dismissal, seeking an explanation for this decision. Mr Venger kept saying that I had been made redundant and that I should not take it personally. I asked whether there were any other jobs for me in the company but Mr Venger said that there was nothing suitable. By the end of the meeting I was very upset.

9   I went home after the meeting. That afternoon I received a letter by courier, confirming that I was being made redundant and enclosing my P45 form and my final payslip. I was told that I was not required to work out my notice and that I would be paid 12 weeks' pay in lieu of notice, statutory redundancy pay and £2,000 as an ex gratia payment.

10   On 1 May 2021, I wrote a letter of appeal to Ms Diana Deane, the managing director. She heard my appeal on 16 May 2021, but she confirmed the decision. She did say that she would give me a very good reference. I asked about my holiday pay. The holiday year starts 1 April and I had not yet taken any holidays this year. I am entitled to four weeks' holiday every year plus bank holidays. Ms Deane said that I would not get pay for my untaken holidays because this was at the discretion of management and I had been paid £2,000 ex gratia.

11   I am not aware of anyone else in the company being made redundant at that time. I do not know why I was made redundant rather than anyone else. I believe I had longer service than any other chef.[4]

After my dismissal

12   I was so shocked by my dismissal that I went to see my GP that same evening. It was the first time that I had seen my GP for nearly ten years. She prescribed me tablets to take for my nerves and for shock. It was the first time that I had been dismissed in all my working life.

13   About two weeks after my appeal, I saw Mr Venger's personal assistant, Patricia Reiss, in Berwick Street market. She told me that my dismissal had not been a complete surprise to her as she remembered writing to the finance

---

3   It is worth emphasising lack of forewarning and consultation, as these may help make the dismissal unfair.

4   Unfair selection can make a redundancy dismissal unfair. An employer need not use length of service as a selection criterion, but in some circumstances it may be a factor which the ET would expect to be taken into account (unless discriminatory).

company cancelling the application for my company car. She thought this was in January.[5]

Trying to find new work[6]

14   Since my dismissal I have been trying without success to secure other employment. In May 2021, I saw a full-page advert in the Hotel and Catering magazine for five different jobs at the Strass Burger House. I could have done any of these jobs but none of them were mentioned to me at the time of dismissal. I have also signed-on at a number of specialist agencies. I have been for a few interviews [*give details*], but I think my age is against me.[7]

Signed: *Jenny Pennant*
Dated: 10 July 2021

---

5   It is a matter of judgement whether to quote what someone else has said if unsure whether they will be a helpful witness for the claimant.

6   Especially in unfair dismissal cases, ETs expect claimants to be ready to deal with the issue of compensation if they win.

7   It is important that the worker can demonstrate that s/he has attempted to mitigate his/her losses. Prior to the hearing it will be necessary to obtain letters from specialist job agencies or the job centre, stating when the worker first signed on, what type of jobs s/he was prepared to do, what vacancies are available in the industry, and whether any jobs were offered. The worker should also keep details of online applications and notifications.

C2 LETTER OF DISMISSAL

Strass Burger House Ltd
153 AVENAL AVENUE, LONDON W1

Ms Jenny Pennant
12 Wesley Place
Hackney
London E8 7ZY

30 April 2021

Dear Jenny,

Further to our meeting today, I very much regret that I have to confirm that your position as head chef is now redundant.

You have been given 12 weeks' pay in lieu of your notice entitlement and in the circumstances you are not required to attend work during this period.

I will endeavour to find you suitable alternative employment within the company. Should any position or vacancy arise we will notify you.

May I take this opportunity to thank you for the considerable service you have given to this company. If you wish to appeal, you may write to the managing director within 14 days.

Yours faithfully

Arthur Venger
Head of Human Resources

C3 INITIAL LETTER TO THE EMPLOYER

The content and style of the initial letter depends on the circumstances. It is common to ask for written reasons for dismissal, where these have not already been clearly set out (see para 20.10). Any sums owing, eg, holiday pay or notice pay, should also be requested. The following letter also asks for the employee's contract and disciplinary procedure because the employee has not retained copies of these. In some circumstances, it may be better for the initial letter to come from the employee him/herself and to be written in informal terms without referring to any legislation.

London Employment Project
12 MALVERN ROAD, LONDON E8 3LT

Arthur Venger
Head of Human Resources
The Strass Burger House Ltd
153 Avenal Avenue
London W1 2GB

1 June 2021

Dear Sir,

Re: Jenny Pennant

I act on behalf of the above named in respect of all matters pertaining to her employment at the Strass Burger House Ltd, and the termination thereof.

In order that I can advise my client further in respect of her several claims against the company, please supply the following:

1 My client's main terms and conditions of employment or her contract of employment. In particular will you supply me with the following particulars:

   (a) My client's contractual right to holiday pay, with sufficient particulars to calculate her entitlement to accrued holiday pay on the termination of her employment. Your attention is drawn to section 1(4)(d) of the Employment Rights Act 1996.

   (b) My client's disciplinary and grievance procedure.

2 Details of the company's redundancy procedure including the selection criteria.

3 The written reasons for my client's dismissal. As you are no doubt aware, if the reasons given in purported compliance of this request are inadequate or untrue, the company will have failed to discharge its legal obligation. Your attention is drawn to section 92 of the Employment Rights Act 1996.[8]

4 All monies which are owed to my client including her holiday pay.

---

8 Even if the employer has supplied the written reasons the adviser is entitled to ask for them pursuant to Employment Rights Act (ERA) 1996 s92 and it will be these reasons which the tribunal will consider. If they are different to the previous statement, both can be referred to.

5   My client's P45.

My client will be seeking an order for reinstatement or re-engagement as her primary remedy before the employment tribunal. To this end please supply me with all vacancies within the company, the terms and conditions attributable to each job and the salary, so that my client can consider applying for the vacancy.[9] Meanwhile, I would invite you to reinstate my client to any suitable vacancy which you identify.

Please supply the above information within the next 14 days.

Yours faithfully

D Rocastle
The London Employment Project

---

9   If the worker wants the job back, it is important that this is made known to the employer at the earliest opportunity. It will also assist in obtaining an additional award from the tribunal (see para 18.15 above) if the employer was put on notice at an early stage.

C4 EARLY CONCILIATION CERTIFICATE

acas

EARLY CONCILIATION CERTIFICATE
Employment Tribunals Act 1996 s18A

ACAS EC Reference Number R00052004/14/49

Prospective Claimant:
Jennifer Pennant
12 Wesley Place, Hackney, London E8 7ZY

Prospective Respondent:
The Strass Burger House
153 Avenal Avenue, London W1 2GB

Date of receipt by ACAS of the EC notification: 22 June 2021
Date of issue by ACAS of this certificate: 13 July 2021
Method of issue – Email

This certificate is to confirm that the prospective claimant has complied with the requirement under ETA 1996 s18A to contact ACAS before instituting proceedings in the Employment Tribunal.

Please keep this certificate securely as you will need to quote the reference number in any Employment Tribunal application concerning this matter.

Lisa Dixon

Lisa Dixon
Conciliator

C5 TRIBUNAL CLAIM (ET1)

The claimant submitted her ET1 on 27 July 2021. The form (see below and following pages) is compulsory. For comments on drafting an ET claim and accessing the standard form, see para 20.60 onwards.

Employment Tribunal

Claim form

You must complete all questions marked with an '*'

Official Use Only			
Tribunal office			
Case number		Date received	

1 Your details

1.1 Title — ☐ Mr ☐ Mrs ☐ Miss ☑ Ms

1.2* First name (or names) — Jennifer

1.3* Surname or family name — Pennant

1.4 Date of birth — ☐☐/☐☐/☐☐☐☐ Are you? ☐ Male ☐ Female

1.5* Address

Number or name — 12

Street — Wesley Place

Town/City — Hackney

County —

Postcode — E8 7ZY

1.6 Phone number
Where we can contact you during the day

1.7 Mobile number (if different)

1.8 How would you prefer us to contact you? (Please tick only one box) — ☑ Email ☐ Post ☐ Fax
Whatever your preference please note that some documents cannot be sent electronically

1.9 Email address — pendy@hotmail.com

1.10 Fax number

1.11 Would you be able to take part in a hearing by video? (Requires internet access). — ☑ Yes ☐ No
Further details on video hearings can be found on the following link https://www.gov.uk/guidance/hmcts-telephone-and-video-hearings-during-coronavirus-outbreak

2 Respondent's details (that is the employer, person or organisation against whom you are making a claim)

2.1* Give the name of your employer or the person or organisation you are claiming against (If you need to you can add more respondents at 2.5)

The Strass Burger House

2.2* Address

Number or name | 153

Street | Avenal Avenue

Town/City | London

County |

Postcode | W 1 2 G B

Phone number |

2.3* Do you have an Acas early conciliation certificate number?

[✓] Yes   [ ] No

Nearly everyone should have this number before they fill in a claim form. You can find it on your Acas certificate. For help and advice, call Acas on 0300 123 1100 or visit www.acas.org.uk

If Yes, please give the Acas early conciliation certificate number.

R00052004/14/49

If No, why don't you have this number?

[ ] Another person I'm making the claim with has an Acas early conciliation certificate number

[ ] Acas doesn't have the power to conciliate on some or all of my claim

[ ] My employer has already been in touch with Acas

[ ] My claim consists only of a complaint of unfair dismissal which contains an application for interim relief. (See guidance)

2.4 If you worked at a different address from the one you have given at 2.2 please give the full address

Address

Number or name | Ashburton Restaurant

Street | Grove Road

Town/City | London

County |

Postcode | W C 2 4 F L

Phone number |

2.5 If there are other respondents please tick this box and put their   ☐
names and addresses here.
(If there is not enough room here for the names of all the additional
respondents then you can add any others at Section 13.)

Respondent 2

Name

Address   Number or name

Street

Town/City

County

Postcode ⌊_⌊_⌊_⌊_⌊_⌊_⌊_⌋

Phone number

2.6 Do you have an Acas early conciliation   ☐ Yes   ☐ No   *Nearly everyone should have this number before they fill in a claim form.*
certificate number?   *You can find it on your Acas certificate. For help and advice, call Acas on*
0300 123 1100 or visit www.acas.org.uk

If Yes, please give the Acas early
conciliation certificate number.

If No, why don't you have this number?   ☐ Another person I'm making the claim with has an Acas early conciliation certificate number

☐ Acas doesn't have the power to conciliate on some or all of my claim

☐ My employer has already been in touch with Acas

☐ My claim consists only of a complaint of unfair dismissal which contains an application for interim relief. (See guidance)

Respondent 3

2.7 Name

Address   Number or name

Street

Town/City

County

Postcode ⌊_⌊_⌊_⌊_⌊_⌊_⌊_⌋

Phone number

2.8 Do you have an Acas early conciliation certificate number? ☐ Yes ☐ No

Nearly everyone should have this number before they fill in a claim form. You can find it on your Acas certificate. For help and advice, call Acas on 0300 123 1100 or visit www.Acas.org.uk

If Yes, please give the Acas early conciliation certificate number

If No, why don't you have this number?

☐ Another person I'm making the claim with has an Acas early conciliation certificate number

☐ Acas doesn't have the power to conciliate on some or all of my claim

☐ My employer has already been in touch with Acas

☐ My claim consists only of a complaint of unfair dismissal which contains an application for interim relief. (See guidance)

3 Multiple cases

3.1 Are you aware that your claim is one of a number of claims against the same employer arising from the same, or similar, circumstances? ☐ Yes ☐ No

If Yes, and you know the names of any other claimants, add them here. This will allow us to link your claim to other related claims.

4 Cases where the respondent was not your employer

4.1 If you were not employed by any of the respondents you have named but are making a claim for some reason connected to employment (for example, relating to a job application which you made or against a trade union, qualifying body or the like) please state the type of claim you are making here. (You will get the chance to provide details later):

Now go to Section 8

5 Employment details

If you are or were employed please give the following information, if possible.

5.1 When did your employment start? `14/1/2000`

Is your employment continuing? ☐ Yes ☑ No

If your employment has ended, when did it end? `30/4/2021`

If your employment has not ended, are you in a period of notice and, if so, when will that end?

5.2 Please say what job you do or did. `Head Chef`

6 **Earnings and benefits**

6.1 How many hours on average do, or did you work each week in the job this claim is about? 65   hours each week

6.2 How much are, or were you paid?

Pay before tax £ 35,000   ☐ Weekly   ☐ Monthly

Normal take-home pay
(Incl. overtime, commission, bonuses etc.) £   ☐ Weekly   ☐ Monthly

6.3 If your employment has ended, did you work (or were you paid for) a period of notice? ☑ Yes   ☐ No

If Yes, how many weeks, or months' notice did you work, or were you paid for? ☐ weeks   ☐ months

6.4 Were you in your employer's pension scheme? ☐ Yes   ☑ No

6.5 If you received any other benefits, e.g. company car, medical insurance, etc, from your employer, please give details.

7 **If your employment with the respondent has ended, what has happened since?**

7.1 Have you got another job? ☐ Yes   ☐ No

If No, please **go to section 8**

7.2 Please say when you started (or will start) work.

7.3 Please say how much you are now earning (or will earn). £

8   Type and details of claim

8.1* Please indicate the type of claim you are making by ticking one or more of the boxes below.

[✓] I was unfairly dismissed (including constructive dismissal)

[ ] I was discriminated against on the grounds of:

    [ ] age   [ ] race

    [ ] gender reassignment   [ ] disability

    [ ] pregnancy or maternity   [ ] marriage or civil partnership

    [ ] sexual orientation   [ ] sex (including equal pay)

    [ ] religion or belief

[ ] I am claiming a redundancy payment

[ ] I am owed

    [ ] notice pay

    [✓] holiday pay

    [ ] arrears of pay

    [✓] other payments

[✓] I am making another type of claim which the Employment Tribunal can deal with.
(Please state the nature of the claim. Examples are provided in the Guidance.)

Section 1 statement of terms and conditions

Written reasons for dismissal

8.2* Please set out the background and details of your claim in the space below.

The details of your claim should include **the date(s) when the event(s) you are complaining about happened.** Please use the blank sheet at the end of the form if needed.

1. The respondent is a public company operating 150 restaurants throughout the United Kingdom. A substantial number of these restaurants are situated in or around London. The respondent has a large personnel department situated at head office employing some 25 full-time employees.

2. The claimant commenced employment on 14 January 2000 with the respondent as a chef at its Felstead restaurant. Thereafter, the claimant was promoted on several occasions and at the time of her dismissal she was employed as the head chef of the respondent's Ashburton restaurant which is the most prestigious in the group.

3. At no time during the claimant's employment did she receive any written or verbal warnings as to her conduct or capability.

4. By letter dated 28 April 2021, the claimant was first informed that there was a redundancy situation and she might be dismissed. The claimant was invited to discuss this matter at a meeting on 30 April 2021 at 10 a.m. with the Head of Human Resources Arthur Venger. The claimant was told at the outset of the meeting that she was to be made redundant, before she was able to express any views. The meeting, which lasted approximately 5 minutes, was not approached by Mr Venger with an open mind. After the meeting, the claimant went home. That afternoon, she received a letter by courier confirming her redundancy.

5. The claimant wrote a letter of appeal to the managing director, Ms Diana Deane, on 1 May 2021. Her appeal was heard on 16 May 2021 and rejected. Ms Deane also stated that the claimant was not entitled to pay for untaken holiday.

6. The claimant's dismissal was unfair under s98 of the Employment Rights Act 1996 in that:
 (a) The dismissal of the claimant was not attributable wholly or mainly to a redundancy situation. The duties which the claimant performed pursuant to her employment contract had neither diminished nor ceased.
 (b) The respondent failed to consult with the claimant prior to the meeting on 30 April 2021 and gave her no warning prior to the letter of 28 April 2021 that there was a redundancy situation or that her job was at risk.
 (c) The respondent unfairly selected the claimant for dismissal. The claimant was the longest serving chef in the company, with vast experience and a very good record.
 (d) Having regard to the nature of the respondent's undertaking, and its size and administrative resources, the respondent failed adequately to discuss, seek or offer the claimant alternative employment.

7. Further or alternatively, the claimant claims the holiday pay which is owed to her. Under the Working Time Regulations 1998, the claimant is entitled to 5.6 weeks' holiday per year including Bank Holidays. The claimant's holiday year starts on 1st April and she did not take any holidays in her final holiday year. The respondent has refused to pay the claimant in lieu of her untaken holiday. The claimant claims the sum due for untaken holidays under reg 30 of the Working Time Regulations 1998 and/or as an unauthorised deduction contrary to s23 of the Employment Rights Act 1996.

8. By letter dated 1 June 2021, the claimant sought the written reasons for her dismissal. To date the respondent has failed to comply with this request. The claimant seeks a declaration as to the reasons for dismissal and compensation.

9. Further, the respondent has never provided the claimant with a statement of terms and conditions as required by s1 of the Employment Rights Act 1996. The claimant therefore requests compensation in accordance with s38 of the Employment Act 2002.

9　**What do you want if your claim is successful?**

9.1　Please tick the relevant box(es) to say what you
want if your claim is successful:

[✓]　If claiming unfair dismissal, to get your old job back and compensation (reinstatement)

[ ]　If claiming unfair dismissal, to get another job with the same employer or associated
employer and compensation (re-engagement)

[ ]　Compensation only

[ ]　If claiming discrimination, a recommendation (see Guidance).

9.2　What compensation or remedy are you seeking?

If you are claiming financial compensation please give as much detail as you can about how much you are claiming and how you have calculated this
sum. (Please note any figure stated below will be viewed as helpful information but it will not restrict what you can claim and you will be permitted to revise the
sum claimed later. See the Guidance for further information about how you can calculate compensation). **If you are seeking any other remedy from the Tribunal
which you have not already identified please also state this below.**

The claimant seeks reinstatement. If that is not possible for her unfair dismissal, she seeks a basic award
and compensatory award comprising
- loss of earnings from her dismissal to the date of the tribunal hearing
- future loss of earnings as she has not yet obtained a new job
- loss of statutory rights - £500
- job hunting expenses (to be calculated).

Holiday pay from 1 April 2021 - 30 April 2021 (calculated on the basis of 5.6 weeks / year).

Four weeks compensation under s38 Employment Act 2002 for failure to provide a s1 statement of terms
and conditions.

10 **Information to regulators in protected disclosure cases**

10.1   If your claim consists of, or includes, a claim that you are making a protected disclosure under the Employment Rights Act 1996 (otherwise known as a 'whistleblowing' claim), please tick the box if you want a copy of this form, or information from it, to be forwarded on your behalf to a relevant regulator (known as a 'prescribed person' under the relevant legislation) by tribunal staff. (See Guidance).   ☐

11 **Your representative**

If someone has agreed to represent you, please fill in the following. We will in future only contact your representative and not you.

11.1   Name of representative   D. Rocastle

11.2   Name of organisation   London Employment Project

11.3   Address
          Number or name   12
          Street   Malvern Road
          Town/City   London
          County
          Postcode   E 8   3 L T

11.4   DX number (If known)

11.5   Phone number

11.6   Mobile number (If different)

11.7   Their reference for correspondence   DA/AFC/JP

11.8   Email address

11.9   How would you prefer us to communicate with them? (Please tick only one box)   ☐ Email   ☑ Post   ☐ Fax

11.10 Fax number

12 **Disability**

12.1   Do you have a disability?   ☐ Yes   ☑ No

If Yes, it would help us if you could say what this disability is and tell us what assistance, if any, you will need as your claim progresses through the system, including for any hearings that maybe held at tribunal premises.

13 Details of additional respondents

Section 2 allows you to list up to three respondents. If there are any more respondents please provide their details here

Respondent 4

Name

Address

    Number or name

    Street

    Town/City

    County

    Postcode

Phone number

Do you have an Acas early conciliation certificate number?

☐ Yes   ☐ No

Nearly everyone should have this number before they fill in a claim form. You can find it on your Acas certificate. For help and advice, call Acas on 0300 123 1100 or visit www.acas.org.uk

If Yes, please give the Acas early conciliation certificate number.

If No, why don't you have this number?

☐ Another person I'm making the claim with has an Acas early conciliation certificate number

☐ Acas doesn't have the power to conciliate on some or all of my claim

☐ My employer has already been in touch with Acas

☐ My claim consists only of a complaint of unfair dismissal which contains an application for interim relief. (See guidance)

Respondent 5

Name

Address

Number or name

Street

Town/City

County

Postcode |___|___|___|___|___|___|___|

Phone number

Do you have an Acas early conciliation certificate number?

☐ Yes   ☐ No

Nearly everyone should have this number before they fill in a claim form. You can find it on your Acas certificate. For help and advice, call Acas on 0300 123 1100 or visit www.acas.org.uk

If Yes, please give the Acas early conciliation certificate number.

If No, why don't you have this number?

☐ Another person I'm making the claim with has an Acas early conciliation certificate number

☐ Acas doesn't have the power to conciliate on some or all of my claim

☐ My employer has already been in touch with Acas

☐ My claim consists only of a complaint of unfair dismissal which contains an application for interim relief. (See guidance)

14 **Final check**

Please re-read the form and check you have entered all the relevant information.
Once you are satisfied, please tick this box. ☑

General Data Protection Regulations
The Ministry of Justice and HM Courts and Tribunals Service processes personal information about you in the context of tribunal proceedings.

For details of the standards we follow when processing your data, please visit the following address https://www.gov.uk/government/organisations/hm-courts-and-tribunals-service/about/personal-information-charter.

To receive a paper copy of this privacy notice, please call our Customer Contact Centre:

England and Wales: 0300 123 1024
Welsh speakers: 0300 303 5176
Scotland: 0300 790 6234
Textphone: 18001 0300 123 1024 (England and Wales)
Textphone: 18001 0300 790 6234 (Scotland)

Please note: a copy of the claim form or response and other tribunal related correspondence may be copied to the other party and Acas for the purpose of tribunal proceedings or to reach settlement of the claim.

15 **Additional information**

You can provide additional information about your claim in this section.
If you're part of a group claim, give the Acas early conciliation certificate numbers for other people in your group. If they don't have numbers, tell us why.

C6 ACKNOWLEDGEMENT AND SERVICE OF ET1 FORM AND CASE MANAGEMENT TIMETABLE

This is the type of letter which may be sent out in an ordinary unfair dismissal case in England and Wales at the time of sending the ET1 to the respondent or soon after. Note that this particular example has several functions – it acknowledges receipt of the ET1; it serves it on the respondent; it gives a hearing date and sets out a timetable for case preparation. In a discrimination claim, it is more likely that a letter will be sent out inviting the parties to a preliminary hearing for case management, at which the hearing date and timetable for case preparation will be discussed orally.

Case number: 20085/21

Claimant	**Respondent**
Jennifer Pennant	The Strass Burger House

Date: 6 August 2021

NOTICE OF CLAIM
NOTICE OF HEARING on 14 January 2022

The claim

The Employment Tribunal has accepted a claim against the above respondent. It has been given the above case number which should be quoted in any communication relating to this case. A copy of the claim is enclosed for the respondent.

Responding to the claim

To submit a response to the claim a prescribed form, a copy of which is enclosed, must be used. Alternatively a respondent may respond online at *[link]*

If a respondent wishes to defend the claim their response must be received at the tribunal office by 2 September 2021. If a response is not received by that date and no extension of time has been applied for and given, or if a respondent indicates that it does not contest any part of the claim, a judgment may be issued and that respondent will only be entitled to participate in any hearing to the extent permitted by the employment judge who hears the case.

The hearing

The claim will be heard by an employment judge sitting alone at tribunal address on 14 January 2022 at 10am or as soon thereafter on that day as the tribunal can hear it. The tribunal may transfer your case at short notice to be heard at another hearing centre within the region. One day has been allocated to hear the evidence and decide the claim. If you think that is not long enough, you must give your reasons, in writing, and your time estimate. Unless there are exceptional circumstances, requests for a postponement or an extension to the hearing length will not be considered before the return date for the response form.

If you wish to rely on written representations at the hearing, they must be sent to the tribunal and to all other parties not less than seven days before the hearing. You will have the chance to put forward oral arguments in any case. It is your responsibility to ensure that any relevant witnesses attend the hearing and that you bring sufficient copies of any relevant documents.

Please advise the tribunal office dealing with your case if you or anyone coming to the tribunal with you has a disability which affects access to the service we provide. We will make reasonable adjustments to the way in which we deliver our service to meet any need identified.

Case management orders

The parties are required to comply with the following case management orders and timetable.

By no later than	The following shall be done
4 weeks from date of this letter	The claimant shall set out in writing what **remedy** the Tribunal is being asked to award. The claimant shall send a copy to the respondent. The claimant shall include any evidence and documentation supporting what is claimed and how it is calculated. The claimant shall also include information about what steps the claimant has taken to reduce any loss (including any earnings or benefits received from new employment).
6 weeks from date of this letter	The claimant and the respondent shall send each other a list of any **documents** that they wish to refer to at the hearing or which are relevant to the case. They shall send each other a copy of any of these documents if requested to do so.
8 weeks from date of this letter	The respondent shall then prepare sufficient copies of the documents for the hearing. The documents shall be fastened together in a **file** so as to open flat. The file of documents shall be indexed. The documents shall be in a logical order. All pages shall be numbered consecutively. The respondent shall provide the other parties with a copy of the file. Two copies of the file shall be provided to the Tribunal at the hearing (and not before).
10 weeks from date of this letter	The claimant and the respondent shall prepare full **written statements of the evidence** they and their witnesses intend to give at the hearing. No additional witness evidence may be allowed at the hearing without permission of the Tribunal. The written statements shall have numbered paragraphs. The claimant and the respondent shall send the written statements of their witnesses to each other. Two copies of each written statement shall be provided for use by the Tribunal at the hearing (and not before).
1 week before the Hearing	Where the claimant and the respondent are both professionally represented, the professional representatives shall prepare a draft statement of issues or questions that are to be decided by the Tribunal at the hearing. The draft **statement of issues** shall be subject to the Tribunal's agreement at the commencement of the hearing.

These Orders are made under rules 29 and 30 of the Employment Tribunals Rules of Procedure 2013. Any person who without reasonable excuse fails to

comply with an Order to which section 7(4) of the Employment Tribunals Act 1996 applies, shall be liable on summary conviction to a fine not exceeding £1,000.

If this Order (including the timetable) is not complied with, the Tribunal, under rule 6 of the Rules of Procedure, may take such action as it considers just which may include (a) waiving or varying the requirement; (b) striking out the claim or response in whole or in part, in accordance with rule 37; (c) barring or restricting a party's participation in the proceedings and/or (d) awarding costs in accordance with rules 74–84.

You may make an application under rule 30 for this Order to be varied or revoked.

Signed,

For the Tribunal Office
cc. ACAS

C7 EMPLOYER'S RESPONSE TO THE TRIBUNAL (ET3)

Employment Tribunal

Response form

	Case number	20065/21

You must complete all questions marked with an '*'

1 Claimant's name

1.1 Claimant's name

Jennifer Pennant

2 Respondent's details

2.1* Name of individual, company or organisation

Strass Burger House Ltd

2.2 Name of contact

Arthur Venger

2.3* Address

Number or name | 153

Street | Avenal Avenue

Town/City | London

County

Postcode | W 1   2 G B

DX number (If known)

2.4 Phone number
Where we can contact you during the day

Mobile number (If different)

2.5 How would you prefer us to contact you? (Please tick only one box)

☐ Email   ☑ Post   ☐ Fax   Whatever your preference please note that some documents cannot be sent electronically

2.6 Email address

Fax number

2.7 Would you be able to take part in a hearing by video? (Requires internet access).

☑ Yes   ☐ No

Further details on video hearings can be found on the following link https://www.gov.uk/guidance/hmcts-telephone-and-video-hearings-during-coronavirus-outbreak

2.8 How many people does this organisation employ in Great Britain?

2000

2.9 Does this organisation have more than one site in Great Britain?

☑ Yes   ☐ No

2.10 If Yes, how many people are employed at the place where the claimant worked?

12

3 **Acas Early Conciliation details**

3.1 Do you agree with the details given by the claimant about early conciliation with Acas? ☑ Yes ☐ No

If No, please explain why, for example, has the claimant given the correct Acas early conciliation certificate number or do you disagree that the claimant is exempt from early conciliation, if so why?

4 **Employment details**

4.1 Are the dates of employment given by the claimant correct? ☑ Yes ☐ No

If Yes, please **go to question 4.2**

If No, please give the dates and say why you disagree with the dates given by the claimant

When their employment started

When their employment ended or will end

I disagree with the dates for the following reasons

4.2 Is their employment continuing? ☐ Yes ☑ No

4.3 Is the claimant's description of their job or job title correct? ☑ Yes ☐ No

If Yes, please **go to Section 5**

If No, please give the details you believe to be correct

5 Earnings and benefits

5.1 Are the claimant's hours of work correct? ☑ Yes ☐ No

If No, please enter the details you
believe to be correct. [   ] hours each week

5.2 Are the earnings details given by the
claimant correct? ☑ Yes ☐ No

If Yes, please **go to question 5.3**

If No, please give the details you believe to
be correct below

Pay before tax £ [   ] ☐ Weekly ☐ Monthly
(Incl. overtime, commission, bonuses etc.)

Normal take-home pay £ [   ] ☐ Weekly ☐ Monthly
(Incl. overtime, commission, bonuses etc.)

5.3 Is the information given by the claimant
correct about being paid for, or working a
period of notice? ☑ Yes ☐ No

If Yes, please **go to question 5.4**

If No, please give the details you believe to
be correct below. If you gave them no
notice or didn't pay them instead of letting
them work their notice, please explain what
happened and why.

5.4 Are the details about pension and other
benefits e.g. company car, medical
insurance, etc. given by the claimant correct? ☐ Yes ☐ No

If Yes, please **go to Section 6**

If No, please give the details you believe to
be correct.

6 Response

6.1* Do you defend the claim?   ☑ Yes   ☐ No

If No, please **go to Section 7**

If Yes, please set out the facts which you rely on to defend the claim.
(See Guidance - If needed, please use the blank sheet at the end of this form.)

1   In April 2021 the kitchen at the Ashburton restaurant was reorganised and decisions regarding menu planning, costing, standards, gross profits and budgets were, in future, to be dealt with by Ms Ethel Mann, the executive director, who was based at the Rusty restaurant.

2   In early 2021 it was also decided that the kitchen of the Ashburton restaurant would be used as a development for senior chefs de partie and junior sous chefs at the Rusty restaurant (the largest of the respondent's restaurants) to develop their management skills. These persons were to assume responsibility for running the kitchen but would report directly to Ms Mann.

3   As soon as the decision was made, a meeting was arranged between the claimant and Arthur Venger, the Head of Human Resources of the respondent company. This took place on 30 April 2021. The claimant was told of the reorganisation of the kitchen and how in future it would be used as a development for senior chefs in the respondent company. This meant that there was no need for a head chef at the Ashburton restaurant and in consequence thereof the position had been made redundant following the reorganisation of the kitchen. Mr Venger told the claimant that every effort would be made to find her alternative employment. These matters were explained again to the claimant by the managing director, Ms Diana Deane.

4   There has been no suitable alternative employment available since this date.

5   The claimant was paid £2000 ex gratia to include outstanding holiday pay. This was fully explained to her by Ms Deane at her appeal on 16 May 2021.

7 **Employer's Contract Claim**

7.1   Only available in limited circumstances where the claimant has made a contract claim. (See Guidance)

7.2   If you wish to make an Employer's Contract Claim in response to
the claimant's claim, please tick this box and complete question 7.3   ☐

7.3   Please set out the background and details of your claim below, which should include all important dates
(see Guidance for more information on what details should be included)

8   Your representative

If someone has agreed to represent you, please fill in the following. We will in future only contact your representative and not you.

8.1	Name of representative	Dan Fishman
8.2	Name of organisation	Hill, Wood & Co
8.3	Address	

Number or name   13 Gillespie House

Street   Hibury Street

Town/City   London

County

Postcode   N W 2   1 P B

8.4	DX number (If known)	
8.5	Phone number	01952 773841
8.6	Mobile phone	
8.7	Their reference for correspondence	
8.8	How would you prefer us to communicate with them? (Please tick only one box)	☑ Email ☐ Post ☐ Fax
8.9	Email address	fishy@gmail.com
8.10	Fax number	

9   Disability

9.1   Do you have a disability?   ☐ Yes   ☑ No

If Yes, it would help us if you could say what this disability is and tell us what assistance, if any, you will need as the claim progresses through the system, including for any hearings that maybe held at tribunal premises.

Please re-read the form and check you have entered all the relevant information. Once you are satisfied, please tick this box. ☐

C8 REQUEST FOR ADDITIONAL INFORMATION, AND DISCLOSURE

Note: As the hearing date is not until 14 January 2022, the claimant has been able to wait until after the date for disclosure under the case management timetable before writing this letter. If the hearing date was sooner, it may be necessary to send this letter, or at least a letter asking for the additional information, as soon as the ET3 is received. This is also the case if there has been no case management timetable sent out.

London Employment Project
12 MALVERN ROAD, LONDON E8 3LT

Dan Fishman
Hill, Wood & Co, Solicitors
Gillespie House
13 Highbury Street
London NW2 1PE

29 September 2021

Dear Sir

Re: Jenny Pennant v Strass Burger House Ltd – Case No: 20085/21

I have now received your client's tribunal response. Disclosure was due on 15 September 2021 under the ordered case management timetable, but although we complied with this, you have only provided the letter of dismissal.

Request for additional information

Please will you forward to this office on or before 12 October 2021[10] answers to the following questions:

1   Under paragraph 2 of the response, what was the precise date in the summer when it was decided that the Ashburton restaurant would be used for this alleged development, who made the decision, and who else was present at the time?[11]

2   Please state (a) the names of all other members of staff who were dismissed on the ground of redundancy as a consequence of this reorganisation, and (b) the selection method.[12]

3   Please state, with dates, the efforts made to secure the claimant alternative employment, who was responsible for this exercise, and the manner and extent of the enquiries made.[13]

10 State a time limit with which to comply; 14 days is fairly standard.

11 It is important to try to ascertain the precise date when the decision was reached to dismiss the employee. From this date the employer would be expected to consult with the employee and consider alternative employment.

12 This information is necessary to ascertain whether the worker was the only person dismissed and, if not, the other types of workers who were dismissed.

13 The failure to find alternative employment can make the dismissal unfair. The tribunal will have to consider the efforts made, in relation to the size and administrative resources of the employer's undertaking. This comparison cannot be made without this information.

4 Please state each and every vacancy within the company and the position and salary attributable to the position in the period 1 January 2021 to 31 July 2021. Please state when each vacancy became available and when it was filled.[14]

Disclosure

Please will you also supply me, within 14 days, with the following documents:

5 A list of all chefs working for the company at any time between 1 January 2021 and 31 July 2021, with dates of employment, job title and location.[15]

6 A list of all job vacancies for kitchen staff within the company from 1 January 2021 to 31 July 2021, the job title, place of employment and the salary.[16]

7 All notes, minutes or memoranda of all meetings at which the reorganisation of the kitchen of the Ashburton restaurant was discussed.[17]

8 Copies of all documents which purport to evidence the claimant's contract of employment.

9 All other documents in your possession which relate in any way to these proceedings, whether or not they are of assistance to the respondent's case or assist the claimant.[18]

If you are unable to supply the above by 26 October 2021, please contact this office in order that a further extension of time can be agreed.[19]

Yours faithfully,

D Rocastle
The London Employment Project
cc Regional Office of the Employment Tribunal[20]

14 The period chosen starts on the date the employer says s/he first contemplated redundancy and ends on the date the employee's notice would have expired, had she been allowed to work it. On receiving the information, consider all the vacancies and list those which the employee could have been offered (ie, within his/her capability). If none of these jobs was offered it will be necessary to ascertain at the hearing the reason why not.

15 Needed to ascertain whether the selection of the worker was unfair. In some circumstances, length of service may be a relevant criterion, provided that it is not indirectly discriminatory in that workplace.

16 Needed for the purpose of determining the question of alternative employment.

17 Needed to ascertain when the decision to dismiss was made, who made it and how it was proposed to deal with those workers being dismissed.

18 This is a standard request to ensure the respondent holds nothing useful back of which the employee is unaware and also that the employee is not surprised by any problematic documents which the respondent first produces at the hearing.

19 This paragraph is optional. It puts pressure on the employer to reply voluntarily, but there is a risk in allowing extensions of time in a region where cases get listed swiftly for hearing.

20 It is useful to copy this letter to the tribunal.

C9 REQUEST FOR ORDER FOR ADDITIONAL INFORMATION AND DISCLOSURE

It is useful, although not required, to explain to the tribunal why the requested information or documents are relevant to the case and in order to meet the over-riding objective.[21]

London Employment Project
MALVERN ROAD, LONDON E8 3LT

London Central Tribunal

15 October 2021

Dear Madam/Sir,

Re: Jenny Pennant v Strass Burger House Ltd – Case No: 20085/21

On 29 September 2021 I requested from the respondent's solicitors additional information of the response, written answers to questions and disclosure of certain documents. Notwithstanding the time limit given, these have not been supplied. A copy of the request is attached. Although disclosure was due on 15 September 2021 under the ordered case management timetable, the respondent only provided my client's dismissal letter. Please will you make an order for those matters sought in my letter of 29 September 2021. It is essential for my client's case to have this information, to establish that she has been unfairly dismissed.

An order for the requested information and disclosure will assist the tribunal in dealing with the proceedings efficiently and fairly for these reasons:

Item 1: This is relevant to the date when consultation with the claimant should have commenced.

Items 2 and 5: These will indicate whether any redundancy selection criteria were applied.

Items 3 and 4: Alternative employment is relevant to the fairness of a redundancy dismissal.

Item 6: This is relevant as to the timing and reasoning behind the dismissal.

Items 8 and 9: These are standard items.

I have copied this letter to the respondents today and informed them that any objection to my application for an order should be sent to the tribunal as soon as possible.

Yours faithfully,

D Rocastle
The London Employment Project
cc Respondent

---

21 See para 20.128 onwards for requesting an order.

C10 LETTER INFORMING RESPONDENT OF REQUEST TO TRIBUNAL FOR AN ORDER[22]

London Employment Project
MALVERN ROAD, LONDON E8 3LT

Dan Fishman
Hill, Wood & Co, Solicitors
Gillespie House
13 Highbury Street
London NW2 1PE

15 October 2021

Dear Sir

Re: Jenny Pennant v Strass Burger House Ltd – Case No: 20085/21

I refer to my letter dated 29 September 2021 requesting additional information and disclosure, to which I have not had the courtesy of a reply. I have therefore written to the tribunal requesting an order for disclosure, copy attached.

You must send any objection to my application to the employment tribunal office as soon as possible. Any objection to my application must be copied to me.

Yours faithfully

D Rocastle

cc Employment tribunal

C11 REQUEST FOR WITNESS ORDER[23]

In obtaining a witness order it is necessary to give the witnesses' full names and addresses (for the purpose of effecting service), a brief statement of their evidence, which must be relevant and necessary, and to state that they are not prepared to attend voluntarily. It may be wise to witness order Ms Reiss only if she has indicated she will be willing to come provided she is subject to an order.

London Employment Project
MALVERN ROAD, LONDON E8 3LT

London Central Tribunal

18 November 2021

Dear Madam/Sir,

Re: Jenny Pennant v Strass Burger House Ltd – Case No: 20085/21

I apply to the tribunal for a witness order for the following person to attend the hearing listed for 14 January 2022.

Patricia Reiss
23 Miller Court
London EC3

Patricia Reiss is employed by the respondent as a personal assistant to the Head of Human Resources. She can give evidence in respect of the respondent's decision to dismiss the claimant.

Ms Reiss is not prepared to attend voluntarily as she is still in the employ of the respondent.

Yours faithfully,

D Rocastle
The London Employment Project

---

23 See para 20.136.

C12 ADDITIONAL INFORMATION

Hill, Wood & Co
GILLESPIE HOUSE, 13 HIGHBURY STREET, LONDON NW2 1PC

D Rocastle
The London Employment Project
12 Malvern Road, London E8 3LT

15 December 2021

Dear Sir,

Re: Jenny Pennant v Strass Burger House Ltd – Case No: 20085/21

You should by now have copies of the documents you requested. In reply to the employment tribunal order of 2 December 2021 to supply additional information and written answers to the claimant's letter of 29 September 2021:

1   The decision was made at a meeting on 10 February 2021 attended by Arthur Venger and Diana Deane. It was a decision reached as part of a reorganisation of the company which was felt to be in the best future interest of all concerned.

2   No other person was dismissed.

3   After 30 April 2021, Arthur Venger personally dealt with this matter. He decided to offer the claimant any future vacancy at head chef level in the larger restaurant. There was no point offering her any other position as she would not have accepted such an offer.

4   The respondent is a large organisation and the turnover of staff in the industry is high. There were many vacancies for other positions within the company, but they were not suitable. The respondent did not take these positions into consideration as they were not relevant.

Yours faithfully,

Dan Fishman

C13 TERMS OF SETTLEMENT[24]

The respondent undertakes:

1   to pay the claimant on or before 2 February 2021 the sum of £15,500 in full and final settlement of all claims that she has arising out of her employment and the termination thereof, save for any claim for personal injury or industrial injury,[25]

2   to supply the following reference and only this reference, if requested for the same, and not to depart from it unless with the express permission of the claimant. If the reference is requested in writing, to supply the same on headed notepaper, dated and duly signed.[26]

'Jenny Pennant has been employed by Strass Burger House Ltd from 2000 until her dismissal on the ground of redundancy on 30 April 2021. She was promoted on several occasions and at the time of her dismissal was employed as the senior head chef. Throughout her employment we found her to be honest, hardworking and enthusiastic. Her timekeeping and attendance were exemplary. She had a pleasant personality and was liked by the other members of staff, as well as by management. We have no hesitation in recommending her for future employment in a similar capacity.'[27]

3   The above reference will also be supplied to the claimant as an open reference on or before 2 February 2022 on headed paper, dated and duly signed, and headed 'To whom it may concern'.

4   The claimant undertakes to withdraw her employment tribunal claim on receipt of the above sum and open reference, and in the meanwhile the case is adjourned generally.[28]

---

24 See paras 20.268 onwards and the settlement checklist in appendix A at A29.

25 Always put in a date for compliance, and always insist that claims for personal injury are excluded with unfair dismissal claims. The Advisory, Conciliation and Arbitration Service (ACAS) will encourage this exception. Also exclude pension rights if these exist.

26 A reference should form part of the agreement (see para 20.278), and this undertaking must be secured from the employer. Consider whether to permit leeway if a reference is sought in a different form or there are follow up questions.

27 Set out the reference in full. It helps when negotiating if the employee supplies the first draft of a reference for agreement. However, many employers only supply factual references nowadays.

28 If the worker undertakes to withdraw the claim only on receipt of the sum, it means that if there is non-payment the worker can return to the tribunal or sue for the agreed sum through the courts. If the worker returns to the tribunal, s/he should apply for costs on the grounds of unreasonable conduct.

Glossary

ACAS

The Advisory, Conciliation and Arbitration Service (ACAS) was founded in 1975 to work towards improving employment relations. An ACAS officer is appointed to employment tribunal (ET) cases to 'conciliate', ie, to act as an independent intermediary to facilitate the parties to settle (see para 20.268). ACAS also run the early conciliation (EC) procedure which claimants must follow before starting a tribunal claim (see para 20.16).

Adjourn, adjournment

This technical word can be used for postponing a hearing date in advance or, once a hearing has started, stopping part-way through and arranging a future date to deal with outstanding matters. It can also be used on what is anticipated to be a permanent basis, eg a case is adjourned pending payment of a settlement sum after an agreed settlement, or while a similar issue is resolved in parallel proceedings in the High Court. See para 20.138 regarding getting a hearing date postponed.

Admissible evidence

Evidence to the employment tribunal may be in documents or oral. Some forms of evidence will not be allowed by the employment tribunal and are termed inadmissible. The employment tribunal operates very lax rules of evidence. Most forms of evidence will be admissible although some may not be given much weight, eg, hearsay, written unsworn statements from absent witnesses, incomplete or unclear tape recordings.

Breach of contract

Breaking or not complying with one of the agreed terms of a contract (of employment). A fundamental or repudiatory breach of contract is an extremely serious breach going to the heart of the employment relationship. If done by the employer, it may entitle a worker to resign and claim constructive dismissal. If done by the worker, it may entitle the employer to dismiss without notice. (See para 6.35 for constructive dismissal.)

Burden of proof

This refers to which party (employer or worker) has the responsibility of proving matters, such as whether a dismissal took place or whether unlawful discrimination happened. The party with the burden of proof cannot simply make an allegation and ask the other party to disprove it. (See paras 9.1 and 16.1.)

Case management; case management discussion (CMD)
Case management concerns the preparation of cases for hearings, eg, disclosing documents, obtaining additional information. Tribunals hold preliminary hearings (which used to be called case management discussions) to deal with these matters, especially in discrimination cases, prior to the full hearing. (See chapter 20.)

Civil courts
Strictly speaking, civil courts are those dealing with civil law, eg, the county court, High Court, Court of Appeal and Supreme Court, as opposed to criminal law, eg, the Magistrates' Court and Crown Court. Technically, employment tribunals are civil rather than criminal courts, but the term is sometimes used to distinguish the county court or High Court with their more formal processes, heavier costs risks and (sometimes) legal aid entitlement, from employment tribunals.

Civil Procedure Rules 1998 (CPR)
These are the rules of procedure applicable in to the High Court, county courts and the civil division of the Court of Appeal. Although they are more formal than tribunal rules, they do have some influence in terms of understanding the scope of orders for documents and additional information (see chapter 20). However, the CPR should not be given too much prominence in employment tribunals, because they are more technical than the usual approach in employment tribunals. The CPR do not apply in Scotland. If anything needs to be done in line with civil court procedure, the Sheriff Court Rules of Procedure apply. The CPR are available at: www.justice.gov.uk/courts/procedure-rules/civil/rules.

Claim
The worker's document which starts the employment tribunal proceedings, usually written on a standard form numbered 'ET1'. (See paras 20.42 and 21.29.)

Claimant
The formal term for the worker in employment tribunal proceedings.

Closing submissions
See Final submissions.

Compromise agreement
See Settlement agreement.

Conciliation, Conciliation officer
Normally refers to the role of an ACAS (Advisory, Conciliation and Arbitration Service) officer once a case has started in liaising between the parties or their representatives off the record, usually on the telephone, to help encourage a settlement (see para 20.268). Conciliation is to be distinguished from mediation which involves different techniques and is not exclusively offered by ACAS.

Consolidation
Where separate cases with one or more of the same parties are combined for the purposes of preparation and a joint hearing. Strictly speaking the term

consolidation is not used in the employment tribunal system and the phrase used is that the cases be 'considered together'.

Constructive dismissal

This is where an employee resigns due to the employer's fundamental or repudiatory breach of the employment contract. See para 6.35.

Contract workers

This is often used to refer to workers employed on fixed-term contracts who may or may not have unfair dismissal rights, according to whether they meet the eligibility criteria (see para 6.26). It is also a precise term with a slightly different meaning under the Equality Act 2010 (see para 12.17).

COT3

The standard form on which an ACAS conciliation officer records an agreement negotiated through him/her. (See para 20.270.)

Court of Justice of the European Union (CJEU)

This comprises the Court of Justice and the General Court. Lawyers still tend to refer to the the European Court of Justice (ECJ), which is the court which generally decides the employment cases. (See chapter 3 for its role.)

CVP (Cloud video platform)

This is the employment tribunal's preferred video platform for remote hearings, although others may be used such as Teams. It is easy for users because all that is necessary is a computer, internet access and reliable wi fi.

Directions

See Case management.

Disclosure of documents

The process of one party disclosing relevant documents to the other. The term 'discovery' is sometimes used in England and Wales. In Scotland, the term used is 'recovery'. (See paras 20.123 and 21.42.)

Discovery

See Disclosure of documents.

Domestic law

This term is usually used to distinguish the national law of an EU member state from European law, ie, law laid down by European legislation and case-law which applies to all member states.

Early conciliation (EC)

Before a worker can start most tribunal claims, including for unfair dismissal, discrimination or pay deductions, s/he must notify ACAS under the EC process. It is not compulsory to further engage in the process and the worker can just ask for a certificate and proceed to an employment tribunal. (See para 20.16 onwards.)

Employee

Different categories of worker are eligible to claim different employment rights. Certain rights can only be claimed by employees. For a definition of employee under the Employment Rights Act 1996, see s229. The definition under discrimination law is wider, see Equality Act 2010 s83 and para 12.12 above.

Employment Appeal Tribunal (EAT)
The first level of appeal from an ET decision.

Employment tribunal (ET)
Originally known as industrial tribunal (IT). Most employment cases are heard in employment tribunals.

ET1, ET3
The ET1 is the standard form on which the claimant's tribunal claim is written. The ET3 is the standard form on which the employer's response is written. These documents are often referred to by the names of the forms rather than their full names. They are called ET1 and ET3.

European Court of Justice (ECJ)
See Court of Justice of the European Union.

Evidence in chief
The evidence given in an employment tribunal hearing by a witness before s/he is cross- examined. The evidence is usually given to his/her own representative, who will be conducting an examination in chief. Most if not all of the evidence in chief is now contained in a witness's written witness statement.

Fact – questions of fact; fact findings
If something is a question of fact for the employment tribunal, it means that the issue is decided on the facts of the particular case as opposed to on the law alone. A fact finding is the employment tribunal's decision on where the truth lies between two conflicting pieces of evidence.

Final submissions
The closing speech in an employment tribunal hearing. The final submissions are sometimes put in writing. They may also be known as closing submissions.

Floating cases; floater
Many employment tribunal centres fix more hearings than they can possible hear, assuming that some will not go ahead, usually because they have settled at the last minute. This is to maximise the use of employment tribunal panels on any given day. An employment tribunal case which has been set for a hearing date, but has been not allocated to a specific employment tribunal panel, is floating or a floater. The problem is that the case can be floating for anything between five minutes and all day; sometimes it may not even be heard that day, which can be very frustrating for unrepresented claimants who were not aware of this process.

Fundamental breach
See Breach of contract.

Grievance, grievance procedure

Grievances are internal complaints made by workers to their employers, complaining that their employers have or have not done something in relation to the worker. The grievance may concern the behaviour of a work colleague or manager. Employers should have their own grievance procedures for the bringing and investigation of such complaints.

Held

Where something is 'held' by a court or tribunal, this is its decision.

Indirect discrimination

This has a specific legal meaning under Equality Act 2010 s19 (see para 13.27 onwards).

Issues

When used as a technical term, this refers to the legal and sometimes factual questions which a tribunal must answer in order to decide the claim. The issues are often itemised as part of case management at a preliminary hearing and are checked with the parties at the start of the final hearing. See document A24 in appendix A for an example of a list of issues.

Judgment

An employment tribunal decision deciding a case or particular issue in the case is a judgment. A decision concerning matter of case management, eg, requiring a party to supply documents, is an order. A judgment can be given orally but must be confirmed in writing. Written reasons for a judgment or order are a separate matter. (See paras 20.224–20.226.)

Jurisdiction

The ET may adjudicate only on certain claims brought by certain workers. These are matters 'within its jurisdiction'. The employment tribunal has no discretion to decide claims outside its jurisdiction, eg, where a worker has insufficient qualifying service to claim unfair dismissal, or a claim completely outside employment tribunal jurisdiction, eg for defamation, withholding a P45 or breach of data protection law.

Liability; hearing on liability

The issue as to whether or not the worker wins his/her case, ie, whether the employer is found 'liable' for unfair dismissal, discrimination, etc, as distinct from the issue of what compensation or remedies the worker should receive.

Listing

When a hearing date is fixed, the case is 'listed' for hearing. (See para 20.138 onwards.)

Lodging documents

This usually refers to lodging the tribunal claim or lodging trial bundles at the employment tribunal. Usually it means delivering the relevant document to the employment tribunal by whatever means. The technical term for lodging the tribunal claim is 'presenting' and the claim will not be accepted as presented if certain requirements are not met.

Mediation, judicial mediation

A form of alternative disputes resolution (ADR). The parties and their representatives hold a meeting, often lasting a whole day, with a view to resolving their dispute. The meeting is chaired by a neutral mediator who may speak to the parties separately or together and facilitate the discussions. The idea is that the parties will focus on what they want rather than the merits of the claim. Mediation is considered particularly suitable where the worker is still employed and in discrimination cases, but its success is very much dependent on the skill of the individual mediator. Mediation may be offered by ACAS or private organisations on a paid basis as well as by the tribunal for no charge (see para 21.53 regarding judicial mediation).

Members, non-legal members

Formerly known as wing members or lay members, together with the employment judge these make up an employment tribunal panel in discrimination and certain other cases including whistleblowing detriment claims. They are chosen for their experience on one or other side of industry (there is an employer panel and an employee panel). A representative from each panel sits on the case, though they take a neutral position.

Merits; merits hearing

This is the same as the hearing on liability (see Liability; hearing on liability above).

Mitigate; mitigation

Mitigation refers to reasonable steps which should have been taken or were taken by a worker to find fresh employment to mitigate (ie, reduce) the loss of earnings resulting from his/her dismissal. (See para 18.34.)

Motion, of its own

An employment tribunal has power to make case management orders and take other steps on its own initiative, ie, of its own motion, as well as at the request of either party.

Obiter

Where a higher court makes a statement of legal principle or interpretation, on which the decision in that particular case does not depend. It is therefore not a binding precedent but is of persuasive authority.

On notice

Where a party takes a procedural step in the employment tribunal having informed the other party.

Open justice

Open justice is regarded as a pillar of a democracy. There is a general principle across all courts and tribunals (with limited exceptions) that members of the public, including journalists, are permitted to watch and report on hearings. This needs to be balanced against the need for privacy and restricted reporting in certain circumstances. (See paras 21.61–21.67 and particularly 21.65.)

Parties

The claimant and the respondent are collectively known as the parties to the case.

Pleadings; to plead

Pleadings are the documents which set out each party's case, ie, the ET1, ET3 and any additional information (in the technical sense – see para 20.116 onwards). To plead something is to put it into any of these documents.

Precedent

The courts decide cases by applying and interpreting the law to given facts. There is a hierarchy of courts and tribunals for employment law purposes, ie in England & Wales, Supreme Court, Court of Appeal, High Court, Employment Appeal Tribunal, employment tribunal. Each level of court/ tribunal is compelled to follow legal principles and interpretations set by higher level courts unless a case can be 'distinguished' on its facts. Where no higher level decision exists, the courts (except the employment tribunal) follow the interpretation of other courts of the same level. Strictly-speaking, decisions by the Court of Session do not bind English and Welsh employment tribunals and EAT, and Court of Appeal decisions do not bind Scottish employment tribunals. However, in practice, Scottish employment tribunals and S(EAT) would only depart from a Court of Appeal decision on a matter of purely Scottish law. Precedent may also be referred to as 'authority'.

Preliminary hearing

Preliminary hearings replace what were previously two different types of hearing, ie case management discussions (CMDs) and pre-hearing reviews. Preliminary hearings are usually held for discrimination or other complicated claims such as whistleblowing in order to decide case management matters so the case is properly prepared for the final hearing. Preliminary hearings can also be held to deal with other matters on any kind of claim, eg to decide a preliminary issue such as whether the claimant is an employee or has sufficient service to claim unfair dismissal, or to decide whether to strike out a claim or order costs because it has no or little reasonable prospect of success. For more detail, see chapter 20.

Presenting the tribunal claim

A claim is presented at the employment tribunal when it is arrives at the central office or one of the employment tribunals nominated for acceptance. However, if the necessary minimum information is missing, the tribunal will return the claim and it will not be taken as presented. (See paras 20.42 and 20.77.)

Privilege

Certain verbal or written communications are private and need not be disclosed to the other side during a case. These are referred to as 'privileged'. The issue tends to come up on disclosure and the definitive rules are set out in the Civil Procedure Rules 1998. The rules can get very complicated, but the most well-known form of privilege is communication between a party and his/her own solicitor. See also Without prejudice.

Protected characteristics
A new term introduced in the Equality Act 2010. It is unlawful to discriminate because of the protected characteristics covered by the Equality Act 2010, ie age; disability; gender reassignment; marriage and civil partnership; pregnancy or maternity; race; religion or belief; sex; and sexual orientation.

Protected conversations
Evidence of pre-termination negotiations cannot be referred to in ordinary unfair dismissal claims, unless any improper conduct was involved. For detail, see paras 9.21–9.24.

Quantum
Financial compensation.

Questionnaire
A special procedure available under the Equality Act 2010, enabling the worker to gather evidence in discrimination claims (see para 21.47). The statutory procedure has been replaced with a non-statutory procedure underpinned by ACAS guidance.

Reconsideration
An employment tribunal can reconsider a decision it has made. This is different from appealing to the EAT and has a shorter time limit (see para 20.236 onwards).

Recoupment
The process by which benefits claimed by the claimant are deducted from his/her award for loss of earnings in a successful unfair dismissal case and repaid by the employer to the Department for Work and Pensions (DWP). (See paras 18.62 – 18.65 for more details.)

Remedies; remedies hearing
Remedies are the compensation in money and other forms which a worker receives if s/he wins. A remedies hearing is sometimes dealt with separately from the hearing on liability, although this is less common in Scotland.

Remote hearings
This refers to preliminary and full hearings held on an audio or video platform as opposed to 'in-person' which means in the tribunal building. These have become far more common due to the Covid-19 pandemic. (See para 20.228 onwards.)

Repudiatory breach
See Breach of contract.

Respondent
This is the legal term for the employer in employment tribunal proceedings.

Response
The employer's reply or defence, usually written on an ET3 form. (See para 20.86.)

Schedule of Loss; Schedule of Remedies and Loss

During the preparation of a case, the claimant is often ordered to prepare a schedule setting out how much s/he has lost by way of earnings and the value of the claim generally. (See para 20.182.)

Serving documents

Delivering or sending documents to the other party.

Settlement agreements

Any agreement to settle a case (ie a negotiated 'deal') can be called a settlement agreement. However, since 29 July 2013, this has been used as a specific term (replacing 'compromise agreement') to indicate a formal agreement which has been made through legal or other authorised representatives and which meets specified requirements. This is so as to be binding on the claimant in respect of ET claims (though others are often included).

Skeleton argument

A written outline of a representative's final speech at the employment tribunal hearing, which s/he will hand to the employment tribunal panel and expand verbally. Sometimes representatives provide skeleton arguments on complex legal points at the outset.

Submissions

An employment tribunal at the hearing may invite a representative to make submissions on a particular point. This usually means the representative is required to make comments or arguments on law or evidence. See also Final submissions.

Summary dismissal

This occurs when an employee's conduct is sufficiently grave as to justify immediate termination of the employment contract without notice. The worker is not entitled to either notice or pay in lieu of notice when summarily dismissed.

Supreme Court

On 1 October 2009, the judicial function of the House of Lords was moved to the Supreme Court. The most senior domestic court, it is the final court of appeal for all UK employment cases. Chapter 3 explains its powers on interpreting EU law both before and after Brexit.

TUPE

This abbreviation is commonly used, especially by trade unions, to refer to the Transfer of Undertakings (Protection of Employment) Regulations 2006. TUPE aims to protect employees' rights when their employer sells the business or contracts out a service. (See chapter 10.)

Unless order

An order, eg for disclosure of documents, which – if it is not complied with by the claimant or respondent – will lead automatic consequences on the date of non-compliance without further consideration by the tribunal. Most commonly, this is that the claim or response (as the case may be) is automatically struck out. (See paras 20.112–20.115.)

Vicarious liability

This is where an employer is responsible for the unlawful acts of his/her employees as if s/he carried them out him/herself, regardless of whether s/he knew or approved of those acts. In the employment field, it is mainly relevant to discrimination law (see para 12.27).

Victimisation

This has a precise legal meaning under the Equality Act 2010. It is where an employer subjects a worker to a detriment because s/he has done a 'protected act', essentially because s/he has complained about discrimination in some way. (For details see para 13.58 onwards.)

Without prejudice

Negotiations between the parties for the purpose of settling a case are off-the-record from the viewpoint of the employment tribunal. To ensure this is so, it is traditional to introduce the conversation by saying the words 'can we speak without prejudice?' Letters regarding settlement should also be headed 'without prejudice'. (See paras 9.18–9.19, 16.34, 20.259.)

Witness order

An employment tribunal can issue a witness order to compel an unwilling witness to attend the hearing. (See para 20.136.)

Witness statement

A statement taken from each witness including the claimant, which it is intended to disclose to the other side in advance of the hearing or at the hearing itself. The witness statement stands as the witness's evidence in chief. Note that the witness must still attend the hearing unless the other side agrees that s/he need not do so. Witness statements are used routinely in England and Wales, but are less common in Scotland. (See paras 20.186 and 21.68.)

Worker

Different employment rights have different eligibility requirements: some are available only to employees and others to 'workers' on a wider basis. These terms can themselves have different definitions according to the employment right concerned. For the definition of 'worker' in the context of the Working Time Regulations, the minimum wage, under the Employment Rights Act 1996 eg for unauthorised deductions claims, and under the Part-time Workers Regulations (see paras 4.5–4.7). See Employment Rights Act 1996 s230 for definitions relevant to rights under that Act.

Redundancy payments table

Age	2	3	4	5	6	7	8	9	10	11	12	13	14	15	16	17	18	19	20
17	1	-	-	-	-	-	-	-	-	-	-	-	-	-	-	-	-	-	-
18	1	1½	-	-	-	-	-	-	-	-	-	-	-	-	-	-	-	-	-
19	1	1½	2	-	-	-	-	-	-	-	-	-	-	-	-	-	-	-	-
20	1	1½	2	2½	-	-	-	-	-	-	-	-	-	-	-	-	-	-	-
21	1	1½	2	2½	3	-	-	-	-	-	-	-	-	-	-	-	-	-	-
22	1	1½	2	2½	3	3½	-	-	-	-	-	-	-	-	-	-	-	-	-
23	1½	2	2½	3	3½	4	4½	-	-	-	-	-	-	-	-	-	-	-	-
24	2	2½	3	3½	4	4½	5	5½	-	-	-	-	-	-	-	-	-	-	-
25	2	3	3½	4	4½	5	5½	6	6½	-	-	-	-	-	-	-	-	-	-
26	2	3	4	4½	5	5½	6	6½	7	7½	-	-	-	-	-	-	-	-	-
27	2	3	4	5	5½	6	6½	7	7½	8	8½	-	-	-	-	-	-	-	-
28	2	3	4	5	6	6½	7	7½	8	8½	9	9½	-	-	-	-	-	-	-
29	2	3	4	5	6	7	7½	8	8½	9	9½	10	10½	-	-	-	-	-	-
30	2	3	4	5	6	7	8	8½	9	9½	10	10½	11	11½	-	-	-	-	-
31	2	3	4	5	6	7	8	9	9½	10	10½	11	11½	12	12½	-	-	-	-
32	2	3	4	5	6	7	8	9	10	10½	11	11½	12	12½	13	13½	-	-	-
33	2	3	4	5	6	7	8	9	10	11	11½	12	12½	13	13½	14	14½	-	-
34	2	3	4	5	6	7	8	9	10	11	12	12½	13	13½	14	14½	15	15½	-
35	2	3	4	5	6	7	8	9	10	11	12	13	13½	14	14½	15	15½	16	16½
36	2	3	4	5	6	7	8	9	10	11	12	13	14	14½	15	15½	16	16½	17
37	2	3	4	5	6	7	8	9	10	11	12	13	14	15	15½	16	16½	17	17½
38	2	3	4	5	6	7	8	9	10	11	12	13	14	15	16	16½	17	17½	18
39	2	3	4	5	6	7	8	9	10	11	12	13	14	15	16	17	17½	18	18½
40	2	3	4	5	6	7	8	9	10	11	12	13	14	15	16	17	18	18½	19
41	2	3	4	5	6	7	8	9	10	11	12	13	14	15	16	17	18	19	19½
42	2½	3½	4½	5½	6½	7½	8½	9½	10½	11½	12½	13½	14½	15½	16½	17½	18½	19½	20½
43	3	4	5	6	7	8	9	10	11	12	13	14	15	16	17	18	19	20	21
44	3	4½	5½	6½	7½	8½	9½	10½	11½	12½	13½	14½	15½	16½	17½	18½	19½	20½	21½
45	3	4½	6	7	8	9	10	11	12	13	14	15	16	17	18	19	20	21	22
46	3	4½	6	7½	8½	9½	10½	11½	12½	13½	14½	15½	16½	17½	18½	19½	20½	21½	22½
47	3	4½	6	7½	9	10	11	12	13	14	15	16	17	18	19	20	21	22	23
48	3	4½	6	7½	9	10½	11½	12½	13½	14½	15½	16½	17½	18½	19½	20½	21½	22½	23½
49	3	4½	6	7½	9	10½	12	13	14	15	16	17	18	19	20	21	22	23	24
50	3	4½	6	7½	9	10½	12	13½	14½	15½	16½	17½	18½	19½	20½	21½	22½	23½	24½
51	3	4½	6	7½	9	10½	12	13½	15	16	17	18	19	20	21	22	23	24	25
52	3	4½	6	7½	9	10½	12	13½	15	16½	17½	18½	19½	20½	21½	22½	23½	24½	25½
53	3	4½	6	7½	9	10½	12	13½	15	16½	18	19	20	21	22	23	24	25	26
54	3	4½	6	7½	9	10½	12	13½	15	16½	18	19½	20½	21½	22½	23½	24½	25½	26½
55	3	4½	6	7½	9	10½	12	13½	15	16½	18	19½	21	22	23	24	25	26	27
56	3	4½	6	7½	9	10½	12	13½	15	16½	18	19½	21	22½	23½	24½	25½	26½	27½
57	3	4½	6	7½	9	10½	12	13½	15	16½	18	19½	21	22½	24	25	26	27	28
58	3	4½	6	7½	9	10½	12	13½	15	16½	18	19½	21	22½	24	25½	26½	27½	28½
59	3	4½	6	7½	9	10½	12	13½	15	16½	18	19½	21	22½	24	25½	27	28	29
60	3	4½	6	7½	9	10½	12	13½	15	16½	18	19½	21	22½	24	25½	27	28½	29½
61+	3	4½	6	7½	9	10½	12	13½	15	16½	18	19½	21	22½	24	25½	27	28½	30

Statutory Redundancy Pay table

Bibliography and other resources

Textbooks and guides

The following books and guides are frequently moved to new web addresses. If you cannot find them, just Google the title.

Butterworths employment law handbook. Edited by Peter Wallington, published by LexisNexis UK. All relevant statutes, regulations, codes and EU directives fully reproduced. No commentary. The book is regularly reissued with latest statutes and amendments to existing statutes. It is invaluable, because it updates statutes and regulations with the amending legislation – something which cannot always be found on the legislation.gov.uk website.

Harvey on industrial relations and employment law. Published by LexisNexis UK. Multi-volume loose-leaf, regularly updated. Also available online. The most authoritative academic text on employment law. Reviews case-law and reproduces key statutes. Popularly known as 'Harvey', it is the textbook which is quoted in the courts and tribunals.

EHRC Employment Code and Equal Pay Code. Available at:
www.equalityhumanrights.com/publication/employment-statutory-code-practice
and:
www.equalityhumanrights.com/en/publication-download/equal-pay-statutory-code-practice.
It is best to look at the pdf version of the code rather than the Word version, since the latter has some mistakes in its paragraph numbering.

Guidance on matters to be taken into account in determining questions relating to the definition of disability, Office for Disability Issues, 2011. This is available at: https://assets.publishing.service.gov.uk/government/uploads/system/ uploads/attachment_data/file/570382/Equality_Act_2010-disability_defini-tion.pdf.

Law reports

Industrial Relations Law Reports (IRLR). Fully reproduced law reports. Essential if using cases in an employment tribunal, but you need to know what you are looking for. The other source of official law reports is Industrial Cases Reports (ICR), but these are less commonly used by advisers. Most judgments can now be found free on the internet (see below). However, the advantage of the IRLR version, if reported, is that it summarises the case and decision in a short head note.

IDS Employment Law Brief. Published twice monthly by Incomes Data Services Ltd. Subscriptions include access to its website plus occasional specialist handbooks. Tel: 020 7449 1107. Used to be called *IDS Brief.*

Legal Action. Published by Legal Action Group. Tel: 020 7833 2931, www.lag. org.uk.

Websites

Access to Law Inner Temple Library's comprehensive listing of available resources including sources of case law and expert witness directories.	www.accesstolaw.com/
Advisory, Conciliation and Arbitration Service (ACAS)	www.acas.org.uk
Case reports	The majority of tribunal and court decisions at appeal level, especially since 2000, but often earlier, are available free online on Bailii, case-law search at: www.bailii.org/
Civil Procedure Rules 1998	www.justice.gov.uk/courts/procedure-rules/civil
Companies House	To do a company search, access the WebCheck service via: www.gov.uk/get-information-about-a-company
Department for Business, Energy and Industrial Strategy (BEIS) – formerly Department for Business Innovation and Skills (BIS), Department for Business, Enterprise and Regulatory Reform (BERR); and the Department of Trade and Industry (DTI). Most government guidance on employment law is now on the GOV. UK site	www.gov.uk
Employment Appeal Tribunal	For appeal forms, judgments and other information as to how to appeal. Start at: www.gov.uk/appeal-employment-appeal-tribunal/overview
	Search for EAT judgments at www.gov.uk/employment-appeal-tribunal-decisions or, pre March 2017, on: www.employmentappeals. gov.uk/public/search.aspx. Also on Bailii at www.bailii.org/uk/cases/UKEAT/

Employment tribunals	General guidance on ET procedure and online ET1 and ET3 forms. Start at: www.gov.uk/employment-tribunals
Health & Safety Executive	www.hse.gov.uk
Information Commissioner	Covers data protection and the Freedom of Information Act. The Information Commissioner and the Scottish Information Commissioner are respectively at: https://ico.org.uk/ and: www.itspublicknowledge.info/home/ScottishInformationCommissioner.aspx
Legislation.gov.uk	Replacing HM Stationery Office (HMSO) and the Office of Public Sector Information (OPSI). Publishes full text of all UK statutes and regulations since 1988 (and some earlier ones) plus drafts. Later amendments to legislation are not always added. A safer place to look for up to date legislation is usually Butterworths or Harvey. www.legislation.gov.uk/
Parliamentary bills	www.parliament.uk/business/bills-and-legislation
Protect (previously called Public Concern at Work)	Informative site about whistleblowing law and cases. https://protect-advice.org.uk/
Supreme Court judgments	www.supremecourt.uk/decided-cases/index.html or on Bailii at: www.bailii.org/uk/cases/UKSC/
timeanddate.com	Useful date calculator when working out compensation. www.timeanddate.com/
TUC (Trades Union Congress)	www.tuc.org.uk/
UNISON (public sector trade union)	www.unison.org.uk/

Index